Criminology

Criminology

Tim Newburn

WILLAN
PUBLISHING

Published by

Willan Publishing
2 Park Square
Milton Park
Abingdon
Oxfordshire, OX14 4RN
United Kingdom

Published simultaneously in the USA and Canada by

Willan Publishing
711 Third Avenue
New York
NY 10017 (8th Floor)
United States

ISBN   978-1-84392-284-1 paperback
         978-1-84392-285-8 hardback

British Library Cataloguing-in-Publication Data

A catalogue record for this book is available from the British Library.

Project managed by Deer Park Productions, Tavistock, Devon
Typeset by Pantek Arts, Maidstone, Kent

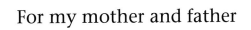

For my mother and father

Contents

Detailed contents	ix
Acknowledgements	xix
Academic review	xxi
Preface	xxiii
List of acronyms	xxv

Part 1 Understanding Crime and Criminology — 1

1	Understanding crime and criminology	2
2	Crime and punishment in history	20
3	Crime data and crime trends	48
4	Crime and the media	82

Part 2 Understanding Crime: theories and concepts — 111

5	Classicism and positivism	112
6	Biological positivism	130
7	Psychological positivism	146
8	Durkheim, anomie and strain	168
9	The Chicago School, culture and subcultures	186
10	Interactionism and labelling theory	208
11	Control theories	226
12	Radical and critical criminology	244
13	Realist criminology	262
14	Contemporary classicism	278
15	Feminist criminology	298
16	Late modernity, governmentality and risk	318

Part 3 Understanding Crime: types and trends — 339

17	Victims, victimization and victimology	340
18	White-collar and corporate crime	370
19	Organised crime	404
20	Violent and property crime	434
21	Drugs and alcohol	472

Part 4 Understanding Criminal Justice   513

22   Penology and punishment   514
23   Understanding criminal justice   540
24   Crime prevention and community safety   564
25   The police and policing   596
26   Criminal courts and the court process   636
27   Sentencing and non-custodial penalties   658
28   Prisons and imprisonment   682
29   Youth crime and youth justice   714
30   Restorative justice   742

Part 5 Critical Issues in Criminology   769

31   Race, crime and justice   770
32   Gender, crime and justice   804
33   Criminal and forensic psychology   836
34   Globalisation, terrorism and human rights   866

Part 6 Doing Criminology   895

35   Understanding criminological research   896
36   Doing criminological research   924

Publisher's acknowledgements   943
Glossary   945
Bibliography   954
Index   1003

Detailed contents

Part 1 Understanding Crime and Criminology **1**

1 Understanding crime and criminology **2**
What is criminology? 4
An interdisciplinary subject 5
Defining criminology 5
Understanding crime 6
Crime and the criminal law 8
Crime as a social construct 8
Historical variation 9
Crime and politics 11
End of the bipartisan consensus 12
Managerialism 13
Centralisation 13
Penal populism 14
Criminology in Britain 15
Further reading 18

2 Crime and punishment in history **20**
Introduction 22
The emergence of a modern criminal justice system 23
Policing 23
The 'new police' 26
Resistance and reform 27
Into the twentieth century 29
The victim and prosecution 30
The formalisation of the prosecution process 31
The courts 33
The decline of the profit motive 33
Punishment 35
Capital punishment 35
Transportation 37
Imprisonment 38
Probation 40
Crime and violence in history 42
Levels of crime 42
Perceptions of crime 43
Questions for further discussion 46
Further reading 46
Websites 47

3 Crime data and crime trends **48**
Introduction 50
Measuring crime 50
Official statistics 51
England and Wales: criminal statistics 52

United States: uniform crime reports 52
Assessing official statistics 53
The impact of legislation 55
Understanding attrition 56
Limitations of official statistics 60
Victimization surveys 61
The British Crime Survey 62
Local crime surveys 65
Other victimization surveys 67
Assessing victimization surveys 67
Comparing official statistics and victimization surveys 68
Crime trends 69
Data on offenders 76
Self-report studies 77
Assessing the self-report method 78
Questions for further discussion 79
Further reading 80
Websites 80

4 Crime and the media **82**
Introduction 84
Academic study of the media 84
Media representations of crime 85
Newsworthiness 85
The crime content in the media 86
Violent crime in the news 88
Are the media criminogenic? 90
Media effects 92
Media and fear of crime 93
Moral panics 94
Mods and rockers 95
Drug use and deviancy amplification 97
Mugging 98
Criticisms of moral panic theory 99
Policing and the media 100
The relationship between the police and the media 101
The representation of policing 102
Crime and the internet 104
Policing cybercrime 107
Representing terror 107
Questions for further discussion 109
Further reading 109
Websites 110

Part 2 Understanding Crime: theories and concepts   111

5   Classicism and positivism   112

Introduction   114
Classical criminology   114
  Beccaria   116
  Jeremy Bentham   117
  The impact of classicism   118
Positivism and criminology   120
  Defining positivism   121
  Cesare Lombroso   122
  Ferri and Garofalo   125
  Charles Goring   126
  Somatyping   127
  The impact of positivism   128
Questions for further discussion   129
Further reading   129
Websites   129

6   Biological positivism   130

Introduction   132
Genetic factors   132
  Eugenics and 'feeble-mindedness'   133
  Twin studies   135
  Adoption   136
  Chromosomal anomalies   137
  Genetics and offending   138
Biochemical factors   138
  Central nervous system   138
  ADHD and brain dysfunction   139
  Neurostrasmitters   140
  Laterality   141
  Autonomic nervous system   141
  Hormones/testosterone   141
  Nutrition   142
Assessing biological positivism   143
Questions for further discussion   144
Further reading   144
Websites   144

7   Psychological positivism   146

Introduction   148
Psychoanalysis and crime   148
  Bowlby and maternal deprivation   150
Learning theories   151
  Differential association   151
  Operant learning   152
  Social learning theory   153
  Rational choice   156
    Routine activity theory   157
Cognitive theories   157
  Yochelson and Samenow   157
  Piaget, Kohlberg, moral

development and offending   159
  Eysenck's biosocial theory   161
  Intelligence and offending   163
Assessing psychological positivism   165
Questions for further discussion   166
Further reading   166
Websites   166

8   Durkheim, anomie and strain   168

Introduction   170
Durkheim and criminology   170
  Durkheim and social change   171
  Durkheim, suicide and anomie   172
  Assessing Durkheim   174
  Merton and anomie   174
    Anomie and the 'American
    dream'   175
  Assessing Merton's anomie theory   178
Later strain theory   180
  Cloward and Ohlin   180
  General strain theory   181
  Messner and Rosenfeld   182
Assessing strain theory   183
Questions for further discussion   184
Further reading   185
Websites   185

9   The Chicago School, culture and subcultures   186

Introduction   188
The Chicago School   188
  Social ecology   190
  Chicago School and crime   190
    The zonal hypothesis   191
    Shaw and McKay: cultural
    transmission   192
    Chicago Area Project   193
  Differential association   193
    Differential reinforcement   194
  Assessing the Chicago School   195
Cultures and subcultures   196
  Albert Cohen   197
  Cloward and Ohlin   198
  David Matza   199
  Subcultural theory   199
  American subcultural theory   199
  British subcultural theory   201
  Assessing subcultural theory   204
Questions for further discussion   207
Further reading   207
Websites   207

10 Labelling and subcultural theory   208

Introduction   210
The emergence of labelling theory   213

Primary and secondary deviance 213
Becker's outsiders 214
   Moral entrepreneurship 214
   Becoming a marijuana user 215
Stigma 217
Self-fulfilling prophecy 218
Deviancy amplification 218
   Folk devils and moral panics 218
Braithwaite and 'shaming' 219
Assessing labelling theories 220
Questions for further discussion 223
Further reading 224
Websites 224

11 Control theories 226

Introduction 228
Reckless's containment theory 229
   Inner containment 230
Neutralisation and drift theory 230
   Drift 231
Social bond theory 231
   Four elements of the social bond 232
   Testing social bond theory 233
Gottfredson and Hirschi's general
theory of crime 234
   Low self-control 234
   Assessing the general theory of
   crime 237
Tittle's control-balance theory 238
   Relating control-balance to crime 239
Assessing control theory 241
Questions for further discussion 242
Further reading 242
Websites 242

12 Radical and critical criminology 244

Introduction 246
   Crime and the underdog 246
Marx and Marxism 246
   Willem Bonger 248
American radicalism 250
   Vold and criminalisation 250
   Austin Turk 250
   William Chambliss 251
   From conflict to peacemaking 252
Radical criminology in Britain 254
   The new criminology 255
   Contemporary radical criminology 256
   Zemiology 258
Assessing radical criminology 258
   Teleology 258
   Determinism 259
   Idealism 259
Questions for further discussion 260
Further reading 260
Websites 260

13 Realist criminology 262

Introduction 264
Left realism 264
   The critique of 'left idealism' 264
   The nature of left realism 266
   What is to be done about law and
   order? 267
   Left realism and method 267
   Assessing left realism 268
Right realism 270
   'Thinking About Crime' 270
   Distinguishing left and right
   realism 270
Wilson and Herrnstein 272
   Murray and the 'underclass' 273
   Assessing right realism 275
Questions for further discussion 276
Further reading 276
Websites 276

14 Contemporary classicism 278

Introduction 280
Rational choice theory 280
   Clarke and Cornish 281
   Bounded rationality 282
   Crime scripts 283
Routine activity theory 286
   Routine activity and crime trends 286
   Routine activity theory elaborated 288
Situational crime prevention 290
   Defensible space and problem-
   oriented policing 290
      Problem-oriented policing 292
   Crime and opportunity 292
Crime science 294
Assessing contemporary classicism 295
Questions for discussion 297
Further reading 297
Websites 297

15 Feminist criminology 298

Introduction 300
Early criminology and the female offender 301
   Lombroso and Ferrero 301
   W.I. Thomas and Otto Pollak 302
   Sociological criminology and the
   continued invisibility of women 303
The development of modern feminist
criminology 305
   Female emancipation and crime 305
   Carol Smart and feminist
   criminology 306
Contemporary feminist criminology 308
   Understanding women's

involvement in crime   309
Women, prison and punishment   311
    The nature of women's
    imprisonment   311
    The criminalisation of women   313
A feminist methodology?   313
    Feminist victimology   314
Assessing feminist criminology   314
Questions for further discussion   316
Further reading   316
Websites   317

**16 Late modernity, governmentality
and risk**   **318**

The transition to late modernity   320
    Surveillance   320
    Changes in property relations   321
    A new regulatory state?   322
Foucault and governmentality   323
    Discipline and Punish   324
    Governmentality theory   325
    The dispersal of discipline   327
    The discipline of Disney World   328
Risk and the new culture of control   329
    Garland and the culture of control   330
    Risk, crime and criminal justice   333
Assessing governmentality, the new
penology and risk   334
    Governmentality   336
    The new penology   336
    Risk   337
Questions for further discussion   338
Further reading   338
Websites   338

**Part 3 Understanding Crime:
types and trends**   **339**

17 Victims, victimization and victimology **340**

Understanding victims and
victimology   342
    The victim of crime   342
    The emergence of victimology   344
        Victim-precipitation   345
        Victim-blaming   346
    Approaches to victimology   346
        Positivist victimology   346
        Radical victimology   347
        Critical victimology   347
The nature of victimization   348
    The extent of victimization   348
        Repeat victimization   349
    Victimization and the vulnerable   351
        Victimization and the homeless   351
        Victimization and the elderly   352
    The impact of victimization   353

Physical impact   354
Behavioural impact   354
Emotional/psychological impact   354
Financial impact   355
Fear of crime   355
Victims policy   358
    Criminal injuries compensation   358
    Court-ordered compensation   359
    Feminism and 'secondary victimization' 359
    Child abuse   361
    Victim support   363
    Victims' rights?   364
        One stop shop and victim
        statements   365
        Rebalancing the criminal justice
        system?   365
Questions for further discussion   367
Further reading   367
Websites   368

18 White-collar and corporate crime   **370**

Introduction   372
    Edwin Sutherland and white-collar
    crime   373
Exploring white-collar crime   377
    Theft at work   378
    Fraud   378
    Employment offences   380
    Consumer offences   381
    Food offences   382
    Environmental crime   383
    State-corporate crime   384
Explaining white-collar and
corporate crime   385
    Differential association   385
    Self-control   385
    Neutralisation   385
    Critical theory   386
    Shaming   387
Understanding white-collar crime   388
    White-collar offenders   388
Victims of white-collar crime   390
The extent of white-collar crime   393
The impact of white-collar crime   394
    Understanding impact: the
    qualitative dimension   395
Controlling white-collar crime   397
    Regulating white-collar crime   399
    Self regulation   401
Questions for further discussion   402
Further reading   402
Websites   403

19 Organised crime   **404**

Defining organised crime   406

Traditional forms of organised crime   408
  The Mafia   408
  Triads   409
  The Yakuza   409
Organised crime in America   409
  The organisation of organised
  crime   411
    An alien conspiracy theory   413
    The ethnic succession thesis   413
  How organised was American organised
  crime?   414
Organised crime in Britain   417
Transnational organised crime   420
  Human trafficking and migrant
  smuggling   421
  Drugs trafficking   425
Transnational crime control   429
  Transnational policing   429
    Europol   430
Understanding organised crime   431
Questions for further discussion   433
Further reading   433
Websites   433

20 Violent and property crime   434

Understanding violent crime   436
Types of violent crime   438
  Homicide   438
    Trends in homicide   439
    Homicide offenders   439
    Victims of homicide   441
    Motive and relationship   442
    Use of weapons   442
    Homicide and social status   444
    Serial killers   444
  Robbery   446
    Armed robbery   446
    Street robbery   448
  Sexual offences   450
    Stalking   451
    Monitoring sex offenders   453
  Violent crime and weapons   454
  Trends in violent crime   456
    Contemporary trends   458
Property crime   458
  Trends in property crime   459
Burglary   460
  Trends in burglary   460
  Distraction burglary   462
  Burglars on burglary   462
  Crimes against retail and
  manufacturing premises   463
  Car crime   465
    Injuries and deaths on the road   465
    Measuring car crime   466
    Joyriding   467
Thinking about violent and

volume crime   469
Questions for further discussion   469
Further reading   470
Websites   470

21 Drugs and alcohol   472

Introduction   474
What are drugs?   475
  Changing official attitudes
  toward drugs   477
Who uses drugs?   480
  Trends in drug use   482
    The normalisation debate   482
Drugs and crime   484
  Drug use causes crime   485
  Crime causes drug use   486
  A common cause?   486
  A reciprocal relationship?   487
  No causal relationship?   487
Drugs and criminal justice   488
  Drug courts, DTTOs and coerced
  treatment   489
  Drug testing   491
  Drugs and policing   493
    Lambeth cannabis experiment   496
Alcohol   498
  Patterns of consumption   498
  Young people and alcohol   504
  Young people, alcohol and moral
  panic   503
    Binge drinking   504
  Alcohol, crime and criminal justice   504
    The legal situation   504
    Alcohol and crime   505
    Costs of alcohol misuse and
    alcohol-related crime   508
    Government alcohol policy   508
Drugs, alcohol and crime   511
Questions for further discussion   512
Further reading   512
Websites   512

**Part 4 Understanding
Criminal Justice   513**

22 Penology and punishment   514

What is punishment?   516
Utilitarian or consequentialist
approaches   518
  Deterrence   518
    General deterrence   518
    Individual deterrence   519
  Rehabilitation   520
  Incapacitation   521
Retributivism   524

Just deserts 524
The sociology of punishment 527
  Emile Durkheim 527
  Max Weber 529
  Marxism 530
  Norbert Elias 531
  Michel Foucault 532
    The impact of Foucault 534
Conclusion: an era of mass
incarceration? 535
Questions for further discussion 537
Further reading 538
Websites 538

23 Understanding criminal justice   540

Government and criminal justice 542
  Home Office 543
    Home Secretary 544
  Ministry of Justice 545
  Office of the Attorney General 545
The criminal justice system 546
  Major agencies, organisations
  and actors 546
    The police 546
    Crown Prosecution Service 546
    Probation Service 546
    Youth Offending Teams 546
    Prisons 546
    Legal Services Commission (LSC) 546
    Criminal courts 546
    Criminal Cases Review
    Commission 547
    Crime and Disorder Reduction
    Partnerships 547
    Criminal Injuries Compensation
    Authority (CICA) 547
    Forensic Science Service (FSS) 547
    Parole Board 548
  Volunteers in the criminal justice
  system 548
  Is it really a system? 549
  The criminal justice process 550
    Fixed-penalty notices 551
  Expenditure and employment 551
Management and oversight in
criminal justice 553
  New public management 553
  Youth Justice Board 554
  Inspectorates 555
    Her Majesty's Inspectorate of
    Constabulary for England, Wales
    and Northern Ireland (HMIC) 555
    Her Majesty's Inspectorate of
    Court Administration (HMICA) 555
    Her Majesty's Crown Prosecution
    Service Inspectorate (HMCPSI) 555

    Her Majesty's Inspectorate of
    Prisons for England and Wales
    (HMIP) 555
    Her Majesty's Inspectorate of
    Probation for England and Wales
    (HMI Probation) 555
    Prisons and Probation
    Ombudsman 556
    Independent Police Complaints
    Commission 556
  Politics and criminal justice reform 556
Understanding criminal justice 557
  Adversarial versus inquisitorial
  systems 557
  Due process versus crime control 559
Questions for further discussion 561
Further reading 562
Websites 562

24 Crime prevention and community safety   564

Defining crime prevention 566
Crime prevention as a policy issue 566
  'Five Towns' and 'Safer Cities' 568
  Neighbourhood Watch 568
  From crime prevention to
  community safety 569
  Crime and Disorder Act 1998 570
  From community safety to crime
  reduction 570
  Reviewing the Crime and
  Disorder Act 573
Anti-social behaviour 574
  Broken Windows 575
  The anti-social behaviour and
  respect agendas 576
Crime prevention in practice 577
Situational crime prevention 578
  Displacement 582
Social and community crime
prevention 583
  Criminality prevention 583
    Risk-focused prevention 584
    The Perry Pre-School Project 584
    Cognitive-behavioural
    interventions with young
    people 585
  Community approaches 585
    Operation Ceasefire 585
    Mentoring 587
Analysis for crime prevention 588
  Hot spots 589
  Repeat victimization 589
    Kirkholt Burglary Prevention
    Project 591

Questions for further discussion	593
Further reading	594
Websites	594

25 The police and policing   596

The organisation of policing	598
Understanding policing	602
What do the police do?	602
Criminal investigation	603
National Intelligence Model (NIM)	604
Investigation and forensics	605
Police powers	606
Stop and search	607
Arrest	607
Detention at the police station	608
Right of silence	610
Models of policing	611
Community policing	612
Problem-oriented policing	612
Intelligence-led policing	612
A brief history of policing	613
Emergence of the 'new police'	613
The Royal Commission on the Police	614
Problems of legitimacy	615
Centralisation	616
Key themes in policing	617
Police culture	617
Zero-tolerance policing	619
Police corruption	622
The causes of police corruption	623
Police governance	626
Plural policing	629
A revolution in policing?	632
Questions for further discussion	634
Further reading	634
Websites	634

26 Criminal courts and the court process   636

Introduction	636
The Crown Prosecution Service (CPS)	638
Sufficient evidence	638
The public interest	639
Downgrading of charges	640
Discontinuance	641
Magistrates' courts	641
The magistracy	641
The Crown Court	642
The judiciary	643
Juries	644
Pre-trial decisions	645
Bail and remand	645
Bail	646
Remand	647

Offending while on bail	648
Mode of trial decision	649
Defendants' rights	650
Pleas and bargaining	651
Charge bargaining	651
Plea bargaining	652
Evidence	653
Disclosure	653
Exclusion	654
Appeals	654
Miscarriages of justice	655
Criminal Cases Review Commission (CCRC)	656
Questions for further discussion	657
Further reading	657
Websites	657

27 Sentencing and non-custodial penalties   658

Introduction	660
Types of sentence	660
Discharges	661
Fines and other financial penalties	661
Community punishment	661
The Community Rehabilitation Order	661
The Community Punishment Order	661
The Community Order	662
The suspended sentence of imprisonment	662
Sentencing policy	663
The Criminal Justice Act 1991	664
Sentencing reform after the 1991 Act	666
The Crime (Sentences) Act 1997	667
Sentencing reform under New Labour	667
The Auld Review of Criminal Courts	668
The Halliday Review	668
Justice For All	669
Criminal Justice Act 2003	669
Trends in non-custodial sentencing	670
Probation	673
Punishment in the community	674
Crime, Justice and Protecting the Public	675
New Labour and probation	676
The probation service and 'what works'	676
A national probation service	677
The Carter Review and the emergence of NOMS	678
Conclusion	680

Questions for further discussion   680
Further reading   681
Websites   681

28 Prisons and imprisonment   682

The rise of the prison   684
  Imprisonment in Britain   685
  Prison security   686
  Strangeways and Woolf   689
Trends in imprisonment   690
  Imprisonment and penal politics   694
International trends   695
  Capital punishment   698
The prison system   700
  Types of prison   700
  Private prisons   701
Life on the inside   702
  Prisoners   703
    Incarceration and social
    exclusion   705
    Violence in prison   705
  Prison officers   707
Release from prison   709
Governance, accountability and
human rights   709
  Independent inspection   710
  Grievance or complaints procedures   710
  Human rights and imprisonment   711
Questions for further discussion   713
Further reading   713
Websites   713

29 Youth crime and youth justice   714

Youth crime   717
  Persistent young offenders   718
  Trends in youth crime   720
  Ethnic minority youth and crime   720
  Drug use and crime   721
  Victimization   724
Youth justice   725
  Childhood and punishment   725
  Emergence of a juvenile justice
  system   726
  The tide turns   727
  The punitive shift   728
  The rise of managerialism   730
  A new youth justice?   731
  Youth Offending Teams (YOTs)   731
  Non-custodial penalties   731
  Anti-social behaviour   732
  Referral orders   733
  Youth Offender Panels (YOPs)   734
Contemporary youth justice   734
  Anti-social behaviour   735
    Criticisms of the anti-social behaviour
    agenda   735

  Young people and imprisonment   737
  Community alternatives   739
  Referral orders and restorative
  youth justice   739
  Young people, crime and justice   740
Questions for further discussion   741
Further reading   741
Websites   741

30 Restorative justice   742

Introduction   744
  Conflicts as property   744
Criminal justice and restorative
justice   746
Defining restorative justice   747
The objectives of restorative justice   748
  Victim involvement   748
  Community involvement   749
  Offender reintegration   750
Types of restorative justice   751
  Court-based restitutive and
  reparative measures   751
  Victim–offender mediation (VOM)   752
  Family group conferencing   753
  Healing and sentencing circles   756
    Healing circles   756
    Sentencing circles   756
  Citizens' panels and community
  boards   757
Assessing restorativeness   758
The limits of restorative justice?   760
  Restorative justice and corporate
  crime   760
  Restorative justice and domestic
  violence   761
Assessing restorative justice   763
Questions for further discussion   767
Further reading   767
Websites   767

Part 5 Critical Issues in Criminology   769

31 Race, crime and justice   770

Introduction   772
Sources of data   772
Ethnicity and victimization   773
  Victimization and risk   773
  Fear of crime   774
  Racist hate crimes   774
    Racist offenders   778
  Community, conflict and cohesion   779
Ethnicity and offending   780
  Self-reported offending   781

'Anti-social behaviour'   783
Drug use   784
Experience of the criminal justice
system   785
    Stop and search   785
        Racism and stop and search   787
    Ethnicity and policing   788
        From Scarman to Lawrence   789
    Cautioning, arrest and sentencing   791
    Ethnicity and imprisonment   793
        Treatment in custody   794
        Deaths in custody   795
    Views of the criminal justice system   796
Minority representation in the
criminal justice system   798
Questions for further discussion   801
Further reading   801
Websites   802

32 Gender, crime and justice   804

Female and male offending   806
    Reasons for offending   808
Women and the criminal justice
process   810
    Cautioning, arrest and prosecution   810
    The use of custody   811
    Women in prison   813
        Mothers in prison   815
    Understanding women and
    criminal justice   817
    Women in the criminal justice
    system: the future   818
Victimization   818
    Fear of crime   819
    Violence against women   819
        Domestic violence   820
        The perpetrators   821
    Policing rape and domestic
    violence   822
        Policy changes   823
    Attrition   825
Women's role in social control   828
    Women in the police   828
    Women in the probation service   830
    Women as prison officers   830
    Women and the legal professions   830
Masculinities, men and victimization   831
    Male victimization   832
Conclusion   833
Questions for further discussion   834
Further reading   834
Websites   834

33 Criminal and forensic psychology   836

Psychology and criminology   838

History of psychology and
criminology   839
Individual factors in crime   840
    Risk factors and crime   841
        Individual factors   841
        Family factors   841
        Socioeconomic, peer, school and
        community factors   842
    Developmental or life course
    criminology   843
        Sampson and Laub   843
        Moffitt's theory of offending
        types   844
Mental disorder and crime   845
    The prevalence of mental disorders   845
    Mental disorder and offending   846
    Understanding mental disorder
    and crime   846
Policing and psychology   847
    Offender profiling   847
        Assessing profiling   850
        Legal and ethical issues   851
    Interrogation   852
        Confessions   853
    Lying and lie detection   854
        Statement validity analysis   856
The courtroom and psychology   856
    Recall/eyewitness testimony   856
    Vulnerable witnesses   857
        Children as witnesses   858
    Juries   859
        Juries and evidence   859
        Juries and other factors   860
        Jury composition   860
        Decision-making   861
Treatment of offenders and
'What Works'   861
        Cognitive skills programmes   862
Questions for further discussion   864
Further reading   864
Websites   864

**34 Globalisation, terrorism and human
rights   866**

Globalisation   868
    Globalisation and criminology   869
    Criminalising migration   869
Terrorism   871
    What is terrorism?   871
    Terrorism in Britain   872
    The new international terrorism   873
    Special powers for special
    circumstances?   874
        Control orders and the PATRIOT
        Act   875

Terrorism and the 'New Wars'   875
   Private military industry   876
   Privatised security in Iraq   877
State crime   878
   Genocide   879
      Cambodia   880
      Rwanda   880
      Bosnia   881
   War as crime and war crimes   882
Human Rights   883
   Origins of human rights   883
      Human rights in the twentieth
      century   884
   Human rights in Britain   886
      The Human Rights Act 1998   886
      The impact of the Human
      Rights Act   888
   Criminology and human rights   890
   Dealing with human rights abuses   891
   Advantages and disadvantages of
   different tribunals   892
Questions for further discussion   892
Further reading   893
Websites   893

Part 6 Doing Criminology   895

35 Understanding criminological research   896

Introduction   898
Research methods   898
   Surveys   899
      Questionnaire design   901
   Interviews   903
   Focus groups   905
   Ethnography   907
   Documentary analysis   910
   Case studies   911
Sampling   911

Random (or probability) sampling   912
   Stratified sampling   912
   Quota sampling   913
   Purposive sampling   913
   Convenience sampling   913
   Snowball sampling   913
Statistics   914
   Descriptive statistics   914
   Numerical and categorical data   915
   Normal distribution   916
   Correlation   916
   Probability and significance   916
Controversy: evaluation and
experimentation   917
   Experimental methods   917
   Quasi-experimental methods   918
   Evaluation research   918
Questions for further discussion   921
Further reading   921
Websites   922

36 Doing criminological research   924

Introduction   926
Choosing a topic   926
Doing a literature review   929
Selecting methods   931
Theory and method   931
   Hypothetico-deductive theory   931
   Grounded theory   932
Negotiating access   933
Research governance/ethics   935
Pilot research   936
Writing   937
   Beginning to write   938
   Write clearly   938
   Decent prose   938
Plagiarism   940
Time management   940
Further reading   942

Acknowledgements

It hardly needs saying that writing this book was a mammoth task and that it would not have been possible without a lot of help and support. A great number of colleagues have provided advice and encouragement – as the list of those who kindly read drafts of parts of this book indicates. For the past five years I have had the good fortune to work at the Mannheim Centre for Criminology at the London School of Economics with a number of wonderful colleagues. I have benefited hugely from conversations with, and teaching alongside: Stan Cohen, David Downes, Frances Heidensohn, Dick Hobbs, Niki Lacey, Jill Peay, Coretta Phillips, Paddy Rawlinson, Robert Reiner, Declan Roche, Paul Rock, Judith Rumgay, Mike Shiner and David Smith.

There is more to producing a text such as this than getting a few words down on paper. A huge amount of planning, organisation, design and research is necessary, and Brian Willan has been absolutely central at every stage. From initial conversations all the way through to final decisions about content and style, Brian has been a hugely creative presence. He has been unfailingly patient and supportive, and always remained outwardly calm when he must have wondered whether I was going to deliver. The description 'publisher' doesn't do justice to Brian's contribution to this project and I would like to record my thanks to him.

There are also a considerable number of people working within, or linked to, Willan Publishing to whom I am enormously grateful. Emma Gubb searched photographic libraries and elsewhere and sourced a range of wonderful images. Along with Rebecca Cheshire, James Lillywhite, Simone Stanbrooke-Byrne and Julia Willan, she also did a huge amount of work in the final stages of compiling the bibliography.

Over a period of six to eight weeks in June/July 2007 I developed a close, electronic working relationship with Nick Hutchins who had the unenviable task of reading and copy-editing the entire typescript. The whole process was done remarkably quickly and with great skill. I know he saved me from many errors, and that he was tactful enough not to draw most of them to my attention. Michelle and Bill Antrobus at Deer Park Productions coordinated the production of the book with their usual efficiency.

My greatest debt is to my family. Whenever one writes a book the temptation is to bang on about it a bit. When it's half a million words long there is every danger that those to whom one is closest will be completely fed up with it long before it is finished. Consequently, I cannot thank my family enough for all they do for me. My wife, Mary, is an inspiration. Her strength and encouragement make everything possible and I'm hugely grateful to be able to share my life with her and our children – Gavin, Robin, Lewis and Owen. To have a large family is an extraordinary privilege, and I would like here to record my thanks to: my brother, David, and Lynne and Alex; Cathy and Terry; Hartley, Pilar and Daniel; Ruth, Hannah and Pablo; Susan, Martin, Rosemary, Harry and Lizzie; Olive, Rufus, Sara and Nigel; and Peter and Nilda. The last year or so has been a very difficult one for both my Mum and Dad and I continue to be amazed by their fortitude, thankful for their love and support, and grateful for their presence. This book is dedicated to them.

Academic review

A large number of people read drafts of individual, and sometimes several, chapters of this book and also reviewed the original scheme for it. Their feedback was enormously helpful, saving me from many errors and oversights and drawing to my attention much work that I would otherwise have missed. Crucially, in a number of cases the strength of their arguments helped reorient the thrust of a chapter and improve it significantly. I am hugely grateful to all of the colleagues listed below for their time, thoughtfulness and expertise. I may not always have succeeded in improving the text precisely as they would have liked but I have certainly sought to do justice to their comments. I thank them all.

Dr Jill Annison, University of Plymouth
Dr Jenny Ardley, De Montfort University
Dr Liz Austen, Sheffield Hallam University
Jamie Bennett, HM Prison Service
Dr Nigel Brearley, Southampton Solent University
Dr Ian Bridgeman, University of Bedfordshire
Dr Fiona Brookman, University of Glamorgan
Anne Brunton, University of Surrey/ London School of Economics
Dr Robin Bryant, Canterbury Christ Church University
Prof Rob Canton, De Montfort University
Cecilia Cappel, Kingston University
Dr Neil Chakraborti, University of Leicester
Helen Codd, University of Central Lancashire
Dr David Cox, Keele University
Dr Don Crewe, Roehampton University
Prof Hazel Croall, Glasgow Caledonian University
Dr Pam Davies, Northumbria University
Prof Nick Dorn, Cardiff University
Rod Earle, London School of Economics
Dr Stephanie Eaton, Kingston University
Dave Edwards, London South Bank University
Prof Nigel Fielding, University of Surrey
Dr Theresa A. Gannon, University of Kent
Dr Jon Garland, University of Leicester
Dr Daniel Gilling, University of Plymouth
Prof Barry Godfrey, Keele University

Prof Penny Green, University of Westminster
Dr Chris Greer, City University, London
Dr Kevin Haines, University of Swansea
Dr Nathan Hall, University of Portsmouth
Dr Lynn Hancock, University of Liverpool
Dr Jamie Harding, Northumbria University
Prof Frances Heidensohn, London School of Economics
Prof Simon Holdaway, University of Sheffield
Dr Katy Holloway, University of Glamorgan
Prof Mike Hough, King's College London
Prof Barbara Hudson, University of Central Lancashire
Prof Gordon Hughes, Cardiff University
Dr Zoe James, University of Plymouth
Dr Janet Jamieson, University of Lancaster
Prof Yvonne Jewkes, University of Leicester
Phil Johnson, The East Lancashire Institute of Higher Education
Dr Helen Johnston, University of Hull
Prof Gerry Johnstone, University of Hull
Dr Jane Jones, University of Chester
Dr David W. Jones, University of East London
Dr Peter Joyce, Manchester Metropolitan University
Dr Maria Kaspersson, University of Greenwich
Paul Kiff, University of East London
Dr Paul Lawrence, The Open University

Dr Maggy Lee, University of Essex
Charlie Lloyd, Joseph Rowntree Foundation
Iolo Madoc-Jones, North East Wales Institute of Higher Education
Emma Martin, University of Teesside
Dr Paul Mason, Cardiff University
Dr Rob Mawby, University of Central England, Birmingham
Prof Rob Mawby, University of Plymouth
Malcolm McDowell, University of Huddersfield
Prof Kieran McEvoy, Queen's University, Belfast
Prof James McGuire, University of Liverpool
Dr Nikki McKenzie, University of the West of England, Bristol
Tanya Miles-Berry, Sheffield Hallam University
Dr Andrew Millie, University of Loughbrough
Dr Aogán Mulcahy, University College, Dublin
Dr Gabe Mythen, University of Liverpool
Dr David Nash, Oxford Brookes University
Prof Mike Nellis, University of Strathclyde
Jane Nolan, University of Glamorgan
Nicola Padfield, University of Cambridge
Dr Francis Pakes, University of Portsmouth
Dr Emma Palmer, University of Leicester
Prof Geoffrey Pearson, Goldsmiths College, University of London
Prof Ken Pease, University of Loughbrough
Dr David Porteous, Middlesex University
Prof Maurice Punch, London School of Economics
Janet Ransom, London Metropolitan University
Dr Declan Roche, Office of the Australian Government Solicitor
Prof Paul Rock, London School of Economics
John Rotherham, St Helens College
Dr Michael Rowe, Victoria University of Wellington

Dr Judith Rumgay, London School of Economics
Dr Teela Sanders, University of Leeds
Dr David Scott, University of Central Lancashire
Dr Kerry Sheldon, University of Gloucestershire
Dr Marisa Silvestri, London South Bank University
Dr Michael Shiner, London School of Economics
Dr Mark Simpson, University of Teesside
Dr Mervyn Sinclair, Buckinghamshire Chilterns University College
Prof Roger Smith, De Montfort University
Dr Jon Spencer, University of Manchester
Prof Peter Squires, University of Brighton
Dr Katie Strudwick, University of Lincoln
Dr Julie Taylor, St Martins College, Carlisle
Prof Nick Tilley, Nottingham Trent University
Prof Steve Tombs, Liverpool John Moores University
Dr Stephen Tong, Canterbury Christ Church University
Dr Barry Vaughan, Institute of Public Administration, Dublin
Dr Dave Waddington, Sheffield Hallam University
Prof P.A.J. Waddington, University of Wolverhampton
Dr Alison Wakefield, City University
Prof Clive Walker, University of Leeds
Prof Sandra Walklate, University of Liverpool
Dr Colin Webster, Leeds Metropolitan University
Dr Nicole Westmarland, University of Durham
Dr Dave Whyte, University of Liverpool
Dr Lorraine Wolhuter, University of Wolverhampton
Dr Dominic Wood, Canterbury Christ Church University
Prof Alan Wright, University of Central England, Birmingham
Prof Richard Young, University of Bristol

Preface

This book is intended for the new, or relatively new, student of criminology. As such the aim is to be accessible and engaging and to this end the book contains a number of features which should help the reader get the most from the text. A look at the shelves of most academic bookshops might reasonably lead you to ask why there is a need for another textbook on criminology. Although the criminology student is now hugely well served by books – both general and specific – it seemed to me that there was still the need for a book that would be as comprehensive as possible, and would introduce students to theory, to research and to some of the crucial aspects of doing criminology for themselves.

What this book covers
The aim, within the confines of this single volume, is to cover as much of the territory that we label 'criminology' as possible. In what follows, therefore, you will be introduced to the full range of criminological theories, as well as to all the main substantive topics you are likely to confront in an undergraduate degree (and a great many you will cover in postgraduate studies). Moreover, the objective has been to try to take a broad approach to criminology itself. Criminology is a multi-disciplinary subject which attracts historians, sociologists, psychologists, lawyers, geographers and others. By training, I am a sociologist and also much influenced by the sociological traditions of contemporary British criminology. The book, however, seeks to pay due regard to psychological approaches to criminology, to the importance of history – to an understanding of the present as well as the past – and to the other main tributaries which make up the subject.

How the book is organised
Each of the chapters is designed to stand alone. The intention is that you should be able to pick a topic – policing, say – and get an overview of the major debates and ideas in that area from reading that single chapter. However, there is also much to be gained from reading 'sideways' – looking for material in other chapters which will support the material in the substantive area you are focusing on. Thus, sticking with policing, there is material on this subject in other chapters, such as those on history, crime prevention and community safety, organised crime and so on. Similarly, there are arguments and debates – for example around such things as risk, late modernity, the position of women or ethnic minorities and many others – that run right through the volume. Wherever appropriate – without it becoming too tedious – I have inserted suggestions in the text about which other chapters one might turn to in relation to each of the major topics.

Graphs and tables
As you will see the book contains a great number of graphs and tables. This is something you will rarely find in criminology textbooks. Much of my career has been spent as a professional researcher – a lot of it outside universities – and I am of the firm belief that it is important for students to be introduced both to theoretical ideas and to empirical data. I have kept the graphs, tables and other data very simple and wherever there is any complexity I have sought to explain it in the text. All data have limitations and you should read the chapters on criminological data and research methods to help you develop the critical tools you need in order to understand these limitations and apply sensible judgements to the material presented. Some of the data will date but again, wherever possible, I have included guides to where research information is available online. Where there is newly published material, by using these guides you will be able to find the most up-to-date information for yourself.

Review questions and questions for further discussion

As I have suggested, each chapter contains a number of special features. There are two sets of questions in each of the substantive chapters. First, there are 'review questions' inserted at strategic points in the chapter. These are designed to pick up on specific issues or ideas that have been raised in the text and to enable you to check that you have spotted them and understood them. In addition, at the end of each chapter there are 'questions for further discussion'. These are generally broader questions which are designed for classroom-style discussion and to prompt you to think and read more widely.

Further reading

Each of the chapters also contains a guide to further reading. In compiling these I have generally relied on the material that I have found most useful and which, in my view, seem to be the most useful, accessible and important pieces of work for you to follow-up. I have limited the number of suggestions I have made for further reading as the intention is simply to provide you with a starting point. At the end of the book there is a very comprehensive bibliography where you can find full details of all the works cited in this book. Part of the fun of learning a new subject or topic is finding some of the reading for yourself. Should you happen to find things that are enormously helpful which you feel it would have been good to have had in the suggestions for further reading do please let me know.

Using the internet

Finally, the most dramatic change in the ways in which we learn these days is the arrival of the internet. A quite astounding amount of material can now be accessed online – from journals and excerpts from books, to original data and research materials, and blogs. In due course a dedicated website will be established for this book and I will post material on it regularly. Each of the chapters in the book contains a short guide to useful websites. Although I have generally only put in links to the most established and trustworthy sites, it is important to be careful how you use web-based information. Nevertheless, this is a truly rich resource and the guides in each chapter will provide you with the basis for some constructive searching. It is an exciting time to be a student (and a teacher) of criminology and I wish you well in your studies.

Tim Newburn
t.newburn@lse.ac.uk

List of acronyms

ABC	Acceptable Behaviour Contract
ABH	Actual Bodily Harm
ACMD	Advisory Council on the Misuse of Drugs
ACPO	Association of Chief Police Officers
ADHD	Attention-Deficit Hyperactivity Disorder
ADR	Alternative Dispute Resolution
ASB	Anti-Social Behaviour
ASBO	Anti-Social Behaviour Order
ASBU	Anti-Social Behaviour Unit
BAWP	British Association of Women Police
BCS	British Crime Survey
BCU	Basic Command Unit
BSC	British Society of Criminology
CAFCASS	Children and Family Court Advisory and Support Service
CAPI	Computer Assisted Personal Interviewing
CASI	Computer Assisted Self Interviewing
CCCS	Centre for Contemporary Cultural Studies
CCRC	Criminal Cases Review Commission
CDRP	Crime and Disorder Reduction Partnership
CICA	Criminal Injuries Compensation Authority
CICS	Criminal Injuries Compensation Scheme
CJ	Criminal Justice
CJS	Crime and Justice Survey
CPO	Community Punishment Order
CPRO	Community Punishment and Rehabilitation Order
CPS	Crown Prosecution Service
CPT	European Committee for the Prevention of Torture and Inhuman or Degrading Treatment or Punishment
CPTED	Crime Prevention Through Environmental Design
CRE	Commission for Racial Equality
CRO	Community Rehabilitation Order
CRP	Crime Reduction Programme
CSC	Close Supervision Centre
CSO	Community Service Order
DAO	Drug Abstinence Order
DAR	Drug Abstinence Requirement
DCA	Department for Constitutional Affairs
DTO	Detention and Training Order
DTTO	Drug Treatment and Testing Order
DVU	Domestic Violence Unit
ELO	Europol Liaison Officer
FGC	Family Group Conferences
FPN	Fixed Penalty Notice

FSS	Forensic Science Service
GBH	Grievous Bodily Harm
HDC	Home Detention Curfew
HMCPSI	Her Majesty's Crown Prosecution Service Inspectorate
HMI Probation	Her Majesty's Inspectorate of Probation for England and Wales
HMIC	Her Majesty's Inspectorate of Constabulary for England, Wales and Northern Ireland
HMICA	Her Majesty's Inspectorate of Court Administration
HMIP	Her Majesty's Inspectorate of Prisons for England and Wales
HSC	Health and Safety Commission
HSE	Health and Safety Executive
ICC	International Criminal Court
ICPC	International Criminal Police Commission
ICPO	International Criminal Police Organization (Interpol)
ICVS	The International Crime Victim Survey
IPCC	Independent Police Complaints Commission
ISSP	Intensive Supervision and Support Programme
JPPAP	Joint Prisons and Probation Accreditation Panel
LASCH	Local Authority Secure Children's Home
LSC	Legal Services Commission
MAPPA	Multi-Agency Public Protection Arrangements
MAPPP	Multi-Agency Public Protection Panel
MBU	Mother and Baby Unit
MoJ	Ministry of Justice
MPA	Metropolitan Police Authority
MPS	Metropolitan Police Service
MUFTI	Minimum Use of Force Tactical Intervention squad
NAPO	National Association of Probation Officers
NAPSA	National Association of Pretrial Service Agencies
NAVSS	National Association of Victims Support Schemes
NCIS	National Criminal Intelligence Service
NCRS	National Crime Recording Standard
NDC	National Deviancy Conference
NDIU	National Drugs Intelligence Unit
NDPB	Non-Departmental Public Body
NFIU	National Football Intelligence Unit
NICS	Northern Ireland Crime Survey
NIM	National Intelligence Model
NOMS	National Offender Management Service
NoS	Notice of Supervision
NPIA	National Policing Improvement Agency
NPS	National Probation Service
NTORS	National Treatment Outcome Research Study
NW	Neighbourhood Watch
NYPD	New York City Police Department
OCJR	Office for Criminal Justice Reform

OCJS	Offending, Crime and Justice Survey
ONS	Office for National Statistics
PACE	Police and Criminal Evidence Act/Code
PAF	Postal Address File
PBA	Probation Boards' Association
PCSO	Police Community Support Officer
PICTS	the Psychological Inventory of Criminal Thinking Styles
PITO	Police Information Technology Organisation
PND	Penalty Notice for Disorder
POA	Prison Officers Association
POP	Problem-Oriented Policing
PRT	Prison Reform Trust
PSNI	Police Service for Northern Ireland
RCOP	Royal College of Psychiatrists
RCS	Regional Crime Squad
RCT	Randomised Controlled Trial
RISE	Reintegrative Shaming Experiment
RJ	Restorative Justice
ROM	Regional Offender Managers
RUC	Royal Ulster Constabulary
SCO	Special Compliance Office
SCS	Scottish Crime Survey
SCVS	Scottish Crime and Victimization Survey
SEU	Social Exclusion Unit
SFO	Serious Fraud Office
SOCA	Serious and Organised Crime Agency
SSO	Suspended Sentence Order
STC	Secure Training Centre
STC	Secure Training Centres
STCs	secure training centres
STOP	Straight Thinking on Probation
TIC	taken into consideration
TOC	Transnational Organised Crime
TWOC	Taking WithOut Consent (of cars)
UNODC	United Nations Office on Drugs and Crime
VOM	Victim-offender mediation
VORP	Victim Offender Reconciliation Project
VS	Victim Support
WIP	'Women in Prison'
WORP	Women's Offending Reduction Programme
YJB	Youth Justice Board
YLS	Youth Lifestyles Survey
YOI	Young Offenders' Institute
YOP	Youth Offender Panel
YOT	Youth Offending Team
ZTP	Zero-Tolerance Policing

Part 1
Understanding Crime and Criminology

1 Understanding crime and criminology

2 Crime and punishment in history

3 Crime data and crime trends

4 Crime and the media

Chapter outline

What is criminology?   4

An interdisciplinary subject   5

Defining criminology   5

Understanding crime   6

Crime and the criminal law   8

Crime as a social construct   8

Historical variation   9

Crime and politics   11

End of the bipartisan consensus   12

Managerialism   13

Centralisation   13

Penal populism   14

Criminology in Britain   17

Further reading   18

1

Understanding crime and criminology

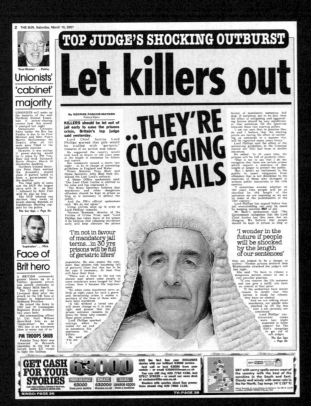

CHAPTER SUMMARY In this chapter we begin the study of criminology. What is this subject, what are its origins and what is its focus? Having considered these questions we move on to look at what is meant by the term 'crime'. As we will see there is a range of ways in which *crime* can be understood. It is, for example, both a legal concept and a socially-constructed one and we will examine these and other ideas. Crime is also something that has become highly politicised in relatively recent times, and we explore elements of the contemporary politics of law and order. The chapter concludes by looking briefly at the history of criminology in Britain, its institutional origins and its recent expansion.

What is criminology?

The fact that we begin with this question assumes that you are new to this subject. Indeed, that is the underlying assumption for this book. The volume is designed as an introduction for students who are studying criminology. I have endeavoured not to make too many assumptions about pre-existing knowledge of the subject and, wherever possible, I will hope to begin from basics and work progressively toward more complex ideas or arguments.

Criminology is a strange beast. With origins in applied medico-legal science, psychiatry, a scientifically-oriented psychology and in nineteenth-century social reform movements, for much of the second half of the twentieth century British criminology has been dominated by sociology. Times are changing again, however, and a new strand of technical and highly policy-oriented 'scientific' criminology is now emerging. During the course of this book you will meet all these variants and should learn how to assess their competing claims.

In a masterly analysis of the emergence and development of criminology in Britain, David Garland (2002: 8) introduces the subject in the following way:

I take criminology to be a specific genre of discourse and inquiry about crime – a genre that has developed in the modern period and that can be distinguished from other ways of talking and thinking about criminal conduct. Thus, for example, criminology's claim to be an empirically-grounded, scientific undertaking sets it apart from moral and legal discourses, while its focus upon crime differentiates it from other social scientific genres, such as the sociology of deviance and control, whose objects of study are broader and not defined by the criminal law. Since the middle years of the twentieth century, criminology has

also been increasingly marked off from other discourses by the trappings of a distinctive identity, with its own journals, professional associations, professorships, and institutes.

In this history, Garland argues that modern criminology is the product of two initially separate streams of work:

- *The 'governmental project'* – empirical studies of the administration of justice; the working of prisons, police and the measurement of crime.
- *The 'Lombrosian project'* – studies which sought to examine the characteristics of 'criminals' and 'non-criminals' with a view to being able to distinguish the groups, thereby developing an understanding of the causes of crime.

During the twentieth century, he suggests, these gradually merged and changed to form the basis for what we recognise these days as *criminology*. The term *criminology* seems first to have been used by Paul Topinard, a Frenchman studying the body types of criminals, though the invention of the term itself is generally credited to an Italian academic lawyer, Raffaele Garofalo. Both are associated with the second stream of work identified above – that Garland names after the Italian scholar, Cesare Lombroso (see Chapter 5). This work, in various forms, was concerned with attempts to identify physical and other characteristics that set criminals apart. Such work varied from the measurement of physical characteristics such as head shape and the shape and size of the jaw and cheekbones, through to work which focused more upon the environmental conditions that produced criminality. Though, by and large, crude attempts to identify and measure characteristics that distinguish criminals from others have largely disappeared, Garland's argument is that one very significant stream of criminology has continued to be concerned with identifying the individual, social and environmental factors that are associated with offending.

An interdisciplinary subject

The first thing that is immediately obvious is just how many disciplinary approaches are utilised within criminology. In this book you will come across work by psychologists, sociologists, political scientists, lawyers, historians, geographers and others, all working within the subject of criminology. Thortsen Sellin, an American criminologist writing in the 1930s, once observed that the 'criminologist does not exist who is an expert in all the disciplines which converge in the study of crime' (Sellin, 1970: 6).

Different disciplines have been dominant at different points in the history of criminology, and there are differing orientations to be found within criminology in different countries. Nevertheless, as you will see as this book progresses, criminology is influenced by, and draws upon, psychology, sociology, legal theory, history and other subjects besides. This raises a number of issues. It means that you will find a number of different approaches being taken to the subject matter within criminology. Moreover, sometimes these approaches will appear rather at odds with each other. This is one of the great challenges within criminology and, though it can occasionally seem daunting, it is one of the characteristics which I think makes the discipline attractive. Linked with this is the question of whether it is appropriate to use the word *discipline* at all. Criminology, as I have suggested draws from disciplines such as psychology and sociology, and there has been quite some debate about whether criminology can lay claim to such status itself.

This is an argument that we cannot resolve here. Indeed, we do not need to spend a lot of time discussing the various positions that have been taken in relation to it. It is enough for current purposes that we are alerted to this issue and bear it in mind as we cover some of the terrain that comes under the heading *criminology*. David Downes once described criminology as a 'rendezvous subject'. He did so precisely to capture the fact that it is an area of study that brings together scholars from a variety of disciplinary origins, who meet in the territory called crime.

There is a further distinction that we must briefly consider, and it concerns *criminology* on the one hand and *criminal justice* on the other. Although the study of the administrative responses to crime is generally seen as being a central part of the criminological enterprise, sometimes the two are separated, particularly in the United States. In America there is something of a divide between those who think of themselves as doing criminology and those who study criminal justice. In fact, the distinction is anything but clear. Criminological work tends to be more theoretically informed than criminal justice studies and also more concerned with crime and its causes. Both, however, have clear concerns with the criminal justice and penal systems. In discussing this distinction, Lacey (2002: 265) suggests that criminology 'concerns itself with social and individual antecedents of crime and with the nature of crime as a social phenomenon', whereas criminal justice studies 'deal with the specifically institutional aspects of the social construction of crime' such as policing, prosecution, punishment and so on. We will consider what is meant by the social construction of crime in more detail below. Before we do so, let us look once more at the parameters of criminology.

Defining criminology

Even the very short discussion so far should have alerted you to the fact that criminology is a complex subject, which has a number of historical roots and, as we will see, a number of quite different approaches in its contemporary guise. On this basis, coming up with a definition of our subject matter is almost certainly not only a difficult task, but quite probably, an impossible one. However, in order to bring a tiny bit more certainty to this rather uncertain terrain, I will borrow an approach to our subject matter first offered by one of the towering figures of twentieth century criminology.

Edwin Sutherland – someone who you will get to meet regularly throughout this book – defined criminology as the study of the making of laws, the breaking of laws, and of society's reaction to the breaking of laws. Whilst this is by no means a comprehensive definition of criminology – criminologists may be interested, for example, in various forms of behaviour that do not involve the breaking of laws but, nevertheless, bring forth some form of social sanction – it does help point us in the direction of what are arguably the three great tributaries that make up the subject:

- The study of crime.
- The study of those who commit crime.
- The study of the criminal justice and penal systems.

Sutherland (1937) went on to argue that the 'objective of criminology is the development of a body of general and verified principles and of other types of knowledge regarding the process of law, crime, and treatment or prevention'. Now, having indicated that this is the general approach that informs much of what follows in this book, I want to pause and look briefly at work that is critical of the very enterprise that is criminology. I do so, not because I think the criticisms that are made are sufficient to make us abandon this project (as you can tell because there are another 1000-odd pages to go before the end of the book), but because they should make us think very carefully about the assumptions that underpin criminology and should make us question the limitations of this particular enterprise.

The critique is associated with what we will come to think of as 'critical criminology' and can be found in various forms since at least the 1970s. A recent exposition (Hillyard and Tombs, 2004) argues for a change of focus away from 'crime' and toward 'social harm'. It does so on the basis of four major lines of criticism:

- *Crime has no ontological reality* – The category 'crime' has no reality beyond the application of the term to particular acts. The acts themselves are not intrinsically criminal. Thus, to kill someone during peacetime may well be treated as murder; to do so on a battlefield will most likely not. We return to this below.

- *Criminology perpetuates the myth of crime* – Despite the criticism above, criminology tends to talk of 'crime' as if the category were relatively unproblematic. The continued attempts to explain the causes of crime are illustrative of this.

- *Crime consists of many petty events* – A great many 'criminal acts' create little physical or financial harm and often involve no victim.

- *Crime excludes many serious harms* – Many things which result in fairly sizeable harm are not dealt with via the criminal law – i.e. are not treated as

'criminal'. One of these might be large-scale tax fraud which is rarely prosecuted.

What is clear from this critique is that criminology's organising focus – *crime* – is potentially a highly contestable and problematic term. In studying criminology this is something we must try not to lose sight of. It was this, in part, that the well-known criminologist Stanley Cohen undoubtedly had in mind, when he said:

> [Criminologists] like leeches, live off a very large body on which they are wholly parasitic. In the same way that our courts, prisons, probation officers and police 'need' crime, so does the criminologist. The gap, though, between the real world of crime and the artificial world of criminology is enormous. One reason for this is that the mere existence of something called criminology perpetuates the illusion that one can have a general theory of crime causation.
>
> (Cohen, 1988: 46)

Understanding crime

Crime, like so many things in our social world, has a certain taken-for-granted or common-sense nature. When we use the term, we assume the category is meaningful; that is, we assume that those to whom we are talking will understand what we're talking about and will tend to use the term in the same way as we do. This, of course, is the basis upon which the social world operates – on assumptions about the taken-for-granted meaningfulness of the vocabulary we use and the behaviours we enact. Yet, as scores of sociologists have illustrated, this shared meaningfulness has to be achieved; it is not *given*.

The apparent orderliness of our world can fairly easily be disturbed. This becomes clear when those with whom we are interacting do not share our assumptions or, alternatively, when they react to what we say or do in ways that we didn't predict, expect or perhaps understand. The word *crime* is used regularly in everyday conversation. That it is used in this manner implies that there is a sufficient level of common understanding. On one level this is undoubtedly the case. However, this masks a number of complexities. As we will see, identifying the boundary between acts that are crimes, and acts which are not crimes is often far from straightforward.

To illustrate this let's consider a couple of examples involving things that might be thought of as *crimes*, both of which involve assault. The first occurs at night time. It is dark and a person is walking alone late at night. They are confronted by a total stranger who asks for money. When refused, the stranger becomes violent. The stranger robs the pedestrian and leaves them needing hospital treatment. There is little doubt that most people, on having this situation described to them, would call what happened 'a crime'. Indeed, in many ways this example represents one of the most common fears that many of us have (Stanko, 1990).

The second example is more unusual. It arises out of the seizure of videotapes during a police raid. One of these videos shows a number of men engaging in fairly extreme sado-masochistic activities, including beatings and genital abrasions. The police launch an investigation (the men in the tape are clearly identifiable) which ends in prosecution despite the fact that the men all argued that they consented to the activities. Indeed, all freely gave statements to the police believing themselves not to have done anything *criminal*. Were they right? This, in fact, is a real case. In what subsequently became known as the 'Spanner case', 16

The Spanner case

During a raid in 1987 the police seized a videotape which showed a number of identifiable men engaging in heavy sado-masochistic (SM) activities including beatings, genital abrasions and lacerations. The police claim that they immediately started a murder investigation because they were convinced that the men were being killed. This investigation is rumoured to have cost £4 million. Dozens of gay men were interviewed. The police learned that none of the men in the video had been murdered, or even suffered injuries which required medical attention.

The verdicts

In December 1990, 16 of the men pleaded guilty on legal advice to a number of offences and were sent to jail, given suspended jail sentences or fined. The men's defence was based on the fact that they had all consented to the activities. But Judge Rant, in a complex legal argument, decided that the activities in which they engaged fell outside the exceptions to the law of assault.

A number of the defendants appealed against their convictions and sentences. Their convictions were upheld though the sentences were reduced as it was felt they might well have been unaware that their activities were illegal. However the Appeal Court noted that this would not apply to similar cases in the future. The case then went to the House of Lords. The Law Lords heard the case in 1992 and delivered their judgment in January 1993. They upheld the convictions by a majority of three to two.

The evidence

The evidence against the men comprised the videotape and their own statements. When they were questioned by the police, the men were so confident that their activities were lawful (because they had consented to them) that they freely admitted to taking part in the activities on the video. Without these statements and

the videotape, the police would have had no evidence to present against the men and would have found it impossible to bring any prosecutions.

The law of assault

In law, you cannot, as a rule, consent to an assault. There are exceptions. For example, you can consent to a medical practitioner touching and possibly injuring your body; you can consent to an opponent hitting or injuring you in sports such as rugby or boxing; you can consent to tattoos or piercings if they are for ornamental purposes. You can also use consent as a defence against a charge of what is called Common Assault, where there is no significant injury involved.

The judgment

The Law Lords ruled that SM activity provides no exception to the rule that consent is no defence to charges of assault occasioning actual bodily harm or causing grievous bodily harm. These are defined as activities which cause injuries of a lasting nature. Bruises or cuts could be considered lasting injuries by a court, even if they heal up completely and that takes a short period of time. Grievous bodily harm covers more serious injury and maiming. Judge Rant introduced some new terms to define what he considered to be lawful and unlawful bodily harm. Judge Rant decreed that bodily harm applied or received during sexual activities was lawful if the pain it caused was 'just momentary' and 'so slight that it can be discounted'. His judgment applies also to bodily marks such as those produced by beatings or bondage. These too, according to him, must not be of a lasting nature. In essence, Judge Rant decided that any injury, pain or mark that was more than trifling and momentary was illegal and would be considered an assault under the law.

Source: http://www.spannertrust.org/documents/spannerhistory.asp

men pleaded guilty on legal advice to assault. Some were jailed, some received suspended prison sentences and others were fined. The judgment was upheld by the Court of Appeal, the House of Lords and the European Court of Human Rights (see box above).

So, how are we to approach the subject matter of criminology? What are the different ways in which we understand crime? An apparently straightforward way is simply to view crimes as being offences against the criminal law. However, even a brief analysis shows that such offences vary enormously historically and culturally, and that the formal application of the criminal law only occurs in relation to a small minority of behaviours that could, in principle, be treated as criminal.

Crime and the criminal law

In some senses the most obvious, and most commonly used, definition of crime is simply to view it as an infraction of the criminal law. Within the criminal law, a crime is conduct (or an act of omission) which, when it results in certain consequences, may lead to prosecution and punishment in a criminal court. Straightforward as this seems there are a number of problems with it. As Zedner (2004) observes, 'crime' may be both a criminal and a civil wrong simultaneously. The legal classification doesn't help tell us why certain conduct is defined as criminal, it merely helps identify it.

She continues: 'To think about crime, as some criminal law textbooks still do, as comprising discrete, autonomous legal categories remote from the social world, is to engage in an absorbing but esoteric intellectual activity' (2004: 61). At its most extreme, a crude legalistic approach to crime implies that if there were no criminal law, then there would be no crime. In its more extreme version it also suggests that no matter what acts someone may have committed, if they are not subject to criminal sanction, then they cannot be considered criminal.

Much of criminology, though aware of some of the problems inherent in legal definitions, nevertheless proceeds on the basis of precisely such an approach to defining crime. Much of what criminologists do uses categories derived from the criminal law and, moreover, uses statistics taken from the operation of criminal justice agencies enforcing or administering the criminal law (see Chapter 3). This led the American sociologist Tappan (1947: 100) to argue that:

> Crime is an intentional act in violation of the criminal law... committed without defence or excuse, and penalized by the state as a felony or misdemeanour [more or less serious criminal acts]. In studying the offender there can be no presumption that ... persons are criminals unless they also be held guilty beyond a reasonable doubt of a particular offence.

Does this mean that there is nothing common to all those things that are the object of our study as criminologists other than they happen currently to be defined as 'criminal'? Can we limit our attention solely to those things that might lead to a conviction in a criminal court? Edwin Sutherland, one of whose major concerns was 'white-collar crime' (see Chapter 18) thought not:

> The essential characteristic of crime is that it is behaviour which is prohibited by the state as an injury to the state and against which the state may react, at least as a last resort, by punishment. The two abstract criteria generally regarded by legal scholars as necessary elements in a definition of crime are legal description of an act as socially harmful and legal provision of a penalty for the act. (1949: 31)

However, as we will see in relation to white-collar crime, he felt that our attention as criminologists should not be limited to those acts that would be punished by the criminal law. There are other forms of punishment and regulation and it is the fact that acts are 'punishable' that makes them fall within our view.

Crime as a social construct

In effect, this position suggests that crime is something that is the product of culturally-bounded social interaction. It is a label applied, under certain circumstances, to certain acts (or omissions). As Edwin Schur (1969: 10) once noted: 'Once we recognise that crime is defined by the criminal law and is therefore variable in content, we see quite clearly that no explanation of crime that limits itself to the motivation and behaviour of individuals can ever be a complete one.' Put a different way, Schur was simply observing that if we take the criminal law to be the thing that defines what is criminal, then the very fact that the criminal law varies – often very significantly – from country to country, makes it immediately clear that there is nothing *given* about crime.

Particularly influential in this regard has been labelling theory (see Chapter 10). Associated with a number of influential American sociologists such as Howard Becker, labelling theory, as its own label implies, places primary emphasis on the definitional power of the application of labels – in our case here, the label 'criminal'. Labelling theory distances itself from the view that defining someone as criminal somehow represents some natural order of events and, rather, analyses such processes as illustrations of the use of power by the state, and others, to define people in particular ways.

In recent times, theorists within criminology have tended not to refer to symbolic interactionism and phenomenology – the roots of labelling theory and related ideas – and it has become fashionable in this general area to talk of 'social constructionism': the idea that crime like other social phenomena is the outcome or product of interaction and negotiation between people living in complex social groups. Central to such an approach is the observation that the power to label certain acts, and certain people, as criminal is one which is restricted and, indeed, keenly contested. Because it involves the exercise of power, the process of labelling acts and people as criminal – generally known as *criminalisation* – tends to reflect power differentials, or particular interests, within society. As we will see in later chapters, there is a radical tradition in criminology, influenced by such insights, which views the criminal law and the operation of the criminal justice and penal systems as clear illustrations of elite or class interests. Put perhaps rather too crudely, it is one means by which the wealthy and powerful discipline and control the poor.

A radical version of social constructionism has recently been offered by the Norwegian criminologist, Nils Christie. In his book, *A Suitable Amount of Crime,* he argues:

> Crime does not exist. Only acts exist, acts often given different meanings within various social frameworks. Acts and the meanings given to them are our data. Our challenge is to follow the destiny of acts through the universe of meanings. Particularly, what are the social conditions that encourage or prevent giving the acts the meaning of being crime? (Christie, 2004: 3)

Historical variation

Similarly, we can gain considerable insight into the socially constructed nature of crime by looking at how our treatment of certain behaviours varies, often considerably, over time. The 1960s in Britain are often referred to as the 'permissive age'. This was intended to convey what was perceived to be a general loosening of moral codes in the period. It was also a time when a series of liberalising laws were passed. The Abortion Act 1967 made it possible for women, under specific circumstances, to have a pregnancy terminated. Prior to 1967 abortion was illegal. Similarly, prior to the passage of the Sexual Offences Act 1967, it was illegal in Britain for men of any age to have consensual sex together. On the other hand, it was perfectly legal to take heroin and cocaine up until the time of the First World War. After that, the use of opiates was restricted, but they could still be prescribed by a doctor. Those of you that have read Conan Doyle's Sherlock Holmes stories will know that the great detective was an opium user – though even by Victorian times it was quite closely associated with criminality. Nevertheless, its consumption wasn't a criminal act.

One of the best examples of historical variation in criminal law is the period of American prohibition. An amendment to the Constitution of the United States – the National Prohibition Act (or Volstead Act) – was passed in 1919 and remained in force until 1933, banning the production and sale of alcohol. Now, as is well known, the Act neither prevented the manufacture nor the sale of alcohol. Indeed, it provided the basis of an extraordinary period in the history of American organised crime. However, what is important for our purposes here is the fact that for a period of 13 years the making and selling of alcohol was illegal, criminal.

Let's consider one final example, again related to substance use, this time illustrating the way in which laws change over time, and vary geographically. Until very recently it was perfectly possible in the United Kingdom to smoke in pubs. However, the law has changed and since March 2004 it has not been possible to smoke in pubs in the Irish republic, similarly in Scotland since

Source: http://www.authentichistory.com/images/1900s/prohibition/closed_sign.html

Above: notice announcing the closure of premises where alcohol was discovered during the prohibition era in the United States. Right: ban on smoking in enclosed work places in Ireland, March 2004 – a similar ban came into effect in Scotland in 2006 and England and Wales in 2007.

March 2006, in Wales since April 2007 and since 1st July 2007 in England, too.

The examples of cultural and historical variation given above all share an implicit assumption: that is that the power to determine what is or is not a crime resides in the nation state. However, we have clearly entered a period of history in which the boundaries between nation states are now rather more porous than they were, say, a century ago. The processes generally understood by the term 'globalisation' mean that the countries and peoples of the world are now increasingly interdependent (see Chapter 34). What happens in one part of the world has greater and more immediate significance for other parts of the world.

Since the Second World War, and the realities of the Holocaust became visible, one question that has repeatedly been asked is under what circumstances is it appropriate or necessary for one or more states to intervene in the affairs of other states? And, linked with this, to what extent is it possible to conceive of a moral order that spans an international community? The last half decade has seen the emergence of

international human rights law, the establishment of an international criminal court and, latterly, the prosecution of war criminals using these international treaties and institutions (see Chapter 34). The processes involved in bringing cases to justice, however, are highly complex and problematic and, in their own way, illustrate some of the problems involved in seeking answers to the deceptively simple question, 'what is crime?' These include:

● There is no international consensus as to what constitutes 'crimes' in the international arena. Thus, for example, nations such the United States, India and China, among others, are not even signatories to the International Criminal Court.

● Securing international co-operation against particular states is often very difficult to achieve.

● Bringing to trial alleged 'war criminals' – often people who occupy, or who have previously occupied, powerful positions – has proved very difficult (see, for example, the cases of General Pinochet and Slobodan Milosevic [Robertson, 1999]).

Demonstrators urge the extradition of the former Chilean President General Pinochet to face murder charges in 1998 – he successfully resisted efforts to bring him to trial for atrocities committed in Chile in the 1970s and 1980s.

- The machinery of justice – in this case the International Criminal Court or other *ad hoc* tribunals – only has a limited capacity. In cases where genocide is alleged there are often hundreds, if not thousands, of perpetrators.

- Where private corporations are involved in alleged war crimes – such as the torture of prisoners in Abu Ghraib prison in Iraq – enforcing the criminal law is often even more difficult.

Indeed, one of the problems with international criminal law is – in some respects like domestic criminal law – that there is not necessarily any consensus as to what constitutes 'rights' on the one hand, or 'crimes' on the other. One of the criticisms sometimes levelled at international endeavour in this area is that rather than reflecting *universal* values it is actually another instance of the West seeking to impose its values and priorities on the world. In such circumstances, we are asked to acknowledge that politics lies behind much of this activity. Discussions of crime,

the operation of criminal justice processes, the application of labels – such as '(war) criminal' – are not neutral activities, but are, in important respects, linked with institutions of power and authority – be those domestic or international.

Crime and politics

Crime, and the study of crime, occurs within a social and political context. You must bear this in mind at all times. What we think about crime, and what we think we know about crime, reflects the times in which we live. As we will see – continually – the ways in which we respond to crime are also very much a reflection of the nature of the contemporary world. Indeed, the work of a number of very distinguished criminologists has focused on using crime and responses to it as a means of understanding the nature of our social order.

End of the bipartisan consensus

Crime and criminal justice policy is now accepted as being a major political issue. That is, not only do we expect politicians to spend a lot of their time talking about crime and criminal justice, but we expect them to disagree. This has not always been the case, and the fact that crime is now highly *politicised* is a very important factor in many of the issues that we will discuss in other parts of this book. As many commentators have noted (for example Brake and Hale, 1992; Rawlings, 1992; Downes and Morgan, 1994; 2007), for many years there existed something approximating a *bipartisan consensus* on issues to do with policing, crime and punishment. By this is meant that there once existed little difference in the general approach to law and order by the two main national political parties.

Now, it is sometimes assumed that 1979 – the election of the first Thatcher government – marked the point at which all this ended. And, whilst the 1979 general election was indeed the first time that a party had successfully used law and order as one of the major elements in its electoral strategy, nevertheless the trend had been toward greater politicisation of crime and justice issues since about 1970 (Downes and Morgan, 1994; Hall *et al.*, 1978). From that point onwards, the major political parties began to blame each other for what was happening in relation to crime, and began to look to make political capital out of their criminal justice and penal policies.

The end of the bipartisan consensus coincided in very rough terms with declining faith in the idea of rehabilitation. Where for much of the twentieth century it has been assumed that one, and perhaps the most important goal, of punishment was to

The 1979 Conservative party manifesto

THE MOST DISTURBING THREAT to our freedom and security is the growing disrespect for the rule of law. In government as in opposition, Labour have undermined it. Yet respect for the rule of law is the basis of a free and civilised life. We will restore it, re-establishing the supremacy of Parliament and giving the right priority to the fight against crime.

The Fight against Crime

The number of crimes in England and Wales is nearly half as much again as it was in 1973. The next Conservative government will spend more on fighting crime even while we economise elsewhere.

Britain needs strong, efficient police forces with high morale. Improved pay and conditions will help Chief Constables to recruit up to necessary establishment levels. We will therefore implement in full the recommendations of the Edmund Davies Committee. The police need more time to detect crime. So we will ease the weight of traffic supervision duties and review cumbersome court procedures which waste police time. We will also review the traffic laws, including the totting-up procedure.

Deterring the Criminal

Surer detection means surer deterrence. We also need better crime prevention measures and more flexible, more effective sentencing. For violent criminals and thugs really tough sentences are essential. But in other cases long prison terms are not always the best deterrent. So we want to see a wider variety of sentences available to the courts. We will therefore amend the 1961 Criminal Justice Act which limits prison sentences on young adult offenders, and revise the Children and Young Persons Act 1969 to give magistrates the power to make residential and secure care orders on juveniles.

We need more compulsory attendance centres for hooligans at junior and senior levels. In certain detention centres we will experiment with a tougher regime as a short, sharp shock for young criminals. For certain types of offenders, we also support the greater use of community service orders, intermediate treatment and attendance centres. Unpaid fines and compensation orders are ineffective. Fines should be assessed to punish the offender within his means and then be backed by effective sanctions for non-payment.

Many people advocate capital punishment for murder. This must remain a matter of conscience for Members of Parliament. But we will give the new House of Commons an early opportunity for a free vote on this issue.

Source: www.conservative-party.net/manifestos/1979/1979-conservative-manifesto.shtml

reform the offender, there was by this stage declining faith that this could be achieved very effectively, and there were growing demands for greater emphasis upon punishment. The Conservative Party was elected in 1979 on a ticket that suggested that the Labour Party was responsible for the increases in crime that had occurred in the latter half of the 1970s and could not be trusted to provide sufficient resources and support for the police. 'Never, ever, have you heard me say that we will economise on law and order' said Margaret Thatcher in 1985 (quoted in Nash and Savage, 1994: 142–3). However, although expenditure on the police in particular was increased markedly in the early 1980s it did not lead to the hoped-for reductions in crime. Far from it: crime rates continued to rise and to do so at a dramatic rate.

Managerialism

Partly as a consequence of the dismay politicians felt at the perceived ineffectiveness of criminal justice agencies in bringing down crime, especially given the sums of money being spent, government policy came increasingly to be dominated by what has come to be called *managerialism*. From the mid-1980s onwards a policy of 'tight-resourcing' was applied not only to the police, but also to the probation service and to the courts system (Raine and Willson, 1993). Through the application of the Conservative government's Financial Management Initiative (FMI), the construction of performance indicators, the use of management information systems and, from later in the 1980s, scrutiny by the Audit Commission and the National Audit Office, radical changes in the management of criminal justice agencies were encouraged.

One of the solutions successive governments have pursued in relation to the problems they have faced in crime and criminal justice has been to seek to make criminal justice agencies more business-like. 'The perceived attributes of the well-run private sector company (of high efficiency, of explicit accountabilities, of clear objectives, and of measured performance)' have increasingly been applied to management in the police, prison and probation services and other agencies (Raine and Willson, 1993: 23). Such changes are often identified using the term New Public Management (NPM). The term is interpreted in a range of ways, though it is generally held to involve an increased emphasis on performance measurement, together

with the use of things like league tables, and an increased likelihood of competition with the private sector and other providers (McLaughlin *et al.*, 2001). Much of the literature, and many speeches made by politicians, also tend to emphasise the idea of devolution of responsibility from the top of organisations down to middle managers and below. Although there has been much talk of devolution of responsibility in relation, say, to the police service, arguably the dominant tendency over the past decade has been toward the progressive centralisation of control.

Centralisation

The gradual accretion of power to the centre can be seen across the criminal justice system (indeed the public sector generally, including universities) and is visible, as we will see in later chapters, for example, in relation to police, probation, prisons and youth justice. For present purposes, a couple of examples will suffice. In relation to probation, what originally emerged from the voluntary sector to become a locally-based service has been radically changed, first to create a *national* probation service and, subsequently, to merge probation with the prison service to create NOMS: the National Offender Management Service. The last 25 years have seen the Home Office seek to extend its control over probation (though this responsibility has now passed to the Ministry of Justice). It initially sought to do so via national standards. When this proved insufficient, the service was turned into a national one and any emphasis on local control was reduced.

In relation to the police, a similar process has been taking place. Indeed, the entire history of the police service can, in part, be read as a continual process of centralisation of control (see Chapters 25 and 27 in particular). Despite what was intended by the Police Act 1964 – which put in place the building blocks for the governance of police which have existed ever since – local police authorities have always occupied a relatively powerless position when compared with chief constables and the Home Office. Since the early 1990s, several reformist and interventionist Home Secretaries have sought to impose their own vision on policing and to ensure that messages emanating from the Home Office are unquestionably the ones that chief constables should pay greatest attention to. Again, through national standards, national inspection systems, shared objectives and the threat of the Home Office taking control of forces if they are deemed to be 'failing', government has progressively extended its reach of what police forces do, and how they do it.

Penal populism

We noted earlier that the 1979 general election was the first in modern times in which 'law and order' was a central plank. It was also the last in which a government pinned faith in the apparently simple equation that spending more on criminal justice would help reduce crime. From the early 1980s onward, criminal justice agencies were encouraged to form partnerships and inter-agency groupings and, more importantly, the wider 'community' was itself encouraged to take responsibility for the fight against crime (Garland, 2001). Prison numbers rose quite substantially as the decade wore on and new legislation concerning sentencing passed in 1991 sought to reorient practices in such a way as to reduce prison numbers and encourage greater use of community penalties.

For a while prison numbers did fall and there was a sense of optimism, fuelled also by the Woolf Report on prisons, that the problems of overcrowding and poor conditions that had bedevilled the prison system for decades might be alleviated. However, penal politics were about to change and to do so dramatically. In early 1993 a young Tony Blair had become Labour Party Shadow Home Secretary and had set about reshaping and repositioning the Party's stance on crime and criminal justice. In particular, having seen how Bill Clinton's Democratic Party had repositioned itself in American politics – in order to shed its previously liberal reputation and become much more hard-line in relation to law and order – Blair wished to achieve something similar in the UK. Initially as Shadow Home Secretary, and then as leader of the Labour Party after John Smith's death in 1995, he was unshakeable in his belief that such changes were necessary if the Labour Party was to have any hope of making itself electable. His most famous soundbite – 'tough on crime, tough on the causes of crime' – expertly captured the shifting stance of the Labour Party.

A few months after Blair became Shadow, Michael Howard was appointed Home Secretary. In his first Party conference speech, Howard announced a new 'law and order' package – one which took a rather different approach from that adopted by previous Home Secretaries, particularly in relation to punishment. The fact that they were under increasing pressure from the Labour opposition was undoubtedly important in this process. The package of measures that Howard announced were punitive in character and involved a reassertion of prison in a range of sanctions he interpreted as having deterrence as their primary aim. The outcome would almost certainly mean a rise in prison numbers. Howard recognised this and welcomed it:

> I do not flinch from that. We shall no longer judge the success of our system of justice by a fall in our prison population ... Let us be clear. *Prison works.* It ensures that we are protected from murderers, muggers and rapists – and it makes many who are tempted to commit crime think twice. (quoted in Newburn, 2003; *emphasis added*)

The speech was a pivotal moment in a recent British law and order politics, ushering in almost three years of almost uninterrupted bidding wars by the two main parties in which each sought to present itself as 'tougher' than the other. Much of this new presentation of law and order politics has been

Tony Blair shortly after becoming Shadow Home Secretary in 1993. Would it be fair to say he was tougher on crime than the causes of crime during his subsequent premiership?

played out in and been stimulated by the popular media. Crime has become staple tabloid newspaper fodder. The stance taken by the two parties has generally come to be characterised as 'penal populism' (Pratt, 2007) or 'populist punitiveness' (Bottoms, 1995). This is an approach to crime and penal policy in which particular policy positions are 'normally adopted in the clear belief that they will be popular with the public (and usually with an awareness that, in general and abstract opinion polls, punitive policies are favoured by a majority of the public ...). Hence, the term "populist punitiveness" is intended to convey the notion of politicians tapping into, and using for their own purposes, what they believe to be the public's generally punitive stance' (Bottoms 1995: 40).

1993 represented an important turning point in British penal politics, therefore. Since that time government and opposition have been locked into a new bipartisan consensus: one that stresses the importance of punishment and deterrence, and that views punitiveness not only as chiming with public views but, crucially, as being critical to electoral success. Being 'tough on crime' is now the political bottom-line for those seeking political office in Westminster and similar trends are visible in many other jurisdictions. Best known of all – no doubt because it represents the most extreme example in the West – is what has occurred in America over the last three decades or so.

In the US, during a period in which 'tough on crime' politics became embedded in national culture, the number of people in prison has expanded from around a quarter of a million in the early 1970s to well over two million today. The US has the highest incarceration rate (i.e. the highest number of citizens sent to prison per head of population) in the world. And, since you must surely be wondering, this cannot be explained as a result of its crime rate. First, for a significant part of the period concerned, crime in most American cities was declining – and quite dramatically at that. Second, the crime rate in America, with the very notable exception of homicide – is really not that different from the crime rate in Britain. Yes, there are some differences – in relation to some crimes the rates are higher in Britain – but in the main crime rates in the big cities in the US and the UK are on a similar scale. Even though Britain is the highest incarcerator in Western Europe, its incarceration rate is only one-fifth (or less) of that in America.

At least two important and related points emerge from this necessarily brief discussion. First, in thinking about crime and crime policy it is always important to bear in mind the cultural and political context in which things take place. Crime is socially constructed, politically-influenced and historically variable. Second, there is no direct link between crime rates and types and levels of punishment. Punishment, like crime, is historically and culturally contingent. We no longer think it appropriate in Britain to hang people. Less than half a century ago we still did so. Many nations still execute citizens. What type of punishment we inflict, how much of it we inflict, and whether or not we inflict it, also depends very much upon the political circumstances of the time. We will return to such observations regularly throughout this book. I want to conclude this chapter, however, by making a similar point about criminology. I want to look briefly at the recent history of criminology in Britain, partly to sketch out one or two of its contours simply so that you will know about them, but also to illustrate the point that criminology – like the things it studies – is a product of its particular historical moment.

Criminology in Britain

The first lectures under the banner of 'criminology' in Britain were delivered in 1921–22 in Birmingham to postgraduate medical students. At that time 'criminology' in the UK primarily involved psychiatrists. It was quite unlike the much more sociologically-influenced subject that it became by the 1970s and, to a significant extent, remains today. The journal, *Sociological Review,* was established in 1908 and carried nothing that was obviously criminological until the late 1930s.

The first professional organisation in the area was established in 1931. Initially called the 'Association for the Scientific Treatment of Criminals' it became the 'Institute for the Study and Treatment of Delinquency' (ISTD) later in the decade (a name it retained until relatively recently). In 1933 it founded the Portman Clinic as the base for the practice of psychoanalytic and psychiatric treatment. Criminology was still not a widespread subject of academic study. By 1948 only three people held jobs in British universities teaching what might be thought of as criminology: Leon Radzinowicz at

2 THE SUN, Saturday, March 10, 2007

'First Minister' . . . Paisley

Unionists' 'cabinet' majority

UNIONISTS will make up the majority of the next Northern Ireland Executive if power-sharing returns later this month, it emerged last night.

Democratic Unionist Party leader the Rev Ian Paisley is due to be First Minister and Sinn Fein's Martin McGuinness his Deputy after all 108 seats were filled in the Assembly election.

However, it was unclear if power-sharing would be in place by PM Tony Blair and Irish Taoiseach Bertie Ahern's March 26 devolution deadline.

Northern Ireland Secretary Peter Hain warned the Assembly would close if parties failed to form a government by the deadline.

The final tally of seats saw the DUP the largest party with 36 — up four — followed by Sinn Fein with 28, also up four.

The DUP insisted any decision they made on power-sharing depends on republicans showing support for the police.

The Sun Says — Page Six

'Inspiration' . . . Mick

Face of Brit hero

A BRITISH commando gunner blown up in a Taliban grenade attack was named yesterday as Sgt Major Mick Smith.

The 39-year-old from Liverpool died after the attack on the UK base at Sangin in Afghanistan's Helmand Province.

He joined the Army in 1985 and 29 Commando Regiment Royal Artillery two years later.

His commanding officer Lt Col Neil Wilson described him as an "inspiration". He said: "His loss is an enormous blow to every one of us."

PM TROOPS SNUB

Premier Tony Blair was thwarted in Brussels yesterday in his bid to recruit more EU troops to fight the Taliban.

TOP JUDGE'S SHOCKING OUTBURST
Let killers out
..THEY'RE CLOGGING UP JAILS

By GEORGE PASCOE-WATSON
Political Editor

KILLERS should be let out of jail early to ease the prisons crisis, Britain's top judge said yesterday.

Lord Chief Justice Lord Phillips warned that jails would be stuffed with "geriatric" inmates if no action was taken.

He suggested the country would look back in shame in 100 years time at the length of sentences for killers and rapists.

His comments caused a storm last night – as he in charge of sentencing guidelines in England and Wales.

Prime Minister Tony Blair and Home Secretary John Reid both dismissed the Law Lord's outburst.

A Home Office spokesman said: "The Lord Chief Justice is entitled to his view and has expressed it.

"The Home Secretary believes that murderers and other dangerous offenders should be kept in prison as long as is necessary to protect the public."

And the PM's official spokesman said: "We do not agree."

Crime victims were up in arms at Lord Phillips' remarks.

Norman Brennan, director of the Victims of Crime Trust, said: "Lord Phillips has taken leave of his senses if he believes that releasing murderers early will help alleviate the prison

'I'm not in favour of mandatory jail terms...in 30 yrs prisons will be full of geriatric lifers'

population. He also makes the comment that prisons risk becoming full of geriatric lifers but that has to be the case if necessary. At least they still have their lives.

"There was a time in the not too distant past where some people or some murderers were hanged for their crimes, then it became life imprisonment.

"So when some murderers serve as little as eight years for such a grave and devastating crime it makes a mockery of the lives of those who have been murdered.

"A life without a loved one will never change so it is only right and proper that the prison sentence remains in place for those who commit these grave crimes."

Lord Phillips sparked outrage when he called for an end to automatic life sentences for killers.

He said: "I'm not i n

favour of mandatory sentences, full stop. If sentences are to be just, then the effect of mitigating and aggravating factors should be very significant, so that sentences fill the spectrum between these two starting points.

"I am not sure that in practice they do and I believe that the starting points are having the effect of ratcheting up sentences in a manner that will be regretted many years hence."

Lord Phillips said the effect of the sentencing guidelines in the Criminal Justice Act 2003 had been to double sentences.

He added: "In 30 years time, the prisons will be full of geriatric lifers.

"That is not to say that I do not recognise that there are certain crimes which require a sentence of that length or longer to protect the public.

"But I detect an incitement to the public to exact vengeance from offenders that is not dissimilar to the emotions of those who thronged to witness public executions in the 18th century.

"I sometimes wonder whether, in 100 years time people will be as shocked by the length of the sentences we are imposing as we are by some of the punishments of the 18th century."

Lord Phillips has argued before that jail overcrowding can only be eased by keeping convicts **OUT** of jail.

Mr Blair's spokesman said: "The Government recognises that the Lord Chief Justice has this view, but we disagree. We believe that people should be kept in prison as long as

'I wonder in the future if people will be shocked by the length of our sentences'

they are judged to be a danger to society." Former prisons minister Ann Widdecombe attacked the judge's call last night.

She said: "To have to release a dangerous person seems to me a very peculiar position.

"If you remove the life sentence and you give a tariff, you have no control at that point.

"If the authorities have severe reason to doubt that this person is ready for release, they have no control.

"And we are talking about murderers, not people who pinched 3p off the bus fare. I am certainly not convinced."

Lord Phillips' controversial views were last night expected to boost support for The Sun's campaign to get rid of soft judges.

The Sun Says — Page Six

'Penal populism' in practice. 'Soft' judges (in this case the Lord Chief Justice, Lord Phillips) have been a particular target for the *Sun* and several other newspapers. Lord Phillips also incurred criticism in the popular press when he sought to popularise community sentences as an alternative to custody (see Chapter 27).

Cambridge, Max Grünhut at Oxford and Hermann Mannheim at the LSE.

The *British Journal of Delinquency* was established by ISTD in 1950. It had three joint editors, two psychiatrists and Hermann Mannheim. The journal was renamed the *British Journal of Criminology* in 1960, though it had the subtitle 'Delinquency and Deviant Behaviour'. According to its editors this was 'to indicate that criminology must be based on the broadest studies of the individual and social determinants of character and conscience'.

It was some considerable time before British criminology took its sociological turn. Terry Morris' *The Criminal Area* was published in 1957 but, arguably, it was not until the publication of David Downes' *The Delinquent Solution* in 1966 followed by a number of other important works that criminology influenced by American sociological theory really began to flourish. There were also a number of important institutional developments around this period that contributed to the further development of British criminology. In the late 1950s the Institute of Criminology at Cambridge was established. In 1957 with both Mannheim and Grünhut about to retire, the Home Secretary, R.A. Butler, approached London and Cambridge universities in order to explore the possibility of establishing a new institute. London University turned him down, but in 1959 the new Institute of Criminology opened in Cambridge under the direction of Radzinowicz. In addition, Butler also helped the university secure independent financial support for the creation of the first chair in criminology. Thus was established the Wolfson Chair in Criminology, held for many years by Radzinowicz and, after his retirement, by Tony Bottoms.

The second major institutional development was the creation of a research unit within the Home Office. The Criminal Justice Act 1948 had given the Home Secretary the power to spend money on research. The sum initially allocated was £2,000. The first external grants were made to the three eminent émigrés: £250 each to Radzinowicz and Grünhut, and £1,500 to Mannheim to begin his famous borstal study. By 1956 the external expenditure on research had risen to £2,500. In 1957 the Home Office Research Unit was established, later becoming known as the Research and Planning Unit – and now the Home Office Science, Research and Statistics Directorate (with other researchers working in research directorates

in the new Ministry of Justice). There are now hundreds of research staff and a budget of millions.

The third of the developments – though they all occurred at roughly the same time – was the establishment of the British Society of Criminology (BSC). ISTD had established a 'Scientific Group for the Discussion of Delinquent Problems' in 1953. However, not everyone was happy with its activities and discussions, in particular with the continued dominance of psychiatric and other clinical perspectives. A number of members broke away in the late 1950s and established the BSC. Though this was intended to herald a shift in perspective, it would not do to exaggerate it. In a paper to the 1971 British Sociology conference, Stan Cohen observed that the BSC was multidisciplinary 'with a heavy bias in a clinical direction'.

Sir Leon Radzinowicz (1906–1999), appointed first director of the Institute of Criminology at the University of Cambridge in 1959. A commanding figure in the history of British criminology, he was also the author of a five-volume *History of English Criminal Law and its Administration from 1750*.

No doubt it was this which, in part, led a group of British sociologists to establish the 'National Deviancy Symposium', later the National Deviancy Conference (NDC). It held its first conference in Autumn 1968 and then for a period of years provided a location in which a more radical British criminology could thrive. David Downes said of the NDC that its great appeal 'was not only to sociologists of crime in search of a congenial forum, but also to younger sociologists who saw in deviance an escape route from the positivist methods and functionalist orthodoxy of much British sociology.' A large number of people were recruited into criminology in the 1960s and 1970s – what Rock (1994) called the 'fortunate generation' – and thereafter recruitment declined substantially.

Since that time, British criminology has expanded massively and also changed in character and focus. Whereas much early, and classic, British criminology took offenders as its focus, there has been a profound shift over the past 20 years or so towards a preoccupation with the operation of the criminal justice system – the rise of what Jock Young called 'administrative criminology'. Arguably, there has also been something of a shift away from theory and theorising.

It is increasingly difficult to characterise British criminology, however; the sheer scale of the expansion now means that it is all the more difficult to grasp, capture and summarise its character. The BSC held its first conference in 1987 – and there were concerns at the time about how much interest there would be. It now hosts an annual conference at which there are usually around 400–500 delegates. The Society has close on 1,000 members. There are upwards of 70 higher educational institutions offering degrees (half or full) in criminology and a further 40 or more running Masters degree programmes. By any standards this is remarkable growth. In the chapters that follow I will endeavour to take you through many of the major issues and debates in contemporary criminology, and to explore with you many of the most important questions that people working within this discipline have grappled with. It is – I hope you will find – an exciting journey.

Further reading

If you want to learn more about the emergence and development of criminology then Garland's (2002) essay, 'Of crime and criminals' in the 3rd edition of *The Oxford Handbook of Criminology* is undoubtedly the place to start. The essay is available online at: http://www.oup.com/uk/orc/bin/9780199205431/01student/chapters/. There is also a wonderful essay by Roger Hood, entitled 'Hermann Mannheim and Max Grünhut' (2004) *British Journal of Criminology*, 44, 469–495.

On more recent developments in British criminology you should look at the range of essays in: Rock, P. (1988) *A History of British Criminology*, Oxford: Oxford University Press; I would also suggest consulting: Downes, D. (1978) Promise and performance in British criminology, *British Journal of Sociology*, 29, 4, 483–502; and Rock P. (1994) The social organisation of British criminology, in Maguire, M. *et al.* (eds) *The Oxford Handbook of Criminology*, 1st edn, Oxford: Oxford University Press.

On understanding what is meant by crime, a very fine introduction and overview can be found in the first section of:

Muncie, J. (2001) The construction and deconstruction of crime, in Muncie, J. and McLaughlin, E. (eds) *The Problem of Crime*, London: Sage

A more focused and developed treatment of the relationship between crime and law is:

Lacey, N. (2007) Legal constructions of crime, in Maguire, M. *et al.* (eds) *The Oxford Handbook of Criminology*, 4th edn, Oxford: Oxford University Press

Lucia Zedner's (2004) *Criminal Justice,* Oxford: Oxford University Press, provides a thorough grounding in the major philosophical debates (and is probably especially valuable for those studying law).

On politics and crime the best overviews and analyses are available in the chapters written by David Downes and Rod Morgan in *The Oxford Handbook of Criminology*. In the most recent (4th) edition, it is called: 'No turning back: The politics of law and order into the new millennium'. Anyone interested in this subject, however, should also consult the essays by these authors in the first three editions.

Chapter outline

Introduction 22

The emergence of a modern criminal justice system 23
  Policing 23
     The 'new police' 26
     Resistance and reform 27
     Into the twentieth century 29
  The victim and prosecution 30
     The formalisation of the prosecution process 31
  The courts 33
     The decline of the profit motive 33
  Punishment 35
     Capital punishment 35
     Transportation 37
     Imprisonment 38
     Probation 40

Crime and violence in history 42
  Levels of crime 42
  Perceptions of crime 43

Questions for further discussion 46
Further reading 46
Websites 47

2

Crime and punishment in history

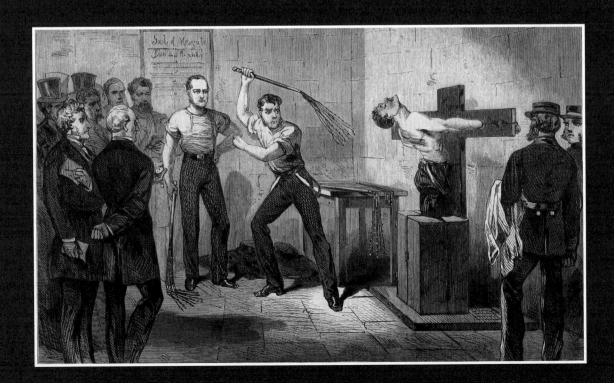

CHAPTER SUMMARY

In this chapter we take a longer historical look at crime and punishment. The aim of the chapter is to provide an historical overview of the origins and development of many of the subjects dealt with in the rest of the book.

It covers:

- the origins of the modern criminal justice system and changes in our understanding of crime from pre-modern to modern times;

- the emergence of modern, formal police forces;

- the growing role of imprisonment as a key response to crime as the use of both capital punishment and transportation declined;

- the changing role of the victim, in particular in relation to the prosecution process;

- what is known about levels of crime in British society prior to the introduction of criminal statistics;

- how attitudes towards, and perceptions of, crime have changed in recent centuries;

- to what extent it is possible to estimate levels and trends in crime in previous eras;

- whether we appear to be becoming a more- or less-crime-ridden society.

Introduction

Why study the history of crime? Well, there are numerous reasons but let's stick with two of the more important. First, it is hard to understand contemporary systems and trends without some grasp of how things were organised in previous eras. Thus, an appreciation of systems of punishment in previous periods may help to provide a better understanding of how we organise our contemporary penal system. A study of the history of crime can do this through the simple process of providing a contrast. By examining systems that are different from those we are used to we may be encouraged to look at our current practices in a new light. Comparative research across differing jurisdictions, but within the same historical period, involves a very similar process. Furthermore, unless we have some grasp of history we are unlikely to be able to understand the *aetiology* – the origins – of current practices. Why are our policing systems organised in the way they are, for example? When and why did we come to use imprisonment as a punishment for serious crime? Asking such questions and seeking answers to them also potentially reveal important things about the nature of society more generally, and how society has changed.

The second major reason for studying the history of crime and punishment is that in focusing on the process of historical change we are reminded – or at least we should be – that things can change. Put another way, the fact that things haven't always been the way they are now should remind us that they don't have to stay the way they are now. Systems of punishment, for example, are the product of historical and political contingency. Not only do they reflect deep, underlying structural changes affecting our society, but they are also a product of political decisions. Consequently, we may remind ourselves that even when our systems of crime control seem locked into a particular path – as in some ways it may feel in relation to the current trend of increasing the number of people in prison, and a growing punitiveness that has gone with this (see Chapter 28) – it is always possible that political decisions may be made which set in train substantial changes in a different direction.

In this chapter we will explore three main topics:

- how the modern criminal justice system emerged, and how crime and deviant behaviour were dealt with prior to the 'modern' age;

- what is known about changing patterns and levels of crime; and

- the way in which attitudes towards, and perceptions of, crime and criminality have changed.

The emergence of a modern criminal justice system

It is arguably the case that it is the period between the mid-eighteenth and the mid-twentieth centuries that saw the establishment of the formal criminal justice system we know today. At the beginning of that period, there was little that could be described as formalised criminal justice – no police forces, no probation service, no court system (as we now understand it) and nothing quite like the contemporary prison – although there is a danger in overstating the degree of novelty of current arrangements (see Morris and Rothman, 1998). By 1950 all this was established and embedded. Godfrey and Lawrence (2005) ask whether if one were attempting to design a criminal justice system to meet the needs of contemporary society it would be at all like the one we have today. It would not, they surmise. The reason is that 'the institutions of criminal justice – the police, prisons and the courts – have all been shaped and influenced by events and ideas over a long period of time'. Our aim in this chapter is to see what is known about crime in history, and how the ways in which responses to crime have changed as the nature of British society has changed. This is a vitally important part of understanding criminology. It is all too easy to imagine that our current way of organising things is roughly the way we have always organised ourselves. In fact this is far from accurate.

Let's take two fairly obvious examples. You might imagine that in keeping order and in preventing and investigating crime we have always relied upon a police force, or something that looks like a police force. If your time frame is the last two centuries then you would just about be right in your assumption. However, if your historical time frame is the last 500 years or 1,000 years, then you would be quite mistaken. Formal police forces, with officers in uniform employed by the state and tasked with maintaining order and preventing crime, are a relatively new phenomenon: the French *Gendarmerie* was established in the 1790s, and the Metropolitan Police, the oldest force in England, won't reach its 200th anniversary until 2029. Police forces are a creation of the modern state; in the sense we understand them now they have only existed since the industrial revolution.

The second example is the prison. Again, you might easily assume that in dealing with serious criminal activity the core method we have always relied upon has been imprisonment. Once more, and like the introduction of formal policing, this would be a quite mistaken assumption. As we will see in some detail, the prison is a relatively modern invention. Indeed, many would argue that the emergence of the prison reflects some hugely important changes in the nature of modern, industrial society. So, again, if one looks at these things through an historical lens, both the apex of our system of punishment – the prison – and the gatekeepers to our justice system – the police – are fairly new phenomena. Understanding something of their history provides an important backdrop to the discussions and debates that follow in the rest of the book.

Policing

Attempting to establish order over an unruly realm, Henry II (1133–1189) established the basis of a system of criminal justice, including a trial and jury system, through the Assize of Clarendon in 1166. Despite this, at this time and for some centuries after, order was generally maintained through a system of local, community-based peacekeeping. This system had a number of facets. The Assize of Arms, introduced in 1181 by Henry II, required all males over fifteen to retain arms in their house for the purpose of preserving the peace; a requirement that varied according to their rank and wealth. With England at this stage a largely rural, agrarian society, responsibility for keeping the peace rested on local householders. In effect a form of medieval neighbourhood watch existed – though community-based and not linked to a 'police force'. A duty to help also existed. If, for example, it was discovered that a thief had been present then the 'hue and cry' would be raised and local men were expected to join the search for the culprit. A failure to assist could be considered a misdemeanour.

Over time, though very slowly, a more formalised system became established. In 1285 the Statute of Winchester introduced a series of reforms aimed at fortifying towns, introducing the formal, though unpaid, role of watchmen to patrol such towns between sunset and sunrise, and even commanding that roads leading to such towns be

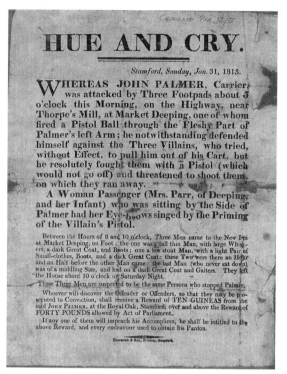

A notice posted in Stamford, Lincolnshire, in 1815, announcing 'hue and cry' following an attack by 'three footpads' on one Mr John Palmer.

regards the inhabitants' to the narrower ideas of law and order that characterise post-industrial revolution Britain. John and Henry Fielding – magistrates based at Bow Street in London – were important proponents of the idea that social control and order could be attained through concerted institutional effort (Rawlings, 1995). They were also of the view that 'the criminal law, poor law, administrative regulation, institutions and philanthropy' could be used to regulate the urban poor – whose numbers increased rapidly as Britain industrialised and urbanised after the mid-1700s.

Partly as a result of concern about general crime levels, but also because of panic over particular crime scares, street patrols by the magistracy and by watchmen became increasingly common in London and beyond in the eighteenth century. There are considerable doubts about their effectiveness, however, and they were regularly criticised in press and pamphlets. In a speech to both Houses of Parliament in 1751, George II called on them:

> … to consider seriously of some effectual Provision to suppress those audacious Crimes of Robbery and Violence, which are now become so frequent, especially about this great capital; and which have proceeded, in a great Measure,

widened so as reduce the likelihood that those intent on highway robbery could conceal themselves. Order in Anglo-Saxon society was underpinned by the principle of Frankpledge in which a small number of households were bound together in a system of mutual responsibility. Certainly up until the late seventeenth century it remained the case that 'for many practical purposes, a large number of communities were virtually self-policing' (Rock, 1983: 193). As Rock explains, part of the explanation for this was the 'peculiar geometry of … relations' in England in this period. The population was small by contemporary standards, and unevenly spread over the country as a whole. Large parts of England were 'an unpoliced wilderness without a system of established roads' in which travel was difficult, leaving many areas cut off for substantial parts of the year. Under these circumstances many communities were self-supporting, and this included the task of keeping order.

However, it was during the eighteenth century that the term 'police' first began to be used regularly. As Rawlings (1995: 138) notes, ideas of governance shifted at this time from the 'regulation and government of a city or country, so far as

Henry Fielding (1707–1754), novelist and author of *Tom Jones*, was also Chief Magistrate, based at Bow Street in London, and an early architect of formal policing.

from that profligate Spirit of Irreligion, Idleness, Gaming and Extravagance, which has of late extended itself, in an uncommon Degree, to the Dishonour of the Nation, and to the great Offence and Prejudice of the sober and industrious Part of my People. (quoted in Rawlings, 1999: 28)

For Henry Fielding, the Chief Magistrate, part of the solution was to be found in regulating gaming houses and alehouses, as well as increasing the powers of magistrates to take action against those dealing in stolen goods or otherwise appearing suspicious. Though he received some support, there remained considerable resistance to increasing magistrates' powers, and even more so to any proposal to formalise policing arrangements. Henry Fielding, and his half-brother John (who on Henry's death became Chief Magistrate), were at the forefront of the movement to put thief taking on a more formal footing and to regularise the collection of information about criminals. Earlier in the century a number of infamous cases – most notably involving Jonathan Wild – in which 'thief taking' was used as a front for often quite highly organised criminal activity (Howson, 1985). A national strategy – the General Preventative Plan – was issued in 1772, in which magistrates and gaol-ers were encouraged to supply information to Bow Street, and Fielding received money from the government to publicise such activities and to post information in the press. Indeed, Fielding published his own newspaper, *The Hue and Cry*, which eventually gave rise to the *Police Gazette*, which was hugely popular in the nineteenth century.

Various initiatives in more formalised policing emerged in the eighteenth century. Among the most famous are the Bow Street Runners associated with the Fieldings, and the establishment of a River Police on the Thames at Wapping by Patrick Colquhoun in 1798. As a major thoroughfare, particularly for commercial trades of various sorts, the River Thames was also the site of considerable theft and other property crime. The officers of this new force initially rowed in galleys and, so far as the official history goes, appear to have had some considerable success in detecting and preventing crime. William Pitt had originally introduced a Police Bill in 1785 five years after the Gordon Riots in 1780. This failed, and subsequent attempts also failed, in part as a result of fears about the possible creation of a form of repressive policing similar to that in post-revolutionary France. In the late eighteenth century Patrick Colquhoun, a merchant and magistrate, wrote *Treatise on the Police of the*

The 'Cato Street Conspirators' – allegedly plotting the assassination of members of the Cabinet – are arrested by Bow Street Runners who stormed their hayloft in Cato Street, near Grosvenor Square in London, 23 February 1820.

Table 2.1	Background to the 'new police'

- End of convict transportation to the colonies in the 1770s
- Gordon Riots, which lasted for five days in 1780
- Rise in radicalism linked to American and French Revolutions
- Napoleonic War (1793–1815): food riots, poor relief and disruption of trade
- Luddite disturbances and demonstrations against the Corn Laws in 1815
- Riots in Manchester's Spa Fields and rural East Anglia in 1816
- Blanketeers march from Manchester in 1817, demanding political reform
- Peterloo massacre in 1819 after political demonstration
- Cato Street conspiracy to assassinate members of the Cabinet in 1820
- Riots among poor wool workers in 1820
- Queen Caroline riots in London in 1820–1821

Source: Rawlings, R. (2002: 106).

Metropolis (1797) and made the case for a full-time, salaried force for the City of London. Though he was successful in creating the River Police on the Thames, it was to be some time before a full-time force was established for the streets of the city.

The 'new police'

Perhaps the most famous date in British policing is 1829, the year when the 'new police' were eventually introduced by Sir Robert Peel. *Eventually*, because he and others had been unsuccessful previously and, even in 1829, there remained considerable scepticism about, and no little hostility towards, this new force. As Emsley (1996: 24) notes, although traditional histories of policing have tended to see a logical progression from the Bow Street Runners, through Patrick Colquhoun's marine police to the eventual establishment of the Metropolitan Police, in fact 'the force which was created in 1829 bore little resemblance to what had gone before in London' or to what had been proposed by Sir John Fielding in the 1770s or Colquhoun in his *Treatise*.

Under the supervision of its two new Commissioners, Lieutenant Colonel Charles Rowan and Richard Mayne, the first instructions for the Metropolitan Police sought to make it clear that they were not primarily a military institution focusing on public order:

> The principal object to be obtained is the prevention of crime. To this great end every effort of the police is to be directed. The security of the person and property will thus be better effected

Sir Robert Peel (1788–1850), Home Secretary in 1829. In the face of considerable opposition Parliament passed the Metropolitan Police Improvement Bill which created the 'new police'.

A group of four 'Peelers' who were amongst the original 3,000 'new police'. Their civilian-style uniform was designed to be clearly distinguishable from that of the army and hence to help allay public fears of a military-style 'state police'.

than by the detection and punishment of the offender after he has succeeded in committing the crime.

To achieve these objectives, a system of beat patrols was established through which the work of the new constables was organised – and, as such, it was little different at first from the activities of the parochial watchmen. The uniform, discipline and organisation of the new Metropolitan Police were all influenced by the already existing Royal Irish Constabulary – a force with which Peel had considerable connections.

Police officers were dressed in blue – to distinguish them from the scarlet of the military – and the architects of the new force ensured through various other means that there was a clear symbolic distinction between police and army. Officers wore tail coats that bore little decoration, none of the epaulettes and braid of military uniforms, as well as top hats. Crucially, and in contrast to the American police forces that would appear during the nineteenth century, they were unarmed (Miller, 1975).

The majority of the new police officers merely carried a wooden truncheon – again an effort by Peel and others to counter public fears of the introduction of a quasi-military force. That said, it is sometimes forgotten that officers carried cutlasses in times of emergency and also more routinely on particularly dangerous beats. Moreover, regulations permitted inspectors to carry pocket pistols.

Resistance and reform

Concern about, and protests against, the new police in the capital did not disappear immediately – far from it. There remained considerable concern about the nature of this new force, most particularly its possible military nature, as well as a generalised reluctance to pay the large sums of money to run an organisation over which local people had no control: the Commissioners being directly accountable to the Home Secretary, not to local authorities. A more specific concern existed amongst the working classes about the treatment they received from the police and the courts.

There was considerable resistance in the provinces to the idea of Westminster-controlled police being introduced locally, and broader fears about the nature of the new police and the cost. The result was that much police reform was piecemeal in the decades immediately after the introduction of the new police in London. The Municipal Corporations Act 1835 created what became known as 'borough police' and subsequent County Police Acts of 1839 and 1840 provided for essentially voluntary introduction of rural forces. The eventual weakening of local resistance came about partly because of concerns about crime as a result of the declining use of transportation, and also because of problems associated with returning soldiers at the end of the Crimean War. The promise of funding from central government also helped to weaken resistance.

From the perspective of central government, police reform was necessary in order to reduce the demands that were still being made on the army when local disorder broke out. It was not until 1856 that the County and Borough Police Act made the introduction of police forces compulsory – there still being somewhere between 6 and 23 areas without a force at this time (Emsley, 1996). Provincial police forces differed considerably in some instances – sporting different uniforms and often being organised along very different lines. The next 150 years (see Chapter 25) have seen the steady, inexorable centralisation and homogenisation of public policing in England and Wales.

The police forces of the nineteenth century gradually acquired a very broad array of functions, including emergency responsibilities for both fire and ambulance services, for controlling traffic, licensing and regulating cabs, and even working as school attendance officers. First and foremost, though, the police constable was a 'domestic missionary', whose duty was to bring decorum and civilisation to the streets of British towns and cities. This meant a focus not simply on theft and violence, but policing drunkenness, prostitution, begging and other matters such as Sunday trading, which was illegal. Not surprisingly such activities led to considerable conflict and, particularly in many working-class areas of the major cities, police officers were regularly assaulted. Indeed, some areas were barely policed at all, the decision being taken by senior officers to attempt to contain, rather than control, the problems that existed. Yet, as Emsley (1996: 80) shows, 'it would be wrong to conceive of the relationship between the working

class and the police in the second half of the nineteenth century as entirely one of mutual hostility'. Although the political rhetoric that the new police were there to serve and protect everyone may have been slightly overblown, nevertheless over the course of the nineteenth century there appeared to be growing acceptance of the police by at least sections of the working class – quite likely those with something that needed protection.

At this point, it is worth pausing and reflecting on police history. How best to understand this momentous development – the introduction of the new police? As a number of authors – perhaps most notably Robert Reiner – have argued, there are two contrasting approaches to police history. There is on the one hand what has variously been called the 'Whig', 'traditional', 'orthodox' or 'cop-sided' view of history. This holds to a general view of social progress in which the new police are not only presented as being a clear advance on previously existing arrangements, but are a necessary response to the general problems of crime and disorder of the period. Such histories are best encapsulated in the writings of Charles Reith (one-time Director-General of the BBC) and, most self-servingly, in an official publication produced by the Home Office in the 1970s called *The Story of Our Police*. This official publication, for example, argues that there can be no doubt:

> ... that right from the start the police force was a great success. It was very well organised and the policemen were a fine and well-disciplined body of men. But people still did not welcome them. At first they were very unpopular and people called them insulting names like 'blue devils' and 'Peel's bloody gang'.

After the sentence 'people still did not welcome them' one can almost hear a whispered 'despite all the benefits – the ungrateful lot'! In this cop-sided view of the world it is impossible to imagine that the new force is there for any other purpose than to protect everyone's interests and to be an utterly impartial keeper of the peace. All that it would take was something to lift the scales from the eyes of the unappreciative:

> After a number of riots, and a number of attacks by the London mobs, the turning-point came in a pitched battle between the police and the London mob at Cold-Bath Fields in 1833. The police were stoned, three of them were stabbed and one killed, but the police baton charges broke up the riot without anyone in the crowd

being seriously injured. The London mob had met their match, and in the end the public supported the police.

The fact that the coroner's jury reached a verdict of 'justifiable homicide' in the killing of the police officer (PC Culley) at Cold-Bath Fields gives a rather different impression from that conveyed above. Although viewed through a more critical lens, this Home Office publication borders on parody, it nevertheless captures some of the core elements of the Whig approach to history, in particular the somewhat apolitical view of the emergence of the police and the more general sense of inevitable progress toward a better world.

The contrasting approach is the 'revisionist', 'radical' or, in Reiner's (2002) terms, 'lop-sided' view of history. In this view, by contrast, the notion that it is possible to conceive of this organisation as *our* police is challenged, initially by a group of radical historians in the 1960s. Beginning from the position that our social order is fractured, particularly along class lines, historians such as Storch argued that the new police were primarily an instrument by which the ruling classes disciplined and controlled the newly burgeoning and non-deferential working classes (Emsley, 2003):

Historians of the police, public order and the criminal law have understandably concentrated on the role of the police in the repression of crime, public disorder, and popular political movements or have studied the police from the point of view of social administration. The police had a broader mission in the nineteenth century however – to act as an all-purpose lever of urban discipline. The imposition of the police brought the arm of municipal and state authority directly to bear upon key institutions of daily life in working-class neighbourhoods, touching off a running battle with local custom and popular culture which lasted until at least the end of the century. Riots and strikes are by definition ephemeral episodes, but the monitoring and control of the streets, pubs, racecourses, wakes and popular fêtes was a daily function of the 'new police'. (Storch, 1976: 481)

Into the twentieth century

Much activity in the nineteenth century was directed toward standardising policing, partly through reducing the number of forces and using the Inspectorate of Constabulary to rationalise policing practices, and also to continuing the process of increasing police legitimacy in the eyes of a far from entirely sanguine public (see Robert Roberts' account of the policing of working-class Manchester below). The two World Wars and the industrial unrest in the first half of the twentieth century further separated police forces from their

Policing in Scotland

An important difference between Scotland and the rest of the UK in the emergence of the police concerns the degree of central influence. Whereas in England and Wales, and indeed in Ireland, central government compelled local areas to introduce police forces, this was not true in Scotland. It was local initiative which was the main impetus, with numerous local areas introducing local police arrangements long before being instructed to do so by government.

Many of these initiatives took place in the early nineteenth century before the introduction of Peel's Metropolitan Police. Thus, new policing initiatives were introduced in Glasgow in 1800 (indeed a force briefly existed in Glasgow as early as 1779), in Edinburgh in 1805 and in Aberdeen in 1818. As they had been in London, the reform efforts of Patrick Colquhoun – the architect of the Thames River Police – were central to the development of policing in Scotland. Colquhoun, a Scot, had been Provost of Glasgow and was brought to London because of his ideas and influence on Scottish urban life.

By 1859, 32 counties and 57 burghs (a local area equivalent to a borough or town) maintained separate police forces. As with England, a process of amalgamation then began. Subsequent years also saw a flurry of legislation and a range of new tasks and responsibilities being allocated to the police – not least as a result of the concerns around crime and social disorder that accompanied growing industrialisation and urbanisation.

The interpretation of 'policing' was also somewhat broader in Scotland than elsewhere, not being constrained by the notion of the prevention and detection of crime and the maintenance of order, but also being concerned with the public good and the public interest. These distinctive origins are held by some scholars (see Dinsmor and Goldsmith, 2005) to have continued to influence the nature of Scottish policing and, in particular, to help explain what they perceive to be the continuing close links between police and community in Scotland.

local authorities. The First World War depleted officer numbers, at least at first, and also increased substantially the responsibilities of the police. There was considerable unrest in the aftermath of the First World War and the Desborough Committee was established in 1919 to consider changes to the recruitment of police officers and to their terms and conditions of employment.

> Altogether, among the lower working class the actions of the police had left them no better loved than they had been before. In 1908 the Chief Constable of Manchester, in his annual report, thought that modern police duty bore 'little resemblance to that of thirty or forty years earlier. Then the policeman dealt largely with the criminal: now he is rendering a public service to all classes.' That he was rendering some sort of service to the poorest of the day there can be not much doubt: during 1908 more than 180,000 of them went to gaol, mostly for miserable little offences, the highest number in decades … nobody in our Northern slum, to my recollection, ever spoke in fond regard, then or afterwards, of the policeman as 'social worker' and 'handyman of the streets'. Like their children, delinquent or not, the poor in general looked upon him with fear and dislike. When one arrived on a 'social' visit they watched his passing with suspicion and his disappearance with relief.

Source: Roberts, R. (1971: 99–100).

The Desborough Committee recommended a substantial rise in police pay and also, importantly, that such matters should be standardised and centrally controlled. Arguably, this was the moment that symbolised the profound shift away from local police authority power and towards increasingly centralised power of the Home Office. This more centralised approach to policing was supported by the use of legal theory in explaining the constitutional position of the police, and the Home Office increasingly sought to 'popularise the theme that the keeping of the King's peace was a Royal Prerogative as old as the monarchy itself' (Morgan, 1987).

Though the problems of police and conditions were not as bad at the end of the Second World War as they had been at the end of the First, the government was nonetheless forced to act to improve matters, and in 1948 established the Oaksey Committee. This was less favourable to the police than Desborough had been, but it did signal the beginnings of a shift away from traditional beat work, and towards a new world dominated by radios and cars. As Emsley (2003) notes, though morale remained low, by this time police–public relations appeared strong, and the positive view of policing was captured in the post-war Ealing studios film, *The Blue Lamp*, which saw the first appearance of PC George Dixon. In fact, as the Oaksey Committee's exploration of the potential of cars and radios illustrated, even by 1950 when the film was released, Dixon was already something of an anachronism. Neither this, nor the fact that Dixon was fatally shot in the film, prevented the character being resurrected in the extraordinarily long-running BBC TV series, *Dixon of Dock Green* (see Chapter 4).

The important point to note here is that, by this point, public trust in policing was extremely high, and the century or so that had passed since the introduction of the new police had witnessed the completion of a remarkable project: the acquisition of legitimacy by an institution that was both widely resisted and largely distrusted when first introduced. Despite this achievement, it would not do to exaggerate matters. Interestingly, or even ironically, a number of scandals hit policing in the 1950s: in 1956 the chief constable and some senior officers in Brighton were charged with corruption and dismissed, and two officers imprisoned; the chief constable of Worcester was jailed for fraud around the same time; a dispute arose in Nottingham between the chief constable, Captain Popkess, and his Watch Committee, leading to his dismissal (though he was eventually reinstated by the Home Secretary). These and other scandals led to the establishment of a Royal Commission in 1960 and signalled the end of the high point of police legitimacy in Britain. We return to this issue in Chapter 25.

The victim and prosecution

In the contemporary criminal justice process (described in detail in Chapters 22–30) the victim plays a fairly passive role. There are currently attempts afoot to make the criminal justice system more 'victim-centred' and yet there are considerable constraints on the extent to which this is possible. However, if we look back over a longer historical period we can see that victims have occupied a rather more active and central role in prosecution of crime, as well as in crime prevention and detection.

As late as the eighteenth century, private actions brought by individuals were more important than actions brought by the state. Three hundred years ago, the state prosecuted relatively few offences and these tended to involve such matters as forgery – convictions for such offences could lead to the death penalty – as well as offences directly against the state like treason and sedition. Indeed, it appears that even in these areas, the government was often slow to get involved, leaving prosecutions to other bodies such as the Bank of England.

In terms of the types of crimes that now fill our courts – offences against individual persons and property – it was not until the creation of formal police forces after 1829 that there was anyone who, in principle, could assume some responsibility for taking them to court, and not until a half century later in 1879 that a public prosecutor was created. In the 1800s, according to Godfrey and Lawrence (2005: 30), 'Tolerance, "rough music" (a form of public shaming ritual often associated with the punishment of henpecked husbands or adulterous couples) and community action were all much more common methods for dealing with minor issues than the constable and the courts' (and see Thompson, 1972). It is highly likely, as the quote indicates, that many 'minor' offences were effectively tolerated – a certain amount of criminality being expected and assumed as a normal part of everyday life. We will return to this idea later in the chapter.

Some punishment might well be meted out by the victim or by the local community. Godfrey and Lawrence quote Henry Mayhew as observing that 'sometimes when these boys are caught pilfering, they are severely beaten especially by the women, who are aided by the men, if the thief offers any formidable resistance' (2005: 31).

It seems attitudes toward violence changed during the nineteenth century. In short, tolerance lessened. Whereas at the beginning of the century it was often accepted as part and parcel of everyday living, and as a means of solving disputes, gradually this gave way to a sense that the state – primarily through the police – should seek to prevent violence. One should not overstate the speed with which this change occurred or, indeed, exaggerate how fully change was achieved. Certainly, in the early decades of the twentieth century, violence within working-class communities was still tolerated in ways that seem unusual by the standards of the early twenty-first century.

The formalisation of the prosecution process

During the eighteenth and nineteenth centuries private prosecutions remained the dominant means of bringing cases to court. Even in more serious cases where the case was heard by a judge, 'the verdict of guilt or innocence was pronounced by a trial jury drawn from minor property owners within the same broad area' (Rawlings, 1999: 16). That said, the cost of bringing cases to court meant that extra-judicial means of dealing with crime remained common. Sometimes, local people would organise themselves into groups – Associations for the Prosecution of Felons – which functioned somewhat like co-operatives, enabling people through the payment of a fee to have their cases supported. The groups were generally small, having between 20–30 members, and generally involved the wealthier sections of community, effectively looking to protect themselves against the poor. To some extent the fact that these Associations existed meant that there was less pressure to introduce a formal police force than might otherwise have been the case (though, as we have seen, there were many other sources of resistance to the introduction of the police). As Philips notes:

> Where property owners had an active Association for the Prosecution of Felons in existence their attitude is easy to understand. They paid their subscription to their Association, which protected their property alone. Why, then, choose to pay [presumably much higher] rates for a police force to serve the whole country, which would spend much of its time policing other people's property? (quoted in Godfrey and Lawrence, 2005: 35)

As we saw above, it is only relatively recently that social control has become something formally associated with the state rather than being largely delegated to the population. To this end the populace was encouraged, via various forms of coercion and bribery, to take on such responsibilities. From the late seventeenth century, rewards were offered by the state – and later by insurance companies and voluntary associations – for successful prosecutions. Indeed:

> Neighbours, friends and associates of the victim might also contribute to particular rewards. It eventually became a matter of course for the victim himself to promise a reward, often by public advertisement. So commonplace did this practice become that a failure to follow it could be construed as a tacit condoning of an offence. The business of crime control became entrepreneurial,

an area to be exploited for gain by small organisations devoted to thief taking. (Rock, 1983: 201)

In the eighteenth century, as we have seen, 'thief taking' became common. Again, however, corruption was rife and Rawlings (1999: 20) suggests that thief takers may 'have blackmailed far more felony suspects than they brought to trial because of the costs involved in a prosecution and because of the risk that an accused would be acquitted or convicted of a lesser charge for which no reward was offered'.

It was not until the mid-nineteenth century and the passage of the County and Borough Police Act 1856 that the police became much more centrally involved in the process of bringing prosecutions. As they did, so the role of the 'victim' changed substantially. It is not that they no longer brought prosecutions – private prosecutions are still possible today, of course – merely that, from this point onward, the balance in bringing prosecutions shifted markedly toward the state.

STEPHEN MACDANIEL,

(Thief Taker.)

Stephen McDaniel, a mid-eighteenth century thief taker who led a gang alleged to have 'preyed on innocent, friendless young men and boys, tempting them into crime only to give them up to the courts and collect the rewards'.

A further way in which the role of the citizen changed in relation to criminal justice is in the use of self-defence. Certainly in the seventeenth and eighteenth centuries there appears to have been significantly greater tolerance of the use of violence in self-defence than might be allowed nowadays. Blackstone, in his classic text on the criminal law, appears to condone the use of violence, so long as it is a fairly immediate reaction to a criminal attack. During the course of the nineteenth century the use of violence in this manner appears to have declined. There are a number of reasons why this might be so.

In part, no doubt, it reflects the gradually increasing visibility and reach of the new formalised police forces. It almost certainly also reflects changing attitudes toward the use of violence by private citizens. Historians such as Beattie (1986), for example, have noted the relatively high level of tolerance of violence in the eighteenth century. In part this may be seen as a long-term process – what the German sociologist Norbert Elias refers to as the 'civilising process' – in which greater and greater control is exercised over a whole range of emotions and bodily functions. Also, it is likely that growing concern about the new industrial working classes, and the potential of revolution, also led to restrictions on the use of violence by private citizens. Such processes continued and gathered pace into the twentieth century as concerns about both communism and fascism emerged and spread.

A further illustration of the role of victims and other citizens in criminal justice in earlier times can be found in the relatively widespread practice of hiring police constables as a form of extra 'private' protection. The hiring of officials such as the Bow Street Runners was widespread prior to the introduction of the new police, and such practices by no means disappeared after 1829. Police officers were hired as watchmen to guard premises. In effect, they were hired as private security guards and, as such, were clear descendants of Jonathan Wild and his like. Well into the second half of the nineteenth century, police forces retained such 'additional constables', and one authority on the subject has estimated that such officers made up close to one quarter of the full strength of some forces in the North of England in the 1860s (Steedman, 1984). Of course they never disappeared. Over time, such practices were no longer allowed to be undertaken by police officers, and such watchmen duties were undertaken by private enterprises – what we would now call 'private security'.

By the mid-twentieth century, many such practices had long been abandoned. However, it was a slow and long-term process of change and by no means a simple reflection of the introduction of police forces. As Godfrey and Lawrence (2005: 45) conclude, 'The emergence of the new police certainly had a great effect over the entire period. But this was no watershed and we cannot categorically say that because a formal policing and prosecuting structure had arrived so the prosecution associations, the need and/or "right" of citizens to defend themselves or extra-judicial initiatives disappeared.'

The courts

As with every other area of criminal justice, the courts system underwent radical overhaul from the late eighteenth century onward. The bureaucratic court system that now exists is, like the police and the prison, a product of modern, industrial society. Criminal cases in the eighteenth century were mainly private prosecutions. Cases didn't involve professional representation by lawyers, and could be held in settings as varied as private rooms or the local inn. Though gradual formalisation took place, in the early nineteenth century even trials at the Old Bailey could still be quick and somewhat chaotic proceedings.

During the eighteenth century there was a substantial increase in the range of cases that could be heard by a single magistrate – i.e. summarily – and the numbers of such cases increased markedly as a result. By the latter half of the nineteenth century most cases were prosecuted by a police prosecutor in police courts. As Paul Rock (2004) outlines, it wasn't until the late nineteenth century that state prosecution, or the role of barrister, came into being, and by the early twentieth century the basis of the modern court system had largely been established.

The history of any aspect of criminal justice involves a number of competing narratives. What I mean by this is that there are at least two quite different ways of presenting the 'story' of the introduction of the police (as we have seen) or, in this case, the gradual emergence of the modern court system. One approach is to construct the story largely in terms of *progress*. Underpinning this approach are two fundamental assumptions. First, there is the notion that the systems that we have today are *better* than those that preceded them. Second, that the gradual improvement that took place was *necessary*; that it somehow met needs that were not previously catered for. The second approach avoids ideas of progress. It tends to look

for another sort of rationale to explain the changes observed. This might be the nature of class society (new means of regulating the working classes) or the changing nature of industrial society and, more particularly, the shift from absolutist monarchy to parliamentary democracy.

Similarly, there are two broadly contrasting approaches to making sense of the evolution of the criminal law during the seventeenth to nineteenth centuries. On the one hand, there is a largely consensual model, again focusing on *progress* and on the rationalisation and bureaucratisation of the legal system, and a more conflictual model that asks 'in whose interests' is the law operating? Godfrey and Lawrence argue that Leon Radzinowicz's path-breaking multi-volume, *History of the English Criminal Law* (published between 1948 and 1986) falls into the former category. In the latter category we find Marxist historians such as Douglas Hay, Edward Thompson, and others.

Intriguingly, it appears that in the late eighteenth and early nineteenth centuries it was relatively rare for violence to be prosecuted unless it resulted in death. There is much disagreement among historians as to the extent to which it is accurate to view the legal system as a means of protecting the rights of the propertied and regulating the lives of the poor. There is considerable evidence to support E.P. Thompson's (1975: 264) contention that 'the law did mediate existent class relations to the advantage of the rulers'. However, other historians such as Beattie have shown that, to a large extent, the interests of the propertied formed a relatively small part of the business of the courts, and although the law was clearly applied unequally, the picture is more complex and nuanced than simple 'class interest' accounts would allow for.

The decline of the profit motive

A system of paid magistrates was established, initially in London, at the end of the eighteenth century. Their emergence was part of a larger shift away from the practice of criminal justice for profit – a shift which saw the decline of so-called 'trading justices' who took a proportion of the fines they imposed, the ending of the 'garnish' in prison (a payment made on arrival) as well as other payments, such as for the use of lighter manacles ('easement of irons') – and reflected, in part, the growing wealth of the UK. At this time there were three main types of criminal court. The most serious cases were heard by the Central Criminal Court (the Old Bailey) which only met a few times a year.

Other serious cases – but not cases that might result in the death penalty – were heard at County quarter sessions. Finally, less serious offences were heard by magistrates within local, petty sessional divisions. These hearings were gradually formalised during the nineteenth century. Indeed, there was a considerable growth in the use of these courts in the early nineteenth century – perhaps as much as sixfold (Gattrell and Hadden, 1972).

The growing importance of the magistracy in the criminal justice process brought forth fears about the decline of the jury and also concerns that magistrates might enforce the law in such a way as to reinforce or protect their own interests (they were primarily men of property at this time). Indeed, according to Godfrey and Lawrence (2005: 61), 'the role of the criminal justice system in supporting the existing status quo (both social and political) is quite evident during the period 1850–1950, albeit not perhaps as clearly as a century before'. The courts, they argue, represented something of a mixture of fairness and support for the existing social order.

During this period, the judiciary and magistrates had an important role in the maintenance of public order – a role that in due course passed to the police. Prior to the police becoming an effective force for the maintenance of order, it was the army that would be used to quell rioting. The 'reading of the riot act' – actually involving the reading of part of the 1715 Act – would be undertaken by a magistrate and would allow the protesters one hour in which to disperse peaceably prior to the army being called upon, assuming existing constables couldn't deal with the incident. Having read out the Act, the offence of 'riot' became punishable by death.

It took much of the nineteenth century for the new police gradually to acquire primary responsibility for quelling large-scale public disorder. According to Emsley (1983: 69), in the 'first ten years of their existence the Metropolitan Police had become something of a national riot squad' operating around the country to suppress disorder and keep the peace at elections. This is not to say that the military were never called upon, but it was increasingly rare. In the Battle of Trafalgar Square in 1887 the Commissioner called for

The Reform League Meeting in Hyde Park, London, in 1866 turns riotous and the police struggle to maintain control. Over 16,000 police officers, mounted and on foot, were drafted in to deal with one of the largest demonstrations to have taken place in the capital. But it was the police, not the army, who were used to control riots.

support from a squadron of Life Guards and two companies of foot guards. This was the first occasion since the mid-1850s that the Metropolitan Police had called for military support and on this occasion there was no military intervention. There were also elements of military organisation about the Metropolitan Police itself, of course. One critical MP in the late 1880s commented that the previous two decades had witnessed the transformation of the police into 'a quasi-military force, drilled, distributed and managed as soldiers ... a cumbrous and badly-organised army' (Bailey, 1981: 106).

Philips (1983: 65–66) in his assessment of 'revisionist' history of this period concludes that the changes can be seen as:

> ... part of the wider process in which the governing class of Britain adjusted to the changes and problems presented by the Industrial Revolution period. There is ample evidence that many of the country gentry would have liked to continue the eighteenth century system of administration and enforcement of the law which ... suited their purposes well ... The rapid growth of large towns and cities ... with their large concentrations of working-class populations removed from face-to-face contact with squire and parson, posed problems for the maintenance of social order that could not be solved by the old methods of control ... New methods of control were needed – in factory discipline and mass education, as well as in the distribution of poor relief and the administration of law, order and punishment. The prison, the workhouse, the factory and the school stand out in nineteenth-century Britain as concrete symbols of the attempts to instil a new sort of discipline and control in the masses of early industrial society.

Review questions

1 What are the main differences in approach in 'traditional' and 'revisionist' histories?

2 In what ways did Robert Peel and the other main architects of the 'new police' seek to minimise the threat they were perceived to pose?

3 What are the main elements of the modern, bureaucratic system of justice?

Punishment

It is in the area of punishment that some of the greatest contrasts can be seen over the past two or three centuries. In the mid-eighteenth century the infliction of very severe punishment on the body of the offender remained relatively common. Seemingly, some of the more severe, non-fatal bodily mutilations that could be carried out on offenders – such as burning the hands of a thief – were beginning to fade out, but whipping and flogging remained fairly common and execution was still public and, on occasion, still completed by the parading of the condemned. A further hundred years on and the death penalty was all but abolished.

Capital punishment

Capital punishment remained relatively common well into the nineteenth century, with even relatively minor offences by today's standards being potentially punishable by death, though such sentences were passed much more often than they were carried out. Gatrell (1994) has argued that there was something of an increase in executions in the early nineteenth century, rather in contrast to much historical opinion which suggests that punishment was becoming less harsh during this period. In this vein, the Bloody Code has often been viewed as a prime illustration of the harshness and violence of much contemporary punishment.

The 'Bloody Code' refers to the large number of statutes passed during the eighteenth century which contained the penalty of death. Historians disagree as to the precise number of such statutes and, indeed, it probably doesn't much matter. We can reasonably estimate that there were somewhere between 150 and 250 such statutes. Intriguingly, the preceding years had seen a fairly significant decline in the numbers of people being hanged. At the end of the sixteenth century, it seems, about one quarter of all those tried for a felony were hanged, but this had dropped to one in ten by the early 1700s (Rawlings, 1999).

Why the decline? There are a number of possible explanations, including the possibility that crime dropped, that concerns about crime declined, that judges were stricter in the interpretation of the law, and that transportation came increasingly to be seen as a useful alternative. So, we then see the odd development in which the numbers of people being executed continues to decline at the same time as parliament passes a large number of new laws involving the death penalty. At least part of this legislative activity was what would be called 'symbolic politics'. It was parliament flexing its muscles and asserting its authority, without necessarily requiring that the law be enforced. In fact, the state was in many respects simply not in a position to enforce such laws much of the time (Rock, 1983). The passing of the legislation was often as much as could be achieved. Indeed, the preamble to the 1752 Murder Act gives something of a flavour of this. The Act aimed to provide 'some further Terror and peculiar Mark of Infamy' and 'to impress a just Horror in the Mind of the Offender, and on the Minds of such as shall be present, of the heinous Crime of Murder' (quoted in Rawlings, 1999: 49).

In this vein, Emsley is critical of some interpretations of the 'Bloody Code'. He is critical of the assumption made by some historians that the large number of statutes is a straightforward indication of the number of offences liable to result in the application of the death penalty. In fact, he suggests, there was a lot of duplication or overlap among the statutes. Second, many of the hangings that took place were actually the result of statutes other than those passed as part of the Bloody Code and, furthermore, that in a very large proportion of cases, the offenders were eventually pardoned.

A public hanging in Smithfield Market in the mid-eighteenth century. A century later Charles Dickens, after attending a public execution, expressed himself horrified by the spectacle.

One of the reasons for the declining faith in the efficacy of public executions was the increasing sense that far from providing a spectacle likely to deter the public from crime, such events were becoming more like carnivals at which entertainment was to be had. Reporting on a public execution in 1849 Charles Dickens reported on:

> … a sight so inconceivably awful as the wickedness and levity of the immense crowd collected … could be imagined by no man … The horrors of the gibbet and of the crime which brought the wretched murderers to it faded in my mind before the atrocious bearing, looks, and language of the assembled spectators. When I came across the scene at midnight, the *shrillness* of the cries and howls that were raised from time to time, denoting that they came from a concourse of boys and girls already assembled in the best places, made my blood run cold. (in Wiener, 1990: 97, quoted in Godfrey and Lawrence, 2005: 72–3)

Although such punishment was progressively seen not only as relatively ineffectual – failing to prevent crime to any extent – and also, as Dickens indicates, as potentially corrupting, it continued to serve an important symbolic function well into the nineteenth century. Although the move to undertaking executions in private has sometimes been interpreted as a civilising move, one of its advocates, Henry Fielding, certainly saw such a move as having the potential to increase the terror associated with executions by removing the sense of familiarity that attached to it (Gatrell 1994). Terrifying the masses could hardly have been helped by cases such as one Rawlings reports in which Thomas Reynolds, in 1736, was hanged and having been taken from the gallows was put in a coffin. He then 'thrust back the Lid, and … clapt his Hands on the Sides of the Coffin in order to raise himself up' (1999: 51). Even though the crowd prevented the hangman from hanging him once more Reynolds didn't survive. Nor did public executions. The gallows at Tyburn were removed in 1759 and the public procession from Newgate to Tyburn ceased in 1783.

As we will see in greater detail below, as the balance of severe punishment began to shift from transportation to imprisonment so confidence in public rituals surrounding the punishment of the body declined. Branding was formally abolished in 1779, and whipping was declining markedly. John Howard, the famous prison reformer, was campaigning vigorously against corporal punishment

Four of the six 'Tolpuddle martyrs' (from a village in Dorset) who were transported to Australia in 1834, having formed a union to protest against the lowering of agricultural wages.

in prison, and the frequency and nature of public executions were changing. After the ending of the Tyburn procession, executions took place within the prison itself. The number of pardons was increasing also and so only a relatively small proportion of those sentenced to death was actually hanged (Radzinowicz 1948). According to Ignatieff (1978: 90), the whole movement:

> ... indicates a loss of confidence in the morality and efficacy of ritual punishments, a growing resistance to the idea that the state should share the infliction of the punishment with the community assembled at the foot of the gallows or around the whipping post. Withdrawing the gallows under the shadow of Newgate and increasing the use of imprisonment denied the offender the opportunity for public defiance and the crowd the chance to turn the ritual to its own purposes. Compared to ritual punishment, imprisonment offered the state unparalleled control over the offender, enabling it to regulate the amount of suffering involved in any sentence, free of the jeers of the populace.

The one major alternative at this time was to use transportation.

Transportation

As with the death penalty, transportation also declined during a similar period. Although there is record of the transportation of prisoners to the West Indies as early as the 1680s, the practice was formalised after 1718. Initially, convicts were sent to America, generally for periods of seven or 14 years. With the War of Independence in the 1770s, America no longer represented a potential destination for Britain's convicts and an alternative was sought. Initially, some convicts were sent to Africa, and closer to home a Hard Labour Bill proposed the creation of what would in effect have been a penal colony in England, though the proposal was defeated. Its defeat indicates that despite the work of reformers like John Howard, England at that stage was still some distance from embracing something like the prison as a standard form of punishment.

The Penitentiary Act as early as 1779 had attempted to stimulate prison building, though unsuccessfully. That said, for a time the government used old battleships that were moored in various English dockyards, including on the Thames, as a temporary site for convicted felons. From 1787 Australia, a six-month voyage from Britain, became the new destination. Conditions in the ships were poor and death rates high. Once ashore, convicts were put to work for local landowners. By the early nineteenth century up to 5,000 prisoners were being sent to Australia each year and in the 70 years from 1787 over 160,000 convicts were sent to Australia.

Transportation declined in popularity during the nineteenth century, for a number of reasons.

- Public opinion slowly turned against the practice.
- Doubts as to its effectiveness increased.
- The colonies themselves began to resent and resist the practice (see Braithwaite, 2001).

Ending the practice was far from easy as some alternative had to be found for the many thousands who hitherto had been sent overseas. In the event that alternative was the prison. Interest in workhouses and houses of correction had existed for some time,

The Fatal Shore

By January 6, 1787, the first convicts were loaded from the Woolwich hulks ... Who were these First Fleet convicts? It was once a cherished Australian belief that at least some of the First Fleet were political exiles – rick-burners, trade unionists, and the like. In fact, though victims of a savage penal code, they were not political prisoners. On the other hand, few of them were dangerous criminals. Not one person was shipped out in 1787 for murder or rape, although more than 100 of them had been convicted of thefts (such as highway robbery in which violence played some part ...).

In all, 736 convicts went on the First Fleet ... The oldest male convict was a Shropshire man, Joseph Owen, who was somewhere between 60 and 66. The youngest boy was John Hudson, a nine-year-old chimney sweep. He had stolen some clothes and a pistol ... The convicts were 'humble, submissive and regular' on this first leg of the voyage ... They had been told 'in the most pointed terms that any attempt ... to force their escape should be punished with instant death'. Escape, however, was unlikely, as they were chained, in shock and monstrously seasick ...

On the evening of January 19 [1788] [they] sighted the coast of mainland Australia ... It had been one of the great sea voyages in English history. Captain Arthur Phillip ... had brought them across more than 15,000 miles of ocean without losing a ship. The entire run had taken 252 days. A total of 48 people had died ... Given the rigours of the voyage and the primitive medical knowledge of the day, the crammed ships and the lack of anti-scorbutics, the poor planning and the bad equipment, it was a tiny death rate – a little over three per cent. The sea had spared them; now, they must survive on the unknown land ...

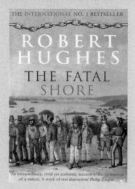

Now the hard work began, and it soon became clear that the colonists were wretchedly equipped for it. Not only was there a dearth of skilled labour, but tools were short ... The only good building timber came from the cabbage-tree palms that grew in profusion around the stream at Sydney Cove ... All were cut down within a year ... The land was not what it seemed. It looked fertile and lovely, but it proved arid, reluctant, incomprehensible ...

The hateful equalizer was hunger. This first democratic experience in Australia spared no-one. It made most of the colonists stupid and some crazy, playing havoc with morale and producing endless displays of petty tyranny ... Only a third of prisoners could work ... More than 50 convicts were too feeble from age and incurable illness to work at all, and many others – slum-raised, utterly ignorant of farming – 'would starve if left to themselves' ...

Source: Hughes, R. (2003: 70–97).

and in some quarters there was growing attraction to the idea of reformation of offenders in penitentiaries. Perceived by some as an American idea and therefore unacceptable (why should Britain wish to import ideas from its former colonies?) the ideas were not especially quick to take hold.

Imprisonment

There was a substantial prison-building programme at the end of the eighteenth century, yet local resistance remained relatively strong and prison conditions remained very poor. At this stage belief in the idea of moral reform – of rehabilitation through hard work and discipline – was growing, and the poor prison conditions were increasingly viewed as likely to undermine this aim. As we have noted the Penitentiary Act in the late 1770s failed. Briefly, Jeremy Bentham's design for the 'panopticon' (see Chapter 5) was embraced by government, but the expense it would entail, especially alongside the cost of transportation, led to its being dropped. It was considered again in 1810 and again rejected. Indeed, Rawlings (1999) suggests that even by that stage the panopticon's time had passed – its central premise of the importance of 'deterrence through theatrical spectacle' was no longer in tune with the dominant ideas of the time.

When eventually new prisons were built – the Millbank penitentiary on the Thames and then Pentonville prison – they were informed by elements of Bentham's plans, not least the idea that the architecture of the institution was crucial in meeting its objectives (though American penitentiaries built in the early nineteenth century were another important influence). Such ideas declined during the nineteenth century as concerns about prison conditions grew and began to dominate decisions about design. Neither of the new prisons

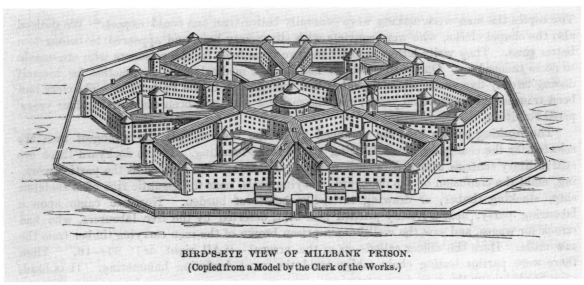

BIRD'S-EYE VIEW OF MILLBANK PRISON.
(Copied from a Model by the Clerk of the Works.)

A model of Millbank penitentiary, built on the shore of the Thames in London where Tate Britain now stands. Building of the new prison was completed in 1821, and incorporated elements of Jeremy Bentham's design for the 'panopticon'.

was deemed much of a success and with transportation continuing, pressure to expand the prison system was muted.

Transportation was formally abolished in 1868. Around the same time the hulks were abandoned and public whipping and hanging ceased. At the same time, interest in the prison grew markedly. The return of troops from the Crimean War and another crime panic stimulated debate about punishment once again. John Howard had published his *State of the Prisons* in 1777, yet there remained considerable resistance to any idea that promoted the role of the state over local government in the provision of justice. It was this that held back not only the emergence of a prison system, but also the introduction of a formal system of policing. As we have seen by the 1830s central government was expanding its reach and confidence in relation to policing, and this was also true of imprisonment.

Gatrell (1994: 10) suggests that 'there has been no greater nor more sudden revolution in English penal history than [the] retreat from hanging in the 1830s'. Again, as with other areas of criminal justice history, it is possible to represent this change – the replacement of the death penalty and transportation with the prison – as 'the march of progress'. Undoubtedly, reformers with sincere humanitarian beliefs play an important part in the story. However, it is equally possible, and in many ways plausible, to argue that the emergence of the prison represents the development of a more subtle, and insidious, form of surveillance and social

control. The Marxist historians, Rusche and Kirchheimer, for example, relate the rise of the prison to the changing economic structure of industrial society. Industrial society, as all societies, discovered punishments which corresponded to its productive relationships, they argued. Unlike medieval society, industrial society required convicts for productive labour and could not easily afford wasteful punishments such as banishment or death.

In part, the ending of public executions in 1868 was a political decision taken by the Liberal government of the day because of concerns about the potential for outright abolition – something it wished to avoid at all costs. By the mid-nineteenth century incarceration had become the major sanction for dealing with adult offenders. In essence it took two forms: 'imprisonment' where sentences of up to two years were served in a local prison; and 'penal servitude' where sentences were five years or more and were served in a convict prison such as Millbank or Pentonville. Early prison regimes had a reformative or rehabilitative purpose. However, according to Godfrey and Lawrence (2005: 75) 'this interest in reform was ... largely abandoned in the period 1865–1895'.

The Penal Servitude Act 1865 restricted the use of remission with the intention that the general level of severity should be increased once more. Although the new measures 'were intended to increase the deterrence value of penal servitude, their ironic effect was to curtail the use of penal

George Smith, a garrotter, receives the sixth of 30 lashes of the cat-o'-nine-tails, 1872.

servitude and to make imprisonment in local prisons the mainstay of the whole system' (Garland 1985: 7). Much punishment in the Victorian era was relatively harsh, though the basis for the more fully rehabilitative approach that emerged in the twentieth century was laid in this period. The reasons for this change are complicated. In part, the shift to what Garland has referred to as 'penal-welfarism' reflects broader social changes related to the problems of poverty in Victorian society, and the rise of voluntary philanthropic bodies dedicated to its removal. In considerably less than a century the penal system had seen a radical overhaul:

> England and Wales entered the twentieth century with a system of judicial punishments which showed, in embryo at least, a number of differing trends. At the centre of the system, practically and symbolically, stood the prison. Hardly thought of as a dominant form of punishment for the serious offender in 1800, by 1900 the prison was firmly established in both the popular consciousness and the practice of the courts as the most potent means by which the generality of offenders might be punished. (Sharpe, 1990: 88)

As was outlined in Chapter 1, it was this period – and by no means coincidentally – which saw the emergence of 'criminology'. In particular, the shift from classicism which approached criminals as rational beings in charge of their own destiny (see Chapter 5) to a criminology that saw the individual offender as buffeted by forces beyond his control, fitted neatly with an increasingly welfarist approach, which sought both to mitigate the circumstances that had led offenders into a life of crime and to save them. Put a different way, there was a significant shift away from seeing crime as a 'moral' issue related to the personality of the offender toward a more 'scientific' approach which was concerned with the conditions in which the individual was created. Radical changes in scientific knowledge, associated with Darwin and others, led to considerable changes in the ways in which the individual was understood. Late nineteenth-century science saw individuals in relatively weak terms, their fate largely determined by heredity and environment. A new army of professionals – psychiatrists, probation officers, medics, and criminologists – emerged to offer various forms of treatment.

Probation

'Probation' has its origins in the Victorian temperance movement and what were then known as *police court missionaries*. Two developments are central to an understanding of the origins and emergence of the probation service: the changing jurisdiction of the magistrates' courts, and increasing concern about drunkenness and the disorderly behaviour that drinking frequently led to. In the second half of the nineteenth century the magistrates' courts became recognisable courts of justice. A number of significant Acts of Parliament resulted in offences which had previously been dealt with in assizes or quarter sessions becoming the business of the magistrates' courts. In addition, new laws also gave the courts greater supervisory powers over juvenile offenders. It was against this background that the idea of supervision of such offenders emerged.

The second half of the nineteenth century had seen a dramatic rise in concern about drunkenness, and in the numbers convicted of and imprisoned for drunkenness and for disorderly behaviour. McWilliams (1983) notes that there were over 88,000 offenders convicted of such offences in 1860 and by 1876 this had risen to over 200,000. In the same period the numbers imprisoned rose from just under 4,000 to almost 24,000. Indeed, McWilliams suggests that, in London, arrests for

drunk and disorderly, drunkenness, and disorderly prostitutes and disorderly characters represented over half of all recorded crime in the capital.

In the 1860s the Church of England Total Abstinence Society was established. Relatively quickly it amended its approach in order to incorporate people other than abstainers, and in 1873 changed its name to the Church of England Temperance Society (CETS). Its membership had reached close on one million by the 1890s. It had three primary goals: the promotion of temperance; the removal of the causes which lead to intemperance; and crucially for our purposes here the reformation of the intemperate. Reforming or 'reclaiming' drunkards through a mission to the police courts was, it is suggested, initially the idea of a printer named Frederick Rainer who, in a letter to the CETS, bemoaned what he saw to be the fate of the drunk facing the courts: 'offence after offence, sentence after sentence appears to be the inevitable lot of him whose foot has once slipped' (quoted in Jarvis, 1972).

The first two police court missionaries, George Nelson and William Batchelor, were both ex-Coldstream Guards men and were appointed in 1876 and 1877. They worked in the Bow, Mansion House, Southwark and Lambeth courts in London. McWilliams (1983: 134) describes their initial efforts in the courts as being 'directed to exhorting offenders to give up drink, distributing uplifting tracts and taking pledges of abstinence'. The work in the courts expanded quickly and came to dominate the activities of the missionaries within the period of a decade. The work was 'unapologetically evangelical', the aim being 'to reclaim the lives and souls of drunks appearing before the courts. They would ask the magistrates to bind individuals over into their care and they would undertake to secure their "restoration and reclamation"' (Mathieson, 1992: 143).

There is one crucial further linking step between the work of the police court missionary and what in the twentieth century we associate with the probation officer. McWilliams (1985: 253) describes it as follows:

> It is important to recall that in their work in the courts the missionaries were not pleading for mercy for all offenders; such a course would undoubtedly have been self-defeating. Rather their pleas were reserved for those offenders deemed suitable for moral reform and this ensured, at least at the beginning, that in addition to intrinsic worth a missionary's plea also had a sort of novelty value. Even with selective application, however, the strong possibility

---

How they came in.

The following are some of the offences which brought the boys admitted last year into the Police Courts:

185 were charged with larceny and embezzlement.

59 were charged with sleeping out or wandering.

Other charges were: house breaking, assault, beyond parents control , &c., while

27 boys were "not charged" but the parents applied for advice to the magistrates.

How they went out.

Situations were found for 69 as Engineers or Munition workers.

41 as Bakers,

52 as Farm workers

Others as Grocers, Butchers, Carpenters, Shoemakers, etc.

NO LONGER TROUBLESOME BOYS

BUT

USEFUL CITIZENS.

958 of our Old Boys are serving in H.M. Forces.

Many have been mentioned in dispatches.

One has won the V.C., five the D.C.M.

Five received commissions.

THE HOOLIGANS OF THE STREETS

HAVE BECOME

HEROES IN THE TRENCHES.

'How they came in' and 'How they went out': the work of the Police Court Mission as presented in their fund-raising brochure 'Saving the Lads', 1919.

existed that special pleading would become a routine … The missionaries began to depend upon a form of justification for their pleas and this was that offenders worthy of mercy could reform under kindly guidance; that is to say that the missionaries' pleas in court began to be linked to the notion of *supervision*, and in particular to the idea that some offenders were suitable for reform under supervision.

As supervisors of offenders deemed to be deserving of mercy, the missionaries increasingly played a part in the process of determining which offenders were to be considered 'suitable for moral reform'. This meant undertaking inquiries prior to sentencing and, although it is not clear when they first undertook such work for the courts, it is likely that they were doing so by the time that the extension of supervision from 'licence holders and habitual criminals' to first offenders at risk of imprisonment was made by the Probation of First Offenders Act 1887.

Jarvis notes that by 1907 – the point at which the modern probation service originates – there were 124 male and 19 female missionaries from the CETS working in the courts, together with a small number of missionaries from other bodies. Despite the central role played by the police court missionaries in the nineteenth and early twentieth century, most commentators are agreed that it would be a gross oversimplification to suggest that the probation service grew directly from such work. The missionaries provided a model for work with offenders, and established the ground whereupon a welfare organisation could work in the courts, but 'the idea which led directly to the passing of the Probation of Offenders Act in 1907 stemmed from American experience and practice, and was actively supported in this country, not from a concern for adult offenders, but from a profound anxiety over the treatment of children by the courts' (Jarvis, 1972: 9). At the same time as probation was introduced, so a separate system of juvenile justice was created, involving both a juvenile court and the gradual emergence of a set of penalties created specifically for young offenders.

Review questions

1 What was the 'Bloody Code'?

2 What were the main reasons for the ending of transportation?

3 What are the main origins of probation?

Crime and violence in history

Underlying all our discussions of the changing nature of criminal justice in British history is, of course, the issue of the nature and level of crime in the same period. Before we move on, it is important to guard against any simple assumption that somehow the nature and level of punishment in society is a straightforward reflection of the nature and extent of crime. This is manifestly not the case, and this is a caution that will be repeated at regular intervals throughout this book. However, it would be equally misleading to suggest that there is no connection between crime and punishment. Consequently, it is worth pausing briefly to consider what it is possible to say about the level of crime at different points in British history.

Levels of crime

As we will see in greater detail in the next chapter, even with the aid of modern crime statistics, understanding levels and patterns of crime with any degree of accuracy is rarely a straightforward business. Official criminal statistics were not collected until the mid-nineteenth century and even then it is doubtful how much value can be placed on them – certainly until some time after the Second World War. Prior to the mid-nineteenth century, therefore, we have to rely on other sources of data in order to get some feel for levels of crime and any changes that may have been taking place.

By and large, historians use court data as the basis for understanding earlier periods. There are a number of difficulties with this, however. Such records are rarely complete, and they are generally only available for particular local areas. Even where records are available, and consistently so over a period of time, there remains the problem that besets all official records: to what extent are they able to tell one anything other than how particular systems operated in certain historical periods? Thus, if there appears to be a substantial increase or decrease in particular types of offence coming before the courts, does this reflect changes in patterns of crime, changes in the operation of the police and/or the courts, or both? Bearing this in mind, what do the historical data suggest?

First, local records suggest something of a diminution in prosecutions from around the 1630s for the next half century or so. For the next century, although there were fluctuations from year to year, there was no substantial overall change in prosecutions for property crimes. They rose in the second half of the eighteenth century and were significantly higher at the close of the century than they were at its beginning. By contrast, homicide appears to drop markedly. According to Sharpe (2001: 127), 'the homicide rate in England ... experienced a massive decrease in the three centuries following the death of Queen Elizabeth I [1603]. Obviously, the strictures that apply to criminal statistics generally must operate here, but one major shift which historians of crime do seem to have established is that there was a major decline in felonious killing as England entered the modern world.'

Official statistics suggest that violent crime declined quite substantially in the second half of the nineteenth century and into the early twentieth century. One important analysis of crime trends in different societies by Ted Robert Gurr (1981: 266–7) suggested that:

> The incidence of serious crime has traced an irregular downward trend for a much longer period of time, in some places for a century or more. When the historical and contemporary evidence are joined together they depict a distended U-shaped curve.

Gurr sought to overcome his reliance on official criminal statistics by focusing only on the most serious crimes (murder and assault), which tend to be more faithfully reported than other less serious crimes. He argues (1976: 37–38) that in London 'rates of convictions for indictable offences for murder, manslaughter, attempted murder, and grievous assault were at their highest recorded levels in the 1840s. They declined between then and the 1920s by a ratio of about 8:1.' However, there is some evidence that the authorities manipulated the system in order to prevent some cases of murder being recognised as such, primarily in order to save money (see Taylor, 1998).

Thus, on the one hand Gurr's data suggests that the nineteenth century saw a sustained drop in levels of violence and, indeed, there is other historical evidence which suggests that violence was higher in previous centuries (Leyton, 1995). On the other hand, Taylor suggests that the police deliberately left many murders and suspicious deaths uninvestigated in order to limit both the number and the cost of prosecutions. Possible further light is thrown on this issue by data on riot and other forms of disturbance during the course of the nineteenth century. There is historical evidence which

suggests that although major disturbances continued on a fairly regular basis well into the nineteenth century – particularly in labour disputes and during political demonstrations – there appears to have been 'a definite trend away from violence and public disorder' in the period between 1835 and 1860 (Philips 1978: 274). Almost certainly, therefore, the Victorians were in large part correct in their portrayal of the era as one of relative orderliness. How any era is understood, however, depends upon more than official estimates of levels of crime. Thus:

> There was more to Victorian perceptions of the orderliness of their society than can be expressed in criminal statistics. In part, one is dealing with attitudes and beliefs which represented a particular moment in social and political development. One crucial perspective for Victorians was that whatever the dangers and difficulties of the past, Britain had escaped the revolutionary upheavals which had affected other nations. (Stevenson, 1979: 298)

Perceptions of crime

As we saw earlier in this chapter, the emergence of what we might understand as the 'modern' criminal justice system – essentially a bureaucratic extension and expression of the nation state – came into being during the eighteenth and nineteenth centuries. Prior to that, 'crime control' was much more a localised matter. The transition toward a centralised state system of justice reflects, in part, changing perceptions of crime or, more accurately, changing perceptions of deviance and, within this, the emergence of something akin to our contemporary notion of 'crime'.

In the seventeenth century and earlier, perceptions of crime were closely tied to ideas of sin and how best it might be suppressed. In other words, crime was not yet a secular term, but was closely bound up with religious morality and the power of the Church. During the eighteenth century this situation gradually changed and it is argued, particularly by radical historians, that ideas of crime and sin rooted in religious teaching were gradually replaced by a set of secular concerns, the most fundamental of which was the need and desire to protect private property. This transition should not be exaggerated, however, for religious ideas and organisations continued to exert a powerful influence throughout the eighteenth and nineteenth centuries – not least through reform programmes aimed at the drunk, the idle and the disorderly.

Nevertheless, as Sharpe (2001: 113) argues, 'the eighteenth century and, perhaps less equivocally, the first half of the nineteenth century did witness the development of what we would consider to be "modern" attitudes to crime and what ought to be done about it', though in all likelihood such 'modern' attitudes have even earlier origins (see Rock, 1994). Nevertheless, in broad terms this meant that crime:

- was increasingly discussed and perceived separately from 'sin';
- was seen as something that should be dealt with via legislation, and should be subject to punishment by the state;
- became a matter of public discussion and debate;
- also increasingly became a staple of popular culture;
- was increasingly seen as comprising murder, rape, theft, robbery, burglary and other more minor offences.

Marxist and radical historians would be quick to point out, however, that there was certainly no consensus in British society at this time over what constituted 'crime'. Indeed, there was considerable conflict around various expressions of working-class cultural activities, which were perceived as perfectly legitimate by their participants and yet were increasingly criminalised by what might be characterised as the 'ruling classes'. In particular, various forms of protest, or what John Stevenson (1992) refers to as 'popular disturbances', are perhaps the best example of this point. A range of historians (see, for example, Thompson, 1975) have argued that, far from being associated with the criminal, the unemployed and the marginal, disturbances such as eighteenth-century food riots, machine-breaking and the 'Captain Swing' episodes of the early nineteenth century, tended to involve a broad cross-section of the working population. In the main they were an expression of economic hardship. Thus, according to Stevenson (1992: 309–313):

> The most striking feature of many English popular disturbances was their essentially defensive character. Whether brought about by high prices, recruiting, new machinery, turnpikes, enclosures, Methodist itinerants, or a myriad of other causes, they occurred most frequently as attempts to resist interference of innovation of some kind ... A similar qualification ought to be made in the case of the violence in popular disturbances; some were undoubtedly violent,

disputes between mobs and press gangs and excise officers particularly so ... Nonetheless, some of the larger disturbances in this period and some of the most frequent occasions of disorder led to very few fatal casualties.

Gradually, as we have seen, during the course of the nineteenth century, forms of protest became more peaceful and orderly. Undoubtedly the introduction of the police made a difference to public order, partly as a visible deterrent and partly through greater surveillance of the streets (Gatrell, 1990; Critchley, 1970). Further, Weiner (1998) argues that the work of the courts also added to the impact made by the police in the second half of the nineteenth century. And yet it does not do to overemphasise the importance or effectiveness of the formal system of crime control, for the historical evidence suggests that increasing orderliness was at least as much a reflection of changes in English culture. In this sense, Stevenson (1992: 323) says, 'the English "mob" tamed itself, at least as much as it was tamed by government or its agents'.

The impression, therefore, and, quite possibly, the reality, was that the period leading up to and including the Victorian era was one of increasing orderliness and stability – certainly in public if not in private. Concerns about the possibility of revolution had largely disappeared and public disorder was coming to be viewed as a 'social problem' rather than as a threat to the political order. According to Gatrell (1990: 248–9):

> Victorian observers would have been struck by their forefathers' relative indifference to crime as a 'problem', and by their relative satisfaction with the apparently arbitrary and capricious mechanisms which contained it. This was not because crime was infrequent then: it is not at all clear that there was less thieving and violence per capita in eighteenth-century cities than in nineteenth. But crime did not as yet appear to threaten hierarchy, and the terms in which crime might be debated as a 'problem' were not yet formed.

Indeed, he goes on to argue that in the earlier era, the very subject simply did not exist in the terms we understand it now. Crime became 'important' over the next half-century and, by the time Sir Robert Peel was establishing the Metropolitan Police, it was increasingly perceived as an indicator of national health and wellbeing.

Terms like 'hooligan' entered common English usage in Victorian times (Pearson, 1983). Although its origins are by no means entirely clear, the term quickly became a shorthand for all manner of youthful misbehaviour, and was associated with street gangs. Certain elements of public opinion were firmly of the view that 'hooligans' represented both a new and terrible threat, and that violence between street gangs had suddenly and dramatically increased. Pearson (1983) cites numerous sources convinced that such 'hooliganism' was indicative of moral decline but, equally, is able to point to similar problems, and similar concerns, in previous historical periods. This was a period of substantial social reform and towards its end saw the emergence of both the probation service and the juvenile court, two further illustrations of the growth of the formal justice system.

Although the second half of the nineteenth century saw some rapid advances in both the spread and legitimacy of the police, and the emergence of social concerns about crime and order that, in many respects, parallel contemporary preoccupations, it is, once again, important not to overstate the degree of consensus that existed around such issues. A study of newspaper reporting of violent disorder in the twentieth century shows that, certainly as late as the 1930s, not only were attacks upon the police far from infrequent, but that they were often reported in the press in a form akin to a spectator sport. The following case, from 1928, illustrates the point.

Fought Four Navvies

Constable Entertains a Crowd

After spending their week's earnings in liquid refreshment, four burly navvies entertained a crowd of 200 people in the Rushes at Loughborough on Saturday night by fighting amongst themselves. A young constable came on the scene and on witnessing the disturbance sent for assistance.

Loughborough's Herculean constable P.C. Norman then arrived, and his part in the entertainment was recognised by the crowd as the star-turn.

He took each navvy in turn, and as each one was rendered hors-de-combat he was handed over to the younger constable and taken to the Police Station.

(*An excerpt from a local newspaper in 1928*)

Source: quoted in Dunning *et al.*, (1987: 34)

As with all history it is possible to identify some important changes as well as important continuities in perceptions of crime and violence in the last two to three hundred years. As we have seen, it is during this period that what we would recognise as the 'modern' concern with crime as a social problem came into being. This was the period in which the 'myth of sovereign crime control' originated (Garland, 1996). From the mid-nineteenth century onward, the state, together with the institutions of civil society such as families, churches and trades unions, gradually succeeded in reducing crime and in establishing a high degree of order. Such success 'helped entrench the image of an effective sovereign state' (Garland, 1996: 449). By the mid-twentieth century, Garland argues, the state was 'promising not just to punish legal violations, and quell internal unrest, but actually to govern in ways which would curb or cure the social problem of crime'.

One linked, gradual change in public attitude concerns levels of tolerance, particularly in relation to violent crime. There is a significant body of opinion, using Norbert Elias' theory of the civilising process as its basis (see Chapter 22), that argues that there is a discernible change in attitude, or mentality, toward the use of violence during the course of the nineteenth century – and indeed over a much longer period. Associated with the formation of the modern nation state and the rise of the modern industrial economy, there developed a set of processes which gradually increased social controls over individuals and, further, ensured that these social controls became internalised as self-controls. These norms covered many aspects of behaviour, including the use of violence. John Pratt in his book on this subject describes the process thus:

> As these internalised controls on an individual's behaviour became more automatic and pervasive … they eventually helped to produce the ideal of the fully rational, reflective and responsible citizen of the civilised world in the nineteenth and twentieth centuries: one who would be sickened by the sight of suffering and, with their own emotions under control, one who respected the authority of the state to resolve disputes on their behalf. (quoted in Godfrey and Lawrence, 2005: 104–5)

Such 'civilising' changes have two major implications for trends in violence and how we might understand them. On the one hand, the general thrust of Elias' theory implies a gradual increase in self-control over various bodily and emotional expressions, including violence. As such, it is compatible with historical data which suggests that, looking back over the past several centuries, the long-term trend has been toward declining levels of violence. On the other hand, his work also suggests that changing perceptions may also be important and that part of this civilising process involves decreasing tolerance of violence – a diminished ability and willingness to put up with such behaviour. One possible implication of this is, arguably, that we have become more likely to seek the suppression of violence, to report it to the police or other authorities, and to expect them to deal with it. The local newspaper article quoted above, which describes quite a lengthy fight between police officers and four navvies largely in terms of its entertainment value, is potentially rather revealing therefore, indicative as it seems to be of a period in which such incidents might be viewed as being exciting rather than necessarily fear-inducing, or requiring moral condemnation. It reminds us that our attempts to understand changes in levels and patterns of crime will come to little unless we give equal emphasis to the importance of attempting to understand how 'crime' is understood socially and why it is responded to in the ways it is.

Review questions

1 What are the main differences between Gatrell's and Taylor's views of what crime statistics tell us about trends in crime?

2 What are the main facets of a 'modern' understanding of crime?

3 In the absence of official criminal statistics, how have historians attempted to assess levels of crime in previous periods?

Questions for further discussion

1 What were the major sources of resistance to the 'new police' and how were they overcome?

2 Are the declining use of capital and corporal punishment in the eighteenth and nineteenth centuries 'a mark of progress'?

3 What is meant by the phrase: 'the myth of the sovereign crime control'?

4 Why might 'Victorian observers [have] been struck by their forefathers' relative indifference to crime'?

5 Assuming it is right to argue that crime, especially violent crime, declined in the second half of the nineteenth century, why might it have done so?

Further reading

There are a number of excellent introductions to the history of crime and its control. Among these are:

Emsley, C. (2005) *Crime and Society in England 1750–1900*, 3rd edn, Harlow: Longman
Godfrey, B. and Lawrence, P. (2005) *Crime and Justice 1750–1950*, Cullompton: Willan
Rawlings, P. (1999) *Crime and Power: A history of criminal justice 1688–1998*, Harlow: Longman
On the history of policing you should consult: Reiner, R. (2000) *The Politics of the Police*, 3rd edn, Oxford: Oxford University Press (ch. 1 and 2); and Rawlings, P. (2001) *Policing: A short history*, Cullompton: Willan

On probation, good introductions to the history of the service can be found in:

Nellis, M. (2007) Humanising justice: the English probation service up to 1972, in Gelsthorpe, L. and Morgan, R. (eds) *Handbook of Probation*, Cullompton: Willan
Vanstone, M. (2007) *Supervising Offenders in the Community*, Aldershot: Ashgate

On the history of the use of imprisonment it is well worth beginning with the essays in:

Morris, N. and Rothman, D. (1995) *The Oxford History of the Prison*, Oxford: Oxford University Press

Websites

There is a lot of information on the Metropolitan Police website: http://www.met.police.uk/history/ though it is important to recognise the nature of the source you are using and treat it with caution.

You can also look directly at proceedings at the Central Criminal Court for the period 1674 to 1884 at: www.oldbaileyonline.org/

There is some useful introductory information on the history of crime and justice at: http://www.learnhistory.org.uk/cpp/ (don't be put off by the fact that it is for GCSE students) which also provides online access to HMIC reports.

Chapter outline

Introduction   50

Measuring crime   50

Official statistics   51
   England and Wales: criminal statistics   52
   United States: uniform crime reports   52
   Assessing official statistics   53
      The impact of legislation   55
      Understanding attrition   56
   Limitations of official statistics   60

Victimization surveys   61
   The British Crime Survey   62
   Local crime surveys   65
      Other victimization surveys   67
   Assessing victimization surveys   67
   Comparing official statistics and victimization surveys 68

Crime trends   69

Data on offenders   76
   Self-report studies   77
      Assessing the self-report method   78
Questions for further discussion   79
Further reading   80
Websites   80

3

Crime data and
crime trends

CHAPTER SUMMARY	In this chapter we focus upon the means by which we measure levels and trends in crime. We look at:

In this chapter we focus upon the means by which we measure levels and trends in crime. We look at:

- the main techniques used and their strengths and weaknesses;

- official statistics and victimization surveys – our two main means of assessing crime levels – and compare their merits;

- the extent to which we can rely upon what we are told about crime, and how we should judge it;

- the major sources of data about crime, and assess their pros and cons;

- recent trends in crime;

- different data sources and what they tell us;

- why this is an area which continues to cause controversy;

- how the criminologist deals with the problem of different data sources appearing to indicate different trends;

- the techniques that can be used for assessing the competing claims of different approaches to measuring crime.

Introduction

David Garland (1994) suggests that for much of its history criminology was dominated by two differing projects: the 'governmental' and the 'Lombrosian' (a reference to Cesare Lombroso – see Chapter 5). The first of these focused primarily on trends in crime and the activities of criminal justice agencies, and its core concern is with the administration of justice. By contrast, the Lombrosian project focused on the causes of crime or, more particularly, in attempting to distinguish the *criminal* from the *non-criminal*. In recent decades, however, these projects have been largely overtaken by a series of broader concerns coalescing around ideas of risk and a calculative, managerialist mentality – concerned with measuring outcomes and managing performance – all of which is set in the context of a much more highly politicised understanding of crime and its control.

Nevertheless, our focus in this chapter is with some of what might be portrayed as the central concerns of the 'governmental' project. The core questions for us are 'how much crime is there?' and 'how do we know?' Now, before proceeding, several words of caution are necessary (and will be repeated regularly). First, and to repeat a message from the very beginning of this book, there is no simple thing 'out there' called *crime*. Though there are *criminal offences*, as defined by the criminal law, we must recognise that these things we call crimes are also

socially constructed. That is to say, whether particular actions or activities come to be labelled 'criminal' depends upon:

- whether anyone knows about them;
- if they know about them, whether they consider them worth doing anything about (such as reporting to the police); and,
- if they do so, whether the police or anyone else acts upon, or is able to act upon, what they decide to report.

The fact that this is so, of course, makes the act of attempting to 'measure' something like crime fraught with difficulties. In recent years, it is fair to say that we have become much more adept at this task. New forms of measurement have appeared and the techniques used have been progressively refined. Nevertheless, as we will see, this remains a highly problematic and often controversial task and our instruments necessarily remain rather blunt in some important respects.

Measuring crime

Broadly speaking there are two main methods used for measuring and tracking trends in crime – both of which we will consider in greater detail later on. One is taken from data collected routinely by law enforcement agencies and concerns crimes reported by the public or otherwise coming to the attention of the authorities. In the United States these are referred to as the Uniform Crime Reports (UCR) and are collected and collated by the FBI. In England and Wales such data are collected by the police and are generally referred to as *recorded crime statistics*. Similar methods of tracking crime via police records are used in most jurisdictions. As we will discuss in greater detail below such data have a number of quite significant shortcomings, not least that there is much crime that never makes it into official records – the so-called 'dark figure' of crime. For much of their history the assumption was that official statistics provided a reasonably sound indication of crime trends. By contrast criminologists have become increasingly critical of such data and some took the view that officially produced statistics had little real value beyond providing an indication of the work undertaken by the main criminal justice agencies. As public and political concern grew in the 1960s and 1970s, so the search for alternative means of estimating crime trends grew.

This resulted in the emergence of the second main approach to crime measurement, which uses survey methods to elicit information from a representative sample of the population about their experiences of crime – primarily as victims, wherever this is the case – usually over the previous 12 months. The US National Crime Victimization Survey (NCVS) was established in 1972 and has been undertaken twice a year since then. In the UK, a similar approach underpins the British Crime Survey (BCS). This was first undertaken in 1981 and has run intermittently since then – though it, too, is now undertaken annually. For a number of reasons it is now generally assumed by most commentators that victimization surveys are a more accurate measure of crime levels and trends than data collected by law enforcement agencies (Farrington and Langan, 2004). As a consequence such surveys are becoming increasingly common in other jurisdictions and, indeed, there are now regular, comparative surveys such as the International Crime Victims Survey (Nieuwbeerta, 2002).

Official statistics

The first national crime statistics were published in France in 1827. Of central importance in the history of official statistics is a Belgian scientist, Adolphe Quetelet, whose career began as an astronomer. He was sent to Paris by the Belgian government to study 'celestial mechanics' (Vold *et al.*, 2002) but

Adolphe Quetelet (1796–1874), astronomer and statistician. One of the first scholars to take a serious interest in criminal statistics, Quetelet became a leading figure in criminology and the social sciences.

quickly became interested in statistics relating to the social world, including crime as a result of the publication of the first French criminal statistics in 1828. Quetelet recognised many of the difficulties involved in measuring 'crime', not least the problem of estimating the extent of the activities that are not recorded ('unknown crimes') using such statistical methods. The size of this 'dark figure' depends on many factors, including the:

> activity of justice in reaching the guilty, on the care which these latter will take in hiding themselves, and on the repugnance which wronged individuals will feel in complaining, or on the ignorance in which perhaps they will be concerning the wrong which has been done them. (quoted in Coleman and Moynihan, 1996: 5)

Similar approaches to collecting crime statistics emerged in Britain later in the nineteenth century, initially through the work of statisticians such as Rawson and Fletcher, then through the work of Henry Mayhew and other campaigning investigators. *Judicial Statistics* – which were essentially sentencing statistics – first emerged in 1856. The first *Criminal Statistics,* drawn from data collected by the police and the courts, were published in 1876.

England and Wales: Criminal Statistics

Published annually as *Criminal Statistics, England and Wales,* this statistical series is compiled from data returned to government by the police and the courts. Although they are subject to changes from time to time – as we will see in greater detail below – they have been produced in a fairly standard format for most of their history. In practice, there are a number of publications published annually (or more frequently) which constitute the 'official statistics' on crime in England and Wales (there are equivalent publications for Scotland and Northern Ireland). The main publications historically have been:

- *Criminal Statistics, England and Wales;*
- *Sentencing Statistics;*
- *Prison and Probation Statistics.*

Until the mid- to late-nineteenth century sentencing statistics were one of the main sources of information about crime. They remain an important data-set in their own right, and also provide the raw data for the Offenders Index (see below) and the Police National Computer (PNC) database of criminal records, both of which provide the bulk of information about criminal careers and reconviction rates. In addition considerable information was collected by both the Prison and Probation Services and published separately as *Prison Statistics* and *Probation Statistics* – covering numbers of people in prison or subject to probation, sentence lengths and so on. With the amalgamation of Prison and Probation (see Chapter 27) the two datasets have also been amalgamated and now appear as *Offender Management Caseload Statistics.*

The annually-published criminal statistics historically came as a main volume and a number of supplementary volumes. Increasingly, such data can be accessed online and provide a wealth of information about crime and the criminal justice system. Since 2005 such publications have been superseded by the annual overview *Crime in England and Wales,* which uses both police-recorded crime data and BCS data to provide a general overview of trends. At the time of writing the most recently published are for 2005/06 and are available at: http://www.homeoffice.gov.uk/rds/crimeew0506.html.

Anyone looking at levels and trends in crime prior to 2005 using official statistics will need to use the older *Criminal Statistics* format. Here, the main volume, for example, contained information on court proceedings, offenders cautioned or found guilty, use of police bail and court remand, and (more recently) offences brought to justice. For the bulk of the period the main report also contained information on notifiable offences recorded by the police. Not all offences are notifiable and some lesser ('summary') offences are excluded. The subsidiary volumes contain more detailed information on proceedings in magistrates' courts, the Crown Court, and by police force area. More recently, government has produced a series of separate publications (generally all published as *Statistical Bulletins*) which provide information about crimes recorded by the police.

United States: Uniform Crime Reports

Collecting systematic data on crime took rather longer to get off the ground in the US than in parts of Europe. Congress initially tasked the Attorney General with reporting crime statistics in 1870. However, the anticipated annual statistics didn't appear and it wasn't until around 1920, as a result of concerns among a number of police chiefs about stories about crime in the press, that a new system emerged. This is what became known as the *Uniform Crime Reports* (UCR) that still forms the basis of crime reporting in America. Under the UCR system, police departments provide information on a limited number of crimes, and these are collated by the FBI. The system is not compulsory and not all police departments – there are almost 20,000 in the US – return data.

The UCR has two parts: Part I covers what are called 'Index offences' and Part II cover non-Index Offences. Part I, generally used as the basis for assessing annual crime rates, comprises eight offences only:

- criminal homicide;
- forcible rape;
- robbery;
- aggravated assault;
- burglary;
- larceny-theft;
- motor vehicle theft;
- arson.

Part II crimes include matters such as other forms of violence (assault) and theft, sex offences, drunkenness, and fraud and only cover those crimes that result in an arrest (which distinguishes them from Part I offences). These generally less serious offences are therefore very significantly underestimated. One of the potential advantages of the UCR system, when compared say with British criminal statistics, is that the Part I offences focus on a clearly identifiable set of crimes that the public would almost certainly agree to be those crimes about which they are concerned (though perhaps not an exhaustive list). By contrast, current criminal statistics in England and Wales contain a very broad range of offences and overall rises and falls in the 'crime rate' reported to the public will not necessarily reflect those things that concern the public most.

On the other hand the UCR system cannot tell us much about the 'overall crime rate' in the United States at all. First, as we have seen it only covers a very limited range of crimes. Second, this limited list is overwhelmingly focused on 'street crime' or conventional forms of crime, and as we have seen doesn't include white-collar crimes and many other fairly serious crimes. Third, because it is not compulsory, it doesn't cover the whole of the country. Finally, it is likely that there remains some variation between police departments in the way in which they record particular crime, despite the existence of guidance about recording procedures. This further limits the reliability of the data.

Assessing official statistics

The most important lesson to be learned in relation to any data-set is that it inevitably has limitations. No data source can tell us with complete accuracy what is happening in relation to crime. Indeed, as Maguire (2007: 254) notes, the fact that there is now a new annual publication on crime which is based on multiple data sources is itself a 'move which amounts to a highly visible acknowledgement of the limitations of police data'. As we will see, each of the major series has its own strengths and weaknesses and awareness of these, together with an ability to recognise where they apply, will enable us to use each source most productively. In what follows we will assess police-recorded crime statistics – official data collected by the police, compiled by government, and published in quarterly statistical bulletins and in the annual overview of crime trends (alongside BCS and other data).

We can begin our assessment by looking at official crime statistics as a 'time series'. As we have already noted, such figures have been collected every year for a century and a half. In principle, therefore, they represent an extraordinary resource for understanding historical trends – something we looked at in the previous chapter. The trend in overall crime over the past century is illustrated in Figure 3.1.

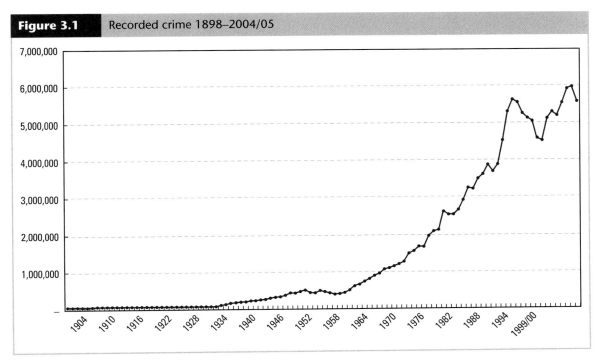

Figure 3.1   Recorded crime 1898–2004/05

Source: *Criminal Statistics, England and Wales* (various).

There are a number of points to note here. First, compared with levels of recorded crime in the twenty-first century, levels in the late nineteenth and early twentieth century were apparently extraordinarily low. Second, they remained so until the late 1950s whereupon crime begins to rise quite quickly. Third, crime rises pretty much every year from the mid-1950s until the early 1990s, at which point there is a brief, but significant decline before crime once again begins to rise. How accurate is this picture? In short, elements of it can probably be taken as a reasonable indicator of what actually happened. Thus, there is relatively little disagreement with the suggestion that crime in England and Wales, and in most other jurisdictions, rose markedly in the second half of the twentieth century – though it is possible that official statistics exaggerate the degree of increase. On the other hand, there is historical data which suggest that Victorian Britain, whilst relatively orderly compared with the first half of the nineteenth century (see Chapter 2), was probably not *more* orderly than Britain in the early decades of the twentieth century (Dunning *et al.*, 1987).

Approximately 100 different notifiable offences are recorded in the official statistics. These are then grouped into nine main categories of crime:

- Theft and handling stolen goods – includes theft of and from motor vehicles and accounts for a large number of offences and, indeed, no doubt for a sizeable element in the growth in crime since the 1960s.

- Burglary – this is now generally subdivided into 'domestic burglary' (i.e. of a household) and 'other burglary'.

- Criminal damage – separate statistics are available for criminal damage to a dwelling, to a building other than a dwelling, and to a vehicle.

- Violence against the person – this is a broad category that ranges from murder, through affray to reckless driving. The bulk of offences recorded in this category come from the more minor end of the spectrum.

- Sexual offences – another broad category covering rape, bigamy, and incest. The majority of recorded offences in this category are indecent assault.

- Robbery – a theft in which force or the threat of force is used. Here again, a distinction can be drawn between robbery of personal property and business property.

- Fraud and forgery.

- Drug offences.

- Other offences.

Table 3.1 and Figure 3.2 provide a graphic illustration of the nature of each of these offences as recorded in the most recent *Criminal Statistics*. Table 3.1 shows the total number of offences falling into each category.

Figure 3.2 illustrates the relative proportions of the different notifiable offences as part of overall recorded crime. The first point to note, very clearly, is that the two main property offences, theft and damage, account for over half of all recorded crime. About one fifth of all recorded crime falls into the category of violence against the person. These three categories account for about three in every five crimes recorded by the police.

There are a couple of important points we might note in relation to the breakdown in the chart above. The first is to reiterate that although violent crime accounts for over a fifth of the total – it is *only* a fifth. So, when we are using general terms like 'crime' it is important to remember that many of the offences recorded are relatively minor, and most do not involve violence. Second, although this pattern is reasonably stable, the breakdown of crime has been changing over time. In particular there has been a substantial rise in two categories of offence: violent crime and criminal damage. Figures for

Table 3.1	Number of crimes recorded by the police in 2005/06
Offence group	**No. (thousands)**
Violence against the person	1,059.9
Sexual offences	62.1
Robbery	98.2
Domestic burglary	300.6
Other burglary	344.6
Thefts of and from vehicles	721.5
Other thefts and handling	1,297.8
Fraud and forgery	233.0
Criminal damage	1,184.7
Drug offences	178.5
Other offences	75.7
Total recorded crime	**5,556.5**

Source: Walker *et al.* (2006).

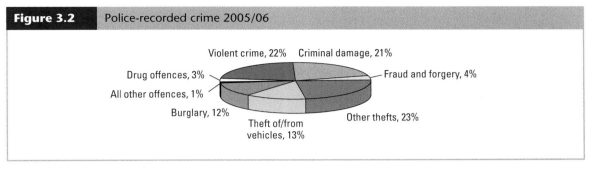

| Figure 3.2 | Police-recorded crime 2005/06 |

Source: Walker *et al.* (2006).

indictable offences recorded by the police in 1975, for example, show that violent crime accounted for approximately five per cent of offences and criminal damage for less than four per cent (HOSB 1/79). As Maguire (2007) notes, the number of criminal damage offences recorded is now over 230 times higher than it was in the 1950s. The apparent proportionate growth in violent crime as indicated by these statistics is actually largely a product of the introduction of the National Crime Recording Standard in 2002 (see below).

When using such statistics, therefore, we must be careful as to how they are utilised. Potentially, such changes may tell us something important about the changing nature of crime over the past half century. Equally, they may also alert us to the possibility that the recording of crimes has changed substantially in the same period. How do we unravel this? In part, we can do so by using other sources of data as a point of comparison. We will return to this later in the chapter. Before we move on, however, we must look in greater detail at the *construction* of official statistics in order to help us assess how useful they are, and what their limitations might be. We can start by considering what influences recorded crime statistics contain. Perhaps the most obvious one concerns the criminal law. The categories we have been discussing so far – burglary, criminal damage, violence against the person, theft of and from vehicles and so on – are all derived from criminal law and form the basis for the definition and identification of the offences that are recorded by the police.

The impact of legislation

Legislation can affect crime in a number of very important ways:

● New legislation creates new offences (crimes that previously did not exist). Successive Race Relations Acts (1965, 1976) have created new offences such as racial discrimination and racial harassment. The Crime and Disorder Act 1998 created a range of new racially- and religiously-aggravated offences. The Health Act 2006 provided the basis for the introduction of a ban on smoking in enclosed public spaces from 1 July 2007 in England and Wales. As new legislation creates new offences it also allows for additional crimes to be recorded in the official statistics.

● Legislation may also be repealed and therefore matters that once would have been seen as crimes will no longer be considered criminal and such offences will no longer appear in the official statistics. Thus, the Sexual Offences Act 1967 made legal homosexual acts in private between consenting adults aged 21 or over. Prior to this, homosexuality had been a criminal offence, and indirectly led to the commission of other crimes such as blackmail. Other changes can affect the way the law is policed. Most obviously, the significant discretion available to the police means that certain laws may be enforced more or less vigorously at different times. There may also be policy decisions which affect enforcement. In recent years the changing categorisation of cannabis has led to some controversy over policing of local drugs markets (see Chapter 21) with critics arguing that the sale of cannabis had effectively been decriminalised in certain areas.

In thinking about the construction of official statistics, therefore, it is always important to bear in mind what impact legislative change may have, and also whether it is possible that changes in policing and/or prosecution policies and practices might lie behind any of the changes identified. Beyond these issues lie a number of other

The ban on smoking in enclosed public spaces means the potential for more crimes to be committed and recorded. This illustration shows part of the government's campaign to publicize the ban ahead of its implementation on 1 July 2007.

important factors influencing what is found in police-recorded crime statistics – most particularly, whether or not 'crimes' are reported to the police and, if so, whether they are then recorded.

Understanding 'attrition'

There are a number of stages in the process by which particular acts come to be defined as 'crimes'. Crimes are not simply 'there', waiting to be included in a statistical summary. First of all, they must be 'known'. Now, this may sound odd, but there are a number of ways in which *crimes* might not be known:

- *The victim may simply be unaware of the offence.* If you had been defrauded of, say, a relatively small sum of money, would you always know about it? How carefully do you read bank statements? Or, if a small sum of money was stolen from your wallet or purse, would you always know? These days we are told to be careful about protecting our personal details as

there is increasing concern about identity theft. When such offences are committed, however, it may be some time, if ever, before the person whose personal details are being used becomes aware of what is happening. Thus, there are circumstances when although a crime may have been committed, you are unaware of it and therefore you cannot tell anyone such as the police about it, and it can therefore never make its way into official records.

- *There may be no victim.* What proportion of cases in which people buy drugs, for example, come to the attention of the police? If a transaction is taking place, to which both people consent, then they will not draw it to the attention of the police. It is likely, therefore, that only a tiny minority of such offences will ever be known by the police – because of proactive operations – and therefore only a tiny minority will potentially be recorded.

The next point at which 'cases' drop out of the system is when crimes are *reported* to the police. Of all those cases in which a victim is aware that an offence has taken place, only a proportion will be reported to the police. Rates of reporting vary markedly by offence with some much more likely to be reported to the police than others. Before we look at the figures we need to raise one question. How do we estimate what proportion of offences are reported to the police? The answer is that we use the BCS as a comparison. The BCS asks respondents about crimes they have experienced in the previous 12 months, and also asks them whether they reported it/them to the police and, if not, why not. Then, using crimes which are covered by both sets of data it is possible to produce estimates of rates of reporting. The 2005/06 BCS estimated that 42 per cent of incidents overall were reported to the police. The reporting rate varied dramatically across offence types (see Figure 3.3).

As Figure 3.3 illustrates, offences such as the theft of a motor vehicle are very likely to be reported. This shouldn't surprise us as by law cars have to be insured before they can be used on the road. By and large insurance claims cannot be made successfully without notifying the police that a crime has taken place. The same is true for household insurance claims – say where a burglary has been committed. However, unlike car insurance there is nothing compulsory about household insurance. Poorer people are less likely to have household insurance (Howarth *et al.*, 1998). As we

will see later (see Chapter 20), as it is those living in the poorest communities who are most likely to experience property crime, one can immediately see how crime has a considerable and differential impact according to wealth.

Why then do people decide not to report matters to the police? There are many reasons, including:

● The victim considers it too trivial.

● The victim feels the police will not be able to do anything about it.

● The victim feels the police will not be willing to do anything about it:
  – they may feel the police will not be interested;
  – they may feel the police won't believe them;
  – they may feel the police are simply too busy.

● The matter is too embarrassing, or is compromising in some other way.

● The victim is too scared to report it.

● The victim would prefer to deal with the matter in another way.

The BCS has for some time found that the feeling that the matter is too trivial is the most commonly cited reason for non-reporting, or that the victim felt that the police could do little about the offence. In relation to violent crime, however, the most common reason given for non-reporting was

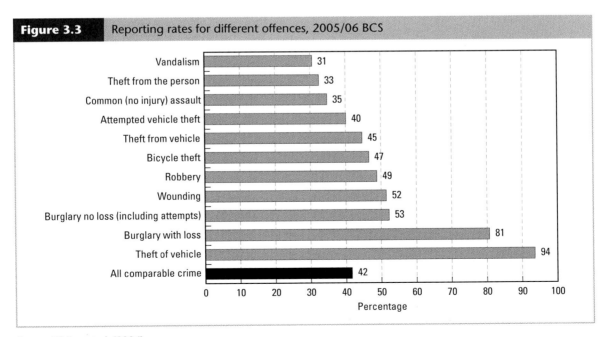

Figure 3.3 Reporting rates for different offences, 2005/06 BCS

Source: Walker *et al.* (2006).

Feminist campaigns to bring greater recognition to violence against women have led to increased reporting of offences such as rape and domestic violence. This picture is of a public protest held in Dublin, Ireland in June 2006.

that victims considered the issue to be a private matter and wished to deal with it themselves, reflecting, it is argued, the personal nature of the offences (Walker *et al.*, 2006).

A further hugely important way in which reporting practices influence levels of crime recorded in official statistics can be seen when social attitudes towards particular offences change. The most obvious example here concerns rape, sexual assault and other domestic violence against women. For many years reporting levels were extremely low – many women being convinced that their experiences would not be treated seriously, that they would be blamed for what had happened to them, or that they would simply not be treated with respect. As a result of much campaigning work over many years, attitudes toward violence against women have changed somewhat, and there have been some substantial changes in police practices in this area (see Chapter 32). One consequence has been significant increases in both reporting (and recording) rates and, therefore, within official statistics, the impression that such offences have been rapidly increasing. In reality, there is little evidence of an increase in such

offences – merely a rise in the number of cases successfully recorded as crimes.

Now, as the previous discussion implies, there is a further stage in the criminal justice process – the *recording* of crime – which also contributes to the attrition process. The uninitiated might assume that once an offence has been reported to the police it is then simply recorded and becomes officially defined as a 'crime'. This is not the case, however. Reporting an offence is not a guarantee that it will be recorded. Again, there are a number of reasons for this:

- The police may not accept the account given to them.

- The police may find insufficient evidence to confirm that an offence has taken place.

- The victim may refuse to press charges.

- The police may judge that the matter reported to them has already been satisfactorily dealt with or resolved.

- The police may simply not wish to pursue the matter and therefore fail to record it (what is often called 'cuffing': the deliberate failure to record an incident in order to save work or to increase clear-ups – see Young, 1991: 323–5).

Audits are now regularly undertaken of police recording practices, and recent estimates suggest that between 70–75 per cent of incidents reported to the police are recorded as crimes. Figure 3.4 illustrates police recording rates for offences in different categories.

Shortfalls in reporting and in recording are the two major factors in what is commonly referred to as the 'attrition rate' in the criminal justice system: the proportion of 'all offences' that eventually end up in the criminal justice system and, more particularly, end with a caution or conviction. Of all those offences recorded by the police, only a very small proportion eventually ends with a caution or a conviction.

At this point we must distinguish between the proportion of offences that end with a caution or conviction and what is generally referred to as the 'clear-up rate'. Historically, the clear-up rate has frequently been used as an indicator of police efficiency. There are a number of conditions which may allow a crime to be defined as having been 'cleared up':

- Someone has been charged or summonsed (though not necessarily convicted).
- Someone has been cautioned.
- The offence has been 'taken into consideration' at court – someone has admitted it even though they haven't been prosecuted for it.

- There is sufficient evidence to prosecute someone, but no prosecution is proceeding (incapacity of the offender, victim, witness and so on).
- Victim is unwilling to give evidence.
- Offender is below the age of criminal responsibility (under ten).
- The offender is already in prison for another offence.

Clear-up rates vary markedly between offence types and, historically, have also varied markedly between police forces. One of the reasons for this – certainly historically – has concerned the use of offences 'taken into consideration' or TICs. These occur when suspects, having been arrested and charged, are asked if there are other offences they will admit to. This is an indirect means of clearing up offences, and differing practices in relation to TICs in different forces has on occasion been an important factor in variations in clear-up rates. In understanding 'attrition' in the criminal justice system, therefore, the major distinctions to bear in mind concern: the proportion of offences reported; of those reported, the proportion recorded; of these how many are 'cleared up'; and, finally, how many result in a caution, a conviction, or a prison sentence. Attrition within the criminal justice system is depicted graphically in Figure 3.5.

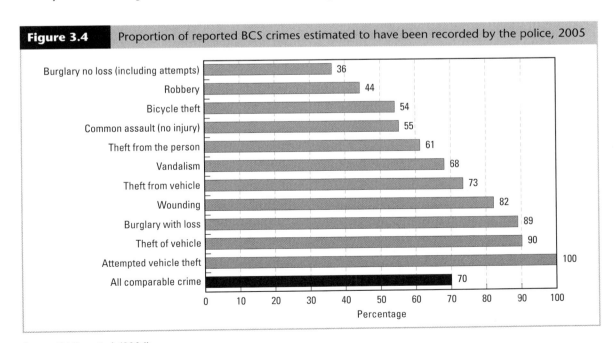

Figure 3.4   Proportion of reported BCS crimes estimated to have been recorded by the police, 2005

Offence	Percentage
Burglary no loss (including attempts)	36
Robbery	44
Bicycle theft	54
Common assault (no injury)	55
Theft from the person	61
Vandalism	68
Theft from vehicle	73
Wounding	82
Burglary with loss	89
Theft of vehicle	90
Attempted vehicle theft	100
All comparable crime	70

Source: Walker *et al.* (2006).

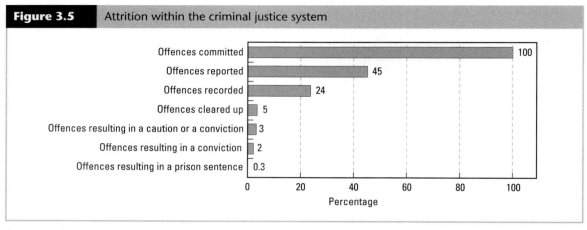

Figure 3.5   Attrition within the criminal justice system

Source: Barclay and Tavares (1999).

Limitations of official statistics

As we have seen, what is included within official statistics can be profoundly affected by what is brought to the attention of the police, and how they then respond to such reports. There are Home Office rules governing police procedures for recording crime and we will look at these in more detail when considering recent trends in crime. These factors are among the main concerns when considering the limitations of this particular source of data. A further limitation of official statistics is that they are generally offence- rather than offender-focused. Furthermore, they are not victim-focused.

Bottoms (1994) has argued that beginning in the 1970s there was something of a shift from the study of the *offender* to the study of *offences*. In part, in the UK this was the result of the increasing influence of Home Office research and an approach to the study of crime that Jock Young has characterised (and possibly caricatured) as 'administrative criminology'. There are a number of potential pitfalls in the counting of offenders and offences using official statistics. If an offender is before the court on three charges then normally only the most serious (the *principal* offence) of these will be recorded in the official statistics. By contrast, an offender who commits three offences at different times may appear in court on three separate occasions and be recorded, therefore, three times. More recently, changes in recording rules further shift the focus of police-recorded crime statistics in the direction of counting offences: where previously cases involving a single victim reporting three offences would have been recorded as a single incident, the police are now required to record all three separately. Official statistics tell us quite a lot about what happens to people as they go through the criminal justice process, but relatively little therefore about the people themselves.

Furthermore, official statistics only contain information about a limited sub-set of offences, not all offences. Police-recorded crime covers all crime reported to, or discovered by, the police and then recorded and *which are required to be reported to the Home Office*. It is for this reason that these are generally known as 'notifiable offences'. Historically, notifiable offences have generally been what would ordinarily be regarded as the 'more serious' crimes. Changes in what are called the 'counting rules' in 1998 also brought some less serious offences into the notifiable category. For the purposes of this discussion, it is what is left out that is important. In the main it is summary offences – relatively minor cases that would be heard in the magistrates' courts – that are not included in police-recorded crime statistics. Whilst they are generally not serious offences – they comprise mainly motoring offences – they are sizeable in number. For this reason, as well as others already outlined, it is a mistake to see police-recorded crime numbers as representing 'all crime'.

Indeed, as Bottomley and Pease (1986: 1) in the introduction to their book on measuring crime, point out: 'It is impossible to give any accurate or straightforward answers to [the question of how much crime there is] ... Not only does everything depend on what is meant by "crime", "criminals" and "victims", but even if there were to be broad agreement on the definition and scope of these basic terms, it is very apparent that most of the extant methods of measuring the nature and amounts of crime, criminality and victimization would be inadequate to the task.' Nevertheless, as Maguire (2002: 334) observes:

Despite the warnings of criminologists and government statisticians alike, these statistics are still treated by many politicians and journalists as an accurate 'barometer' of crime, and any sizeable rise in the figures they produce tends to receive widespread publicity and spark off arguments about police or government ineffectiveness or the need for sentencing changes (falls, conversely, tend to be largely ignored). The figures are also used a great deal at a local level to inform the distribution of police resources and, increasingly, the preparation of crime 'audits' and crime reduction plans, as well as the measurement of police and crime reduction partnerships' 'performance' in comparison with targets and other areas.

Some limitations of *Criminal Statistics*

The numbers of particular crimes, and the overall level of crime, recorded in *Criminal Statistics*, can be profoundly affected by changes in:

- decisions about which offences to include (only 'notifiable' offences are included; this excludes 'summary' offences, as well as those offences recorded by non-'Home Office police forces' such as the British Transport Police, the Ministry of Defence Police, etc.);

- changes in the 'counting rules';

- changes in public attitudes toward the reporting of particular offences;

- changes in police practices toward particular offences (the 'upgrading' or 'downgrading' of particular offences).

In addition, *Criminal Statistics* are a poor tool for:

- understanding the social context of crime (very diverse crimes are included under broad offence headings);

- understanding the relative risks of victimization.

Review questions

1 When were official crime statistics first collected in Britain?

2 What is meant by attrition?

3 What are the main reasons people fail to report crimes to the police?

4 Why might the police decide to, or fail to, record crimes that are reported to them?

Victimization surveys

The essence of the victimization survey is the standard sample survey. The objective is generally to seek to interview a representative sample of a particular population and to ask them a series of questions about their experience of victimization – usually over the past year. As with so many elements of modern social scientific inquiry, the victimization survey began life in America. The product of President Johnson's government in the 1960s, victimization surveys were intended to provide a more accurate measure of the extent of crime, and of trends in crime, than the hitherto standard method of relying on official statistics – the *Uniform Crime Reports*. Of the early studies, it is that undertaken by the National Opinion Research Center (Ennis, 1967) that is most frequently discussed. Based on a sample of 10,000 households, the survey asked a range of questions about household members' experiences of crime. Although the early victimization surveys were somewhat limited, they nevertheless helped to provide an indication of the extent of non-recorded crime (generally three to five times as many as captured by official means) (Coleman and Moynihan, 1996).

The National Crime Victimization Survey (NCVS), originally called the National Crime Survey, was established in the US in 1972. Data for the NCVS are collected twice each year, from a nationally representative sample of roughly 49,000 households comprising about 100,000 people. The data cover the frequency, characteristics, and consequences of criminal victimization in the United States. Originally undertaken by the Law Enforcement Assistance Administration, the survey is now administered by the US Census Bureau (under the US Department of Commerce) on behalf of the Bureau of Justice Statistics (under the US Department of Justice).

The first victimization survey in the UK was included in the 1972 General Household Survey (GHS). As it sounds, the GHS is used to record information about a wide variety of domestic experiences. In the early 1970s the GHS explored the extent of household burglary. The first major victimization survey with a broad focus was also carried out in the early 1970s in three areas of London by Richard Sparks (senior) and colleagues – largely to test the effectiveness of this particular method. Their book, *Surveying Victims* (Sparks *et al.*, 1977), remains an important landmark in British criminology.

The purposes of crime surveys

Sparks and colleagues in the late 1970s identified eight reasons why victimization surveys might provide useful data:

- The ability of victimization surveys to provide a relatively accurate measure of crime rates enables them to be used as a 'social barometer'.
- Such surveys can be used to estimate the size of the gap between reported and unreported crime.
- They can be used to assess public attitudes toward reporting and therefore towards crime and policing.
- They can be used to assess crime prevention effects of particular initiatives.
- They can help direct our attention to the experiences of victims – experiences that might otherwise be ignored.
- They can provide more information about the nature of crime victims.
- They can be used to help assess the veracity of particular criminological theories.
- They can be used to help measure fear of crime and other responses to crime and victimization.

guide to the extent and shape of the problem which the criminal justice system was intended to tackle: police statistics of recorded crime seemed adequate as a measure of police work-load, but – because of unreported and unrecorded crime – deficient as an index of crime …

Another attraction lay in the survey's promise as an antidote to public misperceptions about crime. It was thought within the Home Office that misconceptions about crime levels, trends and risks were widespread among the public. A survey-based index of crime would demonstrate the possibility – if not the reality – that the index of crime based on offences recorded by the police might be subject to statistical inflation by virtue of changing reporting and recording practices … In other words, the survey promised a more informed picture of crime which might help create a more balanced climate of opinion about law and order. Finally, it was felt that a national survey might give a boost for criminological research and theory.

The BCS was undertaken subsequently in 1984, 1988, 1992, 1994, 1996, 1998, 2000, and 2001. Since then it has become an annual survey – essentially conducted on a rolling basis – with a significantly enlarged sample size. The sizeable increase in the BCS sample size meant that analysis could be undertaken at police force level.

The second victimization survey in England was undertaken by Bottoms and colleagues in Sheffield in 1975 (Bottoms *et al.*, 1987).

The British Crime Survey

Within a few years the Home Office had taken the decision to fund a national victimization survey. Although it has always been known as the British Crime Survey (BCS), it was only the first and third surveys that were conducted in Scotland as well as England and Wales. Scotland now has its own survey, as does Northern Ireland. The first BCS was undertaken in 1981/82 and was published in 1983 (Hough and Mayhew, 1983). Based on a representative sample of the population in England and Wales, interviews were conducted with 10,000 respondents aged 16 or over. The authors of the very first BCS described the main reasons for its introduction in the following way (Mayhew and Hough, 1988: 157):

The case for such a survey rested largely in the value to policy-makers of having at least a rough

THE BRITISH
CRIME SURVEY

HOME OFFICE RESEARCH STUDY NO. 76

The very first *British Crime Survey* was published in 1983.

Understanding the British Crime Survey

The BCS increased its sample size to 15,000 in 1996 and then again to 20,000 in 2000. From 2001 onward when it became an annual, rolling survey, the core sample of the BCS was raised to 40,000.

The first three 'sweeps' of the BCS used the electoral register as the sampling frame. The electoral register has a number of shortcomings, leading to the under-representation of minority ethnic groups and transient populations (see Mayhew *et al.*, 1993: 149–151 for details). More particularly, in the 1980s the introduction of the community charge – the 'poll tax' – which used the electoral register as its primary means of identifying those liable for the tax, increased the gaps in its coverage.

Since 1992, the BCS has the used the Postal Address File (PAF) as its sampling frame. The PAF, which also has a number of limitations, has the advantage of being constantly updated, unlike the electoral register which is only updated annually.

Since 1994, the BCS has used CAPI (Computer Assisted Personal Interviewing), with limited use of CASI (Computer Assisted Self Interviewing) for some sensitive questions (see Hough and Maxfield, 2007).

The BCS asks a series of questions covering a list of specified crimes. Respondents are asked whether they have experienced any of the listed crimes in the previous 12 months and, if they answer positively, they are then asked a series of follow-up questions about the incident(s). The remainder of the survey covers other areas, such as (Mayhew and Hough 1988: 158):

First British Crime Survey
- Lifestyle, and other factors affecting risks of victimization.
- Fear of, and beliefs and attitudes about, crime.
- Contact with the police, and attitudes to the police.
- Drinking habits, and knowledge of sanctions for drunken driving.
- Self-reported offending.

Second British Crime Survey
- Assessments of seriousness of crime.
- The impact of crime on victims.
- Perceptions of crime risks and (modified) fear of crime.
- Attitudes to sentencing.
- Attitudes to neighbourhood watch schemes.
- Self-reported offending.

The results of the various 'sweeps' of the BSC are published by the Home Office and the majority are now available online. As we noted in the discussion about official statistics, in recent years the Home Office has taken to publishing an annual 'snapshot' of crime in England and Wales, drawing on data from the BCS, police-recorded crime and other sources. Elements of the BCS are still published separately, but usually when there is a particular subject – such as drug use – being investigated. The major reports from the BCS are listed in the box overleaf.

The first BCS produced some quite startling data. Its authors, faced with the prospect of identifying the level of unreported crime for the first time, also introduced a number of findings that were intended to be somewhat more reassuring. Thus, they (Hough and Mayhew, 1983: 15) suggested that the average citizen could anticipate:

- a robbery once every five centuries;
- an assault resulting in injury once every century;
- the family car to be stolen once every 60 years;
- a burglary in the home once every 40 years.

The authors were subsequently criticised for presenting such 'averages' and thereby masking the very wide variations in likelihood of victimization across different parts of the population. Later crime survey reports avoided such generalisations and have tended to analyse the patterns and risks of victimization by a range of demographic characteristics. We will return to this in later chapters (see, for example, Chapters 20 and 31).

The BCS has provided a wealth of information on criminal victimization over the past 20 years and more. Respondents are asked about a broad range of crimes and, if they have experienced any in the previous year, are then asked a substantial series of follow-up questions to explore the nature of the offence and their response to it (including, as we have seen, whether they reported it to the police). In addition, the BCS carries a series of other modules which explore respondents' experiences and attitudes towards a variety of other

Main Reports from the British Crime Survey

Hough, M. and Mayhew, P. (1983) *The British Crime Survey*, Home Office Research Study No. 76, London: Home Office

Hough, M. and Mayhew, P. (1985) *Taking Account of Crime: Findings from the Second British Crime Survey*, Home Office Research Study No. 85, London: Home Office

Mayhew, P., Elliott, D. and Dowds, L. (1989) *The 1988 British Crime Survey*, Home Office Research Study No.111, London: Home Office

Mayhew, P., Aye-Maung, N. and Mirrlees-Black, C. (1992) *The 1992 British Crime Survey, Home Office Research Study No.132*, London: Home Office

Hough, M. (1995) *Anxiety about Crime: Findings from the 1994 British Crime Survey*, Home Office Research Study No.147, London: Home Office

Mirrlees-Black, C., Mayhew, P. and Percy, A. (1996). *The 1996 British Crime Survey*. Home Office Statistical Bulletin 19/96, London: Home Office

Mirrlees-Black, C., Budd, T., Partridge, S. and Mayhew, P. (1998). *The 1998 British Crime Survey*. Home Office Statistical Bulletin 21/98, London: Home Office

Kershaw, C., Budd, T., Kinshott, G., Mattinson, J., Mayhew, P. and Myhill, A. (2000) *The 2000 British*

Crime Survey. Home Office Statistical Bulletin 18/00, London: Home Office

Kershaw, C., Chivite-Matthews, N., Thomas, C. and Aust, R. (2001) *The 2001 British Crime Survey: First Results*, Home Office Statistical Bulletin 18/01, London: Home Office

Flood-Page, C. and Taylor, J. (2003) *Crime in England and Wales 2001/2002: Supplementary Volume.* Home Office Statistical Bulletin 1/03, London: Home Office

Simmons, J. and Dodd, T. (2003) *Crime in England and Wales 2002/2003.* Home Office Statistical Bulletin 07/03, London: Home Office

Dodd, T., Nicholas, S., Povey, D. and Walker, A. (2004) *Crime in England and Wales 2003/04*, Home Office Statistical Bulletin 10/04, London: Home Office

Nicholas, S., Povey, D., Walker, A. and Kershaw, C. (2005) *Crime in England and Wales 2004/05*, Home Office Statistical Bulletin 11/05, London: Home Office

Walker, A., Kershaw, C. and Nicholas, S. (2006) *Crime in England and Wales 2005/06*, Statistical Bulletin 12/06, London: Home Office

All of the above are available online at the Home Office website: http://www.homeoffice.gov.uk/rds/pubsintro1.html

matters, such as drugs, domestic and sexual violence. Clearly, one of the great advantages that such surveys have over official statistics is that they largely overcome the 'non-reporting' and 'non-recording' problems associated with the latter. Crime, or more accurately, victimization surveys also have some quite significant limitations, however. Thus, for example, the sample for the British Crime Survey:

- does not include under-16s and therefore cannot say anything about the victimization of young people;

- is a household sample, and therefore excludes people not living in a household, such as the homeless, those irregularly living in hostels and those in prisons. Available research suggests that these groups probably have very high victimization rates (see Chapters 17 and 28);

- does not cover businesses and, therefore, commercial and industrial victimization is not included in the BCS's estimate of crime;

- is a study which relies on people to report what they have experienced, by definition it cannot include murder or 'victimless crimes' such as the buying and selling of drugs;

- is insufficiently large (despite increases in sample sizes) to be able to assess offences like rape and sexual assault;

- doesn't include most forms of corporate crime, environmental crime or other offences subject to regulation by bodies such as Revenue and Customs, the Health and Safety Executive and others.

Some of these shortcomings can be overcome, and there have been recommendations recently (Smith 2007) that, if practicable, the BCS should be extended to under-16s and to certain types of group residences (such as university halls of residence) and that the surveys of commercial and industrial victimization that the Home Office has occasionally undertaken ought to be carried out regularly.

It is not just at the national level that victimization surveys have been used. As we will see below they are increasingly being used internationally in order to try to facilitate comparisons across jurisdictions. In addition, there have been a number of influential local crime surveys.

Local crime surveys

For a short but important period in the 1980s and beyond, local crime surveys became a small but influential criminological industry. Adopting a largely identical approach to national surveys, but rather focusing on a much smaller, highly targeted geographical area, local surveys were frequently funded by some of the more radical local authorities (e.g. Islington and Merseyside) that sought to focus attention on the nature, level and shape of local crime problems. Such surveys aimed to correct what their authors saw as two of the main shortcomings of the BCS: its underestimate of the impact of criminal victimization; and its relative ineffectiveness at uncovering 'hidden' crimes such as domestic violence.

The Merseyside Crime Survey was undertaken in 1984 with the first Islington Crime Survey following a year later. Indeed, they were developed together in many ways, sharing overlapping questionnaires and with common staff working as consultants on both surveys. During the period from the mid-'80s to the early '90s crime surveys were undertaken twice in Islington (Jones *et al.*, 1986; Crawford *et al.*, 1990) and also in Merseyside (Kinsey, 1984), Edinburgh twice (Anderson *et al.*, 1990, 1991) and in Glasgow (Hartless *et al.*, 1995). The political context of the emergence of these surveys is interesting. As the authors of the first Islington Crime Survey (Jones *et al.*, 1986: 6) explain:

> It had become increasingly obvious that there was an extraordinary hiatus in Labour Party policy over crime. Despite the fact that socialist administrations control virtually every inner-city high crime area in Britain ... the Labour Party has come to regard law and order as the natural and exclusive realm of Conservatives. The question is how to develop policies which help protect women, ethnic minorities and the working class – those who suffer most from the impact of crime – who are the natural constituents of Labour, whilst refusing to accept the

The Scottish Crime (and Victimization) Survey

The Scottish Crime Survey (SCS) is a repeat, cross-sectional survey which seeks to measure the incidence and prevalence of criminal victimization in Scotland. In 1982 and 1988 the Crime Survey in Scotland was part of the British Crime Survey (BCS) – though the Scottish part of the 1988 BCS was also known as the Scottish Areas Crime Survey. In 1993 the first independent SCS was carried out and then again in 1996, 2000 and 2003. In 2004 the new Scottish Crime and Victimization Survey (SCVS) was launched with a number of changes in design, methodology and sample size from previous surveys. The sample size was increased from 5,000 interviews approximately every three years to an annual sample of 27,000 with continuous interviewing. Second, the survey method was changed in part from a face-to-face survey to a telephone survey (and thus it differs markedly in method from the BCS). In addition to the telephone survey, the research company undertaking the fieldwork in 2004 also undertook a limited face-to-face survey (comprising 3,000 interviews) in order to assess the impact of the change to telephone interviews and to provide some continuity with earlier sweeps of the SCS. A review of the methodology concluded that telephone interviewing was unreliable and the SCVS will revert to face-to-face interviewing from 2007.

The Northern Ireland Crime Survey

The Northern Ireland Crime Survey (NICS) is carried out on behalf of the Northern Ireland Office. Like the BCS and SCVS it is a household survey. It was first carried out as a one-off survey in 1994/5 and was repeated in 1998. It became a biennial survey in 2001 and has been running as a continuous survey since January 2005. The survey involves face-to-face interviews and the sample size of the original surveys was 3,000. This was subsequently increased to 4,000 and now involves approximately 6,500 individuals aged 16 or over from households selected randomly from a list of domestic addresses held by the Northern Ireland Land and Property Services Agency (LPSA). Interviews are now conducted over the course of a calendar year and, consequently, whereas originally the 'recall period' in which respondents were asked about their experiences covered a fixed 12-month period, since 2005 the NICS has asked respondents to recall incidents in the 12 calendar months prior to being interviewed (the BCS has operated in this way since 2001).

Figure 3.6	Major reasons for victim non-reporting to police	
Reasons for not reporting	**Percentage giving reason**	
	British Crime Survey %	**Islington Crime Survey %**
Police unable to do anything	16	38
Too trivial	55	26
Not a matter for police	10	5
Inconvenient	2	13
Fear of police	1	2
Reprisals from offender	1	4

Source: Young (1988: 167).

draconian policing policies and penal practices of the Tories ... The second political circumstance was the need to have objective assessment of police-public relations, a gauge of the efficacy of existing police methods and a measure of public demands as to the sort of service they would ideally want.

One of the core findings of work like the Islington Crime Survey, and something which underpinned the 'left realist criminology' (see Chapter 13) which developed in its wake under Jock Young, was that most people's attitudes toward crime were very much in line with their experiences of crime – with the exception of older, white people.

As I have already noted, the authors of the British Crime Survey report came in for some criticism – particularly from Jock Young, one of the authors of the two Islington Crime Surveys. The thrust of Young's critique was that national surveys tend to miss some important elements in the distribution of victimization which local surveys, because of their geographical focus, are better able to identify. As one example, Young (1988) compared the reasons crime victims gave for not reporting offences to the police. The results from the two surveys can be seen in Figure 3.6.

By using national averages, the BCS masked the fact that triviality was not the main reason for non-reporting in some (high crime) areas and was overwhelmingly the reason in other areas. Subsequent research, such as the Islington Crime Survey, found that the proportion saying they did not report the crime because they felt it was too trivial, was only one quarter. Consequently, as Jock Young argued, a large number of victimizations

'genuinely belong to the "dark figure" as defined by the victims and are seen as a matter for the police' (1988: 167).

The response of the BCS authors to the left realist critique was to amend aspects of the Crime Survey and to seek more effective measures of both patterns of, and the impact of, victimization. Indeed, its original authors defended the BCS robustly arguing that by prompting the development of other work, such as local crime surveys, it had made a significant contribution to increasing knowledge about the rela-

First Islington Crime Survey, published in 1990.

tionship between risks and fear (Mayhew and Hough, 1988). Furthermore, they argued that the rise of victimization surveys such as the BCS, by shifting the emphasis in explaining crime toward the circumstances of the incident and away from perpetrators' motives, had stimulated and helped refine work in the 'situational' or 'opportunity theory' area (see Chapter 14).

Other victimization surveys

National crime surveys tend to be the ones that are most frequently used and cited. Local crime surveys had an important influence in the 1980s and 1990s, but are less commonly used now. In addition to these tools, there are also a number of other victimization surveys that it is worth us briefly reviewing. The major ones are:

- *The International Crime Victim Survey (ICVS)* – an international survey which generates samples of between 1,000–2,000 people through random selection of telephone numbers in most countries. Sample sizes are, therefore, small and some cross-country comparisons are quite difficult as crime categories differ somewhat. Nevertheless, the ICVS provides one starting point for cross-cultural comparison (Van Dijk and van Vollenhoven, 2007).

- *The Commercial Victimization Survey* – first conducted in 1994 and subsequently in 2002 (there was also a Scottish Business Crime Survey in 1998). This was a telephone survey of a subset of businesses, including 3,955 retailing premises and 2,561 manufacturing premises in England and Wales. In the main, interviews were conducted with the person in the business who was responsible for security issues. The survey explored the nature and extent of crime experienced in different business sectors.

Assessing victimization surveys

The great advantage of victimization surveys is that they do not rely on what comes to the attention of the police or any other agency. Second, they enable a lot of questions to be asked about the nature and impact of crime. However, as with any form of data collection – there is no exception – there are a number of limitations to what crime surveys are able to tell us. As we have noted, there are a series of offences that crime surveys don't pick up, including: corporate and organised crime; much

white-collar crime; criminal damage; so-called 'victimless crimes' such as illicit drug use, and certain activities related to sex, pornography and so on.

Surveys, national or local, are invariably household-based, and therefore have little opportunity to ask about work-based offences. As they ask respondents about experiences of victimization they cannot uncover those crimes where there is no obvious victim – possession of cannabis, say, is not going to be uncovered in a household-based victimization survey. Similarly, there are also circumstances under which respondents may be reluctant to answer questions about victimization. Respondents may, for example, be too frightened to report certain events – perhaps they may live with the perpetrator. They may be too embarrassed – being assaulted or robbed whilst visiting a prostitute, for example – or ashamed, perhaps having been unable or unwilling to defend themselves. Hope (2005: 49–50) identifies seven factors that may affect what respondents say to crime survey interviewers:

- *Knowledge of incidents* – only one person in the household is interviewed and they will have limited knowledge of other household members' experiences.

- *Not telling* – as discussed earlier, there may be various reasons why respondents don't, or can't, report everything that might be of relevance to the survey.

- *Memory decay* – respondents may simply forget things that have happened to them.

- *Telescoping* – certain events, especially if serious, may feel as if they occurred more recently than was actually the case (and thus be reported in the wrong year).

- *Education* – the extent of education of the respondent may affect their ability to deal with the questions and willingness to deal with the interviewer.

- *Multiple and serial incidents* – victimization surveys divide experiences into discrete events even when they may not be experienced in quite this way.

- *Interview conditions* – who the interviewer was, the time of day, which day the interview occurs, and whether the interview uses computer-aided questioning are just some of the conditions that may affect the outcome of the interview.

The strengths and weaknesses of crime surveys

Strengths

- Capture incidents not reported to the police.
- Capture incidents reported, but not recorded by the police.
- Rest on victim's understanding of events rather than, say, a police officer's interpretation of what has occurred.

Weaknesses

- There is a range of crimes not effectively captured by such surveys:
    - 'victimless crimes' – drug sale and use;
    - 'hidden crimes' – domestic violence.
- Surveys don't include those that are in institutions such as prisons, hospitals, care homes, student halls of residence, etc.
- There may be other sampling problems.
- There are limits to the accuracy of respondents' memories.

- Focuses on crimes as 'individual events' and therefore generally fails to capture either 'multiple victimization' (see Genn, 1988) or the 'processual' nature of much harassment (see Bowling, 1993). Certain types of offence, such as racial harassment, domestic violence and child abuse, may be difficult to understand as a set of discrete events, when in practice they may be experienced as an ongoing, almost ceaseless set of events – some less serious, some more – but combining and merging over time. These 'series incidents' are argued by some critics to be poorly captured in victimization surveys.
- There is the potential for respondents to feel inhibited in talking about particular types of victimization – sexual assault for example. In an attempt to overcome this the BCS has introduced computer-aided self-interviewing (CASI) in recent years.

Comparing official statistics and victimization surveys

There are a number of difficulties in producing direct and accurate comparisons of these two sources of data. First, as we have seen, the offence categories used by the two sources are not identical; indeed, in some respects they are rather different. Kershaw and colleagues (2001) suggest that in practice only about three-quarters of the offences covered by the BCS can be used in comparison with official statistics. Likewise, there is much captured, albeit partially, in official data-sets that is not covered by the BCS including, for example, shoplifting and burglary from commercial premises, as well as motoring offences and some 'victimless' crimes. This leads Maguire (2002: 352) to conclude that the BCS 'provides an alternative, rather than a directly comparable, overall picture of crime to that offered by police statistics'. That said, there are, of course, areas where comparison can be made and careful contrasts do allow for some estimate of the 'dark figure' of crime to be undertaken (those crimes which are not recorded in official statistics).

Having analysed the data from the first BCS,

Hough and Mayhew (1983) found that 'the survey indicated that there were twice as many burglaries as were recorded by the police; nearly five times as much wounding; twelve times as much theft from the person … The overall ratio for incidents which had been compared was one in four.' More recent surveys find roughly similar proportions of crime being unrecorded in official statistics. As Maguire (2007) cautions, however, it is important to resist the temptation to assume that this can be used as a straightforward indicator of the 'dark figure' of crime. In reality it is an approximation for *only* those offences in the two data sources which can reasonably be compared. It tells us little about the likely levels of crime not captured by crime surveys. Maguire (2007) concludes with five main messages from the BCS and comparisons between the survey and *Criminal Statistics*:

- The BCS clearly indicates that there is a very substantial amount of crime that is never recorded in *Criminal Statistics*.
- Building up a picture from successive BCSs over the past two decades suggests that the increases in crime that occurred up until the early/mid-1990s were less steep than indicated by official figures.

- Nevertheless, the general shape of the overall trend in crime is very similar according to both sources of data.

- Within the overall picture, both the BCS and official records paint a similar picture of the balance between car crime, other property crime and violence against the person.

- The BCS has been much better at measuring offences against private individuals and households that are committed by strangers; it has been less successful at capturing crimes committed within family units or between people otherwise known to each other.

Few criminologists these days are as dismissive of officially recorded crime data as might once have been the case. Though the social constructionist case is now well-embedded in criminological discussions of crime data, there is now at least a degree of acceptance that official data do provide an indication of general trends in crime, albeit that without an alternative against which to assess them, they must still be treated with considerable caution.

Review questions

1   What are the main ways in which the British Crime Survey has changed since it was first undertaken in the early 1980s?

2   Why might local crime surveys differ in their findings from national surveys?

3   Why is it difficult to compare police recorded crime with the findings of victimization surveys?

Crime trends

So far in this chapter we have looked at the two major sources of information we have about levels and trends in crime: police-recorded crime or official statistics on the one hand and victimization surveys – primarily the British Crime Survey (BCS) – on the other. One of their uses is to give us estimates of how much crime there is at any particular point and to help us assess whether crime is rising or falling. What, then, do these data sources suggest has been happening to crime levels in recent decades?

It is widely believed that we live in times of unprecedented levels of crime. Whether such beliefs are accurate rather depends on the time-frame being utilised. It is certainly the case compared with, say, the 1940s, 1950s or 1960s that current levels of crime are very high. However, if we take a longer historical perspective then there is rather reliable evidence to suggest that previous eras were characterised by very high levels of crime and disorder, even by contemporary standards (Gurr, 1989, and see Chapter 2). Indeed, looked at one way there was a reasonably substantial increase in crime during the inter-war years – crime increased by more than one-fifth between 1934 and 1938 for example. With the advent of war in 1939 there were concerns that a crime wave would result and, indeed, there was a substantial rise in indictable offences, an even more significant trend given that many of those most likely to be involved in criminal activity, young males, were abroad fighting the war. Most crime at this time was property crime and rises in violent crime were much shallower than those for theft and burglary.

It was in the mid-1950s that crime began to increase markedly, with recorded crime rising by almost three-quarters between 1955 and 1960. Why might this be so? Well, one important point to note first is that this period saw a very substantial increase in the availability of mass market consumer goods, many of which were portable. Second, as routine activities theorists (see Chapter 14) and others have noted, changes in the labour market saw a substantial increase in the proportion of women going out to work with the consequence that houses were left empty for considerably longer periods than had previously been the case. Third, it is also likely that the police became more assiduous in their recording of crime during this period. As can be seen from Figure 3.1 crime continued to rise fairly markedly and consistently from that period on, all the way through to the mid-1990s from which point it began to fall.

As Maguire (2007) argues, often figures concerning 'trends' in crime are, to put it at its kindest, misleading. Frequently, newspapers will compare this year's figures with last year's on the assumption that any differences between the two are necessarily meaningful. In fact, there are a good number of reasons why they may actually be closer to meaningless. Most importantly, *trends* in crime really need to be understood over a relatively extended period of time. Short-term fluctuations may too easily be affected by temporary, and possibly superficial, changes in organisational practices (changing police priorities; particular public concern with certain forms of behaviour; changes in

MODEL 901

£125 TAX PAID

This new Pam Television receiver is designed for discriminating viewers who appreciate high quality picture definition together with true to life sound reproduction. A 16" diameter Cathode Ray Tube is used giving a clear, steady picture approximately 12" x 10". Operation is extremely simple, there being only two main controls. The cabinet is soundly constructed and beautifully finished to harmonise with either modern or traditional furnishing schemes.

Model 901 is suitable for use on A.C. or D.C. mains and may be used in any B.B.C. Television area.

Crime rates began to increase markedly in the mid-1950s as more and more mass market consumer goods became available – such as television sets, which soon became attractive targets.

counting rules, etc.). Even when a long-term perspective is taken, it remains the case that great care should be taken when interpreting what at first sight appears to be significant change, for changes in recording and reporting can have a substantial impact here also. This is especially the case with trends based on data from *Criminal Statistics*. Maguire (2007) offers seven persuasive reasons why we should be wary of assuming that such data accurately portray changes over time:

- *Coverage* – as we have seen the categories of offence that go to make up *Criminal Statistics* change over time.

- *Counting rules* – these have been altered substantially on three occasions, on each occasion having a significant impact on the number of crimes counted.

- *Redefinitions* – legislative changes may affect what counts as 'theft' or 'burglary'.

- *Behaviour* – it is not certain that the offence categories used in *Criminal Statistics* are necessarily capturing the same forms of behaviour over time. Is 'fraud' in 2007 similar to 'fraud' in 1957?

- *Recording rates* – there may be marked changes in recording rates by police irrespective of changes in the counting rules. Some commentators have argued that the police deliberately manipulate recording rates in order, for example, to make it appear that they are facing particularly difficult times and therefore need more resources or, alternatively, to stimulate government to change the law.

- *Reporting rates* – as we know, public willingness to report particular offences is not static. Where once, domestic violence was considered entirely shameful and was largely hidden, there is now greater openness and, consequently, a greater willingness to report such offences to the police (though all the indications are that the bulk of such violence still remains hidden).

- *At risk populations* – demographic changes can have a considerable impact on the size of various elements of the population, such as those at particular risk of certain types of victimization (the size of the elderly population living alone), or at risk of offending (young males aged under 18 for example).

What then has been occurring to crime in the period for which we have two major data sources available? Figure 3.7 shows levels of recorded crime over the past two and half decades. Police-recorded crime data show crime rising relatively steadily during the 1980s and then increasing markedly from towards the end of the decade until 1992. From that point recorded crime rates declined until 1998/9 when new 'counting rules' were introduced. As the gap between the two sets of 1998/9 figures illustrate, the new counting rules produced an immediate increase in the number of offences recorded and, thereafter, appear to show crime increasing again until 2002/03, whereupon there is a further slight decline.

Data drawn from the various British Crime Surveys in many ways match the general trend visible from police-recorded statistics in the 1980s and early 1990s, though they differ quite significantly in the period since the late 1990s. BCS data, like

| **Figure 3.7** | Overall recorded crime rate, England and Wales, 1981–2005 |

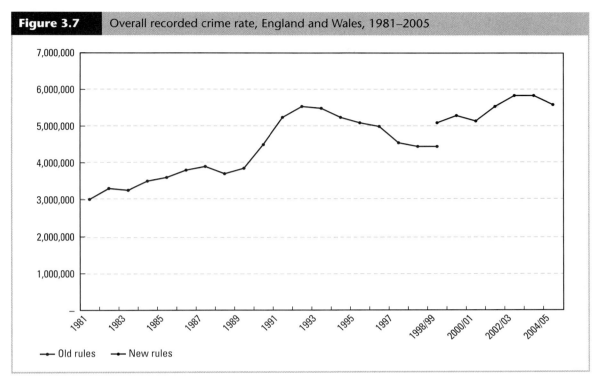

Source: *Criminal Statistics, England and Wales* (various).

| **Figure 3.8** | All crime (British Crime Survey) 1981–2004/05 |

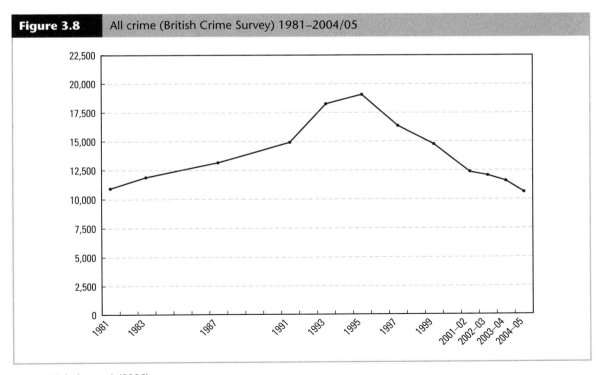

Source: Nicholas *et al.* (2005).

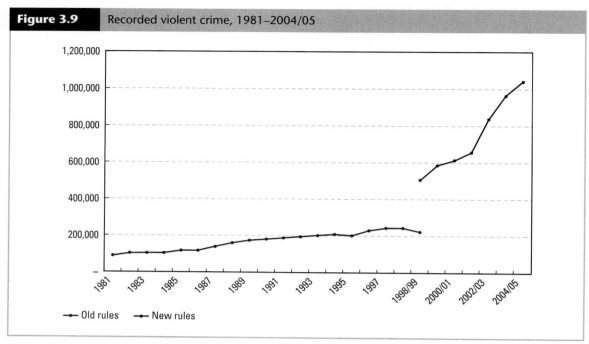

Source: *Criminal Statistics, England and Wales* (various).

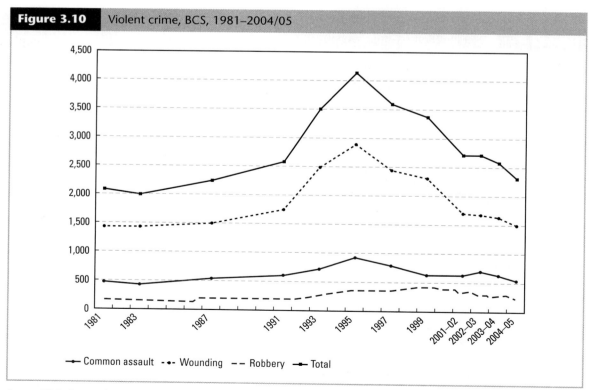

Source: Nicholas *et al.* (2005).

police-recorded crime, show crime rising into the 1990s – in this case to 1995 – and then falling. By contrast with police-recorded crime, the downturn measured by the BCS continues for the whole of the decade since 1995. Indeed, according to the BCS crime has fallen overall by 44 per cent during that decade, and 35 per cent since 1997. By 2005 crime was down slightly below the level recorded in the first BCS in 1981 (see Figure 3.8).

When the two data sources indicate similar trends there is little difficulty. However, when the indicated trends diverge – as they have in recent years – this can quickly become a source of political dispute and controversy. The dispute has concerned the overall trends in crime as well as trends in relation to particular types of offence – particularly violent crime. Indeed, it is in the area of violence against the person that the most significant differences in measured trends are apparent and where, not surprisingly, the most vociferous political debates have focused. Whereas BCS measures suggest that violent crime reached a peak in the mid-1990s and then returned to approximately early 1990s levels, recorded violent crime appears to have increased dramatically in the last five years (see Figures 3.9 and 3.10).

There are a number of reasons why the two sources of data appear to show contrasting trends in recent years. First, as Figure 3.7 indicated, there

was a significant change in 1998–9 in the rules used for 'counting' recorded crime. In particular, these changes to the 'counting rules' expanded the numbers of crimes recorded by including a greater number of more minor, or summary, offences, particularly in the categories of less serious violent crimes (common assault), fraud and drugs offences. There was a further 'counting' change in 2002. This involved the introduction of what was called the National Crime Recording Standard (NCRS). The NCRS sought both to make the process of recording incidents more victim-oriented and to standardise practices across police forces. By 'victim-oriented' what was meant was that in future recording would take greater account of the victim's perception of a crime occurring, rather than relying on police officers' assessments of the situation (Simmons and Dodd, 2003). On the assumption that previously many incidents reported to the police were not recorded as crimes because officers were not satisfied an offence had taken place, this change was expected to lead to an increase in recorded crime.

Given the diverging trends indicated by the BCS and recorded crime statistics, and the general political sensitivities concerning crime measurement, it is important to try to assess the impact of the introduction of the changes to the construction of recorded crime statistics. Clearly the simplest

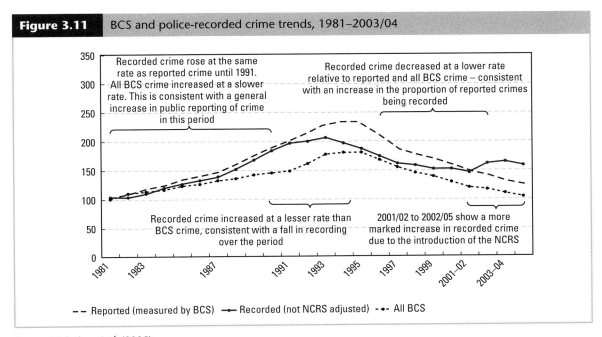

Figure 3.11   BCS and police-recorded crime trends, 1981–2003/04

Source: Nicholas *et al.* (2005).

method would be to compare recorded crime using the old and the new rules. Unfortunately, there is only one year – 1998/99 – when police forces were asked to submit data using both the old and the new counting rules and where a direct comparison of the impact of the new procedures could be made. Since that period the new rules have been applied and no data have been kept using the old counting procedures. As Figure 3.11 indicates, in 1998/99 there was a substantial increase in the number of offences recorded by the police as a result of the introduction of the new rules. In general terms it appears that the NCRS has had a continuing impact on recorded crime trends. The data in Figure 3.11 show that between 1981 and 2000 the trends shown by BCS and police recorded crime data are largely similar, but then depart substantially around 2001/02 when the NCRS was introduced.

In summary, during the period being reviewed here it is clear that crime increased during the first decade or so and then began to decrease. The fact that the two main methods of assessing crime levels produced somewhat differing pictures of the trends since the late 1990s has served to complicate matters and created an opportunity for politicians to present widely varying interpretations of recent changes in crime. A good example of how such disputes can arise can be found in a series of newspaper articles that appeared in the *Guardian* in 2004 and which are reproduced below (Excerpts 1–3). We begin with a piece by columnist Polly Toynbee, in which she argued that the then Leader of the Opposition, Michael Howard, was deliberately misrepresenting crime trends in order to make a particular political point.

The second excerpt is taken from Michael Howard's response. In it he takes Toynbee to task for relying on the British Crime Survey as the basis for what he sees to be her mistaken views on crime trends. As you will see, he suggests that if she had used what he describes as the *most reliable* statistics, police-recorded crime statistics, she would have seen a very different picture.

The third excerpt is taken from a response from Mike Hough, a former Home Office official and one of the originators of the British Crime Survey. Hough

Excerpt 1

A scary night in Brixton

When Michael Howard went on the prowl for a quick-hit crime story he didn't let the facts get in his way
Polly Toynbee, Friday 8 October, 2004, *The Guardian*

The police in Brixton are outraged. The community in Brixton is outraged and the Community Consultative Group, which links police and people together, has written a furious letter to Michael Howard.

It was this section in Howard's conference speech that caused the trouble: 'Three weeks ago on a Saturday night, I went out on the streets of Brixton. I saw the problem their community is up against. In two hours we didn't meet a single policeman, not one. This was inner-city London just before midnight, on a Saturday night. No wonder people feel the police have become distant and remote.'

Leave aside the unpleasant 'black mugger' racist overtones in choosing Brixton in the first place, just look at his failure – yet again – to do the most rudimentary research.
[…]

Here is why they are so angry with him. Crime in Brixton has been dropping like a stone. In the last year alone robbery is down by 21.5% – 330 fewer street robberies. Burglary is down by 16.8% and car crime by 21.9%. There were 2,000 fewer crimes this year and that comes on top of three years of falling figures: robbery dropped by 36% the previous year, remarkable results year after year.
[…]
As attentive *Guardian* readers should know by now, nationally the risk of being a victim of a crime has fallen by 40% since 1995 – the longest continuous fall in crime since 1898. Burglary has fallen by 39% and car crime by 31%. Violence has dropped too, by 24%.

The media and opposition parties get away with pretending it is not so, by quoting the police recorded figures, which have been rising due to improvements requiring the police to record more, not less, crime. All reputable, non-partisan crime experts think that the British Crime Survey findings are the ones that more accurately measure the way things are moving, even if no figures ever catch the whole truth.

Source: http://politics.guardian.co.uk/homeaffairs/comment/0,11026,1322591,00.html

Excerpt 2

Sorry, Polly, you're wrong

Michael Howard, Tuesday 12 October, 2004, *The Guardian*

If you have recently been mugged or burgled, please don't complain. Be positive. According to Polly Toynbee and *The Guardian*, you are living in a virtually crime-free country.
[...]
Her second line of attack was to take refuge in selective statistics. When she talks about crime nationally, Ms Toynbee prays in aid [i.e. uses as supporting evidence] the British Crime Survey. Perhaps she should listen to what the independent Crime and Society Foundation has to say. It argues that there are 'significant flaws' in the BCS and that it 'stretched credibility' to suggest crime is falling. The BCS excludes lots of crimes from its calculations – such as murder, crimes against children under 16, sexual offences, dealing and taking drugs, and shoplifting. It is estimated that around 12 million crimes a year don't even make it on to the BCS radar.

The most reliable crime statistics – those crimes recorded by the police – show that crime in England and Wales has risen by almost 850,000 in the past five years. While burglary and car crime have fallen, gun crime has doubled; robbery has gone up by more than half; and, most damning of all, violent crime has increased by 83%. Last year, it hit the 1 million mark for the first time ever. That is 3,000 violent crimes every day – more than 100 violent crimes every hour.

Source: http://politics.guardian.co.uk/conservatives/comment/0,9236,1325006,00.html

defends the BCS against Howard's attack and argues that the different picture painted by the official statistics, particularly in relation to violent crime, is actually a product of a change in the 'counting rules' (which as we saw above are the administrative rules which govern how the police and other agencies record crime) rather than changes in crime itself.

The most detailed analysis of crime data, comparing BCS and police recorded data, particularly in the most contentious area of trends in violent crime, tends to suggest that the general picture presented by BCS remains the most accurate, with the changes in the counting rules and the introduction of the NCRS having significantly affected

Excerpt 3

Crimes against statistics

As a former home secretary, Michael Howard can't really believe what he is saying about violence in Brixton
Mike Hough, Thursday 14 October, 2004, *The Guardian*

Earlier this week, Michael Howard called Polly Toynbee to task for drawing on British Crime Survey figures about falling crime. 'The most reliable crime statistics – those recorded by the police – show that crime in England and Wales has risen by 850,000 in the past five years', he claimed. He referred to an increase in recorded violent crime of 83% over the past five years nationally, and, in defence of his remarks about Brixton, a rise in violent crime statistics in Lambeth of 10% over the past year.

As a former home secretary, he must be aware that this is a gross misrepresentation of crime trends. Police statistics bear little relation to the reality. The British Crime Survey (BCS) shows unequivocally that major types of crime have fallen dramatically since 1995: vehicle crime down by half, house burglary down by 47%, assault down by 43%, wounding down by 28%, vandalism down 27%. Mugging shows a small fall that is statistically not significant.

Recorded crime has gone up over the past five years because the police have changed the way that they count crime. In particular, they altered their 'counting rules' in 1998, and introduced a national crime recording standard from 2002. They previously rejected victims' reports of crime if they doubted them; now, under the NCRS, these are taken at face value. Both sets of changes have inflated the police count of crime, and this inflation has been greatest for crimes of violence. That is the reason for the 83% rise in violence that Mr Howard cites.

Source: http://politics.guardian.co.uk/conservatives/comment/0,9236,1326685,00.html

police recorded crime. Indeed, Hough *et al.*'s (2005: *vii*) conclusion from their analysis of data on violent crime in England and Wales was that it was 'clear beyond doubt that recorded crime statistics are, in and of themselves, a totally unreliable guide to trends in violent crime since 1998'. Despite the political controversy, particularly around trends in violent crime, most commentators, academic or otherwise, take the view that, overall, crime has continued to decline since peaking somewhere between 1992–1995.

Data on offenders

In discussing criminal statistics we noted that they contained relatively little information about offenders and, rather, tended to focus on offences. Similarly, the nature of surveys such as the BCS means that they focus on victims' experiences and, again, tend to have little to say about perpetrators. We end our discussion in this chapter by looking briefly at some of the main sources of data about offenders and what they have to say about the distribution of offending across different social groups. Much of these data are recent in origin. However, we begin with official data once again, this time derived from something called the *Offenders Index*. This is a database which contains the official criminal histories of people who have been convicted in a criminal court of what are called 'standard list' offences. These offences include all indictable offences and a selection of the more serious summary offences.

Using this information, Home Office statisticians found that over one-third of adult males will be convicted in a criminal court of a relatively serious offence. This, to my eyes at least, is one of the more extraordinary criminological findings. Taking all males born in 1953, the Home Office was able to calculate the proportions of adults that had one or more convictions for a standard list offence. Now, before we move to the detailed findings, let's just remind ourselves that these are the more serious offences – the more minor ones, including traffic offences, are excluded. The results are displayed in Figure 3.12.

What the pie chart shows is that by their 40th birthday, over one-third of males (34%) had a conviction for a standard list offence, and seven per cent had four or more. What these data also indicate is the very substantial differences between men and women in terms of criminal records – a matter we return to in some detail in Chapter 32. In terms of the offences, the same source of data shows theft offences to be the most common, with 16 per cent of males aged 40 having been convicted of such crimes, with burglary being the next most common (see Figure 3.13).

Fascinating though such data are, they have limitations in the same way all data sources do. Thus, they rely upon information that comes to the attention of the authorities – in this case that small proportion of overall cases that reach the criminal courts. All those offences that are not reported, not recorded, or are not 'cleared up' cannot be taken into account. In order, therefore, to gather fuller information about involvement in offending it is necessary to use survey techniques once again – this time to ask people directly whether they have ever been involved in criminal activity. This approach is what is known as the 'self-report study'.

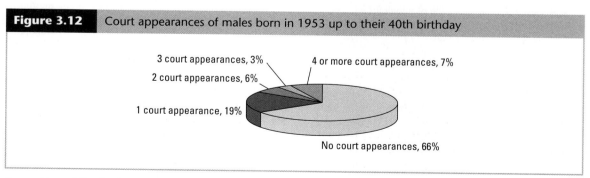

| **Figure 3.12** | Court appearances of males born in 1953 up to their 40th birthday |

3 court appearances, 3%
4 or more court appearances, 7%
2 court appearances, 6%
1 court appearance, 19%
No court appearances, 66%

Source: Home Office Statistical Bulletin 14/95.

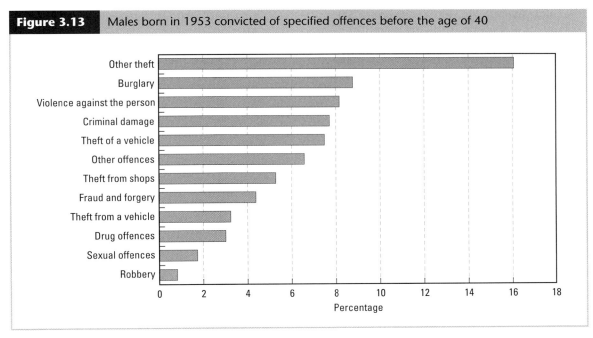

Figure 3.13   Males born in 1953 convicted of specified offences before the age of 40

Source: *Home Office Statistical Bulletin 14/95.*

Self-report studies

Self-report studies may have a number of objectives. One of the aims, at least early aims, of self-report studies was to develop measures of the extent of crime using very similar definitions of crime to those in *official statistics*, but in a way that would overcome many of the shortcomings of such measures. The aim was to develop a more accurate measure of the extent of crime. Such studies may also be used to explore and possibly test theories that seek to explain crime and offending behaviour. Much recent research on 'risk factors' for example has been based around longitudinal self-report studies. A third aim may be to explore the social distribution of crime and offending.

Self-report studies emerged in the 1940s, developed in the 1950s and 1960s and by the 1980s had become an established criminological method. Coleman and Moynihan (1996) suggest the 'breakthrough' for this method came with Nye's (1958) study of delinquency and family relationships. This and other studies he undertook around this time all used the self-report technique, including a 'delinquency checklist' covering such activities as: driving without a licence; skipping school; criminal damage; underage drinking and using or selling drugs. Though using a somewhat erratic and inconsistent measure of 'delinquency', the studies did find a fairly strong relationship between delinquency and social class, as well as reinforcing the clear connections between offending and age (see Chapter 29). This was to remain a strong focus for self-report studies for much of the next two decades (and beyond), to be joined in the 1970s by a focus on gender.

In the 1960s a youth survey was undertaken by the University of Michigan, part of which included a self-report element concerning 'behaviour that would get teenagers into trouble if they were caught'. The researchers constructed a 'delinquency scale' which included the types of offences that had been covered by Nye's study, but also included a range of more serious offences, including assault, drug use, theft of a car and carrying a weapon. The researchers found differences in levels of involvement in crime according to sex, age and race – much as self-report studies have continued to do since that time. The self-report technique has become a standard feature of much research on delinquency, especially longitudinal studies, and subsequent studies such as the National Youth Survey that started in the 1970s, through to the Chicago Neighbourhoods study established in the 1990s have added hugely to our knowledge both of the subject and the methodology.

One of the best-known studies in British criminology that has used a self-report instrument as the core of its approach is the *Cambridge Study in Delinquent Development*, involving a number of academics from the Cambridge Institute of Criminology, but which these days is undoubtedly most closely associated with David Farrington. A longitudinal study of 411 working-class South London males born in the early 1950s and contacted first in 1961–62 when they were eight or nine years old, the study has provided a steady flow of important data for over 40 years. The study has focused on what are now generally referred to as the 'risk factors' associated with offending, as well as providing an insight into the differences between self-report studies and official records as measures of the extent of offending. It is worth highlighting some of the findings from the Cambridge cohort study here:

- Prevalence of offending (the proportion of people who have offended) peaks at age 17.

- Individuals who exhibit 'early onset' (when they begin to offend) tend to accumulate many more convictions over the life-course than those who exhibit later onset.

- Conviction data suggest that male offenders do not specialise in violent offending.

- Offending frequency is the strongest predictor of whether an individual is a violent offender.

- A small group of individuals in the sample is responsible for a sizeable proportion of all offending activity by those in the group. (Piquero *et al.*, 2007)

During the 1980s and 1990s the use of self-report instruments became particularly popular. In the UK, successive Youth Lifestyles Surveys (YLS) (Graham and Bowling, 1995; Flood-Page *et al.*, 2000) have examined self-reported crime, drug and alcohol use by people aged 14 to 25. In addition, a very large longitudinal study was established in Edinburgh in 1998 and is now beginning to produce very interesting results on the offending 'careers' of a cohort of young Scots who were just starting secondary school when the study was first undertaken. Internationally, and especially in the United States, longitudinal studies using self-report instruments have grown markedly in the past decade or more.

Finally, a new survey – the Offending, Crime and Justice Survey (OCJS) – has recently been established in the UK. It is a national longitudinal, self-report offending survey for England and Wales and covers people living in private households. It was first conducted in 2003 and has been repeated

each year until 2006. It has a number of advantages over other surveys, including the YLS, as it includes interviews with children as young as ten and also includes a longitudinal element enabling researchers to follow-up a proportion of respondents in subsequent years (Budd *et al.*, 2005).

Assessing the self-report method

Let us return to the methodological issues raised by self-report studies more generally. We have seen much that is advantageous in using such an approach – particularly when compared with what we can learn about offending from much official data. In short:

- Self-report studies avoid the problems of non-reporting and non-recording associated with police-recorded statistics.

- They do not rely on second- or third-hand accounts, but take information directly from victims/offenders.

- They are not subject to political influence or managerial pressures (they are not, for example, a measure of an organisation's effectiveness).

- When used as part of longitudinal studies, self-report methods can reveal changes in patterns of offending over the life course that would otherwise be hidden.

What, however, are the difficulties and shortcomings of the self-report method? We can identify the following:

- The inclusion of too many, or too many trivial, items in checklists. This was a particular problem in many early self-report studies. Steven Box (1981) was particularly critical of some early self-report studies for focusing on largely trivial matters.

- There can be difficulties in identifying which items to include in checklists – it is rarely possible to include everything that one is interested in as a researcher.

- There may be difficulties in identifying items for checklists that are distinct and don't overlap.

- The reference or time period categories can be problematic/vague. Some early studies used entire school career as the time period. The National Youth Survey referred to earlier focused on the three years prior to the survey. It is now more usual to focus on the previous year only. However, difficulties remain. In relation, say, to self-reported drug use, the reference period options are often: 'in the last month; 'in the last year; and, 'ever'. This doesn't, for example, help identify anyone that might be using daily or who might in other ways be considered a 'frequent' user.

- Questions are often raised about the accuracy of respondent's recall of events that are not particularly recent. Can we recall accurately what happened to us in the past year?

- Although self-report methods may overcome some of the problems associated with official statistics, it cannot be assumed that respondents are always entirely truthful. Are people always willing to disclose what they have done, or what has happened to them? Research suggests that in practice self-report studies have a high level of validity – people tend not to lie/exaggerate/mislead. Nevertheless, there are bound to be limits to the accuracy of such data.

Maguire (2007: 289) offers the following astute general observation:

> [J]ust as victim surveys are vastly more effective in revealing 'hidden' instances of some kinds of crime than of others, so the perpetrators of different kinds of offence are not equally well 'revealed' through the medium of self-report studies. Thus, while respondents tend to be asked in great detail about the relatively visible kinds of anti-social activity which are associated with the court appearances of adolescents, they are not often asked whether they have assaulted their partners or sexually abused their children, nor whether they have perpetrated a significant financial fraud.

His conclusion, therefore, is that there is much to commend the use of self-report surveys and, possibly, they might one day enable us to explore areas of offending – particularly within families and in the commercial and financial sectors – where currently research is somewhat hampered. As such his conclusion reminds us that all sources of data tend to have both strengths and limitations. It is important to understand these so that data can be utilised appropriately. 'Crime' is not something that is, or ever could be, measured with complete accuracy. It is possible, however, to produce reasonable and relatively reliable *estimates* of levels and trends. The fact that such estimates should always be treated with caution should not stop us from always trying to use the best available measures when discussing trends in crime, in seeking constantly to refine the methods of measurement available to us, and from challenging those who use faulty data or make unsupported claims about the nature of crime and crime trends.

Review questions

1 Which two main changes affected official crime statistics after 1998?

2 What is a 'standard list' offence?

3 Approximately what proportion of males have a criminal conviction by their 40th birthday?

4 What sorts of studies use the self-report method?

Questions for further discussion

1 What are the main strengths and weaknesses of official crime statistics?

2 What are the main strengths and weaknesses of victimization surveys?

3 Discuss what is meant by, and what we know about, the 'dark figure' of crime?

4 How are the differing crime trends in recent years that are revealed by these two data sources to be explained?

5 Can we say with any accuracy how much crime there is in our society?

Further reading

Though now out of date it is well worth studying: Bottomley, K. and Pease, K. (1993) *Crime and Punishment: Interpreting the data*, Milton Keynes: Open University Press

Excellent treatments of the issues can be found in:

Coleman, C. and Moynihan, J. (1996) *Understanding Crime Data*, Buckingham: Open University Press

Maguire, M. (2007) Crime data and statistics, in Maguire, M. *et al.* (eds) *The Oxford Handbook of Criminology*, 4th edition, Oxford: Oxford University Press

Hough, M. and Maxfield, M. (eds) (2007) *Surveying Crime in the 21st Century*, Cullompton: Willan

For coverage of slightly different issues you might also consult:

Hope, T. (2005) What do crime statistics tell us? In Hale, C. *et al.* (eds) *Criminology*, Oxford: Oxford University Press

Websites

There really is no substitute for looking at the various Home Office websites. There is an extraordinary amount of information there, ranging from annual publications such as *Criminal Statistics* to specific Statistical Bulletins analysing particular issues and specialised research studies. The best starting points are:

http://www.homeoffice.gov.uk/rds/pubsintro1.html – the homepage of Home Office RDS publications

http://www.homeoffice.gov.uk/rds/pubsstatistical.html – a listing of all statistical publications

http://www.homeoffice.gov.uk/rds/horsarchive.html – the archive of Home Office Research Studies which contains all the early BCS reports

If you want to look at crime data from other jurisdictions there are a number of very good websites you can visit. These include:

Scottish Executive – www.scotland.gov.uk

US Department of Justice – http://www.ojp.usdoj.gov/bjs/

Council of Europe's Sourcebook – http://www.european-sourcebook.org/

Statistics Canada – www.statcan.ca

Australian Bureau of Statistics – http://www.abs.gov.au/

Students who have the inclination and confidence to play around with primary data can get access to the British Crime Survey itself via the ESRC Data Archive at Essex University: http://www.data-archive.ac.uk/findingData/bcrsTitles.asp

Finally it is worth keeping an eye on the website of the Radical Statistics Group for occasional papers providing a different, critical view of the uses (and abuses) of crime data: http://www.radstats.org.uk/crime.htm

Chapter outline

Introduction 84
   Academic study of the media 84

Media representations of crime 85
   Newsworthiness 85
   The crime content in the media 86
   Violent crime in the news 88

Are the media criminogenic? 90
   Media effects 92
   Media and fear of crime 93

Moral panics 94
   Mods and rockers 95
   Drug use and deviancy amplification 97
   Mugging 98
   Criticisms of moral panic theory 99

Policing and the media 100
   The relationship between the police and the media 101
   The representation of policing 102

Crime and the internet 104
   Policing cybercrime 107

Representing terror 107

Questions for further discussion 109
Further reading 109
Websites 110

4

Crime and the media

| **CHAPTER SUMMARY** | Television, radio, newspapers, the internet – these play a significant role in many of our lives. They carry stories about crime, provide us with information about crime, and are a potentially important influence upon the way in which we see the world. In this chapter we explore some of the myriad relationships between crime and the media. In this chapter we look at: |

- 'representations' – how crime and criminals are portrayed on television, in the press and elsewhere;

- how, if at all, these 'representations' depart from reality;

- whether the images portrayed by the media have a negative impact;

- the evidence about 'media effects';

- the limitations of research in this area;

- whether media coverage distorts and exaggerates the threat posed by certain phenomena;

- the notion of 'moral panics';

- how the media are used, and what some of the limitations might be.

We conclude by exploring a number of key contemporary issues relating to crime and the media:

- their relationship with the police;

- the growing importance of the internet;

- the portrayal of terrorism.

Introduction

We are surrounded by electronic and print media (and increasingly print media are themselves available electronically). For most households there are multiple television channels available – for some there are hundreds. Although readership of national newspapers has been declining for some years, there has been a sizeable expansion of the magazine and free paper market, and the arrival of digital broadcasting has meant the relatively easy availability of hundreds of radio stations. The broadcasting of so-called 'rolling news' – 24-hour news stories on a continuous cycle – has become *de rigeur* for most television and radio stations. Moreover, advances in electronic forms of communication mean that pictures and sound can be received on one side of the world pretty much as they are recorded on the other side. The consequences are arguably profound. First, the mass media feel like an almost ever-present element of our contemporary lives. Second, news from around the world arrives on our screens and radios in ways

that make the geographical differences involved all but disappear.

Crime, as we will see, is a staple of the mass media. For television, cinema, magazines, newspapers and books, crime is a central, even dominant, theme. Fiction and non-fiction alike find crime to be irresistible. In previous chapters we looked at changing perceptions and understanding of crime at different periods of history, and also at how our understanding of crime is shaped by the main sources of data on offending. Arguably, however, what we know about crime – or, perhaps more accurately, what *we think* we know about crime, is hugely influenced by what we see on television and film and what we read in newspapers in magazines.

Academic study of the media

The media are – and arguably always have been – a source of many of our contemporary fears. Reiner (2007) identifies two main public anxieties about the media: first that they are in some way subversive and, alternatively, that they are a more or less subtle form of social control. In the former the media are perceived as a source of criminality; in the latter a source of misrepresentation and exaggeration. Both positions rest on the assumption that the mass media have some impact on attitudes and/or conduct. However, as we will see, such effects are difficult to establish empirically. This, as Reiner points out, has led to the accusation that much sociological and criminological writing is based on the assumption that there is no direct relationship between, say, television viewing and everyday behaviour.

Kidd-Hewitt (1995: 1–2) suggests that there have been four main avenues of academic work in the field of crime and the media, investigating:

1 Whether the mass media, particularly television, through depictions of crime, violence, death and aggression, can be proven to be a major cause or important contributory factor in criminal or deviant behaviour.

2 Whether the mass media, particularly the press, construct and present our social world in ways that distort reality, and unjustly stereotype particular groups or individuals, labelling them as 'outsiders', eliminating their credibility and, in the process, exploiting and furthering their own privileged access to powerful state institutions.

3 Whether the mass media engender 'moral panics' and cause people to be fearful by over-reporting criminal and violent events and looking primarily for sensation above accuracy.

4 Whether 'real' crime and fictional crime impact on the viewer in the same manner, particularly in the electronic media.

In what follows we will explore aspects of each of these themes. We begin by looking at how representations of crime in the media may depart from the reality of crime (as we understand it from the research evidence), before moving on to explore the idea that the media themselves may be *criminogenic*.

Media representations of crime

How is crime presented in the media? Why is it presented in this way and what impact, if any, do such representations have? MacDougall (1968: 12) notes that, 'At any given moment billions of simul-

taneous events occur throughout the world ... All of these occurrences are potentially news. They do not become so until some purveyor of news gives an account of them. The news, in other words, is the account of the event, not something intrinsic in the event itself.' How particular events come to be selected depends upon a complex process involving editors, journalists and the broader environment in which they work.

Reiner (2007) identifies two broad approaches to understanding why media representations come to be as they are. The first he refers to as 'crime news as hegemony in action'. Here, the ownership and control of the media, the location and structure of much crime reporting, and the core elements of 'newsworthiness' all contribute to production of crime news in a form that reflects the dominant social ideology and social order: a focus on crimes of the powerless rather than the powerful; sympathetic to the justice system rather than to the offender; and, favouring 'things as they are' rather than 'things as they might be' (Hall *et al.*, 1978).

The second approach, 'crime news as cultural conflict', is a variation on this theme rather than a radically different viewpoint. This attempts to provide a more subtle approach, seeing crime news less as a direct reflection of particular social or economic interests, and more as the product of the interaction between a number of factors, including political priorities, the practice of journalism and everyday pressures. The difference between the two approaches is not necessarily to be found in the outcome – the reproduction of social order – rather in the extent to which this outcome is seen as being inevitable (Ericson *et al.*, 1991).

Newsworthiness

Just as it is only possible for the police to enforce some laws some of the time, so it is only possible for the news media to report some events, and then usually fleetingly. Choices therefore have to be made about which 'stories' to cover and how. This is what we mean by 'newsworthiness' – being considered to meet the necessary criteria for inclusion in a broadcast or in print. A number of authors have outlined what they take to be the core values – the professional ideology – that provide the basis of editorial decisions about which stories to print and to broadcast. In a classic early study by Chibnall (1977) eight 'professional imperatives' were identified as implicit guides to the construction of news stories. They were:

1 Immediacy   (speed/the present)

2 Dramatisation   (drama and action)

3 Personalisation   (cult of celebrity)

4 Simplification   (elimination of shades of grey)

5 Titillation   (revealing the forbidden/voyeurism)

6 Conventionalism   (hegemonic ideology)

7 Structured access (experts, authority)

8 Novelty   (new angle/speculation/twist).

Hall *et al.* (1978), in their study of the moral panic surrounding mugging, argued that violence played an important role in determining the newsworthiness of particular events. They argued (1978: 67–8) that any 'crime can be lifted into news visibility if violence becomes associated with it since violence is perhaps the supreme example of the news value "negative consequences". Violence represents a basic violation of the person: the greatest personal crime is "murder", bettered only by the murder of a law-enforcement agent, a policeman. Violence is also the ultimate crime against property, and against the state. It thus represents a fundamental rupture in the social order.'

Chibnall goes on to suggest that there are at least five sets of further informal rules which govern the reporting of violence and, in particular, help determine what will be considered to be relevant:

1 Visible and spectacular acts

2 Sexual and political connotations

3 Graphic presentation

4 Individual pathology

5 Deterrence and repression.

Building on other work in this area, Jewkes (2004) outlines a slightly revised list of 12 news values that she argues structure crime news. Many of these are similar in all or part to Chibnall's, but three are recognisable additions:

● Risk – in today's more risk-oriented times, she argues, news stories have become more victim-centred and concerned with notions of vulnerability and fear.

● Proximity – this is both spatial and cultural (see also Galtung and Ruge, 1965; Greer, 2003). Spatial refers to geographical proximity (this will vary according to the nature of the media – local, national, international – and according to other aspects of the story – whether it involves celebrity, for example) and cultural proximity to

the apparent relevance of the story to the particular audience.

● Children – the attachment of children to a story gives it a prominence it might not otherwise have. At the time of writing, the story of the missing young girl – Madeleine McCann – has been running for over five weeks. The extent of the coverage of this tragic event is partly an indication of successful news management by the parents of the missing three year-old, but also a clear example of the newsworthiness attached to stories concerning children.

Finally, Greer (2007) has recently added a further news value – the *visual*. As he puts it:

> The rapid development of information technologies in recent decades has changed the terrain on which crime news is produced. Today, crime stories are increasingly selected and 'produced' as *media events* on the basis of their visual (how they can be portrayed in images) as well as their lexical-verbal (how they can be portrayed in words) potential.

The crime content in the media

If events become 'news' in part because they are defined as unusual or extraordinary, then 'deviance' becomes news very easily. As Erikson (1966: 12) argues:

> … confrontations between deviant offenders and the agents of control have always attracted a good deal of public attention … A considerable portion of what we call 'news' is devoted to reports about deviant behaviour and its consequences, and it is no simple matter to explain why these items should be considered newsworthy or why they should command the extraordinary attention they do. Perhaps they appeal to a number of psychological perversities among the mass audience … but at the same time they constitute one of our main sources of information about the normative outlines of our society.

A lot of research has been undertaken exploring the *content* of media coverage of particular issues. Content analysis involves, as the title implies, the analysis of the make-up of particular media. This usually involves the counting of different types of image, story and word usage and then comparing this with other media or with other statistical representations of the world. Thus, this method has been used as the basis for analysing the political content of television news. Is equal time allotted to the main parties? What language is used, and does it differ? How are stories framed and what imagery is used? Similarly, for example, it is possible to analyse the frequency of violence on television and to compare this with what is known about the incidence of such crime in everyday life.

Content analysis is often portrayed as a dispassionate, even 'objective' analysis of media. There are two major problems with such an assumption:

- As with all social research it involves the attribution of meaning, not least in the construction of the categories which are used to guide and frame analysis. Indeed, the categories selected contain assumptions about likely 'effects' or significance – there is little point in selecting the categories otherwise.

- Whilst an image may carry a particular meaning for one viewer – the researcher for example – it may carry a very different one, or many different messages, for others.

How much of what we watch and read involves crime? Of course, the answer depends on what one means by 'crime'. Focusing on the broader category of 'deviance', the Canadian sociologist, Richard Ericson, with his colleagues, found that between two-fifths (45%) and seven-tenths (71%) of quality newspaper and radio content was about deviance and its control (Ericson *et al.*, 1987). In fact, they argued that 'the news institution focuses upon what is out of place: the deviant, equivocal, and unpredictable' (Ericson *et al.*, 1991: 4).

Research on the more tightly restricted category of 'crime' rather than 'deviance' suggests that somewhere between five and ten per cent of space is devoted to crime and justice issues with newspapers in Britain devoting between five per cent and 30 per cent of their news space to crime (Williams and Dickinson, 1993). Although most research has focused on national newspapers, crime is also a staple form of reporting in the local press (Sampson and Phillips, 1992). Perhaps predictably, given what we know about the contemporary prominence of 'crime talk' (Sasson, 1995) in our everyday lives, there is an historical dimension to this, too. Research on the content of the *Mirror* and the *Times* by Reiner and colleagues (2000) found that their respective coverage of crime rose from two and three per cent respectively in 1945–51 to six and nine per cent in 1985–91.

There are a number of other general characteristics of news reporting of crime that lead to a somewhat distorted picture:

- Offenders featuring in news reports in national news media are older and of higher status than is generally the case in the criminal justice system (Reiner *et al.*, 2003).

- Police success in 'clearing up' crimes is exaggerated in news reporting (Roshier, 1973), partly because the police themselves are the source of many stories (and have a vested interest in portraying themselves positively) and also because of the disproportionate focus on violent crime (where clear-up rates are higher).

- News stories tend to exaggerate the risk of victimization, particularly for white, female and higher social status adults (Greer, 2003).

- As Reiner (2007) argues, general news coverage tends to portray crime as a series of discrete

Crime fiction

Books

Any visit to a major bookshop or a railway station bookstall will illustrate the extent to which crime forms the basis of a core part of the market for fiction. Estimates suggest that historically anything between one-quarter and one-third of all paperback titles are 'thrillers' (Mandel, 1984).

Cinema

Similarly, about one-fifth of all cinema films are crime movies and up to half have significant crime content (Allen *et al.*, 1997).

Television

About one-tenth of prime-time television concerned crime and law enforcement in the 1950s. This has increased since, and although there appear to be fluctuations over time, roughly one-quarter of all output is now devoted to crime.

Content

Violence, especially murder, is the staple of crime fiction. Moreover, representations of violence have become graphic and more extensive in the period since the Second World War (Reiner *et al.*, 2003).

incidents rather than having any pattern or structure.

Violent crime in the news

Schlesinger and Tumber (1994) in their study of crime reporting suggest that the nature of crime coverage has changed markedly since the mid-1960s. At that time, they argue, it mainly concerned murder, jewel heists and petty crime whereas, by the early 1990s, it had expanded and altered to include drugs, child abuse, mugging, football hooliganism and terrorism, as well as policy matters. What brought about this change? Some of the key factors, they suggest, include the abolition of capital punishment in 1965 which lessened the impact of murder stories, the rising crime rate leading to a situation in which the sheer weight of stories meant that it had to be something 'special' in order to be reported, together with changes in the nature of crime journalism itself, including the emergence of a range of specialists.

All media appear to exaggerate the extent of violent crime in Britain. This includes newspapers, news and entertainment on television and radio, and crime fiction (Greer, 2005). Content analysis of news media in both America and Britain has found violent crime to be over-represented compared with official statistics. Thus, for example, research by Ditton and Duffy (1983) in Scotland found that 46 per cent of all crime news concerned violent and sexual crime, whereas such crimes made up less than three per cent of police recorded crime. Schlesinger *et al.* (1991) similarly found that, whereas violence against the person accounted for around four per cent of notifiable offences, it made up one-quarter of all crime stories in the 'quality press' and 46 per cent in the 'popular press'. Not only is violent crime much more likely to be reported than property crime (even though there are seven to nine times the number of property offences compared with violent crime), but again this difference appears to be becoming more pronounced over time. Soothill and Walby's (1991) study of the reporting of rape, for example, found that the proportion of cases reported in the press rose from one-quarter in 1951 to one-third in 1985 (see Figure 4.1).

Soothill and Walby's (1991: 32) general conclusion to their review of the reporting of sex crime is that it shows:

> … how pervasive sexual violence has become as a news item, and also how only a very small number of cases are selected as being 'newsworthy'. The examination of rape coverage over time shows in particular how this topic has left the narrow audience of the *News of the World* and has entered the popular dailies on a large scale. Sex crime is both common, and yet the cases are highly selected.

Though we will return to the issue of 'newsworthiness' more generally below, it is worth briefly staying with the study of sex offences as it illustrates very clearly how a process of *selection* underpins what is made available via the media. Soothill and Walby's study suggests that a core theme is this area is the search for the 'sex fiend'. The coverage in the media, they argue, is consistently oriented toward identifying the existence of the 'sex beast'. This is not 'gross misrepresentation' they say, but rather 'a selective portrayal of specific facts' and this is undoubtedly an accurate way of understanding much media coverage of crime more generally.

The primary way in which the idea of the 'sex beast' is encouraged, they argue, is by promoting

Figure 4.1	Coverage of rape cases by six newspapers, 1951–85				
	1951	**1961**	**1971**	**1978**	**1985**
Sun	n/a	n/a	10	32	49
Daily Mirror	1	5	8	26	45
The Times	0	6	3	21	19
News of the World	22	46	62	72	2
Sunday People	1	5	2	1	3
Evening Standard	5	9	8	10	15

Source: Soothill and Walby (1991: 18).

the sense that there are links between sex offences. Thus, they quote examples of newspaper coverage in which a report of one attack contains a note that the police were 'looking into similarities with the rape of a ten year-old girl in Hemel Hempstead five months ago', and another which reported that four other attacks 'were being studied by police to see if there was a link' (1991: 37).

A further method of establishing links in the reader's mind, or of reinforcing previous coverage, is achieved through the application of specific labels beyond those of the generic 'sex beast' style. These may refer to alleged characteristics of the attacker ('the balaclava rapist'; 'lonely heart rapist') or to link the attacker to previous 'fiends' (such as the 'Ripper'). This approach is more typical of the national press, they argue, and increasingly also of television, whereas local newspapers – certainly at the time of their study – were more likely to contain small factual stories. At the national level, newspapers engage in 'a highly selective process by which [they place] certain stories in the public eye and not others' (1991: 44) with the result that events such as spectacular multiple rapes are presented as the rule rather than the exception.

The *News of the World* has led a campaign to press for notification schemes to provide communities with information about convicted sex offenders living locally – a contemporary 'moral panic'?

Another example of this style of reporting concerns the 'discovery' of the 'paedophile' in the 1990s. According to Soothill *et al.* (1998) there was an explosion of interest in this topic in the late 1990s, again with the theme of 'monsters' and 'beasts' being close to the heart of such stories:

THEY SET A SEX MONSTER ON MY CHILDREN

(*Daily Mirror*, 15 August 1994)

BESTIALITY BEYOND IMAGINATION

(*Daily Mail*, 17 May 1996)

BORN A MISFIT, HE BECAME A MONSTER

(*Daily Mail*, 19 July 1996)

MONSTER BAILED THREE TIMES TO ATTACK AGAIN

(*Yorkshire Post*, 23 November 1996)

I'LL NAME THE SEX BEASTS

(*Daily Mirror*, 9 June 1997)

COPS TO UNMASK FIENDS

(*News of the World*, 10 August 1997)

6 MORE CHILD SEX FIENDS TO GO FREE

(*Sun*, 13 March 1998)

CAGE HIM BEFORE HE KILLS AGAIN

(*Daily Mirror*, 14 March 1998)

(quoted in Thomas, 2005: 22)

Thomas (2005) argues that one of the consequences of the concerted attention given to such cases, and in this manner, was something of a 'moral panic' about sex offending and growing demands for the introduction of notification schemes which would provide local communities with information about convicted sex offenders living locally. Such campaigns have drawn particular energy in both America and Britain as a result of high profile cases involving the abduction and murder of young children. Indeed, as Cohen (2002: *xv–xvi*) notes in relation to sex offenders, there is '[o]ne form of sexualised violence against children [that] does not generate counter-claims about its existence nor any moral disagreement: the abduction and sexual killing of children, especially girls'. He goes on:

> This strikes a depth of horror in us all. There is a panicky sense of vulnerability – both in the sense of statistical risk (these events seem to be happening more often) and emotional empathy (how would I feel if it happened to my child?). The script becomes more familiar: child disappears on way home from school; the police set up investigation team; school friends, neighbours, teachers interviewed; frantic, distraught parents make appeals on TV; members of public join police in searching fields and rivers ...
>
> These offenders are pure candidates for monster status.
> (Cohen, 2002: *xvi*)

Are the media criminogenic?

One of the most long-standing debates in post-war public life concerns the potential and perceived ill-effects of the mass media. Violent and sexual imagery, in particular, has been held to be the root cause of contemporary trends in youthful misbehaviour of various forms. Indeed, such concerns have an even longer history than I have implied. Geoffrey Pearson in his study, *Hooligan*, provides numerous examples from the Victorian and Edwardian era of public concern (indeed, *moral panic*) about such media as the 'Penny Dreadful' comics or 'Penny Bloods' as they were sometimes known. Indeed, even earlier he notes:

> Henry Fielding's *Enquiry into the Cause of the Late Increase of Robbers* (1751) would identify 'too frequent and expensive Diversions among the lower kind of People' as one cause which 'hath almost totally changed the Manners, Customs and Habits of the People, more especially of the lowest Sort'. In 1776, Joseph Hanway likewise blamed debasing amusements, deficiencies in parental authority, and luxury and idleness among the common people for resulting in 'the

host of thieves which of late years invaded us.' 'And as to Newspapers, which let us into scenes of villainy,' he thought, 'they were harmful.' (Pearson, 1984: 97)

And there have been regular outbreaks of concern about particular media ever since, including those focusing on 'horror comics' in the 1950s and on 'video nasties' in the 1980s. According to Barker (1984), the campaign against horror comics in Britain originally surfaced as part of a general anti-American backlash by the Communist Party, but was later appropriated and narrowed by a number of other interest groups. The comics became an outlet or scapegoat for a more general threat to what were seen as traditional British values. He quotes one of the campaigners as saying:

> We wanted to get back to some sort of English tranquility. It was a very romantic notion, of countryside, Merrie England, Elgar's music ... And anything that was American was material and brash and vulgar, and that included their comics and motorcars. (1984: 182)

Similarly, a series of campaigns in the 1960s and 1970s were undertaken by the moral entrepreneur Mary Whitehouse and the National Listeners' and Viewers Association against what they perceived to be illustrations of permissiveness and moral decline on the television (Newburn, 1991). More recently, the arrival of mass television ownership, the spread of video and then DVD technology and, subsequently, computer games, have all been regularly castigated (without irony) in the mass circulation press for their powerfully negative effects on those who consume them. In what ways might the mass media *cause* crime? There are a number of possibilities:

- 'Labelling' – helping to define certain acts as harmful, deviant and, eventually, criminal (certain forms of drug use, for example).

- 'Deviancy amplification' – through exaggeration of the extent, or the harmfulness, of particular activities.

- Creation of 'moral panics'.

- Stimulation of desires – say for material goods – that for some can only be achieved illegally.

- Through imitation – so-called 'copycat crimes' (American research on over 200 prison inmates found that 90 per cent 'learned new tricks and improved their criminal expertise' through watching crime programmes on TV (Hendrick, 1977, cited in Meyrowitz, 1985; Jewkes, 2004).

- Through the transmission of knowledge of particular means or techniques.
- Through arousal via the use of violent or sexual imagery.
- Desensitisation through repeated viewing.
- Directly, as a source of valued commodities (televisions, video recorders, DVDs and so on being frequent targets of crime).
- Undermining the credibility of criminal justice agencies ('*Keystone Cops*').
- Glamorising offending.
- Presenting 'moral' views that are insufficiently damning of criminal behaviour.

There has been considerable academic interest in the possible effects of the media. Two major approaches can be discerned: *mass society* approaches and *behaviourism*. The former, which only fully emerged after the Second World War, was at heart an amalgam of various sociological ideas centring on the idea that society was becoming increasingly individualised – social ties breaking down as a result of progressive industrialisation and urbanisation – and disorderly. Under such circumstances the mass media are an increasingly important means of influencing and, potentially, manipulating people's attitudes and behaviour.

By contrast, *behaviourism* has at heart a much more direct link between external stimuli, such as the media, and human behaviour, and much work in this area used experiments to look at whether watching violent or sexual images resulted in a change in behaviour, particularly violent behaviour. Of all the work associated with this approach, arguably the best-known involved an experiment conducted by the American psychologist Albert Bandura in the 1950s and 1960s. Bandura, a social learning theorist (see also Chapter 7), used an experimental study involving 72 children aged between three and six, to explore the extent to which aggression and violence are imitative or learned behaviours.

The experiment involved the children being shown a film in which actors would act aggressively towards an inflatable doll ('a bobo doll') – the actor 'pummels it on the head with a mallet, hurls it down, sits on it and punches it on the nose repeatedly, kicks it across the room, flings it in the air, and bombards it with balls' (Bandura, 1975: 72). After watching the film the children were 'frustrated' by placing them in a room with attractive toys that they were not allowed to touch. They were then taken to a room that had toys identical to those used in the bobo doll film. The results of the experiments suggested that the children who had watched the film were significantly more likely to act aggressively towards the doll than were those who had not seen the film. These results were interpreted by Bandura and colleagues as evidence of the social learning impact of television in relation to violence and aggression.

Despite the existence of a number of famous, indeed occasionally infamous, experiments, there are few persuasive studies that are able to identify any very direct form of relationship between media consumption and behaviour that both the *mass society* and *behaviourism* approaches indicate. That is not to say that such views are discredited, and any regular reader of the popular press will frequently find views being expressed that are clearly underpinned by such assumptions. In recent times examples of such a tendency have focused upon violent films (the film *Child's Play 3* was roundly criticised by the judge in the trial of the two ten year-olds convicted of the murder of James Bulger), violent video games (such as *Grand Theft Auto*) and

The Sun advising its readers to destroy 'video nasties' on the grounds of their effects on children's behaviour – research studies have been much less clear about this relationship.

popular music (Culture Minister, Kim Howells, was highly critical of rap music saying, 'What we are looking at here is a very cynical attempt to romanticise and glorify these idiots who go around carrying guns and knives. What I would like … is for the record industry, which is making a packet out of this, to start thinking very seriously about engaging with their songwriters, singers and bands and saying to them, "Is this what we really want to put out?"') (http://news.bbc.co.uk/1/hi/wales/2752681.stm)

Media effects

Livingstone (1996) raises the question of why we expect to be able to measure media effects in such a straightforward and simple manner. We tend to avoid such simple questions in relation to other areas of the social world. Thus, she says, we don't ask questions as simplistic as 'what is the effect that parents have on children?', for example, and yet we expect to be able to identify the impact the media have upon viewers.

Nevertheless, there is now is a huge body of largely experimental social science that has attempted to study, identify and isolate the effects of the media. Much work in this area concerns viewing sex or violence and seeks to measure, first of all, whether any correlation can be found between viewing and attitudes and behaviour. Although many of the studies do show some effect, in the main the size of the effects is small, particularly where the effect is generally viewed as 'negative' (such as increased aggression or violence). The second question asked in such research is what is the direction of the relationship? There are, for example, three possible answers to this question in relation to the relationship between viewing and aggression:

1 More aggressive people select more violent programmes to watch (selective exposure).
2 Violent programmes make people more violent.
3 Certain social circumstances make people more aggressive and make them more likely to watch more violent television programmes.

The bulk of effects studies focus on the potential for negative effects (Livingstone, 1996); there are few studies of potential pro-social effects. The results of these latter studies suggest that although such programmes are few in number their effects are more sizeable than those measured in relation to harmful

effects. Harold (1986) found the overall effect size to be an extra 50 per cent of pro-social responses following prosocial content compared with 20 per cent of anti-social responses following violent content. The other major criticisms of effects research concern (Gauntlett, 2001; Livingstone, 1996):

- The use of artificial stimuli rather than real programmes (truer of the older studies).
- Measurement of short-term effects rather than anything longer term.
- Crude measures of what constitutes 'violence'.
- Insufficient distinction between different forms of portrayal of violence.
- Absence of follow-up studies.
- The artificiality of many experimental situations.

The artificiality of experiments led researchers to attempt more naturalistic forms of inquiry and, in particular, to explore the use of experiments 'in the field'. In particular, researchers have sought to compare, wherever possible, communities with and without television or, alternatively, communities before and after television is introduced. Research by Hennigan et al. (1982) looked at the introduction of television in the United States in the 1950s.

The spread of television was interrupted by the Federal Communications Commission between 1949 and 1952 providing the possibility of comparing cities which shared many characteristics, but which were separated by their access to television. Comparing the officially-recorded crime rates in these cities they found that, in 1951, larceny (burglary) increased in the sample of 34 cities in which television had just been introduced compared with the 34 cities where television was not available. In 1955 they found that larceny theft increased in the 34 cities that had just gained access to television compared with those cities that had had television access for several years. The increase was approximately five per cent. Here, again, several explanations are possible:

- Television watching has criminogenic features and leads to an increase in crime.
- Television increases materialism and acquisitiveness and leads some who do not have legal access to material goods to find other means (the explanation favoured by the researchers).
- The broader change in culture, of which television was a part, also involved a heightened awareness of crime, increasing people's willingness to report crime.

- The broader change in culture which heightened awareness of crime made the police more crime conscious.

- Some other, unaccounted for, factor lies behind the (relatively small) changes measured.

How to conclude? Livingstone repeats the oft-quoted observation by Schramm *et al.* (1961: 11):

> For some children, under some conditions, some television is harmful. For some children under the same conditions, or for the same children under other conditions, it may be beneficial. For most children, under most conditions, most television is probably neither particularly harmful nor particularly beneficial.

However, she then (2000: 315) goes on to say that 'bland and cautious conclusions ... do not satisfy the strength of public feeling on the issue' and notes that this strength of feeling may well be related to the generalised desire for childhood to be a time of relative innocence – an uncontaminated private sphere.

Media and fear of crime

We have already noted that media representations of crime tend to distort 'reality' in a number of important ways, not least in exaggerating certain risks. It is clearly but a short step from this observation to asking whether fear of crime is itself in part a product of such representations. In other words, is there a 'media effect' in connection with fear of crime?

'Fear of crime' has been a political and policy concern in its own right for over 25 years. It was identified by the early British Crime Survey reports (Hough and Mayhew, 1983) and has been the subject of continuous, and arguably increasing, scrutiny ever since, though critical work in this area in recent years has cast some doubt on the utility of using the term 'fear' in this regard (see Chapter 20). In the late 1980s a Working Group on Fear of Crime, chaired by one-time Director-General of the BBC Michael Grade, reported to the Home Office's Standing Conference on Crime Prevention on the sources and consequences of fear of crime. It argued (1989: 2):

> The effect of crime reporting by the media is almost inevitably to increase fear. This becomes unacceptable when, as so often, crime is reported in an unbalanced way, with a strong emphasis on violent and unusual crimes, and on particular types of victim (notably young women and old people). The public receives only a distorted impression.

The 'cultivation analysis' associated with Gerbner and colleagues in the US has had some influence in

---

Young offenders and the media

Are media consumption patterns among young offenders different from those among young people generally? Some years ago, a small-scale study sought to explore this via interviews with 78 young offenders aged between 12 and 18 and a survey of a representative sample of schoolchildren from approximately the same age range. The young offenders were fairly 'prolific', having committed over 750 offences between them in the year prior to the research. The research, descriptive in character, aimed to see whether there were any significant differences in what the two groups watched and read.

In relation to reading, the key difference was the young offenders read less than did those in the comparison group. The young offenders also had less access to television, video and other equipment than the comparison schoolchildren, and less access to non-terrestrial broadcasting where they lived. By and large the two groups watched roughly similar amounts of television, and similar amounts after the 9pm 'watershed'. Among the young offenders, the most popular programme was the police drama *The Bill*, perhaps reflecting their interests and experiences.

Any variation between the two groups of young people only ever applied to a small number of individuals. In both groups, they did not report anything in the way of watching unusual programmes or films, their choices largely being very mainstream. There was no evidence of any particular attraction to programmes or films with an especially violent content – or, more accurately, the offenders did not appear to be any more attracted to violent television programmes or films than are most children of their age. Case studies of individual offenders suggested that their viewing habits should be assessed in the light of their lifestyles, and that offending and media habits are both single elements in a complicated kaleidoscope of background and behaviour.

Source: Hagell and Newburn (1994b).

relation to the question of what role the media has in affecting levels of fear of crime, finding that 'heavy' users of TV (more than four hours a day) develop a world view that is closer to that being promoted by television than do 'light' users. Heavy viewing is closely associated with the development of higher levels of fear of crime. Mixed results are reported by other research when attempting to explore the same questions, and methodological shortcomings have severely limited much of this work. More recent work that has focused more clearly on the nature of portrayals of violence and on the nature of the audience have found some links with the lives and lifestyles of viewers. Schlesinger *et al.* (1992) suggest that women may be highly sensitised to portrayals of interpersonal crime, particularly sexual crimes.

A small-scale piece of survey research by Schlesinger and Tumber (1992) found 'consistent relations' between individuals' media consumption and their levels of fear of becoming a victim of crime. More particularly, they suggest that it was readers of tabloid newspapers and heavy watchers of television who were more likely to report being particularly worried about becoming a victim of crime, and were especially concerned about the risk of physical attack or 'mugging'.

However, as they readily admit, one cannot assume cause and effect from such an association. It is, for example, perfectly possible that people who are especially fearful are attracted to particular types of media, or that patterns of fear and patterns of media consumption are a product of similar underlying factors. For this reason, Reiner (2002: 401) concludes that 'while it remains a reasonable hypothesis that much public fear of crime is created or accentuated by media exposure, the research evidence remains equivocal about the strength, or even existence, of such a causal relationship'. In this vein, Sparks (1992) is especially critical of the lack of thought given in much research in this area to television 'content' and, in particular, the failure to question assumptions that the meaning of 'violence' is self-evident.

Indeed, as Reiner notes more generally, the main message from empirical inquiry into media effects is that it seems to tell us most about the difficulties involved in rigorous social scientific research in this area. The likely existence of media effects is hardly contested any longer. What remains at issue, however, is how these effects work. Thus, whilst it is perfectly possible to design measures with which to analyse the content of various media, to examine variations among the population and to explore

possible correlations with attitudes (fear of crime for example) or behaviour (offending for example), none of this provides particularly solid evidence of the nature of media effects.

Review questions

1 What are the two main ways identified by Reiner of understanding why media representations of crime come to be as they are?

2 What are some of the main values underpinning the idea of 'newsworthiness'?

3 How has 'media effects' research generally been conducted?

Moral panics

Moral panic is one of those sociological terms that is now part of everyday vocabulary. Kenneth Thompson (1998) in his short book dedicated to the term, opens it with an analysis of a debate about its meaning between Melanie Phillips,

Front cover of the second edition of Stan Cohen's *Folk Devils and Moral Panics: the creation of the Mods and Rockers* – the classic study of 'deviant' subcultures and the 'moral panic' they generated in the media.

Martin Jacques and a number of other columnists/journalists from the *Guardian* and *Observer*. It is a term that is regularly used by social commentators. In the aftermath of the abduction and murder of two year-old James Bulger in 1993, for example, *The Economist* referred to the publicity surrounding the case as a example of 'moral panic' (Thompson, 1998).

The term, however, is lastingly associated with Stan Cohen, who subjected it to its earliest and most thorough-going analysis in his book on the Mods and Rockers in the 1960s – a book which has the distinction of containing two terms, *folk devils* and *moral panics,* which have subsequently entered popular terminology. Cohen's sociology was, arguably, something of an amalgam of American labelling theory and left-leaning British sociology's concern with youth and social class – an approach which was taken up and extended later on by Stuart Hall, Phil Cohen and others at the Birmingham Centre for Cultural Studies (see Chapter 9). Cohen's introduction to his book is worth reproducing:

> Societies appear to be subject, every now and then, to periods of moral panic. A condition, episode, person or group of persons emerges to become defined as a threat to societal values and interests; its nature is presented in a stylised and stereotypical fashion by the mass media; the moral barricades are manned by editors, bishops, politicians and other right-thinking people; socially accredited experts pronounce their diagnoses and solutions; ways of coping are evolved or (more often) resorted to; the condition then disappears, submerges or deteriorates and becomes more visible. Sometimes the object of the panic is quite novel enough, but suddenly appears in the limelight. Sometimes the panic passes over and is forgotten, except in folklore and collective memory; at other times it has more serious and long-lasting repercussions and might produce such changes as those in legal and social policy or even in the way society conceives itself. (1980: 9)

The term, it appears, like so many others, was first used by Jock Young in an article in 1971 talking about public concern about drug use. In it, Young described 'the *moral panic* over drug-taking results in the setting up of drug squads' leading to an increase in arrests. Taking Cohen's definition (cited above), Thompson identifies five key elements or stages in a moral panic (see also Goode and Ben-Yehuda, 1994):

1 Something or someone is defined as a threat to values or interests.

2 This threat is depicted in an easily recognisable form by the media.

3 There is a rapid build-up of public concern.

4 There is a response from authorities or opinion-makers.

5 The panic recedes or results in social changes.

To this we might add that it is young people who are most frequently the subject of such moral concern (they become the 'folk devils'). Whilst writers occasionally disagree over the core characteristics of moral panics, there is general consensus that moral panics involve heightened concern about some behaviour or group, and that this also involves, or results in, increased hostility toward the group concerned. Moral panics are generally volatile – they may disappear as swiftly as they appear and, as the term panic implies, they tend to involve an element of *disproportionality*. By this is meant that the social reaction at the heart of a moral panic is assumed to be greater than the group, behaviour or event would justify if analysed rationally. It is this latter element of moral panic theory that has given rise to much of the criticism levelled at the idea, and we return to this below.

Kidd-Hewitt (1995: 3) rightly cautions that 'the context and significance of Cohen's study has frequently been overlooked and often turned into a pastiche – a mods and rockers soap episode cited by sociology and criminology students without a full sense of its place in the continuity of the media's long association with "the manufacture of news".' That said, let us turn, briefly, to some of the details of Cohen's analysis.

Mods and rockers

Cohen's analysis of the mods and rockers panic in the 1960s involves, among many other characteristics, a clear description of a 'signification spiral' argued to be central to moral panics. The *signification spiral* involves a circular set of interactions between claims-makers, moral entrepreneurs and the mass media in the creation of a panic about a particular *folk devil*. The events themselves are described by Stan Cohen in the following way:

> Easter 1964 was worse than usual. It was cold and wet, and in fact Easter Sunday was the coldest for eighty years. The shopkeepers and stall owners were irritated by the lack of business and

Front page of the *Daily Mirror*, 18 May 1964. It was reporting such as this which led to the developing moral panic about mods and rockers.

the young people had their own boredom and irritation fanned by rumours of café owners and barmen refusing to serve some of them. A few groups started scuffling on the pavements and throwing stones at each other. The mods and rockers factions – a division initially based on clothing and lifestyles, later rigidified, but at that time not fully established – started separating out. Those on bikes and scooters roared up and down, windows were broken, some beach huts were wrecked and one boy fired a starting pistol in the air. The vast number of people crowding into the streets, the noise, everyone's general irritation and the actions of an unprepared and undermanned police force had the effect of making the two days unpleasant, oppressive and sometimes frightening. (Cohen, 1980: 29)

The reaction in the press took on the form of what we now understand as the classic 'moral panic'. Cohen's analysis of the role of the media in the creation of this panic is undertaken under three headings:

- *Exaggeration and distortion* – the exaggeration involved covered the seriousness of the events that weekend, including the numbers involved,

the proportion engaged in violence, the seriousness of the violence and the consequences of the rowdiness and violence; the distortion resulted both from such exaggeration and from the use of sensational and melodramatic language.

- *Prediction* – media coverage regularly assumed, and predicted, that the events they were covering would soon be followed by other, similar events with the possibility of an even worse outcome.

- *Symbolisation* – here the cultural signifiers or symbols of the mods and rockers (their clothes, hairstyles, scooters and bikes) all become negatively portrayed, associated with delinquency and disorder, so that their very mention reinforces the tone of the story. Cohen identifies three main processes here:

  - the mod becomes symbolic of a certain status (deviant or delinquent);

Exaggeration and distortion

The regular use of phrases such as 'riot', 'orgy of destruction', 'battle', 'attack', 'siege', 'beat-up town' and 'screaming mob' left 'an image of a besieged town from which innocent holidaymakers were fleeing to escape a marauding mob'.

During Whitsun 1964 even the local papers in Brighton referred to 'deserted beaches' and 'elderly holidaymakers' trying to escape the 'screaming teenagers'. One had to scan the rest of the paper or be present on the spot to know that on the day referred to … the beaches were deserted because the weather was particularly bad. The 'holidaymakers' that *were* present were there to watch the mods and rockers. Although at other times … there was intimidation, there was very little of this in the Brighton incident … In the 1965 and 1966 incidents, there was even less intimidation, yet the incidents were ritualistically reported in the same way, using the same metaphors, headlines and vocabulary.

The full flavour of such reports is captured in the following lines from the *Daily Express* (19 May 1964): 'There was Dad asleep in a deckchair and Mum making sandcastles with the children, when the 1964 boys took over the beaches at Margate and Brighton yesterday and smeared the traditional postcard scene with blood and violence.'

Source: Cohen (1980: 31–2).

– objects such as hairstyle and clothing come to symbolise the word (mod); and
– the objects themselves become symbolic of the status.

The consequence is that the term mod (and rocker) comes to take on a wholly negative meaning.

Such reporting brings forth a societal reaction, particularly where the behaviour at the heart of the story is perceived in some way to challenge the social order or important social values. As Cohen (1980: 61) puts it, 'Moral panics depend on the generation of diffuse normative concerns, while the successful creation of folk devils rests on their stereo-typical portrayal as atypical actors against a backdrop that is overtypical'. One of the potential consequences under such circumstances is what criminologists, following Leslie Wilkins, have come to refer to as a 'deviancy amplification spiral' (see Chapter 10). In essence, this is a snowballing effect in which a negative social reaction to certain forms of behaviour reinforces, rather than undermines, the 'deviant' activities concerned.

The model of 'deviancy amplification' in Stan Cohen's *Folk Devils and Moral Panics* is graphically illustrated in the following manner (1980: 199):

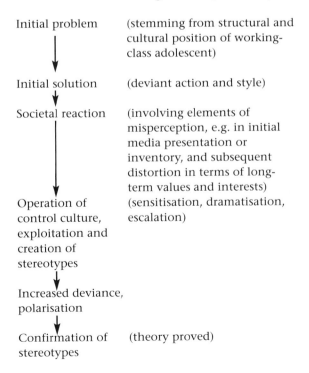

Initial problem — (stemming from structural and cultural position of working-class adolescent)

↓

Initial solution — (deviant action and style)

↓

Societal reaction — (involving elements of misperception, e.g. in initial media presentation or inventory, and subsequent distortion in terms of long-term values and interests)

↓

Operation of control culture, exploitation and creation of stereotypes — (sensitisation, dramatisation, escalation)

↓

Increased deviance, polarisation

↓

Confirmation of stereotypes — (theory proved)

Drug use and deviancy amplification

A further example of this process of deviancy amplification is provided by Jock Young (1973) who examined the social reaction to drug use, particularly cannabis, in Notting Hill, West London in the late-1960s. Young's account begins by examining the relatively socially isolated position occupied by police officers in contemporary society – a form of isolation that means that they are 'particularly exposed to the stereotypical accounts of deviants prevalent in the mass media' (1973: 351). Moreover, there is a close, occasionally symbiotic, relationship between police and media (see below) in which each relies on the other for information or for managing information in particular ways.

In the mid- to late-1960s a moral panic arose around drug use at the heart of which was what Young (1973: 353) describes as a 'fantasy stereotype' of the drug-taker. This he compares with the 'social world of the marijuana smoker' in West London in 1967 (see Figure 4.2).

What then were the effects of the moral panic on drug use in this part of London? According to Young (1973), the intensive action taken by the police served to increase both the organisation and cohesion of the drug-taking 'community'. Members were united by a sense of injustice at the picture painted in the press and at the harsh sentences imposed on those prosecuted. Second, the increase in police action necessitated action by drug-users to protect themselves, primarily by segregating themselves from non-drug users. The deviant norms associated with the bohemian subculture – regular drug use, long hair, unusual dress, lack of a work ethic, and so on – all make re-entry into the mainstream increasingly difficult.

As drug taking becomes increasingly secretive – because of police pressure – so it takes on greater value to the group as a symbol of their solidarity and their resistance to social pressures. Both drug-taking and trafficking become central activities. The price of marijuana rises, and the gains to be made from selling also rise. The importation of the drugs becomes formalised and the street dealer, under pressure, becomes more of a 'pusher' and motivated more by economic concerns. Organised crime becomes more interested in drug markets and the money that can be made.

The user becomes more suspicious – who can he trust? With further police activity the marijuana user and heroin user begin to feel some joint sense

Figure 4.2	Comparing the fantasy stereotype and real social world of the marijuana smoker
Fantasy stereotype	**Real social world**
The isolated drug taker living in conditions of social disorganisation	Bohemian, highly organised with strong friendship networks
Asocial individuals who lack values and are prey to pushers who play on their naïveté	Core values are hedonism, spontaneity, expressivity, disdain for work
Assumed to be the primary concern of such groups	Drug taking tends to be irregular and drugs are an important, but not central, part of bohemian groups
'Pusher' and 'victim' are assumed to be core roles, with the former having close connections with the 'criminal underworld'	'Buyer' and 'seller' are not fixed roles; dealers tend to sell in order to maintain themselves
User seen as essentially immature, psychologically unstable who has been corrupted	Culture consists largely of psychologically stable individuals
Heroin user and marijuana user often indistinguishable	Marijuana user has considerable disdain for the heroin user
Stereotype based on small numbers that come to police attention, but assumption is that numbers are too large and growing	Marijuana users are widely prevalent; a high proportion of young people will have smoked at some point
Exaggerated effects of use include uninhibited pleasure on the one hand and unmitigated misery thereafter	Impact of use include mild euphoria – psychotic effects are rare and temporary

Source: derived from Young (1973).

of injustice and identity. Heroin supply becomes more problematic also and a larger black market begins to grow. The tendency is for the black markets in heroin, methadone, marijuana and other drugs to overlap. A few marijuana users may move on to other drugs. The mass media fan further public indignation and greater police action is demanded. Drug squads are established 'which by their very bureaucratic creation will ensure a regular contribution to the offence figures which had never been evidenced before' (1973: 358–9).

As will be clear, there is more than an element of self-fulfilling prophecy in such spirals. The consequences of mass-media-provoked moral panics and police crackdowns can be the production of the very things that are feared. Moreover, they will be viewed as confirmation that the approach is the correct one: the very fact that there appears to be more drug use – certainly as measured by the number of arrests made by the police – and that some users have moved on to heroin or other drugs, will be interpreted as evidence that the crackdown should have occurred earlier.

Mugging

Thompson (1998) argues that Stuart Hall and colleagues' work on the mugging panic of the early 1970s, *Policing the Crisis,* is most effective in its analysis of the media narratives around street crime and in its careful dissection of the 'signification spiral' at the heart of the panic. In their account, 'news' is understood as the 'end-product of a complex process' of social sorting and construction – along the lines we saw earlier. Thus, 'extraordinariness' is the cardinal news value they suggest. Crucial to understanding the social construction of news is the process by which it is presented to its *assumed* audience. Hall *et al.* (1978: 54) argue:

If the world is not to be represented as a jumble of random and chaotic events, then they must be identified (i.e. named, defined, related to other events known to the audience), and assigned to a social context (i.e. placed within a frame of meanings familiar to the audience). This process – identification and contextualisation – is one of the most important through which events are 'made to mean' by the media. An event only 'makes sense' if it can be located within a range of known social and cultural identifications.

This complex process generally involves the portrayal of the existence of a form of social consensus against which events can be *signified* or given meaning. A vital background assumption in this process concerns the *consensual* nature of society – an assumption that there is a single, overriding perspective and, moreover, that we, the readers or viewers, all share the same interests. Hall *et al.* then examine the ways in which the process of news production serves largely to reproduce elite or class interests. We will look at the broader argument Hall *et al.* advance in relation to the 'politics of mugging' elsewhere in the book (see Chapter 31); here we will focus briefly on what they have to say about the role of the media.

The reproduction and reinforcement of elite interests is not the product of some simple conspiracy – the media are owned and controlled by certain interests and therefore their content reflects those interests – but rather requires us to distinguish between what they term *primary* and *secondary definers* of social events. People in powerful and privileged social positions are those to whom journalists will tend to turn for opinion, and it is these 'spokespeople' who become *primary definers* of social phenomena. It is their interpretation of events that sets the terms of reference for subsequent debates and discussions:

> The media, then, do not simply 'create' the news; nor do they simply transmit the ideology of the 'ruling class' in a conspiratorial fashion. Indeed, we have suggested that, in a critical sense, the media are frequently not the 'primary definers' of news events at all; but their structured relationship to power has the effect of making them play a crucial but secondary role in *reproducing* the definitions of those who have privileged access, as of right, to the media as 'accredited sources'. From this point of view, in the moment of news production, the media stand in a position of structured subordination to the primary definers. (Hall *et al.*, 1978: 59)

A core role for the media, therefore, lies in translating the viewpoints of primary definers into a language and style ready for consumption by various publics. Hall *et al.* (1978) use the example of a statement given by a senior police officer in which he claimed that 'the increase in violent crimes in England and Wales had aroused justifiable public concern'. This was translated by the *Daily Mirror*

into 'a more dramatic, more connotative and more popular form – a news headline which runs, simply, "AGGRO BRITAIN: 'Mindless Violence' of the Bully Boys Worries Top Policeman"' (1978: 61).

'Mugging' as a focus of concern emerges in 1972 and reaches a peak later that year. It breaks as a story, they suggest, because of the application of a new label. It is the label that gives the event its *extraordinary* quality and makes it newsworthy. The label is provided by the police as primary definers. Later on the story is then sustained – once the initial novelty is lost – by two other factors: the bizarre and violence. The former characteristic concerns stories that feature unusual or odd instances, and the latter the generally increased attention given to cases involving violence.

Hall *et al.* then devote considerable space to analysing the media response to a particularly violent attack that took place in Birmingham which occurred in late 1972 and ended with lengthy jail sentences for the three young offenders involved. Here they illustrate how the 'mugging' issue shifted from simply being a news story to being a principal features theme in the press. The features took the victim, offenders and the area where the assault took place – Handsworth – as the main themes. The question being raised – and it was this that enabled the story to become a features issue – was to what extent it was the poor social conditions in the area that were to blame ('Where violence breeds', 'Caught for life in a violent trap' were just two of the headlines). From this emerged a 'public image' – a cluster of images, impressions and ideas – which limits the potential for the emergence of any new explanations. In this case the 'over-arching "public image" which dominated the national papers' feature treatment of the Handsworth case was that of the *ghetto* or *slum'* (1978: 118). The backdrop to the creation of a new 'folk devil' – the black mugger – is established.

Criticisms of moral panic theory

In particular, a number of commentators have been critical of what they take to be the essentially ideological nature of the way in which moral panics are often conceived and presented. That is to say, the main criticism is of the assumption that the concerns identified at the heart of something described as a *moral panic* are, of necessity, seen to be exaggerated and irrational. Waddington, for example, in his response to Stuart Hall and colleagues' work on the moral panic about 'mugging' in the early 1970s, argued that, contrary to their dismissal of the problem as exaggerated, there had, in fact, been a significant increase in street crime in that period. He went on to argue that the term 'moral panic' was best seen as 'a polemical rather than an analytic concept' (1978: 247).

Jewkes (2004) identifies six other substantive problems (see also Goode and Ben-Yehuda, 1994). She suggests:

1 That it is not entirely clear what is the nature of the 'deviance' that is the focus of moral panics (i.e. very different forms of deviant activity may seemingly be the focus of moral panic, thus hiding important differences between them).

2 In parallel, it is not entirely clear whether there is always a moral element in moral panics.

3 There is something of a tendency to 'over-read' the degree of cultural resistance characteristic of youth subcultures in the moral panic literature.

4 An occasional over-reading of the extent of 'panickyness' in media representations.

5 A tendency to exaggerate the cohesion of the 'response' to the perceived threat or problem; media and public reactions are often diffuse; theory also contains the assumption that the focus of the panic is unworthy of such attention.

6 Much moral panic theory makes unrealistic assumptions about the receptiveness of audiences to moral messages.

Some of the more important criticisms of moral panic theory are dealt with by Stan Cohen himself in the introduction to the third edition of the book (Cohen, 2002). First, in relation to the problem of assessing 'disproportionality', Cohen argues that there are cases where it would be possible to assess, empirically, whether a reaction was proportionate or not. And yet, he concedes, 'The problem is that the nature of the condition – "what actually happened" – is not just a matter of just how many mods wrecked how many deck-chairs with what cost … Questions of symbolism, emotion and representation cannot be translated into comparable sets of statistics.'

A second line of critical commentary has noted the increasing rapidity of moral panics – they appear to be arriving, Thompson (1998) suggests, at an ever greater pace – and, where previously they were rather specific (teenagers, young black muggers), they now appear to be all-pervasive (the demise of the family, the loss of community, the breakdown of authority). In this vein, McRobbie

and Thornton (1995: 560) have argued that, far from occurring 'from time to time', moral panics have become:

> … a standard response, a familiar, sometimes weary, even ridiculous rhetoric rather than an exceptional emergency intervention. Used by politicians to orchestrate consent, by business to promote sales in certain niche markets, and by media to make home and social affairs newsworthy, moral panics are constructed on a daily basis.

Cohen (2002) argues that whilst it is undoubtedly the case that the complex, media-interpreted social worlds we now occupy mean that there has emerged a number of long-term anxieties, a *panic* by definition must have temporal boundaries. It is important to hang on to this notion, he suggests, for social reactions – be they over-reaction or under-reaction – are important matters:

> Studying [moral panics] is easy and a lot of fun. It also allows us to identify and conceptualize the lines of power in any society, the way we are manipulated into taking some things too seriously and other things not seriously enough. (Cohen, 2002: *xxxv*)

Review questions

1 What is meant by 'folk devil' and 'moral panic'?

2 Describe how 'deviancy amplification' works.

3 What are some of the main criticisms levelled at moral panic theory?

4 Think of recent examples of 'moral panic'. How well do they fit the theory?

Policing and the media

If crime generally accounts for a substantial proportion of media 'space' then, within this broad subject, the police occupy an important role – both as a source of information and as a subject in their own right. In this section we will look at two themes:

- the nature of the relationship between police and the media – how the two sets of institutions interact; and

- the changing ways in which the police have been represented in the media.

The relationship between the police and the media

Robert Reiner (2003: 259) quotes Sir Robert Mark, Commissioner of the Metropolitan Police in the 1970s, as having referred to the relationship between policing and the mass media as 'an enduring, if not ecstatically happy, marriage'. As he goes on to say, it is in some ways an apposite description for clear tensions in the relationship are revealed from time to time, and yet there remains a mutual dependence between the two. The police are in a powerful position in relation to information. Crime reporters (and others) are in many ways dependent upon the police for information, for leads, and for advanced warning of impending police activity. This enables senior officers often to become 'primary definers' in relation to the presentation of particular stories.

It was not until the early twentieth century, however, that police forces began to develop specialist departments formally to manage their relations with the world outside. The Scotland Yard Press Bureau was established in 1919, though for some years the police more generally remained a largely uncooperative news source and continued to be suspicious of journalists (Chibnall, 1977). Seemingly, this situation began to change somewhat in the 1930s and 1940s, with the expansion of the role of the Press Bureau to include the role of a 'public information officer' (Mawby, 2002). If the immediate post-war years were the high point of police legitimacy (see below, and Chapter 25), then they also marked the point at which police-public relations began to become more problematic, part of which involved the appearance of increasing numbers of hostile stories about the police in the press.

A broad range of changes was occurring around this time. British society was changing – becoming, among other things, less deferential towards authority in many of its guises. The media themselves were changing and, notably, expanding in range and reach. The police, too, were undergoing profound changes, not least as a result of new forms of communication and the shift toward the use of the motor car rather than relying on foot patrol. The period beginning in the 1970s Mawby (2002) characterises as the 'embedding of police public relations', influenced in particular by the appointment of Sir Robert Mark as Commissioner of the Metropolitan Police. After a series of

Media crews await developments outside the home of a suspect at the time of the Ipswich murders in 2006. The relationship between the police and the media has become increasingly professional and interdependent.

corruption scandals, Mark was charged with cleaning up the Yard. Among many innovations, Mark was the prime mover behind a new press policy. Issued in May 1973 the Memorandum opened:

> There is no doubt that the operational effectiveness of the force is to a very large extent dependent upon the goodwill, co-operation and support of members of the general public. There are two main ways in which public backing can be obtained or strengthened. The first is obviously by the adoption of a courteous and helpful attitude at all possible times by every member of the force. The second, *equally important,* is by means of publicity given to the activities of the force in the press and on television and radio. (Mark, 1977: 123, *emphasis added*)

The memorandum went on to note that relations with the press were not as positive as they might be and that in future new facilities would be made available to journalists, and that all officers should be permitted, within acceptable guidelines, to speak with journalists and to provide factual information about cases. Mark's legacy, according to Mawby (2002: 24), was 'to have laid down a template for police–media relations which ... "opens" the police service in that it advocates the free flow of information about the force through the media to the public' – or, at least, to establish this as the image of what the police were doing irrespective of the reality (Chibnall, 1977).

The period since has seen the growing professionalisation of police public-relations. This has involved a complex set of changes including:

- the growing visibility of police representative bodies, including the Police Federation and, especially, the Association of Chief Police Officers (ACPO);
- the establishment of police 'press offices' in all forces;
- the development of proactive press and promotional strategies.

We have reached a stage within a couple of decades where 'the underlying trend, supported by the pressures of the external environment, is towards a future in which image work is significant to the shape of policing' (Mawby, 2002: 185).

The representation of policing

As Robert Reiner has put it 'policing in Great Britain has always been as much a matter of image

as substance' (1994: 11). Going back to the establishment of the police in the early nineteenth century (see Chapter 2) he reminds us of the careful work done by Robert Peel and others in presenting the force in a way that might reduce some of the public concerns about the threat to their freedom and liberty they felt the new police presented.

For the next century or so the police strove, largely successfully, to increase their legitimacy and public standing. This reached its high point in the decade and a half or so after the end of the Second World War and was most vividly represented by the figure of PC George Dixon of Dock Green. The mass media thus played an absolutely central role in the development of 'police fetishism' – the sense that the police are absolutely crucial to social order. For the first half of the twentieth century the police legitimisation project benefited hugely from the largely positive and deferential attitude struck in the press, the cinema and, latterly, television.

Much debate about policing has concerned the nature of their role and, more particularly, the balance in police work between the maintenance of order on the one hand and crime control on the other. In *The Blue Lamp* and *Dixon of Dock Green* the police are presented straightforwardly as a caring organisation. Indeed, Reiner describes Dixon as a 'superannuated boy scout' (1994: 23). Parts of this image remained in the next major cop show, *Z-Cars* (broadcast initially between 1962 and 1965), in which elements of 1960s television realism were mixed with a somewhat rose-tinted portrayal of the police as a form of social glue. It had an edgy quality, partly as a result of its being shot live, partly its Northern location, and partly through its grittier stories and flawed cops, which set it apart from Dixon. A former senior police officer, Sir John Woodcock, talking on television in the 1990s, reflecting back, said: 'When *Z-Cars* came along we were really dismayed that they'd portrayed a police officer as being brutish and violent, and violent domestically as well as in relation to duties' (quoted in Leishman and Mason, 2003).

The style of *Z-Cars*, and indeed some of the characters, found their way into *Softly, Softly,* the BBC's next major police drama (1965–70).

The major change in the presentation of British policing came with the arrival of an ITV show, *The Sweeney,* a fictional portrayal of detectives in the Metropolitan Police's 'Flying Squad' (the title using rhyming slang: Sweeney Todd/Flying Squad). No longer were the police social workers with powers

The Blue Lamp and Dixon of Dock Green

Of all the fictional representations of the British police officer there is one that stands out. PC George Dixon (later promoted to Sergeant) of the fictional London district of Dock Green has become the most celebrated symbol of the 'British bobby'. PC George Dixon was very much a product of an era when it was regularly and confidently asserted that the British police force was the 'best in the world'.

Dixon first appeared in the 1950 Ealing Studios film, *The Blue Lamp*. Indeed, he only appears in the film for 20 minutes before being shot and killed by the film's villain, Tom Riley, played by Dirk Bogarde. Where previously police officers had almost always been portrayed as 'bumbling simpletons', Dixon and his fellow officers are unashamedly heroic figures in *The Blue Lamp*, and Dixon's death, McLaughlin (2005) argues, represents the final point of the English bobby's transformation into an idealised representation of Englishness.

This might have been the end of this particular story were it not for the fact that in 1955 the BBC resurrected George Dixon and gave him his own series, *Dixon of Dock Green*. By the early 1960s it was one of the most popular programmes on British television and Dixon's parting shot at the end of each episode of 'Evenin' all', together with the theme tune, *An Ordinary Copper,* became the show's trademarks.

The final episode of *Dixon of Dock Green* was broadcast in 1976, with Jack Warner, the actor who played Dixon in both film and television, by then in his late 70s. Despite its obvious datedness, and the fact that it was superseded by ever more realistic portrayals of policing – from *Z-Cars*, through *Softly, Softly, The Sweeney*, to *The Bill*, and others – Dixon has remained an enduring cultural icon, not least for police officers and politicians seeking solace in a bygone era. Debates about community policing, even in the early twenty-first century, are still regularly accompanied by references to Dixon of Dock Green, despite the fact that the numbers that will remember this fictional copper must fast be diminishing.

PC George Dixon played by Jack Warner. The character originally appeared in the film *The Blue Lamp* and subsequently the long-running (1955–1976) television series *Dixon of Dock Green*.

of arrest *à la* Dixon, but hard-nosed, often brutal cops whose only concern was in preventing or detecting crime. This is cop as vigilante.

Since the time of *The Sweeney,* cop shows have proliferated on TV. Police dramas have changed as the social and political environment has changed. That is not to say that the shows are a simple reflection of the times – they clearly are not. However, just as Dixon was partly a reflection of the search for consensus and order in the aftermath of the Second World War, so Detectives Regan and Carter in *The Sweeney* reflect both the changing public conception of policing from the 1960s onward (there had been numerous corruption scandals and the hard-earned police reputation for honesty, integrity and working within the law had come under serious pressure) as well as the changed social circumstances where rapidly rising crime rates were increasingly met by a punitive brand of law and order politics.

Contemporary cop shows run the gamut of representations, from the old-fashioned, rural Dixon-like world of *Heartbeat* through the initially realistic, now more far-fetched soap opera of *The Bill,* to harder-edged dramas such as *Prime Suspect* and *Cracker*. Even the gentler programmes now tend to present police officers as morally more complex creatures than George Dixon was ever allowed to become. Nevertheless, as Reiner (2003: 276) notes:

The police seem to be a 'Teflon service' that has survived a long period of increasing revelations of failure and malpractice to remain a powerful political and cultural force. Although the media have increasingly highlighted scandals and controversy about policing, they have also perpetuated the myth of police fetishism ... Media stories of morally flawed but courageous and determined cops as shields against victimization continue to reproduce police fetishism.

In addition to factual news reporting on the one hand, and fictionalised accounts of policing on the other, the other format in which representations of policing are regularly made available is through various forms of 'reality television' and 'infotainment' programmes which combine real life footage with reconstructions and participants' accounts of events. Programmes such as *Police, Camera, Action!*, *Cops*, *World's Craziest Police Chases* and others in the genre rely upon surveillance footage to follow police officers on chases, busts and the like. Like much reality television, they are relatively cheap to make and appeal to viewers' more voyeuristic characteristics. It is arguable whether they have much impact on public attitudes to policing. In terms of police PR, however, probably the most successful of all programmes in recent times has been *Crimewatch UK*, though it has not been without controversy.

Crime and the internet

As we saw earlier in the chapter, the arrival of 'new' media is usually greeted with concern, if not outright moral panic. Comics, radio, television and video have all been the subject of scare stories focusing on their likely impact on public morals. However, arguably, no new medium has generated as much concern as the internet. This may be testimony to its power and reach or may reflect the extent of the dangers it brings.

Changes are often described as 'revolutionary'. In this case the adjective may be apposite, certainly as regards the speed of the arrival of this new form of communication. Early experiments with a worldwide computer network began in the 1960s and 1970s. Netscape and Microsoft Internet Explorer were not launched until the 1990s and it was in the middle of that decade that full-scale commercialisation of the internet took place. By mid-2007 there were well over one billion internet users (http://www.internetworldstats.com/stats. htm) with

the numbers expected to double before the end of the decade (Castells, 2002). As access and usage has grown, so concerns have developed about the misuse of this form of communication. The term 'cybercrime' has now entered everyday language and is defined by Thomas and Loader (2000: 3) as 'computer-mediated activities which are either illegal or considered illicit by certain parties and which can be conducted through global electronic networks'.

Wall (2001) sub-divides cybercrime into four primary categories:

1 *Cyber-trespass* – crossing boundaries into other people's property and/or causing damage, e.g. hacking, defacement, viruses.

A variety of activities are found under this general heading. 'Hacking' itself comes in many guises, but includes the straightforward offence of gaining unauthorised access to a computer system. There is then a range of activities that may occur once access has been gained, from theft to sabotage. In a recent case a British man, Gary McKinnon, has been extradited to the United States on various charges including hacking into NASA and the US military computer system and of rendering the 'US military district of Washington' inoperable. Though McKinnon denies such charges, the case illustrates one of the great contemporary fears: that there will be groups or individuals with sufficient expertise to threaten national or international security by hacking into computer systems. Such threats include: attacks on systems that control power grids; crippling transport systems such as air or rail; and, stealing information about defence and national security systems (Yar, 2006).

2 *Cyber-deceptions and thefts* – stealing (money, property), e.g. credit card fraud, intellectual property violations (aka 'piracy').

One of the basic features of the internet – the ability to contact very large numbers of people and to disguise or misrepresent one's identity – provides considerable opportunity for fraud. Most internet users will be familiar with various 'scams'. I mention only the two that are most frequently found in my own email inbox:

- Advanced fee frauds – Often known as '419 fraud' after the relevant part of the Nigerian penal code, this is a very old scam, now often associated with Nigeria because of the large number of cases emanating from there. The scam usually begins with the announcement that large sums of money are deposited in an account and help is required in order to release them. The recipient of the email is asked to make their account available so that

the money can be deposited. In return they are promised a very substantial reward. The next stage is then for the email recipient to be asked to advance some money as unexpected

Nick Ross, presenter of the BBC TV programme, *Crimewatch UK*, from 1984 to 2007. In 1999, *Crimewatch* itself became newsworthy as one of its presenters, Jill Dando, was murdered outside her home in West London.

Crimewatch UK

Apparently the inspiration came from a 1970s German TV programme called *Aktenzeichen Ungelöst XY* ('File XY Unsolved'). *Crimewatch* began in 1984, initially for three programmes only. The BBC describe its early days in the following terms: 'Initially the police were distrustful of the media and only a few forces would take part in the first programme. Indeed no arrests resulted at first and it was not until the last episode in the commissioned run of three that *Crimewatch* had its breakthrough, solving a rape in the New Forest.'

Within a year it had become plain that *Crimewatch* could solve cases when other methods had failed, and detectives were queuing to get onto the programme. *Crimewatch* has featured more than 2,900 cases, including most of the major crimes of the last two decades.' (http://www.bbc.co.uk/crimewatch/how_it_began.shtml)

The programme has held to a consistent format – with a small number of 'reconstructions' of particular crimes, interviews with senior investigating officers, and public appeals. Nick Ross presented the programme from its inception to 2007. *Crimewatch* has been criticised for exploiting and exaggerating public fears (Kidd-Hewitt, 1995; Schlesinger and Tumber, 1994), for generating hostility toward particular social groups, and for failing to comply with programme guidelines in relation to the use of reconstructions (Pengelly, 1999).

What is clear is that the programme is hugely dependent upon the police for both information and for co-operation. Clearly this is a mutually beneficial relationship and Jewkes (2004: 163) suggests that police involvement in *Crimewatch* 'has proved to be one of the most effective public relations exercises at [their] disposal'.

difficulties have arisen. This goes on for as long as the recipient remains convinced that it is worthwhile – for some of those that get trapped, the more money they hand over, the greater the pressure they place themselves under to believe they are acting appropriately. According to the Metropolitan Police: 'Victims' individual monetary losses can range from the low thousands into multi-millions. True figures are often impossible to ascertain, because many victims, embarrassed by their naïveté and feeling personally humiliated, do not report the crime to the authorities. Others, having lost so much themselves, become "part of the gang" recruiting more victims from their own country of residence.' (http://www.met. police.uk/fraudalert/419.htm)

As I was writing the paragraph above, the email below arrived in my inbox!

DEAR SIR,
I AM MR, PRINCED CHARLES FROM SUDAN. I JUST I SAW YR YAHOO MAIL AT ABOUT AN HOUR AGO, AS REGARD MY CONSIGNMENT AT THE KOTOKA INT. AIRPORT HERE IN GHANA ACCRA, I HAVE YOUR CONTACT FROM THE NET ON LINE, AND I WANT YOU TO BE MY BENEFICIARY SO AS TO HELP RECIEVE MY CONSIGNMENT
ON ARRIVAL IN YOUR COUNTRY, THIS CONSIGNMENT CONTAINTS ARE ($20.MILLION DOLLARS) AND I ALSO WANT YOU TO CONTACT THE HEAD OF LOGISTICS IN CHARGE OF SHIPMENT, HON. BARR. JJ. KWAME, TEL+ 233-24265-2748, HE SPECIALISE IN ALL KIND OF SHIPMENT AS REGARD DIPLOMATIC TRANSFER OF LUGGAGIES AND CONSINMENT TO ANY WHERE AROUND THE WORLD, EVERY NESSESARY PAYMENT HAS BEING MADE AS REGARD THIS SHIPMENT, AND ALL THE NESSESARY DOCUMENTS AS REGARD'S MY CONSIGNMENT HAVE BEING DEPOSITED ALSO WITH THE LOGISTICS DEPARTMENT, I WILL APPRECIATE IF YOU CONTACT HIM FOR INTRODUCTION AS MY BENEFICIARY ABROAD, AND SEND TO HIM YOUR CURRENT DETAILS AND ADDRESS FOR DELIVERY, SO AS TO ENABLE THE ASSIGNED DIPLOMAT TO DELIVER TO YOU SUCCESFULY TO YOUR DOOR STEP, HE WILL SEND TO YOU THE AIR-WAY BILL AND FLIGHT SCHEDULE, AS EARLY AS HE RECIEVED YOUR INFORMATIONS FOR DELIVERY, HERE IS HIS CONTACTS BELOW, HON. BARR. JJ. KWAME,

,
EMAIL;- PRINCEED_CHAR@XXXXX.COM
PLEASE YOU MAY CONTACT ME AS YOU RECIEVE THIS MESSAGE,
REGARDS,
princeed charles

- Phishing – these are large-scale email frauds that use what on the surface appear to be legitimate electronic letters from banks and building societies. The message contains an alert, warning the recipient that security measures are being checked, updated, changed and so on. There is then a form to complete which requires the individual's banking details. Having handed over such details, of course, any bank or building society accounts are at risk. In addition to gaining illegal access to bank accounts, such phishing gangs also trade in personal details, selling them on to others for advertising and other purposes. In one case the Metropolitan Police reported that:

> Recent attempts have the caller pretending they were from the local Primary Care Trust calling about requests for Emergency Services. The caller states that a call has been made for an emergency doctor and they are returning the call to arrange an appointment. The caller then asks a number of questions in an attempt to get the correct name, address, date of birth and telephone number. Mail order accounts have then been set up in their names. (http://www.met.police.uk/ fraudalert/news/phishing2.htm)

3 *Cyber-pornography* – breaching laws on obscenity and indecency.

Here we are dealing largely with long-standing criminal offences but a new means of transmission and sale. There are various estimates of the number of pornographic websites on the internet which range from about two per cent up to 12 per cent of all websites. Whatever the reality there is no doubting the size of the business involved. As with debates over pornography generally, one of the central issues in relation to cyber-porn concerns what types of image are considered 'obscene' and worthy of policing. The definition contained in the Obscene Publications Acts 1959 and 1964 (and amended by the Criminal Justice and Public Order Act 1994) is not explicit about what is 'obscene' (matters likely to deprave and corrupt) and makes intervention in this area far from straightforward. Cyber-porn is inherently more difficult to police – and prosecute – than other forms of publication, because the very nature of 'publication' is less easy to define.

Undoubtedly the major concern in this area, and one where there is something closer to agreement about the unacceptability of the material, is that of child pornography. According to Jewkes (2003c) it was concern about pornography involving minors on the one hand and children gaining access to pornographic websites on the other that was the primary driver behind the establishment of the National Hi-Tech Crime Unit, the Internet Watch Foundation and the European Commission's hotlines for the reporting of illegal content on the Net.

The highest profile police operation in this area in the UK has been 'Operation Ore', launched in 2002, after details were passed by the FBI to the National Criminal Intelligence Service of over 7,000 British people who had accessed a Texas-based subscription child pornography site. Over 200 arrests were made, though only a small number of cases ever came to court, and it was alleged that many of the credit card details that had been used to access the site had been fraudulently obtained in the first place.

4 *Cyber-violence* – doing psychological harm to, or inciting physical harm against, others, thereby breaching laws relating to the protection of the person, e.g. hate speech, stalking.

Johnson (2003) defines 'cyberstalking' as 'unwanted, threatening or offensive email or other personal communication over the computer that persists in spite of requests by the victim that it be stopped'. It may also be indirect – aimed at a particular person, but not sent directly to them. She argues that it is like 'off-line stalking' in that it often involves a desire to exert control over the victim. Most perpetrators are men and the majority of victims are women (see Chapter 20). According to Yar (2006: 129) cyberstalking appears to differ from more general stalking in that it is 'more likely to remain mediated and at a distance. In other words, it is less likely to entail direct, face-to-face harassment in which perpetrator and victim are physically co-present.' Cyberstalking tends to remain online – though this does not necessarily diminish its impact.

Policing cybercrime

The recently-formed Serious and Organised Crime Agency (SOCA) is now the home to what was originally established as the National Hi-Tech Crime Unit (referred to above) in 2001. With a sizeable budget, considerable publicity, and some apparently notably successes, it has actually been far

from plain sailing for the policing of cybercrime. Indeed, Jewkes (2003b: 502) suggests that the 'sheer size and scope of the internet, the volume of electronic traffic it facilitates, the varying legal responses to cybercrime in different countries and other inter-jurisdictional difficulties combine to ensure that the police feel they remain in a perpetual game of "catch-up" with the vast number of criminally-minded individuals who lurk in the shadowy corners of cyberspace.'

In practice, much responsibility for policing the Internet lies with users and with Internet Service Providers (ISPs) – just as the bulk of 'policing' of other parts of our social world is undertaken by individuals, families, community groups and others. Cyberspace is monitored by ISPs and, indeed, they can be held criminally responsible for the posting of various forms of illegal content. In addition, there are a number of other independent bodies and pressure groups that 'patrol' the web and campaign for greater regulation, including the Internet Watch Foundation, Cyberangels, and Working to Halt Online Abuse (WHO@).

In relation to more formal policing there are a number of substantial challenges facing local, national and trans-national forces (Jewkes 2003b):

- *Volume* – the scale of the material on the internet makes it extremely difficult to police.

- *Jurisdiction* – as with terrestrial crimes which cross international boundaries there can be many problems in applying domestic criminal laws.

- *Under-reporting* – the fact that victims may be unaware that they have been victimised or unwilling to report internet-based crimes restricts what the police can do.

- *Police culture* – the relatively high-tech, desk-bound nature of much cyber-policing puts it somewhat at odds with what are often viewed as the more exciting and high profile elements of police work (see Chapter 25).

- *Limited resources* – arguably until such crime becomes a core policing priority it is unlikely to command significant resources.

Representing terror

We finish by briefly considering current representations of the so-called 'War on Terror' and international terrorism, as this is perhaps the best method of illustrating some of the ways in which the globalised and complex role of the media now operates. A number of aspects of this conflict provide vivid examples of some of the newer characteristics of the mediatised world we now inhabit – from the live broadcasting of the planes crashing into the World Trade Center towers, through the use of the internet by Jihadists to publish films of the execution of hostages, to the digital photographs of the abuse of prisoners in Abu Ghraib jail. Each of these shows how central the media have become to the promulgation of such conflict – and a world away from the moment in 1985 when the British Prime Minister, Margaret Thatcher, announced that 'democracies must find a way to starve the terrorists and hijackers of the oxygen of publicity on which they depend'. Within a couple of years a broadcasting ban had been introduced which meant that representatives of particular organisations, such as Sinn Fein, had their words spoken by an actor rather than being able to appear themselves.

Cottle (2006: 153) describes the broadcasting of the images of the jets flying into the World Trade

The Guardian's reaction to 9/11 the day after – in no doubt at all about the significance of the event or the role the media were likely to play in the 'War on Terror'.

Center towers as 'a calculated act of political communication enacted on a global stage'. What they communicated, he argues, was that mainland United States was not immune from attack, and that aspects of American foreign policy in the Arab World would be violently opposed. The subsequent war in Iraq has also been fought in part *through* the media, from the initial 'Shock and Awe' bombing campaign in Iraq which lit up the night sky and provided dramatic television and newspaper pictures, to the symbolic toppling of the statues of Saddam Hussein and the images of his eventual capture and execution.

Wars have always involved the use of propaganda. There has been something of a social revolution in warfare, however, and the emergence of the 'new wars' (Kaldor, 1999) has seen the role of the media transformed. The 'embedding' of journalists so that they worked alongside troops, potentially providing 'rolling news' coverage as the war unfolded in Iraq was a substantial departure from most previous conflicts, and raised questions about media independence. On the other hand, so concerned was the US government about the broadcasts of the Arabic satellite television network, al-Jazeera, that it is alleged that plans to bomb its headquarters were discussed at a meeting between President Bush and Tony Blair in 2004 ('Blair faces questions over alleged US plan to attack al-Jazeera', *Guardian*, 12 May, 2007).

It was not just the US government and others involved in the coalition that have exploited the propaganda potential of the new 'mediatised' wars. Dramatically, 'insurgent' groups began taking hostages, filming them begging for their lives and then being executed – the films later being posted on the internet. The imagery of death is generally kept from television screens, even in times of war. It is widely accepted, for example, that photographs and television pictures of returning coffins, draped in the flag, bringing American servicemen back from Vietnam, were a major factor in declining trust in President Lyndon Johnson and in declining public support for the war.

On the eve of the Iraq War a directive was issued that there would be no media coverage of the return of military personnel who had been killed. Under such circumstances, the broadcasting of beheadings of captives by insurgent groups has enormous potential, and one that was quickly understood and exploited. Crucially, perhaps, what the use of information technology in this way illustrates is that in the modern era, the changes that have taken place in access to the media 'have reduced the ability of national governments to define events for their citizens' (Brown, 2003: 56). Part of the conflict now is therefore over occupying the role of 'primary definer' of events. As Cottle (2006: 166) concludes:

> In a world of globally communicating images, the costs of not winning the image war can be high and the efforts at control are not always successful. The historical transformation of visibility has recently taken a new turn, at once both democratizing and tyrannical. Democratizing in so far as the availability of new digital technologies, ease of visual recording and access to communication systems now enfranchises everyone from foot soldiers to torturers who potentially bear witness to acts of inhumanity (including their own) anywhere in the world; and tyrannical in so far as these same means and

developments have produced a new 'amoral economy' where the production and circulation of symbolic violence and violent symbolism increasingly becomes staged in the battle for symbolic ascendancy and political impact.

Review questions

1 In what way might 'an enduring, if not ecstatically happy, marriage' be a good description of the relationship between the police and the media?

2 What are some of the difficulties involved in policing the internet?

3 In what ways might the 'War on Terror' illustrate the changing relationship between war and the media?

Questions for further discussion

1 In what ways might the media be criminogenic?

2 What are the main problems characteristic of 'media effects' research?

3 In what ways might the idea of 'newsworthiness' distort what is presented in the media on the subject of crime?

4 On what basis can we judge something to be a 'moral panic'?

5 How have representations of the police changed over the past half century?

6 Applying what you have learned, in what ways might the representations of imprisonment have changed over the past half-century?

Further reading

Good introductions to, and overviews of, the literature in this area are contained in:

Jewkes, Y. (2004) *Media and Crime,* London: Sage

Reiner, R. (2007) Media-made criminality, in Maguire, M. *et al.* (eds) *The Oxford Handbook of Criminology,* 4th edn, Oxford: Oxford University Press

On moral panics, there is no substitute for reading Stanley Cohen's original:

Cohen, S. (2002) *Folk Devils and Moral Panics,* 3rd edn, London: Routledge

and following up with:

Thompson, K. (1998) *Moral Panics,* London: Routledge

On policing and the media, a good starting point is:

Leishman, F. and Mason, P. (2003) *Policing and the Media: Facts, fictions and factions,* Cullompton: Willan

Mawby, R.C. (2002) *Policing Images: Policing, communication and legitimacy,* Cullompton: Willan

Reiner, R. (1994) The dialectics of Dixon: The changing image of the TV cop, in Stephens, M. and Becker, S. (eds) *Police Force, Police Service,* Basingstoke: Macmillan

Reiner, R. (2003) Policing and the media, in Newburn, T. (ed.) *Handbook of Policing,* Cullompton: Willan

On the internet:

Jewkes, Y. (ed.) (2003) *Dot.Cons: Crime, deviance and identity on the internet,* Cullompton: Willan

Jewkes, Y. (ed.) (2007) *Crime Online,* Cullompton: Willan

Yar, M. (2006) *Cybercrime and Society,* London: Sage

Websites

Two sites from the Centre for Crime and Justice Studies provide regular updates on the media and crime:

http://www.crimeinfo.org.uk/
http://www.kcl.ac.uk/depsta/rel/ccjs/

A number of newspapers and broadcasters also have sites that are hugely informative:

http://www.guardian.co.uk/
http://bbc.co.uk

Part 2

Understanding Crime: theories and concepts

5 Classicism and positivism

6 Biological positivism

7 Psychological positivism

8 Durkheim, anomie and strain

9 The Chicago School, culture and subcultures

10 Labelling and subcultural theory

11 Control theories

12 Radical and critical criminology

13 Realist criminology

14 Contemporary classicism

15 Feminist criminology

16 Late modernity, governmentality and risk

Chapter outline

Introduction   114

Classical criminology   114
   Beccaria   116
   Jeremy Bentham   117
   The impact of classicism   118

Positivism and criminology   120
   Defining positivism   121
   Cesare Lombroso   122
   Ferri and Garofalo   125
   Charles Goring   126
   Somatyping   127
   The impact of positivism   128

Questions for further discussion   129
Further reading   129
Websites   129

5

Classicism and positivism

| CHAPTER SUMMARY | In this chapter we look at the origins of contemporary criminology. Two contrasting philosophical approaches are identified and compared: |

- the first, classicism, rests on the assumption of free will and rational choice and reflecting this, and also reacting against the unpredictability of punishment in the sixteenth and seventeenth centuries, proposed greater certainty and the proportionate infliction of pain on the offender;

- the second, positivism, was founded on the belief that there were other factors – either intrinsic to the individual or to be found in the immediate environment – which could be identified and which would help distinguish the criminal from the non-criminal.

In outlining these two contrasting approaches we consider the works of the main thinkers associated with each, in particular:

- Beccaria;

- Bentham;

- Lombroso;

- Ferri.

Introduction

David Garland (2002) argues that the new 'science of criminology' emerged about 130 years ago and only became an independent discipline 60–70 years ago. Most accounts of the birth of criminology begin with what is now generally referred to as the classical school or classical criminology. In this vein, Garland argues that the emergence of criminology was the product of the convergence of two 'projects': the 'governmental project' – effectively classical criminology and its concerns with the administration of criminal justice – and the 'Lombrosian project' – concerned with identifying the major differences between offenders and non-offenders.

Classical criminology, as we shall see, proceeded from the assumption of free will and, consequently, assumed that criminal activity was the result of the rational choice and of the hedonistic impulses of the individual. By contrast, what might be thought of as the early *positivist* school of criminology focused much more strongly on factors and features within the individual to explain criminal behaviour.

Before moving on, however, we need to set the emergence of classical criminological thought in its historical context. This context is what might be referred to as the 'pre-enlightenment period' and it is often France which is used as a particularly extreme example of the modes of thought and ways of behaving associated with this period. The pre-enlightenment world (by which is generally meant, Europe) was one in which individual rights were not generally recognised, where punishment was frequently arbitrary and where torture was routinely used as the means of securing confessions (see Chapter 2). Crime was generally believed to be the product of evil. Much of what we will discuss in this chapter was in part a reaction to such arbitrary and cruel systems of punishment and 'justice'. Modern conceptions of justice and the principles associated with *due process* are one of the outcomes of this process of change.

Classical criminology

According to Garland (1994: 25), 'Modern criminology, like other academic specialisms, consists of a body of accredited and systematically transmitted forms of knowledge, approved procedures and techniques of investigation, and a cluster of questions which make up the subject's recognised agendas.' The age of enlightenment saw the first formal theorising about crime and punishment and sought to identify rational means of delivering justice. More broadly, the predominant model of human conduct around the eighteenth century held that there were few or no limitations on the choices individuals could make. In this vein, at the heart of the classical school of criminological thought is the assumption that the criminal is someone exercising free will and rationality. As we will see, the question of whether individuals are or are not rational decision-makers is a central fault line separating different traditions of criminological theorising. What is frequently referred to as the 'classical' tradition in criminological theory rests on the assumption that humans are rational actors; that they make decisions about courses of action on the basis of some form of cost-benefit analysis. In essence, when making decisions we ask ourselves whether particular courses of action 'make sense' – are they worthwhile?

In general terms, the emergence of classical conceptions of law and criminal justice can be seen as a product of the more general shift from feudal to industrial society. Feudal societies, based on land ownership and the concentration of wealth and power into relatively few hands, rested on a combination of tradition (things are done this way because they've always been done this way) and harsh, repressive systems of justice (just see what can happen if you stray). At the heart of such systems were kings and queens whose authority was believed to derive from God and who were thus able to rule with absolute power – or, more realistically, at least attempt to give the impression that they had such power. Looked at the other way around, most citizens enjoyed few *rights* and many aspects of systems of justice in this period depended on circumstance. Whether or not people were prosecuted, were likely to be found guilty, and how they were punished, was highly variable and far from predictable.

Systems of punishment for much of the seventeenth and eighteenth centuries were bloody and cruel; they rested on ideas of revenge or retribution. The death penalty and banishment by transportation were the major forms of punishment by the state and there were many other punishments which, by today's standards, would be considered to be particularly barbaric, though this should not be overstated (see Chapter 2). Burning of the hands, the use of the ducking-stool – though Sharpe (1990) suggests it was probably used infrequently – and flogging were all fairly standard punishments in the sixteenth to eighteenth centuries. According to Sharpe (1990: 23) 'whipping was normally carried out in public, with the offender either tied to a whipping post or to the end of a cart. The instrument used to inflict

the punishment seems to have been some sort of cat-o'-nine-tails, and the punishment was obviously no light one. The number of strokes to be inflicted was rarely stated, but it was usually made clear that blood should be drawn.' This may possibly have been so in eighteenth-century England, but in convict Australia in the early years of transportation, flogging was undoubtedly brutal:

> Most floggings by [the 1820s] were confined to 25, 50, 75, 100 or, on very rare occasions, 150 lashes. By the standards of earlier days when punishments of 500 lashings were handed out ... such inflictions may sound light. But they were not; and in any case, a magistrate could stack up separate floggings for different aspects of the same deed ... Even 25 lashes (known as a *tester* or a *Botany Bay dozen*) was a draconic torture, able to skin a man's back and leave it a tangled web of criss-crossed knotted scars. (Hughes, 2003: 427–28)

In the eighteenth century, so-called 'classical' thinking emerged largely in response to the arbitrary and cruel forms of punishment that continued to dominate. Campaigns for individual rights saw the power of monarchs progressively circumscribed and great upheavals such as the American and French revolutions led to the creation of new institutions in which political decisions were made. Writers such as Voltaire and Montesquieu both became involved in campaigns for more enlightened approaches. Cesare de Beccaria (see box below) and Jeremy Bentham (see box below), two of the most important enlightenment thinkers in this area, though coming from very different philosophical positions, both sought to limit the barbarity of eighteenth-century systems of justice. In addition to such philosophical arguments, demands for more predictable forms of legal regulation also resulted from the nature of industrial society itself. The process of industrial production and exchange needed legal rules to ensure a sufficient amount of predictability and regularity in the system. Property needed to be protected, systems of production maintained, workers disciplined and urban centres given a degree of order.

For utilitarians such as Bentham, punishment – the infliction of pain – had always to be justified in terms of some greater good. At the heart of much writing in this tradition there is, therefore, the understanding that crime is a normative category – it encapsulates certain social norms and values – indicating that certain forms of behaviour should be subject to *censure*. Some of the crucial normative questions for criminologists, therefore, concern which forms of behaviour should be defined as 'criminal' and what the form and extent of punishment that should be related to them should be.

Beccaria

The core principles of classical jurisprudence as outlined by Beccaria can be briefly summarised as follows (see Valier 2002; Vold *et al.*, 2002):

- The law should restrict the individual as little as possible.

- The law should guarantee the rights of the accused at all stages of the criminal justice process.

- Punishment is only justified to the extent that the offender has infringed the rights of others or injured the public good. As Beccaria (1764/1963: 93) put it, 'It is better to prevent crimes than to punish them'.

- The seriousness of the crime should be determined by the harm it inflicts on others.

- The severity of the criminal law must be drastically curtailed. Penalties should be proportionate to the crime committed, and no more than what is necessary to deter both the offender and others from committing crimes (see Chapter 2 on the decline of public hanging and the birth of the prison).

- Excessive punishment is inefficient in that it not only fails to deter, but is also likely to increase crime.

- The written law should clearly advertise what acts were forbidden, as well as the different sanctions imposed for committing each crime.

- Punishment must be inflicted swiftly and with certainty, in order to create a close association in people's minds between a crime and its inevitable penalty.

- The infliction of punishment upon an offender must be free of corruption and prejudice.

Much of Beccaria's approach to the prevention of crime is often distilled down to three ideas: that it is fundamentally a product of:

- *certainty* (how likely punishment is to occur);
- *celerity* (how quickly punishment is inflicted);
- *severity* (how much 'pain' is inflicted).

Cesare Bonesana, Marchese di Beccaria.

These factors need to be appropriately manipulated in order to produce the most effective results. Successful *deterrence* in Beccaria's view first of all required punishment to be *certain*. The more likely one is to be punished for one's actions, the less likely one is to engage in deviant behaviour. The law must be clear and must be enforced consistently. Second, the swiftness of the punishment also has a positive impact on the violation of rules. The shorter the period between the misdeed and the punishment, according to Beccaria, the 'stronger and more lasting in the human mind is the association of these two ideas, crime and punishment; they then come insensibly to be considered, one as the cause, the other as the necessary inevitable effect' (*ibid*, 56). Third, the severity of the punishment must be significant enough to deter further misconduct, but no more severe than is necessary to bring about that effect. In this connection Beccaria proposes forms of punishment that are quintessentially modern: long-term prison sentences for example rather than capital or corporal punishment.

At the heart of his philosophy is the rational actor. 'For a punishment to attain its end, the evil which it inflicts has only to exceed the advantage derivable from the crime ... All beyond this is superfluous and for that reason tyrannical' (*ibid*, 43). The aim of punishment is to prevent crime. According to Beccaria:

Cesare Bonesana, Marchese di Beccaria (1738–1794)

A mathematician and economist, Beccaria was born into an artistocratic Italian family. He completed his doctorate at the age of 20. Anyone looking to Beccaria's biography for clues to the development of his particular philosophy may possibly need look no further than the fact that he was refused permission to marry Teresa Blasco by his father. Fathers had enormous, almost unlimited, powers over their children at this stage, and Beccaria was placed under effective house arrest for three months in an effort to dissuade him. It was unsuccessful and eventually Beccaria and Blasco married, though they lived in much reduced circumstances for some time thereafter.

His most famous work, *Essay on Crimes and Punishments*, was published in 1764, and has been described by Marvin Wolfgang as 'the most significant essay on crime and punishment in Western civilisation' (Wolfgang, 1996). In fact the book was first published anonymously – Beccaria fearing he would be viewed as a revolutionary. Though banned in some countries initially, it quickly gained a reputation and was translated into English and French. Voltaire, the French philosopher, wrote a commentary on it, and the two essays have often been published in a single volume. Beccaria argued forcibly against the excessive and inconsistent use of the criminal law, and was especially critical of the use of torture and capital punishment.

The work made Beccaria famous, and became hugely influential, stimulating reform in numerous jurisdictions.

Beccaria had been much influenced by the case of Jean Calas in France in 1762. Calas had been sentenced to death for murdering his son. It was argued in the case that Calas had committed the crime as a result of his son's conversion to Roman Catholicism. Voltaire, however, was able to present evidence that the son had in fact committed suicide and that the case was a result of religious intolerance. Voltaire's subsequent treatise on tolerance was a particular inspiration for Beccaria's work.

A flavour of Beccaria's prose can be found in the following passage:

> Laws are the conditions of that fellowship which unites men, hitherto independent and separate, once they have tired of living in a perpetual state of war and of enjoying a liberty rendered useless by the uncertainty of its preservation. They sacrifice a portion of this liberty so that they may enjoy the rest of it in security and peace … Punishments which go beyond the need of preserving the common store or deposit of public safety are in their nature unjust. The juster the punishments, the more sacred and inviolable the security and the greater the liberty which the sovereign preserves for his subjects. (Beccaria, 1764: 11–13)

The end of punishment, therefore, is no other, than to prevent the criminal from doing further injury to society, and to prevent others from committing the like offence. Such punishments, therefore, and such a mode of inflicting them, ought to be chosen, as will make the strongest and most lasting impression on the minds of others, with the least torment to the body of the criminal. (*ibid*, p.43)

This led to Beccaria's general theorem:

> That a punishment may not be an act of violence, of one, or of many against a private member of society, it should be public, immediate and necessary; the least possible in the case given; proportionate to the crime, and determined by the laws. (quoted in Cullen and Agnew, 2006: 25)

Jeremy Bentham

Classical thinking developed further as a result of the other major figure associated with such work: the British philosopher Jeremy Bentham. Although some of the extremes of punishment associated with parts of continental Europe were not to be found in Britain, nevertheless there remained relatively high rates of capital punishment and a very large number of crimes for which death was the stated penalty.

At the heart of Bentham's writing was the pleasure–pain principle: more particularly, the idea that human behaviour is generally directed at maximising pleasure and avoiding pain. Individuals broke the law, he felt, in order to gain excitement, money, sex or something else that was valued. The trick for criminal justice, therefore, is to try to ensure that any pleasure to be derived by crime is outweighed by the pain that would be inflicted by way of punishment – though only outweighed just enough to ensure compliance.

There were some differences between Beccaria and Bentham. Both rejected the death penalty – though Bentham argued that it could be used in cases of murder – arguing that in almost all cases its negative consequences outweighed any positive ones that might ensue. Bentham was a firm believer in the efficacy of the prison. He also argued, in contrast to Beccaria, that increased penalties for recidivist offenders were to be justified because of the potential offences committed by such criminals. At the heart of Bentham's utilitarian philosophy – the assumption that social action should be guided by the objective of ensuring the greatest happiness for the greatest number – was the idea that offences must, if they are to be considered worthy of punishment, produce 'evil' – in essence, unhappiness or pain. As such, he was drawing a distinction between offences that might reasonably be considered *criminal* and those that were merely offences against morality.

Punishments themselves are viewed by Bentham as essentially negative and they, therefore, must be restricted so as only to produce the desired outcome. They should also operate on a scale so as to be proportionate to the crime, but also to be understandable and predictable to the offender. If two offences of widely differing seriousness were punished by the same penalty – as was often the case in sixteenth- and seventeenth-century England – the reasoning criminal, Bentham argued, has little incentive not to commit the more serious of the two. Bentham was particularly critical of certain types of punishments:

- Where there is no ground for the punishment – either where there has been consent to an act or where any harm is outweighed by the good, such as in justifiable homicide.

- Where the punishment is limited in its effect – where for example the offender is mentally incapacitated or where the behaviour concerned seemed to be involuntary.

- Where the punishment is unprofitable because its 'evil' outweighs that of the offence.

- Where it is unnecessary because the ends it seeks to bring about can be achieved more easily by other means, such as education or instruction. (Geis, 1960)

Bentham is lastingly associated with the idea of the 'panopticon', a circular prison arranged in such a way that the prison officer(s) in the central watch tower could observe prisoners in surrounding cells at all times (see also Chapter 2). Bentham argued that such prisons should be built near the centre of cities so that they would be a visible reminder of the consequences of criminality, and within the prison the regime was to be one characterised by the segregation of inmates, the teaching of trades and regular religious instruction. In this way, idleness was to be discouraged, and every waking moment of the prisoner's day was to be occupied in ways that would encourage reflection and bring about moral reform.

Bentham was never successful in his campaign to have such a prison built in England, although penitentiaries using some of these ideas were built in the United States. One of these, Stateville prison in Illinois, which opened in the 1930s was described by one architect as 'the most awful receptacle of gloom ever devised and put together with good stone and brick and mortar' (quoted in Geis, 1960: 65). Moreover, Geis quotes a former inmate's description of one of the potential drawbacks of the panoptic reach of Stateville:

> I stood in the cell looking out through the bars, which were panelled with glass. In the centre of the house was a tower of tubular steel. On top of it was a round porchlike affair with large oblong openings. Through these openings the guard kept constant watch on the cells surrounding him.
>
> I remembered what Carl had said: 'They figured they were smart building them that way. They figured they could watch every inmate in the house with only one screw in the tower. What they didn't figure is that the cons know all the time where the screw is, too.'

The impact of classicism

Classical thinking has had a significant impact on criminological theory and, arguably, an even greater impact on criminal justice practice. Classical thought had a great impact on jurisprudence (the theory of law) across Europe and America, and ideas such as punishments being appropriate to the nature of the crime became foundational ideas for 'modern' criminal justice systems. The use of capital punishment declined, as did that of torture and corporal punishment, and the second half of the eighteenth and the

Jeremy Bentham (1748–1832)

Born in London, Bentham was studying law at Oxford by the age of 12. His career in the law was brief, however, and he gave it up in order to pursue his life as a writer. He never married, seemingly only having had one romantic attachment in his life, and is described as having been somewhat eccentric. He didn't get on well with others and 'shrank from the world in which he was easily browbeaten to the study in which he could reign supreme' (quoted in Geis, 1960). Money, inherited from his parents, enabled him to devote himself to his writing. His most famous work, T*he Principles of Morals and Legislation,* was published in 1781 and was inspired in part by Beccaria.

Like Beccaria, Bentham viewed humans as rational, calculating actors:

> Nature has placed mankind under the governance of two sovereign masters, pain and pleasure. It is for them alone to point out what we ought to do, as well as determine what we shall do. On the one hand the standard of right and wrong, on the other the chain of causes and effects, are fastened to their throne. They govern us in all we do, in all we say, in all we think: every effort we can make to throw off our subjection, will serve but to demonstrate and confirm it. In words a man may pretend to abjure their empire: but in reality he will remain subject to it all the while. (Bentham, 1789/1973: 66)

Bentham had numerous critics, one of the most trenchant of whom was Karl Marx, who observed of Bentham's philosophy that 'in no time and in no country has the most homespun commonplace ever strutted about in so self satisfied a way' (quoted in Geis, 1960: 51).

Like Beccaria before him, Bentham was generally positive towards imprisonment as a form of punishment. One of Bentham's most famous ideas was that of the panopticon. Though never built, elements of its design found their way into some early British prisons. The design had more impact in the United States, where a number of penitentiaries, including Richmond and Pittsburgh, reflected Bentham's ideas.

After his death Bentham's body was (as requested in his will) preserved and stored in a wooden cabinet, termed his 'Auto-Icon', at University College London (UCL). It has always had a wax head, as Bentham's head was badly damaged in the preservation process. The real head was displayed in the same case for many years, but became the target of repeated student pranks. Bentham's actual mummified head is now kept in the safe at UCL.

Jeremy Bentham, inventor of the panopticon and proponent of the pleasure–pain principle.

nineteenth centuries saw the establishment and growth of the prison as a core element in modern systems of punishment (see Chapter 2).

On criminological thought, classical ideas can be seen in those theoretical approaches which view offenders as rational actors (see Chapter 14). More particularly, much of our system of justice, particularly those aspects to do with due process and the rights of the accused in the criminal justice system, derive from the ideas of thinkers like Bentham and Beccaria. Taylor *et al.* (1973: 7) quote one nineteenth-century assessment of Beccaria's influence as suggesting:

> Whatever improvement our penal laws have undergone in the last hundred years is due primarily to Beccaria, and, to an extent that has not always been recognised. Lord Mansfield [a famous judge] is said never to have mentioned his name without a sign of respect. Romilly

[Solicitor-General and famous law reformer] referred to him in the very first speech he delivered in the House of Commons on the subject of law reform. And there is no English writer of that day who, in treating of the criminal law, does not refer to Beccaria.

In addition, elements of classical thought can be seen in many of the ideas, such as *deterrence,* that continue to infuse our systems of punishment and which underpinned the principles of Sir Robert Peel and his first Commissioners, Rowan and Mayne, in the establishment of the Metropolitan Police (see Chapters 2 and 25).

What are the potential problems with such classical thinking? One set of criticisms of such approaches focuses on problems of fairness and equity. Classical thought, in treating all individuals as rational, is argued to overlook the problems of incapacity of various forms. What of impaired ability to make decisions? Such theories pay scant regard to the problems of, say, mental illness, learning difficulties and other forms of impairment, or simply ignore matters of maturity, implying that children should be treated in the same way as adults. Treating actors as rational, but making allowance for matters such as age and mental state, is often referred to as 'neo-classicism'.

Second, there is the problem of power. If individuals act entirely according to the principles of rationality and free will, why is it that the poorest tend to be those who predominate in the criminal justice system? Is rationality somehow related to wealth and power? Those who argue that social inequalities of various sorts are important in helping us understand the operation of justice systems regard classical thinking as lacking in some fundamental ways. As Jeffrey Reiman (1979) once wryly observed, 'the rich get richer and the poor get prison'.

Thus, although classical thought has been of enormous influence, there are also very substantial limits to the implementation of classical principles in criminal justice. According to White and Haines (2004) classical thinking came under three sets of challenges when put into practice:

- The first is the question as to how to make such ideas serve the interests of justice and equality when faced with a particular defendant in court. By this they are referring to the potential difficulties involved when the differences between defendants become clear: in practice not all defendants in court appear to be acting

rationally and of free will. What about the particular circumstances of crimes? Can they not be taken into account?

- The second challenge is that posed by the growth of criminal justice bureaucracies – professional police, courts and others – with the possibility that growing efficiency may not always be compatible with an emphasis on equal justice.

- The third challenge is to the powerful – for whom the rationalisation of the legal system potentially meant some reduction in their power.

The emergence of classical models of justice has been anything but straightforward as a consequence. As Radzinowicz (1966: 123) observed:

Had our system of dealing with crime been confined within the pattern laid down [in the classical school] ... virtually all the reforms of which we are most proud would have been excluded because they would have conflicted with the principle that punishment must be closely defined in advance and strictly proportionate to the offence. There would have been no discharge, no adjustment of fines to the means of offenders, no suspended sentences, no probation, no parole, no special measures for young offenders or the mentally abnormal.

Review questions

1 What are the main features of classical criminology?

2 What three factors did Beccaria identify as being central to the prevention of crime?

3 What is utilitarianism and how is it applied to punishment?

4 What is the pleasure–pain principle?

5 Of what types of punishment was Bentham particularly critical?

Positivism and criminology

Classicism had been the dominant approach to thinking about crime for about a century. In the late nineteenth century it came under sustained attack as a particular form of 'scientific criminology' emerged alongside many other scientific developments.

Darwin's great works had been published between the 1850s and the 1870s and had a profound impact both on scientific thought and, more generally, on the ways in which human behaviour was viewed. In his books, *On the Origin of the Species* and *The Descent of Man,* Darwin outlined his ideas concerning evolution in which he proposed a theory of human development based on natural selection rather than, say, the influence of a god or gods.

In general terms, scientific thought now placed increased emphasis on ideas asserting that human behaviour was determined by factors such as biology and physiology. In this period, writers such as Auguste Comte laid the foundations for what they hoped would be the scientific study of society: sociology. Similarly, positivist criminology is very much a product of this era – an era in which it was assumed that progress was to be gained as a result of the dispassionate study of cause and effect (including in human conduct). As we saw in Chapter 3, it was during this time that the first criminal statistics started to be collected regularly, and in which scientists like Quetelet began to use such statistics as the basis for research inquiry.

For some of its key proponents, the mission of such positivistic criminology was the creation of a better society through the application of scientific principles. According to one of its foremost advocates, Enrico Ferri:

> The historical mission of the [Classical] School consisted in a reduction of punishment ... We now follow up the practical and scientific mission of the classical school with a still more noble and fruitful mission by adding to the problem of the diminution of penalties the problem of the diminution of crimes. (quoted in Taylor *et al.,* 1973: 10)

Defining positivism

So the mission of positivism was the reduction, or even elimination, of crime. What, however, is meant by positivism? This is a term that causes much confusion within criminology. Bottoms (2000: 25–27) summarises the main assumptions of positivist or the 'scientific approach' to criminology as follows:

i The methods of the natural sciences should be applied, and could be applied, to the social world.

ii The foundation of our knowledge of the world (our *epistemology*) is data derived from

observation. The basis of scientific knowledge is 'facts' collected dispassionately by the scientist.

iii Facts must be distinguished from values.

iv The core method involved the collection of data, the development of hypotheses, and the testing of these for verification or falsification (*hypothetico-deductive reasoning*).

v The combination of natural scientific methods and deductive reasoning led to a 'powerful preference' for quantitative over qualitative data.

Now such assumptions, as we will see, have been severely criticised and, in some cases, completely rejected. Indeed, the whole idea of 'positivism' has become surrounded by a certain controversy and the term is sometimes used in books almost entirely disparagingly. This is not necessarily helpful, and before moving on to consider early positivist criminology in more detail, it is important to be reminded of why it is necessary to think carefully about this, as indeed, all philosophies of approach and method. In this regard Bottoms (2000: 29) provides a sensible reminder:

> In some criminological circles, the term 'positivism' is now never used without strongly pejorative connotations. This is descriptively unhelpful, but more importantly it can serve to deflect attention from the strengths of the so-called 'scientific approach' in criminology. Whatever the defects of positivism (and it has many), it has bequeathed to contemporary criminologists a fine tradition of careful observation of the natural and social worlds, and a tradition also of the scientist's duty to report his/her data dispassionately, even if he/she finds them personally unwelcome. For those of us who argue that there is an external world which is in principle capable of being described (albeit not without difficulties), these are important legacies.

In many respects therefore such 'positive' criminology was very different from many of the classical ideas that had preceded it, not least in the focus it gave to the importance of causes beyond the individual human actor. And although the contrasts between the two approaches are arguably more important that any similarities, it would be an exaggeration to treat them as 'opposites' for both are concerned with the causes of crime and, indeed, many commentators have argued that it is perfectly possible to see important continuities between the classical and positivist approaches (Gottfredson and Hirschi, 1987; Beirne, 1993). The

Figure 5.1	Comparing classicism and positivism	
	Classicism	**Positivism**
Object of study	The offence	The offender
Nature of the offender	Free-willed Rational, calculating Normal	Determined Driven by biological, psychological or other influences Pathological
Response to crime	Punishment Proportionate to offence	Treatment Indeterminate, depending on individual circumstances

Source: Adapted from White and Haines (2004).

major differences between classicism and positivism are summarised in Figure 5.1.

Early biological theories of criminality focused on physical attributes and appearance (you may well see such work referred to as 'biological positivism' – to distinguish it from 'psychological positivism'). In particular, criminality was associated with abnormality or defectiveness, the assumption being that it was those that were somehow biologically inferior who were most likely to become involved in deviant activities. The best known approaches to such activity are probably *physiognomy* and *phrenology*. As early as the sixteenth century the seeds of individual positivism had been sown by an Italian physician, Giambattista della Porta, whose interest was in the study of human physiognomy, or facial features. In such work, della Porta argued that thieves tended to have sharp vision and large lips (for a discussion see Gibson, 2002). Such work was expanded upon in the eighteenth century by a number of scholars who focused more upon the shape of the skull and any distinguishing bumps or other features.

The assumption in phrenology was that the external shape of the skull was indicative of the size, shape and nature of the brain inside. Both approaches assumed that conclusions could be drawn from such study – of faces or skulls – about the behaviour of the individuals concerned. An Austrian physician, Joseph Gall (1758–1828), argued that the size and nature of the brain, as well as the contours of the skull, provided many clues to understanding criminality and, at one stage, even identified what he argued was a 'murder organ' in the brains of murderers and a 'theft organ' in those of convicted thieves. Phrenology remained popular in some circles into the twentieth century, and phrenological analyses of the famous – such as Napoleon Bonaparte – were undertaken and published.

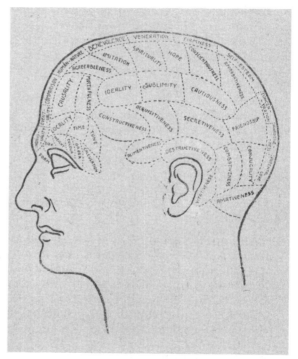

A phrenology head from a late nineteenth-century manual, showing what were believed to be the different aspects of personality within the brain.

Cesare Lombroso

Positivism in criminology is associated with writers like Cesare Lombroso (see box below), someone who has been referred to as 'the father of modern criminology' but whose work is now largely discredited. His most famous works were published in the second half of the nineteenth century: *The Criminal Man* in 1876 (though it wasn't translated into English until the early 1900s) and *The Female Offender* in 1895. Some of his early work resulted from autopsies he had performed on male criminals, though for his subsequent work he relied on examinations of living respondents – in the case of one of his most famous works, *L'uomo Delinquente* [*The Criminal Man*], on an examination and comparison of almost 400 non-criminal Italian soldiers and 90 'lunatics'.

As Marvin Wolfgang (1960: 168) noted, 'In the history of criminology probably no name has been eulogised or attacked so much as that of Cesare Lombroso'. A psychiatrist, Lombroso viewed criminals as throwbacks to a more primitive stage of human development – this atavism being found both in a variety of inferior physiological features associated with lower primates, and with biological regression involving a less civilised form of mentality and behaviour. Such an idea had previously been proposed by Darwin, who argued, 'With mankind some of the worst dispositions which occasionally without any assignable cause make their appearance in families, may perhaps be reversions to a savage state from which we are not removed by many generations' (quoted in Taylor *et al.*, 1973: 41).

For Lombroso the criminal was almost a separate species exhibiting a variety of mental and physical characteristics setting them apart. These included:

... deviation in head size and shape from the type common to the race and religion from which the criminal came; asymmetry of the face; excessive dimensions of the jaw and cheek bones; eye defects and peculiarities; ears of unusual size, or occasionally very small, or standing out from the head as do those of the chimpanzee; nose twisted, upturned, or flattened in thieves, or aquiline or beaklike in murderers, or with a tip rising like a peak from swollen nostrils; lips fleshy, swollen, and protruding; pouches in the cheek like those of some animals; peculiarities of the palate, such as a large central ridge, a series of cavities and protuberances such as are found in some reptiles, and cleft palate; abnormal dentition; chin receding, or excessively long or short and flat, as in apes; abundance, variety and precocity of wrinkles, anomalies of the hair, marked by characteristics of the hair of the opposite sex; defects of the thorax, such as too many or too few ribs, or supernumerary nipples; inversion of sex characteristics in the pelvic organs; excessive length of arms; supernumerary fingers and toes; imbalance of the hemispheres of the brain (asymmetry of cranium). (quoted in Wolfgang, 1960: 186)

As the passage indicates, Lombroso's approach was to assume that being criminal was somehow to be explained through identifying particular characteristics of individuals. Criminals were born, not made. As such there is a link between Lombroso's ideas and earlier work in the field of *phrenology* in which the shape of the head was held to offer a guide to the personal characteristics of the individual. In fact Lombroso went beyond the straightforward idea of atavism to explore the possibility that other pathological conditions might explain criminal and other behaviour, eventually settling on epilepsy as the 'uniting bond' linking the criminal and the moral imbecile.

Where his early work had focused primarily on biological factors, as it developed he also incorporated greater consideration of broader environmental factors. Lombroso identified a series of different types of criminal including the *epileptic criminal,* the *insane criminal* and the *born criminal,* being those with atavistic characteristics. To these he added *occasional criminals* (divided into three sub-types: *pseudo-criminals* who commit crimes involuntarily

Fig. 19. Tipo di razza inferiore - Parricida.

Fig. 22. Tipo criminale comune - Associazione di malfattori.

Fig. 20. Tipo di razza inferiore - Ladro abituale.

Fig. 23. Tipo comune di ladro - Ladro abituale.

Fig. 21. Tipo di razza inferiore - Ladro abituale e feritore.

Fig. 24. Tipo comune di ladro (degenerato) - Borsaiolo.

An illustration from Lombroso's classic study *The Criminal Man* (1876): top left is a murderer; the others he described as 'habitual thieves'.

Cesare Lombroso (1835–1909)

Born in Verona in Italy, of Jewish origin, Lombroso's first qualification was in medicine. He worked as an army doctor and subsequently in asylums for the mentally ill. In 1876 he became a Professor at the University of Turin, practising in psychiatry. Lombroso married in 1867 and had two daughters, both of whom did much work for and with him in later life.

His original insights came in the 1860s when he was employed as army doctor. Taken particularly by the frequency with which the soldiers were tattooed, and also by the nature of the tattoos, Lombroso began a study of the physical characteristics of Italian soldiers. His major works included *The Criminal Man, The Legal Medicine of the Corpse, The Female Offender* and *Crime: Its Causes and Consequences.*

Enrico Ferri (1900:12) reports Lombroso's early breakthrough in his studies as occurring during a postmortem in which:

> … on laying open the skull I found on the occipital part, exactly on the spot where a spine is found in the normal skull, a distinct depression which I named *median occipital fossa*, because of its situation precisely in the middle of the occiput as in inferior animals, especially rodents … At the sight of that skull, I seemed to see all of a sudden, lighted up as a vast plain under a flaming sky, the problem of the nature of the criminal – an atavistic being who reproduces in his person the ferocious instincts of primitive humanity and the inferior animals.

Of Lombroso and his work, Thorsten Sellin observed, 'Any scholar who succeeds in driving hundreds of fellow-students to search for the truth, and whose ideas after

Cesare Lombroso, 'the father of modern criminology'.

half a century possess vitality, merits an honourable place in the history of thought' (1937: 898–99) (see also Rafter, 1992: 525).

In his will, Lombroso left his body to the laboratory of legal medicine and his brain to the Institute of Anatomy at Turin University.

through passion or some other emotion, *criminaloids* for whom opportunity to commit crime plays a greater part than other criminal types, and *habitual criminals* who have few if any serious anomalies but, rather, fall into primitive tendencies because of factors such as poor education and training). The relationship between these groups Lombroso presented as follows:

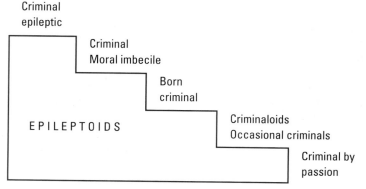

Source: Wolfgang (1960: 190).

Women were held by Lombroso and Ferrero (Lombroso's son-in-law) to be less advanced from their primitive origins than men and, consequently, to be morally more deficient and have greater evil tendencies than men:

> … women are big children; their evil tendencies are more numerous and more varied than men's, but generally remain latent. When they are awakened and excited they produce results proportionately greater.
>
> Moreover, the born female criminal is, so to speak, doubly exceptional, as a woman and as a criminal. For criminals are an exception among civilised people, and women are an exception among criminals, the natural form of retrogression in women being prostitution and not crime. The primitive woman was impure rather than criminal.
>
> As a double exception, the criminal woman is consequently a monster. Her normal sister is kept in the paths of virtue by many causes, such as maternity, piety, weakness, and when these counter influences fail, and a woman commits a crime, we may conclude that her wickedness must have been enormous before it could triumph over so many obstacles.
>
> (quoted in Wolfgang, 1960: 192)

Even during his own lifetime – he died in 1909 – Lombroso's ideas were declining substantially in influence, though he has remained a major figure in criminology textbooks even if, in large part, this was as the most important figure in a school of thought that is generally disparaged and discredited (Rock, 2007). Though Lombrosian notions of criminals as throwbacks to earlier stages of evolution may be easy to ridicule from a contemporary standpoint, it is worth remembering that, as we saw earlier, as respectable a figure as Charles Darwin had argued that certain human dispositions might best be viewed as reversions to some form of savage state.

Such ideas were very much a product of their era – as indeed most ideas are. Though now entirely abandoned, the broader approach project attempted by Lombroso and others – the identification of factors associated with criminality through the application of scientific methods – has had a huge impact on criminology. What was referred to earlier, following Garland, as the 'Lombrosian project' continues to be one important strand of contemporary criminological activity.

Valier argues that numerous works in popular culture were inspired by the work of Lombroso and others in the same tradition. Bram Stoker's *Dracula* for example, with 'massive eyebrows, sharp and protruding teeth, red lips, a cruel mouth, pointed ears, broad and squat fingers, and long sharp nails' (2002: 18) was indicative of the idea of the criminal that was to be found in criminal anthropology and the eugenics movement which emerged in the late nineteenth/early twentieth century, and which sought either to create circumstances in which the reproduction of the fittest would be maximised or, more radically, the reproduction of the least fit would be prevented.

Ferri and Garofalo

Lombroso's work was continued and elaborated by two other Italian scholars, Enrico Ferri (1856–1929) and Raffaele Garofalo (1852–1934). Described by Sellin (1960: 277) as 'one of the most colourful and influential figures in the history of criminology', Ferri was a criminal lawyer, member of parliament, editor of a socialist newspaper, university professor and in his latter years had given up socialism in favour of support for Mussolini's fascist government. In Ferri's work much greater attention is paid to, and influence attributed to, social and environmental factors in the explanation of criminality than can be found in Lombroso's studies.

Indeed, Sellin (1968: 17–18) cites an exchange between the two scholars in which Ferri, hearing

Enrico Ferri (1856–1929). In *The Positive School of Criminology* (1901) and *Criminal Psychology* (1905) Ferri emphasised the importance of social and environmental factors in explaining criminality, as well as developing ideas of crime prevention.

that Lombroso had accused him of not being positivist enough, replied 'What! Does Lombroso suggest that I, a lawyer, should go and measure the heads of criminals in order to be positivist enough!'. In his work with Lombroso, Ferri broadened the search for the causes of crime. Very much in the classical tradition, these were not to be found in the choices made by rational individuals:

> How can you still believe in the existence of free will, when modern psychology, armed with all the instruments of positive modern research denies that there is any free will and demonstrates that every act of a human being is the result of an interaction between the personality and the environment of man? ... The positive school of criminology maintains ... that it is not the criminal who wills: in order to be a criminal it is rather necessary that the individual should find himself permanently or transitorily in such personal, physical, and moral conditions, and live in such an environment, which become for him a chain of cause and effect, externally and internally, that disposes him toward crime. (1917: 54)

The third of the major figures of the Italian school of criminology was Raffaele Garofalo. Like Ferri he was convinced of the importance of scientific methodology to the study of crime. His book, *Criminology,* was published in 1885 when Garofalo was 33 years old, and was described by Allen (1960: 255) as a 'product of certain important intellectual currents which profoundly affected social thought during the last half of the nineteenth century'. These were 'social Darwinism' (a form of social survival of the fittest associated with writers like Herbert Spencer), a belief in the inevitability of social progress and an assumption of the essentially benign nature of political power. In the book he introduced the notion of 'natural crime', which was defined by two essential characteristics: offending the moral sentiment of pity (revulsion against the voluntary infliction of suffering on others) and probity (respect for others' property rights).

The identification of natural crimes was, for Garofalo, the basis upon which the important task of identifying criminals was to be based. Given that crime is essentially the transgression of basic moral sentiments, the criminal in Garofalo's terms was someone who is lacking in concern for others and in this, and possibly other ways, may be considered developmentally deficient – particularly with regard to their 'altruistic sensibilities'. He then identified four classes of criminal: the murderer (in whom altruism is wholly lacking); the violent criminal (characterised by a lack of pity); thieves (characterised by a lack of probity) and, finally, lascivious criminals such as some sexual offenders (characterised by a low level of moral energy and deficient moral perception).

Garofalo, Allen (1960) argues, worked very much in the positivist tradition. He was convinced of the importance of scientific method, and was much more concerned with social interests than individual rights. And, yet, in his writing he also reflected elements of the classical tradition. He paid close attention to the nature of the penalties that should attach to particular types of crime or criminal, thought that these penalties should be ordered in some manner, and was also a qualified supporter of the idea of deterrence. Garofalo's work, among other things therefore, is a good illustration of the simple but important point that positivism was never a complete replacement for classicism. Strains of both traditions can be found running through much criminology.

Charles Goring

Lombroso's work gave rise to strong feelings, and led him to throw down various challenges to his most vociferous critics. Charles Goring, author of *The English Convict,* first published in 1913, distanced himself from some of the cruder ideas of criminal anthropology, but espoused ideas clearly influenced by eugenics. His study, which took 13 years, examined 3,000 English convicts together with a control group of non-convict males, and concluded that there were no significant physical differences between the two groups.

> We have exhaustively compared, with regard to many physical characters, different kinds of criminals, with each other, and criminals, as a class, with the law-abiding public ... Our results nowhere confirm the evidence [of a physical criminal type], nor justify the allegation of criminal anthropologists. They challenge their evidence at almost every point. In fact, both with regard to measurements and the presence of physical anomalies in criminals, our statistics present a startling conformity with similar statistics of the law-abiding class. Our inevitable conclusion must be that there is no such thing as a physical criminal type.
> (Goring, 1913: 173, quoted in Sutherland, 1939)

However, he continued to argue that measured differences in stature and body weight meant that criminals were biologically inferior:

There is no such thing as an anthropological criminal type. But despite this negation, and upon the evidence of our statistics, it appears to be an equally indisputable fact that there is a physical, mental, and moral type of normal person who tends to be convicted of crime … the criminal of English prisons is markedly differentiated by defective physique … by defective mental capacity … and by an increased possession of wilful anti-social proclivities. (Goring, 1913: 370, quoted in Valier, 2002: 19–20)

As the passage makes clear, Goring distanced himself from many of Lombroso's arguments, yet continued to work in ways that were far from entirely dissimilar. As indicated by Lilly *et al.*, (2002: 22) 'the search for a constitutionally determined criminal man did not stop with Goring's conclusions'.

Somatyping

In the 1930s an American anthropologist, Earnest Hooton, though critical of Goring's methods nevertheless concluded his own research by arguing that:

Criminals are organically inferior. Crime is the resultant of the impact of environment upon low-grade human organisms. It follows that the elimination of crime can be effected only by the extirpation of the physically, mentally and morally unfit, or by their complete segregation in a socially aseptic environment. (quoted in Brown *et al.*, 2004: 249)

He went on to argue that human progress would best be assured by the ruthless elimination of inferior types, thus ensuring that evolution was dominated by superior types. This would progressively eliminate human problems. Crime could be eradicated, he argued, and war would eventually be forgotten.

The response to Hooton's work was highly critical. Although his statistical procedures were robust he was criticised for having poor data, not least the size and unrepresentativeness of his control group. Moreover, he was attacked for failing to provide criteria by which to assess the notion of biological inferiority. This, it was suggested, was something he merely assumed.

A number of other studies in Germany and the USA ploughed a similar furrow well into the 1950s. A German psychiatrist, Ernst Kretschmer, distinguished between three major physical types: the asthenic (lean and slightly built); the athletic (medium-to-tall in height, and strong); and, the pyknic (rounded, large neck and broad face). Each type was related to particular psychic disorders such as depression and schizophrenia. Subsequently, a study of 200 men in Boston by William Sheldon (1949) looked at 'body types' or *somatypes* and distinguished a number of basic forms:

- *Endomorph* – Soft and round, short tapering limbs, velvety skin.
- *Mesomorph* – Muscular, large trunk, heavy chest, large wrists and hands.
- *Ectomorph* – Lean, fragile, delicate body, droopy shoulders, little body mass.

Each of these bodily forms was argued by Sheldon to be related to particular personalities or temperaments. The three temperament types were:

- *Viscerotonic* – A comfortable person, likes luxury, extrovert.
- *Somotonic* – Active, dynamic, aggressive.
- *Cerebrotonic* – Introverted, characterised by skin complaints, fatigue, suffering from insomnia.

All individuals possess elements of all three body types, but in differing proportions. Delinquent

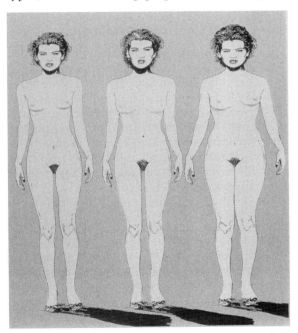

An illustration of somatypes, or body shapes, in women. *Left*: ectomorph (lean and delicate build). *Centre*: mesomorph (compact and muscular build). *Right*: endomorph (soft, round build with high proportion of fat tissue).

males were found to be low in ectomorphy and high in mesomorphy.

A famous study by Sheldon and Eleanor Glueck (1950), in a somewhat similar vein, compared male delinquents and non-delinquents, finding a number of physical differences between the two groups (delinquents, for example, having wider chests, and bigger forearms and upper arms) – in particular that there was a substantially higher proportion of mesomorphs (60%) in the delinquent than non-delinquent group (31%). Like William Sheldon they linked the body types to various personality traits, finding that mesomorphs were generally 'more highly characterised by traits particularly suitable to the commission of acts of aggression (physical strength, energy, insensitivity, the tendency to express tensions and frustrations in action), together with a relative freedom from such inhibitions to anti-social adventures as feelings of inadequacy, marked submissiveness to authority, emotional instability and the like' (1956: 226). For many years their work was dismissed, in part as a result of their apparent connection with an earlier style of increasingly discredited work. However, there was much else besides in the Gluecks' work and, largely as a result subsequently of work by Robert Sampson and John Laub, it has become an important early influence on developmental or life course criminology. In this vein, for example, the Gluecks found the delinquents in their study to be:

> ... less adequate than the non-delinquents in capacity to operate on a fairly efficient level and have less emotional stability ... they are more dynamic and energetic, much more aggressive, adventurous, and positively suggestible, as well as stubborn ... more inclined to impulsive and non-reflective expression of their energy-drives ... Such temperamental equipment is in itself highly suggestive of the causes for their greater inclination to ignore or readily break through the bonds of restriction imposed by custom or law (1950: 251–2).

Criminal career research, and the emerging body of work referred to as developmental criminology (see Chapter 33), is becoming increasingly important as a result of work like the Gluecks'. Indeed, Sampson and Laub (2005: 14) argue that the Gluecks' 'is one of the most influential research projects in the history of criminological research'. The fact that until recently the Gluecks' work was little discussed within criminology is a result, Laub and Sampson (1991) argue, of the rise to dominance of a sociologically-informed perspective within the subject.

More particularly, they suggest that it is the dominant figure of Edwin Sutherland in twentieth-century criminology that is the most significant cause of this oversight. Sutherland became increasingly concerned, they suggest, to establish the primacy of a form of sociological positivism within criminology and, to this end, 'deemed it necessary to attack the Gluecks' work' (1991: 1420). The consequence, Laub and Sampson (1991: 1434) argue, is that 'to this day sociological positivism is dominant and the Gluecks are often seen as relics of a distant past'.

The impact of positivism

Positivism within criminology has been enormously influential and comes in for substantive and sustained criticism. Critics of individual positivism such as David Matza (1964) argue that it draws on three problematic sets of assumptions (Tierney, 1996):

- *Determinism* – The assumption that there are things beyond the individual that impel or constrain people in ways that lead to crime. These factors may be biological, psychological or social. The problem of such views is that they fail to take account of human decision-making, rationality and choice. In policy terms it tends to lead to an emphasis on treatment and to avoid consideration of individual responsibility.

- *Differentiation* – The assumption that offenders can be separated from non-offenders; that they have some characteristic(s) that will help identify them as criminal or non-criminal (much positivist criminology has focused around the search for precisely these characteristics).

- *Pathology* – The assumption that the difference between offenders and non-offenders is the result of something having gone wrong in the lives or circumstances of the former.

In the early decades of the twentieth century much positivist criminology was dominated by a concern with attempting to understand genetically-determined psychological characteristics such as 'feeble-mindedness' and 'moral degeneracy' (Tierney, 1996). As we have seen, work by Charles Goring in the first decade of the century concluded that, in contrast to the views of Lombroso and others, there was no identifiable 'physical criminal type'. Nevertheless, he largely rejected the possibility that social inequality or other environmental factors might have explanatory power so far as criminality was concerned.

Similarly, research on youth by Cyril Burt in the 1920s, which had sought to explore and predict delinquency, was also strongly supportive of the argument that hereditary factors were crucial in explaining how some people rather than others came to be offenders. Though cruder forms of individual positivism have declined in popularity and influence, the search for characteristics which will allow us to separate offenders from non-offenders have continued to dominate criminological thought for much of the twentieth century. In the next three chapters we explore elements of biological, psychological and sociological positivism, three important tributaries that have flowed into and helped to shape contemporary criminology.

Review questions

1 What are the main features of positivistic criminology?

2 What is meant by 'atavism'?

3 What is 'somatyping'?

4 What are the three main body types identified by William Sheldon?

Questions for further discussion

1 To what extent do you think crime is the product of individual free will?

2 Is the classical criminological assertion that 'the law should restrict the individual as little as possible' feasible in modern society?

3 If Marvin Wolfgang's observation that 'In the history of criminology probably no name has been eulogised or attacked so much as that of Cesare Lombroso' is accurate, why might this be so?

4 What are the main differences between what Garland calls the Lombrosian and governmental projects?

5 In what ways might body shape influence behaviour?

Further reading

Beccaria, C. (1764/2003) On Crimes and Punishment, in McLaughlin E., Muncie J. and Hughes G. (eds), *Criminological Perspectives: Essential readings*, London: Sage

Garland, D. (1985) The criminal and his science, *British Journal of Criminology*, 25, 2, Oxford: Oxford University Press

Lombroso, C. and Ferrero, W. (1895/2003) The criminal type in women and its atavistic origin, in McLaughlin E., Muncie J. and Hughes G. (eds.), *Criminological Perspectives: Essential readings* London: Sage

Rafter, N. (2006) Cesare Lombroso and the Origins of Criminology: Rethinking criminological tradition, in Henry S. and Lanier M. M. (eds), *The Essential Criminology Reader*, Boulder, CO: Westview Press

Taylor, I. *et al.* (1973) *The New Criminology*, London: Routledge and Kegan Paul (ch. 1)

Websites

Project Gutenburg (www.gutenberg.org/wiki/Main_ Page) provides online versions of books and other materials that are now out of copyright. Some of Enrico Ferri's work, for example, is available to download.

There is a lot of useful information, including guides to further reading, at:

http: //www.crimetheory.com/

Chapter outline

Introduction   132

Genetic factors   132

    Eugenics and 'feeble-mindedness'   133

    Twin studies   135

    Adoption   136

    Chromosomal anomalies   137

    Genetics and offending   138

Biochemical factors   138

    Central nervous system   138

    ADHD and brain dysfunction   139

    Neurostransmitters   140

    Laterality   141

    Autonomic nervous system   141

    Hormones/testosterone   141

    Nutrition   142

Assessing biological positivism   143

Questions for discussion   144

Further reading   144

Websites   144

Biological positivism

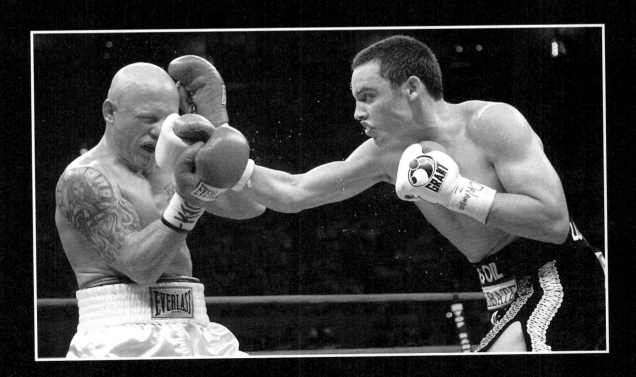

CHAPTER SUMMARY

As we saw in the previous chapter the early positivist criminology, associated with the likes of Lombroso and Ferri, looked at a variety of physical characteristics and sought to link them with criminal propensities. Although such work was heavily criticised and fell out of favour fairly swiftly, being largely displaced by a much more sociologically-oriented approach to crime and its causation, a body of work exploring aspects of biology, and more particularly the interaction between biological and social factors, continues to this day. Indeed, arguably a new biologically-oriented and influenced criminology is now beginning to emerge (Rose, 2000).

In this chapter we:

- explore some of that work;

- examine its main findings;

- consider future possibilities in this field;

- ask why many such ideas continue to attract such criticism and controversy.

Introduction

Many explorations of crime and biology begin by discussing the work of Cesare Lombroso. Growing interest in physiognomy (the study of facial features) and phrenology (the study of the shape of the skull) in the eighteenth and early nineteenth centuries led to much theorising about the possible relationship between particular physical features and the likelihood of engaging in crime. Lombroso was one of the most famous scholars working within this general tradition and although most of his work is now largely discredited, his influence over the development of criminology is undeniable. Similarly, William Sheldon's theory of *somatypes,* linking body shape to behaviour, is now largely discredited, though he has also found favour in some quarters, perhaps most famously in James Q. Wilson and Richard Hernnstein's (1985) work, *Crime and Human Nature* (see Chapter 13). Both Lombroso's and Sheldon's work was discussed in some detail in the previous chapter and so there is no need to review it again here.

Work in the biological positivist tradition developed relatively swiftly after Lombroso and there is a considerable distance between today's work and earlier attempts to identify the crucial characteristics of criminals via the measurement of the skull or the study of other physiological features. In this chapter we explore a range of biological, biochemical and physiological factors which may have some link with offending.

As we noted in the previous chapter, the work of Lombroso is no longer taken seriously. Whilst there are many reasons for rejecting Lombroso's theories, we should not jump to the simple conclusion that any search for biological influences on criminal behaviour is similarly likely to be flawed. Work in this area is no longer based on a simplistic search for a direct connection between physical characteristics and behaviour. In relation to the influence of heredity, for example, scholars are not searching for a single gene that might be identified as the 'criminal gene'. Rather, research on genetic influences tends to focus on this as one of a range of influences on behaviour. Thus, Hollin (1992: 30) quotes Plomin (1990) as observing that, 'Genes are chemical structures that can only code for amino acid sequences. These amino acid sequences interact with all of what we are and can thus indirectly affect endpoints as complex as behaviour, but there is no gene for a particular behaviour.'

Genetic factors

For centuries scholars have been interested in the possible links between the body and the mind. In this vein, one possible way of explaining conduct, including criminal conduct, is to look for inherited characteristics that might dispose people to behave in particular ways. In an early form, such exploration of genetic factors was called *eugenics* and, crudely, it linked physiological inadequacy of some form to criminality. Eugenic thought has taken various forms and has a dubious history, not least because of the eugenic philosophy adopted by the Nazis in 1930s Germany.

Eugenics and 'feeble-mindedness'

Darwinian-influenced social theories had a profound impact on nineteenth-century thought. So-called 'social Darwinists' believed that a process akin to natural selection, if left largely undisturbed, would result in an increasingly healthy society. Welfare programmes designed to support those perceived as morally less deserving were felt to put such social development at risk.

Arguably the most extreme version of such an approach was the eugenics movement which enjoyed considerable popularity in the late nineteenth and early twentieth century. Eugenic – meaning 'well-born' – was a term coined by Francis Galton, a cousin of Darwin's, and eugenics sought to explain human behaviour through genetics. In essence, those traits that led either to success or to failure in life were believed to be transmitted from generation to generation.

Some of the major benefactors in the USA established centres for the study of eugenics at leading universities, their objective being to study the nature of the nation's 'stock' (Lilly *et al.*, 2002). Katz and Abel (1984) suggest that the primary characteristic identified with individual failure was 'feeble-mindedness'. This, eugenicists came to believe, was linked with pauperism, promiscuity and criminality. The next logical question is, assuming this to be true, what is the appropriate policy response? Katz and Abel distinguish between what they call 'positive' and 'negative eugenics'. Positive eugenics focused its policy prescriptions on attempts to improve the gene pool – essentially through encouraging the genetically well-endowed to reproduce more frequently.

Negative eugenics is where the greatest controversy lies. In this connection, they suggest, there were four main policy initiatives. These were:

1 permanent segregation;
2 sterilisation;
3 restrictive marriage restraints;
4 restrictive immigration policies.

A now famous study, *The Jukes: A Study in Crime, Pauperism, Disease and Heredity* by Richard Dugdale (1895), first published in the late 1870s, explored the lives of the descendants of the eponymous (Ada) Jukes. Large numbers of criminals, paupers and others suffering various forms of malady, including venereal disease, were found among the 1000 and more relatives studied. The pattern was held up as evidence of what was known as 'bad blood' – the passing from generation to generation of various characteristics including criminality (see also Estabrook, 1916). In the hands of the eugenicists, evidence of families such as the Jukes – and also the Kallikaks (another fictitious name for a real family) subsequently studied by Goddard (1912) – was used to call for sterilisation, imprisonment, the use of shock therapies and lobotomies and even extermination.

Though responses such as shock treatment and sterilisation may seem extreme, such practices were not uncommon well into the twentieth century. In 1927 for example the US Supreme Court ruled that the State of Virginia had the authority to administer involuntary sterilisation on those deemed to be 'feeble-minded' or otherwise 'unfit' if the superintendent of a state institution deemed it to be in the best interests of the state. Up to a further 30 states passed such legislation and over 65,000 Americans were compulsorily sterilised over the next decade and a half. The Supreme Court ended the practice in the early 1940s, though many laws remained on the statute books for decades afterward. The law was not repealed until 1974.

Nevertheless, according to Rafter (1998: 210) 'eugenic criminology' – the confinement, and possibly treatment' – of *born criminals* in specific institutions lost its impetus from around the 1920s. In particular, advances in intelligence testing made it increasingly problematic to define individuals as 'feeble-minded' and developments in genetics undermined the geneticists' views of heredity.

The Jukes and *The Kallikak Family* were relatively unsophisticated works, and were highly moralistic. Subsequently, a range of more rigorous studies have, nevertheless, found family to be an important influence on criminal conduct. A study by Osborn and West in the 1970s found that two-fifths of boys whose fathers had criminal records had criminal records themselves, compared with just over one-eighth of boys whose father had no

The Kallikaks: What is to be done?

GREAT-GRANDCHILDREN OF "OLD SAL."

CHILDREN OF GUSS SAUNDERS, WITH THEIR GRANDMOTHER.

Illustrations from *The Kallikak Family: a study in the heredity of feeble-mindedness* (1912), which sought to identify how criminality and other characteristics were passed from generation to generation in particular families – in response eugenicists advocated sterilisation and imprisonment amongst other supposed forms of treatment.

What *can* we do? For the low-grade idiot, the loathsome unfortunate that may be seen in our institutions, some have proposed the lethal chamber. But humanity is steadily tending away from the possibility of that method, and there is no probability that it will ever be practiced.

But in view of such conditions as are shown in the defective side of the Kallikak family, we begin to realize that the idiot is not our greatest problem. He is indeed loathsome; he is somewhat difficult to take care of; nevertheless, he lives his life and is done. He does not continue the race with a line of children like himself. Because of his very low-grade condition, he never becomes a parent.

It is the moron type that makes for us our great problem. And when we face the question, 'What is to be done with them – with such people as make up a large proportion of the bad side of the Kallikak family?', we realize that we have a huge problem.

The career of Martin Kallikak Sr. is a powerful sermon against sowing wild oats. Martin Kallikak did what unfortunately many a young man like him has done before and since, and which, still more unfortunately, society has too often winked at, as being merely a side step in accordance with a natural instinct, bearing no serious results …

The real sin of peopling the world with a race of defective degenerates who would probably commit his sin a thousand times over, was doubtless not perceived or realized. It is only after the lapse of six generations that we are able to look back, count up and see the havoc that was wrought by that one thoughtless act. Now that the facts are known, let the lesson be learned …

Others will look at the [chart of the family history] and say, 'The difficulty began with the nameless feeble-minded girl; had she been taken care of, all of this trouble would have been avoided.' This is largely true. Although feeble-mindedness came into this family from other sources in two generations at least, yet nevertheless these sources were other feeble-minded persons. When we conclude that had the nameless girl been segregated in an institution, this defective family would not have existed, we of course do not mean that one single act of precaution, in that case, would have solved the problem, but we mean that all such cases, male and female, must be taken care of, before their propagation will cease. The instant we grasp this thought, we realize that we are facing a problem that presents two great difficulties; in the first place the difficulty of knowing who are the feeble-minded people; and, secondly, the difficulty of taking care of them when they are known.

Source: Goddard (1912: 102–104).

criminal record. The finding that criminal conduct tends to run in families may be an indicator of the influence of heredity, but might equally be an indicator of the influence of environmental factors such as socialisation and peer group. Put differently, just because fathers with criminal records are more likely to have sons with criminal records is not in itself evidence of any genetic link. Second, Osborn and West's (1979) findings also suggest that 60 per cent of boys whose fathers had criminal records *did not* have criminal records themselves (and see Farrington *et al.*, 1996).

Research in the area of genetics and crime/anti-social conduct has grown markedly in recent years and some solid empirical findings are now available. Moffitt (2005) argues that the 100 or so studies of the genetic influence on anti-social behaviour that have been conducted 'conclude that genes influence 40% to 50% of population variation in anti-social behaviour'. According to Moffitt the clearest ways of testing for such effects is to see whether family members are more similar in their behaviour than would be explained by their genetic make-up or, alternatively, are less similar in their behaviour. The main ways in which this is done is by looking at identical or non-identical twins or at children adopted at birth.

Twin studies

The nature versus nurture debate – whether in understanding human conduct it is the physical/psychological make-up of the individual or their social context that is most important – is the source of considerable controversy. One way of getting an interesting angle on the potential impact of heredity on human behaviour is thought to be to study twins. Twins share a genetic make-up, but may differ in their wider social experiences. There are two types of twins: identical (monozygotic) twins (MZ) who are genetically identical, being the product of a single egg and a single sperm; and, dizygotic (non-identical) twins (DZ) who are the product of two eggs that are fertilised at the same time by two sperm and thus are no more likely to be genetically alike than other siblings born at different times.

The basic theory underlying such research is that if MZ twins demonstrate greater similarity in their behaviour than DZ twins or, alternatively, that twins generally demonstrate greater similarity in their behaviour patterns than non-twin siblings, then this is evidence for the possibility of a genetic influence.

However, such findings are complicated, indeed possibly undermined, by the fact that twins growing up together are subject to similar social influences. Thus, some studies have sought to study twins separated at birth and growing up in different family environments. The theory here is that identical twins, separated at birth, should display similar offending patterns if it is inherited traits that are most important in explaining behaviour.

Perhaps the first study was that by Lange published in 1929 and entitled *Crime as Destiny*. Based on a study of 30 pairs of adult male twins, Lange found what he claimed to be considerable similarity in offending patterns among the identical twins in the sample. An early study in the 1930s found a fairly high degree of similarity or overlap – generally referred to as *concordance* – between monozygotic twins. That is, a higher proportion of identical twins were found both to have prison records than were a comparison group of non-identical twins. Early studies were limited by a number of methodological problems, not least that the samples were often at least partly drawn from prisons or psychiatric clinics hence biasing them from the outset.

Subsequent studies have tended to be more sophisticated. A large-scale study in Denmark by Christiansen (1977) focused on all twins born between 1881 and 1910 (so long as the twins lived to age 15). This identified around 6,000 pairs. The study also found a high rate of criminal concordance – 36 per cent for identical males compared with 12 per cent for non-identical males (see also Eley *et al.*, 1999). However, Christiansen admitted that it was all but impossible even in this study to separate heredity from other factors, and argued that some of the concordance he found might be the product of shared environments:

> Nothing in these results, however, can be interpreted as indicating that a higher twin coefficient in [identical] than in [non-identical] twins, or in pairs with more serious than in pairs with less serious forms of criminality, is due to … the quite preponderant part played by heredity in the causation of crime. (quoted in Vold *et al.*, 2002: 41)

Another Scandinavian study, by Dalgaard and Kringlen (1976), studied 139 pairs of male twins and also found some significant differences between the concordance rates for MZ and DZ twins – at 26 per cent and 15 per cent respectively. However, they explained this difference by suggesting that the identical twins shared a particularly close psychological bond and that it was this rather than their genetic make-up which explained the apparent similarity in their behaviour.

Such early studies tended to use official records as the basis for their analysis of patterns of offending and also often had unreliable methods of determining genetic make-up of the twins in the sample. More recently, as it has become more usual to use improved methods of determining 'zygosity' and to use self-report methods to assess levels of offending (see Chapter 3), these studies have tended to show less dramatic results. Thus, the Ohio twin study conducted by Rowe and Rogers, which studied same-sex and mixed-sex twins, argued that their study suggested that genetic influences partly affected the behaviour of both same-sex and MZ twins, but accepted that the similarities were mediated by social and psychological factors (Williams, 2004). Raine (1993) analysed the results from ten studies of identical twins, and reported that the overall finding was of a relatively high level of concordance among identical twins.

There are a number of points worth bearing in mind in assessing such work. First, as indicated, there are a number of methodological limitations to many of the studies. Second, the level of concordance detected – often somewhere between 25 per cent and 33 per cent – is relatively low, suggesting that even if there is some genetic effect there are undoubtedly a range of other, very powerful influences at work. Third, whilst MZ twins are always same sex, it is possible for DZ twins to be of different sexes. Given that there are well-established gender differences in offending, some of the measured differences between identical and non-identical twins may reflect this gender imbalance. There is also the possibility with identical twins that both labelling processes (one sibling getting a reputation because of the other) and mistaken identity could affect whether or not siblings are identified as 'offenders'.

Moreover, concordance doesn't necessarily demonstrate a genetic impact for it remains possible that similarity in behaviour may still be explained by broader environmental factors such as similarities in socialisation. That is to say, most of the twins that have been the subject of such studies have grown up in the same household. Identical twins may be particularly close, and may be treated very similarly by parents. It is therefore all but impossible to separate out environmental and genetic influences. In this vein Blackburn (1993: 139) concluded that the 'available twin data favour some genetic influence on criminality, but are inconclusive in the absence of twins reared apart'. Some studies have therefore sought to explore the impact of genetics whilst attempting to control for environmental factors by investigating the experiences of siblings who haven't grown up together.

Adoption

In this context adoption provides another means of testing elements of the nature/nurture controversy. Here the focus tends to be on children who have been adopted soon after birth by non-family members. The assumption in such work is that if adopted children resemble biological rather than adoptive parents in some important respects, then this is potentially evidence of a genetic influence. Once grown up, for example, an adoptive child's criminal record or offending history can then be compared, say, with the biological and adoptive parents' records in an attempt to isolate the more important source of influence. Work by Hutchings and Mednick (1977) found some evidence that adoptees with criminal records had a higher proportion of biological mothers and fathers with criminal records than adoptees with no criminal record.

Similarly, a study by Crowe (1974) found that adopted children whose biological mothers had criminal records had higher offending rates than those whose mothers had no record. A Danish study examined the criminal histories of over 14,000 adoptees (Mednick et al., 1984). When both biological and adoptive parents had criminal records, approximately one-quarter of sons also did, compared with one-fifth where only the biological parent had a criminal record and nearer to one in seven when only the adoptive parent was criminal (see Figure 6.1). According to Mednick, the conclusions of these studies:

> ... irrefutably support the influence of heritable factors in the etiology of some forms of antisocial acts. Because we can only inherit biological predispositions, the genetic evidence conclusively admits biological factors among the important agents influencing some forms of criminal behaviour. (quoted in Gottfredson and Hirschi, 1990: 53)

Similarly, a study by Bohman (1995) found that in cases where the biological and adoptive parents had criminal records there was a 40 per cent chance the child would develop a criminal record compared with a 12 per cent chance where the

Figure 6.1	Percentage of male adoptees with criminal records according to the criminality of the parents (after Mednick *et al.*, 1983a)

| Adoptive parents | Biological parents | |
	Criminal	Non-criminal
Criminal	24.5% (*n* = 143)	14.7% (*n* = 204)
Non-criminal	20.0% (*n* = 1,226)	13.5% (*n* = 2,492)

Source: Hollin (1989).

adoptive parents had no criminal record. Overall, Gottfredson and Hirschi (1990: 58) conclude that they 'would not be surprised to learn that the true genetic effect on the likelihood of criminal behaviour is *somewhere between zero and the results finally reported by Mednick [et al.].* That is, we suspect that the magnitude of this effect is minimal' (*emphasis in original*).

There are numerous limitations to such studies that must be borne in mind when assessing such evidence. First, it is possible, and in some jurisdictions reasonably likely, that children who are adopted are placed in environments that resemble those from which they were taken in some important respects. Second, it is by no means the case that children are always adopted immediately after birth. Some may be adopted only after several months, or in some cases, years, have passed. In such cases there is considerable potential for early formative influences to take place and to affect later behaviour patterns. Third, and certainly in early studies before genetic testing was easier, there was very significant potential for the mis-classification of 'twins' (i.e. wrongly defining some siblings as twins and vice versa). Finally, there has been much dispute about the nature of the data used, particular when official records rather than self-report measures have been used to identify levels of offending.

Chromosomal anomalies

A further approach to potential genetic effects on criminal behaviour is to be found in the study of chromosomal anomalies – cases in which there is some departure from the normal complement of chromosomes. Men and women normally have 46 chromosomes in 23 pairs, one of which is a pair of sex chromosomes: the Y denotes the male chromosome and X the female. Under normal circumstances men have an XY pair and women an XX pair. Research in the early 1960s found a new chromosomal configuration: a male with XYY chromosomal make-up (not to be confused with Klinefelter's Syndrome which refers to men with an extra X chromosome). Such anomalies are rare, but have been linked with various behavioural disorders.

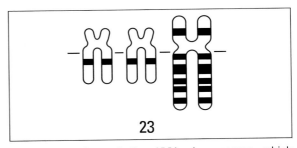

A representation of the XYY chromosome which approximately one in 1,000 males are born with. Research has failed to establish a conclusive link between the possession of an extra Y chromosome and the likelihood of increased criminality.

Research in the 1960s was able to identify a number of XYY males among a sample of mentally-disordered, male offenders in Scotland (Price *et al.*, 1966). Responsible for some serious crimes, a picture developed of some form of hyper-masculine offender, labelled the 'supermale syndrome', who was especially aggressive and somewhat lacking in intelligence. Some circumstantial evidence was offered in support of the theory – most suggestively that an American serial murderer, Arthur Shawcross, had such a genetic make-up. Subsequent research in the UK and in Denmark in the 1970s found some association between the extra Y chromosome and offending behaviour, but not violent crime. However, such studies also found those with the extra chromosome to be of lower intelligence and consequently argued that any genetic influence was indirect or non-specific (for more recent results see Götz *et al.*, 1999).

Such overall conclusions led Hirschi and Gottfredson (1990: 62) to conclude that the history of XYY chromosome research is a story of 'extraordinary effort expended to document the possible existence of a small effect, the significance of which is unclear even to those pursuing it'. Indeed, in Ainsworth's (2000) view, what is interesting about the XYY story is not to be found in what it can tell us about offending behaviour, but rather in the public fascination with such possibilities. In this case, he notes, 'the public reacted to it [in] much the same way as the public greeted news of Lombroso's findings 80 years earlier' (2000: 66). The implication is that there appears to be an enduring public fascination with, and possibly desire to believe in, the notion that criminals are somehow different from other people.

Genetics and offending

There has been much interest in possible genetic influences on offending and a few authors have argued strongly that there is an important biological hereditary element in offending (Raine, 1993). There are immense methodological difficulties in separating out biological and environmental influences and most scholars interested in genetic influences will now argue that it is a combination of biology and environment – and in particular the interaction between the two – that is important in explaining human behaviour.

The question left in all this is what is the mechanism in any genetic influence? As has been suggested, the idea of a 'bad' or 'criminal' gene has all but been abandoned. Any suggestion of direct influence has great difficulty in accounting for links with the enormously varied behaviours that can be labelled as 'criminal', and also with the fact that the majority of people who offend tend to do so in their teenage years and largely cease to do so as they grow older.

How, then, might genetic make-up influence behaviour? It is to more indirect connections that researchers now look. One intervening variable is alcoholism. Research by Bohman (1978) suggested a genetic predisposition to alcoholism which, in turn, increases the likelihood of criminal behaviour. Recent research suggests that there may be some genetic basis for ADHD and impulsivity

(Sherman *et al.*, 1997). It is possible, some argue, that 'poor heredity' may exacerbate the difficulties encountered in particular social circumstances, thereby increasing the likelihood of offending. Put differently, it is possible that genetic make-up provides individuals with particular *predispositions*, but that these only become realities under particular social/environmental circumstances. Thus, there are various forms of mental illness that are felt to operate in a similar manner: certain individuals are more highly predisposed to particular illnesses, schizophrenia for example, but this predisposition does not lead inevitably to the disease developing. Rather, there appear to be particular environmental factors which magnify the likelihood. Ainsworth (2000: 72) puts it as follows:

If there is a link between genetics and criminal behaviour it is perhaps that some aspects of personality have a genetic component. Thus, what is inherited is not a tendency to commit criminal acts as such, but rather a predisposition to develop certain aspects of personality, some of which may be linked to criminal behaviour.

Review questions

1 What is meant by 'eugenics'?

2 In what ways might the study of identical twins be useful in the study of crime?

3 What is the link thought to be between the possession of an extra Y chromosome and criminal behaviour?

Biochemical factors

There is a range of other potential biological factors that have been explored in relation to explaining various aspects of human behaviour, including criminality. In this section we consider the central and autonomic nervous systems and related biochemical factors, including the influence of hormones and nutrition.

Central nervous system

The central nervous system (CNS) comprises the brain and the spinal cord, and studies in this area are focused upon brain function and the transmission of information through the CNS. Brain functioning has traditionally been measured using an electroencephalogram (EEG). The EEG records brainwave patterns from the continuous electrical signals coming from the brain and these are used to detect various abnormalities.

Electrical disorganisation in the brain may lead to recurrent seizures, a condition known as epilepsy (as we saw in the previous chapter, Lombroso was perhaps the first major scholar to draw a link between epilepsy and crime). General estimates suggest that perhaps 0.5 per cent of the population suffer from epilespy. Research in prisons has found higher levels – Gunn and Bonn (1971) found a prevalence rate of 0.71 per cent, while research in America found over two per cent of prisoners had a history of seizures (Whitman *et al.*, 1984). If indeed there is any associaton, the question that arises is what link might there be with criminality. Two main hypotheses have been explored: the idea of *automatism* in which offences are committed without the perpetrator being aware of it and, second, the possibility that certain forms of epilepsy are linked with increased aggression and violence. In relation to the latter, research provides little evidence of heightened aggression or violent offending, nor any concrete illustrations of automatic offending during seizures.

A number of early research studies appeared to detect some link between abnormal brain activity and serious crimes such as murder by the insane (Hollin, 1992) and, whilst considerable doubt is placed on some of these findings, more recent research has shown inconsistent findings in possible links between abnormal EEG patterns and criminality. Hollin (1992: 37), however, quotes one sizeable and rigorous recent study (Hsu *et al.*, 1985) as concluding that there is 'no compelling reason to believe that epilepsy and abnormal EEGs are major determinants of juvenile delinquency'.

ADHD and brain dysfunction

Beyond the direct measurement of central nervous system functioning via EEG there are a number of other ways in which data are collected on brain activity. One set of ideas, which remains controversial, relates to the notion of 'minimal brain dysfunction'. This is a syndrome, associated with children and adolescents in particular, which consists of a group of factors associated with abnormal or inappropriate behaviour and cognition. Already the use of terms here like *abnormal* and *inappropriate* indicate that there are some quite substantial judgements being made about what is *normal* and *appropriate* conduct.

The term most commonly used in relation to such brain dysfunction currently is attention-deficit hyperactivity disorder (ADHD). ADHD is characterised by impulsivity (acting without thinking through the consequences), hyperactivity (excessive activity) and inattentiveness (failure to concentrate or pay attention). Children with ADHD may find interacting with others problematic. The problems and frustrations they experience may lead to aggression and violence. ADHD is associated with biological causes such as a genetic predisposition, brain damage and neurological immaturity (Wender, 2002).

Research by Farrington *et al.* (1990) has found a significant connection between typical ADHD measures of conduct problems (low attention span, hyperactivity, etc.) and offending patterns (see also Unnever, 2003). Attention deficits were found to be linked with low cognitive abilities and low IQ and were found in young men coming from large families, with parents likely to have a criminal history, and who were most likely to progress to lengthy and chaotic criminal careers. By contrast, other ADHD-related conduct problems were associated with young men who had more mundane criminal behaviour as adolescents, but progressed later to persistent adult offending.

Once again, there are limitations to the existing research in this area, which are important in assessing its impact. First, much work in this area has focused on males and, therefore, is limited in its general application. Like so much of criminology it can tell us little about female behaviour and offending. Second, whilst there may be some link between brain dysfunction and certain types of behaviour, this is not the same as saying that one is the cause of the other, and certainly not to the exclusion of other, social factors. Thus whilst there is indeed 'a substantial body of research that suggests that *some* delinquents are characterised, to a greater or lesser extent, by CNS impairment or dysfunction' (Hollin, 1992: 43), research by Farrington and others suggests that such individual factors are strongly mediated by other, social influences (Piquero *et al.*, 2007).

In addition to various forms of brain dysfunction (what are referred to as 'soft' neurological signs) there is also the possibility that tissue damage resulting from some form of physical injury may have an impact on later behaviour. Recent research has pointed to the possible influence of complications in pregnancy and delivery as having some impact on later conduct. A study by Kandel and Mednick (1991), looking at children born in Copenhagen in the late 1950s whose parents suffered from schizophrenia, psychopathy or a number of other disorders, also considered the potential impact of factors in pregnancy and childbirth.

Kandel and Mednick (1991) found that complications in pregnancy (e.g. infections, jaundice) appeared not to be linked to later offending, whereas complications in delivery (ruptured perineum or uterus) did appear to be linked, though only when combined with other factors. Four-fifths of violent offenders had greater than average delivery problems, compared with under half of non-offenders and one-third of property offenders. Similarly, a later study by Raine and colleagues (1997) found that a combination of delivery complications and maternal rejection in the first year of life was connected with a heightened risk of involvement in serious violent crime at the age of 18. Work by Terri Moffitt on what she refers to as 'life-course persistent offenders' (see Chapter 14) suggests that the behaviours associated with this pattern of offending – persistent and, often, increasingly serious – is associated with factors including drug use and poor nutrition during pregnancy, birth complications resulting in minor brain damage and, like Raine, deprivation of affection or abuse in early childhood (see also Brennan et al., 1999).

A review of studies (Miller, 1999) of head injuries found offenders to be more likely to have suffered such damage than non-offenders, though whether the injury leads to the offending or the offending to the injury remains unclear. Further research by Raine and colleagues (1994) has found some linkage between brain abnormalities and homicide. Indeed, his research has been used in defence cases seeking a verdict of 'not guilty by reason of insanity' in the USA. In interpreting his data, however, Raine is careful to avoid reductionism, observing:

> ... the neural processes underlying violence are complex and cannot be simplistically reduced to single brain mechanisms causing violence in a direct causal fashion. Instead, violent behaviour probably involves disruption of a network of multiply interacting brain mechanisms that predispose to violence in the presence of other social, environmental, and psychological predispositions. (quoted in Rose, 2000: 16)

In examining research on brain dysfunction, and particularly studies in which brain injury is linked with later violent conduct, Howitt (2002) notes a number of significant methodological difficulties related to such research. He argues that:

- People who are violent and get into fights are more likely to suffer brain damage (this, of course, doesn't undermine the potential explanatory power of brain injury during birth).
- Some of the research may have been based on samples with higher than average levels of disadvantage – which is what explains the disproportionate levels of offending.
- Pre/post injury studies tend to be based on the most seriously injured people – and may therefore be unrepresentative.

Neurotransmitters

These are chemicals that enable electrical impulses within the brain to be transmitted and which form the basis for the processing of information. There is some limited evidence that three neurotransmitters – serotonin, dopamine, and norepinephrine – may have some link with anti-social behaviour (though there are numerous other neurotransmitters about which relatively little is yet known).

Serotonin is assumed to reduce aggressiveness by inhibiting responses to external emotional stimuli, whereas dopamine and norepinephrine counteract the inhibitory impact of serotonin. Normally, the three are in some sort of equilibrium, but a disturbance of this equilibrium can lead to aggressive or unpredictable conduct. A meta-analysis by Raine (1993) suggests that studies consistently find lower levels of serotonin in people described as 'anti-social', though the findings in relation to the other two neurotransmitters were less clear cut.

There are several issues affecting such research, however. One is the potential for mediating or confounding factors to complicate the findings. Thus, alcohol in sufficient quantities can also affect neurotransmitter levels and is itself linked with aggressiveness. Similarly, and intriguingly, neurotransmitter levels can also be affected by diet, another area of growing interest in the general area of the socio-biological study of criminality. Furthermore, it is not at all clear in some of the studies what measures of aggressiveness or violence are being used, and whether these are used consistently between experimental and control groups (see Chapter 35 for an explanation of the use of experimental and control groups).

Laterality

This term refers to the bilateral symmetricality of human physiology: the two mirror images at the heart of the human body. In particular, the forebrain is divided into two cerebral hemispheres, the left and right cortical hemispheres, and most people display a preference for one or the other. One of the ways in which this is displayed is through being left- or right-handed and footed. Some early studies claimed to detect some linkage between left-sidedness and delinquency, though much of this may simply have reflected social responses and other environmental factors. Importantly, left-handedness was, until relatively recently, openly discouraged and treated as abnormal. Under such circumstances it might not be surprising if such stigma and labelling had other adverse consequences, including some delinquent behaviour.

Another possibility concerns the association between certain cognitive and personality factors and the predominance of one hemisphere over the other. Thus, it is argued that language abilities are located in the left hemisphere and it is possible, therefore, that left-handed people – on the assumption that they tend to be right-hemisphere dominant – might be less verbally able. Such skills are linked with levels of self-control and this in turn is argued to be linked to anti-social conduct. According to Hollin (1992: 40), though 'conceptually neat, the empirical evidence in support of such a path of events remains to be gathered'.

Autonomic nervous system

The autonomic nervous system (ANS) connects several of the body's organs to the CNS. It is a motor system with an important role in the regulation of breathing, the heart rate and the operation of various glands. Much research in this area focuses on the rate of functioning of the ANS. One common application of ANS measurement is the use of lie detectors. Generally measuring ANS activity via the sweat glands in the hands, lie detectors measure the degree of arousal – the working assumption being that people are more likely to be aroused (nervous, tense, anxious, fearful, frightened) when lying.

ANS responsiveness is also linked to offending in other ways. Thus, slow responsiveness is interpreted as cases in which individuals require strong stimuli to arouse them, and is linked to poor learning skills, particularly in relation to *aversion,* i.e.

avoiding circumstances likely to lead to harmful outcomes. Such slow responsiveness is argued by some researchers to be characteristic of offender groups. Thus, for example, Raine (1996) provides some evidence to suggest that anti-social individuals are characterised by under-arousal and that aggressive children may be stimulation seekers who are relatively fearless.

Hormones/testosterone

Why are men more likely to become involved in violence than women, and why are some men apparently particularly violent? One possibility, explored in a number of studies, is that the hormone that produces male secondary sex characteristics, *testosterone,* is in some way implicated. Certainly, there is considerable evidence from research on animals that testosterone is an important factor in aggressiveness (Raine, 1993). What might be the link in humans? According to Hollin (1992), such thinking is based on a number of assumptions. These include the idea that as both delinquency generally, and aggressiveness more particularly, tend to be pronounced during and just after puberty, then it may be the changes in hormonal activity that explain such changes in behaviour.

Why are men more likely to be involved in violence than women? Levels of testosterone have been one of the factors investigated in research studies.

The research evidence in relation to humans is rather trickier to interpret than that on animals. Research by Persky *et al.* (1971) found a correlation between the rate of production and level of testosterone and measures of hostility in males. A study of over 4,000 military personnel (Booth and Osgood, 1993) found a link between testosterone levels and adult offending. However, once they had controlled for 'social integration' they found that the strength of this connection lessened markedly. Controlling for offending behaviour further lessened the link.

Some research has found a tendency toward abnormally high testosterone levels in violent male sex offenders, though there are often a number of important intervening variables, notably alcohol consumption, that make judging the impact difficult (Booth and Osgood, 1993). Finally, there has been some limited research on the impact of hormone levels on women's behaviour and, in particular, the role they play in the menstrual cycle and the potential psychological and behavioural consequences that result. Research by Herbert and Tennent (1974) found that disturbed women in a security hospital were more likely to be confined as a result of behavioural problems during the pre-menstrual week. Although the research evidence is inconclusive, the idea of pre-menstrual tension

(PMT) has been used successfully in mitigation in criminal trials (Allen, 1984).

There are several potential difficulties with research, and the interpretation of data, in this area. One is that the relationship between hormone levels and aggression may potentially work in both directions: higher hormone levels leading to greater aggressiveness, and heightened aggression raising hormone levels. In addition, there may be situational factors that also lead to increased hormone levels, resulting in heightened aggression, though the link wouldn't show up in research conducted under 'normal' circumstances.

Nutrition

Anyone who watched the first Jamie Oliver *School Dinners* TV series may have been struck by the scenes in which parents, having been persuaded to change their children's diets, later reported what on the surface appeared to be some dramatic changes in behaviour. In particular, children were reported to have become calmer and more stable. Far from scientific, nevertheless these programmes link with a growing belief in contemporary society that diet and nutrition are important not only in terms of general health, but also in that they may have some more immediate impact on conduct.

Healthy school dinners or junk food? Diet and nutrition have become recognised as important not just for general health and development, but also in relation to behaviour and potential delinquency.

Recent years have seen increasing interest in nutrition, or diet, and its potential impact on crime. In particular, prisons (where it is possible, within limits, to both control and change diet, and to observe behaviour) provide an interesting location for research in this area. It is felt by some that prison studies are particularly important as the behavioural gains that are anticipated are most needed in the context of prisons.

There are various ways in which links may potentially be made between nutrition and crime:

- Low blood-sugar, or hypoglycaemia, has been associated with a number of behavioural problems including violence, alcoholism, hyperactivity and learning difficulties (Tuormaa, 1994).

- Food allergies, and food additives have been associated with hyperactivity and attention-deficit disorder (Tuormaa, 1994).

- Some have suggested that vitamin and/or mineral deficiencies or excesses may be linked with criminality or anti-social behaviour (Gesch et al., 2002). The most commonly suggested links focus on excess levels of lead in the bloodstream (which is linked with slow learning ability, hyperactivity, and low intelligence), and a deficiency of vitamin B complex which is linked with aggression and erratic behaviour.

As the introduction to this section implied, much of the argument in this area is based on supposition and anecdotal evidence, though some recent research appears more reliable. There is considerable doubt in some quarters about the impact of processed 'junk foods', especially those with high sugar content. A series of studies conducted in the 1980s examined the impact of changes in diet on juveniles held in detention. The changes involved replacing sugar with honey, soft drinks with orange juice and snack food with fruit and peanut butter. It was claimed (Schoenthaler, 1983) that the changes led to a substantial decline in reported incidents of violence. However, this and similar studies have been criticised for their poor scientific design – not using control groups and failing clearly to quantify the changes in sugar intake.

More recent research by Gesch and colleagues (2002: 26) found that 'supplementing prisoners' diets with physiological dosages of vitamins, minerals and essential fatty acids caused a reduction in anti-social behaviour to a remarkable degree'. However – and this is important for both this and later discussions in the book – the authors go on to acknowledge that they are not arguing that the

measured changes were solely a product of the nutritional changes involved in the experiment. There may have been other factors – to do with the nature of prison life for example – which had some form of mediating effect on behaviour.

Although this is an area in which solid empirical research is in short supply, the results of recent research like that conducted by Gesch et al. (2002) suggests that there is some potential for dietary interventions in relation to anti-social behaviour. However, it is important to bear in mind that the research evidence remains relatively slim at this stage. Moreover, even if some link between diet/nutrition and offending behaviour could be demonstrated, it would still be necessary to explain the nature of the link and in what way cause and effect work.

Assessing biological positivism

Such a wide range of ideas has been briefly explored in this chapter, covering the role of heritable characteristics, the biochemical functioning of the brain and nervous system, and the impact of such factors as nutrition, that it is arguably difficult to reach anything approaching a solid conclusion as to its contribution to our understanding of criminal conduct. That said, most reviews of evidence in this area tend to conclude by making three general points:

- Biological factors almost certainly have some role in the determination of criminal conduct.

- The extent of this role is generally (very) small.

- Such effects are heavily mediated by, or only occur in interaction with, broader social or environmental factors.

Such summaries, and the approach they imply, are some distance from the biological positivist model adopted by Lombroso and his successors which sought a direct link between physical characteristics and criminality. As we have seen, contemporary approaches are much more likely to talk of the possibility of heritable characteristics, or biochemical influences, as predisposing factors, potentially affecting the likelihood of subsequent behaviours.

Even the relatively modest claims that much research in this tradition is able to make are qualified by a number of methodological limitations. As we have seen, much research on genetics has been bedevilled by problems of sampling and of

comparison and has experienced particular difficulties in understanding and measuring crime. It is
this shortcoming that led Gottfredson and Hirschi
(1990) among others to dismiss the applicability of
anything approaching the strict application of biological positivism in the study of crime:

> Acceptance of the state's definition of crime ... led
> [biological positivism] to search for the *biological
> causes of state-defined* crime, an ostensibly empirical
> enterprise that was actually massively constrained
> by *a priori* principles. As a result, biological posi-
> tivism has produced little in the way of meaningful
> or interpretable research. (1990: 61–62).

Review questions

1 What might the links be between ADHD and
offending behaviour?

2 What are the main methodological difficulties in
trying to establish a link between brain
dysfunction and criminality?

3 In what ways might nutrition and diet be linked
to criminality?

Questions for further discussion

1 Is there any evidence that criminals are physically
different from non-criminals?

2 What problems might you have to overcome in
comparing the biological characteristics of *criminals*
and *non-criminals?*

3 Are biological and sociological approaches to understanding crime compatible?

4 What, if any, are the dangers of suggesting that biological characteristics may help to explain
criminality?

5 Assuming some genetic or similar cause of crime
could be identified, what do you think the policy
implications would be?

Further reading

There is a broad range of introductory, and not so introductory, books that will provide further information on
the areas covered here. Among the ones that I have
found helpful are:

Ainsworth, P. (2000) *Psychology and Crime,* Harlow:
Longman (ch. 4)
Blackburn, R. (1993) *The Psychology of Criminal Conduct,*
Chichester: Wiley (ch. 6) (this is quite an advanced
book)

Hollin, C. (1992) *Criminal Behaviour: A psychological
approach to explanation and prevention,* Hove:
Psychology Press (ch. 3)
Vold, G. *et al.* (2002) *Theoretical Criminology,* New York:
Oxford University Press (ch. 3)

Websites

http: //www.eugenicsarchive.org/eugenics/branch.pl –
provides a lot of useful information on the movement
in support of, and later abolition of, involuntary sterilisation of criminals and other practices.

http: //crime-times.org – is intended as a forum in which
those involved in research on biological/physiological
factors in crime can share information, and where the
general approach is advertised and promoted.

Chapter outline

Introduction 148

Psychoanalysis and crime 148
  Bowlby and maternal deprivation 150

Learning theories 151
  Differential association 151
  Operant learning 152
  Social learning theory 153
  Rational choice 156
    Routine activity theory 157

Cognitive theories 157
  Yochelson and Samenow 157
  Piaget, Kohlberg, moral development and offending 159

Eysenck's biosocial theory 161

Intelligence and offending 163

Assessing psychological positivism 165

Questions for further discussion 166
Further reading 166
Websites 166

7

Psychological positivism

In this chapter we consider:

- various forms of *psychological positivism*: theories that focus on the personality and psychological make-up and learning processes of individuals, and how these have been thought to relate to crime and anti-social behaviour;

- what these theories share with many of those outlined in the previous two chapters;

- the assumption that it is possible to identify causes of crime beyond the control of the individual – factors that constrain and mould individual behaviour.

Introduction

Howitt (2002) argues that it is probably fair to suggest that forensic and criminal psychology have contributed less by way of theory to criminology than have many other disciplines. Indeed, for much of the twentieth century – certainly its second half – there was something of a rupture between psychology and criminology, the latter becoming increasingly dominated by sociological concerns. This is now beginning to change, in part because there is an increasingly vibrant body of psychological research on crime and anti-social conduct, and also because there are growing numbers of criminologists seeking to build bridges between the sociological and psychological aspects of the subject (see, for example, Gadd and Jefferson, 2007).

There is a range of psychological theories that might be brought to bear on criminological topics, and Howitt offers a tabular illustration of a range of theories and of the types of psychology that each involves (see Figure 7.1). We covered biological theories in the previous chapter and we will cover social theories in later chapters. Here we focus primarily on psychoanalytic theories, learning theories, and personality theories. We begin with some of the classic psychological theories – associated with Freud, Bowlby and others, before moving on to more contemporary approaches.

Psychoanalysis and crime

As Valier (1998) notes, psychoanalysis has had relatively little to say directly about crime. That said, psychiatric and psychoanalytic ideas have been important in the history of British criminology

Figure 7.1	Some theories of crime and the types of psychology they involve

Theory	Biological	Psychoanalytic	Cognitive	Individual differences	Learning	Social
Neuropsychology	✓	✗	✗	✗	✗	✗
XYY	✓	✗	✗	✗	✗	✗
Intelligence	✓	✗	✓	✓	✗	✗
Bowlby's attachment	✓	✓	✗	✗	✗	✓
Eysenck's biosocial	✓	✗	✗	✓	✓	✓
Learning theory	✗	✗	✗	✗	✓	✓
Social constructionism	✗	✗	✗	✗	✗	✓

Source: Howitt (2002).

Sigmund Freud (1856–1939), the 'father of psycho-analysis', whose ideas and work have been highly influential in a number of different fields.

and criminology more widely. Indeed, as we saw in Chapter 1, such ideas were in many respects dominant within work on crime in much of the first half of the twentieth century. Work in this area derives from Freud's psychoanalytic theories, at the heart of which humans are conceived as inherently anti-social, having pleasure-seeking impulses that conflict with the broader interests of social groups. Psychoanalytic theory emphasises irrational and unconscious motivations in explaining criminal conduct. In this, three concepts distinguished by Freud are central to psychoanalytic theory:

- *Id* – An aspect of personality that is unconscious, includes primitive and instinctual behaviours and is the primary component of personality. It is driven by the *pleasure principle* and seeks the immediate gratification of desires.

- *Ego* – That element of the personality which enables the id to function in socially acceptable ways, based around the *reality principle*. The ego also helps to discharge tensions created through unmet desires.

- *Superego* – Originally conceived as part of the unconscious mind, it is now more usually seen as part of the conscious mind also. Contains all the internalised moral and social standards which guide behaviour. Composed of two parts: the *ego ideal* containing all those socially-approved standards; and the *conscience* which includes

information about negative views of particular behaviours. It is the source of feelings of guilt.

As already indicated, Freud viewed humans as inherently anti-social. What makes them social, what enables them to survive, is the regulation or control of their pleasure-seeking impulses. This is done in two main ways. The id is opposed by the functioning of the ego guided by the *reality principle*. Second, the ego itself is guided by the superego as part of the process of regulating the id. In contemporary psychoanalytic theory the superego is partly conceived of as a *conscience* which works to neutralise impulses that run contrary to internalised moral rules. In this manner, the superego represents the internalisation of group norms and it is the inadequate formation or functioning of the superego that is generally central to psychoanalytic accounts of crime.

Three main sources of crime are identified in such work and these relate to harsh, deviant or weak superegos. The existence of a harsh superego may lead to extreme guilt, and to acting-out behaviour which subconsciously invites punishment. Such behaviours are akin to *neuroses* and in one version of the theory such criminality is a product of unconscious guilt over infantile desires. Alternatively, such behaviour may represent a substitute for security or for status needs not met elsewhere.

The second source relates to the weak superego and this tends to be associated with self-centredness, impulsivity and, therefore, psychopathy. Here individuals are portrayed as egocentric and lacking in guilt. The primitive and instinctual needs displayed by the id are subjected to insufficient regulation by the superego. Some neo-psychoanalytic work, such as that by John Bowlby, which focused on such issues as 'maternal deprivation' and linked it to juvenile delinquency, talked of such individuals as displaying an 'affectionless character' (we return to this below).

The final source of delinquent conduct results from the deviant superego – where the superego standards develop normally, but the standards are deviant (reflecting *deviant identification*) – possibly as a result of close attachment between a child and a criminal parent. The consequence of such attachment is an absence of guilt about particular types of behaviour. Though such ideas have had relatively little direct influence on criminological theory they have, as Howitt argues, had a more significant impact in directing some criminological researchers toward the issue of the impact of early life experiences, such as parenting, on criminality.

According to Blackburn (1993) such psychodynamic theories rest on three major claims:

1 Socialisation depends on the internalisation of society's rules during early childhood.

2 Impaired parent–infant relationships are causally related to later criminal behaviour.

3 Unconscious conflicts arising from disturbed family relationships at different stages of development – particularly the oedipal stage – are the causes of *some* criminal acts.

The first of these assumptions is pretty much common to most psychological and all sociological theorising. The second assumption is also present in much criminological work in some form, and certainly informs current risk and protective factors research, for example. It is the third assumption that distinguishes psychoanalytic approaches from most other attempts to explain criminal conduct. Furthermore, it only attempts to account for particular types of criminality, particularly those identified in some way as involving irrational behaviour.

Whilst potentially helpful, in Blackburn's (1993) view, psychoanalysis fails to account for a number of important features of criminal behaviour and, in particular, the age distribution of offending. Thus, whilst using such a perspective might be used to account for the emergence of various behaviours in puberty, it would not be able to explain the generalised desistance from delinquency that occurs in late adolescence. Nor, he argues, can such approaches easily account for the higher rates of offending among males given that in psychoanalysis females are argued to have weaker superegos.

Bowlby and 'maternal deprivation'

Working broadly in the psychoanalytic tradition, one of the better known psychological theories of delinquency is John Bowlby's notion of 'maternal deprivation'. In Bowlby's view, children require consistent and continuous care from a primary care-giver until the age of five. Disruption to this relationship may have harmful consequences, in particular that the child may have difficulty later in establishing relationships. Bowlby's research draw on the experiences of 44 young people referred to child guidance clinics because of delinquent behaviour (theft) and a matched group of 'non-delinquents'. Almost two-fifths (39%) of the delinquent group had experienced significant disruption in their relationships with their mothers (at least six months of separation) prior to the age

of five compared with only five per cent of the comparison group. One of Bowlby's cases involved a child who was hospitalised for almost a year beginning before he reached the age of one. This child was reported to have called his mother 'nurse' when he returned home and had profound difficulties in establishing affectionate relationships with his family. His experience captures the essence of the maternal deprivation thesis.

The thrust of Bowlby's theory was later encapsulated in arguments about the role of 'broken homes' and 'latchkey children' in delinquency, and about family dysfunction more generally. There is now much evidence which links problems within the family to delinquency in children, though it tends to point to factors other than separation from parents, and generally posits a more complex relationship between family functioning and crime.

However, Bowlby's work has been criticised for a number of methodological and empirical reasons. These included the nature of his sample which was argued to be unrepresentative and was anyway very small, and also his research design, which had a poorly matched control group. Famously, Barbara Wootton (1959) criticised Bowlby's thesis on three other grounds:

- That no evidence had been offered to suggest that any damage done by the experience of separation was irreversible.

- That maternal separation is not uncommon among the population more generally and that the theory therefore over-predicts delinquency.

- That separation is not the same as deprivation – that is to say that it is the quality of the relationship that is important.

One critic, Michael Rutter, challenged Bowlby's emphasis on the importance of physical separation in childhood, arguing that empirical research challenged this finding. However, the same research did show important associations between family discord and delinquency (Rutter, 1972; Rutter and Giller, 1983). It remains the case, however, that early socialisation experiences are shown in many longitudinal studies to be closely linked with later behavioural outcomes. A study in the north of England (Kolvin *et al.*, 1988) found that boys experiencing divorce or separation before the age of five had almost double the risk of conviction before the age of 32 (53% as against 28%). Similarly, Henry *et al.* (1996) in their New Zealand-based study found that boys from single-parent families had a heightened risk of later conviction (see also McCord, 1982).

Indeed, more generally psychoanalytically-influenced theories have become less popular as a means of explaining delinquency. According to Rutter and Giller (1983: 257) this is not because empirical research has provided powerful evidence that such theories are wrong, but rather that 'the theories have not proved to be particularly useful either in furthering our understanding of crime or in devising effective methods of intervention'.

Learning theories

An important approach within psychology sees offending, like all behaviours, as something that is learned. Perhaps the best known forerunner of behavioural learning theory – and one of the few psychological experiments that most people will have heard about – is the work of Ivan Pavlov (1849–1936). His Nobel prize-winning work illustrated how behaviour, in this case reflexes, could be modified through experience. Famously, he showed how dogs presented with food accompanied by the ringing of a bell could eventually be made to salivate simply through the ringing of the bell on its own. This he termed *conditioning* and is sometimes referred to as *Pavlovian* or *classical condi-*

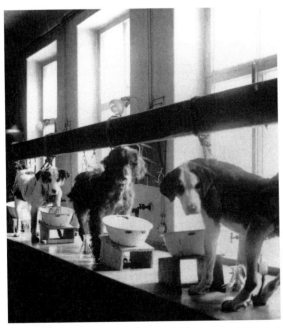

'Pavlov's Dogs.' Now one of the most famous conditioning experiments, they were carried out in Pavlov's laboratory in St Petersburg, Russia, in the 1890s and 1900s.

tioning. In addition, psychologists have identified what they call *instrumental conditioning* – or *operant conditioning* – where behaviour is influenced by the consequences that follow, or are anticipated to follow, from it, such as rewards or punishments.

From theories of *classical conditioning* onward, psychologists and others have looked to explain human behaviour as a consequence of the interaction of the individual and the world in which they live. Modern learning theories understand behaviour to be a consequence of contact with others, particularly via primary sources of socialisation such as the family and peer groups. One approach to learning that has been particularly influential within criminology is Edwin Sutherland's theory of differential association. We will encounter this in greater detail in Chapter 10, though it is important to outline its major features here before moving on to other learning theories.

Differential association

At the heart of Sutherland's theory is the idea that conduct is learned through coming into contact with social norms. The nature of one's conduct is therefore influenced by the norms present in the particular groups of which one is a member and other members of which one comes into contact with on a regular basis. Through learning and imitation such contact helps to mould individual behaviour. Group norms include attitudes toward the law and its transgression, and Sutherland's theory postulated that it was the balance in human interactions between contact with attitudes favourable to socially acceptable conduct and attitudes favouring deviance that influences behaviour itself.

Now it will be immediately clear that this is not straightforwardly classifiable as a psychological theory. Sutherland was a sociologist and one of the key figures of the Chicago school (see Chapter 9). His theory of differential association, however, involved both individual and social factors and, as such, another reason for Sutherland's importance is the attempt he made via this theory to bring both psychological and sociological matters to bear on the question of how to understand criminal conduct.

'Becoming deviant' for Sutherland is, therefore, a fairly mundane process involving the learning of attitudes and values that affect choices in just the same way all behaviours are learned. The term *differential association* quite specifically points in the direction of the two central elements of the theory: that criminal behaviour is learned, and that it is learned in association with others (not necessarily people who are themselves involved in crime) – what is learned tending to reflect the balance of 'definitions' favourable or unfavourable towards breaking the law.

One of the great advantages of the theory is its relative simplicity. There are, however, a number of difficulties also, and Sutherland's theory has come in for sustained criticism. One concerns the question of why in apparently similar circumstances, where individuals should be subject to a similar 'balance of definitions', some choose to deviate and others don't. The idea, favoured by Sutherland, that it should be possible to quantify pro-criminal or anti-criminal definitions or values that people come into contact with, is almost certainly impossible in practice, even should someone show any desire to try. In a similar vein, others have pointed to the difficulty within Sutherland's theory of distinguishing between the quantity of definitions favouring particular courses of action versus the quality or power of particular definitions. In other words, is it not possible that the opinions and views of one or two very powerful or influential people will outweigh the views of numerous other, less influential people?

Operant learning

The principles of operant learning underpin what has come to be known as *behaviourism* within psychology. This approach is overwhelmingly associated with the work of B.F. Skinner (1953), an American psychologist who studied how the consequences of particular actions shape future behaviour (see box below).

At the heart of operant learning theory is the apparently simple idea that behaviour resulting in consequences felt to be desirable will tend to increase in frequency, whereas behaviour that results in undesirable outcomes will decrease. The former behaviour has been *reinforced* whereas the latter has been *punished*. At the core of Skinner's behavioural theory – the ABC of behaviourism – are three elements:

- the Antecedent conditions prompt particular
- Behaviour, which in its own turn produces the
- Consequences.

There are two types of reinforcement and two types of punishment. Positive reinforcement produces rewarding consequences thereby encouraging similar behaviour in the future. Negative reinforcement also encourages similar behaviour, but in this case by removing consequences that are adverse. Punishment leads to declining frequency of particular forms of behaviour, either positively by producing negative consequences, or negatively through the removal of some desirable goal.

B.F. (Burrhus Frederick) Skinner (1904–1990)

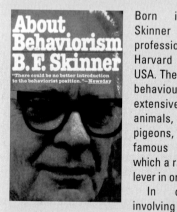

Born in Pennsylvania, Skinner spent most of his professional career at Harvard University in the USA. The founder of modern behaviourism, Skinner did extensive research with animals, notably rats and pigeons, and invented the famous Skinner box, in which a rat learns to press a lever in order to obtain food.

In one experiment involving rats, Skinner discovered that the frequency with which they engaged in particular behaviours, such as pressing a bar in order to get food, was influenced not by prior factors – as Pavlov thought to be the case – but by what happened as a result of the particular action. This he called *operant behaviour* and he spent much of his early career studying *operant conditioning* in various organisms.

Along with Freud he is perhaps the best known psychologist of the twentieth century.

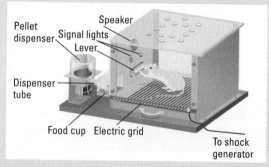

A rat in a Skinner box – or 'operant conditioning chamber' – learning to press a lever in order to release food.

Now, it should be clear why such ideas are included under the heading of psychological *positivism*. In operant learning theory behaviour is fundamentally shaped by factors outside the individual, factors that can be identified and measured and, consequently, treated as *causes* of particular types of conduct. Equally, however, the potential shortcomings of such an approach are also straightforward to discern. At least in the form presented so far, there appears little scope for individual agency or choice. If our behaviour results from positive and negative reinforcements external to us, in what ways do our own thoughts and emotions affect any decisions we may make?

A variation on operant learning can be found in Jeffery's work on *differential reinforcement* (Jeffery, 1965). Adapting Sutherland's ideas of differential association using the theory of operant conditioning, Jeffery argued that criminal behaviour is learned as a result of the reinforcing consequences of particular behaviours. An individual's learning history therefore becomes vital in understanding their decisions in relation to crime (to engage in criminal activity, or not). Crime may have a number of benefits as well as negative consequences and, in the main, it is to the balance of particular rewards and punishments that we should look in attempting to explain patterns of offending:

> The theory of differential reinforcement states that a criminal act occurs in an environment in which in the past the actor has been reinforced for behaving in this manner, and the aversive consequences attached to the behaviour are of such a nature that they do not control or prevent the response. (quoted in Hollin, 1989: 42)

Social learning theory

Social learning theory emerged in the 1970s as the product of two hitherto largely separate theories: behaviourism (which sought to mould psychology into a hard, 'objective' science and, arguably, is responsible for many of the misgivings about psychology currently held by many criminologists) and cognitive psychology. There was seemingly relatively little contact between behaviourists and cognitive psychologists for the bulk of the twentieth century (McGuire, 2004) with something of a thawing beginning in the 1970s. The emergence of social learning theory and the work of Albert Bandura and colleagues illustrated how the two traditions might be married in some ways – social learning theory combining the ideas that observa-

tional learning and direct conditioning are both important in understanding human behaviour. Out of such combinations came a new set of interventions known as *cognitive-behavioural therapies*.

There are three linked psychological concepts at the heart of cognitive social learning theory: learning, social and cognition. The term *learning* indicates that an important element in the theory is the assumption that many things humans do are learned, including very basic apparently physical functions. However, unlike most other species such learning takes place in a *social* context. The crucial distinction between humans and other species, though, is undoubtedly the complex nature of the human brain – the basis of our consciousness and of processes such as perception, understanding, imagining, and dreaming. These and other processes are known generally as *cognition*. McGuire (2004: 59) defines cognition as 'mental events which each of us directly experiences, but which we cannot directly observe in others'.

In fact, the roots of social learning theory are to be found in the work of the French sociologist Gabriel Tarde and his three laws of imitation (Tarde, 1903), the first of which – that people engage in imitation of others in proportion to the degree of contact they have with them – had influenced Edwin Sutherland. Social learning theory is associated primarily with Bandura (1977). The approach uses and extends notions of operant learning and, via the work of others such as Ron Akers, also amplifies Sutherland's theory of differential association.

The core difference between operant and social learning theories is that whereas the former stressed the importance of the environment – social reinforcements and punishments – the latter maintains that it is also possible to learn cognitively through observing the behaviour of others, what Bandura called *models*. Having been learned then environmental reinforcements and punishments come into play in the fashion suggested by Skinner and others. Social learning theory also includes a consideration of *motivation,* and here Bandura pointed to three types:

- *external reinforcement* (from the environment);
- *vicarious reinforcement* (from observing others);
- *self-reinforcement* (as a result of taking pleasure or pride from one's own actions).

In this sense we learn from observing others, and are likely to be particularly influenced if they are high status (rather like Tarde's second law of imita-

Illustrations from Bandura's famous Bobo doll experiment. Here both the model and the children are shown hitting the Bobo doll with a mallet.

tion) and our behaviour is then moulded by the nature of the external influences and reinforcements that occur.

One of Bandura's best-known studies was briefly described in Chapter 4. In what has become known as the 'Bobo doll study', Bandura sought to examine and measure the impact of watching filmed images of aggression on children. This has become one of the best known experiments in the 'media effects' field, and is illustrative of aspects of Bandura's social learning theory (see also Chapter 4). It also illustrates the way in which experimental designs have been used in psychological research for a long time (the results of Bandura's experiment being published in 1961) even though they are only now beginning to be used to any extent within criminology.

The Bobo doll experiment

The subjects were 36 boys and 36 girls enrolled in the Stanford University Nursery School. They ranged in age from 37 to 69 months, with a mean age of 52 months. Two adults, a male and a female, served in the role of model, and one female experimenter conducted the study for all 72 children …

Subjects were divided into eight experimental groups of six subjects each and a control group consisting of 24 subjects. Half the experimental subjects were exposed to aggressive models and half were exposed to models that were subdued and nonaggressive in their behaviour.

In the first step in the procedure subjects were brought individually by the experimenter to the experimental room and the model … was invited by the experimenter to come and join in the game … After having settled the subject in his corner, the experimenter escorted the model to the opposite corner of the room which contained a small table and chair, a tinker toy set, a mallet, and a 5-foot inflated Bobo doll. The experimenter explained that these were the materials provided for the model to play with and, after the model was seated, the experimenter left the room.

With subjects in the *non-aggressive condition*, the model assembled the tinker toys in a quiet subdued manner totally ignoring the Bobo doll.

In contrast, with subjects in the *aggressive condition*, the model began by assembling the tinker toys but after approximately a minute had elapsed, the model turned to the Bobo doll and spent the remainder of the period aggressing toward it … [I]n addition to punching the Bobo doll, a response likely to be performed by children independently of demonstration, the model exhibited distinctive aggressive acts which were to be scored as imitative responses. The model laid Bobo on its side, sat on it and punched it repeatedly in the nose. The model then raised the Bobo doll, picked up the mallet and struck the doll on the head. Following the mallet aggression, the model tossed the doll up in the air aggressively and kicked it about the room. This sequence of physically aggressive acts was repeated approximately three times, interspersed with verbally aggressive responses such as, 'Sock him in the nose ... ,' 'Hit him down ... ,' 'Throw him in the air ... ,' 'Kick him ....'

Subjects were tested for the amount of imitative learning in a different experimental room ... Prior to the test for imitation, however, all subjects ... were subjected to mild aggression arousal to insure that they were under some degree of instigation to aggression ...

Subjects in the aggression condition reproduced a good deal of physical and verbal aggressive behaviour resembling that of the models, and their mean scores differed markedly from those of subjects in the non-aggressive and control groups who exhibited virtually no imitative aggression ... Subjects in the aggressive condition also exhibited significantly more partially imitative and non-imitative aggressive behaviour and were generally less inhibited in their behaviour than subjects in the non-aggressive condition.

Source: Bandura *et al.* (1961: 575–582).

Thus, in social learning theory, it is assumed that particular stimuli may gave rise to a number of different consequences depending on the nature of the intervening processes such as attention, memory and understanding. It has three elements or 'domains' – behaviour, thoughts and feelings – and is often presented using the following mnemonic (McGuire, 2004):

S = Stimulus: the external event or conditions impinging on the person.

O = Organism: the internal state of the individual, including current representations of the external world, and their history.

R = Response: the behavioural or motor reaction.

C = Consequences: the pattern of reinforcers or punishers which follow.

At the core of this model lies the processing of information and sequences of action. Such processing may be *automatic,* i.e. largely automatic, or *controlled,* which calls for significantly more awareness, attention and effort – as in the solving of problems. The importance of all this for the criminologist, McGuire argues, is that it aids an understanding of both processes and individual differences. Internal psychological events are involved in all behaviours, including criminal ones. That is to say, 'crime events consist of, or are the result of, individual acts linked to other activities such as thoughts, feelings, attitudes or interpersonal exchanges' (2004: 71). Moreover, he suggests that different categories of crime can be placed on a continuum related to the degree to which individual differences have contributed to them.

A version of this approach has been utilised in the study of crime, principally by Ron Akers. From this perspective criminal behaviour occurs as a result of either operant conditioning or imitation. Such imitation or modelling occurs within the family, peer group and so on as well as through media and other cultural sources of information. Social responses to criminal behaviour, depending on their nature, will reinforce the behaviour negatively or positively, as will the impact that the behaviour has upon personal feelings of pride and self-esteem. This led Burgess and Akers (1966: 146) to revise Sutherland's set of propositions about criminal behaviour. They argue:

1 Criminal behaviour is learned according to the principles of operant conditioning.

2 Criminal behaviour is learned both in non-social situations that are reinforcing or discriminative and through that social interaction in which the behaviour of other persons is reinforcing or discriminative for criminal behaviour.

3 The principal part of the learning of criminal behaviour occurs in those groups that make up the individual's major source of reinforcement.

4 The learning of criminal behaviour (including specific techniques, attitudes, and avoidance procedures) is a function of the effective and available reinforcers and the existing reinforcement contingencies.

5 The specific class of behaviours that are learned and their frequency of occurrence are a function of the reinforcers that are effective and available and the rules or norms by which these reinforcers are applied.

6 Criminal behaviour is a function of norms that are discriminative for criminal behaviour, the learning of which takes place when such behaviour is more highly reinforced than non-criminal behaviour.

7 The strength of criminal behaviour is a direct function of the amount, frequency, and probability of its reinforcement. These interactions rely on norms, attitudes, and orientations.

Hollin (1992: 61) describes Akers' approach as 'perhaps the most psychologically complete mainstream theory in criminology', and he quotes Akers as saying:

> The full behavioural formula in social learning theory includes both positive and negative punishment and positive and negative reinforcement. It also includes schedules of reinforcement, imitation, associations, normative definitions (attitudes and rationalisations), discriminative stimuli, and other variables in both criminal and conforming behaviour.

More recently Akers has revised his theoretical approach further and has offered what he terms a *social learning and social structure* model of crime. This acknowledges what Akers takes to be the important role of social structures in the determination of criminal behaviours, but argues that these are mediated by social learning processes. He identi-

fies four dimensions of social structure that provide the context for social learning (see Figure 7.2):

● *Differential social organisation* – Those aspects of community – age, population density, etc. – that affect crime rates.

● *Differential location in the social structure* – The social and demographic characteristics that identify people's social status.

● *Theoretically defined structural variables* – Social disorganisation, anomie, class relations, patriarchy and other theoretical ideas.

● *Differential social location* – People: membership of family, peer groups and other social groups.

Rational choice

Although we deal with rational choice theory in greater detail in Chapter 14, a brief discussion here is necessary as there are connections between rational choice and learning theories. Indeed, some commentators view rational choice as simply one version of learning theory. The primary link is the emphasis in learning theories on the importance of reinforcement – positive or negative – as the basis on which certain behaviours are selected. In such a view, courses of action occur, in fact are chosen, because of the benefits or deficits that are anticipated to result. Similarly, in rational choice theory, the underlying assumption is that actors make cal-

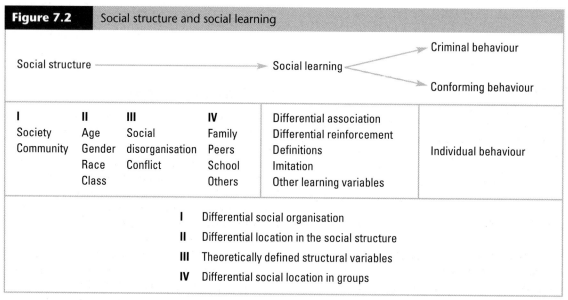

Figure 7.2 Social structure and social learning

Social structure ⟶				Social learning ⟨ Criminal behaviour / Conforming behaviour	
I Society Community	**II** Age Gender Race Class	**III** Social disorganisation Conflict	**IV** Family Peers School Others	Differential association Differential reinforcement Definitions Imitation Other learning variables	Individual behaviour

	I	Differential social organisation
	II	Differential location in the social structure
	III	Theoretically defined structural variables
	IV	Differential social location in groups

Source: Akers (1998).

culations about future courses of action on the basis of some assessment, however incomplete or inadequate, of the balance between the benefits or problems that will result.

Not all commentators are comfortable with the link between rational choice and learning theory, and Akers (1998), for example, queries whether rational choice is really a theory at all. On the other hand, for some of its proponents, rational choice theory is more attractive than learning theory because it is argued to be less deterministic in that it allows for greater initiative and choice on the part of the individual.

There is now a substantial body of evidence derived from research applying rational choice theory – particularly in the field of crime prevention. Studies, varied in approach, have shown, for example, that:

- Changing the design of products ('design against crime') – making cars more difficult to break into – can reduce crime markedly (Ekblom, 2005).
- Urban graffiti and theft can be substantially reduced as a result of increased surveillance (van Andel, 1989; Poyner, 1991).
- Reducing opportunities for trading in stolen goods not only reduces such activities but also reduces theft and burglary (Sutton, 2005).
- Increased natural surveillance through the trimming of hedges and trees and the enhancement of street lighting can reduce residential burglary (Ramsay, 1991).
- 'Target removal' can have a very substantial impact on crime – for example through cash reduction measures on public transport (Clarke and McGrath, 1990).

Routine activity theory

Linked with rational choice theory but focusing more broadly on what its proponents argue are the three core components in the commission of crime, routine activity theory is again an amalgam of psychological and sociological insights. Cohen and Felson (1979) argue that there are three necessary elements for the commission of most crimes:

- suitable targets (things worth stealing, attacking, etc.);
- a motivated offender (understood through rational choice theory);
- the absence of a 'capable guardian' (someone or something that might ordinarily deter the crime).

Broadly speaking, routine activities and linked ideas are classified as 'opportunity theories', focusing as they do on the ways in which opportunities affect decision-making by actual or potential offenders and how such opportunities can be manipulated so as to reduce or prevent crime. (Both rational choice and routine activities are discussed in detail in Chapter 14.)

Review questions

1 What did Bowlby mean by 'maternal deprivation' and how was this thought to link with crime?

2 What is the fundamental idea in 'operant learning' theory?

3 In what ways is 'differential association' a psychological theory?

4 What was being tested in the Bobo doll experiment?

5 In what ways might we consider offenders to be rational actors?

Cognitive theories

We have already seen, for example, how Akers' theory aims to take account of human cognition (at its simplest, this simply means 'thinking') in the social learning process. There are a number of theoretical approaches within psychology which focus centrally on the relationship between cognition and crime. Again, such ideas have close connections with elements of rational choice theory.

Yochelson and Samenow

Based on research with male offenders, some of whom were young offenders identified via community clinics, but the majority of whom were adult offenders committed to hospital for psychiatric evaluation, Yochelson and Samenow claimed to have identified the 'thinking patterns' that they suggested characterised all criminals. At the heart of their study, *The Criminal Personality*, is the suggestion that there are a number of identifiable flawed ways of thinking that are common to criminals. What turns someone into a criminal is a series of choices they make from early in life.

Whereas most people are able to make rational decisions, the criminal personality features a range

Figure 7.3	Yochelson and Samenow's 'thinking errors' in the criminal personality		
	Character traits	**Automatic errors of thinking**	**Errors associated with criminal acts**
Types of error	• Pervasive fearfulness • Feelings of worthlessness • Need for power and control • Perfectionism • Need for sexual excitement	• Lying • Poor decision-making • Lack of trust • Secretiveness • Failure to understand others' positions • Failure to assume obligations • Fantasies of anti-social behaviour	• 'Corrosion' of internal and external deterrents • Super-optimism

Derived from: Putwain and Sammons (2002); Blackburn (1993).

of thinking errors. There are something between 40–50 of these, and they can be grouped into three categories: character traits; automatic errors; and, errors associated with criminal acts (see Figure 7.3).

At least three possible shortcomings of Yochelson and Samenow's personality theory can be identified:

- The definition of 'criminality' is value-laden and is essentially based on a subjective distinction between those taken to be behaving responsibly and 'criminals' who are treated effectively as a different breed.

- No attempt was made by Yochelson and Samenow to show that the thinking errors they claim to have identified in criminals are not also made by others – there was, for example, no comparison or control group.

- Their sample is unrepresentative (including many individuals who were in institutions having been judged 'not guilty by reason of insanity'), and yet their claims are generalised to the offending population more broadly.

Stanton Samenow on his study with Samuel Yochelson

In 1970, two years after receiving a doctorate in clinical psychology from the University of Michigan, I joined Samuel Yochelson, a psychiatrist and psychologist, in his Program for the Investigation of Criminal Behavior located in Washington D.C. ... Serving as a clinical research psychologist, I collaborated with Dr Yochelson in what turned out to be a 17 year research-treatment study of career criminals ...

The findings of the study were highly controversial, largely because they ran counter to pervasive thinking in the United States about the causes of crime ... The prevailing thinking was (and still is in many quarters) that people are influenced or forced into crime by poverty, divorce, abusive parents, peer pressure, and other environmental factors. We found this not to be so. More critical than specific environmental factors is how human beings choose to deal with the environment in which they find themselves ...

Some critics dismissed our work out of hand by asserting that there is no such entity as a 'criminal mind' – that under sufficiently adverse circumstances anyone can become a criminal. Although hypothetically this may be so, in reality this contention is glib and absurd ... The youngster with the incipient criminal personality reacts to consequences differently from his responsible counterpart. Every boy who steals a candy bar does not become a one-man crime wave. For most young first-time shoplifters who are caught and punished, that is the end of the thievery. Not so for others, who conclude that the next time they need to be slicker to avoid detection.

Dr Yochelson identified the 'errors in thinking' that we all make from time to time. The individual who is extreme in these thinking errors pursues excitement by doing the forbidden and builds himself up at the expense of others. Human relationships are seen by these people as avenues for conquest and triumph. Any means to self-serving ends, including deception, intimidation and brute force, are employed without considering the impact on others ...

Dr Yochelson did more than describe the criminal's patterns of thinking in meticulous detail: he piloted a program to help offenders change. By knowing their fears and vulnerabilities, a change agent can get his foot in the door and begin a constructive dialogue with an offender who long has sought to control others while regarding himself as the hub of a wheel around which all else revolves.

Source: Samenow (2006: 71–7).

Nevertheless, though not directly drawn from Yochelson and Samenow's work, there is now a strong body of work that focuses directly on offenders' decision-making processes as part of the process of 'rehabilitation'. Thus, 'cognitive skills training' programmes focus on ways of enabling offenders to develop their abilities in relation to considering and resolving everyday decisions and problems. The probation service in the UK regularly uses a number of tools, such as PICTS (the Psychological Inventory of Criminal Thinking Styles) which draws on related cognitive theory by Ross and Fabiano (1985) as part of the process of assessing the impact of interventions with groups of offenders.

Piaget, Kohlberg, moral development and crime

By contrast with Yochelson and Samenow's focus on cognitive development, Piaget and Kohlberg's concern was with moral development. Piaget's concern was with the process of maturation and how cognition is structured and operates. He argued (Piaget, 1952) that the child's reasoning goes through four main stages, distinguishing primarily between young children who view moral rules in fairly fixed ways and older children who are able progressively to apply a more flexible form of understanding (Palmer, 2003):

- *Sensorimotor stage* (birth to 18 months) – A stage in which the child depends upon sensory and motor skills.
- *Preoperational stage* (18 months to six years) – A period during which the child is able to form mental images as well as understand things physically. The child begins to learn to classify objects through identifying similarities and differences.
- *Concrete operational stage* (six years to early adolescence) – A period in which children are able to use abstract rules and categories and to use inductive logic (drawing broad lessons from particular experiences).

Jean Piaget (1896–1980), a Swiss biologist who originally studied molluscs and published scientific papers while still at school, later became one of the world's best-known developmental psychologists. He famously identified four stages in child development.

- *Formal operational stage* (early adolescence onwards) – A stage characterised by the ability to use complex problem-solving.

Following Piaget, Kohlberg identified a set of levels and stages of moral development. Kohlberg identified three levels and six stages of moral development (see Figure 7.4). Each of the three levels represents a changing relationship between self and society, the first of which characterises pre-adolescent children, the second being reached by most adults and the third only by a minority of adults. Progression from one stage to another depends on cognitive development.

Underpinning each of the stages identified by Kohlberg – and differentiating this theory from Piaget's – is a conception of social perspective-taking (how the child/adolescent views the world).

Figure 7.4	Levels and stages of moral development (Kohlberg)

Level 1: Pre-conventional or pre-moral

> *Stage 1 – Obedience and punishment orientation* – Right action consists of obedience to rules backed by punishment administered by powerful others.

> *Stage 2 – Instrumental purpose and exchange* – Right action is what serves someone's immediate interest. Emphasis on meeting one's own needs while recognising those of others.

Level 2: Conventional

> *Stage 3 – Interpersonal accord and conformity* – Right action consists of living up to one's expected roles. Behaviour judged in terms of good intentions, trust, loyalty, concern.

> *Stage 4 – Social accord and system maintenance* – Right consists of fulfilling one's agreed duties, upholding laws and contributing socially.

Level 3: Post-conventional or principled

> *Stage 5 – Social contract* – Right action is what upholds general rules and values as part of the social contract.

> *Stage 6 – Universal ethical principles* – Right is defined in terms of self-chosen and universal ethical principles of justice, human rights and dignity.

Source: Blackburn (1993).

The respective perspectives of the different stages are as follows:

Stage 1: Concerned with how the self relates to perceived authority figures.

Stage 2: Interests are understood in relation to the interests of others.

Stage 3: Behaviour is understood as being located within a network of other relationships.

Stage 4: Involves an understanding of the wider social system.

Stages 5/6: Involve an understanding of underlying moral principles.

In essence, therefore, the argument is that the relationship between the individual and social rules and norms differs depending on the stage of moral reasoning that has been reached:

- *Preconventional* – Rules and social expectations are seen as being external to the person.
- *Conventional* – Rules and expectations are internalised.
- *Postconventional* – Self and social rules and expectations are differentiated. The individual defines their own values using selections from universal moral principles (Palmer, 2003).

Kohlberg's theory can be applied to the study of delinquency. Offending behaviour, in this view, is associated with less mature moral development. Delinquents in Kohlberg's terms are more likely to display pre-conventional moral reasoning. The logical implication of this is that the restricted ability to think in more complex moral terms restricts individual decision-making and, in combination with other factors, makes rule-breaking more likely.

Kohlberg focused on 'moral reasoning' rather than 'moral conduct' and one potential limitation of his theory concerns whether there is any necessary link between reasoning and behaviour. That is to say, it is perfectly possible in principle for someone to be able to reason very effectively in the abstract, and yet behave according to different principles in practice. Nevertheless, whilst Kohlberg's theory was not, strictly speaking, a theory of criminal behaviour, there is empirical support for the idea that immature moral development is related to delinquent conduct. However, this is not a consistent finding in research and there remain doubts as to whether moral reasoning is a potential explanation for offending or simply one of several factors that it is important to take into consideration.

There are numerous ways in which moral reasoning may be related to offending:

- Moral development is likely to be heavily influenced through the nature of interaction with peers, parents and others.
- Parenting processes may affect moral reasoning through:

– the type and extent of discipline used;

– the extent and type of supervision;

– the nature of interaction within the family (affected by family size, for example);

– family structure, such as the presence/absence of two parents.

As a consequence, quite a broad range of intervention programmes have been developed in recent years which focus on offenders' reasoning. These include parenting programmes, anger-management or control training, and multi-modal interventions such as the 'Reasoning and Rehabilitation' programme developed in Canada (Ross *et al.*, 1988) and the 'Think First' programme from England and Wales (McGuire, 2005). Cognitive programmes are discussed further in Chapter 33.

Eysenck's biosocial theory

Eysenck's personality theory is *biosocial* in the sense that his aim was to combine biological, individual and social factors in a theory of criminal behaviour. Eysenck believed that the study of twins provided strong evidence for the importance of genetics in explaining crime, citing evidence from a comparison of monozygotic (identical genetic make-up) and dizygotic (some genetic make-up shared) twins which appeared to show that identical twins were much more likely to be similar in terms of their offending than were non-identical twins. As we saw in the previous chapter, there are a number of problems with such arguments, not least that they fail fully to deal with all the other potential influences which might go to explain such similarity and difference – such as the social contexts in which such twins grow up.

Eysenck also argued that there were physical differences between criminals and non-criminals. Picking up on work by Sheldon which identified three different body types, Eysenck went on to argue for the existence of three different components of personality which he considered to be linked to criminality. As we saw in Chapter 7, Sheldon's three different body types were:

- *endomorphs* (people who tend toward being fat around the stomach/abdomen and whom he believed to be sociable and good at communicating);

- *ectomorphs* (people with an overabundance of sense organs in their nervous system and brain

Hans Jurgen Eysenck (1916–1997)

Born in Berlin, Eysenck left Germany in the 1930s seeking exile first in France and then England.

In England he studied under Cyril Burt and after the Second World War founded the Psychological Department at the newly created Institute of Psychiatry in London.

He was responsible for the introduction of clinical psychology as a profession in the UK. Highly prolific, he wrote over 50 books and over 900 articles and was also the founding editor of the journal *Personality and Individual Differences*.

His research was often controversial and included such subjects as personality, race and intelligence, behavioural genetics, the health hazards of smoking, and astrology.

In the 1970s and 1980s in particular Eysenck's writings on race and IQ (for example in *Race, Intelligence and Education*, 1971) aroused widespread opposition, with demonstrations taking place at institutions where he was asked to speak.

Eysenck was also a contributor to the *Black Papers* (1971), a series of polemical – and highly influential – pamphlets that sought to reverse the 'progressive' educational policies of the time.

compared to their body mass and whom he believed to be adventurous, desirous of power, risk-taking and ruthless);

- *mesomorphs* (whom he took to be thin, bony and, possibly, muscular and whom he believed to be private and solitary, not especially sociable and sensitive to pain).

Eysenck identified three personality components which show some obvious links to Sheldon's model (the characteristics listed apply to people scoring highly on the particular dimension):

- *Extroversion (E)* – Assertive, creative, dominant, active and sensation-seeking.
- *Neuroticism (N)* – Anxious, depressed, emotional, low self-esteem, moody, shy.
- *Psychoticism (P)* – Aggressive, anti-social, egocentric, impulsive and lacking empathy.

Each of these three characteristics is a separate element of personality. In Eysenck's view, criminals display higher levels of all three characteristics, though it is the combination of the levels rather than the dimensions on their own that he took to

be important. Higher levels of psychoticism are almost a given in that, by definition, psychoticism tends to involve criminal conduct. The reasoning behind the association of high E and N with criminal behaviour links to the notion of *conditioning* or, more particularly, the process by which children come during socialisation to associate anti-social behaviour with punishment. Over time children develop a fear response which progressively restricts anti-social impulses. The biological basis of the theory lies in Eysenck's argument that this process – conditioning – works to differing extents in different people and that this is largely genetically determined. Offenders are characterised by low conditionability (see Figure 7.5).

Eysenck's theory has been widely tested and, although the results are perhaps predictably mixed, there seems to be evidence that offenders will consistently score high in relation to psychoticism, and will tend to score higher on neuroticism (Eysenck and Gudjonsson, 1989; Bartol, 1999). Evidence in relation to extroversion is inconsistent. Though discussion to date has talked of 'offenders' as a single group, Eysenck also suggested that research might

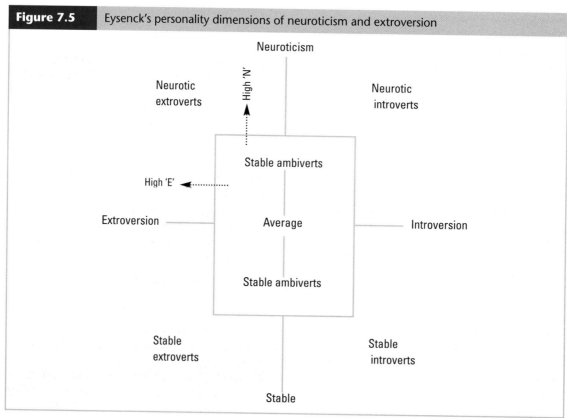

| Figure 7.5 | Eysenck's personality dimensions of neuroticism and extroversion |

Source: Hollin (1992).

profitably be conducted in order to look at personality variation among offenders:

> Now it seems unlikely in the extreme that there are no personality differences between different types of criminals ... Gang crimes would appear likely to involve high E personalities; aggressive crimes and crimes involving unnecessary cruelty seem to carry implications of high P; the ineffectual crimes often committed by aging recidivists might be due to the social incapacities of the introvert. It would seem to follow that by paying attention to differences *within* the criminal group in respect to P, E and N, i.e. by constructing a *typology* of crimes to take its place beside our typology of *people*, we should be able to get much greater differences between controls and *homogenous* groups of criminals that we have obtained from our *total* group of criminals. (Eysenck, 1970: 236)

Critics of Eysenck's work have focused on the biological basis of the theory, the lack (some allege) of empirical support for its main propositions, and its positivistic assumptions which imply clear and consistent differences between 'criminals' and 'non-criminals'. Eysenck's biological positivism can be clearly seen in his use of somatyping as a component in his explanation. Thus, in *Crime and Personality* (1977: 146–7) Eysenck argued 'that criminals, on the whole, tend to be athletic in body build, that is stocky and muscular rather than fat, and that they tend to show a temperamental tendency towards extraversion, particularly towards impulsiveness'.

Eysenck's determinism and biological positivism can also be seen in the tendency in some of his work to assume that it is possible to treat criminals and non-criminals as two distinct social groups. In one study, for example, the Eysencks compared a group of 603 prisoners from two prisons and a remand centre with two control groups, one of what are described as 'male non-prisoners ... selected in the course of an investigation of the relation between personality and sport' and a group of university students. Reporting the results of the study the Eysencks use the terms 'prisoner' and 'criminal' interchangeably even though the sample included remand prisoners who, by definition, have not yet been convicted, and assume the university students and other control group adults to be 'presumably largely non-criminals, although proof for this assertion would be difficult to furnish' (Eysenck and Eysenck, 1970: 231).

Intelligence and offending

Much early criminological writing classically described the offender as lacking in intelligence, as feeble-minded or some such similar euphemism. A number of writers in more recent times have argued that low intelligence is linked with crime. Herrnstein and Murray (1994), for example, have suggested that those with limited cognitive skills are significantly more likely both to experience and to be otherwise involved in various social ills. The difficulty with such an argument – even if such a correlation can be shown – is that IQ is largely determined by social rather than hereditary factors and, consequently, it is almost impossible to separate out IQ from other possible social explanations for the behaviours in question. More recent work by Cullen and colleagues (1997) suggest that IQ is only weakly related to criminality and that other identifiable factors, such as income and education, are significantly more important to any explanation. Similarly, meta-analyses of work on this area find correlations of between 0.1 and 0.2 between measures of intelligence and crime, whereas they find correlations closer to 0.5 in relation to other risk factors.

There are many ways, in theory, that intelligence could be linked with criminality:

- Lower intelligence, for example, might lead to poorer decision-making as a result of a limited ability to envisage the consequences of action.
- Lower intelligence might be linked with frustration and an inability to control behaviour.
- Lower intelligence is linked with low educational achievement – a key predictor of life chances.
- Higher intelligence might result in an understanding of social rules and laws, and an accurate assessment of the risks involved in engaging in crime.
- In a less direct sense, intelligence is linked with a range of other key *risk* and *protective factors* related to offending (see Chapter 33).

This is a controversial area, however, and has frequently resulted in raised tempers (metaphorically at least).

Although there has been renewed interest in the possible role of intelligence in relation to offending in recent years, for much of the twentieth century this area was largely ignored. Hirschi and Hindelang argue that much of this is to do with the discrediting of medically-dominated approaches to criminology in the early twentieth century being superseded by sociological criminology as the century wore on. Indeed, the backlash was fairly quick, they suggest (1977: 580):

> Less than two decades after Goring estimated 0.6553 as a 'minimum value' for the correlation between mental defectiveness and crime, Sutherland (1931) was poking fun at the absurdities of 'mental testers'. His negative view of their research was so influential that the 'modern' or 'recent' position on IQ ... appears to have been firmly established at that time, i.e. 45 years ago.

The measurement of intelligence owes much to a French psychologist, Alfred Binet, and to a colleague, Theodore Simon, who devised a scale of tasks for use as the basis for assessing intelligence of Parisian school pupils. The Binet-Simon scale has remained very influential, though adapted and modified by others, particularly in America, and forms the basis for the measures we continue to use today.

One of the most controversial findings of research in this area is that which shows differences in scores in IQ tests by race. Research in the US has found that, on average, African Americans score approximately 15 points lower on IQ tests than do European Americans. Now, there are a number of reasons why this might be. It has been argued that the nature of the tests themselves is such that it favours particular skills – rather than 'intelligence' – and these skills are differentially distributed in the population. The tests, it has been suggested, are culturally biased. Even if such tests *do* measure intelligence, the question then remains as to whether the recorded differences between groups are somehow inherent or are the product of social and environmental factors.

Nevertheless, despite these difficulties, some researchers have taken the data from IQ tests more or less at face-value as actually measuring intelligence, and have used this to construct arguments about the differing levels of offending measured among different ethnic groups. An article by Jensen in the late 1960s (Jensen, 1968) argued that 80 per cent of the measured differences between groups was to do with inherited characteristics rather than environmental factors. Perhaps the most famous recent treatment of the role of intelligence in relation to crime is Herrnstein and Murray's (1994) *The Bell Curve*. Hugely controversial, they argued that people of low intelligence, as measured by IQ, were

more heavily predisposed to commit crime, as well as to be much more likely to fail educationally, become unemployed, live on welfare, and have illegitimate children. This argument, and the responses to it, are dealt with in greater detail in Chapter 13. However, it is worth setting out the brief outlines here as the arguments relating to intelligence relate quite strongly to other elements of at least some of the earlier biologically-influenced theories.

Herrnstein and Murray (1994) had found that offenders scored 92 on average in IQ tests. Having controlled for such factors as education, socio-economic background, and race, they found that the link with offending continued to be strong. The responses to the research have been critical of the approach used (for example, for failing to conduct primary research), of the form of analysis and the failure to explore different types of crime and the impact of the criminal justice system. Crucially, responses have also been extremely hostile to what is seen by some as the *political* nature of the research. Hauser (1995: 149), for example, concluded that '*The Bell Curve* is a massive, ideologically driven and frequently careless or incompetent assemblage of good science, bad science and pseudo-science that is likely to do great damage both in the realm of public policy and in the conduct of social research'.

Nevertheless, a review of existing research by Hirschi and Hindelang (1977) presents evidence from a range of studies which appear to show a strong association between IQ and delinquency. The authors consequently make a strong case for reintroducing IQ as an important factor in explaining delinquency and pull no punches in criticising those who had ignored it for so long:

> The assertion that IQ affects the likelihood of delinquent behaviour through its effect on school performance is consistent with available data. The corollary descriptive assertion that delinquents have lower IQs than non-delinquents is firmly established ... IQ is doubly significant in that it represents an entire class of variables traditionally ignored by sociological students of crime and delinquency. Variables in this large residual category (virtually everything beyond class, culture and official processing) will not lose their status as alternative hypotheses simply by being ignored, and they will continue to restrict and even embarrass sociological theory until some effort is made to incorporate them. (1977: 584–5)

Given the apparent strength of the evidence linking IQ with delinquency, the important question they raise in their review, of course, concerns the nature of the mechanism that links IQ to delinquency. Hirschi and Hindelang state, again very firmly, that the available evidence shows no *direct* impact of IQ on delinquency and argue, rather, that the most likely linking mechanism is school performance. As such IQ is perfectly compatible with existing sociological theories which, whether they are strain, control or other theories (see Chapters 8, 9 and 11) tend to place considerable emphasis on education and school achievement. Others, sharing the view that IQ is an essentially inherited characteristic, focus on other factors such as the child-rearing practices and abilities of low-IQ parents (Gordon, 1987).

Review questions

1 What are the three main types of 'thinking error' identified by Yochelson and Samelow?

2 In what ways might 'moral development' be linked with offending behaviour?

3 What are the three main personality components identified by Eysenck?

4 How might intelligence be linked to crime?

Assessing psychological positivism

The more radical forms of positivist explanation – generally some of the earlier psychological approaches to criminality – now elicit relatively little support. In fact, as McGuire (2004: 11) puts it: 'very little of contemporary psychology can be described as positivistic in any meaningful sense'. Cruder forms of behaviourism and those biological approaches that take human behaviour not only to be rooted in, but in some ways determined by, biology, such as Eysenck's theory, are not representative of contemporary psychology. Rather, a number of psychological approaches, not least various applications of cognitive social learning theory, now approach the task of understanding individual differences in the way in which environmental factors influence offending behaviour.

One question which arises is whether psychology has an equal role to play in relation to all forms of offending. It is possible, for example, that volume crimes, such as various widespread and fairly mundane property crimes, are unlikely to be explained psychologically over and above a general interpretation of the processes and actions involved. In this manner, psychology may be limited in relation to those crimes that require 'little in the way of effort, planning, preparation or skill' (Gottfredson and Hirschi, 1990). However, McGuire suggests that there are elements of social learning theory that may be relevant to an understanding of property offending. More particularly, he suggests that psychology may have even more to offer in helping us understand the group dynamics and interpersonal processes that may surround some property offending – there being evidence, for example, of the importance of membership of delinquent peer groups in explaining rates of such offending (Matsueda and Anderson, 1998).

Psychology may have more to offer in relation to the explanation of interpersonal violence. For example, a review of research by Olweus *et al.* (1986) shows considerable continuity in patterns of aggression between infancy, later childhood, adolescence and into adulthood. Aggression in childhood is linked with later problems, such as offending and other conduct problems. The development of aggressiveness is strongly linked with a number of family-based socialisation processes involved in parenting and child-rearing. A large body of research has explored how certain patterns of socialisation and interaction between adults and children may make later aggressiveness in children and adolescents more likely. Important factors include cruel, authoritarian and inconsistent discipline, the use of shaming and degradation in the expression of authority, and physical methods of restraint and control. Finally, there also appears to be some evidence linking patterns of social information processing to the likelihood of aggression.

Where more unusual forms of offending are involved, then the likelihood, McGuire suggests, is that psychological factors and individual differences will be able to play a greater role in explanation. These process and individual difference 'dimensions of psychological factors can help to bridge the gap between environmental and social variables and the acts we call crime' (2004: 72). Indeed, contemporary psychology contributes significantly to many aspects of criminal justice and punishment policy, and we discuss these in greater detail in Chapter 33.

Questions for further discussion

1 How might the personalities of 'offenders' differ from 'non-offenders'?

2 In what ways might childhood experiences affect behaviour in adolescence and adulthood?

3 How might separation from parents in early childhood contribute to later anti-social behaviour?

4 Take three different types of crime, e.g. theft from a shop, burglary, and robbery, and think about how each of these behaviours might be encouraged or discouraged by previous experiences.

5 What is the relevance of 'thinking processes' to the study of crime?

Further reading

Ainsworth, P. (2000) *Psychology and Crime,* Harlow: Longman

Akers, R. (1998) *Social Learning and Social Structure: A general theory of crime and deviance,* Boston: Northeastern University Press

Blackburn, R. (1993) *The Psychology of Criminal Conduct,* Chichester: Wiley

Hollin, C. (1989) *Psychology and Crime,* London: Routledge

Hollin, C. (1992) *Criminal Behaviour,* Hove: Psychology Press

Howitt, D. (2006) *An Introduction to Forensic and Criminal Psychology,* 2nd edn, Harlow: Pearson

A hugely helpful review of work on moral reasoning, crime and interventions is:

Palmer, E. (2003) *Offending Behaviour: Moral reasoning, criminal conduct, and the rehabilitation of offenders,* Cullompton: Willan

Websites

The British Psychological Society has a lot of information on its website, including an archives and history section: www.bps.org.uk

There are helpful, bite-sized chunks of information at the Encyclopedia of Psychology: http://www.psychology.org/

There is a crime and psychology blog which has interesting news and updates from time to time. As with all such sites, try to cross-check any information you take from it: http://www.crimepsychblog.com/

Chapter outline

Introduction   170

Durkheim and criminology   170

    Durkheim and social change   171

    Durkheim, suicide and anomie   172

    Assessing Durkheim   174

    Merton and anomie   174

      Anomie and the 'American dream'   175

    Assessing Merton's anomie theory   178

Later strain theory   180

    Cloward and Ohlin   180

    General strain theory   181

    Messner and Rosenfeld   182

Assessing strain theory   183

Questions for further discussion   184

Further reading   185

Websites   185

Durkheim, anomie and strain

CHAPTER SUMMARY

In previous chapters we have explored some ways in which positivism has shaped and influenced criminology. In particular, the last two chapters were concerned with approaches that were predominantly individualistic in focus – biological and psychological positivism. Here we shift focus to look at the emergence of sociological criminology. Of the three main 'founding fathers' of sociology it was only Emile Durkheim who discussed the subject of crime at any length.

In this chapter we explore:

- elements of Durkheim's thought and the influence this has had on later criminological writing;

- the linked concepts of *anomie* and *strain*;

- how these concepts have been utilised by various writers to help us organise our thinking about the nature of crime in modern society.

Introduction

Though Marx has had a considerable influence on criminological thought, he had little directly to say about crime. Emile Durkheim, by contrast, had a considerable amount to say about crime. His ideas can be said to have had a significant bearing on the Chicago School (see Chapter 9), on Robert Merton and strain theory, and upon more contemporary theories of punishment (see Chapter 22). As with the rest of his work, Durkheim's preoccupation was with the ways in which the *social* aspects of phenomena might be understood and illustrated. His major writings on crime emerge from his work on the division of labour and on the nature of social solidarity.

Durkheim and criminology

Crime, for Durkheim, was those actions that offended against collective feelings or sentiments. Crime is not something that is unchanging, or has some essence. Rather, the notion of 'crime' reflects particular social conventions and these vary according to time and place. Moreover, it is not the case that 'crimes' are everywhere equally harmful to society; that is, crimes cannot be conceived as matters which are specifically injurious to the wider community. Rather, they are best understood, he argued, as violations of a moral code – what he referred to as the *conscience collective* of society. It is because this moral code is violated that punishment is required. As Garland (1990: 30) explains it:

The criminal act violates sentiments and emotions which are deeply ingrained in most members of society – it shocks their healthy consciences – and this violation calls forth strong psychological reactions, even among those not directly involved. It provokes a sense of outrage, anger, indignation, and a passionate desire for vengeance.

According to Durkheim a certain amount of crime is normal in any society:

Crime is present not only in the majority of societies of one particular species but in all societies of all types. There is no society that is not confronted with the problem of criminality. Its form changes; the acts thus characterized are not the same everywhere; but, everywhere and always, there have been men who have behaved in such a way as to draw upon themselves penal repression. (1938: 65–6)

Crime, for Durkheim, plays a number of important functions. First, it has an *adaptive* function in that it introduces new ideas and practices into society thereby ensuring that there is change rather than stagnation. It also has a *boundary maintenance* function, reinforcing social values and norms – crudely, through its stimulation of collective action against deviance it helps to reaffirm the difference between right and wrong. To this extent crime should be considered to be a *normal* element in any properly functioning society.

Let us make no mistake. To classify crime among the phenomena of normal sociology is not to say merely that it is an inevitable, although regrettable phenomenon, due to the incorrigible wickedness of men; it is to affirm that it is a factor in public health, an integral part of all societies. (1938: 67)

His phrase – crime 'is a factor in public health' – seems odd at first sight. Surely, crime is bad, negative, unhelpful, destructive? Durkheim's argument was intended as a corrective to those views that took crime to be entirely anti-social, strange or parasitic. Rather, he pointed out that it had a social role. However unpalatable it may seem, sociologically we must recognise the functions it performs. It is, for example, part of our social 'glue'. By proscribing certain forms of behaviour we simultaneously indicate what acceptable behaviour looks like. By punishing, we reinforce legal and moral rules. Thus, too little crime, by implication, could be as concerning as too much. This is an observation of huge importance to criminologists. As Durkheim observes in an important passage, there is no prospect of crime disappearing:

> In a society in which criminal acts were no longer committed, the sentiments they offend would have to be found without exception in all individual consciousnesses, and they must be found to exist with the same degree as sentiments contrary to them. Assuming that this condition could actually be realized, crime would not thereby disappear; it would only change its form, for the very cause which would thus dry up the sources of criminality would immediately open up new ones. (1938: 67)

In the opening chapter of this book we discussed what is meant by this thing we call 'crime'. Very quickly it becomes clear in such a discussion that crime has no *essence*. It varies by time and by place. The sociological study of crime, therefore, immediately must become much more than simply looking at patterns and trends, discussing practical responses to crime and how they might be altered or improved. Crime, in the hands of a sociologist such as Durkheim, becomes an important tool that can tell us much about the nature of the social order in which we live. The types of behaviours that we legislate against – and call crimes – and the specific ways in which we respond to them – the types and amounts of punishment – are indicators of the nature of our society.

One of the clearest illustrations of this style of sociological thinking can be found in Durkheim's focus on the importance of the nature of social reactions to crime. Here, Durkheim was highlighting what has become an important criminological truth:

> We must not say that an action shocks the conscience collective because it is criminal, but rather that it is criminal because it shocks the conscience collective. We do not condemn it because it is a crime, but it is a crime because we condemn it. (Durkheim, 1972: 123–4)

As we will see in subsequent chapters (and Chapter 10 in particular) this observation runs through much criminological theory, not least labelling theory, some radical criminologies and, indeed, control theory.

Durkheim and social change

If crime and punishment have the ability to provide us with important insights into the nature and functioning of society, the periods of dramatic social change will surely be reflected in the penal sphere. In *The Division of Labour in Society* Durkheim analysed and sought to understand the profound changes affecting modern industrial societies. What occurred as relatively primitive societies were superseded by more complex ones. In his analysis, Durkheim identified two ideal typical social formations which he terms 'mechanical' and 'organic', each typifying differing forms of social solidarity.

Ideal types are abstractions designed to help identify and explain patterns that appear in the real world, rather than straightforward, faithful descriptions of that world. Weber described ideal types as one-sided accentuations, and as syntheses of particular phenomena, arranged in order to provide a unified construct useful for analysis. These terms – 'mechanical' and 'organic' solidarity – and other ideal types that we will meet, are best seen as didactic models, used to help us understand particular social phenomena by focusing on certain core characteristics.

In more primitive societies, characterised by mechanical solidarity, there is, he argued, a relatively undifferentiated division of labour. People live fairly common, shared lives in which work is generally identical and values are shared. Under conditions of mechanical solidarity, he argued, the social order was largely organised through similarity, and social norms were enforced through retributive sanctions. Such sanctioning served to identify and exclude offenders, to treat them as outsiders.

Such societies are gradually superseded by more complex formations characterised by what Durkheim referred to as organic forms of solidarity. Within such societies there is a relatively highly-differentiated division of labour, and social solidarity is organised around difference rather than similarity. Such social transformation is reflected in the systems of law and punishment characteristic of the different types of social solidarity. Under mechanical solidarity the primary function of law is to enforce uniformity and to limit or even prevent deviation from the common pattern. Under conditions of organic solidarity on the other hand the primary function of law is to regulate the interactions between the different parts of society and between members.

What we have here, then, is a sophisticated attempt to examine how social bonds are reciprocal ties and obligations are maintained (a) in times of very rapid social change, and (b) in societies which are highly internally differentiated. Durkheim was writing in the aftermath of the industrial revolution, in a period in which all major writers (as varied as Karl Marx and Charles Dickens) were struggling to understand the nature of the social transformation in front of them. In this regard, Durkheim confronted head-on one of the great questions of the moment: what is it that will provide social solidarity and coherence in these new times? One can see similar questions being asked of globalisation now. Is the new global order breaking down all the old certainties? Will these new social arrangements bring with them the collapse of social structures? Are we losing the ability to regulate behaviour and maintain order?

The transformation of social systems toward those characterised by organic solidarity is accompanied by a decline in retributivism. This is viewed by Durkheim as involving an increasing valuation of human dignity – akin to what Elias (1978) referred to as a 'civilizing process' (see Chapter 22). Now, for Durkheim, the modernisation of society, involving a shift from mechanical to organic solidarity, is far from straightforward. In particular, there is a danger, Durkheim argued, that the forms of regulation that bound less complex societies together wouldn't be replaced quickly and effectively enough by new forms of moral regulation. One potential consequence of this is *anomie*, where moral constraints are insufficient effectively to limit individual desires. The link with crime and deviance is clear. We return to anomie below.

Durkheim, suicide and anomie

For our purposes here Durkheim's other centrally important piece of work concerned suicide and how this apparently most individual of acts might be used as an indicator of how sociological analysis might be undertaken. Suicide was chosen as a subject of study for a number of reasons. At the time Durkheim was writing, suicide was a crime in most of Europe – and was generally considered a deviant act. Moreover, as remains the case today, it was generally viewed as an individual rather than a

Emile Durkheim (1858–1917)

Born in eastern France, Durkheim was the son of a Rabbi. Indeed, not only his father, but his grandfather and great-grandfather had been Rabbis also, and it was expected that Emile would also follow this path.

He studied at the Ecole Normale Supérieure and in his early 20s became a teacher of philosophy. By the age of 29 he got a job at the University of Bordeaux where he taught the very first sociology course in France. It wasn't until 1902, when Durkheim was 44 years of age, that he became a Professor of Philosophy and Education at the University of Paris.

The Division of Labour in Society, arguably Durkheim's greatest work, was published in 1893, and this was quickly followed by *The Rules of Sociological Method* (1895), *Suicide: A Study in Sociology* (1897) and, later, *The Elementary Forms of the Religious Life* (1912).

Durkheim died in 1917 not long after his son, also a gifted academic, had been killed in the First World War.

Emile Durkheim, one of the 'founding fathers' of sociology.

social phenomenon. Suicide, for Durkheim, therefore provided the basis for illustrating the sociological aspect of even the apparently most individualised forms of deviance.

Durkheim's focus was upon *suicide rates*, using official records, and he sought to explain how patterns of suicide might be explained by reference to such sociological phenomena as religion, social structure, economic conditions and so on. The study of suicide rates threw up a number of interesting features. He found, for example, that:

- Rates of suicide were higher in Protestant than Catholic countries.

- Single people were more prone to suicide than those who were married.

- Suicide among military personnel was higher than among civilians.

- Suicide rates drop in times of war.

- Suicide rates were higher in times of economic crisis than stability.

In explaining the patterns he observed, Durkheim identified four 'ideal types' of suicide. We met this term earlier in relation to the two main types of social solidarity identified by Durkheim. Consequently, these types, he argued, are rarely found in their 'pure' form. The four types he called *altruistic, egoistic, anomic* and *fatalistic* (though he felt this last type to be of little importance at the time he was writing). The rates of suicide, he argued, could be explained by the degree of social solidarity, and he distinguished two aspects of solidarity: *integration* into social groups and *regulation* by social norms (see Figure 8.1).

Anomic suicide, as the figure above suggests, arises where the degree of regulation is insufficient (as also happens potentially during the shift from mechanical to organic solidarity). Central to Durkheim's sociology was the assumption that one of the keys to successful social integration was the regulation of

human desires and that, where this was problematic, individuals experienced a form of 'normlessness'. This had, he felt, an obvious link to suicide:

> With increased prosperity, desires increase ... Overweening ambition always exceeds the results obtained, great as they may be, since there is no warning to pause here ... since this race for an unattainable goal can give no other pleasure but that of the race itself ... once it is interrupted the participants are left empty-handed ... How could the desire to live not be weakened under such conditions? (1897/1951: 253)

To reiterate, Durkheim's view was that social solidarity was a product of two forces:

- *Integration* – Social cohesion brought about by shared beliefs and practices; the forces of attraction that bring people together.

- *Regulation* – The constraints which limit human behaviour and desires.

He related this to the study of suicide by showing how variation in integration and regulation (too much or too little of each) is linked with rates of suicide at particular times. Too little regulation – where the individual is insufficiently regulated by the group – produces high levels of what he called *anomic* suicide. However, Durkheim also uses the term anomie in another context, and arguably in a slightly different way. For Durkheim, regulation becomes increasingly important as societies become more complex. In times of rapid social change – such as that from mechanical to organic solidarity – systems of regulation may be insufficient. Where this is so, what emerges is a state of anomie or the anomic form of the division of labour. This, in some respects, is a critique of modern industrialism and the failure of its systems of moral regulation to keep pace with changes in the economic and occupational structure of society. Individual desires, ambitions and appetites are stimulated but insuffi-

Figure 8.1	Durkheim's typology of suicide	
Type of suicide	**Degree and nature of solidarity**	**Example**
Egoistic	Lack of integration	Suicides of Protestants and single people
Anomic	Lack of regulation	Suicides during economic crisis
Altruistic	Excessive integration	Suicides in primitive societies, military suicides
Fatalistic	Excessive regulation	Suicide of slaves

ciently controlled or limited. It is this argument as we will see below that, largely as a result of the work of Robert Merton, has become deeply embedded in contemporary criminology.

Assessing Durkheim

It is not only through the notion of anomie that Durkheim has exerted a very particular and profound influence over criminological theory. More generally, his observation about the 'normality' of crime, and the importance of societal reaction in framing what is to be considered criminal, are now cornerstones of the sociological approach to the study of crime and crime control. Smith and Natalier (2005) suggest that we might take three general lessons from Durkheim's work:

- The need to think about the criminal justice system in the wider context of the problem of social order and its general social location, rather than as autonomous spheres largely independent of their social context.

- That the law and the criminal justice system reflect deeply embedded beliefs and values, and are not simply the straightforward product of reason.

- The importance of understanding the symbolic functions of punishment. Distinguishing right from wrong, legal from illegal, sends messages about justice, morality and collective values.

Before moving on, however, there are a number of criticisms of Durkheim's work that have been made and which we must briefly consider. First, Durkheim's work arguably underplays the way in which systems of punishment are shaped by the nature and distribution of power within society. That is to say, it is possible, as radical critics might argue, that rather than punitive responses tending to be directed at actions which transgress generally held social norms, it is possible that it is actions which run counter to the interests of particular groups that tend to be punished. Second, but relatedly, the assumption of consensus which underpins the notion of conscience collective is precisely that, an assumption, rather than something that Durkheim demonstrated empirically.

Third, it is debatable whether Durkheim's arguments about the functional utility of crime actually apply to all types of crime. Thus, it is possible to identify criminal acts that simply don't call forth the type of moral outrage that Durkheim took to be illustrative of challenges to

the collective conscience. Finally, critics have also pointed to the circularity in the functionalist character of elements of Durkheim's explanation of why laws are enacted and criminals punished. As Garland (1983: 52–53) notes:

> The discussion of crime reproduces all the circularity of Durkheim's basic arguments. We are told that crime consists in acts 'universally disapproved by members of each society'. Clearly, as an empirical statement this is questionable; one must presume that the offenders themselves do not wholly partake in this universal spirit of disapproval. However, Durkheim tells us that he refers only to healthy consciences, that is, to those which share the sentiments of the collective conscience. But since violation of the collective conscience is the very quality which gives certain acts the attribute of criminality, the appeal to 'healthy consciences' as a proof is an empty form of tautology.

Review questions

1 What are the main characteristics of *mechanical* and *organic* solidarity?

2 Why does anomie occur in the process of social change?

3 What are the four main types of suicide identified by Durkheim?

Merton and anomie

One influential commentator judged Robert K. Merton's anomie theory 'the single most influential formulation in the sociology of deviance' (Clinard, 1964: 10). It has however fallen 'distinctly out of fashion, perhaps permanently so in any explicit form. Like functionalism, from which it derives, it has become a routine conceptual folly for students to demolish before moving on to more rewarding ground' (Downes and Rock, 2003: 104). Indeed, Downes and Rock argue that it has been Robert Merton's version of anomie theory that has been subject to the most vociferous criticism, rather than Durkheim's approach.

Although Durkheim was by no means entirely consistent in his portrayal of anomie, as we have seen he viewed it as the product of rapid social change unaccompanied by corresponding growth in systems of moral regulation. Anomie for Durkheim, then, is that state of affairs brought about by insufficient normative regulation. Building on this idea, but within the specific context of having lived through the depression experienced by America in the 1930s, Robert Merton saw anomie as resulting from the absence of alignment between socially-desired aspirations, such as wealth, and the means available to people to achieve such objectives. Merton, like the researchers of the Chicago School that we will meet in the next chapter, sought a more sociological explanation of crime as a corrective to the generally individualised explanations that still tended to dominate. Merton's aim was to:

> ... discover how some social structures exert a definite pressure upon certain persons in the society to engage in non-conforming rather than conforming conduct. If we can locate groups peculiarly subject to such pressures, we should expect to find high rates of deviant conduct in these groups, not because the human beings comprising them are compounded of distinctive biological tendencies but because they are responding normally to the social situation in which they find themselves. (1969: 255)

Merton's theory was built on a critique of particular elements of American culture. The emphasis on consumption and the tendency towards greed, ever-increasing material desires and dissatisfaction, which some critics would take to be defining negative characteristics of modern capitalism, also lie at the heart of much of anomie theory's portrayal of the sources of deviance. It was this focus that distinguished it from the ecological approach adopted by many of the Chicago School sociologists with their concern with neighbourhoods and the social structure of the city. In an oft-quoted statement, Merton observed that 'a cardinal American virtue, ambition, promotes a cardinal American vice, deviant behaviour' (Merton, 1949: 137, quoted in Downes and Rock, 2003: 94). At the heart of this is the 'American dream'.

Anomie and the 'American dream'

At the core of the ideology of the American dream was the idea that prosperity and success were available to all those who worked hard. The depression of the 1930s, however, had given the lie to the idea of America as a prosperous, egalitarian society,

Crowds form outside as the Brooklyn branch of the Bank of the United States closes its doors, 11 December 1930. The mismatch between aspiration and reality was central to the development of sociological concepts of anomie and strain theory during the period of the depression in the United States.

though President Roosevelt's New Deal sought to maintain faith in the vision of opportunity for all. Mertonian anomie theory emerged in this period. It got a further boost in the early 1960s from the Kennedy government and its concern with civil liberties and opportunity. According to Merton any society identifies certain culturally preferred goals. In American society this is material success:

> It would of course be fanciful to assert that accumulated wealth stands alone as a symbol of success just as it would be fanciful to deny that Americans assign it a high place in their scale of values. In some large measure money has been consecrated as value in itself ... [However it is] acquired, fraudulently or institutionally, it can be used to purchase the same goods and services. (Merton, 1968: 190)

However, not everyone can realistically achieve such goals. There is not the means for everyone to succeed. The dissonance between socially desired ends and limited means produces a 'strain to anomie' – effectively a range of behavioural adaptations to these social and psychological circumstances. In Merton's terms this strain to anomie is the product of the 'contradiction between the cultural emphasis on pecuniary ambition and the social bars to full opportunity'. Merton summarised his argument as follows:

> The dominant pressure of group standards of success is, therefore, on the gradual attenuation of legitimate, but by and large ineffective, strivings and the increasing use of illegitimate, but more or less effective, expedients of vice and crime. The cultural demands made on persons in this situation are incompatible. On the one hand, they are asked to orient their conduct toward the prospect of accumulating wealth and on the other, they are largely denied effective opportunities to do so institutionally. The consequences of such structural inconsistency are

psychopathological personality and/or anti-social conduct, and/or revolutionary activities. (Merton, 1938: 71)

The bulk of individuals will continue to conform, he suggested, despite the strain to anomie. However, 'certain phases of social structure generate the circumstances in which infringement of social codes constitutes a "normal" response' (Merton, 1938: 672). The strain to anomie is stronger for certain social groups than others. The social structure effectively limits the possibilities for some groups more than it does for others – in short, the lower classes. In this fashion, it has been argued that Merton is forwarding a *cultural* argument to explain the nature of crime in American society and a *structural* argument to explain its uneven distribution (Vold *et al.*, 2002).

For those who don't conform there are four *deviant adaptations*: innovation, ritualism, retreatism and rebellion. These are distinguished by whether culturally prescribed goals and institutionally available means are accepted or rejected. The five sets of relationships can be illustrated as follows (see Figure 8.2).

Innovation is the application of illegitimate means to the achievement of socially approved and legitimate ends. The innovator accepts the social goal of material success, but has not the legitimate means for achieving it: 'such anti-social behaviour is in a sense "called forth" by certain conventional values of the culture *and* by the class structure involving differential access to the approved opportunities for legitimate, prestige-bearing pursuit of the culture goals' (Merton, 1938: 679). Deviance is the consequence.

In this sense, much organised crime shares both the overall aims, and indeed many of the means, of standard capitalist activity. It differs in that it operates outside the law in some important ways. Innovators accept the cultural goals, but don't use the standard institutionalised means. The protago-

Figure 8.2	Merton's typology of modes of individual adaptation		
	Mode of adaptation	*Culture goals*	*Institutionalised means*
I	Conformity	+	+
II	Innovation	+	−
III	Ritualism	−	+
IV	Retreatism	−	−
V	Rebellion	+/−	+/−

Marlon Brando as Don Corleone in the film *The Godfather*: a man with seemingly traditional values and many legitimate aspirations, all achieved through violence and racketeering – an example of 'innovation' in terms of Merton's typology.

nists in a number of Hollywood portrayals of American Mafiosi – Francis Ford Coppola's *Godfather* movies and Scorsese's *Goodfellas*, for example – continue to espouse many traditional values and goals whilst using culturally illegitimate means for their achievement. Confronted with the 'absence of realistic opportunities for advancement' Merton argued, some people are particularly vulnerable to the 'promises of power and high income from organized vice, rackets and crime' (Merton, 1968: 199).

Arguably, it is in the area of corporate and white collar crime that this particular adaptation often appears. Accounts of insider trading, corporate fraud, major failures in industrial health and safety are all replete with illustrations of individuals focused upon achieving material and career success, whilst failing to operate within rules and laws. Protagonists like Gordon Gekko in the 1987 movie *Wall Street* and Sherman McCoy in Tom Wolfe's novel *Bonfire of the Vanities*, published in the same year, captured the greed and rampant materialism of that era – a period many critics felt promoted the idea of success at all costs (Downes, 1989).

By contrast, *ritualism* concerns those circumstances in which the cultural goals disappear – they are lost sight of – whilst attachment to the institutional means becomes seemingly ever stronger. It is deviant because, although the means conform to social expectations, the search for the socially-valued goal of financial success has been abandoned. This is a routinised nature of elements of bourgeois life, a sticking to the rules at all costs, and a scaling down of aims to the point where they can be achieved effortlessly. Merton's example here was the bureaucratic mindset.

Retreatism, according to Merton the least common of the adaptations, involves the rejection of both the objectives and means, and concerns people who 'are in society but not of it'. Merton's examples are the hobo, the drugtaker and elements of the tramp played so famously by Charlie Chaplin: 'always the butt of a crazy and bewildering world in which he has no place and from which he constantly runs away into a contented do nothingness' (Merton, 1949: 251). As such it may be characterised by drug use/addiction, alcoholism, homelessness and so on. It is an adaptation, Merton felt, that tends not to involve

Merton saw Charlie Chaplin's comic tramp figure as a supreme form of 'retreatism' in terms of his typology – rejecting both society's goals and the means of achieving them, and hence unlikely to engage in criminal activity.

the victimization of others, and is often a private, rather than a public, response. Retreatism became something of a subcultural style in the 1960s with the advent of the hippie movement.

The final adaptation is *rebellion*. This is a more radical alternative, seeking to replace both the means and the ends as a way of resolving the strain to anomie. This might be the political radical proposing an entirely new set of culturally approved goals and means for their achievement. Unlike some criminological theories, Merton was explicit in his acknowledgement that anomie theory was 'designed to account for some, not all, forms of deviant behaviour customarily described as criminal or delinquent' (Merton, 1968: 195).

Assessing Merton's anomie theory

Despite its enormous influence, it was some two decades before Merton's famous article began to resonate powerfully through criminology. It did so partly as a result of Albert Cohen's *Delinquent Boys,* Richard Cloward and Lloyd Ohlin's *Delinquency*

and Opportunity, as well as Merton's reworking of the original article. As Downes and Rock argue, anomie theory has had an odd shelf-life: for its first few decades after Merton's original exposition in 1938 it was accepted rather uncritically. Since the early 1960s, however, the reverse has been true with its rejection arguably being more critical than is deserved. Again, rather like functionalism, anomie theory may not be referred to explicitly very much these days, but seasoned observers can see its footprints everywhere:

> It has an anonymous presence in Jock Young's essay in labelling theory, *The Drugtakers,* and appears under its own name as one of the principal themes in his account of the making of left realism in the 1980s. It is the invisible prop to the Birmingham Centre for Contemporary Cultural Studies' radical work on class, youth, and deviance in Britain. (Downes and Rock, 2003: 105)

Numerous potential shortcomings have been identified in Merton's anomie theory (we return to this at the end of the chapter). Some of the criticisms

Robert King Merton (1910–2003)

Born Meyer Robert Schkolnick in Philadelphia on American Independence day 1910, Merton's parents were working-class Jewish immigrants from Eastern Europe. The family lived above the father's dairy products shop in South Philadelphia. It was common at this time to Americanize names and Merton initially changed his to Robert K. Merlin (as a young man he worked as a magician) before a friend advised him that it was rather 'hackneyed'.

Inquiring as to why Merton should have focused his attention of the unintended consequences of the American dream, Lilly and colleagues point to his social origins. Born into considerable poverty, Merton gained a scholarship to Temple University in Philadelphia, published his famous article 'Social Structure and Anomie' whilst teaching at Harvard University, aged 28, and became a Professor at Columbia University three years later. Though speculative, 'this personal journey', they suggest, 'may have helped focus Merton's attention on the prominent role in the national culture of social ascent' (Lilly *et al.*, 2002: 53).

Among others, he coined the phrases 'self-fulfilling prophecy', 'role model' and 'reference group'. Merton is also credited with being the creator of the idea of focus groups as a research tool. Merton's son, Robert C. Merton, won the Nobel Prize for Economics in 1997.

Robert K. Merton (1910–2003): born into impoverished circumstances in Philadelphia, he captured part of the dark side of the American dream in his work on anomie.

of Mertonian anomie theory reflect differences between Merton's use of the notion and Durkheim's. There was, as we have seen, something of a shift in the use of the term anomie, which is neatly captured in the following passage from Steven Box (1981: 97–98):

> Merton's analysis … appears to follow Durkheim's usage of the concept of anomie. But the appearance is, I think, deceptive, for during the argument Merton shifts *his* meaning of anomie away from a Durkheimian position towards one which is peculiarly his own. Initially, Merton appears to be discussing the *emphasis on normative means* of achieving cultural values … However, later in his analysis, Merton appears to shift the focus of his attention away from an *emphasis on normative means to differential access to opportunity structures*, such as schools and employment organizations, through which cultural values can be properly and legally realized … The emphasis on normative means is fundamentally Durkheimian because, by implication, it suggests that human aspirations have to be regulated and channelled.

Merton's initial use of the term was faithful to this conception, Box argues, in that at its core the emphasis is upon an overriding cultural goal – worldly material success. The difficulty for Merton was how to explain the apparent over-involvement of people from lower social classes in criminal and deviant activity if this cultural goal was universally accepted.

> Merton needed to transform the conception of anomie; he did this by shifting from an under-emphasis on normative means to a discussion on the differential access to legitimate opportunity structures, particularly education and occupational opportunities. Anomie was no longer a condition of deregulation or normlessness, but one of *relative deprivation*. Individual motivation behind deviant behaviour emerged out of the frustrations of such deprivations and these emotions existed because individuals had internalized the 'American Dream'. (Box, 1981: 99–100)

Competition and frustration around status has been suggested as being a key to understanding youthful delinquency – and stealing from cars is seen as a means of achieving status for young people who feel excluded from more conventional means of doing so.

Later strain theory

It was Albert Cohen's work which picked up on Merton's theory and introduced the notions of culture and subculture to the study of delinquency. Cohen was critical of Merton's approach because of its failure in his eyes to explain the nature or content of juvenile delinquency. Relative deprivation, identified as the major impetus to adult deviance in Merton's usage of the term anomie, is less useful, Cohen argued, in explaining juvenile motivations. Crucially, rather than being oriented towards the legitimate goals of adult society, many young people engage in behaviour which is 'non-utilitarian, malicious and negativistic' (1955: 25). It is not material success that delinquents are searching for, but meaning in some other way. We return to this idea in greater detail in the next chapter when we consider subcultural theory.

Rather than anomie, Cohen suggests that competition and frustration around status is the key to understanding youthful delinquency. It is here the parallels with Merton are visible. Cohen argues that in contemporary society issues of status are largely settled according to criteria such as educational success. However, not everyone is equally placed in this competition. The terms and criteria used by teachers and others are far from straightforwardly objective and they distinguish between children in both moral and social terms, i.e., crudely, according to middle-class standards. Significant proportions of working-class children are therefore faced with a number of status difficulties and linked feelings of shame or guilt on the one hand and resentment on the other. These young people are placed under severe strain. The issue is how such difficulties can be resolved. One solution is to form attachments with others in similar situations, to form gangs or other groupings and to reject some of the core adult values. This is the basis, in Cohen's terms, for the formation of delinquent youth subcultures.

Cloward and Ohlin

Influenced by Merton and by Albert Cohen, as well as by Edwin Sutherland's notion of differential association, the next milestone in strain theory was Richard Cloward and Lloyd Ohlin's *Delinquency and Opportunity*, published in 1960. Their debt to Merton can be seen in one of their central questions (1960: 32): 'Under what conditions will persons experience strains and tensions that lead to delinquent solutions?' At the heart of their answer is the observation that in 'a system that stresses ability as the basis of advancement, the failures who view themselves as equal in ability to those who succeed tend to feel unjustly deprived' (1960: 117). That is to say, where people are led to believe that the ability they have will enable them to gain access to education and thereby to occupational success, but where opportunities are limited and decisions are frequently based on other criteria such as class, ethnicity and sex, the outcome is that a proportion of the population feel anger at their unreasonable exclusion. The solution again is the rejection of core middle-class values.

However, as we noted earlier, Cloward and Ohlin also sought to incorporate elements of Sutherland's differential association theory. They do so by arguing that there are numerous means of resolving the adjustment or *strain* problems. The particular delinquent solution adopted will depend upon the nature of illegal or criminal means available in the particular environment. In this way:

> The concept of differential opportunity structures permits us to unite the theory of anomie, which recognizes the concept of differentials in access to legitimate means, and the 'Chicago tradition', in which the concept of differentials in access to illegitimate means is implicit ... The approach permits us to ask, for example, how the relative ability of illegitimate opportunities affects the resolution of adjustment problems leading to deviant behaviour. (Cloward and Ohlin, 1960; reproduced in Jacoby, 2004: 286–287)

We return to Cloward and Ohlin and the subcultural elements of the approach in Chapter 9.

Strain theory was remarkably influential in its time. Lloyd Ohlin, for example, was appointed by Robert Kennedy when he was Attorney General, to help develop Federal crime policy, and his and Cloward's work later formed the basis for much of President Lyndon Johnson's action in the war on poverty in the mid-1960s. The apparent lack of success of many of these programmes led President

Nixon to abandon them and led many critics to focus their attention on strain theory.

General strain theory

More recently, Robert Agnew has sought to build on Merton's ideas. Agnew suggests that there are at least four reasons why strain theory had declined in popularity:

- It has tended to focus on lower-class delinquency.
- It has neglected all but the most conventional goals (middle-class status and wealth).
- It overlooked barriers to achievement other than social stratification (these might include gender, race, intelligence and many others).
- It has found it difficult to explain why some people who experienced strain didn't turn to criminal activity. Arguably, strain and frustration are experienced by many who continue to conform.

As a consequence Agnew sought to develop a more general strain theory, though his specific focus was upon adolescent delinquency and drug use. His extension and elaboration of strain theory involves the identification of two types of strain over and above the central problem of failing to achieve one's personal goals. The first, slightly at variance with Merton's theory, he suggests arises from the 'actual or anticipated removal (loss) of positively valued stimuli from an individual' (1992: 57). The withholding of something that is valued – privileges, opportunities, relationships – is the source of strain. The second form of strain is the result of 'actual or anticipated presentation of negative or noxious stimuli' (1992: 58) such as relationships at home, work or elsewhere, that are abusive.

The greater the extent of strain, the more likely the adaptive response is to be deviant. In this context, delinquency and drug use are means of coping with negative relationships and emotions. The likelihood of deviant adaptations may be offset, Agnew argues, by the existence of support from other sources, the availability of alternative goals, and personal characteristics such as high levels of self-control and fear of adverse consequences. Relatedly, Agnew (2001) identifies a number of factors that increase the likelihood that strain will lead to crime and delinquency:

- Where the strain is perceived to be 'unjust'; where people feel that they have been treated unfairly they are more likely to become angry, and anger, according to Agnew's strain theory, is linked with increased likelihood of offending.
- When strain is high in magnitude it is more difficult to ignore and to manage in ways that are legitimate.
- Where the strain is caused by, or is associated with, low social control it is more likely to result in a deviant adaptation.

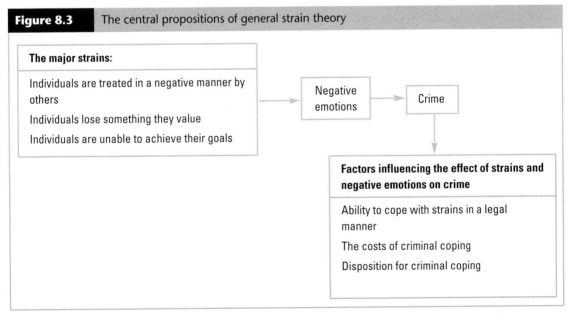

Figure 8.3   The central propositions of general strain theory

Source: Agnew (2006: 19).

- Strains may also lower levels of social control.
- Where the strain creates pressure to engage in 'criminal coping' – such as strain induced by criminal victimization leading to a desire for revenge.

What is particularly problematic is chronic or repeated strains. Agnew argues that such chronic strains are likely to create a predisposition to crime. They do this in a number of ways. Through repetition they reduce the ability of individuals to cope with strain. Thus, if one is regularly bullied it may, over time, become increasingly difficult to resist resorting to violence in response. Chronic strains may lead to the development of negative emotional traits such as anger, depression, fear and frustration, each of which may be conducive to crime. Agnew quotes a passage from Elijah Anderson's *Code of the Street* in support of this:

> Frustrations mount over bills, food, and, at times, drink, cigarettes, and drugs. Some tend toward self-destructive behaviour; many street-oriented women are crack-addicted ('on the pipe'), alcoholic, or repeatedly involved in complicated relationships with the men who abuse them. In addition, the seeming intractability of their situation, caused in large part by the lack of well-paying jobs and the persistence of racial discrimination, has engendered deep-seated bitterness and anger in many of the most desperate and poorest blacks, especially young people ... the frustrations of persistent poverty shorten the fuse in such people, contributing to a lack of patience with anyone, child or adult, who irritates them. (Anderson, 1990: 10–11)

Agnew summarises these arguments in the following diagram:

Messner and Rosenfeld

A variant on Agnew's general strain theory, called *institutional anomie theory,* is proposed by Messner and Rosenfeld (2001). Focusing, like Merton, on the 'American Dream' they suggest an anomic society has been created which privileges success over all other socially-approved goals:

> A primary task for noneconomic institutions such as the family and schools is to inculcate beliefs, values and commitments other than those of the marketplace. But as these noneconomic institutions are relatively devalued and forced to accommodate to economic considerations, and as they are penetrated by economic standards, they are less able to fulfil their distinctive socialization functions successfully. (2001: 150)

At its simplest, their argument is that 'the American Dream itself exerts pressures toward crime by encouraging an anomic cultural environment, an environment in which people are encouraged to adopt an "anything goes" mentality in the pursuit of personal goals' (2001: 61). There are a number of specific features of the American dream, they suggest, that are crucial. These are:

- the emphasis on *achievement* and on the winner takes all mentality;
- the *individualism* that focuses attention of rights rather than responsibilities;
- the *materialism* that fetishises wealth;
- the fact that these values permeate the whole of society – which they call *universalism*.

The effect of these cultural values is to privilege economic goals over others – for example, education

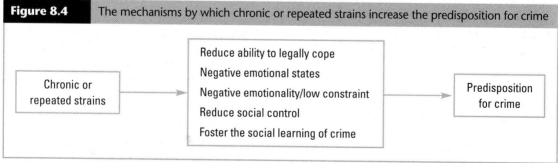

| **Figure 8.4** | The mechanisms by which chronic or repeated strains increase the predisposition for crime |

Chronic or repeated strains →

Reduce ability to legally cope
Negative emotional states
Negative emotionality/low constraint
Reduce social control
Foster the social learning of crime

→ Predisposition for crime

Source: Agnew (2006).

becomes increasingly devoted to servicing the labour market and the family becomes increasingly dominated by work. The tendency to focus on ends rather than means makes it increasingly difficulty for institutions such as schools and families to exert appropriate social control. Messner and Rosenfeld's argument owes much to earlier strain theory but also reflects the critical criminologist's discontent with the nature of contemporary capitalism. In addition, they reflect Durkheim's central point about the *normality* of crime:

> There is nothing necessarily 'sick', pathological, dysfunctional, or disorganized about a society organized to produced high rates of crime ... a particular level and type of crime are a normal outcome of a specified set of cultural and social arrangements ... A *low* level of predatory crime would be a sign of 'something wrong' with a society that places a premium on the individual competitive pursuit of financial gain, encourages people to create ever more efficient means of besting others, and offers comparatively little protection or comfort to the unsuccessful. We would be on the lookout for something out of the ordinary, something abnormal, about unusually low or falling crime rates in a society organized for crime. (Rosenfeld and Messner, in Henry and Lanier, 2005: 168)

In contemporary society crime, for Messner and Rosenfeld, is a product of the dominance of free-market economics, its elevation of material success above all other goals, and its cultural tendency toward anomie. Social controls are weakened and the use of illegitimate means to attain culturally-desired goals increases as such means themselves become progressively legitimised. They argue that societies which protect their members from the worst excesses of free-market economics therefore tend to have lower crime rates than others where there is less restriction on the market. Recent research (Downes and Hansen, 2006; Cavadino and Dignan, 2006) tends to provide support for just such a proposition. Thus, Downes and Hansen (2006) in a study of crime rates and welfare spending across 18 societies concluded that:

> ... countries that spend a greater proportion of GDP on welfare have lower imprisonment rates and that this relationship has become stronger over the last 15 years. The consistency in these findings across the United States and the other 17 countries studied makes it difficult to believe that this relationship is simply accidental or coincidental.

> **Review questions**
>
> 1 What are *strains*? Give some examples.
>
> 2 What are the central components of general strain theory?
>
> 3 Why do strains increase the likelihood of crime?
>
> 4 What are the main characteristics of *institutional anomie theory*?

Assessing strain theory

As we noted at the outset, in many respects strain theory has fallen out of fashion. It had major influence in the 1960s but has waned since, though Agnew's general strain theory has revitalised discussion of such ideas in some quarters. Nevertheless, strain theories contain a number of important features and it is important to recognise them.

- They draw our attention to the social, cultural and economic circumstances that lead to crime.
- They point to the *necessary* relationship between particular forms of social organisation and particular levels of crime.
- Merton's formulation drew attention to the unintended consequences of the social goal of individual economic achievement. Critics of the market society and of consumer capitalism are in many respects working in a similar tradition.
- Anomie and strain theory's predominant concern with the vulnerability of working-class or poorer communities sits comfortably with the liberal sensibilities of much sociological criminology and, undoubtedly, accounts for some of its intuitive appeal.

There are, however, numerous criticisms of strain theory:

- The tendency to rely on official statistics as an indicator of the nature and distribution of crime and, connected with this, the tendency generally to focus on lower-class crime is argued to be misleading. Strain theory tends to ignore the crimes of the powerful for example, or simply the crimes of the middle classes.
- It is argued that anomie theory exaggerates the consensus that surrounds financial success as a socially and culturally defined objective; there are other, competing means by which success can be measured. Indeed, Merton clearly

recognised the existence in American society of a range of 'counter-cultures' (lower middle-class preference for security over competition; the craftsman's emphasis on skill and 'expressivity' over financial reward) but nevertheless assumed a generalised acceptance of the American dream.

- For the radical theorist, anomie theory fails to look closely enough at the socio-political circumstances of crime. Thus, according to Taylor, Walton and Young, the major shortcoming of Merton's analysis was its failure to go beyond the identification of the central contradiction of American capitalism to ask why the situation existed and continued. They quote Laurie Taylor (1971: 148):

  > It is as though individuals in society are playing a gigantic fruit machine, but the machine is rigged and only some players are consistently rewarded. The deprived ones then either resort to using foreign coins or magnets to increase their chances of winning (innovation) or play on mindlessly (ritualism), give up the game (retreatism) or propose a new game altogether (rebellion). But in the analysis nobody appeared to ask who put the machine there in the first place and who takes the profits. Criticism of the game is confined to changing the pay-out sequences so that the deprived can get a better deal ... What at first sight looks like a major critique of society ends up by taking the existing society for granted. The necessity of standing outside the present structural/cultural configurations is not just

the job of those categorized in the rebellion mode of adaptation – it is also the task of the sociologist.

- In a similar vein, it is argued, again notably by Taylor *et al.*, that anomie theory over-predicts lower-class crime (and, arguably, lower-class *strain*) but it is less clear whether anomie theory is able to account for crimes of the middle class and wealthy.

- It is similarly unclear that the theory can deal with the very wide variety of forms of offending (the wide variety of *adaptations*) that exist – are sexual violence and theft the product of the same strain to anomie that leads to vandalism, for example?

- Early strain theory tends to focus on structural conditions and, consequently, pays relatively little attention to human agency – Agnew's general strain theory endeavours to deal with this criticism.

- The theory underplays the importance of social control (and self-control) in the production and moulding of deviance, i.e. it pays insufficient attention to the particular social circumstances and opportunities which affect crime.

- Merton ignored the possibility of achievements exceeding expectations, rather than simply failing to reach them – what Downes and Rock call the 'anomie of success' (2003: 137).

- Some deviance, rather than being the product of 'strain', appears rather to be part and parcel of the routine operation of work or organisations, or even the state. How, for example, might anomie theory deal with state human rights abuses?

Questions for further discussion

1 In what ways might crime be considered *normal* in society?

2 What are the main differences between Durkheim's and Merton's use of the term *anomie*?

3 In what ways is Merton's argument *structural* and in what ways is it *cultural*?

4 Is it right to say that strain theory over-predicts working-class deviance?

5 In what ways might a society be considered to be criminogenic?

6 Does general strain theory solve the problems identified in earlier strain theories?

Further reading

Agnew, R. (2006) Pressured into Crime: General strain theory, in Cullen F.T. and Agnew R. (eds), *Criminological Theory Past to Present: Essential readings,* 3rd edn, Los Angeles, CA: Roxbury

Cloward, R. A. and Ohlin, L. E. (2006) Delinquency and Opportunity, in Cullen F.T. and Agnew R. (eds), *Criminological Theory Past to Present: Essential readings,* 3rd edn, Los Angeles, CA: Roxbury

Durkheim, E. (1938) *The Rules of Sociological Method,* New York: Free Press (ch. 3)

Downes, D. and Rock, P. (2007) *Understanding Deviance,* 5th edn, Oxford: Oxford University Press (ch. 5)

Garland, D. (1990) *Punishment and Modern Society,* Oxford: Oxford University Press (ch. 2)

Merton, R. K. (1938) Social Structure and Anomie, *American Sociological Review,* 3,5, 672–682, Columbus, OH: The Ohio State University, Department of Sociology

Websites

There are a number of websites worth visiting. On Durkheim's life and work, the Emile Durkheim archive has lots of useful material – http: //durkheim.itgo.com. It is also worth looking at: http: //emiledurkheim.com. There are some interesting materials on Merton and anomie on the Crime Theory website: http: //www.crimetheory.com/Merton/index.html.

Chapter outline

Introduction	188
The Chicago School	188
Social ecology	190
Chicago School and crime	190
The zonal hypothesis	191
Shaw and McKay: cultural transmission	192
Chicago Area Project	193
Differential association	193
Differential reinforcement	194
Assessing the Chicago School	195
Cultures and subcultures	196
Albert Cohen	197
Cloward and Ohlin	198
David Matza	199
Subcultural theory	199
American subcultural theory	199
British subcultural theory	201
Assessing subcultural theory	204
Questions for further discussion	207
Further reading	207
Websites	207

The Chicago School, culture and subcultures

CHAPTER SUMMARY	For half a century, from the First World War onwards, criminology was increasingly dominated by sociologists and sociological thought. Initially, via a group of scholars working in, or trained at, the Department of Sociology in the University of Chicago the focus of much criminology was upon the nature of the city, its structures and processes, and how these related to patterns of crime and delinquency.

This chapter looks at how:

- such sociology was based on rich ethnographic studies of the everyday lives of Chicagoans;

- this tradition bred a further set of detailed empirical studies focusing on the cultural context and social meaning of deviant activity;

- initially in the US, and subsequently in Britain, attention turned to the notion of *subcultures*.

Introduction

In the previous four chapters we looked at some of the roots of what we now understand as criminology. By the 1930s – the period we begin from in this chapter – criminology was still not a term that was widely used. However, this was soon to change, and what has subsequently become known as the Chicago School is central to that process. Indeed, according to Leon Radzinowicz (1962: 117–118):

> In the years between the two world wars, the significance of criminological studies in the United States of America increased out of all recognition. The European influence was transcended ... American criminology entered upon its germinal phase ... It became an independent discipline, unmistakably original in its approach and conclusions, full of explanatory vigour, attracting minds of outstanding ability.

Indeed, Lewis Coser (1979: 311–2) says 'It seems no exaggeration to say that for roughly 20 years, from the first world war to the mid-1930s, the history of sociology in America can largely be written as the history of the Department of Sociology of the University of Chicago.'

The Chicago School

Chicago University has a special place in the history of criminology. The reason for this dates back to 1892 when it took the decision to establish the first major sociology department in the United States. By the 1930s the department was a large and vibrant home for a particular brand of sociology – one based on direct experience and observation (generally referred to as 'ethnography') – and a massive amount of work which focused on the city in which the University was located.

Some of the most important names in American sociology – Walter Reckless, Frederick Thrasher, Everett Hughes, Robert Park, Edwin Sutherland and later Clifford Shaw, Henry McKay, Louis Wirth and Gerald Suttles – studied Chicago's immigrant and minority communities, its vice and organised crime, its homeless and, crucially, the make-up of the city itself.

Though generally referred to as the Chicago *School* the work of the Chicago sociologists isn't uniform or particularly systematised (Heidensohn, 1989). If the establishment of the first sociology department was an important factor in this history, the siting of it in Chicago was vital. At the time, Chicago was America's second largest city and it was undergoing rapid and significant change. The rapid industrialisation of the United States saw the growth of steel mills, railroads and other major manufacturing concerns in Chicago and alongside this, swift demographic changes as African Americans from the South and white immigrants from Europe arrived in large numbers. Half of the population of Chicago in 1900 had been born outside the USA.

It was such changes, Lilly *et al.* (2002: 32) argue, that 'made the city – and not the "little house on the prairie" – the nation's focal point'. Just as sociology itself was the product of the rapid social,

The influence of the Chicago School

Albion Small

Founder of the Sociology Department in Chicago and also of the *American Journal of Sociology*

Clifford Shaw and Henry McKay

Authors of some of the Chicago School's best-known work

W.I. Thomas

Ethnographer and author of *The Polish Peasant*, with:

Florian Znaniecki

Louis Wirth

Enormously influential urban sociologist

Frederic Thrasher

Author of *The Gang*, a huge and influential study of Chicago's gangs

Herbert Blumer

Coined the term 'symbolic interaction'

Edwin Sutherland

Arguably the most famous criminologist of the twentieth century

Gerald Suttles

Author of numerous studies of urban life including *The Social Order of the Slum*

Walter Reckless

Deviser of 'containment theory'

Erving Goffman

Hugely influential sociologist; author of *Stigma, Asylums*, and *The Presentation of Self in Everyday Life*

Everett Hughes

Studied occupations, author of *Men and their Work*

Howard Becker

A graduate of the Chicago School and author of *Outsiders: Studies in the sociology of deviance*

economic and cultural changes of the eighteenth and nineteenth centuries so sociologically-informed criminology was itself profoundly influenced by the significant social changes of the early twentieth century – not least urbanisation and mass migration. Increasingly, crime came to be seen, at least in part, as a *social* problem.

Social ecology

The studies of the city itself are often referred to using the term 'ecology' – a biological metaphor pointing to the importance of natural patterning produced by differing species within some form of overall ordered universe. In this case, the universe was the city and the ecological focus was upon how the city grew and developed. Much of the Chicago School work was heavily influenced by Durkheim and, in particular, the view of crime levels as being linked to social organisation, and also

by Georg Simmel's (1903) picture of the city as a source of liberation and alienation.

According to Savage and Warde (1993: 13, quoted in Valier):

> The work of the Chicago School is best seen as an extended empirical inquiry into the nature of social bonding in the modern, fragmented, city. The city interested them for empirical, rather than conceptual reasons. It was where the division of labour was most elaborate and developed, and hence where the fragmentary nature of modern life could most profitably be studied.

Chicago School and crime

Though elements of the Chicago School research was statistically based, this group of sociologists is best known for their detailed ethnographic work,

---

Robert Ezra Park (1864–1944)

Robert Park, originally a newspaperman, turned urban ethnographer.

Born in Pennsylvania, Park grew up in Minnesota on the banks of the Mississippi. Graduating from the University of Michigan in 1887, Park became a newspaperman and worked on daily papers for the next decade in Minnesota, Detroit, Denver, New York, and Chicago.

According to Burgess and Bogue (1964: 3) Park 'was interested in the newspaper, its power of exposing conditions and arousing public sentiment, and in taking the lead against slums, exploitation of immigrants, or corruption in municipal affairs'.

In the mid-1890s he began to study philosophy at Harvard University and subsequently became a postgraduate student in Germany where, though he was not formally studying sociology, he was influenced by Georg Simmel.

'Dr Park found that, while newspaper publicity aroused a great deal of interest and stirred the emotions of the public, it did not lead to constructive action. He decided that something more than news was needed, that you had to get beneath the surface of things' (Burgess and Bogue, 1964: 3). His academic career then started in 1914 at the age of 50.

I expect I have actually covered more ground tramping about in cities in different parts of the world than any other living man. (cited in Lilly *et al.*, 2002: 33)

It is probably the breaking down of local attachments and the weakening of the restraints and inhibitions of the primary group, under the influence of the urban environment, which are largely responsible for the increase of vice and crime in great cities. (Robert Park, 1915)

using participant observation in order to produce what Matza (1964) later called 'appreciative' accounts of people's everyday lives. Shaw and McKay's (1942) work in Chicago uncovered two important patterns concerning the social and geographical distribution of crime and delinquency. The first was neighbourhoods tended to be relatively stable in their statuses as high, medium or low crime areas. That is, over a 20–30-year period, neighbourhoods would remain as high-crime, say, or low-crime areas despite changes in their racial and ethnic compositions.

Second, they found that crime and delinquency rates tended consistently to be lower in areas of high socio-economic status and higher in areas of relative socio-economic deprivation. This led them to conclude that the factors that helped to explain socio-economic differences were also important in explaining social and geographical variation in crime and delinquency. This is not the same as saying, however, that poverty *causes* crime.

The zonal hypothesis

At the heart of the Chicago School's explanation of urban development was their *zonal hypothesis*, the idea that the city evolved through a series of concentric circles, each being a zone of social and cultural life. The natural element to all this is the fact that it is not, or at least not *entirely,* planned. Moreover, the nature of each of the areas comes increasingly to resemble the character and qualities of the inhabitants: 'The effect of this is to convert what was at first a mere geographical expression into a neighbourhood, that is to say, a locality with sentiments, traditions, and a history of its own' (Park, quoted in Downes and Rock, 2003: 64).

Early work in Chicago by Ernest Burgess had sought to produce a social map of the city, and this work in the mid-1920s included the first exposition of the idea of concentric circles as the basis for understanding the social organisation of the city. For Burgess the growth of cities is far from haphazard, but actually is heavily patterned in ways that can be understood sociologically. He argued that cities tended to grow outwards in a series of concentric circles or rings.

As Burgess suggests, and Figure 9.1 illustrates, at the heart of the concentric circles is the business district (Zone I) – a zone that has high property values and a small residential population. Outside this is, for criminological purposes at least, arguably the most important zone (Zone II), known as the *zone of transition*. This is an area which has a more transient population, one which is poor, living in inadequate and deteriorating housing. Beyond this zone lay four residential zones each of which was broken down into a number of subsections, Burgess's argument being that newcomers gradually moved outward into more prosperous zones as they became integrated into American cultural life. Zone III is a zone of relatively modest residential homes occupied by people who have escaped Zone II. Zone IV, another residential district, is more affluent and occupies the space up to the city limits. Beyond this are suburban areas which make up Zone V.

According to Burgess (1925: 51):

This chart brings out clearly the main fact of expansion, namely, the tendency of each inner zone to extend its area by the invasion of the next outer zone. This aspect of expansion may be called *succession*, a process which has been studied in detail in plant ecology. If this chart is applied to Chicago, all four of these zones were in its early history included in the circumference of the inner zone, the present business district. The present boundaries of the area of deterioration were not many years ago those of the zone now inhabited by independent wage-earners, and within the memories of thousands of Chicagoans contained the residences of the 'best families'.

In the zone of transition there were copious examples of *deviant* behaviour and social problems: crime, prostitution, high infant mortality and poor health and, of course, poverty. Such problems were by no means confined to the zone of transition, but they were disproportionately concentrated there. Such deviance is, in effect, largely an effort to create order in an area of disorganisation. This zone was portrayed by the Chicago sociologists as disorganised and unruly, though others such as Matza and Whyte were critical of what they saw as the failure to *see* the nature of social order and organisation in the diversity and hubbub of this transitional zone.

Thomas and Znaniecki (1918) had earlier argued that 'The stability of group institutions is ... simply a dynamic equilibrium of processes of disorganization and reorganization. This equilibrium is disturbed when processes of disorganization can no longer be checked by any attempts to reinforce the existing rules.' Building on this, Shaw and McKay argued that rapid population changes resulted in a degree of social disorganisation in which established values lost their hold with predictable consequences for crime and delinquency.

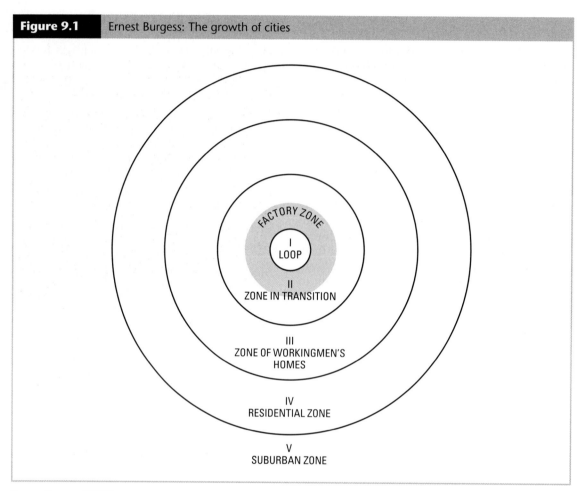

Figure 9.1   Ernest Burgess: The growth of cities

FACTORY ZONE

I
LOOP

II
ZONE IN TRANSITION

III
ZONE OF WORKINGMEN'S
HOMES

IV
RESIDENTIAL ZONE

V
SUBURBAN ZONE

Source: Burgess (1925).

Shaw and McKay: cultural transmission

Burgess's work was tested by Shaw and McKay in the early 1940s. Their work (Shaw and McKay, 1942), using Chicago's juvenile court records over several decades, explored the ecological patterning of such offending. They found that the parts of the city with high delinquency rates were also characterised by:

- A high percentage of 'foreign born' and African-American heads of households.
- A high percentage of families on welfare.
- A low rate of home ownership, and greatest number of condemned buildings.
- Decreasing population.
- High rates of infant mortality, tuberculosis, insanity, adult criminality and truancy.

These parts of the city are characterised by different value systems from those held by other parts, they argued, and this can have important consequences for the ways in which people behave:

> In the areas of high economic status where the rates of delinquency are low there is, in general, a similarity in the attitudes of the residents with reference to conventional values ... In contrast, the areas of low economic status where the rates of delinquency are high, are characterized by wide diversity in norms and standards of behaviour ... Children living in such communities are exposed to a variety of contradictory standards and forms of behaviour rather than to a relatively consistent and conventional pattern.
>
> (1942: 170–172)

Their research supported Burgess's ecological thesis and they argued that the high levels of juvenile delinquency found in the zone of transition were a product of *social disorganisation* in that part of the city. This social disorganisation was characterised by poverty, residential mobility and racial heterogeneity. In addition, Shaw and McKay introduced the idea of *cultural transmission*. Their argument was that values, including delinquent values, are transmitted from generation to generation, and it is through such processes that particular areas become established as delinquent areas despite the turnover of people in the area. In such communities there develops a tradition in which various criminal activities are learned by young boys from the older ones in the area, with particular offences such as shoplifting, car theft and jackrolling (stealing) being passed from generation to generation.

> This tradition is manifested in many different ways. It becomes meaningful to the child through the conduct, speech, gestures, and attitudes of persons with whom he has contact. Of particular importance is the child's intimate association with predatory gangs or other forms of criminal or delinquent organization. Through his contacts with these groups and by virtue of his participation in their activities he learns the techniques of stealing, becomes involved in binding relationships with his companions in delinquency, and acquires the attitudes appropriate to his position as a member of such groups. (Shaw and McKay, 1942: 436)

Anticipating control theory-related ideas that were to follow in succeeding decades, Shaw and McKay argued that in the wealthier parts of the city children were more closely and carefully supervised and that such supervision was more difficult to achieve in those areas where traditional institutions such as schools, churches and the family itself were under greater pressure from rapid urban change. In this manner, *social disorganisation* is a significant breeding ground for delinquency and criminality.

Chicago Area Project

Clifford Shaw's academic studies had a practical component and consequence also. In the early 1930s he established the Chicago Area Project, a series of neighbourhood centres situated around the city. Their function was to co-ordinate community resources (churches, schools, local associations and clubs) in tackling local problems. In addition, they acted as a forum for generating funds to sponsor programmes for adults and young people, again with a view to responding to local problems and, crucially, involving local people in this process. The projects ran for over 20 years and spawned a number of imitators and, whilst there is little evidence that they had any profound effect on local

Much of the work of the Chicago sociologists focused on first-hand accounts of life in some of the most run-down parts of the city.

levels of juvenile delinquency, such models continue to exert some influence on much local community crime prevention activity.

Differential association

Shaw and McKay's ideas were taken up and modified by Edwin Sutherland, another criminologist who studied and, briefly, worked at Chicago University. His focus was less upon the fairly negative idea of social disorganisation. Rather, he explored how differential forms of organisation led to different cultural influences and mechanisms, and he sought to understand criminal behaviour as learned behaviour. His theory argued that, as with all behaviour, criminal conduct is learned in interaction with others, being communicated between groups and, indeed, generations. In this, he was much influenced by work by the French sociologist, Gabriel Tarde and his 'laws of imitation', and also by George Herbert Mead's influential work on symbolic interactionism. In a manner similar to

Sutherland's later work, Frederick Thrasher (1927) had argued in *The Gang* that ideas about behaviour were passed from generation to generation of males on the streets. At the core of the idea of differential association is the notion that if an individual is exposed to more ideas that promote law-breaking than they are ideas that act as barriers to such conduct, then criminal conduct becomes highly likely.

In Sutherland's words *differential association* is based on the hypothesis that 'a person becomes delinquent because of an excess of definitions favourable to violation of law over definitions unfavourable to violation of law' (Sutherland, 1947: 6). Shaw's work in books such as *The Jackroller* (Shaw, 1930) had shown the important influence of friends and peers on juvenile delinquency. For Sutherland, such learning covers the techniques of committing crime (which may be more or less complex) and what he refers to as 'the specific direction of motives, drives, rationalizations, and attitudes'. Differential associations vary in intensity, frequency, and duration and it is those, he argued, that last longer, are more intense, and occur earlier in life that are likely to be more influential.

Sutherland's ideas have been criticised for failing to explain why people develop the associations they do. Insofar as friendship groups are concerned it might be argued that the explanation is actually more to be found in peer *selection* than peer influence, i.e. people who are disposed toward delinquency search out delinquent peers precisely so as to provide a sympathetic context for their behaviour. Indeed, a number of criminologists, particularly those working in the control theory tradition (Hirschi, 1969) have proposed precisely this. However, in terms of the importance of *association,* the 'selection' criticism is obviously more difficult to sustain if the relationships concerned are, say, family relationships. The theory of differential association went through a number of forms, eventually being summarised in a set of nine propositions in 1947 (Sutherland and Cressey, 1947):

1 Criminal behaviour is learned.

2 Criminal behaviour is learned in interaction with other persons in a process of communication.

3 The principal part of the learning of criminal behaviour occurs within intimate personal groups.

4 When criminal behaviour is learned, the learning includes (a) techniques of committing the crime, which sometimes are very complicated, sometimes very simple; [and] (b) the specific direction of motives, drives, rationalisations, and attitudes.

5 The specific direction of motives and drives is learned from definitions of legal codes as favourable and unfavourable.

6 A person becomes delinquent because of an excess of definitions favourable to violation of law over definitions unfavourable to violation of law. This is the principle of differential association.

7 Differential associations may vary in frequency, duration, priority, and intensity.

8 The process of learning criminal behaviour by association with criminal and anti-criminal patterns involves all the mechanisms that are involved in any other learning.

9 While criminal behaviour is an expression of general needs and values, it is not explained by those general needs and values since non-criminal behaviour is an expression of the same needs and values. Thieves generally steal in order to secure money, but likewise honest labourers work in order to secure money. The attempts by many scholars to explain criminal behaviour by general drives and values, such as the happiness principle, striving for social status, the money motive, or frustration, have been, and must continue to be, futile, since they explain lawful behaviour as completely as they explain criminal behaviour. They are similar to respiration, which is necessary for any behaviour, but which does not differentiate criminal from non-criminal behaviour. (1970: 75–76)

Differential reinforcement

Criminologists such as Akers (see Chapter 7) and others have sought to extend Sutherland's ideas in a fairly direct form, using social learning theory to explore how criminal learning is undertaken. Akers' theory of 'differential reinforcement' takes Sutherland's ideas of 'definitions', and distinguishes between the 'general' (overall beliefs about what is good and bad) and the specific (particular conditions under which things are considered to be good or bad or right or wrong). This introduces the possibility that certain forms of criminal behaviour might generally be considered to be wrong, but may be permitted under certain circumstances.

Differential reinforcement relates to the anticipated consequences of particular actions, i.e. whether they are likely, for example, to result in punishment. We tend to do things that will not result in punishment, but in choosing courses of action we are influenced by what others do through a process that Akers refers to as *imitation.* Akers' expansion of Sutherland's ideas leads to the proposition that initial delinquent activity results from a combination of differential association and imitation. This initial participation will be differentially reinforced – meaning that it may be continued if the reinforcement is positive, or it will cease if the reaction is experienced as negative. These reinforcements may be directly experienced – say in the form of punishment – or observed in others.

Edwin Sutherland's ideas have had a lasting impact on various aspects of criminology. His theory of differential association was arguably crucial in moving criminology away from theories dominated by those who sought their answers in human biology, physiology or through psychiatry, and his 'legacy to criminology is not his specific learning theory but his argument that criminal behaviour is normal learned behaviour' (Vold *et al.*, 2002: 175). On a more general level, however, as Downes and Rock (2007) note, differential association theory's influence was in acting as a bridge between the early work of the Chicago School and what later became known as subcultural theory. This was true not just of American subcultural theory but also of British work in this area in the 1960s and 1970s. Before we turn our attention to subcultural theory we must look at some of the criticisms levelled at Chicago School sociology.

Assessing the Chicago School

One of the most oft-proffered negative views of the Chicago School is that the work is somewhat atheoretical. Some critics view the work of the Chicago sociologists as being rather overly descriptive and lacking in clear, theoretically-based, testable hypotheses. Downes and Rock quote Joseph Gusfield's reminiscence that he and his colleagues harboured an 'indifference, even disdain, for the endless efforts of sociologists to develop refined theory or methodological rigour' (2003: 76). It is important not to overstate such criticism however. By contrast, Lewis Coser (1979: 313), discussing the work of Chicago School has argued that:

> … it must be stressed that their reputation as atheoretical fact-finders and empty-headed empiricists is by no means deserved. The members of the early generation possessed well-furnished theoretical minds and were very much conversant with social theory, whether European or homegrown. Simmel, Durkheim, the Austrian conflict theorists, but also Marx (though not Weber) were part of the theoretical

toolkits of most Chicago sociologists of the first generation, and also, though less uniformly so, of the second.

Second, some commentators have been critical of the idea of the ecological model itself, in particular for its downplaying of those structurally determining factors within cities that were planned and far from 'natural'.

Third, the idea of *social disorganisation* itself is by no means always clearly distinguished from the phenomena it is used to explain, such as crime and disorder. That is, there appears sometimes to be an element of *teleology* in aspects of Shaw and McKay's explanation.

A fourth criticism concerns the idea of cultural transmission which, though persuasive and important, is argued to be unclear in some respects. Thus, it is not always clear how particular cultural formations, e.g. criminal (sub)cultures, come into being.

Fifth, much of the Chicago work is regularly criticised for having used official measures of crime as the basis for understanding different parts of the city and for doing so rather uncritically (for a critique of such official statistics see Chapter 3).

Sixth, elements of the Chicago sociology came close to structural determinism, placing too little emphasis on individual decision-making, and over-emphasising the influence of place.

Seventh, some of the work is said to have assumed too close a 'fit' between delinquent values and lower-class status or, the reverse, non-delinquent values and middle-class norms and lifestyles.

Finally, critics question whether ideas such as differential association and cultural transmission can explain *all* forms of crime. Can they, for example, explain impulsive or emotive offences where offenders may have had little contact with deviant values or ideas?

Whatever its shortcomings may have been, the detailed ethnographic work of the Chicago School 'prepared the basis for some of the principal sociological stances that were to come' (Downes and Rock, 2003: 80). Crucial amongst these were more recent studies of neighbourhoods and networks that have explored issues of 'social capital' and 'collective efficacy'. According to Bursik (2000: 94) these *systemic* theories of neighbourhood crime rates build on insights originating with Chicago School studies and suggest that:

- The levels of residential instability and population heterogeneity will be highest in economically-deprived neighbourhoods.

- Private and parochial networks will be smaller, be less dense, and have less breadth in neighbourhoods with high levels of residential instability and population heterogeneity.

- Public networks will be smaller, be less dense, and have less breadth in economically-deprived neighbourhoods.

- Crime rates are a function of the ability of private, parochial, and public networks to transfer the types of social capital that are necessary for the effective control of crime.

- The total effects of economic deprivation, residential instability, and population heterogeneity on crime are mediated by these intervening systemic factors.

One body of work that owes a substantial debt to the Chicago School and has sought to build on many of its insights, is Robert Sampson's work on local neighbourhoods and crime and, more particularly, on the idea of 'collective efficacy'. Sampson and colleagues' research in Chicago neighbourhoods found that a combination of poverty, family instability and high residential mobility tended to be associated with relatively high levels of violent crime (Sampson *et al.*, 1997). This they related to 'social disorganisation', defined as the community's inability to realise its objectives. The notion of 'collective efficacy' is almost the reverse of this, being the community's ability to maintain order through overt action. This can only successfully occur when there is 'mutual trust' and sufficient shared expectations about intervening to maintain order. Essentially, it refers to social cohesion – a form of social capital – based on shared values.

Although there are a number of important and very substantial differences between the social ecological approach of the Chicago School and later cultural and subcultural theorists, it is also the case that it is in some of this later work that the influence of the Chicago School can most obviously be seen. The developing interest in modern urban life and its opportunities can be seen early on in the work of Robert Park who set the tone of much that followed:

The processes of segregation establishes moral distances which make the city a mosaic of little worlds which touch but do not interpenetrate. This makes it possible for individuals to pass quickly and easily from one moral milieu to another, and encourages the fascinating but dangerous experiment of living at the same time in several different contiguous, but otherwise widely separated worlds. All this tends to give to city life

a superficial and adventitious character; it tends to complicate social relationships and to produce new and divergent individual types. It introduces, at the same time, an element of chance and adventure which adds to the stimulus of city life and gives it, for young and fresh nerves, a peculiar attractiveness. (Park, 1925: 40–41)

Review questions

1 What is meant by an *ecological* approach?

2 Explain what is meant by the *zone of transition* and what its importance was held to be.

3 What is *differential association*?

4 Why might critics have suggested that Chicago sociology was atheoretical?

Cultures and subcultures

Core features of Chicago School sociology – the focus on the city, the ethnographic and appreciative approach to research, and concern with the cultural basis of crime – all find their way into the subcultural approaches which emerged initially in America and later Britain after the Second World War.

As was suggested in the previous chapter it was actually Albert Cohen's work that initially built on Merton's theory and which, as importantly, introduced the notions of culture and subculture to the study of delinquency. Culture, for Cohen (1955), is systematised 'traditional ways of solving problems' transmitted across time. Cohen, who had been a student of Merton's at Harvard and Edwin Sutherland's at Indiana, drew on strain theory and the idea of cultural transmission as a means of explaining the development of delinquent subcultures.

'Subcultures' emerge as means of solving problems created by the incompatible demands of structure and culture. Though conducted much earlier, an early and path-breaking study of Chicago gangs by Frederic Thrasher saw such groupings as being characterised by a quest for excitement among other features. Thrasher's immense empirical study of 1,313 gangs in the city led him (1927: 57) to define the gang as:

… an interstitial group originally formed spontaneously, and then integrated through conflict. It is characterised by the following types of behaviour: meeting face-to-face, milling, movement

Street-corner boys in New York in the 1950s. Gangs, their organisation and operation, have been a long-running theme in American criminology.

through space as a unit, conflict and planning. The result of this collective behaviour is the development of tradition, unreflective internal structure, *esprit de corps,* solidarity, morale, group awareness, and attachments to a local territory.

Thrasher's view of gangs as the product of socially disorganised environments has been particularly influential, not only on subsequent studies of gangs, but also in the area of delinquency more generally.

Albert Cohen

Albert Cohen was also drawn to the concentration of delinquency within gangs, and in his model viewed gang delinquency as a form of solution to the contradictions, or strains, faced by many young men, in particular as a result of their failure within the educational system. According to Downes and Rock (2007), the way of life outlined in Cohen's theory of delinquency had six major features:

1 Economic rationality is largely absent.

2 Much delinquent activity is characterised by 'malice'.

3 The behaviour involves a rejection of dominant values.

4 Gang activity is hedonistic and emphasises instant gratification.

5 Delinquents are not specialists – their delinquent behaviour is varied.

6 Primary allegiance is to the gang rather than other groups.

Young people who have no immediate access to respectable status by virtue of their families, and who fare poorly in the competition for achieved status, can either continue to conform to middle-class values despite their low-status position, or they can find an alternative source of status: the gang. The gang inverts traditional values – hard work, respectability – as a means of creating an alternative world within which status can be achieved. In this sense it is perhaps closest to elements of Merton's 'rebellion' adaptation to strain. In a passage resonant of Merton, Cohen (1955: 137) observed that:

> Those values which are at the core of the 'American way of life', which help to motivate behaviour which we most esteem as 'typically American', are among the major determinants of that which we stigmatize as 'pathological' … the problems of adjustment to which the delinquent subculture is a response are determined, in part, by those very values which respectable society holds most sacred.

What Cohen called the 'corner boys' were poorly prepared and equipped to compete with their higher-class peers. The limited access they have to the status that is valued in American society means they are confronted with a 'problem of adjustment'. In effect, lower-class boys are handicapped, in part by the limitations of their own socialisation and also by the middle-class attitudes and values which are socially esteemed and by which they will inevitably be judged. They are 'denied status in the respectable society because they cannot meet the criteria of the respectable status system' (1955: 121).

According to Cohen, to the extent that they care about this they will feel some 'shame' and will experience 'status frustration'. Faced with such problems of adjustment, there is a search for a 'solution'. The response of the 'delinquent boy' is to join together with others in a similar position, forming the basis for the development of a delinquent subculture. Such reaction formation leads to a response that is hostile to middle-class values and rejects middle-class status and middle-class values. This process, argues Cohen, provides a more realistic basis than strain theory (see Chapter 8) for understanding the generally negative and non-pecuniary nature of much lower-class delinquency.

A number of criticisms have been levelled at Cohen's theory. First, some have been critical of the argument that middle-class values are as widely accepted by lower-class boys as Cohen suggests. Other critics, such as Downes (1966), have questioned the extent to which lower-class delinquent boys are hostile to middle-class norms and values.

Cloward and Ohlin

An attempt to build on and test Cohen's theory was the work undertaken by Cloward and Ohlin (1960) in a book entitled *Delinquency and Opportunity*. Again, much influenced by elements of strain theory, Cloward and Ohlin sought to build not only on Merton's work but also on Edwin Sutherland's notion of differential association (Cloward had been a student of Merton's at Columbia, Ohlin a student of Sutherland's as well as studying at Chicago).

Cloward and Ohlin asked 'under which conditions will persons experience strains and tensions that lead to delinquent solutions?' (1960: 32). In part, the answer was that 'the disparity between what lower-class youths are led to want and what is actually available to them is the source of a major problem of adjustment' (1960: 86). Where Cohen had emphasised the importance of schooling and education failure, Cloward and Ohlin's analysis was in some ways closer to Robert Merton's original picture of anomie, emphasising economic failure within a culture that idealised financial success.

However, into this mix they add elements of cultural transmission theory in order to illustrate how different forms of deviance develop. In essence, they argue that there exists an illegitimate opportunity structure (in parallel to the legitimate one), with some having greater access to this than others. Different groups, and different neighbourhoods vary in their access to resources and to opportunities – both legitimate and illegitimate. Adaptation to strain is mediated by the availability of particular means therefore:

> The concept of differential opportunity structures permits us to unite the theory of anomie, which recognizes the concept of differentials in access to legitimate means, and the 'Chicago' tradition, in which the concept of differentials in access to illegimate means is implicit. We can now look at the individual, not simply in relation to one or the other system of means, but in relation to both legitimate and illegitimate systems. (Cloward and Ohlin, 1960: 151)

They argued for the existence of greater specialisation in delinquency than Cohen had allowed for and, utilising Sutherland's ideas identified three types of delinquent subculture:

- *Criminal* – In which gangs worked largely for financial gain through robbery, theft and burglary; such subcultures he argued were more likely to emerge in organised slum areas where established offenders could act as role models to the younger generation.

- *Conflict* – Where the primary form of delinquency was violence; such subcultures were more likely to arise in disorganised areas where access to criminal role models was more restricted and where offending was therefore more to do, at least initially, with establishing social status.

- *Retreatist* – Where much delinquent activity involved drug use, arising out of the 'double-failure' to achieve success through legitimate or illegitimate avenues. Drug use is a 'solution' to the status dilemma posed by such failure.

Each of these represents a specific form of adaptation to anomie/strain:

Types of adaptation	Conventional goals	Legitimate means	Illegitimate means
Criminal	+	−	+
Retreatist	−	−	−
Conflict	+/−	+/−	+/−

Source: Cloward and Ohlin (1960).

The criminal subculture is likely to arise, they argued, when individuals facing blocked opportunity structures seek – and find – illegitimate means for achieving conventional goals. As Cloward and Ohlin describe it (1960: 171), it arises in circumstances where:

> ... a neighbourhood milieu characterized by close bonds between different age-levels of offenders, and between criminal and conventional elements. As a consequence of these integrative relationships, a new opportunity structure emerges which provides alternative avenues to success-goals. Hence the pressures generated by restrictions on legitimate access to success-goals are drained off. Social controls over the conduct of the young are effectively exercised, limiting

expressive behaviour and constraining the discontented to adopt instrumental, if criminalistic, styles of life.

David Matza

A critique and reworking of strain theory can be found in the work of David Matza. In his own work, and in his joint work with Gresham Sykes (Matza, 1969; Sykes and Matza, 1957; Matza and Sykes, 1961), Matza was critical of strain theory for its over-prediction of delinquency – a straightforward reading of the theory implying that in fact there is far more delinquency than is actually the case. As such Matza and Sykes shared something of the perspective of control theorists (see Chapter 11) in that their focus was upon the apparent conventionality and conformity of many young delinquents. More particularly, Matza and Sykes departed from the assumptions of much strain and subcultural theory in rejecting the idea that delinquent values should necessarily be understood as oppositional to mainstream values.

Rather, the constraints of the dominant value system are merely loosened; delinquent values enable some distance to be created from dominant values through the adoption of what they term 'subterranean values'. Such values include excitement, maschismo, toughness and a rejection of the world of work, and they are to be found in all parts of society. Delinquent activity itself is justified through what he terms *techniques of neutralisation*. These are effectively rationalisations or justifications. In order to continue with a decision to break the law, individuals need to able to convince themselves that what they are doing is not really deviant, is not really wrong. The application of such techniques, and the necessity of doing so, is an illustration of the power of non-delinquent values. They include:

- Denial of responsibility ('It wasn't my fault', 'I wasn't to blame').

- Denial of injury ('They were insured anyway', 'No-one will ever miss it').

- Denial of the victim ('They were asking for it'; 'It didn't affect them'; 'No-one got hurt').

- Condemnation of the condemners ('They were just picking on me, I didn't do anything that others don't do').

- Appeal to higher loyalties ('I was only protecting my family'; 'I was only obeying orders').

Critics have taken Matza to task for underplaying offending behaviour: 'Unfortunately in setting out to remedy theories which he saw as "over-predicting" delinquency, Matza over-corrects to the point at which his own theory *under-predicts* both its scale and, in particular, its more violent forms' (Downes and Rock, 2003: 149).

Subcultural theory

Cultural or subcultural theories proceed from the basis that behaviour can be understood as a largely rational means of solving problems thrown up by existing social circumstances – and, in this, they share something with strain theory. At the heart of such approaches there lies the comparison of the 'dominant' cultures and deviant subcultures – these subcultures being conceived as a solution (a *delinquent solution*) to the dilemmas posed by the dominant culture. In early Chicago School work the cultures of the criminal area were distinct from mainstream values, and the process by which such values were learned was one of 'cultural transmission'.

Later writers such Cloward and Ohlin focused more on the internalisation of middle-class values and the reaction formation that occurred as a result of rejection by middle-class society. In later subcultural theory, the rather consensual model of social organisation implied by the idea of a dominant culture was replaced with a greater focus on dissensus and conflict and, particularly in British subcultural theory, in an emphasis on social class. There have been, therefore, effectively two *waves* of subcultural theory (Young, 1986). The first an American structural-functionalist wave appearing in the 1950s and 1960s, later followed by a largely British Marxist wave in the late 1970s. As Stan Cohen (1980: *iv*) noted, despite any differences, the two waves shared a great deal:

> Both work with the same 'problematic' (to use the fashionable term): growing up in a class society; both identify the same vulnerable group: the urban male working-class late adolescent; both see delinquency as a collective solution to a structurally imposed problem.

American subcultural theory

An early attempt 'to give a new slant' to the field (Laub, 1983: 174) was Thorsten Sellin's (1938) idea of culture conflict. Sellin, building on Chicago School work, focused on the way in which the nature of local neighbourhoods or communities could lead to the development of social attitudes that conflicted with legal rules and norms. In particular he was interested in which localised normative systems could come into conflict with more general social normative systems – as expressed in law. Crudely, therefore, it is possible that adherence to local, community norms may have the effect of leading individuals into conflict with wider social expectations and rules: a form of conformity that leads to crime.

An extension of these ideas was proposed by Wolfgang and Ferracuti (1967) in *The Subculture of Violence*. Their focus, in particular, was on the most expressive or emotional forms of violence, those conducted in the heat of the moment rather than activities that were planned and calculated. Earlier, Marvin Wolfgang had argued:

> A male is usually expected to defend the name or honour of his mother, the virtue of womanhood ... and to accept no derogation about his race (even from a member of his own race), his age, or his masculinity. Quick resort to physical combat as a measure of daring, courage or defence of status appears to be a cultural expression, especially for lower socio-economic class males of both races. When such a culture norm response is elicited from an individual engaged in social interplay with others who harbour the same response mechanism, physical assaults, altercations, and violent domestic quarrels that result in homicide are likely to be common. (1958: 188–89)

Wolfgang and Ferracuti (1967) argued that the differences between the parent culture and a subculture of violence were only partial, not total. The crucial difference was the reliance, in some circumstances, on violence as a response to these circumstances. This might involve challenges to honour, respect or some other form of challenge, but was expected to be met with physical force rather than some other form of reaction. Thus, one can easily imagine in some communities, slights or perceived threats to a man's honour or social standing would be likely to prompt a violent response. These circumstances are indicative of a *subculture of violence* and are often class-related. Violence tends to be viewed as normal and expected, and thus is not perceived as wrong or something which should result in a feeling of shame or guilt.

Needless to say, *subcultures* of violence are often associated with lower-class/working-class environments. Elijah Anderson (1990) in his *Code of the Street* argued that competition among the poor for very limited job opportunities, and with plentiful illegitimate opportunities, led to the development of a sense of alienation and despair. This in turn generated a code of the street which was a set of rules governing public behaviour, at the heart of which is 'respect'. It is the failure to show respect which lies at the heart of much violence he argues:

> Manhood in the inner city means taking the prerogatives of men with respect to strangers, other men and women – being distinguished as a man. It implies physicality and a certain ruthlessness. Regard and respect are associated with this concept in large part because of its practical application: if others have little or no regard for a person's manhood, his very life and those of his loved ones could be in jeopardy ... For many inner-city youths, manhood and respect are flipsides of the same coin; physical and psychological well-being are inseparable, and both require a sense of control, of being in charge. (reproduced in Cullen and Agnew, 2006: 158)

Walter B. Miller's (1958) ethnographic research concentrated on the behaviour and attitudes of male gang members from a relatively poor area near Boston and explored the extent to which such groups displayed and adhered to norms and values that were distinguishable from those of mainstream cultural values. For Miller (1958), there were six distinguishing concerns in such cultures:

1 *Trouble* – There is a particular preoccupation with 'getting into trouble' and the potential consequences of doing so.

2 *Toughness* – The dominance of female role models within the family in such cultures leads to the valorisation of certain aspects of other aspects of masculinity in other environments, none more so than toughness.

3 *Smartness* – In the sense of being 'street smart' is highly prized, in contrast to being 'book smart'.

4 *Excitement* – Daily routines of work can be exceedingly monotonous and are compensated for by the active search for excitement in other arenas.

5 *Fate* – The future tends to be viewed in fatalistic terms rather than as something that can be manipulated or in any way controlled.

6 *Autonomy* – Strong resentment of outside interference and intervention is a sign according to Miller of a sense of autonomy in life – albeit one that is undermined by the other focal concerns of such subcultures.

In this view, working-class culture is a 'generating milieu' for delinquency. The absence of male role models can lead to the development of exaggerated masculine styles, and overcrowded conditions push males out on to the street where gang activity becomes more likely. It will be immediately obvious that one of the important contrasts between subcultural theory – at least in this particular form – and strain theory is that, unlike strain theory it sees lower-class cultural values as being quite distinct from those of the mainstream. In this case crime is not a product of a failure to meet middle-class expectations, but more a product of conformity to working-class norms.

There are problems, of course, with both positions. Critics have argued that strain theories overemphasise the importance of middle-class values and, in doing so, adopt a somewhat patronising attitude toward 'lower' social classes. On the other hand, whilst subcultural theory largely avoids such faults, some have argued that by contrast one of its shortcomings is that it is based on a stereotyped view of working-class cultures.

Much American subcultural theory has been preoccupied with gangs or similar organised groupings within which delinquent activity takes place. By contrast, as we will see, British subcultural theory has questioned the extent to which delinquency really takes place within such settings or, at least, have questioned the applicability of such ideas to the British context.

British subcultural theory

David Downes (1966) in his landmark study, *The Delinquent Solution,* noted that British criminology, with its preoccupations with penology, the psychology of crime and legal and statistical studies of delinquency, had 'involved the almost complete neglect of the very questions with which American sociologists preoccupy themselves'. As David Matza observed in the introduction to the book, 'Downes was a most un-English criminologist'. In the late 1950s/early 1960s, influenced by American sociological criminology, studies such as John Barron Mays' *Growing Up in the City* and Terry Morris' *The Criminal Area* began to emerge, and they formed the basis of a distinctly British form of sociological criminology which really took off from the late 1960s after the publication of Downes' work.

Heavily influenced by the Chicago School, Mays' work was based in a poor neighbourhood in Liverpool and examined the subculture of the area and its relationship with the culture of the city more generally. Delinquent values were learned, he argued, and much of the behaviour he recorded he inter-

David Downes stumbled into criminology, as so many criminologists do, when 'not even knowing of the existence of the subject' (Downes, 1998). He applied to enter the London School of Economics (LSE) hoping to become a social worker and was told how people studied such subjects as 'drug-taking, white-collar crime and delinquency'. David Downes went on to become one of the leading British criminologists, specialising in the study of delinquency and comparative penal policy.

preted as that of relatively deprived young people seeking to cope with their restricted circumstances. Morris' study of a Croydon suburb saw this 'delinquent area' as the product of housing policies and the social concentration of 'problem families' in particular areas. The consequence, borrowing elements of differential association and cultural transmission theory, is the emergence of a delinquent subculture in which many will adopt delinquent values but some will remain relatively resistant – largely because of their socio-economic and family circumstances.

Willmott's (1966) study of adolescent boys in Bethnal Green in East London also explored youthful delinquency. Willmott rejected the idea of 'status frustration' as being at the heart of much delinquent activity and argued instead that the more serious offending behaviours were partly at least a product of a search for excitement and an expression of group values and solidarity. Simultaneously, David Downes was also doing his doctoral research in the East End (in Stepney and Poplar).

In Downes' view, delinquency is not at heart rebellious, but conformist. The conformity is to working-class values. Consequently, he effectively rejected the idea – so far as the area he was

East London, 1960. The site of a number of important studies – notably David Downes' *The Delinquent Solution* – forming the basis for the British subcultural tradition.

studying was concerned – of delinquent subcultures and, rather, saw delinquency as a 'solution' to some of the structural problems faced by young men. In this, in part, he was aligning himself with American sociologists such as Matza and Sykes. For Downes, many of the young people he studied dissociated themselves from school and work and emphasised leisure goals:

> In the absence of work-orientation and job-satisfaction, and lacking the compensations accruing from alternative areas of non-work, such as home-centredness, political activity and community service, the 'corner boy' attaches unusual importance to leisure. There is no reason to suppose that the delinquent 'corner boy' does not share the more general, technically classless 'teenage culture', a culture whose active pursuit depends on freedom from the restraints of adult responsibility, but which reflects the 'subterranean values' of the conventional adult world. There is some reason to suppose, however, that the working-class 'corner boy' both lays greater stress on its leisure goals, and has far less legitimate access to them, than male adolescents differently placed in the social structure. This discrepancy is thought to be enough to provide immediate impetus to a great deal of group delinquency, limited in ferocity but diversified in content. (Downes, 1966: 250)

British subcultural studies really took off in the 1970s and much of the most important work emanated from the Centre for Contemporary Cultural Studies (CCCS) at Birmingham University. Funded initially with money from Sir Allen Lane of Penguin Books, the first Director of CCCS was Richard Hoggart whose (1957) book, *The Uses of Literacy,* has been described as one of the two 'foundational texts' for British (sub)cultural studies – the other being Raymond Williams' (1958) *Culture and Society 1780–1950.*

Subculture, for the Birmingham School writers, was viewed as an expression of an 'imaginary relation' – something expressed via symbols and feelings. The cultural and political stance of various youth groupings was therefore 'read' by cultural theorists through an examination of dress, music, style and elements of behaviour. In a seminal CCCS article, Phil Cohen (1972: 23) argued that subcultures could be considered:

> … as so many variations on a central theme – the contradiction, at an ideological level, between traditional working-class Puritanism, and the new hedonism of consumption; at an economic level between the future as part of the socially mobile elite, or as part of the new lumpen. Mods, Parkers, skinheads, crombies, all represent, in their different ways, an attempt to retrieve some of the socially cohesive elements destroyed in their parent culture, and to combine these with elements selected from other class fractions.

Beginning with the Teds in the 1950s a succession of white working-class subcultures followed with what appeared to be increasing speed. These included 'mods' – of various sorts – whose style was 'sharp but neat and visually understated' (Hebdige, 1976: 88) and broad enough to encompass sharp-suits, parkas, and the seemingly ubiquitous Vespa (Cohen, 1972). In opposition, sometimes literally, always stylistically, were the Rockers. Similar to the Teds, in that they originated from lower down the social scale than the mods (Barker and Little, 1964), they were unfashionable, unglamorous, and associated with leather, motor bikes, and an aggressive, often violent, masculinity (Willis, 1978).

Perhaps the most starkly aggressive of all subcultural styles were the skinheads, who appeared in the late 1960s, but resurfaced in the mid-1970s. The skinheads espoused traditional, even reactionary, values and, through their association with football violence and attacks on ethnic minorities and gays, quickly obtained folk devil status. Their racism, defence of territory, opposition to hippie values, their social origins (unskilled working class) and particular construction of style or 'bricolage' (Clarke,

British subcultural studies, and especially the 'Birmingham School', were preoccupied with readings of 'style' such as the scooters and parkas of the mods (1960s) and the cropped hair, braces and Doc Martens of the skinheads (seen here at a National Front rally in London in 1988).

1976b) – Doc Marten boots, cropped hair, braces – were seen by subcultural theorists as representing 'an attempt to recreate through the "mob" the traditional working class community' (Clarke, 1976a: 99).

The emergence of a distinctly British school of subcultural theory was in part a response to the perceived shortcomings of *anomie* theory, but also because North American theory was felt inapplicable to the British context in a number of ways (Downes and Rock, 1982). As British subcultural theory developed, so its focus moved gradually away from delinquency and increasingly towards leisure and style (the main exceptions being Patrick (1973), Parker (1974), and Gill (1977). Parker's is a study of criminal subculture in which theft from cars provided a profitable adolescent interlude before the onset of a more respectable adult life or a more serious and long-term criminal career. Both his and Patrick's study – in which the focus was on the machismo of the 'hard man' – brought insights from labelling theory to bear on the study of subcultures. Parker's 'boys' used theft as a means of dealing with some of the problems they faced, dissociating themselves in part from the values of the dominant social order and, like the delinquents in Downes's (1966) study, responding within the physical and material conditions which constrained their range of choice and freedom.

Subcultures emerged not just as a response to the problems of material conditions – their class circumstances, schooling, and so on. They were also taken to represent a symbolic critique of the dominant culture in which 'style' was read as a form of resistance. Subcultures, at least from the viewpoint of the more radical commentators of the 1970s, were essentially oppositional rather than subordinate. In Phil Cohen's (1972: 23) terms, the latent function of subculture was to 'express and resolve, albeit "magically", the contradictions which appear in the parent culture'.

The solution, however, is largely expressed through style rather than crime. The style of each subculture involves the creation of identities and images built upon objects appropriated from other cultures and eras. It was at this point that the vocabulary of cultural studies met various strands of the sociology of deviance. Discerning 'the hidden messages inscribed in code on the glossy surfaces of style, to trace them out as maps of meaning' (Hebdige, 1979: 18) became the key task.

Though the bulk of youthful styles in the 1960s were of working-class origin, the last years of the decade also saw the development of a middle-class counter-culture which, associated with both permissiveness and drug use, was guaranteed a hostile reaction from 'respectable' society. Brake argues that hippie culture in Britain was made up largely of students and ex-students and 'provided a moratorium for its members of approximately five years in which to consider one's identity and relationship to the world' (1985: 95).

Through the late 1970s and into the 1980s, social and economic conditions for many young people became dramatically tougher. The key defining features were unemployment and racism, and it was against this background that African-Caribbean cultural resistance burgeoned and that 'punk' appeared. As the world of work retreated as a realistic prospect for many, so, it is argued, lifestyles dominated by consumption have come closer to the foreground. This was reflected in youth culture in the 1980s which 'became more of an advertising medium than ever before; it was notable not for opposition, but for its role in selling everything from Levi 501 jeans to spot cream' (Redhead, 1990: 105).

In such circumstances, 'respectable fears' about young people become exacerbated, especially around drug use. The late 1980s and 1990s saw the emergence of dance-based, drug-associated, youth cultural styles, to which the acid house subculture and subsequent rave 'movement' or 'scene' were central. With its origins in Chicago House music and Euro-Pop (the Balearic Beat), acid house enjoyed a brief moment of approbation in the media before its drug connections led to inevitable backlash. Acid house parties and, more particularly, the use of ecstasy were the focal point of moral campaigns. Such partying – or 'hedonism in hard times' (Redhead, 1993: 4) – was somewhat in contrast with the drabber youth culture of the late 1970s and early 1980s. Where 'punk had rejected such obvious pleasure a decade before ... youth hedonism was now back, with a vengeance. A fortnight's holiday in the sun became packed into a single weekend – then the next weekend and the next' (McKay, 1996: 105).

Resistance through Rituals (1975), one of the key publications from the Centre for Cultural Studies in Birmingham – a central concern in the work of the Centre was the investigation of youth subcultures.

From the 1970s onwards, as structural circumstances changed and, more particularly, youth unemployment rose, youth cultures fragmented. If anything, this served further to reinforce the view that adolescence was a problematic period in the life-course, and that adolescents themselves were a problem. The arrival of spectacular youth cultures also gave rise to a brief flourishing of subcultural theory which, though it has been largely out of favour for a long while, is now seeing something of a revival in elements of what is currently referred to as *cultural criminology*. In most respects cultural criminology is not a substantial departure from the types of subcultural theory that emerged in America and Britain in the 1950s to the 1970s and has developed in various ways since then. Rather, it appears more a (welcome) reassertion of the importance of sociologically-informed criminology at a time when administrative concerns and the new 'crime sciences' are seeking to impose their less theoretically-oriented approaches to the subject.

One of the themes that runs through both much of strain theory and of subcultural theory (and reappears later in cultural criminology) is excitement. Excitement is related to delinquency in a number of ways: as one of its primary causes or consequences or, relatedly, as a close correlate (delinquency being a by-product of other *exciting* activities). However, it is very much taken-for-granted in much strain theory that the search for excitement exists, at least in part, to make-up for lost opportunities elsewhere. However, with the gradual uncovering of middle-class 'delinquency' such an explanation becomes trickier. The consequence, as Downes and Rock (2003: 154) point out, was that 'these theories lost some of their force. Labelling theory assumed greater plausibility' (see Chapter 10).

Assessing subcultural theory

No study of youthful delinquency can now easily proceed without utilising many of the insights of subcultural theory. As numerous commentators have observed, subcultural theorists pointed to the collective nature of much delinquency, drawing our attention towards groups and gangs and away from more individualised notions of deviance. Second, subcultural theorists were insistent that deviance was to be understood in social and political contexts, not as something which is a product of biology or psychology. Such approaches also point us to the very particular socio-economic circumstances of the working classes and the important role this potentially plays in our understanding of 'deviant activity'.

Nevertheless, there have been a number of substantive criticisms aimed at subcultural theory. Heidensohn (1989) lists five major sets of criticism:

- *Determinism* – Subcultural theory has been criticised for its tendency to overemphasise the influence of structural and cultural constraints, underplaying the conscious choices made by individuals. This is arguably particularly true of the more Marxist-influenced elements of British subcultural theory.

- *Selectivity* – British subcultural theory in particular has been criticised for focusing on the most stylistically outrageous and unusual subcultures whilst ignoring the more mundane and, arguably, conforming youthful styles. This is linked with a later criticism – that of generally ignoring women in such work. Interestingly, it was the feminist subcultural theorists who, later, paid greater attention to more mundane aspects of everyday teenage life, not least through studies of girl's bedrooms and popular magazines (McRobbie and Garber, 1991).

- *Conformity* – One of the problems with subcultural theory, as Matza and others have pointed out, is that of over-prediction. That is to say that even in the poorest working-class communities, crime is not ever-present in all lives. Not everyone is delinquent or, more particularly, involved in serious delinquency.

- *Gender*

Subcultures: the feminist critique

According to its feminist critics, the bulk of subcultural theory was blind to gender. Indeed, in the book that came closest to being a *manifesto* for British subcultural studies, *Resistance through Rituals* (Hall and Jefferson, 1976), McRobbie and Garber (1976: 209) noted that the 'absence of girls from the whole of the literature in this area is quite striking and demands explanation. Very little seems to have been written about the role of girls in youth cultural groupings in general. They are absent from the classic subcultural ethnographic studies, the 'pop' histories, personal accounts, or journalistic surveys. When they do appear, it is either in ways which uncritically reinforce the stereotypical image of woman with which we are now so familiar ... or they are fleetingly and marginally presented.'

Angela McRobbie

Why is this, they ask? Is it because girls are not really active or present in youth subcultures or is it a product of a particular form of academic research? Their conclusion was that because of their position within public and private worlds, girls tend to be pushed to the periphery of social activities, and much 'girl culture' becomes a culture of the bedroom rather than the street (see also Frith, 1983). It is this McRobbie (1980: 40) argues that most subcultural theorists ignore:

> in documenting the temporary flights of the Teds, mods or rockers, most subcultural theorists 'fail[ed] to show that it is monstrously more difficult for women to escape (even temporarily) and that these symbolic flights have often been at the expense of women (especially mothers) and girls. The lads' ... peer group consciousness and pleasure frequently seem to hinge on a collective disregard for women and sexual exploitation of girls.'

- *Anomie* – Much subcultural theory focuses on the supposedly anomic circumstances of delinquent lives and yet, as Downes and others show, delinquent youth share much of the value system of the mainstream adult and middle-class world.

One of the most serious criticisms of British subcultural theory concerns the issue of imputation – in effect 'reading off', or assuming, particular attributes from specific ways of living, dressing and behaving.

The question is, how reliable are such readings and how do we or can we know? Stan Cohen points to three areas in which this problem arises:

- *Structure* – Cohen is critical of the tendency in such writing to explain the problems of the present by reference to the historical past. He is, he says (2002: liii-liv) 'less than convinced that any essentialist version of history – such as the dominant one of a free working class interfered with since the eighteenth century by the bourgeois state apparatus – is either necessary or sufficient to make sense of delinquency or youth culture today.'

- *Culture* – Meaning is attributed to all manner of artefacts from the important all the way through to the mundane. However, Cohen is critical of the tendency to treat them all as if they were signs of 'resistance' when some could just as easily be symbols of conservatism and support. Then there is the question of intent. How do we know what the symbols mean? Here, he says (2002: lix) 'my feeling is that the symbolic baggage the kids are being asked to carry around is just too heavy, that the interrogations are just a little forced.' Moreover, the analyses offered by the likes of Hebdige and others are undoubtedly an imaginative way of reading the style, but how can we be sure, he asks, that they are also not imaginary?

- *Biography* – A number of important questions are hardly addressed by subcultural theory. Why, Cohen (2002) asks, is it that the case that some individuals exposed to particular pressures behave one way and others, subject to the same pressures, behave in a different manner, as with the problem of structure, so with biography. Why do some conform and others rebel? Subcultural theory is of little help here.

Related to these criticisms outlined by Cohen is a more general methodological and epistemological criticism made by Downes and Rock. In their view the failure to explore the difficulties of imputation is illustrative of a broader failure to consider the 'taxing methodological problems involved in exploring, describing and analysing entities so complicated and intangible as "culture" and "subculture"' (2003: 175). Subcultural theorists, they suggest, have tended to go about their work with only a passing acknowledgement of the sociology of knowledge and the niceties of cultural anthropology.

The final line of criticism concerns what Downes and Rock refer to as 'differential magnification'; the sense that subcultural theory, and those approaches that emphasise class conflict most particularly, are excessively concerned with subordinate cultures and largely ignore dominant cultures and the deviance that is associated with them. 'In these works, the worlds of teachers, social workers, policemen (*sic*), prison officers, employers and even academics are treated with the very disregard for ambiguity, complexity and resistances to ideology that would be (rightly) impugned if applied to working-class or delinquent cultures' (Downes and Rock, 2003: 174–5).

Review questions

1   What are the three main forms of subculture identified by Cloward and Ohlin?

2   What are the main *techniques of neutralisation*?

3   In what ways do subcultures offer 'magical' solutions to structural problems?

4   What are the main criticisms of subcultural theory?

Questions for further discussion

1 In what ways might understanding the ecology of the city be helpful in understanding crime today?

2 What differences are there between differential association and subcultural theory?

3 Is the study of subcultures of any relevance in understanding women's lives?

4 Does membership of a subculture imply rejection of mainstream social values?

5 What are the main differences between American and British subcultural theory?

Further reading

The following seven pieces provide a good introduction to the Chicago School and subcultural theory:

Anderson, E. (1999/2006) The code of the streets, in Cullen, F.T. and Agnew, R. (eds), *Criminological Theory Past to Present: Essential readings.* 3rd edn, Los Angeles, CA: Roxbury

Clarke, J. *et al.* (1976) Subcultures, cultures and class, in Hall, S. and Jefferson, T. (eds), *Resistance through Rituals,* London: Hutchinson

Cohen, A. (1955) *Delinquent Boys: The culture of the gang,* New York: Free Press (ch. 2, A general theory of subcultures)

Cohen, P. (1972) Subcultural conflict and working-class community, *Working Papers in Cultural Studies No. 2,* University of Birmingham: CCCS; reprinted as ch. 2 in Cohen, P. (ed.), *Rethinking the Youth Question,* Basingstoke: Macmillan

Cohen, S. (2002) *Folk Devils and Moral Panics,* 3rd edn, London: Routledge (esp. Introduction to the 3rd edn)

Shaw, C.R. and McKay, H.K. (1942/2006) Juvenile delinquency and urban areas, in Cullen, F.T. and Agnew, R. (eds), *Criminological Theory Past to Present: Essential readings,* 3rd edn, Los Angeles, CA: Roxbury

Sykes, G. and Matza, D. (1957) Techniques of neutralization: A theory of delinquency, *American Sociological Review,* 22, 6, 664–670, Columbus, OH: The Ohio State University, Department of Sociology

Arguably the two early classic British studies of male delinquency (they still hold up enormously well despite the years that have passed since their initial publication) are:

Downes, D. (1966) *The Delinquent Solution,* London: Routledge and Kegan Paul

Parker, H. (1974) *View From the Boys,* London: David and Charles

Websites

Some of the history of the Chicago Area Project as well as up-to-date information about its operation can be found at – http://www.chicagoareaproject.org/

There is material on the history of the Chicago University Sociology Department at – http://sociology.uchicago.edu/dep_hist.html

Chapter outline

Introduction 210

The emergence of labelling theory 213
Primary and secondary deviance 213

Becker's outsiders 214
Moral entrepreneurship 214
Becoming a marijuana user 215

Stigma 217

Self-fulfilling prophecy 218

Deviancy amplification 218
Folk devils and moral panics 218

Braithwaite and 'shaming' 219

Assessing labelling theories 220

Questions for further discussion 223
Further reading 224
Websites 224

Interactionism and labelling theory

CHAPTER SUMMARY

In the 1960s, the view that the response to crime might itself be criminogenic took hold. From this viewpoint the reaction to deviant conduct becomes a crucial factor in understanding the behaviour itself. Indeed, in some of the more extreme versions of labelling theory there is little to distinguish deviant behaviour from the social reaction. Such work has, as we will see, a number of key characteristics:

- it is concerned with what happens after an act is committed, not what happens before;

- it argues that deviance doesn't reside in the act, but in the reaction to it;

- it pays great attention both to how this reaction may consist of the application of labels, and the impact that such labels may have on the person concerned.

Although the bulk of work in this tradition focuses on the negative impact of labelling, some more recent criminological work has considered the positive potential of 'shaming'.

Introduction

Much of the criminological theory discussed in previous chapters, in its discussion of the causes of crime, has focused on matters prior to the criminal act. Moreover, positivist criminology in particular has tended to treat the notion of 'crime' relatively unproblematically. By contrast, the approaches discussed in this chapter start from the assumption that there is no essence to this thing we refer to as 'crime'. Deviance is simply those things we describe as such. Consequently, in such work the focus shifts away from the nature of deviant acts, and the 'nature' of the people that commit such acts, to look much more closely at how and why particular people come to be defined as 'deviant'. The focus is therefore more upon the social reaction to deviance. This is not entirely novel, for commentators had long observed the potentially negative impact of punishment. However, as Downes and Rock (2003: 154) argue, it was in the 1950s and 1960s that scholars such Howard Becker, Edwin Lemert and Aaron Cicourel were among 'the first to approach the social reaction to deviant behaviour as a *variable* not a constant'.

Much influenced by the Chicago School, the social psychology of George Herbert Mead and by the work of Herbert Blumer, the sociologists who are of central importance to this chapter came to focus on the importance of meaning in social interaction. The focus here is upon the world as a socially-constructed reality. The core task for the sociologist working in this tradition is to uncover such meanings, to examine how particular features of the social world are negotiated and are understood. The central argument is that it is this that makes us human – the fact that we are able to invest our actions with meaning. We act, and react, on the basis that actions have meanings.

Such observations require us to pay great attention to the ways in which human actors are active in the creation of their world, and are not simply products of it. Human action is invested with meaning. It is not static or unchanging. Nor are human actions necessarily easily understood. The same set of behaviours may be understood in different ways by different people, or may be understood differently depending on the cultural or historical context. The social-psychological perspective associated with Mead, Cooley and others (see Mead, 1934) sees the self as the crucial distinguishing characteristic of humans. Humans can make objects of themselves. That is, we can think of ourselves when acting, just as we can think of others. According to Herbert Blumer (1969: 12) the idea of self in this sense simply means:

> ... that a human being can be an object of his own action. Thus, he can recognize himself, for instance, as being a man, young in age, a student, in debt, trying to become a doctor, coming from an undistinguished family and so forth. In all such instances he is an object to himself; and he acts toward himself and guides himself in his actions toward others on the basis of the kind of object he is to himself.

Human interaction is undertaken with the aid of symbols – things which can be used to signify other things. In particular, we use language – and words

George Herbert Mead (1863–1931)

Born in Massachusetts, Mead was the son of a Congregationalist Minister. He studied philosophy at Harvard and began work on a PhD thesis in philosophy and physiological psychology at the University of Leipzig in Germany where he studied with Wilhelm Wundt and G. Stanley Hall.

He joined the University of Chicago, in the Philosophy Department, in 1894 and stayed there the rest of his career. Much of his most important work focused on the idea of 'the self' and his approach stressed how the self was constructed in interaction with others. That is to say, it is not something that we simply take with us to our social interaction, but rather is constantly negotiated and constructed through such interaction.

George Herbert Mead (1863–1931). A highly influential social psychologist, concerned in particular with issues of 'the self'.

such as *book, pen, computer, tutorial, lecture, university, pub* – to signify activities, institutions and ideas. If the meanings of these things are sufficiently shared then social life can proceed with a certain degree of orderliness and predictability. However, there is no guarantee that this will necessarily be so and we constantly monitor our own actions and those of others

to check that our understanding of *things* tallies with what it appears others assume. From this perspective, the nature of reality is constructed through the use of symbols and the interpretation of the meaning of (inter)actions. We tend to act on the basis of things that we believe to be true. This led the Chicago sociologist W.I. Thomas to coin the famous dictum that if we 'define situations as real, they are real in their consequences' (Thomas and Thomas, 1928: 572). This dictum resonates through the criminological ideas that have been influenced by interactionism and related sociological approaches.

The criminological ideas discussed in this chapter focus on the social reaction to crime. In addition to symbolic interactionism the other major influence on such work was a form of sociology informed by *ethnomethodology* and *phenomenology* and associated with scholars such as Alfred Schutz and Harold Garfinkel. Phenomenology is concerned with the ways in which people's subjective experience may be understood and, in particular, one aim is to uncover those underlying structures or rules which guide behaviour.

Ethnomethodologists such as Garfinkel focused on the ways in which everyday activities are made meaningful and on occasion this was done through shock tactics – by disturbing the social world one would help uncover its taken-for-grantedness. Thus, in one famous example, Harold Garfinkel instructed a group of his students that when they returned home, instead of behaving as they normally would, they should behave as if they were staying in a hotel and to record their parents' reactions. Predictably, the parents were often more than a little bemused as the background assumptions upon which their relationship with their children existed failed to help them make sense of what was happening:

> Family members were stupefied. They vigorously sought to make the strange actions intelligible and to restore the situation to normal appearances. Reports were filled with accounts of astonishment, bewilderment, shock, anxiety, embarrassment, and anger, and with charges by various family members that the student was mean, inconsiderate, selfish, nasty or impolite. (Garfinkel, 1967: 47)

Though there are varieties of phenomenology and many subtleties and nuances in such perspectives, for our purposes here the main impact has been in the development of what these days are often referred to as *social constructionist* approaches to understanding crime and deviance. Here the emphasis is placed upon the importance of seeing the social world as a product of long chains of individu-

Alfred Schutz (1899–1959). Born in Vienna, but left for America in 1939, where he settled in New York becoming one of the key influences in the development of the phenomenological perspective in social science.

Harold Garfinkel (1917–), sociologist who coined the term 'ethnomethodology'.

als' actions and interactions. Although this may have the appearance and feel of something that is solid and relatively unchanging, it is dynamic and constantly changing. Everything we wish to study as criminologists – laws, rules, behaviour defined as illegal, immoral, deviant and so on – must be approached as socially constructed achievements. It is to the processes and meanings of such social constructions that our attention should be trained.

Interactionist sociology is concerned with the minutiae of social worlds and social interactions. Moreover, much interactionist sociology, and therefore criminology, is focused on the attempt to understand the meanings involved in social interaction. The language of theatre – a dramaturgical analogy – pervades interactionist writing. There is much talk of actors, roles and audiences. The following oft-quoted remarks illustrate the point:

> Forms of behaviour *per se* do not differentiate deviants from non-deviants; it is the responses of the conventional and conforming members of society which identify and interpret behaviour as deviant which sociologically transforms persons into deviants. (Kitsuse, 1962)

> [D]eviance is *not* a quality of the act the person commits, but rather a consequence of the application by others of rules and sanctions to an 'offender'. (Becker, 1963: 9)

> The critical variable in the study of deviance ... is the social audience rather than the individual actor, since it is the audience which eventually

determines whether or not an episode of behaviour or any class of episodes is labelled deviant.
>
> (Erikson, 1966: 11)

> Older sociology ... tended to rest heavily upon the idea that deviance leads to social control. I have come to believe that the reverse idea, i.e. social control leads to deviance, is equally tenable and the potentially richer premise for studying deviance in modern society. (Lemert, 1967: v)

The last quote, from Edwin Lemert, illustrates an important and challenging aspect of the approaches to deviance discussed here. What they share is a concern with social reaction – not just for its own sake – but as a means of understanding deviance itself. This potential shift of focus involved in the so-called 'new deviancy' theories is illustrated in Figure 10.1.

The new deviancy theories, of which labelling theory was a prime example, were subversive, 'though what was subverted was not so much the wider society as academic criminology' (Tierney, 1996: 126). Breaking with orthodox, somewhat more positivistic criminology, the new deviancy theories adopted a more appreciative stance toward *deviants* and a more critical stance toward the state and the system that defined them as *deviant*. Sometimes such appreciation crossed the boundary into out and out admiration – in which lawbreakers became latter-day Robin Hoods redistributing wealth from the rich to the poor – and it was this normative stance that eventually led to a sociological and criminological reaction against such radical positions.

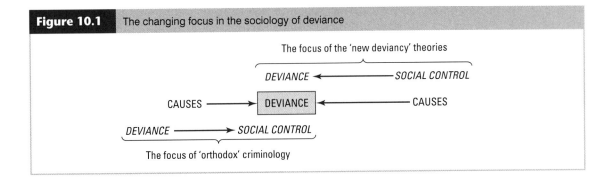

Figure 10.1   The changing focus in the sociology of deviance

The emergence of labelling theory

In the late 1930s Frank Tannenbaum's work on juvenile delinquency contained some of the elements of what would later become recognised as 'labelling theory'. Using the symbolic interactionist work on 'the self' – associated with scholars such as George Herbert Mead (the self as a social construct) and Charles Cooley (the looking-glass self) – Tannenbaum argued that delinquents are not inherently different from non-delinquents. Rather, it is the process of defining someone as a juvenile delinquent that arises out of conflict over the definition of particular activities or situations which (usually involving relatively minor forms of infraction by the young person concerned) which is important. Over time this leads to a hardening of local opinion, and attitudes change not just toward the behaviour concerned but also toward the young person. The changed attitudes lead to changes in behaviour – in interaction between the community and the young person – and eventually to the 'tagging' of the youth:

> The process of making the criminal is a process of tagging, defining, identifying, segregating, describing, emphasising, making conscious and self-conscious; it becomes a way of stimulating, suggesting, emphasising and evoking the very traits that are complained of ... The person becomes the thing he is described as being ... The way out is through a refusal to dramatise the evil. (Tannenbaum, 1938: 20)

Delinquents in this picture are good kids doing bad things, they become labelled as bad kids and continue in that vein.

Primary and secondary deviance

Edwin Lemert, an early advocate of this sociological approach, argued that amongst the vast range of acts of rule-breaking and deviance, it was those that generated a social response that should be the object of inquiry. Moreover, the social response may lead the 'offender' to make adjustments to their self-conception – their perception and understanding of themselves. Crucially, it may lead them to begin to see themselves as *deviant* and to act on this basis – that is, to adopt this as their *master status*. When they do, according to Lemert, their deviance is *secondary*.

Secondary deviance occurs 'when a person begins to employ his deviant behaviour or role based upon it as a means of defense, attack, or adjustment to the overt and covert problems created by the consequent societal reaction to him' (Schur, 1951: 76). As such it is distinguished from *primary deviance* which is the simple commission of a prohibited act. This is something that pretty much everybody does and most of the time is unlabelled, meaning that the people concerned don't develop a deviant identity. As Lemert (1972: 48) outlined:

> Primary deviance is assumed to arise in a wide variety of social, cultural, and psychological contexts, and at best [it] has only marginal implications for the psychic structure of the individual; it does not lead to symbolic reorganization at the level of self-regarding attitudes and social roles. Secondary deviation is deviant behaviour or social roles based upon it, which becomes a means of defense, attack, or adaptation to the overt and covert problems created by the societal reaction to primary deviation. In effect, the original 'causes' of the deviation recede and give way to the central importance of the disapproving, degradational, and isolating reactions of society. (Lemert, 1967: 17)

At least part of the importance of such insights is that they alert us to the fact that there is nothing *essential* about the bulk of deviant activity. It is not the fact that it happens *per se*, rather its extent, where it occurs and what precisely it consists of that is likely to be crucial in determining the response – formal or otherwise – that it calls forth. As such, therefore, such insights should caution against simplistic formulations about the inevitability of the exercise of state power and, moreover, of the inevitability of the consequences of state action should power be exercised. Certainly it highlights the unpredictability of the social world. Into this mix, as we will see, Becker introduced the idea of *moral entrepreneurship*: the activities of those members of society who seek to have rules enforced or the moral constitution of society somehow protected.

Review questions

1 What was Garfinkel attempting to illustrate when he asked his students to behave as if they were in a hotel when they went home?

2 How might social control create deviant activity?

3 What is the difference between *primary* and *secondary* deviance?

Becker's outsiders

Possibly the most influential writer of the period, Howard Becker was crucial in shifting attention away from crime and toward *deviance*. This shift acknowledged the inherently problematic and contested nature of much activity defined as criminal, and sought to explore how deviancy was created and understood. Becker's central contention, that deviance is 'a consequence of the application by others of rules and sanctions', is, according to Downes (1979: 3) 'superficially a banal and even trivial assertion'. Nevertheless, it 'caused an explosion in the petrified forest of criminology'. The sea change in criminology was from a position that took for granted the nature and status of legal codes and their enforcement, to one that treated such things as socially constructed and therefore problematic.

Many criminologists working in the interactionist tradition have focused particular attention on the ways in which particular laws, rules and regulations come into being. In many cases at the heart of the process of rule creation there lie the actions of individuals or groups who have a particular interest in seeing certain behaviours proscribed or subjected to some form of penalty. Such people Becker referred to as *moral entrepreneurs*:

> The prototype of the rule creator, but not the only variety ... is the crusading reformer. He is interested in the content of rules. The existing rules do not satisfy him because there is some evil which profoundly disturbs him. He feels that nothing can be right in the world until rules are made to correct it. (1963: 147–48)

Moral entrepreneurship

In a famous study of moral entrepreneurship, the sociologist Joseph Gusfield examined the history of the American temperance movement and the campaigns that lay behind the passage of the Prohibition laws in the US in the 1920s. His argument suggests that, in part, the prohibition movement was driven by white Protestant groups who were declining in social status and felt themselves threatened in particular by immigrant Irish Catholics. Their anti-alcohol campaigns were partly a symbolic attempt to reassert authority and social status in the face of such perceived threats, by demonstrating their continuing power to influence social mores. Moral entrepreneurs in general seek to impose their values or moral rules on others:

> Moral crusaders typically want to help those beneath them to achieve a better status. That those beneath them do not always like the means proposed for their salvation is another matter. But this fact – that moral crusaders are typically dominated by those in the upper levels of the social structure – means that they add to the power they derive from the legitimacy of their moral position, the power they derive from their superior position in society. (Becker, 1963: 149)

There are a number of important qualities in this excerpt from Becker. First is the emphasis on human agency. In discussing many other criminological approaches we have encountered the criticism that they present an overly-socialised, or deterministic, view of human behaviour (in which we, as individuals, are respectively the product of our biology, our psychology or our social environment). Labelling theory puts human creativity and decision-making at the centre of its concerns.

Second, as other sociologists had done in relation to other aspects of social behaviour, Becker introduces the idea of *career*. Third, Becker shifts

Moral campaigners from different eras. *Left*: Mary Whitehouse who sought to reduce the amount of sex and violence shown on television in the 1960s and 1970s. *Right*: Peter Tatchell, campaigner on human rights and gay rights – seen here attempting a citizen's arrest on Robert Mugabe, the President of Zimbabwe, when he visited London in 1999.

attention from the rule breaker to the audience – deviance, as we heard earlier, being the consequence of the application of rules and sanctions. A fuller quote is useful:

> Social groups create deviance by making the rules whose infraction constitutes deviance, and by applying those rules to particular people and labelling them as outsiders. From this point of view, deviance is *not* a quality of the act the person commits, but rather a consequence of the application by others of rules and sanctions to an 'offender'. The deviant is one to whom that label has been successfully applied; deviant behaviour is behaviour that people so label. (Becker, 1963: 9)

In effect, then, Becker argues that rule-breaking is generally the result of the three-stage process:

1 Rules are created by social groups, and it is the infraction of these rules that creates deviance.

2 The rules are applied to particular people.

3 Those to whom the rules are applied are then labelled as 'outsiders' (the selection of particular people or groups is dependent on *career contingencies*).

This process creates the deviant. At the heart of interactionist understandings of deviance, and labelling theory in particular, is the argument that what is crucial to the creation of deviance is the application of labels – *not* the breaking of rules.

Becoming a marijuana user

Becker's most famous essay, 'Becoming a Marijuana User', illustrates his argument that deviant 'motivation' (why we decide to do things that are socially proscribed) can often be understood as things that are developed in the course of experience with that deviant activity. Becker (1963: 42) argues that 'instead of the deviant motives leading to the deviant behaviour, it is the other way around; the deviant behaviour in time produced the deviant motivation' and then goes on to explore the emerging 'career' of the marijuana user (see box). He concludes, however, that 'learning to enjoy marijuana is a necessary but not sufficient condition for a person to develop a stable pattern of drug use'. In addition, there is the question of dealing with those forces of social control that attempt to prevent such activity.

How are the social sanctions against marijuana use rendered ineffective? There are three stages in the career of the marijuana user he argues:

● the *beginner* who is using for the first time;

● the *occasional user* whose use is sporadic and opportunistic;

● the *regular user* who uses systematically and, perhaps, daily.

In examining social controls, Becker focuses on access and supply, on the need for secrecy, and on the fact that such behaviour is socially defined as immoral.

Becoming a marijuana user

A young Howard Becker, on piano, in the Bobby Lain Trio at the 504 Club in Chicago *circa* 1950.

In his book *Outsiders* Howard Becker (1963) devotes two chapters to the subject of marijuana use. In the first he explores what he calls the 'career' of the marijuana user: 'the sequence of changes in attitude and experience which lead to *the use of marijuana for pleasure* (p. 43). By this he means the 'non-compulsive' and generally casual nature of such behaviour.

His work is based on 50 interviews with users undertaken through his contacts in the music business (Becker worked as a professional dance musician). His account begins with the person who has arrived at the point at which they are willing to try marijuana. There then follow three main stages:

- *Learning the Technique* – Learning the 'proper way to smoke the drug'. This may happen directly whilst participating with others or through observation and imitation. Learning the technique was vital if marijuana was to be seen as something that could bring pleasure.

- *Learning to Perceive the Effects* – Becker suggests that 'being high' consists of two elements: the presence of particular symptoms and the ability to recognise these symptoms. 'It is only when the novice becomes able to get high in this sense that he will continue to use marijuana for pleasure' (p. 51). As experience increases, the user becomes more familiar with the effects of the drug and develops a set of mechanisms for recognising and appreciating its impact.

- *Learning to Enjoy the Effects* – These effects are not necessarily or immediately pleasurable. The taste is a socially acquired one, 'not different in kind from acquired tastes for oysters or dry martinis' (p. 53). The initial effects of use may often be experienced as frightening, unpleasant or highly unusual. Unless these can be redefined as pleasurable then continued use is unlikely.

In relation to supply what is required is joining a group in which marijuana is used. This provides opportunity and access. It also provides the basis for *occasional* use. It will also likely provide the necessary connections in due course to make the necessary purchases to support *regular use*. Purchase carries latent dangers (such as arrest), but this may be re-estimated once a transaction has been successfully completed. In this way 'participation in groups in which marijuana is used creates the conditions under which the controls which limit access to it no longer operate' (1963: 66).

Because of social disapproval (perhaps stronger at the time Becker was writing) the marijuana user must manage their use in ways that ensure that non-users remain unaware that they are doing so. Again, experience of use, with others, gradually enables the user to recognise that there is no reason why others should find out so long as the behaviour is regulated in certain ways: 'persons limit their use of marijuana in proportion to the degree of their fear, realistic or otherwise, that non-users who are important to them will discover they use drugs and react in some punishing way' (1963: 72).

Finally, what of moral controls? There are a number of ways in which these can be circumvented. One is through what Becker refers to as 'rationalisations and justifications', but which are rather like 'techniques of neutralisation'. These include arguments such as suggesting that non-users often engage in much more harmful practices (alcohol misuse, for example), that the effects of cannabis are beneficial not harmful, and that use is limited and doesn't affect the user's life in any important way. 'In short, a person will feel free to use marijuana to the degree that he comes to regard conventional conceptions of it as the uninformed views of outsiders and replaces those conceptions with the "inside" view he has acquired through his experience with the drug in the company of other users' (1963: 78).

Stigma

Another concept which appears regularly in the new sociologies of deviance is *stigma* or what Goffman (1963) referred to as 'spoiled identities' and which he defined as 'an attribute that is deeply discrediting within a particular social interaction' (1963: 3). Such attributes may include physical and mental characteristics as well as various statuses associated with particular types of behaviour. According to Goffman (1963: 1) in ancient Greece stigma referred to:

> ... bodily signs designed to expose something unusual and bad about the moral status of the signifier. The signs were cut or burnt into the body and advertised that the bearer was a slave, a criminal or a traitor – a blemished person, ritually polluted, to be avoided, especially in public places.

Perhaps nowhere is such stigmatisation clearer in the contemporary criminal justice context than within prisons. In his account of the New Jersey State Prison in the 1950s, Gresham Sykes (1958) reflected on the variety of ways in which prisoners are reminded of their status through degradation ceremonies:

> The signs pointing to the prisoner's degradation are many – the anonymity of a uniform and a number rather than a name, the shaven head, the insistence on gestures of respect and subordination when addressing officials, and so on. The prisoner is never allowed to forget that, by committing a crime, he has forgone his claim to the status of a full-fledged, *trusted* member of society. (in Jacoby, 2004: 513)

Recent proposals from government ministers that offenders should be made to wear uniforms whilst undertaking work as part of their community penalties are an indicator that such symbols of degradation are not confined to the prison.

One of Goffman's central questions concerned how people manage such spoiled identities. Within institutions such as prisons – what Goffman (1961) called 'total institutions' – such debasements are a prelude to what is often a profound series of shifts in the inmate's *moral career*. Although on release some of the losses that have been experienced and incurred can be remedied, this is not possible for all. Some rights may be permanently lost, and elements of the redefinition of self that takes place in the process of adjustment and institutionalisation may have permanent consequences. On a more mundane level, parallel processes of stigmatisation are of potential relevance to the study of deviance, including the ways in which deviant careers may

Erving Goffman (1922–1982), sociologist, famous for his studies of human interaction. The title of one of best-known books, *The Presentation of Self in Everyday Life*, is indicative of his sociological perspective.

Former *Culture Club* singer, Boy George, in overalls cleaning up streets in Lower Manhattan as part of his community service, August 2006, after being found guilty of wasting police time (falsely reporting a robbery). Should such offenders wear uniform?

start and may either be reinforced or restricted by the criminal justice system.

Self-fulfilling prophecy

Part of the process of labelling is captured by Merton's term, 'self-fulfilling prophecy'. This, he described, as 'in the beginning, a *false* definition of the situation evoking a new behaviour which makes the originally false conception come *true*' (1968: 477). Much labelling theory, therefore, proceeds from the premise that many offenders are falsely defined as such or, if not falsely defined, have their moral character degraded as well as their behaviour judged. Put crudely, not only is their behaviour defined as 'bad', but their character too. Judged as being bad, and labelled as such, there is an enhanced likelihood that this will become that person's *master status* or will promote behavioural choices – which friends to hang around with, what forms of conduct are reasonable, appropriate or legitimate – which predispose toward increased criminality in the future.

As I am writing this, a radio programme is discussing the life of a former heroin addict and is following his attempts to leave his former life as an addict behind and to become a drugs counsellor. In describing the difficulties of doing this, the man concerned has talked not only of the physical problems associated with cessation of drug use – difficult enough – but also of what, from his account of it, sounds like the even greater challenge of ridding himself of the image that local people have of him as what he describes as a 'scumbag'. He says his previous life had left him with a reputation, and for a long time no matter what he did, people would continue to act toward him as if he were unchanged. What he is describing is precisely the problem of ridding himself of a label. Moreover, in recounting his *recovery* he talked powerfully of his desire not only to change his behaviour, but also the wish to change others' opinions of him. We return to this below in relation to what Braithwaite has called 'reintegrative shaming'.

Deviancy amplification

Related to Lemert's distinction between primary and secondary deviance, and the elaboration of such ideas within interactionist approaches to the sociology of deviance, is the notion of *deviancy amplification*. Associated initially with Leslie Wilkins (1964), deviancy amplification points to

the way in which the transmission of information about deviance may lead to both distortion and exaggeration and, in turn, to an adaptive behavioural reaction (see Chapter 4). That is to say, the reaction by agents or agencies of social control may lead to an escalation, rather than a diminution, of deviancy. Wilkins (1964: 90) summarises the general process of deviancy amplification as follows:

Less tolerance leads to →
  more acts being defined as crimes
    leads to →
  more action against criminals
    leads to →
  more alienation of deviants
    leads to →
  more crime by deviant groups
    leads to →
  less tolerance of deviants by conforming groups
      and round again

Folk devils and moral panics

Such ideas find expression in slightly altered form in, for example, Stan Cohen's *Folk Devils and Moral Panics*, notably in the social reaction to the dress and behaviour of the mods and rockers. Cohen's (2002: 8) explanation of the amplification process is as follows:

An initial act of deviance, or normative diversity (for example, in dress) is defined as being worthy of attention and is responded to punitively. The deviant or group of deviants is segregated or isolated and this operates to alienate them from conventional society. They perceive themselves as more deviant, group themselves with others in a similar position, and this leads to more deviance. This, in turn, exposes the group to further punitive sanctions and other forceful action by the conformists – and the system starts going round again.

As Cohen goes on to argue, there is no *necessity* to this process. It doesn't have to happen, just as primary deviation need not necessarily lead to secondary deviation or to the incorporation. What the argument about deviancy amplification does is illustrate how a potential sequence of events may lead to a spiral in which the behaviour of particular groups becomes subject to public attention, and that this may lead to a reaction which, in turn, fosters more behaviour of the kind that was the initial focus of public hostility. The job of the criminologist is to investigate such processes and explain how the sequence works in practice. This is what Cohen explored in his famous treatment of the

Stan Cohen, author of the path-breaking study of social reaction which showed how *folk devils* are created, and around whom *moral panics* are built.

case of the mods and rockers in *Folk Devils and Moral Panics*.

Earlier in this book (Chapter 4) we looked at Cohen's work and some of the classic moral panic literature, focusing on mods and rockers in the 1960s, drug use in the 1960s/1970s and mugging in the 1980s. More recent work by Goode and Ben-Yehuda (1994) identifies three theories of moral panics which vary in the way they explain why such phenomena come into being and which social groups are prime movers behind them:

- *The grassroots model* – in which it is suggested that the panic originates with the general public and where the threat about which concern develops is widespread and genuinely held (even if mistaken). Panics around crime often fall into this category.

- *The elite-engineered model* – in which the panic is deliberately engineered by a powerful social group in order that the broader public become concerned about some political or social issue. President Reagan's 'war on drugs' falls into this category, Goode and Ben-Yehuda (1994) suggest.

- *Interest-group theory* – involves the argument that many moral panics result from the activities of moral entrepreneurs. The panic that grew up around the issue of 'satanic ritual abuse' in Britain in the 1980s arguably is an example of such a development (Jenkins, 1992).

Does the identification of these different models have any purpose other than the descriptive one of helping explain different types of panic? According to Goode and Ben-Yehuda (1994: 142–43) the model does indeed have a broader purpose:

It is that the grassroots provide fuel or raw material for a moral panic, organizational activists provide focus, intensity, and direction; and it is that issues of morality provide the *content* of moral panics and interests provide the *timing* … No moral panic is complete without an examination of all societal levels, from elites to the grassroots, and the full spectrum from ideology and morality at one pole to crass status and material interests at the other.

Braithwaite and 'shaming'

The issue of the relationship between social reaction and offending is examined and given an original twist by John Braithwaite in his book, *Crime, Shame and Reintegration*. In addition to exploring the effect highlighted by labelling theorists – that social reaction can be criminogenic – Braithwaite considers the conditions under which certain forms of social reaction can produce responses that enable offenders to become law-abiding, respectable citizens. At the heart of this process is shaming – expressions of 'disapproval which have the intention or effect of invoking remorse in the person being shamed and/or condemnation by others who become aware of the shaming' (1989: 9). He identifies two forms of shaming:

- *Disintegrative shaming* – a form of shaming that stigmatises and excludes the person being shamed. This is the process identified or implied in the bulk of labelling theory literature, and involves not merely the labelling of particular acts, but labelling of the actor as well.

- *Reintegrative shaming* – in which social disapproval is followed by processes that seek to 'reintegrate the offender back into the community of law-abiding or respectable citizens through words or gestures of forgiveness or ceremonies to decertify the offender as 'deviant' (1989: 100–101).

It is this theoretical approach – a potentially positive version of labelling processes – that underpins much work on restorative justice: a field in which Braithwaite has been enormously influential over the past two decades and more (see Chapter 30). At its core, Braithwaite's argument is that crime rates tend to be higher in circumstances in which disintegrative shaming is dominant and lower where reintegrative shaming is the preferred mode of responding to offending.

The historical backdrop is one in which rapidly industrialising societies are characterised by a diminishing ability to exert social control through interdependence and tend as a consequence to engage in forms of stigmatising shaming which tend to have negative effects, particularly on people who have few or inadequate social bonds to mainstream society. More effective crime control can be brought about, he argues, through the stimulation of reintegrative shaming. Such shaming works in the following ways (Braithwaite, 1989):

1 Through specific deterrence and the shame associated with detection.

2 Through general deterrence of others who wish to avoid such shame.

3 Shaming work best with those with most to lose – those strongly integrated into local networks.

4 By contrast, stigmatising works less well as it may involve the breaking of attachments to those who might shame future criminality.

5 Shaming is the social process which encourages the belief that certain forms of action are wrong (and this is more effective than both sorts of deterrence).

6 A combination of shame and repentance – especially when undertaken publicly – reaffirms social commitment to the law.

7 Such processes are participatory and therefore build the social conscience.

8 This process reinforces the impact of conscience as a means of controlling conduct.

9 Shaming is therefore the process that builds consciences and the mechanism used when consciences fail to restrict behaviour.

10 Gossip is an important source of material for building consciences because much crime does not occur within the local neighbourhood.

11 Public shaming puts pressure on parents, teachers and others to engage in private shaming.

12 Public shaming works on general principles and adapts these to new forms of transgression.

13 The transition between family socialisation processes and wider social control is smoother in cultures where there is considerable emphasis on reintegrative shaming.

14 Direct confrontation is not always necessary for shaming to work. Often people will know when they are the subject of gossip or some disapproval.

15 The effectiveness of shaming is sometimes advanced by directing it more generally at the family or other important members of the offender's social circle, rather than simply at the offender themselves.

Braithwaite's theory is a sociological approach that combines elements of social disorganisation theory, control theory and labelling among others. Indeed, as he observes overly modestly, 'there is therefore no originality in the elements of this theory, simply originality of synthesis' (1989: 107). He provides a graphic illustration of the processes involved (see Figure 10.2) and suggests that the top left of the diagram cover the key parts of control theory; the top right the main elements of opportunity theory; the middle and bottom right of the diagram cover elements of subcultural theory; and, the bottom left covers learning theory. The box in the middle covers labelling theory – the right hand part of the box is the argument as presented by traditional labelling theory, the left hand part Braithwaite's use of labelling insights in his theory of reintegrative shaming.

Review questions

1 How did Becker define deviance?

2 What is a self-fulfilling prophecy?

3 How does the process of deviancy amplification work?

4 What is meant by *disintegrative* and *reintegrative* *shaming*?

Assessing labelling theory

Labelling theory had a profound effect on much thinking in criminal justice in the 1970s and 1980s. In Britain, this was perhaps most visible in juvenile justice where many social workers became convinced that an important part of their role was to limit the extent to which juvenile offenders became entangled in formal criminal justice processes. *Diversion*, as practices associated with such ideas became known, meant that, wherever possible, juvenile justice workers would endeavour to ensure that young people were cautioned rather than prosecuted or, if prosecuted, were kept out of custody. The most extreme interpretation of labelling theory

| Figure 10.2 | Summary of the theory of reintegrative shaming |

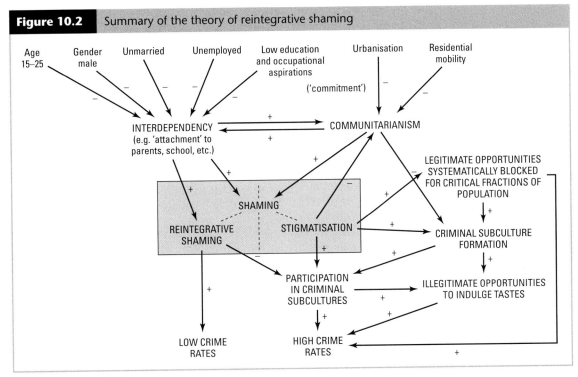

Source: Braithwaite (1989).

was arguably Edwin Schur's (1973) book entitled, *Radical Nonintervention,* which, as its title implies, recommended that young people who broke the law should not be punished. The experimentation involved in delinquency was, he argued, an important part of adolescent development.

Grounded in labelling theory and informed by arguments that offending by young people is relatively 'normal' and, if left alone, young people would 'grow out of crime', it was held that not only did state intervention not prevent reoffending (at least not very effectively), it contained the potential to reinforce patterns of offending through the establishment of delinquent identities. In 1988, for example, a Home Office green paper stated:

> Most young offenders grow out of crime as they become more mature and responsible. They need encouragement and help to become law abiding. Even a short period in custody is quite likely to confirm them as criminals, particularly as they acquire new criminal skills from the more sophisticated offenders. They see themselves labelled as criminals and behave accordingly.

As late as 1990 the Home Office was describing prison as 'an expensive way of making bad people worse' (Home Office, 1990a). However, despite the

importance of the insights stemming from such work, Downes and Rock (2003: 195) have argued that interactionist-influenced approaches have tended to follow the typical pattern of sociological ideas: 'the extraordinary has become ordinary and then banal'. Accordingly, there is a range of critical responses to interactionism and labelling that we must consider.

It is argued that interactionist inquiry, based on ethnographic fieldwork, is difficult to substantiate or refute. Moreover, it tends to avoid questions of power and inequality and underplays the importance of social structures in framing human activity. Thus Taylor *et al.* (1973: 169) argued that social reaction theorists in attempting to problematise the idea of social consensus, 'chose to ignore the way in which deviancy and criminality are shaped by society's larger structure of power and institutions'.

In a similar vein, some radical critics have accused interactionists of empiricism. Pearce, for example, argued that:

> A major aim of political action is to assist the proletariat to identify itself as a class over and above whatever, ethnic, religious or geographical identifications already exist. Thus, one does not

automatically start from the already-present group identifications. To do so is a form of empiricism, a central characteristic of symbolic interactionism. Whether they accept the judgements of the powerful or give a sympathetic ear to the complaints of the oppressed, deviancy theories [such as labelling theory] allow their field of study to be circumscribed by the given-ness of social definitions. (1978: 45)

There are a series of further criticisms aimed at labelling theory's explanatory power. Such work, it is argued, tends to be preoccupied with secondary deviance and, by contrast, is not only relatively unconcerned with the causes of primary deviance, but often largely unable to explain it. Thus, in its concern with the application of labels, there is a tendency to ignore the circumstances under which people actively seek out a deviant label. By contrast, for example, some subcultural theory pays greater attention to the active embracing of particular 'deviant identities' and labels. Moreover, as the work of Braithwaite illustrates, not all labelling results in further deviance. In fact, some labelling/punishment may result in a reduction in deviant activity. Work on restorative justice and on police arrest policy in domestic violence cases (Sherman, 1992) suggests that there are circumstances in which criminal justice interventions may have reinforcing consequences that are positive.

One question which is therefore important, but largely unanswered in labelling theory, is why some sanctions are likely to increase deviance, why some reduce it, and why some have little or no impact? In this context, Sherman developed a theory of what he termed 'defiance', focusing attention on the 'net increase in the prevalence, incidence, or seriousness of future offending against a sanctioning community caused by a proud, shameless reaction to the administration of a criminal sanction' (1993: 459). Defiance, he says, may occur under four conditions:

1 The offender defines a criminal sanction as unfair.

2 The offender is poorly bonded to, or alienated from, the sanctioning agent or the community the agent represents.

3 The offender defines the sanction as stigmatising and rejecting a person, not a lawbreaking act.

4 The offender denies or refuses to acknowledge the shame the sanction has actually caused him to suffer.

In short, he argues that three main factors associated with a sense of unfairness or injustice will likely lead to further offending:

● where offenders are poorly integrated into the local community;

● where offenders feel they and not simply their offending, have been stigmatised;

● where shame is denied.

In its more overstated forms, labelling theory exaggerates the importance of societal reaction, implying that without it deviance would not exist. As Akers (1967) has argued,

One sometimes gets the impression from reading this literature that people go about minding their own business, and then – 'wham' – bad society comes along and slaps them with a stigmatized label. Forced into the role of deviant the individual has little choice but to be deviant.

In this vein, a number of more specific questions might be raised:

● Is it really not possible for deviance to exist in the absence of application of a label? Can an individual who commits a serious human rights violation, but is not sanctioned, really be considered not to have deviated?

● Is the nature of the action really as unimportant as labelling theory sometimes implies? As Taylor, Walton and Young (1975: 147) argue, 'With the exception of entirely new behaviour, it is clear to most people which actions are deviant and which are not deviant ... We would assert that *most deviant behaviour is a quality of the act,* since the way we distinguish between *behaviour* and *action* is that behaviour is merely physical and action has meaning that is socially given.'

Much interactionist or labelling theory is preoccupied with the underdog and, critics have argued, in explaining away deviance as merely the product of the interventions and reactions of the authorities. Ian Taylor and colleagues, for example, were critical of Howard Becker for precisely this reason. They suggested (1973: 142):

Becker's confusion stems from his desire to preserve the category deviant for those people who are labelled deviant, but, to do this, is to imply at the outset that rule-breakers, and rule-breakers who are labelled (i.e. deviants), are fundamentally different from each other.

A few critics have, probably rather unfairly, suggested that labelling theory carries an implicit view of the deviant as a fairly helpless or hapless stooge, reacting and responding to the whims of social control agents. In practice, although labelling theory sees the application of labels as a crucial factor in understanding deviant behaviour, it generally stops well short of suggesting that the application of the label actually *causes* such deviant behaviour. That said there is a powerful sociology of the underdog in much labelling theory. In a presidential address to the Society for the Study of Social Problems, entitled 'Whose side are we on?', Howard Becker (1967: 247) defended the necessity of taking sides 'as our personal and political commitments dictate, use our theoretical and technical resources to avoid the distortions that might introduce into our work, limit our conclusions carefully ... and field as best we can the accusations and doubts that will surely be our fate'.

His stance provoked a strong reaction from Alvin Gouldner (1968: 37–8):

> Their pull to the underdog is sometimes part of a titillated attraction to the underdog's exotic difference ... equivalent to the anthropologist's (one-time) romantic appreciation of the noble savage ... Becker's school of deviance is redolent of romanticism. It expresses the satisfaction of the Great White Hunter who has bravely risked the perils of the urban jungle to bring back an exotic specimen. It expresses the romanticism of the zoo curator who preeningly displays his rare specimens. And like the zookeeper, he wishes to protect his collection; he does not want spectators to throw rocks at the animals behind the bars. But neither is he eager to tear down the bars and let the animals go. The attitude of these zookeepers of deviance is to create a comfortable and humane Indian Reservation, a protected social space, within which these colourful specimens may be exhibited, unmolested and unchanged.

The final question for us here is whether labelling theory is really a *theory*. Arguably this perspective has never been fully developed as a theory. As Ditton (1979) once observed, had it been, it might have been called *contrology*. In the absence of such contrology, labelling and allied approaches have had a limited impact on mainstream approaches he argued (1975: 5):

> The total rejection of positivism by followers of the labelling perspective either had no effect at all on the institutionalized study of crime or, at best, the massive theoretical critique was distilled into an additional factor ('the reaction') to be henceforth co-opted in the unchanged rhetoric of mathematical calculation. It has always been content instead to snipe at convention from the theoretical sidelines – happy to stand on the lunatic fringe and lob distracting stories of strippers, nudists, gays, teddy boys, nutters, dwarfs, and druggies at the central juggernaut of state-sponsored criminology.

Thus, although the term *theory* has been used throughout this chapter there is a strong case to be made that the ideas discussed here are more appropriately thought of as a *perspective* (Plummer 1979). Certainly, some of the insights of the labelling approach have been utilised by others – amongst them Braithwaite and Sherman – as one part of a theory of deviance, but none of the scholars working in this field have either identified themselves as a *labelling theorist* or presented their work as a theory of deviance. The intention was to apply important, and somewhat neglected, insights to the field. Moreover, as Plummer (1979: 120) quite rightly observes, 'Labelling perspectives, symbolic interactionism and political economies of crime do not have to rival each other. They each raise their important problems and they each deserve serious attention.'

Questions for further discussion

1 In what ways might the concept of 'the self' be important to an understanding of deviance?

2 How might the process of stigmatisation have negative or positive consequences for the prevention of crime?

3 What are the policy implications of labelling theory?

4 Is prison just an expensive way of making bad people worse?

5 In what ways are the ideas of 'folk devil' and 'moral panic' helpful in understanding contemporary problems of crime and disorder?

Further reading

Becker, H.S. (1963/2003) Outsiders, in McLaughlin, E. Muncie, J. and Hughes, G. (eds) *Criminological Perspectives*: *Essential readings*, London: Sage

Braithwaite, J. (1989) *Crime, Shame and Reintegration*, Cambridge: Cambridge University Press

Cohen, S. (2002) *Folk Devils and Moral Panics*, 3rd edn, London: Routledge

Lemert, E. (1951/2006) Primary and secondary deviance, in Cullen, F.T. and Agnew, R. (eds) *Criminological Theory Past to Present*: *Essential readings*, 3rd edn, Los Angeles, CA: Roxbury

Plummer, K. (1979) Misunderstanding labelling perspectives, in Downes, D. and Rock, P. (eds), *Deviant Interpretations*, Oxford: Martin Robertson

Websites

Howard Becker maintains an excellent homepage full of material relevant to this and other chapters, and much else besides: http: //home.earthlink.net/ ~hsbecker/

The Mead Project contains a lot of information on history of social psychology: http: //spartan.ac. brocku.ca/~lward/

Chapter outline

Introduction   228

Reckless's containment theory   229
   Inner containment   230

Neutralisation and drift theory   230
   Drift   231

Social bond theory   231
   Four elements of the social bond   232
   Testing social bond theory   233

Gottfredson and Hirschi's general theory of crime   234
   Low self-control   234
   Assessing the general theory of crime   237

Tittle's control-balance theory   238
   Relating control-balance to crime   239

Assessing control theory   241

Questions for discussion   242
Further reading   242
Websites   242

1

Control theories

Control theory permeates criminological thinking. Ideas associated with control theory can be found in the majority of approaches to the understanding of crime and deviance. What distinguishes the theories discussed in this chapter from many of those in preceding and succeeding ones is the emphasis placed upon the importance of controls or, conversely, the implied lack of attention paid to the *causes* of crime. Put at its simplest, in this perspective crime is something we would all engage in were it not for internal or external controls preventing us from doing so. Control theories come in many forms.

In this chapter we will consider:

- Walter Reckless's *containment theory*;
- Sykes and Matza's *neutralisation theory*;
- David Matza's *drift theory*;
- Travis Hirschi's *social bond theory*;
- Gottfredson and Hirschi's *self-control theory*;
- Charles Tittle's *control-balance theory*.

Introduction

Control theory proceeds from a different question from much criminological theory. Rather than focusing on deviance and seeking to explain the causes of crime, control theory focuses on conformity and asks why most of us don't commit crime more often. Its central argument, as the phrase implies, is that crime is a normal phenomena and is something that should be expected in the absence of adequate controls. Control theory also takes a rather different view of human nature than some other criminological theories. Baldly put, control theory tends to assume that human conduct is driven by desires and needs and that, therefore, we are all predisposed to deviance. Social order is maintained by bringing such desires under control. The central concern of control theory is *conformity* rather than *deviance*.

Control theory became popular within criminology in the late 1950s and 1960s, though, as Downes and Rock note, it never assumed the ascendancy achieved by either strain theories in the 1950s or labelling theories in the decade afterward. Indeed, they ask why it is that until fairly recently such approaches have been thoroughly unfashionable in criminology and the sociology of deviance. The answer, they suggest, lies partly in the implicit normative position of most control theory: the fact that it is apparently comfortable with, and supportive of, greater punishment and regulation.

The period in which control theories began to emerge with some force also saw the beginnings of counter-cultural movements. It was a time in which traditional sources of authority were coming under increasing scrutiny and question. Just as the beatniks gave way to the hippies so control theory was eventually overtaken in some quarters, temporarily at least, by the radical theories associated with the left. That said, its decline in popularity should not be taken as evidence of a lack of influence. As we will see, in various forms control theory has continued to exert an important influence on contemporary criminology – and still does today.

This leads us to a second observation: there is no single control theory. There are many. Quite possibly control theories are the best example of the difficulty of attempting to maintain some form of analytical separation between different theories of deviance. In practice, there is an element of 'control theory' in much theorising about crime, even if it isn't a dominant feature. Moreover, and as I hope to demonstrate, it would be very odd if this were not the case. Cohen and Short (1961) in their critical examination of the basis of control theory, for example, observed:

> They [culture conflict and social disorganisation theories] are both *control* theories in the sense that they explain delinquency in terms of the *absence* of effective controls. They appear, therefore, to imply a model of motivation that assumes that the impulse to delinquency is an

inherent characteristic of young people and does not itself need to be explained; it is something that erupts when the lid – i.e., internalized cultural restraints or external authority – is off. (quoted in Hirschi, 1969: 32; *emphasis in original*)

In what follows we will explore several variations on the theme of control and conformity, notably Reckless's *containment theory*, Sykes and Matza's *neutralisation theory*, Matza's *drift theory*, Hirschi's *social bond theory*, Gottfredson and Hirschi's *self-control theory* and Tittle's *control-balance theory*. Before we move on, a word or two about terminology. Downes and Rock (2007) helpfully distinguish between three different usages of the term 'control' within criminology:

1 Control theories which focus on the presence or absence of controls as *the* key variable in explaining deviance.

2 Controls as a substantive phenomenon: the sanctions that are, or could be, brought to bear on deviant activity.

3 The element of all theories of deviance that deals with the question of control – whether explicit or otherwise (whether, as in labelling theory, as a cause of deviation or, as in radical theories, as a means of sustaining the viability of the state).

The focus in this chapter centres primarily upon the first of the three areas of control: the influence of controls as the key variable in helping to explain deviant activity. So what is control theory? In what is often regarded as a classic statement of control theory, Reiss (1951: 196) argued:

Delinquency results when there is a relative absence of internalized norms and rules governing behaviour in conformity with the norms of the social system to which legal penalties are attached, a breakdown in previously established controls, and/or a relative absence of or conflict in social rules or techniques for enforcing such behaviour in the social groups or institutions of which the person is a member.

As Lilly *et al.* (2002) note, Reiss's view was clearly influenced by the social disorganisation tradition (see Chapter 9) – viewing the breakdown of controls under particular social conditions as being the basis for understanding crime. In this he was, as were many control theorists, much influenced by Durkheim's sociological analysis of the problems of individualism and anomie. Reiss's observation was based on research which involved

a study of court records of over 1,000 young white males on probation. He had found that juveniles diagnosed psychiatrically as having 'weak ego or superego controls' (in crude terms, less self-control) were more likely to have their probation revoked. Poor attendance at school was also associated with low levels of success on probation. In this view 'delinquency and delinquent recidivism may be viewed as a consequence of the failure of primary groups to provide the child with appropriate non-delinquent roles and to exercise social control over the child so these roles are accepted and submitted to in accordance with needs' (1951: 198).

Reiss's sociological approach, influenced by Freudian psychology, was one of the earliest formulations of what has become known as control theory. A number of other authors such as Jackson Toby (1983) and F. Ivan Nye (1958) similarly focused on the importance of the school and of the home as sources of control and conformity. Setting out one of the fundamental tenets of much control theory, Nye (1958: 5) argued that 'in general being prescribed as delinquent or criminal need not be explained in any positive sense, since it usually results in quicker and easier achievement of goals than the normative behaviour'. The goal is therefore to explain why there is not more deviance. Another early and influential form of control theory is found in Walter Reckless's 'containment theory'.

Reckless's containment theory

Another product of the University of Chicago, Walter Reckless was seemingly much influenced by Durkheimian sociology (as were Reiss, Nye and other control theorists) and, in particular, by the view that increasingly complex forms of social organisation brought with them problems of containment and control. Like Durkheim, he was concerned with the problems associated with the increasingly complex division of labour characteristic of modern, industrialised societies and with the associated problem of 'individualisation of the self' (see Chapter 8) that was its potential consequence:

In a fluid, mobile society which has emphasised freedom of action for its individuals, the person is able to soar like a balloon without the ballast of social relationships. He can readily aggrandize himself at the expense of others. His society does not easily contain him. He no longer fits into expected roles ... He plays his major themes in life without agreed-upon ground rules. (1967: 21)

Reckless's primary focus was on the question of why, given all the opportunities and pressures toward deviance in the modern world, the primary response remained conformity. His underlying assumption was that individuals are subjected to varying forces or influences, and that some of these push people toward crime ('social pressures' or 'pulls') whilst others protect against involvement in crime. That is to say, despite the apparently ubiquitous pushes and pulls toward crime that exist in modern society, many people appear 'immune' or 'resistant'. These protective factors he called 'inner containment' and 'outer containment'. In relation to the latter he identified meaningful roles and activities and a number of other 'complementary variables' such as reinforcement by social groups and the existence of supportive relationships. Groups, organisations and associations, he argued, that seek to stay in existence need reasonable conformity on the part of their members. They therefore work toward this end – 'containing' their members – and do so with differing degrees of success.

Walter C. Reckless (1898–1988) was particularly interested in the idea of 'containment' – in particular how 'inner containment' enabled individuals to resist pressures that might otherwise push them towards crime or delinquency.

Inner containment

The core of Reckless's analysis, however, focused on inner containment for, at least in part, this would tend to regulate the individual no matter what the circumstances externally, i.e. even where organisations, associations and other factors were relatively ineffective at the job of containment. The key elements of inner containment included:

- *Self-concept* – the possible existence of an image of oneself as law-abiding and obedient is something that will tend to insulate individuals against deviance.

- *Goal-orientation* – an orientation toward legitimate goals as well as aspirations that are realistic will tend to lead toward conformity (unlike in strain theory where deviance may also be a consequence of striving to achieve legitimate goals).

- *Frustration tolerance* – different people have different capacities for coping with socially-induced frustration.

- *Norm-retention* – the 'adherence to, commitment to, acceptance of, identification with, legitimation of, [and] defence of values, norms, laws, codes, institutions and customs' (1967: 476).

Reckless's ideas have been much criticised, not least for being difficult to examine empirically and, relatedly, for seeming somewhat vague. Nevertheless, they had an important influence on later variants of control theory and on key proponents such as David Matza and, later, Travis Hirschi.

Neutralisation and drift theory

As we saw earlier (Chapter 10) David Matza and Gresham Sykes built on existing strain theory by exploring the ways in which what they termed 'neutralisation techniques' were used to justify and legitimise deviant activity. There is a link here also with control theory for the impact of such techniques is to reduce the impact of social and self-controls so as to enable the possibility of delinquent activity. Matza later went on to argue that delinquents were not especially committed to their illicit activities – no more than any other activity – but, rather, through a process of *drift* they became involved in such behaviour.

Sykes and Matza's early work was in part stimulated by questioning why it appeared to be the case that many people involved in delinquent activities were otherwise relatively conventional and conforming in their lives. Moreover, there was also considerable evidence that delinquent activity was a temporary state – engaged in during adolescence and early adulthood, but generally diminishing thereafter despite, presumably, continuing pressures pushing in that direction. An alternative means of understanding delinquency, therefore, is to view it as an unusual and temporary state of affairs, rather than something fundamental in most individuals' lives. In this vein, Sykes and Matza proposed the idea of techniques of neutralisation (see Chapter 10) as a means of understanding how social norms could be abandoned on a temporary basis, thus allowing deviant activity to be undertaken. The delinquent in this view continues to adhere to important social norms, but has techniques that allow this adherence to be temporarily, indeed fleetingly, suspended.

Drift

As we have noted, Sykes and Matza were particularly critical of theories that sought to differentiate delinquents and non-delinquents. Theories that assumed that any identified differences (be they biological, psychological or social) and viewed these as constraints leading to delinquency, tended to over-predict deviance, Matza argued. Most of the time 'delinquents' are not engaged in delinquent activity, they are law-abiding, and engaged in everyday, mundane behaviour, as are 'non-delinquents'. As opposed to a focus on differentiation therefore, Matza's concern was with similarity and freedom. Delinquency, where it occurred, was in his view often a matter of *drift*. The idea of drift is intended to capture situations where controls have loosened making it easier for the person concerned to be influenced by social forces – be they criminal or conventional:

> Those who have been granted the potentiality for freedom through the loosening of social controls but who lack the position, capacity, or inclination to become agents in their own behalf, I call drifters, and it is in this category that I place the juvenile delinquent. (1964: 29)

There is considerable emphasis in Matza's theory, therefore, on contingency – the fact that particular behaviours may be influenced in one direction or another by quite specific social forces. In this view

much delinquency is unpredictable or accidental. This is not to say that there aren't people whose involvement in criminal activity is more embedded, simply that much delinquency doesn't follow such a pattern. Put a different way, much of the thrust of Matza's (1964) argument is that delinquent behaviour is not dependent on commitment to delinquent values. Such behaviour may be understood by the person concerned to break moral injunctions, but means can be found to justify it or 'neutralise' the guilt. It is the loosening of the sense of guilt, or of other controls, that forms the basis of the drift into delinquency.

Social bond theory

As we have seen, Reckless distinguished between external and internal controls in his *containment theory* and, more particularly, took the view that it was inner containment that was crucial in understanding deviance. Travis Hirschi, initially via his *social bond theory,* and later with his work jointly with Michael Gottfredson, is probably the best known of all control theorists. By contrast with Reckless and with his later work, Hirschi's (1969) initial writing on control theory placed greater emphasis on social influences. He suggests that the response of early control theory was simply to use the idea that we are all subject to animalistic impulses. The argument of the early control theorist was:

> ... *not* that delinquents and criminals alone are animals, but that we are all animals, and thus all naturally capable of committing criminal acts ... The chicken stealing corn from his neighbour knows nothing of the moral law; he does not want to violate rules; he wants merely to eat corn ... No motivation to deviance is required to explain his acts. So, too, no special motivation to commit crime within the human animal was required to explain his criminal acts. (Hirschi, 1969: 31)

Such views became less acceptable and fashionable. In the end, Hirschi argues, the question 'Why do they do it?' is not a question that control theory is designed to answer. The important question, he says, is 'Why don't we do it?' (1969: 33).

Control theories, according to Hirschi, assume that deviance occurs when 'an individual's bond to society is weak or broken' (1969: 16) and, in this vein, he argued that Durkheim was himself a control theorist for 'both anomie and egoism are conditions of "deregulation"' (1969: 3). Control

What is the motivation?

The most disconcerting question the control theorist faces goes something like this: 'Yes, but *why* do they do it?' In the good old days, the control theorist could simply strip away the 'veneer of civilization' and expose man's 'animal impulses' for all to see. These impulses appeared to him (and apparently to his audience) to provide a plausible account of the motivation to crime and delinquency. His argument was *not* that delinquents and criminals alone are animals, but that we are all animals, and thus all naturally capable of committing criminal acts ...

Times changed. It was no longer fashionable (within sociology, at least) to refer to animal impulses. The control theorist tended more and more to deemphasize the motivational component of his theory. He might refer at the beginning to 'universal human needs', or some such, but the driving force behind crime and delinquency was rarely alluded to ...

There are several additional accounts of 'why they do it' that are to my mind persuasive and at the same time generally compatible with control theory. But while all of these accounts may be compatible with control theory, they are by no means deductible from it. Furthermore, they rarely impute built-in, unusual motivation to the delinquent: he is attempting to satisfy the same desires, he is reacting to the same pressures as other boys ... In other words, if included, these accounts of motivation would serve the same function in the theory that 'animal impulses' traditionally served: they might add to its persuasiveness and plausibility, but they would add little else, since they do not differentiate delinquents from non-delinquents.

In the end, then, control theory remains what it has always been: a theory in which deviation is not problematic. The question 'Why do they do it?' is simply not the question the theory is designed to answer. The question is 'Why don't we do it?' There is much evidence that we would if we dared.

Source: Hirschi (1969: 33–4).

theory has often been contrasted with strain theory, it being suggested that the latter proceeded from the assumption that man was essentially moral (and only deviated as a result of strain), whereas control theory began from the assumption that man is essentially amoral (and therefore needs to be controlled). This contrast is a false one, Hirschi (1969: 11) argued, for control theory 'merely assumes variation in morality: For some men, considerations of morality are important, for others they are not'.

Four elements of the social bond

Hirschi identifies four elements – variously described as 'control variables, each [representing] a major social bond' (Lilly *et al.*, 2002: 90), 'social bonds' or 'elements of the social bond' which explain conformity:

1 *Attachment* – According to Hirschi (1969: 18), 'The essence of internalization of norms, conscience, or superego thus lies in the attachment of the individual to others'. To the extent that we are at all concerned about what others think of us, and react towards us, then we are under an element of control. Hirschi argued that this element of his theory was similar to F. Ivan Nye's notion of 'internal control' and to Reiss's notion of 'personal controls'. For Hirschi, attachment was crucial for the simple reason that, 'If a person does not care about the wishes and expectations of other people – that is, if he is insensitive to the opinion of others – then he is to that extent not bound by the norms. He is free to deviate' (1969: 18). Of all the four elements of Hirschi's model, it is attachment that has been treated as being the most important.

2 *Commitment* – This refers to the investment of time, energy, etc. that people put into particular activities. In doing so, Hirschi felt, we weigh up the investment we are making and the likely consequences before we act (there is an element of rational choice in this). The calculations we make in relation to some actions are indicative of our commitment to the conventional social order – or what Toby referred to as our 'stake in conformity'. We are unlikely to do things that lower our standing in conventional society if we have such commitment to the conventional social order:

> The idea, then, is that the person invests time, energy, himself, in a certain line of activity – say, getting an education, building up a business, acquiring a reputation for virtue. When or whenever he considers deviant behaviour, he must consider the costs of this deviant behaviour, the risk he runs of losing the investment he has made in conventional behaviour. (1969: 20)

3 *Involvement* – This refers to the assertion that being heavily involved in conventional, non-deviant, activities will most likely serve to insulate people from deviance: 'To the extent that he [*sic*] is engrossed in conventional activities, he cannot even think about deviant acts, let alone act out his inclinations' (1969: 22). In many ways this element of Hirschi's

argument is an opportunity theory. He suggests that people may simply be so bound up in other conventional activities that they have no time or opportunity for delinquent activity. There are links here with Matza and Sykes' arguments about delinquency and leisure-oriented values.

4 *Belief* – This element concerns the strength of our commitment to particular beliefs. We may be commonly attached to various cultural goals, but we will not all be equally attached to them. Straightforwardly, the stronger our belief in conventional values, the less likely we will be to offend. This element of control theory makes explicit the assumption that there is a common value system in society – or group – whose norms are violated. For Hirschi the assumption is 'that there is *variation* in the extent to which people believe they should obey the rules of society, and, furthermore, that the less a person believes he should obey the rules, the more likely he is to violate them' (1969: 26, *emphasis in original*). In this regard he was distinguishing himself from Sykes and Matza who argued that techniques of neutralisation were necessary in order to release individuals from the controls exercised by belief in social norms.

Testing social bond theory

When added together, attachment, commitment, involvement and belief describe in prototypical terms the mindset and behaviour of the non-deviant. By contrast, the delinquent is freer of such controls, especially attachment. Hirschi's theory was tested using a self-report survey of approximately 4,000 Californian high school pupils, together with an analysis of school records. He found little evidence of a social class effect and few racial differences among the sample. However, controlling for such factors he found that young people reporting strong attachment to parents reported fewer acts of delinquency than those reporting less strong attachment. Such a finding seemingly supports Hirschi's particular brand of control theory, and tends to fly in the face of cultural theories which might explain offending as a result of close attachment to delinquent peers and others involved in deviant activity.

Hirschi also found that those reporting higher rates of delinquent activity also tended to have lower educational aspirations and less investment in educational achievement. Again, this seems consistent with control theory's view of education as a source of social control. There was less empirical

According to Hirschi the social bond forms early in life and involves the internalisation of social norms expressed in part through attachment to others – the family was one of the key factors in this process.

support in his study for the third element: involvement. Although boredom was linked with delinquency, there was also evidence that boys who were in work and heavily involved in other conventional activities also reported relatively high levels of criminal activity. In relation to 'belief', Hirschi asked his respondents whether they agreed or disagreed with the statement 'It is alright to get around the law if you can get away with it'. Fairly strong correlation was found between self-reported offending and agreement with this statement, leading Hirschi to reject Sykes and Matza's argument in relation to 'techniques of neutralisation'.

Although Hirschi's theory has had its supporters, there have also been a number of criticisms aimed at the central parts of his argument. The major shortcomings are held to include:

- There is a chicken and egg problem. Is delinquency a product of weak attachment to cultural norms, or is weak attachment a product of delinquency? Hirschi's theory proposes one answer, but the other is also perfectly plausible and, indeed, a case could easily be made for the potential for an iterative relationship between attachment and delinquency in which they are mutually reinforcing (positively or negatively).

- There is evidence, contradicting social bond theory, that offenders are not weakly attached to conventional social norms – and as we will see such a view is precisely what underpinned Matza and Sykes' notion of neutralisation.

- It is, at best, a partial theory. Although it proposes a set of criteria by which we may understand and test the idea of a social bond, it doesn't explain the basis of weak attachment or low levels of belief which, if correct, are the basis of delinquency. Why do social bonds vary in strength?

- Like many control theories the underlying assumption that deviance is natural – and would undoubtedly occur unless controlled – is difficult to sustain.

- Even if it could account for deviant behaviour, it cannot explain why particular forms of deviant behaviour occur. As Braithwaite (1989: 13) put it, it cannot explain 'why some uncontrolled individuals become heroin users, some become hit men, and others price-fixing conspirators'.

- As already suggested, research evidence has found reasonably strong support for two of Hirschi's four variables – attachment and commitment – but much less for involvement and belief.

- There were relatively few serious delinquents in his sample; had there been more it is possible that the results would have been different.

- Control theories, including this, tend to treat criminal behaviour as a 'given' – a naturally occurring phenomenon – requiring no explanation beyond the fact that they bring satisfaction. This may be true of some criminal activity, but is not necessarily a convincing explanation of all such activity.

Review questions

1 What, for Reckless, are the main differences between inner and outer containment?

2 In what way is the idea of 'techniques of neutralisation' linked with control theory?

3 What did Matza mean by the idea of 'drifting' into delinquency?

4 According to Hirschi, what are the four main elements of the social bond?

Gottfredson and Hirschi's general theory of crime

More recently, Gottfredson and Hirschi (1990) have offered a 'general theory of crime' that builds on Hirschi's earlier work – though shifting a long way from it – and reinserts the importance of internalised self-control as the basis for understanding deviance and conformity. In some senses, therefore, the general theory of crime returned control theory to some of its roots. Their approach, they argue, takes its stimulus from the failure of existing criminological theory to focus on the fact that it is well established that problematic behavioural patterns are often embedded and are frequently then fairly consistent over the life course:

> Thus no currently popular criminological theory attends to the stability of individual differences in offending over the life course. We are left with a paradoxical situation: A major finding of criminological research is routinely ignored or denied by criminological theory. After a century of research, crime theories remain inattentive to the fact that people differ in the likelihood that they will commit crimes and that these differences appear early and remain stable over much of the life course. (1990: 108)

Low self-control

In Gottfredson and Hirschi's model it is stable, underlying individual differences – 'persistent

Michael R. Gottfredson and

Travis Hirschi

A GENERAL

THEORY OF

CRIME

A General Theory of Crime (1990): 'One of the most important contributions to criminology in years' – in the view of John Hagan, a leading Canadian sociologist. Later critics queried whether it really helped to explain white-collar or corporate crime.

heterogeneity' – that provide the basis for explaining stability over the life course. At the heart of their 'general theory' is self-control – 'concern for the long-term consequences of one's acts' (Hirschi and Gottfredson, 2000: 64). It is self-control that allows us to resist temptation, including the temptations of criminal opportunity. Their theory covers a range of forms of behaviour therefore – not just crime – including promiscuity, alcohol use and smoking.

They argue that the self-control required to govern behaviour needs to be instilled early in the life course and it is the parental failure to inculcate such attributes that leads to children that tend to be 'impulsive, insensitive, physical (as opposed to mental) risk-taking, short-sighted, and nonverbal, and they will tend therefore to engage in criminal and analogous acts' (1990: 90). What is meant by low self-control? For these purposes it is generally held to include: impulsiveness, risk seeking, physicality, self-centredness and low temper threshold. For Gottfredson and Hirschi, these characteristics are derived from the nature of crime itself:

- It offers immediate gratification and quick thrills. Those with low self-control indulge in a variety of behaviours, including offending, drug use, and illicit sex. 'People lacking self-control tend to lack diligence, tenacity, or persistence in a course of action' (1990: 89).

- Crime is risky, exciting or thrilling and those with low self-control tend to seek the forms of excitement associated with such risk. By contrast, those with higher levels of self-control 'tend to be cautious, cognitive, and verbal'.

- Crime provides few long-term gains and tends to be incompatible with those lifestyle features that require long-term investment: work, family life, and so on. Those with low self-control tend not to have established careers and stable families, but rather have unstable profiles.

- Crime generally requires little expertise or planning and is compatible with the relatively low educational and general cognitive skills of people with low self-control.

- Crime brings pain and suffering to others; those with low self-control are generally self-centred and less affected by the difficulties experienced by others.

There is another important factor, for low self-control doesn't automatically lead to offending. Opportunity is also required. The combination of criminal opportunities and low self-control is what leads to offending. In discussing this they cite Cohen and Felson's argument that crime requires a motivated offender, the absence of a capable guardian, and a suitable target. They argue that most criminological theory has made the mistake of focusing the majority of its attention on the first of these three criteria. Rather, they suggest, if one uses some understanding of targets and guardians as the basis for constructing a model of the offender then a rather different picture emerges as a result. That is of an offender with the desire to seek fairly immediate gratification of particular desires and who is lacking in the controls necessary to contain them. In their view the offender:

> ... is neither the diabolical genius often portrayed by the police and the media nor the ambitious seeker of the American dream often portrayed by the positivists. On the contrary, the offender appears to have little control over his or her own desires. When such desires conflict with long-term interests, those lacking self-control opt for the desires of the moment, whereas those with greater self-control are governed by the restraints imposed by the consequences of acts displeasing to family, friends, and the law. (1990: xv)

The final major question for the general theory of crime is what *causes* low self-control? Why do some people display low self-control compared with others? The answer they give is ineffective childrearing. More particularly, those with low self-control have parents who generally fail to monitor their behaviour, are poor at recognising inappropriate behaviour and either do not punish such behaviour, or do so only inconsistently. By contrast, effective childrearing tends to involve consistent monitoring of behaviour and the punishment of deviation, leading to high levels of self-control. The key age is around eight years. By this stage, they argue, if a reasonable level of self-control hasn't been reached, then that shortcoming is likely to be visible – stable – for the rest of the individual's life:

> All that is required to activate the system is affection for *or* investment in the child. The person who cares for the child will watch his behaviour, see him doing things he should not do, and correct him. The result may be a child more capable of delaying gratification, more sensitive to the interests and desires of others, more independent, more willing to accept restraints on his activity, and more unlikely to use force or violence to attain his ends. (1990: 97)

How and why does this go wrong? They reject the idea that what they describe as 'unsocialised' behaviour is the result of deliberate socialisation by parents as they say is suggested in cultural or subcultural theories of deviance. Rather, they suggest a number of alternative possibilities arise:

- The parents may not care for the child.
- Even if they care for the child the parents may not have the time or energy to monitor the child's behaviour.

- Even if they care for the child and monitor its behaviour, they may not notice or see anything wrong in the child's behaviour.
- Even if this is not the case they may not have the ability or the inclination to impose sufficient discipline or punishment on the child.

As implied by the title of their book, *A General Theory of Crime,* Gottfredson and Hirschi hold that this focus on individual self-control can explain almost all forms of criminality, including 'acts of force or fraud undertaken in pursuit of self-interest'. Their book begins with a consideration of crimes as varied as burglary and murder, and they argue later that many of the distinctions between *types* of crime made by criminologists are unhelpful – certainly so far as theorising is concerned. In this vein they examine the idea of 'white collar crime' (see Chapter 18) and argue that their 'general theory of crime accounts for the frequency and distribution of white collar crime in just the same way that it accounts for the frequency and distribution of all other forms of crime, including rape, vandalism, and simple assault' (1990: 181). How so?

Using data from Uniform Crime Reports (see Chapter 3), and adjusting for 'opportunity', they argue that the age-sex-race correlates of white collar crime are no different from 'ordinary crime'. Moreover, they suggest that the individual self-control theory of offending would tend to predict a relatively low rate of offending among white collar workers and – despite what some criminological research has purported to show – they argue that the most reliable empirical data back up this view.

Michael Gottfredson and Travis Hirschi, whose general theory of crime rests on a picture of the offender as someone who has relatively little control over their desires, and who tends to opt for short-term gratification over longer-term satisfaction.

Assessing the general theory of crime

What has been the response to Gottfredson and Hirschi's general theory? A number of empirical studies appear to demonstrate a link between low self-control and delinquency, though the strength of the association has often not been all that great. In addition a number of elements of the general theory – in particular the argument that self-control is largely fixed by age eight – have not as yet been subject to much empirical scrutiny. A number of more specific criticisms have been levelled at different elements of Gottfredson and Hirschi's general theory:

- The idea of 'self-control' is difficult to research. In more technical language it is difficult to operationalise empirically. How are we to measure it? Is there really one thing called self-control or is it actually made up of several different facets?

- As with other control theories, some critics have suggested that Gottfredson and Hirschi's general theory is *tautological*. That is to say it is circular. Crudely, in arguing that low self-control is central to explaining delinquency, there is a real danger that we will use the fact of offending as an indicator of low self-control. It is hard to see each independently of the other. Hirschi and Gottfredson (1993: 52–3) reject such a charge, arguing instead:

    In our view, the charge of tautology is in fact a compliment; an assertion that we followed the path of logic in producing an internally consistent result ... We started with a conception of crime, and from it attempted to *derive* a conception of the offender ... What makes our theory *peculiarly* vulnerable to complaints about tautology is that we explicitly show the logical connections between our conception of the actor and the act, whereas many theorists leave this task to those interpreting or testing their theory ... But what would a [nontautological] theory look like? It would advance definitions of crime and of criminals that are independent of each other.

- A third line of criticism has focused on the claim that the theory is 'general'; that is, capable of explaining *all* crime. More particularly, some critics (Reed and Yeager, 1996) have argued that the notion of low self-control seems a better bet as an explanation of some violent and property crimes (opportunistic theft/burglary) for example, than it is in explaining white collar or corporate crime (a matter specifically refuted by Gottfredson and Hirschi).

- Some critics have focused on Gottfredson and Hirschi's argument about stability of low self-control across the life course and queried why, if this is the case, crime should decline as age increases.

- Scholars such as Sampson and Laub (see Chapter 33) have identified what they believe are multiple pathways to crime rather than the more stable and consistent pattern that is predicted by the general theory of crime. Gottfredson's and Hirschi's (2000) response is that the complexity of analysis offered by Sampson, Laub and others does little to add clarity to our thinking in explaining crime. Indeed, given the predictive ability of early offending behaviour, they specifically reject the idea that longitudinal research is especially useful in understanding crime over the life course.

- Sampson and Laub (1993) have also argued that their research provides evidence that social bonds in adulthood may act to direct people away from offending and other problematic behaviours.

- The theory has been criticised for ignoring the role of gangs on the behaviour of adolescents and the role of spouses on adults. Hirschi and Gottfredson's (2000) rejoinder to such criticisms is that the correlation between an individual's delinquency and that of their peers is largely a product of selection effects (people associating with like people) and a number of measurement errors.

- Critics such as Currie (1985) have argued that control theory underestimates the role of socio-economic factors in criminality. He refers to the emphasis on self-control in such theories as the 'fallacy of autonomy'.

- Finally, concern is raised about the relationship between low self-control and opportunity in explaining crime and, more particularly, the possibility that opportunity might actually be the more important of the two factors.

For many critics, the major difficulty that control theory has, however, is that whilst it helps explain why people *don't* offend, it is less good at providing an explanation of why they *do*, except that it is argued to be some form of natural impulse that is kept generally in check by external controls. For Hirschi, as we have seen, this is seemingly relatively unproblematic for the theory is primarily concerned with the question of 'why don't we do it?' rather than the reverse.

Tittle's control-balance theory

Though generally discussed as a control theory, strictly speaking control-balance theory is an attempt at what is called 'integrated theory'. It was developed in the mid-1990s by Charles Tittle largely as an example of what could be achieved in combining the best elements of more than one existing theoretical approach. Thus, although it contains elements of what are generally thought of as control theories, there are also elements of rational choice, routine activities, differential association, strain and labelling theory visible in parts of Tittle's argument.

What Tittle shares with control theory is the notion that too little control may lead to deviance. Where he departs is in offering the reverse observation also: that too much control may also lead to deviant activity. Charles Tittle's addition to control theory was the observation that people are *agents* as well as *objects* of social control. That is we both control and are controlled. Humans strive to be autonomous, yet of necessity are subject to a variety of controls.

Control-balance theory suggests that 'the amount of control to which an individual is sub-

ject, relative to the amount of control that he or she can exercise, determines the probability of deviance occurring as well as the type of deviance likely to occur' (1995: 135). The balance between the exercise of control and being subject to control he referred to as the *control ratio*. The control ratio is 'the extent to which an individual can potentially exercise control over circumstances impinging on him, relative to the potential control that can be exercised by external entities and conditions against the individual' (Cullen and Agnew, 2006: 566). In summary, according to Tittle (1995: 142):

> The central premise of the theory is that the amount of control to which people are subject relative to the amount of control they can exercise affects their general probability of committing some deviant acts as well as the probability that they will commit specific types of deviance. Deviant behaviour is interpreted as a device, or manoeuvre, that helps people escape deficits and extend surpluses of control.

Control-balance is associated with conformity; control-imbalance with deviance. The argument is that where control isn't balanced – that is when someone's ability to exercise control is either exceeded by the degree of control to which they are subject, or the reverse – then the likelihood of deviance increases. Moreover, the existence of a deficit or a surplus of control determines what sort of deviance is likely to result. In order for deviance to occur at all a number of causal elements must be present:

- A predisposition toward being motivated for deviance.
- Situational provocation that reminds a person of control imbalance – that is, the person concerned must be aware of the control imbalance and must experience a 'negative emotion' in this connection such as a feeling of humiliation or denigration.
- The transformation of predisposition into actual motivation for deviance – the individual must recognise the possibility that deviance will affect this control imbalance.
- Opportunity for deviant response.
- The absence or relative weakness of restraint so that the mental process of 'control balancing' will result in a perceived gain in control. Constraints such as situational risks, moral inhibitions and social bonds must be overcome. (Tittle, in Cullen and Agnew, 2006: 566)

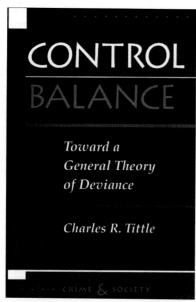

Control Balance, by Charles Tittle (Professor of Sociology at North Carolina State University), published in 1995, attempts to provide an integrated criminological theory.

Relating control-balance to crime

How does this theory explain why certain people commit certain forms of crime? According to Tittle, because certain types of opportunity for deviance – theft from shops, for example, damage to property, drinking to excess – are almost always present, people with motivation have a high probability of engaging in some deviant activity. However, this is not any kind of deviance. Rather, they will engage in what is reasonable for them given their control ratio, their degree of motivation and the nature of the opportunity. The person with motivation and opportunity is likely to engage in those deviant acts that hold out the greatest possibility of having some effect. By *effect* Tittle meant actions which most effectively lead to short-term change in control.

Tittle identifies six major forms of deviance, the first three of which are more likely when there is a control deficit, and the latter three when there is a control surplus:

- *Predation* – Theft, rape, homicide, fraud, sexual harassment.
- *Defiance* – Vandalism, political protests, etc.
- *Submission* – Passive obedience, allowing oneself to be abused, etc.
- *Exploitation* – Corporate price-fixing, profiteering, endangering workers.
- *Plunder* – Organisations pursuing their own interests without due regard to others.
- *Decadence* – Debauchery, irrational pleasure.

These he arranged in a sequence, with conformity in the centre, to illustrate how each is related to control imbalances (see Figure 11.1).

What is at first sight a somewhat complicated diagram summarises much of Tittle's control-balance theory. There are a number of features of the diagram that it is important to note. At the top of the diagram there are two arrows extending horizontally outwards. They indicate increasing control imbalance – either a deficit (to the left) or a surplus (to the right). The two diagonal arrows indicate the seriousness of the anticipated deviance. As the diagram indicates, on the deficit side the seriousness of likely offending is negatively associated with the extent of the imbalance. That is to say, it is those with the smaller control deficits who are likely to commit the most serious forms of 'repressive' deviance. Those with much greater deficits are only likely to commit less serious acts as these are the only forms that they can contemplate. By contrast, on the surplus side the relationship is a positive one: the greater the control surplus, the more serious the likely deviant conduct because such individuals are able to contemplate serious offending with the least chance of 'counter control'. Finally, in the middle of the diagram is a zone in which control ratios are balanced and where conformity – 'behaviour consistent with social norms that is undertaken with full awareness of possible alternative, nonacceptable behaviour' – is likely.

Thus far the theory seems somewhat deterministic – implying that given a certain set of

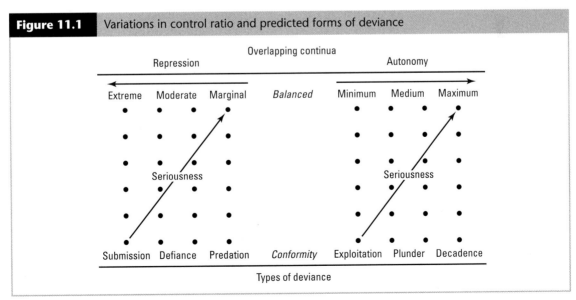

| **Figure 11.1** | Variations in control ratio and predicted forms of deviance |

Source: Tittle (in Cullen and Agnew, 2006).

circumstances particular types of deviant activity are likely to result. However, Tittle is careful to argue that such outcomes are not inevitable. In particular, certain conditions, or *contingencies*, may intervene to affect the outcome. These contingencies generally fall into three categories:

- *Personal* – Moral feelings, habits, personality, desire to commit deviant acts and prior deviance.

- *Organisational* – Subcultural affiliations.

- *Situational* – Variations in opportunity, risk and provocation.

If, therefore, at the heart of this theory is the idea that deviance emerges in situations in which individuals become aware of, and are made to feel humiliated by, a control imbalance, the way in which this plays out in practice is influenced by a wide range of contingencies.

Control-balance theory has met with a number of favourable responses. Braithwaite (1997: 78) in an early review suggested that, 'If it can be shown that both control surpluses and control deficits explain deviance, it may be that crime in the suites [white collar crime] can be explained by control surplus, crime in the streets by control deficit, so that control imbalance structured into a society becomes a common cause of both types of crime.' However, it has also met with some criticism:

- According to Savelsberg (1999) the 'achilles heel' of control-balance theory is its definition of deviance. The definition – 'any behavior that the majority of a given group regards as unacceptable or that typically evokes a collective response of a negative type' (p. 124) – has difficulty in accounting for differing standards of behaviour (what is unacceptable to one group may be acceptable to another) and also in dealing with cases in which even though the majority may disapprove an influential majority may condone, even reward, the behaviour concerned.

- How is the distinction between those deviant acts which are 'repressive' and those which are 'autonomous' to be determined (Braithwaite, 1997)? In response to this criticism, Tittle (2000) later abandoned the idea of two separate continua (of repressive acts on the one hand and autonomous acts on the other) and argued instead that control balancing should be seen in relation to a single continuum of deviant acts, but that at different points on that continuum acts would be distinguished by what he came to call their *control balance desirability*. This he defined as referring to:

... a quality possessed in different degrees by various potential deviant acts. In empirical terms, it is a composite variable composed of two indicators: (1) the likely long-range effectiveness of the deviant act in question for altering a control imbalance; and (2) the extent to which a given form of misbehavior requires the perpetrator to be directly and personally involved with a victim or an object that is affected by the deviance.

- The desire for autonomy isn't a sufficiently all-encompassing explanation for human motivation to be convincing in all circumstances. What of the motivation favoured by earlier control theories, namely the quest for excitement and self-gratification?

- Arguably, Tittle's theory incorporates so many different features and factors that it becomes difficult if not nigh impossible to test (though see Piquero and Hickman, 1999). This is particularly the case in relation to the influence of what he refers to as *contingencies*.

The ideal of good parenting as represented in this picture. In part inspired by control theories, parenting programmes are now a popular form of crime-related intervention.

Assessing control theory

As we noted at the beginning of this chapter, it is only relatively recently that control theory – of various sorts – has become especially influential. This can be seen particularly in relation to situational control theories which are dealt with in Chapter 14. However, the variety of control theories discussed in this chapter has also enjoyed considerable influence in policy circles in modern industrial societies. In particular, the emphasis on control via family and education, and the notion that self-controls are established early in life, has given rise to a variety of early intervention policies aimed at stimulating pro-social conduct. Programmes that provide support to families, that focus on parenting skills, that seek to improve young people's self-esteem, and that seek to bolster conventional values and norms are all, in part, influenced by control theory.

Nevertheless, control theory is far from uncontroversial and by no means unproblematic. As implied earlier, its focus on systems of control, and its apparent comfort with proposals to increase control in order to reduce deviance, has not sat easily with the liberal predisposition of much sociological criminology. One consistent criticism of control theory, therefore, is that its focus may lead to oppressive and repressive policy responses – increasing controls, restraints and prohibitions. Control theory raises important normative questions about how much intervention is appropriate.

What then are the other main lines of criticism aimed at control theory? First and foremost, arguably, is the suggestion that some control theory overstates its ability to explain the matter at hand: crime. Thus, whilst controls are undoubtedly important – most criminological theories contain an element of control theory – proposing such an approach as a 'general theory' ignores the claims of other approaches such as differential association, strain, anomie and other factors. In this manner it is sometimes argued that control theory is not a theory of crime causation at all. Rather, according to some critics all control theory is able to do (itself not unimportant) is to explain the conditions that make crime a possibility rather than an actuality.

Another related criticism of control theory is that by focusing on the immediate and the apparently malleable, it may direct attention away from deeper and more intractable, but at least as impor-

tant, factors in the aetiology of crime, such as social inequality. In this manner, Hirschi's social bond theory notwithstanding, control theory tends to underplay the role of social structures and deeper social controls in the explanation of criminality. As noted earlier, Elliott Currie refers to this as the 'fallacy of autonomy', the assumption that 'what goes on inside the family can usefully be separated from the forces that affect it from outside: the larger social context in which families are embedded for better or worse' (1985: 185).

A criticism of much control theory is that it helps little in the job of explaining why people engage in particular forms of deviant activity rather than others – though Tittle's control-balance theory attempts to overcome this. By taking the central question of much criminological theory – the motivation for offending – as essentially a given, control theories generally tell us little about why offending takes the forms it does and why, on occasion, it takes forms we don't expect. In this sense, as Downes and Rock observe, 'control theorists make far too little of both deviance and conformity' (2007: 224).

Finally for our purposes here, there is arguably also something slightly deterministic in some control theory – the implication (or explicit argument in some cases) that without particular controls or inhibitors crime is inevitable. In the end, this is as much a philosophical question as one that is likely to be resolved empirically. Are we by nature predisposed to deviance unless held in check, or are we propelled into deviant activity by forces beyond our control? At the very least the underlying assumptions of control theory are contestable. The bulk of sociological criminology, in contrast to most control theory, has taken the question of motivation to be the central matter for theory rather than something that can be assumed to be straightforward and relatively constant.

Review questions

1 What do Gottfredson and Hirschi mean when they call their approach to explaining crime a 'general theory'?

2 What are the main lines of criticism of Gottfredson and Hirschi's general theory of crime?

3 What is a control ratio?

Questions for further discussion

1 How does Sykes and Matza's notion of techniques of neutralisation fit with Matza's idea of drift?

2 Occasionally famous people, such as fairly high-ranking politicians, are exposed for having engaged in some deviant activity – often sexual or criminal. How do you square their behaviour with control theory and, in particular, Hirschi's argument about 'commitment' and 'involvement'?

3 In one of their published responses to their critics, Hirschi and Gottfredson (2000) report having received a number of letters from undergraduate students describing cases that appeared to run contrary to their general theory – cases in which it appeared low self-control in one area of life were not manifested in other areas, or which were exhibited when young, but not likely to be similarly exhibited later in life. Can you (a) think of a few such examples yourself, and (b) imagine what Gottfredson and Hirschi's response was?

4 What do you think is the relationship between Hirschi's social bond theory and Gottfredson and Hirschi's general theory of crime?

5 In what ways are theories other than control theory visible in Tittle's control-balance theory? Give examples.

Further reading

Most textbooks provide fairly comprehensive coverage of control theories. Two of the very best discussions are those in Downes and Rock's *Understanding Deviance* (5th edn, Oxford University Press, 2007) and Lilley *et al.*'s *Criminological Theory* (3rd edn, Sage, 2002). As ever, there is no substitute for looking at the original sources. Of these, you might reasonably start with:

Hirschi, T. (1969) *Causes of Delinquency*, Berkeley, CA: University of California Press (ch. 2)

Hirschi, T. and Gottfredson, M.R. (1994) *The Generality of Deviance*, New Brunswick: Transaction, pp. 1–23

(reprinted in McLaughlin, E. *et al.* [eds] *Criminological Perspectives*)

Sykes, G. and Matza, D. (1957) Techniques of neutralization: A theory of delinquency, *American Sociological Review*, 22, 664–673 (abridged in McLaughlin, E. *et al.* [eds] *Criminological Perspectives*)

Tittle, C. (2006) Control balance theory, in Cullen, F.T. and Agnew, R. (eds) *Criminological Theory Past to Present: Essential readings*, Los Angeles, CA: Roxbury

Websites

Once again, Bruce Hoffman's crime theory website is probably the best, reliable source of web-based information in this area: http://www.crimetheory.com/

Chapter outline

Introduction 246
  Crime and the underdog 246

Marx and Marxism 246
  Willem Bonger 248

American radicalism 250
  Vold and criminalisation 250
  Austin Turk 250
  William Chambliss 251
  From conflict to peacemaking 252

Radical criminology in Britain 254
  The new criminology 255
  Contemporary radical criminology 256
    Zemiology 258

Assessing radical criminology 258
  Teleology 258
  Determinism 259
  Idealism 259

Questions for further discussion 260
Further reading 260
Websites 260

Radical and
critical criminology

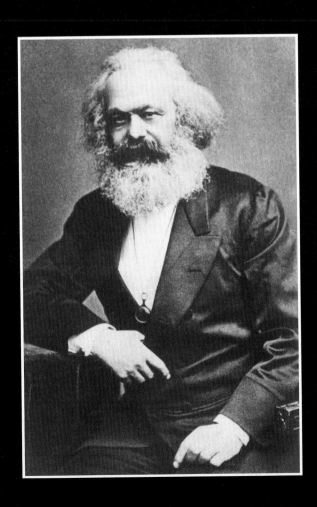

CHAPTER SUMMARY

Stimulated by the social and political upheavals of the 1960s a group of more radically-orientated criminologists began to look beyond questions of strain and anomie toward the structural inequalities and power relations of capitalist societies. Building on some of the insights of interactionism and labelling theory a variety of radical criminological theories focused on the nature of *criminalisation*: the process by which certain people become identified as criminal and what this has to tell us about the nature of contemporary social relations.

This chapter:

- outlines the main contours of these radical theories;

- explores their similarities and differences;

- highlights the ways in which they continue to influence contemporary criminology;

- examines the main lines of criticism aimed at such work.

Introduction

Much of what we discussed under the heading of 'control theories' in the previous chapter rested on the assumption that offenders are self-interested individuals who commit crimes when opportunities arise and circumstances make such criminal activity seem 'worth the risk'. Such approaches differ markedly from early sociological theories which place much less emphasis upon individual decision-making and, rather, focus on the social and cultural context in which crime is to be found. In this chapter we will examine a number of theoretical approaches which, again, differ in many ways from control theories, not least in the emphasis they place upon the *meaning* of crime.

Taylor, Walton and Young, at the forefront of radical criminology in Britain in the 1970s, took anomie theory and other approaches to task for 'predicting too little bourgeois and too much proletarian criminality' (1973: 107). In part, what they meant by this was that such approaches tend to focus upon those social conditions that are held to produce the types of crime that the working classes or poorer members of society are most likely to engage in, whilst paying little attention to other offences such as white-collar and corporate crime.

Crime and the underdog

As we have seen (Chapter 10), labelling theory generated something of a debate about the nature and limitations of what has been referred to as *underdog sociology*. An early extension of labelling theory by

Horowitz and Leibowitz (1968) increased the emphasis on the political nature of some deviant activity. They took the view that certain types of deviance could be seen as forms of social protest. Commenting on this work, Pearson (1975: 96) suggested that the implication was that deviant behaviour 'should be accorded political status. Or, more specifically, that deviance should be grasped as a primitive crypto-political action.'

Though this possibly overstates the case somewhat, it was nevertheless the case that in Britain in particular, a movement developed within one particular strain of sociological criminology which sought to adopt a more explicitly politicised position in relation to deviance and to see an element in it of resistance to existing social conditions. More generally, a radical criminology developed as a reaction in part to the functionalist sociology that had dominated up to this point with its assumptions, implicit or otherwise, about the necessity of policing and punishment. By contrast:

> Critical scholars refused to practise criminology as an auxiliary discipline to criminal law enforcement, and saw it as their task to examine the functioning of the criminal justice system as an instrument of the state to keep power relations as they are. (van Swaaningen, 1997: 79)

Marx and Marxism

Unlike Durkheim, Marx appears to have been relatively unconcerned by crime as a subject. That is not to say that Marxist thought has not been influential in criminology, merely that the influence is a result of Marx's general sociological theory rather than any direct observations he may have made about crime and criminality. Marx was a political economist/sociologist whose concern was with the nature of social divisions and the distribution of power within society. For Marx, it was to the *relations of production* that one should look in the search for the answers to such questions. Within industrial societies, the relations of production can be understood as a dyad, involving a capitalist class (or *bourgeoisie*) that owns the *means of production* and a working class (or *proletariat*) that has to sell its labour in order to survive. All other aspects of society come to reflect this basic division and the major state institutions work toward the maintenance and reproduction of this uneven and unequal system.

As Marx put it:

> In the social production of their existence, men inevitably enter into definite relations, which are independent of their will, namely relations of production appropriate to a given stage of development of their material forces of production. The totality of these relations of production constitutes the economic structure of society, the real foundation, on which arises a legal and political superstructure and to which correspond definite forms of social consciousness. The mode of production of material life conditions the general character of the social, political, and intellectual life. It is not the consciousness of men that determines their existence, but their social existence that determines their consciousness. At a certain stage of development, the material productive forces of society come into conflict with the existing relations of production ... Then begins an era of social revolution. (Marx, 1976: [1857] 5–6)

Here Marx sets out many of the fundamental ideas of his political economy. Societies can be seen to have gone through different stages of development (he was writing at the time of the growth of industrial capitalism). The economic structure of society is the basis on which all other aspects depend and, moreover, it is this that moulds and shapes human consciousness (what we think and believe). However, there are contradictions within the system. Capitalist society, for Marx, is one in which property and wealth become progressively concentrated in fewer and fewer hands. Society polarises into two groups – or classes – whose interests are fundamentally in opposition. Eventually, the con-

Karl Marx (1818–1883), philosopher and revolutionary and author of *Das Kapital* and *The Communist Manifesto*. Though he had relatively little to say directly about crime, his ideas have had a profound impact on radical criminology.

tradictions of capitalism will become so serious that, following revolution, it will be replaced by a wholly new social system – *communism*.

For Marx, the essence of human nature was to be found in productive work – this is an essential part of what he referred to as our 'species being'. The denial of productive work, as happens to ever-larger numbers of people under capitalism, leads to demoralisation. Indeed, it leads to the emergence of a class of people, he argued, who are typified by criminal conduct and other forms of vice-ridden behaviour. This he termed the *lumpenproletariat*. The law, however, is not some neutral expression of what the philosopher Rousseau called 'the social contract' – that thing which binds free individuals together in an expression of collective interest. For Marx, the law is not something which upholds the rights and interests of all citizens, but is an expression of class domination: representing the interests of the dominant class.

One relatively simple – some might suggest *simplistic* – approach to crime that can be drawn from such an approach, is to see offending straightforwardly as a form of resistance by the disenfranchised to the capitalist order. The American political scientist James Q. Wilson (1975: xiii) caricatured such portrayals of crime as the 'expression of the political rage of the dispossessed, rebelling under the iron heel of capitalist tyranny'. It is true to say that Marx had been particularly concerned with working-class resistance to elements of industrial capitalism and, indeed, his collaborator, Engels, had argued in his most famous work, *The Condition of the Working Class in England,* that 'theft was the most primitive form of protest' (1969 [1892]: 240). This is sometimes referred to as the *primitive rebellion* thesis and, although you will rarely find it in crude form these days, you may still find echoes of such views in some contemporary accounts of some criminal activity.

Generally though, it is a subtler reading of Marx's ideas that tends to find its way into modern criminology. Arguments such as the centrality of class conflict to an understanding of social order, the notion that the dominant ideas of the moment are the ideas that serve the interests of the 'ruling class' (however such a thing is to be defined), and the centrality of property and the economy to class relations, all underpin radical, or conflict, theories of crime and criminal justice. All draw their inspiration more or less directly from Marx.

Willem Bonger

The Dutch scholar, Willem Bonger (see box), was one of the first criminologists to utilise the the theory of political economy of Marx and his collaborator, Friedrich Engels. Bonger studied crime rates in Europe in the late nineteenth and early twentieth centuries and was highly critical of the form of social organisation he saw emerging. Capitalism, he argued, 'is a system of exploitation in which, in place of the exploited person being robbed he is compelled by poverty to use all his powers for the benefit of the exploiter' (1969: 28).

For Bonger, the economic inequalities found in contemporary capitalism, and the emphasis on financial success and the individualised, selfish pursuit of pleasure produced a form of 'egoism' which increased criminal conduct. Rather in parallel with Durkheim, Bonger identified the insufficient control of individuals in the new division of labour as a core problem of modern industrial times (what Durkheim sought to capture in his notion of *anomie* – see Chapter 8). However, unlike Durkheim, Bonger didn't see the solution to this as something to be found in more effective controls – as these controls reflect the nature of the society itself.

Like Marx, Bonger took the view that there was something fundamentally unjust about capitalist social organisation for 'hardly any act is punished if it does not injure the interests of the dominant class' (Bonger, 1969: 9). That is to say, the operation of the law in capitalist society acts to punish the poor whilst allowing the wealthy to act in selfish and greedy ways without fear of punishment. By contrast, in a socialist society crime would eventually be eliminated as the law would protect the interests of all rather than merely the propertied.

In a similar vein (see Chapter 18), Edwin Sutherland in the 1930s noted the extent to which major corporations were involved in activities that were, in principle, 'criminal' but which avoided being defined as such because of the economic and political muscle the organisations enjoyed. At approximately the same period, Thorsten Sellin (1938) published a book, *Culture Conflict and Crime,* which, though not Marxist in orientation, focused on conflict between dominant and subsidiary cultures as a means of understanding deviant activity. The law, Sellin argued, tends to reflect dominant cultural norms rather than some broader social consensus. This was not a class-based analysis but a theory which focused on differing normative standards among different communities and neighbourhoods. Much influenced by the work of the Chicago School (see Chapter 9) and by Edwin Sutherland's notion of differential association (see Chapter 7) he observed how conformity to one set of cultural norms may bring people into conflict with the institutions of the criminal justice system.

What we have in the radical or critical criminologies which draw at least some of their inspiration from Marx, therefore, is work that is especially concerned with power relations in society and how crime and the criminal law relate to such power differentials. One of the core ideas running through much such work is that of *criminalisation*. According to Spitzer (1975: 642, quoted in Box, 1983):

> Problem populations tend to share a number of social characteristics but most important among these is the fact that their behaviour, personal

Willem Bonger (1876–1940)

The youngest of 10 children, Bonger grew up in Amsterdam, where his father worked in insurance. He studied law at the University of Amsterdam where he came under the influence of scholars interested also in sociological thought and issues of crime and justice.

The author of a number of books, including *Race and Crime* (1939) and *An Introduction to Criminology* (1932), he is perhaps best known for *Criminality and Economic Conditions,* which was published in 1916. He was an influential author and academic and it has been argued that it 'was due to him that criminology in Holland became a separate field of science' (van Bemmelen, 1960).

Bonger was a fervent critic of oppressive regimes generally, and the Nazis in particular. He was identified by the Third Reich as an arch-enemy of the German state and, despite accepting that a German invasion of Holland would almost certainly end with his death, he refused to emigrate. When the German army entered Holland in early 1940 he wrote to his son, 'I don't see any future for myself and I cannot bow to this scum which will now overmaster us.' He committed suicide not long afterward.

Willem Bonger (1876–1940). A key figure in the emergence of criminology in the Netherlands, Bonger was fiercely critical of the operation and application of the criminal law in capitalist societies.

qualities, and/or position threaten the social relations of production ... In other words, populations become generally eligible for management as deviant when they disturb, hinder, or call into question ... capitalist modes of appropriating the product of human labour ... the social conditions under capitalist production takes place ... patterns of distribution and consumption ... the process of socialization for productive and non-productive roles ... and ... the ideology which supports the capitalist state.

More particularly, radical theory is *critical* precisely because it begins from the normative premise that current arrangements are unequal, exploitative and in need of substantial (radical) overhaul. Most criminological work that comes under this heading therefore is *structuralist* in character, seeing the deep-seated structural inequalities in society as the basis from which an analysis of crime and justice must proceed.

Although *radical* and *conflict theories* are largely discussed together in this chapter, there are a number of differences between them in practice.

Generally speaking, it is held that conflict theory assumes human nature to be amoral whereas radical theorists hold a more benign view in which human nature is more positive, but the circumstances in which individuals find themselves shape behaviour in less acceptable ways. Conflict theories tend to view society as being divided into numerous groups whose interests differ, whereas the bulk of radical theorists, drawing at least in part on Marxism, tend rather to see the division as being primarily between two groups – differentiated by their relationship to property.

Review questions

1 What is meant by 'criminalisation'?

2 What is the 'primitive rebellion' thesis?

3 What is meant when we describe radical sociological theories as generally *structuralist* in character?

American radicalism

A body of radical criminological work influenced by Marxist theory emerged in the US in the late 1960s. It was associated with three people in particular: William Chambliss, Richard Quinney and Austin Turk. However, a survey of American radical criminology must begin somewhat earlier with the work of George Vold. Writing in the 1950s, and building on work by Edwin Sutherland, and by the German sociologist, Georg Simmel, Vold focused on the centrality of political conflict in contemporary society and how group conflict is often the source of criminal activity. In this view the uneven distribution of power is vital. Vold felt that, although the idea of group conflict had some general relevance, it was most applicable to four types of crime:

- crimes arising from labour disputes;
- crimes arising from political protests;
- crimes arising from disputes between and within competing unions;
- crimes arising from racial and ethnic clashes. (Brown *et al.*, 2004: 402)

Vold and criminalisation

The issue raised implicitly by Vold in the quote earlier is that of 'criminalisation' – the assignment of the status *criminal* to particular individuals – and, more particularly, the socially uneven way in which this occurs. What are the consequences of the uneven distribution of power and the fact, therefore, that some people have authority over others? Vold's approach began from the assumption that people in general are group-oriented and that they tend to develop strong attachment to particular groups. Groups inevitably come into conflict because of their differing interests, and this is a normal part of the functioning of any society.

Criminal activity is often something carried out for the benefit of a particular group, or indeed may be committed by groups, and can be understood in part as something that arises in the context of social and political inequality. Industrial or labour conflicts, for example, between management and workers have often led to the criminalisation of certain forms of behaviour – secondary picketing is one example – often reflecting the balance of power between the groups involved. As Vold argued in the first edition of his textbook, *Theoretical Criminology:*

> The whole political process of law making, law breaking, and law enforcement becomes a direct reflection of deep-seated and fundamental conflicts between interest groups and their more general struggles for the control of the police power of the state. Those who produce legislative majorities win control over the police power and dominate the policies that decide who is likely to be involved in the violation of the law. (1958: 209)

The task for the critical criminologist, therefore, becomes the analysis of the ways in which such conflicts of interest are played out to the detriment of the least powerful in our society, and the role of the criminal justice system in this process.

Austin Turk

Like Vold, Turk's conflict-oriented theory was stimulated by his perception that existing theories were unable to explain many of the problems and conflicts besetting contemporary American society. In the preface to his book *Criminality and Legal Order*, published in 1969, he said that:

> Embarrassment provided much of the initial push that led to the writing of this book. I was embarrassed at my lack of good answers when confronted by students who wondered, somewhat irreverently, why criminology is 'such a confused mish-mash' … Some of these students were especially bothered by the 'unreality' of criminological studies, by which they meant the lack of sustained attention to connections between the theories and statistics about crime, and what they heard every day about relations among social conflicts, political manoeuvres, and law violation and enforcement. (quoted in Taylor *et al.*, 1973: 239)

Turk's sociology was heavily influenced by the work of the British sociologist Ralf Dahrendorf. In his conflict theory, Dahrendorf (1959) argued that members of society occupied one of two positions in any relationship: one of *domination* or one of *subjection*, and that these were not straightforwardly a reflection of property relations (as in traditional Marxist theory). Consequently, people see each other differently, conflict is inevitable, and both social norms and institutions develop in such a way as to protect the social status of those in dominant positions. Following Dahrendorf's reworking of Marxist theory, Austin Turk's conflict theory, rather than focusing on class conflict result-

Austin Turk, an influential figure in American radical criminology – when conflict emerges, he argued, criminalisation is the inevitable consequence.

ing from unequal access to property and the means of production, was concerned with the unequal distribution of authority in contemporary societies. He argued that:

> The stability of an authority relationship appears to depend far less upon subjects' conscious or unconscious belief in the rightness or legitimacy of the rank order than upon their having been conditioned to accept as a fact that authorities must be reckoned with as such.
>
> (1969: 43)

The nature of social life is to be understood in part as a constant negotiation by individuals in different social positions as to how to behave in relation to each other. This learning of authority positions enables the social order to continue to exist. There are circumstances, Austin Turk argued, in which conflicts will arise between 'authorities' and 'subjects' and where criminalisation will be the consequence. Echoing elements of Becker's labelling theory (see Chapter 10), he argued that 'Nothing and no one is intrinsically criminal; criminality is a definition applied by individuals with the power to do so, according to illegal and extra-legal, as well as legal criteria' (1969: 10). He identified four types or levels of conflict:

- *Organised and sophisticated* – such as corporate and some organised crime.

- *Organised and unsophisticated* – such as youth offending and youth gangs.

- *Unorganised and sophisticated* – such as the con artist or fraudster.

- *Unorganised and unsophisticated* – such as thieves.

He argued that such conflict is most likely where the subjects are *highly organised* and *relatively unsophisticated* (such as in the case of delinquent gangs) and least likely where subjects are *unorganised* and *sophisticated* (such as in the case of professional con artists). A further mediating factor was the relative power of those seeking to enforce norms and those resisting them. In short, he argued that the greater the power differential, the greater the probability of criminalisation.

William Chambliss

Chambliss's work, especially his later work, is more explicitly Marxist in orientation than that of Turk, arguing that as the gap between the bourgeoisie and proletariat widens in contemporary capitalism, so it becomes necessary to use increasingly punitive measures to maintain order. Chambliss provides one of the clearest personal statements about the origins of his radical views:

> After I graduated from (UCLA) [University of California, Los Angeles], I hitchhiked across the country again to see my father. It was 1955, and in short order I was drafted into the army and sent to Korea with the Counter Intelligence Corps (CIC). I learned a lot about crime during that period. American and Korean soldiers raped, stole, assaulted, intimidated, and generally terrorised the Koreans. Because they had the power, nothing was done about it ... How could crime be understood from the paradigms I learned in psychology and sociology? (*The Criminologist*, 12, 1–9, quoted in Lilly *et al.*, 2002: 140)

Pursuing a Marxist-influenced analysis of crime and society, Chambliss and Seidman (1971) argued that the popular view that the law represents general social values and operates in the best interests of society is mistaken, indeed naïve. Rather, they argued that:

> Every detailed study of the emergence of legal norms has consistently shown the immense importance of interest group activity, not the 'public interest', as the critical variable in determining the content of legislation. To hold to the

Korean War Veterans Memorial, Washington DC. The experience of abuses committed by soldiers during wartime was a crucial radicalising experience for the American criminologist, Bill Chambliss.

notion of natural laws emerging from the needs of society requires that we accept the highly questionable assumption that somehow interest groups operate in the best interests of society. It may be true that 'what's good for General Motors is good for society', if all the members of society benefit from the triumph of special interests. Rarely does this happen. Laws inevitably improve things for some people and make things worse for others. (1971: 73)

They went on to argue that the more socially stratified a society becomes, the greater is the necessity for dominant social groups to enforce their supremacy through the coercive regulation of the conduct of others. By the mid-1970s Chambliss's position had further radicalised and he argued that 'crime diverts the lower classes' attention from the exploitation they experience and directs it toward other members of their own class rather than toward the capitalist class or economic system' and, furthermore and even more contentiously, that 'crime is a reality which exists only as it is created by those in the society whose interests are served by its presence' (1975: 152–3).

Some of Chambliss's most important work concerned the crimes of the powerful. In his book, *On the Take: From Petty Crooks to Presidents*, he studied the relationship between organised crime and organised bureaucracy in Seattle. Based on participant observation in and around the city's bars Chambliss eventually built a picture of a network of powerful people and groups involved in illegal activities.

In a radical criminological version of C. Wright Mills' (1956) *The Power Elite* Chambliss interpreted organised crime as a form of quintessentially capitalist activity, elements of which were protected from police intervention by the very fact of links with other powerful social interests. This is long-standing, he suggests, for 'The first President of the United States, George Washington, used the office of the presidency to enhance his personal fortune. A precedent was established that one way or another has characterized every administration since' (1978: 201). In the conclusion the influence of Marxism on Chambliss's radical criminology is clear:

> Criminal behaviour is generated because of the contradictions that inevitably arise in the course of the working out of the particular form of social, political, and economic structures. The types of crime, the amount of crime, and the distribution of crime in a particular historical period and society depend on the nature of existing contradictions, and conflicts that develop as people respond to the contradictions, and the mechanisms institutionalized for handling the conflicts and dilemmas produced by the contradictions. (1978: 209)

From conflict to peacemaking

In addition to Turk and Chambliss, the third important figure in American radical criminology in this period is Richard Quinney. Quinney's work has undergone a number of mutations over the years, beginning as a form of conflict theory not unlike that of Turk and Chambliss, subsequently radicalising under the influence of the Frankfurt School, latterly transforming into his more recent advocacy of what he terms 'peacemaking criminology' – influenced as much by theological writings as Marxist political economy. In his early work Quinney, like other conflict theorists, was preoccupied with the social construction of crime and how this related to the distribution of power in contemporary society. Thus, for Quinney (1970: 16) 'criminal definitions describe behaviours that conflict with the interests of segments of society that

Chambliss on the laws of vagrancy

Chambliss's paper concerns the introduction of vagrancy laws in England and America. The laws in England compelled people to work, imposed a standard wage and limited the movement of workers.

[T]here has been a severe shortage of sociologically relevant analyses of the relationship between particular laws and the social setting in which these laws emerge, are interpreted, and take form ...

There is general agreement among legal scholars that the first full fledged vagrancy statute was passed in England in 1349 ... The prime-mover for this legislative innovation was the Black Death which struck England about 1348. Among the many disastrous consequences this had upon the social structure was the fact that it decimated the labour force. It is estimated that by the time the pestilence had run its course at last 50% of the population of England had died from the plague ... Even before the pestilence, however, the availability of an adequate supply of cheap labour was becoming a problem for the landowners ...

The immediate result of these events was of course no surprise: wages for the 'free' man rose considerably and this increased, on the one hand, the landowners' problems and, on the other hand, the plight of the unfree tenant. For although wages increased for the personally free labourers, it of course did not necessarily add to the standard of living of the serf, if anything it made his position worse because the landowner would be hard pressed to pay for the

personally free labour which he needed and would thus find it more and more difficult to maintain the standard of living for the serf which he had therefore supplied. Thus the serf had no alternative but flight if he chose to better his position. Furthermore, flight generally meant both freedom and better conditions since the possibility of work in the new weaving industry was great and the chance of being caught small.

It was under these conditions that we find the first vagrancy statutes emerging. There is little question but that these statutes were designed for one express purpose: to force labourers (whether personally free or unfree) to accept employment at a low wage in order to insure the landowner an adequate supply of labour at a price he could afford to pay...

...these laws were a legislative innovation which reflected the socially perceived necessity of providing an abundance of cheap labour to landowners during a period when serfdom was breaking down and when the pool of available labour was depleted...

This analysis of the vagrancy statutes... has demonstrated the importance of 'vested interest groups in the emergence and/or alteration of laws. The vagrancy laws emerged in order to provide the powerful landowners with a ready supply of cheap labour. When this was no longer seen as necessary and particularly when the landowners were no longer dependent upon cheap labour nor were they a powerful interest group in the society, the laws became dormant.

Source: Chambliss (1964: 67–77).

---

have the power to shape public policy'. By the mid-1970s Quinney's position had become even more straightforwardly Marxist, as summarised in the following six propositions:

1 American society is based on an advanced capitalist economy.

2 The state is organised to serve the interests of the dominant economic class, the capitalist ruling class.

3 Criminal law is an instrument of the state and ruling class to maintain and perpetuate the existing social and economic order.

4 Crime control in capitalist society is accomplished through a variety of institutions and agencies established and administered by a governmental elite, representing ruling class interests, for the purpose of establishing domestic order.

5 The contradictions of advanced capitalism – the disjunction between existence and essence – require that the subordinate classes remain oppressed by whatever means necessary, especially through the coercion and violence of the legal system.

6 Only with the collapse of capitalist society and the creation of a new society, based on socialist principles, will there be a solution to the crime problem. (1974: 16)

He summarised his position in the following way:

The reality of crime that is constructed for all of us by those in a position of power is the reality we tend to accept as our own. By doing so, we grant those in power the authority to carry out the actions that best promote their interests. This is the politics of reality. The social reality of crime in a politically organised society is constructed as a political act.

In *Class, State and Crime* Quinney (1977) outlined a typology of crime in which he distinguished between:

- *Crimes of domination* which included:
  - *crimes of control* such as crimes committed by the police;
  - *crimes of government*;
  - *crimes of economic domination* such as white-collar or organised corporate crime.
- *Crimes of accommodation and resistance* which included:
  - *predatory crimes* such as burglary and theft;
  - *personal crimes* such as robbery and homicide.
- *Crimes of resistance* such as political crimes and terrorism.

By the time of the second edition of the book, although Quinney continued to advocate responses that would be identified as socialist, he also 'increasingly emphasised the *religious* nature of the goal, going so far as to reject Marxist materialism' (Lilly *et al.*, 2002: 152) arguing that political consciousness in late capitalism 'is increasingly accompanied by a consciousness about matters of ultimate concern' (Quinney, 1980: 112). Within a short period Quinney's approach had shifted significantly away from his earlier Marxist position and gradually coalesced, in part through his work with Hal Pepinsky, into what he came to refer to as 'peacemaking criminology'. Though continuing from the baseline assumption that conflict is a root cause of crime, peacemaking criminology seeks solutions that do not involve the further infliction of violence and pain and, rather, stresses conflict resolution, mediation and conciliation. Thus, the traditional approach of the criminal justice system, according to Quinney, is to impose a form of 'negative peace' through the use of threats and sanctions. Peacemaking criminology involves a search for means of establishing 'positive peace':

> There can be no peace – no positive peace – without social justice. Without social justice and without peace (personal and social), there is crime. And there is, as well, the violence of criminal justice ... Criminal justice keeps things as they are. Social policies and programs that are positive in nature – that focus on positive peace-making – create something new. They eliminate the structural sources of violence and crime. A critical, peacemaking criminologist is engaged in the work of positive peace. (1997: 117)

Quinney's later peacemaking criminology was, in his words, more influenced by socialist humanism than Marxism and took as its objective being 'kind to one another, to transcend the barriers that separate us from one another, and to live everyday life with a sense of interdependence' (Quinney, 2000: 26). It took much of the language of pacifism, and elements of Buddhism, to mount a critique of the violence that was perceived to lie both at the heart of our responses to crime as well as framing the way we talk about crime. It rejected retributive forms of punishment and sought to direct attention to the need to improve social and individual relationships as the basis for solving conflict. More recently, Fuller (2003) has outlined what he calls a 'peacemaking pyramid paradigm' in an attempt to use the perspective as the basis for constructing practical programmes to address the problem of crime. The paradigm has six major characteristics:

- *Non-violence* – Peacemaking attempts to eschew violence and is, therefore, against capital punishment.
- *Social justice* – It aims to be anti-discriminatory.
- *Inclusion* – Involving those from the most affected communities, and including victims and others in criminal justice processes.
- *Correct means* – Protecting due process and ensuring that coercion isn't used.
- *Ascertainable criteria* – Everyone involved in criminal justice processes should understand and be aware of rules, regulations and procedures.
- *Categorical imperative* – Everyone should be treated with respect and dignity.

Similar practical and normative features can be found in much conflict resolution and restorative justice theory and practice and, indeed, peacemaking criminology has strong links with both the alternative dispute resolution movement and with restorative justice (for further discussion, see Chapter 30).

Radical criminology in Britain

Somewhat later than it had appeared in the United States, radical criminology began to emerge in the UK. Once again, though, this development was very much a child of the times, reflecting the emergent radical political developments of the period; developments which sought to challenge established ways of thinking and behaving and, not least, which sought to challenge the established forms of authority.

According to Jock Young (1988: 159) 'British criminology in the late 1960s was at a cross-roads. The social democratic positivism which had been dominant in the post-war period entered into a period of prolonged crisis, out of which emerged the two major contending paradigms: radical criminology and administrative criminology.' By administrative criminology, Young meant a form of inquiry that was largely empiricist and narrowly policy-oriented in its focus. By contrast, radical criminology was 'that part of the discipline which sees the causes of crime as being at core the class and patriarchal relations endemic to our social order and which sees fundamental changes as necessary to reduce criminality' (1988: 160).

In the UK the organisational home of radical criminology was the National Deviancy Conference which was established in the late 1960s and disappeared in the late 1970s. Jock Young describes its thrust as follows:

> Positivism was perhaps the main enemy: its ontology was seen to take human creativity out of deviant action, its sociology erected a consensual edifice from which deviants were bereft of culture and meaning, its methodology elevated experts to the role of fake scientists discovering the 'laws' of social action and its policy, whether in mental hospitals, social work agencies or drug clinics, was self-fulfilling and mystifying. (Young, 1998: 17)

Crucial to this development was the 'impact of the West Coast labelling theory centring around Howard Becker which set the creaking chariot of radical criminology off on its course' (Young, 1988: 163) and also to the social movements and politics of the 1960s (Scraton and Chadwick, 1991). Labelling theory had identified the source of deviance in social reaction and pointed to the importance of understanding the way in which the power to label was utilised. Out of an amalgam of Durkheimian sociology, interactionism, labelling theory and Marxism there emerged a new criminology in Britain that was intent on achieving a radical break with previous theoretical approaches.

The new criminology

In 1973 Ian Taylor, Paul Walton and Jock Young published their manifesto for a critically engaged criminology: *The New Criminology*. In the book and through their critique of existing criminological theories, they suggested that what they wished to develop was a fully 'social theory of deviance'. Although forewords to books are probably slightly unreliable guides to the import of what follows – the author of the foreword is naturally positively inclined toward the merits of the work – Alvin Gouldner's assessment of *The New Criminology* is nevertheless worth repeating:

> If any single book can succeed in making 'criminology' intellectually serious, as distinct from professionally respectable, then this study, remarkable for its combination of the analytical with the historical, will do it ... What this important study does then, is this: it redirects the total structure of technical discourse concerning 'crime' and 'deviance'. (Gouldner, 1973: *ix*)

Not only did the new criminology seek to make a radical break with what it took to be positivist criminology, it also sought to develop a highly politicised position, taking the view that 'any criminology which is not normatively committed to the abolition of inequalities of wealth and power, and in particular of inequalities in property and life-chances, is inevitably bound to fall into correctionalism' (1973: 281). The task, according to the authors, was 'to create a society in which the facts of human diversity, whether personal, organic or social, are not subject to the power to criminalize' (*ibid*).

The New Criminology: described by the American criminologist, Elliott Currie, as 'the first truly comprehensive critique of the totality, of past and contemporary, of European and American, studies of "crime" and "deviance"'.

By contrast, a fully social theory, such as that they were attempting to construct must, they said, break entirely with correctionalism, in which they included even the social reform efforts advocated by and engaged in by the Chicago School theorists. Lanier and Henry (1998) summarise the radical theory offered in *The New Criminology*, and by other radical criminologists such as Spitzer, Quinney (in his earlier guise) and Chambliss, in the following six statements:

1 *Capitalism shapes social institutions, social identities, and social action* – The mode of production shapes the nature of social institutions and the behaviour and activities of individuals within those institutions.

2 *Capitalism creates class conflict and contradictions* – The nature of contemporary capitalism impoverishes the working class and restricts their ability to resist or change the system.

3 *Crime is a response to capitalism and its contradictions* – Crime is a logical or rational response to the structural position people find themselves in under capitalism and, in some cases, a form of resistance or rebellion.

4 *Capitalist law facilitates and conceals crimes of domination and repression* – The focus on the behaviour of the subordinated class deflects attention from the crimes of the powerful (including by the state itself).

5 *Crime is functional to capitalism* – Crime provides work (for those in criminal justice) and legitimises the operation of the system of law and justice.

6 *Capitalism shapes society's response to crime by shaping law* – The content of the criminal law reflects the need to control subordinated social classes and protect the property of the powerful; the law enables the continuation of the capitalist system of production, in part by protecting the interests of the powerful and by shaping the behaviour of the powerless. As Scraton and Chadwick (1991: 181) put it, 'The criminal justice process and the rule of law assist in the management of structural contradictions and the process of criminalization is central to such management.'

Taylor *et al.*, (1973) rejected the passive view of the offender that appeared in much criminology – what Gouldner referred to as 'man on his back' – and started out from the view of the deviant as 'a decision-maker who actively violates the moral and legal codes of society' (1973: 163). Building on

Marxist foundations, they examined and developed a critique of the criminogenic consequences of capitalism. They argued explicitly that 'much deviance is in itself political' (as, indeed, was their project in response: see below). However, as Tierney (1996: 157) notes, two years later 'by 1975, with the publication of a follow-up collection of readings, *Critical Criminology* (Taylor *et al.*, 1975), Jock Young was already starting to review his position'. Tierney (1996: 183) suggests that the position adopted by Taylor, Walton and Young in *The New Criminology* can be summarised in five main points:

- They adopted and espoused a commitment to a *normative* criminology – their work was part of a larger political project. This project was to 'argue for a criminology which is normatively committed to the abolition of inequalities of wealth and power [and] ... to attempt to create the kind of society in which the facts of human diversity are not subject to the power to criminalise' (Taylor *et al.*, 1975: 44).

- They envisaged a socialist future in which crime as we currently understand it, would be absent.

- They sought to create a sociological criminology that was simultaneously anti-positivist yet avoided the relativism that some of the more subjectivist accounts of crime fall into.

- Great emphasis was placed upon the structural constraints and determinants of human action, not least the impact of class society.

- A central feature of their explanation was the role of the state and the main powerful institutions of society – in this explanation crime was a rational response to the social arrangements of a capitalist political economy.

The new criminology was both normative and highly idealistic. Its authors argued that 'close reading of the classical social theorists reveals a basic agreement; the abolition of crime *is* possible under certain social arrangements' (1973: 281). The task for the new criminology, they argued, 'is to create a society in which the facts of human diversity, whether personal, organic or social, are not subject to the power to criminalize' (1973: 282).

Contemporary radical criminology

Although there has been a marked turn away from Marxist theory in contemporary criminology, elements of such thinking can still regularly be found. In particular, the work of Antonio Gramsci (see box below) and his notion of 'hegemony' remains of considerable importance. Building on Marx's notions of class conflict, Gramsci sought to explain how ruling classes maintain their position of dominance without relying on force. His argument, in brief, was that the consent and co-operation of the masses was secured through *hegemonic strategies*. These strategies – which are cultural and ideological – generate and maintain popular support for existing relations. Subordinate groups are, in effect, persuaded of, rather than forced to accept, the normality and legitimacy of current social arrangements. The means by which hegemony is achieved, and consequences of challenges to hegemony, have been important tools in elements of radical criminology.

As one example, Beckett and Sasson (2000) use elements of Gramsci's theory as the basis for analysing changes in the nature of American crime control policy from the New Deal in the 1930s to the present day. From the 1930s, they argue, the US used social policies focused on poverty-reduction and tackling related social problems, together with a partially welfarist criminal justice policy in which rehabilitation was an important facet, as its primary means of governing the population and maintaining order and stability. However, the upheavals of the late 1960s/1970s brought various challenges to the established order – not least via the civil rights movement, the campaign against the war in Vietnam and the rise of the youth counterculture. Together, 'these protest movements constituted a serious "counter-hegemonic" challenge to prevailing social and economic arrangements' (2000: 66).

The consequence, Beckett and Sasson (2000) argue, was a political reaction which sought to re-establish hegemony by abandoning the 'inclusionary' social policies that had developed since the 1930s and, instead, sought to discredit the socially marginal. The new model of governing shrank the welfare state and expanded what one might think of as the 'security state'. At the core of this new strategy were the 'war on drugs' and the 'war on crime' and the shift toward the use of incarceration as a standard means of dealing with offending. This, together with the introduction of mandatory minimum ('three strikes') sentences, the scaling back of parole, and the revival of the

Antonio Gramsci (1891–1937)

Born in Sardinia in 1891, one of seven children, Antonio Gramsci initially left school at 11 in order to work to help support his impoverished family (his father had been imprisoned after being accused of embezzlement). He continued to study and eventually was able to return to school and in 1911 won a scholarship to the University of Turin. He studied linguistics, humanities and courses in the social sciences, also joining the Italian communist party and becoming involved in radical politics. By 1915 he was working as a journalist and became an important radical voice on both the local and national political scene. In the early 1920s he spent 18 months living in Russia as an Italian delegate to the Communist International (also known as Comintern, an organisation set up in 1919 to support international communism). Gramsci met his future wife whilst working as delegate to Comintern. In November 1926 he was arrested and imprisoned by Mussolini's fascists. He remained in hospital until 1933, his poor health leading to his transfer to a clinic and then hospital subsequently – though always under guard. He died in 1937 from a cerebral hemorrhage. It is his *Prison Notebooks* and the idea of 'cultural hegemony' for which he is now chiefly remembered.

Antonio Gramsci (1891–1937). Italian journalist and political philosopher, imprisoned by Mussolini's fascists, his *Prison Notebooks* had a huge impact on twentieth-century radical thought.

death penalty was, Beckett and Sasson (2000: 68) suggest, 'a hegemonic project of the ruling class, spearheaded by political conservatives (neoliberals and social conservatives) in response to the various challenges of the late 1960s and early 1970s'.

Zemiology

More recently a number of radical criminologists have also begun once again to question the entire criminological enterprise. Given that one of the fundamentals of much radical scholarship is to treat categories such as *crime* as being deeply problematic, this raises awkward issues for the criminologist and, they suggest, should make one ask 'what is the theoretical rationale and political utility of retaining a commitment to the analysis of crime, (criminal) law and the criminal justice system?' (Hillyard *et al.*, 2004b: 1).

Their response is to offer an alternative focus for such scholarship: social harm. The intention is to broaden the focus of inquiry beyond crime to various social phenomena that cause harm (irrespective of whether or not they are currently defined as criminal). At one stage such an approach was known by the label *zemiology,* though in recent times the terminology appears to have been dropped. A recent important collection (Hillyard *et al., 2004)* designed to illustrate the breadth and strengths of such an approach, includes a range of thoughtful and provocative articles on topics such as state harms, migration, workplace injury and death, and poverty. It is perhaps particularly in the area of corporate (mis)conduct that the potential strength of an approach that is not limited by a concern with 'crime' is clearest.

Since 1980 the US prison population has more than quadrupled and is now over two million: incarceration, as radical criminologists have argued, has become the standard means of dealing with offending.

Zemiology, or whatever the study of social harms comes to be called, is unlikely to displace criminology, at least not in the short-term. Nevertheless, it presents a healthy reminder to criminologists of one of the more obvious limitations of their subject as well, potentially, as being a focus for what will likely stimulate important and provocative research.

Assessing radical criminology

The influence of Marx and Engels runs through criminology just as it does through sociology. Though they had relatively little to say about crime – particularly Marx – their analysis of social organisation, power and exploitation have had a powerful impact upon much twentieth century criminology, particularly in the post-war period. More particularly, the idea of *criminalisation* has been a hugely important organising idea in both radical/critical and what are sometimes referred to as social constructionist theories of crime. And, yet, despite this influence, radical criminology is, currently at least, somewhat marginalised within contemporary scholarship.

In part this is a reflection of the times; the political context in which criminology is practised. However, it is also because, intellectually, elements of radical criminology have been subjected to sustained and substantive criticism, sometimes from within. Three criticisms have been voiced most frequently, those of teleology; determinism; and idealism.

Teleology

First, in certain versions of critical criminology there is a teleological, almost conspiratorially functionalist quality. Put in simpler language, it appears that some radical theories view crime or deviance as a straightforward product of capitalism and the operation of the criminal justice system as seamlessly meeting the needs of capitalism. Working-class resistance is criminalised – the process of criminalisation being an important part of the maintenance of the capitalist system. At its worst the argument is entirely circular. Criminal law as currently constituted is vital in sustaining class domination. Crime is therefore *functional* so far as capitalism is concerned. But showing that something has a social function is not the same as explaining why it occurs or exists (as Durkheim observed). The historian E.P. Thompson was particularly critical of some Marxist theory which he felt overlooked the 'difference between arbitrary power and the rule of law. We ought to expose the shams and inequities which may be concealed beneath this law. But the rule of law itself ... seems to me to be an unqualified human good' (1975: 266).

Determinism

Second, some critics have argued that the new criminology suffered from just the sort of determinism for which its authors had criticised others. In particular, the structural features of capitalism appear to produce effects that allow for little human agency or resistance. In some radical theorising the contradictions of capitalism, or the structural imbalance between social classes, appears to be the crucial determinant of criminal conduct, overriding all other considerations and in which the individual actor, as Taylor *et al.* (1975: 108) said of Mertonian anomie theory, 'boxed into a fixed social position – is rarely seen to evolve a solution to his problem in his own terms.'

One of the most trenchant critics of *The New Criminology* was Paul Hirst (1975a; 1975b) who argued that crime and deviance were not proper objects of study. He was also critical of the 'crime as resistance and rebellion' thesis that appeared to lie at the heart of much conflict theory:

> The romanticisation of crime, the recognition in the criminal of a rebel 'alienated' from society, is, for Marxism, a dangerous political ideology. It leads *inevitably* ... to the estimation of the lumpenproletariat as a revolutionary force.
>
> (1975a: 218)

Some critics have also argued that there is little empirical support for radical criminological ideas. Klockars (1979) suggested that Marxist criminologists appeared like 'true believers' in a 'new religion' and argued that such ideas were able to explain neither the relatively low crime rates in some capitalist societies nor the problems that existed in communist societies. Klockars accuses such theorists of utopianism and critical irresponsibility:

> By presenting itself as an ideal and as inevitable, of inexorably moving toward a crime-free, unexploitive, unrepressive, unoppressive future, Marxist theory relieves itself of all responsibility for the exploitation, crime and human abuse which has been and continues to be perpetuated in its name. (1979: 506)

Though less a criticism of critical criminology than simply a reflection upon the state of affairs in British criminology in the early 1980s, Stan Cohen noted its lack of impact:

> There are more corners and cavities than ten years ago, but for the most part the institutional foundations of British criminology remain intact and unaltered, for the establishment saw the new theories as simply fashion which eventually pass over or as a few interesting ideas which could be swallowed up without changing the existing paradigm at all. (Cohen, 1981: 236)

Idealism

As was implied in the earlier discussion, some Marxist treatments of crime appear somewhat idealistic, not least in their portrayal of the possibility of a crime-free society. Similarly, the tendency in elements of critical criminology to view criminal activity as a form of resistance – as a political or quasi-political act – arguably led to the under-estimation of the impact of crime on the working classes. Indeed, this observation was one of the stimuli for the development of left realism (see Chapter 13). Jock Young, one of the most important figures in radical criminology in Britain also became one of its most vocal critics. In outlining the case for a realist criminology, he and Roger Matthews (Matthews and Young, 1986: 1) were highly critical of its failures:

> The tide is turning for radical criminology. For over two decades it has neglected the effect of crime upon the victim and concentrated on the impact of the state – through the process of labelling – on the criminal. There was nothing wrong with this *per se*. It was a necessary antidote to orthodox criminology ... But radical analysis also lost touch with the most obvious focus of criminology – crime itself. It became an advocate for the indefensible: the criminal became the victim, the state the solitary focus of attention, while the real victim remained off-stage.

Review questions

1 What is peacemaking criminology?

2 By describing itself as 'new' what was the 'new criminology' distinguishing itself from?

3 What did Gramsci mean by the term 'hegemony'?

4 What is 'zemiology' and why are its proponents critical of traditional criminology?

Questions for further discussion

1 Is a crime-free society possible?

2 Is it accurate to think that the operation of the criminal justice system favours the powerful and disadvantages the powerless? Give examples.

3 'Poverty and exploitation is at the root of most crime.' Discuss.

4 What is the importance of radical or critical criminology?

5 What is the relevance of Marxist criminology to contemporary society?

Further reading

McLaughlin, E. *et al.* (eds) (2003) *Criminological Perspectives,* 2nd edn, London: Sage (contains some wonderful selections from the original materials; an indispensable companion)

Scraton, P. and Chadwick, C. (1991) The theoretical and political priorities of critical criminology, in Stenson, K. and Cowell, D. (eds) *The Politics of Crime Control,* London: Sage (abridged in McLaughlin *et al., Criminological Perspectives*)

Taylor, I. *et al.* (1973) *The New Criminology,* London: Routledge and Kegan Paul (ch. 8)

van Swaaningen, R. (1999) Reclaiming critical criminology: Social justice and the European tradition, *Theoretical Criminology,* 3, 5–28

Vold, G. *et al.* (2002) *Theoretical Criminology,* 5th edn, New York: Oxford University Press (especially ch. 13 and 14)

Young, J. (1988) Radical criminology in Britain, *British Journal of Criminology,* 28, 159–183

Websites

You can find useful information on the website of the Critical Criminology division of the American Society of Criminology at: http://www.critcrim.org

John Fuller maintains a website that is a useful resource for anyone interested in peacemaking criminology: http://peacemakingandcrime.blogspot.com/

There is a lot of information about Gramsci at the International Gramsci Website: http://www.italnet.nd.edu/gramsci/index.html

Chapter outline

Introduction   264

Left realism   264
   The critique of 'left idealism'   265
   The nature of left realism   266
   What is to be done about law and order? 267
   Left realism and method   267
   Assessing left realism   268

Right realism   270
   Thinking About Crime   270
   Distinguishing left and right realism 270
   Wilson and Herrnstein   272
   Murray and the 'underclass'   273
   Assessing right realism   275

Questions for further discussion   276
Further reading   276
Websites   276

Realist
criminology

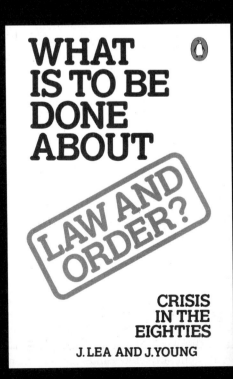

WHAT
IS TO BE
DONE
ABOUT

LAW AND
ORDER?

CRISIS
IN THE
EIGHTIES

J. LEA AND J. YOUNG

CHAPTER SUMMARY   Realist criminology takes a number of forms. In America in the 1970s a right-wing critique of the 'great society' programmes emerged which advocated greater emphasis on personal responsibility and identified the breakdown of marriage and the growth of single-parenthood as sources of a number of contemporary social ills including crime. By contrast, primarily a British development, left realist criminology grew out of a critique of elements of radical and Marxist approaches. At a time in which right-wing governments were increasingly dominant on both sides of the Atlantic, and neo-liberal economic policies were becoming fashionable, a number of scholars argued that critical criminology had little to say of any practical value and, worse still, had ignored the very real impact of crime on the most vulnerable members of society.

Introduction

The Reagan and Thatcher governments that emerged in America and Britain in the 1970s and which, via their successors, dominated politics for a considerable period, represented a significant break with much previous post-war politics and public policy. Both favoured free market economics and were critical of the social welfare programmes that had developed in previous decades, arguing that they encouraged people to rely on others rather than taking responsibility for themselves and to assume that the state should provide for them if they were unable, or unwilling, to do so themselves. Put at its most basic, right realism was part of this larger critique, whereas left realism was a reaction to it and to the perception that existing radical theories had little influence upon or relevance to the new political and economic situation.

Left realism

Downes and Rock describe the process that gave rise to left realism as 'a revolution within radical criminology itself' (2003: 284). Why did left realism emerge? Downes and Rock, with tongue only slightly in cheek, suggest that 'One influence must have been the sheer tedium which inventive minds experienced in emphasizing again and again arguments about the class-bound nature of crime, the forgotten importance of political economy and criminology's scandalous neglect of Marx, Engels and Pashukanis' (2003: 285).

A second and hugely important influence on the emergence of left realism was the general impact that feminism had on radical theorising

(see Chapter 15). The rise up the political agenda of concerns about sexual and domestic violence made political positions which naturally sympathised with those caught up in the criminal justice 'net' increasingly difficult to sustain. Thus, portrayals of the justice system as simply a reflection of class interests did not always sit comfortably with scholars whose concerns, for example, were focused upon uncovering the extent of domestic violence and other violence against women, and in creating effective political and policy responses to such problems.

A third reason concerns the changing political circumstances in which radical criminologists found themselves working in 1970s and 1980s Britain – not least with radicalised local authorities seeking advice from local academics about problems of crime and victimization set against a broader context of the dominance of right-wing political ideas (see Chapter 3). If earlier radical criminology was *socialist*, then left realism was *social democratic* in its ambition and approach. As Jock Young observed in the mid-1970s:

> It is unrealistic to suggest that the problem of crime like mugging is merely the problem of mis-categorization and concomitant moral panics. If we choose to embrace this liberal position, we leave the political arena open to conservative campaigns for law and order – for, however exaggerated and distorted the arguments conservatives may marshal, the reality of crime in the streets *can be* the reality of human suffering and personal disaster. (Young, 1975)

The mention of Britain above was deliberate for this was a very British development. Though there were important sightings of left realism in the US – not least in the work of Elliott Currie (1985) – these were generally few and far between.

Dekeseredy and Schwartz (1991) suggest that the general marginalisation of radical thought in America and the more particular absence of any dominant radical tradition in American universities were largely responsible for its relative absence there. In Britain, left realism was built on a critique of previous radical criminological approaches and, in particular, what Jock Young, memorably called 'left impossibilism'.

The critique of 'left idealism'

The left realists (Matthews and Young, 1992b; Young and Matthews, 1992) mounted a fierce critique of radical criminology, or what they referred to as *left idealism*. Left idealism, they argued, assumed that crime occurred within the working class because of the poverty, and that crime was an attempt to redress their balance in our inequitable society. To blame the poor for their criminality is to blame the victim and it is the crimes of the powerful, rather than the powerless, that should preoccupy us. The crimes of the powerless are, in fact, generally petty and the fact that it is such crimes which are the predominant focus of the criminal justice system illustrates the way in which the criminal law functions to protect the interests of the wealthy. The core of the critique focused on left idealism's:

- *Utopianism* – It has continued to adhere to the view that some form of crime-free future is possible if only social structural conditions could be changed. One consequence of this is that left idealism is accused of focusing on unrealistic and unachievable political change, and of failing to focus on more practical policy changes which would improve people's lives.

- *Romanticism* – Left idealism has continued to view much crime as a form of primitive rebellion, has excused it and failed to understand and appreciate the harm caused. As David Matza (1969: 44) put it, 'Romance, as always, obscures the seamier and more mundane aspects of the world.'

- *Naïve anti-empiricism* – Left realists accuse their *idealist* colleagues of ignoring evidence not only about the impact of criminal victimization, but also about its extent. Whereas idealists are scornful of data suggesting that crime had been increasing during the 1970s and 1980s, realists, not least via local crime surveys, adopted a position that, whilst it retained a scepticism about official measures, nonetheless accepted that crime had been increasing.

- *Naïve abolitionism* – It has clung to the view that the closure of institutions and the limiting of the criminal justice system would be an uncritical good.

Margaret Thatcher (Prime Minister, 1979–1990) and Ronald Reagan (President of the United States, 1981–1989), seen here at a summit meeting in Venice in 1987. 'Realist criminology' was very much a product of the political times in which it emerged – a period which saw the rise of free-market liberalism and associated social policies.

One of the interesting features of left realism is that its main proponents described themselves as *criminologists*, many having previously largely avoided the term, tending to prefer the label *sociologists of deviance*. A third impetus, therefore, for the emergence of left realism was the apparent irrelevance of much criminology to contemporary political and policy debates about crime. As John Braithwaite (1989: 133) had noted:

> The present state of criminology is one of abject failure in its own terms. We cannot say anything convincing to the community about the causes of crime; we cannot prescribe policies that will work to reduce crime; we cannot in all honesty say that societies spending more on criminological research get better criminal justice policies

than those that spend little or nothing on criminology. Certainly we can say some important things about justice, but philosophers and jurists were making a good fist of those points before ever a criminological research establishment was created.

Jock Young (1992) identifies a series of linked processes which, he suggests, transformed criminological thinking and led to the emergence of left realism:

- *The aetiological crisis* – Although it had been assumed that economic restructuring and improved conditions would lead to a drop in crime, in reality the reverse occurred. 'Slums were demolished, educational standards improved, full employment advanced, and welfare spending increased: the highest affluence in the history of humanity achieved, yet crime increased' (Young, 1997: 482). The aetiological crisis led both 'left idealism' and what Young called 'administrative criminology' (situational prevention, rational choice among others) to ignore questions of causation: both assuming that such a search was fruitless, rehabilitation largely impossible, and that crime control via social justice was mistaken (see Chapter 14).

Jock Young, arguably the prime mover behind the emergence of 'left realism', had been central to much of the British radical criminology which preceded it.

- *The crisis in penality* – Despite increasing the size of the police force and the capacity of the prison system, crime had been rising year on year. Young describes this and the aetiological crisis as 'the palpable failure of the two main staples of criminological theory, neo-classicism and social positivism' (1997: 482).

- The increased awareness of victimization and of crimes which previously been 'invisible'.

- A growing public demand and criticism of public service efficiency and accountability.

The nature of left realism

The central tenet of left realism is to reflect the reality of crime, that is in its origins, its nature and its impact. This involves a rejection of tendencies to romanticize crime or to pathologize it, to analyze solely from the point of view of the administration of crime or the criminal actor, to underestimate crime or to exaggerate it … Most importantly, it is realism which informs our notion of practice: in answering what can be done about the problems of crime and social control. (Young 1986: 21)

Tierney (1996: 282) identifies four main strands to left realism:

- The attempt to develop an empirically-based picture of local crime and its impact.

- A focus on causal explanations of crime.

- Exploring the relationship between offenders, victims and formal and informal controls.

- Attempting to develop realistic policies aimed at reducing the frequency and the impact of victimization.

Figure 13.1	'The square of crime'

Police, multi-agencies		Offender
Social control		**The criminal act**
The public		Victim

Source: Young (1992).

At the heart of realist criminology Young argues that there are two dyads: a *victim* and an *offender,* and one of *actions* and *reactions,* or crime and its control. This, in turn, leads to the identification of four 'definitional elements' of crime: a victim, an offender, formal control and informal control. This then leads to what Young calls the 'square of crime' which involves the interaction between police and other institutions and agents of social control, the offender, the public and the victim:

Young's argument is that crime rates are generated by the *social relationships* between the four points in the square and that any explanation which ignores one of the four points is bound, by definition, to be incomplete. The intention is also to draw attention to what is necessary within a realist response to crime:

> To control crime from a realist perspective involves intervention at each part of the square of crime: at the level of the factors which give rise to the putative offender (such as structural unemployment), the informal system (such as lack of public mobilisation), the victim (such as inadequate target hardening), and the formal system (such as ineffective policing). (Young 1988b: 41)

What is to be done about law and order?

The closest the left realists came to a manifesto is John Lea and Jock Young's *What is to be Done about Law and Order?* Here they set out their critique of existing approaches, outline their view of the current state of crime and justice and set out details of a 'realistic' approach to law and order. This involved six major premises:

1 Crime really is a problem – more particularly, 'working-class crime is a problem for the working class' (1984: 264).

2 We must look at the reality behind appearances – by which they intended that attention should be paid both to the causes of crime (relative deprivation) and to the need to understand its impact.

3 We must take crime control seriously – here they advocated 'demarginalisation' (non-exclusionary forms of punishment), pre-emptive deterrence (situational and social 'target-hardening'), and the minimal use of prison (only to be used when there is a danger to the community).

4 We must look realistically at the circumstances of both the offender and the victim – to hold offenders to account and to protect victims.

5 We must be realistic about policing – the creation of democratic policing and enhanced public co-operation.

6 We must be realistic about the problem of crime in the present period – with rising relative deprivation, and rising discontent as a consequence, there is the need to stimulate a new politics of crime control.

Left realism and method

At the heart of much early left realist activity was research using local crime surveys – what Jock Young (1992) considered to be the basis for the 'democratic measurement' of crime (see Chapter 3). By this he meant that whilst crime is not something that can ever be measured *objectively*, it is nevertheless important to look for 'common measuring rods' by which the seriousness of crime can be understood, particularly as it affects the poorer and most vulnerable sections of the population.

What Young (1986: 23) suggested left realists were looking for was an 'accurate victimology' that could be counterposed 'against those liberal and idealist criminologies, on the one side, which play

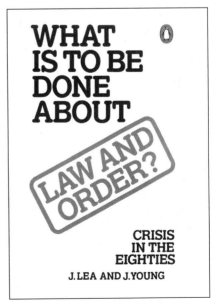

The seminal publication in British left realism, Lea and Young's *What is to be Done about Law and Order?* was published as an accessible paperback by Penguin in 1984.

down victimization or even bluntly state that the 'real' victim is the offender and, on the other, those conservatives who celebrate moral panic and see violence and robbery as ubiquitous on our streets'. The realist victimology proceeded from two assumptions: first, that crime is geographically and socially focused on the most vulnerable parts of the community; and, second, that the impact of criminal victimization was the product of the extent of the risk combined with the degree of vulnerability of the victim:

> Realism starts from problems as people experience them. It takes seriously the complaints of women with regards to the dangers of being in public places at night, it takes note of the fears of the elderly with regard to burglary, it acknowledges the widespread occurrence of domestic violence and racist attacks. It does not ignore the fears of the vulnerable nor recontextualise them out of existence by putting them into a perspective which abounds with abstractions such as the 'average citizen' bereft of class or gender. It is only too aware of the systematic concealment and ignorance of crimes against the least powerful. (Young, 1986: 24)

For Young and colleagues this meant engaging in theoretically-grounded empirical work. The sea change that this involved should not be underestimated. As Downes and Rock note of left realism, '[w]here once radical criminologists would have disparaged surveys as positivist and action as correctionalist, they now embarked on a programme of policy-making as vigorous as that of any government department' (2003: 289). They go on to note that much of what was recommended was hard to distinguish from the recommendations that might have been made by the Home Office and, as a consequence, as it has evolved, left realism 'has become more and more a practical administrative criminology of the left' (*ibid*: 290).

A significant element of the left realist approach to beginning with 'problems as people experience them' drew on local crime survey data on fear of crime. Early British Crime Surveys had drawn attention to the apparent gap between some people's estimates of the risks they faced and the 'real' risks as measured in victimization surveys. Young women and the elderly, for example, have lower rates of violent victimization (as measured by crime surveys) than young men, and yet they tend to report being more fearful. The realist response was to question what was being measured in such surveys and to highlight the fact that the impact of crime upon the elderly and on women is likely to be greater than on young men, adding to this the fact that national crime surveys were generally poor at recording domestic violence, thereby significantly underestimating the extent of female victimization (particularly within high crime areas).

The left realist portrayal of fear of crime came in for a certain amount of criticism however. Sparks (1992a) was particularly critical of the tendency, as he saw it, for left realism to treat fear of crime as 'rational' only if it appeared to coincide with some measure of objective risk. He went on to argue that there was no substantive basis for this assumption and, moreover, that it was anyway a simplification of the ways in which people think about and experience the world. In fact, a 'rational fear' may be something which cannot be established empirically:

> Crime presents people with certain dangers of which they must take account as best they may. In taking account of these dangers each of us engages in some version of risk analysis. But the resources available to us in making the necessary judgements are both enormously extensive, varied and complex and inherently incomplete. We are not really reckoning probabilities bounded by known parameters: we are facing up to possibilities surrounded by uncertainty ... Why then should it *not* be the case that the fears which preoccupy us most would not be those which are most likely to come to pass? (Sparks, 1992a)

Assessing left realism

Although the primary thrust of much penal policy in Britain over the past decade and longer has, arguably, been punitive and exclusionary, it is nonetheless the case that left realist thinking has accorded with much that has happened during this period. Certainly, at the level of rhetoric, there is much in the 'third way' speeches of New Labour that contain more than an echo of left realist thought. In a similar vein, there appears to have been a period in the late 1980s/early 1990s when left realist thinking began to have some influence in parts of Australia. In New South Wales in particular, a number of academics developed a variant on left realist thinking and, like their counterparts in the UK, placed policy-influence high on their agenda (White and Haines, 2004). Attempts at influence were largely undermined, or limited, by the rightwards shift in politics and penal policy that occurred after 1995.

By contrast, at the level of substantive policy, one can identify a number of policy developments in the UK that sit relatively comfortably with left realism. Thus, the Crime and Disorder Act 1998, which introduced what were then called multi-agency *Crime and Disorder Partnerships* (see Chapter 24) very much reflected the community safety-orientation recommended in a number of left realist texts. The first Labour administration's emphasis on social inclusion, though somewhat short-lived, also reflected some of the central arguments Lea and Young had advanced in *What is to be Done about Law and Order?* Arguably, however, during a decade in power from 1997, Labour governments have shifted progressively from a position that was reasonably sympathetic to left realist thinking to one that is much more comfortable with right realist theory. The emphasis on social inclusion is now much more muted, and moralistic underclass theory, with its emphasis on the feckless and irresponsible, has come much more to the fore.

Left realism, though born out of a critique, has itself been subject to considerable criticism. These include:

- *Essentialism* – In that it takes the term 'crime' largely at face value. Thus, in moving away from the 'left idealist' emphasis on the social construction of crime, left realists arguably went too far in accepting standard definitions of crime as if they were self-evidently meaningful.

- Its failure to focus sufficiently on the political and ideological sources of crime and its control. Stan Cohen (1986: 131), for example, argued that left realists 'have retreated far from the theoretical gains of 20 years ago. Their regression into the assumptions of the standard criminal law model of social control – criminalization and punishment – is premature.'

- Its over-concentration on crime and victimization within poor communities, and its failure to focus on crimes of the powerful and, related to this, its over-reliance on the local crime survey (Walklate, 1989).

- Through its failure to focus on corporate and organised crime, left realism is accused by some of having an 'incomplete aetiology' – a model of crime causation that even if it helps explain volume crimes such as burglary, is of limited utility in the task of explaining 'crimes of the suites' (Pearce and Tombs, 1992).

- Its tendency to talk about victims and offenders as if they were hermetically sealed, rather than overlapping and blurred, categories (Walklate, 1992).

- Relatedly, its assumption that the power relationship between offender and victim is always one in which the former is more powerful than the latter (Ruggiero, 1992).

- Their general rejection of the possibility that *some* working-class 'criminal' activity may be understood as a means of managing and coping with the limited opportunities allowed by current social arrangements.

In terms of what left realism is in practice, Downes and Rock (2003: 290) suggest that 'it is now difficult to discern quite what distinguishes it from a combination of anomie, interactionist and subcultural theories with a covert superaddition of social and situational control theories'. As we will see below, there are elements of what is often referred to as 'right realism', an approach to criminological questions that appeared around the same time as left realism but, as the label implies, built on quite different political assumptions, which appear very similar to elements of left realism.

One of the most famous pieces of right realist writing is an article written by James Q. Wilson and George Kelling (1982), published in the magazine *Atlantic Monthly*, called 'Broken Windows'. In it the two authors use the metaphor of untended broken windows as the basis for arguing that the failure to deal with relatively minor matters such as graffiti,

Symbol of a world falling apart? Run-down council housing in Lewisham, South London – the kind of scene that led Wilson and Kelling's 'Broken Windows' theory to be applied in the UK.

vandalism and minor disorderliness tend to lead to the commission of more serious offences. The following passage from *What is to be Done about Law and Order* is strongly resonant of Wilson and Kelling's discussion of the day-to-day realities of crime:

> The run-down council estate where music blares out of windows early in the morning; it is the graffiti on the walls; it is aggression in the shops; it is bins that are never emptied; oil stains across the streets; it is kids that show no respect; it is large trucks racing through your roads; it is always being careful; it is a symbol of a world falling apart. (Lea and Young, 1984: 55)

Review questions

1　What feature of earlier radical theories led Jock Young to characterise them as 'left impossibilism'?

2　What are the four main parts of the 'square of crime'?

3　Why did left realists embrace the crime survey as a useful research method?

4　What have been the main criticisms of left realism?

Right realism

The emergence of a form of realist criminology in America is associated with the work of a group of authors on the right of the political spectrum – generally referred to as 'right realists' in contrast to the left realists that emerged on both sides of the Atlantic, though sometimes called 'new realists' by the 'left realists'. Like left realism, such views developed at a time when it was becoming increasingly clear that post-War prosperity and the Great Society and welfare state programmes in the US and UK were not resulting in declining rates of crime.

Right-wing governments, committed to *laissez-faire* economics were elected on both sides of the Atlantic and neo-liberal economics and neo-conservative politics gained a considerable foothold in both America and Britain – captured in Andrew Gamble's phrase 'the free economy and the strong state'. *Realism* in criminology can, at least in part, be seen as part of that shift – either directly as a part of the change in the ideological climate, or in response or reaction to it. Left realism, as we have seen, was an attempt to build a social democratic criminological response to the politics of the 1970s and 1980s. By contrast, right realism in criminol-

ogy was very much of a political mainstream in this period. Central to the shift of criminological attention in the direction of right realism was the American political scientist James Q. Wilson and his hugely influential book, *Thinking About Crime*.

Thinking About Crime

In the opening to his book, Wilson summarises much of the approach that came to be known as right realism. Underpinning it is precisely the aetiological crisis that Jock Young and British left realists were also reacting to, albeit rather differently (see box on next page).

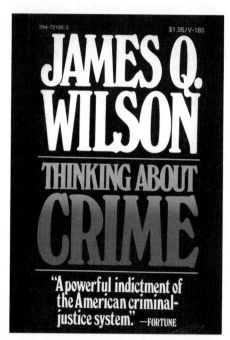

Published in 1975 and still in print over 30 years later, James Q. Wilson's *Thinking About Crime* has been both influential and controversial.

Distinguishing left and right realism

Both left and right realists borrowed or developed elements of control theory in order to develop more *realistic* policies for the prevention or reduction of crime. Moreover, both shared 'a concern with the corrosive effects which crime can have on communities and with the formulation of workable policies, but they are ultimately oppositional and competing positions' (Matthews and Young, 1992). That is to say, whilst both share a common origin – the desire to produce a policy-relevant criminology – there is much that distinguishes them. For

Thinking About Crime

If in 1960 one had been asked what steps society might take to prevent a sharp increase in the crime rate, one might well have answered that crime could best be curtailed by reducing poverty, increasing educational attainment, eliminating dilapidated housing, encouraging community organisation, and providing troubled or delinquent youth with counselling services. Such suggestions would have not only a surface plausibility, but some evidence to support them …

Early in the decade of the 1960s, this country [USA] began the longest sustained period of prosperity since World War II, much of it fuelled, as we later realized by a semi-war economy. A great array of programs aimed at the young, the poor, and the deprived were mounted. Though these efforts were not made primarily out of a desire to reduce crime, they were wholly consistent with – indeed, in their aggregate money levels, wildly exceeded – the policy prescription that a thoughtful citizen worried about crime would have offered at the beginning of the decade.

Crime soared. It did not just increase a little; it rose at a faster rate and to higher levels than at any time since the 1930s and, in some categories, to higher levels than any experienced in this century. The mood of contentment and confidence in which the decade began was shattered, not only by crime, but by riots and war …

In fact, rising crime rates were not the only sign of social malaise during the 1960s. The prosperity of the decade was also accompanied by alarming rises in welfare rates, drug abuse, and youthful unemployment. During the 1960s we were becoming two societies – one affluent and worried, the other pathological and predatory …

It all began in about 1963. This was the year, to over-dramatize a bit, that a decade began to fall apart. (Wilson, 1975: 3–5)

Matthews and Young a number of characteristics of right realism distinguish it from left realism. Right realism, they suggest:

● Takes conventional definitions of crime for granted.
● Ignores the importance of socio-economic context in explaining crime.
● Over-emphasises control and containment.

Right realism has two major characteristics:

● first, it tends to take an individualised view of crime, looking for explanations in individual choices rather than in broader social or structural conditions;
● second, right realist responses to the crime problem tend to be couched in terms of greater controls and enhanced punishments.

Figure 13.2	Right and left realism compared
Right realism	**Left realism**
Rejection of utopianism in favour of neo-conservatism	Rejection of utopianism in favour of democratic socialism
Acceptance of legal definitions of 'crime'	Acceptance of legal definitions of 'crime'
Primary focus on 'crime' as represented by official statistics	Primary focus on 'crime' as perceived by victims
Fear of crime as rational	Fear of crime as rational
Reworking of genetic and individualistic theories	Reworking of subcultural, anomie and structural conflict theories
Crime caused by lack of self-control	Crime caused by relative deprivation, social injustice and marginalisation
Prioritising order (rather than justice) via deterrent and retributive means of crime control	Prioritising social justice via programmes of crime prevention

Source: Muncie (2004: 143).

In the view of the right realists the breakdown of moral values and social controls associated with permissiveness was central to understanding rising crime rates. Thus, Wilson and Herrnstein (1985) focused on inadequate socialisation of young children in families, particularly one-parent families, with the consequent failure to develop an appropriate moral conscience. As we will see in connection with Wilson and Herrnstein's work below, they also place a certain emphasis on the biological bases of human behaviour, arguing that certain groups and individuals are predisposed toward offending.

Elements of the right realist approach were clearly influential in the rise of situational crime prevention theories. As James Q. Wilson (1975: xiv) argued:

> If objective conditions are used to explain crime, spokesmen who use poverty as an explanation of crime should, by the force of their own logic, be prepared to consider the capacity of society to deter crime by raising the risks of crime. But they rarely do. Indeed, those who use poverty as an explanation are largely among the ranks of those who vehemently deny that crime can be deterred.

Wilson and Herrnstein

Wilson and Herrnstein's own theory of criminal behaviour is biosocial in character, focusing on what they called the 'constitutional factors' that they argued underpinned criminality (and as such is reminiscent of the biological positivist theories reviewed in Chapter 6):

> The existence of biological predispositions means that circumstances that activate behaviour in one person will not do so in another, that social forces cannot deter criminal behaviour in 100% of the population, and that the distribution of crime within and across societies may, to some extent, reflect underlying distributions of constitutional factors. Crime cannot be understood without taking into account predispositions and their biological roots. (1985: 103)

Though they do at one stage point to the existence of physiological differences that distinguish criminal from others, the basis of their explanation is genetic and social rather than physiological. The genetic element concerns the 'constitutional factors' that predispose individuals

toward crime; the social element is those mediating factors that explain how these factors are translated into particular forms of behaviour. Their theory has been described as 'operant utilitarianism' (Gibbs, 1985); one in which individual biological or genetic differences influence individual understandings and interpretations of rewards and punishments:

> The larger the ratio of the rewards (material and nonmaterial) of noncrime to the rewards (material and nonmaterial) of crime, the weaker the tendency to commit crimes. The bite of conscience, the approval of peers and any sense of inequity will increase or decrease the total value of crime; the opinions of family, friends, and employers are important benefits of noncrime, as is the desire to avoid the penalties that can be imposed by the criminal justice system. The strength of any reward declines with time, but people differ in the rate[s] at which they discount the future. The strength of a given reward is also affected by the total supply of reinforcers.
> (1985: 261)

In a subsequent variant of right realism, the psychologist Richard Herrnstein reappears as the co-author of another controversial and influential book, this time with the notable American social commentator, Charles Murray. In their book, *The Bell Curve,* Herrnstein and Murray (1994) proposed the idea that intelligence was the best indicator of social behaviour, including criminal behaviour. Those of lower intelligence have always been at a disadvantage, however under contemporary conditions where cognitive skills are of increasing importance, those who are 'cognitively disadvantaged' will face a particular struggle.

Using data from a large, longitudinal study (the National Longitudinal Survey of Youth) they argued that those with lower IQ scores were more likely to report having been involved in crime, irrespective of social status. Social class and poverty are not therefore important in the explanation for crime, even though they are clearly associated with offending. Rather, Herrnstein and Murray (1994: 251) argued, although 'many people tend to think of criminals as coming from the wrong side of the tracks. They are correct insofar as that is where people of low cognitive ability disproportionately live.' As a consequence, they argued, 'much of the attention now given to problems of poverty and unemployment should be shifted to another question altogether: coping with cognitive disadvantage' (1994: 251).

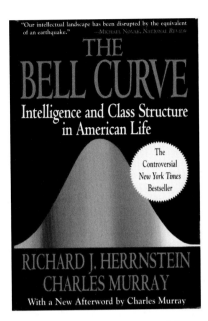

In their hugely controversial book, *The Bell Curve*, Richard Herrnstein and Charles Murray argue that it is not social class or poverty that we should look to in explaining criminality, but low intelligence.

Herrnstein and Murray's work generated considerable controversy and has been subjected to sustained, and sometimes vituperative, criticism (Fraser, 1995), not least as a result of Herrnstein and Murrays' claim that measured differences in IQ between ethnic groups were a reflection of genetic differences. A number of major criticisms have been levelled at their work. Significantly, subsequent analysis of numerous data sets suggests that differences in measured IQ scores account for only a very small part of the variation in self-reported crime rates (generally between 1% and 3%). At the very most, critics suggest, cognitive disadvantage plays only a minor role in crime causation (Lilly *et al.*, 2002).

In a review of the book, Stephen Jay Gould (1995: 6) said, 'Disturbing as I find the anachronism of *The Bell Curve*, I am even more distressed by its pervasive disingenuousness. The authors omit facts, misuse statistical methods, and seem unwilling to admit the consequences of their own words.' Second, critics argued that there was little empirical support for the policy responses that Herrnstein and Murray recommended on the basis of their study, and no necessary link between their finding and their policy recommendations.

Murray and the 'underclass'

Charles Murray (1990) also made a further significant contribution to the debate on crime through his work on what he termed 'the underclass'. Conjuring up nineteenth-century notions of the dangerous classes and the undeserving poor, a consistent element of right realist writing has been the need to reinforce personal responsibility for behaviour. Murray describes what he says are 'two kinds of poor people':

One class of people was never even called 'poor'. I came to understand that they simply lived on low incomes, as my own parents had done when they were young. There was another set of people, just a handful of them. These poor people didn't just lack money. They were defined by their behaviour. Their homes were littered and unkempt. The men in the family were unable to hold a job for more than a few weeks at a time. Drunkenness was common. The children grew up ill-schooled and ill-behaved and contributed a disproportionate share of the local juvenile delinquents. (Murray, 1990: 1)

In this work Murray goes on to articulate his view of what has gone wrong in American and British society since the 1970s (in America somewhat before Britain, he suggests). In short, traditional means of socialising the young have broken down, there has been a decline in appropriate role models for young people, and young men in particular, with the consequence that many refuse to work, and our willingness to tolerate such behaviour in our midst undermines the social solidarity so necessary for an orderly society:

Crime is the next place to look for an underclass, for several reasons. First and most obviously, the habitual criminal is the classic member of an underclass. He lives off mainstream society without participating in it. But habitual criminals are only part of the problem. Once again, the key issue in thinking about an underclass is how the community functions, and crime can devastate a community in two especially important ways. To the extent that the members of a community are victimized by crime, the community tends to become fragmented. To the extent that many people in a community engage in crime as a matter of course, all sorts of the socializing norms of the community change, from the kind of men that the younger boys choose as heroes to the standards of morality in general. (Murray 1990: 15)

In his book, *Losing Ground,* in the early 1980s Murray argued that welfare dependency was one, if not *the,* key problem for American public policy. Welfare, he argued, encourages people to behave irresponsibly and fecklessly and has resulted in large numbers of single-parent families incapable of appropriate socialisation of young children, especially young males. Murray interpreted the decline in marriage as a major factor in rising crime. Traditionally males have proved themselves through marriage and supporting a family. Young males are essentially barbarians he argued and without the responsibilities and constraints of marriage, turn to various destructive alternatives, including crime.

The final variant of *right realism* is again the product of conservative America and a series of social commentators associated with the Reagan and Bush administrations: William Bennett, John Dilulio and Ronald Walters. In their book *Body Count* (1996) they outline their view that 'moral poverty' is the primary cause of soaring crime in the United States:

> It is the poverty of being without parents, guardians, relatives, friends, teachers, coaches, clergy, and others who *habituate* (to use a good Aristotelian word) children to feel joy at others' joy; pain at others' pain; satisfaction when you do right; [and] remorse when you do wrong. It is the poverty of growing up in the virtual absence of people who teach these lessons by their own everyday example and who insist that you follow suit and behave accordingly. In the extreme, it is the poverty of growing up surrounded by deviant, delinquent, and criminal adults in a practically perfect criminogenic environment – that is, an environment that seems almost consciously designed to produce vicious, unrepentant predatory street criminals. (1996: 13–14)

As the lengthy quote illustrates Bennett and colleagues' argument is itself primarily a moral one. It offers little new to criminology, but rounds up many of the usual suspects – delinquent peers, dysfunctional families, inconsistent discipline – and sets them within a conservative political framework (*moral* rather than *economic* poverty) as the basis for understanding what became one of the major folk devils of the 1990s: the predatory street criminal. Where the arguments in both *The Bell Curve* and *Crime and Human Nature* required their authors to make something of a leap in order to recommend and justify punitive policies as a result of their analyses, no such difficulty arises for the authors of

Charles Murray is closely associated with arguments about the existence of an 'underclass'. The habitual criminal is the classic member of an underclass, Murray has argued, because 'he lives off mainstream society without participating in it'. (Murray, 1990)

Body Count. Its entire thrust is to identify permissiveness, moral laxity and failures of discipline as the primary causes of the crime problem. The solution is to reassert such values and principles.

What then of the right realist position on what to do about crime? In *Thinking About Crime* James Q. Wilson (1975: 233) argued strongly that attempting to respond to the causes of crime was not something that could any longer be indulged:

> Though intellectually rewarding, from a practical point of view it is a mistake to think about crime in terms of its 'causes' and then to search for ways to alleviate those causes. We must think instead of what it is feasible for a government to do, and then try to discover … which of those things will produce, at acceptable costs, desirable changes in the level of criminal victimization.

He went on to conclude that for certain classes of person, the only possible response was incarceration – something, he implied, that we had been afraid to use sufficiently for too long:

> Wicked people exist. Nothing avails except to set them apart from innocent people. And many people, neither wicked nor innocent, but watchful, dissembling and calculating of their

opportunities, ponder our reaction to wickedness as a cue to what they might profitably do. We have trifled with the wicked, made sport of the innocent, and encouraged the calculators. Justice suffers, and so do we all. (1975: 235–236)

Assessing right realism

Right realism has been politically influential but academically controversial. Some of its best known proponents – James Q. Wilson, Charles Murray, Lawrence Mead – have enjoyed considerable attention from successive American presidents, have rarely been short of an audience in the UK and have had considerable influence beyond. The stress on individual responsibility within right realist criminology has chimed with the penal policies of so-called 'third way' governments such as the New Labour administrations in Britain. However, right realism has been regularly and vociferously criticised by academic researchers from other perspectives. Many of these criticisms are close in content to the criticisms often levelled at classical criminological approaches: that they are essentialist, avoid dealing with structural influences and inequalities, over-emphasise individual differences and underplay issues of power thereby overstating the importance of rationality in human conduct.

Much of the critical response to right realism has focused on *The Bell Curve* and *Crime and Human Nature*. Both have been regularly criticised for the inadequacy of their 'science'. Wilson and Herrnstein, for example, have been criticised for the vagueness of some of their conceptual tools and the consequent difficult of testing their theory, for focusing largely upon violent and predatory crimes rather than taking a broader focus (Gibbs 1985). A number of critics drew attention to what they took to be Wilson and Herrnstein's selective use of evidence in support of their argument (Kamin 1985). Even then the evidence is not particularly convincing, some have argued. Thus, in relation to Herrnstein and Murray's argument about IQ and crime, although it is the case that offenders tend to score less highly in intelligence tests than non-offenders, it remains the case that such scores are actually a very poor predictor of criminality.

Indeed, many commentators reject the whole enterprise of attempting to distinguish criminals from non-criminals. Thus Gottfredson and Hirschi, in outlining their general theory of crime point to the 14 different dimensions of personality that Wilson and Herrnstein claim that delinquents

score higher on than non-delinquents – including fearlessness, aggressiveness, extroversion, psycopathy – and argue that 'all of these "personality" traits can be explained, without abandoning the conclusion that offenders differ from non-offenders only in their tendency to offend' (1990: 109). They are actual *empirical tautologies* they argue – a finding that two measures of the same thing are related to each other.

However, as Lilly *et al.* (2002: 213) quite rightly note, 'much criticism aimed at *Crime and Human Nature* occurred because many criminologists were themselves ideologically opposed to biological theorising, again because of the repressive policies that, historically, such thinking had justified' as well as the generally conservative political stance adopted by its authors. In particular, Wilson and Herrnstein took an unashamedly punitive stance when outlining the policy choices that they took to flow from their work, and argued that even though it was clear that crime had causes, it was nevertheless the case that the cause of deterrence required 'that the courts act *as if* crime were wholly the result of free choice' (1985: 529, *emphasis added*).

In a similar fashion, Herrnstein and Murray's policy implications from *The Bell Curve* were to advocate clear rules about acceptable behaviour and to place greater emphasis on the importance of certain and severe punishment, rather than seeking to promote social policy aimed at stimulating the cognitive abilities of those at risk. 'The policy prescription', they said, 'is that the criminal justice system should be made simpler. The meaning of criminal offences used to be clear and objective, and so were the consequences. It is worth trying to make them so again' (1994: 544). Many politicians have clearly agreed.

Review questions

1 What are the main differences between left and right realism?

2 Why, according to James Q. Wilson, did crime increase so markedly after the Second World War?

3 How did Herrnstein and Murray link IQ and crime?

4 According to Charles Murray, what is the connection between crime and the underclass?

Questions for further discussion

1 Should we be more concerned about street crime or corporate crime?

2 To what extent is 'tough on crime, tough on the causes of crime' a (left or right) realist statement?

3 How distinctive are left realism and right realism?

4 Is rising crime a sign of moral decline in our society?

5 What is meant by the term 'underclass'?

6 Why might right realist ideas have caused so much controversy in criminology?

Further reading

Cullen, F.T. *et al.* (1997) Crime and the bell curve: lessons from intelligent criminology, *Crime and Delinquency,* 3, 4, 387–411, London, Sage Journals

Downes, D. and Rock, P. (2003) *Understanding Deviance,* Oxford: Oxford University Press (ch. 10 and 11)

Matthews, R. and Young, J. (1992) Reflections on realism, in Young, J. and Matthews, R. (eds) *Rethinking Criminology: The realist debate,* London: Sage

McLaughlin, E. *et al.* (eds) (2003) *Criminological Perspectives,* 2nd edn, London: Sage (contains some wonderful selections from the original materials; an indispensable companion)

Sparks, R. (1992) Reason and unreason in left realism: some problems in the constitution of the fear of crime, in Matthews, R. and Young, J. (eds) *Issues in Realist Criminology,* London: Sage

Wilson, J.Q. (1975) *Thinking About Crime,* New York: Basic Books (abridged as 'on deterrence' in McLaughlin, E. *et al.* [eds] *Criminological Perspectives*)

Young, J. (1986) The failure of criminology: the need for a radical realism, in Matthews, R. and Young, J. (eds) *Confronting Criminology,* London: Sage

Websites

The website 'Crime Theory' at www.crimetheory.com is a very good resource.

Chapter outline

Introduction   280

Rational choice theory   280
   Clarke and Cornish   281
   Bounded rationality   282
   Crime scripts   283

Routine activity theory   286
   Routine activity and crime trends   286
   Routine activity theory elaborated   288

Situational crime prevention   290
   Defensible space and problem-oriented policing   290
     Problem-oriented policing   292
   Crime and opportunity   292

Crime science   294

Assessing contemporary classicism   295

Questions for discussion   297
Further reading   297
Websites   297

Contemporary classicism

| CHAPTER SUMMARY | The theoretical approaches covered under the heading of contemporary classicism are included because, to some degree, they share 'classical' criminology's assumption that offenders are essentially rationally-calculating actors. From the late 1960s, and especially during the following decades, a number of criminological theories emerged that placed great emphasis on the importance of understanding the choices made by offenders in different circumstances or locations and, consequently, how offenders' decision-making, and how particular locations or opportunities, might be manipulated as a means of reducing crime. |

Introduction

The various approaches covered in this chapter have enjoyed growing popularity since the 1970s. This, Garland (2000) argues, represents a fairly marked break with the criminological orthodoxy that held sway for most of the twentieth century. The reason for their emergence, and their popularity, lies in the growth of the sense that 'nothing works' in the same period. Previously, great faith had been invested in the expectation that increasing prosperity and improving living conditions would lead to declining crime rates and, also, that where crimes were committed ameliorative interventions would be found which could be used successfully to rehabilitate those who contravened the law.

However, faith in rehabilitation receded from the 1960s onward and, consequently, greater emphasis began to be placed on deterrence and on 'justice' approaches to sentencing and sanctions (see Chapter 28). As we saw in relation to the rise of both left and right realism in the previous chapter, there was a reaction in various quarters to growing penal pessimism and there emerged a growing sense that existing theoretical approaches were of little relevance to those with responsibility for matters of crime and justice.

In parallel with this, criminologists from various perspectives were increasingly looking for approaches to intervention that would have some fairly immediate policy and practical relevance. It was in this context that theories that stressed the possibility of manipulating environments rather than humans, or of deterring offenders prior to the act rather than rehabilitating them afterward, began to become much more popular. As one their main exponents, Ron Clarke (1980: 136) has argued:

> With some exceptions ... criminological theories have been little concerned with the situational determinants of crime. Instead, the main object of

these theories (whether biological, psychological, or sociological in orientation) has been to show how some people are born with, or come to acquire, a 'disposition' to behave in a consistently criminal manner. This 'dispositional' bias of theory has been identified as a defining characteristic of 'positivist' criminology, but it is also to be found in 'interactionist' or deviancy theories of crime developed in response to the perceived inadequacies of positivism. Perhaps the best known tenet of at least the early interactionist theories, which arises out of a concern with the social definition of deviancy and the role of law enforcement agencies, is that people who are 'labelled' as criminal are thereby prone to continue in delinquent conduct. In fact ... a dispositional bias is prevalent throughout the social sciences.

Clarke (1980: 138) goes on to argue that some of the theoretical difficulties he suggests confront contemporary criminology 'could be avoided by conceiving of crime not in dispositional terms, but as being the outcome of immediate choices and decisions made by the offender. This would also have the effect of throwing a different light on preventive options.' Following this line of thinking, situational approaches focus on the opportunities for crime and the risks involved. As we will see, at their heart, often, is some variant of rational choice theory. More or less explicitly, therefore, they not only seek to manipulate the environment – the situation – but also influence the actual or potential offender.

Rational choice theory

Rational choice theory is based on the idea of 'expected utility', assuming that individuals proceed on the basis of maximising profits and minimising losses. Rational choice theory allows the difficult question of criminal motivation to be reformulated as a calculation – a balancing of costs and benefits. In this manner, what some have come to see as a form of control theory, shifts attention somewhat away from the offender toward the criminal event. Its advantage in so doing is that it effectively abandons any sense that there is any utility in seeking to differentiate between criminals and non-criminals/offenders and non-offenders. As control theorists generally argue – we are all capable. One fairly obvious short-coming of such approaches is the lack of attention paid to motivation, beyond the straightforward assumption that all that is required is some benefit to the offender. Nevertheless, rational choice-influenced and opportunity-focused theories have been hugely influential in the last quarter decade or more. Some of the earliest approaches focused particularly on the manipulation of the environment as a crime-preventive strategy.

The intellectual origins of much of this work can be traced to the classical theorists of the eighteenth and nineteenth centuries, and more recently to the American Nobel Prize-winning economist, Gary Becker. Becker (1968) argued that individuals will commit offences if the 'expected utility' of doing so is positive, and will not do so if it is negative. The expected utility in this context essentially means benefits, and the theory assumes that offenders will commit crimes when the benefits outweigh the risks or losses.

As we saw in Chapter 5, classical approaches to the explanation of crime assumed that individuals were rational beings who made decisions about how to behave and should be held to account for those decisions. The positivist movement which arose in the late nineteenth century and dominated much of the first three-quarters of the twentieth century reacted against such a view and argued, by contrast, that there were other factors – physiological, psychological, economic and social – that affected and indeed constrained human behaviour and needed to be taken into account in understanding crime.

Clarke and Cornish

Recent times – the final quarter of the twentieth century – have seen renewed interest in the idea of the 'rational actor'. Undoubtedly, the most impressive and influential application of rational choice theory within criminology has been that by Clarke and Cornish (Clarke and Cornish, 1985; Cornish and Clarke, 1986). Rather than a simple choice,

they argue that a sequence of choices has to be made, and that these choices are influenced by a number of social and psychological factors that individuals bring with them to the situation. These factors can be understood as 'criminal motivations' which incline or dispose individuals, more or less, toward criminality. Under these conditions, rational choice theory then becomes the study of why particular people make decisions to behave in particular ways under certain circumstances.

Cornish and Clarke (2006) summarise the basis of their rational choice perspective in the following six basic propositions:

1 Crimes are purposive acts, committed with the intention of benefiting the offender.

2 Offenders try to make the best decisions they can, given the risks and uncertainty involved.

3 Offender decision-making varies considerably with the nature of the crime.

4 Decisions about becoming involved in particular kinds of crime ('involvement' decisions) are quite different from those relating to the commission of a specific criminal act ('event' decisions).

5 Involvement decisions comprise three stages – initiation, habituation, and desistance. These must be separately studied because they are influenced by quite different sets of variables.

Ron Clarke, head of the Home Office research unit in London in the 1970s and early 1980s, now teaches at Rutgers University in the United States.

6 Event decisions involve a sequence of choices made at each stage of the criminal act – for example: preparation, target selection, commission of the act, escape, and aftermath.

Crime in this perspective is treated as 'purposive'; it is never 'senseless'. That is to say, there is always some anticipated or intended benefit to the offender. Whilst in the most obvious cases the benefit may be some material reward, benefits may also include excitement, prestige, fun, sexual gratification, as well as the defiance or dominance of others. Thus:

> A man might 'brutally' beat his wife, not just because he is a violent 'thug' but also because this is the easiest way of making her do what he wants. 'Senseless' acts of vandalism or gang violence might confer considerable prestige on the perpetrators among their peers. The term 'joyriding' accurately conveys the main reason why cars are stolen – juveniles enjoy driving around in powerful machines. (Cornish and Clarke, 2006: 20)

Bounded rationality

Even in cases which on the surface may seem irrational, they argue, such as those where there is some clinical delusion or pathological compulsion, there is still some degree of rationality involved, although it may be limited. Thus, for Cornish and Clarke behaviour is rational, but *bounded*. It is limited in its understanding of possibilities, potentials and consequences (see Figure 14.1).

Offenders 'are generally doing the best they can within the limits of time, resources, and information available to them. This is why we characterize their decision-making as rational, albeit in a limited way' (Clarke and Cornish, 2001: 25). From this perspective the assumption is that all offenders think before they act, even if this is only momentary and is based on some immediate assumptions and hoped-for benefits rather than any longer-term strategic thinking. The conditions under which decisions about offending are made can be summarised, they say, as follows:

- Offenders are rarely in possession of all the necessary facts about the risks, efforts and rewards of crime.

- Criminal choices usually have to be made quickly – and revised hastily.

- Instead of planning their crimes down to the last detail, criminals might rely on a general approach that has worked before, improvising when they meet with unforeseen circumstances.

- Once embarked on a crime, criminals tend to focus on the rewards of the crime rather than its risks; and, when considering risks, they focus on the immediate possibilities of being caught, rather than on the punishments they might receive. (Cornish and Clarke, 2006: 20–21)

Figure 14.1	Bad decisions are still bounded 'rational' choices
Type of decision	**Example/Caricature**
Quick decision (not thought through)	It seemed like a good idea at the time I wasn't really thinking – I just did it Now I regret it
Decision based on imperfect information	I didn't know they had a dog I didn't know they would hit me back I didn't know they had a silent alarm I didn't know I was on CCTV At the time, I didn't think of the consequences
Impaired decision (including emotional decision)	I wasn't thinking straight It was the alcohol acting, not me

Source: Farrell and Pease (2006: 187).

A number of consequences flow from adopting the rational choice perspective. First, the centrality of decision-making in this approach requires that the criminologist focus on specific types of crime, rather than talking about crime in the abstract. Choice by offenders is linked to the nature of the particular offence and the specific benefits that are felt likely to accrue. Second, as was suggested earlier, it is important to distinguish between two types of 'criminal choices': those related to 'involvement' and those related to the 'event'. 'Event choices' concern such things as decisions about particular targets (which house to burgle) and ways of reducing risks (when to do it, etc.). 'Involvement decisions' are sub-divided into three stages:

1 Whether the person is ready to begin committing crime in order to obtain what they want (*initiation*).

2 Whether, having started offending, they should continue to do so (*habituation*).

3 Whether, at some stage, they ought to stop (*desistance*).

Not only are decisions taken at different stages of a 'career', but they are affected by different factors. These include 'background factors' (personality, upbringing), current life circumstances, routines and lifestyles, and 'situational variables' (needs, motives, opportunities and inducements). Background factors are likely to be most important at the initiations stage, current life circumstances at the habituation stage and at the desistance stage. However, 'during all stages … it is the immediate influence of situational variables, such as needs, motives, opportunities, and inducements, that trigger the actual decision about whether or not to commit a particular crime' (2006: 23).

Crime scripts

Once this is understood it is possible to construct what they call basic 'crime scripts', which are

Figure 14.2	A simple crime script: residential burglary in the suburbs	
Stages		**Actions**
1.	Preparation	Get van, tools, co-offender (if needed)
		Take drugs/alcohol
		Select general area for crime
		Assume appropriate role for setting
2.	Enter setting	Drive into development
3.	Precondition	Drive around and loiter in development
4.	Target selection	Scan for cues relating to rewards, risks and effort (e.g. potential 'take', occupancy, surveillability and accessibility)
5.	Initiation	Approach dwelling and probe for occupany and accessibility
6.	Continuation	Break into dwelling and enter
7.	Completion	Steal goods
8.	Finish up	Load up goods and drive away from house
9.	Exit setting	Leave development
10.	Further stages (if applicable)	Store, conceal and disguise goods
11.	Further crime scripts (if applicable)	Market and dispose of stolen goods

Source: Cornish and Clarke (2006).

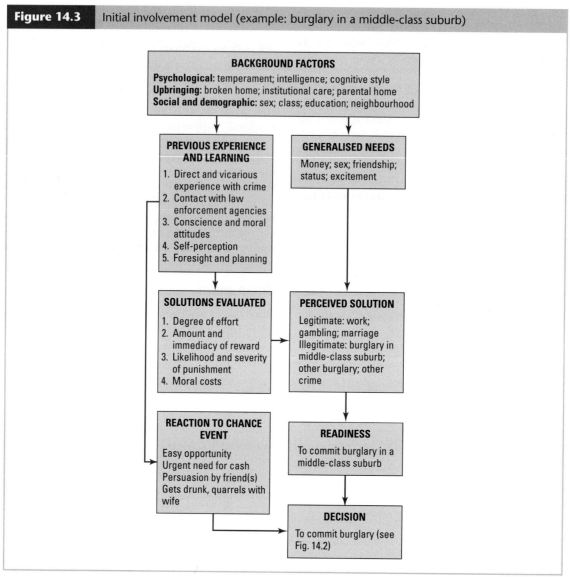

Figure 14.3   Initial involvement model (example: burglary in a middle-class suburb)

Source: Cornish and Clarke (2006).

essentially step-by-step accounts of the procedures and decision-making processes involved in particular events. The term 'scripts' indicates that these are essentially stories, often using offenders' accounts, to identify both the decisions and the situational context in which particular crimes come about. They provide an example of a script involving residential burglary.

One of the advantages of the rational choice perspective, Clarke and Cornish argue, is that it enables the criminologist to begin to deal with the variable and contingent nature of so much offending. It is not unchanging, but varies according to

the needs, wants and desires of offenders, as well as according to the opportunities offered them. As such it places great emphasis on the situational context of offending and has, its proponents stress, great policy-relevance. We return to this below in relation to *situational crime prevention* – a set of techniques that build on both rational choice and routine activity theories.

Rational choice theory is sometimes presented as if it were simplistic in the extreme, reducing our understanding of offending to a very straightforward set of decisions made by individuals. This is to underestimate the approach. We will come to criticisms of rational choice theory in due course. Before that, however, a brief discussion of the detail of an example given by Cornish and Clarke illustrates the range of factors they suggest should be taken into consideration in considering the involvement, habituation and desistance stages of a hypothetical 'criminal career'. They do this using three illustrations (see Figures 14.3 to 14.5).

Figure 14.3 above illustrates the decision-making process in relation to initial involvement, including the offender's evaluation of their readiness according to various generalised needs, their personal traits and their evaluation of the likely benefits accruing from particular courses of action. The actual decision involved in the commission of the crime itself is captured separately in the 'script' that was outlined earlier. Figure 14.4 examines the offender's continuing involvement and includes a series of variables which influence the decision to continue with this particular type of burglary – a decision which the diagram suggests is constantly re-evaluated. The variables include the possible increased professionalism of the offender, changes in their lifestyle, and changes in friendship and peer groups.

Finally, Figure 14.5 illustrates the decision-making process in relation to potential desistance from such offending. There are two main classes of variable: life-events such as marriage and family, and others that are more closely tied to the criminal events. Again, each of these is evaluated regularly and has a cumulative effect.

Review questions

1 Why might approaches to understanding crime which focus on opportunity and rational choice rather than, say, strain, anomie or labelling, have become popular since the 1970s?

2 What is meant by 'bounded rationality'?

3 What is a 'crime script'?

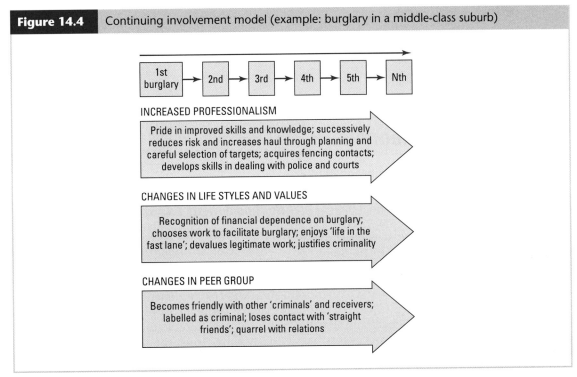

Figure 14.4   Continuing involvement model (example: burglary in a middle-class suburb)

Source: Cornish and Clarke (2006).

| **Figure 14.5** | Desistance model (example: burglary in a middle-class suburb) |

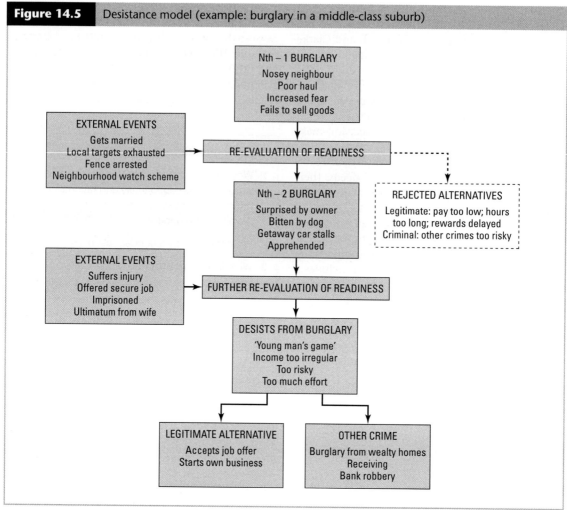

Source: Cornish and Clarke (2006).

Routine activity theory

Routine activity theory is magnificent. While easy to grasp, it can be almost universally applied to provide insight for crime prevention. It is arguably the simplest theory of crime, but astonishing in its flexibility: it is deceptively powerful and insightful and, to be blunt, a downright useful way of thinking about both crime and its prevention. (Farrell and Pease, 2006: 180)

Developed originally by Cohen and Felson (1979), in recent times routine activity theory has been elaborated by, and is now associated primarily with, the American criminologist Marcus Felson. Routine activity theory is arguably a variant of con-

trol theory. In this case it argues that attention should be focused on the situation in which offending takes place, rather than on the offender.

Routine activity and crime trends

Routine activity theory was originally an attempt to make sense of rising crime rates in the post-war period, though it has developed and changed somewhat since its first formulation. Cohen and Felson's (1979) argument, simply put, was that social and cultural changes during this period had produced opportunities for crime that did not previously exist. Thus, the increase in crime in the post-War period may be in part a product of the greatly increased number of targets for crime together with some reduction in the availability of

Marcus Felson, Rutgers University, USA, wrote the original article with Lawrence Cohen which set out the basis of routine activity theory, and has subsequently elaborated the basic idea in articles and his book *Crime and Everyday Life*, now in its third edition.

people watching or guarding those targets. In short, changes in 'routine activities' have created new opportunities for offending. The argument is worth exploring in greater detail.

Cohen and Felson's original article (1979) begins with a conundrum. Why, when the major social indicators generally associated with crime (poverty, educational failure, unemployment) appear to be improving, has crime been increasing? Existing criminological theory implied that crime should have declined. Cohen and Felson's answer is that much of the increase in crime experienced in America between 1960 and 1975 could be explained by reference to changes in 'routine activities'.

Routine activity theory treats as important the distinction between criminality and crime or a crime *event*. The motivation to offend is important, but not all-important, for other factors need to be present for a crime event to take place. Routine activity theory, like other control-style theories, starts from the assumption that a key question is 'Why do people *not* commit crime?'

Cohen and Felson's focus was upon what they called 'direct-contact predatory violations', by which they meant illegal acts in which 'someone definitely and intentionally takes or damages the person or property of another' (1979: 589). Structural changes in routine activity patterns influence crime rates, they argue, when three elements of such predatory offences come together in time and space. These three elements are:

- Motivated offenders.
- Suitable targets (likely to reflect such things as value, portability, symbolic desirability of property or physical capacity/capability of persons).
- The absence of capable guardians.

They summarise this element of the argument thus:

> Each successfully completed violation minimally requires an *offender* with both criminal inclinations and the ability to carry out those inclinations, a person or object providing a *suitable target* for the offender, and *absence of guardians* capable of preventing violations. (Cohen and Felson, 1979: 590)

This is what Felson subsequently came to call the 'chemistry for crime' (Felson, 1998: 52). The lack of any one of these three elements is potentially sufficient to prevent the successful completion of a predatory offence. Suitable targets may shift in location as a result of everyday activities, as may the presence or absence of capable guardians. One of the central questions for the routine activity theorist, then, is what is known about how these three factors come together.

What separates routine activity theory from straightforward situational crime prevention approaches is its broader argument that the likelihood of these three factors being found together is dependent on the social conditions at the time. That is to say these three factors must *converge in time and space* if transgressions are to occur. The most significant influence on whether such convergence takes place is the *routine activities*: 'any recurrent and prevalent activities which provide for basic population and individual needs, whatever their biological and cultural origins' (1979: 593). In this manner opportunity for the commission of crime is profoundly affected by the routines of everyday life.

Using this approach Cohen and Felson (1979) argued that the substantial rise in predatory crimes in the US since the Second World War was partially because of a major shift of routine activities away from the home as a result of changes in the labour market. With properties untended, burglary became easier and, similarly, contact crimes increased as the greater mass of people out and about increased the probability that they would come into contact with motivated offenders. More particularly, they argue that there were important changes in this period in relation to the:

1   *Circumstances and location of offences* – 'The risk of criminal victimization varies dramatically among the circumstances and locations in which people place themselves and their property' (1979: 595). Two examples will suffice. Cohen and Felson using national crime victimization data show that personal theft (with contact) is 350 times higher at the hands of strangers in streets than at the hands of non-strangers at home. Second, looking at motor-vehicle thefts they show that there were two per million vehicle-hours parked at or near home, 55 per million vehicle-hours in streets, parks, playgrounds, school grounds and parking lots, and 12 per million vehicle-hours elsewhere.

2   *Target suitability* – There were some significant changes in this area linked to the spread and availability of particular types of consumer goods ('portable and movable durables [stereo equipment, televisions, etc.] are reported stolen in great disproportion to their share of the value and weight of goods circulating' (1979: 596).

3   *Family activities and crime rates* – Changes in family structures – the rise of single-person households of various types – tends to lead to changes in routine activities and, in particular, to an increase in time spent outside the home. Burglary and robbery victimization rates in the US in the 1970s were about twice as high for persons living in single-adult households as for others in the same age group.

4   *Trends in human activity patterns* – There has been a dispersion of activities away from the home, caused by more women going out to work, the rise of two-person working households, the increase in the time spent on holiday and in overseas travel.

5   *Related property trends and their relation to human activity patterns* – The dispersion of the population across a greater number of households enlarges the market for consumer goods (televisions, cars, etc.) as well as the purchase of such goods for use away from the home. The same period saw changes in the nature of such consumer goods also (the average weight of televisions dropped from 17kg in 1960 to 7kg in 1970).

6   *Composition of crime trends* – Cohen and Felson argue that if the circulation of people and property are related to crime trends, then the trends should reflect this. In the period 1960–1975 they found that commercial burglaries declined from 60% of the total to 35%, while daytime residential burglaries increased from 16% to 33%.

Cohen and Felson (1979) also conduct various analyses which, they argue, show that the trends in crime they seek to explain are not a product of demographic changes (numbers of people aged 16–25, for example) or of changes in poverty or unemployment. Rather, they suggest, 'the convergence in time and space of three elements (motivated offenders, suitable targets, and the absence of capable guardians) appears useful for understanding crime rate trends' (1979: 604).

Routine activity theory elaborated

Subsequently, Felson extended routine activity well beyond such contact crimes. For example, Felson takes the commission of 'vice' – such as the buying and selling of drugs, prostitution, and so on. What is required, he argues, is a favourable setting ('a slice in time and space') and the absence of a place manager (capable guardian), plus the addition, where possible, of some 'camouflage' such as a crowd or similar. This is simply a variant on the basic routine activity theory outlined earlier. All crimes have their own 'chemistry', Felson suggests. Understanding such chemistry involves:

●   Understanding who and what must be present and absent for a crime to occur.

●   Finding out what slice of space and time (setting) makes this likely.

●   Determining how people move into and out of the setting when committing an offence.

The dynamics of vice, for example, he illustrates using the following diagram that Felson (1998: 68) explains in the following way:

[It] shows how drugs, money, and people move quickly toward a transfer. The first requirement is a favourable setting, a slice in time and space.

Perhaps its main characteristic is the absence of a place manager [a 'capable guardian'] to interfere with an illegal exchange ... Illegal merchants and their customers may also prefer some sort of camouflage for their transactions, such as distracting crowds, turbulent movements, concealing foliage, or protective crannies. The buyer and seller of illegal goods or services enter from different directions, commit the illegal transaction (!) and depart in different directions.

Figure 14.6 Vice dynamics

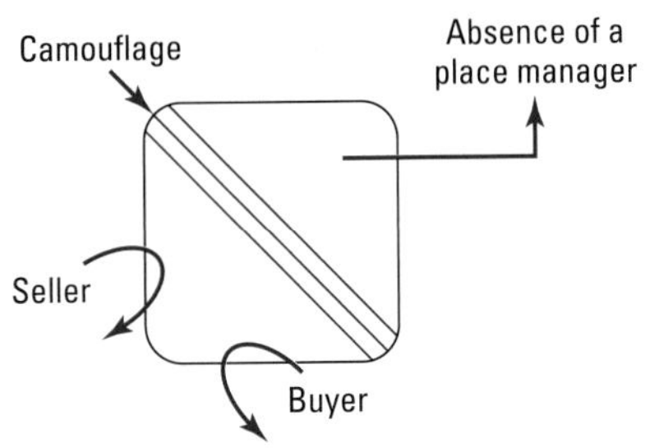

Source: Felson (1998: 68).

One of the key factors that distinguishes routine activity theory from other criminological theories is the relative absence of emphasis on the offender. The commission of the offence depends on two presences and one absence: the presence of an offender and a target, and the absence of a capable guardian.

> Offenders are but one element in a crime, and perhaps not even the most important. Predatory crimes need targets with guardians absent. Fights thrive on audiences and troublemakers without peacemakers. Illegal sales depend on settings where buyers and sellers can converge with camouflage present and place managers absent. (1998: 73)

Felson is quick to point out that most of the time the capable guardian is not a police officer or a security guard but, rather, is a family member, friend or someone else exercising some form of informal oversight or surveillance. Felson then goes to argue that a target's suitability for attack is dependent on four criteria, which he summarises using the acronym VIVA:

- *Value* – The *worth* of the target from the viewpoint of the offender; what it is worth to them.
- *Inertia* – The extent to which the article or target can be realistically removed, taken, robbed or moved.
- *Visibility* – How visible the target is to the offender.
- *Access* – How easy it is to gain access to the target.

Figure 14.7 How to modify criminological concepts to meet scientific standards, using the routine activity approach

Vague criminological concept	More precise and useful statement
Criminogenic social roles (changes over the life course)	More time away from home brings more offending and less guardianship
Differential association	An offence is easier to carry out with help from friends
Social strains	Nearly empty streets invite muggings
Shaming and social control	Keeping an eye on the likely offender discourages further misbehaviour
Marxist materialism	Study who owns what, who watches what, and which things are easy to steal
Offender emotions	Learn the timing and settings for emotional outbursts of crime
Labelling, secondary deviance	Find out exactly how one offence sets up another in time and space
Racial inequality	Find out how easily-burgled housing is distributed by race

Source: Felson (1998).

Felson (2000: 209) summarises this viewpoint using the example of residential burglary:

> A burglar tries to find a suitable household that is empty of guardians or within which the guardians are asleep or indisposed. The burglar seeks a place containing valuables easy to remove. Easy access and visibility draw the burglar further. The larger community structure offers the burglar crime opportunities by producing more lightweight but valuable goods and getting people out of their homes for work, school, or leisure. While they are out, the burglar goes in.

So confident is Felson in the power of the routine activity theory that he illustrates its centrality to other theoretical approaches. He summarises its relevance as shown in Figure 14.7.

Review questions

1　How do Cohen and Felson link changes in routine activities to post-war trends in crime?

2　What are the three components necessary for the commission of a crime according to routine activity theory?

3　In relation to target suitability what does VIVA stand for?

Situational crime prevention

Strictly speaking, 'situational crime prevention' is not a separate theoretical perspective, but one that builds on rational choice and routine activity theory. Nevertheless, such a substantial body of work, and argument about crime and its causes, has developed under this heading that it is deserving of separate consideration (it is also discussed further in Chapter 24). Situational prevention has been defined by its leading scholar, Ron Clarke, as:

> ... comprising measures directed at highly specific forms of crime that involve the management, design, or manipulation of the immediate environment in as systematic and permanent a way as possible so as to reduce the opportunities for crime and increase its risks as perceived by a wide range of offenders. (Clarke, 1983: 225)

The recent history of the development of situational prevention theory begins with a body of work undertaken by the Home Office in the 1970s, which illustrated how opportunities for offending could be manipulated in ways which would prevent or reduce crime. It quickly grew in popularity in part, as suggested in the introduction of this chapter, because of growing disenchantment with alternative, more sociological perspectives that focused on social structural conditions leading to crime. By 1983 the Home Office had set up a 'Crime Prevention Unit' and was conducting an increasing amount of research in this area. Such work had also been influenced by two cognate developments in America: Oscar Newman's idea of 'defensible space' and Herman Goldstein's work on 'problem-oriented policing'.

Defensible space and problem-oriented policing

One of the best known studies which focuses on manipulating situations, and reducing opportunities, through design, is that by Oscar Newman. In outlining his theory he defined *defensible space* as:

> ... a model for residential environments which inhibits crime by creating the physical expression of a social fabric which defends itself ... 'Defensible space' is a surrogate term for the range of mechanisms – real and symbolic barriers, strongly defined areas of influence, and improved opportunities for surveillance – that combine to bring an environment under the control of its residents. (1972: 3)

Newman argued that a sense of 'ownership' of spaces was important to their security – and that public spaces needed to be both observable and used in order for social control to flourish. It is possible, Newman (1972: 4) argued, to develop:

> ... extremely potent territorial attitudes and policing measures, which act as strong deterrents to potential criminals ... [by grouping] dwelling units to reinforce associations of mutual benefit; by delineating paths of movement; by defining areas of activity for particular users through their juxtaposition with internal living areas; and by providing opportunities for visual surveillance.

With echoes of Jane Jacobs' (1961) discussion of informal social control in cities and, indeed, Wilson and Kelling's (1982) ideas about social decline outlined initially in their 'Broken Windows' article, Newman's work was hugely influential. He identified four key areas of design that would encourage the development of social control and consequently likely reduce crime (Crawford 1998):

- *Territoriality* – defining space in particular ways so as to encourage residents to protect their areas, to indicate authority and to discourage outsiders from entering.
- *Surveillance* – designing building in such a way as make the observation of territorial areas easy and effective, and to encourage residents to do so.
- *Image* – designing building and areas in ways that help avoid stigma and the suggestion of vulnerability.
- *Environment* – juxtaposing public housing with 'safe zones' in adjacent areas.

In addition to defensible space, a further raft of design-related ideas developed in the 1970s which became known as 'crime prevention through environmental design' (CPTED). Though similar to Newman's ideas, CPTED was rather broader in focus and encompassed not just design principles, but also a combination of biological and psychological theories in an attempt to manipulate behaviour by

Defensible space. Writers such as Oscar Newman have drawn attention to the importance of design and physical characteristics in inhibiting crime – as in this diagram of a housing cul-de-sac, recommended as good practice in crime prevention literature in the UK in the 1990s.

changing environments. Both as a consequence of its association with biological theories and an enormous government-funded evaluation which showed no impact, CPTED was long considered a total failure and is felt by some to have held back the development of situational crime prevention in the US for some time (Clarke, 1995).

Oscar Newman's theory, although apparently more successful and more influential than CPTED, has also been heavily criticised:

- It has been argued that the reputation that particular areas develop over time is an important element in explaining levels of offending in high crime areas, and is something ignored by Newman (the importance of stigma).
- Housing policies, which are also argued to be significant in determining local rates of crime and disorder, are generally absent from Newman's work (Mayhew, 1979).
- Similarly, it is suggested he largely ignored the impact of different policing tactics – both in reducing and, possibly, exacerbating recorded local crime rates (the importance of formal social control) (Crawford, 1998).
- Newman's work has been criticised for giving the impression that space is to be defended from 'others', rather than offenders being those just as likely to occupy the spaces as the respectable non-offender (Mawby, 1977).

In the UK, Newman's work was further developed by Alice Coleman (1985) who produced what she called a 'design disadvantagement' index against which it was argued it was possible to identify and then rectify problems of design that were leading to crime and anti-social behaviour. The ideas proved popular with government, and the Department of Environment in the late 1980s invested considerable resources into improvements in residential estates driven by Coleman's ideas. Work by Poyner (1983) suggested extensions of Newman's notion of defensible space beyond residential communities to city centres, public transport and schools, and design-related prevention remains generally popular with policy-makers. A recent review of work in this area suggested that there 'is much common-sense in a "designing out crime" approach, but also a danger of overstating its impact and slipping into a design-determinist philosophy whereby people are seen as mere automatons whose behaviour is entirely conditioned by the environment they find themselves in' (Shaftoe and Read, 2005).

Problem-oriented policing

Clarke (1995) also draws attention to the importance of the idea of problem-oriented policing (POP) in the development of situational prevention ideas. POP is associated with the work of Herman Goldstein (see Chapter 25) who argued that greater efficiency in policing was not to be found (or found primarily) in reorganisation of the police service or in better management, but rather through having a more 'problem-oriented' approach to the job itself. In his view the police service needed to be less reactive, and to think more about the problems with which it was confronted. Analysis was required to understand why some problems re-occurred and why particular places appeared especially crime-prone.

Thus, rather than simply returning again and again to the same places and people, the police ought to attempt to devise solutions to the underlying problems. As such Goldstein's ideas were broadly in line with elements of situational prevention, though important differences between them also existed: 'In particular, problem-oriented policing is a management approach designed to make the most efficient use of police resources, while situational prevention is a crime control approach open not just to the police, but also to any organisational or management structure' (Clarke, 1995: 97).

Crime and opportunity

Building on rational choice, routine activity, ideas of defensible space and crime prevention by design, an opportunity-based 'theory' of crime prevention has come to the fore on both sides of the Atlantic in the last 20 years. Its advocates describe it is as providing a 'scientific framework' for practical thinking about crime and, as we will see below, recent years have seen the emergence of a group of academics who increasingly portray themselves as 'crime scientists' rather than criminologists. Practical situational crime prevention-oriented research consists of action research in five sequential stages:

1 Collection of data about the nature and dimensions of a specific crime problem.

2 Analysis of the situational conditions that permit or facilitate the commission of the crimes in question.

3 Systematic study of possible means of blocking opportunities for these particular crimes, including analysis of costs.

4 Implementation of the most promising, feasible, and economical measures.

5 Monitoring of results and dissemination of experience. (Clarke, 1995: 93)

According to Clarke (1995) this opportunity theory – rather like routine activity theory – has three components:

- *targets* (e.g. cars, shops, ATM machines);
- *victims* (women alone, drunks, strangers);
- *crime facilitators* (tools such as guns and cars and disinhibitors such as alcohol and drugs).

The nature and supply of targets is a function of the physical environment and the lifestyle and routine activities of the population. Such factors influence the existence, number and effectiveness of capable guardians. The supply of facilitators is also determined by the physical environment. Although the focus is on opportunity, the broader social and economic environment does make an appearance in opportunity theory:

> Physical environment and lifestyles and routine activities are themselves determined by the broader socioeconomic structure of society, including demography, geography, urbanisation and industrialisation, health and education policy, and legal and political institutions. The numbers of potential offenders and their motives are also determined partly by the socioeconomic structure of society through many of the mechanisms (alienation, subcultural influence, neglect, and lack of love, etc.) identified by traditional criminology and partly by lifestyle and routine activities which affect the nature of social control afforded by 'intimate handlers' in other ways. (Clarke, 1995: 102–3)

More recently, a more radical form of opportunity-theory has been advocated by Felson and Clarke (1998). This theory of 'crime settings', they say, rests on a single principle: 'that easy or tempting opportunities entice people into criminal action' (1998: 2). The approach, they argue, has 10 principles:

1 Opportunities play a role in causing all crime.

2 Crime opportunities are highly specific.

3 Crime opportunities are concentrated in time and space.

4 Crime opportunities depend on everyday movements.

5 One crime produces opportunities for another.

Figure 14.8   The opportunity structure for crime

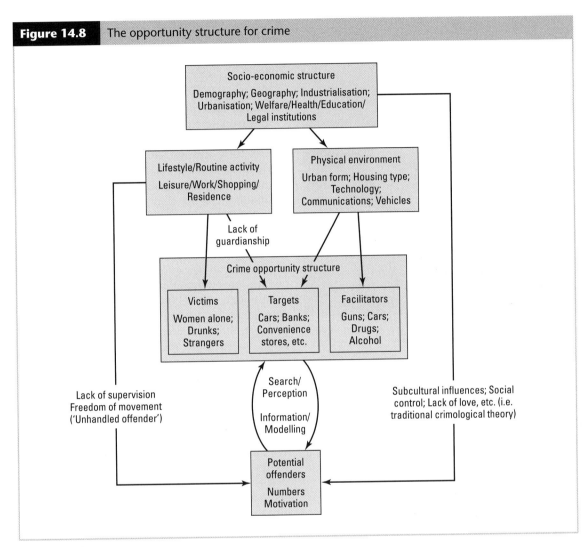

Source: Clarke (1995).

6 Some products offer more tempting crime opportunities.

7 Social and technological changes produce new crime opportunities.

8 Opportunities for crime can be reduced.

9 Reducing opportunities does not usually displace crime.

10 Focused opportunity reduction can produce wider declines in crime.

This approach, its proponents argue, has the twin benefits of freeing criminologists from their preoccupation with abstractions and their discussions of deep-seated factors such as race, class or intelligence and, second, providing a police and practice-relevant set of tools with which to make an immediate difference. As such, these ideas 'do not merely complement existing efforts to diminish individual propensities to commit crime through social and community programmes or the threat of criminal sanctions. Rather, the newer policies operate on circumstances much closer to the criminal event and thus have much greater chance to reduce crime immediately' (Felson and Clarke, 1998: 33).

Although some of the criminologists – Clarke in particular – working within these general frameworks (rational choice, routine activity, opportunity) are careful to acknowledge that their arguments are compatible with broader sociological theories about the impact of socio-economic factors, it is not

Valuables left on back seats of cars are tempting targets. Criminologists such as Marcus Felson and Ron Clarke stress the importance of opportunity in explaining crime.

immediate matters that can be manipulated and which might have some practical benefit. Related to this, criminology also has a particular 'political' problem he argues (2004: 59):

> The belief that crime is the product of discrimination and disadvantage has had another unfortunate effect. It has led criminologists to align themselves habitually with the criminal underdog and ignore the harm he inflicts on victims and society ... Instead of always sympathizing with the criminal's plight, criminologists should recognize that crime is fuelled by greed and selfishness as much as by any other cause.

The shift he and others recommend, therefore, is to pay much less attention to the causes of crime and much more on *how* crime is committed and, consequently, how it might be prevented.

Although Clarke and others push the case for criminology reorienting itself in this direction there is, as yet, little sign that such a sea change is occurring. Indeed, in anticipation of considerable resistance within criminology to such approaches, Clarke and others deliberately chose the term 'Crime Science' to characterise the work, and the first university-based Institute specialising in such activity – the Jill Dando Institute of Crime Science at University College, London – was deliberately placed in an institution with no department of criminology 'to hinder its growth' (Clarke, 2004: 62).

difficult to detect the frustration they clearly feel with those criminologists who remain wedded to other approaches and who are sceptical or even dismissive of opportunity-related approaches. In recent years this frustration has led to the emergence of a group of scholars who define themselves as 'crime scientists' rather than criminologists.

Crime science

Much of the work that has developed under this heading is an amalgam of rational choice theory, routine activity and situational control theories. It is worth considering in its own right, however, for its major proponents see it as being a body of work that is to be understood very differently from traditional criminology (see Figure 14.9).

One of its main advocates, Ron Clarke, argues that traditional criminology has defined itself as being primarily interested in and concerned with explaining and understanding crime. Important though this might be, he suggests, it has meant that the subject has generally been of limited utility to those who have responsibility for controlling or reducing crime. Rather than focusing on distant causes such as poverty and social inequality – which have generally proved rather resistant to change – criminologists should look to the more

It is possible that 'crime science' may one day become an inclusive term under which opportunity theories of crime are encapsulated or, as some of its proponents suggest, it may become an even more general category covering all activities related to reducing crime just 'as medical science is about reducing ill-health' (Laycock, 2005: 6). Given its current stance, it seems likely that in the immediate future it will have a difficult, often fractious relationship with criminology. In part, this is an inevitable consequence of the critical comments made by criminologists and crime scientists about each other. More fundamentally, the different *epistemological* (ideas about how the world is to be understood) positions adopted by each other will undoubtedly continue to separate them. Crime scientists generally adhere, or say they adhere, to the standards and values of the natural sciences and the application of these to the goal of crime control. Criminology, or at least parts of criminology, with its roots in critical social sciences, has a much more difficult relationship with the idea of crime control, the role of the state and, indeed, the notion of *crime* (see Chapter 1).

Figure 14.9	Differences of emphasis between criminology and crime science

Criminology	Crime science
	Mission
Understand criminals	Understand crime
Long-term social reform	Immediate crime reduction
Help the criminal underdog	Reduce harm to victims
'Pure'	'Applied'
Theory-led	Problem-led
Shun policy	Embrace policy
	Theory
Distant causes paramount	Near causes paramount
Opportunity secondary	Opportunity central
Crime pathological	Crime normal
The WHY of crime	The HOW of crime
Criminal dispositions	Criminal choice
Criminal motivation	The rewards of crime
Anomie, subcultures and conflict theory	Routine activities, rational choice
Sociology, psychiatry, law	Economics, geography, biology, planning, computer science
	Research methods
Cohort studies	Crime patterns
Criminal careers	Hot spots
Regression analysis	Crime mapping
Self-reported delinquency	Victim surveys
Randomised control trials	Crime-specific case studies
Long-term studies in depth	Rapid appraisal techniques
	Applications and audience
Crime and delinquency in general	Specific crime and disorder problems
Sentencing/treatment/social prevention	Detection/deterrence/situational prevention
Social workers/probation officers	Police, planners and security industry
Social policymakers	Business and management
Scholarly treatises	Policy briefs
Careers in academia	Careers in prevention/security/policy

Source: Clarke (2004).

Assessing contemporary classicism

There can be little doubt that the approaches reviewed in this chapter represent one of the more significant developments within criminology in recent decades. As I explained at the outset, routine activity theory, rational choice, situational preven-tion and opportunity-focused criminology have their roots in growing pessimism about positivist and correctionalist criminology from the 1970s onward. These new approaches are what Garland (2001) has called 'the new criminologies of every-day life'. What they have in common, he argues (2001: 128), is that:

... they each begin from the premise that crime is a normal, commonplace, aspect of modern society. Crime is regarded as a generalized form of behaviour, routinely produced by the normal patterns of social and economic life in contemporary society. To commit an offence thus requires no special motivation or disposition, no abnormality or pathology ... Crime comes to be viewed as a routine risk to be calculated or an accident to be avoided, rather than a moral aberration that needs to be specially explained.

In this vein, one of the critical responses to rational choice theory has been that, despite its claims, it generally fails to explain offender motivation – indeed it is largely unconcerned with it. Like much control theory, the underlying assumption in the application of rational choice theory to crime is that most of us would do it if we thought we could get away with it. The fact that we don't is explained by the control theorist by some combination of internal and external controls, and by the rational choice theorist by the fact that the perceived gains from offending are, in some way, outweighed by the costs.

Is it realistic, however, to make such assumptions? Do offenders actually behave in this manner? What about the excitement, the thrills, the bravado involved in certain types of crime? Some offenders may decide to engage in certain forms of crime in the face of overwhelming evidence of its likely 'success' in such rational terms. Tunnell (1992) for example has argued that it is not unusual for individuals to make decisions that are not obviously in their own best interests. In particular, for various reasons they may not be in a position to assess the pros and cons of particular courses of action. To this extent, those operating within what we are referring here to as 'contemporary classicism' tend to work with a model of 'bounded' or 'limited rationality'.

As with classical theories generally, one consistent criticism of rational choice and related approaches is that they fail to take sufficient account of the structural conditions within which individual decision-making takes place. True enough, most of the models make some reference to social conditions, but few then go on to spend much time exploring these in detail and relating these to offending patterns. Indeed, this is far from the concern of the rational choice theorist who generally has more pressing policy and practical concerns. Tilley and Laycock (2002: 30) illustrate this preoccupation in their analysis of the importance of 'opportunity' as the key to crime reduction:

[T]he meaning of 'root causes' [of crime] is not clear. At one level if there were no laws there would be no crime, but this approach would not take us very far. Accepting that crime is a legal construct, research shows that the 'causes' of crime are many and varied – poor parenting, lack of education, poverty, greed, drug addiction, genetic predisposition, and so on. The most significant is, however, opportunity. If there were no opportunities there would be no crimes; the same cannot be said for any of the other contributory causes.

Situational prevention – which tends to draw on some of the theoretical approaches covered in this chapter – has been subject to a number of criticisms. One frequent observation is that such interventions don't prevent crime they merely *displace* it from one place to another. Indeed, in addition to such geographical movement there are numerous other ways in which crime may be displaced:

- It can be moved from one time to another (doing it later rather than now).
- The target may change (different types of household may be targeted).
- The means used may change (using the internet for fraud rather than paper-based systems).
- The crime 'type' may change ('fencing' rather than stealing for example).

There has been much research on the possibility and nature of displacement, much of which challenges the assertion and argues that the extent of such impact is much less than critics believe (see Chapter 24). However, the logic of the 'opportunity theory' approach is that it is the opportunity which makes the thief (Felson and Clarke, 1998). Consequently, if opportunities are reduced or removed then particular crimes will reduce or disappear.

Other criticisms include a series of arguments about the utilisation of such theoretical approaches and, in particular, the possibility that they may act *repressively* and/or *regressively* (Downes and Rock, 2007). By this is meant the possibility that emphasis on situational controls may lead to the use of surveillance, limitations on basic freedoms (speech, privacy, movement) which, even if effective in preventing crime, are nevertheless detrimental to the overall quality of life, and also to the possibility that such measures may place undue burdens on citizens, not least financial burdens. For some there is a clear link here with the generally risk-oriented drift of contemporary penal policy (see Chapters 22 and 28):

The cost-driven turn of economic analysis is mirrored also in the increasingly prudential orientation of crime policies concerned less with responding to crime as a moral wrong than with estimating, preventing, and minimizing losses and insuring against harm. (Zedner, 2006)

Situational prevention and allied approaches are viewed by some as diverting attention and resources away from important social interventions focusing on improving local conditions and lives. Finally, a linked criticism of opportunity-related theories is that they strip away what makes individuals 'social' and treat them simply as calculating individuals:

> We now have only the criminal as consumer and market actor – someone who not only has more rationality than the determined creatures of sociological enquiry, but has *nothing* but choice and rationality. Disembodied from all social context – deprivation, racism, urban dislocation, unemployment are airily listed as – 'background factors' – they take their risks, assess their opportunities, have their targets hardened and stay away from others' 'defensible spaces'. (Cohen, 1996: 5)

Questions for further discussion

1 Rational choice, routine activities and situational crime prevention all suggest that a specific crime focus is important in understanding offending. Illustrate why this might be so by using the examples of domestic burglary, fraud, and street robbery ('mugging').

2 Cut out half a dozen crime stories from some recent newspapers. In what ways do you think the offenders in these stories might have weighed up the costs and benefits of their actions?

3 How might you use a routine activities approach to reduce crime in a public car park?

4 Is situational crime prevention a theory or simply a set of practical tools for manipulating the environment?

5 Are all types of crime explicable in terms of rational choice and routine activities?

6 Why are the approaches covered in this chapter referred to as *contemporary classicism*?

Further reading

Clarke, R.V.G. (2003) 'Situational' crime prevention: theory and practice, in McLaughlin, E. *et al.* (eds) *Criminological Perspectives*, 3rd edn, London: Sage

Cohen, L. and Felson, M. (1979) Social change and crime rate trends: A routine activity approach, *American Sociological Review*, 44, 588–608, Columbus, OH: The Ohio State University, Department of Sociology

Downes, D. and Rock, P. (2007) *Understanding Deviance*, 5th edn, Oxford: Oxford University Press (ch. 9)

Felson, M. (2002) *Crime and Everyday Life*, 3rd edn, Thousand Oaks, CA: Pine Forge Press

Felson, M. and Clarke, R.V.G. (1998) *Opportunity Makes the Thief: Practical theory for crime prevention*, London: Home Office

Garland, D. (2001) *The Culture of Control*, Oxford: Oxford University Press (ch. 5)

Smith, M.J. and Tilley, N. (eds) (2005) *Crime Science: New approaches to preventing and detecting crime*, Cullompton: Willan Publishing

Websites

There is a huge amount of material available on the Home Office website, particularly in the Crime Prevention and Police Research series: http://www.homeoffice.gov.uk/rds/pubsdiscontinued.html

The Center for Problem-oriented Policing website contains masses of downloadable material, crime prevention guides and publications: www.popcenter.org

The Design Against Crime Association has a growing website of potentially useful material: http://www.doca.org.uk/

Chapter outline

Introduction   300

Early criminology and the female offender   301
  Lombroso and Ferrero   301
  W.I. Thomas and Otto Pollak   302
  Sociological criminology and the continued
    invisibility of women   303

  The development of modern feminist criminology   305
  Female emancipation and crime   305
  Carol Smart and feminist criminology   306

Contemporary feminist criminology   308
  Understanding women's involvement in crime   309
  Women, prison and punishment   311
    The nature of women's imprisonment   311
    The criminalisation of women   313
  A feminist methodology?   313
  Feminist victimology   314

Assessing feminist criminology   314
Questions for further discussion   316
Further reading   316
Websites   317

Feminist criminology

CHAPTER SUMMARY	Criminology, historically, has been dominated by men. For much of the twentieth century the majority of practising criminologists – in universities and elsewhere – were men. Moreover, the bulk of criminological scholarship, both theory and research, focused on male offenders. Women, undeniably, have been all but invisible for much of criminology's history. This is less true today though, arguably, criminology remains male-oriented. The growing visibility of women – as professional criminologists and as the object of criminological study – is largely the result of the feminist movement that emerged in the second half of the twentieth century. The changes this has brought are the subject of this chapter (and of Chapter 32).

This chapter considers:

- the way in which female offenders were presented and understood in early criminological theory and research;

- the rise of feminist criminology;

- some of the variety of work undertaken within feminist criminology;

- the impact that feminism has had on criminology more generally.

In addition to highlighting concerns around female offenders and women's victimization, feminist scholarship's great project has been to attempt to put questions of gender firmly at the centre of criminology.

Introduction

This chapter considers the emergence, nature, and impact of feminist criminology. Like all the other perspectives we have considered in other chapters it is very much a product of a particular time. Straightforwardly, the scholarship covered in the main sections of this chapter was a product of the re-emergence of feminism from the late 1960s onwards. In part, feminist criminology was a reaction to pre-existing ways of 'doing' criminology:

[T]he reaction was against an old, established male chauvinism in the academic discipline. Women were either invisible to conventional criminologists or present only as prostitutes or marginal or contingent figures. Further, when women were discussed it was in crude sexist stereotypes which were widely and thought-lessly disseminated. Feminist criminology has been quite successful in developing and establishing this critique, although it has been much more difficult to get it taken into mainstream criminology. (Heidensohn, 1996: 161–2)

Later in the book (Chapter 32) we consider female offending and the treatment of women in the criminal justice context in more detail. These two chapters are probably best read in conjunction as many of the theoretical arguments outlined here are illustrated by the greater empirical detail contained in the later chapter. The focus here is upon criminological theory and, in particular, how it has been influenced by feminist scholarship. Arguably the most important development in critical criminological theory in the past 30–40 years, feminist theory has transformed thinking in this area. There are continuing debates about what constitutes feminist criminology, but what seems undeniable is that feminist scholarship has had a substantial impact on criminology in recent decades.

Developing in the United States in the late 1960s and in the UK in the 1970s, feminist scholarship has been heavily critical of much mainstream criminological theorising. Heidensohn (1996: 111) put it starkly when she observed: 'criminology, mainstream and tributary, has almost nothing to say of interest or importance about women'.

Early criminology and the female offender

Early criminology, often characterised as 'biological positivism' or something similar (see Chapter 6), is in some ways unusual. It is unusual less for its emphasis on matters such as biology and physiognomy than for the fact that it did actually pay some attention to women. In this it may be distinguished from much that followed which was, as we will see, almost wilfully blind to female offending and female victimization. There are two key aspects to work on female offending from within this tradition: it is seen as particularly influenced by biology – more so than male offending – and it is highly sexualised.

Lombroso and Ferraro

For Lombroso, women were especially influenced by their biology (see Chapter 6). Lombroso and Ferraro's work on the female criminal concluded that there were far fewer 'born female criminals' than males. The reason that women commit less crime, they argued, is that they are less highly developed than the male. They are more primitive, the consequence of which was that they have less scope for degeneration. The most common form of regression for the woman, Lombroso and Ferraro argued, was prostitution.

Rock has argued that the primary reason that Lombroso's work continues to be referred to in contemporary criminology is as a result of his role as the primary *bête-noir* of feminist criminology – as 'the man they loved to hate' (Rock, 2007: 125). According to many feminist critics, it was not just in the early twentieth century that views of women as outmoded as Lombroso's were expressed, but that they could be found within contemporary criminology too. Heidensohn (2002) argues that Lombroso and Ferraro's work had a significant influence on women's penal treatment. Similarly, Carol Smart (1976) suggested the work of Lombroso, though considered by many to be archaic and desperately outdated, remained typical in its attitude toward and portrayal of women. Ironically, it appears that whereas much of what Lombroso had argued was largely discredited and abandoned, the relative invisibility of female crime meant that many of the assumptions that underpinned Lombroso's work continued to exert influence long afterward.

16 Gabriella Bompard. Source: Lombroso, *La donna delinquente*, 1893. *Editor's note*: Lombroso considered Bompard, a French prostitute convicted of premediatated murder, to be an example of the full born criminal type.

17 Berland (2 views). Source: Lombroso, *La donna delinquente*, 1893. *Editor's note:* Lombroso describes this criminal as lascivious, homicidal, and virile in appearance.

18 Thomas (2 views). Source: Lombroso, *La donna delinquente*, 1893. *Editor's note:* In this photo, Lombroso detected the wrinkles, protruding ears, twisted nose, and overall virility that he considered typical of female born criminals.

Illustrations from Lombroso and Ferrero's *La Donna Delinquente* (1893), now republished in a new translation (Lombroso and Ferraro: 1893/2004).

Lombroso and Ferraro on the 'female born criminal'

While the majority of female criminals are merely led into crime by someone else or by irresistible temptation, there is a small subgroup whose criminal propensities are more intense and perverse than even those of their male counterparts. These are the female born criminals, whose evil is inversely proportionate to their numbers ... The extreme perversity of female born criminals manifests itself in two characteristics: the variety of their crimes and their cruelty.

Variety of crimes

Many female born criminals specialize in not just one but several types of crime and often in two types that in males are mutually exclusive, such as poisoning and murder ... In history we find Agrippina, an adulterer, incest offender, and party to homicide, and Messalina, a prostitute, adulterer, accomplice in homicide and thief.

Cruelty

Second, the female born criminal surpasses her male counterpart in the refined, diabolical cruelty in which she commits her crimes. Merely killing her enemy does not satisfy her; she needs to watch him suffer and

experience the full taste of death ... In short, while female born criminals are fewer in number than male born criminals, they are often much more savage. What is the explanation?

We have seen that the normal woman is by nature less sensitive to pain than a man. Because compassion is an effect of sensitivity, if one is lacking, the other will be too. We have also seen how women have many traits in common with children; that they are deficient in the moral sense; and that they are vengeful, jealous, and inclined to refined cruelty when they take revenge ...

In addition, the female born criminal is, so to speak doubly exceptional, first, as a woman and then as a criminal. This is because criminals are exceptions among civilized people, and women are exceptions among criminals, women's natural form of regression being prostitution, not crime. Primitive woman was a prostitute rather than a criminal. As a double exception, then, the criminal woman is a true monster. Honest women are kept in line by factors such as maternity, piety, and weakness; when a woman commits a crime despite these restraints, this is a sign that her power of evil is immense.

Source: Lombroso and Ferraro (1893/2004: 182–185).

By and large, the idea that it is biological differences that are the primary cause of the distinctive patterns of male and female offending has disappeared from criminology, though Gelsthorpe (2002) points to the work of Maccoby and Jacklin (1975) as an exception to this, as is the work of Dalton (1977) on the link between menstruation and crime.

W.I. Thomas and Otto Pollak

W.I. Thomas was another who propounded a view of female deviance that emphasised sexuality, with promiscuity being regularly equated with delinquency. Much of Thomas's focus was upon prostitution and soliciting, and these activities were seen as typical of female deviance. The female criminal, according to Thomas (1923), was cold, calculating and amoral. They had failed, in essence, to learn appropriate female roles and required greater control and oversight. In an echo of Durkheim (see Chapter 8) he argued that the rapid social transformations taking place resulted in the undermining of previously existing social constraints and the development of greater awareness of the deprivations that people, and women in particu-

lar, were forced to suffer. This frustration led to the disorganisation of women's lives and potentially to delinquency (often defined as sexual delinquency).

A similar, sex-based theory was that developed by Otto Pollak (1961). He sought to explore the phenomenon of hidden female crime – being convinced that the relatively low official rates of female offending disguised the real situation. In part, this is a reflection of the lenient way in which women are treated by the criminal justice system, he argued. It also reflects the fact that women are in many ways manipulative and deceitful, this being a reflection of the nature of their sexuality and biology. In particular, women's passive role in sex, he argued, forms the basis for women's skill in deceit:

Not enough attention has been paid to the physiological fact that man must achieve an erection in order to perform the sex act and will not be able to hide his failure. His lack of positive emotion in the sexual sphere must become overt to the partner and pretense of sexual response is impossible for him, if it is lacking. Woman's body, however, permits such pretense to a certain degree and lack of orgasm does not prevent her ability to participate in the sex act. (1961: 10)

Women therefore have a different relationship with the truth. In particular, through sexual intercourse, women are able to develop both the ability and the confidence to deceive men. As Smart (1976) argues, rather than ask what might lie behind women's experience of sex, Pollak assumes that such behaviour is illustrative of fundamental characteristics – characteristics that are played out in relation to crime also. Much male offending, he argued, is actually stimulated or instigated by women. Crimes committed by women tend to reflect their nature and may often be hidden (poisoning, infanticide), or reflect the psychological make-up of women (kleptomania, for example) or their sexuality (prostitution, sexual blackmail).

Heidensohn (1987: 17) says that 'what is striking about [Lombroso's, Pollak's and Thomas's] theories is not merely their sexism, or even their misogyny, but their resilience and persistence.' Indeed, she points out that a second generation of writers (Cowie *et al.*, 1968; Richardson, 1969; Gibbens, 1971) continued to advance very similar ideas and such views had a practical impact on women's treatment in prison in particular (Dobash *et al.*, 1986). Nevertheless, though the work of the likes of Lombroso, W.I. Thomas and Pollak is much discredited now, there are at least two important reasons for studying them (Heidensohn 1996):

- Such theories have been used to lend 'intellectual respectability' to long-standing folk ideas about women and women's behaviour.

- Until relatively recently such work was rarely questioned or criticised.

Sociological criminology and the continued invisibility of women

By contrast with the earlier work of the likes of Lombroso, W.I. Thomas and Pollak, the female offender hardly appears at all in much of the classic criminological theory of the mid-twentieth century, such as the work of the Chicago School, in strain, subcultural or control theory or, indeed, in much later 'radical' work. In a path-breaking article in 1968 in the *British Journal of Sociology* Frances Heidensohn drew attention to the notable failure to examine and research female deviance. This, she said, was remarkable for at least three reasons:

- Deviance in general (male and female) has long aroused much sociological and other academic interest (from at least the time of Durkheim). It is surprising therefore that the actual or potential deviance of approximately half the members of any society elicits such little concern.

- Interest in other aspects of women's experiences and social position has been very substantial, and has included almost every 'type' of sociologist.

- The differences between male and female offending have also long been noted, and these differences appear to occur with the kind of regularity and uniformity that normally attracts the interest of the social scientist.

This is not to say that mid-century sociological criminology made no reference to gender. It is merely to observe that, as a number of feminist scholars have argued, such work often relied on a set of assumptions about gender and took as its core concern the behaviour of men. Heidensohn (1996: 127) quotes the eminent mid-century criminologist Herman Mannheim making just such a point:

Hitherto female crime has, for all practical purposes, been dealt with almost exclusively by men in their various capacities as legislators, judges, policemen; and ... the same was true of the theoretical treatment of the subject ... This could not fail to create a one-sided picture ... this centuries-old male predominance in theory.

One of the big differences between early criminological thought and the more sociologically-informed theorising that succeeded it was the abandonment of the idea that crime is abnormal or pathological, and its replacement with a more understanding and appreciative set of approaches which sought to make sense of the circumstances in which offending took place and of the view of the world as it was seen through the eyes of the offender (see, for example, Chapters 9 and 10).

It is precisely this appreciative sociology, Heidensohn argues, that led male researchers to ignore or exclude women from their studies: 'treating delinquency as normal made female delinquency problematic because it was both statistically unusual and also deemed role-inappropriate' (1996: 129). Delinquency is viewed as unfeminine, precisely because it is *male* behaviour. Moreover, Heidensohn argues it was not just that male sociologists were concerned to study male delinquency that was important, it was that their appreciative stance led them to *celebrate* it that reinforced the short-sightedness so far as women were concerned.

Heidensohn provides a number of examples, including the following from Albert Cohen's *Delinquent Boys* (1955: 140):

> The delinquent is the rogue male. His conduct may be viewed not only negatively ... [but also] ... positively ... as the exploitation of modes of behaviour which are traditionally symbolic of untrammelled masculinity, which are renounced by middle-class culture because incompatible with its ends, but which are not without a certain aura of glamour and romance.

Neither labelling theory nor British subcultural theory had much to say about female crime. As we saw in Chapter 9, the dominant focus of British subcultural theory in the 1970s was on white, working-class, male culture (Dorn and South, 1982). There were, at least in the earliest years of such writing, few attempts to understand either female delinquency or the styles associated with female subcultures, though the work of Angela McRobbie was both an early and a consistent exception to this (McRobbie and Garber, 1976; McRobbie, 1980, 1991).

According to McRobbie and Garber (1976), because of their position within public and private worlds, girls tend to be pushed to the periphery of social activities, and much 'girl culture' becomes a culture of the bedroom rather than the street (see also Frith, 1983). It is this, McRobbie (1980: 40) argues, that most subcultural theorists ignore:

> ... in documenting the temporary flights of the Teds, Mods or Rockers, they fail to show that it is monstrously more difficult for women to escape (even temporarily) and that these symbolic flights have often been at the expense of women (especially mothers) and girls. The lads' . . . peer group consciousness and pleasure frequently seem to hinge on a collective disregard for women and sexual exploitation of girls.

The 'lonely, uncharted seas of human behaviour', as Heidensohn (1968) described female deviance, were consequently long overdue serious academic consideration. Where is the equivalent of Shaw's *The Jackroller* or Sutherland's *The Professional Thief* she asked? What is needed, she suggested, 'is a crash programme of research which telescopes decades of comparable studies of males.' Such work when it begins must avoid treating its subject matter either as if it must be understood simply as a question of sex, or simply in comparison with men. A start would be to develop a 'natural history'

of female deviance, in which knowledge of the parameters, types and nature of such activities would be a central focus.

Why such silence in criminological theory in relation to female offending – or, indeed, female conformity? Heidensohn (1996) suggests that there at least four important reasons:

1 What she terms the 'delinquent machismo tradition' in criminology treated male deviance as heroic and romantic – 'the "college boys" became fascinated by the "corner boys"' (1996: 141).

2 This was reinforced by male dominance in academic life (the emphasis on 'founding fathers'; the preponderance of men in senior positions; and the 'ideology of gender' which constructs reality in sexually stereotyped ways).

3 The relative infrequency and relatively mundane nature of female offending made its public profile much lower.

4 The primary theoretical concerns in mainstream criminology are easier to sustain if one ignores the issue of sex differences in offending.

In the main, both American and British subcultural theory, like all mainstream criminology of the time, ignored girls and women.

The development of modern feminist criminology

Feminist criminology proceeds from the assertion, therefore, that women at best have been marginal in criminology, are all too often entirely invisible, and, even when they are the focus of attention this is rarely undertaken in a sympathetic or rounded fashion. At the heart of feminist criminology lies a critique of extant criminology for a number of highly significant oversights. These include:

- The failure to theorise or to engage in the empirical study of female offending.

- The neglect of female victimization and, particularly, male violence against women.

- The over-concentration on the impact of the criminal justice system on male offenders.

The period since the early 1970s has seen the emergence of new feminist and/or feminist-influenced criminologies. In fact, as we will see, there has been a considerable debate as to whether a 'feminist criminology' is desirable or even possible. Nevertheless, what is undeniable is the huge expansion of work in this area during this period. Writing in 1990, Carol Smart observed, 'some ten years ago it was *de rigueur* to start any paper on this topic [feminism and crime] with a reference to a dearth of material in the field. Now it is difficult to keep up with the production of papers and books' (1990: 71).

Female emancipation and crime

Two books published in America in 1975 set the tone for much that was to follow. In *Sisters in Crime* Freda Adler argued that changes to women's roles were leading to greater aggressiveness, competitiveness and criminality. In short, as women were leaving traditional housebound roles they were becoming more involved in violence and other forms of offending. The differences between the sexes in this regard were declining. Similarly, Rita Simon in *Women and Crime* also considered some of the changes in female criminality, but argued that it was the new opportunities that came with women's new roles, rather than some fundamental change in women themselves, that was crucial in understanding what was occurring. However, as Gelsthorpe (2002: 22) observes:

A major assumption underlying the suggestion that increased opportunities lead to increases in women's crime is that women's roles have changed, that women now play an equal part in social, economic and political life. Moreover, women's earnings continue to be lower than those of men, and women remain a minority in high-ranking positions in society. Women also continue to bear the brunt of domestic and childcare responsibilities even when they are in full-time employment. Thus, women may be more involved in crime than hitherto, but this may be due to reasons of poverty, economic marginalisation and so on, and not due to women's emancipation.

Nevertheless, she suggests that there are at least two reasons to think that the 'emancipation thesis' had value:

1 It focused attention on female crime.

2 The feminist critique of existing theories made an immense contribution in stimulating a proper evaluation of theories and their importance and relevance in explaining women's crime. (Gelsthorpe, 2002: 24)

Moreover, it is far from the case that arguments that link alleged or actual changes in women's social position and social roles to female offending have disappeared. Heidensohn (2006) suggests that media preoccupation with female (mis)conduct seems even more disproportionate than it was previously and, in a recent volume, Alder and Worrall (2004) detail the apparent rise of public concern about violence by young women and the suggestion in the media and elsewhere that alleged increases in such behaviour are evidence of the emergence of a new breed of violent young women. Worrall (2004a: 47) describes the build-up of a moral panic in the late 1990s focusing on 'younger and younger girls becoming increasingly aggressive, mushrooming girl gangs, increased use of drugs and, especially, alcohol, and the wilful abandonment of gender role expectations'.

Although the early focus of much feminist work was on the changing social position of women and the impact, often assumed, that this was having on female criminality, it was fairly quickly superseded by theories that were more concerned with patriarchy and male domination. Carol Smart (1976: xiii), for example, argued that criminology tended to adopt 'an entirely uncritical attitude towards sexual stereotypes of women and girls'. In this context, 'patriarchy' has been defined as 'a sex/gender system in which men dominate women and what is considered masculine is more highly valued than what is considered feminine. Patriarchy is a system of social stratification, which means that it uses a wide array of social control policies and practices to ratify male power and to keep girls and women subordinate to men' (Chesney-Lind, 2006: 9).

Feminist scholarship in criminology has a number of characteristics that distinguish it from traditional male-dominated work. Daly and Chesney-Lind (1988: 504) suggest that there are five key elements underpinning feminist work:

- Gender is not a natural fact, but rather a complex social, historical and cultural product; it is related to, but not simply derived from, biological sex differences and reproductive capacities.

- Gender and gender relations order social life and social institutions in fundamental ways.

- Gender relations and constructs of masculinity and femininity are not symmetrical, but rather are based on an organising principle of men's superiority and social and political-economic dominance over women.

- Systems of knowledge reflect men's views of the natural and social world; the production of knowledge is gendered.

- Women should be at the centre of intellectual inquiry, not peripheral, invisible, or appendages of men.

A number of questions are raised by this. Most obviously, is whether theories derived from the study of, and designed to aid understanding of, male offending can be used or applied to female offending. This approach to theorising has been referred to as the 'generalisability approach', or the 'add women and stir approach' (Heidensohn, 2006; Chesney-Lind, 2006). Miller (2000) suggests there have been two main lines of criticism of the generalisability approach.

The first suggests that it overlooks ethnic and economic inequality, failing to focus on the very different structural circumstances occupied by men and women and ignoring the racial and class inequalities that are important in explaining patterns of offending. Thus, for example, Lisa Maher's (1997) study of a Brooklyn drug market illustrates the highly gendered and racialised division of labour in the local drug economy – a division of labour that in important respects replicates and reinforces women's typically disadvantaged position in relation to men.

The second line of criticism is that whatever the benefits in using traditional criminological theory in attempting to explain female offending, what it is clearly unable to do is address the pivotal issue of the differential rates of male and female offending.

Carol Smart and feminist criminology

The book that has perhaps had greatest impact on this debate, both in stimulating much of it, and in setting the parameters for many successive arguments, is Carol Smart's (1976) *Women, Crime and Criminology*. In the preface to the book she raised two crucial concerns: first, that there was a particular danger that studying women separately from men would lead to continued marginalisation and to the perpetuation of a male-dominated criminology; and second, that increasing academic attention on female crime could have the unintended, and arguably undesirable consequence of increasing public and criminal justice attention on such activities.

In the text, Smart argued that women offenders were treated as being *doubly deviant* because they were perceived as having not only broken the law, but also as having transgressed their gender roles. Early research by Eaton (1986) found that female defendants in court were simultaneously located and understood as dependants within the family setting and also as being responsible for their own behaviour and for that of other family members. As Edwards (1984: 213) put it:

> Female defendants are processed within the criminal justice system in accordance with the crimes which they committed and the extent to which the commission of the act and its nature deviate from appropriate female behaviour.

Though making an enormously important contribution to the development of feminist scholarship in this area, Smart has been generally sceptical about elements of the project, particularly more recent attempts to develop a policy-oriented and pragmatic 'feminist criminology':

> The problem which faces criminology is not insignificant, however, and, arguably, its dilemma is even more fundamental than that facing sociology. The whole *raison d'être* of criminology is that it addresses crime. It categorises a vast range of activities and treats them as if they were all subject to the same laws – whether laws of human behaviour, genetic inheritance,

Women, Crime and Criminology

Carol Smart's 1976 book is one of the most important contributions to feminist scholarship in this area. The book began life as a Master's dissertation and it was at this time that Smart says she 'became aware of the overwhelming lack of interest in female criminality displayed by established criminologists and deviancy theorists' (1976: *xiii*).

In the book Smart discusses the nature of female offending and examines classical and modern criminological work. Existing work, where it considers women at all, is generally inadequate and may be divided into two main categories: those that make an explicit reference to female criminality and those in which it remains implicit. Women generally remain invisible within criminology, she suggests, and, more particularly, their victimization is especially ignored.

The silence around women's victimization raises the question, she suggests, 'whether the victims of these offences being women has influenced the criminologist's or sociologist's interest, especially where the majority are male' (1976: 180). Not only is it vital for there to be more research on female criminality, Smart argued, but that such research should be situated in the broader moral, political, economic and sexual spheres which influence women's position in society.

If criminology and the sociology of deviance are truly to play a significant role in the development of our understanding of crime, Smart concludes, then they must 'become more than the study of men and crime' (1976: 185).

economic rationality, development or the like. The argument within criminology has always been between those who give primacy to one form of explanation rather than another. The thing that criminology cannot do is deconstruct crime. It cannot locate rape or child sexual abuse in the domain of sexuality, nor theft in the domain of economic activity, nor drug use in the domain of health, to do so would be to abandon criminology to sociology, but more important it would involve abandoning an idea of a unified problem which requires a unified response – at least at the theoretical level. (1990: 77)

Smart's questioning of the criminological enterprise stimulated a considerable debate within feminism (Edwards, 1981; Heidensohn, 1985; Rafter and Stanko, 1980; Young, 1996). Pat Carlen (1992: 53) described the idea of feminist criminology as neither 'desirable nor possible' but, as we will see, still considered it possible for feminists to study 'women and crime'. Gelsthorpe and Morris (1990: 2) suggested that criminology 'has for many feminist writers and researchers been a constraining rather than a constructive and creative influence'. Maureen Cain (1989: 3), another long-standing critic of the limitations of the traditional criminological project, argued that:

Crimes, criminals, victims, courts, police officers, lawyers, social workers may be objects of investigation, but our explanations must reach beyond and encompass all of them, as life histories and the victim studies, the continuity studies and the ideology studies already strain to do. I am arguing that, in a sense, feminist criminology is impossible; that feminist *criminology* disrupts the categories of criminology itself.

Cain's argument was that work in this arena should question the assumptions of traditional criminology and, in particular, should seek to examine how gender is constructed by official bodies and also more broadly within social life. Despite the scepticism voiced in the quote above, Cain (1989) was by no means entirely dismissive of a feminist criminology. Carlen (1992), though similarly sceptical, nonetheless defended the potential within feminist scholarship to transcend the existing limitations of the discipline of criminology as it was currently constituted.

The left realist response to Smart's critique of the criminological enterprise is to suggest that it leads to 'infinite regress'. If deconstruction is the key, when does one stop? Everything eventually disappears because it is argued to have no essence. More particularly, they suggest that the critique is inconsistent, on the one hand criticising criminology for its *essentialism* in treating crime as if it were a meaningful category, and on the other using terms like *rape* and *child sexual abuse* as they too could not be subject to the same criticism (Matthews and Young, 1992). The deconstructionist impulse, and the antipathy toward grand theory displayed in the radical feminist critique 'too easily lead towards nihilism, cynicism and conservatism', they argue (1992: 13).

Nevertheless, as we saw in Chapter 13, feminist criminology had an important impact on left realism and the perspectives are in many ways much more compatible than the 'debate' between Smart and Matthews and Young might imply. In part, the existence of disagreement is more a reflection of the fact that there is no single feminist criminology (Gelsthorpe, 1988). Rather, there are a number of different forms of feminist scholarship that can be identified within recent criminology, and although there have been a number of attempts to categorise these (see, for example, Harding, 1987), such is the wealth of scholarship available now that it is debatable whether such distinctions are especially helpful.

> ### Review questions
>
> 1. What did Lombroso and Ferrero suggest were the major indications of the 'extreme perversity' of the female born criminal?
>
> 2. What is the 'emancipation thesis'?
>
> 3. What was Carol Smart's major criticism of the idea of a feminist criminology?

Contemporary feminist criminology

Rather than reworking existing criminological theories in ways which incorporate consideration of female offending, a substantial strand of feminist scholarship has focused on the development of new theoretical tools and on the utilisation of particular methodological approaches. Leonard (1982: *xi–xii*) describes it as follows:

> Initially I thought it might be possible simply to add what had been overlooked, and to elaborate an analysis of women in terms of existing theory. I quickly discovered that this is impossible. Theoretical criminology was constructed by men, about men. It is simply not up to the analytical task of explaining female patterns of crime. Although some theories work better than others, they all illustrate what social scientists are slowly recognizing within criminology and outside the field: that our theories are not the general explanations of human behaviour they claim to be, but rather particular understandings of male behaviour. A single theoretical canopy has been assumed for men and women, although their social realities are extremely diverse. (quoted in Valier, 2002: 132)

A range of feminist responses has begun to fill this void. Daly (1997) identifies three modes of conceptualising sex/gender in feminist theory, and the implications of each for criminology. The three she identifies as: 'class-race-gender', 'doing gender' and 'sexed bodies'.

Class-race-gender has also been referred to as 'multiple inequalities'. This perspective, Daly says, conceptualises inequalities as intersecting, interlocking and contingent matters, rather than as being discrete or separate. Despite the terminology, such approaches are not restricted to the main inequalities of class, race and gender, but also incorporate age, sexuality and physical ability/disability. Attempting to show how multiple inequalities work has resulted in the utilisation of particular methods, such as literary and story-telling forms. The relevance and contribution of this perspective to criminology 'is an insistence that everyone is located in a matrix of multiple social relations', i.e. that race and gender are just as relevant to an analysis of white men as they are to black women. With an emphasis on contingency, one can explore the varied positions of 'black women' – as offenders, victims and mothers and wives of offenders and victims – to 'white justice' (1997: 35; and see Johnson, 2003).

The second mode is what she refers to as 'doing gender', a phrase taken from West and Zimmerman in which gender is conceived not as the property of individuals, but as:

> An emergent feature of social situations ... an outcome of and a rationale for ... social arrangements ... a means of legitimating [a] fundamental division ... of society. [Gender is] a routine, methodical, and recurring accomplishment ... not a set of traits, nor a variable, nor a role [but] itself constituted through interaction. (quoted in Daly, 1997: 36)

Such a view has been an important influence on feminist writing and, more recently, has particularly informed the growing body of work on 'masculinity' (Newburn and Stanko, 1994). As the quote suggests, in this view gender is viewed as a social accomplishment – something constructed and attained in particular social settings. As such, crime, like other activities, may be viewed as a practice or set of practices through which particular articulations of gender – particular styles of masculinity or femininity – are 'done'. One of the difficulties that authors such as Messerschmidt (1993) who work in this tradition encounter 'is how to conceptualize crime as a gendered line of action without once again establishing boys and men as the norm, differentiating themselves from all that is "feminine"' (Daly, 1997: 37).

The third mode Daly identifies is what she refers to as 'sexed bodies'. This is work which builds on Foucault's analysis of the body as a site of 'disciplinary practices' (see Chapter 22) together with feminist work which seeks to acknowledge sex differences whilst avoiding biological essentialism (that these sex differences *determine* gendered differences in behaviour, status and similar). What is the relevance of this position to criminology? Building on work by Katz (1988), Daly (1997: 40) argues that it enables us, among other things, to:

> ... explore how the 'sensual attractions' of crime are differently available and 'experienced' by male/female bodies and masculine/feminine subjectivities. We could analyse the variable production of sexed (and racialized, etc.) bodies across many types of harms (not just rape) or for other sites of legal regulation such as family law. We could take Howe's (1994) theoretical lead by investigating women's bodies as the object of penality.

Crucially, she says, such a perspective allows that the allegedly gender-neutral penal policies and practices are tied to specific male bodies. The danger of such a perspective lies in the prominence given to sex differences, and the possibility that these may come to dominate other aspects of social life and practice.

Understanding women's involvement in crime

Given the failures of traditional criminology in this area, it can be of little surprise that a substantial element in feminist criminology has involved attempts to understand the nature of female offending and, linked with this, the treatment of women within the criminal justice process. In particular, feminist work has been concerned to examine what has variously come to be called 'the gender gap' or the 'sex–crime ratio': the generally higher levels of offending among men. We look in greater detail at the empirical research in these areas in Chapter 32. Here we look more briefly at some of the key theoretical developments of recent decades. By the late 1980s, Frances Heidensohn (1987) was able to examine the growing body of research and identify four characteristics of many of the female offenders that had been the subject of recent research. These were:

- *Economic rationality* – In contrast to earlier portrayals, such as those of Lombroso, Pollak and others, which took female criminality to be illustrative of irrationality and the influence of biology, feminist research had produced considerable evidence that women offenders were predominantly involved in property crimes and were motivated by economic concerns.

- *Heterogeneity of their offences* – 'Women commit fewer crimes than men, are less likely to be recidivists or professional criminals and contribute very little to the tariff of serious violent crime' (Heidensohn, 1987: 19). Moreover, the differences between male and female offending derive not from the innate characteristics of men and women, but from social circumstances, differing opportunities, the socialisation process and the differential impact of informal and formal social control.

- *Fear and impact of deviant stigma* – The process of criminalisation has a differential impact on men and women, producing a greater sense of what Goffman (1968) called 'spoiled identity' among female offenders. The fact that female offending is considerably less extensive than male offending, together with the generally more sensational treatment it receives by public authorities and especially the media, produces a greater sense of stigmatisation.

- *The experience of double deviance and double jeopardy* – The experience, highlighted earlier, of being damned for being criminal, and doubly damned for behaving 'unlike a woman'. Such double deviance produces the potential for double jeopardy – excessive intervention by the criminal justice system which not only punishes the crime but, often justified in paternalistic terms, seeks also to impose particular controls over women's behaviour, together with the potential for additional informal sanctions from family and community (Heidensohn, 2006).

So, where are we left in attempting to understand female offending? As we have seen, much critical feminist scholarship has emphasised the role of patriarchy (Edwards, 1984) in explaining the role of criminal justice in women's oppression, and the importance of women's economic marginalisation (Carlen, 1985) in making sense of why some women make the decisions that they do (and see recent work by Hansen, 2006).

More recently it is perhaps control theory that has proved to have the greatest resonance for some feminist scholars. With its emphasis on conformity rather than deviance, control theory offers possibilities for understanding the lower levels of female offending compared with male offending, together with the specific nature of female offending. Heidensohn (1996: 199) argues that 'If we start from the broader issues of conformity and control and observe and analyse how these affect *all* women to some degree and *some* groups of women

Frances Heidensohn, a pioneer in feminist perspectives in criminology. In 2004, she won the Sellin Glueck Award of the American Society of Criminology for contributions to international criminology.

more than others, we can then learn rather more about those who become involved in crime as compared with other kinds of activities which might be available to them.'

In essence, her position rests on the argument that it is crucial to understand the varied and multiple ways in which women's lives are ordered and controlled. From this point of view it becomes important to acknowledge the varied and often subtle ways in which women's lives are subjected to high levels of informal social control (Feeley and Little, 1991). Female roles and behaviour are fundamentally shaped, she argues, at four levels:

- *The home* – There is a considerable sociological literature (e.g. Gavron, 1966) detailing the multiple ways in which women's lives are constrained in the private, domestic world of the home.

- *In public* – Here Heidensohn suggests that there are three separate, but linked, aspects to the control of women's behaviour:

  - the male quasi-monopoly of force and violence – note the very high (relative) levels of fear reported by women in relation to physical attack and sexual violence in particular;

- the notion of reputation and 'name' – the ways traditionally girls and women have been 'kept in their place' through male control over reputation;

- the ideology of separate spheres – the notion that men and women operate in different ways in the public and private realms and are subject to different rules.

● *At work* – Again Heidensohn notes three ways in which the normative constraints on women are either greater or different from those on men:

- most women have to cope with both home and work;

- the bulk of supervisors of women's work are male;

- women have to deal with sexual harassment at work.

● *In social policies* – A range of social policies – not least welfare benefits – have traditionally been organised in ways which reinforce women's roles.

The essence of Heidensohn's argument, therefore, is that in these many ways we can begin to understand the highly constrained and controlled environments that women have generally inhabited in modern society, and that this should be helpful to us in understanding their (more limited) offending behaviour. Moreover, they 'face distinctively different opportunity situations and ... an additional series of controls' (1996: 198). Thus, the predominance of property offending in female crime is likely related, she argues, to women's general powerlessness and economic marginality.

One further question raised by such an analysis concerns how such controls are to be understood normatively: i.e. whether they should be perceived as benign or malign. In this regard, Carlen (1995) is clear that there is much here that is far from benign, and argues consequently that a more appropriate term to capture such processes might be 'anti-social control':

> ... a variety of malign institutionalized practices that may either set limits to individual action by favouring one set of citizens at the expense of another so as to subvert equal opportunities ideologies in relation to gender, race and class (or other social groupings); or (in societies without equal opportunities ideologies) set limits to individual action in ways that are anti-social because they atrophy an individual's social contribution and do so on the grounds of either biological attributes or exploitative social relations. (Carlen and Worrall, 2004: 122)

Women, prison and punishment

The body (or soul) upon which punishment is inflicted is gendered and, yet, as Carlen (2002) has noted, it is relatively rare within criminology that the words 'women' and 'punishment' are brought together. The reason for this, she suggests, is in part a product of a more general need to deny or repress knowledge about the social inequalities between those that impose punishment and those upon whom it is imposed. In addition, however, there are a number of more specific reasons:

● Women commit fewer crimes than men and commit fewer serious crimes than men. Consequently, 'the nightmarish and murderous felon in the shadows has not traditionally lurked in female form' (2002: 4).

● One result of this is that, traditionally, women have tended to be controlled through informal rather than formal means.

● When women are prosecuted there has been a tendency not to view them, simply, as criminal and rather to see them as mad or as subject to forces beyond their control (Zedner, 1991).

● Finally, Carlen (2002) argues that connecting women with punishment has potential sexual or pornographic connotations and that this has served to inhibit discourse in this area.

From the outset therefore feminist penology was grappling with a set of difficult problems. As a consequence, there is a number of questions which have become central to this area. They begin with the core question of whether women are treated differently from men in the penal sphere and, if so, in what ways? Relatedly, feminist scholarship also asks whether women *should* be treated differently. In relation to imprisonment, feminist writers inquire as to its purpose, why it takes the forms that it does and whether, in most cases, it is an appropriate setting for female offenders.

The nature of women's imprisonment

Carlen and Worrall (2004) identify four themes which, they argue, are central to answering the question, 'why do women's prisons take the forms they do?'

● *Prisonisation* – An idea with a long history in the study of imprisonment, which suggests that inmates take on a set of behaviours and values that reflect the culture of the institution (Sykes, 1958). Feminist work has identified a number of problems particular to women's imprisonment, notably that prisons and prison systems are

Holloway prison in London, perhaps the best-known women's prison in the UK, as it is today. Completed in 1985, it replaced the original Victorian prison where suffragettes were imprisoned and Ruth Ellis was hanged.

usually organised in relation to men's needs and are often very poorly equipped to deal with the often very different needs of female prisoners. Moreover, feminist work suggests that female prisoners are more adversely affected by the separation brought about by imprisonment. In relation to 'prisonisation', studies have tended to focus on how women adapt to the experience of imprisonment and to what extent their behaviour 'inside' is a product of the nature of the regime and the culture of the prison itself.

- *Discrimination* – Focusing on the way in which female prisoners are treated differently from male prisoners, 'though not usually in ways which have been to their advantage' (Carlen and Worrall, 2004: 82; see also Zedner, 1991). In this connection they quote an historical study by Rafter looking at women's imprisonment in nineteenth and early-twentieth century America, in which she noted that:

> The custodial model was a masculine model: derived from men's prisons, it adopted their characteristics – retributive purpose, high-security architecture, a male-dominated authority structure, programmes that stressed earnings and harsh discipline ... women's custodial institutions treated women like men. (Rafter, 1985: 21)

As Carlen (1983) and others have noted elsewhere, although women may be treated somewhat as if they are men, their experience of imprisonment is generally different from men's:

- They tend to be imprisoned at greater distances from home than male prisoners (because of the smaller number of women's prisons).

- The nature and range of regimes tends to be more restricted (for the same reason).

- Women prisoners tend to suffer greater social stigma than men – largely as a result of being perceived as being doubly deviant.

- *Resistance* – In contrast to the idea of prisonisation, one theme in feminist work on women's imprisonment has explored and stressed ways in which women can and do resist aspects of the experience of imprisonment, including using femininity as a tool (Bosworth, 1999) and in developing vibrant, highly-organised inmate cultures (Barton, 2005; Denton, 2001).

- *Carceral clawback* – A term coined by Pat Carlen (2002; 2004) to capture the ideological project engaged in within prison systems to promote the idea that prisoners *need* to be kept inside. Without this, prisons lose one, if not the, central reason for their continued existence. The consequence of this ideological project is that reform programmes which challenge prison security and traditional prison functioning tend to be modified, reformed or even suppressed. This is one of the key barriers to the development of regimes that are better suited to women's needs (Hannah-Moffat, 2002; Hayman, 2006).

The criminalisation of women

As we have seen, feminist scholars have been concerned with why women are criminalised less than men. Beyond the straightforward empirical observation that women commit less crime than men (which we explore in greater detail in Chapter 32), one consistent line of argument has focused around how women are 'constructed' and 'presented' within criminal justice. In particular, a number of authors have argued that one element of the criminal justice process involves rendering female offenders harmless by (re)locating them within traditional gendered roles:

> The female lawbreaker is routinely offered the opportunity to neutralise the effects of her law-breaking activity by implicitly entering into a contract whereby she permits her life to be represented primarily in terms of its domestic, sexual and pathological dimensions. The effect of this 'gender contract' is to strip her lawbreaking of its social, economic and ideological dimensions in order to minimise its punitive consequences. (Worrall, 1990: 31)

One consistent theme running through many of the chapters in this book concerns the growing punitiveness visible at the end of the twentieth century and the beginning of the twenty-first. Arguably, this has affected women at least as much, if not more, than men (see Chapter 32). Worrall (2002) argues that the politicisation of crime control, and the emergence of new forms of actuarial justice (the new penology – see Chapter 16), have seen what she refers to as a 'search for equivalence' in relation to female offending. Such equivalence blurs or ignores the differences between men and women (and male and female offenders) and serves to make women punishable, and requiring of punishment. 'The political and moral justification for such punishment is that either more women are committing punishable acts or more women are being *discovered* committing punishable acts' (Worrall, 2002: 48). One consequence of this, Worrall argues, has been a retreat from the medicalisation, welfarisation, sexualisation and domestication that has traditionally characterised responses to much women's offending.

A feminist methodology?

Much feminist scholarship, especially from the 1980s onward, was particularly critical of aspects of traditional, mainstream criminology's approach to inquiry (Stanley and Wise, 1979; Cain, 1986). By contrast, feminist work promoted appreciative, generally qualitative methodologies (Gelsthorpe, 1990) and was highly critical of claims to objectivity and neutrality (Kelly, 1978). In large part, this reflected the fact that much feminist writing was located – indeed, often deeply embedded in – practical, political campaigning activity (Stanko, 1990). More recently, Chesney-Lind (1997) has written of the importance of seeing female offenders as 'people with life histories' (Gelsthorpe, 2002). A recent edited collection on gender and justice (Heidensohn, 2006) illustrates that contemporary scholarship in this area is still predominantly characterised by qualitative research methods, though by no means exclusively so (also see Oakley, 2000).

Gelsthorpe (1990) identifies four major themes in debate around the nature of feminist methodology:

- *Choice of topic* – This, Gelsthope suggests, has generally meant selecting objects of study that are linked to women's oppression and, in particular, seeking to identify topics of political and practical importance that have the potential to contribute to ending that oppression. Within this context one area of debate has concerned the extent to which it is appropriate for men to be involved in the enterprise (Stanley and Wise, 1983; Cain, 1986).

- *Process* – Also, in particular, the strengths and weaknesses of quantitative and qualitative approaches to research (see Chapter 35) has been debated. As suggested above, there has been a consistent view put forward that qualitative methods are in many respects best suited to feminist research studies. It is not quantitative methods *per se* that Gelsthorpe (1990: 91) says are the problem, but 'insensitive quantification'.

- *Power and control* – Here the focus is on the nature of the relationship between the researcher and those they are researching. Gelsthorpe quotes Stanley and Wise's (1983: 170) observation that the traditional relationship 'is obscene because it treats people as mere objects, there for the researcher to do research "on". Treating people as objects – sex objects or research objects – is morally unjustifiable'. One consequence of this has been to attempt to engage the subjects of research more fully in the project itself (Ramazanoglu and Holland, 2002).

- *The subjective experiences of doing research –* Feminist researchers have been concerned to attempt to record elements of the research experience, to be open about what is involved, and emphasising the personal aspects of research. Again, as with the three other themes, this arises from the importance of personal experience to all aspects of research, captured in McRobbie's (1982: 52) observation that 'Feminism forces us to locate our own autobiographies and our experience inside the questions we might ask'.

Although work in this area has given rise to a number of potentially contentious debates – in particular around how feminist criminology should be conducted, and who should do it – Heidensohn and Gelsthorpe (2007: 385) in their recent review of the area conclude that a close reading reveals 'no fixed "absolutes" beyond the need for sensitivity in the research task, for personal reflexivity – to reflect on the subjectivities of all involved – and commitment to make the research relevant to women'.

Feminist victimology

One very important strand of feminist scholarship has been what might be called feminist victimology (this is also explored in Chapters 17 and 32). The focus of this work is on uncovering, assessing and responding to the victimization of women and, in particular, men's violence against women. Historically, relatively little attention had been paid to rape, sexual assault and to domestic violence. The private world of the family, and the behaviour of men within it, was subject to little critical scrutiny. Moreover, there was tacit acceptance of much male violence against women and a range of justifications or rationalisations for such behaviour.

From the 1970s onwards there was a substantial growth in work – both practical and intellectual – in these areas. Campaigning around, and research on, domestic violence (Dobash and Dobash, 1979), and violence against women more generally (Hanmer *et al.*, 1989) began significantly to challenge many mainstream (sometimes referred to as 'malestream') ideas in criminology. Feminist work in this area had a number of themes and objectives:

- Making visible forms of victimization that hitherto had been largely ignored.
- Illustrating the extent to which violence against women was primarily an issue of men's violence against women.

- Illustrating that whilst popular representations highlight the idea of 'stranger danger', in practice women have been most at risk 'within the home'. As Stanko (1990: 6–7) put it:

  While other criminological works concern themselves only with the potential threat posed by strangers outside the home, I do not assume that the home is safe. The place where people are supposed to find solace from the perils of the outside world should not be presumed to provide a respite from interpersonal violence. For far too many, menace lurks there as well. The prevalence of battering among women's experiences of intimate relationships with men, the growing awareness amongst adult women of potential and actual sexual danger from male intimates, acquaintances and friends, and the memories of adults of physical and sexual abuse during their childhoods shatter the illusion of the safe home.

- Arguing that sexual violence by men against women was not primarily an issue of sex, but one of power (Daly and Chesney-Lind, 1988).

- Illustrating the ways in which the criminal justice system failed to respond appropriately to women's victimization and how this was frequently the result of the male-dominated and oriented nature of the system, and the stereotyped views of women that structured the working of the major agencies such as the police and the courts.

- Identifying aspects of secondary victimization – the negative consequences of the criminal justice process for women complainants, often experienced as further victimization (Stanko, 1985).

Assessing feminist criminology

It is impossible to deny that feminist scholarship has had anything but an important impact on criminological thought in recent decades. As a consequence of its impact it is no longer the case that criminology is gender blind – though some critics might quite reasonably claim that it continues to be dominated by discussion of male offending and by theories that are more concerned with men than women. Carlen and Worrall (1987: 9) have argued that a focus on gender has had three crucial consequences for criminology:

1 It has called into question previous theories of law-breaking and/or criminalisation.

2 It has suggested new lines of investigation for empirical research programmes.

3 It has either provoked new uses for old concepts, or has displaced old theories with new ones.

Feminist scholarship had an important impact in refocusing elements of criminological attention on the impact of the criminal justice system (Heidensohn, 1968). Examining the ways in which the police, the courts and the prisons dealt with women, such work argued that there were numerous structural disadvantages faced by women – in contrast to the oft-held assumption that, in fact, the criminal justice system tended to treat women more leniently (an assumption that one can still hear repeated regularly – for assessments of the arguments see Hedderman and Hough, 1994; Hedderman, 2004).

In terms of its more particular impact, Downes and Rock argue that the 'study of victimization constitutes the sole area in which gender has transformed research' (Downes and Rock, 2007: 265). They go on to argue, nevertheless, that there are four substantive areas where feminist scholarship has led to significant work:

1 Mounting a significant challenge to the 'female emancipation leads to crime' debate.

2 Challenging and undermining the hypothesis that women are treated more leniently than men by the criminal justice system.

3 The development of a gender-based theory of both male and female delinquency focusing on differential or segregative social control systems.

4 The raising to greater prominence of the female victim and, indeed, of the plight of victims generally – male or female. As Chesney-Lind (2006: 7) remarks: 'the naming of the types and dimensions of female victimization had a significant impact on public policy, and it is arguably the most tangible accomplishment of both feminist criminology and grassroots feminists concerned about gender, crime, and justice.'

Intriguingly, one of the more recent areas that has developed from the insights derived from feminist scholarship is that which has led a number of criminologists to focus on ideas of 'maleness'. This is a relatively recent development and traditional criminology has tended to ignore the issue of masculinity, leading Heidensohn (1987: 23) to refer to this as the 'lean-to' approach to gender and deviance in which:

> Gender is no longer ignored ... but it is consigned to an outhouse, beyond the main structure of the work and is almost invariably conflated with *women*; males are not seen as having gender; or if their masculinity does become an issue, it is taken-for-granted and not treated as problematic.

In fact, as Renzetti (1993: 232) has observed, 'the goal of feminism is not to push men out so as to bring women in, but rather to gender the study of crime'. Underpinning much work on masculinity is the idea that much extant criminology has tended to treat men in a somewhat stereotypical and uni-dimensional form – as if there were only one way of *being* male. Borrowing from Connell (1987), Messerschmidt (1993) focuses on the way in which men are socialised into a form of 'hegemonic masculinity'. This term, utilising Gramsci's notion of 'hegemony' (see Chapter 12), has proved something of a mixed blessing in relation to understanding maleness and crime. At heart, it picks up the idea that there are certain core attributes – toughness and other forms of physical prowess, authority, heterosexuality, competitiveness – which are associated with a dominant model of how to be a man. Such hegemonic masculinity is contrasted with 'subordinated masculinities' (associated with other ways of being male such as being bi-sexual or gay) and with femininity.

Certainly, early usage of the idea of hegemonic masculinity added little to the existing literature on male offenders, doing little other than identifying characteristics that had long been associated with young, particularly working-class males (Willis, 1977). Moreover, in some of the literature the links between 'doing masculinity' and crime were far from clear. One attempt at clarification, by Messerschmidt (1993), argued that deviance is a core method by which men who experience goal blockages use to communicate their masculinity. There is no single method of achieving this, but many, mediated by race and class, that have differing effects on offending behaviour. At one extreme, therefore, domestic violence is a 'resource for affirming "maleness"' (1993: 173). In an echo of strain theory, he argues that such offending will be more common about lower-class males because of the problems they face in securing the necessary resources for constructing their masculinity.

The concept of 'hegemonic masculinity' was criticised on a number of accounts:

- *Essentialism* – Under-emphasising the fluid, contested and changing nature of masculinity (Hearn, 1996).

- *Inconsistency* – What does hegemonic masculinity actually mean? Is it an ideal-type, not found in reality, or is it an attempt to identity the attributes of particular types of men, or men in certain situations or positions – 'Is it John Wayne or Leonardo DiCaprio; Mike Tyson or Pelé?' (Connell and Messerschmidt, 2005: 838).

- *Emphasising the negative* – Treatments of hegemonic masculinity, especially within criminology, have tended to focus on negative male attributes rather than positive ones (Collier, 1998).

Connell and Messerschmidt (2005) have responded to these and other criticisms. They argue for the retention and reformulation of the concept. They defend the idea that there exists both a plurality and a hierarchy of masculinities, and they suggest it is important to emphasise that the 'hegemonic' form of masculinity need not be the commonest pattern of masculinity, its characteristics being established through exemplars such as sports and pop stars. Despite some far-reaching criticisms of both the theory and its application (see also Hood-Williams, 2001), the sense persists that the study of masculinities has potential explanatory power within the field of criminology even if, as yet, this potential remains some distance from realisation.

Feminist writing has had an impact, therefore, on our understanding of women's offending, their victimization – particularly at the hands of men – and their treatment by the criminal justice system. Feminist emphasis on the idea of 'doing gender' has also given rise to a growing concern with masculinities and how such a notion might be linked to the ways in which we understand and research male offending. Although feminist scholarship has undoubtedly fallen far short of the impact on criminology that many of its most important advocates would wish (Smart, 1990; Heidensohn, 1996), and criminology remains male-dominated and male-oriented, it is important not to underestimate the ways in which feminism resonates through criminological work. It can be seen in criminological theory, in the nature and style of criminological methods, and in all the major policy debates of the moment. Nevertheless, in attempting to wield *influence* (changing the nature of the enterprise), there is the constant danger of *incorporation* (simply becoming absorbed into the mainstream – or 'malestream'). No doubt this is the balancing act that feminist criminologists will continue to confront for the foreseeable future.

Review questions

1 What does Carlen mean by the term 'carceral clawback'?

2 What are the main characteristics of a feminist methodology?

3 What have been the major impacts of feminism in the area of victimology?

4 What is meant by 'hegemonic masculinity'?

Questions for further discussion

1 Is a 'feminist criminology' possible?

2 Do we need to consider biology at all when discussing women and crime?

3 What has been the main impact of feminism on criminology?

4 If feminist criminology began 'as a reaction', is it more than that now?

5 Is it true to say that mainstream criminology had nothing of interest to say about female offenders and offending (prior to the second wave of feminism in the 1970s onward)?

Further reading

Heidensohn, F. and Gelsthorpe, L. (2007) Gender and crime, in Maguire, M. *et al.* (eds) *The Oxford Handbook of Criminology*, 4th edn, Oxford: Oxford University Press

Heidensohn, F. (1996) *Women and Crime*, 2nd edn, Basingstoke: Macmillan (esp. ch. 8–10)

Miller, J. (2000) Feminist theories of women's crime: Robbery as a case study, in Simpson, S. (ed.) *Of Crime and Criminality*, Thousand Oaks, CA: Pine Forge Press

Smart, C. (1990) Feminist approaches to criminology or postmodern woman meets atavistic man, in Morris, A. and Gelsthorpe, L. (eds) *Feminist Perspectives in Criminology*, Milton Keynes: Open University Press, (abridged in McLaughlin, E. *et al.* [eds] *Criminological Perspectives*)

Walklate, S. (2004) *Gender, Crime and Criminal Justice*, 2nd edn, Cullompton: Willan

There is also a relatively new journal, *Feminist Criminology* (London: Sage Journals), which is well worth consulting.

Websites

There are a number of campaigning organisations which maintain good websites that contain a lot of useful information and campaigning material. They include:

Justice for Women website: http: //www.jfw.org.uk/
The Fawcett Society: www.fawcettsociety.org.uk

Rights of Women: www.rightsofwomen.org.uk
Griffins Society: www.thegriffinssociety.org

There is a multidisciplinary Feminist Crime Research Network with a sizeable website: http: //www.perc. plymouth.ac.uk/solon/fcrn/

Chapter outline

The transition to late modernity   320
  Surveillance   320
  Changes in property relations   321
  A new regulatory state?   322

Foucault and governmentality   323
  Discipline and Punish   324
  Governmentality theory   325
  The dispersal of discipline   327
  The discipline of Disney World   328

Risk and the new culture of control   329
  Garland and the Culture of Control   330
  Risk, crime and criminal justice   333

Assessing governmentality, the new penology and risk   334
  Governmentality   336
  The new penology   336
  Risk   337

Questions for further discussion   338
Further reading   338
Websites   338

Late modernity, governmentality and risk

CHAPTER SUMMARY

The world appears to be changing remarkably quickly. Terms such as *postmodernity* and *globalisation* (and a host of others) have risen to prominence in the search for means of capturing these changes. Each focuses on different aspects of the shift from one stage of history – *modernity* – to another. The sociologist Zygmunt Bauman describes the nature of this change by suggesting that in comparison with the relatively 'solid state' of the modern era, we are now living in an age of *liquid modernity*.

In this chapter we explore:

- some of the ways in which criminological theory has focused upon such shifts;

- how the changing nature of criminal justice and penality is understood.

The transition to late modernity

Central to the many accounts of the changing nature of the contemporary, developed world is the idea that the nation state is somehow being undermined by a combination of globalising and localising forces. As the nation state is generally understood to be one of the defining features of modern times, such a fundamental transition represents, some argue, evidence of a shift into a qualitatively new historical era. Much of this is to do with the changing nature of capital and business, which have been progressively internationalised or transnationalised, and which increasingly lie beyond the control of individual nation states.

It is not just global, but also local pressures which are important in this regard. This is captured well by David Harvey (1989: 271) who has argued that 'the free flow of capital across the surface of the globe ... places strong emphasis upon the peculiar qualities of the spaces to which that capital might be attracted. The shrinkage of space that brings diverse communities across the globe into competition with each other implies localised competitive strategies and a heightened sense of awareness of what makes a place special and gives it a competitive advantage'. The consequence of these dual processes of globalisation and localisation, some argue, is to 'hollow out' the state from two directions.

Surveillance

A second feature of this 'new' modernity is the globalisation of surveillance. The new technologies of communication extend surveillance far beyond the borders of nation states. According to theorists like Daniel Bell (1973) and Anthony Giddens (1990) these new information technologies have the consequence of 'foreshortening time'. This, together with the impact that communication and transport developments have on distance, means that we are increasingly joined together with people previously considered far distant.

These changes have led some theorists to describe the rise of what they call the 'information society' (Bell, 1973). More recently, Manuel Castells (1996) has expanded this idea into a broader thesis about the ways in which information, people, symbols, money, goods and so on move across borders under conditions of globalisation. What he refers to as the 'network society' is characterised by networks and 'flows' which alter the nature of spaces and places in relation to each other. Such ideas are quite closely linked to another school of thought, in this case one focused on processes of production, called 'post-Fordism' (Jessop, 1995). At heart, such ideas contrast traditional forms of mass production (Fordism) with new, more flexible forms and means of production that are not tied to particular geographical locations and which tend to involve smaller organisations using sophisticated new technologies. This is the basis of the new consumer society. For the criminologist, one of the important features of this is the progressive commodification of surveillance and security – the expanding market for goods and services sold to those who wish to buy protection of various forms (Jones and Newburn, 1998). The implications for how we live our lives in 'maximum surveillance society' (Norris and Armstrong, 1999b) are potentially far reaching:

The combination of digital photography, image recognition and matching software brings with it the very real prospect of a mass surveillance society – a society in which movements and interactions in public spaces are regularly monitored, recorded and logged. Maybe, therefore, public and civic life can no longer be viewed as carrying with it an expectation of anonymity. Every journey, meeting and encounter may now be officially recorded, stored and matched to other centrally held records – social security, health and criminal records, to name but a few. (Norris and Armstrong, 1999a: 93)

Changes in property relations

A further set of hugely important changes are connected with the nature of property and space. One very significant trend, picked up by Shearing and Stenning (1981) initially in the 1980s, is the increasing extent to which life is now lived in settings that are in large part manufactured. These spaces are neither straightforwardly 'public' (i.e. places to which we all have the right of access) nor 'private' (where access is very restricted). Rather, 'hybrid' spaces have emerged which are privately owned but where there is general and routine public access. These spaces, Shearing and Stenning refer to as 'mass private property'.

Shopping malls – the new giant out of town centres of consumption – are one prime example of such spaces. These are places that are almost exclusively privately-policed and often subtly controlled through careful design features. In part, these new areas have arisen as a consequence of the major changes affecting traditional urban centres (Shearing and Stenning, 1983). The decline of manufacturing brought about relatively rapid de-industrialisation of many urban areas. The social geography of the city has been transformed in many respects, therefore. All these changes potentially have far-reaching consequences for crime and social order. The negative aspects of such changes were captured most graphically by Mike Davis (1990) is his dystopian vision of contemporary Los Angeles:

> The American city … is being systematically turned inside out – or, rather, outside in. The valorized spaces of the new megastructures and super-malls are concentrated in the centre, street frontage is denuded, public activity is sorted into strictly functional compartments, and circulation is internalized in corridors under the gaze of private police. (1990: 226)

Garland and Sparks (2000) summarise the transition from modernity to late modernity in 'two intertwined transformative dynamics'. The first of these concerns five sets of social, economic and cultural changes:

1   Changes in the nature of production and consumption including the impact of globalisation on markets and the new insecurity of employment.

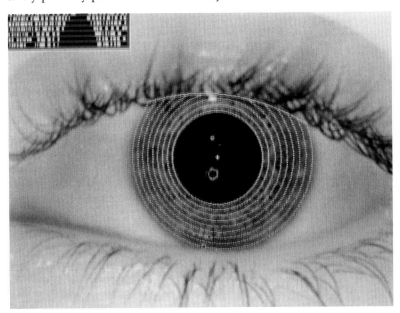

'Maximum surveillance society'? Surveillance technology in action. *Left*: Computer screen image of the iris of an eye being scanned as part of a computer recognition programme. *Right*: Multiple CCTV cameras record people walking down a street. The UK has more CCTV cameras per head of population than anywhere else in the world.

2 Changing nature of families and households including increasing female employment, rising divorce rates and so on.

3 Changes in social ecology, including to time and space as a result of transport and communications.

4 The social impact of the electronic mass media.

5 Democratisation in social life (declining deference and diminishing power ratios between men and women, social groups, etc.).

The second set of dynamics they identify concerns the changing nature of class relationships and, in the US in particular, of race relations. The rise of free-market economics, of cultural conservatism and what they call 'anti-welfare social policy', changed public perceptions of and discourses around both crime and welfare. In particular, the rebirth of the idea of an undeserving underclass, together with the emergence of new insecurities, progressively led high crime rates and related issues to be interpreted as problems of control rather than of welfare (see Chapter 13). Politicians come to talk about crime in a new, populist and emotional manner. No longer are criminal justice and penal policy matters that can be safely delegated to experts and officials. Rather, they have become a key political priority – one that can make or break political careers.

The transition to late modernity, it is argued, also has other profound consequences for the places and spaces within which we live. Thus, whilst we continue to make appeals to the idea of *community*, this is something whose moorings have loosened and which cannot be understood in any simple, fixed sense. Jock Young (2007: 195) suggests that the late modern community has the following eight features:

1 *Difference* – It is plural in terms of age, gender, class, ethnicity and other features.

2 *Fragmentation, cross-cutting and hybridisation* – Pluralism may lead to fragmentation, but it also produces new cross-cutting alliances and points of connection.

3 *Intensity* – This, too, is varied: some subcultures may be intense and concentrated; other parts of the 'community' may be withdrawn and atomised.

4 *Transience* – Subcultures are not fixed, they change in terms of their composition, intensity and coherence.

5 *Mediated* – The local is penetrated by the global and many activities cease to be defined by their location.

6 *Actuarial* – The absence of information and the lack of knowledge of others leads to a wariness and rise in calculative relationships.

7 *Internecine conflict* – This involves a wide variety of opinion, chaotic spread in wealth and status and widespread relative deprivation.

8 *Reinvention* – The history of communities is constantly reworked and reinvented.

A new regulatory state?

Many of the changes referred to above in connection with the 'coming of late modernity' rest upon what are held to be significant transformations in the nature and the operation of the nation state. This shift is captured by Braithwaite (2000) as involving a shift, initially from the 'Nightwatchman State' to the 'Keynsian State' and thence from that to the 'New Regulatory State'.

In summarising the differences between the forms of political order he uses Osborne and Gaebler's (1992) distinction between the activities of *steering* and *rowing*. In this formulation, steering refers to policy decisions and rowing refers to service delivery. Whereas previously governments had often attempted to play a significant role in both steering and rowing, under contemporary conditions the two sets of activities were increasingly being separated. Braithwaite's summary describes the change as shown in Figure 16.1.

It is important to bear in mind that these are ideal types – and are therefore not to be found in pure form. Nevertheless, in this model the Nightwatchman State is that pre-industrial model in which the general regulation of social life was undertaken locally within communities – prior to the introduction of the new police, for example (see Chapter 25). The nineteenth century sees the gradual emergence of the modern nation state and what Braithwaite calls the Keynesian State (after the economist Maynard Keynes) comes into being with the New Deal in America in the 1930s and the birth of the welfare state in Britain in the 1940s. Both involved a substantial expansion of the role and remit of the state:

> Under the ideology of the Keynesian State, the response to every outbreak of disorder was to increase central state policing resources. Social workers, probation officers and other welfare workers employed by the state also acquired ever more resources and powers under the same Keynesian disposition. (Braithwaite, 2000: 49)

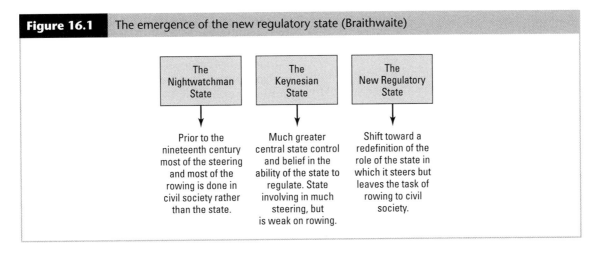

Figure 16.1   The emergence of the new regulatory state (Braithwaite)

The Nightwatchman State	The Keynesian State	The New Regulatory State
Prior to the nineteenth century most of the steering and most of the rowing is done in civil society rather than the state.	Much greater central state control and belief in the ability of the state to regulate. State involving in much steering, but is weak on rowing.	Shift toward a redefinition of the role of the state in which it steers but leaves the task of rowing to civil society.

The New Regulatory State comes into being with the emergence of the Reagan and Thatcher governments of the new right. A combination of privatisation and new forms of regulation emerged to set new limits to the role of the state, particularly in relation to rowing. Oftel, Ofgas, OfWat and many other organisations were established to regulate the privatised utilities and a raft of inspectorates, auditing bodies and ombudsmen have been created to oversee and govern the operation of matters that hitherto were largely within the remit of the Keynesian State. Such changes can also be witnessed within the criminal justice state, not least through the interlinked processes of privatisation and managerialism.

We will return to the subject of globalisation, and some of its defining features, in Chapter 34. Our focus here is on those criminological theories that take as their focus the changing nature of modernity, and what numerous social theorists have come to term 'late modernity'.

Foucault and governmentality

It was not until the late 1970s that the work of the French philosopher, Michel Foucault, began to influence British criminological theory (see also Chapter 22). Foucault's ideas attracted many seeking an alternative way of capturing the power of the state without recourse to Marxist views of the primacy of the economic sphere and the concentration of power in the hands of the few.

Foucault's view of power as being dispersed throughout state and civil society and through all relationships and, more particularly, his concern with discourse, provided a nuanced alternative to what, for some, increasingly felt rather rigid and ideological approaches to sociological analysis. In his early work, *Madness and Civilization*, Foucault (1989) argued that the emergence of mental institutions as a gradual replacement for prisons as the means of regulating the mentally ill actually involved an expansion of state power. That is, contrary to the line of argument that presented such processes as a largely civilising measure, according to Foucault this was, at least in part, an expression of a more subtle, nuanced and far-reaching form of social control.

Foucault's analysis of power in society shifts attention away from class relationships and the central importance of the ownership and control of capital, towards a model of power as a set of relationships which order, manage and facilitate as well as constrain and oppress. Valier (2002) suggests that Foucault's analysis of the relationship between power and knowledge rests on two related propositions:

- That without the exercise of power there is no knowledge.
- That similarly there is no power without knowledge.

His work was dominated by an analysis of the changing relationship between power and knowledge: a topic which is explored – as well as elsewhere – in what has probably become his most famous work, *Discipline and Punish*.

Discipline and Punish

In *Discipline and Punish* Foucault looks at the birth of the prison and the processes by which brutal systems of punishment focused on the infliction of pain on the body were gradually replaced by systems directed more toward the souls and minds of offenders. That said, the analysis could be extended to many other areas of life – the sphere of punishment simply happens to be the one Foucault used. However, as he noted (1979: 228), 'Is it surprising that prisons resemble factories, schools, barracks, hospitals, which all resemble prisons?'

Up until the 1700s (see Chapter 2), much punishment was inflicted in public, and involved considerable pain and terror. Executions were relatively common. Torture was used, as were various forms of humiliation. From the public hangings at Newgate, through the use of branding, whipping, the stocks and, from a contemporary perspective, other hugely cruel techniques, punishment of criminals in this period was focused upon the body, and was inflicted in such a manner as to involve public spectacle. Foucault's argument is that the function of punishment in this period was not deterrence – general or specific – but to illustrate the power of the state, or more precisely, the monarch. At this time in history, when the modern nation state was coming into being, control over the populace was exercised by illustrating that state power was absolute – it could be arbitrary and extreme, but in being so it could not be doubted.

Gradually, this arbitrary, cruel and public system of punishment came under a number of pressures. Far from being cowed by such spectacles, the crowds that gathered at executions became more and more boisterous. Protests at the inconsistencies of punishment began to grow. Spectacular punishment, focused on the body, gradually gave way to the prison. Punishment happened behind closed doors and was increasingly bureaucratic in its operation. Foucault famously illustrates this dramatic change with two examples: the execution in 1757 of Damiens the regicide (who was hanged, drawn and quartered in the most brutal fashion) and the highly bureaucratic system of discipline shown in a timetable from 1838 (for details of both see Chapter 22).

Although less than a century separates these two examples the contrast appears clear. Brutal and public forms of punishment have been replaced by private and apparently more civilised forms of regulation. Foucault describes this as a shift from a corporal to a carceral system of discipline. In considering this history there are a number of temptations we should resist, Foucault suggests. One, already alluded to, is the temptation to see this as somehow a simple illustration of growing civilisation – the straightforward development of more humane forms of punishment. Rather, this new form of punishment – what Foucault refers to as 'discipline' – based around surveillance, uses a variety of subtle techniques to control and manage the offender in ever more finely graded ways. Rather than occasional bursts of (by today's standards) quite horrific forms of bodily punishment, the system that replaces aims to control and regulate at all times.

The second mistake we must avoid concerns the assumption that it was our growing knowledge of the nature of delinquency that led to the creation and elaboration of imprisonment as a means of punishment. Rather, he suggests, we should recognise that the *invention* of delinquency and the birth of the prison are part and parcel of the same process:

> The penitentiary technique and the delinquent are in a sense twin brothers. It is not true that it was the discovery of the delinquent through a scientific rationality that introduced into our old prisons the refinement of penitentiary techniques. Nor is it true that the internal elaboration of penitentiary methods has finally brought to light the 'objective' existence of a delinquency that the abstraction and rigidity of the law were unable to perceive. They appeared together, the one extending from the other, as a technological ensemble that forms and fragments the object to which it applies its instruments. (1979: 255)

The rise of the disciplinary prison rose simultaneously with the emergence of a new form of knowledge about the criminal. This body of knowledge – part of which eventually came to be known by the term *criminology* – involved the study, in great detail, of the criminal and delinquent and underpinned a variety of practices which through the utilisation of these new forms of expertise – psychiatry, psychology, criminology, social work and others – disciplined the body and mind of the offender.

Jeremy Bentham, a utilitarian philosopher (see Chapter 5) was also much interested in the design of prisons. He is famously associated with the design of an inspection house – the panopticon – which, though never fully realised in the form he intended, nevertheless had some impact over prison design.

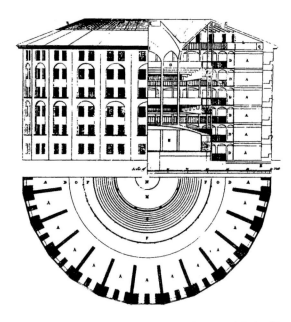

Although the panopticon is commonly associated with Jeremy Bentham it was originally his brother Samuel's invention. Jeremy got the idea during a visit to his brother in the 1780s and subsequently spent many years trying to put it into practice. Samuel Bentham was responsible for the construction of a panopticon in Russia in 1806, and saw the beginnings of its development before he left the country. His brother Jeremy never saw a panopticon built. See: http://www.ucl.ac.uk/Bentham-Project/journal/cpwpan.htm

The panopticon had a central tower around which were arrayed the prisoners' cells. The central inspection tower was designed in such a way that the prison guards could, at all times, see into the prisoners' cells. However, the reverse was not true and the inmates could not see the guards in the central inspection tower. The theory was that this constant visibility would bring about a sense of vulnerability and, in turn, would lead to self-control on the part of the prisoner. Foucault uses Bentham's idea of the panopticon as a metaphorical representation of this emergent enveloping disciplinary gaze of what he called the 'age of panopticism':

> The panopticon is a machine for dissociating the see/being seen dyad: in the peripheric ring, one is totally seen, without ever seeing; in the central tower, one sees everything without ever being seen. (Foucault, 1979: 202)

What is important here for Foucault is that the inmates themselves are caught up in the exercise of power over themselves. The panoptic system does not require that power is exercised over inmates by others at all times; indeed, progressively the exercise of power over the inmate should become unnecessary as they exercise self-discipline. In addition to being an illustration of the changing techniques of punishment this, for Foucault, is illustrative of wider changes.

The principles captured in the operation of the panopticon can be found operating in other spheres of social life. Indeed, in the grander claims in *Discipline and Punish* Foucault appears to suggest that such practices are now so widespread and embedded that it is possible to talk of a 'disciplinary society' and numerous other authors have talked of the 'surveillance society' or 'maximum security society' (Lyon, 2001) and the like. Indeed, it is in focusing attention on and providing tools for the analysis of the nature and spread of surveillance and the subtle techniques of governing and disciplining populations – held by some to be core characteristics of contemporary society – that, arguably, Foucault's influence on criminological theory has been greatest.

Governmentality theory

In a series of essays written not long before his death, Foucault explored the nature of government. This was not, however, the study of government through an analysis of the state but, rather, a study of the nature and rationalities of particular social and political *practices*. Governmentality, in this conception, refers to the ways in which we think about the process of governing. Governing, according to Foucault, is about the 'conduct of conduct' (1982: 220–1).

What cannot be stressed too often is that Foucault's analysis of the conduct of conduct sought to break with state-centred analyses. It involves attempting to understand systems of thought, bodies of knowledge, the social practices of a broad range of governing authorities – family, church, schools, prisons and the state – that work to shape individual behaviours, beliefs and values in ways that are both predictable and unpredictable.

Critically, Foucault also wished to place at the centre of such an approach the figure of the *active subject* – individuals capable of thought and preference. The image in much of Foucault's work is of individuals selecting choices, making decisions that are in line with the broader aims of governing bodies. This is not a conspiracy theory in which citizens are duped into courses of action that favour the interests of the state – a kind of large-scale 'find the lady' trick in which we believe we have a free choice of which card to choose, but end up selecting the one the dealer wishes us to. Rather, Foucault's approach stresses the multiple ways in which individual subjectivities are organised and created, and the ways in which we act to shape our own conduct.

What is important to the criminologist in this approach is its shift away from a focus on punishment and control as the imposition of government authority on individual citizens, toward one which stresses both the more disparate sources of power and authority. It is also centrally concerned with the ways in which individual actors are involved in their own governance. As Rose (2000: 185–6) puts it:

> ... 'the state' is neither the only force engaged in the government of conduct nor the hidden hand orchestrating the strategies and techniques of doctors, lawyers, churches, community organisations, pressure groups, campaigning groups, groups of parents, citizens, patients, survivors and all those others seeking to act upon conduct in the light of particular concerns and to shape it to certain ends. And mobility and contestability is further enhanced by the fact that contemporary strategies for the government of conduct, far from seeking to crush and eliminate the capacities for action of those persons and forces they act upon, on the contrary seek to foster and shape such capacities so that they are enacted in ways that are broadly consistent with particular objectives such as order, civility, health or enterprise.

There is a link between such ideas and earlier discussions of late modernity. A number of authors have argued that these new conditions – referred to by some as 'advanced liberalism' – involve a series of changes which recast the ideal role of the state from one as guarantor of security to one in which rule is progressively undertaken 'at a distance' from the state. Under such conditions, the state becomes a facilitator, organiser, partner, co-ordinator, supervisor or enabler.

Similarly, in seeking to understand the conduct of conduct our attention shifts from its previous preoccupation with the formal architecture of the state – such as the criminal justice and penal system – to broader questions of how conduct is governed via strategies in the areas of health, education and welfare, as well as non-state organisations and agents in the criminal justice sphere.

Michel Foucault (1926–1984)

Born in Poitiers, France, the son of a surgeon. Foucault studied philosophy under Maurice Merleau-Ponty. He held various academic appointments, in the 1950s teaching French at the universities of Uppsala, Warsaw, and Hamburg. His PhD thesis, *Madness and Unreason,* was published in 1961. His book *The Order of Things* was published in 1966 and became a bestseller.

With others he formed the Prison Information Group in 1968 – an organisation enabling prisoners to communicate about problems they faced. His *Archaeology of Knowledge* was published in 1969 and a year later he was elected to the Collège de France as Professor of the History of Systems of Thought. In the 1970s Foucault's ideas gained increasing currency in the English-speaking world, and he gave a number of lectures in America. He also travelled to Iran in the late 1970s, coming out in support of the new interim government after the ousting of the Shah. He died of Aids in 1984, having destroyed most of his manuscripts.

Michel Foucault (1926–1984), French philosopher and sociologist. His books on madness, sexuality and punishment had a profound impact on twentieth-century thought.

Two examples of how such a Foucauldian approach works will suffice. First, governmentality theory points us toward the growing importance and dispersal of surveillance techniques. Rather than focusing our concerns on the activities of the police for example, such approaches direct us toward the multiplicity of other forms of overseeing and moulding everyday conduct through the increased monitoring of conduct involving such means as computerised surveillance, credit checking, assessment of performance, and the associated growth of enormous databases covering matters as varied as insurance, credit-worthiness, criminal activity and DNA.

Second, as indicated earlier, this approach stresses the importance of citizen involvement in the governance of their own conduct. Criminological work influenced by Foucault has given rise to a number of terms that build on this insight. The first is *prudentialism*. Pat O'Malley, in particular, has written in some detail of the ways in which individuals, organisations – a range of bodies beyond the state – take upon themselves responsibility for security and protection (O'Malley, 1992; 2000). Indeed, such activity is encouraged increasingly by the state. As individual citizens, we are increasingly encouraged to consider matters of crime prevention, to insure against particular forms of risk and loss, and to link with others in an attempt to stimulate a greater sense of local security. Such processes are often referred to using the term *responsibilisation*. According to Garland (2001: 124):

> It involves a way of thinking and a variety of techniques designed to change the manner in which governments act upon crime. Instead of addressing crime in a direct fashion by means of the police, the courts and the prisons, this approach promotes a new kind of indirect action in which state agencies activate action by non-state organizations and actors. The intended result is an enhanced network of more or less directed, more or less informal crime control, complementing and extending the formal controls of the criminal justice state.

Consequently, much greater criminological attention is now paid to the role of private agencies in policing and the delivery of security, and on citizen involvement in self-protection, crime prevention and what is referred to as the 'co-production of security'.

Review questions

1 How might you distinguish between the Nightwatchman State, the Keynesian State and the New Regulatory State?

2 How was it intended that the panopticon should work?

3 What evidence can you see of the dispersal of surveillance techniques in modern society?

4 What is responsibilisation?

The dispersal of discipline

Foucault's influence has been remarkable in contemporary criminology and can be seen in a number of ways. One of the more important has seen a number of significant writers focus their attention on what are argued to be the emergence of systems of social control that are, in some ways, more subtle in their impact, and yet are more extensive than previously existing sources. In this manner, Stan Cohen, for example, talked of the 'dispersal of discipline' brought about by the spread of community corrections and other means of social control. In explaining this process Cohen (1985: 41–3) uses what has become one of the best-known metaphors in contemporary criminology:

> Imagine that the entrance to the deviancy control system is something like a gigantic fishing net. Strange and complex in its appearance and movements, the net is cast by an army of different fishermen and fisherwomen working all day and even into the night according to more or less known rules and routines, subject to more or less authority and control from above, knowing more or less what the other is doing. Society is the ocean … Deviants are the fish … Our interest is in the operation of this net … First, there are matters of *quantity*: size, capacity, scope, reach, density, intensity. Just how wide are the nets being cast? Over a period of time, do they get extended to new sites, or is there a contraction? … Second, there are questions about *identity*. Just how clearly can the net and the rest of the apparatus be seen? Is it always visible as a net? Or is it sometimes masked, disguised or camouflaged? … Third, there is the *ripple* problem. What effect does all this activity … have on the rest of the sea? Do other non-fish objects inadvertently get caught up in the net?

In answering these questions Cohen argues that three linked sets of changes can be seen as having occurred in the great transformation from nineteenth century systems of control to those visible in the late twentieth century. Continuing with his metaphor, he describes these as:

- *Net-widening* – The expansion of community control alongside the continuing use of custody means that increasing numbers of people are being caught up in the criminal justice system. In part, this results in the 'wrong' populations being swept up in the net. Thus, he argues, from the 1970s onward a whole series of diversionary measures were instituted with the aim of keeping young people out of the reach of the juvenile justice system generally and penal institutions in particular. In practice earlier and earlier intervention has meant that groups of young people that would not previously have been subject to penal sanctions are now targeted for treatment. The increasing numbers caught in the system also results from mesh thinning, as detailed below.

- *Mesh thinning* – Once drawn into the net the intensity of intervention tends to increase. As Cohen puts it (1985: 53) 'populations who once slipped quickly through the net are now retained much longer; many innovative alternatives become adjuncts to established sanctions such as probation and fines'. There has been a proliferation of programmes, he argues, that look and sound benign – social work-oriented interventions – but which, because of their nature, tend to be used both more extensively and more intensively.

Cohen goes on to outline a number of other changes to contemporary systems of social control that are bound up in the process by which increasing numbers are caught up in formal systems. There is a *blurring of boundaries* in which distinctions between such ideas as inside/outside, guilty/innocent, freedom/captivity, and imprisoned/released are now much less easy to understand than was once the case. So fine are some of the distinctions that now operate, he argues, that it is sometimes difficult to tell where the prison ends and the community begins. Anyone wishing to explore this might look at the Criminal Justice Act 2003 and its use of the terms 'custody plus' and 'custody minus', together with recent use of electronic monitoring, the registration of offenders and so on, to get some sense of what Cohen was getting at.

Related to this is the blurring of the boundary between the public and the private. The modern conception of crime control as the responsibility of the state is now changing substantially as the private sector comes to play an ever-larger role and in which community punishments are increasingly delivered by an amalgam of public and private agencies. Under such circumstances the techniques of control begin to change markedly.

The discipline of Disney World

A further classic example of criminological insight built on elements of Foucault's analysis of the conduct of conduct, and another terrific example of the use of metaphor, can be found in Clifford Shearing and Phillip Stenning's (1987) use of the example of Disney World as a means of understanding the power and reach of informal techniques as the basis of control within private security.

Shearing and Stenning's argument picks up on a critique of Cohen's dispersal of discipline thesis made by Tony Bottoms. In short, Bottoms (1983) argued that although Cohen was right to identify a broadening of interventions as a result of greater use of community-based punishment, many of these latter developments were not *disciplinary* in the way suggested by Cohen (and intended by Foucault). That is to say these forms of punishment do not involve the training of the self that is central to the use of the prison (as exemplified in the panopticon as we saw earlier), but is aimed more at conveying messages about harm and blame.

In this vein, Shearing and Stenning (1987) contrast what they call the 'moral discipline' of the prison system with the 'instrumental discipline' of private control systems. To illustrate this distinction they use the example of Disney World in the way Foucault offered the example of the panopticon. The Disney control system is apparent the moment one arrives as a visitor:

As one arrives by car one is greeted by a series of smiling young people who, with the aid of clearly visible road markings, direct one to one's parking spot, remind one to lock one's car and remember its location and direct one to await the rubber-wheeled train that will convey visitors away from the parking lot. At the boarding location one is directed to stand safely behind guard rails and to board the train in an orderly fashion. While climbing on board one is reminded to remember the name of the parking area and the row number in which one is

Disney World, used by Clifford Shearing and Philip Stenning as an example of the 'instrumental discipline' of modern, private control systems.

parked (for instance 'Donald Duck 1'). Once on the train one is encouraged to protect oneself from injury by keeping one's body within the bounds of the carriage and to do the same for children in one's care. Before disembarking one is told how to get from the train back to the monorail platform and where to wait for the train to the parking lot on one's return. At each transition from one stage of one's journey to the next one is wished a happy day and a 'good time' at Disney World (this begins as one drives in and is directed by road signs to tune one's car radio to the Disney radio network). (in McLaughlin *et al.*, 2003: 429–30)

And on it goes. As Shearing and Stenning (1987) note, the system of control is deeply embedded in both the architecture of the site and within other systems so that much of it appears relatively invisible. And, yet, it is ever-present and all-pervasive. Moreover, the system is consensual. The visitor buys (literally) into it. The systems that are

designed to protect and control children also serve to control adults who, simultaneously, regulate themselves and their children. Their picture of Disney World is one of a coercive system of control just below the surface, which becomes visible when anyone seeks to behave in ways contrary to expectation. Failure to comply results in exclusion:

> In summary, within Disney World control is embedded, preventative, subtle, co-operative and apparently non-coercive and consensual. It focuses on categories, requires no knowledge of the individual and employs pervasive surveillance. (in McLaughlin *et al.*, 2003: 431)

It is disciplinary in a Foucauldian sense, they argue, except that this is an instrumental discipline designed to further the interests of the Disney Corporation rather than a moral discipline which shapes and sustains a particular social order. The importance of the Disney World example lies in what it might be able to tell us about the nature of control in contemporary society. As we saw earlier, Shearing and Stenning argue that, increasingly, our lives occur in private spaces governed by private authorities operating with our consent, and in which conformity is brought about by seduction and persuasion at least as much as it is through threat and punishment.

Risk and the new culture of control

According to Ericson and Carriere (1994: 102–3) 'It is now possible to contend that we live in a "risk society" ... There is a drift in the public agenda away from economic inequality to the distribution and control of risks. The values of the unsafe society displace those of the unequal society.' This thesis is associated first and foremost with the German sociologist, Ulrich Beck, and his book *Risk Society*. Here he argues that the optimistic modernist belief in the power of scientific rationality to produce security, improved welfare and prosperity has gradually given way to a pessimistic focus on the risks that are produced by scientific and technological developments:

> This book is, then, about 'reflexive modernisation' of industrial society. This guiding idea is developed from two angles. First, the intermingling of continuity and discontinuity is discussed with the examples of *wealth production*

and *risk production*. The argument is that, while in classical industrial society the 'logic' of wealth production dominates the 'logic' of risk production, in the risk society this relationship is reversed ... The gain in power from techno-economic 'progress' is being increasingly overshadowed by the production of risks ... At the centre lie the risks and consequences of modernization, which are revealed as irreversible threats to the life of plants, animals and human beings. Unlike the factory-related or occupational hazards of the C19 and first half of the C20, these can no longer be limited to certain localities or groups, but rather exhibit a tendency to globalization which spans production and reproduction as much as national borders, and in this sense brings into being supranational and non-class-specific global hazards with a new type of social and political dynamism. (Beck, 1992: 12–13)

In Beck's thesis, risk is conceived as something that used to be the means by which the future was organised and controlled. However, we increasingly worry about our impact on the future. Advances in medical knowledge in the nineteenth century helped reduce the risks associated with a wide variety of diseases (smallpox, typhoid and so on) and the emergence of new scientific knowledge since then has put astronauts on the moon, split the atom and led to Crick and Watson revealing the structure and properties of DNA. However, there is a downside to such developments, Beck argues. The new technologies and knowledges are themselves producing risks – risks that are potentially devastating.

As a consequence, the challenge is now less about how we can use knowledge and skill to exploit nature for our benefit, and more about how we deal with the actual and potential problems created by our technological and economic 'progress': pollution, global warming, BSE, nuclear power, superbugs, avian flu and the like. Crucially, these are risks that are frequently global in nature – events happening in one part of the world may have dramatic impacts on other, distant locations. They are also risks that are not necessarily diminished or mitigated by wealth. Just because you are wealthy and powerful doesn't mean you can insulate yourself from them.

These changes can also be seen in the world of politics. No longer is it the case that the primary aim is the creation of the 'good society' – the construction and implementation of policies aimed at bringing about a set of idealised social objectives. Rather, we embrace the much more limited objective of avoiding catastrophe. However, this is in itself a difficult objective for the apparently intractable and global nature of many of the risks we face means that the nation state ceases to be a particularly effective guarantor of security. It is now increasingly a manager – often a *crisis* manager.

The changes involved in the shift from classical modernisation to the risk society also result in declining trust in what are called expert systems or expertise (Giddens, 1990). Modernity, as already argued, was characterised by a faith in the ability of scientific knowledge to manipulate and manage the external world. Increasingly, however, the demands for security outstrip the ability of expert systems to deliver. The reflexive nature of modernity means that expertise is increasingly called into question and challenged – in the criminal justice sphere as in others.

What are the implications of the risk society thesis for our understanding of crime and criminal justice? The question is probably most easily answered by conceiving of risk, and risk-related ideas and practices, as one important part of the more general shift that, it is argued, we are witnessing as *modernist* conceptions of crime control are progressively replaced or displaced by a new crime control complex. The best-known account of these changes is undoubtedly to be found in David Garland's (2001) *Culture of Control*. In short, Garland argues that a set of social, economic and cultural transformations, captured with the phrase the 'coming of late modernity', are accompanied by a set of quite fundamental changes in the discourses, practices and politics of contemporary crime control.

Garland and the Culture of Control

Though such matters can never be settled, arguably the most important and influential book in Western criminology in the past ten years has been David Garland's *The Culture of Control*. At the heart of the book is an analysis of changes in the field of crime control in America and Britain. Both societies have seen some remarkable and, in many respects, parallel changes in the last 30 or so years – parallel, but not identical:

My argument will be that the strong similarities that appear in recent policies and practices in these two societies ... are evidence of underlying patterns of structural transformation, and that these transformations are being brought about by a process of adaptation to the social conditions that now characterize these (and other) societies. I make no claim that the pattern of developments to be found in these two societies is universal: there are important national differences that distinguish the specific trajectory of these policy environments from one another and from those of other societies. (Garland 2001: 7)

Garland identifies twelve indices of the changes that have taken place in connection with the emergence of this new culture of control:

1 *The decline of the rehabilitative ideal* – For much of the twentieth century the ideal of rehabilitation was a profound influence on responses to crime. The assumption that people could be reformed – or as Winston Churchill put it, the existence of 'an unfaltering faith that there is a treasure, if you can only find it, in the heart of every man' – fell quickly out of fashion from the 1970s onward and as it did so, so many of the assumptions that had underpinned criminal justice began to fall away.

2 *The re-emergence of punitive sanctions and expressive justice* – Punishments that were straightforwardly harsh or retributive were perceived as having little place in criminal justice. However (see Chapter 28) retributive

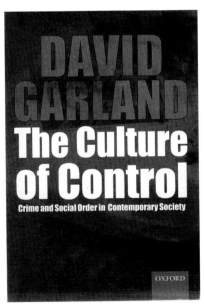

David Garland's *The Culture of Control* (2001), which examines the changing nature of contemporary crime control, was described by one reviewer as the most important book in the field since Foucault's *Discipline and Punish*.

forms of justice – just deserts – have been re-emerging and it has become progressively easier for politicians to call for and justify punitive sanctions as well as those that are strongly emotive in character, including naming and shaming, boot camps and chain gangs.

3 *Changes in the emotional tone of crime policy* – Apparently growing 'fear of crime' and generalised insecurity has created a situation in which politicians and others now talk about crime and its control in much more openly emotive terms. Where once many discussions of crime were relatively dispassionate, they have now in part been replaced by a 'phone-in programme' style of debate.

4 *The return of the victim* – The victim has become a more important figure in contemporary criminal justice (see the discussion of this argument in Chapter 17). Reference to victims' rights and needs are regularly made by people justifying new, punitive legislation and laws named after particular victims (Megan's Law, the Brady Bill) have become more common in America. In many respects the victim is a symbolic figure, standing in for widespread concerns about crime and disorder.

5 *Above all, the public must be protected* – Protecting the public is a central part of all systems of crime control. What is different now, Garland argues, is the urgency and stress on this factor. Using the prison to stop offending occurring (through incapacitation rather than rehabilitation); probation and parole as means of managing risk; and sex offender registers and notifications schemes for highlighting future dangers, are all indications of the overriding importance of public protection in contemporary crime control.

6 *Politicisation and the new populism* – The end of the 'bipartisan consensus' (see Chapter 1) has changed the way in which crime is talked about and policy is made. Where once major political parties departed little from each other in their diagnosis of crime and their models of punishment, and much policy-making centrally involved expert opinion, now crime and criminal justice are major areas for political contest, and much such debate is now heavily *populist*. Expert opinion is ignored and crude measures of public opinion are used to justify new measures.

7 *The reinvention of the prison* – The espousal of the idea that 'prison works' represents a major shift away from the view that dominated much of the twentieth century. During this time, dominant approaches sought alternatives to using custody and the proliferation of community sanctions is testimony to this. In America since the 1970s, and Britain since the early 1990s, there has been a profound shift toward viewing expanding prison numbers as a necessary and important part of a successful criminal justice system.

8 *The transformation of criminological thought* – Criminology up until the 1970s was dominated by a variety of approaches which saw criminality as a product of faulty adaptation or social injustice and inequality (deprivation, poor socialisation, inadequate treatment of psychological or mental problems, etc.). The period since has seen the rise of theories which see inadequate controls as being the core issue. These control theories take many forms (see Chapter 11), but they differ from earlier ideas in that they contain a less positive view of 'human nature', viewing crime as normal and to be expected in the absence of suitable controls. One consequence of such ideas is that they shift attention away from the criminal (and how they might be treated or rehabilitated) toward the criminal act (and how it might be prevented). In such a vision, social welfare is not a core issue.

9 *The expanding infrastructure of crime prevention and community safety* – A huge new crime control establishment covering such matters as Neighbourhood Watch, local crime prevention programmes, Business Improvement Districts have developed alongside criminal justice, but with objectives focused on harm and fear reduction, loss prevention and security rather than those of traditional criminal justice. Crucially, many of them are exclusionary rather than inclusionary.

10 *Civil society and the commercialisation of crime control* – A number of processes have increased the emphasis on preventative actions by citizens in the control of crime, and related developments have seen a signficant expansion in the private security industry. Policing is something that is now undeniably provided through a mixed economy of public and private bodies (see Chapter 25), and security has become progressively 'commodified' (something that is bought and sold in the marketplace).

11 *New management styles and working practices* – Criminal justice, like many areas of public life, have become progressively subject to a set of pressures which collectively are known as 'managerialism'. These include increasing financial oversight and control by government and other auditing bodies, the establishment and use of performance indicators and league tables, and the use of cost-effectiveness as a primary value in service delivery.

12 *A perpetual sense of crisis* – Criminal justice and penal systems are gripped by a sense of impending crisis, as being 'unfit for purpose' and being unable to cope with the pressures placed upon them. One consequence is that professional experience and expertise have become increasingly discredited, as both politicians and the public have lost confidence in them to ensure security and safety.

In exploring these changes in detail, Garland charts the way in which what he calls 'penal-welfarism' (that punishments should, wherever possible, also seek to reform) went into decline as it was subject to criticism from both ends of the political spectrum as being either inefficient, by failing to show that its measures actually *did* rehabilitate, or unfair, because it gave rise to systems in which huge discretion was left to sentencers to impose 'treatments' in ways that were discriminatory and repressive.

Simultaneously, a set of profound changes was affecting the social order of modern societies. These changes, including the make-up of families, the social organisation of cities, the power of the electronic media, and the extent of 'democratisation' in social life, provided the conditions in which a new 'culture of control' could emerge. As Garland (2001: 103) puts it, 'Late modernity and the new politics to which it gave rise, changed how organisations thought about crime and punishment, justice and control, just as it changed the terrain on which these organisations operated.'

The emerging apparatus of control, he argues, is characterised by two major strategies: one that is pragmatic and *adaptive* and a second that is primarily *expressive* and which seeks 'to denounce the crime and reassure the public' (2001: 133):

- *Adaptive responses* include:
  - The commercialisation of justice and what has been referred to as the 'reinvention of government' in which the state progressively becomes the 'steerer' rather than the 'rower' in crime control policy.
  - A focus on the consequences rather than the causes of crime.
  - A strategy of *responsibilisation* in which state agencies activate non-state organisations and actors (including individual citizens) to work as partners and to take responsibility for action against crime, and for prevention in particular.
  - The development of the *new criminologies of everyday life* such as rational choice, situational crime prevention and routine activities (see Chapter 11) which tend to view crime prospectively (what may happen in the future) and in aggregate (e.g. hot spots).

- *Non-adaptive responses* include:
  - *Denial* – In the face of evidence of the limits of sovereign authority in controlling crime, and evidence that harsh punishment is a relatively ineffective means of control, governments argue ever more loudly that what is needed is increased punitiveness and state intervention.
  - *Acting out* – Impulsive, almost knee-jerk reactions to underlying problems – 'three strikes and you're out' mandatory sentences; Megan's Laws (American paedophile notification schemes nearly imported to Britain as 'Sarah's Laws' in the aftermath of the murder of Sarah Payne) and the like, introduced as much for their symbolic and expressive effect as any impact they may have on crime.

The result is the gradual emergence of a new culture of control characterised by a distinctive mixture of attitudes and assumptions. Societies such as America and Britain now see and experience high crime as a 'normal social fact' and in part respond to that fact emotionally and expressively. Crime, as a consequence, becomes an important element of political debate and dispute, within which victims of crime increasingly dominate. As traditional criminal justice responses are increasingly perceived to be ineffective, new privatised forms of defence and protection, such as CCTV, gated communities, and security guards, come to

the fore. One consequence of this mixture of developments, in America at least, has been the rise of the 'mass incarceration'. With well over two million people in prison the United States is the world's primary incarcerator, and all the signs are that many other countries are heading in a not dissimilar direction (see Chapter 28).

Risk, crime and criminal justice

In a similar vein, but with different emphases from those in Garland's thesis, O'Malley (2001) argues that there are close links between the socio-economic changes associated with neoliberalism and a host of changes in contemporary crime control. Indeed, he suggests this relationship is an 'elective affinity' (in which two parallel sets of developments or practices appear to be bound by a similar rationality and, consequently, reinforce each other). In particular, O'Malley (2001; 2006) draws attention to the:

- rise of predictive, rational-choice models and the gradual displacement of more socially-oriented approaches to the explanation of causation (see Chapter 14);
- emergence of such practices as 'truth in sentencing', and the gradual prioritisaton of deterrence over rehabilitation and welfare;
- emphasis on individual responsibility and the gradual devolution of responsibility for crime prevention to the citizenry;
- rise of rationalities of cost-effectiveness and consumerism in crime control.

The growing importance and visibility of risk-oriented thinking and practice can be seen across the whole of the criminal justice system. Here we briefly consider a few of these in outline by way of illustration of some of the more important characteristics of such developments.

- *Sex offenders* – Growing concern about sexual offending, particularly against children, has led to the emergence of a series of strategies for managing people convicted of such offences. Much media coverage, and public concern, in this area is dominated by the image of the predatory paedophile. Policy developments in this area illustrate well some aspects of the risk-oriented style of many contemporary developments:
  - The Sex Offenders Act 1997 introduced a sex offender register which was to be used to monitor such offenders, to track their movements.

– Multi-Agency Public Protection Panels were introduced by the Criminal Justice and Court Services Act 2000. These engage in risk assessment and classify offenders according to the potential danger they pose.

– There have been consistent calls, so far resisted, for the introduction of sex offender notification systems akin to the Megan's Laws that operate in the United States and which allow residents access to information about the location of convicted sex offenders living in local communities.

● *Crime prevention* – New discourses and practices aimed at engaging communities and citizens in preventative activity very much have the feel of risk-oriented strategies. From the selling of new security-oriented lifestyles in gated residential communities, the burgeoning markets in security devices such as CCTV and alarms, to the hiring of extra police or private security, this 'new infrastructure is strongly oriented towards a set of objectives and priorities – prevention, security, harm-reduction, loss-reduction, fear reduction – that are quite different from the traditional goals of prosecution, punishment and "criminal justice"' (Garland 2001: 17).

● *Policing* – The influence of risk-oriented practices can be seen in two major areas within policing:

– In the strategies employed by the police organisation such as increasing use of surveillance, proactive targeting of people and places, and the rise of 'problem-oriented policing', 'intelligence-led policing' and related approaches (see Chapter 25).

– On the police organisation itself. In an influential book Ericson and Haggerty (1997) argued that police work is increasingly focused on the collection and dissemination of information, and that the police might well be seen as 'information brokers' as well as 'crime fighters'.

Inside a gated community in Hampstead, London. Increasing numbers of people are living in residential areas that are sealed off by walls and gates, often accompanied by guards and closed-circuit television surveillance.

Assessing governmentality, the new penology and risk

In a seminal article published in 1992, Malcolm Feeley and Jonathan Simon advanced the idea that we have been witnessing the emergence of a 'new penology'. At heart, this new penology:

> … is neither about punishing nor rehabilitating individuals. It is about identifying and managing unruly groups. It is concerned with the rationality not of individual behaviour or even community organization, but of managerial processes. Its goal is not to eliminate crime but to make it tolerable through systemic coordination. (1992: 455)

They argue that one clear indicator of this shift of objectives is the declining significance of recidivism. Under previous systems, recidivism was almost always used as a key criterion for assessing the effectiveness of penal sanctions. New penology continues to use recidivism rates, but does so in different ways. Now the tendency is to use such terms in looser ways, and generally in the context of offender management. Where once reference to parole failure would most likely have been discussed negatively as an indicator of a system failing to reform offenders, now the tendency is to use it as a positive indicator of the way in which the system manages this difficult population. Feeley and Simon (1992: 456) note that this:

... also reflects the lowered expectations for the penal system that result from failures to accomplish more ambitious promises of the past.

The penal system under such circumstances measures flows through the system, numbers processed, speed of processing, and the like rather than more difficult objectives such as offender reintegration. Progressively, the system distances itself from the social purposes of punishment:

> In contrast the new penology is markedly less concerned with responsibility, fault, moral sensibility, diagnosis, or intervention and treatment of the individual offender. Rather it is concerned with techniques to identify, classify and manage groupings sorted by dangerousness. The task is managerial not transformative. (1992: 452)

In addition to these new objectives, the new penology involves a new discourse and a set of new techniques. The new language involves a shift away from clinical or moral descriptions of individuals towards an actuarial language which is applied to populations. The adjective *actuarial* here refers to the type of statistical or probabilistic language that is used in the insurance industry. Such thinking, they suggest, has gradually come to permeate both legal discourses and the language of criminal justice and penal policy. Although this shift in language is less spectacular than the policy emphasis from rehabilitation to crime control, it is no less significant.

At the heart of the new penology is a set of reworked techniques which place greater emphasis on cost-effectiveness and the identification and classification of risk. These include electronic monitoring ('tagging') and the use of statistical techniques for assessing and predicting risk and dangerousness. This can be seen in the revivification of incapacitation as a prominent penal philosophy. Less emphasis is now placed on ends such as rehabilitation, and much greater prominence is given to social protection through incapacitation:

> These new forms of control are not anchored in aspirations to rehabilitate, reintegrate, retrain, provide employment, or the like. They are justified in more blunt terms: variable detention depending on risk assessment. (1992: 457)

At heart the new penology is about the management of populations rather than the reform of individuals. Imprisonment in such a system is increasingly focused on the incapacitation of particular types of offender – in particular those defined as 'persistent' or 'high rate'. Assessments of 'risk' therefore come to play a progressively central role within the new penology as the focus of the justice system shifts away from the idea of tailoring interventions to fit the requirements of particular cases, toward the identification and sorting of populations into categories (such as dangerous, persistent) on the basis of risk.

This 'new penology' is directed less at responses to offending and more at using knowledge to identify risks – indeed *risky* populations – and then through intervention or moral suasion to reduce or prevent anticipated offending. Anticipating the future, assessing risks, and preventing crime are increasingly dominant characteristics of the late modern crime control system. Ever a clever predictor of future trends, the science fiction writer Philip K. Dick anticipated some of these ideas in his short story, *The Minority Report* (see overleaf).

Feeley and Simon's (1992, 1994) vision of a new penology is not intended as a description of the way things *are*. Rather, it is an attempt to describe some of the dominant characteristics of an emergent system of punishment – one that is increasingly visible, even if its major characteristics are yet some way from dominating our current system of punishment. It is one way of helping us see what they consider to be the direction our penal systems may be heading.

Review questions

1   What was Cohen attempting to convey with his fishing metaphor?

2   According to Shearing and Stenning how does social control work within Disney World?

3   What other examples can you think of in which control systems are largely informal and rely on co-operation rather than punishment?

4   What are the main characteristics of the 'new penology'?

Minority Report

Originally published in 1956 in the magazine *Fantastic Universe*, Philip K. Dick's short story, *The Minority Report*, will be best known to many readers now as a result of the Steven Spielberg film starring Tom Cruise.

Dick, a prolific science fiction writer, has had his work translated into movies on numerous occasions, including *A Scanner Darkly*, *Blade Runner* and *Total Recall*.

Minority Report is set in a Washington DC policing agency in 2054. Its central character, John Anderton, is the head of a police agency called *Precrime*. The agency is able to foresee future criminal activity through the powers of 'precogs' – three psychics kept in a chamber in the agency's headquarters. As a result of its advance warning it is able successfully to prevent crime and has all but eliminated serious felonies.

However, Anderton finds that he has been accused of 'pre-murder' and the story concerns his attempt to prove his innocence.

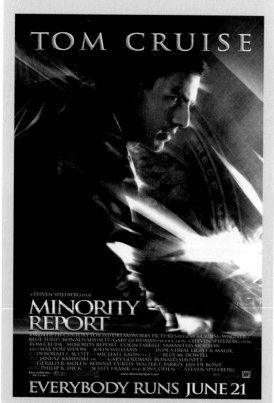

Minority Report: Stephen Spielberg's adaptation of Philip K. Dick's short story, in which serious crimes are prevented through an ability to see the future.

In this chapter we have considered a number of theoretical ideas in criminology which all owe something to the work of Michel Foucault. Foucault's work, as we have seen, has been of considerable significance in recent times to the study of deviance and particularly punishment.

Govermentality

One scholar, David Garland (1997), himself influenced by elements of Foucault's work, also points to a number of limitations to the governmentality approach:

- The terminology can be confusing. Thus, governmentality theory places considerable emphasis upon the need to think 'beyond the state' in considering the operation of power. However, as the term *government* in conventional usage implies the state, there is considerable danger of confusion here.

- Although Foucault raises a number of potentially intriguing links between the practices and mentalities characteristic of previous centuries and those of today, the nature of these links remains somewhat unclear. Arguably, it is the absence of precisely such a 'history of the present' in the field of crime control that led Garland (2001) to produce *The Culture of Control*.

- Foucault's history tends to deal in abstractions – not as the basis for grounded, empirical analysis, but as ends in themselves. There is a tendency in his work, therefore, to avoid answering detailed questions about how particular systems function in practice, and how they may have unintended or unanticipated consequences.

- The Foucauldian approach tends to focus its attention on instrumental rationalities and underplays some of the more emotive and expressive elements of contemporary penality. As an example of this, Garland cites Feeley and Simon's recent work on the new penology. In contrasting older style rehabilitative approaches with new actuarial, managerial styles, they pay insufficient attention to the continuities and, in some ways, interlocked and mutually supportive relationships between old and new penologies.

The new penology

A number of other criticisms have been directed at the 'new penology' thesis. Feeley himself (2006) identifies and responds to three main strands of criticism. These are:

- That there is 'nothing new' about the 'new' penology.

- Despite new language and even some new actuarial technologies, practices are largely unchanged. In this regard, Garland (2003: 65) notes that a 'focus upon the differential risks posed by classes and categories, a notion of criminality as an aggregate phenomenon, and a concern to manage populations were all characteristic of the eugenics movement at the turn of the century, a movement that influenced both criminological discourse and penal policy at that time.'

- The 'technology' of the new penology has been ineffective: for all the talk of risk management, in practice penal policy has been dominated by populism and retributivism.

In responding to such criticisms, Feeley tells the story of bail reform in the United States. Though bail reform is, perhaps, not the biggest story in American criminal justice in the last 30 years, Feeley argues that it illustrates some of the powerful consequences of the rise of actuarialism. He also suggests that a similar story would be told if the focus were on other aspects of penal change such as 'three strikes', career criminals or sentencing guidelines. Although the work undertaken by the National Association of Pretrial Service Agencies (NAPSA) falls well short of the promised ability to predict appearance at trial, or to predict dangerousness, Feeley (2006: 229) argues that 'once the aspiration [to do these things] was legitimized, [NAPSA] was authorized to engage in a host of activities that would not be permitted under a more traditional rights regime.' These new activities – requiring clients to 'check in', home visits by staff, new powers to allow detention and the forcible return of clients who had failed to appear, as well as a host of monitoring and supervisory functions (of clients who have not yet been convicted) – are described by Feeley as being a 'weak conception of the new penology', but nevertheless 'certainly [as being] alive and well in the pretrial process in the United States'. Moreover, this is only the beginning he suggests, and in the relatively-near future there are likely to be developments in a similar vein which will transform the criminal process in its entirety into an administrative system.

Risk

The final development we considered in this chapter was the growing importance of risk and related ways of thinking and behaving. Again, such approaches have become increasingly influential within criminology. They, too, have been subject to debate and Kemshall (2003: 10) suggests that criticisms of the risk society argument tend to cluster around four main themes:

- *The contention that the distinction between traditional and late modern risks is overstated.* To what extent, some critics ask, is it really the case that the major risks we face are global and new? As one example, contemporary news broadcasts discussing bird flu epidemics will tend to talk about previous pandemics that have affected the globe. On average there have been three each century, including the twentieth century. The outbreak in 1918–1919 killed an estimated 40 million people.

- *The thesis that risks are under-regulated and weakened social control of technology has contributed to risk proliferation is incorrect.* Again, it is possible that elements of the alleged ineffectiveness of contemporary regulation have been exaggerated. Braithwaite (2000), for example, argues that in the aftermath of the Three Mile Island nuclear disaster the American nuclear industry established an industry-based self-regulatory system that appears to have been more successful than state regulation was on its own.

- *The claim that the end of traditional bonds exacerbates risk is overstated.* The processes of individualisation and fragmentation that characterise late modernity are held to result in a loss of traditional certainties, and the replacement of old inequalities with new differences in ability to manage risk. However, much research seems to shows that old inequalities of wealth and power appear to be surviving these changes.

- *The multiplication of risk is overemphasised.* Beck's answer to his own question as to whether risks are changing in nature or are now different in extent is that it appears that both are true. Risks are multiplying and changing in nature. It is unclear to what extent this diagnosis is accurate, however. Most commentators accept that there have been some important changes in the nature of risk and, certainly, there appear to be significant alterations in perceptions of risk. However, are risks really proliferating? As Kemshall (2003: 14) puts it, 'Is the risk society about new risks, or merely a new way of looking at risk?'

Although there have been a number of important, and in some cases, far-reaching criticisms of governmentality theory, of notions of risk and of the assertion that we are witnessing the gradual emergence of a new penology, it is undeniably the case that these ideas have been enormously important in shaping our understanding of trends in contemporary criminal justice. Similarly, although there have been some trenchant criticisms of David Garland's culture of control thesis (see for example Zedner, 2002; Zimring, 2001) it has now firmly established itself as the basis of, and often the framework for, all thoughtful discussions of crime control under conditions of late modernity.

Questions for further discussion

1 What did Foucault intend to convey in arguing that we have witnessed a shift from a *corporal* to a *carceral* system of punishment?

2 Give examples of the *widening of the net* and the *thinning of the mesh*.

3 Are current trends in the nature of punishment an indication of a process in which discipline is being dispersed?

4 In what ways can elements of the 'risk society' be seen in contemporary criminal justice?

5 To what extent have we witnessed the emergence of a new culture of control?

Further reading

Dick, P.K. (2000) *Minority Report: The short stories of Philip K. Dick,* New York: Orion Books

Feeley, M. and Simon, J. (1992) The new penology: notes on the emerging strategy for corrections, *Criminology,* 30, 4, 449–75, Columbus, OH: Blackwell Journals (abridged in McLaughlin, E. *et al.* [eds] *Criminological Perspectives*)

Garland, D. (1990) *Punishment and Modern Society,* Oxford: Oxford University Press (ch. 6 and 7)

Garland, D. (1997) 'Governmentality' and the problem of crime: Foucault, criminology, sociology, *Theoretical Criminology,* 1, 2, 173–214, London: Sage Journals

Garland, D. (2001), *The Culture of Control: Crime and social order in contemporary society,* Oxford: Clarendon

Kemshall, H. (2003) *Understanding Risk in Criminal Justice,* Buckingham: Open University Press

Mythen, G. and Walklate, S. (2006) *Beyond the Risk Society: Critical reflections on risk and human security,* Maidenhead: Open University Press

Rose, N. (2000) Government and control, in Garland, D. and Sparks, R. (eds) *Criminology and Social Theory,* Oxford: Oxford University Press

Young, J. (1999) *The Exclusive Society,* London: Sage (ch. 2)

Websites

Foucault Info is a website with numerous original texts (or excerpts from texts) by Foucault – http: //www.foucault.info/documents/

There is also a lot of material on Foucault at Foucault Resources – http: //www.michel-foucault.com/index.html

Part 3

Understanding Crime: types and trends

17 Victims, victimization and victimology

18 White-collar and corporate crime

19 Organised crime

20 Violent and property crime

21 Drugs and alcohol

Chapter outline

Understanding victims and victimology   342
    The victim of crime   342
    The emergence of victimology   344
       Victim-precipitation   345
       Victim-blaming   346
    Approaches to victimology   346
       Positivist victimology   346
       Radical victimology   347
       Critical victimology   347

The nature of victimization   348
    The extent of victimization   348
       Repeat victimization   349
    Victimization and the vulnerable   351
       Victimization and the homeless   351
       Victimization and the elderly   352
    The impact of victimization   353
       Physical impact   354
       Behavioural impact   354
       Emotional/psychological impact   354
       Financial impact   355

Fear of crime   355

Victims policy   358
    Criminal injuries compensation   358
    Court-ordered compensation   359
    Feminism and 'secondary victimization'   359
    Child abuse   361
    Victim support   363
    Victims' rights?   364
       One stop shop and victim statements   365
       Rebalancing the criminal justice system?   365

Questions for further discussion   367
Further reading   367
Websites   368

Victims, victimization and victimology

CHAPTER SUMMARY	What does it mean to be a victim of crime? Criminologists have slowly come to pay increasing attention to the issue of victimization – partly as an alternative means of measuring crime and partly in order to attempt to understand the impact of crime. This has given rise to its own subsidiary area of study within criminology, known as victimology. In this chapter we look at:

- the rise of victimology;

- the nature and impact of victimization, including the much discussed idea of 'fear of crime';

- government policy in relation to victims of crime;

- debates about victims' 'rights';

- the recently-expressed government ambition of 'rebalancing' the criminal justice system more in favour of victims.

Understanding victims and victimology

It is now standard practice to observe that the 'victim' has long been the forgotten party in criminal justice. Occasionally victims would appear on the scene as complainants and applicants for compensation, or as witnesses, perhaps to give evidence in court, but thereafter they were often largely neglected. This situation has now changed – somewhat. Certainly, victims now form the focus of a substantial area of inquiry within criminology. And yet there remains a sense in many quarters that insufficient attention is paid to the needs – and for some the *rights* – of crime victims. We return to this sense of neglect at various stages later in the chapter. We begin, however, by looking at the term 'victim' itself, and the ways in which it is used and applied.

The victim of crime

Earlier in the book (in Chapter 10, in particular) we looked at labelling theory and the concern that some criminologists have with how it is that some acts, and individuals, come to be defined as crimes and criminals. In parallel with this, a set of questions can be posed in relation to victims of crime. Under what circumstances are some people treated as victims, and are there particular consequences from having such a label attached (or denied)? What anyway do we understand by the term 'victim'? The 1985 United Nations Declaration of Basic Principles of Justice for Victims of Crime and Abuse of Power offers a definition of 'victims':

[1] 'Victims' means persons who, individually or collectively, have suffered harm, including physical or mental injury, emotional suffering, economic loss or substantial impairment of their fundamental rights, through acts or omissions that are in violation of criminal laws operative within Member States, including those laws proscribing criminal abuse of power.

[2] A person may be considered a victim, under this Declaration, regardless of whether the perpetrator is identified, apprehended, prosecuted or convicted and regardless of the familial relationship between the perpetrator and the victim. The term 'victim' also includes, where appropriate, the immediate family or dependants of the direct victim and persons who have suffered harm in intervening to assist victims in distress or to prevent victimization. (http://www.unhchr.ch/html/menu3/b/h_comp49.htm)

An alternative approach, developed by the Norwegian criminologist Nils Christie (1986), involved an attempt to develop an idealised picture of the crime victim, i.e. a model or stereotype designed – no doubt with some irony – to illustrate the ideological ways in which 'victims' and 'offenders' are generally discussed. Christie's *ideal victim* has six major attributes:

1 The victim is weak in relation to the offender – the 'ideal victim' is likely to be either female, sick, very old or very young (or a combination of these).

2 The victim is, if not acting virtuously, then at least going about their legitimate, ordinary everyday business.

3 The victim is blameless for what is happening.

4 The victim is unrelated to and does not know the 'stranger' who has committed the offence (which also implies that the offender is a person rather than a corporation; and that the offence is a single 'one-off' incident).

5 The offender is unambiguously big and bad.

6 The victim has the right combination of power, influence or sympathy to successfully elicit victim status without threatening (and thus risking opposition from) strong countervailing vested interests.

Public campaigns involving victims of crime

On 29 July 1994, a seven year-old girl, Megan Kanka, living in New Jersey, was raped and murdered by a two-time convicted sex offender. The offender, Jesse Timmendequas, had been convicted for a 1981 attack on a five year-old child and an attempted sexual assault on a seven year-old. The fact that the community were unaware of the presence of convicted sex offenders living locally quickly gave rise to a public campaign for reform of the law. New legislation, known as 'Megan's Law', was passed which ensured that, in future, the community would be made aware of the presence of a convicted sex offender if he poses a threat to the public. The law requires convicted sex offenders to register after their release from custody and guarantees both public access and the dissemination of this registration information.

More recently, there has been pressure to introduce similar legislation in Britain. Again, the campaign involved the case of a young victim of a convicted sex offender. In this case, eight year-old Sarah Payne was abducted from a Sussex village on 1 July 2000. It was two weeks before her body was found and in the interim a major publicity campaign was under way. When it later emerged that the man convicted of the crime had previous convictions for sexual offences, and had recently been released from prison where he had been serving a sentence for child abduction, momentum built for a campaign for the introduction of what, before long, became known as 'Sarah's Law'. Though such legislation has not yet been passed, the *News of the World* and others continue to campaign vigorously and in June 2007 the government announced a variety of measures to allow parents access to information about convicted sex offenders.

The *News of the World* has run a campaign for the introduction of a paedophile notification scheme to the UK since the abduction and murder of Sarah Payne in July 2000.

If you read newspaper coverage of, say, violent crimes, you will frequently be able to spot aspects of this stereotype, not least the idea that victims are, or are supposed to be, *innocent*. However, and we will look at this in more detail below, the reality is often far more complex. One illustration will suffice. The ideal-typical victim is often presented as being quite different from, and quite separate from, the offender. Thus, as in Christie's model, they are blameless whereas the offender is not, they are relatively weak, and they are a generally sympathetic character. Put simply, from this perspective, offenders and victims are assumed to be largely separate groups.

Empirical research, however, illustrates the limitations of this view. In a review of studies across the world Fattah (1991: 123) concluded that 'criminals are more frequently victimized than non-criminals' and that victims of violent crime themselves have considerable criminal involvements' (arguably what Wolfgang was arguing some decades earlier). More recent research by Dobrin (2001) found that people who had ever been arrested were significantly more likely than those who had never been arrested to become victims of homicide. Comparing the general adult population with a sample of 105 homicide victims, Dobrin found that likelihood of being murdered (which is, of course, very small) increased markedly according to the number of times someone had been arrested (see also Bottoms and Costello, 2001). It is important not to overstate the links between victimization and offending. On the other hand, it is equally important not to lose sight of the fact that the categories we use – 'victim' and 'offender' – are not simple indicators of different *types* of people.

Christie's outline of the 'ideal victim' is particularly useful in understanding and helping us 'deconstruct' public portrayals of victims. This can be especially valuable when the idea of the victim is being used to promote or to defend some new criminal justice or penal policy. For example, in many jurisdictions, perhaps most famously America, idealised portrayals of victims have been used as the centrepoint of campaigns for various legislative changes – from laws to publicise the whereabouts of convicted sex offenders to campaigns for tougher sentencing of violent and sexual offenders. One of these cases, involving campaigns for the introduction of sex offender notification schemes, is described above.

The emergence of victimology

The link between *victims* and *crime* is now firmly fixed in the public mind. However, historically, the term victim has had a broader meaning relating to misfortunes of many sorts, not just suffering caused by crime. Dignan (2005) identifies six major factors that have contributed to the rising public profile of the victim and issues of victimization:

1 The interests of victims were championed by penal reformers, such as Margery Fry, who not only campaigned for better conditions for, and treatment of, offenders but also sought to improve services for victims, principally because victims were portrayed as unreasonable obstacles to enlightened penal reform in the late 1940s (Rock, 1990).

2 The mass media have helped highlight the plight of victims – or at least certain categories of victim.

3 The increasing recognition since the late 1960s of particular vulnerable groups – women suffering domestic violence, children subject to abuse inside and outside the home – gave rise both to public campaigns and to increased general recognition of criminal victimization.

4 High-profile cases of domestic and foreign political violence have drawn attention to the plight of victims.

5 Increasing knowledge through victimization surveys (such as the British Crime Survey) allow better estimates to be made of the nature and extent of criminal victimization.

6 Academic criminology, belatedly, has also recognised the importance of studying and understanding victimization and has thereby increased public recognition and knowledge. Such academic study is generally referred to as *victimology*.

The term 'victimology' is generally credited to Beniamin Mendelsohn in 1947, though some suggest that Frederick Wertham first used the term in 1949 (Fattah, 1992). The precise origins of the term are probably of relatively little importance. What its emergence indicates is that this particular area of criminology has about half a century behind it now. From slightly strange origins it is now an eminently respectable sub-area of criminology with its own journals and conferences.

Tierney (1996) identifies two major early traditions in victimology. First, an initial approach associated with Von Hentig and Wertham and others, which focused primarily on psychological characteristics and social circumstances. Second, and largely superseding the first, a body of work which focuses more on attempts to measure the extent of victimization. Both of these might broadly be described as forms of *positivist victimology*.

Victim-precipitation

The first approach has, to a degree, been discredited because of its association with victim-blaming and victim-precipitation. In Hans Von Hentig's work, victims were classified according to how 'victim prone' they were and, indeed, how 'culpable' they could be considered to be. His concern was to attempt to understand the relationship between perpetrator and victim:

> In a sense the victim shapes and moulds the criminal. The poor and ignorant immigrant has bred a peculiar kind of fraud. Depressions and wars are responsible for new forms of crimes because new types of potential victims are brought into being. It would not be correct nor complete to speak of a carnivorous animal, its habits and characteristics, without looking at the prey on which it lives. In a certain sense the animals which devour and those that are devoured complement one another. Although it looks one-sided as far as the final outcome goes, it is not a totally unilateral form of relationship. They work upon each other profoundly and continually, even before the moment of disaster. To know one we must be acquainted with the complementary partner. (Von Hentig, 1948, reproduced in Jacoby, 2004: 27)

Building on this insight, Wolfgang and colleagues undertook a major study of 'victim-precipitated criminal homicide'. Using police records, they examined 588 consecutive cases of homicide that occurred in Philadelphia between 1948 and 1952. Of these, they identified 150 to have involved victim-precipitation. The researchers then compared these cases with the non-victim-precipitation cases in the remainder of their sample in order to isolate the characteristics of this particular type of homicide.

Such work has a number of shortcomings. First, Wolfgang's study was heavily dependent on police records of criminal events and, therefore, police inter-pretations of those events. To what extent such versions of cases of homicide are in any way accurate must be open to doubt. Second, the approach generally carries with it a set of *normative* implications that many commentators have criticised. In particular, the idea of victim-precipitation can, under some circumstances, come very close to absolving offenders of responsibility for their actions. As many feminist critics have observed, such reasoning has often been used to discredit female victims in rape and sexual assault cases – arguing that they had, through their behaviour, somehow brought their victimization upon themselves. A student of Wolfgang's, Menachim Amir (1971), had applied the idea of victim-precipitation to a study of forcible rape, concluding that up to one-fifth of the rapes he studied might be defined as involving some precipitation by the victim. Many of the weaknesses of such an approach, and in particular its limiting assumptions about the nature of victimization, were exposed by more recent work which has uncovered many of the social patterns of victimization.

Classic work in the 1970s by Richard Sparks (senior) and colleagues looked at a number of factors including vulnerability, neighbourhood characteristics and various features of lifestyle, all of which were linked to geographical and social differences in the level and type of victimization. Subsequent to his London research, Sparks (1982) developed a six-fold typology of victim proneness:

- *Precipitation* – Where one may precipitate or encourage one's own victimization.

- *Facilitation* – Putting oneself, deliberately or otherwise, at risk of crime – failing to lock the front door, leaving car windows open and valuables on the seat, etc.

- *Vulnerability* – Physical attributes which increase risk.

- *Opportunity* – You cannot have things stolen that you do not possess, and you can reduce the risk by keeping them somewhere safe (tourists are regularly advised not to carry large sums in cash and when they do carry cash, to keep it somewhere where it is not especially easy to steal).

- *Attractiveness* – Displays of wealth may draw attention.

- *Impunity* – You may be perceived as a relatively 'easy target' – you won't complain or seek retribution.

Walklate (1989) is critical of the approach, arguing that it pays too little attention to the structural circumstances within which people find themselves and too much to individual events and choices. She argued then, and has done so since (Mawby and Walklate, 1994), for a more radical or 'critical victimology'.

Victim-blaming

Victim-precipitation theories in their benign form simply acknowledge that in some crimes there is a 'relationship' between perpetrator and victim, and identify the fact that that relationship might be important in understanding those crimes. However, such approaches can also take a somewhat less attractive form, tipping over into blaming victims for what has befallen them and implying that, were it not for their own culpability, no crime would have been committed.

Victim-blaming is still to be found in connection with various forms of crime. Despite consistent feminist criticism for several decades, violence against women still sometimes carries overtones of victim-blaming. Court cases in which the female victim's behaviour becomes the focus of scrutiny are by no means unknown. Another area, much less studied, but seemingly equally prone to victim-blaming, is what have been referred to as 'safety crimes'. Defined as 'violations of law by employers that either do, or have, the potential to cause sudden death or injury as a result of work-related activities' (Tombs and Whyte, 2007: 1) such incidents have long been explained by reference to 'accident prone' workers. According to Tombs and Whyte (2007) such ideas allow attention to be deflected away from structural deficiencies and to be focused, rather, on the actions of individuals – often, those who have suffered. In this way, they argue, workers come to be viewed as a group that is prone to accidents as a result of incompetence, laziness or some other negative attribute:

> Accidents are linked with workers. Those on the scene of accidents are held, automatically, as responsible. In a generalised sense, then, 'workers' become the problem at the heart of occupational safety – and this in turn is the basis for worker, and often victim, blaming in discourse and practice around occupational safety. (Tombs and Whyte, 2007: 75–6)

The consequence of such approaches is effectively to deny victim status. If the victim is portrayed as culpable in some way for the 'accident'

that has occurred, they are no longer 'innocent' and, consequently, do not measure up to the ideal that forms the basis of our understanding of what a victim is. Any more fundamental causes are thereby partially or fully hidden from view, protecting employers and investors from investigation and action. It is arguably the case that the victim retains a largely marginal status within much criminology, still perceived as having little claim to any formal role within criminal justice. As Rock (forthcoming) puts it, '[i]t is as if victims are still sometimes thought to be held barely in check, near-feral, angry creatures of a Hobbesian world, restrained only by the legal apparatus of the State whose failure would lead to a reversion to "wild justice"'.

Approaches to victimology

As Rock (2007) notes, it has become commonplace to observe that much work in the victimological arena has tended to be theoretically thin. Indeed, he argues that given the variety of concerns and phenomena that fall within the scope of victimology, it is difficult to imagine what a coherent and consolidated theoretical approach might look like. For our purposes here we can distinguish between what are possibly best thought of as *orientations* to the issues within victimology. Three major approaches are identifiable: generally referred to as positivist, radical and critical victimologies.

Positivist victimology

We have already come across one part of what is often referred to as *positivist* victimology. According to Miers (1989: 3) such an approach involved:

> the identification of factors which contribute to a non-random pattern of victimization, a focus on interpersonal crimes of violence, and a concern to identify victims who may have contributed to their own victimization.

Although much of the work associated with von Hentig and others is now largely discredited, there remains a strong body of work which focuses on patterns of victimization and how these may be related to crime prevention or crime reduction initiatives. One body of work that has been an important element in the development of victimology is what is generally referred to as 'routine activities theory'.

Routine activities theory is dealt with in greater detail elsewhere (see Chapters 14 and 24). Here we merely sketch out its most basic features. According to the key thinker in this area, Marcus Felson, criminal acts have three what he calls *almost-always elements*:

- a likely offender;
- a suitable target;
- the absence of a capable guardian against the offence.

As you can immediately see this adds a third element – the capable guardian – to the perpetrator–victim dyad that was the focus of the work of von Hentig, Wolfgang and others. The concern in this approach is to examine how these elements come together in time and space and, in principle, how such things might be manipulated so that the opportunities for crime are reduced. In relation to 'potential victims', therefore, routine activities and related approaches focus on how lifestyles might be altered so as to reduce opportunities or risks.

A number of criticisms are frequently levelled at such approaches:

- They tend to underplay structural inequalities in the distribution of victimization, being more likely to focus on more immediate characteristics of criminal events.
- Much work in this area tends to concentrate either on direct contact, predatory crime or on burglary and is not necessarily therefore easily or fully applicable in other situations.
- In particular, such approaches tend to be based on conventional definitions of crime and therefore pay insufficient attention to other forms of 'harm' such as crimes committed by corporations (though see Felson, 2002) or even by states.

Radical victimology

In Chapter 12 we considered the influence of radical theorising within criminology. So-called radical victimology is a product of the same era and same ideas. As with radical criminology more generally, this approach to victimology has focused on the vulnerability of particular groups. It has also sought to draw attention to the crimes of the powerful, including the state, and the frequent failure to recognise the victimization that results, though to what extent this, therefore, actually constitutes a new perspective is somewhat open to doubt.

At the heart of radical criminology is a concern with structural inequalities and how these come to shape and mould the distribution of victimization. We are not uniformly vulnerable, and local crime surveys in the 1980s for example were used precisely

to uncover the often extremely high levels of victimization within some of the poorer neighbourhoods in the UK. A central plank of left realism (see Chapter 13) was the assertion that criminology had failed to take victimization seriously, and that henceforward an accurate or realist victimology was a crucial part of the enterprise. As such it was highly critical of what it took to be the uncommitted stance of 'administrative criminology' (criminological work that was solely concerned with the effective operation of the criminal justice system) with its neutral calculations of the likelihood of victimization across the population as a whole.

Predictably, however, radical victimology has in turn been criticised for its narrow preoccupation with social class relationships and its portrayal of victimization as a system of oppression. In this regard it is viewed as failing to deal with other sources of structural inequality such as gender, ethnicity and age. As a result of this, critics such as Mawby and Walklate (1994) argue that it has largely failed to develop a coherent research agenda, leaving victimology in the grip of positivist approaches. It is this, it is argued, that 'critical victimology' seeks to address.

Critical victimology

Borrowing from labelling theory, much critical victimology has focused on the process of becoming a victim through the application of the label (and its reverse, the denial of victim status through a refusal to attach the label, or to accept the label). In this fashion, Miers (1990: 224) observes, 'Many groups and individuals may claim the label, but the key questions for a critical victimology are who has the power to apply the label and what considerations are significant in that determination'. Much feminist victimology might reasonably be located under this heading, focusing on hitherto neglected areas of women's victimization at the hands of men.

Mawby and Walklate (1994) argue that a critical victimology should be organised around three key concepts:

- rights;
- citizenship;
- the state.

The first question, therefore, concerns whether victims have needs *or* rights. Their preferred response is that a critical victimology should be based on the presumption that victims' rights are a crucial basis for future policy-making and, in particular, in getting away from previous policy positions that have cast the victim in a subservient role as simply the recipient of services. This, in turn, they argue implies a particular conception of citizenship – one that goes beyond what they suggest are limited conceptions emphasising responsibilities rather than rights. Finally, then, such a critical perspective demands explicit recognition of the ideological role of the state in the construction of victims policies.

The nature of victimization

Whilst early victimological work used victims as another means of understanding crime, more contemporary work has focused on the nature of victimization itself. This includes matters as varied as attempting to estimate both the extent of criminal victimization and seeking to understand its effects.

The extent of victimization

What do we know about victims of crime? Who is victimized? How likely is it? Our primary source of statistical information about victimization is the British Crime Survey (BCS). As we saw in Chapter 3, the BCS is a large household survey which asks a series of questions of its respondents about their experiences, generally over the previous 12 months. The path-breaking work in this area, in the UK, was undertaken by Sparks and colleagues' survey of victimization in London. Subsequently the BCS, which was first run in 1981 (and published in 1982) has provided a very substantial body of knowledge about the distribution of (various types of) crime. We will consider the nature of victimization in relation to particular crime types (violent crime and property crime, for example) in subsequent chapters. Our concern here is with the general pattern that is revealed by crime victimization data.

The 2005–06 BCS estimated that there were approximately 10.9 million crimes against adults living in private households. Calculating 'general risks' suggested that the chance of becoming a victim of crime was approximately 24 per cent (taking all crimes measured by the BCS into account). Now, such risks differ markedly according to the nature of the crime concerned. The overall risk of being a victim of household crime was just over 18 per cent whereas the risk of becoming a victim of violence was under four per cent.

Such general figures also disguise different levels of risk among different social groups. Taking violent crime as an example, 5.5 per cent of men aged

25–34 had been a victim at least once compared with 12.6 per cent of men aged 16–24. We look at these patterns in greater detail in Chapter 20. The important observation here is to note that criminal victimization is socially unevenly distributed. There are a number of ways of measuring this. One is to look at the geographical distribution of different types of crime and see to what extent this varies according to particular social characteristics. In the most recent BCS (Walker et al., 2006) an example is given using the rate of domestic burglary in different parts of Coventry in the East Midlands (see box below). What the shaded diagram shows is that those areas with the highest rates of burglary were the poorest areas of the city (using measures of deprivation and housing type as indicators). Put at its crudest, therefore, victim survey data suggest that it is those with the fewest material possessions who are most at risk from burglary.

Using data from the 1992 BCS and the 1991 Census, Hope (2001) calculates the incidence of property crime in different geographic areas according to levels of deprivation. To illustrate the differences areas are grouped in 'quintiles' – or fifths – and the incidence of property crime (i.e. the number per 100 households) is calculated for each. Those in the bottom quintile (the 20 per cent

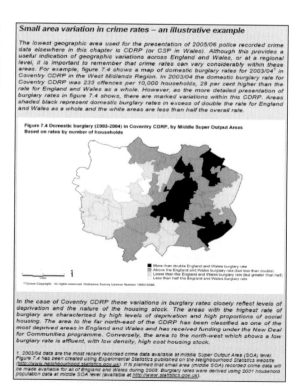

Small area variation in crime rates – an illustrative example

The lowest geographic area used for the presentation of 2005/06 police recorded crime data elsewhere in this chapter is CDRP (or CSP in Wales). Although this provides a useful indication of geographic variations across England and Wales, or at a regional level, it is important to remember that crime rates can vary considerably within these areas. For example, figure 7.4 shows a map of domestic burglary rates for 2003/04[1] in Coventry CDRP in the West Midlands Region. In 2003/04 the domestic burglary rate for Coventry CDRP was 233 offences per 10,000 households, 28 per cent higher than the rate for England and Wales as a whole. However, as the more detailed presentation of burglary rates in figure 7.4 shows, there are marked variations within this CDRP. Areas shaded black represent domestic burglary rates in excess of double the rate for England and Wales as a whole and the white areas are less than half the overall rate.

Figure 7.4 Domestic burglary (2003-2004) in Coventry CDRP, by Middle Super Output Areas. Based on rates by number of households

In the case of Coventry CDRP these variations in burglary rates closely reflect levels of deprivation and the nature of the housing stock. The areas with the highest rate of burglary are characterised by high levels of deprivation and high proportions of social housing. The area to the far north-east of the CDRP has been classified as one of the most deprived areas in England and Wales and has received funding under the New Deal for Communities programme. Conversely, the area to the north-west which shows a low burglary rate is affluent, with low density, high cost housing stock.

1. 2003/04 data are the most recent recorded crime data available at middle Super Output Area (SOA) level. Figure 7.4 has been created using Experimental Statistics published on the Neighbourhood Statistics website (http://www.neighbourhood.statistics.gov.uk). It is planned that small area (middle SOA) recorded crime data will be made available for all of England and Wales during 2006. Burglary rates were derived using 2001 household population data at middle SOA level (available at http://www.statistics.gov.uk).

Source: Walker et al. (2006: 114).

of areas that are least deprived) had a property crime incidence rate of 17, compared with an incidence rate of 49 in the top quintile (the 20 per cent of areas that are most deprived). Even more dramatically, this leads him to calculate that:

> ... around one-fifth of the victims of household property crime live in the ten per cent of the residential areas with the highest crime rates, and suffer *over one-third* of the total of household property crime ([and household property crime] constitutes just under one half of all victimization recorded in the BCS). (Hope, 2001: 209)

We have considerable evidence, therefore, that there is a considerable geographical and social patterning to crime. Moreover, studies of offending patterns show that a great many offenders commit their offences within a short geographical distance of their own homes (Wiles and Costello, 2000). Consequently, therefore, in a great many cases, offenders and victims are drawn from the same communities. In the case of violent crime, in something close to one-half of cases, perpetrator and victim know each other. According to the most recent BCS, one-third of violent incidents reported in the survey were classified as 'acquaintance violence' and a further 15 per cent were incidents of domestic violence (Walker *et al.*, 2006).

Repeat victimization

One of the most important facets of the uneven social and geographical distribution of crime is referred to by the term 'multiple' or 'repeat victimization' (see also Chapters 20 and 24). This refers to the important criminological finding that some people suffer much more crime than others – they are multiply or repeatedly victimized. There has been something of an explosion of work on repeat victimization since the late 1980s. Much of the work in this area proceeds from the understanding that when it comes to victimization, this is an area of life where the dice are loaded. When rolling a die, anyone with a passing understanding of probability knows that the fact that you have just rolled a 'six' has absolutely no bearing on the likelihood that you will roll a six next time around (even if we *feel* that it is somehow *less* likely).

What researchers working on repeat victimization have found is that this is not how things work in relation, for example, to burglary. If you have recently been burgled you might reasonably assume that the likelihood that it will happen to you again is reduced (or, if you're a mathematician, that the probability has stayed the same). Burglars might assume that you'll be more vigilant. There may be less to take next time around. And so on. However, this appears not to be the case. In fact,

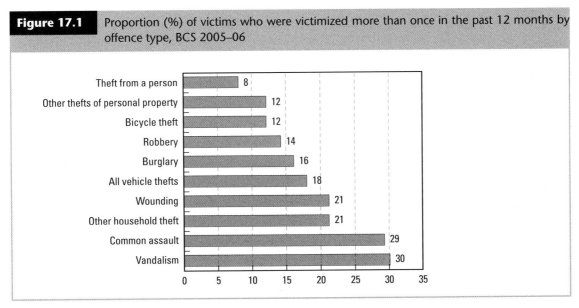

Figure 17.1 Proportion (%) of victims who were victimized more than once in the past 12 months by offence type, BCS 2005–06

Source: Walker *et al.* (2006).

your chances of being burgled again are in all likelihood increased – perhaps substantially.

Some of the credit for uncovering this uncomfortable finding must go to Sparks and colleagues' survey in London in the 1970s. Their finding that a minority of their respondents were experiencing a disproportionate amount of crime was important, they argued, because it could 'make it possible to identify particular sub-groups defined by attributes associated with relatively high rates of multiple victimization … which may be obscured by an overall comparison of victims and non-victims' (1977: 94).

Similarly, the 2006 BCS found that victims of vandalism (30%) and assault (29%) were the most likely to suffer repeat victimization (see Figure 17.1). However, within the general offence categories, domestic violence had the highest rate of repeat victimization. Over two-fifths (43%) of victims of domestic violence reported being attacked more than once, and almost one-quarter (23%) had been attacked on at least three occasions in the previous year.

Crime surveys, however, are something of a blunt instrument when it comes to trying to reveal the impact of repeat victimization for, somewhat inevitably, they tend to treat victimization as one or a series of discrete events rather than, as is sometimes the case, a more or less continuous feature of everyday life (Bowling, 1993). This is brought home most forcefully in a qualitative study by Hazel Genn in one London housing estate (see box below).

Maureen

Maureen is 32 years old, of English and Asian parentage. She is medium build, has short, untidy black hair, and not a tooth in her head. She looks at first sight at least 45 years old … In the original interview (as part of the Sparks' study) [Maureen] reported six violent offences and seven property offences during the previous year.

DAILY LIFE
Mid-June
Great excitement when I arrived. The police were on the landing asking questions about a robbery in the local post office. Maureen was in high spirits. She was detained by the police yesterday. She says they called on her in the afternoon and told her to come with them to the station because she failed to pay her fine for not having a television licence.

Late June
They had a party last night which was a success but the next door neighbour complained to the police about the noise and the police subsequently called and warned Maureen she must keep the peace … Next excitement – Kath's boy enters with minor injury to arm and Kath follows in near hysteria saying that he has been hit by a small girl. Kath had gone downstairs and found the girl's father holding her son. She hurled abuse at him and warned him she would kill him if he laid a finger on her child … She said if she had had the walking stick with her she would have beaten him (I believed her) …

Late July
Endless stream of neighbours coming in and out. Aggression is very noticeable. There are many mock fights both between women and between men and women. There is some pride in the extent to which women are knocked about by men. During the afternoon when Kath mentioned the new bruises on her arm, a neighbour took down her trousers to reveal a sizeable bruise on her thigh …

Early August
Morning mostly spent discussing last night's fight. Everyone was very excited …

KATH: I heard the screaming and I said 'Oh she's off again' and I turned over. I thought 'I'm not going to bother this time'. He'll roll out later on laughing, you watch – as if nothing has happened.

SUE: Brenda likes her drink too much. I mean I feel guilty in as much as she's got a beating, but I mean it's not my fault. She should keep her mouth shut. I suppose she must have said something to him about me and he's started. Well, I mean it's nothing to do with me.

KATH: He's probably told her to keep her mouth shut and she's kept it up.

SUE: He did hit me once – I bloody shit myself. He slung me from the bedroom to the bathroom and then back to the bedroom and I did a somersault over the bed.

MAUREEN: He's done that to Brenda you know. I've seen him do it.

HAZEL GENN: Why does she put up with it?

KATH: She likes him.

SUE: You know when you get cut with glass the blood spreads and you think it's more than what it is.

MAUREEN: I don't know if it was the glass because they said that he had some kind of hammer or axe with him. Marilyn was screaming up here 'He's gonna kill her. Oh God Maureen, quick.' It's madness though isn't it? Fucking two o'clock in the morning. Might get it again over the weekend. Any time there's a party and Cliff wants to feel a bit free, bam bam bam on her and that's it.

Source: Genn, H. (1988: 93–98)

Although only a short excerpt it gives a flavour of what appears to be an almost continuous round of arguments, fights, and other forms of conflict that permeated 'Maureen's' life and that of her family, friends and neighbours. This is not something that is easily captured by victimization surveys. As Pearson *et al.* (1989: 135) observe:

> For white people, for example, racial harassment and racial attacks are undoubtedly merely incidental, one-off events which are rarely, if ever, encountered. For black and minority ethnic groups, on the other hand, these are areas of experience which are part and parcel of everyday life. A black person need never have been the actual victim of a racist attack, but will remain acutely aware that she or he belongs to a group that is threatened in this manner. In much the same way that the high levels of 'fear of crime' among women can be better understood when experiences of subordination and daily harassments, from the subliminal to the blatant are reconnected, so the reconnected experiences of racism from a black and minority ethnic perspective shift the ground of how to define a 'racial' incident and what it is to police 'racism'. (quoted in Bowling, 1993: 240)

One of the most famous pieces of research in this area, known as the 'Kirkholt Project' after the estate in Rochdale in which it was conducted, focused on the prevention of burglary through concentrating on repeat victimization. It did so based on the fact that the researchers found that houses that had already been burgled were four times more likely to be burgled again than were houses that had not experienced a burglary. The reason that the Kirkholt Project became famous is that it found that through the tactic of focusing on repeat victimization, rather than the community as a whole, burglary was reduced by three-quarters over three years (see Chapter 24).

Victimization and the vulnerable

Crime, as has been illustrated, is socially very unevenly distributed. Nevertheless, it is often the case that 'vulnerability' has been defined very narrowly as physical vulnerability. In fact, and as we will see when we come to consider fear of crime, research shows people's assessments of risk to be heavily influenced by demographic factors such as where one lives and works, as well as physical characteristics, and also by some assessment of the likely impact of victimization should it occur.

The bulk of our information about victimization comes from large-scale surveys. However, whilst they have added enormously to our understanding, they also have some significant limitations. In particular, there are certain sections of society that are not well covered by household surveys – by definition, those that do not live in conventional 'households'. Some of these groups also happen to be some of the most vulnerable. To illustrate this we consider two here: the homeless and the elderly.

The homeless are especially vulnerable to violence, theft and harassment but are largely invisible, making little use of support services for victims of crime.

These two groups occupy the bottom rungs on what Carrabine *et al.* (2004) refer to as the 'hierarchy of victimization' – groups that have to struggle to have their victimization treated seriously and frequently feel under-protected.

Victimization and the homeless

Of all the groups in our society, arguably the homeless are most at risk from crime. Ironically, however, their marginal status makes this vulnerability largely invisible. The homeless tend not to report crime in any numbers and they make relatively little use of support services for victims. Indeed, the police are more likely to encounter the homeless as offenders than as victims. The BCS does not include the experiences of the homeless and, in the main, specific surveys of the homeless population tend not to ask about crime. However, a recent study based on a survey of over 300 homeless people in London, Oxford and Cambridge provides some evidence of the extent of criminal victimization among this population (Newburn and Rock, 2006).

First of all, the research indicates very high levels of victimization:

● Two-thirds (67%) of respondents said they had experienced theft in the last year compared with just over 1% of adults in England and Wales.

- 43% of the homeless reported having suffered damage to property compared with 7% of households in England and Wales.

- One-fifth (20%) of the homeless had suffered a burglary compared with 3.2% of households in the BCS.

- The picture was the same in relation to violence. Approximately half had experienced threats and/or violence compared with 4% of the population covered by the BCS.

- Finally, almost one-tenth (8%) of the homeless had been sexually assaulted, whereas the BCS encountered too few cases 'to count'.

In short, the homeless live in a very different world from most of us so far as crime is concerned. As one respondent put it:

> Describing it to people that don't, the general public, it's … completely [different] … it's a rite of passage, it's a very, very extremely intense period of one's life that can either destroy you or make you. It is very, very hard and it changes you immensely … if you're a decent person or if you've got, if you're not built for this sort of lifestyle, I mean you to sort of like toughen up very, very quickly because it's very, physical, very, very rough, very difficult. And if you don't fit in, you'll just go under (Newburn and Rock, 2006: 8).

Respondents were also asked about anti-social behaviour, including harassment on the street and during their time staying in hostels. Almost two-thirds reported having been insulted publicly whilst sleeping rough and one-tenth said that someone had urinated on them (see Table 17.1).

One very striking finding from the research was that in most major categories of criminal victimization – burglary, violence, threats, sexual assault and

criminal damage – the homeless reported that the perpetrator had been a member of the public. The exception was theft where other homeless people appear slightly more likely to have been the perpetrators than were members of the public. Violence, threats, intimidation and abuse from the public, particularly where the latter are intoxicated, appear to be an everyday reality for the homeless population.

It also seems clear from this research that the homeless not only experience very high levels of victimization, but they also feel that they receive very inadequate support from the police. By contrast, they are stopped and questioned relatively frequently and felt themselves to be simultaneously over-controlled and under-protected.

Victimization and the elderly

It is only relatively recently that criminology has begun to pay attention to the experiences of older members of society. In part, this is because of the expanding prison population, some of which involves what is sometimes referred to as a 'greying' of the prison population: as people are sentenced to longer and longer terms of imprisonment, so the proportion of the prison population that is elderly expands. Interest has also been stimulated by developments in victimology and the move beyond crude measures of 'risk' and vulnerability.

Criminology's failure to pay sufficient attention to the victimization of the elderly is attributed by Brogden and Nijhar (2006) to six factors:

- *Legality* – Much victimization of the elderly is not captured by the criminal law and is thus beyond the scope of traditional criminology.

- *Opposing paradigms* – The victimization of the elderly has long been dominated by social work and gerontology, both of which tend to have different approaches or philosophies from criminology.

Table 17.1	Experience of anti-social behaviour by the homeless	
Type of behaviour	**Number**	**%**
Harassed by others at a hostel	128	45
People throwing things at you	125	42
People insulting you publicly	192	64
Intimidated/harassed by drug dealers	114	38
Someone urinating on you	30	10

Source: Newburn and Rock (2006).

- *Private space* – The lives of the elderly are protected from scrutiny, because they are largely confined either to private households or to privately-run care homes.

- *Homogeneity* – The elderly, they argue, are less easily recognisable as a category than, say, the young, males and females, or even ethnic groups.

- *Gender* – Whilst drawing attention to women's victimization, one unintended consequence of the influence of feminism may have been to divert attention from the experiences of the elderly.

- *Structural location* – The elderly are socially excluded and marginal to political processes. This further marginalises their experiences.

A number of scholars have begun to challenge this lack of interest (see the essays, for example, in Wahidin and Cain, 2006). Research in a sample of nursing homes in Germany, for example, reveals what might be considered to be relatively high levels of experience of abuse. Based on interviews with nursing staff – and therefore quite likely to be an underestimate of the extent of various forms of abuse behaviour – the study nevertheless revealed that over two-thirds of nurses said that they had behaved abusively or neglectfully at least once, or had observed such behaviour (Görgen, 2006). A self-report study among nursing staff in 27 nursing homes found that 71 per cent reported having witnessed at least one incident of abuse in the previous 12 months, the most common of which were verbal aggression and neglectful care (see Table 17.2).

The results led Görgen to conclude that whilst the evidence fell short of suggesting that serious incidents against the elderly in care homes are common, they clearly do happen. It appears that night shifts are critical periods. However, there are many barriers not only for criminological researchers attempting to explore the vulnerability of the elderly in greater detail – including willingness and ability to discuss victimization – but also for the police and other agencies in attempting to investigate or respond. Moreover, 'these barriers are even higher when residents suffer from dementia which at the same time renders them extremely vulnerable to many forms of victimization' (2006: 88).

The impact of victimization

What is the impact of crime on its victims? Clearly, crimes vary in their nature and likely impact as do, presumably, victims in their ability to withstand whatever the impact may be. Goodey (2005: 121–2) lists a range of emotional, material and social needs that victims may need to have met in the aftermath of crime:

- reassurance and counselling;

- medical assistance;

- financial and practical assistance to secure property;

- information about case progress;

- guidance about what to expect in court;

Table 17.2	Victimization of residents in previous 12 months, Germany 2001			
	Self-reported		*Observed*	
Behaviour	Yes	%	Yes	%
Physical abuse	85	23.5	126	35
Psychological abuse/verbal aggression	194	54	223	62
Inappropriate use of mechanical restraints	102	28	142	39
Inappropriate use of chemical restraints	20	5.5	45	12.5
Neglectful care	194	54	215	60
Psychosocial neglect	107	30	123	34
Sexual abuse, sexual harassment	0	–	4	1
At least one of the above behaviours	258	71.5	257	71

Source: Görgen (2006: 84).

- the chance to express how the crime has affected them;
- assistance with filling out a form for state compensation;
- information about the release date of 'their' offender.

In terms of relatively immediate 'needs', the most pressing are likely to include needing to have property repaired or made secure, attention to physical injuries that require some form of attention, and emotional reassurance or comfort. The police and health services will generally deal with the first two of these. Emotional support in the aftermath of crime may well be provided by friends and family. In addition, formal services are provided by a voluntary organisation called Victim Support which offers help via home visits and telephone contact and, through its Witness Service, support before and during trial proceedings, to victims whose crimes have been reported to the police (we discuss Victim Support in greater detail later in this chapter).

In relation to longer-term impacts of criminal victimization, we may summarise these under four main headings: physical, behavioural, emotional or psychological, and financial.

Physical impact

Burgess and Holmstrom (1974) have described rape as less a sexual act than an 'act of violence with sex as the weapon'. Consequently, physical injury is a very common consequence of such violence. Most research suggests that the proportion of rape victims who suffer lasting injuries is small – perhaps around five per cent – though estimates of what are referred to as 'serious injuries' are often far higher, sometimes reaching close to 20 per cent (Williams and Holmes, 1981). Minor injuries are a common result of other forms of violent crime. The Islington Crime Survey (Jones *et al.*, 1986) found that over 96 per cent of victims of domestic violence had sustained black eyes or other forms of bruising, almost two-thirds had been scratched, just under half had suffered cuts and almost one-tenth had bones broken. Research also suggests that victims of sexual assault and domestic violence may experience a number of linked reactions such as headaches and general fatigue, stomach pains and loss of appetite in the aftermath of victimization (Stanko and Hobdell, 1993). Even in what is predominantly a property crime – burglary – physical injury may occur in a small minority of cases (Repetto, 1974).

Behavioural impact

Researchers studying the effects of rape, domestic violence, child (sexual) abuse and burglary have noted a number of behavioural consequences. A number of studies have shown sexual and marital problems to be relatively frequent in the aftermath of rape and sexual assault (Ellis *et al.*, 1980; Tufts, 1984). Research on the impact of other forms of violence have found changes in sleeping and eating patterns, feelings of helplessness (Burgess and Holmstrom, 1974) and increased security-consciousness. Problems of 'social functioning', including potential difficulties at home and school, as well as longer-term problems of substance abuse, are reported among child sex abuse victims (Anderson *et al.*, 1981; Briere, 1984).

Emotional and psychological impact

More has been written about this aspect of the aftermath of particular forms of crime than other consequences. Serious criminal victimization, such as rape, frequently results in feelings of depression (Burgess and Holmstrom, 1974; Indermaur, 1995), though full-blown clinical depression is relatively rare (Katz and Mazur, 1979). Reviews of the impact of child abuse have found somewhat different effects at different ages, with substantially higher proportions of children registering 'serious disturbance' in the seven to 13 age range compared with younger children (Friedrich *et al.*, 1986). Fear, guilt and shame are commonly reported among adult and child sexual assault victims. Research by Morgan and Zedner (1992) found that almost half the children in their sample that had been assaulted continued to be fearful of further attacks. One parent speaking three to four months after the incident said of their son:

> He does not go out in the evening any more ... He just thinks about it a lot. He very rarely goes out on his own – just outside the house or one of us accompany him. He goes to school and returns in the company of friends so that he is not alone.

Moreover, there is also a fairly strong body of evidence to suggest that victims of some property crimes such as residential burglary suffer considerable emotional effects. Maguire (1980), for example, found that approximately two-thirds of the burglary victims he interviewed said that the incident was still having an effect on their lives and that, most commonly, this took the form of unease or insecurity.

There is also the question of what are referred to as 'indirect victims' such as parents, children and others close to a victim. There is evidence, for example, that the partners of sexual assault victims may themselves suffer considerable distress as a result of the incident and that this may compound the problems faced by the primary victim. Studies of the relatives of murder victims, for example, have noted a number of physical and psychological symptoms at the acute stage of grieving (Burgess, 1984). Though conducted some time ago, Pynoos *et al.*'s (1987) study of the reactions of children who witnessed a sniper attack provides considerable insight into this issue. Based on interviews conducted one year after the attack, the researchers found that children and adults responded similarly in terms of the nature and frequency of their grief reactions, that many of the children continued to have grief-related dreams and some, particularly those who knew the victim, no longer played games that reminded them of the victim.

Financial impact

There may be financial consequences for victims of crime, both directly as a result of the crime and indirectly also. Recent research by Victim Support (2005) provides information about the financial impact of a range of crimes. It found that:

- 86% of victims said that they had possessions stolen during burglary. Of these:
  - 30% estimated that the value of the property lost through the burglary was in excess of £1,000;
  - a further 50% lost property worth between £100 and £999.
- Half of victims said that there was damage to their property as a result of the burglary, for example to doors, windows or furniture. In these cases:
  - over half estimated the cost of damage to be between £100 and £999;
  - over one-tenth suffered damage to property costing in excess of £1,000.
- Over a quarter of burglary victims don't have insurance, the research suggests.

There are also indirect costs. Thus, although an assault may not involve robbery, the indirect costs associated with the investigation, court proceedings and any hospital care that may be necessary, may also place substantial financial burdens on the victim. Research on victims of violence (Shapland *et al.*, 1985) showed that those victims who went to the police station to make a statement, provide evidence, or went to court, not only had the cost of transport to cover, but frequently also had to take time off work, arrange for someone to look after children and so on. Victims of rape and sexual assault may move house subsequent to victimization, and this and other changes in lifestyle are usually costly and generally borne entirely by the victim.

Fear of crime

In the last decade or two the idea of 'fear of crime' has become an important, if often misleading, notion within criminology. Indeed, so established has it become as an idea that it has often been referred to as 'a problem in its own right'. Certainly, there is evidence that people make decisions about their behaviour based on assumptions about crime and victimization. To repeat, however, this is a relatively new subject. It was not until the 1960s in the US and the 1970s in the UK that politicians and other commentators (including criminologists) started to talk of *fear of crime*.

Academic interest in this subject grew partly as a result of the development of victimization survey methodology, and partly as a consequence of the wider emergence of what is often referred to as 'administrative criminology'. We have noted elsewhere (see Chapter 3) that one of the very first BCS reports was much criticised for using 'average risks' as a measure of the likelihood of victimization and, more particularly, for seemingly accepting at face value the 'apparent paradox that those who are most fearful are least often victims' (Mayhew and Hough, 1988: 160). Jock Young (1988b: 165) was especially critical of such an approach to understanding fear of crime and, in particular, to the idea that the:

> ... 'irrationality' of the public [could be] demonstrated by tabulating real risks of crime against fears. Thus the first BCS report included a table ... in which two groups, the elderly and women, were seen to be particularly disproportionately worried. This kind of table ... stands at the centre of the fear of crime debate.

What is necessary, he argues, is an alternative approach which avoids using abstract crime rates as a core measure and, rather, focuses on the concrete predicaments that people actually face. Such criticisms led to considerable refinement of the approach taken in subsequent national crime surveys and also led directly to further investigation via local crime surveys.

Understanding 'fear of crime' is something that victimization surveys have continued to grapple with. The initial approach in the BCS was to ask a series of questions focusing on how safe people felt 'being out alone in this area after dark'. The full question reads:

ASK ALL: How safe do you feel walking alone in this area after dark? Would you say (READ OUT)

- Very safe
- Fairly safe
- A bit unsafe
- Very unsafe

(NOTE: IF RESPONDENT NEVER GOES OUT ALONE AT NIGHT, PROBE ... 'How safe *would* you feel ...). (reproduced in Lee, 2007: 90).

There are a number of potential problems with such an approach:

1 The question doesn't actually ask about crime.

2 It is not specific about time (when is 'after dark'?) or place (what is 'in this area'?)

3 Their feelings may have little or nothing to do with the *actual* risks of particular types of victimization.

4 Answers may reflect previous experiences or other fears.

5 Responses may not actually be about 'fear' at all.

Indeed, in terms of measurement, Hale (1996: 92) also points to the danger posed by conflating attempts at measuring risk with assessments of fear or anxiety:

... fear of crime refers to the (negative) emotional reaction generated by crime or associated symbols. It is conceptually distinct from either risks (judgements) or concerns (values). Of course fear is both an effect of, and caused by, judgements of risk but to confound the two is to confuse the relationship.

Indeed, Goodey (2005: 77) suggests that:

The apparent paradox that often lies with victimology's search for corresponding levels of risk and emotional response is partially explained by the problematic use of the term 'fear of crime'. Given the range of responses that people can

have to the same crime it would appear that the employment of the term 'fear' has been highly detrimental for the advancement of the 'science' of victimological inquiry.

Recent British Crime Surveys have sought to measure 'worry about crime'. The 1994 BCS reported particularly high levels of worry: one-quarter of the population reported that they were 'very worried' about burglary and rape, and that these worries were greater than many other broader concerns such as job loss, road accidents, illness and debt (see Farrall and Gadd, 2004). Work in the USA has found that women tend to worry about crime because of its links with the possibility of sexual assault (Ferraro, 1995) and that concerns about risk are linked to the potentially serious consequences of uncommon events as well as the less serious consequences of more frequent events (Douglas and Wildavsky, 1982). Later British Crime Surveys have reported consistently lower levels of concern and, moreover, there appears to have been some decline in worry around three of the main forms of crime in recent years (according to this type of measure – see Figure 17.2).

Within these overall measures, clear differences were apparent within the population:

- Women were more likely than men to worry about violent crime and burglary, but not car crime.

- Women were at least twice as likely to worry about violent crime as men, but this was especially pronounced in younger age groups.

- People from non-white groups overall were more than twice as likely to have high levels of worry about violence, burglary and car crime.

There has been a lot of important academic work in the area of 'fear of crime' in recent years, the bulk of which has been seeking subtler means of understanding public attitudes and feelings about crime. Feminist work, developing in the late 1980s and early 1990s, sought to shift the debate away from 'fear' – with its implications of passivity and helplessness – toward the issue of 'safety'. The work of scholars, such as Stanko (1990) in particular, pointed to the 'unsafety' that was a core part of aspects of women's everyday lives and in which men were particularly visible as perpetrators. In this manner, abstract notions of risk were replaced by gendered depictions of safety and, in particular, picked up on the high levels of violence against women that had been revealed in research over the

Figure 17.2   Worry about crime, 1988–2005/06 BCS

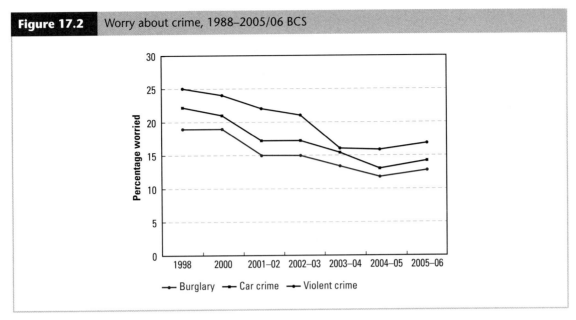

Source: Walker *et al.* (2006).

previous decade or so (see Chapter 32). There is a link between such work and another approach to crime victimization which sought to place it within a broader context of anxieties that formed part of the fabric of late modern society.

Subsequently, however, two further bodies of research have begun to appear which have introduced other issues into the study of fear of crime. First is the issue of *frequency*. As we have seen, surveys tend to pose standard questions which ask whether or not people feel fearful, not how often they do so (if they do). Exploring the issue of frequency, Farrall and Gadd (2004) found that whilst a little over one-third (37%) of people said they had been fearful in the past year, only 15 per cent had felt a high level of fear and only eight per cent experienced such a feeling more than once a quarter. They conclude, therefore, that the *incidence* of the fear of crime is actually quite low.

A second body of work, associated with Ditton and colleagues (e.g. Ditton and Farrall, 2000; Ditton *et al.*, 1999), started from the observation that what respondents to crime surveys were being asked to do was to summarise what were likely to be a wide variety of feelings, and have these captured as 'fear'. To explore this, the researchers began with a qualitative pilot study and asked respondents a series of open questions about their experiences of crime. This threw up the possibility that it was in fact 'anger' that was a more common response to crime than was being 'afraid'. This was

then formally tested in a random survey of 1,629 Scottish householders (see Figure 17.3).

The overall finding, that 'anger' is more commonly felt than being 'afraid', was found for all age groups and for men and women. The authors argue consequently that it seems likely that it is anger rather than fear that is the prime reaction of most people to the experience of criminal victimization. Indeed, they suggest much previous work on 'fear' may simply be a product of the kinds of questions asked in crime surveys, rather than an accurate indicator of what people actually feel. Finally, following their own experience in uncovering the

---

Review questions

1 What are the main differences between *positivist* and *critical* or *radical* victimology?

2 In what ways is criminal victimization unevenly distributed?

3 What is meant by 'multiple' or 'repeat victimization'?

4 What is the range of potential consequences of criminal victimization?

5 Why is crime experienced by the homeless or the elderly relatively invisible?

6 What is meant by the idea that fear of crime is a 'problem in itself'?

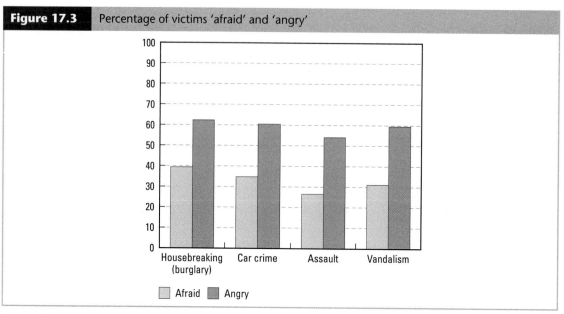

Figure 17.3 Percentage of victims 'afraid' and 'angry'

Source: Ditton *et al.* (1999).

importance of anger, they argue for the necessity of a combination of qualitative and quantitative methods in conducting research in this area.

Victims policy

We opened this chapter by repeating the observation that victims have, until recently, been a somewhat invisible part of the criminal justice system. Dignan (2005) has characterised the period prior to the developments of the last two decades as the 'era of disenfranchisement'. From the early nineteenth century, he argues, when the state began to take formal responsibility for the prosecution of offenders, the approach towards victims of crime has been characterised 'at best by neglect and at times by insensitive and harsh treatment' (2005: 63) as well as by distrust of the victim (Rock, 2004b).

Another illustration of this neglect is that it is only in recent decades that it has become possible to talk of such a thing as 'victims policy'. However, progressively over the past 20–30 years, increasing government attention has come to be paid to victims of crime and there now exists a reasonably substantial raft of services and other initiatives aimed at meeting victims' needs or, more challengingly, at protecting victims' rights.

Duff (1988) argues that there are two discernible trends which illustrate the worldwide impact the 'victim movement' has had on the criminal justice process: the first is the introduction of state-funded compensation schemes (with the aim of strengthening the relationship between the offender and the state) and, second, the adoption of compensation by the offender to the victim into the criminal justice system (thereby increasing the importance attached to the victim–offender relationship). In many respects the story of the 'victims' movement' in the UK begins with the introduction of criminal injuries compensation, for it was through the introduction of that scheme that the needs of victims were first formally recognised.

Criminal injuries compensation

In 1959, the government published *Penal Practice in a Changing Society*, which, whilst it focused primarily on the penal measures, also considered obligations to victims of crime, and resulted in the setting-up of a working party to examine the proposal to introduce a scheme for the payment of compensation to victims of crimes of violence. In the event there was relatively little political opposition to the idea and the Criminal Injuries Compensation Scheme (CICS) came into operation on 1 August 1964. In its first year of operation it received over 500 applications for an award. In its first full year of operation the scheme paid out almost half a million pounds in compensation.

Although the introduction of the scheme had come about as part of a process of penal reform, it was perceived to be the righting of a wrong in the criminal justice system, and not as the start of a long-term programme on behalf of victims. The scheme was amended in 1969, and again in 1979, and eventually was put on a statutory footing as a result of the Criminal Injuries Compensation Act 1995 (whereupon it became the Criminal Injuries Compensation Authority – CICA).

The CICA has been amended in recent years and is now based on a 'tariff system' in which injuries are separated by severity into different bands. These are then translated into different levels of payment. The system is less generous than it used to be as it tends not to provide compensation for loss of earnings or expenses. One of the important characteristics of the state-based compensation system is the model of the 'innocent victim' that it uses. The terms of the scheme are such that an award may be refused or reduced because of the applicant's conduct before, during or after the events giving rise to the application – most usually in cases where the applicant was being aggressive or was engaged in actual or attempted criminal conduct.

The Authority may also refuse or reduce an award because of the applicant's character as shown by his criminal convictions. Moreover, there does not have to be any connection between the convictions and the incident from which the claim is being made. Indeed, the use of this notion of the innocent or blameless victim as the basis for the operation of criminal injuries compensation is quite explicit. Miers' (2007) description of the Authority's operations makes clear the link with an idealised view of victim status:

> Prior to and since its inception, both the [CICA] and the Home Office have repeated that the Scheme applies to the 'blameless' victim (CICA, 2004: 4; Home Office, 2005: 15). But 'blame' in this context does not refer to a victim's actions in respect of the criminal injury, but to his or her moral worth as a person who should properly be the beneficiary of public money.

Court-ordered compensation

The other major source of compensation for victims is via the courts. Such compensation has quite a long history in England and Wales, at least as far back as the Larceny Act and the Malicious Damage Act of 1861. It was the Criminal Justice Act 1972 which enabled compensation to be ordered by the courts, giving magistrates' courts and the Crown Court a general power to order offenders to pay compensation for loss, damage or personal injury resulting from a criminal offence. Initially, the compensation order was an *ancillary* order which had to be made in conjunction with another penalty – it could not be made on its own – though this was eventually made possible by the Criminal Justice Act 1982.

Much research has shown the delivery of compensation via the courts to be a rather haphazard process. Only a minority of victims ever receive compensation from an offender via the court system, and fewer still will receive anything from the CICA. In addition, the two systems of compensation do not mesh and, indeed, are not intended to fit together. The two compensation systems cover predominantly different offences, operate at different financial levels and have quite distinct threshold criteria. Even in the area of criminal injury there appears to be little correspondence between the court system and the CICA. As it stands at the moment, victims of crime tend to receive sums of compensation from magistrates' courts which, because in practice claims are generally small and many offenders have limited means, are generally far below the lower limit operated by the CICA. Although, theoretically, compensation orders should cover injuries up to and over the minimum threshold at CICA, in practice there exists a considerable gulf between awards from the scheme and awards from the court.

Feminism and 'secondary victimization'

We consider the importance of feminist scholarship in our understanding of women's victimization in some detail in Chapter 32. Here, we focus more on the notion of 'secondary victimization' and how feminism in particular has played a role in campaigns to reform the way in which the justice system treats certain types of victim of crime. The term 'secondary victimization' refers to the situation in which victims feel so poorly treated by the criminal justice system that the experience was akin to being victimized all over again. This has been the case for many victims, but is an experience that has been very clearly illustrated in relation to many female victims of rape and sexual assault who were forced to relive their experiences in court and who

Campaigners in London in the 1970s highlight the problem of men's violence against women.

were often treated as if they had invited the assault, or were in some other way to blame for what had happened to them.

The increasing recognition of women as victims of sexual assault or domestic violence, and the changes this has brought about, have their roots in the re-emergence of the feminist movement in the 1970s. There is evidence from the late 1970s and early 1980s that women reporting sexual assault to the police were, on occasion, treated as if they were responsible for their own victimization. Public attention was focused sharply on such issues in early 1982, when a judge imposed a fine rather than a prison sentence on a man convicted of rape on the grounds that the victim was guilty of what he called 'contributory negligence'. This was followed shortly after by a BBC television 'fly-on-the-wall' documentary about Thames Valley Police, one episode of which concerned the interview of a woman who was reporting that she had been raped. So intimidating was the investigating officer's approach that a considerable public furore followed the broadcast (see box below). Much concern was voiced about the lack of sensitivity and sympathy being given to the victim's rights and

feelings. As Adler (1987) put it some time later: 'All but the most transparently flawless victim was liable to be bullied by interrogators and prosecutors, exposing her to a form of secondary victimization'.

There have been a number of practical developments in response to these issues. The Women's Movement has been instrumental in setting up rape crisis centres and women's refuges in many towns and cities in the UK. The first refuge was set up in 1971 (Pizzey, 1974) and there were over 150 by 1978 (Binney *et al.*, 1981). The centres operate telephone counselling services and offer emergency and, to some extent, continuing support and advice for any woman or girl who has been raped or sexually assaulted – irrespective of whether or not the offence is reported to the police.

Pressure for change remained high and, as far as the police were concerned, it was the Metropolitan Police that led the way. During 1985, they set up a working party to look into the problems of policing domestic violence. Reporting in 1986 it recommended a more active arrest and prosecution policy, better collection of statistics on the nature and extent of domestic violence, and the introduc-

Police (BBC Television, 1982)

Director: Charles Steward; Producer: Roger Graef

Police (1982) was another tele-verité exercise by the BBC to lift the lid on British institutions, following *Sailor* (1976), *Hospital* (1977) and *Strangeways* (1980). Filmmakers Roger Graef and Charles Stewart were given the keys to Reading police station, and spent a year trailing the bobbies of Thames Valley's E Division. Consent came from senior officers and the Home Office itself, who were anxious to stem a growing mistrust of the police, particularly among Britain's inner city ethnic minorities. Shooting on the series wrapped in early 1981; that summer the police fought pitched battles in Brixton, Toxteth and Bristol during Britain's worst race riots. When *Police* was finally transmitted in January 1982, the public stakes had been raised immeasurably.

Police was quintessential fly-on-the-wall fare. Favouring long takes over fast editing, and shorn of commentary, background music or interviews, the series offered instead the drama of real, unpredictable, life and challenged the fictional stereotypes that had dominated television police drama. While the cop-show scenario of an armed standoff in episode one proved a false alarm, the drama of a disciplinary hearing, in which a plainclothes officer was returned to uniform, and reduced to tears, was almost unbearable.

Police showed the force as all too human but sometimes far from humane. In episode three, 'A Complaint of Rape', a woman with a history of psychiatric treatment claims she has been raped by three strangers and is, in turn, bullied and cajoled by three male officers who dismiss her story out of hand. "This is the biggest bollocks I've ever heard," erupts one officer. The woman remains unseen as the camera assumes her point-of-view, trapped in the claustrophobic confines of the interrogation room. As she is subjected to the most hostile questioning, the accusing officers fill the frame in penetrating close-ups and the viewer gains some sense of her double violation.

Transmitted soon after an infamous court decision (in which a judge had accused a hitchhiker of "contributory negligence" in her own rape), 'A Complaint of Rape' caused a public outcry and led to a change in the way police forces handled rape cases. Within months, a new rape squad of five female officers was formed in Reading. "The most we can hope is that people will rethink their assumptions – including policemen," said Graef. *Police* showed that the fly-on-the-wall doesn't just watch the world. It can change it too.

Joe Sieder, British Film Institute

http://www.screenonline.org.uk/tv/id/464502/

---

tion of improved training for the police officers who deal with such incidents. It was particularly critical of existing training which, it said, 'perpetuate[d] current terminology ("domestic dispute") which ... trivialise[d] marital violence rather than treating it as an allegation of crime'. A Force Order encouraging arrest was issued in 1987, and the Metropolitan Police quickly set up a number of specialist domestic violence units, being followed in later years by a small number of provincial forces. A broad range of initiatives have followed and some of these are explored in greater detail in Chapter 32.

Child abuse

Developments in the area of child abuse occurred around about the same time as recognition about violence against women grew, and were in many respects very much part of the same feminist-inspired critique of criminal justice. Again, it was the repercussions of specific, highly-publicised incidents of abuse which did as much as anything to raise the profile of the issue in Britain. The first major case was that of Maria Colwell in 1973. Maria was seven years old when she was killed by her stepfather. She had previously been removed from her home by social services for fostering, but had later been returned and had been both beaten and starved before eventually being murdered. It was this case, and the ensuing public outcry, which led to the acceptance of the term 'child abuse' and to the establishment of a new system of child protection in the UK – involving area child protection committees, inter-agency case conferences, and the development of specific training.

However, it was not until the early 1980s that the idea of *sexual* abuse of children, as opposed to physical abuse, gained any sort of real recognition. In 1984, a further notorious case involving the abuse and later murder of a young girl by her stepfather was crucial in bringing the issue to public attention. Jasmine Beckford and her sister had been placed in care soon after their births because of evidence of physical abuse. However, they were later returned and Jasmine died, aged four, in 1984. The subsequent public enquiry recommended that the primary aim of social work in this area was to protect the child, rather than keep the family together. The pressure on the police around this time to introduce more sympathetic means of dealing with adult victims of sexual violence was quickly extended to children.

Two other crucial developments in the late 1980s brought further attention to the issue of child abuse in the UK. The first was the setting-up of a telephone helpline, 'Childline', in 1986 by the television presenter Esther Rantzen. Tens of thousands of calls were made on the first day of Childline, and although the service was not without its critics, the publicity that surrounded its operation did as much as anything to draw public attention to the issue of

Established in 1986 by Esther Rantzen, Childline is a free helpline for children and young people in the UK. She is seen here with the former boxer, Chris Eubank.

sexual abuse of children. It was the 'Cleveland affair' in 1987 which really brought the issue of sexual abuse to the forefront of public debate. The scandal involved two local paediatricians who, over a period of months, had been instrumental in bringing over 100 children into care on place of safety orders. On the basis of a particular physical test, the doctors argued that many of the children had been anally abused. Before long stories of large numbers of children being taken into care in Cleveland began to surface in the national press and, after a successful campaign by parents, a public inquiry was established. Chaired by Judge Elizabeth Butler-Sloss it was surrounded by massive media and public attention. The report (Butler-Sloss, 1988) made a number of detailed recommendations including:

- Procedures for joint investigation of child abuse cases by police officers and social workers.
- Joint training of police and social workers.
- New interview techniques.
- A network of communication between all the involved agencies.

A decade and a half later multi-agency child protection work remains hugely difficult and an area which has continued to cause controversy, not least in cases such as that of Victoria Climbié who died in 2000 after multiple failures by both police and social services.

In contrast to the instances of physical abuse noted above, the main criticism of social workers in the Cleveland case was that they had been over-zealous in their desire to take action to protect children. Crucially, the report recommended that it was the interests of the child that should form the primary focus of any policies established to deal with the problem and that general philosophy formed the basis of the subsequent 1989 Children Act.

Much of the focus on child victims of crime has been upon the potentially traumatic consequences for those who have to give evidence in court. Powerful arguments have been advanced in favour of limiting the range of cases that come to court and thereby protecting the child. The 1988 Criminal Justice Act abolished the requirement that unsworn evidence from a child be corroborated, and the 1991 Criminal Justice Act introduced the use of video recordings of testimony. More recently screens and video links in court have been established to prevent direct contact between child witnesses and the accused. Court procedures have been amended to take the needs of young victims and witnesses into account largely as a result of the Youth Offending and Criminal Justice Act 1999. Its provisions included:

- Screening the witness from the accused.
- Giving evidence by live link.
- Ordering the removal of wigs and gowns when the witness testifies.
- Giving evidence in private (in sexual cases involving intimidation).
- Video recording of evidence-in-chief; video recording of cross-examination and re-examination.
- Examination through an intermediary.
- The provision of aids to communication for young or incapacitated witnesses.

Such measures were intended to provide special treatment not only to child witnesses, but also to those with learning disabilities or a mental illness, to those that have suffered intimidation, and for complainants in sexual cases. Goodey (2005: 102), however, suggests a number of reasons why the provisions in the Act may not be fully realised:

- There is the significance given over to the discretionary powers of the judiciary, to decide whether a victim should be considered as a vulnerable or intimidated witness and afforded certain safeguards.
- There is a lack of consistent service provision between and within agencies that should consistently recognise and respond to the needs of vulnerable or intimidated witnesses.
- The deep-rooted traditions of the adversarial trial (see Chapter 26) in England and Wales continue to work against alternative means for presenting evidence such as pre-recorded evidence and the use of live television links.

Victim support

What have often been referred to as 'victims' movements' have developed in both America and Britain over the past 30 years or so. Goodey (2005: 102) notes three main factors in the rise of these reform movements:

- A rising crime rate and, at the same time, a rejection of the rehabilitative criminal justice model as a response to offending.

- The emergence of the centre-right in British and North American politics and, with it, a tough approach to law and order.
- Growth in the feminist movement, and, with this, an emphasis on women and children as victims of interpersonal patriarchal violence.

There are, however, some distinctive differences between these victims' movements, not least in the much more highly politicised nature of developments in America (Rock, 2005). The more politically neutral nature of much of the victims' movement in the UK is best captured in the history of what is now the largest victims' organisation in the UK, Victim Support (VS). It had its origins in Bristol in the early 1970s, when the first local project, Bristol Victims' Support Scheme, started visiting victims in January 1974. They quickly found that they became almost overwhelmed by the nature and size of the demand for support. To cope they started hiring volunteers, and that has formed the basis of the VS model ever since. However, they also found that there were significant problems with fund-raising; in short it was difficult to keep the service going (Rock, 1990).

Nevertheless, by May 1977 there were 13 schemes in England and Wales and two years later when a National Association was set up, there were 30. At around this time NACRO, the prisoner resettlement and crime prevention charity which was providing support for the developing organisation in a number of ways, approached the Home Office with a view to securing some financial backing for a national association for the victim support movement. In mid-1979 this was successful, and the Home Office promised £10,000 a year for three years.

From there the movement expanded rapidly. The 30 schemes running when the National Association (known originally as the National Association of Victims Support Schemes or NAVSS) was officially launched in 1979 more than doubled to 79 by the end of the following year. This increased to 159 by September 1983 and to over 300 by 1987. Referrals increased at a faster rate than did the schemes: from 18,000 in 1979 to 65,000 in 1983 and 257,000 in 1986–7 (Rock, 1990). The work increased not only in quantity but also in range, taking on, for example, victims of rape and sexual assault, and of serious assault and even murder.

Part of the success of Victim Support has been in successfully managing its public image. There are a least four elements to this.

1 It was crucial that the movement was, and was seen to be, non party-political.

2 From the outset the organisation decided against getting involved in penal politics of any sort. It steadfastly refused to comment on criminal justice issues unless they directly affected victims or victim services. 'This single issue approach was a deliberate device to avoid distractions and to guard against co-option by the developing political theme of "law and order"; particularly, we wanted to avoid reinforcing illusions that victims benefit from tougher sentencing' (Holtom and Raynor, 1988: 24).

3 In many respects it fought shy of publicity, particularly by campaigning around the plight of particular victims, even when the resulting publicity might, in the short-term at least, have helped it raise the funds it often desperately needed.

4 The Association encouraged very close ties with the police. Schemes relied upon the police for referrals, and that meant that without their cooperation the organisation simply could not function. In addition, being a very powerful and influential body, the police also carried great weight with other agencies and bodies that NAVSS wished to influence, so close relationships were doubly advantageous.

5 The adoption of a co-operative, partnership approach to working, not just with the police but also with the probation service and other agencies (Mawby and Walklate, 1994).

In 1986 government took the decision to provide core funding to Victim Support with a grant of £9 million over a period of three years. In the first years the work of victim support schemes focused mainly on the victims of 'conventional' crimes such as burglary and theft. During the 1980s, they became progressively more involved in providing support for a wider variety of victims, including victims of racial harassment, families of murder victims, and victims of rape and serious sexual assault. More recently, Victim Support has broadened out in a variety of new areas.

Researchers identified one area in which victims required support as being that of the court process itself (Shapland *et al.*, 1985; Shapland and Cohen, 1987). A longitudinal study undertaken by Shapland and colleagues charted a continuous decline in levels of satisfaction reported by victims as they passed through the criminal justice system. Crucially, they found that facilities in the courts were sadly lacking, with victims and defendants frequently having to share the same waiting spaces in court, and little information available to victims or witnesses about court dates. By 1990, Victim Support were running a series of pilot victim/witness support programmes in seven Crown Court centres and the organisation now provides a witness service in every criminal court in England and Wales (Rock, 1993).

Victims' rights?

The first Victims' Charter was published in 1990. Rock (2004) describes it as a 'maverick', being published a full year before the Citizens' Charter. It was the first acknowledgement that some victims might have entitlements (not *rights*) because of their victimization. However, Dignan (2005: 69) describes some of the charter's standards as being 'so platitudinous as to be virtually worthless'. Nevertheless, it did try to improve victims' access to information and the extent to which criminal justice agencies such as police and courts should feel obliged to keep victims in touch, and reflected growing interest in victims' needs – if not rights.

The publication of the second Victims' Charter in 1996 (Home Office, 1996) made a significant impact on the status of victims. The charter covered police responsibilities for providing information to victims, familiarisation visits to courts, together with details of complaints procedures if the standards set out were not met. The charter suggested that victims of crime could in future expect:

● To be given the name and phone number of a police officer or 'crime desk' responsible for their case.

- To be given a leaflet called 'Victims of Crime' as soon as they report a crime in person at a police station.
- To be told if someone has been caught, cautioned or charged, and to be asked if they require further information. If so, they will be told of any decision to drop charges, the date of the trial and the final result.
- To have the chance to explain how they have been affected by the crime.
- To be told when an offender serving a sentence of life imprisonment, or a custodial sentence for a serious sexual or violent crime, is likely to be released.
- To be treated with sensitivity when attending court as a witness, and to receive support from the Witness Service before, during and after the trial.
- To be paid travel and other expenses for attending court.
- (In the case of child witnesses) to have special arrangements made including the provision of a TV link.
- To be offered emotional and practical support by Victim Support and, where appropriate the Criminal Injuries Compensation Agency.

Treating victims as customers in this fashion was largely unaffected by the change of government that occurred in 1997. As Rock (2004: 166) notes:

> Citizens' charters may have been John Major's creation, but the New Labour administration's preoccupation with modernisation, articulate standards, and active citizenship melded well with his ideology of the consumer-citizen, and the charter programme was endorsed and boosted by the new government.

One stop shop and victim statements

As part of the process of developing the services outlined by the revised charter, two pilot projects were launched by the Home Office. The first, generally referred to as the 'One stop shop', covered the new procedures within which the police were to collect, collate and disseminate information on the progress of cases to victims of crime. This was the latest in a series of initiatives attempting to improve the experience of crime victims, long shown by research to have considerable difficulty in eliciting information about 'their' cases from criminal justice agencies (Maguire, 1982; Shapland et al., 1985).

The second pilot project was the victim statement scheme in which victims may opt to make written statements about the impact of a crime or crimes upon them and, in principle, to have these read out in court. Although what are often referred to as 'victim impact statements' are permitted in certain jurisdictions (South Australia, Canada and many States in the USA), there has been considerable scepticism about, and resistance to, them in the UK. Their function is generally seen as being 'to inform a decision-maker of any physical or emotional harm, or any loss of or damage to property, suffered by the victim through or by means of the offence, and any other effects on the victim' (Ashworth, 1993).

The One stop shop and victim statement initiatives were linked. The pilot projects involved an opt in element; victims were asked whether they wished to opt in to receiving further information after their initial contact with the police (Hoyle et al., 1998). The police were to write to victims after charge and before papers were passed to the CPS (Crown Prosecution Service) inviting them to opt in. For those who did, the police then had a responsibility to see that certain information was passed to them. In addition, a combined compensation/victim statement form was also sent. There was no obligation to make a statement, but victims were told that if they did it would be added to the case papers and that they could, potentially, be cross-examined on it at court.

These pilot projects raised a number of interesting issues. First, and in line with previous research, they suggested that citizens have rather imprecise expectations when they become victims and make a report to the police. They generally are keen to receive information, but are rather unclear as to what this might mean. The pilots, however, suggested that expectations appeared to have been raised, sometimes beyond what services could offer. The researchers concluded that the receipt of information from one point only may create as many problems as it solves (Hoyle et al., 1998). The evaluation of victim statements found that police officers occasionally exaggerated the possible impact such a statement might have on the court process and, of those victims who did make such a statement, only a small minority had any idea what use had been made of it subsequently.

Rebalancing the criminal justice system?

In 2002 a White Paper, *Justice For All*, was published by the Home Office. Its aim, it said, was to 'rebalance the [criminal justice] system in favour of victims, witnesses and communities'. Subsequently, the Domestic

Violence, Crime and Victims Act 2004 paved the way for the publication of a Code of Practice for Victims of Crime which formed the basis for the government's claim that it is 'reforming the justice system so that the needs and rights of victims and witnesses are placed at the heart of what we do' (http://www.home-office.gov.uk/crime-victims/victims/Victims-rights/). The new code of practice was launched on 3 April 2006, and applies to all police forces, the CPS and the Courts Service, Prisons and Probation Services, CICA, Parole Board and others. Among others, it sets out the following requirements:

- A right to information about the crime within specified time scales, including the right to be notified of any arrests and court cases.

- A dedicated family liaison police officer to be assigned to bereaved relatives.

- Clear information from the Criminal Injuries Compensation Authority (CICA) on eligibility for compensation.

- All victims to be told about Victim Support and either referred on to them or offered their service.

- An enhanced service for vulnerable or intimidated victims.

- The flexibility for victims to opt in or out of services to ensure they receive the level of service they want.

The Act also made provision for the introduction of a Commissioner for Victims and Witnesses though, to date, no appointment has been made.

What should we make of the changes to the criminal justice process as a result of the growing acknowledgement of the role of the victim of crime? Does it amount to a radical overhaul? Does it, as government has suggested it should, achieve a 'rebalancing' of the criminal justice system in favour of the victim? The answer from most academic experts is a fairly unequivocal 'no'. Walklate (2007) describes the changes as 'tinkering with adversarialism' and Dignan (2005: 85) argues that the changes 'so far constitute a partial enfranchisement at best':

- Victims tend now to be kept better informed than previously, but information still tends to be incomplete and is often late.

- Opportunities to discuss the experience of victimization and to have it acknowledged are limited.

- Involvement in decision-making, such as at court, other than offering information, remain prohibited.

- Influence over forms of redress, assuming there is redress, is very limited.

- Only certain types of victim are recognised in policy-making (rarely, for example, are victims of regulatory offences or of corporate crimes acknowledged).

- The influence of Christie's *ideal victim* can still be seen in some policy initiatives (victim policies are often established as a means of indicating tough criminal justice credentials rather than a means of supporting victims *per se*).

Indeed, he goes on to argue that traditional criminal justice has failed victims in three important ways:

1 It hasn't acknowledged the special status of victims as those who have personally suffered harm as a result of an offence.

2 It has denied victims a formal role in proceedings except under limited circumstances where victims are necessary to the achievement of broader criminal justice goals (though in some European systems it is possible for victims to be auxiliary prosecutors or *partis civiles* (see Brienen, M. and Hoegen, 2000)).

3 It has failed to provide material redress for personal harm.

Is the notion of victims' *rights,* however, a good idea? To what extent should there be limits to reforms aimed at 'rebalancing' the criminal justice system? Although the idea clearly attracts politicians, legal scholars are frequently much more sceptical. Thus, for example, Ashworth and Redmayne (2005) offer a number of important criticisms of the way in which government discussion of victims' rights has become bound up with the idea of *rebalancing* the justice system. This metaphor – the idea of changing the *balance* in the criminal justice system – is misleading in a number of important respects, they argue. First, it implies that defendants have too many rights and that somehow the position of defendants needs to be worsened in order to improve the situation of victims. On the contrary, they argue, there are many things that can be, and have been, done for victims that have no bearing at all on defendants' rights. In other words, this is not a 'zero-sum' game. Improving things for one party needn't (and shouldn't) necessitate making them worse for others.

Second, even where there is some closer connection in which reforms affect defendants' experiences of criminal justice, such as the rules governing cross-examination of vulnerable witnesses, there is still no necessary clash between the rights of defendants and those of victims or witnesses (though for a different view see Sanders and Jones, 2007). Again, quite the reverse, they say: 'Even the most controversial of these reforms, that involving a restriction on the ability of defendants to cross-examine witnesses in sexual assault cases, there is a shared assumption on both sides of the debate that defendants have the right to adduce all relevant evidence; the dispute has been over just what is relevant' (2005: 42). The bottom line in this position is that there are certain basic rights enjoyed by defendants and these should not be undermined by any policies designed to improve the lot of victims.

The final reason they say the 'rebalancing' metaphor is misleading is that it implies that it is somehow in the interest of victims to see increased conviction rates, irrespective of how such an increase is brought about. Not true, they say. Victims gain nothing, they argue, if any of the fundamental principles of criminal justice are compromised. Their argument, put simply, is that political campaigns which set 'victims' rights' against 'defendants' rights' are misleading and potentially dangerous. We should not think of criminal justice in this way. Our concern, they imply, should be with the general principles that underpin the system of criminal justice or, put differently, the rights that *everybody* should share. This sentiment was eloquently captured by Dubber (2002: 342) when he said: 'Victims' rights will be vindicated only after we abandon the concept of victims' rights and reform our law to vindicate instead the rights of persons'.

Review questions

1 What are the main differences between positivist and critical or radical victimology?

2 In what ways is criminal victimization unevenly distributed?

3 What is meant by 'multiple' or 'repeat victimization'?

4 What is the range of potential consequences of criminal victimization?

5 Why is crime experienced by the homeless or the elderly relatively invisible?

6 What is meant by the idea that fear of crime is a 'problem in itself'?

Questions for further discussion

1 To what extent is people's level of fear of crime irrational?

2 To what extent is the adversarial nature of the criminal justice system the main difficulty faced by victims?

3 To what extent should the state ensure that only 'deserving' victims receive compensation?

4 Are victims' rights and defendants' rights fundamentally incompatible?

5 What did Dubber mean when he said, 'Victims' rights will be vindicated only after we abandon the concept of victims' rights?'

Further reading

There is a good selection of very fine essays in Walklate, S. (ed.) (2007) *Handbook of Victims and Victimology,* Cullompton: Willan. (Particularly worthwhile in the context of the issues discussed in this chapter are the chapters by Booth and Carrington, Hope, Miers, Rock, Sanders and Jones, and Whyte.)

There are now a number of good textbooks covering the general area of victimology. Among the best introductions are:

Goodey, J. (2005) *Victims and Victimology: Research, policy and practice,* Harlow: Longman

Spalek, B. (2006) *Crime Victims: Theory, policy and practice,* Basingstoke: Palgrave

Walklate, S. (2007) *Imagining the Victim of Crime,* Maidenhead: Open University Press

In relation specifically to the history and politics of the fear of crime, there is a very useful book by Murray Lee (2007) *Inventing Fear of Crime,* Cullompton: Willan

Anyone wanting to know about the recent history of criminal justice policy in this area should consult Rock, P. (2004) *Constructing Victims' Rights: The Home Office, New Labour and victims,* Oxford: Clarendon Press

Websites

There is some useful material on academic victimology at the International Victimology website: www.victimology.nl

Both the Home Office (www.homeoffice.gov.uk/crime-victims) and the Victim Support (http://www.victimsupport. org/) websites contain a lot of useful information.

Chapter outline

Introduction   372
   Edwin Sutherland and white-collar crime   373
   Distinguishing between white-collar and corporate crime   376

Exploring white-collar crime   377
   Theft at work   378
   Fraud   378
   Employment offences   380
   Consumer offences   381
   Food offences   382
   Environmental crime   383
   State-corporate crime   384

Explaining white-collar and corporate crime   385
   Differential association   385
   Self-control   385
   Neutralisation   385
   Critical theory   386
   Shaming   387

Understanding white-collar crime   388
   White-collar offenders   388

Victims of white-collar crime   390

The extent of white-collar crime   393

The impact of white-collar crime   394

Understanding impact: the qualitative dimension   395

Controlling white-collar crime   397
   Regulating white-collar crime   399
   Self-regulation   401
Questions for further discussion   402
Further reading   402
Websites   403

White-collar and corporate crime

CHAPTER SUMMARY

Much of criminology is focused upon those activities that fill our criminal courts: burglary, vandalism, theft, violence – often minor – as well as some more serious offences. It is comparatively rare, however, for matters like embezzlement, fraud and other crimes by apparently respectable, professional people to end up in court. Still less common are prosecutions brought against major corporations – or even smaller companies – for criminal activities. Generally speaking this is not because such activities are rare, but because they are policed in different ways and, arguably, subject to different standards. Criminologists, albeit a minority of them, have long been interested in what is variously called 'white-collar' or 'corporate' crime.

In this chapter we explore:

● what is meant by such terms;

● what types of criminal activity it covers;

● what impact it has;

● how it is regulated or otherwise controlled.

Introduction

Now, a very great man once said That some people rob you with a fountain pen. (Bob Dylan, *Talking New York* © 1962)

Business has a dirty side. On those occasions when the veil of corporate respectability and probity is lifted, we are able to witness a world where managers lie, cheat, manipulate, dissemble, and deceive. (Punch, 1996: 1)

The title of this chapter is 'white-collar and corporate crime'. This is something of a fudge for, in one sense, it represents a failure to find a term that will encompass crimes *within* and *by* businesses. There is an ongoing debate within criminology as to how such activities are to be described and the fact that this has been by no means resolved is reflected in the chapter title. Students exploring this subject should not be put off by the very broad range of terminology available. This includes, at least, 'crimes of the powerful' (Pearce, 1976), 'organisational deviance' (Punch, 1996), 'occupational crime' (Quinney, 1977), 'business crime' (Clarke, 1990), elite crime, an 'abuse of occupational trust' (Shapiro, 1990) and 'state-corporate crime' (Michalowski and Kramer, 2006b) as well as white-collar crime and corporate crime. All have their advantages and disadvantages. The distinctions between some of them can be important, but the subject matter is too important to spend too long getting bogged down in terminology. We begin

below by looking at debates over the use of these terms and then will simply use 'white-collar crime' as a convenient (if not entirely accurate) shorthand for the range of crimes discussed in this chapter.

As almost everyone who has written in this field has noted, this is a minority interest within criminology (in the sense that only a small proportion of criminologists research and write in this area). Traditional criminology has been dominated by a concern with crimes such as burglary, theft, assault, criminal damage and the rest and, in so doing it reflects dominant social values. By and large, there is much less attention paid by politicians, policy-makers, journalists and concerned citizens to matters we might describe as white-collar or corporate crime than there is to things like mugging and burglary.

Criminology has been regularly, roundly and rightly criticised for this preoccupation: a concern with the crimes of the powerless rather than the powerful, with the 'crimes of the streets' rather than the 'crimes of the suites' (Timmer and Eitzen, 1989). This is not to say that criminologists have entirely ignored such activities, and there are a number of honourable exceptions to the general picture I have painted so far, scholars who have sought to reorient criminology – or, at least, balance its concern with crime as ordinarily understood – with a focus upon a range of other 'harms' (Hillyard *et al.*, 2004). These concerns include matters as varied as environmental pollution, health and safety violations, fraud, consumer affairs, money laundering and food regulation.

Why, we might ask, has this area of study remained somewhat at the margins of criminological attention? A number of reasons seem likely:

- There is less social and political interest in these areas of activity – and much criminology tends to reflect powerful interests.
- Media attention paid to white-collar and corporate crime is very different from conventional crime:
  - Generally, there is far less space devoted to white-collar and corporate crime.
  - Coverage of white-collar and corporate crime is often also less prominent.
  - Some of the time corporate crime is confined to the specialist press, or to the business pages of the mainstream press.
- It is difficult to research; much activity of this kind is 'private' and hidden.
- Relatedly, these forms of activity are not things that are generally captured by crime statistics – either in recorded crime, through victimization surveys or, given how infrequently prosecutions are brought, via court records.
- Understanding such behaviour often involves forms of knowledge – of the financial sector for example – that is way outside the experience of most criminologists.
- It has been argued that the marketisation and commodification of knowledge (through increased market and competitive pressures on universities and academics) has reduced the willingness of criminology – which was not great anyway – to challenge authority (Tombs and Whyte, 2007a).

Edwin Sutherland and white-collar crime

Despite the general failure to focus on such issues in the mainstream of criminology, it is, nevertheless, the case that interest in this area has a fairly lengthy history. As early as 1912, Thorstein Veblen noted the similarity between the successful captain of industry and the successful delinquent in his 'unscrupulous conversion of goods and persons to his own ends, and a callous disregard for the feelings and wishes of others, and of the remoter effects of his actions' (1912: 237). The towering figure in this field, however, is Edwin Sutherland (see box). Almost without exception – and I'm certainly not going to start differently – discussions of white-collar crime will begin with Sutherland's work. This is right and proper, for two reasons. First, it is effectively the case that criminological work in this area actually began with Sutherland. It was he who coined the term and sought to introduce its study into criminology. Second, we must start with Sutherland because his work has been of lasting influence and, though much criticised in some respects, set the parameters for much that followed.

Edwin Sutherland (1883–1950) – coined the term 'white-collar criminal' in 1939, a concept developed ten years later in his monograph *White-Collar Crime*.

In a book and a number of academic papers in the 1940s, Sutherland sought to direct criminology's attention away from its misleading preoccupation with the crimes of people of low social status and toward those committed by the 'respectable'. If one took criminal statistics at face value, he argued, it would be reasonable to assume that most criminal activity was concentrated among the poorer sections of society. However, this is a false picture and it is to the unequal application of the criminal law that we should turn in seeking an explanation for its creation. In looking at what he came to call 'white-collar crime' Sutherland took a broad view that included acts that were defined as 'socially injurious' in law, but not confining himself to infractions of the criminal law.

Edwin Sutherland and white-collar crime

Criminal statistics show unequivocally that crime, as popularly understood and officially measured, has a high incidence in the lower socio-economic class and a low incidence in the upper socio-economic class. Crime, as thus understood, includes the ordinary violations of the penal code, such as murder, assault, burglary, robbery, larceny, sex offences and public intoxication ... Persons who are accused or convicted of these ordinary crimes are dealt with by the police, juvenile or criminal courts, probation departments, and correctional institutions.

The concentration of crimes, as conventionally understood, in the lower socio-economic class has been demonstrated by two types of research studies. First, the analysis of case histories of offenders and of their parents shows a high incidence of poverty in such cases ... The second method of demonstrating the concentration of crimes in the lower socio-economic class is by statistical analysis of the residential areas of offenders; this is ordinarily called the 'ecological distribution of offenders' ...

The thesis of this book is that these social and personal pathologies are not an adequate explanation of criminal behaviour. The general theories of criminal behaviour which take their data from poverty and the conditions related to it are inadequate and invalid, first, because the theories do not consistently fit the data of criminal behaviour; and second, because the cases on which these theories are based are a biased sample of all criminal acts ...

The thesis of this book, stated positively, is that persons of the upper socio-economic class engage in much criminal behaviour; that this criminal behaviour differs from the criminal behaviour of the lower socio-economic class principally in the administrative procedures which are used in dealing with the offenders; and that variations in administrative procedures are not significant from the point of view of the causation of crime ...

These violations of law by persons in the upper socio-economic class are, for convenience, called 'white-collar crimes'. This concept is not intended to be definitive, but merely to call attention to crimes which are not ordinarily included within the scope of criminology. White-collar crime may be defined approximately as a crime committed by a person of respectability and high social status in the course of his occupation ... The financial cost of white-collar crime is probably several times as great as the financial cost of all the crimes which are customarily regarded as the 'crime problem'.

Source: Sutherland (1983: 3–9).

In a great many respects Sutherland's work was before its time. His identification of 'white-collar crime' and the deviance of high-status individuals came a great many years before labelling theorists drew attention to the biases in criminal justice systems and the hugely important observation that the nature of a 'crime' is to be found in the social response to the act, not intrinsically within the act itself (see Chapter 10). Nevertheless, Sutherland's approach has come in for considerable criticism. Tappan (1947), for example, took a much more straightforwardly legalistic approach. In his view:

> Crime is an intentional act in violation of the criminal law (statutory and case law) committed without defence of excuse, and penalised by the state as a felony or misdemeanour. In studying the offender there can be no presumption that arrested, arraigned, indicted, or prosecuted persons are criminals unless they also be held guilty beyond a reasonable doubt of a particular offence. (quoted in Slapper and Tombs, 1999: 5)

Slapper and Tombs identify three main lines of criticism in Tappan's response to Sutherland's work:

- He was concerned about Sutherland's attempt to label people who had not been convicted in a court of criminal law as 'criminal'. How are we to make such judgements?

- In Tappan's view the offences that are typically committed by people in organisations are different from the bulk of criminal offences.

- Much of what Sutherland regarded as 'deviant' actually falls within the framework of normal business practice.

However, as they go on to note, Sutherland took the view that, whilst many practices might be perceived as 'normal business', this did not mean they were not socially injurious:

> The law is pressing in one direction and other forces are pressing in the opposite direction. In business, the 'rules of the game' conflict with the legal rules. A businessman who wants to

obey the law is driven by his competitors to adopt their methods. This is well illustrated by the persistence of commercial bribery in spite of the strenuous efforts of business organisations to eliminate it. (1999: 6)

There are further problems, however, with Sutherland's definition of white-collar crime, not least that it covers very different kinds of offence, offender and victim. Sutherland's term 'white-collar crime' is built on the *overlap* between three different types of misbehaviour (crimes). These are:

- Crimes committed by people of high status (whether or not the crime is committed in the course of their occupation).
- Crimes committed on behalf of organisations (irrespective of the status of the person committing the crime).
- Crimes committed against organisations (whether or not the person works in the organisation, or irrespective of whether they work for any organisation at all).

Nelken (1994) has consequently argued that the definition lacks internal coherence and he uses a Venn diagram (see Figure 18.1) to illustrate this point.

Nelken's criticism is that it is perfectly possible that what unites actions that fall into the central category of 'white-collar crime' may be no stronger than what they share with forms of behaviour which fall outside the core category. Although there are a number of difficulties raised by Sutherland's definition, it continues to provide a useful starting

point for discussion in this area. Before we move on, there remain a number of questions raised by Sutherland's argument (Nelken, 2007; Levi, 1988; Slapper and Tombs, 1999):

- Is it the social status of offenders or the occupational context of the offending that should be the focus of attention?
- How is 'high social status' to be defined (and are similar crimes committed by those who fall outside this definition therefore of no interest)?
- Should the focus be on major organisations (as was the case in Sutherland's work) or on any businesses?
- Is it restricted to infractions of the criminal law (Sutherland argued not) and, if not, what are the definitional limits?

Such questions continue to frame discussions in this field and they should be kept in mind throughout the rest of this chapter. The difficulties in this area led Friedrichs (2007: 165) to counsel that the term white-collar crime 'is best treated as a heuristic term, to which various specific forms of illegal and harmful activity are best viewed as cognate, hybrid, or marginal forms of white-collar crime'. Before we move on, however, there is a further important issue to note in relation to white-collar and corporate crime. That is the very limited role played by the formal criminal justice system in relation to offending in this area. As the earlier discussion indicated, whilst there is much activity within and by corporations that is appropriately described as 'criminal',

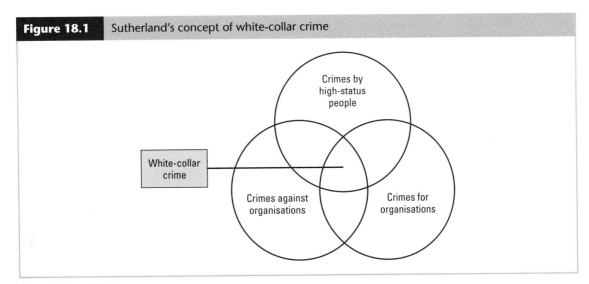

Figure 18.1 Sutherland's concept of white-collar crime

Source: Nelken (1994).

there is also a great deal of activity that might be considered to be harmful which is not criminalised. Moreover, even when corporations are prosecuted, it is often the case that the penalties that attach to the offences that are charged bear little relation to the scale of the harms caused, and corporations are often especially well-placed to defend themselves against any charges that are brought:

> Large companies are able to hire the best lawyers, secure professional expert witnesses, and engage in delaying tactics that will outlast the political pressure that prompted the government to initiate a prosecution in the first place. Given the difficulties in securing a conviction, the tendency is for parties to engage in a form of 'plea-bargaining' where the company agrees to try to do better in the future and the government agrees not to prosecute for offences committed in the past. The lesson seems to be that the criminal justice system, as presently constituted, is simply not a viable forum for tackling corporate wrongdoing. (Gobert and Punch, 2003: 9)

What we have, therefore, is an area in which there is considerable misconduct, much of which is never prosecuted or otherwise dealt with. Corporate crime remains largely invisible, and even when made visible, is often subject to comparatively minor penalties. The questions you should have in your mind, therefore, as you proceed through this chapter are:

- Why is it that white-collar and corporate crime are subject to relatively little attention by criminal justice agencies?

- Why, even when punishment is imposed, are the penalties often relatively slight?

- Why do such questions remain largely marginal to the preoccupations of mainstream criminology?

Distinguishing between white-collar and corporate crime

In attempting to make sense of, and delineate, our subject matter, one potentially useful distinction is that between *occupational* and *organisational* crimes. Crudely put, the former are crimes committed by people *within* corporations or businesses (such as embezzlement); the latter are crimes *by* corporations or businesses (such as failure to observe health and safety legislation). As we have seen, this distinction

has been argued to be somewhat confused in Sutherland's work. Another way of using this distinction is to see the former as *white-collar crime* and the latter as *corporate crime*. Such a distinction is, of course, an analytical one, rather than something that seeks to reflect some hard and fast distinction in society. In practice, businesses and corporations are made up of individuals making decisions, and much corporate gain may be individual gain also. Nevertheless, it is very important not to reduce the activities of organisations entirely to the actions of the individuals who work within it. As we will see, organisational culture and practice are important elements in understanding corporate crime:

> ... the pursuit of organisational goals is deeply implicated in the cause(s) of corporate crime. But it is important to realise that these goals are not the manifestation of personal motives cast adrift from organisational moorings, neither are they disembodied acts committed in some metaphysical sense by corporations. Rather, organisational goals are what they are perceived to be by officials who have been socialised into the organisational 'way of life' and who strive in a highly co-ordinated fashion to bring about collectively their realisation. (Box, 1983: 21)

Nevertheless, there are some potentially important distinctions between these two forms of activity, one of which may be the sanctions that apply to them in practice. As Croall (2001) and others note, the typical social construction of what 'crime' is, is more easily applied to those forms of rule-breaking undertaken by individuals within organisations than it is to the illicit activities of organisations themselves: 'Organisational crimes are therefore often perceived to be less "criminal" than those of individuals, and patterns of victimization are less direct, whereas individual offences may attract stronger public reaction and heavier sentences' (2001: 12).

Before we move on, it is useful to think slightly more concretely about our subject matter. In doing so, we can draw on a typology provided by Punch which outlines the major forms of deviance that are commonly found within organisations:

1 *Informal rewards* – Perks, fiddles, tipping, discounts, presents, use of company phone/post, etc. These practices may be widespread, and are technically against company rules, they may also be tolerated or even accepted.

2 *Work avoidance/manipulation of work situation* –
   Activities designed to make work conditions
   more comfortable and acceptable (arriving late,
   skiving, undertaking leisure activities in company
   time, etc.) Likely to be encountered at all levels,
   but often defined as a 'blue-collar' problem.

3 *Employee deviance: against the organisation* –
   Stealing, absenteeism, neglect and sabotage are
   often viewed as being largely confined to lower
   levels. Embezzlement and fraud often occur at
   middle and upper levels. 'Private justice' is
   often applied in order to protect the reputation
   of the business.

4 *Employee deviance: for the organisation* – Bending
   rules, cutting corners, failing to observe
   regulations in order to improve performance.
   These activities can be seen as minor, virtually
   unavoidable, near universal, but essentially
   positive.

5 *Organisational deviance: for the organisation* – Acts
   of commission or omission which are
   supported, overtly or covertly, by senior
   management which involve deception, stealth,
   etc. to achieve organisational goals.

6 *Managerial deviance: against the organisation* –
   The deliberate victimization of the company by
   senior managers for personal gain. (Punch,
   1996: 56–57)

Using the distinction we drew before, the first four
of these categories probably belong under the heading 'white-collar crime' or 'occupational crime'; the
latter two fall more clearly into 'corporate crime'.
However, this division is by no means hard and fast
and the distinction is, anyway, very hard to maintain – indeed, we will cease using it in a minute.

In practice, distinctions between corporate or
white-collar crime and other forms of offending
are themselves far from clear, and point to general
attributes rather than specific differences. In the
main in this chapter we focus on the more serious
forms of offending rather than what Karstedt and
Farrell (2007) have referred to as the 'crimes of
everyday life' – though there is no suggestion in
doing so that the latter are not of significance. As
we have seen, it is certainly possible to identify
characteristics of white-collar crime or corporate
crime. However, it remains equally true that not all
forms of white-collar or corporate crime exhibit *all*
of the characteristics. This leaves us with a slightly
ill-defined area of study, covering a range of activities from 'fiddles' on the job to large-scale
industrial fraud, and with a choice of various terms
with which to try to describe it.

Although there are felt to be very significant
problems with the term 'white-collar crime' – not
just Sutherland's particular definition – a number
of influential commentators have argued for its
continued usage. John Braithwaite (1985: 3), for
example, suggests the term 'is shared and understood by ordinary folk as more meaningful than
occupational crime, corporate deviance, commercial offences, economic crime or any competing
concept'. It is largely on this basis – convenience
rather than any assumption of overall accuracy –
that I will continue to use it throughout this chapter. Bear in mind, however, that when white-collar
crime is being discussed hereafter, we are talking
about activities that other authors might very reasonably categorise differently.

In this chapter we begin by looking at the
nature of white-collar crime: what types of offence
does this term cover and what are its major forms?
We then move on to look at explanations and
impact and, in particular, what is the scale of harm
caused by such offences? Finally, we look at the
question of regulation and control.

Exploring white-collar crime

How does white-collar crime differ from other
forms of criminal activity? In numerous ways, in
practice. White-collar crime:

● Generally takes place in private.

● 'Offenders' are usually quite legitimately present
  at the scene.

● It tends to involve an abuse of trust inherent in
  the occupational role.

● It often involves some form of 'insider'
  knowledge.

● Often there is no complainant or, where there is,
  the complaint is often made long after the event.

● Because generally it involves no immediate
  physical threat, it is less a source of fear or
  anxiety than some other forms of crime.

● Determining responsibility may be extremely
  problematic (because of the nature of
  organisations).

● It tends to have an ambiguous legal and
  criminal status. (Croall, 2001)

As we have already discussed, a very broad range of
crimes is potentially captured by this term *white-
collar crime* and other linked terms. Before we move

on to discuss the causes of such crime, its impact, and how it is regulated, we must begin by looking in a little more detail at some of the major types of white-collar crime. In doing so we will use a helpful general categorisation of white-collar crime developed by Croall (2001). She identifies seven main types of white-collar crime, to which an eighth might be added:

● Theft at work.
● Fraud.
● Corruption.
● Employment offences.
● Consumer offences.
● Food offences.
● Environmental crime.
● State-corporate crime (Michalowski and Kramer, 2006b).

Theft at work

This covers a range of activities from the relatively minor – small-scale employee theft and 'fiddling' – to very large-scale cases of embezzlement. Studies of theft at work illustrate the nature of this 'grey area' as an accepted and 'normal' 'perk' rather than theft. Research by the British retail consortium found that theft by staff accounted for losses of well over £350 million, or approximately one-quarter of the losses from all crime (Barclay and Tavares, 1999). Recent research by Karstedt and Farrell (2007), based on a survey of over 1,000 people in England and Wales aged between 25 and 64 asked respondents whether they had ever committed offences such as paying in cash to avoid taxation, keeping money when 'over-changed', avoiding paying a TV licence, falsely claiming refunds, and the like. They found that 61 per cent admitted committing at least one such offence, and over three-fifths of those had committed three of more such offences.

Some of the flavour of relatively small-scale employee theft is captured in the title of a wonderful book by Jason Ditton (1977) called *Part-Time Crime*. In it, Ditton describes elements of life in the 'Wellbread Bakery', the name he gave to a factory-production bakery he worked in after graduating. He describes a number of 'fiddles' practised by the men delivering bread to households and businesses, which ranged from stealing bread from work to 'adding a bit on to the bill' of customers. New recruits to such activity were often puzzled,

he reports, by a distinction drawn by management between stealing from work and stealing from customers. But, says Ditton, the rationale is obvious: the management simply cared more about being stolen from than they did about any fiddles directly affecting their customers. In fact, these activities are best viewed as a subculture of legitimate commerce, Ditton argues. They share many features with business, differing largely in the particular emphasis they place on certain values: 'Fiddling, like selling, *epitomises* the capitalist "spirit"' (Ditton, 1977: 174).

Fraud

This covers a variety of activities which involve some form of misrepresentation in order to gain financial or other material advantage. Levi *et al.* (2007: 13–15) provide the following outline of some of the most common types of fraud:

● *Benefit fraud* – Frauds upon the social security system, ranging from working and claiming, through housing benefit fraud and failure to notify benefit officials of changes in circumstances.

● *Charity fraud* – In which donations are taken from fictitious or unregistered charities or are embezzled from registered charities.

● *Cheque fraud* – Most frauds on individual accounts are covered up to a set limit.

● *Consumer frauds* – A broad category including lottery/prize scams, telemarketing frauds, the misrepresentation of products and services and gaming frauds (fixed races and so on).

● *Counterfeit intellectual property and products* – Including medicines, vehicle parts, art and antiques, computer software, CDs/DVDs, etc.

● *Data-compromise fraud* – Frauds on both companies and individuals – sometimes called 'phishing' and 'pharming' – in which financial details are fraudulently gained and used (see Chapter 4).

● *Embezzlement* – Frauds against all businesses, government departments and professional firms by staff ranging from clerical to senior management. Generally involves either accounts manipulation, or the construction of false invoices.

● *Gaming frauds* – Fixed matches or races particularly in relation to spread betting.

'Fiddling'

Skill at 'fiddling' customers is a major criterion of unofficial status amongst Wellbread salesmen ... In transactional terms, a successful fiddle refers to over-charging: the practice by salesmen of invisibly altering the ownership of goods in transactions with customers to cover expropriations from a money (or equivalent) source within the fiddler's control ...

Even over-charging can be of two sorts. Firstly, the price is simply increased to unknowing customers; although the 'price of bread' is heavily invested with moral and symbolic significance, few people actually know *what* it is. Secondly, the price, but not the size of the delivery remains constant ...

Customers lose money in sales transactions in clear, simple and easily specifiable ways. The fiddled retail customer either gets the ordered number of items at a higher price (over-charge) or a reduced number of items for the standard price (short deliver). Whist this is occurring, the customer may unwittingly accept insufficient change (short change). The percentage made is simply physically diverted from the cash bag (a large leather pocket hung by a leather thong from the neck down to the waist) to the salesman's own pocket.

[One retailer remembers:] You know, I once went with this bloke from the Superloaf bakery ... he said

'Short change them, yeah, but never overcharge them, you're daft if you do, it's against the Trades Descriptions Act' ... he'd been on that round for about five years, and he was a fly bugger! He used to count the change so fast ... then he'd say 'Sorry, ma'am, it's a shilling short', she'd give him the other shilling, and then he'd turn his hand over, just to me, and he'd have it tucked between his fingers underneath ... and he used to take the money, and then ask if she had a pound note, as he had so much change, and then he used to take the money *again*, and give her a whole load of two bob bits to make up for it, ... you know, so it looked a lot! ... he made five pounds in a morning, think what he made in a week.

He [the previous roundsman] ... never used to give credit for returns from the shops, that's how he used to make his cover, ... or sometimes, he'd make twelve loaves look like fourteen on a tray, if you hold it up high, or grip it close to your belly, they don't know that you haven't got fourteen on a tray ... that's the best way, you walk past, and say 'here's a tray', and carry it above your head ... I often do that.

Source: Ditton (1977)

- *Insider dealing/ market abuse* – Generally share trading using commercially-sensitive information that is not in the public domain/known to others engaged in the trading. May not have any directly attributable victims, but may affect the market and can be seen as a fraud against the public.

- *Insurance fraud* – Where frauds are perpetrated against insurance companies either by businesses (arson for profit; maritime fraud; from piracy to the misdescription of lost goods) or individuals (inflated or false claims).

- *Lending fraud* – Fraudulent bankruptcy (long-firm fraud), consumer credit (involving fictitious invoices), and mortgage frauds (involving the manipulation of prices).

- *Pension-type fraud* – The embezzlement of pension and national insurance funds.

- *Procurement fraud* – Fraud and corruption in the purchasing process, including price-fixing and the abuse of inside information.

- *Tax fraud* – The failure to pay direct (income tax, corporation tax), indirect (such as VAT) and excise (duty on alcohol, tobacco and other goods) taxes. One recent example of such activity is what has become known as 'carousel fraud'. In its simplest form this involved traders importing goods, such as mobile phones, from somewhere where there is no Value Added Tax (VAT). The phones are then sold in the UK with VAT added on. The VAT is collected, but never handed over to the government. A more sophisticated version, which led to the application of the name 'carousel fraud', began as the example above with the import of phones. The phones would then be re-exported, using a different paper trail, and the fraudsters would reclaim the VAT. Once exported, the phones would be re-imported and the merry-go-round would begin again. Estimates (*Guardian*, 21 September 2006) have suggested that this type of activity might cost as much as £34 billion a year in the European Union – effectively as much as the entire Common Agricultural Policy budget.

Nick Leeson, former derivatives trader, being arrested at Frankfurt Airport in Germany in 1995. He incurred over £800m of losses in unauthorised trading and caused the collapse of his employer, Barings Bank.

Some large-scale frauds are well-known, such as that associated with Nick Leeson and the collapse of Barings Bank in 1995. Fraud is to be found well beyond the private sector. There have been some very significant cases in the public sector and particularly within local authorities and the National Health Service. Croall (2001: 28) reports a number of cases involving fraud against the NHS including frauds perpetrated by:

- *GPs* – False claims in relation to staff, numbers of patients, night visits and vaccinations, including one GP who, it was claimed, had made £700,000 in five years from the writing of bogus prescriptions.

- *Opticians* – False claims in relation to dispensing glasses, sight tests and tinted lenses.

- *Pharmacists* – False claims for emergency opening, colluding in prescription frauds, processing bogus prescriptions and collecting charges for drugs that cost less than the prescription charge.

- *Dentists* – False claims for non-existent patients.

So far, we have considered a range of offences that accord fairly closely with traditional notions of crime – theft and fraud – but happen to take place in a business-related environment or by people in positions of corporate responsibility. There is, however, a range of other acts that result in some form of social harm that might also be considered in the context of a discussion of white-collar and corporate crime. These include political and economic corruption, offences relating to employment, and to health and safety. In addition, a number of authors – most particularly recently, Steve Tombs – have urged us to focus attention on injuries that are sustained at work.

Employment offences

There is now extensive legislation covering various aspects of business practice and aspects of working life, ranging from employment, health and safety to low pay. A large number of people are injured, and many are killed, at work. The available evidence suggests that this burden falls disproportionately on people in the lowest socio-economic groups. According to Tombs (2004), the Health and Safety Executive (HSE) recorded over 1,600 deaths from mesothelioma, an asbestos-related cancer, in 2000 and 186 deaths officially involving asbestosis, though it suggests that this significantly underestimates the extent of such deaths. In 2001/02 the HSE recorded 633 fatal occupational injuries, and almost 130,000 injuries resulting in a minimum of three days off work. The Health and Safety Commission has estimated the cost of workplace injury and ill-health at £18 billion a year (Tombs, 2004).

Again, this is an area that until recently has not been much studied by criminologists. In the first full study, however, Tombs and Whyte (2007b) begin to rectify this oversight. Focusing on what they refer to as 'safety crimes', they use a variety of case studies – from the Bhopal disaster to the *Herald of Free Enterprise* capsizing – to illustrate what appear to be many shared characteristics of such 'crimes'. These include: aggressive management; (global) market pressures; casual labour, and victim-blaming; this leads them to observe that whilst:

> ... these common themes are refracted differently in specific case studies, have more or less significance and combine with other context-specific factors ... taken together, [they] indicate causes that reside in systems of management, in features of wider industry and market contexts which provide the conditions from which those crimes are produced, and in systems of law and regulation, which create opportunity structures for such offences. (Tombs and Whyte, 2007b: 34)

It is wrong, consequently, to portray such events as 'accidents' or as events which are the result of 'human error'.

'Employment offences' or 'safety crimes'? *Left*: workers removing asbestos, the greatest single cause of work-related deaths in the UK, from an office building. *Right*: Collapsed scaffolding around an office block in Cardiff in the aftermath of high winds.

Consumer offences

This covers that range of activities which involve the 'violation of laws and regulations that relate to the production, distribution and sale of goods and services' (Croall, 2001: 36). Television programmes such as *That's Life, Watchdog, Moneybox,* and more specific programmes like *Britain's Worst Builders* and their like, are very much focused on consumer offences covering such matters as building safety, compliance with health regulations, pricing irregularities, and failures to meet advertising standards. In the nature of such programmes, they are frequently focused on crimes against specific, targeted individuals. One very common form of consumer offence involves the sale of counterfeit goods. A visit to almost any large town market will find stalls selling what appear to be 'designer clothing' at prices that are way below those on the high street. With the huge growth in demand for 'labelled' clothing and footwear in recent years a sizeable business has grown in counterfeit goods in this area.

However, we should not forget those consumer offences that are more general failures by compa-

nies to regulate their behaviour resulting in often very serious outcomes. One of the most infamous cases in this regard concerned the release on to the market in the USA of the Ford Pinto.

Facing strong foreign competition in the late 1960s, the Ford Motor Company launched a new 'compact' – a relatively small car produced cheaply. The petrol tank was placed behind the rear axle and tests found that in certain types of accident there was a danger that the tank would rupture, leading to the petrol igniting. The car went into production in 1970 and during the course of the early 1970s a number of rear-end collisions resulted in horrific accidents in which drivers and passengers died in flaming vehicles. Ford was taken to court on charges of 'reckless homicide' though the prosecution was unsuccessful. Civil cases followed, and a class action suit, which eventually led to the recall of the Pinto despite the company publicly continuing to defend the car.

The case is 'one of the most widely debated ... in business ethics' (Punch, 1996: 23). The primary reason for its notoriety concerns information that later came to light about the cost-benefit analysis conducted by Ford in relation to its decision to

A gleaming new Ford Pinto, launched in 1970 – all were eventually recalled after they revealed an alarming tendency to burst into flames in accidents, causing a number of fatalities.

continue to allow the car to be produced. The calculations suggested that the defect in the car would have cost Ford approximately £11 per vehicle to correct or £137 million in all to recall all the Pintos that had been manufactured and to make the necessary changes. By contrast, it was calculated that the likely insurance claims from those anticipated to be killed or injured was likely to total £49.5 million (Slapper and Tombs, 1999).

Slapper and Tombs (1999: 142) argue that this 'sort of cost–benefit analysis, which relegates human life below the considerations of profit, is not peculiar to the Ford Motor Company or to recent developments. It is a feature endemic to the system of commerce.' Nevertheless, Punch (1996: 23) cautions that the 'difficulty in interpreting many business decisions that have led to intense public debate and even court cases is that you cannot fully reconstruct the motives and interaction of executives in a board-room meeting. Motives may be mixed, documents which appear in the public arena and are held to have been influential may not have played a highly significant role.'

Food offences

In recent years, concerns about 'mad cow disease', 'bird flu' and E-coli have focused most people's attention on the fact that there exists a range of laws, regulations and regulatory bodies – including the Food Standards Agency, the Office of Fair Trading and a number of government departments such as the Department for Environment, Food and Rural Affairs – governing food production. Regulations range from controls over how animals are kept, slaughtered and butchered to the cleanliness of kitchens, restaurants and shops. Failure to comply can have significant consequences, as we have seen. In terms of the sale of food, there are regulations governing how it should be labelled, packaged and stored and, indeed, what it should contain. Fraudulent and other practices have involved price-fixing, false advertising, and false or deceptive packaging. Croall (2007) offers the following overview of offences and problems in this area:

- **Food production**

  - *Farming* – There is a range of offences linked with the growing of genetically modified crops, the misuse of pesticides, the misappropriation or fraudulent claiming of subsidies, and inhumane practices associated with factory farming.

  - *Gang masters* – The case of the 23 cockle pickers who died in Morecambe Bay in 2004 highlighted the problems associated with the absence of control of gang masters, and the apparent involvement of 'organised crime' in the use of illegal immigrants in this and similar work. In this particular case the gang master was convicted of 21 counts of manslaughter, but this successful prosecution is viewed by many commentators as the exception rather than the rule.

  - *Fishing* – In particular the fishing in prohibited waters or of prohibited fish stocks, and the failure to declare catches, are major problems.

- **Food manufacture**

  - The illegal, fraudulent or misleading use of additives and other substances in the production of food.

- **Food distribution**

  - Including such activities as 'meat laundering' in which food that is not meant for human consumption is repackaged and sold on to hospitals, schools and supermarkets.

- **Food preparation**

  - Deliberate avoidance of regulations around hygiene and packaging. Again, Croall notes that although breaches of regulations are common, prosecutions are rare.

- **Selling, marketing and packaging**

  - Confusing or misleading labelling of foodstuffs, particularly in relation to disguising the amount of fat, sugar, water, and so on in products.

As Croall (2007: 223) argues, there is much about food crime that mirrors other areas of corporate crime, including 'how the definition of crime and criminalisation can be related to the interests of powerful business lobbies' and how 'these groups, despite claims of corporate social responsibility, also seek to evade the "letter of the law"'.

Environmental crime

Here we might include everything from 'fly-tipping' to major industrial disasters such as Bhopal. Three varied examples of environmental crime will help illustrate its nature and its impact:

- *Bhopal* – On 2 and 3 December 1984, a Union Carbide plant in Bhopal, India, began leaking the gas methyl isocyanate. The safety systems in the plant all failed to operate and something close to 30 tons of gas spread throughout the city. Half a million people were exposed and some estimate that up to 20,000 have died to date as a result. Perhaps six times that number continue to suffer as a result of exposure, with the symptoms including blindness, breathing difficulties and gynaecological disorders. Campaigners argue that the site has never been properly cleaned up. (You can find more details at: http://www.bhopal.org/whathappened.html)

- *Waste dumping* – In 1998 in Cambodia, a shipment of waste packed in plastic sheets was deposited outside a village some 15 miles or so from the southern port where it had arrived. The plastic sheeting, considered useful and valuable in such a poor country, was quickly taken by local villagers, and others further away. Within a few days, people began falling sick with symptoms that included headaches, fever, skin rashes, dizziness, coughing, stomach aches and chest pains. It was estimated that up to half of the 1,200 residents fell sick. The Taiwanese company from which the waste had come claimed it was not poisonous. In the event the material was found to have levels of mercury four times the legal limit (in Taiwan). There were also found to be discrepancies between the quantity of the material itemised in the ship's

Fire at the Union Carbide plant in Bhopal in India in 1984, following an explosion which released poisonous gases – one of the world's worst industrial disasters.

log, and the quantity that eventually arrived in Cambodia, leading to suspicions that some had been dumped at sea.

- *Pollution* – In the United States one of the cases that led eventually to the passage of environmental legislation occurred in Donora, a small industrial town south of Pittsburgh on the Monongahela River in Pennsylvania. In October 1948, a noxious smog grew and covered the town. The cloud, it turned out, was a poisonous mixture of sulphur dioxide, carbon monoxide and metal dust, which came from the smokestacks of the local American Steel and Wire Company zinc works. At first no one realised the smog was poisonous. During the course of the next week 20 residents died and half the town's population – 7,000 people – were hospitalised. It was 1970 before the Clean Air Act was passed in the US.

State-corporate crime

The term is used to refer to 'serious social harms that result from the interaction of political and economic organisations' (Michalowski and Kramer, 2007: 200). The necessity for such a term, Michalowski and Kramer argue, derives from work on events such as the explosion of the space shuttle *Challenger* (Kramer, 2006) in which crimes were identified that were a product of the joint actions of a state agency and a business corporation.

The *Challenger* space shuttle exploded shortly after take-off in January 1986. Kramer (2006) argues that the disaster was the collective product of interaction between the US National Aeronautics and Space Administration (NASA) and a private corporation, Morton Thiokol, Inc (MTI). The history of the development of the space shuttle involved a series of major compromises involving budget restrictions, several of which had profound safety implications. In addition, NASA was increasingly working in conditions which magnified the likelihood that unreasonable risks might be taken. Some of the factors involved in the *Challenger* explosion therefore included (Kramer, 2006):

- Development restrictions which led to the use of solid-fuelled rockets rather than the more expensive, but safer, liquid-fuelled engines, and other 'design compromises'.
- Pressure to make the shuttle cost-effective which increased the number of flights being undertaken.

- Growing political and military imperatives around the 'Star Wars' initiative which placed further pressure on NASA to speed up production and to increase flights, even when there were concerns about safety.
- Poor communication between NASA and MTI – the private corporation contracted to manufacture solid rocket boosters for the shuttle – as well as within NASA itself, which meant that vital information about potential failings in the seal of one of the joints on the rocket was not always delivered to decision-makers within NASA.
- When the problem eventually became clear, MTI failed to take action because to do so would have meant stopping shuttle flights and putting their contract at risk, and NASA didn't do so because of the economic, military and political pressures they were under.
- Those responsible for safety within NASA were 'insufficiently independent' within the structure of the organisation.

This leads Kramer (2006: 43) to conclude that the *Challenger* story indicates that 'the explosion of the shuttle was not an "accident" ... [Moreover] This disaster cannot be attributed solely to the actions of one organisation. The misconduct occurred as an institution of political governance pursued a goal in direct cooperation with an institution of economic production.' More generally, Michalowski and Kramer (2007: 212) suggest that the notion of state-corporate crime is valuable in directing criminologists 'to engage in inquiries that identify, describe and explain the variety of social harms that emanate from the intersection of business and government' (see also Chapter 34).

Review questions

1 What have been the main criticisms of Edwin Sutherland's definition of white-collar crime?

2 How might you distinguish between corporate and white-collar crime?

3 What are the main forms of white-collar crime?

4 Can Ditton's observation that fiddling 'epitomises the capitalist spirit' be applied to white-collar crime generally?

5 What is meant by the term 'state-corporate crime'?

Explaining white-collar and corporate crime

Although we devoted considerable attention to criminological theory earlier in the book (see Chapters 5 to 16) we return briefly to it now. The reason for this is that criminological theory has tended to focus its attention on the individual, often youthful and male, offender. It has paid relatively scant attention to white-collar or to corporate crime. Consequently, it is worth thinking again about what criminology may have to offer in making sense of these particular areas of criminological activity.

Differential association

As we have seen, one of the few criminologists to have expressly engaged in theorising about white-collar crime is Sutherland. His starting point was that classical, individualistic explanations of crime are of little help in this area. One could only jokingly argue, he said, that 'the crimes of the Ford Motor Company are due to the Oedipus Complex … or those of the US Steel Corporation to Frustration and Aggression!' Sutherland, by contrast, offered differential association theory as a means of explaining both street crime and white-collar crime. They 'differ in incidentals, rather than essentials', he argued (1949: 7). At the heart of differential association theory is the notion that the offender (a person or an organisation) has been subject to a greater number of normative influences that support offending than those that reject or resist it:

> Criminal behaviour is learned in interaction with other persons in a process of communication … When criminal behaviour is learned, the learning includes (a) techniques of committing the crime, which are sometimes very complicated, sometimes very simple; (b) the specific direction of the motives, drives, rationalisations, and attitudes … (Sutherland, 1947: 6–7)

Though differential association is no longer much used in theorising white-collar or corporate crime, and has been roundly criticised (see Braithwaite, 1985), it is perfectly plausible that the type of social learning that Sutherland outlined is a significant factor in much offending, including corporate misconduct. In this vein, Geis's (1968) study of the electrical equipment industry found that many manufacturers encouraged price-fixing by their employees, through promotions and other inducements, as a means of coping with market pressures.

Geis described such activities as an 'established way of life', with participants learning attitudes and rationalisations that favoured and supported such misconduct.

By contrast, there is much criminological work, including classic works by Clinard (1946) and Cressey (1953) which cast doubt on the importance of such learning in activities such as price regulation violations and embezzlement. Perhaps the central reason that a theory such as differential association is important in this context is that it invites questions about the nature of the corporate environment and how this might relate to offending behaviour and practices: crudely, what is it about some organisations and their environments that leads to particular forms of crime?

Self-control

The other 'general' theory of crime that has been advanced with a view to explaining not just conventional crime but also white-collar crime is Hirschi and Gottfredson's work on human nature and the importance of gratification. Essentially, their 'self-control' theory assumes that people pursue self-interest and short-term gratification and the avoidance of pain. Crime in this model becomes a means by which some people maximise pleasure and minimise pain, and white-collar criminals are no different, they assert, from those involved in burglary or car theft. The involvement of some people and not others in criminal activities is a result of the different weight they give, or the greater 'attachment' they have, to the feelings of others. The relative absence of such attachment would then help explain differential involvement in activities such as price-fixing, embezzlement, environmental pollution or health and safety violations.

This notion has been heavily criticised, most notably by Steffensmeier (1989) who argued that Hirschi and Gottfredson's two major claims – that the demographic distribution (age, sex, ethnicity) of white-collar crimes and conventional crimes are very similar, and that white-collar crime is relatively rare – are demonstrably false. And, so, their claim that it is possible to identify a single, underlying cause of all criminality is also highly contestable.

Neutralisation

By contrast, Matza and Sykes' notion of 'techniques of neutralisation' (see Chapter 8) has enjoyed some popularity in relation to corporate crime. The five techniques they identified were as follows:

- Denial of responsibility ('It wasn't my fault', 'I wasn't to blame').
- Denial of injury ('They were insured anyway', 'No one will ever miss it', 'I was only borrowing it').
- Denial of the victim ('they deserved it').
- Condemnation of the condemners ('Everyone's at it').
- Appeal to higher loyalties ('I was protecting the gang's reputation').

There are numerous illustrations in the literature on white-collar and corporate crime of the operation of such forms of denial. Thus, Cressey's previously mentioned research on embezzlement found that many of those involved used words such 'borrowing' and talked of their intention to 'put the money back'. Studies of employee theft have regularly documented justifications based on being paid too little, of being mistreated (and therefore the employer 'had it coming').

In a slightly different vein, a form of denial frequently used by corporations found to have been engaged in wrongdoing is to claim that the activities were the fault of a few 'rotten apples' or maverick individuals. This, traditionally, has also been the way that police forces have responded to allegations of corruption (see Chapter 25). In parts of the business world there is evidence that the characteristics found in successful, legitimate entrepreneurial activity are also those that may be found in the characters of those engaged in high level fraud and, similarly, some of the most corrupt police officers have also had highly successful careers, for example as detectives. 'Bad apple' theories are roundly rejected by critical theorists.

Critical theory

A further general theory arises from Marxism and critical theories, including left realism. Put at its simplest, such approaches take the view that it is to the unequal structure of our society that we should look in seeking explanations for crime. For those working in this tradition, it is capitalism itself that is criminogenic. Though the terminology varies, approaches that invoke notions of late capitalism, market societies and other cognate terms, point to the importance of changes that, among other things, appear to have promoted individualism over the general good, have deregulated markets and stressed the importance of profit and success over ethical practices, have progressively reduced the availability of secure employment and have increased levels of relative deprivation and undermined informal systems of social control. Croall (2001: 93) quotes Elliott Currie's argument that:

> Market society promotes violent crime in part by creating something akin to a perpetual state of internal warfare in which the advancement of some is contingent on the fall of others and in which a corresponding ethos of unconcern – of non-responsibility for others' well-being – often legitimized under the rubric of beneficent competition, pervades the common culture and the interactions of daily life.

In a similar vein, Pearce (1976), Slapper and Tombs (1999) and others argue that the structural make-up of contemporary capitalism is an important explanatory factor in understanding corporate crime. There is much to commend such an approach – not least in the way it locates corporate misconduct within general cultural norms about socially approved forms of behaviour. However, there are important ways in which corporate crime is hardly *functional* for capitalist society. The undermining of the credibility of financial markets – which certainly could occur if there were a sufficiently large-scale set of frauds – would hardly be conducive to the continuing successful operation of financial trading. Second, such approaches have difficulty explaining the absence of such offending – or the absence of more such offending. Why do so many organisations apparently choose to operate within the law and other regulatory schemes? Given how shallow and weak many regulatory systems have apparently been, it can hardly be the threat of prosecution.

A critical perspective is also advanced by Punch who argues that business is criminogenic. He quotes Clarke (1990: 8) making a similar case, saying, 'crime and misconduct are endemic to business and that the key to understanding lies in recognizing the structure that the business environment gives to misconduct, both in terms of opportunities and in terms of how misconduct is managed'. At the heart of this view is the argument that corporate crime is simultaneously normal and deviant. It is normal in the sense that such activities are sometimes fairly rational responses to the nature and pressure of business and, in many respects, little different from many normal, licit activities.

And yet, on the other hand, it is deviant in that it violates rules, regulations, norms and, often, laws. Punch argues that corporate misconduct should, at least in part, be seen as a response to the internal and the external pressures that are to be found in the business world. Many of these internal pressures are simply the circumstances of 'people trying to survive, to succeed, or simply to get things done without making waves' (1996: 217). As Box (1983: 42) put it, 'it might be more realistic to argue that corporate officials are frequently placed in a position where they are required to choose between impairing their career chances or being a loyal organizational person'.

Punch (1996) identifies a range of variables that help explain why some companies turn to deviant solutions to particular situations or problems and why managers and others become involved in illicit practices. He orders these into three main groups: structure, culture and personality/identity.

1 **Structure** – Broadly speaking, the structural circumstances or conditions within which companies work:

   – *Markets* – Although the relationship is difficult to specify, there would appear to be some circumstances in which competitive pressures lead to misconduct.

   – *Size/complexity* – The size and complexity of organisations can produce circumstances in which oversight and control are difficult.

   – *Goals* – Pressure to achieve particular objectives may increase the likelihood of deviance (a form of 'strain' in which not everyone can succeed by legitimate means).

   – *Opportunity structures/rewards* – It is possible that the temptations increase as the rewards increase.

2 **Culture** – The possible existence of corporate cultures that sponsor rule-breaking mentalities:

   – *Fun/excitement* – Whereby some managers actively come to enjoy the competitive, risk-taking excitement of rule-breaking.

   – *Risk-taking* – The cultural encouragement of risk-taking and idealisation of the successful gambler in certain business environments.

   – *Corporate heroes* – The veneration of those who will do whatever it takes to succeed (Punch quotes the golfer Ben Hogan's observation that 'Nice guys come last').

   – *Dirty workers* – Arguably some business environments need 'dirty tricks' as, infamously, occurred when British Airways was alleged to have hacked into Virgin's computer systems in order to poach customers, and then sought to tarnish the reputation of its competitor when the allegations were made public.

3 **Personality/identity** – The social psychological factors associated with corporate misconduct:

   – *Depersonalisation* – Referring to circumstances in which managers within corporations may feel cut off from the consequences of their actions (a 'win at all costs' mentality).

   – *Ideology/rationalisations* – This refers to Sykes and Matza's work (see above) on 'techniques of neutralisation' – the vocabularies of motive that provide a set of reasons for neutralising the harm or negative impact of particular actions.

Shaming

The final general theory for us to consider comes from John Braithwaite. As he put it (1991: 40):

> Unlike many contemporary criminologists, I continue to be motivated by the goal that Edwin Sutherland set for us of developing criminological theory of maximum possible generality. Like most contemporary criminologists, I accept that Sutherland's revelation of the nature and extent of white-collar crime creates some acute problems for traditional criminological theories. And as Sutherland so convincingly argued, the dominant tradition of criminological theory that excises white-collar crime from its explanatory scope lays the foundations for a class-biased criminology and criminal justice policy.

He then goes on to argue, against Sutherland, that it is possible to have both poverty and inequality as important explanatory variables in a theory of white-collar crime. His explanation combines elements of strain theory, subcultural theory and labelling theory. In short, he suggests that strain – blocked opportunities – can be applied not only in the case of the poor and restricted opportunities to have *needs* met, but also to the wealthy and restricted opportunities for *greed* to be satisfied. Under these conditions, illegitimate avenues may be used. In both circumstances, criminal subcultures may develop 'to communicate symbolic reassurance to those who decide to prey on others, to sustain techniques for neutralising the evil of crime' (1999: 48). Finally, he takes Jack Katz's (1988) work on humiliation and the emotion of crime, to argue that stigmatisation may play as important a role in white-collar crime as street crime. Provocatively, he observes (1991: 54):

> In the same year that Edwin Sutherland introduced white-collar crime into our lexicon, the greatest white-collar criminal of our century set the world alight. His name was Adolf Hitler. Thomas Scheff points out that 'Every page of Hitler's *Mein Kampf* bristles with shame and rage' … War crimes are partly about blocked legitimate opportunities to achieve national economic objectives. But they are also about being humiliated, wanting to humiliate, and fear of being humiliated on both sides of a conflict.

Understanding white-collar crime

We have looked at the nature of white-collar crime, and considered briefly some attempts to explain it. What then of its impact? Who are the white-collar offenders? Who are its victims and what type of impact does it have on individuals and on society more generally?

White-collar offenders

The observations we have already made about the difficulties associated with studying corporate and white-collar crime apply particularly strongly to research on those responsible for such offending. Relatively few are processed through the criminal justice system, and systematic information on the background on offenders is difficult to come by. As we saw earlier, according to Edwin Sutherland, one of the crucial factors in distinguishing white-collar crime from other sorts of offending is precisely the social status of the offender, and some criminologists describe this area of activity as 'elite crime'. As others have noted, however, it is not necessarily helpful to think of such offenders as being inevitably of a higher socio-economic status, despite the fact that the stereotype of the white-collar criminal is that of 'advantaged older men from stable homes living in well-kept communities' (Weisburd *et al.*, 1991: 47). Levi's (1988) research that we came across earlier, found that a significant proportion of fraud in large companies was perpetrated by relatively junior employees and research by Hagan in Canada has tended to confirm this general picture.

Much of the literature in this area suggests – or sometimes simply assumes – that the vast majority of offenders are male. Few women are prosecuted for serious fraud, for example (i.e. proportionately fewer than are found in high level financial occupations, Levi, 1994), though some have argued that it is women's structural, socio-economic position that largely explains their lack of involvement. There is some suggestion that high status offenders enjoy considerable protection from prosecution because of their social status and because of the generalised view that criminal prosecution is often not the most advantageous way of dealing with many forms of corporate offending. Again, the prosecution of Conrad Black in 2007 for racketeering and fraud might be seen as another exception to the more general trend in which elite offenders tend to manage to avoid prosecution and conviction. Croall (2001) suggests that something of a typology of offenders is possible, distinguishing 'individual' offenders according to their social status and corporate or organisational offenders according to the size of the organisation (see Figure 18.2).

Arguably, it is the 'middle classes', white-collar workers, the 'petty bourgeois' and rogue traders who are most likely to be prosecuted, in part because they enjoy less protection as a result of their social status, but also because their offending behaviour is often easier to investigate – crudely, their frauds are 'simpler'.

Conrad Black, British life peer and former proprietor of Telegraph newspapers: found guilty of criminal fraud charges in a US district court on 13 July 2007, and facing a maximum possible sentence of 35 years in prison.

Figure 18.2	A typology of white-collar offenders	
Individual offenders		**Organisational offenders**
'Elite offenders'		*'Corporate offenders'*
This group would include owners and partners in businesses and corrupt politicians. The stories of Ivan Boesky and Michael Milken and, more recently, of Conrad Black would be key examples. This category also, arguably, includes what Croall calls 'entrepreneurs and mavericks': individuals whose status in organisations is unusual/ problematic, but who are often 'classic self-made entrepreneurs'.		There has been no shortage of cases involving some of the world's largest corporate bodies in various forms of misconduct. From Sutherland's research in the 1940s onward, major companies have been found to be in breach of both the criminal law and other regulations.
'The middle classes'		*'Petty bourgeois' and small businesses*
Middle managers, professionals, civil servants. It is people in these positions whom research often finds to be responsible for much tax offending and fraud.		Smaller companies, often operating more locally, involved in failures in relation to health and safety, food standards, etc.
'White-collar workers'		*'Rogue and cowboy' businesses*
Clerical workers and others in the lower echelons of organisations, involved in embezzlement/theft.		The classic rogue traders currently to be found in many television programmes. Involved in various forms of misrepresentation, fraud and counterfeiting activity.

Source: Based on Croall (2001).

Thus far, however, in the main we have reverted to talking of 'offenders' as individuals. Many scholars working in this area caution precisely against such assumptions. Thus, Punch (1996), for example, as in the quote at the beginning of this chapter, focuses much more on the 'corporation' and corporate culture as being the primary focus of our attention when thinking about offending. As he puts it we 'must cast our gaze *upwards*' (1996: 1). In parallel to his and others' work on police corruption, the argument is that we should drop our preoccupation with 'bad apples' and, instead, look at the moral, managerial and business aspects of human behaviour within organisations. Others, such as Slapper and Tombs (1999) and Tombs and Whyte (2007) take a more overtly Marxist position, and argue in relation to safety crimes, for example, that 'under-regulation and an absence of safety crime controls appears to be as much an embedded feature of capitalist social orders as safety *crime* itself is' (2007: 214).

In this vein, according to Punch (1996) the major corporate crimes of the twentieth century have at least three main lessons at their heart:

1 The financial capitalism of the 1980s (the 'casino economy') created a series of new opportunities for such deviant activity:

a Having expanded, Western economies went through difficult times in the 1970s and 1980s.

b Deregulation, and a series of takeovers, mergers, etc. began to restructure the financial sector.

c Globalisation and the rapid growth of global, electronic financial markets created new opportunities and, in some respects, less (effective) oversight.

2 The reduction in regulatory oversight which took place at this time 'spawned an incredible array of cases of mismanagement, undue risk-taking, speculative investment, looting, fraud, and creative accounting' (1996: 21).

3 A number of cases, but the 1980s Savings and Loan scandal in the US particularly, reshaped our perception of corporate crime as something which was done for the good of the business. As he shows in some detail, quite the reverse may be true. The example Punch uses is that of Robert Maxwell, the publisher and newspaper magnate, who systematically defrauded his own companies and their pension schemes.

The consequences of the particular era of financial capitalism discussed above are possibly best illustrated by reference to one specific case – and a company that has become intimately linked with global deregulated markets: Enron. Referred to as the 'Enron stage of capitalism' (Nelken, 2007) or 'Enron-era economics' (Michalowski and Kramer, 2006a), the 1990s saw a number of huge corporations bankrupted after having engaged in a variety of unethical or illegal practices, many of which were designed artificially to inflate the value of corporate stock. Enron, at its height, was the seventh- largest company in the United States, employing over 20,000 people across 40 countries. Put at its simplest, the company published false information relating to its profits and systematically hid many of its debts. Between 1990 and 1998 the company's stock had risen by slightly over 300 per cent – slightly better, but not dramatically so, than other large and successful corporations in the USA. After that the stock skyrocketed. It increased by 56 per cent in 1999 and 87 per cent in 2000 (Healy and Palepu, 2003). By the end of 2001 it had filed for bankruptcy at one trillion dollars – the largest in history (Nelken, 2007). Its collapse, together with the accounting firm Arthur Andersen who had been responsible for the auditing of the company, led to huge monetary losses for shareholders, and very large numbers of lost jobs and pensions. There were, therefore, countless thousands of victims of the activities – some legal, some criminal – that brought Enron to collapse.

Victims of white-collar crime

In noting its breadth, Levi (1988: 1) observes that the victims of fraud 'range from the very wealthy to the very poor. It includes swindles by "professional criminals" against suppliers of goods on credit, banks and credit card companies, mail-order purchasers, and people willing to pay money upfront for a promised job or loan; by "criminal professionals" against their clients' accounts held in trust or against building societies and banks supplying mortgages for their imaginary clients; and by businesspeople against consumers and employees'.

It is important to note, therefore, that corporate and white-collar victimization do not fit, or do not easily fit, the standard patterns associated with conventional crimes (on victimization more generally, see Chapter 17). First, a significant element of the impact of corporate crime is upon communities or society more generally, rather than *individual*

victims. Thus, if we take the example of the large-scale VAT frauds that are believed to have been occurring in the UK in recent times, there are no obviously identifiable individual victims. These are crimes against the Exchequer – though arguably all citizens suffer as a result of losses to the Exchequer. The scale of such offences, of course, is often calculated in a way that estimates the effect on individual citizens. Similarly, government corruption often works to the general detriment of the population rather than specific individuals.

In addition, many of the victims of corporate crimes are, of course, organisations rather than individuals. Large-scale frauds against banks are not aimed at individual employees, even though they may have an effect on individual employees. Frauds against organisations generally take one of three main forms (Levi, 1988):

- *External frauds* – Emanating from outside a business, such frauds frequently involve the abuse of credit facilities. One type is the 'long-firm fraud' in which companies are established or acquired with the intention not of trading, but of building up large quantities of goods on credit, failing to pay for them and then selling them on. Having done so, the business is then abandoned or destroyed.

- *Internal frauds* – The illicit electronic transfer of funds or fraudulent conversion of cheques stolen from a company into personal bank accounts, as well as expenses frauds.

- *Collusive frauds* – In which employees or managers collude with people outside the organisation to perpetrate fraud.

Another important feature of much corporate or white-collar offending is that it is characterised by a denial of 'harm'. The counterfeiting of expensive designer sports gear, or the copying of CDs and DVDs, is often presented as if it were simply a case of making available goods to people who otherwise wouldn't be able to afford them. This is, of course, a classic *neutralisation technique* (see Chapter 10). However, white-collar and corporate crime can have very significant consequences for individuals, corporations and communities:

- Large numbers of employees were permanently denied their pension entitlements as a result of Robert Maxwell's embezzlement of funds from the Mirror Group.

- Almost 200 people drowned when the *Herald of Free Enterprise* sank off the coast of Belgium.

- Over 8,000 children in 46 countries were born with physical disabilities because of the use of the drug Thalidomide.
- 167 workers were killed aboard the Piper Alpha oil platform in the North Sea in 1988.

Many frauds against individuals are investment frauds and, though variable in nature, are based on the underlying principle that they are 'too good to be true' (Levi, 1988: 6). Promising very high returns on investment, growth in the value of property, and other bargains such as misrepresented time share offers, pyramid selling deals and the like, such fraud exploits the gullibility of the victim. One example of this is telemarketing fraud. This involves mass marketing techniques via telephone in order to defraud individuals – often the elderly. According to the FBI (2005), this type of fraud, emanating primarily from Canada, produces estimated losses to US citizens exceeding $500 million per year. There are a number of variations of this type of fraud, including:

- *Fraudulent telefunding for charitable donations* – Where the caller presents themselves as phoning on behalf of what sounds like a well-known charity (but perhaps with a word in the title changed) and solicits donations for whichever good cause it is. Tragedies and natural disasters are often followed quickly by fraudulent, as well as legitimate, fund-raising activities.

- *Fraudulent sweepstakes* – The telephone call announces that you have won a prize, but there is a small promotional item you are required to buy in order to claim your prize (the prize is worth far in excess of the promotional item, you are told). In practice the reverse is true. This is a standard scam used by fraudulent market traders.

- *Lotteries* – On this occasion you receive notification through the post that you have won a prize. You ring a number in order to claim it. The scam, straightforwardly, is that it is a high-rate telephone call, it takes you many minutes to eventually get through the system and, when you do, you find you've won one pound (if you're lucky).

A recent study of fraud in the UK (Levi *et al.*, 2007) illustrates the complexity involved in attempting to understand the impact of such activities. Adopting what they refer to as a 'victim-centric' approach, Levi and colleagues sought to produce a typology of victims of all major types of fraud. The typology (see Table 18.1) covers 'private' and 'public' victims, of which there are several sub-types.

The table indicates that certain types of fraud imply certain types of victim, whereas others can be perpetrated against a range of victims. Benefit frauds are perpetrated against the welfare or social security system. Tax fraud – a failure to pay direct or indirect taxes – is directed against the Exchequer (though, as a result, everyone suffers indirectly). Cheque and credit card fraud may be directed at organisations or at individuals. However, as Levi *et al.* (2007: 10) note, 'individuals (the public-at-large) are ultimately the victims of most fraud, as they generally bear the costs of fraud through higher insurance premia, reduced dividends or pensions, higher credit card fees or interest rates, higher fees for banking services, higher taxes and so on'.

The Piper Alpha oil platform on fire in the North Sea in July 1988. The enquiry into the disaster found that Occidental, who operated the platform, had inadequate maintenance procedures.

Table 18.1	A typology of fraud by victim		
Victim sector	**Victim sub-sector**	**Examples of fraud**	**Estimated losses**
Private	**Financial services**	Cheque fraud Counterfeit intellectual property and products sold as genuine Counterfeit money Data-compromise fraud Embezzlement Insider dealing/market abuse Insurance fraud Lending fraud Payment card fraud Procurement fraud	**Total: £2.826 billion**
	Non-financial services	Cheque fraud Counterfeit intellectual property and products sold as genuine Counterfeit money Data-compromise fraud Embezzlement Insider dealing/market abuse Insurance fraud Lending fraud Payment card fraud Procurement fraud	**Total: £0.934 billion**
	Individuals	Charity fraud Consumer fraud Counterfeit intellectual property and products sold as genuine Counterfeit money Investment fraud Pension-type fraud	**Total: £2.75 billion**
Public	**National bodies**	Benefit fraud Embezzlement Procurement fraud Tax fraud	**Total: £6.434 billion**
	Local bodies	Embezzlement Frauds on council taxes Procurement fraud	**Total: £0.04 billion**
	International (but affecting UK public)	Procurement fraud (by UK against non-UK companies to obtain foreign contracts) EU funds fraud	**No figure given**

Source: Levi *et al.* (2007).

The extent of white-collar crime

For fairly obvious reasons, criminal statistics are of little use in the task of assessing the extent of corporate crime. The fraud statistics do provide a little information, but in reality tell us about how little corporate crime ever gets as far as the criminal courts. The other major source of data on levels and trends in crime – the British Crime Survey – is based entirely on individuals' experiences of victimization and doesn't ask about crimes potentially committed by organisations. The Home Office has undertaken a separate victimization study – of crimes *against* businesses (see Chapter 3). The Second Islington Crime Survey (Crawford *et al.*) did include some questions relating to health and safety, and pollution offences. The main available data on corporate crime comes from the major regulatory agencies such as the Health and Safety Executive and suffer, like all such agency data, from the fact that they tell us at least as much, if not more, about the work of the agency, and its priorities, than they do about this particular form of crime.

There have been two large-scale quantitative attempts to map the extent of white-collar crime. The earlier and most famous is that by Sutherland. He analysed the decisions taken against the '70 largest manufacturing, mining and mercantile corporations'. This covered what he called their 'life careers' which spanned on average 45 years. The analysis focused on restraint of trade, misrepresentation in advertising, infringement of patent, trademarks and copyrights, 'unfair labour practices', rebates, financial fraud and violation of trust, violations of war regulations (up to and including treason) and other miscellaneous offences (1983: 13–14).

Overall, Sutherland found that these 70 corporations had a total of 980 decisions against them. There was not a single one that had no decisions against it, and only two had a single decision against them. The average was 14 and the maximum 50 which was against Armour and Company (12 for restraint of trade; six for misrepresentation; two for infringement; 11 for unfair labour practices; and 13 other offences). General Motors were third in the list and Sears Roebuck fourth with 40 and 39 decisions respectively. In other circumstances, this is what might be called 'serious and persistent offending'. Of course, the bulk of these decisions were not made by criminal courts, but by other regulatory bodies, where often the burden of proof is less stringent. Nevertheless, as Sutherland (1983: 23) noted:

> Even if the present analysis were limited to these decisions by criminal courts, it would show that 60 per cent of the large 70 corporations have been convicted in criminal courts and have an average of four convictions each. In many states persons with four convictions are defined by statute to be 'habitual criminals'. The frequency of these convictions of large corporations might be sufficient to demonstrate the fallacy in the conventional theories that crime is due to poverty or to the personal and social pathologies connected with poverty.

The second large-scale study was undertaken by Clinard and colleagues and was based on the records of actions taken against 582 of the largest manufacturing, retail and service corporations in the world over a two-year period. The violations included:

- *Administrative violations* – Non-compliance with agency or court requirements, for example failure to obey an agency 'order to institute a recall or to construct pollution control facilities', and various 'paperwork violations'.
- *Environmental violations* – Air and water pollution, violations of permits.
- *Financial violations* – Illegal payments, issuing of false statements/information, various transaction offences, and tax violations.
- *Labour violations* – Discrimination in employment, health and safety violations, unfair labour practices, wage/hour violations.
- *Manufacturing violations* – Mainly related to product safety, labelling and the provision of information, and product defects.
- *Unfair trade practices* – Various competition offences, as well as false advertising. (1980: 113–116, quoted in Slapper and Tombs, 1999)

Once again, as with Sutherland's study, there are many reasons to assume that there is considerable under-recording involved in the process of relying on such records, and that the totals discovered by Clinard and colleagues should be treated as a conservative estimate of corporate crime. They found that:

> A total of 1,553 federal cases were begun against all 582 corporations during 1975 and 1976, or an average of 2.7 federal cases of violation each. Of the 582 corporations, 350 (60.1%) had at

least one federal action brought against them, and for those firms that had at least one action brought against them, the average was 4.4 cases ... Only 33 (2.1 per cent) of the actions instituted were later discovered to have been dismissed during the period covered by the study. (Clinard and Yeager, 1980: 113)

Important though these studies are, as with all research, they have limitations. Slapper and Tombs point to three in particular:

1   Both studies focus on the largest corporations and are, therefore, by no means representative of commercial practices generally (or cannot be assumed to be).

2   Sutherland's research focused exclusively on US corporations, and Clinard's work also had a bias in this direction, and it is, therefore, problematic to assume that the findings are necessarily applicable to corporations in other jurisdictions.

3   The studies focus on very different timescales – Sutherland's on a period of many decades, Clinard's on two years – and have little to say about annual corporate crime. As a consequence, any comparison with other crime data, levels and trends becomes all but impossible (though it would be highly problematic anyway).

The impact of white-collar crime

In the late 1970s Conklin (1977) compared the costs of a number of white-collar and 'conventional' crimes in the US. He estimated the total cost of robbery, theft, car theft and larceny at between $3–4 billion. By contrast, the estimated cost of consumer fraud, illegal competition and deceptive practices was approximately $40 billion. Barkan (1997) estimated the annual cost of white-collar crime to be over $400 billion compared, for example, with the estimated cost of street crime of $13 billion.

In the UK, the Serious Fraud Office (SFO) was established in 1987 to investigate cases of serious and complex fraud (defined as involving sums in excess of £1m). Since that time it has held a caseload of approximately 40–80 cases per year. In its annual report (2005–06) the SFO reported that it had worked on 88 cases during the course of the

year and of the 63 that were ongoing at the year end, the sum at risk was £2.47 billion.

In a similar vein, a decade or so ago, Levi (1995: 184) compared various reported crimes with fraud, noting that 'During 1990, in the whole of England and Wales, the police recorded "only" 123 robberies, 419 burglaries and 819 thefts over £50,000, very few of which would have been significantly over that amount ... The alleged frauds in any one of the most serious cases – those involving Bank of Credit and Commerce International (BCCI), Barlow Clowes, Guinness, Maxwell, and Polly Peck – approach or exceed [these combined totals].' An assessment undertaken for the Home Office and the Serious Fraud Office in 2000 (NERA) estimated that the cost of fraud to the main agencies was between £4 and £7 billion (see Table 18.2)

More recently, work undertaken by Levi and colleagues (2007) for the Association of Chief Police Officers estimates that the direct losses from frauds of all types was at least £12.98 billion and that 'it would be surprising if the "true total" was not much larger than this'. Two decades ago, Levi (1987) estimated that evasion of payment of Value Added Tax (VAT) cost the exchequer somewhere between £300–500 million. More recent estimates by HM Revenue and Customs have suggested the annual figure may now be near £7 billion (http://news.bbc.co.uk/1/hi/uk/5178788.stm).

Though the financial costs are useful because they help quantify impact, there are other consequences of course, including injury and loss of life, such as in Bhopal. Slapper and Tombs provide data on deaths at work. The Royal Society for the Prevention of Accidents provide an estimate of the number of road traffic deaths involving people at work, and have argued that as many as 1,000 people may die annually in these circumstances. To this total they add those deaths occurring in the course of commercial fishing, merchant shipping and those arising from the supply or use of flammable gas, bringing the overall number to over 1,300. This may be compared, for example, to the number of homicides annually, which is generally substantially under 1,000 – and was 765 in 2005–06 (including those killed in the July terrorist attacks). They also note that trade union research suggests that upward of 10,000 people may die annually from work-related medical conditions.

Work in the United States has drawn comparisons between the impact of street crime and corporate or organisational crimes. In the mid-1980s, official statistics recorded 19,000 deaths as a

Table 18.2	The cost of fraud		
		£ million	
Agency	Number	Low estimate	High estimate
Home Office police stats.	312,151	no data	no data
Serious Fraud Office	94	512	1,281
Dept. of Work and Pensions	1.5 million	2,000	3,000
Civil Service	580	3	
Audit Commission	638	10.8	
NHS		4.7	6
Customs and Excise		885	2,500
Inland Revenue		1.8	19.4
Insurance	430,000	645	650
Financial fraud		221.7	
Retail fraud	393,000	147.2	
Total		**4,431.2**	**7,838.1**

Source: Doig (2006).

result of street crime in the US. According to Mokhiber (1988), by contrast, white-collar crime includes the following facts:

- Nearly 800 people die in the US every day from diseases related to smoking.
- Approximately 8,000 people per year die from asbestos-related cancers.
- Up to 85,000 cotton textile workers suffer breathing problems due to brown-lung disease from cotton dust.
- The numbers killed as a result of product-related accidents are estimated as being in the tens of thousands.

One-off cases may result in very significant loss of life. The description of some of the factors leading to the sinking of the *Herald of Free Enterprise*, which resulted in the deaths of 197 people, details how these particular 'unlawful killings' came about:

> Another aspect of the accident had to do with the question of why the water entered through the open [bow] doors, which were several metres above sea level. Here it appeared that the 'Herald' was originally designed for the Dover–Calais connection. The ramp in Zeebrugge differed from the ramp in Calais; at

high tide it was not possible for the cars to reach the upper deck. Therefore, the nose of the ship had been lowered a few metres through the filling of the ballast tanks. The ballast pumps did not have a sufficient capacity for emptying the tanks in a short time. The 'Herald' had docked in Zeebrugge five minutes late, but was requested to arrive in Dover 15 minutes early. Therefore, there was no time for waiting till the ballast tanks were empty. Instead the 'Herald' left the harbour with the nose 3 metres down, and at full speed, which created a high bow wave. And so the 'Herald' capsized, in perfect weather, and on a practically waveless sea. (Wagenaar, quoted in Punch, 1996)

A criminal prosecution for 'corporate manslaughter' followed, but was unsuccessful, illustrating the difficulty often encountered in bringing criminal cases against organisations. We return to this issue below.

Understanding impact: the qualitative dimension

Although the scale of the impact of white-collar crime can be convincingly demonstrated using quantitative measures, there is also an argument for using various types of qualitative data as the basis

'Accident' or 'unlawful killing'? The *Herald of Free Enterprise* on its side after capsizing outside Zeebrugge harbour in Belgium in 1987.

for capturing its consequences. Slapper and Tombs (1999) identify three general approaches to qualitative studies of corporate crime, each of which provides important insights into the subject matter:

1 **Case studies of particular crimes** – Much research on corporate crimes has been based around case studies of particularly revealing cases. These include:

   a *Dalkon Shield* – This was an intra-uterine device which went on the market in the early 1970s. It quickly became a leading product in the contraceptive market, but within a relatively short time it appeared to be much less effective than had been claimed, as well as potentially being dangerous. By the mid-1980s the corporation producing the Dalkon Shield had paid out almost £400 million in lawsuits and in due course went bankrupt. Nevertheless, it was claimed to be still in use in Latin America a year after having been withdrawn elsewhere (Punch, 1996).

   b *The Savings and Loan crimes* – This particular scandal 'represents almost certainly one of

the greatest cases of mismanagement and fraud in [the twentieth] century' (Punch, 1996: 15). Savings and Loan schemes or 'thrifts' was a system for buying and arranging loans on property. In a competitive, financial environment, but one where regulations controlling the making of loans was liberalised, there was widespread malpractice. Indeed, so widespread were the frauds that the total value represented 'a monetary loss greater than the direct cost of crime over a lifetime for all but a very small fraction of American individuals or families' (Zimring and Hawkins, 1993: 256).

   c *The Maxwell pensions case* – Involving the publisher, Robert Maxwell, who, after his death, was found to have fraudulently taken nearly £800 million from his own companies and over £400 million from their pension funds. Punch suggests that the Maxwell case is a good illustration of two important facets of corporate crime:

   i It dispels the notion that such activity is undertaken 'for the good of the company'.

ii The fraud had multiple victims: banks, investors, employees and the pensioners who lost their pensions.

It also illustrated just how many failures of scrutiny, oversight, control and accountability are often involved in major corporate crimes. As the Select Committee noted:

> If the regulators had acted with a proper degree of suspicion, if the directors had carried out their duties fully, if professional advisers' common sense had been commensurate to their fees, if insiders had been brave enough to resign and talk, if newspaper editors had been prepared to stand up to Maxwell's bile and legal attacks, if brokers and merchant bankers had cared about their tasks as much as they did about their fees, if parliament had not been so beguiled by its own rhetoric about the special status of trust law, the Maxwell pension funds would have been secure. (quoted in Punch, 1996: 8)

d *BCCI* – The Bank of Credit and Commerce International was established in 1972 and from relatively modest beginnings grew to be the world's seventh-largest bank. Far from behaving ethically, however, it systematically appropriated investors' funds, kept false accounts and acted as a conduit for funds from the Colombian Medellin drug cartel, as well as various arms dealers.

2 *Categories/types of crime* – Studies have often taken a particular category or type of crime as their focus. These include:

a *Financial crimes* – Including illegal share dealings, tax evasion, bribery and false accounting. As in most areas of corporate crime there is much more work in America in this field than there is the UK. However, Levi's (1987) research on long-firm fraud is an important exception.

b *Crimes against consumers* – Such as the sale of unsafe goods, the misrepresentation or mislabelling of goods and the faulty or fraudulent testing of the safety of particular items.

c *Crimes against employees* – Including discrimination, violations of employment protection, wage laws and rights to industrial action, and health and safety offences.

d *Crimes against the environment* – Including pollution, waste dumping and environmental destruction.

3 *Industry-specific case studies* – These are attempts to provide an overview of a particular industry and, not surprisingly given the scope of such an enterprise, are relatively rare. An exception is Braithwaite's (1984) study of the pharmaceutical industry in which he uncovered a broad range of crimes:

> … bribery is probably a larger problem in the pharmaceutical industry than in almost any other industry. Of the 20 largest American pharmaceutical companies, 19 had been embroiled in bribery problems during the decade before the publication of the book … Product safety offences such as the sale of impure, overstrength, out of date or nonsterile products were also shown to be widespread. Anti-trust offences kept some of the wonder drugs financially out of the reach of most of the world's population for many years, causing countless lives to be lost needlessly. Misrepresentations in printed word and by word of mouth were common offences … The pharmaceutical industry also had its share of tax offenders and fraudsters who duped shareholders and creditors. But the most serious corporate crimes in the pharmaceutical industry were, and still are, in the safety testing of drugs. (Braithwaite, 1995: 13)

Controlling white-collar crime

Despite the very substantial harms that result from white-collar crime, we have noted at various stages during the course of this chapter that such offences are generally much less visible than conventional crime, and also that social attitudes toward such crimes are less straightforwardly condemnatory than they tend to be against what we might think of as conventional crime. For these reasons, among others, corporate crime tends to be subject to different forms of control than conventional crime. Frequently, many of the offences covered in this chapter are not referred to as 'crimes' at all. Rather, terms like 'rule-breaking', 'violations of codes' and 'malpractice' are used. Such activities tend to be 'regulated' rather than 'policed'. As a consequence, there is a range of agencies involved in the investigation of corporate crime, and the police in many respects play a relatively minor role.

In this regard our relatively crude distinction between white-collar and corporate crime has some benefit. Corporate crime – illicit actions by corporations or by individuals working on behalf of corporations – cannot easily be punished in the same way that individuals can. The phrase 'no soul to damn and no body to kick' is attributed to Lord Thurlow and outlines one of the central problems in the prosecution and punishment of corporate crime. Historically, corporations have enjoyed considerable protection from the criminal law. In an attempt to strengthen the law in this area, a Corporate Manslaughter and Corporate Homicide Bill was introduced to Parliament in 2006. By mid-2007, however, after numerous delays, the Bill had still not received Royal Assent.

One of the central difficulties has been establishing responsibility: how is this key element of criminal responsibility – the *mens rea* (the 'guilty mind') – to be established? One approach has been to attempt to establish the responsibility of certain key individuals in an organisation, and then impute these to the corporation more broadly – identifying the 'controlling minds' of the organisation.

In practice, the diffusion of responsibility throughout complex organisations makes it difficult successfully to identify individuals with sufficient authority, influence and control to hold them responsible for particular actions taken by the organisation itself. Consequently, successful prosecutions in this area are rare. In the case brought against P&O European Ferries (the boat was operated by Townsend Thoresen at the time of the sinking) after the sinking of the *Herald of Free Enterprise*, it was established that corporations, and not just specified employees, could be prosecuted for serious crimes (though P&O were acquitted). OLL Ltd, a much smaller, less complex (and less powerful) company, was the first company to be convicted of homicide. The company, which ran outward bound courses for schools, and its managing director were found guilty of manslaughter after four teenagers died on a canoeing trip. Peter Kite, the managing director, was sentenced to three years' imprisonment and the company was fined £60,000.

There can be particular difficulties in regulating business activity that crosses national boundaries and where issues of ownership and control of commercial interests is, at best, complex. The globe provides a range of tax havens, inaccessible bank accounts, and poorly-regulated regimes that make various forms of corporate misconduct possible, as well as making the task of regulatory agencies more difficult. Punch repeats a description of a case of corporate fraud that involved the disappearance of an oil tanker:

> It concerned a Liberian registered ship with Greek officers and a Turkish crew. The oil, loaded in Kuwait through an Italian company, was sold in turn to a British-Dutch concern (Royal Shell) and was supposed to be delivered in France. It was in fact unloaded in South Africa, the ship was deliberately scuttled in international waters off the Senegal coast, and involved were, among others, an American, a German and a Dutchman. (Bakker, quoted in Punch, 1996)

Generally speaking, even where responsibility can be determined in some way, the range of penalties for corporate crime is more restricted and cannot easily include imprisonment. Even when this is the case, the terms are often relatively modest in comparison with, say, the sentencing of conventional crimes. By 2000 the *average* sentence length for those imprisoned for burglary was 18 months. By contrast, in the prosecutions of Ernest Saunders, Gerald Ronson and others involved in the Guinness share price scandal in 1990 the longest prison sentence imposed for theft, conspiracy and false accounting was 30 months. All defendants went to open prison and one was spared imprisonment because of his age (74). Nevertheless, alongside multi-million pound fines, these were stiff sentences for white-collar crime. The judge passing sentence said:

> The sentence I pass must send a clear message that persons who seek commercial advantage by acting dishonestly can expect little mercy from the courts ... The vice with which we are dealing is the corruption of public and commercial life. (quoted in Punch, 1996: 175)

However, when prosecutions are brought as a result of regulatory offences they will most usually result in a fine. One frequent criticism has been that fines tend to be relatively small compared with the assets available to those fined. As Tombs and Whyte (2007) illustrate, the majority of safety crimes are punished through the magistrates' courts where the maximum fine is £20,000.

Although the trend in the size of fines has been sharply increasing over the past decade, the average remains less than £14,000. Similarly, the fines imposed following work-related fatalities have also been increasing, but the average remains under £45,000, a figure unlikely to make a substantial impact on a large multinational. There is some, limited, evidence that fines are increasing, especially in the most serious cases. Tombs and Whyte (2007b) give the following examples:

- In 1999, Balfour Beatty was fined £1.2 million after the collapse of a tunnel during the construction of a new rail link to Heathrow (a record fine for incident where there were no fatalities).

- In 1999, Great Western Trains was fined £1.5 million for their role in the Southall rail crash which killed seven people and injured a further 150.

- In 2005, the gas company Transco was fined £15 million for killing a family of four in a gas explosion.

- In 2006, Balfour Beatty was fined £10 million for the four deaths and 102 injuries in the Hatfield train crash.

However, they go on to argue that reliance on fines as a means of punishing such offences is problematic:

- Even large fines such as these are relatively insignificant when compared with the profits that such corporations make.

- The fact that fines are generally low means that it is the small firms that suffer disproportionately.

- Fines tend to reflect the gravity of the breach of the law rather than the gravity of the outcome of the breach of the law.

- Fines are levied on the company, rather than individuals, and they can therefore be absorbed. Indeed, the costs may even be passed on to workers rather than managers.

- Fines are ineffective when applied to government departments and the public sector – it simply means money is shuffled around.

In a similar vein, the sentences handed out to those convicted of fraud have also been criticised for relative leniency. There are a number of potential explanations for the tendency to treat such offenders leniently:

- It is often difficult to prove intent (defendants may claim, say, that the 'accident' was just that and that they were acting in good faith).

- Defendants may argue that they took steps to prevent what occurred happening (and therefore have their sentence reduced).

- Defendants' character and prospects may also be used in mitigation.

- The difficulty of detection (and the resources devoted to it) mean that few defendants have prior convictions.

- Some offences may not be viewed as especially serious – particularly where there is no 'direct' victim.

Regulating white-collar crime

The difficulties in controlling corporate and white-collar crime via conventional criminal justice methods, together with the generalised view that such activities are somehow intrinsically different from conventional crime, have meant that a separate set of regulatory systems have emerged in response to such offending. The regulation of business practices – of conditions at work, and with the production and distribution of food – all developed in the nineteenth century, and grew markedly during the twentieth century. The Factory Acts, the Trades Descriptions Acts, and so on attempted to strike some form of balance between business interests and those of workers and consumers.

Clarke's research on the regulation of business crime identifies a number of shortcomings. First, it is corporate interests that have traditionally regulated corporations: the boundary between poachers and gamekeepers has, at best, been blurred. The deregulatory movement in financial markets that took off in the 1980s and the scandals that followed made reform of the system increasingly likely. Privatisation added further to these pressures, and a series of new regulatory bodies – the Serious Fraud Office (SFO), the Health and Safety Executive (HSE) and others (see box below) – came into being.

There are important differences between bodies like the SFO, which are involved in what we might think of as 'policing' activities, and regulatory agencies such as the HSE. The latter are not engaged in the same form of policing but, rather, seek to engage in preventative activity in the main and, through persuasion, to increase compliance with regulatory systems. These are often referred to as *compliance strategies*. As Croall (2001: 105) notes, 'Regulatory agencies are not seen as, nor do they see themselves as, "industrial police officers" but as expert advisers or consultants whose aim is to

Some major regulatory agencies

HM Revenue and Customs (formerly *Inland Revenue* and *HM Customs and Excise*)
Focusing on VAT fraud and other tax offences, this new agency (HMRC) places greater emphasis on compliance and settlement than on investigation and prosecution. Its primary goal is revenue maximisation – ensuring that as much tax is paid to the state as possible. The Agency contains a number of other specialist groups including the Special Compliance Office (SCO) dealing with complex fraud, the Special Office, dealing with complex tax avoidance, and the Insolvency and Confiscation Group which deals with insolvency and confiscation as a result of criminal cases.

Financial Services Authority
Established in 1998, the FSA regulates all financial services in the UK, including the activities of banks, building societies, insurance and the London Stock Exchange. It is a huge concern with over 2,000 staff and with far-reaching objectives:

- Market confidence: maintaining confidence in the financial system.
- Public awareness: promoting public understanding of the financial system.
- Consumer protection: securing the appropriate degree of protection for consumers.
- The reduction of financial crime: reducing the extent to which it is possible for a business to be used for a purpose connected with financial

crime. (http://www.fsa.gov.uk/pages/About/ Aims/ Statutory/index.shtml)

In relation to financial crime, its approach is to attempt to make such activity more costly for those that engage in it and, using a risk-based approach, to provide an effective regulatory regime.

Health and Safety Executive (HSE) and Commission (HSC)
Established by the Health and Safety at Work Act 1974, the HSE and HSC are non-departmental public bodies with statutory responsibilities in relation to health and safety. Their initial responsibilities covered local government, education, and hospitals, but this has subsequently been extended to cover asbestos licensing, genetic modification, gas safety, transport of dangerous goods by road, pesticides, rail safety, nuclear safety research and off-shore safety.

Department for Trade and Industry's (DTI) Companies Investigation Branch
Investigates complaints about the conduct of companies, including fraud, insider dealing or trading and other matters associated with insolvency. It has about 100 staff and also uses private sector lawyers and accountants. The DTI also has an arms-length agency called the Insolvency Service which investigates the causes of business failure and is mainly involved in work connected with compulsory bankruptcy and the winding-up of companies.

---

secure compliance to laws and regulations.' This is not to say that prosecutions will not be brought, rather that they tend to be a 'last resort' when other approaches appear to have failed, an approach characterised by Braithwaite (1984) as 'walking softly while carrying a big stick'.

The contrast between the traditional policing approaches to conventional crime and the regulatory approach to corporate and white-collar crime raises a number of questions. First, there is the question of effectiveness. Do regulatory approaches lead to compliance? Second, is the more normatively-oriented question as to whether it is fair. Why should one group of offenders be subject to criminal sanctions when others are not? One of the strongest advocates of an approach that combines self-regulation with sanctions, John Braithwaite, bases part of his argument on the political realities confronting us:

[C]orporate crime is responsible for more property loss and more injuries to persons than is crime in the streets. Yet we know it is politically and fiscally unrealistic to expect that our generation will see the public resources devoted to corporate crime control approach anything near those expended on crime in the streets. Thus, the relevance of assessing how much private enforcement might contribute to corporate crime control. (Braithwaite and Fisse, 1987: 221)

Elements of this contrast can be seen in the contemporary policing of fraud. Though it is increasingly treated seriously, research by Levi and others has pointed to the shortcomings of policing activities in this area. Punch summarises Levi's work on enforcement in four general points:

1 British enforcement styles have tended to be more reactive, cautious and accommodating

than their US counterparts. They have also tended to be poorly staffed.

2 The police have traditionally been poorly trained for work in this area and have tended to accord it a relatively low priority.

3 Fraud trials tend to be expensive, sometimes complicated and prone to failure.

4 There are forms of 'private policing' such as self-regulating organisations that operate to maintain standards in some areas of professional practice.

Self-regulation

The problems associated with the policing and prosecution of corporations has led some scholars increasingly to explore the possibilities of self-regulation in the corporate sphere. Gobert and Punch (2003: 336) argue that 'the best way to combat corporate crime is to prevent it before it can occur, and that the best way to prevent it before it can occur is through a regime of individualised self-regulation in which every company takes responsibility for policing itself'.

There are a number of reasons why self-regulation is attractive. First, it is cheap, the cost being borne by the organisation itself rather than the police or some other investigative agency. Second, arguably, the organisation knows more about its own operation than any outsider. It is therefore well-placed to scrutinise itself. The dangers, of course, are either that such regulatory regimes will be insufficiently rigorous, or that they will eventually be diverted from their aims by other priorities. Nevertheless, there are argued to be some highly successful examples of self-regulation. On the basis of their research, Braithwaite and Fisse argue that companies that are effective at self-regulation share the following characteristics (1987: 225):

1 A great deal of informal clout and top management backing is given to their compliance personnel (safety inspectors, in the case of mine safety).

2 Accountability for compliance performance is clearly defined and placed on the line managers.

3 Performance is monitored carefully and managers are told when it is not up to standard.

4 Compliance problems are effectively communicated to those capable of acting on them.

5 Training and supervision (especially by front-line supervisors) for compliance are not neglected.

Regulatory bodies often have the difficult balancing act of investigating and controlling an industry on the one hand, and protecting its interests on the other. As a consequence, the strategy of many is to seek to control through persuasion and co-operation, rather than through the bringing of prosecutions or the imposition of some other form of sanction. According to Tombs (2004), the vast majority of reported deaths at work are not investigated by the HSE. Moreover, the likelihood of investigation varies significantly according to the nature of the industry concerned. About one-third of investigated cases result in a prosecution, and again these vary markedly by industry (almost half of investigated manufacturing deaths resulted in prosecution, compared with one-tenth of agricultural fatalities). On the basis of his analysis, Tombs (2004) reaches two conclusions. First, that for all its limitations, the criminal law and criminal sanctions continue to play an important role, especially symbolically, in signifying which acts are considered injurious and unacceptable. Second, notwithstanding this, criminalisation is too narrow a focus and an alternative, based on the notion of 'social harms', provides a more all-encompassing standpoint for understanding and responding to the negative outcomes of business practices.

There seem to be a number of options for controlling corporate crime, each of which may have some advantages but also shortcomings. The options include:

- *Self-control* – In which businesses seek to control their own behaviour as a form of enlightened self-interest. This can work, but there are numerous examples where existing self-controls have not been sufficient.

- *Whistle-blowing* – Attempts to encourage employees to report dubious practices have met with mixed success.

- *Government control* – There are numerous problems here, not least that often there is no report or knowledge of misconduct for a government agency to investigate (much such activity is hidden).

- *Legal controls* – Often considered to be a very ineffective instrument for regulating corporate activity, but may be practically important in some cases and symbolically so in many others.

- *Media* – Though inconsistent, and not without conflicts of interest, the media can be a powerful tool in regulating business activity.

- Other forms of regulation:
  - *Deterrence* – Rather like legal controls, there are numerous problems in imposing sanctions upon companies/organisations.
  - *Shaming* – John Braithwaite has argued strongly in favour of the use of reintegrative shaming theory (see Chapter 30) in the context of corporate offending.

Although formal systems of criminal justice and government regulation are seen as being, at best, only partly effective, they are likely to remain an important part of the overall jigsaw. Most commentators in this area, however, in identifying the limits of formal systems of control, also consider the possibility of various forms of self-regulation or less formal means of ensuring compliance. Thus, Ayres and Braithwaite (1992) in their work on 'responsive regulation' (see also Chapter 30) and Gobert and Punch (2003) on the 'socially responsible company' explore a range of alternative means by which cor-

porations are persuaded to behave like good citizens. In this world Gobert and Punch (2003: 345) argue, 'directors would be held to account by "stakeholders", who either would be accorded a place on the company's board of directors or who would be able to institute legal proceedings as representatives of the public interest to hold directors to their fiduciary obligations, including those owed to society'.

> ### Review questions
>
> 1 What are the main theoretical approaches to understanding white-collar crime?
>
> 2 What are the problems with the 'bad apple' theory of corporate offending?
>
> 3 Why should we be concerned about fraud if many of the losses are covered by insurance?
>
> 4 Why are legal controls considered to be so ineffective against white-collar crime?

Questions for further discussion

1 Does the fact that there is 'no soul to damn and no body to kick' make punishing organisations impossible?

2 Is white-collar crime, crime?

3 Does white-collar crime require an entirely different set of criminological theories from other forms of offending?

4 To what extent does the field of corporate and white-collar crime illustrate some of the limits of criminology?

5 Why do we talk about regulating rather than punishing white-collar crime?

Further reading

Reading in this area should probably start with Edwin Sutherland's (1983) *White-collar Crime: The uncut version,* New Haven, CT: Yale University Press.

There are a number of textbooks that provide an overview of the subject area. I found the most helpful to be:

Croall, H. (2001) *Understanding White-collar Crime,* Buckinghamshire: Open University Press

Punch, M. (1996) *Dirty Business: Exploring corporate misconduct,* London: Sage

Slapper, G. and Tombs, S. (1999) *Corporate Crime,* Harlow: Longman

There are also a number of slightly more specialised books which contain a lot of useful material:

Gobert, J. and Punch, M. (2003) *Rethinking Corporate Crime,* London: Butterworths

Pontell, H. and Geis, G. (eds) (2007) *International Handbook of White-Collar and Corporate Crime,* New York: Springer-Verlag

Tombs, S. and Whyte, D. (2007) *Safety Crimes,* Cullompton: Willan

Of the British criminologists in recent years who have studied white-collar and corporate crime it is undoubtedly Mike Levi who has had the greatest impact. You can look up any of his work in your university library and it will almost certainly be of use in the study of this subject. As a pointer you might start with:

Levi, M. (1987) *Regulating Fraud: White-collar crime and the criminal process,* London: Tavistock

Websites

A lot of information and news reports can be found on a number of campaigning websites:
www.corporatewatch.org
http://paulsjusticepage.com/elite-deviance.htm

The Centre for Corporate Accountability provides information and advice on safety, law enforcement and corporate criminal accountability issues: www.corporateaccountability.org

There are also a number of government websites which provide information about the major regulatory agencies. You can go to individual government departments (Department for Business, Enterprise and Regulatory Reform) or individual agencies (HSE) or begin with the official guide to government website and navigate from there:
www.direct.gov.uk

Finally, you can find a number of useful links at:
http://www.ex.ac.uk/~RDavies/arian/scandals/fight.html

Chapter outline

Defining organised crime 406

Traditional forms of organised crime 408
  The Mafia 408
  Triads 409
  The Yakuza 409

Organised crime in America 409
  The organisation of organised crime 411
    An alien conspiracy theory 413
    The ethnic succession thesis 413
  How organised was American organised crime? 414

Organised crime in Britain 417

Transnational organised crime 420
  Human trafficking and migrant smuggling 421
  Drugs trafficking 425

Transnational crime control 429
  Transnational policing 429
    Europol 430

Understanding organised crime 431

Questions for further discussion 433
Further reading 433
Websites 433

Organised crime

CHAPTER SUMMARY	In Chapter 18 we looked at criminal activities by and within corporations. Here we consider the related subject of 'organised crime' – often viewed as the criminal activities of syndicates or even 'families'.

We look at:

- what is meant by organised crime;
- the history of organised crime;
- the types of organised crime currently to be found in our society and beyond.

In our globalised world there is increasing concern that organised crime is undertaken across national boundaries and that, consequently, it is necessary to create cross-national means of responding to such crime.

We conclude the chapter by looking at the growth of transnational policing.

Defining organised crime

Here we enter territory where terminology is tricky and the subject-matter all but impossible to define. A report produced jointly by the EU and Europol in 2001 sought to develop means of identifying organised criminal activities. They identified eleven criteria, the first four of which must all be present for something to be defined as 'organised crime', as must at least two of the seven others:

1 Collaboration of more than two people.

2 Taking place over a prolonged or indefinite period of time.

3 Suspected of the commission of serious criminal offences.

4 Having as its central goal, the pursuit of profit and/or power.

> Mandatory criteria

5 Having a specialised division of labour.

6 Utilising a system of discipline and control.

7 Using violence and other means of intimidation.

8 Having a commercial or business-like structure.

9 Involved in money-laundering.

10 Operating internationally, across national borders.

11 Exerting influence over politics, judicial bodies, media, the economy.

> Optional criteria

How helpful is this? Levi (2002) notes that many of the optional criteria are fairly easy to satisfy: there are few major forms of criminal activity, for example, that can take place without there being some money-laundering, or some form of division of labour among the participants. As such it is certainly not a foolproof way of enabling us to distinguish 'organised' criminal activities from the rest of criminal activity. Nevertheless, it provides a reasonably reliable indicator of what are often taken to be the central characteristics of the forms of criminal activity that we will discuss in this chapter.

'Organised crime' is sometimes referred to as 'syndicated crime' (particularly in America) because, in part, it refers to what are held to be the activities of *criminal syndicates*. Thus, for example, there is a sizeable body of work focusing on forms of gangsterism associated with particular ethnic groups – the Italian *Mafia*, Japanese *Yakuza*, Chinese *Triads* and so forth. This is the model of organised crime best known to popular culture through the activities of the Corleone family in the *Godfather* movies and, more recently, in the television portrayal of the New Jersey-based racketeering in *The Sopranos*. This picture of organised crime – essentially a stereotype developed in the United States to describe what was believed to be the nature of such activities in America in the early- to mid-twentieth century – has come to dominate both criminological and popular understandings in this area. We will spend some time in this chapter looking at both the history of this particular 'paradigm' for understanding organised crime, as well as looking at its limitations.

There is relatively little suggestion that this model of organised crime was ever terribly applicable to

Britain in the twentieth century. Rather, domestic organised crime has tended to be associated with racketeering by criminal gangs which frequently were not ethnically-based, and whose activities were linked with the control of particular forms of illegal enterprise within a given geographical area: the race-course gangs in Sheffield and elsewhere in the 1930s, the Krays and Richardsons in different parts of London in the 1950s and 1960s, and so on. The nature of their activities led some commentators to talk of 'professional and organised crime' (Hobbs, 1994). The Krays and others were 'professional' criminals in the sense that crime was a full-time occupation rather than an occasional activity that punctuated otherwise ordinary, legitimate lifestyles. It is not – or not simply – the nature of their activities – violence, extortion, protection rackets, and so on – that necessarily distinguishes them, it is the structure (the *organisation*) of these activities that sets them apart.

Both of these styles and forms of activity have now been largely displaced – both in the criminological literature and also, to a degree, 'on the ground' – by criminality that is international or transnational in character, and which involves more or less complex networks of actors. Gone is the preoccupation with hierarchically-structured *mobs;* now the concern is with loosely structured, complex networks which are generally fluid both in organisation and activity. These may involve Mafia-style groups, but will often not. Rather, it is the simple fact that their activities are complex – they require a high degree of organisation – which leads them to be categorised in this way.

This by no means exhausts the range of activities that may be referred to in discussions of organised crime. It serves to illustrate that there is no easily identifiable 'essence' to this thing sometimes called organised crime, and also to indicate the approach taken in this chapter. If we are going to study it and discuss it, then we have to try to be clear about what it is we are examining, where we set our boundaries, and so on. Now, if you are reading this chapter having already read the previous one, then a further difficulty may already have occurred to you. What is the distinction between the activities covered here and those we described earlier as corporate and white-collar crime? A number of commentators have argued against bothering to attempt to maintain any such distinction. The critical criminologist, Bill Chambliss (see also Chapter 12) has argued, for example, that 'one of the reasons we fail to understand organised crime is because we put crime into a category that is separate from normal business. Much crime does not fit into a separate category. It is primarily a business activity' (1978: 53). Similarly, Lyman and Potter (2004: 476) argue that the Savings and Loan scandal in America in the 1980s (a huge fraud estimated to have 'cost' every American citizen $6,000) points to three often-ignored facets of organised crime:

- There is relatively little difference between those perceived as law abiding and those who are viewed as deviant.

- Corporate finance and corporate capital are characterised by criminality and misconduct at least as much as any poor neighbourhood.

- The distinctions between business, politics and organised crime are in many ways artificial and meaningless. 'Rather than being dysfunctions, corporate crime, white-collar crime, organised crime and corruption are mainstays of US political-economic life.'

Nevertheless, for our purposes, a general analytical distinction can be used. Whereas the matters described in Chapter 18 were largely made up of the activities of corporations or people working within corporations, the bulk of activities we focus upon in this chapter do not involve, at their heart, legitimate corporations or businesses. Organised crime – as we shall use the term here – may use corporations as 'fronts' for other activities, or as means of laundering money from illegal activities but, in the main, the organisations in organised crime are not registered businesses or multinational corporations. The chapter unfolds as follows. We begin by looking at what might be called various 'traditional' forms of organised crime – what have often been referred to as Mafia (or equivalents). We do so as these terms, and some of the ideas linked with them, regularly reappear in the literature on contemporary organised crime. We then turn our attention to organised crime in America and how this has been understood.

Traditional understandings of American organised crime rest on two fundamental assumptions: that it involved an 'alien other' (the modern stereotype being Italian immigrants, particularly from Sicily); and, that the organisations involved were characterised by a formal, hierarchical structure. Having questioned these assumptions, we will move on to consider the nature of organised crime in Britain in the twentieth century and examine the extent to which this mirrors or departs from the 'American model'. Finally, we turn our attention to transnational organised crime. Our late modern world – as a result of the processes of globalisation (see Chapter 34) – is characterised by ease of movement and communication, leading to new criminal opportunities. Though Transnational Organised Crime (TOC) is a relatively new term (Woodiwiss, 2003) it is now the focus of considerable (inter)governmental activity. We conclude by looking at the transnational policing structures – many of which are emerging in response to the perceived threat posed by TOC.

Traditional forms of organised crime

The Mafia

Banditry was relatively commonplace in the middle ages. It was the growing power of the nation state and the gradual formalisation of policing and criminal justice that put paid to much such activity. It was in the south of Italy, where the state remained relatively weak, and family ties remained predominant, that the Mafia emerged and flourished. The term was unknown before the 1800s but has generally come to represent at least three distinct things:

- A code of behaviour based on courage and toughness, which recognises no obligation except those of the code of honour or *omertà* (manliness), the core of which was the unwillingness to pass any information to the authorities.

- A local system of power in which a private magnate or boss organises a network of influence using patronage and providing protection to those on the 'inside'.

- The control of a community's life through a secret, or officially unrecognised, system of gangs. (Hobsbawm, 1959: 32–3)

With their origins in Sicily, the Mafia grew in the nineteenth century as a form of protection for both landowners and peasants – for peasants against absentee landlords and for landlords against the state and its private 'armed companies'. According to Hobsbawm, the rise of the Mafia in Sicily marked the transfer of power from a feudal to a rural middle class. It served numerous purposes:

In a sense, it grew out of the needs of all rural classes, and served the purpose of all in varying degrees. For the weak – the peasants and the miners – it provided at least some guarantee that obligations between them would be kept, some guarantee that the usual degree of oppression would not be habitually exceeded; it was the terror which mitigated traditional tyrannies. And, perhaps, also, it satisfied a desire for revenge by providing that the rich were sometimes fleeced, and that the poor, if only as outlaws, could sometimes fight back. (Hobsbawm, 1959: 40–41)

Though disparate and fragmented in this period, from the early twentieth century there tended to be greater co-ordination and power-sharing. According to Ianni and Ianni (1972: 31–2) it was the impact of Don Vito Cascio Ferro that led to a situation in which:

... all crimes became organised and the *società* controlled them all directly or through licencing arrangements. He devised the *Mafia* system of demanding tribute – of *fari vagnari a pizzu* ('wetting the beak') by dipping into every business venture. He also maintained rigid discipline.

The Mafia's power has arguably been diminishing since the Second World War as government, police and trades unions all reinforced their position in Italian society. An Anti-Mafia Commission was established in 1963 and operated for over a decade when other measures were also introduced. More recently, however, it is suggested that the Mafia has changed in character, becoming more international in scale and focus, as its traditional role in Italian society shrank. Although it is easy to overstate the extent to which Mafia families traditionally distanced themselves from activities such as drugs trafficking and prostitution (Gambetta, 1993), it appears that recent decades have seen greater involvement in such areas of criminality. This has been accompanied by changes to the structure of the organisation itself, involving (Wright, 2006: 105–6):

- A shift away from protection activity towards more diverse goals.

- Horizontal financial integration ('gangster capitalism').

- Control of political/economic clients; not using them for mediation.

- Vertical integration by inclusion of extra-familial members.

- Violence used for tactical control, rather than for strategic coercion.

By such accounts, the Sicilian Mafia has mutated somewhat. According to Gambetta (1993) it has remained primarily Sicilian, and largely concentrated in the Western part of the island. Why, he asks, was it not exported to the rest of Italy? It cannot be because of an absence of economic opportunities. Rather, he says, one must conclude that it is because it is a difficult business to export as it depends heavily on local circumstances. In particular, the establishment of such business requires the ability to 'exploit independent networks of kinship, friendship, and ethnicity' (1993: 251). Those Mafiosi in Northern Italy that existed were there largely because they had been confined there and had little choice (though see Varese, 2006). Moreover, on this same basis Gambetta argues that Mafia families were not exported to America – a common assumption as we will see. Rather, they 'emerged spontaneously, as it were, when the supply of, and the demand for, protection met: when, in other words, a sufficient number of emigrants moved there for independent reasons, some bringing along the necessary skills for organizing a protection market, and some were able to exploit these when certain events, notably the Great Depression and Prohibition, opened up a vast and lucrative market for this commodity' (1993: 251–2).

Triads

Originating in the Fujian province in China, the Triads were originally a secret society organised in opposition to the Manchu dynasty. It was only later that such groups became involved in protection, extortion and corruption. After the Communist Party took power in China in the late 1940s many Triad members fled to Hong Kong, and later dispersed to the West. There, their activities included protection rackets, illegal gambling, prostitution, loan sharking and drug trafficking (Bresler, 1980) and subsequently has expanded to include human smuggling (Zhang and Chin, 2002).

The Yakuza

With origins – possibly – in seventeenth-century Japanese gambling gangs, the Yakuza had moved into gambling, and protection by the late-nineteenth century. According to Hill (2003: 2) by the 1980s 'the Yakuza apparently enjoyed a position of wealth, security and acceptance inconceivable for organised crime groups in other advanced liberal democracies'. Seemingly highly organised in a pyramidal fashion, Hill estimated there to be over 86,000 people involved in the Yakuza by the late-1980s, divided into over 3,000 separate groups, of which almost half were attached to one of three large, national syndicates.

Organised crime in America

As Walker (1988) has argued, for as long as there have been major urban areas in America, there has been demand for alcohol, gambling and prostitution. Where such demands exist, it is likely that they will be met in an increasingly organised manner. Until prohibition, he argued, vice entrepreneurs had generally been small-scale operators. 'Prohibition completely transformed the industry. By creating a vast new market for illegal alcohol, it fostered the growth of large-scale enterprises that could monopolize production and distribution, just as a few large corporations dominated the steel, oil and automobile industries' (1988: 158). You might at this point return to the sections earlier in the book on interactionist and labelling theories (especially Chapter 10) and apply Howard Becker's observation that 'deviance is *not* a quality of the act the person commits, but rather a consequence of the application by others of rules and sanctions to an "offender"' to the impact of prohibition.

Anyone who has seen Martin Scorsese's rather overblown cinematic version of Herbert Asbury's book *Gangs of New York* will at least have a sense of the types of gang activity that characterised the larger American cities in the nineteenth and early twentieth centuries. Though such gangs were undeniably *disorganised* in many respects, they nevertheless sought to maintain control over particular illicit activities within particular territories, and sometimes had a degree of structure to them. The most famous figure in American organised crime is Al Capone – and again much of this is to do with the power of the media and of the recreation in print and in film of one of the most famous eras in modern American history: prohibition.

Although one of the enduring images of Capone is as head of a large criminal network, the more prosaic truth is that he was one of a number of figures who had a prominent role in what was more likely a relatively loose confederation of groups, gangs and networks (Repetto, 2005). Organised

Scene from Martin Scorcese's film *Gangs of New York* (2002), starring Leonardo di Caprio and Daniel Day-Lewis. Set in the mid-nineteenth century, it explores the familiar pattern of rivalry between established and immigrant gangs – replicated in many other contexts.

crime in Chicago was little affected by Capone's eventual imprisonment in the early 1930s. He was succeeded by Sam Giancana and his organisation, 'The Outfit', was dominant in Chicago's organised crime for several decades. If Capone is the best-known individual, it is the apparent growth of Italian-American organised crime that has dominated Hollywood over the last 30 years. In particular, Francis Coppola's *Godfather* films, together with Martin Scorsese's *Goodfellas* and Sergio Leone's *Once Upon a Time in America* have popularised the idea of the transplantation of Sicilian family-based organised crime to twentieth-century America. And, indeed, figures like Vito Genovese, Charles 'Lucky' Luciano and, more recently, John Gotti and Paul Castellano give a certain credence to elements of such stories.

The Hollywood portrayal of organised crime in this period of American history is based in large part on many of the same sources that influenced the dominant academic picture of organised crime. In particular, the idea of 'crime families', with highly organised internal structures is heavily influenced by the work of the American criminologist, Donald Cressey.

In fact, the idea of a national crime syndicate (the Mafia) poisoning American public life and threatening American democracy had initially been promoted in a Senate report investigating committee not long after the Second World War (Kefauver, 1951). According to Woodiwiss (2005: 73) 'The Kefauver Committee's most significant legacy was to misrepresent the problem of organised crime and commit the federal government to becoming more involved in the policing of gambling and drugs.' This view of organised crime as Mafia-led and that much of the activity had foreign origins, was further reinforced by the report of the President's Commission on Law Enforcement in the late 1960s (thanks to the influence of Cressey, who was a member of the Commission). In the 1960s, Valachi argued that the Mafia had been superseded by another grouping, the *Cosa Nostra* ('our thing'). This he alleged had a highly formalised structure comprising 24 or more families, each linked to by understandings, agreements and 'treaties' and by mutual attachment to a 'Commission'. Using the memoirs of one important participant, Joseph Valachi (see Maas, 1969), Cressey detailed the means by which initially a 'boss of bosses' emerged (originally Giuseppe Masseria, and after his assassination, Salvatore Maranzano), later to be replaced by a '*consiglieri* of six' – made up by the six most influential heads of syndicates in the US.

Prohibition and the birth of the *Cosa Nostra*

Al Capone

Joe Masseria

Organised Italian racketeering really did not begin to be a national force until the 1920s. Prohibition, of course, was the catalyst. In addition to those old standbys – prostitution and gambling – there was now a new illicit commodity that millions of Americans craved: alcohol. And it brought the racketeer riches and respectability beyond his wildest dreams; in effect most of the nation became his accomplice. The entire underworld, then monopolized by the Irish, Jews, and, to a lesser extent, Poles, cashed in on the Prohibition bonanza. But for Italian racketeers, especially, it was a chance at last to move into the big time. Bootlegging was something they knew about. For years, Prohibition or not, thousands of home distilleries had been operating in the ghetto-like neighbourhoods that Italian immigrants, like other

ethnic groups before them, tended to crowd into after landing in [America]. Thus they had a running start in the huge – and thirsty – market that had opened up, and from then on they bowed to no one.

By the end of the decade, despite the latter-day publicity given to Alphonse (Scarface Al) Capone, a vain, chunky little man named Giuseppe (Joe the Boss) Masseria had emerged as the most powerful single figure in Italian crime. Allied with him, besides Capone, was an awesome collection of mobsters of future note, including Charley (Lucky) Luciano, Vito (Don Vito) Genovese, William (Willie Moore) Moretti, Joseph (Joe Adonis) Doto, and Francesco (Frank Costello) Castiglia.

Source: Mass (1969: 77–8).

The organisation of organised crime

Cressey, who advised the President's Commission on Law Enforcement and the Administration of Justice in the late 1960s, argued that organised crime in America was dominated by a tightly-knit network of 'Mafia families', and that these groupings had a largely formal, hierarchical structure: 'The structures of formal organisations are rational. They allocate certain tasks to certain members, limit entrance, and influence the rules established for their own maintenance and survival' (1972: 11). This view of organised crime, though, as we will see, much criticised, has had a huge impact on thinking in this area. Cressey was influenced by testimony given by Joseph Valachi – a self-confessed Mafia member – this testimony providing

detailed information (over 300,000 words, according to his editor, Maas, 1969) on the alleged operation of American organised crime. According to Cressey (1969: 109):

Since 1963, when Joseph Valachi testified before the McClellan Committee, there has been a tendency to label America's nationwide criminal cartel and confederation '*Cosa Nostra*' and then to identify what is known about *Cosa Nostra*'s division of labour as the structure of 'organized crime' in the United States. I have followed this tendency, believing that the *Cosa Nostra* organization is so extensive, so powerful, and so central that precise description and control of it would be description of all but a tiny part of all organized crime.

Police emptying barrels of beer during the prohibition period in the US in the 1920s.

According to Cressey, the *Cosa Nostra* was headed by something called the 'Commission' or *Consiglio d'Amministrazione*. Like a board of directors, it was actually rather like a court of arbitration, settling disputes and making rulings. Although crime 'families' from different cities were not formally represented on the Commission, he argued that it was likely that they had a designated member. Below the Commission, in some parts of the country, were 'councils' which were made up of the more experienced members of the 'families'. The council was headed by a 'Don' or 'chairman' and members of the council were elected from among the families.

Beneath the 'councils', Cressey said, there were at least 24 crime families each with its own boss. The bosses' primary functions were to maintain order and to maximise the amount of money earned. Of these, the richest were in New York, New Jersey, Illinois, Florida, Louisiana, Nevada and Rhode Island. Families varied in size from only 20 people up to about 800. The families were interlinked, he argued, with the bosses knowing each other and arranging deals between the families. Below them, on the next rung of the ladder was the 'underboss' or *sottocapo*. At the same level as the underboss, there would also often be an adviser or *consigliere* – made famous in the *Godfather* movies in the shape of Robert Duvall as 'Tom Hagen'. Also at the same level is someone playing the role of 'buffer', communicating with those lower down and insulating the boss from any direct contact with those carrying out his orders.

Below the underboss, working effectively as a works or sales manager, is the 'lieutenant', 'captain' or simply, *capo*. All men occupying this position within the family are of equal rank irrespective of how many men they have working for them. Beneath them are 'section chiefs' or 'group leaders', and on down the line the structure goes to the 'soldiers' or 'wise guys' at the bottom. According to Cressey, in the late 1960s there were around 5,000 men belonging to crime families fitting this description and being part of the larger organisational structure he referred to as the *Cosa Nostra*. In effect, through the President's Commission on Law Enforcement and the Administration of Justice, this became the 'official' picture of organised crime. In the Commission's words (1967: 187):

> Organized crime is a society that seeks to operate outside the control of the American people and their governments. It involves thousands of criminals, working within structures as complex as those of any large corporation, subject to laws more rigidly enforced than those of legitimate governments. Its actions are not impulsive but rather the result of intricate conspiracies carried on over many years and aimed at gaining control over whole fields of activity in order to amass huge profits.

An alien conspiracy theory

Cressey's account of the Sicilian origins and basis for such activities presents American organised crime as a largely alien affair, imported to the US, and operating in a highly bureaucratised, almost conspiratorial form. Cressey argued that organised crime groups in the US at this time, though modelled on the Sicilian Mafia, were not simply a direct transplant from the mother country. Rather, they had undergone a process of change as they entered the new cultural setting. This process of 'Americanization', which accounted for the main differences between the Sicilian Mafia and the *Cosa Nostra*, was a result of three conditions:

1 The short period of time since the main thrust of Italian-Sicilian immigration.

2 Fragmentation of the native extended family by migration to the host country of only a part of that family.

3 Location of the immigrants in the urban areas of a rapidly industrializing nation rather than in the rural areas of an agricultural nation. (Cressey, 1969: 151)

The ethnic succession thesis

Ethnicity has generally been seen as one of the primary driving forces in organised crime. In addition to the association of organised crimes with 'alien others', there is a thesis which associates such activities with the more marginal elements of the population – those most likely to experience 'strain' (see Chapter 8). As particular ethnic groups become gradually assimilated to the mainstream, they are replaced in organised crime by other, more recent arrivals. This ethnic succession thesis has been applied particularly to the case of America, though it can also be found in relation to organised crime in other jurisdictions. The Iannis (Ianni and Ianni, 1972: 49) described the process in America as follows:

> The Irish came first, and early Irish gangsters started to climb the ladder. As they came to control the machinery of the large cities, the Irish won wealth, power and respectability ... In organized crime, the Irish were succeeded by Jews ... The Jews quickly moved on up the ladder into the world of business, a more legitimate means of economic and social mobility. The Italians came last and did not get a leg up on the rungs of crime until the late Thirties.

And so the process continues. Writing some time later, Levi (1998: 338) wrote 'nowadays there is hardly an Italian name on the FBI's "most wanted list" of targets. Cuban refugees, Colombians and, increasingly, Mexicans have come to dominate the distribution of narcotics in the southern States, and other ethnic groups – Puerto Rican, Japanese and Chinese – as well as white motorcycle gangs are involved in organized crime in the United States.' Though a number of authors have cast doubt on the accuracy of the idea of ethnic succession (Block, 1983), the thesis helpfully draws attention to the importance of locating an understanding of organised crime within the broader context of the social, political and economic circumstances of the times.

How organised was American organised crime?

Although official inquiries such as the President's Commission in the 1960s were convinced of the existence of an American Mafia, others were much more sceptical. According to Daniel Bell:

> Neither the Senate Crime Committee in its testimony nor Kefauver in his book presented any real evidence that the *Mafia* exists as a functioning organization. One finds police officials asserting before the Kefauver committee their belief in the *Mafia*: the Narcotics Bureau thinks that a worldwide dope ring allegedly run by [Lucky] Luciano is part of the *Mafia*, but the only other 'evidence' presented – aside from the incredulous responses both of Senator Kefauver and Rudolph Halley when nearly all of the Italian gangsters asserted that they didn't know about the *Mafia* – is that certain crime bears 'the earmarks of the *Mafia*'. (quoted in Wright, 2006: 28)

'Lucky' Luciano (1897–1962). *Mafia* godfather in New York in the 1920s and 1930s – amassed a fortune from protection rackets and control of the heroin trade.

Thus, in contrast to the view of organised crime as being hierarchically organised, syndicated and increasingly monopolistic, there developed an alternative model which focuses more on organised crime as 'enterprise' (Block and Chambliss, 1981; Passas and Nelken, 1993). In this view, organised crime is seen as much more flexible and opportunistic, organised in different ways at different times according to the markets it is related to. Thus, Block (1983) found considerable evidence of organised crime syndicates, but nothing of the scale of the alleged *Cosa Nostra*. Indeed, Block argued that there were actually two types of syndicate in operation at the time: *enterprise* syndicates focusing on illegal trades of various sorts, and *power* syndicates which used violence as the basis for extortion and for maintaining power. Such power syndicates run, for example, by 'Lucky' Luciano among others, used very serious violence (and the threat of it) up to and including murder, as the basis for protection rackets.

Albini (1971: 288), another of Cressey's critics, using the example of organised crime in Detroit, argued that: 'rather than being a criminal secret society, a criminal syndicate consists of a system of loosely structured relationships functioning primarily because each participant is interested in furthering his own welfare.' In this view he was joined by the Iannis, whose study of Italian-American crime groupings in the US in the late 1960s/early 1970s remains of lasting importance in this field. Ianni and Ianni (1972: 153) argued:

> Secret societies such as the *Mafia*, however, are not really formal organizations ... They are not rationally and consciously constructed; they are responsive to culture and patterned by tradition. They are not hierarchies of organizational positions which can be diagrammed and then changed by recasting the organizational chart; they are patterns of relationship among individuals which have the force of kinship and so they can only be changed by drastic, often fatal action.

In their view, *Mafia* families were just that, *families*. As such they were to be understood as a kinship network, and the rules were those of such a network (Ianni and Ianni, 1972: 154):

1. The family operates as a social unit with social organization and business functions merged.

2. The group assigns all leadership positions based on kinship, down to the 'middle management' level.

3. The higher the position in the organization, the closer the kinship relationship.

4. The group assigns leadership positions to a central group of family members, all of whom have close consanguineal or affinal relationships, which fictive godparental relationships reinforce.

5 Members of this leadership group are assigned primarily to either legal or illegal enterprises, but not both.

6 Transfer of monies from illegal to legal and back into illegal activities takes place through individuals rather than companies and is part of the close kin-organization of the family.

In the Iannis's (1972) view, the crime family can be considered a 'quasi-corporate being'. It demands loyalty, and its members must always subjugate their individual desires to the larger whole. However, it is a much more fluid entity that the almost stereotypically corporate model outlined earlier by Cressey. The origins of these family-style structures lie in Italy they argue, not in North America. In Italy, certainly in its southern reaches, the family formed the basis of the social order, and loyalty to family was the basis of honour.

Subsequently, a number of American research studies, such as Chambliss's (1988) in Seattle and Reuter's (1983) in New York, found relatively low levels of 'organisation' in organised crime – certainly as far as hierarchically-managed groups were concerned. More recent research on the involvement of Chinese organised crime in human smuggling in the United States tended to reinforce this view:

> From our many conversations and interactions with Chinese human smugglers, we have found that the best way to describe smuggling organizations is that they are amorphous. Although Chinese human smuggling rings have previously been described as complex and highly organized, we have not been able to establish any clear hierarchical order resembling that of a formal social organization. Although we talked to a few successful snakeheads (smugglers), none would consider themselves as occupying a commanding position in their smuggling network and able to exercise a high level of authority. They would describe themselves as working with their 'friends'. (Zhang and Chin, 2002: 750)

Zhang and Chin (2002: 754–55) go on to say that they 'found human smuggling in general to be haphazard in its business formation, irregular in its planning and execution, and uncertain in its outcome.' It also depends upon the existence of corrupt public officials in order for it to occur. In this regard, Chambliss, Block and other critics were especially dismissive of the idea that organised crime was somehow entirely separate from, and a threat to, the existing political order. On the contrary, they argued, criminologists should be exploring the complex interconnections between, and in many cases mutual dependence of, organised crime and what is presented as being the legitimate business and political world.

This critical view of American organised crime sees it as embedded within the otherwise apparently legitimate power structures of American political life. Block and Chambliss's picture of organised crime ran contrary to the implication drawn by Cressey that somehow such activities were alien to American culture. Quite the reverse: scholars like Chambliss saw such activities as being deeply embedded at all levels of American culture. The title of his book on the subject – *On The Take: From petty crooks to presidents* – illustrates his position (see also Chapter 12).

Chambliss was highly critical of the picture of organised crime that dominated popular culture, and some academic writing, and argued that it was based on the slimmest of evidence – what he described (1978: 4–5) as a 'few imaginative and talkative persons, usually facing felony charges and long prison sentences, [who] gain immunity from prosecution on at least some of the charges by "telling it all"'. By contrast, Chambliss undertook five years of fieldwork, based on observation and interviewing, in an attempt to study the criminal networks in the American city of Seattle. This led him to two conclusions that ran directly against the dominant grain of thinking in this area. First, he concluded that organised crime was not controlled by some form of national syndicate who exercised a feudal-like control over their underlings across the nation. Second, his research did not support the idea that there was some 'godfather' or even a group of private citizens running these rackets. Rather, he suggested, it is 'a coalition of businessmen, politicians, law enforcers and racketeers (see Figure 19.1) who have a greater interest in the rackets than anyone else, who stand to lose the most if the operation is exposed, and who also have the power to do something when it is called for' (1978: 73).

Figure 19.1	Seattle's crime network

Financiers

Jewellers
Realtors (estate agents)
Contractors

Attorneys
Businessmen
Industrialists

Bankers

Organisers

Businessmen	**Politicians**	**Law-enforcement officers**
Restaurant owners	City councilmen	Chief of police
Cardroom owners	Mayors	Assistant chief of police
Pinball machine licence holders	Governors	Sheriff
Bingo parlour owners	State legislators	Under-sheriff
Cabaret and hotel owners	Board of supervisors members	County prosecutor
Club owners	Licensing bureau chief	Assistant prosecutor
Receivers of stolen property		Vice squad commanders
Pawnshop owners		Narcotics officers
		Patrolmen
		Police lieutenants, captains and sergeants

Racketeers

Gamblers	Pimps	Prostitutes	Drug distributors	Usurers	Bookmakers

Source: Chambliss (1978).

As will be obvious, Chambliss was painting a very different picture of organised crime from the *Cosa Nostra* model. By contrast to the picture that emerges from Valachi's and Cressey's accounts, Chambliss says that he:

> ... believed that organised crime nationally and internationally consisted of hundreds or perhaps even thousands of networks that sometimes co-operated and sometimes competed with one another. I also suspected that these networks were coordinated and managed by legitimate business people, law enforcement agencies, and politicians. At the very least, I was convinced from my Seattle research that a symbiotic relationship between politics, law enforcement, legitimate business, and organized crime was absolutely necessary for organized crime to survive and flourish as it does in America. (1978: 154)

As a result of criticism from Chambliss, Block and others, Cressey's model of American organised crime is now generally regarded by criminologists

as overblown and somewhat naïve. There have been perhaps three main lines of criticism:

- To the extent that there were identifiable families or syndicates involved in organised illegal activity they were significantly less bureaucratically organised (Albini, 1971):
  - Internally – the structure was less predictably organised than Valachi's description.
  - Generally – there was at least as much competition between families/groups as there was co-operation.

- There has never been an ethnically-based monopoly in any of the main areas of organised criminal activity – prostitution, drugs, gambling, and so on.

- The idea of organised crime posing a threat to the 'non-criminal' world ignores the often-close relationships that exist between the so-called 'underworld' and apparently legitimate worlds of politics and finance.

Despite the fact that the bulk of research that has been conducted in the last 40 years tends to support such lines of criticism, the message of such work 'has sadly been buried by the endless repetition of Mafia myths or updated variations' (Woodiwiss, 2005: 77).

Organised crime in Britain

The alien conspiracy theory and the notion of highly organised Mafia-style gangs have never gained much purchase in Britain. That said, many of the major players in Britain's gangland activities in the 1940s–1960s were held to be of Italian, Jewish or Maltese origin and, more recently, the threat of 'Russian Mafias', Turkish gangs and of 'Yardies' with their origins in the Caribbean have been used as one of the justifications for establishing new policing bodies whose focus is serious and organised crime. Levi (1998: 338) suggests that organised crime groups have not developed in the same way in Britain as they did, say, in America, partly because of a more conservative social and political system (see also Hobbs, 1995), but principally because the supply and consumption of alcohol, the opiates, gambling and prostitution remain legal, but partly regulated. This reduces the profitability of supplying them criminally.

For much of the twentieth century much organised crime in Britain appeared highly local in character. In the 1960s two of the most famous 'gangs' – the Krays and the Richardsons – both operated almost entirely in London, but one north and one south of the Thames (though the Richardsons did spread their activities later in their 'career'). In practice, it is only relatively recently that 'organised crime' has been much talked about in Britain – it certainly was not a term applied to the Krays at the time they were operating.

The twentieth century has numerous examples of what might be thought of as organised or syndicated crime involving groups of people. In the 1920s and 1930s a number of local gangs fought over various criminal spoils, notably the money made from gambling at racecourses. Racecourse gangs were a source of considerable speculation and consternation, and one account of their activities in Sheffield notes that the area became known as 'Little Chicago' because of the nature and scale of the violence. According to Bean (1981: 133) 'gang warfare in Sheffield began as a result of violent competition for the exclusive and lucrative rights to the Sky Edge tossing ring'. This was the best-known place in Sheffield where one of the simplest forms of gambling – pitch and toss – took place. Bean (1981: 7–8) describes pitch and toss as follows:

> Three coins are placed on the ends of the first two fingers and tossed spinning, into the air. Bets are made on the proportion of heads to tails – or vice versa – as they fall to the ground.

> … The boss was known as the 'towler' or 'toller', as he collected a toll on bets made … Round the toller hung a number of satellites, chief of whom were known as the 'ponter' and 'pilners', or scouts. The latter were also known as 'pikers' or 'crows' because, like the sentinel crows on a rookery, they were constantly on the lookout for the approach of danger. The business was known as a 'joint' and the ring itself a 'pitch'. Out of the tolls the toller paid his henchmen and virtually guaranteed the ring against police raids …

> The action commenced with the toller shouting 'Heads a pound', or whatever the amount might be, and someone coming with an equivalent sum to 'Tail' it. The stake money was placed in the centre of the ring and the toll – paid only by the person initiating the bet – in the toller's pocket … Picking up the coins after they had fallen, the ponter officially announced the result, head or tails; winnings were paid out by the toller and re-betting began …

> Generally, the organised tossing rings were run on sound sporting lines – the gambler being expected to take his fate, whatever it may be … However, when quarrels did erupt they were by no means gentle affairs. Out of one … sprang a bitter feud that was to result in one man being killed, two hanged for murder, and many law-abiding citizens reduced to a state of terror.

If the years after the First World War were dominated by gangs competing for control of lucrative gambling operations, the privations of the Second World War opened up a whole new set of opportunities. The shortages of the wartime economy meant boom time for organised crime. A substantial 'black market' in food, clothes, coupons, alcohol, petrol and anything that was in limited supply soon emerged and a number of gangs emerged at this time and continued their illegal operations well after the war had ended. During the war, much of the contraband came from the

The Kray twins

The Kray twins in 1966, relaxing over tea after spending 36 hours 'helping the police with their enquiries' into the murder of George Cornell.

Although there was an older brother, Charlie, it was the twins, Ronnie and Reggie who came to dominate organised crime in the East End of London in the 1960s. Born in 1933 in Hoxton, both became schoolboy boxing champions as teenagers. They were also heavily involved with local gangs and were arrested on numerous occasions, serving their first prison sentence for assaulting a police officer whilst on the run from the army (having been called up for national service).

After leaving the army they took control of a snooker club in Bethnal Green. From this point their empire expanded, taking in a variety of clubs in the East End and in Central London. For quite some time the Krays were not a particular focus of police attention. It was only when the violence became impossible to ignore that major police operations were launched.

By the mid-1960s there were considerable tensions between the Krays and the South London Richardson gang. On one occasion an associate of the Richardsons, George Cornell, insulted Ronnie and later one of the Kray gang was shot in a club in South London. In March 1966 Ronnie Kray, on hearing that Cornell was drinking in an East End pub, *The Blind Beggar,* walked in and shot and killed Cornell. Although the identity of the killer was hardly a secret, no-one was prepared to give evidence, further strengthening the twins' feeling that they were untouchable. Their activities continued and the violence escalated.

In 1966, the Krays were involved in the escape of 'Mad Axeman' Frank Mitchell from Dartmoor prison. After his escape he was kept in a flat in East London whilst the gang campaigned for his release. They were unsuccessful and were left with an escaped convict on their hands. It was later alleged that Mitchell was killed by the Krays, though his body was never found. In 1968 Jack 'the hat' McVitie was murdered by Reggie Kray after he had claimed to have cheated the brothers out of money they had paid him to kill a former financial adviser.

In the end it seems it was Ronnie Kray's deteriorating mental state that led to their downfall. The twins were arrested in May 1968 after a lengthy police operation and by the time they came to trial seven months later their whole empire had collapsed. No longer in a position to intimidate witnesses, many came forward to testify or turned Queen's evidence. Both Krays were sentenced to life imprisonment with a recommendation that they serve at least 30 years. Ronnie Kray died in 1995, Reggie Kray in 2000.

armed forces, and highly organised systems for theft from army stores and similar locations have been documented (Thomas, 2003).

From the 1920s to the 1940s one of the most powerful groupings had been run by the Sabini family. However, they were interned during the war leaving a space for new gangs to emerge. Two of the criminals that emerged in the post-war period were Jack 'Spot' Comer and Billy Hill: 'both made their names as neighbourhood men of violence in the 1930s, made their money in the 1940s, and made the Kray twins in the 1950s' (Hobbs 1994: 451). Involved in gambling, prostitution and protection, both employed Ronnie and Reggie Kray at various points, before eventually being succeeded by the twins. The Kray twins are undoubtedly the best-known faces in post-war British organised crime. Immortalised in film and numerous books, and a source of constant interest in the tabloid press until their deaths, the Krays combined a range of licit and illicit activities, always accompanied by the threat of, or use of, violence.

The demise of the Krays and the Richardsons in the late 1960s was accompanied by concerted police efforts to attempt to ensure that similar enterprises didn't quickly replace them. According to Hobbs (1994: 453), at this time 'British organised criminals used traditional neighbourhood bases to exploit a multitude of market opportunities. There was no unifying structure and no unifying market.' A range of new or expanding markets – in pornography, video piracy, counterfeiting, VAT fraud and, of course, drugs – provided opportunities for the entrepreneurially-minded. Although the trafficking of drugs in particular, together with various forms of computer-based fraud, have affected the nature of criminal enterprise, it remains the case, according to Hobbs (1994: 455), that the 'outstanding feature of British organised crime is its conservatism and consistency with the past.' Much such activity remains locally-rooted, even if it may now exploit the opportunities raised by the growing international trade in various forms of criminality. In Hobbs's (1995: 115) view, professional crime 'has moved from an occupational foundation of neighbourhood-oriented extortion and individualistic craft-based larcenies towards an entrepreneurial trading culture driven by highly localized interpretations of global markets.' The recent case of the Adams family (see box) is undoubtedly an illustration of this.

End of the road for the other A Team

By Chris Summers, the Old Bailey
BBC News, 9 March 2007

One of Britain's most powerful criminals has been jailed for seven years for money laundering. Terry Adams was the leader of a gang known as the A Team, which for years operated a hegemony over London's underworld ... The Adams Family, or the A Team as it was often known, was feared and respected by many in London's underworld throughout the 1980s and 90s. The gang is suspected of involvement in a number of murders, but so far this remains only speculation ...

To bring him down the police combined forces with MI5 ... Like many London gangsters they started off in petty crime and graduated to armed robbery before diversifying into a more lucrative and less risky trade – drug trafficking.

[The prosecution] said Terry Adams had made so much money from crime he was able to retire at the age of 35. From then on the former meat porter sat back and set about laundering his ill-gotten gains, estimated at up to £11m. The scheme involved inventing sham companies and claiming to work for them as a business consultant.

But things began to go wrong for Terry Adams in the late 1990s after a series of setbacks. One of the A Team's 'enforcers' was Gilbert Wynter, who had been acquitted in 1994 of murdering former British high-jump champion Claude Moseley, after a key witness refused to give evidence. Wynter disappeared in March 1998, and underworld sources suggest he may have been killed after 'double-crossing' the family. In September of that year Tommy Adams, who had previously been acquitted of handling the proceeds of the 1983 Brinks Mat robbery, was jailed for seven-and-a-half years for smuggling cannabis worth £2m. He was also fined £1m.

Last month Terry Adams pleaded guilty on the eve of his trial to one sample charge of money laundering. Police had been planning special measures to protect jurors in the case ... Judge Pontius made a £750,000 confiscation order against him and ordered him to contribute a further £50,000 towards the costs of the £1.7m prosecution.

Source: http://news.bbc.co.uk/1/hi/uk/6342521.stm

The Adams family were alleged to have made much of their money through drug and gun-running from Eastern Europe to Britain and Ireland. Like another well-known figure, Curtis Warren, they were apparently involved in a complex, international trade network with very different forms of organisation from their 1960s 'underworld' predecessors. The marketplace has changed and with it has come a new form of entrepreneurialism in organised crime, the emergence of new international networks (Ruggiero, 1996) in which those involved can be viewed as 'fluid sets of mobile marauders in the urban landscape alert to institutional weakness in both legitimate and illegitimate spheres' (Block, 1983: 245). For many commentators, it is precisely the growth of international networks and the emergence of 'transnational organised crime' which represents the greatest change in this field in recent times.

> **Review questions**
>
> 1 In relation to organised crime what is meant by an 'alien conspiracy theory'?
>
> 2 What is meant by 'ethnic succession' in relation to organised crime?
>
> 3 What have been the main criticisms of the Mafia-conspiracy thesis?
>
> 4 In what ways were the conditions in which organised crime took place different in America and Britain in the mid-twentieth century?

Transnational organised crime

As with so many subjects discussed under the heading of globalisation (see Chapter 34), it is the end of the Cold War that is often seen as marking an important point in at least the recent history of Transnational Organised Crime (TOC). Although the term itself can be found in use from the mid-1970s, it is the fall of communism which resulted in a degree of instability in Eastern Europe and also opened up borders that had previously been particularly hard to cross. At the very least, these changes have heightened concern about criminal activity that crosses national borders. Central to increased governmental concern has been the trafficking of drugs, in particular stimulated by America's 'war on drugs'.

A word of caution before we move on. The great danger in this field is to be seduced into thinking

that all this is somehow new. As Woodiwiss (2003: 13) observes, 'Piracy, cross-border brigandage, smuggling, fraud and trading in stolen or forbidden goods and services are ancient occupations that increased in significance as nation states were taking shape.' Moreover, the influences on criminal justice have never been solely from *within* particular nation states. Britain borrowed the idea of the penitentiary from the United States. It also exported its policing models – Peel's Royal Irish Constabulary as well as his Metropolitan Police – around the Empire. The great prison reformer, John Howard, spent much of the latter half of his life visiting prisons around Europe and beyond and, indeed, eventually died during such a trip to Russia.

However, it would be equally absurd to deny that there isn't much that has also changed in the international arena. In particular, recent decades have seen the emergence of a number of important international organisations that have some responsibility for responding to crime and other security matters that transcend particular national boundaries. Such concerns were formally acknowledged by the passage of a number on international agreements, crucially the United Nations Convention Against Transnational Organised Crime. We look at some of the main organisations involved in transnational crime control in greater detail in the next section.

What then do we know about transnational crime? It has been argued to consist of three main sets of activities (Reuter and Petrie, 1999: 11–12):

- Smuggling
  - Commodities
  - Drugs
  - Protected species.
- Contraband (goods subject to tariffs or quotas)
  - Stolen cars
  - Tobacco products
  - Alcohol.
- Services
  - Immigrants
  - Prostitution
  - Indentured servitude
  - Money laundering
  - Fraud.

In what follows we look briefly at two examples of TOC: human trafficking and drugs trafficking.

Human trafficking and migrant smuggling

The trafficking of people – with or without their consent – appears to be a growing trade. In particular, the rise of conflicts around the world, together with the relative ease of travel, has led to growing numbers of people fleeing war zones in search of safer havens. Freilich *et al.* (2002) point to six primary reasons for the increasing international flow of people:

1 Geographic differences in supply and demand for labour which encourage decisions to move and to make more money in the new 'host' country.

2 Benefits of additional markets and other benefits in the target country.

3 Demands by developed countries for cheap labour.

4 Feedback: perpetuation of migration by existing networks of immigrant families in the host countries and by organisations there which promote migration.

5 Environmental degradation, where the physical or agricultural environment in the home country no longer proves acceptable.

6 Involuntary migration caused by civil war or oppression.

Earlier in the chapter we briefly mentioned the slave trade. Its existence reminds us that the trafficking of humans around the globe is far from a new phenomenon. Nevertheless, it is in the latter decades of the twentieth century that changing migration patterns and political circumstances combined to provide new opportunities for criminal exploitation. In this area there are two related sets of activities that can be identified – and, indeed, are formally distinguished by the United Nations in a protocol against trafficking which came into force in 2004:

● *Trafficking* – According to the UN, this is the 'recruitment, transportation, transfer, harbouring or receipt of persons, by means of threat or the use of force or other forms of coercion, of abduction, of fraud, of deception, of the abuse of power or of a position of vulnerability or of the giving or receiving of payments or benefits to achieve the consent of a person having control over another person, for the purpose of exploitation'. The exploitation involved covers such activities as prostitution or other sexual exploitation, forced labour or services, slavery, and the removal of organs.

● *Smuggling* – The 'procurement, in order to obtain, directly or indirectly, a financial or other material benefit, of the illegal entry of a person into a state party of which the person is not a national or a permanent resident'. (see also Arlacchi, 2002)

A family of would-be illegal immigrants aboard a truck bound for Dover in December 2000 – discovered by Calais ferry terminal security agents before leaving France.

In short, then, migrant smuggling consists of aiding the illegal movement of people between countries, whereas human trafficking involves the forced movement of people in order that they can be exploited sexually, for their labour, or in some other way. People being smuggled have generally consented to the activity, whereas those being trafficked have not, or have not in any meaningful way. Smuggling is always transnational but, whereas this is also largely true of trafficking, it need not be. Some trafficking occurs within a single country.

What are the factors that help account for these activities in the modern world? Broadly, they can be divided into three:

1 *'Push' or 'supply' factors* – those factors which create a sizeable population of people looking to leave their own country and seek better circumstances elsewhere.

2 *'Pull' factors* – which make foreign destinations attractive to migrants.

3 *'Demand' factors* – which underpin illegal trades.

- *Supply*
  - The existence of large numbers of impoverished and vulnerable people.
  - Political instability and civil wars – the existence of weak states.
  - Religious and ethnic conflict – as extreme as genocide in some cases.
  - Natural disasters.
- *Pull* (for migrants)
  - Availability of relatively well-paid work.
  - Welfare systems.
  - Relative wealth and stable economies.
  - Political stability and security.
- *Demand*
  - Demand for cheap and vulnerable labour.
  - Demand for 'embodied' labour services (people of a particular age, ethnic origin, in relation to their suitability for domestic labour or, more usually, involvement in different aspects of the sex trade. (Anderson and O'Connell Davidson, 2004)

As suggested in relation to the supply factors outline above, the characteristics that tend to link the victims of such activity are poverty and vulnerability. It is those who are most desperate to leave their current living circumstances who are most at risk and most likely to be exploited.

The data used to produce Figure 19.2 below rely upon reports collected by the UN on human trafficking. The totals are somewhat hard to interpret as the percentages don't add up to 100 – and the categories used overlap quite considerably. Nevertheless, what the figure does make clear is that women and girls are overwhelmingly the focus of human trafficking, and that it is sexual exploitation, rather than forced labour, that is the most common aim of such activity.

The business of moving migrants illegally is generally understood as being divided into three stages: *recruitment, transfer* and *entrance*. Recruitment usually takes place in the country of origin and clearly involves different processes depending on whether the activity involves smuggling or trafficking. Smugglers may recruit via adverts or simply word of mouth, and then tend to require a fee – often very substantial – from the recruit. Traffickers will use similar methods in order to recruit, but generally work by offering employment in a destination country.

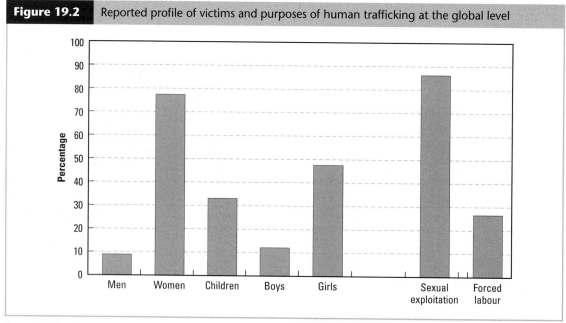

Figure 19.2   Reported profile of victims and purposes of human trafficking at the global level

Source: UNODC (2006).

Recruitment

UNODC research in Brazil shows the use of different recruitment methods for different types of victim:

> In the human trafficking cases involving the recruitment of several victims simultaneously (in general, these were women already working as sex professionals), there was usually no previous acquaintanceship between the victims and the accused traffickers. The majority of recruiters were male, and victims were often aware the offer of employment was in the sex industry. In human trafficking cases in which the victims were not previously prostitutes, previous acquaintanceship and even blood relations predominated. The job offers made to such victims tended to be false, and to not indicate the form of exploitation they would be subjected to.

Analysis of the cases investigated also showed the traffickers carefully chose their victims, who were mostly young women. Other criteria used by traffickers included physical characteristics, artistic talents, colour of the skin and a lack of inhibition. Many of the victims were unmarried and uneducated.

Source: UNODC (2006).

Transportation is discussed in greater detail below, but is often complex in terms of route and varies substantially in nature at its end point, depending on whether immigration is legal or illegal. Tourist and student visas may be used to enable legal entry; illegal entry may mean extraordinarily uncomfortable and dangerous journeys by road, sea and air, either crossing borders without anyone's knowledge or with the help of corrupt officials. Once the journey is completed, people who have been smuggled will generally be abandoned and left to look after themselves; those who are being trafficked will be taken to wherever they are to be put to work.

In terms of patterns and flows of this activity, North America, Western Europe, parts of the Middle East and Australia are the most common destinations for people being trafficked. Latin America, parts of West Africa and Eastern Europe are the most common sources of people being trafficked. In addition a number of countries in the Far East, including Thailand, China, and Cambodia, rate highly as countries of both origin and destination in human trafficking (see Figure 19.3). There are a number of well-established routes, including a *Baltic* route that starts in Asia, passes through Baltic states ending in Scandinavia, and an *East Mediterranean* route which runs from Turkey to Italy, sometimes stopping in Greece or Albania en route (Di Nicola, 2005).

| **Figure 19.3** | Reported human trafficking: main origin, transit and destination countries |

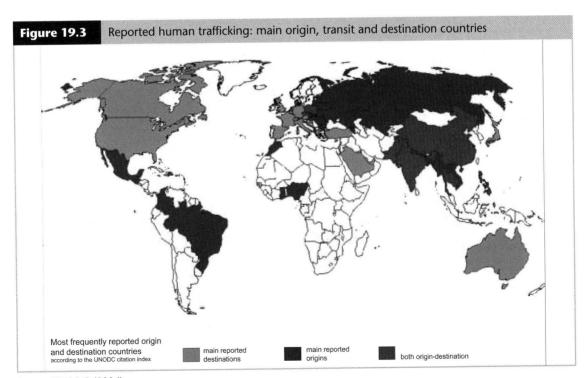

Source: UNODC (2006).

Table 19.1	Sending countries and trafficking routes to the UK	
Region of origin	**Sending countries**	**Routes**
South America	Brazil	via Lisbon
South-East Asia	Thailand, Philippines, Malaysia, Hong Kong, Singapore	Air direct into Heathrow or via mainland Europe, and rail via Eurostar
Central/Eastern Europe	Lithuania, Hungary, Ukraine, Belarus	Various trans-Europe routes by air, sea and rail, e.g. through Greece and Italy, then to the UK
East and West Africa	Nigeria, Ghana, Kenya, Uganda	Air direct or via mainland Europe

Source: Kelly and Regan (2000).

Graycar (2002) analyses the methods by which smuggling and trafficking are carried out. Again, as with other areas of organised criminal activity, there appears to be a range of approaches. He identifies:

- *Amateur traffickers* – who are those that specialise in occasional, sometimes one-off jobs in helping people cross borders and possibly find work.

- *Small groups of organised criminals* – who specialise in leading people from one country to another using recognised routes.

- *International trafficking networks* – who provide a broad range of services including fake documents, accommodation, employment, and so on.

A recent report by the United Nations Office on Drugs and Crime (2006) reported that two main types of group could be detected working in human trafficking. First, were what they called *hierarchical* groups, which were highly organised, had strong lines of control and discipline and tended to be involved in a broad range of other activities in addition to human trafficking, including the trafficking of drugs and other goods, smuggling and kidnapping. They tended to have a strong social or ethnic identity and used violence as a central tool. The others they called *core* groups. These tended to have a small, highly organised core surrounded by a loose network of associates. They rarely had a strong social or ethnic identity, tended to focus their activities on human trafficking and were extremely violent. At the more sophisticated end of the spectrum there may be a more- or less-highly developed division of labour, including:

- *Arrangers/investors* – who direct and finance operations.

- *Recruiters* – who arrange customers.

- *Transporters* – who assist the movement of immigrants at departure and destination.

- *Corrupt public officials* – including police/law enforcement officers who may obtain travel documents or overlook illegal transit.

- *Informers* – who provide information on border controls and other factors.

- *Guides/crew members* – who help move the migrants between specific points.

- *Supporting personnel and specialists* – who provide accommodation and other assistance.

- *Debt collectors* – who collect trafficking fees in the destination country.

- *Money movers* – who launder the proceeds of the transactions.

How sizeable is the problem? One of the few studies in the UK estimated that in 1998 a minimum of 71 women had been trafficked into the UK to work in prostitution and were known to the police, and that the minimum figure for the previous five years was 271. The authors recognised that this was almost certainly an underestimate and, using a variety of non-police data sources, estimated that the 'true' figure could be as high as 1,400 women a year (Kelly and Regan, 2000). The US State Department (2004) has estimated – and because of the nature of the phenomenon most such estimates are no better than educated guesses – that, worldwide, the number of people trafficked across national border is between 600,000 and 800,000 (of whom 70% are female and half are minors) and that there could be up to four times that number if people trafficked within national boundaries were included.

Drugs trafficking

There are a number of differing approaches to conceptualising drugs trafficking. Wright (2006) identifies three main approaches:

- The pyramidal model in which high-level dealers distribute goods downwards through 'middle markets' to lower level dealers and eventually to users (as outlined by the Broome Report on the drugs market – see Chapter 21).
- The supply- and value-chain model which is based on the assumption that drugs trafficking is organised along the lines of most commercial enterprises.
- A typology of traffickers that recognises greater diversity than this (see Dorn and South below).

Although the pyramidal model has influenced much government and criminal justice policy in this area, much of the research evidence points to a more complicated or varied structure. Dorn *et al.* (1992) identify a range of different types of trafficker, for example, in the British drugs market:

1 *Trading charities* – Enterprises involving an ideological commitment to drugs with profit as a secondary motive.

2 *Mutual societies* – Involve friendship networks of user dealers who support each other and sell or exchange drugs amongst themselves.

3 *Sideliners* – Licit business enterprises that begin to trade in drugs as a sideline.

4 *Criminal diversifiers* – Existing criminal enterprises that diversify into drugs.

5 *Opportunistic irregulars* – Those who get involved in activities in the irregular economy, including drugs.

6 *Retail specialists* – Enterprises with a manager who employs others to distribute drugs to users.

7 *State sponsored traders* – Enterprises that operate as informers and that continue to trade.

As we have noted throughout this chapter there is a tension in the organised crime literature between those who see such activities as being highly organised into hierarchically-based Mafiosi-style groupings and those who emphasise looser networks of co-operating entrepreneurs. According to Pearson (2007: 85) it is likely that the international trade in drugs trafficking resembles the latter rather than the former, although 'tightly organised clan and kinship-based networks with a global reach undoubtedly do exist'. The example he gives is what he refers to as the Turkish networks that currently control the supply of heroin into Europe. These have:

> ... separate sub-divisions or cells that deal with different aspects of the organisation such as the provision of finance, the purchasing of opium or morphine base from producers or middle men, the processing of heroin laboratories, arrangements for the purchase of precursor chemicals, transportation of heroin throughout Europe, warehousing of bulk shipments, trading to lower-level 'middle market' drug brokers, and the laundering of financial assets.

According to the United Nations Office on Drugs and Crime (UNODC) there are three major trafficking routes for opiates (heroin, morphine and opium). Although it is difficult to monitor such traffic, the UNODC uses information on drugs seizures as an indicator of the major sources and movements of drugs. The three primary routes it suggests are:

- From Afghanistan to neighbouring countries, the Middle East and Europe.
- From Myanmar/Lao PDR to neighbouring countries in South-East Asia (notably China) and to Oceania (mainly Australia).
- From Latin America (Mexico, Colombia and Peru) to North America (notably USA), (see Figure 19.4).

According to UNODC the bulk of heroin and other opiates in Western Europe are trafficked from Afghanistan to Turkey and then along various branches of what is called the Balkan route. In the main this has meant routes from Turkey via Bulgaria, Romania and Hungary to Slovakia, the Czech Republic, Germany and the Netherlands, or via Hungary and/or Slovakia to Austria and then to Germany and the Netherlands. However, such routes change rapidly in response to policing efforts.

Figure 19.4   Trafficking in heroin and morphine 2006 (countries reporting seizures of more than 10kg)

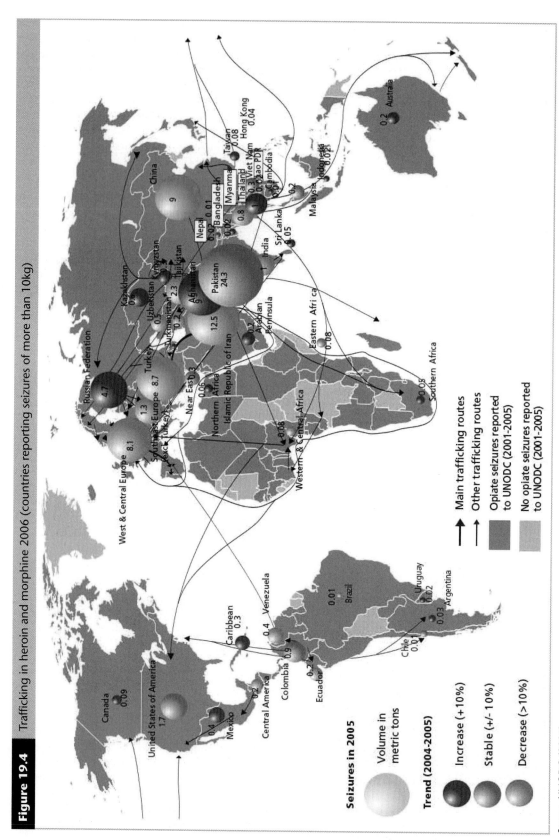

Source: UNODC (2006).

The bulk of the existing literature suggests that the nature, the trafficking routes and the forms of organisation of the international drugs trade varies and changes depending on the social and political circumstances in which it operates. However, a recent review identified three fairly consistent forms of organisation:

- *Insurgent groups* and/or *paramilitaries* in some source zones impose 'taxes' on producers/traffickers or involve themselves in trafficking directly, supporting their political and military activities out of the proceeds. These 'politico-military' traffickers are most commonly hierarchical in structure and may persist for decades. Current examples include the FARC in Colombia, regional commanders in Afghanistan and elements in ex-Yugoslavia, Spain and Northern Ireland. Whilst the headquarters and main operations of most such groups are usually outside the UK and other European Union countries, small and discreet European branch offices, cells or representatives exist.

- *Business criminals* are driven by financial considerations. Their aspirations are limited to their own quiet enjoyment of the proceeds of crime and they do not seek wider political change. The principals may continue in business for many years, drawing in other human and technical resources as required for particular jobs. They typically adopt the structure described here as 'core group'. Examples from the past include Cali traffickers and some in Medellín in Colombia. Today there are a multiplicity of loosely co-operating enterprises in South America, South East Asia and Europe, bringing drugs though transit zones, their principals being located in source zones, transit zones or the EU.

- *Adventurers* are involved in the trade in a variety of positions, working for self, working for others, drifting around seeking opportunities, generally on a relatively precarious basis. For them, a relatively high level of risk-taking is the norm, either because they experience little choice (due to debt and/or coercion), or because challenge and beating the authorities are as important to them as financial aims. The roles taken by these individuals may vary by the month. Examples include Afghan villagers trying their luck as traffickers, Latin American and Caribbean-based individuals, and migrant and other 'give it a try' traffickers in Spain, Italy, Germany, the Netherlands, the UK and elsewhere.

- Variants on the above types include alliances, mixed types, and one type 'nesting' within another in positions of domination or subordination.
(from: Dorn *et al.*, 2005: 35)

Contemporary international drugs trafficking cannot be understood without reference to the so-called 'war on drugs' fought by the United States since the 1960s. Since the time of the Presidency of Richard Nixon, domestic and foreign policy in the United States has been based on the assumption that a 'drug-free' society is imaginable. It was from such assumptions that terms like 'zero tolerance' were first popularised. Although initially the emphasis was on drugs control within national borders, it was soon expanded to include attempts to prevent drugs reaching American soil. Consequently, for the last 40 years the United States has attempted to impose its own view of drugs control on the rest of the world. As Nadelmann (1993: 470) put it:

> The modern era of international law enforcement is one in which U.S. criminal justice priorities and U.S. models of criminalization and criminal investigation have been exported abroad. Foreign governments have responded to U.S. pressures, inducements, and examples by enacting new criminal laws regarding drug trafficking, money

Heavily armed fighters from FARC (Revolutionary Armed Forces of Colombia), a guerilla movement which controls large areas of Colombia in South America – supported by the proceeds of large-scale drug cultivation and trafficking.

laundering, insider trading, and organised crime and by changing financial and corporate secrecy laws as well as their codes of criminal procedure to better accommodate U.S. requests for assistance. Foreign police have adopted U.S. investigative techniques, and foreign courts and legislatures have followed up with the requisite legal authorizations. And foreign governments have devoted substantial police and even military resources to curtailing illicit drug production and trafficking ... By and large, the United States has provided the models, and other governments have done the accommodating.

An armed police officer keeping guard as officials eradicate poppy fields near Kandahar in Afghanistan – source of most of the world's heroin.

Huge efforts, and even larger sums of money, have been spent attempting either to prevent the production of various crops – the production of opium and cocaine in particular – or in attempting to intervene in the movement of goods around the globe. It is far from clear that any of these efforts has had any lasting impact on the international trade in illicit drugs. What is important here for our purposes is the role that the US has played in the establishment and promotion of a particular view of organised crime. In particular, the end of the 'cold war' provided the opportunity for the rise of a new global threat and, until the emergence of the new international terrorist threat, organised crime served to fill the gap.

According to Woodiwiss (2005), an American-reporter with close links to the CIA promoted the view that the world's heroin trade was controlled by the Mafia in co-operation with various terrorist groups and with the support of Colombian drug 'cartels'. Though such arguments were dismissed by many experts, they chimed with the views of the American intelligence community and have subsequently been echoed by many influential politicians and policy-makers. Woodiwiss (2005: 156) quotes the Secretary-General of the United Nations, Boutros Boutros-Ghali, as saying in 1994:

> Organised crime has ... become a world phenomenon. In Europe, in Asia, in Africa and in America, the forces of darkness are at work and no society is spared ... it scoffs at frontiers and becomes a universal force. Traditional crime organisations have, in a very short time, succeeded in adapting to the new international context to become veritable crime multinationals.

Such views, as Woodiwiss and others argue, deflect attention from the corrupting influence of global neo-liberal capitalism. In their view the drugs war/drugs prohibition approach has had no success in reducing demand and only limited and very temporary successes in affecting supply. For such critics the international war against drugs has achieved precisely the opposite of its stated aims. For those living in poverty, the drugs trade has become increasingly attractive. According to the campaigning organisation *Drug Police Alliance,* drug trafficking across the world exists as a $400 billion trade – drug traffickers earn gross profit margins of 300% (www.drugpolicy.org). Peter Andreas summarised this element of the problem in testimony to the US House of Representatives Subcommittee on Crime in 1996:

> The unleashing of market forces has unintentionally encouraged and facilitated not only legal economic activity, but illegal economic activity as well. Part of the problem is that legal and illegal markets are increasingly intertwined ... The logic of liberal economic theory, after all, is for the State to conform to the dictates of the market. Although illegal, the drug economy should be seen as part of this process. Neoclassical economics suggests that countries should specialize in exports in which they enjoy a comparative advantage. For some countries this has meant their market niche in exporting illegal drugs. (quoted in Sheptycki, 2000: 212)

Transnational crime control

Predictably, the growing visibility of various forms of transnational criminal activity has been paralleled by a set of changes in the organisational response to crime. Crime that crosses national boundaries poses particular problems for domestic law (fraudsters operating in the Caribbean, in West Africa or simply in other parts of Europe cannot easily be prosecuted under English criminal law) and domestic law enforcement (how it is possible to track the activities of global traffickers whose activities may cross several continents?). Consequently, groups of nations develop treaties for extradition and, beyond that, begin to co-operate in the sharing of information and intelligence and, eventually, the prospect of the establishment of bodies that are international in scope and draw their legitimacy from somewhere other than individual nation states becomes something akin to a reality. It is these bodies that are truly *trans*national.

A series of international conventions has been established in recent years in the field of organised crime. The United Nations established a Commission for Crime Prevention and Criminal Justice in the early 1990s and subsequently held a ministerial conference in Naples at which Boutros-Ghali made the speech quoted earlier. Out of this emerged a Global Action Plan and in 2000 a UN Convention against Transnational Organised Crime which sought to harmonise legal systems and set standards for domestic laws in tackling organised crime. A year later the EC launched the European Forum on Organised Crime Prevention and the G8 has also produced a whole series of recommendations on organised crime. The last decade or more has seen a lot of activity in this area, most notably in relation to policing, and in the following section we look at the development of transnational policing bodies.

Transnational policing

Transnational policing structures have a history that dates back to the latter half of the nineteenth century. However, the first permanent international agency – the International Criminal Police Commission (ICPC) – was established in the wake of the First World War. It was later to become known as the International Criminal Police Organization (ICPO) – or more popularly, Interpol. Interpol was never intended as an operational police force, but was designed to act as a clearing-house for information and intelligence between participating police forces and as a network forum for senior officers or a 'policeman's club' (Anderson, 1989).

Over the years, membership has expanded markedly, and technological developments have aided its growth. In February 1987 a computerised Criminal Information System replaced the previous manual system and an Electronic Archive System was introduced in 1990. More recently Interpol further rationalised its organisational structure with the creation of a separate European Unit. At the 54th General Assembly in 1985, Interpol's involvement in anti-terrorist activity was established with the creation of a specialised group within the then Police Division to 'co-ordinate and enhance co-operation in combating international terrorism'. It was not, however, until 1987 that the group became operational.

A number of problems have been identified with Interpol. First, there have been persistent doubts about the security of Interpol's communications network (House of Commons, 1990). Second, the ineffectiveness or inadequacy of Interpol's structures for tackling terrorism in the 1970s in part prompted European states to make other arrangements, notably the establishment of the Trevi Group and the European Police Working Group. Despite improvements in organisational structure Walker (2003) maintains that Interpol remains the 'paradigm case of an *inter*national police organisation' that remains largely parasitic on national police forces.

The Schengen Convention has been described by Hebenton and Thomas (1995) as the 'most complete model ... of international police co-operation within Europe' (59–60). Its origins lie in the Schengen Agreement 1985. Five EC member states (France, Germany, Belgium, the Netherlands and Luxembourg) originally signed up to the agreement. An Implementation Agreement enabled the signing of the Convention in 1990 and over the following two years Spain, Portugal, Italy and Greece also signed up. Schengen now covers all EU-member states with the exception of Britain and Ireland (Maas, 2005). The Schengen arrangements were eventually incorporated by the Amsterdam Treaty into the new Area of Freedom Security and Justice. To a large extent, Schengen has been overshadowed by developments that resulted in the establishment of the EU's own policing body, Europol.

Europol

The platform for the launch of Europol was the Trevi group, formed in 1976. Originally established as a European intergovernmental forum to tackle terrorism, its remit was eventually expanded 'to look ... at the mechanics of police co-operation in the European Community across the whole range of crime, the use of liaison officers and the creation of a common information system' (Hebenton and Thomas, 1995: 71). By the early 1990s the Trevi group was already far advanced in the development of a rapid and protected communications system for collecting and disseminating information on terrorism and other forms of cross-border criminality. At the European Council meeting in Luxembourg in 1991, the Group presented plans for a common information system that was able to compensate for the erosion of borders and with the capacity to tackle international organised crime (Hebenton and Thomas, 1995), and in a meeting later that year the European Police Office – or Europol as it is more commonly known – was created.

Europol started limited operations in early 1994, specifically in relation to drugs (with the creation of the Europol Drugs Unit in 1993), though it didn't become fully operational until 1999. Its mandate was extended in 1998 to include counter-terrorism (Rauchs and Koenig, 2001). Europol supports member states by:

- Facilitating the exchange of information, in accordance with national law, between Europol Liaison Officers (ELOs). ELOs are seconded to Europol by the member states as representatives of their own national law enforcement agencies.

- Providing operational analysis in support of member states' operations.

- Generating strategic reports (e.g. threat assessments) and crime analysis on the basis of information and intelligence supplied by member states, generated by Europol or gathered from other sources.

- Providing expertise and technical support for investigations and operations carried out within the EU, under the supervision and legal responsibility of the member states concerned.

Europol's mandate has been extended since 9/11 to allow it to investigate murder, kidnapping, hostage-taking, racism, corruption, unlawful drug trafficking, people smuggling and motor vehicle crime, amongst other offences (Lavranos, 2003).

The European Union has also significantly enhanced the level of its co-operation with the United States in the sharing of information and intelligence. This has occurred primarily through Europol, but also through the establishment of Eurojust – the EU inter-governmental institution responsible for judicial co-operation around crime.

Dubois (2002: 328) quotes the European Council of 21 September 2001 as agreeing that 'The member states will share with Europol, systematically and without delay, all useful data regarding terrorism'. Moreover, criminal investigations involving two or more member nations have been facilitated since June 2002 by an EU Council decision to enable the creation of 'joint investigation teams' comprising terrorist experts, members of Europol and Eurojust and, potentially at least, US officials also. Despite such developments we are, arguably, still some way short of seeing the introduction of something akin to a European FBI (Lavranos, 2003). However, this appears to be the direction in which European transnational policing is heading. The twin threats of international terrorism and organised crime would appear to be the primary driving force.

The perceived threat of organised crime is also being felt at an organisational level in domestic policing. In 2005 the Serious and Organised Crime Agency (SOCA) was established, bringing together previously-existing bodies like the National Crime Squad and the National Criminal Intelligence Service, together with staff from HM Revenue and Customs and the UK Immigration Service. Officially launched in early 2006, SOCA initially comprised 4,500 staff. The official description is that the agency will be 'intelligence-led, and have as its core objective the reduction of harm caused to the UK by organised crime' (NCIS, 2005). SOCA has a number of other important characteristics that set it apart from the main constabularies in the UK. Although its first director general was drawn from the police service, its first chair, Sir Stephen Lander, was previously the Head of MI5, indicating the emergence of a hybrid agency working as a policing body, but specialising in covert and intelligence-gathering activity. SOCA will have officers permanently stationed abroad working with and within intelligence agencies in other jurisdictions and, similarly, will house investigators from other agencies within the UK. It represents a substantial departure in domestic policing arrangements.

Understanding organised crime

There are at least four areas of debate and dispute that we can identify that run through the preceding discussion of organised crime, its history and development. First, it is and remains an area that is highly problematic to define and delimit. Any discussion of organised crime will almost certainly impinge upon and, most likely, have to take into account, matters such as corporate deviance, crime sponsored by states (sometimes referred to as 'state corporate crimes'), and a range of other harms. Organised crime links with criminological discussions of drugs and alcohol, of sex crimes, violent crime and corruption. Drawing some boundary between those things we might label organised crime and other criminal activities is not straightforward. Indeed, there are those who doubt the usefulness of the term entirely arguing, for example, that 'we need to be clearer about which segments of the criminal market we are referring to before we can be sure we are discussing the same thing when we use the term "organised crime". In fact, it might be better not to rely on the term or alternatively to rely on the fact that it does not have a stable meaning' (Levi, 2007: 799).

Bearing this in mind, we can move to the second problem which concerns the nature of 'organisation' in organised crime. As we have seen, popular conceptions of organised crime are deeply affected by the 'Mafia conspiracy theory' and its variants. This model views organised crime as being under the control of a number of highly structured, identifiable groups, often rooted in transplanted versions of traditional forms of racketeering such as the Sicilian Mafia, Japanese Yakuza and so on. There are a number of problems with this thesis. Even for the particular period it was designed to explain – Prohibition and post-Prohibition era America – the evidence suggests that it is a poor fit. In reality it appears organised crime groups were much more fragmented than this model proposed. Moreover, they were often involved in considerable, and violent competition rather than co-operation. Crucially, such groups are better viewed as *participating* in criminal markets rather than *controlling* them. Finally, as critics such as Block and Chambliss (1981) pointed out, the traditional Mafia conspiracy model presented such activities as if they were almost entirely cut off from the respectable worlds

of politics and finance. In practice, as Chambliss's (1988) study of Seattle sought to demonstrate, these worlds were much more closely intertwined with so-called organised crime.

Third, as we have seen, the dominant discourse in relation to organised crime now makes the word 'transnational' ubiquitous in debates in this area. It is undoubtedly the case that there now exist a large number of complex, international networks created in order to facilitate criminal activity across jurisdictions. Again, however, one needs to be slightly careful with this idea. In part, this is because talk of TOC can easily become a modern variant of the traditional alien conspiracy theory. It is not the nature of domestic institutions, politics or people that is at fault, but outsiders who seek to exploit or subvert our social order. It is also the case that globalisation or transnationalisation theses tend to ignore, or at least underplay, the role of the nation state. In doing so, once again the risk is that organised crime will be presented and understood as being entirely separate from respectable institutions. In this connection, Chambliss (1988: 182–83) observed:

> In Seattle it was not obvious how the various rackets ranked in order of importance. Drugs, gambling, fraud, and stolen property were as intertwined as straw in a bale of hay. When I began investigating national and international crime networks, however, it became clear almost immediately that smuggling narcotics and military weapons was head and shoulders above other forms of organized criminality in importance … On the national and international level … the smuggling of arms and drugs is the foundation on which rests a mammoth enterprise which amounts to hundreds of billions of dollars annually. It is an enterprise which not only affects millions of lives directly, it affects international relations, governments and war.

The other difficulty with all this talk of TOC is that it ignores or underplays the other side of the globalisation coin: localisation. Thus, as Hobbs (1998: 405) argues, empirical research indicates 'that ever-mutating interlocking networks of *locally-based* serious criminality typify the current situation' (emphasis added). In making this observation, Hobbs is not in anyway seeking to deny the existence or importance of transnational criminal networks, merely to point out that much of what occurs still needs to be understood within its local, and locally-changing context. This is both a socio-logical point (that is, it should affect how we seek to analyse and understand things), and also a prac-tical point. That is to say, it is a corrective against any easy acceptance of any single model of crime control in response to the perceived threat of organised crime. This leads us to the final point.

The growth of transnational law-enforcement bodies is generally presented as a response to the growing threat of TOC. This is the 'master narra-tive' in this field (Andreas and Nadelmann, 2006). However, as Andreas and Nadelmann (2006: 7) go on to suggest, this explanation is 'at best incom-plete and at worst misleading'. Just as the traditional American Mafia conspiracy thesis can be argued to have been used as a means of creating and justifying a particular law enforcement response to organised crime from the 1930s onward so, similarly, a particular picture of mod-ern, transnational threats can be viewed in a similar way. As Nadelmann (1993), for example, argues, the 'war on drugs' rhetoric has been used not only as a justification for the creation of new organisations but also, as some critics would sug-gest, as a means of promulgating a particularly American model of international policing:

> The modern era of international law enforce-ment is one in which U.S. criminal justice priorities and U.S. models of criminalization and criminal investigation have been exported abroad. Foreign governments have responded to U.S. pressures, inducements, and examples by enacting new criminal laws regarding drug traf-ficking, money laundering, insider trading, and organized crime and by changing financial and corporate secrecy laws as well as their codes of criminal procedure to better accommodate U.S. requests for assistance. Foreign police have adopted U.S. investigative techniques, and for-eign courts and legislatures have followed up with the requisite legal authorizations. And for-eign governments have devoted substantial police and even military resources to curtailing illicit drug production and trafficking ... By and large, the United States has provided the mod-els, and other governments have done the accommodating. (1993: 469–70)

In understanding the growth and spread of the new transnational law enforcement bodies, Andreas and Nadelmann (2006) suggest that there are a number of other factors that we need to take into account beyond the question of the threats posed by organised crime. First, is the issue of *crim-inalisation*. A wide range of once legal cross-border activities have progressively been made illegal. This process of criminalisation means that the 'policing face of the state is becoming more and more prominently displayed, with its gaze increasingly extending beyond national borders' (2006: 225). The second is the growing fusion between criminal justice and security concerns, a process that has gathered pace since 9/11 as a variety of public pol-icy issues have increasingly been defined as 'security concerns'. As a consequence of these and other developments, they argue, 'state capacities to detect, deter, and detain transnational law evaders have, if anything, grown substantially... Moreover, one should not lose sight of the fact that it is the very existence of state controls that makes it necessary for smugglers and other criminalized transnational actors to try to devise such creative and elaborate means to evade and circumvent them' (2006: 246). As other chapters in this book have illustrated, as criminologists we should view with scepticism all claims that the state is uniquely threatened by some particular or new crime problem, not least because such claims usually form the justification for the creation for extend-ing the reach of law enforcement and other criminal justice agencies. (Transnational) organised crime is no exception.

Review questions

1 What is the main difference between human *smuggling* and *trafficking*?

2 What are the main ways of conceptualising drugs trafficking?

3 What have been the main lines of criticism of some of the work on transnational organised crime?

4 What is meant by the phrase *transnational policing*?

Questions for further discussion

1 How organised is organised crime?

2 In what ways is 'organised crime' different from other criminal activities?

3 Why does there appear to have been a growth in human trafficking in the last two decades?

4 Why has transnational policing expanded in recent decades?

5 What might be the negative consequences of the 'war on drugs'?

Further reading

Alan Wright (2006) *Organised Crime,* Cullompton: Willan, provides a good overview of the key debates and developments. An up-to-date review of organised crime literature, set in a broader context, can be found in: Levi, M. (2007) Organised crime and terrorism, in Maguire, M. *et al.* (eds) *The Oxford Handbook of Criminology,* Oxford: Oxford University Press. Finally, well worth a read is: Woodiwiss, M. (2005) *Gangster Capitalism,* London: Constable

In relation to organised crime in Britain, and in particular the changing nature of policing, there is no better place to start than Dick Hobbs (1989) *Doing the Business,* Oxford: Oxford University Press and John Pearson's (1973) *The Profession of Violence,* London: Panther

Peter Maas's (1969) *The Valachi Papers,* London: Panther and Donald Cressey's (1969) *Theft of the Nation,* New York: Harper and Row, provide the account of American organised crime that has since permeated popular culture through Mario Puzo's novels and a raft of Hollywood movies. By way of contrast, it is well worth reading Chambliss, W. (1978) *On The Take,* Indiana: Indiana University Press, and Albini, J. (1971) *The American Mafia,* New York: Appleton-Century-Crofts.

A very useful collection of essays can be found in: Edwards, A. and Gill, P. (eds) (2003) *Transnational Organised Crime,* London: Routledge

For my money the best books on policing and related developments in the global arena are:

Nadelmann, E. (1993) *Cops Across Borders*: *The internationalization of U.S. criminal law enforcement,* University Park, PA: Pennyslvania State University Press; and

Andreas, P. and Nadelmann, E. (2006) *Policing the Globe*: *Criminalization and crime control in international relations,* New York: Oxford University Press

Websites

There are numerous websites with all sorts of material on American and British organised crime. The vast majority are best approached with a healthy degree of scepticism. Thus, there is a wealth of information on www.thekrays.co.uk, for example, but much of it has the flavour of a fan club.

The UNODC has a lot of research information on both drugs trafficking and human trafficking: http://www.unodc.org/unodc/index.html

In relation to international drugs policy more generally there is much good material on the website of the Drugs Policy Alliance: www.drugpolicy.org

The Standing Group on Organised Crime is one of the European Consortium for Political Research standing groups and manages a useful website and blog: www.scog.blogspot.com/

For developments in Europe the *Statewatch* website is absolutely invaluable: http://www.statewatch.org/

Chapter outline

Understanding violent crime   436

Types of violent crime   438
  Homicide   438
    Trends in homicide   439
    Homicide offenders   439
    Victims of homicide   441
    Motive and relationship   442
    Use of weapons   442
    Homicide and social status   444
    Serial killers   444
  Robbery   446
    Armed robbery   446
    Street robbery   448
  Sexual offences   450
    Stalking   451
    Monitoring sex offenders   453
  Violent crime and weapons   454
  Trends in violent crime   456
    Contemporary trends   458

Property crime   458
  Trends in property crime   459

Burglary   460
  Trends in burglary   460
    Distraction burglary   462
  Burglars on burglary   462
  Crimes against retail and manufacturing premises   463
  Car crime   465
    Injuries and deaths on the road   465
    Measuring car crime   466
    Joyriding   467

Thinking about violent and volume crime   469

Questions for further discussion   469
Further reading   470
Websites   470

20

Violent and property crime

CHAPTER SUMMARY

Earlier in the book (Chapter 4) when we discussed the role of the media as one of our major sources of information about crime, we noted that one consistent misrepresentation is the exaggeration of the extent of violent crime. Given the propensity of drama to rely upon violent crime – and often very serious violent crime – as the basis for its representation of the world we live in, it is all the more important to think carefully about its nature and extent. There are many questions we need to ask including what is meant by the term 'violent crime', what is known about its extent and how this has changed over time.

In this chapter we consider:

- the meaning of violent crime;

- how much violent crime there appears to be;

- whether violent crime is rising or falling (and how we know);

- how the criminal justice system responds to violent crime;

- various forms of 'property crime', notably burglary and car crime, the latter of which constitutes a large proportion of overall crime, but is little studied by criminologists;

- why property crime is little studied;

- what is known about property offenders and about the impact of property-related crime.

Understanding violent crime

The way in which we understand violence is much influenced by culture and history. If you have read the chapter on punishment (Chapter 22) you will have come across a number of examples of the infliction of pain that would be considered pretty much unthinkable in our society these days. We live in times when debates about the notion of 'torture' are once again a major political issue. Centuries ago those techniques we now condemn as torture would have been used routinely against certain types of offenders. Standards change over time – and vary between cultures. Although we no longer use corporal or capital punishment in Britain, we did so until relatively recently and others continue to do so. In thinking about violence, therefore, we need to think carefully about the context in which it is used. The subject of the first two-thirds of this chapter – violent *crime* – alerts you to the fact that we are talking about the use of violence in circumstances in which it is considered illegal.

Let us begin, therefore, by asking what we mean by 'violent crime'. What does the term cover? It is, as Levi and Maguire (2002: 796) note, a 'slippery term' that covers a very wide range of activities, including:

- Terrorist attacks.

- Youth gangs fighting and intimidating each other.

- Single and small group fights, usually same-sex and between acquaintances or strangers from similar backgrounds, in and around pubs and clubs.

- Domestic violence (from homicide and rape to assaults involving minor physical injuries) against women in the home, most commonly by intimates.

- Street robberies in which items such as handbags, wallets or mobile phones are taken by threats or assault.

- Intimidation on the grounds of race or sex, both person-specific and general.

Though it may seem odd to ask what we mean by violent crime, it is particularly important when levels and trends in such crime are being considered. When using various data sources to think about violent crime, it becomes crucial to look at the definitions that are used in each particular case. By and large, violent crime can be divided into three main categories:

- Violence against the person.
- Sexual offences.
- Robbery.

Each of the three categories is captured in differing ways in recorded crime statistics and by the British Crime Survey (BCS), (see the box below).

Despite this variety of offences, 'violent crime' is often talked about as if it were a fairly homogenous *thing*. Although talking of trends in violent crime may reveal something important, it is just as likely that using the general category actually hides as much as it reveals. Before we move on to look at trends, therefore, let us look more closely at violent crime itself. How is it made up? What proportion of violent crimes involves the most serious forms of violence? Data from police recorded crime and from the BCS suggest that robbery accounts for something in the region of one-tenth of all violent offences. Homicide represents only one-tenth of one per cent of all recorded violent crime. In counts of violent crime, incidents that involve no injury at all make up almost one-quarter of all recorded crime and well over a third of BCS violence (see Figures 20.1 and 20.2).

It is worth noting that in the case of police recorded crime, one-quarter of cases involve no injury, and this is the case for 40% of BCS violent crime. Indeed, common assaults accounted for over three-fifths (61%) of BCS violent crime in 2003/04 and of this, 39% involved no injury and the other 22% involved minor injury. Arguably, this has added to public confusion about levels of violent crime. When headlines talk of 'violent crime' it is likely that the picture conjured up involves significant injury. As explained above, however, there are many offences that are defined as violent which involve the threat rather than the use of force. Where force is used, it may not result in injury, such as in threats during an armed robbery. None of this should necessarily be taken as arguing that such cases should not be treated as 'violent', merely that some clarity in reporting such statistics is undoubtedly required. A recent report on the

Violence against the person

Recorded crime includes a wide range of offences. The more serious offences include homicide, threat or conspiracy to murder, and serious wounding inflicted intentionally (i.e. Grievous Bodily Harm [GBH] with intent). The 'less serious wounding' category includes less serious injury (such as assault occasioning Actual Bodily Harm [ABH]) or GBH without intent. It also includes offences that are generally viewed less seriously by the courts, such as common assault, harassment and possession of weapons.

Common assault

Until 2002 assaults resulting in injury no more serious than grazes, scratches, abrasions, minor bruising, swellings, reddening of the skin, superficial cuts or black eyes were recorded as common assaults. Since 2002 the definition of common assault used for recorded crime statistics changed and now only includes assaults involving no injury. The BCS definition did not change in April 2002 and includes assaults involving at most minimal injury (broadly in line with the previous recorded crime definition).

Sexual offences

Recorded crime covers most unlawful sexual activity, including rape, buggery, indecent assault, incest, unlawful sexual intercourse with an under-age girl, and gross indecency with a child. It also includes kerb crawling and procuration (i.e. pimping), but excludes prostitution and indecent exposure. Not all offences included are violent, e.g. bigamy.

The number of sexual offences picked up by the BCS is too small to provide reliable estimates.

Robbery

Robbery is included as a violent crime, although the category can include a wide variety of different events including, in police recorded robbery offences: bank robbery, mobile phone robbery, street mugging and violence between schoolchildren over small amounts of money or property.

Recorded crime offences distinguish between robbery of personal property and business property. A robbery of business property is where goods stolen belong to a business or other corporate body (such as a bank or shop), regardless of the location of the robbery.

Robbery is an offence in which force or the threat of force is used either during or immediately prior to a theft or attempted theft. If there is no threat of force, an offence of theft from the person is recorded.

In the BCS, mugging is comprised of snatch theft (where there is no threat of force), robbery and attempted robbery.

Source: Dodd *et al.* (2004).

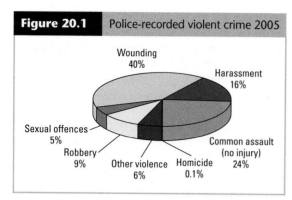

Source: Nicholas *et al.* (2005).

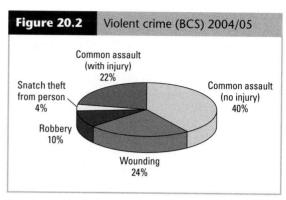

Source: Nicholas *et al.* (2005).

future of criminal statistics (Smith, 2007) recently recommended that a distinction be made between violent offences causing injury and violent offences where there was no injury – though as the example of the armed robbery makes clear, this distinction is by no means a clear guide to offence seriousness.

Types of violent crime

We have not the space to look at every type of violent crime in detail, so we will focus on three main types of offence: homicide; robbery; and sexual offences. We do not consider domestic violence in this chapter as we look at it in greater detail in Chapter 32.

Homicide

This is the most serious of forms of violence. It refers to the killing of another human being, whether that killing is lawful or unlawful. Using the term here is slightly misleading as *homicide* is not a specific category of crime in Britain. Within common law, the term homicide covers two crimes: *murder* and *manslaughter*. A range of other offences that come under the heading of homicide have been created by various Acts of Parliament. These include: *causing death by reckless driving* and *manslaughter on the grounds of diminished responsibility*. There is also the crime of *infanticide* – which applies when a woman causes the death of her own (biological) child (Brookman, 2005). It is intended that someone found guilty of such an offence should be dealt with as though guilty of voluntary manslaughter.

The crucial difference between murder and manslaughter concerns the degree of fault attached to the offence and the presence of any mitigating circumstances. The most often quoted definition of murder is that of Sir Edward Coke:

Murder is when a man of sound memory, and of the age of discretion, unlawfully killeth within any county of the realm any reasonable creature *in rerum natura* under the King's peace, with malice aforethought, either expressed by the party or implied by law, so as the party wounded, or hurt, etc. die of the wound or hurt, etc. within a year and a day after the same.

The 'year and a day' rule came into being because of difficulties associated with proving that a defendant's actions had led to the death of the victim where a considerable time had elapsed between the offence and the death. Advances in medicine eventually made this redundant and the law was amended in 1996 to remove the rule.

Manslaughter is divided into the two main categories of 'voluntary' or 'involuntary'. It is voluntary where the offender:

- Was provoked to kill (that is that there existed some sort of *provocation* such that a jury would be convinced that a reasonable person would have been unable to control themselves in similar circumstances).

- Was suffering an abnormality of the mind such that might plead 'diminished responsibility' (where the defendant's ability to exercise self-control is substantially affected by their mental condition).

- Killed in pursuance of a suicide pact (should they survive they are liable to be convicted of the manslaughter of the other person in the pact).

Involuntary manslaughter covers those cases where there is no malice aforethought or mitigating circumstances but the death was caused by recklessness, or was intentional but the offender lacked sufficient awareness of the consequences of his or her actions for it to be treated as murder.

In the US, homicide is usually broken down into four categories: murder, manslaughter, excusable homicide, and justifiable homicide. The differences, crudely, are that 'first degree' murder requires both *premeditation* (planning to kill) and *malice aforethought* (a desire to kill), 'second degree' murder only malice aforethought and manslaughter neither. Excusable homicide covers deaths as a result of accidents and justifiable homicide when the death is caused in the line of duty, as may be the case on certain occasions, say, by a police officer.

Trends in homicide

Before we come on to the actual numbers, cast your mind over the television and cinema you have watched in the last year. Now, very approximately, how many homicides/murders do you think you have 'seen' in various dramas in that period? Ten? A hundred? A thousand? More? Personally, being of a generally squeamish disposition, and yet a fan of programmes like *NYPD Blue*, *The Sopranos*, *The Shield* and the rest, I reckon I'd have to answer 'several hundred' and even then it might be a serious underestimate (I haven't included cartoon violence like Itchy and Scratchy in *The Simpsons*). So, how many homicides are there in Britain each year? The answer is under 1,000. In 2003/04 the figure recorded by the police was 853 and in 2004/05 it was 839. Figure 20.3 illustrates trends in homicide (including a 'spike' in 2002/03 as a result of the Harold Shipman case) since just after the Second World War.

Homicide varies significantly between different countries. In Europe, for example, homicide rates in 2003 varied from 21.9 (per 100,000) in Russia, 9.5 in Lithuania and 8.5 in Albania down to 1.0 in Switzerland and Slovenia and 0.6 in Austria. The mean was 2.7, with the homicide rate in the UK being 1.6 in England and Wales, 1.9 in Northern Ireland and 2.1 in Scotland (Aebi *et al.*, 2006). By comparison, the homicide rate in the USA was 5.7 in 2003, substantially higher than the European average and approximately three times the rate in the UK. We return to this comparison below in relation to the use of weapons.

Homicide offenders

There are few British studies of homicide. Mitchell (1990), for example, studied a random sample of 250 cases of people convicted of murder between 1978 and 1982, or approximately one-third of the convictions for murder during that period. Data were drawn from files held by the Home Office on 50 cases in each year, 41 of whom were adult males, two were adult females and seven were young offenders. The gender breakdown slightly under-represented women, in that earlier research by Morris and Blom-Cooper (1979) found that between 11–16% of offenders during the 1970s were female. More recent research by Brookman (2005), involving analysis of the Homicide Index and examination of police murder files, found males to comprise 90% of homicide offenders. She

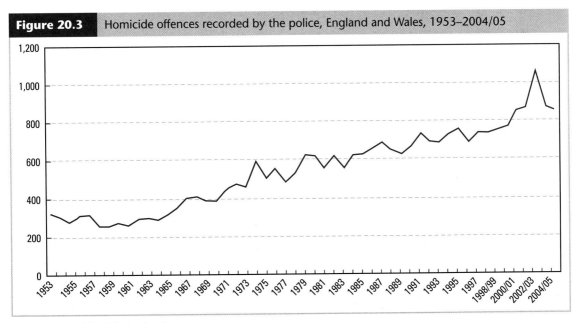

Figure 20.3 Homicide offences recorded by the police, England and Wales, 1953–2004/05

Source: *Criminal Statistics* (various).

found that further data from Scotland and Northern Ireland suggested even greater over-involvement of males.

Brookman's and Mitchell's data confirm that those who commit homicide are often relatively young. Morris and Blom-Cooper's (1979) study had suggested that two-fifths of those charged with murder were aged between 15 and 24 and Mitchell (1990) found that over three-fifths (62%) were aged under 29, and 85% were aged under 39. Brookman's (2005) study suggests that the peak age of offending for homicide perpetrators is 31–35. Both Mitchell's and Blom-Cooper's studies appear to find that women convicted of murder are generally older than male offenders.

With some understatement, Mitchell (1990: 46) says that it 'appears that those convicted of murder are unlikely to be people pursuing professional careers.' Four of the 250 people in his sample fell into that category. Approximately half the men in the sample (48%) were in non-professional occupations or were unemployed (46%) at the time of the offence. Research by Dobash et al. (2001) on male homicide offenders found that:

> When compared to the general population, a greater proportion of these offenders had problems as children, including disrupted caretaking, physical and/or sexual abuse, substance abuse and early onset of offending. As adults they were likely to be undereducated and unemployed.

Nearly one half had problems with alcohol while one quarter had problems with drugs and a similar proportion had mental health problems. (quoted in D'Cruze et al., 2006: 15)

Research by Dobash et al. (2002) found that of the 180 male convicted murderers they interviewed in prisons in England and Scotland:

- 61% had problems at school.
- 39% were from 'broken homes'.
- 24% came from families in which the father used violence against the mother.
- 26% had been in care.
- 25% had problems with alcohol as children.
- 10% had learning disabilities.
- 25% had mental health problems.

As with most crime types, once again we have found that murder is committed predominantly by men. That female murderers are therefore relatively unusual might explain why there are times when such cases come to public attention that they appear to engender particular horror. There is a tendency to talk of female murderers as if they are either 'mad' or especially 'bad'. The horrific case of the Moors Murders in the 1960s, in which four young people aged between ten and 16 were murdered and buried on Saddleworth Moor near Manchester, illustrates this point well. Two people, Ian Brady and Myra Hindley, were convicted of the

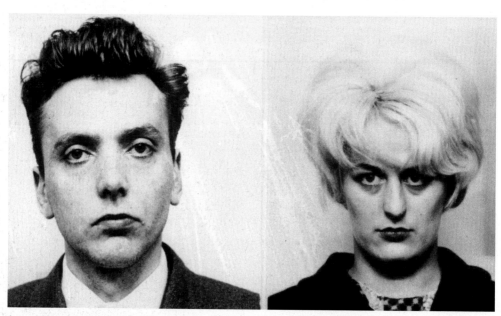

Ian Brady and Myra Hindley, guilty of the notorious Moors Murders in the 1960s. Although the vast majority of homicide perpetrators are male, the media show a particular fascination with women convicted of murder.

murders in 1966. The death penalty having not long been abolished, both were imprisoned for life.

However, as D'Cruze *et al.* (2006: 48) observe, 'over the ensuing decades, it has been Hindley, rather than Brady, who was repeatedly cited as the prime exemplar of evil, and it has been her image from the original police photograph that appeared recurrently in the media until her death in 2002.' The alternative to this form of demonisation is to portray women offenders as 'mad' and historically certain classes of female have been identified as somehow less than fully rational. D'Cruze *et al.* give the example of the crime of *infanticide*, created by the Infant Life (Preservation) Act 1929, which assumed that there was sufficient potential for mental disturbance in childbirth that women in such circumstances were to be treated as being of diminished responsibility.

Finally, we cannot conclude this section without a brief mention of those unusual occasions when murder is committed by very young children. Such homicides are rare – there were 254 cases of child-perpetrated homicide in the decade 1992–2001 (Brookman, 2005) – though predictably they are subject to considerable media scrutiny when they do occur. Such acts stand in stark contrast to the idealised picture of childhood innocence that most of us hold and, because of this, tend to elicit shocked and highly moralistic responses from public and media alike. The abduction and murder of two year-old James Bulger in Liverpool in 1993 provides a dramatic example. However, such reactions may also tell us something about our national culture and psyche, for there is evidence that the responses are far from identical in other countries (see box below).

Victims of homicide

A body of existing research has found that the victims of unlawful killing are fairly evenly divided between men and women (for example Gibson, 1975). The proportion in Mitchell's (1979) study

---

The cases of James Bulger and Silje Redergard

James Bulger was two years old when he was abducted and murdered in Merseyside in February 1993. CCTV images broadcast around the country appeared to show James leaving the shopping centre, where he had been with his mother, in the company of two older boys. Six days later, two ten year-old boys were arrested and charged with the offence. Early appearances of the two boys in court were accompanied by crowds on the streets threatening violence against them. In November that year they appeared in an adult court where in due course they were convicted and sentenced to eight years in prison – later increased to ten. On their eventual release from prison, the two men assumed new identities and, it is assumed, now live outside the UK.

There are some similarities in the case of Silje Redergard, but also some dramatic differences. In this case, which occurred in the Norwegian city of Trondheim in 1994, a five year-old girl was murdered by two six year-old boys. As in the Bulger case it appears that considerable violence was involved in the attack. There was considerable national shock and concern at the crime. However, the media reaction was very different as was the criminal case that ensued. The two children who had killed Silje were below the age of criminal responsibility and couldn't be prosecuted. Indeed, according to news reports they were back in kindergarten within weeks, and were generally treated with compassion by the local community.

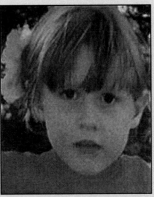

Various sources including BBC World Service (http://www.bbc.co.uk/worldservice/people/highlights/001109_child.shtml)

was lower – 59% of victims were male and 41% female. However, Brookman (2005) found 70% of homicide victims between 1997 and 2001 were male, and it is this latter figure which is probably the most accurate. There were differences between them, however. Thus, whereas just over half the married or widowed victims were female, over 70% of the single victims were male (Mitchell, 1990).

Like the offenders, the victims of murder tend to be found in the younger age groups. According to Brookman (2005) it is those aged 31–35 who are most vulnerable, followed by those aged 26–30 and 21–25. Morris and Blom-Cooper (1979) found that one-fifth of murder victims were aged between 15 and 24 and a further 15% were aged between 25 and 34. Mitchell's (1990) research found that 38% of victims were aged under 30 and 71% were aged under 50. Within this general finding there is evidence which suggests that it is very young children (aged under 1) who are most at risk (Brookman and Maguire, 2003). Finally, but importantly, current data also suggest that ethnic minorities are most at risk. In the period 1995–2001 almost one-tenth of victims of homicide were black, even though they comprise only just over two per cent of the population as a whole. For this same period Asians constituted 4.4% of the population, but 6% of homicide victims. By contrast, over 90% of the British population was white, but only 75.5% of victims of homicide were white (Brookman, 2005).

Motive and relationship

Why does murder occur? As Brookman (2005: 56) comments, 'few commentators believe that homicide, or any other crime – violent or otherwise – has a single cause' (for reviews see Brookman, 2005; Polk, 2004). There is a broad range of theories rather paralleling more general criminological theory (see Chapters 5 to 16). Consequently, this chapter is best read in conjunction with earlier discussions of crime and its possible causes.

According to Mitchell (1979: 58) 44% of the male victims and almost all the female victims were killed during the course of some dispute with someone they knew, and this led him to conclude that, 'whether the victim be male or female, it seems that the most common motive for unlawful homicide is some sort of personal emotional reason; that is, the offence is committed in the course of a quarrel or fit of temper'. Similarly, Gibson (1975) found that over half of male victims were killed by acquaintances, and that over a third of female victims were killed by their husbands.

Morris and Blom-Cooper (1979: 10), summarising existing evidence, concluded:

> Earlier studies of homicide established that murder was overwhelmingly a domestic crime. More than half of the persons indicted for murder each year have a familial relationship, and up to two-thirds of all have had a personal relationship of some duration and/or intensity with the victim. Only about a quarter of the total number of murder victims have been total strangers to their victims.

Mitchell's (1979) data tend to confirm this general pattern. Among his sample in only 22% of cases was the offender a stranger. In over three-quarters of cases, therefore, the victim and offender had some form of relationship. The most common were friend/acquaintance (40%) and spouse/cohabitant or former spouse/cohabitant (15%). Collating homicide data leads Brookman (2005: 50) to develop a typology of homicide in which she distinguishes offences according to both victim/offender relationships, and context (see Table 20.1).

Use of weapons

For some time now there has been concern that use of weapons is increasing – both the use of knives and guns. We consider this in greater detail later in the chapter in relation to crime generally. However, in connection with homicide, the evidence suggests that there has been some increase in the use of firearms over the past decade. However, it is the use of 'sharp instruments' – usually a knife – that is the most common method of killing (see Figure 20.4). Morris and Blom-Cooper (1979) found that in under 10% of the 4,000 cases they studied had the victims been shot. However, they found that somewhere between 22% and 40% of those indicted for murder between 1957 and 1977 had used some form of sharp instrument in the course of the offence. Mitchell's (1990) small sample also found that almost two-fifths (39%) of cases involved a sharp instrument, 22% involved strangulation, and a further fifth (19%) involved a blunt instrument. Twenty-one cases (8%) involved shooting. Recent Home Office data shows that shooting is the method of killing in less than one-tenth of cases, whereas the use of a sharp instrument accounts for nearly one-third (very much in contrast with the United States for example where the use of handguns accounts for a much higher proportion of homicides).

Table 20.1	Homicide in England and Wales 1997–2001 by victim–offender relationships and context				
Type of offence	**Number**	**%**	**Total number**	**Total %**
Domestic homicide			1,287	**31**
Sexual intimacy	**717**	17.3		
Current or former spouses/lovers	704			
Sexual rivals	13			
Family intimacy	**570**	13.8		
Parent/child	348			
Child/parent	96			
Other (e.g. siblings/in-laws)	126			
Homicide in the course of other crime			294	**7**
Robbery	147	(50)		
Burglary	60	(20)		
Other gain	28	(10)		
Sex attack (unrelated individuals)	53	(18)		
Resisting/avoiding arrest	6	(2)		
Gang homicide			43	**1**
Confrontational homicide (unrelated individuals)			888	**22**
Jealousy/revenge (unrelated individuals)			94	**2**
Reckless acts (unrelated individuals)			248	**6**
Racial violence			14	**<1**
'Other' unspecified circumstances (unrelated individuals)			117	**3**
Context/motive unknown			967	**23**
Unusual cases			171	**4**
Serial murder	80			
Mass homicide	58			
Terrorism	4			
Homicide amongst children (under 17) (unrelated)	29			
Total			4,123	**100**

Source: Brookman (2005).

| **Figure 20.4** | Method of killing, England and Wales, 1995–2001 |

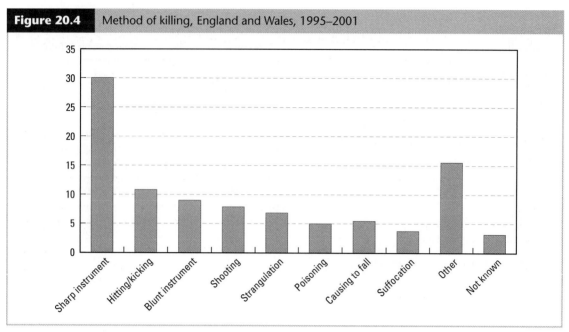

Source: Brookman (2005).

Homicide and social status

Looking beyond explanations for homicide as an act of individual violence, a more general question can be asked about overall levels of homicide. These vary society to society and also vary over time. A fascinating analysis of recent homicide trends has been conducted by Dorling (2004) and although a summary of elements of his argument appear in the box below, I would urge you to look at the original for it tells a very interesting story in not much over ten pages.

Serial killers

In recent times there has developed a public fascination with the 'serial killer'. Railway bookstalls are now full of 'true crime' books and many of these are devoted to the subject of serial murder: those cases in which a single offender is responsible for a series of murders. This is by no means an entirely new fascination, as the 'Jack the Ripper' case from Victorian London confirms. Nevertheless, there is a sense from contemporary popular culture that, somehow, we are uniquely threatened by such crimes. Before we move on it is important to distinguish between a number of different 'types' of multiple killing:

- *Mass* killings – When a number of people are killed in a single episode (an example in the UK would be the case of David Copeland the 'Soho nail bomber').

- *Spree* killings – When there are multiple victims and the deaths take place over a longer time period but are still considered to be one event.

- *Serial* killings – Over a much more extended time period, often with long periods between events.

The term 'serial killer' itself appears to have emerged in the United States in the 1970s and to be linked to a number of cases that became notorious and, in particular, to that of Ted Bundy. Although no-one knows when he first started killing, he later admitted a number of murders going back to 1974. He was arrested in 1975 and convicted of kidnapping in early 1976. He escaped from jail twice in 1977. On the first occasion he was recaptured quickly, but on the second occasion was at large for several months during which time he committed another series of murders. In 1979 he was sentenced to death, and eventually executed in 1989. Though estimates vary, Bundy is believed to have killed between 20 and 30 women.

There are various typologies of serial killing, with that by Holmes and Holmes (1998) which includes four main types perhaps the best known:

- *Visionary* – Responding to voices/hallucinations. Probably psychotic.

- *Missionary* – Rid the world of particular problem groups.

Prime suspect: Murder in Britain (Dorling, 2004)

Dorling's fascinating article begins with five questions:

1 Who is murdered?

2 When were they murdered?

3 Where were they murdered?

4 With what were they murdered and, finally,

5 Why were they murdered?

In the best traditions of murder mysteries he says that he will reveal the identity of the killer at the end of the article. So, read on.

The answer to the first question – who is murdered – is answered by analysing data on all homicides between 1981–2000. This shows that the murder rate for men is roughly twice that of women, and that a quarter of all murders are of men aged between 17–32.

The number of murders and the rate of murders have doubled since the late 1960s. Intriguingly, looking at the changing murder rate reveals that for all women except infants the rate has either stayed stable or fallen, and the same is true for men over 60. It is males aged between 5–59 for whom the murder rate has risen, and has done so dramatically. At its most extreme, the murder rate has doubled for male victims aged 20–24.

Asking where they were murdered reveals that it is the nature of the place in which people live that is arguably the crucial factor influencing risk of male homicide. The poorer the area, the higher the murder rate. Dorling is then able to show that the people living in the ten per cent poorest areas in Britain were four and a half times more likely to be murdered than those living in the richest ten per cent. This means that the rise in murder has, in fact, been concentrated almost entirely among working-age men living in the poorest parts of Britain.

With what were they murdered? Tempting as it might be to believe the headlines and think it was largely due to an increase in gun crime, Dorling shows this not to be the case. Much of this increase was as a result of traditional conflicts – fights in which knives, broken glass or other sharp implements were used. Why were they murdered? This is where the analysis becomes more complicated and slightly more speculative. Dorling shows that, contrary to the normal pattern of homicide rates declining as young males mature, there is an identifiable cohort of men – those born in the mid-1960s – for whom the murder rate is actually increasing as they age. Why should this be? Dorling's answer is that this was the generation who reached the school-leaving age as the recession of the early 1980s began in earnest, and for whom work was very scarce. The increase in murder, he argues, is largely concentrated within this group of men who were most likely to be affected by the absence of jobs, and who live in circumstances of 'inequality, curtailed opportunities and hopelessness [which] have bred fear, violence and murder'.

As to the identity of the killer, well at the very least you have to turn to the original and look at the conclusion.

Source: Dorling (2004).

- *Hedonistic* – Those who kill for lust, thrills or comfort. The sexual dimension is most obvious in this group but may be present in other cases.

- *Power and control* – To have power over life and death (taken from D'Cruze *et al.*, 2006).

The extent of serial killing is not really known. There have been some outlandish estimates of the likely number of homicides resulting from such offenders, but these tend to be based on assumptions about unsolved cases. By contrast, research based on data from known cases of serial murder tends to provide much more conservative estimates. Jenkins (1988) suggests that there were a dozen cases between 1940–1985 in England and Wales in which someone was suspected or convicted of serial homicide (more than three victims) and that, in total, this accounted for less than 2% of all homicide in the period. Gresswell and Hollin (1994) identify 52 cases between 1982–1991 (more than two victims) involving 196 victims, accounting for approximately 3% of all homicides in the period.

We have in our recent past one of the most extreme examples of serial murder in the case of Harold Shipman, the Manchester GP who was convicted of the murder of 15 of his patients in 2000, but is believed to have murdered many more. The official inquiry into the Shipman case considered 887 deaths in all. In 394 cases it found compelling evidence that the patient had died a natural death, leaving 493 about which questions remained. According to the inquiry further investigation found evidence that in 210 of these cases there was evidence to show that death was from natural causes. However, there was sufficient evidence that Shipman killed 200 patients in addition to the 15 for which he was convicted, and there were a further 45 cases in which there was a real cause to suspect that Shipman might have killed the patient. The case also

The typical Shipman murder

The following picture of a typical Shipman murder emerged. Shipman would visit an elderly patient, usually one who lived alone. Sometimes, the visit would be at the patient's request, on account of an ailment of some kind; sometimes, Shipman would make a routine visit, for example to take a blood sample or to provide repeat prescriptions; sometimes he would make an unsolicited call. During the visit, Shipman would kill the patient. Afterwards, he behaved in a variety of ways and had a variety of typical explanations for what had happened. Sometimes, he would claim that he had found the patient dead when he arrived.

If asked how he had gained entrance, he would say that the patient had been expecting him and had left the door 'on the latch'. Sometimes, he would stay at the premises and telephone relatives or call upon neighbours and reveal the death to them. He might say that he had found the patient close to death or he would sometimes claim that the patient had died quite suddenly in his presence. Sometimes, he would leave the premises after killing the patient, closing (and thereby locking) the door behind him. Either then or later, he would go in search of a neighbour who held a key, or to the warden if the patient lived in sheltered accommodation, and together they would go to the premises and 'discover' the body. On other occasions, he would leave the body unattended and would wait for a relative or friend to discover the death.

Shipman's usual method of killing was by intravenous injection of a lethal dose of strong opiate. Sometimes, mainly if the patient was ill in bed, he killed by giving an intramuscular injection of a similar drug. I suspect that, on occasions, he also gave overdoses of other drugs, such as Largactil, with the intention of putting a patient

Harold Shipman, the Manchester GP convicted in 2000 of the murder of 15 of his patients, but believed to have been responsible for the deaths of over 200 others.

into a deep sleep from which he or she would be unlikely to awake. There is no reliable evidence that he killed other than by the administration of a drug.

In addition to these serious offences against the person, Shipman must have committed drugs offences virtually every day he was in general practice, in that he was almost always in possession of controlled drugs without lawful authority. He obtained large quantities of pethidine and diamorphine by illegal, dishonest means, using deception and forgery.

Source: *The Shipman Inquiry*, First Report (http://www.the-shipman-inquiry.org.uk/fr_page.asp?ID=188).

---

raises a number of other issues, not the least of which is the unknown number of deaths that may have been homicides but have not been identified as such – or not yet identified as such. This point is worth bearing in mind given the trust that is generally placed in the accuracy of homicide data.

Robbery

As we saw earlier in the chapter, the term 'robbery' can cover a broad range of offences covering such things as bank robbery, mobile phone robbery, street mugging and violence between schoolchildren over small amounts of money or property. Here we will focus on two of the main categories: armed robbery and street robbery (or 'mugging').

Armed robbery

Armed robbery is generally considered a very serious offence and there are numerous famous cases – such as the Great Train Robbery in 1963 – that remain in the public consciousness to this day. Armed robbery has changed over the years as the technologies for protecting money have changed. According to Matthews (2002), at the beginning of the twentieth century the 'smash and grab' raid was the preferred method for stealing from banks and other premises. Between 1920 and 1960 safe-cracking became more common, with various forms of explosive being used once the safes became difficult to unlock. From the early 1960s the difficulties involved in robbery led to a more direct approach in which banks, building societies,

Figure 20.5 Robberies in which firearms were used, England and Wales, 1988–1999, by location of offence

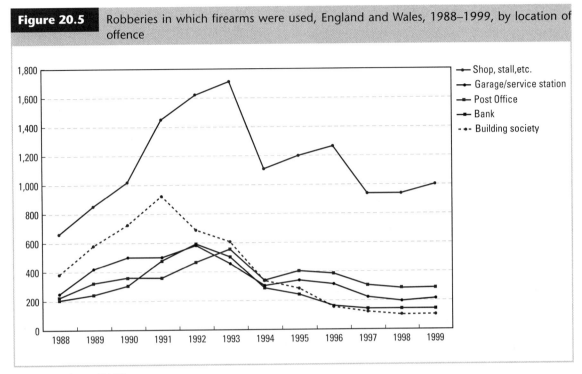

Source: Matthews (2002).

post offices, etc. were robbed during working hours by armed men often carrying sawn-off shotguns. There appears to have been a substantial increase in armed robbery in the 1970s and 1980s, but something of a decline since the early 1990s as banks and building societies in particular have made their premises more secure (see Figure 20.5).

There are a number of reasons for this apparent trend. As already suggested, a number of forms of 'target hardening' were employed by banks, building societies, post offices and other premises which appear to have had some impact. These included intruder alarms, more complex locks, toughened glass, reinforced doors, security lights, fake note detectors, intercom entry and internal CCTV. Particularly elaborate methods were introduced to protect cash-in-transit, including dummy boxes and bags (full of shredded paper rather than bank notes) and cash boxes filled with dye that would mark the cash if they were incorrectly opened. The consequence, according to Matthews (2002: 138), has been that:

> The most noticeable change that has occurred over the last decade has been the demise of the more professional and career robbers and, subsequently,

a greater proportion of those currently involved in commercial robbery are more inexperienced, younger, more desperate, more criminally diverse and more spontaneous in their actions.

Matthews distinguishes between what he calls 'amateurs', 'intermediates' and 'professionals' in armed robbery. The largest group, particularly given the trend outlined above, is the amateurs, not the professionals of folklore. In the main they are poorly organised, often operate alone, and often rob for relatively small amounts of money. Professional and persistent robbers are an 'elite group' and robbery is a core part of their lives. They tend to be much better organised, often work in groups, and plan to steal substantial sums of money. This group was visible in Wright and Decker's (1997) in-depth interview-based study. Based on interviews with 87 robbers, they found that approximately one-third said they had committed almost 50 robberies in their lifetime. Most usually committed street robberies, the remainder holding up fuel stations, liquor stores and the like. The intermediate group is comprised of robbers who are much better organised than the amateurs, but less 'dedicated' than the professionals.

Armed robbery: a robber threatens staff with an axe at a MacDonald's restaurant in Birmingham in 2006.

Street robbery

If this is simply a modern term for what was once known as 'highway robbery' then one can immediately see that what is now often referred to as 'mugging' has a long and varied history. Moreover, it is something about which there has long been public concern. Pearson (1983) describes in detail the 'garrotting' panic of the mid-nineteenth century. According to *The Times* of 10 June 1863, this 'modern peril of the streets created something like a reign of terror' in which 'whole sections of a peaceable city community were on the verge of arming themselves against sudden attack' (quoted in Pearson, 1983: 128–9). According to contemporary accounts garrotting gangs worked in threes – two who worked as look-outs and a third, the 'nasty man', who attacked from the rear:

> The third ruffian, coming swiftly up, flings his right arm around the victim, striking him smartly on the forehead. Instinctively he throws his head back, and that movement loses every chance of escape. His throat is fully offered to the assailant, who instantly embraces it with his left arm, the bone just above the wrist being pressed against the 'apple' of the throat. At the same moment the garrotter, dropping his right hand, seizes the other's left wrist; and thus supplied with a powerful lever, draws his back upon his breast and there holds him. The 'nasty man's' part is done. His burden is helpless from

the first moment, and speedily becomes insensible; all *he* has now to do is be a little merciful.

> (Pearson, 1983: 129)

Such panics continue to this day – though their focus and the terminology may change slightly. Nevertheless, street robbery remains a constant source of public concern. From the 1970s onward the term 'mugging' increasingly came to be applied to such activity and, in particular, became associated with the idea that this was a crime particularly likely to be carried out by African-Caribbean youth (see the account of *Policing the Crisis* in Chapter 31). In *Recorded Crime Statistics* 'mugging' is made up of robbery, attempted robbery and snatch theft from the person.

Although crime generally declined from the early to mid-1990s onward and, indeed, violent crime has declined for much of that period, there have been increases, particularly, recently in recorded street robbery. Thus, between 1981 and 2000 whilst there was a 21% drop in both burglary and other theft and an 11% drop in wounding, robbery rose by 14% (Kershaw, 2000), (see Figure 20.6). It is worth remembering, however, that such offences account for only approximately 2% of all recorded crime.

The reasons for rising rates of street robbery are undoubtedly complex. However, one factor that has been much discussed is the importance of valuable consumer goods such as mobile phones and subsequently iPods/MP3 players as a particularly attractive item for robbers. Recent research by Harrington and Mayhew (2002) found that trends in street robbery had indeed been much influenced by the increasing availability of mobile phones:

- The rise in phone robberies between 1998/99 to 2000/01 was generally greater than for other offences involving phones, and much greater than other offences of robbery that did not involve the theft of a phone.

- The upward trend in robbery since 1990 can be redrawn to show a levelling off between 1998–2000 when robberies involving the theft of a mobile phone are removed from the calculation. Harrington and Mayhew (2002) also excluded those robberies where a mobile phone is the only item stolen, in an effort to identify cases in which victims were being specifically targeted for their phones, as opposed to the theft being just part of the opportunistic trawl. The redrawn trend in robbery, excluding mobile only robbery, estimated an increase of 8% between 1999/00 to 2000/01 and not the 13% reported in the official statistics.

| **Figure 20.6** | Recorded robbery in England and Wales, 1990–2001/02 |

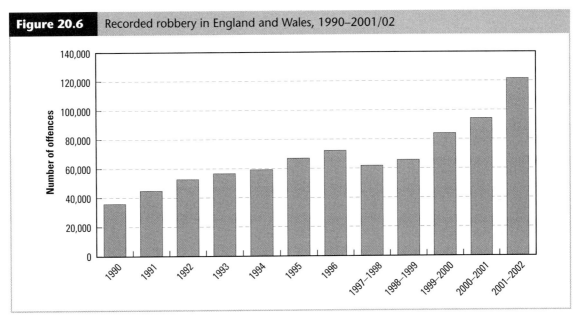

Source: Smith (2003).

The easy availability of portable consumer goods such as iPods, MP3 players and mobile phones have been linked with rising rates of street robbery in recent years.

Smith's (2003) research suggests that personal robbery generally involves males. Over three-quarters of victims (76%) and the vast majority of suspects (94%) are male. It is a crime that is often carried out in small groups. Three-fifths (62%) of all recorded robberies have two or more suspects, and the younger the victim the more likely this is to be the case, with 71% of cases involving victims aged under 20 having two or more suspects. Indeed, it is young people – especially young males – who predominate as both offenders and victims of street robbery. Current estimates suggest that slightly more than half of street robbery suspects are aged 20 or under and, though the age profile of victims is less stark, 45% are aged 20 or under. Nevertheless, there is a stark trend toward the victimization of younger age groups – the number of victims aged 11–15 and 16–20 increased threefold between 1993 and 2001 – and a similar trend in which it appears that younger offenders are also becoming more common: the 11–20 age group accounted for 56% of offenders in 1993 and this had increased to 78% by 2000 (Harrington and Mayhew, 2002).

As we have already noted (see Chapter 4) the politicisation of street crime in the 1970s and 1980s focused particularly on claims that this was predominantly an offence committed by young, black men. Not surprisingly, therefore, this remains a contentious issue and one that is difficult to resolve. The offending profile of street robbers varies markedly by area – predictably, given that the populations of those areas vary. It is the case that visible ethnic minorities are over-represented in some areas and not in others. In Smith's research the pattern was complicated: in some cases approximately reflecting the make-up of the local population, but in others – notably Lambeth – being substantially over-represented despite a very large black population in the borough. Research by Fitzgerald *et al.* (2003) suggests that black young people are more than three times as likely as whites to have been found guilty of robbery (although they were only half as likely to have been convicted of burglary).

Smith (2003) identifies five main types of street robbery which vary according to how the victim(s) are initially approached by the suspect. These are:

- *Blitz.* Violence is used to overwhelm, stun or control the victim prior to the removal of any property or prior to any demands to hand over property. Violence is the first point of contact between the victim and the suspect. There is no prior verbal exchange between victim and offender, though threats and abuse may follow the initial assault [25% of cases involving male victims and 25% of cases involving female victims].

- *Confrontation.* A demand for property or possessions is the initial point of contact between the victim and offender, e.g. 'Give me your money and your mobile phone'. This may be followed through with threats and, on occasion with force [41% of cases involving male victims and 25% of cases involving female victims].

- *Con.* The suspect 'cons' the victim into some form of interaction. This typically takes the form of some spurious conversation, e.g. 'Have you got a light/the time mate?' This is the initial approach to the victim regardless of how the robbery subsequently develops [25% of cases involving male victims and 12% of cases involving female victims].

- *Snatch.* Property is grabbed from the victim without prior demand, threats or physical force. This is the initial contact between the victim and the suspect. Physical force is used to snatch property from the victim, which is nearly always on display, e.g. handbag. There is no physical search of the victim by the suspect [6% of cases involving male victims and 37% of cases involving female victims]. There is a further important gender difference in victimization, however. For men, rates of snatch theft drop steadily as they age, though this is not the case for women where risk increases following middle age as they become older.

- *Victim-initiated.* The victim initiates contact with the suspect and becomes the victim of a robbery, e.g. a drug deal, procuring sex, etc. [3% of cases involving male victims and 1% of cases involving female victims].

Street robbery is highly geographically concentrated, being overwhelmingly found in the major urban conurbations, especially London. When the government launched its 'street crimes initiative' in 2001 – designed to stem the rising rate of street robbery – it focused its attention on the ten areas with the highest rates of such crime (see Chapter 25).

Sexual offences

A variety of crimes come under the heading 'sexual offences'. They include rape and indecent assault, indecent exposure, 'stalking', child sexual abuse, the creation and dissemination of child pornography. What many offences share is an absence of 'consent', either because of coercion, the age of one of the parties or because of the nature of the relationship (between father and daughter, for example). What we refer to as the 'age of consent' is 16 in the UK. This means that people below that age are not necessarily considered able to consent to sex and the younger the child, the more likely that is to be the case. There are additional protections beyond the age of consent: teachers are not permitted to have sex with their pupils whatever the age of the pupil and other adults caring for children are under similar restrictions.

Accurate information about sexual offences is extremely difficult to get. First, sexual offences are significantly under-reported to the police and to other organisations. There are many reasons for this, not least the shame and stigma that are often still attached to such offences. Police recorded crime statistics are therefore a very significant under-estimate of the number of sexual offences committed. The BCS is even less reliable. The number of sexual offences recorded by the BCS is too small to allow for reliable estimates to be made and therefore such figures are often excluded from publications analysing BCS data.

Specific estimates made by the BCS suggest that 26% of women and 17% of men aged 16 to 59 have experienced at least one incident of non-sexual domestic abuse, threat or force since they were 16. Furthermore, Walby and Allen (2004) found that 17% of women and 2% of men had been sexually assaulted at least once since they were 16. Indeed, 4% of women had been raped and 1% had experienced another type of serious sexual assault since the age of 16. In all, therefore, the BCS estimates suggest that a minimum of 5% of women have suffered a very serious sexual assault.

Figure 20.7 Prevalence of sexual assaults (including attempts) since age 16

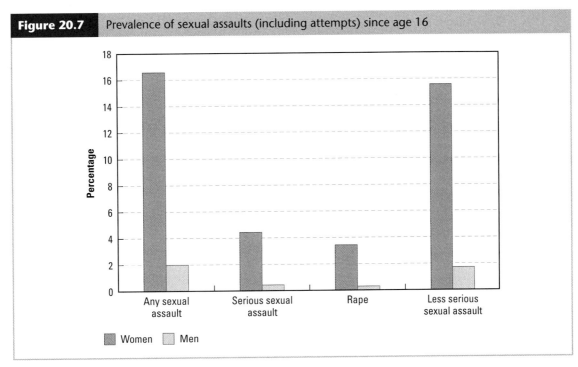

Source: Walby and Allen (2004).

The BCS provides a more detailed breakdown of what it refers to as 'interpersonal violence' (see Table 20.2). It distinguishes between 'serious' and 'less serious' sexual assaults. 'Less serious' sexual assaults were categorised as those that caused 'fear, alarm or distress'. The typology is much more explicit than any previous scale. In part this is to reflect changes in legislation since 2003 which extended the definition of rape to include penetration of the mouth by a penis without consent, and also to include the offence of 'assault by penetration' (penetration of the vagina or anus by other body parts or by objects without consent). The naming of particular orifices was undertaken as it was believed that offences would otherwise be significantly under-reported.

Table 20.2 shows that the most common of the forms of less serious sexual assault in the previous year was unwanted sexual touching that caused fear, alarm or distress, and that this affected an estimated 172,000 women. In relation to serious sexual assault, the extension of the legal definition of rape in 2003 (including penetration of the mouth by penis without consent) led to a slight increase in the number of reported rapes.

Stalking

Table 20.2 also contains information on 'stalking'. The term itself doesn't appear in the criminal law, but an offence was created by the Protection from Harassment Act 1997 following a series of high profile 'stalking' cases and most other European countries now also have stalking laws. There is considerable debate as to whether stalking constitutes a crime of violence (Finch, 2002) and, relatedly, what the appropriate forms of punishments are for such offences. Research suggests that stalking can have a significant impact on its victims, with one study suggesting that 71% of people reporting having been stalked saying that they undertook a major lifestyle change as a result of the experience (Budd and Mattinson, 2000).

Although this generally involves a sequence of events, it is counted as one course of conduct of harassment in the BCS. Respondents were asked about three types of stalking or harassment: the receipt of unwanted letters/messages; someone hanging around near the victim's home or work; and interference with, or damage to, property. The most common form was that of phone calls or written notes or other material that had been left for

Table 20.2	Detailed prevalence of inter-personal violence

Percentage victims once or more

	Women				Men			BCS
Nature of violence	Ever	Since age 16 in last year (000s)	Last year	Est'd no. of victims	Ever	Since age 16	Last year	Est'd no. of victims in last year (000s)
Sexual assault								
Serious sexual assault	**7.0**	**4.5**	**0.5**	**79**	**1.5**	**0.5**	**0.1**	
Rape (1994)	5.2	3.6	0.3	47	0.9	0.4	<0.0	
Penetrated your vagina with a penis	3.8	2.7	0.2	25	***	***	***	***
Penetrated your anus with a penis	0.9	0.7	<0.1	5	0.6	0.2	<0.1	
Attempted to penetrate your vagina with a penis	1.3	0.8	0.1	21	***	***	***	***
Attempted to penetrate your anus with a penis	0.3	0.2	<0.1	2	0.3	0.2	<0.1	
Rape (2003)	5.5	3.7	0.3	52	1.2	0.4	<0.0	
Penetrate your mouth with a penis	0.9	0.6	0.1	10	0.2	<0.1	<0.1	
Attempted to penetrate your mouth with a penis	0.2	0.1	<0.1	2	0.2	<0.1	…	
Assault by penetration (2003)	2.9	1.6	0.3	42	0.4	0.2	<0.0	
Penetrated your vagina with an object (incl. fingers)	2.0	1.1	0.2	25	***	***	***	***
Attempted to penetrate your vagina with an object (incl. fingers)	0.8	0.4	0.1	1.5	***	***	***	***
Penetrated your anus with an object (incl. fingers)	0.4	0.2	<0.1	5	0.3	0.1	<0.1	
Attempted to penetrate your anus with an object (incl. fingers)	0.1	0.1	<0.1	2	0.1	<0.1	<0.1	
Less serious sexual assault	**22.3**	**15.3**	**1.9**	**293**	**3.9**	**1.8**	**0.2**	**24**
Indecently exposing himself (flashing) in a manner that caused fear, alarm or distress	12.8	8.0	0.5	80	1.2	0.5	0.1	11
Touching you sexually in a manner that caused you fear, alarm or distress (e.g. groping, touching breasts or bottom, unwanted kissing)	10.7	7.0	1.1	172	2.3	1.1	0.1	10
Sexually threatening you in a manner that caused you fear, alarm or distress (e.g. demanding sex when you didn't want it, following or cornering you in a sexually threatening way)	4.9	3.8	0.6	90	0.8	0.4	<0.1	4

Table 20.2	*Continued*								
Percentage victims once or more									BCS
	Women					**Men**			
Nature of violence	Ever	Since age 16 in last year (000s)	Last year	Est'd no. of victims	Ever	Since age 16	Last year	Est'd no. of victims in last year (000s)	
Stalking	18.9	…	7.8	1206	11.6	…	5.8	888	
Received a series (i.e. two or more) phone calls or written letters that were obscene, a significant nuisance or threatening or had been left obscene, offensive or distributing material.	13.5	…	4.9	758	5.3	…	2.7	410	
Someone loitered regularly outside my house/work place/place I regularly visit or persistently followed me around (at least twice)	3.7	…	1.1	167	1.0	…	0.4	54	
Someone deliberately interfered with/damaged my property on at least two occasions.	5.0	…	2.5	385	6.5	…	3.1	477	

Notes:
1. Source 2001 BCS
2. '…' not available
3. '***' not applicable
4. '.'indicates no cases in this category
5. Estimated number of victims are rounded to the nearest 1,000.
6. Number of victims are not available for male serious, sexual assault due to the small number of cases.
7. Prevalences estimates are based on the total sample including those who said they did not know or did not want to answer the question.

Source: Walby and Allen (2004).

the respondent that were obscene, offensive, disturbing, a significant nuisance or threatening. This was experienced by almost 5% of women and something under 3% of men in the previous year. Deliberate interference with, or damage to, property was experienced by 2.5% of women and 3.1% of men in the previous year. The least common of the three forms was regular loitering at the victim's home or place of work or persistently following them. This was experienced by just over 1% of women and 0.4% of men in the previous year.

Monitoring sex offenders

In the last decade or more, sexual offences against children – particularly cases in which children are targeted by adult male offenders – have become one of our great contemporary concerns. The term *paedophile* is used, often very loosely, to describe such offenders and to convey public concerns. As we saw in Chapter 16 contemporary criminal jus-tice is argued to be increasingly risk-oriented and to be concerned with prevention, management and monitoring of offenders. One of the areas in which this can most clearly be seen is in relation to sex offenders. According to Kemshall and Maguire (2001) the British government was in some ways following the American lead when it introduced the Sex Offenders Act 1997, though there had been growing concern about the issue of child sexual abuse since the 1980s, with a major public enquiry into high numbers of children taken into care in Cleveland in the late 1980s as a result of allegations of sexual abuse (Campbell, 1988).

From the 1990s onwards, there were a number of media stories involving the alleged 'ritual abuse' of children. The most notorious of these was in Nottingham (where police and social workers publicly disagreed about the approach to investigating cases of alleged 'satanic' abuse) and the Orkney Islands (where police and social workers were required to return a number of children they had taken into care because of suspected sexual abuse). There were also a number of high profile investigations of sexual abuse in children's homes, most notably in Leicestershire and North Wales (Jones *et al.*, 1994).

In due course, new legislation – the Sex Offenders Act 1997 – required persons who had been convicted of certain sexual offences to notify the police of their name and home address, together with any subsequent changes of residence or name. The obligation to register continues for a variable period – five years to life – depending on the nature of the offence and sentence length. Subsequently, the Crime and Disorder Act 1998 introduced sex offender orders and extended supervision of sex offenders. Amendments made by the Sexual Offences Act 2003 required sex offenders on the register to report each year to the police to verify their details and tightened up the time periods in which changes of address and other details had to be notified.

Although public access to information from the sex offender register was specifically excluded, the subject has been on the public agenda since the abduction and murder of an eight year-old girl, Sarah Payne, from a Sussex village in July 2000. It later emerged that the man who was eventually convicted of the crime had previous convictions for sexual offences, and had recently been released from prison where he had been serving a sentence for child abduction. The case provided momentum for a campaign for the introduction of what, before long, became known as 'Sarah's Law' (see Chapter 4). This was essentially a campaign for full public rights of access to the sex offenders' register. Although the campaign has some weighty supporters – including the *News of the World* and *Sun* newspapers – and initially attracted support in some political circles, there was significant and sufficient resistance from among influential criminal justice professionals to prevent any early action being taken.

However, a series of changes has been made, and the Criminal Justice and Court Services Act 2000 introduced a package of measures including a new statutory duty upon the police and probation to establish arrangements for assessing and arranging the risks posed by sex offenders. The new arrangements were to be called Multi-Agency Public Protection Panels (MAPPPs). The Sexual Offences Act 2003 also introduced the possibility for magistrates' courts to lay down restrictions on the travel, both within the UK and abroad, of an offender convicted of sexual offences against a child aged

below 16. If the court believes that the behaviour of the offender since the first relevant conviction for a sexual offence is such that it is reasonable to believe that he poses a threat of serious sexual harm to children, then a travel order can be issued that forbids travel to a specified country, or any foreign travel at all, for a period of up to six months. Despite this activity, as recently as April 2007 newspapers were reporting that the Home Office was still considering the introduction of a 'Sarah's law', though at the time of writing (June 2007) both the police service and the major children's charities continue to argue against the idea of a register to which the public have access.

Violent crime and weapons

To what extent are weapons used in violent crime? News reports from time to time carry stories of amnesties being called by the police during which knives can be handed over without fear of prosecution and there has been considerable concern in recent years that gun crime is on the increase in Britain. On the other hand, Britain has often portrayed itself as a place in which there are relatively strict gun controls. What is the reality? In examining the data below it is important to bear in mind that evidence about what type of weapons are alleged to

Concern about the increasing possession and carrying of weapons has led the police on many occasions to announce amnesties in which knives and other dangerous items can be handed over without fear of prosecution.

have been used in particular crimes is not always accurate, weapons are not always recovered, and police recording practices are sometimes inconsistent.

As has already been intimated in relation to homicide, the use of knives is far more common than the use of guns in violent crime and, moreover, knives result in a greater number of deaths than do guns. In 2005/06, 31% of male homicide victims and 23% of female victims died in an incident involving a 'sharp instrument' compared with 8% and 4% respectively who died in incidents involving firearms (Coleman *et al.*, 2007). Moreover, although there have been increases in firearms offences in the last decade, the most recent figures have actually shown a drop. The number of recorded crimes involving firearms in 2005/06 was 21,521 a fall of 6% on the previous year. About half of these crimes involve air weapons, and 78% of these offences (i.e. around 37% of all crimes involving firearms) were cases of criminal damage – not violent crimes at all. Excluding air weapons, offences involving firearms account for 0.2% of all recorded crime, or one in every 500 offences.

The phrase 'firearms being used/involved' is also potentially misleading, for guns can be used to threaten and also as a 'blunt instrument'. In cases in which non-air weapons were used they were only fired in 43% of cases. Furthermore, in half of these cases the firearms involved were imitations that only fired blanks or pellets (though they can still result in fatal injury). Handguns were fired in 14% of the crimes in which they were involved. Of those cases in which a non-air weapon was used, handguns accounted for 42% and imitation firearms for 30%. Although the overall level of crimes involving firearms declined between 2004/05 and 2005/06, there was an increase in the use of handguns (see Figure 20.8).

In all, there were 50 fatalities in 2005/06 as a result of the use of firearms. There were a further 595 cases resulting in serious injury and the number of injuries caused by firearms has been increasing markedly – and doubled between 1998/99 and 2005/06. Firearms offences are quite geographically concentrated, with over half of non-air weapon firearm offences occurring in three police force areas. Over a third (35%) of firearms offences in 2005/06 occurred in the Metropolitan Police area, 11% in Greater Manchester and 9% in the West Midlands.

How do we compare with other countries? First, gun ownership is low in the UK. Data from the International Crime Victims Survey found that 2.5% of respondents said that they owned a gun, compared with 11% in Denmark, 24% in Finland, 30% in Switzerland and 33% in the USA (Tseloni and Bass, 2002). Interestingly, there appears to be no clear connection between overall crime victimization levels in particular countries and levels of gun ownership. However, where there does appear to be a closer connection is in levels of 'lethal violence'.

In an important and provocative book entitled *Crime is Not the Problem: Lethal violence in America*, Zimring and Hawkins (1997) argued that what separates America from other developed nations is not

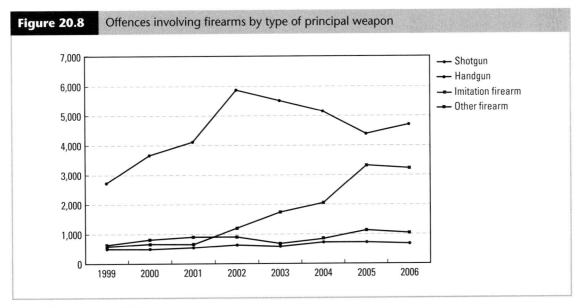

Figure 20.8   Offences involving firearms by type of principal weapon

Source: Coleman *et al.* (2007).

| Figure 20.9 | London crime rates (per 100,000) compared with New York City |

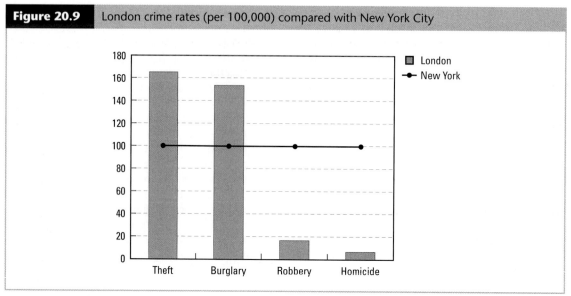

Source: Zimring and Hawkins (1997).

its crime rate but, rather, the level of lethal violence in its cities. To illustrate this, take the following illustration they provide which contrasts various types of crime in New York City with those in London (though once again bearing in mind the limitations of police-recorded statistics). The level in New York is represented by the line across the chart, and in London by the bars. The New York level is set at 100 so that it can be compared with levels in London. As is quickly visible, levels of robbery and homicide are significantly higher in New York, but levels of theft and burglary (much more common forms of crime) are significantly higher in London.

Put at its simplest, the fundamental problem they argue is the availability and use of firearms. Another comparison makes the point. London and New York have populations that are roughly similar. If robberies and burglaries are counted together, then at the time Zimring and Hawkins were doing their research the two cities had roughly the same number of offences. Where the two cities differ is in the number of people who die in the course of such crimes. In London in 1992 there were five deaths during the course of robberies and two during burglaries. The figures for New York were 357 and 21 respectively.

Although the differences between the two cities cannot simply be reduced to firearms, Zimring and Hawkins (1997: 46) conclude that 'the use of guns in robbery in New York City alone seems to be responsible for more than three-quarters of all the deaths that result from robbery and burglary'. Despite such contrasts, there remains considerable concern about levels of gun crime in Britain, and particular con-

> ### Review questions
>
> 1 What are the main forms of violent crime?
>
> 2 What proportion of overall crime does violent crime account for?
>
> 3 What are the advantages and disadvantages of the two main methods of measuring levels of violent crime?
>
> 4 Why is stalking considered to be a crime of violence?
>
> 5 Are we right to show such concern about levels of gun crime?

cerns surrounding the apparent ease with which guns are now available in parts of Britain. Research on arrestees by Bennett and Holloway (2004) found that one-quarter of those interviewed had got hold of a gun at some point in their lives and that one-tenth had done so in the previous year. The most common reason given for gun possession was needing protection, with drug dealing and drug purchasing a common reason for needing protection.

Trends in violent crime

For various reasons it is obviously difficult to say a great deal about trends in violence over extended historical periods. Indeed, the usefulness of more recent official data as a reliable source for understanding historical trends has been severely questioned by Howard Taylor. Examining homicide statistics in the early part of the twentieth century he observed:

> Between 1900 and 1909 there were 1,500 murders, giving an average of exactly 150 per year for that decade. There were also 150 murders in 1923 and 1924. The range of figures is just as remarkable. In only five of the 104 years between 1862 and 1966 were there either fewer than 120 murders or more than 179, i.e. the number of murders was kept within a tight band of 20 per cent (30 murders) on either side of the average of 150. (Taylor 1998: 585)

He goes on to argue that there may well have been some form of rationing taking place, the implication being that police force returns for various forms of criminal conduct may say more about the police service and its resources than about levels and trends in crime. Although identifying crime levels over broad sweeps of history is a difficult task, there are a number of pieces of historical research which provide us with a decent guide to long-term changes.

The best known is that by Ted Robert Gurr. Using data on homicides Gurr (1981) demonstrated what he took to be a long-term process of decline in the frequency of homicide and, indeed, of aggression more generally. More recent research by Eisner (2001) using a variety of official data sources provides a similar picture. In the thirteenth and fourteenth centuries, he argues, according to these sources the average homicide rate was around 23–24 per 100,000 population. There is then a gap in the data of about 150 years, but once information is available again in the sixteenth century the homicide rate appears to have dropped to between 3–9 per 100,000. There is then a further, continuous decline for the next three and a half centuries. Using similar data in other jurisdictions, Eisner is able to show that similar trends can also be found in other parts of Europe (see Table 20.3).

These long-term historical declines in homicide are explained by Gurr, Eisner, Spierenberg and others in part by reference to Norbert Elias' theory of

Table 20.3	Homicide rates per 100,000 in five European regions, 13th–20th centuries				
	England	**Netherlands and Belgium**	**Scandinavia**	**Germany and Switzerland**	**Italy**
13th and 14th centuries	23	47	–	37	(56)
15th century	–	45	46	34	(73)
16th century	7	25	21	11	47
17th century first half	6.2	(6.0)	24	11	(32)
17th century second half	4.3	9.2	12	(2.4)	–
18th century first half	2.3	7.1	2.8	(2.5)	(12)
18th century second half	1.4	4.1	0.7	5.5	9
1800–1824	1.5	1.5	1.0	3.2	18
1825–1849	1.7	–	1.4	4.1	15
1850–1874	1.6	0.9	1.2	2.0	12
1875–1899	1.3	1.5	0.9	2.2	5.5
1900–1924	0.8	1.7	0.8	2.0	3.9
1925–1949	0.8	1.3	0.6	1.4	2.6
1950–1974	0.7	0.6	0.6	0.9	1.3
1975–1994	1.2	1.2	1.2	1.2	1.7

Figures in brackets are considered particularly unreliable as they are based on fewer than five separate estimates. Figures in italics are based on national statistics; the others are based on a variety of local statistics.

Source: Eisner (2001).

the civilising process (see Chapter 22) which argued that the process of nation formation and democratisation brought with it changing sensibilities and attitudes toward violence and aggression as part of a heightening of self-control through social control. It is not only homicide, but a wider set of changes in which violent practices such as the use of the scaffold and other forms of public demonstrations of punishment come increasingly to be viewed as abhorrent.

Contemporary trends

As we saw in Chapter 3, although there is no single source of data on crime levels and trends that might be considered entirely accurate, it is generally argued by most academic commentators that victimization surveys such as the British Crime Survey are a more accurate measure of crime trends than data collected by the police. That said, it is often worth comparing what the two main sources of crime data have to say: do they back each other up or do they contradict each other? For the most part the BCS and recorded crime statistics have indicated largely similar trends in crime over the last two decades or so. However, violent crime in the last decade is the one major exception to this.

Whereas BCS measures suggest that violent crime reached a peak in the mid-1990s and then returned to approximately early 1990s levels (see Figure 3.8), recorded violent crime appears to have increased dramatically in the last five years (see Figure 3.9). Recorded crime statistics show violent crimes increasing throughout the 1980s and the first part of the 1990s, peaking around 1997/8, before rapidly rising once again. There are a number of reasons why the two sources of data appear to show contrasting trends in recent years. In the main, it has been two major methodological changes – changes in the counting rules in 1998/99 and the introduction of the National Crime Recording Standard (NCRS) in 2002 – that lie behind the inflation of violent crime figures. It is possible also that increases in both the *reporting* and *recording* of violent crime may have contributed to the divergent trends since 1998/99 (Smith and Allen, 2004).

Given its newsworthiness, the extent to which it forms the basis of public fears, and how often politicians offer misinformed statements about violent crime, it is important to think carefully about what 'violence' means, how it is measured and what the trends in such offending are. All this is explored in greater detail in Chapter 3.

Review questions

1   What has been the general trend in violent crime over the last 500 years?

2   What is meant by the idea of a 'civilising process' in relation to historical trends in violent crime?

3   What has been the general trend in violent crime over the past 15 years?

4   What are the main factors affecting the measurement of recorded violent crime in the last 15 years?

Property crime

As we have seen, there is a tendency in public discourse – understandable in some ways – to focus on violence when discussing crime. It is in many respects what people fear most. The impact can be devastating. However, we must never lose sight of the fact that the vast majority of crime does not involve violence against the person. The most recent British Crime Survey (BCS) (Walker *et al.*, 2006) suggests that violent crime comprises just over 22% of all crime, and violent crime involving injury just 12%. In this chapter we discuss elements of what is often referred to as 'volume crime' (although this sometimes includes street robbery and drugs offences which we deal with elsewhere) focusing in particularly on what might broadly be thought of as property crime.

The main categories of property crime are burglary, theft, handling stolen goods, fraud and criminal damage. Figure 20.10 shows the breakdown of the offence types for both recorded crime and the BCS. According to both measures, criminal damage accounts for a significant proportion of property crime (between a quarter and a third) and non-vehicle-related theft represents approximately another third.

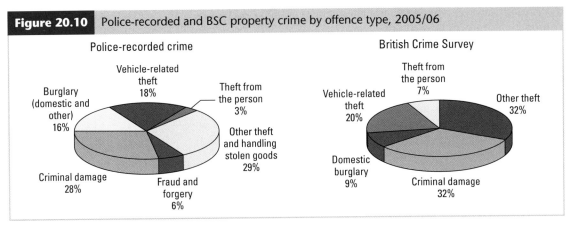

Figure 20.10 Police-recorded and BSC property crime by offence type, 2005/06

Source: Walker *et al.* (2006).

Trends in property crime

The long-term trend in recorded crime was upwards for most of the twentieth century – at a rate of approximately 5% per year (see Figure 20.11). As property crime has always constituted the substantial majority of recorded offences, we can state with some certainty that until the crime rate peaked and began to drop in the mid-1990s, the twentieth century was characterised by very substantial rises in property crime, decade after decade, especially household crimes.

A number of commentators have linked this extraordinary rise of household and other property crime to a number of changes in the nature of mod-

ern society – or to what Cohen and Felson (1979) have called the 'modernisation of risk'. According to Hope (2001), a number of rapid changes to people's homes and lifestyles may help us understand at least one important element in the escalating property crime rate (see also the discussion of this by Cohen and Felson in Chapter 14):

● *Environment* – Expressed in physical forms which combine *privacy* – for example, the degree to which the property is not under the surveillance of others – with *accessibility* – for example, the ease with which it is possible to gain physical access to all parts of the residential property.

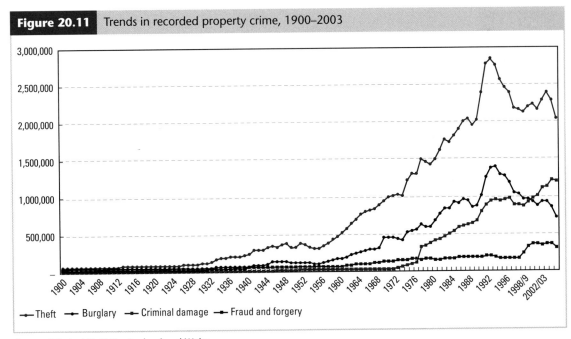

Figure 20.11 Trends in recorded property crime, 1900–2003

Source: *Criminal Statistics England and Wales*.

- *Occupancy* – The extent to which domestic property is unoccupied and unguarded due to the routine activities of people's lives in work and leisure away from the home environment.

- *Value* – The extent to which domestic property is 'valuable' as a commodity which can be exchanged illicitly for other commodities (e.g. cash, drugs) – the most valuable commodities in this regard (including cash itself) usually have a high exchange value relative to their portability.

- *Security* – The extent to which domestic property is guarded by physical, electronic or human means which deny or increase the risk of unauthorised access and appropriation.
(Hope 2001: 199)

As Hope then goes on to explore, and we considered in Chapter 14, these changing aspects of lifestyle and routine activity may work differently for the 'rich' and for the 'poor'. In short, the rich and poor occupy different 'risk positions', he argues, and the one strategy that would be most effective at reducing risk for the poorest in our society – moving their home in order to live in an affluent area – is, of course, not open to them. The fundamental point, and we will revisit this as we look at different types of property crime, is that the uneven social distribution of crime disproportionately affects the least well off in our society. The richest tend to suffer least.

Burglary

Forced entry – burglary is one of the more common crimes, accounting for approximately one-tenth of property offences according to the British Crime Survey.

Trends in burglary

Burglaries are generally divided into two broad types: domestic and non-domestic. Non-domestic burglaries include those of businesses, including

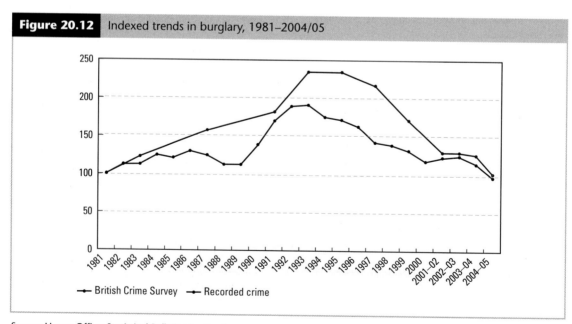

Figure 20.12 Indexed trends in burglary, 1981–2004/05

Legend: British Crime Survey — Recorded crime

Source: Home Office *Statistical Bulletins* (various).

hotels and the like, as well as some break-ins to sheds and outhouses where these are not obviously connected to a house that has people living in it. By contrast, domestic burglaries include break-ins to all 'inhabited dwellings' – whatever the intention behind the break-in, including such dwellings as caravans, houseboats and holiday homes, and garages, sheds and outhouses that are connected to the dwelling. In 2005/06 the police recorded 300,555 domestic burglaries and a further 344,563 non-domestic burglaries.

The BCS estimates that there was a 59% fall in burglary between 1995 and 2004/05, and then the rate appeared to stabilise in the year to 2005/06. It is not just the BCS which indicates that the general trend is downward. Police recorded crime figures for burglary also peak in the mid-1990s and then begin to fall steadily for the next decade (see Figure 20.12). In the figure below, trends are indexed – that is to say, any rises or falls are calculated as a proportion of the level at the beginning of period. Thus, the figure begins in 1981 and levels are represented as being at 100. Both BCS and recorded statistics show rates rising until somewhere around 1993 and then beginning to fall. By the end of the period in 2004/05 levels of burglary are roughly what they were 25 years earlier.

The risk of being burgled overall is relatively low (though remember what we have learned in earlier chapters about the danger of talking of 'averages' and 'overall risks' in relation to victimization). The BCS estimates that between 2% and 3% of households experience burglary in any one year. However, the risks are not evenly distributed in practice and there are various characteristics associated with elevated risk (Walker *et al.*, 2006):

- Home security seems to be important. Households without security measures are ten times as likely to be burgled as houses in which measures such as deadlocks on doors and window locks have been installed.

- Households in owner-occupied properties had much lower risks of victimization (1.8%) than those in other tenure types such as renting (4.2%).

- Reinforcing one of the assumptions of routine activities theory (capable guardianship – see Chapter 14) the BCS data suggest that households that were left unoccupied for five hours or more a day were significantly more likely to have been burgled (2.9%) than those unoccupied for shorter lengths of time.

- Households with an overall income of less than £5,000 were more likely to have experienced at least one burglary in the past year (4.1%) compared with families with incomes over £30,000 (2.4%).

- Finally, households in areas where perceived physical disorder was high were more likely to be victims of burglary (5.3%) than those in a low level area (2.2%).

Figure 20.13 illustrates some of the comparative risk factors associated with burglary.

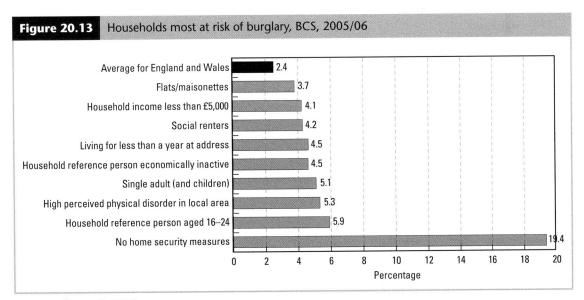

Figure 20.13 Households most at risk of burglary, BCS, 2005/06

Source: Walker *et al.* (2006).

Distraction burglary

Although constituting a relatively small proportion of overall burglaries, there is one particular form we have not yet mentioned that can have a dramatic impact on its victims: distraction burglary. This refers to those cases where the offender somehow tricks their way inside the victim's home. The victims are generally elderly – often very elderly. A common method is for offenders to present themselves as visiting on behalf of some organisation – the water board or gas board, for example – or as being gardeners, repairmen, or in urgent need of help. A combination of politeness (not wishing to appear rude by refusing people entry) and/or a failure to recognise the importance of asking to see identification enable offenders to gain entry. In a sizeable proportion of cases (perhaps as many as two-fifths) even when the offender is refused entry they will then simply walk into the house. Although there has been relatively little research on the impact of such crimes, a study by Thornton *et al.* (2003) found:

- Higher reported levels of post-traumatic stress disorder scores among victims of distraction burglary than among those who had successfully repelled such callers.

- Forty per cent of victims and repellers reported that the incident had had a significant impact on their quality of life.

- Participants in the research reported greater concern over national and local crime than those interviewed for the British Crime Survey (Kershaw *et al.*, 2001). Victims reported the greatest fear of crime where the offender gained entry uninvited.

Burglars on burglary

As Mawby (2001) notes, there has been quite a lot of research on burglary victims, and on the ways in which people are affected by such offences, but comparatively little work on offenders. The bulk of work on offenders has tended to use samples of people convicted for burglary. It is possible that such groups are unrepresentative of burglars in general – they may simply be those who are least good at it. Nevertheless, the small number of studies that have been undertaken do provide a number of useful findings about the nature of such offending:

- Interview-based research by Wright and Decker (1994) found that much burglary was prompted by financial need, with many offenders needing

Distraction burglary – a crime often targeting the elderly and disabled, and which may have a dramatic impact on its victims.

money to pay for alcohol and drugs, or simply to cope with the levels of debt they are in. Although this appears consistent with rational choice theory, and particularly with the idea of 'bounded rationality', Wright and Decker nevertheless argue that such approaches pay insufficient attention to the emotional aspect of offending and how this affects the offender's decision-making processes. Recent research by Hearnden and Magill (2004) on 82 burglars found that the most common reasons given for committing their first and their most recent burglary were: the influence of friends; to fund drug use; and boredom.

- There is a division between those burglars who plan their activities by watching potential targets before breaking in, and those who are more opportunistic in their activities (Maguire, 1982; Nee and Taylor, 1988). Bennett and Wright (1984: 47) distinguish between two types of 'planned offence':

> In the first, there is no time gap between the decision to offend and the selection of the target. This type of offence might occur when an offender discovers a target by chance, but, instead of committing the offence there and then, returns later. Similarly, an offender might be 'tipped off' about a desirable target. In this case, a time gap will occur between

selection of the target and the offence, even if he travels to the chosen site almost immediately. In the second, there is a time gap between the decision to offend and the selection of a target. Offences of this type occur when the decision to offend is made independently of the discovery of a target. It differs from the search in that the offence is not committed immediately upon locating a suitable place to burgle.

- There also seems to be a division between those who 'specialise' in burglary (Farrington and Lambert, 1994) and those that burgle as part of a broad repertoire of offending activity (Maguire, 1982).

- 'External cues' are important in decision-making. The cues include the nature and size of the house, the presence or absence of people, cars and dogs, as well as security devices such as alarms. According to Cromwell *et al.* (1991) three main sets of clues include: *surveillability* (the extent to which the site is overseen); *occupancy* (whether there are any signals that indicate the site is occupied); and, *accessibility* (how easy it is likely to be to gain entry).

- Despite fears about night-time burglary, most such offences are committed during daylight hours when homes are most likely to be empty.

- The Kirkholt project (see Chapter 24) found that the majority of offenders were male and lived in council accommodation (95%) and that almost three-quarters were unemployed (Forrester *et al.*, 1988).

- Mawby (2001) found that the vast majority of his sample of burglars (though admittedly from Plymouth which does not have a large black population) were white (97%) and relatively young (one-quarter were aged under 20), (see also Farrington and Lambert, 1994).

- Burglary rates tend to be highest where burglars live and there is considerable evidence to suggest that offenders do not travel great distances to commit offences (Baldwin and Bottoms, 1976; Wiles and Costello, 2000) though Mawby (1979) questioned the extent to which evidence from local burglary rates could be taken as an indicator that the burglars were necessarily local (see also Maguire, 1982).

Crimes against retail and manufacturing premises

The bulk of writing about crime victims focuses on the experiences of individuals. Of course, it is not just individual citizens who are victimized and, indeed, when considering property crime there is an argument for paying particular attention to crimes against businesses. The difficulty, however, is that data on such crime is not collected regularly, though it may become more regular in the future. The most up-to-date information is that contained in the second sweep of the Home Office's 'commercial victimization survey' (Shury *et al.*, 2005). The survey was based on a large-scale telephone survey of over 6,500 manufacturing and retail premises with 250 employees or fewer, a follow-up qualitative survey of 40 establishments which had experienced a range of crimes, and a postal survey of head offices.

Perhaps predictably, levels of reported victimization were high. Three-quarters of all retailers and a half of all manufacturers had experienced at least one crime in the previous year. Property crime was of course much more prevalent than violent crime, though over one-fifth of all retailers had experienced some form of violent crime (see Table 20.4).

In general terms it tended to be the larger retailers and larger manufacturers that were most likely to have been victimized – across almost all crime types (being offered stolen goods being the exception for retailers). The larger retailers and individual parts of chain stores were more likely to experience:

- theft at the premises;
- fraud by employees or outsiders;
- theft of vehicles;
- burglary;
- violent crime.

Most retailers that experienced crime in the previous year had experienced more than one crime type. Almost one-quarter had experienced at least four different crime types (as defined in Table 20.4). Such results are largely in line with previous research. Thus, for example, a study by Johnston *et al.* (1994) looking at commercial burglary on industrial estates found that approximately one-third of all units had been burgled in the preceding two years and a quarter had experienced attempted burglary. Similarly, an assessment by Tilley (1993) also

Table 20.4	Victimization rates in retail and manufacturing premises, 2005	
	Retail premises	**Manufacturing premises**
Any crime	74	53
Any property crime	70	48
Theft by customers	43	3
Vandalism	23	16
Theft by persons unknown	20	10
Fraud by outsiders	18	8
Theft by employees	10	5
Theft by outsiders	9	7
Theft from vehicles	8	11
Fraud by employees	4	2
Theft of vehicles	3	4
Any burglary	25	22
Attempted burglary	17	14
Burglary	16	14
Any violent crime	23	7
Threat, assaults, intimidation	20	6
Robbery or attempted robbery	6	2
Being offered stolen goods	10	6

Source: Shury *et al.* (2005).

found burglary to be commonly experienced by small businesses. Such experiences are by no means confined to the UK, although the international crime survey has recorded rates of commercial burglary ranging from 14% in Italy to 40% in the Netherlands (quoted in Mawby, 2001).

As with crime generally, there are some victims who suffer repeated victimization and therefore are disproportionately affected by crime. Repeat victimization was most common in relation to non-vehicle theft, fraud by outsiders, and threats and assaults. According to the survey, those retailers who suffered theft by customers – and over two-fifths did – were highly likely to do so frequently. Almost six in ten such victims experienced at least six thefts of this type. A similar pattern was visible in manufacturing premises. Thus, for example, almost one-quarter (23%) of victims of theft by employees among manufacturers had suffered six or more incidents in the

previous year. Added together, these incidents accounted for 70% of all employee thefts among the manufacturers responding to the survey.

What of the consequences of commercial burglary? A study by Redshaw and Mawby (1996) identified a number of significant areas of impact among victims:

- One-quarter (26%) identified having to meet the cost of damage caused to their premises as a major factor.
- Twenty-two per cent said that their insurance didn't cover all the costs of stolen items.
- A similar proportion (21%) identified loss of business as one of the primary impacts.
- One-fifth (20%) identified the increasing cost of insurance premiums as a consequence of burglary.
- Seven per cent said that they had to invest in extra security as a result of victimization.

Research by Shury *et al.* (2005) reinforces this view of the costs borne by commercial enterprises suffering criminal victimization. Table 20.5 outlines the extent of these costs for the six most frequently reported types of offence in the Home Office's commercial victimization survey.

Car crime

As was illustrated in Figure 20.10 above, vehicle-related theft represents a substantial proportion of all property crime – probably in the region of one fifth. And yet, crimes involving motor vehicles seem far from a political or a criminological priority. Why? Corbett (2003) suggests that the primary reason is our value system: we are practically and emotionally dependent on the car and consequently reluctant to admit, let alone embrace, the problems associated with its use. Much car crime is not perceived as *real* crime. And yet, as we will see, the social costs are significant. Corbett (2003) identifies five main reasons why car crime is not treated as seriously as many other forms of crime:

- *The legal view* – Many of the consequences of illegal behaviour in cars is not intended, has no premeditation and does not involve personal gain. Such behaviour is therefore different from some other illegal acts.

- *The critical criminological view* – The state encourages use of the car, is often unwilling to punish the middle classes and tends, therefore, to prioritise 'theft of and from vehicles' over other forms of car crime.

- *The role of gender* – Traffic laws were conceived by men, men dominate car usage and it is men who appear to enjoy the risks and thrills associated with high speeds on the roads. In this manner masculinity may be linked to the general downplaying of car crime.

- *Neoliberalism* – The Thatcher governments of the 1980s sought to stimulate private transport and, arguably, reinforced existing cultural views that drivers should not be subject to stringent policing.

- *The power of the electorate* – There is a strong body of opinion, backed by some of the tabloid press, which regularly rails against traffic policing and can be heard arguing that 'surely the police have better things to do?' Given the power of the motoring lobby, politicians are often reluctant to attempt to impose tougher sanctions.

Injuries and deaths on the road

The bare facts of traffic injuries and deaths are quite startling. In 2005 in Britain:

- A total of 3,201 people were killed.
- The number seriously injured was 28,954 (7% lower than in 2004).
- Total casualties were 271,017 (3% lower than in 2004).
- Of those killed, 141 were children. The total number of children killed or seriously injured was 3,472.

Table 20.5	Financial cost of the last incident of crime to retailers						
				% of retailers with costs falling in each range			
Offence	Retailers suffering this crime type (%)	Median cost (£)	Maximum cost (£)	Up to £500	£501–£1,000	£1,001–£10,000	£10,000 plus
Theft by customers	43	35	26,000	94	2	3	<1
Vandalism	23	250	250,000	73	13	13	<1
Theft by persons unknown	20	60	150,000	86	6	7	1
Fraud by outsiders	18	100	260,000	81	7	10	2
Attempted burglary	17	100	80,000	81	10	9	<1
Burglary	16	1,350	180,000	33	12	46	8

Source: Shury *et al.* (2003).

Of course, by no means all these incidents involve the commission of a criminal offence – they are 'accidents'. Nevertheless, even though a minority of cases appear to involve some criminal action, the absolute number remains large. Thus, estimates from 2005 suggest that 560 people were killed in incidents involving drink driving (remember, the number of people murdered in the same year was 839). According to Corbett (2003), research suggests that about one-third of road fatalities result from drivers using excessive speed. This, she says, is the equivalent of 75,000 people being injured as a result of someone breaking the law, of whom around 1,100 are killed.

Measuring car crime

This general category of *car crime* covers a range of offences. Corbett (2003: 7) suggests that, in practice, 'no correct way exists of defining what should be deemed "criminal" or "crime" in a motoring sphere, but ... the boundaries [can be] drawn in line with Sutherland's view that crimes are acts causing social harms or injuries.' In practice, as we have already noted, official discussion of car crime tends to reduce it largely to 'theft of and from a vehicle'. Even so this is the largest 'single' element of recorded crime and is estimated to cost over £3.5 billion every year (Corbett, 2003). Car-related theft offences are classified rather differently depending on which data series is being used (recorded crime statistics or the BCS). The major categories of car-related theft are:

Police recorded crime:

- *Thefts and attempted thefts of vehicles* – where the intention is to permanently deprive the owner of the vehicle.

- *Unauthorised taking of a vehicle* – where there is no evidence that there was any intention of permanently depriving the owner of the vehicle. Joyriding would be an example.

- *Aggravated vehicle taking* – where the stolen vehicle is driven dangerously, damaged or has caused an accident.

- *Thefts and attempted thefts from a vehicle* – in which there is actual or attempted theft of property in the vehicle.

- *Vehicle interference* – including attempts to drive away with a car, but where there is no intention to permanently deprive the owner.

British Crime Survey:

- *Thefts of vehicles* – where a vehicle and its contents are stolen.

- *Thefts from vehicles* – where parts from a vehicle are stolen or the contents are stolen.

- *Attempted thefts of and from vehicles* – where someone has attempted to do one of the above.

Vehicle-related theft has followed a roughly similar pattern to other types of crime over the past two decades or so (see Figure 20.14). All forms of vehicle-related theft rose during the 1980s, reached

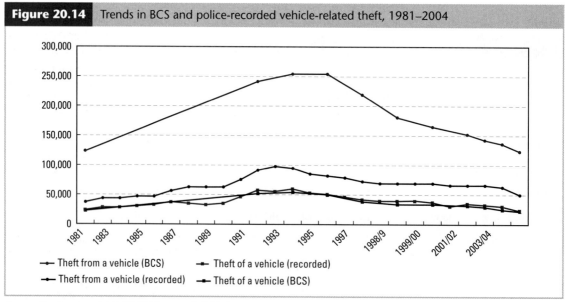

Figure 20.14 Trends in BCS and police-recorded vehicle-related theft, 1981–2004

Legend:
- Theft from a vehicle (BCS)
- Theft of a vehicle (recorded)
- Theft from a vehicle (recorded)
- Theft of a vehicle (BCS)

Source: Kershaw *et al.* (2001); Walker *et al.* (2006).

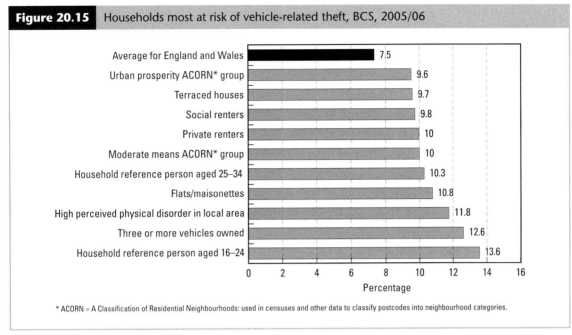

Figure 20.15   Households most at risk of vehicle-related theft, BCS, 2005/06

* ACORN = A Classification of Residential Neighbourhoods: used in censuses and other data to classify postcodes into neighbourhood categories.

Source: Walker *et al.* (2006).

a peak somewhere between 1990 and 1995 and have generally declined since. This is despite the fact that the number of vehicles on the roads has increased by 12%.

According to the most recent BCS, approximately 7.5% of all vehicle-owing households experienced some form of vehicle-related crime in the course of the last year (including vandalism). However, as with all other forms of crime, the risks of victimization are not evenly distributed. Thus, the households most at risk of such crime were those in which what the BCS calls the 'household reference person' (in effect the head of household) was aged between 16 and 24. Almost 14% of these households had experienced vehicle-related crime in the previous year. The number of cars owned by household was also related to likelihood of victimization – predictably, the more vehicles owned, the more likely the household is to have been victimized (see Figure 20.15).

A helpful classification of types of vehicle theft is provided by Clarke and Harris (1992), building on a model developed by Challinger. This involves a threefold distinction between thefts for recreation, for transport, and for financial gain. Theft for recreational purposes includes such things as joyriding, whereas transport-related thefts are where cars are stolen to complete a journey or for use in another crime. Finally, thefts for property include 'stripping' (stealing equipment), 'chopping' (where cars are broken up for re-use) and insurance frauds. They also use Challinger's distinction between what he calls 'opportunity takers' (those simply exploiting a situation) and 'opportunity makers' who actively seek out and create circumstances in which theft can occur. The latter (see Figure 20.16) are found in increasing proportions as one progresses through the three main categories of theft.

Joyriding

Generally prosecuted – when it is prosecuted – as vehicle theft ('Taking WithOut Consent' or sometimes TWOC-ing) or aggravated vehicle theft if it involves a crash causing damage or injury, joyriding is one of the few terms that captures an important emotional element of the offence it describes. For many of the young men – and it is generally young men (Buckley and Young, 1996) – who are involved in this type of behaviour, its essence is to be found in the excitement, thrill and display involved. This is not to deny the seriousness of the offence and the consequences it may engender, merely to recognise that the stealing of cars for the purpose of driving at high speeds, often in front of 'spectators' is, for some, an undoubtedly exciting activity. Research on joyriders in West Belfast led McCullough *et al.* (1990: 11) to describe the protagonists as 'expert show-offs'. One respondent from Kellett and Gross's (2006: 47) study described the feeling in the following way:

... and then when I was getting ready, if I had a screwdriver in me hand and that yeh, it were that weird yeh, I used to have to feel like I used to have to go to the toilet, you know with the rush and that, and if I was going to take a car and that, I had to go for ... I had to go for like a piss and that after ... I used to get really excited and that (...) I used to get dead excited, then ... and as we were getting close to it man (phew) you know what I mean, and then we'd see a car and that, and that's it (...) put some screwdrivers in the door, sweating and that, you know what I mean, and used to get that much of an adrenaline rush, when I'd be sitting at traffic lights, when I'd just took a car and be sat at lights. Me foot was like that [demonstrates] shaking on the clutch, you know what I mean?

A significant component of much joyriding concerns 'performance driving' – driving a car to its limits in terms of speed, manoeuvrability and road holding. Light *et al.* (1993: 30) suggest that, as well as the usual driving skills, 'use is also made of some motor sport techniques, the most common being to spin the car through an angle of 180 degrees so that it ends up facing and can be driven off in the opposite direction.' In terms of 'joyriding careers' Light *et al.* (1993) found that the majority of car

Emergency services deal with the aftermath of a joy-riding episode. Although car-related offences account for a very substantial proportion of overall crime, it is a subject that has been largely ignored by criminologists.

thieves began such offending around the age of 14 or 15, and then usually in the company of more experienced offenders. Their 'apprenticeship' rarely lasted more than six to 12 months as they quickly became competent. Moreover, as they grew used to it and material rewards were revealed, some would go on to have a more 'professional' relationship

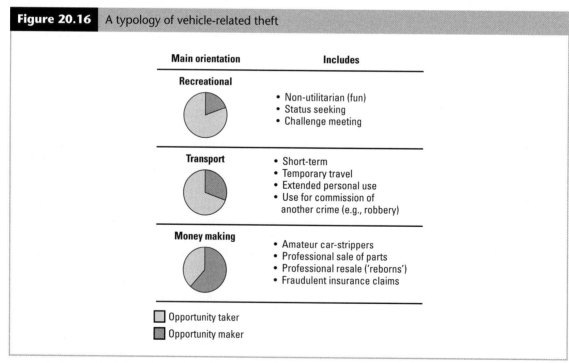

Figure 20.16   A typology of vehicle-related theft

Main orientation	Includes
Recreational	• Non-utilitarian (fun) • Status seeking • Challenge meeting
Transport	• Short-term • Temporary travel • Extended personal use • Use for commission of another crime (e.g., robbery)
Money making	• Amateur car-strippers • Professional sale of parts • Professional resale ('reborns') • Fraudulent insurance claims

☐ Opportunity taker
■ Opportunity maker

Source: Clarke and Harris (1992).

with car theft. Nearly half of Light *et al.*'s sample were 'ramraiders or professionals' and 'stripping and ringing cars, and destroying cars for insurance purposes, began as early as age 16' (1993: 45).

Thinking about violent and volume crime

In this chapter we have looked briefly at a variety of different forms of criminal activity – varying from homicide to joyriding. Sticking with these two examples we might note first of all that they appear to have rather little in common – except that they share this general term 'crime'. This points us to one of the fundamental problems facing criminologists and, indeed, facing criminology. Looked at in this manner, its subject matter has relatively little coherence: it happens to focus on those activities that are socially defined as 'criminal'. Not only is it the fact of the very great range of matters that can fall into this category – from graffiti to gun crime – but, as we have repeatedly observed, what we consider to be criminal varies historically and culturally.

And, yet, the difference between homicide and joyriding is not necessarily as great as it may first appear. Joyriding – if it involves dangerous driving in public places – can cause death by reckless driving. Homicides and joyriding may take place when the offender is under the influence of drugs or alcohol. Moreover, we may see patterns in the commission of such offences – say in terms of rises or falls over time, or in the social distribution of offenders and/or victims. Similarly, much research on offenders' 'criminal careers' shows that few are specialists and most are generalists. Drawing, or attempting to draw, hard and fast distinctions between crimes we think of as violent and those that are aimed at property is inherently problematic. Although it is undoubtedly possible, and in some respects sensible, to think and talk about different forms of crime separately, it is equally important not to invest any distinctions with greater importance than they deserve. Thus, in thinking about violent and volume crime there is much to be gained by drawing connections between them, just as there is from remaining aware and analysing the contrasts. At the very least, therefore, there should be sufficient here to interest and intrigue the criminologist.

Review questions

1 What proportion of overall crime is made up of property crime?

2 Who is most at risk from burglary?

3 What have been the main trends in property crime over the last two decades?

4 Should we be concerned about car crime?

Questions for further discussion

1 What are the main problems in defining what is meant by 'violent crime'?

2 In what ways is gender relevant to a discussion of violence?

3 Why does there appear to be so much concern these days about 'serial killers'?

4 How might we explain the differences between the pictures painted by the British Crime Survey and recorded crime statistics in relation to recent trends in violent crime?

5 Thinking about the material you have read in Chapters 5 to 16, which criminological theories do you think are most applicable in attempting to understand violent crime *or* property crime?

6 Why do you think criminologists have paid relatively little attention to car crime?

7 Following the data sources that have been described and used in this chapter, what can you find out about trends in crimes we have not discussed in detail such as arson and shoplifting?

Further reading

Much work on violence tends to focus on particular types of violent crime: homicide; sexual violence/violence against women and so on. There are two sources that provide useful overviews of the general territory however:

Jones, S. (2000) *Understanding Violent Crime*, Buckingham: Open University Press

Levi, M. *et al.* (2007) Violent crime, in *The Oxford Handbook of Criminology*, 4th edn, Oxford: Oxford University Press

In addition, there are many specialist works which are well worth looking at. Among them I would recommend:

Brookman, F. (2005) *Understanding Homicide*, London: Sage

Eisner, M. (2001) Modernization, self-control and lethal violence, *British Journal of Criminology*, 41, 618–638, Oxford: Oxford Journals

Hallsworth, S. (2005) *Street Crime*, Cullompton: Willan

Matthews, R. (2002) *Armed Robbery*, Cullompton: Willan

Thomas, T. (2005) *Sex Crime*, Cullompton: Willan

Among the most useful recent texts on property crime are:

Corbett, C. (2003) *Car Crime*, Cullompton: Willan

Gill, M.L. (2000) *Commercial Robbery: Offenders' perspectives on security and crime prevention*. London: Blackstone Press

Mawby, R. (2001) *Burglary*, Cullompton: Willan

Websites

There is a huge amount of information on violent and volume crime on government websites, notably the Home Office RDS publications site: http://www.homeoffice.gov.uk/rds/pubsintro1.html and the Scottish Executive website: www.scottishexecutive.gov.uk

A large number of research projects were undertaken as part of a Violence Research Programme run by the ESRC. You can find details, data and discussion at: www.esrcsocietytoday.ac.uk/ESRCInfoCentre/research/research_programmes/violence.aspx?ComponentId=9259&SourcePageId=9102

There is a lot of (some variable) material on Paul Leighton's Stop Violence website: http://stopviolence.com/

The Home Office has a vehicle crime website which contains both information and links: www.homeoffice.gov.uk/crime-victims/reducing-crime/vehicle-crime/

The crime reduction website – useful for many types of crime – has a good section on burglary and its prevention: www.crimereduction.gov.uk/toolkits/db00.htm

Chapter outline

Introduction | 474

What are drugs? | 475
Changing official attitudes toward drugs | 477

Who uses drugs? | 480
Trends in drug use | 482
The normalisation debate | 482

Drugs and crime | 484
Drug use causes crime | 485
Crime causes drug use | 486
A common cause? | 486
A reciprocal relationship? | 487
No causal relationship? | 487

Drugs and criminal justice | 488
Drug courts, DTTOs and coerced treatment | 489
Drug testing | 491
Drugs and policing | 493
Lambeth cannabis experiment | 496

Alcohol | 498
Patterns of consumption | 498
Young people and alcohol | 501
Young people, alcohol and moral panic | 503
Binge drinking | 504
Alcohol, crime and criminal justice | 504
The legal situation | 504
Alcohol and crime | 505
Costs of alcohol misuse and alcohol-related crime | 508
Government alcohol policy | 508

Drugs, alcohol and crime | 511
Questions for further discussion | 512
Further reading | 512
Websites | 512

21

Drugs and alcohol

CHAPTER SUMMARY	In this chapter we discuss a range of substances that are controlled under the Misuse of Drugs Act 1971, together with another substance which may be legally purchased and where the only major restrictions concern the age at which it may be consumed – alcohol.

In this chapter we explore:

- the history of the criminalisation of drug use;

- the legal position in relation to drugs and alcohol;

- trends in the use of drugs and arguments relating to the idea of 'normalisation';

- the nature and patterns of consumption of alcohol and their impact;

- the relationship between drugs, alcohol and crime;

- how the criminal justice system operates in relation to substance use, and drug and alcohol-related crime.

Introduction

Illicit drugs are one of our greatest contemporary concerns. However, taking the long sweep of history, this is a fairly recent development. Most of the drugs now criminalised have only been so for something less than a century and in many cases much less than that. Two hundred years ago there was much more concern about alcohol, and drinking was seen as a much more significant threat to individual morals and social well-being.

By contrast, in the nineteenth century, Britain was heavily involved in the international opium trade, in particular between India and China, and fought wars against China in a bid to secure its interest in what was a hugely profitable business.

Drug control gradually became an international issue during the first half of the twentieth century – stimulated in large part by the United States. In the UK at this time drug use was increasingly treated as a medical concern, and the Rolleston Committee report in 1926 recommended that drugs such as heroin continue to be available on prescription. They affirmed that addiction was a disease and that heroin prescription was an appropriate form of medical treatment. It is really the post-Second World War era, and the period since the 1960s more particularly, that has seen the policy of a gradual criminalisation of drugs.

Attitudes toward alcohol have been somewhat different. Drink was the focus of much moral reform activity in the nineteenth century. The probation service, for example, has its historic origins in the Church of England Temperance Society, and worries about the deleterious effects of alcohol framed much work with offenders as well as the destitute and out of work during this period. The only major attempt at complete restriction occurred in the United States in the prohibition era between 1920 and 1933. Although there is some evidence that alcohol consumption dropped during the early years of prohibition, eventually it began to increase (see Figure 21.1) and its production and sale became closely associated with 'organised crime' (see Chapter 19).

One of the reasons that criminologists are interested in drugs and alcohol is the possibility of a link between their consumption and crime. So far as alcohol is concerned it is the possibility that alcohol consumption may be associated with criminal activity – particularly violent crime – that tends to be the primary issue. In relation to drugs there are also concerns that usage may be linked with criminality, particularly acquisitive crime, but there are also the problems of supply and possession. There are ongoing debates about the most appropriate and effective ways to respond to the 'drugs problem' and, as we will see, there is a tension between law enforcement models that stress the importance of investigation, detection and punishment and medically-oriented models which place greater stress on treatment and harm reduction.

| **Figure 21.1** | Per capita consumption of alcoholic beverages (gallons of pure alcohol per year), United States, 1910–1929 |

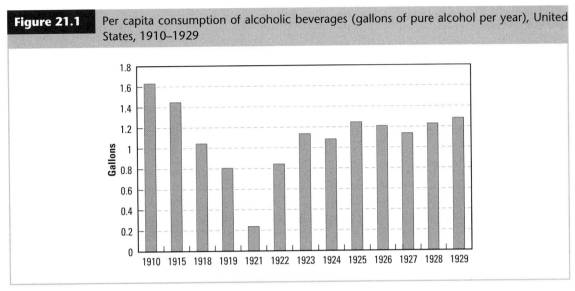

Source: Warburton (1932)

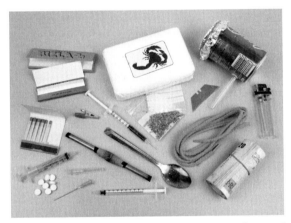

Items and equipment associated with various forms of drug use.

What are drugs?

In the main we can distinguish two main ways of categorising drugs: a *pharmacological* approach and a *legal* approach. Pharmacology divides drugs into:

- *Stimulants* – ('Uppers') which activate the nervous system (crack, cocaine and amphetamines).

- *Depressants* – ('Downers') which, on the contrary, depress the nervous system and are generally used to reduce anxiety and induce sleep (barbiturates and benzodiazepines).

- *Analgesics* – Which are mainly used in pain relief (opium, morphine, heroin).

- *Hallucinogens* – Which tend to alter perceptions and emotions (LSD, magic mushrooms and ecstasy).

One substance missing from the above list is cannabis. This is sometimes, arguably somewhat inaccurately, classified as an hallucinogen, but it doesn't fit straightforwardly into the pharmacological categorisation.

By contrast, the legal classification in England and Wales divides illicit drugs into three categories or 'Classes' (A, B and C) according to their perceived harmfulness. The current classification – with Class A being those drugs perceived to represent the greatest harm – is shown in Table 21.1.

The purpose of a legal classification is to identify, and to distinguish among, 'illicit' drugs. Such drugs are effectively those prohibited under the Misuse of Drugs Act 1971. 'Prohibition' in this sense covers such activities as production, supply, importation and exportation, possession and cultivation. It does not prohibit consumption. The offences defined by this Act include possession of a controlled drug, possession with intent to supply, the production, cultivation and manufacture of a controlled drug, and allowing premises to be used for the consumption, production and supply of a controlled drug. Within the UK, the most severe legal sanctions are placed on those substances that are seen to be the most harmful, though recent legislative change (the Criminal Justice Act 2003) has substantially increased the penalties relating to Class C drugs.

Table 21.1	The legal classification of illicit drugs
Class A	Cocaine, crack (a form of cocaine), ecstasy, heroin, LSD, methadone, methamphetamine ('crystal meth'), magic mushrooms containing ester of psilocin and any Class B drug which is injected.
Class B	Amphetamines (not methamphetamine), barbiturates, and codeine.
Class C	Cannabis (in resin, oil or herbal form), anabolic steroids and minor tranquillisers.

Source: Hough and Roberts (2004).

The basis of current drugs law was reviewed by the *Independent Inquiry into the Misuse of Drugs Act 1977* (The Police Foundation, 2000). The inquiry upheld the existing role of harmfulness which it defined in terms of:

- acute (i.e. immediate) physical harm, including risk of overdose;
- physical harm from chronic (i.e. longer-term) use;
- the ease with which drug may be injected;
- the likelihood of the drug leading to dependence and addiction;
- physical withdrawal symptoms;
- psychological withdrawal symptoms;
- the risk of social harm through intoxication;
- the risk of causing other social problems;
- the risk of medical costs arising.

This framework was applied to illicit drugs and to alcohol and tobacco which were included in order to 'put things in perspective' (The Police Foundation, 2000: 46). The inquiry's conclusions can be seen in Table 21.2.

A number of potentially important points arise from this work. First, alcohol was assessed as being more harmful than tobacco and cannabis and was classified alongside heroin and cocaine which are considered to be the most harmful of the illicit drugs. Second, another relatively freely available substance, tobacco, was assessed as being sufficiently harmful to require classification as Class B – above cannabis, for example. Such findings raise important questions about our attitudes toward different substances, our assessment of different social harms, and about the policies that might be adopted in relation to the management of these problems.

More recently, work by Nutt *et al.* (2007) has cast doubt on the current threefold classification of drugs. The authors assessed various substances in relation to three types of harm – physical, dependence, and social – and then ranked them accordingly. The authors concluded that if a three-category classification were to be retained then, as with the Police Foundation report, alcohol would be classed as A and cannabis as C. However, their more general argument is that the differences in harms between different substances are much more finely graded (see Figure 21.2).

Table 21.2	Harmfulness of illicit drugs, alcohol and tobacco	
Class A	**Class B**	**Class C**
Cocaine	Amphetamines (non-injectable)	Cannabinol and cannabinol derivatives
Heroin	Barbiturates	Benzodiazepines
Methadone	Buprenorphine	Cannabis
Other opiates in pure form	Codeine	
Amphetamines (injectable)	Ecstasy and ecstasy-type drugs	
Alcohol	LSD	
	Tobacco	

Source: The Police Foundation (2000).

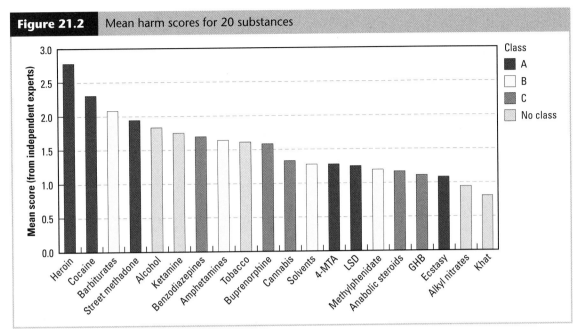

Figure 21.2 Mean harm scores for 20 substances

Source: Nutt *et al.* (2007).

Changing official attitudes toward drugs

In the opening chapter of this book we observed how those things we consider to be 'criminal' vary hugely according to time and place. One of the clearest examples of this simple point is to be found in relation to drugs and drug use. For the bulk of human history those drugs we now classify and criminalise have been neither illegal nor morally condemned (assuming they were known about). Up to the nineteenth century opium-based products were fairly widely available as were items utilising hashish and cannabis. In the eighteenth and nineteenth centuries there was a variety of opium-based products on sale for use as 'baby quieteners' (Booth, 1996).

Such acceptance began to change toward the end of the nineteenth century and moral and legal condemnation grew throughout the twentieth century. This coincided initially with a process of *medicalisation* in which professionals and specialists gradually gained control over how, for example, opiate use would be viewed and, if necessary, treated. Beginning with the Arsenic Act 1851, legislation to restrict access to drugs was implemented in the second half of the nineteenth century. In 1868 the Pharmacy Act gave pharmacists a monopoly over the distribution of opium and morphine derivatives – legislation that is generally considered a landmark in the development of legal control. The 1920 Dangerous Drugs Act permitted doctors to prescribe such drugs for medical treatment. Soon after, the Rolleston Committee made a series of recommendations which strengthened the grip of the medical profession on the management of drug use.

A bottle of laudanum, one of a number of opium-based patent medicines in the nineteenth century – prescribed for a wide range of ailments. Samuel Taylor Coleridge, John Keats and Charles Dickens were amongst those reputed to be addicted to it.

Some major drug policy developments

1800	Napoleon bans cannabis use among occupying French troops in Egypt arguing that 'habitual drinkers and smokers of this plant lose their reason and are victims of violent delirium'.
1858	The Poisons Act in Britain regulates the supply of poisonous substances. Forms the basis for later drugs prohibition.
1868	The Pharmacy Act.
1906	Amendment to the UK Pharmacy Act regulates the supply of opium.
1910	British end India–China opium trade.
1912	MDMA first synthesised by Merck Pharmaceuticals.
1914	Harrison Act limits sale of opium and cocaine (USA).
1916	Defence of the Realm Act (UK) introduces new regulations to limit the sale and possession of cocaine and opium.
1920	Passage of the Dangerous Drugs Act (first formal drugs legislation in the UK). New controls on tincture of cannabis, and outright ban on cocaine following stories of 'crazed soldiers'.
1926	Rolleston Committee emphasises addiction in understanding and responding to drug use; recommends that prescription of heroin and morphine be permitted for the cure of addiction by gradual withdrawal and for incurable addicts (unlike the USA which was still taking a largely punitive line).
1928	Amendment to the Dangerous Drugs Act introduces the offence of the possession of cannabis.
1938	Lysergic Acid Diethylamide (LSD) first synthesised in Switzerland.
1942	Methadone patented (Germany). From 1947 it is used in the US as a low cost painkiller.
1953	Opium Protocol (New York) starts process of consolidation of international agreements.
1961	Single Convention on Narcotic Drugs.
1961	Brain Report reinforces the findings of the Rolleston Committee.
1963	Methadone maintenance treatment pioneered in the US.
1964	Dangerous Drugs Act. Introduces schema for classifying drugs which, though amended, is still in force today. Creates new offence of cultivation of cannabis.
1966	Drugs (Prevention of Misuse) Act Modification Order 1966 prohibits LSD.
1971	President Nixon launches the American 'War on Drugs'. Misuse of Drugs Act (UK).
1977	Amendment to the Misuse of Drugs Act 1971 to include MDMA (Ecstasy) as a Class A drug.
1984	Launch of 'Just Say No' movement in the USA.
1995	Publication of *Tackling Drugs Together*.
1998	Appointment of first UK 'drugs tsar', Keith Hellawell; publication of *Tackling Drugs to Build a Better Britain*; Crime and Disorder Act introduces DTTOs.
2000	Publication of Police Foundation Report on the Misuse of Drugs Act 1971 (the 'Runciman Report').
2001–02	Lambeth cannabis experiment.
2002	UK reclassifies cannabis to Class C.
2006	Ketamine made illegal following a recommendation from the Advisory Council on the Misuse of Drugs.

Sources: Police Foundation Commission (2000) and website of Transform (http: //www.tdpf.org.uk/Policy_Timeline.htm).

It was at this stage that a shift began away from medicalised control and toward the criminalisation of drug use though, as Bennett and Holloway (2005: 21) argue, 'for most of the twentieth century drug use was viewed as both a medical and a criminal problem'. Nonetheless the second half of the century saw a distinct shift towards a criminal justice-led approach and this was partly a response to evidence of an escalating problem. First, the number of registered addicts began to show signs of increase. Second, there was also evidence that cannabis use was on the increase as was the use of amphetamines during the 1960s. In response, two new pieces of legislation were introduced in 1964 which restricted the cultivation of cannabis and criminalised the possession of amphetamines. A further raft of new laws in 1967 restricted GPs' prescribing practices – particularly the prescribing of heroin – and also established the 'clinic system' in which drug dependency units were set up. Crucially, however, much of this legislation was overtaken by the Misuse of Drugs Act 1971 – the Act that remains the main piece of British legislation in this area.

According to Bennett and Holloway (2005), three general phases in drugs policy are visible since the 1980s: supply reduction in the 1980s; demand reduction in the mid- to late-1990s and, more recently, harm reduction (though, as we will see, the reality is arguably more complex than this):

● *Supply reduction* – Involving measures to: reduce supply from abroad; increase deterrents and domestic controls and develop preventative measures.

● *Demand reduction* – By the mid-1990s the focus had begun to shift toward attempts to reduce demand through supporting young people to resist drug use, and to enable those with drug problems to overcome them.

● *Harm reduction* – Popular prior to the 1980s, harm reduction has recently come back into favour, particularly in relation to those elements of the population most at risk of contracting HIV or hepatitis B.

It is not possible to draw hard and fast distinctions between such approaches in terms of the times they were prominent in government policy toward drugs. As Bennett and Holloway's outline implies, elements of each of these approaches have been visible during the past 20–30 years of government policy, albeit to differing degrees. Moreover, one of the prominent discourses for the whole period, particularly in the international arena, has been the enforcement-focused language and tactics of the so-called 'war on drugs'. Announced by President Nixon in the 1960s, and renewed by President Reagan in the 1980s, the rhetoric of American governments since that time – and a substantial element of policy and practice also – has involved attempts to control drugs through enforcement initiatives.

In Britain there has been a succession of drugs *strategies* which have set out the government's approach to tackling drugs. The initial document, *Tackling Drug Misuse*, published in 1985, outlined a combination of enforcement, prevention and treatment (South, 2002). Subsequent strategy documents in 1995, *Tackling Drugs Together*, and in 1998, *Tackling Drugs to Build a Better Britain*, have been fairly broad-based in their approach to prevention, although government expenditure has continued to give priority to criminal justice-based approaches to drugs-abuse prevention (see also South, 2007 for a discussion of this shift). The one approach to drugs that has received very little official consideration in recent times is 'legalisation'. Although, as we will see below, there have been brief experiments in dealing with cannabis offences informally, the idea of controlling drugs as we control other substances such as alcohol has tended not to be treated as a matter for serious debate.

Should drugs be legalised?

Much of this chapter focuses on some of the harms associated with the use or possession of illicit drugs. There is one strand of thought which suggests that a more effective response to the problems posed than policing and punishment is legalisation. What are the arguments in favour?

1 That the current laws appear not to be working – the first laws to prohibit drugs were introduced almost a century ago. Some estimates suggest that illegal drug use has increased by at least 300% in the last 40 years, hardly an overwhelming success.

2 The trade in illicit drugs creates hugely lucrative opportunities for criminals, and creates markets characterised by violence. Estimates suggest the drug market may be worth up to £300 billion a year.

3 Drug users often have to resort to crime in order to support their habits. Government estimates suggest over half of robberies, up to three-quarters of burglaries and the vast majority of street prostitution is drug-related.

▶

4 Keeping drug use illegal increases the risks of harm associated with such practices.

5 The global 'war on drugs' has 'fuelled corruption and conflict, contributing to political and economic instability all over the world'.

It would be more effective, campaigners argue, to seek to regulate drug use through prescription from doctors and licensed retailing through pharmacy sales and off-licences.

Source: Transform (Drug Policy Foundation) at: http://www.tdpf.org.uk/Transform_leaflet.pdf

Who uses drugs?

As with crime, the nature of measurement is far from straightforward. How do we know who uses drugs and when? What forms of measurement can we use? The most frequently-used current method is the self-report survey (see Chapter 35). These generally involve sample surveys of either the population or some sub-sample of it. Respondents are then asked a series of questions covering such things as their knowledge of drugs, their experience of taking drugs, and the nature and frequency of their use (if relevant). The largest domestic survey to do this is the British Crime Survey which, since 1994, has had a self-report element focusing on illicit drug use. The Scottish Executive also publishes regular results from self-report surveys.

All surveys show cannabis to be the most commonly-used drug. In terms of *who* takes drugs, the BCS shows that usage is clearly age-related, certainly as far as cannabis is concerned.

The most recent BCS found that one-quarter of 16–24 year-olds reported having used an illegal drug in the last year and eight per cent had used a Class A drug (see Figure 21.4).

Figure 21.5 shows the general pattern of drug use among 16–59 year-olds as reported to the BCS.

The broader results from the most recent BCS are as follows (Roe and Man, 2006).

● Approximately 35 per cent of 16–59 year-olds have used one or more illicit drugs in their lifetime; ten per cent have done so in the last year and six per cent in the last month.

● Cannabis is the most frequently-used drug – just under nine per cent of 16–59 year-olds have used this in the past year; cocaine is the next most frequently-used drug.

● Between 1998 and 2005/06 the use of any illicit drug in the past year decreased, reflecting a decline in cannabis use.

● Class A drug use increased during the same period, due primarily to the increase in use of cocaine powder.

● Approximately 45 per cent of 16–24 year-olds have used one or more illicit drugs in their lifetime, and a quarter have done so in the past year.

● Overall drug use by young people declined between 1998 and 2005/06 though Class A drug use remained stable.

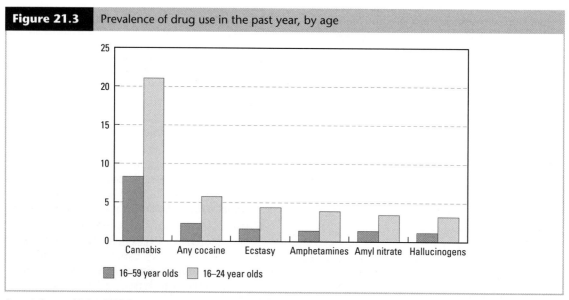

Figure 21.3 Prevalence of drug use in the past year, by age

■ 16–59 year olds   □ 16–24 year olds

Source: Roe and Man (2006).

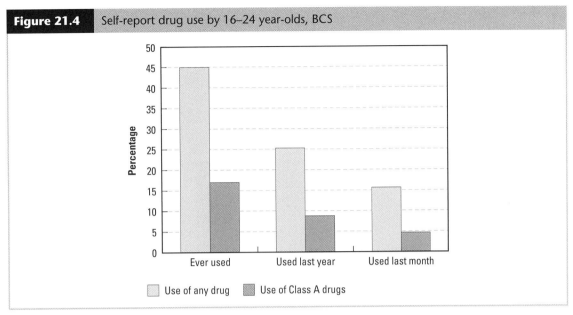

Figure 21.4   Self-report drug use by 16–24 year-olds, BCS

Source: Roe and Man (2006).

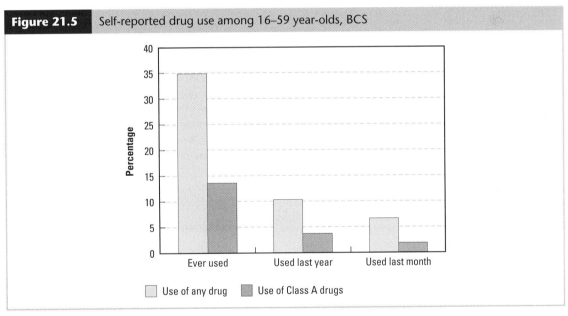

Figure 21.5   Self-reported drug use among 16–59 year-olds, BCS

Source: Roe and Man (2006).

Data on drug use are also available from a large survey of schoolchildren conducted by the National Centre for Social Research and the National Foundation for Educational Research. The 2006 survey found that under one-fifth (17%) of 11–15 year-old respondents had used at least one illicit drug in the past year (down two per cent on 2005) and that four per cent had used Class A drugs during this period (NFER, 2007). There are also a number of more specific surveys such as the Youth Lifestyles Survey (YLS) which has been conducted on two occasions by the Home Office. Most forms of drug use tend to decrease with age. Males are more likely to use than females (see Figure 21.6).

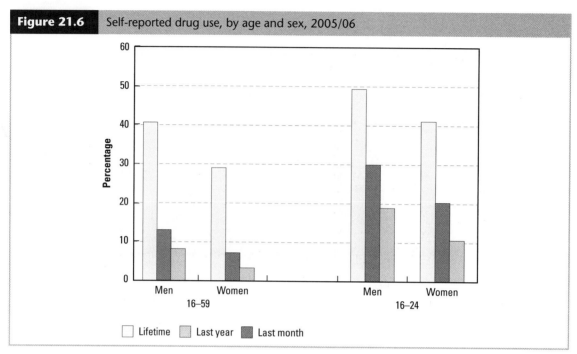

Figure 21.6   Self-reported drug use, by age and sex, 2005/06

Source: Roe and Man (2006).

Given that some popular representations link certain forms of drug use with particular ethnic groups, the differential rates of usage according to ethnicity are of interest. The 2000 BCS found that one-third (34%) of white respondents reported having used an illicit drug at some point in their lives compared with 28 per cent of black respondents, 15 per cent of Indian respondents and 10 per cent of Bangladeshis.

How does this compare with the situation in other countries? According to a report by the UK Drugs Police Commission (Reuter and Stevens, 2007), the UK has high rates of drug use. Thus, estimated lifetime prevalence of cannabis use is higher in England and Wales than in any other country in Europe (except France), though lower than the USA and Australia (see Figure 21.7). Two other measures – the prevalence of 'problem drug use' and the rate of acute drug-related deaths – are both lower than those in America but higher than in the rest of Europe.

Trends in drug use

The proportion of the adult population using drugs increased during the late 1980s through to the mid- to late-1990s, but has subsequently remained fairly stable, with some evidence of decline. Data from the BCS suggest that in the period since 1998 there

has been some increase in the use of cocaine, but there has been decreasing use of cannabis, amphetamines, hallucinogens/LSD, and methadone. Use of heroin, crack cocaine, steroids and tranquillisers appears to have been relatively stable (see Figure 21.8). Evidence increasingly suggests something of a shift toward heroin and cocaine use by problem drug users – the proportion of arrestees testing positive for cocaine, for example, increased from 15 per cent to 23 per cent between 1999 and 2001 (Bennett and Holloway, 2005).

The normalisation debate

In the late 1980s and into the 1990s there appeared to be a steady rise in drug use, particularly among young people, although prevalence levels have stabilised in recent years. Not only did youthful drug use increase, but reported levels were generally higher in the UK than in many other European countries. In an attempt to understand what has been happening in the UK, the work of Howard Parker and colleagues has been enormously influential. Beginning in the early-1990s a series of primarily school-based surveys of youthful drug use conducted in the North-West of England found comparatively high and increasing levels of drug use among teenagers. By the time the majority of their respondents had reached 16 years of age they

Figure 21.7   Prevalence of last year drug use reported by adults, by country

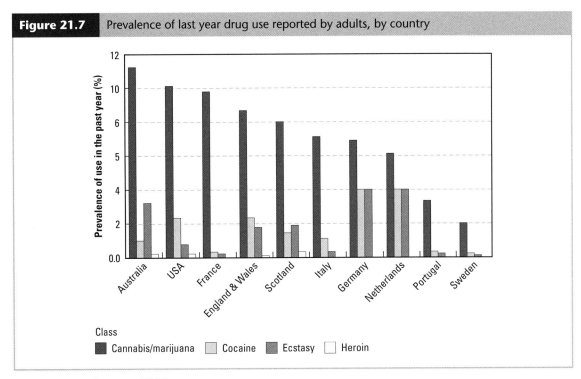

Source: Reuter and Stevens (2007).

Figure 21.8   Self-reported drug use by 16–24 year-olds, by drug type, 1996–2005/06

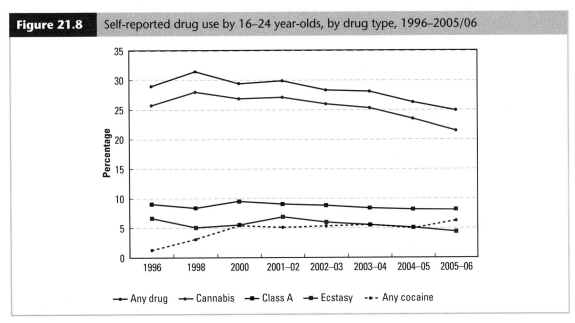

Source: Roe and Man (2006).

reported a lifetime drug use prevalence of 51 per cent (Parker *et al.*, 1995; 1998). This led the authors to argue that drug use among young people was undergoing a process of 'normalisation'.

What did they mean by this? In its initial formulation, the 'normalisation thesis' argued that 'for many young people taking drugs has become the norm' with predictions that 'over the next few years, and certainly in urban areas, non drug-trying adolescents will be in a minority group' (Parker *et al.*, 1995: 26). This thesis has been criticised (Shiner and Newburn, 1997, 1999; see also Manning, 2007) and has subsequently been somewhat refined. The critique argued that the early formulation of the thesis was too crude. In particular, the thesis was criticised for:

- Relying on 'lifetime' measures of drug use.
- Failing to distinguish between 'poly-drug' use and one-off use.
- Failing to distinguish between current and ex-users.
- Talking about 'drugs' rather than distinguishing between those (few) substances that are used by a substantial number of young people and those substances that are very infrequently used.
- For reading off 'normalcy' too easily from measures of frequency. That is to say, it is perfectly possible to be a very occasional user of a substance without it becoming a 'normalised' and accepted activity – perhaps by deploying *techniques of neutralisation* (see Chapter 9).

Some academics have argued that youthful recreational drug use is so widespread as to have become 'normalised'.

Subsequent versions of the 'normalisation thesis', although never acknowledging this critique, do appear to have been influenced by aspects of it. The revised versions discuss a more limited repertoire of drug usage (generally 'recreational drugs' such as cannabis and some other Class B drugs), use more sophisticated measures of drug prevalence and are clearer about linking the idea of normalisation to cultural attitudes rather than simply to behaviour. This leads the authors to more restrained conclusions, albeit still cast in the language of normalisation, and more recently, for example, Parker *et al.* (2002) have concluded – rather more defensibly – that their data support

'the notion that "sensible" recreational drug use is continuing to be gradually further accommodated into the lifestyles of ordinary young Britons' (for an exploration of 'normal drug use' among adults see Pearson, 2001; and for an extended discussion Simpson *et al.*, 2007).

Drugs and crime

There are a number of ways in which we can think about and classify the negative impact of illicit drugs. For our purposes here we might reasonably distinguish individual from social consequences of drug use.

Individual problems are generally referred to using terms such as *addiction*, *dependence* or *tolerance*. Addiction occurs when there is an increased tolerance for a particular drug, when there are signs of physical or psychological dependence and when there is experience of withdrawal following cessation of use.

Such problem drug use is not evenly spread through society. The General Household Survey (Singleton *et al.*, 2001) found the lifetime prevalence of drug dependence to be about four per cent. By contrast, over one-third (35%) of arrestees have been found to be 'problem drug users', with about two-thirds of such offenders being dependent on heroin (Holloway and Bennett, 2004).

The social problems associated with drugs are varied and include a number of health-related problems (HIV, hepatitis C) and, crucially for our purposes, include criminality (over and above the fact that possession of such drugs is in itself a criminal offence).

Some of the more serious health risks associated with drug use are linked with intravenous injection, particularly where injecting equipment is being shared. The risks include the aforementioned HIV and hepatitis C as well as blood clots, blood poisoning and risk of overdose. Department of Health research found 1 in 27 male and 1 in 34 female injecting-drug users to be HIV-infected (DoH, 2002) and by 2005 almost six per cent of all UK cases of HIV were attributed to injecting drug use (HPA *et al.*, 2006). Hepatitis C infection as a result of injecting drug use rose from fewer than 350 known cases in 1992 to over 9,000 in 2005 (Reuter and Stevens, 2007). Official data show that the number of drug-related deaths increased up until 2000; it then declined somewhat and appears now to be increasing once again (EMCDDA, 2003; Reuter and Stevens, 2007). One London study found the mortality rate for heroin users to be 17 times higher than that for non-heroin users (Hickman *et al.*, 2003).

As has already been alluded to, offenders are more likely than non-offenders to report using drugs:

- Almost three-quarters (73%) of prison inmates report having taken an illicit drug in the 12 months prior to imprisonment (Ramsay, 2003) and 57 per cent have done so in the past month (Boreham *et al.*, 2006).

- Almost half of prison inmates report having used crack or heroin in the same period (Ramsay, 2003).

- Four-fifths (80%) of arrestees at police stations report having used an illicit drug in the past year (Holloway and Bennett, 2004) compared with just over one-tenth of the general population.

- One third (32%) of arrestees report having used heroin in the past year compared with just one per cent of the general population (Holloway and Bennett, 2004); 17 per cent of male arrestees and 22 per cent of female arrestees had used heroin in the past month (Boreham *et al.*, 2006).

What then is the nature of the relationship between drugs and crime? There are basically five main hypotheses that are investigated by researchers:

1 Drug use might cause crime.

2 Crime might cause drug use.

3 Both drug use and crime might have some other common cause.

4 Drug use and crime are reciprocally related.

5 There is no relationship between drug use and crime.

Whilst accepting that the first four hypotheses are not mutually exclusive (Hough, 1996), let us look at each briefly in turn.

Drug use causes crime

Bean (2004) and McSweeney *et al.* (2007) cite a variety of research evidence that might be used to support the argument that drug use causes crime. For example:

- An American drug-monitoring study in 1998, based in 35 cities, found that between two-fifths and four-fifths of all arrestees tested positive for at least one drug.

- US Bureau of Justice statistics shows that over a fifth of all federal prison inmates and one-third of state prison inmates convicted of robbery, burglary or motor vehicle theft reported being under the influence of drugs at the time of their arrest.

- A study in England between 1997 and 1999 found that over two-thirds of arrestees tested positive for at least one drug (Bennett and Sibbett, 2000).

- The NEW-ADAM survey which is based on drug-testing samples of people who have been arrested, found that almost two-thirds of arrestees tested positive for some type of illicit substance (Bennett *et al.*, 2001) and a quarter (24%) tested positive for opiates.

There are a number of ways in which it is theoretically possible for drug use to lead to crime. The most obvious, and direct, is through the chemical or (psycho)-pharmacological effects of the drug: that is that the properties of particular drugs lead directly to certain forms of offending behaviour. The clearest possibility is violence. Drugs and alcohol might conceivably do this by reducing inhibition, altering an individual's cognitive abilities or perceptions, reducing their attention and concentration and/or altering their judgement. Although there is some evidence of such links, particularly in relation to alcohol, the nature of this link tends to be less direct, being at least partly dependent on, or mediated by, the characteristics and disposition of the individual as well as more general cultural expectations.

In addition to pharmacological explanations, there are economic or financial explanations for the drug–crime link. Indeed, these are the explanations that are given most attention in the research literature. Again, such arguments may take various forms, but the most common is that based on the idea of 'economic necessity'. This argument rests on the suggestion that the drug user is unable to control their consumption and unable to fund their use through regular employment. As a result they turn to crime in order to pay for their drug habit. It is often assumed that heroin-, cocaine- and crack-use may be linked to crime, particularly property crime, in this way. There is evidence from self-report studies that some criminality is undertaken to support drug habits. Over three-quarters (78%) of the past year heroin- and/or crack-cocaine-users in the NEW-ADAM study felt that there was some link between their drug use and their offending (Bennett *et al.*, 2001). It is possible, of course, that, at least in some cases, admitting to some link between drug use and criminality is a form of *post-hoc* rationalisation – what we have seen referred to elsewhere as a *technique of neutralisation* (see Chapter 9).

Finally, there are 'lifestyle' or 'systemic' explanations. These explanations link drug use with crime through broader contextual factors such as the inherent dangers associated with buying and selling Class A drugs. One of the ways in which drug use is linked with crime is through the problems associated with drugs markets. Violence, minor and serious, has been found to be associated with competition for drugs territories and also with the enforcement of drug debts. Bean (2004: 42) building on the work of Reiss and Roth (1993) identifies four distinct forms of systemic crime:

- Organisational crime, involving territorial disputes over drug selling, the enforcement of organisational rules and norms, informers and conflict with the police.

- Transaction-related crime, involving theft of drugs or money from a buyer or seller, the collection of debts and the resolution of disputes of drug quality.

- Third party-related crime, involving bystanders to drugs disputes in drugs markets or related markets such as prostitution, protection or guns.

- Secondary crime activities which are a consequence of the development and growth of drugs markets, e.g. police corruption.

Crime causes drug use

Again, it is possible to identify chemical, economic and lifestyle variations in this form of explanation. Psycho-pharmacological approaches focus on the pleasure associated with drug use and, in this context, the use of drugs to celebrate or mark successful criminal activity. There is a link here with cultural criminological explanations – of both criminality and drug use – which focus on the pleasure, the 'carnival' involved in such behaviours (Presdee, 2000). The alternative form of this explanation focuses on drug use as a means by which offenders build up the nerve necessary to commit crime. The economic form of explanation focuses on the fact that the profits from crime may be used to buy drugs – funds which might not be available were it not for criminal activity. Finally, the lifestyle or systemic argument simply inverts the addiction argument outlined earlier. Here, rather than suggesting that drug use breeds crime, it is argued that a 'criminal lifestyle' tends to involve drug use, either via sub-cultural values, through available opportunities, or as a result of self-medication.

A common cause?

Here, the idea that drug use leads to crime or vice versa is abandoned in favour of arguments that there are other factors which help to explain both forms of behaviour. Again, such factors may take various forms including aspects of personality or temperament, aspects of a person's interpersonal social world (family, friends, peers) or some feature of the social environment in which they live, such as access to education, training or employment. A sizeable body of research evidence has been collected in recent years, largely from longitudinal research, which focuses on what are referred to as 'risk factors' connected with 'problem behaviours' such as criminality and illicit drug use. Many of the risk factors that are linked with criminality are also linked with increased likelihood of drug use, especially problematic drug use (see also Dillon *et al.*, 2006).

A more sociological version of this idea of 'common cause' is a variant on the idea of sub-cultural values mentioned above. From this perspective, drug use is viewed as one part of a learned lifestyle. In effect, conduct or behavioural norms are learned and passed from generation to generation, leading individuals within particular families or social groups to continue particular patterns of behaviour across the generations. In a fascinating article based on an ethnographic study of highly disadvantaged New York families, Dunlap *et al.* (2002) provide a moving account of how four generations of women led lives punctuated by drug abuse, sexual exploitation and violence, and how their social circumstances minimised the likelihood that they might avoid such a 'fate'. The authors illustrate this process of generational transmission with the following 'family tree'. In explaining how such behaviours are passed from generation to generation, Dunlap *et al.* (2002: 17) argue:

> Young girls learn (unhappily) to accept violent physical and sexual assault, substance abuse and sales, and unstable households as the effective conduct norms in their households while growing up. In essence, their sense of self and any possible hope and preparation for a mainstream lifestyle seem to die in the face of the realities of their households. This socializes them to internalize the prevailing conduct norms, accept and expect abuse relationships, and treat their children no better than they had been treated as children. This generational training process initializes and maintains the intergenerational transmission process of drug abuse/sales, sexual exploitation, and violence.

A reciprocal relationship?

This approach is very similar to the arguments outlined above but, rather than going in one direction, the relationship goes in two directions. That is, in essence drug use and criminality are considered to be causally interrelated: drug use might lead to offending and offending to drug use. Neither fully explains the other, but they are clearly bound together in important ways. Chaiken and Chaiken (1990), for example, suggest that their research shows that high-frequency drug users are also likely to be persistent or frequent offenders. In this manner, Walters (1994) and De Li Periu and MacKenzie (2000) have explored such reciprocal relationships in which offending both makes drug use possible and helps maintain such behaviour, while drug use simultaneously maintains involvement in crime.

No causal relationship?

This final possibility is a variant on the third and fourth hypotheses and, in essence, rests on the idea that there is essentially only a correlation between drug use and crime, not a causal connection. Connected with this is the 'policy and prohibition' model (Bean, 2004) which posits that the primary linkage between crime and drugs is the fact that public policy makes certain forms of drug use *criminal* (in parallel to the way we have used the term *criminalisation* in other parts of the book). Attempting to assess such claims is difficult. A number of conclusions seem possible. First, the links between drug use and crime that are most robustly established are those involving street heroin users. Second, in most cases such evidence as there is falls some way short of supporting the idea of a direct causal link between drug use and crime. Third, there is less evidence to support the 'crime leads to drug use' thesis than there is the 'drug use leads to crime' argument.

Talking of *causes* is highly problematic. Although people who use illicit drugs are more likely to offend than those who do not, there is no conclusive evidence of a causal link between drugs and crime in the lives of most drugs users. What is difficult to deny is that the very fact of criminalisation of drug use *creates* a relationship between drugs and crime. Proponents of legalisation argue strongly that breaking at least part of the connection between drugs and crime would be one of the substantial benefits of responding to drug use as, say, a public health rather than a 'crime' problem. However, there is also considerable evidence that it is not just the fact that certain substances are illicit that links their use with criminal activity. As McSweeney *et al.* (2007: 106–7) note:

> A small proportion of problem users – unlikely to exceed 100,000 in number – finance their use through crime and are extensively involved in the criminal justice system. Frequent estimates suggest that this group of users spend in the region of £400 each week on drugs, despite limited legitimate incomes. Shoplifting, burglary and selling drugs are common fund-raising strategies. This group also report long parallel careers in offending and drug use. The majority of those who steal to buy drugs were involved in crime before their drug use became a problem for them.

It is important in thinking about drugs and crime, therefore, to distinguish between the 'overwhelming majority of drug users [who] do not cause apparent significant damage to themselves or others' and that 'small minority ... who develop frequent and dependent patterns of use [and who] cause a large amount of harm to themselves and wider society' (Reuter and Stevens, 2007: 47). Of all the wider 'harms' that are caused it is undoubtedly crime that is the most costly.

When thinking about drugs and crime, is it all drug use we should be concerned about, or just frequent and dependent patterns of use?

Drugs and criminal justice

As we have seen, the Misuse of Drugs Act remains the most important piece of legislation in this area. A host of potential charges can be brought in relation to illicit drugs, including:

- Possession of a controlled drug.
- Possession with intent to supply another person.
- Production, cultivation or manufacture of controlled drugs.
- Supplying another person with a controlled drug.
- Offering to supply another person with a controlled drug.

- Import or export of controlled drugs.
- Allowing premises to be used for the consumption of certain controlled drugs (smoking of cannabis or opium, but not use of other controlled drugs) or supply or production of any controlled drug.

In the main, drugs offences fall into two major categories: *possession* and *supply*. The penalties attaching to either possession or supply vary significantly according to the classification of the drug concerned. The current legal situation is shown in Table 21.3.

Table 21.3	Penalties for possession and dealing	
	Possession:	**Dealing:**
Class A	Up to seven years in prison or an unlimited fine or both.	Up to life in prison or an unlimited fine or both.
Class B	Up to five years in prison or an unlimited fine or both.	Up to 14 years in prison or an unlimited fine or both.
Class C	Up to two years in prison or an unlimited fine or both.	Up to 14 years in prison or an unlimited fine or both.

Table 21.4	Persons found guilty, cautioned or dealt with by compounding* for drug offences, by class of drug, England and Wales, 2004								
	Class A						Class B	Class C	
	Heroin	Cocaine	Crack	Ecstasy	LSD	Meth-adone	Ampheta-mines	Anabolic steroids	Cannabis
Unlawful production	20	40	10	10	0	20	20	0	2,480
Unlawful supply	1,800	750	480	290	–	30	150	10	880
Possession with intent to supply	1,620	1,235	670	830	20	10	520	10	2,200
Unlawful possession	7,110	6,290	1,370	4,350	70	330	5,230	160	45,490
Unlawful import or export	50	690	10	20	–	–	0	0	320
Dealing	3,420	1,980	1,150	1,120	20	40	670	10	3,070
Permitting premises to be used for unlawful purposes	40	30	20	10	–	0	10	–	230
TOTAL	14,060	11,015	3,710	6,630	110	430	6,600	190	54,670

Source: Mwenda (2005).
* 'Compounding' is an administrative process involving a financial penalty imposed by HM Revenue and Customs.

Figure 21.9 Sentences for drug offences by drug type, 2004

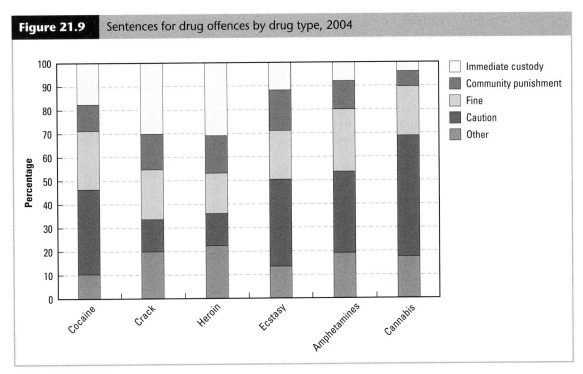

Source: Mwenda (2005).

In 2004, a total of 105,570 drug offences were dealt with in England and Wales by the police, courts and HM Revenue and Excise. Of these, 34 per cent were Class A drug offences, seven per cent were Class B offences and 56 per cent were class C offences. Although cannabis was downgraded to a Class C drug (from Class B) in 2002, unlawful possession of cannabis continued to account for a very substantial proportion of all prosecutions for drugs offences in 2004 and, indeed, possession offences represent the bulk of all drugs offence proceedings (see Table 21.4).

We have seen what the maximum penalties are for offences in relation to drugs in Classes A, B and C. But what is the range of available penalties and what happens in practice? In addition to custodial penalties there is a range of community-based orders that can be used, as well as fines and cautions. In 2004, 11 per cent of drugs offences resulted in a prison sentence. The likelihood of custody varied substantially according to the nature of the drug involved and the nature of the offence. Thus, whereas 29% of heroin and 22% of crack offences resulted in immediate custody, only 12% of cannabis offences did so. Similarly, whilst 93% of import/export offences and 61% of dealing offences resulted in immediate custody, only 5% of possession offences did so (see Figure 21.9).

Drug courts, DTTOs and coerced treatment

Drug treatment has been available as part of a community sentence since 1973, but for much of this period was not widely used by the probation service and was not especially attractive to treatment providers. It is only with the arrival of the Drug Treatment and Testing Order (DTTO), as part of the 1998 Crime and Disorder Act, that coercion into treatment as part of a community penalty has become at all widespread. The DTTO can be imposed for between six months and three years and includes:

A requirement (the treatment requirement) that the offender shall submit, during the whole of the treatment and testing period, to treatment by or under the direction of a specified person having the necessary qualifications or experience (the treatment provider) with a view to the reduction or elimination of the offender's dependency or propensity to misuse drugs.

During the course of the order the offender is subject to drugs testing, of a form and frequency determined by the treatment provider. An evaluation of the piloting of DTTOs (Turnbull *et al.*, 2000) found substantial reductions in drug use and very sharp drops in expenditure on drugs (from an average of £400 per week down to £25 in the first weeks of the order) for those who remained in the programme (though there was a high drop-out rate). As part of the introduction of the generic Community Order created by the Criminal Justice Act 2003, DTTOs have been phased out and replaced with Drug Rehabilitation Requirements, initially for adults only and, from April 2007 onward, for 16 and 17 year-olds also.

As with so many recent developments in British criminal justice, part of the inspiration for the DTTO lies in the American drugs courts. According to Bean (2004), though this is not officially acknowledged, there are at least three core elements of the American drug court that have found their way into the DTTO:

- Treatment is provided by agencies outside the criminal justice system.
- Treatment is underpinned by drug testing.
- Treatment is reinforced by regular supervision – generally by the probation service.

The history of drug courts in the US goes back to the late 1980s. Established initially in Miami, Florida, drug courts have spread across the US and beyond in recent times. Bean (2004) cites ten main components of drug courts as highlighted by the US National Association of Drug Court Professionals:

1 They integrate alcohol and other drug treatment services with criminal justice system processing.

2 They are non-adversarial, and prosecution and defence seek to promote public safety whilst having regard to the due process rights of participants.

3 There is an emphasis on early intervention after arrest.

4 Drug courts provide access to a very broad range of alcohol, drug and other treatment and rehabilitation services.

5 Abstinence is monitored by frequent drug testing.

6 Careful attention is paid to constructing a co-ordinated strategy for managing participant compliance (seeking to manage non-compliance in a firm but realistic way).

7 Ongoing interaction between the judge and the other participants is vital.

8 Monitoring and evaluation are used to assess the efficacy of the programme.

9 Effective drug court operations require continuing interdisciplinary education.

10 Forging partnerships among drug courts, public agencies and community-based organisations enhances the effectiveness of drug courts and generates local support.

There are, however, a number of important differences between drug courts and DTTOs. Turnbull *et al.* (2000) and Bean (2004) provide a useful summary in Table 22.5:

Table 22.5	Differences between Drug Courts and DTTOs
Drug court	**DTTO**
Aim is abstinence. That may include alcohol	Aim is harm reduction, especially heroin or cocaine
Treatment providers are employed by the court	Treatment providers work for the probation service
Judge conducts the supervision	Probation service conducts the supervision
Adversarial system replaced by team approach	Adversarial system remains intact
Judge can impose multiple sanctions	Court restricted to breach proceedings defined in legislation
Drug test results sent to the judge immediately	Drug test results take up to 5 days before arriving at court
Courtroom procedure is less formal	Formal procedures remain
Offender may be required to pay for treatment	Treatment is part of NHS provisions
Drug court judge concentrates on drug offenders	Judges retain full range of offenders
Probation service has only a minor part to play	Probation service is central to the order

Source: Bean (2004).

Britain itself has more recently begun to experiment with drug courts. The first were in Scotland and were established in late 2001. Much of the Miami drug court model was adopted in Glasgow, but then adapted to suit the Scottish criminal justice system. Like American drug courts the Scottish court has dedicated judges, dedicated supervision and treatment teams and powers to impose a range of sanctions prior to final disposal. Overall, the system has a number of features that distinguish it from the DTTO system (Bean, 2004: 134; McIvor *et al.*, 2003):

1 It has a specialist bench consisting of a sheriff who develops a considerable measure of expertise.

2 A multi-agency team oversees the operation of the drug court.

3 Regular and random testing of all orders, including offenders on probation.

4 Regular review of the offender's progress.

5 A multi-disciplinary screening group and inter-agency working.

6 Fast-track court procedures to get the offender into treatment quickly.

7 Initiation of breach proceedings by the bench.

8 Use of summary sanctions at reviews.

The rise of drug testing in the context of criminal justice, and the development of drug courts and interventions such as the DTTO and its successor all raise questions about how much coercion is appropriate in seeking to get problem drug users into treatment. As we have seen, there has been a shift in recent years whereby the role of the criminal justice system has been progressively emphasised in the tackling of drugs problems. Bodies such as the Audit Commission have argued that research evidence suggests that drug users in the criminal justice system who are coerced into treatment achieve similar outcomes as those seeking treatment on a voluntary basis (see also Reuter and Stevens, 2007). Increasingly, however, authors are coming to question the usefulness of the distinction between 'voluntarism' and 'coercion':

> The shift towards criminal justice-based treatment cannot be understood simply in terms of a shift from voluntarism towards coercion. For a

start, coercion has been a strong feature of medical, harm reduction and counselling approaches, outside the criminal justice system ... The perceived short-termism and coercion inherent in court-led drug treatment orders (that are said to ignore motivation, and impose drug treatment programmes over the course of a sentence, rather than according to clinical and social need) can be matched by similar shortcomings of short-term and inappropriate treatment in non-clinical approaches and agencies. (Webster, 2007: 153)

Drug testing

Drugs policy has placed increasing emphasis on *forcing or coercing* offenders into treatment in recent years. This policy has its origins in the 1995 Drugs Strategy, *Tackling Drugs Together: A strategy for England 1995–8*, which established Drug Action Teams and committed the government to increasing treatment facilities. It was subsequently reinforced by the national drug strategy published in 1998, *Tackling Drugs Together to Build a Better Britain*. The Department of Health's National Treatment Outcome Research Study (commonly known as NTORS) highlighted the potential benefits of increased treatment, though much government policy appeared still to be driven by the Home Office and by a criminal justice agenda.

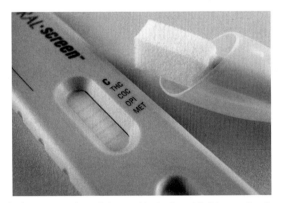

A drug screening stick used to test oral fluid samples for the presence or absence of drugs. Mandatory drug testing is now found at various parts of the criminal justice process – from arrest to imprisonment – and is also used, on a voluntary basis, by researchers trying to investigate patterns of drug use.

Compulsory drug testing in the criminal justice system

The Criminal Justice and Court Services Act 2000 sets out provisions for the use of drug testing for specified Class A drugs for individuals aged 18 and over. The objective in doing so is 'to deter drug misuse whilst under criminal justice supervision and to identify offenders who should be receiving treatment and monitoring their progress'.

The police can test detainees who have been charged with what are called 'trigger offences' (these include property crime, robbery and specified Class A drug offences). Detainees charged with a non-trigger offence can also be tested if authorised by a police inspector ('Inspector's discretion') if drug misuse is suspected as a contributing factor in the crime committed. The legislation allows for the drug test result to be used 'in assisting the court in deciding whether to grant bail in criminal proceedings' and 'helping a court to decide on the appropriate sentence following conviction'.

In addition, courts can order the probation service to test individuals aged 18 or over who have received the following:

- An order from the court to conduct a pre-sentence test for any specified Class A drug, when considering the imposition of a community sentence.
- A Drug Abstinence Order (DAO) for those in a specified target group for whom an alternative community sentence is not appropriate, involving twice a week testing for a period of 13 weeks, with discretion for this to be reduced to once a week if the offender is responding well.
- A Drug Abstinence Requirement (DAR) as a condition of a community sentence, which involves twice a week testing for 13 weeks, with discretion for this to be reduced to once a week if the offender is responding well.
- A drug-testing requirement as part of a condition of release from prison on licence or under Notice of Supervision (NoS) (for 18–22 year-olds). Offenders are tested twice a week for 13 weeks following release, with discretion for this to be reduced to once a week if the offender responds well.

Testing interventions and the route through the criminal justice system

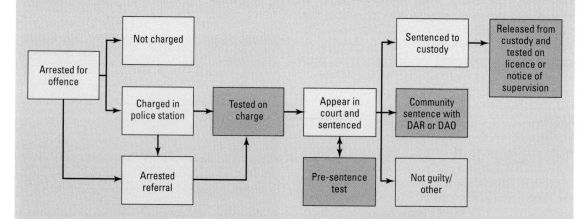

In addition, mandatory drug testing was introduced for all prisons from February 1996. All prisoners are subject to the random testing programme and prisons are required to test five to ten per cent of their population each month. Refusal by a prisoner to be tested will lead to up to 28 days' loss of remission.

Source: Matrix Research and Consultancy and NACRO (2004).

Drug testing has expanded rapidly over the course of the last decade and potentially provides a basis for directing people into treatment or keeping them there. Such testing is often mandatory, such as that which takes place in prisons, and can take a number of forms (see Bean, 2004; (http://www.lindesmith. org/law/drugtesting/; http://www.drugscope.org.uk/ druginfo/):

● *Sweat patches* – A test involving the placement of a patch on the arm for up to two weeks. It can detect the presence of drugs in the bloodstream, but cannot determine the amount consumed.

● *Saliva tests* – Tests for the presence of alcohol using saliva have been available for decades. Now similar tests can be used to detect the presence of opiates, amphetamines and cocaine. It is neither as intrusive nor as unpleasant for those administering tests such as urine testing, but has the disadvantage of being less accurate.

● *Blood tests* – Blood tests are expensive, obviously invasive and have to be administered under highly controlled conditions – which generally requires hospitalisation.

● *Hair tests* – The advantage of hair tests is that they are virtually tamper-proof and can provide indications of the quantity of drugs consumed. However, they are expensive, more so than blood tests, and have to be administered in a laboratory or similar environment.

● *Eye tests* – In theory, certain substances should have an effect on the eye's reactions to light and with specialist equipment these can be detected and the substance identified. If there is a sufficient number of tests to be administered there is the potential for this to become a relatively cheap option, though it is currently rarely used. Its other potential advantage compared with some other tests is that it would measure current intoxication.

● *Urine tests* – These remain the most commonly used tests for drugs (they are used as the basis for prison drug-testing regimes, for example) and are an approved and certified method. They are relatively inexpensive and have a fairly high degree of accuracy.

There are two major shortcomings of such tests. One is the creation of what are called *false positives*. This simply means wrongly identifying someone as having taken an illicit drug. None of the test types is entirely accurate and the 'cut-off point' – the point below which a test is considered negative –

has an important effect on accuracy: too low and it will produce more false positives, too high and the second major problem will result – *false negatives*. Any readers at all familiar with athletics and a number of other major sports will be familiar with debates over drugs testing and the difficulties associated with detecting drugs on the one hand, whilst on the other being sufficiently sure that the tests accurately reflect the behaviour of the person being tested.

Drug testing at work has become more common in recent years and provides an interesting illustration of some of the technical and practical problems of testing, as well as raising interesting legal and human rights questions. A recent independent inquiry into drug testing at work (JRF, 2004) found a lack of evidence for a strong link between drug use and accidents in safety-critical industries, such as transport, engineering, quarrying and mining. Although acknowledging the potential risks associated with drug- and alcohol-induced intoxication, it argued that other factors may well have a greater impact on safety, productivity and performance, including bad working conditions, sleeping and health problems, excessive workloads and work-related stress (see Chapter 18 and also Tombs and Whyte, 2007).

One of the difficulties with drug testing at work is that it measures certain types of drug consumption – through traces in the blood or urine – but can say little or nothing about current levels of intoxication. It appears that relatively few employers currently use such testing. A survey by the independent inquiry found that four per cent of respondents said they currently used such testing and a further nine per cent said that they might introduce testing in the next year.

Drugs and policing

Until relatively recently the policing of drugs markets was organised according to a three-tier strategy set out in the 1985 Broome Report (ACPO, 1985):

1 Regional crime squads policing the trafficking of drugs at a national level, and occasionally international level.

2 Force-level drugs squads responsible for the policing of middle-level markets and co-ordinating force-level intelligence.

3 Officers at divisional- or basic command unit (BCU)-level responsible for street-level local policing.

As Bean (2004: 169) slightly acerbically notes:

> The Broome strategy was based on the belief that drug markets operated according to a model derived from a police officer's view of the structure and importance of policing (i.e. allowing the most important traffickers to be dealt with by the most important police officers, the less important with the less important officers and so on).

Since 2005 these arrangements have been superseded by the creation of a new national-level body, the Serious and Organised Crime Agency (SOCA) and, as we have seen, drugs policing has been one of the driving forces behind the growing visibility of trans-national policing organisations (see Chapter 34). According to Kleiman and Smith (1990), there are four main objectives to drugs policing:

1 Limiting the number of persons who use various illicit drugs and the damage suffered as a result – psychological, physical, moral, etc.

2 Reducing the violence connected with drug dealing and the property and violent crimes committed by users, whether to obtain money for drugs or as a result of that intoxication.

3 Preventing the growth of stable, wealthy, powerful criminal organisations.

4 Protecting the civility of neighbourhoods, and thus their attractiveness as places to work and live, from the disorder caused by drug dealing, open or otherwise.

Domestically, a considerable amount of police attention has always been trained on seeking to seize illegal drugs as they enter the country (as well as the attention of other organisations such as HM Revenue and Customs). Seizure statistics are often used as an indicator of police performance as well as a signal of the nature of, and changes in, the drug problem. Whether either of these uses is especially helpful is somewhat doubtful. Only a very small proportion of drugs entering the country is ever seized, and given that it is all but impossible to know what proportion the seized drugs actually represent, interpreting the figures is fraught with problems (South, 2002).

The other major areas of policing enforcement activity take place in relation to supply on the streets and possession. In relation to supply, much activity is focused on what are generally referred to as 'drugs markets'. Much discussion in this area adopts a language similar to that used by the Broome Report, and distinguishes between 'high level', 'middle level' and 'street level' or 'retail level' drugs markets. The markets that have been least studied, for fairly obvious reasons, are the middle- and high-level ones. Access is difficult and in some cases undoubtedly dangerous. Much of the literature in this area is concerned with organised crime and examines networks, often international in nature, in which people occupying fairly distinctive and differentiated roles combine to move goods across jurisdictions and eventually sell on the streets.

Combating illegal drugs. *Left*: A drugs squad officer logs bags of cocaine, part of a consignment with a street value of £10m, seized by the Metropolitan Police. *Right*: Officers from Hertfordshire Constabulary carry out a raid at the home of a known drug dealer.

There is a variety of ways of understanding 'middle markets'. The definition preferred by Pearson and Hobbs (2001: 17) for the purposes of their research – one of the few studies in the UK – 'is something that happens between importation and retail supply to consumers'. One of the key roles in such markets, they suggest, is the 'middle-market drugs broker'. These brokers tend to have a regular customer base made up primarily of retail dealers, or intermediaries who operate just above retail level. The broker regularly buys drugs in relatively large (multi-kilo or tens of thousands of pills) quantities. An illustration of the position occupied by a multi-commodity broker (not all brokers deal in the full range of drugs – some refusing, for example, to have anything to do with heroin) can be seen in Figure 21.10.

Retail level drugs markets are 'those who supply drugs to end-point consumers, sometimes by means of intermediaries where drug users club together to make bulk purchases' (Pearson, 2007: 77). Researchers have distinguished between 'open'

and 'closed' retail-level markets (Edmunds et al., 1996). Open markets are street-level and tend to be available to most people in the vicinity who might wish to buy drugs – though they are not necessarily always localised. By contrast, closed retail markets tend to operate from private premises and to be used by those who are known to the dealer or who have a prior appointment – though mobile phones are changing the nature of such markets (May and Hough, 2004). Often dealers will operate across the 'boundary' between open and closed markets. Pearson (2007: 80) describes the activities of one such dealer:

> Gary is sitting in his usual spot at the end of the bar in the King Cole, nursing a pint of lager and smoking roll-up cigarettes. Immediately behind him is the juke-box, a slot-machine, a cigarette machine, and the entrance to the bar's toilets. This means that there is a constant traffic of people around him, and that customers often have to lean over him to order their drinks from

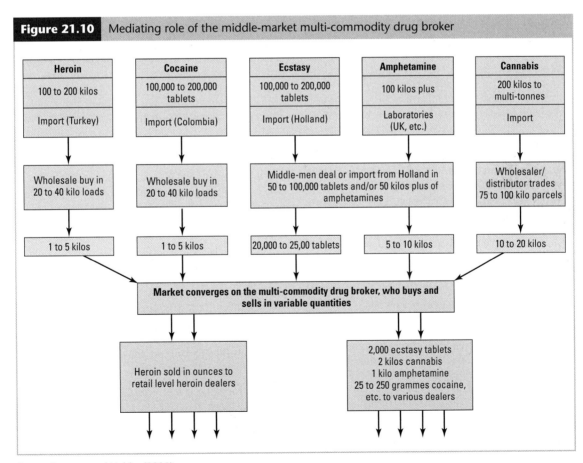

Figure 21.10   Mediating role of the middle-market multi-commodity drug broker

Source: Pearson and Hobbs (2001)

the staff behind the bar. Other people might find this the most inconvenient place to sit at the bar, but this doesn't worry Gary because it enables some customers to have a surreptitious conversation with him and makes his trade less conspicuous. For example, a customer orders a couple of drinks and hands a £20 note across the bar which reliably results in some small change together with two notes, a ten and a five. The small change pocketed, the £15 is slipped to Gary who exchanges the favour with an eighth of cannabis resin wrapped in cling-film. Deal completed.

Lambeth cannabis experiment

As noted above, cannabis was downgraded from a Class B to a Class C drug in 2002. For some time prior to this there had been a public debate about how much police time was being spent on the polic-ing of cannabis and whether, given the discretionary nature of much policing activity, this was the most effective or economic use of police time. From 2001 a pilot project was undertaken by the Metropolitan Police in the London borough of Lambeth in which anyone found in possession of small amounts of cannabis was to be cautioned rather than arrested. The scheme ran for approximately a year, at the end

---

Cannabis and recent government policy

The Police Foundation (Runciman) Inquiry, which reported in 2000, recommended that cannabis be reclassified from Class B to Class C. At the time that would have meant that cannabis ceased to be an 'arrestable offence'. The inquiry also recommended that cannabis possession ceased to be an imprisonable offence. The proposals were swiftly rejected and condemned by the then Home Secretary, Jack Straw, and his drugs tsar, Keith Hellawell.

Shortly after becoming Home Secretary in mid-2001, David Blunkett called for an 'adult, intelligent debate' on the reform of the law on cannabis. He asked the Advisory Council on the Misuse of Drugs (ACMD) (a standing body of experts in the field) to review the status of cannabis. Around the same time an experiment in Lambeth was taking place in which the police were warning, rather than arresting, anyone found in possession of small amounts of cannabis. Perhaps predictably, the experiment gained significant media exposure and caused considerable controversy.

The ACMD report, published in early 2002, recommended the reclassification to Class C. Two months later, a report on the government's drugs strategy by the parliamentary Home Affairs Select Committee (comprising politicians from all the major parties) also supported the proposal to reclassify cannabis. Although the government announced the reclassification of cannabis to Class C in June 2002, media reporting of the Lambeth experiment and of the cannabis debate more broadly was becoming increasingly hostile to the government's proposals.

The reclassification meant that the maximum penalties for trafficking/supply were reduced and that possession ceased to be an arrestable offence. However, the Criminal Justice Act 2003 effectively

overturned this – leaving cannabis classified as Class C, but increasing the penalties for trafficking/supply and once again making it an arrestable offence. Nevertheless, media reporting of drugs policy continued to assert that the reclassification was evidence of 'softness' in this area and that the police no longer had sufficient powers in relation to cannabis offences.

After David Blunkett's resignation in late 2004, Charles Clarke took over as Home Secretary and once again the ACMD was asked to review cannabis policy and there were suggestions that government favoured returning cannabis to Class B (doing so might have had a symbolic impact, but it would have made little difference in practice). Reporting in late 2005, the ACMD recommended that the position of cannabis remain unchanged (i.e. that it remain Class C and possession remain an arrestable offence). In due course the Serious and Organised Crime and Police Act 2005 made all offences arrestable. Is this the end of it? Apparently not. In the aftermath of revelations of his cannabis smoking during his days at Eton, David Cameron announced that he favoured reclassifying cannabis as Class B and this has subsequently become official Conservative Party policy.

Despite very mixed messages from government, there has been a general shift in policing policy toward the increased use of street warning for cannabis possession and away from the presumption of arrest (though practice is variable). This has proven popular with police officers, and with the public, and can save time and money (May *et al.*, 2007).

[*I am particularly grateful to Charlie Lloyd for his account of these changes.*]

of which officers were once again given the discretion to arrest people found in possession of cannabis. The pilot was undertaken partly because of concerns that the police were being diverted from more important work, and also because of worries stimulated by a recent disciplinary case in which the informal police practice of not arresting had been subject to legal challenge.

Brian Paddick, the high-profile Metropolitan Police commander of the London borough of Lambeth at the time of the 'cannabis enforcement' controversy in 2002.

An evaluation conducted for the Metropolitan Police Authority found that 'the scheme saw a 110% increase in the number of interventions for cannabis possession during the pilot period with a total of 1,390 warnings being given, in contrast to the 661 arrests in the preceding year. Each of these warnings has been calculated at a time saving of three hours, which equates to 4,170 hours saved or

2.75 officers per annum' (MPA, 2002). Moreover, although controversial in some quarters, the scheme also attracted a fair level of public support. A survey conducted by the Police Foundation found that the vast majority of residents supported the scheme outright (36%) or supported it conditionally (47%). Only eight per cent disapproved of it (Police Foundation, 2002).

The Lambeth experiment raises many issues. First is the practical question of how best this particular form of retail drug market can be policed. Second, if the answer is felt to be to attempt to do so informally as far as possible, then there is the issue of how this is to be communicated. More particularly, is it possible to signal that possession of small amounts of cannabis will always be dealt with informally, whilst at the same time maintaining that the drug is illegal and that supply may be dealt with much more severely? During the Lambeth experiment there was certainly evidence of some confusion, not least among some political commentators. Third, how will such practices be perceived? Although the Police Foundation survey found high levels of public support, this was contingent on the police spending more time tackling serious crime (32%) or even reducing serious crime in the borough (15%). Laudable as such aims may be, neither – especially the latter – are a inevitable product of such an experiment. Moreover, what the experiment appears to point out is the rather mixed cultural position that cannabis continues to occupy in British public life – relatively high levels of use combined with sometimes restrictive attitudes (at least among parts of the population).

The different policing practices in relation to cannabis across Europe are no doubt in part a reflection of different cultural attitudes toward the drug (see Figure 21.11).

Figure 21.11	European approaches to cannabis possession offences
Country	**Approach**
Italy	Personal possession is not a criminal offence. Civil sanctions such as the suspension of a driver's licence are, however, applied. Effectively, Italy has 'decriminalised by law'.
Netherlands	Possession, selling and growing small amounts are not prosecuted. Small amounts (5g or less) are sold through 'coffee shops'. The Netherlands' approach could be viewed as 'grudging toleration'.
Portugal	An individual found in possession of a small amount (not specified) has the drug seized from them and they are referred to a local commission. The commission's remit is to (where possible) divert the individual from prosecution and into treatment. Effectively, Portugal has 'decriminalised by law'.

Figure 21.11	Continued
Country	Approach
Spain	Personal possession of less than 50g is not a criminal offence. It may attract a civil penalty or fine. When an individual is caught in possession, the drug is seized and they are referred to the administrative authorities. Effectively, Spain has 'decriminalised by law'.
Sweden	No distinction is made between drugs that are considered 'hard' and those considered 'soft'. Usual court sentences are a fine or imprisonment for a maximum of six months. Sweden is widely known for its tough stance against drugs and it would appear that cannabis possession will remain – for the foreseeable future – within the criminal law.
France	Both simple possession and (uniquely) use are prohibited and punishable by one year's imprisonment and/or 4,000 Euros. However, in practice, those found in possession of small amounts receive a warning, which is often accompanied by a suggestion (from the police) to attend a social or health service. This process is termed 'no further action with orientation'.
Germany	Possession is a criminal offence. However, the Public Prosecutor retains the right not to prosecute where the amount is small and for personal use and it is not in the public interest to prosecute.

Source: May et al. (2002).

Review questions

1 What is meant by 'normalisation' in the context of youthful drug use?

2 What are the main possible connections between drug use and crime?

3 How might you distinguish between high-level, middle-level and retail-level drugs markets?

4 What is the difference between 'open' and 'closed' retail drugs markets?

Alcohol

We switch our attention now to the consumption of a substance that is legal – and is therefore not obviously an immediate concern for criminologists. Plant and Plant (2006: 27) in their analysis of trends in alcohol consumption note that it 'is clear that the UK has a long tradition of both moderate and not so moderate drinking'. Clearly, anyone who has listened to radio or television or been a regular reader of newspapers in recent years will have noticed that there is now considerable concern expressed about levels of alcohol consumption, particularly among young people, and how this is thought to be linked to crime, disorderliness and anti-social behaviour. One question for us as criminologists is the extent to which this reflects changes in patterns of consumption, changing attitudes toward alcohol use, or whether it is simply the product of a generalised moral panic about drinking and/or youth.

Patterns of consumption

The first thing to note is that, in general terms, levels of alcohol consumption in the UK appear to be on the rise. Looking over the last century or so, data from the British Beer and Pub Association (2006) suggests that levels of alcohol consumption dropped during the First World War, remaining relatively low (by turn of the century standards) during the inter-war years, and then began to rise in the aftermath of the Second World War. Barring a few moderate falls, per capita alcohol consumption has been rising for the past half century.

Looking cross-nationally it is possible to see rather different patterns in different countries. Figure 21.12, taking selected European countries only, shows a fairly substantial decline in per capita alcohol consumption in France, Spain and Italy, a fairly stable or slight decline in Austria and Germany, and rising rates in the Netherlands and the UK (in fact the data suggest on this general measure that the differences between the countries are slowly disappearing). It is worth noting, however, that the UK has comparatively high levels of alcohol consumption compared with other English-speaking countries such as the USA, Canada or Australia, but lower levels than many other European nations.

Contrasting drinking styles – a bar in Paris (*left*) and London (*right*). Styles of alcohol consumption in parts of continental Europe are often perceived to be very different from those in the UK where there has been concern in recent years about 'binge drinking'.

However, such general measures can only tell so much about the 'drinking cultures' in different societies and, in particular, they tell us little about such things as 'binge drinking'. Drinking cultures are often classified as 'wet' or 'dry' to reflect general attitudes toward alcohol and its use. A wet culture is one in which alcohol appears as an everyday item, often, if not routinely, served with meals, and where rates of abstinence are low. Dry cultures, by contrast, tend to have much more restrictive views and higher rates of abstinence. One of the 'ironies' of dry cultures is that despite such restrictions they are often characterised by high rates of excessive consumption.

| **Figure 21.12** | Alcohol consumption in selected nations (litres of pure alcohol per inhabitant, 1999) |

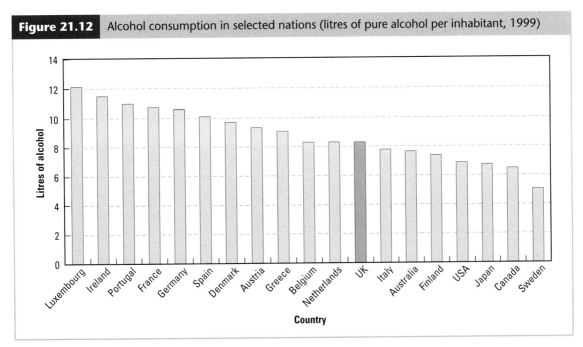

Source: Strategy Unit (2003).

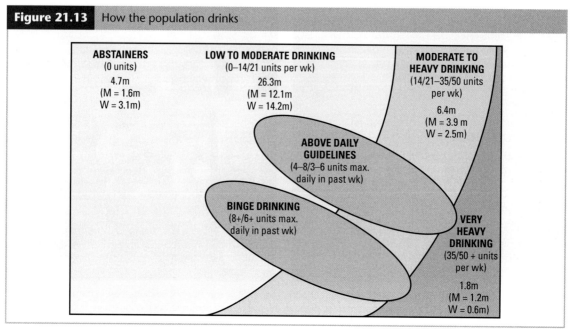

| Figure 21.13 | How the population drinks |

Source: Strategy Unit (2003).

In the UK, half the adult population drinks less than the recommended maximum unit intake per week as recommended by government, and a sizeable minority (almost five million people) do not drink at all. However, over six million people drink up to 35 units (women) or 50 units (men) per week, and a further 1.8 million people drink more than these amounts. Finally, as illustrated in Figure 21.13 there are two overlapping groups who 'binge' drink – these days commonly defined as drinking very heavily on some occasions. Recent debates about alcohol controls in the UK have focused on the problems associated with excessive or 'binge' drinking, and there have been numerous calls for changes that might bring about a shift toward what is often thought of as a more 'continental' attitude towards alcohol – characteristic of southern European 'wet' cultures.

There are considerable differences in patterns of alcohol consumption according to age. Highest levels of consumption are to be found in the 16–24 year-old age category, though this consumption is more likely to be concentrated into fewer instances of drinking. As age rises, so alcohol consumption tends to decline, but also tends to become more regular (see Figure 21.14).

Not only are the late teens and early twenties the period of highest consumption, but it appears that levels of alcohol use are increasing amongst this age group. The proportion of people in the age category who are drinking is not increasing markedly, rather it is the quantity being drunk by those who do

drink that is changing. The average number of units of alcohol drunk by school pupils almost doubled from 5.3 in 1990 to 10.5 in 2002 (Strategy Unit, 2003). A BBC *Panorama* programme in November 2006 used NHS data to suggest that the number of hospital admissions of under-18s linked with drinking had risen by 20 per cent between 2004–05.

This increase was linked to other research evidence which suggests that young people in the 16–24 year-old age category are the most likely to report 'binge drinking'. Indeed, it is this pattern of drinking that appears to distinguish us most from our continental neighbours. Thus, in the UK, 'binge drinking' (defined by government as drinking at least double the recommended daily guideline – i.e. six units for women and eight for men) accounts for 40 per cent of all drinking occasions by men, and 22 per cent by women, compared with nine and five per cent respectively in France. The term 'binge drinking', of course, is far from straightforward:

> Since alcohol will affect different people in different ways, there is no fixed relationship between the amount drunk and its consequences. So although many people understand 'bingeing' to mean deliberately drinking to excess, or drinking to get drunk, not everyone drinking over 6/8 units in a single day will fit this category. Similarly, many people who *are* drinking to get drunk, will drink far in excess of the 6/8 units in the unit-based definition. (Strategy Unit, 2003: 11)

Figure 21.14   Drinking frequency by days per week, age and sex in Britain, 2002

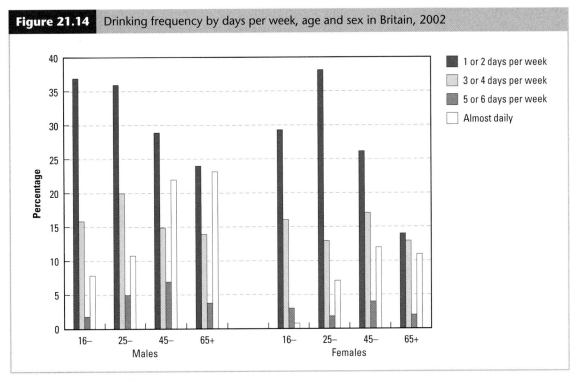

Source: Strategy Unit (2003).

As the figures above illustrated there are also some substantial and continuing differences in men's and women's patterns of alcohol consumption – not least that men tend to drink more. Women are less likely to drink than men and are also less likely to drink above the recommended limits. That said, the levels of alcohol consumption by women are rising, and are doing so more quickly than they are for men.

Young people and alcohol

Drinking by young people is often considered to be akin to a form of delinquency or deviant behaviour. This conceptualisation is particularly strong in the United States of America where the literature tends to be dominated by a paradigm in which alcohol use by young people is seen to be necessarily problematic and dysfunctional (Wright, 1999). It would be wrong to suggest, however, that such a view is limited to North America. In the UK traces of this view are evident in concern about the drinking habits of those who are variously described as 'excluded' or 'alienated'. An emphasis on exclusion was evident in the report from the Royal College of Physicians and British Paediatric Association (1995: 34–5):

Young people who feel excluded from society because they are out of work or in boring, humdrum jobs are more likely to drink heavily than those studying or in interesting occupations.

'Excessive' drinking has been seen to be prevalent among 'delinquent youth' and 'damaged minorities' (Brain *et al.*, 2000: 5) and there is some evidence of heightened levels of alcohol consumption among young people who may be considered to be 'alienated'. According to Craig (undated) measures of alienation have been found to be significantly correlated with a range of heath risk behaviours including lack of exercise, smoking, drinking and drug use. Based on her own study, she also reported that, for sixth formers, 'alienation' – measured on the basis of feelings about school and future plans – was strongly correlated with 'frequent' and 'excessive' drinking. No such link, however, was evident among young people in further education or on Youth Training Programmes.

The influence of parents and peers on young people's drinking has provided an important focus for research and it is often suggested that, as young people go through their early- and mid-teens, the family influences become less important and peer influences become more important

(Wright, 1999). Notions of peer groups and peer pressure are closely tied to understandings of deviant behaviour as they offer a way of dividing young people into 'good' and 'bad' and provide a way in which 'bad' behaviour by 'good kids' can be explained – i.e. by providing a neutralisation technique (Davies, 1992: 29–32).

While it has been shown repeatedly by cross-sectional studies that young people's drinking – or non-drinking – habits reflect those of their friends (Royal College of Physicians and British Paediatric Association, 1995; Ianotti *et al.*, 1996; Wright, 1999) this does not necessarily indicate causation. Such patterns may be explained by peer selection rather than peer pressure: that is, rather than pressuring those around them to behave in certain ways, young people seek out others who think and behave like them (Davies, 1992; Coggans and McKellar, 1994).

What is the impact of alcohol consumption? Several European surveys have reported relatively high levels of problems associated with youthful drinking (see Table 21.5).

Much of the research on alcohol and family life has been conducted on the basis of parents who are problem drinkers and who may, as a result, be in contact with support services (Royal College of Physicians and British Paediatric Association, 1995; Wright, 1999). Research in the US provides the extraordinary estimate that about one in eight children have at least one parent who is a problem drinker (MacDonald and Blume, 1986). Recent estimates in the UK suggest that between 780,000 and 1.3 million children are affected by parental alcohol misuse (Alcohol Harm Reduction Strategy, 2004) or approximately one in eleven children (Turning Point, 2006). In practice, it is far from straightforward to assess the impact of parental alcohol misuse on children, as such parents frequently have other 'problems'. The problem of co-morbidity, as we shall see, runs throughout consideration of most aspects of the impact of alcohol (mis)use on young people. In summary, however, research has found:

- Insecure patterns of attachment at one year among infants born to women with high alcohol use before and during pregnancy (O'Connor *et al.*, 1987).

- Cognitive deficits and poor school performance among children of problem drinkers when compared with other children (Nordberg *et al.*, 1993; von Knorring, 1991).

Table 21.5	UK teenagers' problems caused by own drinking (self-report)	
Type of Problem	**Boys (%)**	**Girls (%)**
Engaged in sex you regretted next day	9	12
Engaged in unprotected sex	6	11
Scuffle or fight	12	11
Victimized by robbery or theft	2	2
Trouble with police	9	11
Performed poorly at school	3	4
Damage to objects or clothing	21	28
Loss of money or valuables	16	22
Accident or injury	14	17
Hospitalised or admitted to the emergency room	2	3
Quarrel or argument	13	18
Problems in relationship with friends	8	11
Problems in relationship with parents	6	10
Problems in relationship with teachers	1	1

Source: Hibbell *et al.*, 2004, reported in Plant and Plant (2006).

- Raised prevalence of behavioural and emotional disorders (West and Prinz, 1987).
- Some evidence of association between heavy alcohol use by parents and physical abuse of children (Oliver, 1985).

In addition, it has been estimated that young people with alcoholic parents are approximately five times more likely to develop alcohol-related problems than are those with non-alcoholic parents (Pickens *et al.*, 1991). This link appears to reflect a range of biological and environmental factors. The role of genetic influences has been discussed in relation to a variety of 'anti-social behaviours' including heavy drinking (Rutter *et al.*, 1998) and it has been estimated from studies of identical and non-identical twins that 30 per cent of the familial transmission of alcoholism in males can be attributed to genetic factors (Merikanges, 1990; Pickens *et al.*, 1991; see also Lloyd, 1998). The link between parents' and children's drinking cannot, however, be reduced to biology. Thus, for example, although the children of heavy drinkers have an increased likelihood of becoming heavy drinkers themselves, it appears to be the case that the children of non-drinkers are also at an increased risk of becoming heavy drinkers. This has led some commentators to emphasise the importance of 'sensible' drinking by parents as a model of appropriate behaviour for young people (McKechnie *et al.*, 1977; Orford, 1990; Wright, 1999).

Family support, family control and family drinking styles have all been identified as having an important influence on young people's drinking. Low parental support, low parental control, heavy parental drinking and attitudes that condone such behaviour are associated with heavy drinking by young people. Moderate levels of support and control, attitudes which support sensible drinking by young people and a model of sensible parental drinking provide an environment which is most conducive to the development of 'socially competent drinking behaviour' by young people (Foxcroft and Lowe, 1991, 1997; Lowe, Foxcroft and Sibley, 1993).

Young people, alcohol and moral panic

Whilst there are regular attempts to deploy the 'drinking as deviance' argument in the UK, by and large such a view has been rejected. Thus, Sharp and Lowe (1989, 305) have argued that to see youthful drinking as necessarily problematic 'runs the risk of turning what is essentially normal behaviour into something deviant'. Similarly,

Wright (1999: 1) suggests that 'British researchers have challenged this perspective, arguing that adolescent drinking in Britain is essentially normal behaviour, which is part of the process of socialisation and reflects adult norms and drinking practices within a wider cultural setting'.

Underage drinking: normal adolescent behaviour or potentially 'deviant'?

As a consequence, recent research in the UK has tended to concentrate on the inappropriateness of public policy responses in this area and on the essentially rational nature of much alcohol consumption by young people. Within this literature it is argued that while alcohol use is problematic for a small minority of young people, for the majority it is functional and purposeful:

- May (1992) argued that there had been a succession of 'moral panics' about young people's use of alcohol during the 1970s, '80s and '90s and that they made little sense in view of research which emphasised the stability of young people's use of alcohol during this period. He went on to suggest that research highlighted the 'normality' of alcohol consumption among young people, most of whom drank in moderation.
- Brain *et al.* (2000: 5) offer an 'appreciative' analysis whereby young people's use of alcohol was framed 'as they perceive it – as consumption rather than "abuse"'. They argue that young people consume licit and illicit drugs in order to

seek a 'buzz' (intoxication) and that this profile of 'hedonistic/functional consumption' extends far beyond a small delinquent or damaged core of adolescents, and is apparent among 'otherwise conventional, conforming youth' including higher education students and professional groups. They conclude that policy initiatives and theoretical explanations should adjust to 'post-modernity' so that such consumption can be better socially managed.

Although young people's drinking has, within the UK, increasingly come to be seen as a form of 'consumption', the limits of this perspective have been noted. Research by Coleman and Cater (2005) detailed the multiple motivations behind youthful alcohol consumption, including increased confidence in social and sexual situations, enabling young people to 'escape' or forget problems, and simply to get a 'buzz'. Furthermore, while Dorn (1983) and Gofton (1990) also discuss the positive reasons that young people give for drinking alcohol, it is not only British-based researchers who have rejected the idea that young people's drinking is necessarily problematic. Thus, for example, Pape and Hammer (1996) concluded that, among young males in Norway, getting drunk for the first time in mid-adolescence seemed to be an ingredient in the normal developmental process.

Binge drinking

As well as providing a focus for adult concern about young people, 'binge drinking' is a growing concern among professionals with regard to alcohol consumption by adults. Nevertheless, as we have noted, there is a lack of agreement as to what the term means. This lack of consensus reflects differences in public and professional perceptions, as well as technical debates about the amount of alcohol consumed and the period of time during which it is consumed.

Clinically, binge drinking refers to continuous drinking over a day or more to the point of unconsciousness, but the term is now used more generally to describe heavy drinking sessions. The amount of alcohol involved is a matter of debate, though British studies tend to define binge drinkers as men who consume at least eight units and women at least six units in a day. North American studies tend to use a lower threshold of five or more drinks in a row for men and four for women. Unit-based definitions have been challenged by some commentators who favour subjective approaches which define binge drinking as that

resulting in at least partial drunkenness (Institute of Alcohol Studies, 2005). The Health Education Authority generally avoids defining binge drinking in terms of units per session:

> If you drink most days of the week and you regularly drink more than the benchmark, then you could be said to be a regular heavy drinker ... [and] if you drink a lot on some occasions, perhaps every weekend or less often, and you usually get drunk then you could be described as a *binge drinker*. (quoted in Newburn and Shiner, 2001)

Research by the Department of Health suggests that mean alcohol consumption among those young people who say that they have drunk in the last week increased steadily between 1990 and 1998, from 5.3 units a week to 9.9 units a week. Mean alcohol consumption has fluctuated between 9.5 and 10.5 units a week since 1998, and was 9.5 units in 2003 (Boreham and Blenkinsop, 2004). A survey of English, Scottish and Welsh adults in 1996 classified 12 per cent of young men and six per cent of young women as heavy drinkers, and a national survey of English adults in 1997 also highlighted the greater rate at which young adults engaged in heavy drinking (Goddard, 1998). National surveys of the general population also confirm that binge drinking – defined as drinking above the recommended daily limits – is most common among young age groups (see Figure 21.15).

The fact that much research on binge drinking uses official guidelines about alcohol consumption as its definitional guide is an indication that there are considered to be both health as well as social costs to excessive consumption. One of the alleged social harms is crime, and it is to this we turn next.

Alcohol, crime and criminal justice

The legal situation

Alcohol offences differ from drugs offences. Though there are age restrictions, the possession of alcohol is not generally an offence. However, though legal, the manufacture, sale, distribution and purchase of alcohol are carefully circumscribed by the Licensing Act 1964. The laws restricting the consumption of alcohol are, of course, quite different from those restricting use of heroin, cocaine, amphetamines and other banned substances. As a general outline the legal situation in relation to alcohol is as follows:

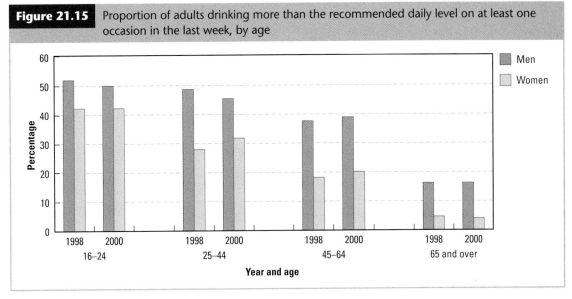

Figure 21.15 Proportion of adults drinking more than the recommended daily level on at least one occasion in the last week, by age

Source: ONS, *Health Survey for England, 2000*.

- A child under the age of five may not be given alcohol except on medical orders.
- Children between five and 18 may consume alcohol at home, but not on licensed premises.
- Adults over the age of 18 may purchase and consume alcohol in licensed premises as well as elsewhere.
- Under 14s may not be present in the bar of licensed premises unless accompanied by a person over 18, it is before 9pm and a children's certificate for the bar is in force.
- A 14 year-old can go into a pub alone but not consume alcohol.
- Under 16s can be present in a restaurant, etc. where alcohol is served with a meal and, at the licensee's discretion, may consume (but not purchase) alcohol bought by a parent or guardian.
- A 16 year-old can buy and consume beer, port, cider or perry (but not spirits) in a pub if having a meal in an area set aside for this purpose.
- It is an offence for a vendor knowingly to sell alcohol to an under-18 year-old.
- In some areas there are bylaws restricting the drinking of alcohol on the streets at any age. Police also have powers to confiscate alcohol from under 18s who drink in public places, and to contact their parents.

Clearly, there are a number of offences that are linked directly to alcohol consumption: drunkenness; being drunk and disorderly and so on. As Wright (1999: 124) notes, offences of drunkenness in England and Wales rose steadily throughout the 1970s and 1980s, peaking in 1989. The number of offences decreased from the peak of 93,000 in 1989 to 42,500 in 1995, though it is likely this reflects changes in the nature of policing rather than alcohol consumption. The rate of convictions for drunkenness peaks at 18 for both men and women. Greater public concern is generally reserved for the role of alcohol in other, often more serious, forms of offending.

Alcohol and crime

The repeated finding of an association between alcohol consumption and a problematic event explains very little about the relationship between the two phenomena. Nevertheless, the tendency to assume cause from association pervades much of the literature. Indeed, the presence of alcohol, where it is found, is often treated as the sole cause for criminal events which are, in their sober manifestations, recognized to be complex, multi-factored phenomena. (Rumgay, 1998, quoted in Dingwall, 2006: 59)

There is now considerable research that shows that younger people are more likely to be both perpetrators and victims of violence – at least violence in public places (see Chapter 20) – and that alcohol is implicated in much of this offending (see, for example, Hindelang *et al.*, 1978). According to the BCS, 47 per cent of victims of violence said the offender 'had been drinking' (Flood-Page *et al.*,

2003). The BCS suggests that approximately two-fifths of violent crimes involve alcohol (over half of violence by strangers, 45% of violence by acquaintances, 32% of domestic violence and 17% of muggings), (Budd, 2003).

Shepherd and Brickley's (1996) study of an Accident and Emergency (A&E) department found that 85 per cent of 18–35 year-old males injured in urban city centre violence were involved in assaults that either took place in a bar or shortly after leaving one (see also Warburton and Shepherd, 2006). Not only is drinking associated with offending, it is also linked to victimization. People injured in cases of assault are more likely to have been drinking at the time than those injured in other ways (Hayden, 1995), and those assaulted are likely themselves to be occasionally 'heavy' or 'binge' drinkers (Yates, 1987; Shepherd and Brickley, 1996; Strategy Unit, 2003).

As with illicit drugs the precise nature of the relationship between alcohol and crime is difficult to determine. At the very least, we may state with some certainty that alcohol is *associated with* a considerable amount of crime (Marsh and Fox Kibby, 1992; Parker, 1996). Thus, for example, Newcombe *et al.*'s (1995) study of adolescents in the North-West of England found a strong relationship between offending and the frequency and amount of alcohol consumed. Cookson (1992), in a self-report survey of over 600 convicted male offenders, found that one-quarter reported being drunk at the time of the offence, and a further 16 per cent said they had been drinking, but were not drunk. She found 'habitual drunkenness' to be associated with self-reports of all major types of offending.

The young offenders in McMurran and Hollin's (1989) sample, reported drinking an average of 58 units a week, and they found alcohol to play a similar role in both property and violent offending. Similarly, Ferguson *et al.*'s (1996) longitudinal study found that both male and female 15–16 year-olds who drank heavily, frequently or problematically were at increased risk of committing both violent and property crimes. Not only would there appear to be a general association between offending and alcohol consumption, but some studies have also detected a more specific link between drinking and persistent offending. Data from the Youth Lifestyles Survey (Flood-Page *et al.*, 2000) show a clear relationship between the level of alcohol consumption and serious or persistent offending. A higher proportion of offenders aged 12–17 than non-offenders were frequent drinkers (36% compared with 20%) (see also Hagell and Newburn, 1994; Audit

Commission, 1996; Parker, 1996). This pattern held across the age range. Relatedly, Parker's (1996) study of 'persistent young adult offenders' found that their drinking and offending careers overlapped and interacted in complex ways.

As has been implied, however, explaining the link between alcohol use and crime (like drug use and crime) is not straightforward. Longitudinal research tends to suggest that offending and drunkenness share common 'risk factors' (parental substance use, conduct problems in middle childhood and affiliations with 'delinquent peers'). Thus, Ferguson *et al.* (1996) found statistically significant relationships between both alcohol misuse and juvenile offending as well as:

- social disadvantage;
- family adversity throughout childhood (a range of items including poor parenting, family instability and conflict);
- a family history of alcohol or drug and/or alcohol abuse;
- individual factors, such as early tendencies toward conduct problems;
- affiliations with 'delinquent peers' at age 15.

Much of the literature on alcohol and crime is couched in the language of 'shared risk factors'. Thus, there is some support for the idea that aggressive behaviour may be a precursor to later heavy drinking and alcohol-related aggression (White and Hansell, 1996), though some have found evidence for the reverse relationship (alcohol use leading to aggression) and for a 'shared risk factors' explanation (see also Coggans and McKellar, 1995). In a similar vein, McMurran and Hollin (1989), from a survey of 100 incarcerated young offenders, suggest that there is a 'functional relationship' between drinking and delinquency. That is, they say, alcohol use may be both an antecedent to offending and a consequence of it. Farrington (1996), acknowledging this, points out that a factor such as alcohol misuse can be both a symptom and a cause simultaneously.

Whilst a number of studies have drawn broad links between alcohol use and offending in general, evidence of causality is stronger in relation to aggression and violence. There is now considerable evidence that aggression and violent offending are linked with heavy drinking and drunkenness (Graham *et al.*, 1998). There is, in addition, evidence that increases in the total consumption of alcohol are associated with changes in the levels of recorded violent crime (Smith, 1990). Studies of police records show that a significant proportion of violent offenders are either persistent heavy drinkers or were drunk when the violent offence occurred (Wiley and Weisner, 1995).

Even if some connection between alcohol consumption and aggression can be found, this still leaves the question of the nature of the 'causal' relationship. Rossow *et al.* (1999) speculate that alcohol intake increases the risk of aggression in situations of frustration or in response to provocation. Age, however, is crucial:

> In early adolescence drinking and intoxication is still rather infrequent and deviant and ... early onset of drinking tends to be a predictor or symptom of other problem behaviours. Among older adolescents, however, there was still a small but statistically significant net effect of intoxication on violent behaviour when all potential confounders were taken into account. (1999: 1029)

Shepherd (1996: 501), commenting on this connection, suggests that it is consistent with evidence of a link between injury and high binge consumption in young men (see also Shepherd *et al.*, 1990). Finally in this regard, Cookson (1992) argues that focusing on the role of alcohol in particular violent events, rather than on its role in individual offending behaviour, highlights its role as a contributory factor. Thus, she says, 'when criminals are the focus of the study it seems from all data sources that drinking and delinquency go together, and that this is true for all types of crime. When criminal incidents are examined, alcohol is clearly involved more frequently in crimes of violence than in crimes of acquisition' (1992: 359).

It is important, however, not to be uncritical in accepting such links. Parker (1996) in his study of young adult offenders in the North-West of England, illustrated a number of difficulties in attempting to isolate alcohol use as a key variable. He noted:

> Our respondents interchanged alcohol and illicit drugs, they used different drugs such as cannabis and amphetamine for different purposes at different times. They also emphasized how their preferred lifestyles, which embraced drinking and drug use, changed through time, affected by a range of contingencies – the most important of which was income generated by acquisitive crime. Drinking careers and criminal careers overlapped in complex ways. In short, these respondents remind us that alcohol is an accessory, but both to crime and to a lawful good time. There is perhaps no definitive criminological message in a bottle. (1996: 296)

In recent times many town and city centres have been quite substantially transformed both by efforts at regeneration but also by, often linked, developments in the leisure/pleasure industry. The emergence of what is now generally referred to as the 'night-time economy' has seen a spectacular set of changes in the way in which youthful leisure is performed, how alcohol is consumed and how much of it is consumed. In the past 25 years, during which there has been a substantial decline in the number of pubs in rural areas, there has been a 30 per cent increase in the number of licensed premises overall reflecting the huge change in our major urban centres (Hobbs *et al.*, 2003).

Town centre violence – encouraged, it has been argued, by a 'night-time economy' that has made the consumption of alcohol central to young people's leisure. Are 'alcohol-free zones' one answer?

The changing nature of such premises – with the rise of the 'superpub', a huge variety of themed premises and the emergence of chameleon bars that operate as one thing during the daytime and quite another at night – have brought with them a number of regulatory challenges. As Hobbs *et al.* (2003: 28–36) put it: 'We are currently witnessing the rapid development of differentiated centres of economic power in the form of leisure outlets catering to a range of audiences, but with a hard core of alcohol-based dance music bars and clubs designed predominantly for young heterosexuals ... Alcohol is the vital lubricant that aids the propulsion of young people into this carnivalesque and consumer-oriented world.' Crucially, this carnivalesque world is one that is regularly punctuated by violence.

> Acutely aware of the visceral pleasures and seductive hedonism of the night-time carnival, our respondents overwhelmingly held the opinion that violence was simply a part of the show in the same way that it has for a long time been an organic 'fairground attraction' in village shows and traditional village 'football' matches. It was perhaps an unwanted digression from the central business of purchasing and consuming pleasurable experiences, seeking sexual encounters ... but for the most part the young people we talked to accepted it as an unavoidable aspect of the night-time scene. (Winlow and Hall, 2006: 96)

Costs of alcohol misuse and alcohol-related crime

In terms of the estimated harms, the government's Strategy Unit report (2003) estimated that every year:

- Alcohol dependence syndrome accounts for over 30,000 hospital episodes.
- 150,000 people enter hospital as a consequence of alcohol.
- Around 20,000 people die prematurely.
- There are an estimated 1.2m alcohol-related violent incidents.
- 480 deaths result from drink-driving.
- Up to 17m days are lost from alcohol-related absence and up to 20m due to alcohol-related reduced employment activity.
- Up to 1.3m children are affected by family drinking.
- There are up to 20,000 street drinkers.

A study conducted by the Cabinet Office sought to estimate the costs of alcohol misuse, including the costs incurred as a result of alcohol-related crime (see Table 21.6). It is worth bearing in mind when looking at such figures that identifying a link between alcohol and crime is often problematic and therefore it is often no more than an assumption that certain forms of crime can be straightforwardly attributed to alcohol consumption. With this caveat in mind, the estimate covers three main categories of cost: an estimate of the

worth of property damaged or stolen; the victim support and emotional impact costs; and, the loss of productive output – through being unable to work, etc. – by victims of crime. As Figure 31.6 suggests, the estimated total costs of alcohol-related crime are over £8 billion per annum at 2001 prices. When drink driving is added, the estimated costs rise to approximately £12 billion a year. This includes estimated costs of almost £2 billion for the criminal justice system to process such offences, £2.5 billion in property/health and victim services costs and £1 billion in lost productive output (Cabinet Office, 2003).

Government alcohol policy

In addition to restricting the sale of alcohol and its consumption on licensed premises to people aged 18 and over, a number of initiatives have been introduced by government to limit or manage drinking, particularly by young people. In the main it has been local bylaws that have been used. A bylaw passed in Coventry in 1989 banned public drinking – i.e. on the street – in the city centre and was claimed by some to have resulted in a significant drop in alcohol-related disorder made up of low level incivilities, but not mugging or assault (Ramsay, 1990). A number of other experiments around the same time were undertaken in Bath, Chester, Scarborough, Stockton-on-Tees, Aldershot and in Newquay/St Austell. These were less closely monitored by government, but still appear to have provided a model for 'alcohol-free zones' in other parts of the country.

More recently, the Criminal Justice and Police Act 2001 gave local authorities extended powers to ban public drinking. Local authorities can now designate certain public places as areas in which alcohol may not be consumed in public if they are satisfied that there has been nuisance or annoyance to members of the public, or a section of the public, or there has been disorder associated with the consumption of alcohol. Designated Public Place Orders give the police powers to confiscate alcohol.

The Anti-Social Behaviour Act 2003 gave the police the power to disperse groups and take people under 16 home in areas designated as dispersal zones. The zones are designated with the consent of the local authority where the police officer has reasonable grounds for believing that groups of two or more individuals are causing people alarm or distress, or that anti-social behaviour is a significant or persistent problem. Finally in this regard,

Table 21.6	Costs as a consequence of alcohol-related crime, England and Wales 2000/01				
	Alcohol-related	Average costs (£)			
Type of offence	Cases	Property/victim	Lost output	Emotional	Total costs
Homicide	319	5,000	370,000	0	125,322,932
Common assault	841,770	10	20	240	238,133,374
Wounding	309,730	1,206	2,000	12,000	4,934,706,373
Sexual offences	18,848	1,206	2,000	12,000	300,297,666
Burglary in business	159,998	1,200	40	0	207,893,734
Criminal damage	3,151,896	440	30	0	1,552,146,640
Robbery from individual	43,440	506	420	2,400	151,382,307
Robbery from business	9,185	1,550	120	590	21,749,834
Burglary in a dwelling	168,470	834	40	550	251,359,685
Theft from a person	80,080	130	4	100	19,633,737
Theft of a pedal cycle	50,050	127	4	100	12,113,764
Theft of vehicle	42,900	3,060	60	890	180,245,621
Theft from a vehicle	202,800	300	10	180	104,118,305
Attempted vehicle theft	91,910	120	7	120	23,786,075
Other theft and handling	192,920	127	4	100	46,693,055
Total costs (£)					8,169,563,102

Source: Cabinet Office (2003).

the Violent Crime Reduction Act 2006 introduced what are now known as *Alcohol Disorder Zones* in which publicans and owners of off-licences and clubs in designated areas will be issued with a warning where there is a problem of crime/anti-social behaviour, and if they fail to take steps to deal with the problem they face having to pay for extra policing, street cleaning and hospital costs.

The increasing powers available to police and to local authorities have been introduced at the same time as there has been considerable liberalisation of the licensing laws in England and Wales. Prior to the introduction of new arrangements by the Licensing Act 2003, pubs ceased serving alcohol at 11pm. Many argued that this led to drinking being compressed into relatively short periods, particularly as 'last orders' approached, and a strong body of opinion supported the extension of the period in which pubs and clubs could open. Under the new arrangements, licensees have been able to apply for permission to operate flexible opening,

with the possibility of operating 24 hours a day. Applications for such licences had to take into account the potential impact on local residents and businesses. The results of a Home Office assessment of the impact of changes to the licensing laws can be seen in the extract below.

For the first time in 2004 the Government produced a formal alcohol policy, its title, *Alcohol Harm Reduction Strategy*, giving a sense of what was driving it. The strategy, updated in 2007 (HM Government, 2007) had four key aims:

- To improve the information available to individuals and to start the process of change in the culture of drinking to get drunk.
- To better identify and treat alcohol misuse.
- To prevent and tackle alcohol-related crime and disorder and deliver improved services to victims and witnesses.
- To work with the industry in tackling the harms caused by alcohol.

Impact of the Licensing Act 2003 on violent crime and criminal damage

The introduction of the Licensing Act 2003 in November 2005 allowed flexible opening hours for licensed premises. The Home Office has undertaken an assessment of the change in the timing and volume of violent offences from October 2004 onwards. Detailed information on the occurrence of the offences by time of day was collected from 27 police forces in England and Wales. Of these, 23 forces have provided data up to March 2006.

Information was collected on selected offences in five groups.[7]

The data from the subset of forces shows a similar pattern in violent offences to that for England and Wales as a whole. The number of violent offences with injury in both datasets fell by 10 per cent between the quarters August – October 2005 and November 2005 – January 2006. There was a similar rise in the two datasets for violent offences without injury and criminal damage, although the proportion was higher for the subset of forces: a rise of 3.6 per cent for the subset, compared with a rise of 1.2 per cent for all forces combined. This is due to the greater proportionate rise

in two forces, Durham and South Yorkshire, following the amendments to the recording of common assault (see Section 5.4 Other offences against the person).

The total number of offences recorded in the subset has remained largely stable at around 80,000 offences per month since October 2004. The Figure below shows the proportion of violent offences and criminal damage occurring between 11pm and 2am by offence type over the period October 2004 to March 2006. The trend for each offence group shows little overall change but seasonal variations do occur with peaks in December and in the summer months in particular. Since the introduction of the Act in November 2005, the proportions of offences for each type occurring between 11pm and 2am are consistent with the same months in the previous year.

The data show no indication of a rise in the overall level of offences or a shift in the timing of offences as a result of the change in the opening hours of licensed premises. More detailed results will be published in due course.

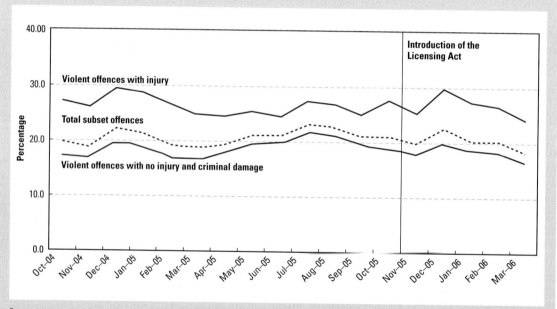

[7]Five offence groups: more serious violence against the person (offence codes 1, 2, 4, 1, 5); other offences with injury (8A, 8D); other offences without injury (excluding harassment) (104, 105A, 105B); harassment (8C, 8E); criminal damage (5O, 58A–58H). These offences have been combined into two groups: 'Violent offences with injury' (groups 1 and 2), and 'violent offences with no injury and criminal damage' (groups 3–5). Figures are also presented for the 'total subset offences' (groups 1–5).

Source: Walker et al. (2006)

The harms associated with excessive drinking include a range of health problems, lost work productivity, family problems and a number of crime-related concerns including violent crime and, in particular, domestic violence. From the point of view of the issues covered in this chapter, one of the assessments made by government leading up to the publication of its alcohol strategy concerned the relative contribution made by different factors to what it called the 'disease burden' (the health costs) in developed nations. The greatest of these was tobacco at 12.2 per cent followed by high blood pressure at 10.9 per cent. Alcohol was the third most significant factor at 9.2 per cent and illicit drugs only eighth of those listed at 1.8 per cent. Though both belated and arguably rather marginal, the shift in attention that appears to be taking place away from illicit drugs and towards alcohol appears somewhat overdue.

Review questions

1   What are the main legal restrictions on the purchase and consumption of alcohol?

2   What does the term 'binge drinking' mean?

3   What are the possible relationships between alcohol and crime?

4   What are the main 'harms' associated with alcohol consumption?

Drugs, alcohol and crime

Most public statements by politicians on the subject of crime and its control these days are likely to make some reference to drugs, and increasingly likely to mention alcohol. Over the past 20 years there has been a very sizeable expansion in the criminal justice-based interventions aimed at drug users and, in particular, those users considered to be drug dependent or problematic. Although successive drugs strategies have talked about taking a broad-based approach, with terms like prevention and harm reduction used regularly, the bulk of expenditure in this area has been devoted to criminal justice and enforcement.

Like so many aspects of criminal justice, or related topics, drug use is also an area in which public debate is often characterised by more heat than light. Moral panic is not uncommon and it is still politically problematic, for example, for politicians to admit that they have ever smoked cannabis, even though survey evidence suggests that a very substantial number of people will do so in their lifetime. The contrast with alcohol is stark. Legally available for purchase and consumption over the age of 18 there is growing evidence that excessive alcohol consumption has both significant effects on health and is also linked with violence and disorder (though this chapter should make you think carefully about cause and effect in this area) and yet its regulation is dealt with very differently from a range of other substances – some of which are assessed by experts to be less harmful.

The various attempts that have been made recently to assess the harmful impacts of a range of different substances – licit and illicit – have all suggested that alcohol and tobacco are more harmful than, say, cannabis. What should the response be? The Police Foundation Inquiry (Runciman, 2000) resisted the suggestion that these substances should be subject to legal prohibition on the basis that:

> It is simply a fact that the use of alcohol and tobacco is so widespread and familiar that an attempt to prohibit their supply by law would lead to widespread resentment and law breaking … Although it [alcohol] is a dangerous drug and causes enormous social costs and harm, it is also used by many people moderately and non-destructively. It is strictly the misuse of alcohol that needs to be prevented, and while the ways in which this can best be done may be debated, control under the [Misuse of Drugs Act] is not one of them. (Police Foundation, 2000: 50)

If one accepts such an argument, then it necessarily raises the reverse question of whether there are some substances currently prohibited by the Misuse of Drugs Act that would be best regulated by other means.

Questions for further discussion

1 What would a drugs policy based on 'harm reduction' look like?

2 What are the pros and cons of drugs legalisation?

3 Is it appropriate to coerce people into drugs treatment through the criminal justice system?

4 Are contemporary concerns about 'binge drinking' just another moral panic?

5 Do you think the law should be changed to make the availability of drugs like that of alcohol, the availability of alcohol like that of drugs, or neither?

Further reading

There are a number of extremely helpful books and reports on the subject of drugs and alcohol. Readers are recommended to consult:

Bennett, T. and Holloway, K. (2005) *Understanding Drugs, Alcohol and Crime*, Maidenhead: Open University Press

Bean, P. (2004) *Drugs and Crime*, 2nd edn, Cullompton: Willan

Dingwall, G. (2005) *Alcohol and Crime*, Cullompton: Willan

Plant, M and Plant, M. (2006) *Binge Britain: Alcohol and the national response*, Oxford: Oxford University Press

Reuter, P. and Stevens, A. (2007) *An Analysis of UK Drug Policy: A monograph prepared for the UK Drug Policy Commission*, London: UKDPC

South, N. (2007) Drugs, alcohol and crime, in Maguire, M. *et al.* (eds) *The Oxford Handbook of Criminology*, 4th edn, Oxford: Oxford University Press

There are a number of useful essays in Simpson, R. *et al.* (eds) (2007) *Drugs in Britain*, Basingstoke: Palgrave, notably those by Newcombe; Pearson; McSweeney *et al.*; and Webster.

On the 'normalisation debate' the pieces to begin with are:

Measham, F. *et al.* (1994) The normalisation of recreational drug use amongst young people in North-West England, *British Journal of Sociology*, 45, 2, 287–312, Oxford: Blackwell Publishing

Shiner, M. and Newburn, T. (1997) Definitely, maybe not? The normalisation of drug use amongst young people, *Sociology*, 31, 3, 511–529, London: Sage Journals

On the new 'night-time economy' there is no better and more informative read than:

Hobbs, R. *et al.* (2003) *Bouncers*, Oxford: Oxford University Press

Websites

The charity *Drugscope* maintains an extremely helpful website with lots of research reports and access to a very sizeable library: www.drugscope.org.uk

Similarly, *Alcohol Concern's* website also contains a lot of useful information: www.alcoholconcern.org.uk

Part 4
Understanding Criminal Justice

22 Penology and punishment

23 Understanding criminal justice

24 Crime prevention and community safety

25 Policing

26 Criminal courts and the court process

27 Sentencing and community penalties

28 Prisons and imprisonment

29 Youth crime and youth justice

30 Restorative justice

Chapter outline

What is punishment?	**516**
Utilitarian or consequentialist approaches	**518**
Deterrence	518
General deterrence	518
Individual deterrence	519
Rehabilitation	520
Incapacitation	521
Retributivism	**524**
Just deserts	524
The sociology of punishment	**527**
Emile Durkheim	527
Max Weber	529
Marxism	530
Norbert Elias	531
Michel Foucault	532
The impact of Foucault	534
Conclusion: an era of mass incarceration?	**535**
Questions for further discussion	537
Further reading	538
Websites	538

Penology and punishment

CHAPTER SUMMARY

The eight chapters that follow this one all explore different aspects of the criminal justice process – the end point of which involves the imposition of punishment. In this chapter we consider the idea of punishment – what it involves and how it is to be understood. In the main, the chapter focuses on two sets of debates:

● the first, a largely philosophical discussion, focuses upon the nature and rationale for punishment: is it primarily imposed in order to prevent criminality in the future, or is it a penalty imposed for misconduct in the past?

● the second set of debates is primarily sociological and concerns how we are to conceive of the place of punishment within society and to understand punishment as a set of social practices.

What is punishment?

There are a number of criteria that can be laid down in order to distinguish punishment in the sense that interests us as criminologists from other forms of unpleasant forms of pain. According to various experts (Hudson, 2003b; Zedner, 2004) these include:

1 The involvement of an evil, and unpleasantness to the person on whom the punishment is inflicted.

2 It must be for an offence, actual or supposed.

3 It must be of an offender, actual or supposed.

4 It must be the work of personal agencies.

5 It must be imposed by an authority conferred through or by the institutions against the rules of which the offence has been committed.

6 The pain which is inflicted must be intentional, not accidental or coincidental (Hudson, 2003).

7 To interest criminologists, the punishment should be imposed in response to a 'criminal offence'.

8 It should be imposed by a judicial authority.

Not surprisingly punishment can and does take a variety of forms, particularly if one looks cross-culturally. Until relatively recently most liberal democracies still used the death penalty. However, during the course of the twentieth century most abandoned it. The United States remains the great exception – but even within America there is significant variation, state by state, in the use of the death penalty (Zimring, 2003). In this opening section we will quickly look at some of the central issues in discussions of punishment; what these days is generally referred to as 'penology'. Having provided a brief overview we will then look at ideas of punishment in greater detail.

In the context of criminal justice, Zedner (2004) says there are six key questions in relation to punishment:

1 What are the prerequisites of formal punishment? Two basic principles govern punishment:

a there can be no crime without law; and

b there can be no punishment without law.

2 What are its component parts? Two components appear key to most, though not all, definitions of punishment:

a censure (the expression of disapproval); and

b sanction ('pain').

However, as we will see, particularly in relation to what is called 'retributivism', it is sometimes easier to find a justification for the censure than it is for the sanction.

3 By whom is punishment imposed?
Is it by the state only or by other bodies as well? Sometimes there is a distinction drawn between the allocation of punishment on the one hand and the delivery of punishment on the other (allocation usually remains in the hands of the state whereas, say in the case of private prisons, the delivery may be via private corporations).

4 Upon whom, and when, is punishment to be imposed?
Must the imposition of punishment follow conviction? If so, what of informal punishment or the infliction of pain for civil wrongs – are they punishments? In this regard the recent move toward the increasing use of 'on-the-spot' penalties and civil penalties such as ASBOs is an interesting development (see Chapter 29).

5 What social roles does punishment fulfil?

As we will see, these may vary and may include bolstering what Durkheim referred to as the collective conscience, through to maintaining the position of the powerful.

6 And with what justification or to what end is it inflicted?

Why should offenders be punished? This is the matter that will form the major focus of our concerns in this chapter. Why do we inflict punishment? What are we trying to achieve? And, on what basis are we justified in so doing? There are numerous answers to this question including to:

a Discourage people from offending.

b Make amends for what they have done.

c Protect us from those who are dangerous.

d Reinforce social values and bonds.

e Simply because they deserve to be punished.

However, as we will see, there are a number of practical problems involved. Centrally, the aims of punishment may be several, but they may also conflict. What someone 'deserves' may not be the same as what is judged necessary to protect society. The literature generally asks two questions: on what grounds can the state inflict pain, and how much pain is the state justified in using in any particular case? There are no 'final' answers to these questions, but exploring the arguments helps us understand the basis of our (and others') system of punishment, and provides a philosophical and normative basis upon which we can debate and discuss how we think our penal system should operate in the future.

It is at this stage that we begin to encounter quite a number of philosophical terms which help us identify different positions in relation to punishment and, most particularly, help us to understand the different responses that there are to Zedner's sixth question outlined above. In thinking about justifications for punishments, approaches are generally divided into two main camps. These are *consequentialists* on the one hand and *retributivists* (after 'retribution') on the other.

Retributivism is backward-looking rather than directly considering the future good. Retribution implies the imposition of something (punishment) in response to actions already undertaken. By contrast, consequentialist approaches tend to justify punishment on the basis of what it will achieve in the future. That is to say it is frequently aimed at the prevention of future offending – and, as we will see, there are a variety of means that it can use to do this. These forward-looking theories are generally based on utilitarianism – itself often summarised in Jeremy Bentham's words as the 'greatest happiness of the greatest number'. On this basis, the 'good' brought about by the infliction of punishment must outweigh the pain imposed.

In addition to philosophical approaches to the study of punishment there is a developing field, heavily influenced by sociological theory, which focuses on punishment as a set of socio-cultural practices. This field – now generally referred to as *penology* or the study of *penality* – examines the structures and systems of punishment and asks what these have to tell us about the nature of particular social systems. Why, for example, did industrialising societies progressively abandon

One of the key concerns in penology is the relationship between punishment and society – and understanding why, for example, contemporary western societies prefer prisons to the stocks.

forms of punishment that were public and spectacular – public executions, floggings, the stocks, and so on – and replace them with the prison? What does the nature of punishment have to tell us about contemporary social change? We will return to these questions later in the chapter. First, we turn to matters of penal philosophy.

Utilitarian or consequentialist approaches

Although there is by no means complete overlap between utilitarian philosophy and consequentialist approaches to punishment, much of what we will encounter in this section has been informed or influenced by utilitarian theory. As we saw above, this is often linked as a starting point with Bentham's advocacy of the idea of the promotion of the sum of human happiness. The utility or goal of punishment – the consequence it seeks to promote – is generally the prevention or reduction of crime. It can do this in three main ways: through deterrence (putting people off), rehabilitation (improving people) or incapacitation (reducing or removing the possibility of offending). We will take each of these in turn.

Deterrence

From Bentham onwards a distinction has been drawn between two types of deterrence: *individual* and *general* deterrence (sometimes referred to as *specific* and *general* deterrence). The former refers to the aim of deterring those who have already offended from doing so again. The latter is the more general aim of imposing punishment so as to deter other potential offenders. In this regard, according to Bentham, 'The punishment suffered by the offender presents to every one an example of what he himself will have to suffer, if he is guilty of the same offence' (quoted in Hudson, 2003b: 19).

General deterrence

General deterrence has arguably been the predominant justification for punishment and it is something that also benefits from having intuitive appeal. Most of us understand, and may well also believe, that imposing punishment on someone is a

sensible way of showing others that such behaviour is unacceptable. A distinction is often drawn between the *certainty* and the *severity* of punishment. Historically – certainly in pre-industrial times – severity was the basis of the system of punishment. Penalties were often arbitrary and, by contemporary standards, would seem often to be extraordinarily severe. One only has to look at the Bloody Code or the history of transportation, and apply contemporary standards, to see the way in which severity of punishment was a key organising principle up until the eighteenth century (see Chapter 2). As reliance on the death penalty and transportation declined, so the underlying basis of the penal system shifted toward the *certainty* of punishment.

Important in this regard were the writings of Cesare Beccaria (see Chapter 5). Believing that offenders made decisions based on 'rational choice', and were therefore largely uninfluenced by their social and personal conditions, Beccaria argued that the extent of punishment should be limited by what was necessary to prevent crime, and that the system of punishments should be graduated to fit the severity of the crime and not the nature of the individual criminal:

> The purpose of punishment is not that of tormenting or afflicting any sentient creature, nor of undoing a crime already committed ... Can the wailings of a wretch, perhaps, undo what has been done and turn back the clock? The purpose, therefore, is nothing other than to prevent the offender from doing fresh harm to his fellows and to deter others from doing likewise ... [P]unishments and the means adopted for inflicting them should, consistent with proportionality, be so selected as to make the most efficacious and lasting impression on the minds of men with the least torment to the body of the condemned. (Beccaria 1767/1995: 31)

As such, as we will see, such ideas have much in common with the 'tariff' approaches to punishment that have been used in Britain and elsewhere in recent decades.

There are a number of potential difficulties with the idea of general deterrence (von Hirsch *et al.*, 1999):

- How does one decide how severe punishments have to be in order to make people decide not to commit offences?

- Is the same level of severity appropriate for everyone (are we deterred by different things)?

- Are all offences rationally assessed? What about those offences where there is a significant degree of emotion?
- Is it the case that all those people one might wish to deter will actually know about punishments that have been imposed?

In the 1970s the Home Office undertook a review of existing studies of deterrence. The conclusion to the review (Beyleveld, 1979: 136; quoted in Hudson, 2003) was that:

> There exists no scientific basis for expecting that a general deterrence policy, which does not involve an unacceptable interference with human rights, will do anything to control the crime rate. The sort of information needed to base a morally acceptable general policy is lacking. There is some convincing evidence in some areas that some legal sanctions have exerted deterrent effects. These findings are not, however, generalizable beyond the conditions that were investigated. Given the present state of knowledge, implementing an official deterrence policy can be no more than a shot in the dark, or a political decision to pacify 'public sentiment'.

Individual deterrence

Let us move now from general to *individual* deterrence. Individual deterrence, or what is sometimes referred to as 'special' deterrence, is again often to be found in contemporary justifications of punishment. Let us take two examples. In the early 1980s

William Whitelaw, Home Secretary in Margaret Thatcher's first administration, announced, in a speech to the 1983 party conference the introduction of a new regime in juvenile detention centres which would provide a 'short, sharp, shock' to those on the receiving end and, consequently, would be more effective in preventing future offending. There have been similar experiments in the United States with what are generally referred to as 'boot camps'. Unfortunately for those who place their trust in such initiatives, the research evidence is not good. The Home Office's own evaluation of the short, sharp, shock initiative was that the regimes were no more effective than those they had replaced. The most recent review of research evidence on boot camps concludes that the 'evidence suggests that the military component of boot camps is not effective in reducing post-boot camp offending' (Wilson *et al.*, 2005: 18).

A second example would be the raft of 'three strikes and you're out' sentences that were introduced in America, and to a lesser extent elsewhere, in the 1980s and 1990s. The reasoning that lies behind such sentences is that the extent of punishment increases as the number of previous offences rises with a cut-off – usually of three – which triggers an exemplary sentence. Huge numbers of offenders have been sentenced to lengthy periods of imprisonment, especially in states such as California, and yet there is little evidence of any particularly significant impact on crime (Zimring *et al.*, 2001).

'Three strikes and you're out'

The American baseball term 'three strikes and you're out' came to be applied in the 1990s to a particular form of mandatory minimum sentencing – a form of sentencing which specifies a minimum term that someone must serve if they are a repeat offender. Though the laws vary, as the term suggests there tends to be an increase in sentence severity up to the point at which a three-time offender receives what is often a life sentence. In some states the impact of three-strikes laws has been particularly dramatic and has led to the formation of a number of campaigning groups, such as Families Against Mandatory Minimums, that have been seeking repeal of the legislation.

Families Against Mandatory Minimums

Finally, in addition to questions of efficacy (whether such approaches work) there are also questions of acceptability (whether they are fair or right). Hudson (2003b) notes three types of moral objection:

- It allows for the innocent to be punished (the principle is simply that some punishment must be meted out in order to remind others of its existence).

- It allows for punishments to be imposed that are in excess (often well in excess) of the harms done by the offence (in one infamous case in California a twice-convicted felon received a 'third strike' life sentence of 25 years to life for the theft of a slice of pizza from a group of children. The sentence was reduced to six years on appeal).

- It allows for the punishment of crimes that have not yet been committed.

Of course, in addition to moral difficulties there is the no small matter of evidence for the effectiveness of deterrence. Writing in the 1970s, Robert Martinson famously queried whether much at all had been learned in this area:

> We know almost nothing about the 'deterrent effect', largely because 'treatment' theories have so dominated our research, and 'deterrence' theories have been relegated to the status of a historical curiosity. Since we have almost no idea of the deterrent functions that our present system performs or that future strategies might be made to perform, it is possible that there is indeed something that works – that to some extent is working right now in front of our noses, and that might be made to work better – something that deters rather than cures, something that does not so much reform convicted offenders as prevent criminal behaviour in the first place. (1974: 50)

Weisburd *et al.* (1995) examined the behaviour of a group of white-collar criminals in order to test for the possibility of individual deterrence. They found few differences in re-arrest rates for those who had been imprisoned compared with those who had not. By contrast, though in connection with a very different form of offending, the Minneapolis Domestic Violence Experiment appeared to show some impact of arrest – though doubts were later thrown on these findings. One of the more innovative studies was that conducted by Chambliss in the 1960s. Changing procedures so as to increase markedly the certainty and severity of punishment linked to violation of parking regulations on a university campus, Chambliss (1966) found that there were some significant reductions in violations of the rules.

Rehabilitation

If the highpoint of deterrence was around the eighteenth century, then it is to the nineteenth and twentieth centuries that we must turn in looking for the era when rehabilitation was at its height. As we discussed in greater detail in Chapter 2, there are a number of core reasons why deterrence-based approaches to punishment declined in influence and the aims of rehabilitation and reform gained precedence. In part, the change was a consequence of the very significant social changes that took place in this period. The processes of industrialisation and urbanisation lent weight to views that suggested that social and political circumstances were important in understanding human behaviour. Industrialisation also created a vastly increased demand for labour and, consequently, pressure increased to find ways of ensuring that offenders were made available for work rather than, for example, being transported for use as forced labour in the colonies.

Second, as implied initially, positivistic-influenced social sciences began to develop. They questioned the idea of crime as simply rational choice and focused rather on notions of individual pathology, seeking to distinguish criminals from non-criminals according to their physical features or other aspects of their circumstances. As Zedner (2004) notes, 'At its height, punishment was recast as a means of restoring the offender to good citizenship through programmes of training, treatment, counselling, psychotherapy, drug and even shock treatment'. By and large, however, there was relatively little distinction drawn between 'types' of offender in the nineteenth century, and 'treatments' were not generally geared to individual differences or perceived needs.

Again, a number of shortcomings in rehabilitative approaches to punishment can be identified. As Zedner (2004) and others (see, for example, Ward and Maruna, 2007) note, rehabilitative approaches rely on a number of core assumptions, each of which is at least challengeable:

- *Delinquency has causes that are discoverable.* As we saw in Chapters 5 to 15 there is a long-standing debate within criminology between those who, largely working in the positivist tradition, assume that the causes of delinquency are discoverable and that this is an appropriate aim for criminology, and others working in *critical* and *constructivist* traditions who tend to be more concerned with the ways in which state power is used to criminalise particular sections of the population.

- *These causes are open to treatment.*
  For a considerable period it was assumed that offenders could be reformed or rehabilitated. From the 1970s onward considerable doubt was thrown upon such claims, not least as a result of the publication of a review of existing research evidence by Robert Martinson. Though it was entitled *What Works*, Martinson's (1974) work is generally credited with ushering in a period in which faith in rehabilitation declined almost to invisibility, leading to the use of the term 'nothing works' to describe the new era.

- *If not treated they will get worse.*
  Labelling theorists (see Chapter 10) would argue quite the reverse. There is much evidence that the criminal justice process is itself criminogenic. Many who come into contact with the criminal justice system will, in fact, go on to display more extensive patterns of offending than might otherwise be the case.

- *Treatment, even if coerced is not punitive as it is for the offender's good.*
  However, considerable criticism has been aimed at indeterminate sentencing and of what are justified as being 'welfare-oriented interventions for their punitive and inequitable nature'. One example of this concerns the use of 'care orders' in juvenile courts during the 1970s in particular. Designed to allow intervention by social workers in response to the young person's particular welfare needs, they also had the effect of increasing any subsequent punishment. As Morris and Giller (1987: 101) noted, 'While one can understand the benign motives of those who used a care order for a juvenile who had committed an offence in order to facilitate social work ends, their contribution in producing as an unintended consequence severe responses by magistrates when the juvenile returned to the juvenile court cannot be minimised'.

- *Overlooks the fact that much offending is opportunistic.*
  Thus, rather than taking the view that there are deep, underlying causes that must be 'treated', there are schools of thought within criminology (particularly those we discussed under the heading of 'contemporary classicism' in Chapter 14) which take the view that, even if this is the case, such causes have not shown themselves to be especially amenable to manipulation and, consequently, we are better advised to manipulate the circumstances in which offending takes place.

In addition, rehabilitative approaches are criticised for holding to an overly-determined view of behaviour, of placing too much emphasis on social and cultural conditions, and too little on the ability of individuals to make decisions and choices. Much of the history of traditional criminological approaches to female offending, for example, has rested on sexist assumptions about how women's biology is a crucial determinant of their behaviour (see Chapter 15). One, if not *the*, core aim of feminist scholarship in this area has been to challenge such views and to assert the importance of individual agency in decision-making.

For a whole host of reasons, rehabilitative ideas have had a rough ride over the past 30 years. And yet, as Ward and Maruna (2007) argue, perhaps in this period the wrong question has been asked. Rather than obsessing about 'what works?', they suggest that a much more practical and realistic question is 'what helps people go straight?' Although on the surface the difference between the two may not seem great, this is deceptive:

> For one thing, it is easy to declare that 'nothing works' when 'works' implies some degree of predictable consistency (i.e. 'reliably works every time'). Nothing 'works' for every offender in every circumstance. Yet it would require an extremely unusual view of the social world for someone to declare 'Nothing *helps* people go straight'. Although many things might hinder this process, surely some things can help it. (2007: 12)

Incapacitation

This approach at preventing or reducing crime holds no assumptions about our ability to rehabilitate offenders, includes nothing which seeks to bring about reform and shows no interest in the harm caused by crime other than the general displeasure signalled by the imposition of the punishment. As Hudson (2003: 31) puts it:

> If general deterrence and individual rehabilitation are difficult to achieve, it perhaps seems a plausible goal to protect potential victims from further crime by known offenders through physical incapacitation, either by rendering criminals physically harmless, or by removing them from circulation.

This approach is based upon the assumption that the state has a duty to protect and that, in the absence of other approaches that can be shown to work, such protection can be provided through some form of incapacitation. Incapacitation may take various forms. When Michael Howard as Home Secretary announced in 1993 that 'prison works', he did so not on the basis of a belief in its ability to rehabilitate offenders but, rather, because he felt that there were good reasons to think that it might deter offenders and, even if it did not, it would certainly incapacitate:

> Let us be clear. Prison works. It ensures that we are protected from murderers, muggers and rapists – and it makes many who are tempted to commit crime think twice.

At its most extreme, of course, the death penalty is the ultimate form of incapacitation. The death penalty was abolished in Britain in the mid-1960s and the vast majority of developed countries have also ceased using execution as a punishment for crime. One of the major exceptions is the United States which had a moratorium on executions between 1967 and 1977, but since that time – in some states – has once again begun using the death penalty regularly.

A number of other forms of incapacitation exist. One area where there is considerable debate concerns sex offending and whether there is anything that can be done to prevent further offending. Some countries still use surgical castration – the removal of the testicles – but this is regarded by many as being in contravention of the Convention on Human Rights. There are countries which use what is euphemistically termed 'chemical castration' of sex offenders whereby drugs are used artificially to lower the production of testosterone in the body (see box below) and, indeed, the possibility of introducing such approaches was briefly mooted in the UK in 2007.

'Chemical castration' in Denmark

In Denmark ... the Herstedvester Institute for Abnormal Offenders is a closed prison that serves the Danish Department of Prisons and Probation as an institution for offenders who require psychiatric or psychological treatment. Denmark has a long history of castrating sexual offenders and was the first country in Europe to legalise surgical castration, performing its first procedure in 1925 and enacting legislation in 1929. In the period 1935–1970, surgical castration was offered on a voluntary basis to sexual offenders in lieu of a prison sentence. Although surgical castration was combined with psychiatric treatment, it was eventually deemed to be inhumane and it was banned. In 1973 chemical castration was implemented as a last resort after other therapeutic measures have failed.

[...] In 1989, 33 offenders were referred for chemical castration at Herstedvester. Three of those referred refused castration, 2 of whom were later released and committed further sexual offences that were serious and resulted in further preventative detention. Of the 30 offenders who commenced treatment, 7 had their treatment discontinued, one after release. Twenty-four offenders underwent treatment in the period of study (including the one who discontinued after release), and were rewarded with the lifting of liberty-related restrictions. Of the 24 who commenced treatment, 5 are still detained, with privileges, 12 have been released on probation and continue to undergo treatment, one has

been released on probation but has recently stopped treatment and is under continued supervision ... One was released and had treatment discontinued following aggressive behaviour associated with the treatment, and 5 were released on probation with a limited period of supervision, all of whom discontinued treatment at the expiry of the supervision period. Of the 5 who discontinued treatment, one has committed a further sexual offence and has been sentenced to further preventative detention and 4 have been without treatment for an average of 2.5 years and have not re-offended. There has been no re-offending by those who have continued treatment.

[...] The sample of offenders is small and the duration of the study is short, but the Institute is optimistic about the treatment regime. Offenders who are treated are reported to be content with the treatment, although in one case treatment was discontinued due to it causing an increase in aggression. Other offenders have experienced negative physiological side effects from the treatment ... [I]t is the policy of the Institute to engage an offender in therapy before and after chemical castration treatment. Offenders typically spend one year in treatment and parole is not contemplated until at least 5–6 months after the chemical castration.

Source: Scottish Executive, *A Review of the Literature on Serious Violent and Sexual Offenders*, available at: http://www.scotland.gov.uk/cru/kd01/green/s-off-10.htm

In England and Wales, high-risk sex offenders who have served their sentences are managed and monitored by Multi-Agency Public Protection Arrangements (MAPPA) and a variety of techniques including supervision, surveillance, curfews and restrictions on various activities are used. As yet, 'chemical castration' has not been used to any significant extent in the UK (Harrison, 2007).

Much contemporary policy interest in incapacitation has centred on the belief – underpinned by a considerable body of research evidence – that a small proportion of offenders are disproportionately responsible for a significant proportion of crime. Estimates vary, and are all probably fairly inaccurate, but the general idea is captured by former American President, Gerald Ford:

> The crime rate will go down if persons who habitually commit most of the predatory crimes are kept in prison for a reasonable period ... because they will not then be free to commit more crimes ... one obvious effect of prison is to separate law breakers from the law-abiding society. (quoted in Zimring and Hawkins, 1995: 18)

The problem lies not in the logic, but in the practice. What is problematic is the process of identifying the 'habitual' or 'persistent' offender. In a study conducted in one Midlands county in England in the mid-1990s when interest in this idea was particularly high in government, Hagell and Newburn (1994) examined how the use of different means of defining a 'persistent' offender might work in practice. They applied three similar, but slightly different definitions, to a sample of young offenders. The three definitions were:

- *Definition 1* – The most active ten per cent of offenders in terms of number of arrests and offences.

- *Definition 2* – Frequency of known and alleged offending over any three-month period during the course of one year.

- *Definition 3* – (The government's preferred definition): any juvenile who has committed one imprisonable offence whilst subject to a supervision order, and who has committed two other similar offences.

Applying the three definitions produced the result shown in Figure 22.1.

Figure 22.1 shows that there was relatively little overlap between definitions and that only three juve-

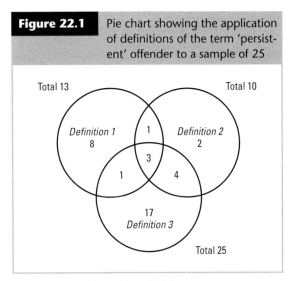

Figure 22.1 Pie chart showing the application of definitions of the term 'persistent' offender to a sample of 25

Source: Hagell and Newburn (1994).

niles were identified as 'persistent' according to all three. The researchers concluded that 'The fact that a discrete group of persistent offenders cannot be identified in this manner suggests that any definition of persistence will inevitably be arbitrary' (1994: 122). Put another way, what this finding points to is a constant problem with incapacitation: the difficulty of 'false positives'. This was described by Norval Morris (1974: 72–73) in the following way:

> Even when a high-risk group of convicted criminals is selected, and those carefully predicted as dangerous are detained, for every three so incarcerated there is only one who would in fact commit serious assaultive crime if all three were released ... [A]s a matter of justice we should never take power over the convicted criminal on the basis of unreliable predictions of his dangerousness.

The false positive problem raises both practical and moral problems. Not only can it not be shown to work – at least not without considerable 'collateral damage', but it is also difficult to justify imposing particularly harsh terms of imprisonment on people who are highly likely *not* to offend in future. Nevertheless, as we have seen with the rise of mandatory minimum sentencing (along the lines of 'three strikes and you're out'), incapacitative sentencing has proved popular with contemporary politicians and has clearly played a role in the very substantial rises in prison populations in England and beyond (Newburn, 2007; Zimring *et al.*, 2003).

Retributivism

Perhaps the most straightforward expression of retributivism is to be found in *lex talionis* – 'an eye for an eye, a tooth for a tooth, a life for a life' (*Exodus* 21, 23–5). Is this simple idea a potential basis for organising our system of punishment? Bluntly, no. Lacey (1988) suggests that there are two fundamental problems:

- Although this sort of equivalence might help us in relation to some offences – say murder – it provides us with no guidance as to the appropriate punishment for other offences such as fraud or blackmail.

- It pays scant regard to the notion that punishment should only be inflicted upon those that are held to be *responsible* for an offence (i.e. whether a killing was an accident or a deliberate act).

Following Immanuel Kant, retributivists hold that punishment should not be a means to an end, but an end in itself. Clearly by contrast anything that is *consequentialist* – concerned with consequences – is a means to an end. In relation to retributivism the justification for punishment is because the offender is held to deserve it – it has no purpose beyond that.

Retributivism in criminology has an interesting history. Until relatively recently it was regarded as a less promising basis for sentencing than consequentialist approaches which allowed for aims such as rehabilitation and reform. However, as doubts grew about the efficacy of rehabilitative programmes and, at least as importantly, concerns grew about the unfairness of indeterminate sentencing, so there developed renewed interest in a particular form of retributive thinking known as 'just deserts' or 'desert theory' – in short, the argument that the punishment ought to be proportionate to the harm caused. We will return to this shortly, but first it is worth saying a little more about the reasons for declining faith in rehabilitative sentencing.

The attack on rehabilitative sentencing came from both ends of the political spectrum. On the 'liberal left' there was increasing concern about the inequities and excesses of indeterminate sentencing. Indeterminate sentencing exists where the length of sentence is left to the discretion of the sentencer. Such approaches were viewed as a necessary part of a rehabilitative approach in order to allow sentencing to be moulded to fit the type of 'treatment' imposed. However, the absence of any obvious direct relationship between the offence and the scale of punishment was viewed by many as being an inappropriate basis for sentencing. It also allowed for considerable variations in the punishments imposed upon people who had ostensibly committed similar offences.

Moreover, the lack of clarity that often existed in rehabilitative sentencing about the precise length of the sentence – because of the vagaries of the parole system – led to inequity and in some well publicised cases not only to resentment but also to prisoner unrest.

At the other end of the spectrum there was increasing criticism of rehabilitative sentencing for its apparent ineffectiveness, and commentators from the 'new right' increasingly called for tougher incapacitive sentencing. In some respects the emergence of mandatory sentencing – 'three strikes' and the like – was a product of precisely such calls for exemplary measures, especially against repeat offenders.

Just deserts

It was against this background that what has been referred to as the new retributivism emerged. Also known as the 'back to justice' movement, it grew in popularity from the mid-1970s onward. The key text in the new movement was called *Doing Justice* (von Hirsch, 1976). At the heart of this approach was the assertion that punishment should be linked to the nature of the crime that had been committed; that is, it should be *proportionate*. There are two distinct elements to proportionality, however. The first concerns the need to rank offences hierarchically according to their seriousness. This is generally referred to as *ordinal proportionality*. In addition, there is the question of the overall scale of punishments. This is generally referred to as *cardinal proportionality* and refers to the question of what the most serious punishment in the scale is to be. The death penalty? Imprisonment? The answer to this question is obviously crucial in establishing the basis on which ordinal scale is constructed.

According to von Hirsch (1993) the argument for proportionality involves three steps:

1 The state's sanctions against proscribed conduct should take a punitive form; that is, visit deprivations in a manner that expresses censure or blame.

2 The severity of a sanction expresses the stringency of the blame.

3 Hence, punitive sanctions should be arrayed according to the degree of blameworthiness (i.e. seriousness) of the conduct.

There are a number of points to note here. First, the justification for punishment is that it is necessary for the state to express censure. Desert theorists proceed on the assumption that offenders are free willed and can therefore be held morally to account for their actions. Second, that censure is connected with a crime that has been committed. There is no reference to, or concern with, any future offending. Third, according to von Hirsch, therefore, sanctions should be ordered, in a schedule, in order to correspond with the seriousness of the crimes concerned. Such a schedule is often referred to as the *tariff*. By making punishment proportionate, desert theory aims to make punishment certain, consistent and fair.

This raises a further question, however, which is how are offences to be ranked? How is seriousness to be assessed? Sometimes, indeed most often, this has been left to sentencers. An alternative is to establish a formal body to construct guidelines which can be used to structure sentencing. The most famous case of this was in the American state of Minnesota which took effect in 1980. Essentially, such guidelines (see Table 22.1) comprised a grid with two axes. Down one axis is the 'offence score' indicating the gravity of the particular offence and along the other axis is the 'criminal history score' indicating the number and gravity of prior convictions. The grid contains a line that distinguishes the point above which prison would be the usual sentence and below which a different type of penalty would be used. In the illustration below the boxes marked 'NP' are those which result in lesser sanctions than prison. The other boxes contain numbers indicating the expected duration of the prison sentence (in months).

In England and Wales, the just deserts-influenced 1991 Criminal Justice Act contained a somewhat simpler attempt at grading punishments, dividing them into three groups according to seriousness: those warranting a fine or discharge; those that should result in a community punishment; and those that are so serious that a custodial sentence is necessary.

There are a number of problems relating to proportionality. First, in relation to ordinal proportionality it seems clear that some offences are obviously easy to rank in relation to one another (serious assault versus theft from a car, for example) but in other cases this is less straightforward, perhaps especially in relation to minor offences (Zedner, 2004). In relation to cardinal proportionality one of the major problems concerns the basis on which the decision is made. As Hudson (2003: 45) puts it, 'the problem is that deserts theory can help with the graduation of punishments within the most severe and least severe points, but can do nothing to tell us what those anchoring points should be'. The consequence is that cardinal proportionality tends to have been much influenced by political considerations.

What then of the reason *why* offenders should be punished? As with von Hirsch's three steps outlined above, the core of punishment concerns the expression of blame. Social disapproval is indicated through such censure.

> Censure addresses the victim. He or she has not only been injured, but *wronged* through someone's culpable act. It thus would not suffice just to acknowledge that the injury has occurred or convey sympathy (as would be appropriate when someone has been hurt by a natural catastrophe). Censure by directing disapprobation at the person responsible, acknowledges that the victim's hurt occurred though another's fault.

> Censure also addresses the act's perpetrator. He is conveyed a certain message concerning his wrongful conduct, namely that he culpably has injured someone, and is disapproved of for having done so. (von Hirsch, in Duff and Garland 1994: 119)

Of course punishment generally involves more than just censure. In desert theory a distinction is often drawn between the censure (the expression of disapproval) and the *sanction*, the *deprivation* or the *hard treatment* (the 'pain' that is inflicted as a consequence). The justification in desert theory for the use of sanctions varies, but in general terms tends to rest on the idea that the censure must be backed up by a *prudential disincentive* – something extra, as it were, to persuade us to resist the temptation to offend. The censure or blame is the primary reason, but it is backed up by sanctions.

Crucially, within this approach it is argued that these sanctions – penalties – must not be too severe or it will be fear rather than the moral sense of being wrongful that will become the primary reason for obeying the law. A variant of this form of desert theory sees punishment as a form of moral communication. So-called 'penal communication' theories find the justification for punishment in the communicative power of censure backed up by 'hard treatment' (Duff, 2003). The serving of the sentence is an indication of the fact that the offence has been accepted as being wrong; in this

Table 22.1   Minnesota sentencing guidelines grid (presumptive sentence lengths in months)

SEVERITY LEVEL OF CONVICTION OFFENSE (Common offenses listed in italics)		CRIMINAL HISTORY SCORE						
		1	2	3	4	5	6 or more
Murder, 2nd Degree *(intentional murder, drive-by-shootings)*	XI	306 *261–367*	426 *278–391*	346 *295–415*	426 *312–439*	426 *329–463*	406 *346–480[2]*	426 *363–480[2]*
Murder, 3rd Degree *Murder, 2nd Degree* *(unintentional murder)*	X	150 *128–180*	165 *141–198*	180 *153–216*	195 *166–234*	210 *179–252*	225 *192–270*	240 *204–288*
Assault, 1st Degree *Controlled Substance Crime, 1st Degree*	IX	86 *74–103*	98 *84–117*	110 *94–132*	122 *104–146*	134 *114–160*	146 *125–175*	158 *135–189*
Aggravated Robbery, 1st Degree *Controlled Substance Crime, 2nd Degree*	VIII	48 *41–57*	58 *50–69*	68 *58–81*	78 *67–93*	88 *75–105*	98 *84–117*	108 *92–129*
Felony DWI	VII	36	42	48	54 *46–64*	60 *51–72*	66 *57–79*	72 *62–86*
Assault, 2nd Degree *Felon in Possession of a Firearm*	VI	21	27	33	39 *34–46*	45 *39–54*	51 *44–61*	57 *49–68*
Residential Burglary *Simple Robbery*	V	18	23	28	33 *29–39*	38 *33–45*	43 *37–51*	48 *41–57*
Nonresidential Burglary	IV	12[1]	15	18	21	24 *21–28*	27 *23–32*	30 *26–36*
Theft Crimes (Over $2,500)	III	12[1]	13	15	17	19 *17–22*	21 *18–25*	23 *20–27*
Theft Crimes ($2,500 or less) *Check Forgery ($200–$2,500)*	II	12[1]	12[1]	13	15	17	19	21 *18–25*
Sale of Simulated Controlled Substance	I	12[1]	12[1]	12[1]	13	15	17	19 *17–22*

☐ Presumptive commitment to state imprisonment. First Degree Murder is excluded from the guidelines by law and continues to have a mandatory life sentence. See section II.E. Mandatory Sentences for policy regarding those sentences controlled by law.

▨ Presumptive stayed sentence; at the discretion of the judge, up to a year in jail and/or other non-jail sanctions can be imposed as conditions of probation. However, certain offenses in this section of the grid always carry a presumptive commitment t state prison. See sections II.C Presumptive Sentence and II.E Mandatory Sentences.

Source: http://www.msge.state.mn.us/Guidelines/guide06.DOC

process the offender demonstrates that they accept general social values about the nature of wrong doing.

What are the problems with just deserts? A number of criticisms have been made of retributivism and of just deserts more particularly (Braithwaite and Petit, 1990; Hudson, 2003b; Zedner, 2004):

- Is it always appropriate for proportionality to be the primary aim of sentencing? Are there not cases – exceptional perhaps – where matters of public protection outweigh individual rights?

- Is it really possible to order offences, and those matters which might act as aggravating or mitigating factors, in a way that is clear and just? What is to prevent the creation of ever more finely graded punishments and creating a system which is overly complex and possibly incoherent?

- A danger with retributivism is that it is easily subverted by repressive and punitive political intentions.

- More generally, radical critics have argued that retributivist theory pays insufficient regard to the social conditions that produce criminality; it individualises and over-rationalises offending behaviour.

Review questions

1 What are the main philosophical justifications for punishment?

2 What are the main differences between utilitarian and retributive approaches to punishment?

3 What is meant by 'just deserts'?

4 What is the difference between *ordinal* and *cardinal proportionality*?

The sociology of punishment

Thus far in this chapter we have looked at some of the main ways in which legal philosophers have talked about the justifications for both the imposition of punishments and the nature and scale of those punishments. We turn now to another body of work, this time emanating from sociology. By contrast with philosophical questions, this is more concerned with what punishment has to tell us about the nature of society, about the functions or roles that punishment plays, and how the changing nature of punishment is related to broader and deeper socio-cultural changes. Readers who have already worked their way through earlier chapters (8 and 16 in particular) will have encountered some of these ideas already. In what follows we look at the ideas associated with what are often referred to as the 'founding fathers of sociology' – Durkheim, Weber and Marx – and conclude with a brief discussion of the more recent sociology of punishment associated with Norbert Elias and particularly with the work of Michel Foucault.

Emile Durkheim

As we saw in Chapter 8, Durkheim's particular concern in analysing the emergence of modern industrial society focused on the nature of social solidarity. Durkheim's concerns with punishment were, like most sociologists who have subsequently worked in this area, to understand what the nature of punishment says about social order and what functions it plays, particularly in relation to social solidarity. To recap briefly, Durkheim in *The Division of Labour in Society* distinguished between two ideal typical representations of social solidarity which he called *mechanical* and *organic solidarity*.

Mechanical solidarity was characteristic of pre-industrial societies where the division of labour is far from advanced and, indeed, most people are engaged in the same jobs or tasks. In such societies solidarity is based on this absence of differentiation; it is based on similarity. There are shared values, norms and beliefs and social rules are likely to be broadly accepted by all. In industrial society, by contrast, which is characterised by a much more highly differentiated division of labour with people undertaking very specialised jobs and tasks, solidarity is based on difference. Within such organic solidarity, beliefs are not shared in the way they are within simpler forms of social order.

Emile Durkheim (1858–1917)

Born a year after the death of August Comte, in Alsace-Lorraine, in France, Durkheim was the son of a rabbi and, indeed, his father was one of a long line of rabbis. It initially looked as if young Emile would follow this tradition. However, alongside his religious education he also received a strong educational grounding in secular schools and, after a brief flirtation with Catholicism in his teens, turned away from formal religion.

He completed his formal education at the age of 24 and became a professor of philosophy at various institutions in France. He taught the first course in sociology in France at the University of Bordeaux (1887–1902) and later joined the University of Paris (1902–17). His most famous works include: *The Division of Labour in Society* (1893), *Rules of Sociological Method* (1895), *Suicide* (1897), and *Elementary Forms of Religious Life* (1915).

Durkheim then proceeded to examine the implications of his analysis of social solidarity for punishment. In societies characterised by similarity, he argued that law would tend to be repressive in order to signify that collectively agreed norms had been breached. By contrast, in more complex societies, where there is no such collective agreement about rules, it is necessary for law to reconcile differences and repair harms among people with differing opinions and sentiments. In consequence, it will tend to be less repressive and more restitutive.

As such he argued that the use of prison – which is largely absent in primitive societies – would tend to replace death and torture as the main form of penalty in industrial societies. In societies characterised by mechanical solidarity, where repressive sanctioning is typical, punishment is meted out by and on behalf of the group, and its primary purpose or function is to uphold moral values through indignation. By contrast, under conditions of organic solidarity, where restitutive law is the norm, crime and deviance disturb social order rather than moral sentiments and rehabilitative, restorative action by officials is necessary in order to restore the *status quo*.

What has been made of Durkheim's ideas? There have been a number of criticisms. One important strand of criticism concerns the argued shift from generally punitive or repressive measures to more restitutive measures. On the one hand, some critics have noted the continuing importance of repressive law and sanction in modern, industrialised societies. On the other hand, others have also pointed to the apparent importance of restitutive systems of conflict resolution in traditional societies (Spitzer, 1979). A second line of criticism concerns the teleological element of Durkheim's analysis – the danger of confusing the functions that a social institution plays, with the reasons for the development of that institution. Durkheim himself recognised this danger. As he (1938) put it so elegantly:

> To show how a fact is useful is not to explain how it originated or why it is what it is. The uses which it serves presuppose the specific properties characterizing it, but do not create them. The need we have of things cannot give them existence, nor can it confer their specific nature upon them. It is to causes of another sort that they owe their existence … We must seek separately the efficient cause which produces it and the function it fulfils.

Nevertheless, Garland (1983) argues that Durkheim still falls foul of this problem. The difficulty lies in Durkheim's claim that 'crime shocks sentiments which, for a given social system, are found in all healthy consciences' (1964: 73). In response, Garland (1983: 53) says:

> Clearly, as an empirical statement this is questionable; one must presume that the offenders themselves do not wholly partake in this universal spirit of disapproval. However, Durkheim tells us that he refers only to healthy consciences,

that is, to those which share the sentiments of the collective conscience. But since violation of the collective conscience is the very quality which gives certain acts the attribute of criminality, the appeal to 'healthy consciences' as a proof is an empty form of tautology.

Nevertheless, Durkheim's sociology of punishment has been hugely and lastingly influential. In particular, Garland (1990) argues that Durkheim's legacy includes the way in which we now understand and focus at least some of our attention on the way in which punishment has an expressive, emotional and moral element above and beyond any instrumental, crime-control function. Moreover, as Durkheim observed, even if punishment has a very limited capacity in relation to crime control, it is able to play an important political role in the maintenance of particular forms of authority.

Max Weber

It is Weber's work on authority that is of primary importance to us here. Weber differentiated three types of authority: *traditional*, *charismatic* and *rational–legal*. Again, these are ideal types – heuristic devices designed to aid analysis and understanding, rather than attempts at faithful descriptions of things as they are.

- *Traditional authority* – Where rulers govern as of right, through heredity, and where rules are obeyed because of tradition.

- *Charismatic authority* – Depends upon the particular or special qualities of the ruler or ruling elite.

- *Rational–legal authority* – Weber sees as being the form of authority associated with complex, modern societies. In such systems authority is governed by rules and is organised by and through bureaucratic forms of organisation.

For Weber, as societies become more complex they are increasingly governed through rational–legal forms. In this regard punishment is not exceptional – it has become progressively rationalised and subject to bureaucratic rule.

As such, Weber's work is something of a forerunner for what Foucault would later have to say about the development of formal regulation and control. More generally, Weber's work on the emergence and development of the modern nation state has had a massive and continuing impact on debates about policing, security and the control of violence. A series of shifts from medieval to modern times saw the emergence of formal property rights, the rise of bureaucratic organisations such as police, police replacing older and, to modern eyes, more barbaric forms of punishment, and the rise of the idea of sovereignty and the concentration of power at the centre – initially in the hands of a monarch (Giddens, 1981). In this way, the monopolisation of the legitimate use of violence has become one, if not *the*, defining characteristic of the modern nation state.

Max Weber (1864–1920)

Weber, one of the great figures in sociology, had relatively little to say about crime, law or punishment. Born in Germany, he studied law and went on to do graduate work with a dissertation on medieval trading companies in Italy and Spain. He was appointed to a chair in political economy at Freiburg University in 1894 and to another chair in political economy at Heidelberg in 1896.

He suffered a nervous breakdown in 1898 and did not continue his scholarly work until 1904. From 1904 on he was a private scholar, mostly in Heidelberg. Weber's fascination with the subject of authority is sometimes linked by some commentators to his relationship with his authoritarian father and to his later discomfiture with life in the Kaiser's Germany.

Describing Weber's early life, Lewis Coser (1977) noted that he 'joined his father's duelling fraternity and chose as his major study his father's field of law. He became as active in duelling as in drinking bouts, and the enormous quantities of beer consumed with his fraternity brothers soon transformed  the thin and sickly looking young man into a heavy-set Germanic boozer proudly displaying his fencing scars.'

Marxism

Karl Marx also had little directly to say about punishment. Nevertheless, Marx and Engels' work on the nature of capitalist societies has had a significant and lasting influence on the sociology of punishment. Central to such work is the class-based nature of capitalist society and, more particularly, the notion that elements of society's ideological *superstructure* – including punishment – will tend to reflect the class interests of the economic *base*. The primary function of punishment, therefore, is the maintenance of the social order. Marxist scholars have moved beyond the idea that punishment is a repressive tool for repelling threats to the system, to argue that it also plays a fundamental role in the organisation of labour. Here the work of Rusche and Kirchheimer in *Punishment and Social Structure*, first published in the late 1930s, has become highly influential since it was republished in the late 1960s. They set out the basis of their approach in the following way:

> The transformation in penal systems cannot be explained only from changing needs of the war against crime, although this struggle does play a part. Every system of production tends to discover punishments which correspond to its productive relationships. It is thus necessary to investigate the origin and fate of penal systems, the use or avoidance of specific punishments, and intensity of penal practices as they are determined by social forces, above all by economic and then fiscal forces. (quoted in Jacoby, 2004: 381)

In tracing this history they identify three epochs: the early Middle Ages, the later Middle Ages, and the seventeenth century. Each had a different system of punishment influenced by the economic and social structure of the period. The use of penance and fines were the dominant modes of punishment in the early Middle Ages, a time when work was fairly plentiful and consequently conditions for the lower classes were relatively good. Punitive treatment by landowners therefore was unlikely to be especially productive. In the later middle ages, after the plague, social conditions produced a surplus of labour. This both drove the value of labour down and produced an increasing group of poor without work. This was the era in which punishment generally became more brutal and capital punishment was used extensively. In the seventeenth century there was once again a considerable labour shortage and it was this period

onward that we see, they argue, the rise of the prison and the use of prison labour to help make up for the shortfall.

As should be clear from this briefest of summaries, at the core of Rusche and Kirchheimer's thesis is the argument that the severity of punishment varies with the availability of labour. More generally, they argued that 'Every system of production tends to discover punishments which correspond to its productive relationships' (1968: 5) and that, in this regard, it was the prison that most obviously reflected the productive relationships typical of industrial capitalism. In explaining the centrality of the prison, writers working within a predominantly Marxist framework have offered varying explanations, from those like Rusche and Kirchheimer who viewed the prison as a source of labour through to those like Melossi and Pavarini who see in the prison and the factory a shared disciplinary style: 'for the worker the factory is like a prison (loss of liberty and subordination); for the inmate the prison is like a factory (work and discipline)' (1981: 188).

The implications of Marxist theory for an understanding of punishment – not just the prison – should be reasonably clear. By drawing attention to the ways in which systems of punishment are linked

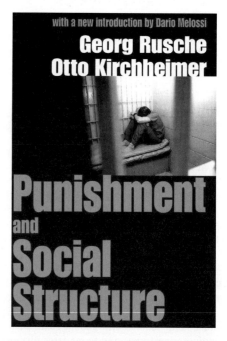

One of the key texts in applying Marxist ideas to an understanding of punishment – a recent new edition testifying to its continuing impact since publication in 1939.

with the functioning of capitalist society, such work invites us to think about how the unequal distribution of power within society might be reflected in the ways in which certain forms of behaviour are criminalised. Police cells, courts and prisons are filled with suspects, defendants and inmates who are predominantly drawn from the poorest parts of our society. By contrast, it is rare for the wealthy, the powerful and the influential to find themselves the focus of prosecution and punishment. At this stage you might want to dip into some of the discussions in Chapter 18 and ask why this is so.

Norbert Elias

Though a prolific author, it is Elias's two-volume history entitled *The Civilizing Process* that has received most attention within criminology. Elias's study focused upon changing social mores or standards of conduct and, in particular, he explored what he took to be the increasing social control, and socially-induced self-control, over various bodily functions.

Relatedly, one of Elias's central arguments concerns the gradual process through which violence is brought under control. The last five hundred years, he argues, have seen declining levels of violence as social conventions have increasingly come to emphasise the need for restraint, for forethought and planning and for greater abhorrence of physical cruelty. Gradually, public expressions of violence – bear baiting and other cruelty to animals, the punishment of criminals – have become increasingly private. This is true also of bodily functions such as defecation, urination and sexual conduct.

Elias's explanation for this goes to the heart of his idea of the 'civilising process', and it is to do with the changing nature of social and political authority and the rise of the nation state. Or, in Elias's terms, it is to do with the changing nature of human interdependencies – what he came to call 'figurations'. This long-term process has seen an increasing differentiation of social functions as societies become more complex. Alongside this process there has been the centralisation of power in the hands of the state, and changes in what he refers to as the 'triad of basic controls' (Elias 1978: 156). The stage of development of any human society can be understood by looking at the extent to which there is control over:

1 'natural events';

2 interpersonal or 'social' relationships;

3 the self (it is in this third area that greater control is called by Elias a 'civilising process').

As societies develop, according to Elias, they require organisation and long-term planning, and therefore there is increasing need for self-control among citizens. By contrast, 'the less amenable a particular sphere of events is to human control, the more emotional will be people's thinking about it; and the more emotional and fantasy-laden their ideas; the less capable they will be of ... gaining greater control over them' (1978: 156–7).

An important contribution to the sociology of punishment, using insights from Elias' *Civilizing Process*, is to be found in Pieter Spierenburg's (1984) *The Spectacle of Suffering*. In this he examines the changing nature of punishment in Europe between the fifteenth and nineteenth centuries. The growing interdependence of society during this period, with courtly elites coming closer to the masses, was accompanied by a set of gradual changes in the nature of punishment:

> The two elements, publicity and suffering, slowly retreated. The disappearance of most forms of mutilation of non-capital convicts constituted the clearest example. An equally important expression of the retreat was the spread of houses of correction; a theme which could not be discussed here. A slight uneasiness about executions among the elites in the second half of the seventeenth century has also been shown. These developments all anticipated the more fundamental change in sensibilities which set in after the middle of the eighteenth century: an acceleration which led to the privatization of repression. The acceleration after the middle of the eighteenth century had a parallel in other areas of the history of mentalities. Processes of privatization are notably reflected in the rise of the domesticated nuclear family.

In particular, he shows how punishment was gradually transformed from private into public vengeance and later still led to the development of a system of punishment which lost both its public character and the personal and violent nature. As we will see below, such arguments about the changing 'sensibilities' surrounding punishment also chime closely with the work of the French sociologist, Michel Foucault.

Norbert Elias (1897–1990)

Norbert Elias was born in Breslau, then in Germany, but now part of Poland. He served in the German army in the First World War. After the war he studied medicine whilst completing his military service. He later switched to philosophy and received his PhD in 1924. In 1930 he became an assistant to Karl Mannheim, then Professor of Sociology at Frankfurt. Sociology at Frankfurt University largely came to an end when the Nazis came to power in 1933.

Fleeing Germany, Elias initially settled in Paris. A business venture there failed and he emigrated to England in 1935. At the time he could read English but not speak it and, unable to get a job, he buried himself in the library of the British Museum in London. Here he focused on books of etiquette and manners, using these as the basis of a study of changing standards of behaviour. Elias introduced his study as follows:

> Central to this study are modes of behaviour considered typical of people who are civilized in a Western way. The problem they pose is simple enough. Western people have not always behaved in the manner we are accustomed to regard as typical or as the hallmark of 'civilized' people. If a member of present-day Western civilized society were to find himself suddenly transported into a past epoch of his own society, such as the medieval-feudal period, he would find there much that he esteems 'uncivilized' in other societies today.

Elias illustrates this with numerous examples concerning such things as manners at the dinner table, the use of the fork and, in the following extracts, on bodily functions:

1530 From *De civilitate morum peurilium* by Erasmus
Listen to the old maxim about the sound of wind. If it can be purged without a noise that is best. But it is better that it be emitted with a noise than that it be held back ... To let a cough hide the explosive sound: Those who, because they are embarrassed, want the explosive wind to be heard, simulate a cough. Follow the law of Chiliades: Replace farts with coughs.

1570 From the Wernigerode Court Regulations of 1570
One should not, like rustics who have not been to court or lived among refined and honourable people, relieve oneself without shame or reserve in front of ladies, or before the doors or windows of court chambers or other rooms. Rather, everyone ought at all times and in all places to show himself reasonable, courteous, and respectful in word and gesture.

Michel Foucault

The word 'discipline' is also central to Foucault's analysis of the nature and use of punishment (see also the discussion of Foucault's life and work in Chapter 16). In this case it is not presented as being attached to, or reflective of, class interests. Rather, Foucault uses his particular historical method to uncover what he presents as technologies of power which define two different penal styles and how these operate to discipline human bodies and human societies. He uses two defining examples to illustrate these differing styles. The first concerns the execution of Damiens the regicide in the mid-eighteenth century; the second, the rules from a house for young prisoners in Paris in the mid-nineteenth century (see boxes below).

Foucault's argument is that though the public execution and the prison timetable punish different crimes, what is important about them is that each defines a certain penal style. The earlier period is one where the monarch has considerable power over citizens and, more particularly, over

Damiens the regicide

On 2 March 1757 Damiens the regicide was condemned 'to make the *amende honourable* before the main door of the Church of Paris', where he was to be 'taken and conveyed in a cart, wearing nothing but a shirt, holding a torch of burning wax weighing two pounds'; then 'in the said cart, to the Place de Grève, where, on a scaffold that will be erected there, the flesh will be torn from his breasts, arms, thighs and calves with red-hot pincers, his right hand, holding the knife with which he committed the said parricide, burnt with sulphur, and, on those places where the flesh will be torn away, poured molten lead, boiling oil, burning resin, wax and sulphur melted together and then his body drawn and quartered by four horses and his limbs and body consumed by fire, reduced to ashes and his ashes thrown to the winds.

Finally, he was quartered ...This last operation was very long, because the horses used were not accustomed to drawing; consequently, instead of four, six were needed; and when that did not suffice, they were forced, in order to cut off the wretch's thighs, to sever the sinews and hack at the joints.

Discipline and Punish, p.3

Faucher's House of young prisoners

Eighty years later, Léon Faucher drew up his rules 'for the House of young prisoners in Paris':

Art.17. The prisoners' days will begin at six in the morning in winter and at five in summer. Two hours a day will be devoted to instruction. Work and the day will end at nine o'clock in winter and at eight in summer ...

Art.20. *Work.* At a quarter to six in the summer, a quarter to seven in winter, the prisoners go down into the courtyard where they must wash their hands and faces, and receive their first ration of bread. Immediately afterwards, they form into work-teams and go off to work, which must begin at six in summer and seven in winter ...

Art.26. Supper and the recreation that follows it last until five o'clock: the prisoners then return to the workshops ...

Art.28. At half-past seven in summer, half-past eight in winter, the prisoners must be back in their cells after the washing of hands and the inspection of clothes in the courtyard; at the first drum roll they must undress, and the second get into bed.

Discipline and Punish, pp.6–7

their bodies. The public execution, and especially the brutality of it, illustrate and serve to reinforce that power. Eighty years later and the modern sovereign no longer has such power over their subjects and, rather than inflicting pain upon the body, a different form of regulation is imposed. This new system of discipline seeks to govern the mind or the 'soul'. It aims to inculcate self-government or self-control through surveillance.

Foucault uses Bentham's panopticon as an illustration of this principle. The panopticon (as detailed in Chapter 5) was a prison design – never fully realized in England – in which the prisoners' cells were all to be visible from a central watch-tower. The guards in the watch-tower, however, were not visible to the inmates. This provided the two basic principles of panoptic surveillance: that it should be visible and unverifiable. Prisoners have in front of them the outline of the central tower, but do not know whether they are being observed, though they know they may be. According to Foucault (1979: 201) the major effect

of this is to, 'induce in the inmate a state of conscious and permanent visibility that assures the automatic functioning of power'. Crucially, he argues, 'it is at once too much and too little that the prisoner should be constantly observed by an inspector: too little, for what matters is that he knows himself to be observed; too much, because he has no need in fact of being so' (*ibid*).

In talking of 'panopticism' Foucault is doing more than attempting an analysis of the changing nature and function of punishment. Rather, as with other social theorists, he is asking what the changing nature of punishment can tell us about social change. What we are witnessing, he argues, is the emergence of a 'disciplinary society', not in the sense that the disciplinary form of power illustrated by the panopticon has replaced all other forms but, rather, because it increasingly infiltrates all others it makes 'it possible to bring the effects of power to the most minute and distant elements' (1979: 216). His work has given rise to considerable scholarship on subjects such as surveillance, which provide one of the most obvious contemporary illustrations of disciplinary power.

Foucault's work has been highly influential. However, it has also been subject to criticism from a number of quarters. Hudson (2003) identifies four main sources of criticism:

1　A number of authors have been critical of Foucault's historical accuracy arguing, for example, that the shift from corporal and capital punishment to the prison is far less clear than his argument would imply.

2　Foucault, it is suggested, overstates the instrumental aspects of punishment – how it disciplines the human body – at the expense of its emotional, expressive content.

3　Elements of his argument confuse consequences for functions and in so doing they overstate the efficacy of the prison.

4　He overstates the extent to which the disciplinary society has effected ever greater control over human lives.

The impact of Foucault

As the earlier discussion implied, the work of Michel Foucault has had a great impact on the contemporary study of punishment (see, for example, Chapter 16). Most centrally, a body of work has appeared in recent years, generally referred to as 'governmentality theory' that has built on some of Foucault's ideas in this area. Ideas in this area arise out of Foucault's stress not on *government*, but on forms of *governing* or, typically, *governance*. In essence what is being referred to are the complex strategies and techniques through which technologies of power govern individual and social conduct – what is sometimes referred to as the 'conduct of conduct'.

Analyses of crime control that proceed from this starting point focus considerable attention on organisations, structures and processes in civil society and the private sector, as well as within government, in an attempt to make sense of the complex – and, arguably, increasingly complex – systems for governing that currently exist. One example of how this approach can be utilised can be found in the French sociologist Jacques Donzelot's history of the policing of families. In his book *The Policing of Families* (1977), Donzelot outlines how a range of professionals and campaigners – doctors, psychiatrists, social workers, educators and others – worked to shape the modern family. Through a variety of techniques, the argument goes, individuals are persuaded to accept responsibility for the man-

agement of their own behaviour in ways which are socially approved. Nikolas Rose (1999: 74) describes the process as follows:

> The government of freedom, here, may be analysed in terms of the deployment of technologies of *responsibilization*. The home was to be transformed into a purified, cleansed, moralized, domestic space. It was to undertake the moral training of its children. It was to domesticate and familialize the dangerous passion of adults, tearing them away from public vice, the gin palace and gambling hall, imposing a duty of responsibility to each other, to home and to children, and a wish to better their own condition. The family, from then on... links public objectives for the good health and good order of the social body with the desire of individuals for personal health and well-being.

The family is just one site through which processes of responsibilisation occur. Responsibilisation strategies involve indirect government activity, via non-state agencies and organisations, to stimulate new forms of behaviour. The indications of such processes in the crime control arena include the increasing visibility of the private security sector, increasing emphasis on *partnerships* and *multi-agency activity*. The central message in such activity is that the state alone cannot (or cannot any longer) be responsible for controlling crime. The strategies that flow from this are quite different from those, say, that characterised penal-welfarism. No longer is there any objective to bring about social change. Rather the emphasis becomes one of the *management* of social problems rather than their alleviation (Garland 1996). In this context the idea of *risk* becomes of increasing importance.

The shift away from concerns with causes and towards the management and administration of crime problems has led some commentators to argue that we are witnessing the emergence of a distinctive form of criminal justice policy that they characterise as a 'new penology' (Feeley and Simon, 1992). Such strategies are risk-oriented and based on actuarial calculations rather than individual diagnoses, and future preventive-orientation rather than the imposition of sanctions *ex poste ante*. Such strategies are clearly compatible with the broader neo-liberal political project which seeks to roll back the welfare state, both resting on a view of those caught in poverty, offending and drug dependence as straightforwardly feckless and morally culpable.

The result in the crime control arena is policies dominated by rational choice models, the ratcheting-up of penalties and hazards attendant on behaviour deemed to fall short of required standards, together with vast increases in the technologies of surveillance available to monitor populations of risk.

Conclusion: an era of mass incarceration?

In this chapter we have looked at the main philosophical explanations of and justifications for punishment, and then turned our attention to the sociology of punishment. The latter discussion raises questions about what systems of punishment have to tell us about the societies in which they are found. Different systems of punishment have different philosophical justifications. They are also put into practice in diverging ways. That this is so is in part a reflection of the changing social relations that produce them and that they reproduce. If, therefore, we turn our attention to contemporary systems of punishment what do we find?

Arguably, the most influential work in this general field in recent years – though it is about much more than simply punishment – is David Garland's *The Culture of Control* (Garland, 2001). This thesis is one we also consider in some detail in Chapter 16 and it is worth reading this chapter in conjunction with that. In *The Culture of Control* Garland argues that in both America and Britain two contrasting policy strategies have been introduced, first and more vigorously in the USA, but subsequently in the UK. The first concerns the introduction of pragmatic or 'adaptive' approaches to the crime problem, such as the introduction of private sector management techniques to the criminal justice systems, the promotion of management reforms and privatisation, rigorous systems of performance measurement, and the active 'responsibilisation' of a range of private, voluntary and community agents in the field of crime control.

The second involves the simultaneous (and paradoxical) adoption of policies of 'denial' in which governments have adopted primarily expressive law enforcement and sentencing policies, the object of which is 'to denounce the crime and reassure the public' (2001: 133). This new 'expressive justice' is simultaneously symbolic and instrumen-

tal, is populist and politicised and, Garland argues, at its heart there is a projected, politicised *victim* used as justification for increasingly harsh treatment of offenders. The consequences of these changes are seen most visibly in the penal landscape of the United States.

For most of the twentieth century the incarceration rate in the USA, though on the high side internationally, remained relatively stable at around 100 to 120 per 100,000 population. It started to rise steadily in the 1970s, however, and by 1995 had reached 600 per 100,000. By comparison, in 1995 the rate per 100,000 in Japan was 37, in Germany and Italy 85 and around 100 in England and Wales. The incarceration rate in the US is now over 700 per 100,000. Where in 1972 there were under 200,000 Americans in federal and state prisons, this figure has now risen to over 1.5 million. Add the 700,000 prisoners incarcerated in local jails and well over two million Americans are now imprisoned and a further five million are under some form of supervision – probation, parole, etc. – by the criminal justice system (see Figure 22.2).

The sheer scale of imprisonment in the US now means that commentators routinely refer to this aspect of penal policy in the US as *mass incarceration* (see Garland, 2001b). Although the pace of change has been less dramatic in Britain there has nonetheless been a significant expansion in the numbers of people in prison over the past decade or so (see Figure 22.3).

Why have such changes taken hold in America, Britain and elsewhere? The reasons are complex, but one important factor concerns the growing politicisation of crime and its control (dealt with in more detail in Chapter 1). Crime and criminal justice is now accepted as being a major political issue. Not only do we expect politicians to spend much of their time talking about crime and criminal justice, but we also expect them to disagree. It hasn't always been this way. For much of the twentieth century there existed something close to a *bipartisan consensus* (agreement between the two main political parties) about how best to respond to crime both in the US and the UK (Downes and Morgan, 2007). Broadly speaking, the consensus view was that a set of strategies aimed simultaneously at punishing and reforming – what Garland has called 'penal welfarism' – was the most appropriate and effective way in which the modern state could maintain order and reduce crime.

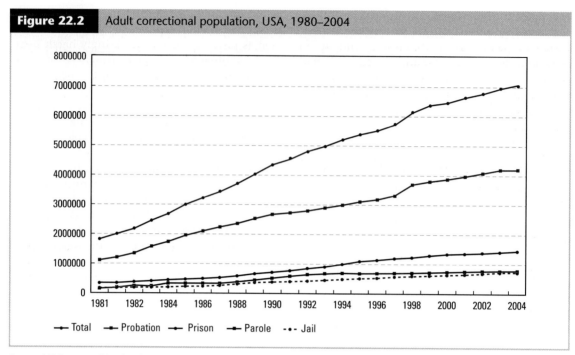

Source: US Bureau of Justice Statistics (2006).

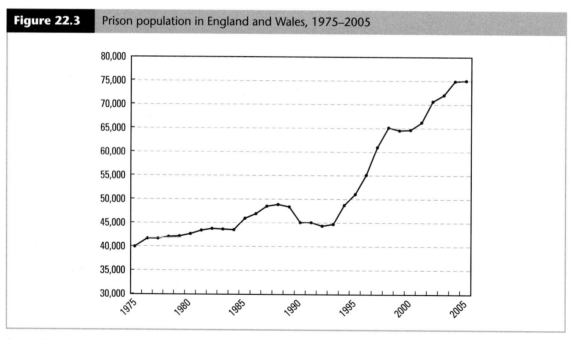

Source: Prison Statistics and NOMS caseload statistics (various).

In recent times, the general trend appears to be away from penal welfarism and towards a set of highly punitive and exclusionary strategies. Indeed, it seems a new political consensus has emerged around 'tough on crime' rhetoric and practice. At the heart of much of this is the language of risk. In discussing the politics of crime control, Simon (1997) has described the strategy of 'governing through crime'. Simon's central argument is that advanced industrial societies are experiencing a crisis of governance (rather than a crisis of crime) and that the response to this has been to prioritise crime and punishment as the preferred contexts for governance. As a consequence, he argues that crime currently casts a 'disproportionate shadow over what we primarily identify with governance, i.e. politicians and the electoral process of democracy' (1997: 174).

One possible explanation for the rise up the political agenda of crime policy generally, and punitive policies particularly, is what Beckett (1997) calls the 'democracy-at-work' thesis. This thesis suggests that the significant increases in crime that have occurred have led to increases in public fear of crime. Heightened fears put crime on the political agenda; in turn this leads to demands for harsher punishments for offenders and eventually to a significant growth in the number of people incarcerated. She quotes James Q. Wilson (1975) arguing along these lines that 'public opinion was well ahead of political opinion in calling attention to the rising problem of crime'.

In fact, using public opinion data during the US war on crime period (1964–1974) and the war on drugs era (1985–1992), she is able to show that, in practice, it was political initiatives in relation to crime and drugs that were a significant factor in

shaping public concerns, rather than the other way around. Moreover, the assumption that there is a close link between levels of public concern and the reported rate of crime and drug use is also shown to be much more complex than the 'democracy-at-work' thesis would allow. In Garland's view, as the 'limits of the sovereign state' become more visible, so part of the response appears to have been to engage 'in a more expressive and more intensive mode of punishment that purports to convey public sentiment and the full force of state authority' (2000: 349). The result is a set of arrangements for dealing with criminality that pays precious little regard to root causes, and has little interest in punishment beyond its utility as a means of reducing threats and managing risks. It is to contemporary practices of criminal justice that we turn our attention in the remainder of this section of the book.

Review questions

1 Why, according to Durkheim, has there been a shift from repressive to restitutive sanctioning?

2 What did Rusche and Kirkhheimer mean when they said, 'Every system of production tends to discover punishments which correspond to its productive relationships'?

3 What did Elias mean when he talked of a 'civilising process'?

4 What is the importance of the 'panopticon' to Foucault's ideas?

5 Are contemporary commentators right to talk of 'mass incarceration'?

Questions for further discussion

1 What do you think the limits on punishment should be? And why?

2 How might you apply Marxist ideas to contemporary trends in punishment?

3 What evidence is there in the twentieth and twenty-first centuries for and against the idea of a civilising process?

4 To what extent do you think it is accurate to argue that we live in a 'disciplinary society'?

5 Are rising incarceration rates in places like America and Britain just a reflection of public intolerance of crime?

Further reading

There are a number of books in this connection that I have found immensely helpful. They include:

Garland, D. (1990) *Punishment and Modern Society*, Oxford: Oxford University Press

Garland, D. (2001) *The Culture of Control*, Oxford: Oxford University Press

Hudson, B. (2003) *Understanding Justice*, Buckingham: Open University Press

Smith, P. and Natalier, K. (2005) *Understanding Criminal Justice*, London: Sage

Valier, C. (2002) *Theories of Crime and Punishment*, Harlow: Longman

Zedner, L. (2004) *Criminal Justice*, Oxford: Oxford University Press

A number of other more specific or specialised works are also likely to be helpful to you:

Lacey, N. (2007) Legal constructions of crime, in Maguire, M. *et al.* (eds) *The Oxford Handbook of Criminology*, 4th edn, Oxford: Oxford University Press

Lacey, N. *et al.* (2003) *Reconstructing Criminal Law: Critical perspectives on crime and the criminal process*, 3rd edn, Cambridge: Cambridge University Press

Loader, I. and Sparks, R. (2007) Contemporary landscapes of crime, in Maguire, M. *et al.* (eds) *The Oxford Handbook of Criminology*, 4th edn, Oxford: Oxford University Press

The journal *Punishment and Society*, London: Sage Journals, contains relevant and up-to-date material and is well worth consulting regularly.

Websites

There is useful material on Durkheim at: http://www.hewett.norfolk.sch.uk/curric/soc/durkheim/durk.htm

A lot of useful material on Weber, including the text of the Lewis Coser article on his life and work at: http://www.faculty.rsu.edu/~felwell/Theorists/Weber/Whome.htm

The Critical Criminology Division of the American Society of Criminology runs a website that is updated fairly regularly and often contains material relevant to the discussions in this chapter: http://critcrim.org/node?page=3

The Foucault Resources website has some unusual material, and some great photos: http://www.michel-foucault.com/cof.html

Chapter outline

Government and criminal justice   542
  Home Office   543
    Home Secretary   544
  Ministry of Justice   545
  Office of the Attorney General   545
The criminal justice system   546
  Major agencies, organisations and actors   546
    The police   546
    Crown Prosecution Service   546
    Probation Service   546
    Youth Offending Teams   546
    Prisons   546
    Legal Services Commission (LSC)   546
    Criminal courts   546
    Criminal Cases Review Commission   547
    Crime and Disorder Reduction Partnerships   547
    Criminal Injuries Compensation Authority (CICA)   547
    Forensic Science Service (FSS)   547
    Parole Board   548
  Volunteers in the criminal justice system   548
  Is it really a system?   549
  The criminal justice process   550
    Fixed-penalty notices   551
  Expenditure and employment   551
Management and oversight in criminal justice   553
  New public management   553
  Youth Justice Board   554
  Inspectorates   555
    Her Majesty's Inspectorate of Constabulary for England, Wales
      and Northern Ireland (HMIC)   555
    Her Majesty's Inspectorate of Court Administration (HMICA) 555
    Her Majesty's Crown Prosecution Service Inspectorate (HMCPSI) 555
    Her Majesty's Inspectorate of Prisons for England and Wales (HMIP) 555
    Her Majesty's Inspectorate of Probation for England and Wales
      (HMI Probation)   555
  Prisons and Probation Ombudsman   556
  Independent Police Complaints Commission   556
Politics and criminal justice reform   556
Understanding criminal justice   557
  Adversarial versus inquisitorial systems   557
  Due process versus crime control   559
Questions for further discussion   561
Further reading   562
Websites   562

23

Understanding criminal justice

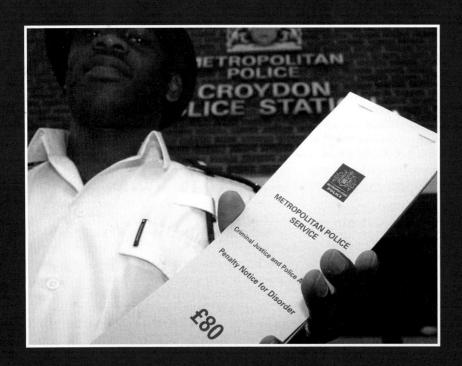

Government and criminal justice

Parliament is the highest legislative authority in the United Kingdom and is the body responsible for the passage and repeal of law, including criminal law. In addition to making laws, parliament controls finance (it approves proposals for taxation and expenditure) and is a forum for scrutinising government proposals and action. In addition to debates within the two main houses of parliament – the House of Commons and the House of Lords – discussion of proposals and activity in relation to crime and justice take place within the Home Affairs Select Committee. The Select Committee describes its responsibilities as: 'examining the expenditure, policy and administration of the Home Office and its associated public bodies; and the administration and expenditure of the Attorney General's Office, the Treasury Solicitor's Department, the Crown Prosecution Service and the Serious Fraud Office'. In addition to specific committees established to investigate activities in Scotland, Wales and Northern Ireland there are a number of other parliamentary committees that are supposed to monitor government activities in the general area of criminal justice and penal policy. They include:

- *Constitutional Affairs Select Committee* – Covering those areas of activity now the responsibility of the Ministry of Justice (MoJ).

- *European Scrutiny Committee* – Covering European Union legislation and activity.

- *Public Accounts Committee* – Covering value for money and 'economy, efficiency and effectiveness' by government departments and public bodies (for example, the police).

There are three main government departments relevant to matters of crime and justice. The first, and until recently the largest and most important, is the Home Office. For the bulk of its history, the Home Office had responsibility for police, prisons, probation and a number of other smaller bodies (see below). Since May 2007 a new Ministry of Justice has been established and incorporates what was previously known as the Department for Constitutional Affairs (DCA). The new Ministry of Justice has responsibility for all those areas of activity previously the responsibility of the DCA – the magistrates' courts, the Crown Court, the appeal courts and the Legal Services Commission – as well as incorporating a set of responsibilities which previously belonged to the Home Office – including prisons, probation (now jointly referred to as the National Offender Management Service) and sentencing. Finally, there is the Office of the Attorney General, which oversees the Crown Prosecution Service, the Serious Fraud Office and the Revenue and Customs Prosecutions Office.

In addition, there is a cross-departmental government body which is responsible for coordinating activity across these three bodies. This is called the Office for Criminal Justice Reform (OCJR). One of the topics we will discuss later on in the chapter is *managerialism*: the increasing subjection of public and other bodies to performance measurement and management. The OCJR is part of a relatively new system of management of the criminal justice system. It has responsibility for attempting to ensure that improvements identified by the National Criminal Justice Board (a body made up of government ministers, senior civil servants and other civil service officials) are put into practice. We look briefly at each of the elements of government with criminal justice responsibility below.

Home Office

A little over a century and a half ago, in 1848, the Home Office employed only 22 permanent officials at a total cost of £13,406 per annum (Pellew, 1982). The Home Office is now one of the great government departments, with thousands of employees and a broad range of responsibilities. The Home Office is headed by the Home Secretary. The day-to-day running of the Home Office is in the hands of the senior civil servant in the department, otherwise known as the Permanent Secretary. The Home Office has its central headquarters in Marsham Street in central London. It is made up of the Immigration and Nationality Directorate – which manages requests to live or work in the UK – and a number of other elements covering crime reduction and community safety as well as the government's Respect Agenda (see Chapter 24). The Home Office is responsible for a number of other services and public bodies, including three Executive Agencies: the Criminal Records Bureau; the Identity and Passports Service; and the Border and Immigration Agency.

As we will see below there are a number of inspectorates linked to the criminal justice system. Following reorganisation, the Home Office is now linked only with Her Majesty's Inspectorate of Constabulary. Finally, there is a host of what are known as *Non-Departmental Public Bodies* (NDPBs) that are linked to the Home Office. NDPBs are public bodies that, although not part of government departments, carry out functions on behalf of sponsor departments, who fund them and ensure they are effective. Those linked to the Home Office include: the Security Industry Authority; the Independent Police Complaints Commission; the Office of the Immigration Services Commissioner; and, the Serious and Organised Crime Agency (see Chapter 19).

The Home Office currently lists seven key objectives: They are to:

- Help people feel safer in their homes and local communities.

- Support visible, responsive and accountable policing.

- Protect the public from terrorist attack.

- Cut crime, especially violent, drug and alcohol-related crime.

- Strengthen our borders, fast track asylum decisions, ensure and enforce compliance with our immigration laws, and boost Britain's economy.

- Safeguard people's identity and the privileges of citizenship.

- Work with our partners to build an efficient, effective and proportionate criminal justice system.

As other chapters will illustrate, many of these are far from straightforward and by no means uncontroversial. What, for example, is meant by *accountable* policing? To whom should the police be accountable and how should such processes work? These are fraught questions and have been the subject of considerable debate and disagreement over many decades (see Chapter 25). Similarly, the last objectives suggests that the criminal justice system should be 'efficient, effective and proportionate'. However, as we will see during the course of this chapter and others that follow, the goals of efficiency and proportionality can come into conflict. Thus, the increasing emphasis on financial efficiency within criminal justice can lead to proposals to restrict expenditure in ways that affect defendants' rights (for example, by limiting jury trial).

As we have already noted, there has recently been very significant reorganisation of government responsibilities in relation to criminal justice. The idea of splitting the Home Office into two ministries had been discussed on a number of occasions previously. Many jurisdictions – including France and the Netherlands – distinguish between what is often referred to as a Ministry of Justice on the one hand and a Ministry of the Interior on the other. The principle is that the former takes responsibility for criminal justice and penal policy, and for the management of offenders, whereas the latter has responsibility for policing and security.

On arrival in the Home Office in May 2006 the new Home Secretary, John Reid, described it as 'not fit for purpose' and promised some radical reforms. By early 2007 he was seeking to persuade political colleagues that the Home Office be split in two. In a short space of time, and without significant parliamentary debate or public discussion, proposals were accepted by Cabinet and the reforms rushed through in May 2007. The consequence is that the Home Secretary now has substantially reduced responsibilities from those traditionally associated with the post.

'Not fit for purpose?' John Reid, the last Home Secretary (2006–2007) to have had responsibility for prisons and probation before these became part of a new Ministry of Justice.

Home Secretary

Until the end of the eighteenth century, the business of government was managed by two geographical departments. At that point a secretary of state for domestic and colonial affairs and one for foreign affairs were created. When responsibility for war and military affairs was split from other domestic matters, a secretary of state for home affairs finally emerged. Through the course of the nineteenth century the Home Secretary, as the office holder continued to be called, gradually acquired numerous functions – the 1829 Police Act and the 1832 Prison Act in particular both added major new responsibilities.

The amount of legislation passed by the Home Office has gradually increased during the course of the twentieth century. However, it is only in relatively recent times that the position of Home Secretary has become highly politicised (see Chapter 1). Thus, writing in 1976 a senior Home Office official was able to observe:

> In general, however, it is unusual for an incoming government to bring with it anything approaching a detailed blueprint of penal policy. This is not really surprising. Although the maintenance of law and order remains a basic task of any government, the methods of performing it *are simply not of great political importance* in comparison with the major economic and social issues of the day which rightly preoccupy the political parties and other organs of society. (Moriarty, 1976: 132–3, *emphasis added*)

Moriarty went on to talk about the largely 'bipartisan' nature of much criminal justice and penal policy – the fact that this was not generally an area on which the main political parties disagreed all that fundamentally. With some foresight, he then went on to comment that the 'politicization of penal policy issues could well encourage the development of crude policies and the raising of expectations which, given the intractable nature of the crime problem, no Government could fulfil' (1976: 133). This is close to the situation that we find ourselves in today. Crime and penal policy has indeed become highly politicised. The process has its origins in the late 1960s/early 1970s, and the 1979 General Election was arguably the first in which 'law and order' played a central, and possibly

Table 23.1	British Home Secretaries since 1979		
William Whitelaw	C	(5 May, 1979 – 11 June, 1983)
Leon Brittan	C	(11 June, 1983 – 2 September, 1985)
Douglas Hurd	C	(2 September, 1985 – 26 October, 1989)
David Waddington	C	(26 October, 1989 – 28 November, 1990)
Kenneth Baker	C	(28 November, 1990 – 10 April, 1992)
Kenneth Clarke	C	(10 April, 1992 – 27 May, 1993)
Michael Howard	C	(27 May, 1993 – 2 May, 1997)
Jack Straw	L	(2 May, 1997 – 8 June, 2001)
David Blunkett	L	(8 June, 2001 – 15 December, 2004)
Charles Clarke	L	(15 December, 2004 – 5 May, 2006)
John Reid	L	(5 May, 2006 – 28 June, 2007)
Jacqui Smith	L	(28 June, 2007 –

decisive role. Home Secretaries since that time have become increasingly high-profile politicians.

In his first party conference after becoming Home Secretary in 1993, Michael Howard made a speech announcing a raft of almost 30 new policy proposals. He followed this up a year later with further controversial policy proposals, undoubtedly in an attempt to shake off the extremely visible Shadow Home Secretary, Tony Blair. Blair, by this time, had formulated his 'tough on crime, tough on the causes of crime' approach to home affairs and was challenging pre-existing Conservative dominance of the law and order agenda by shifting the Labour Party to the right. In this he was highly successful, and the first four Labour Home Secretaries since 1997 have sought to maintain such a profile and to make considerable political capital out of tough law and order pronouncements (at the time of writing it is too early to reach a judgement about the fifth and, in a similar vein, whether the reform of the role of the Home Office will have an impact upon the way in which the Home Secretaries position themselves).

Ministry of Justice

Prior to the 2007 reorganisation, the Department for Constitutional Affairs (DCA) was responsible for magistrates' courts, the Crown Court and the Court of Appeal. In addition it appointed magistrates and advised on the appointment of the professional judiciary. The DCA also funded a number of bodies which play an important role in the functioning of the criminal justice system:

● *The Legal Services Commission* – Responsible for the provision of publicly-funded criminal defence services within both magistrates' courts and the Crown Court.

● *The Judicial Studies Board* – An independent body established to provide training for judges and to provide guidance on the training of magistrates.

● *The Law Commission* – Another independent body responsible for reviewing laws and recommending reform.

All these responsibilities have passed to the newly-created Ministry of Justice (since May 2007). In addition, a number of major areas of criminal justice and penal policy responsibility have moved over from the Home Office. These include responsibility for the emergent National Offender Management Service (NOMS) – what previously were the separate Prison and Probation Services – as well as the Youth Justice System, sentencing policy and human rights. As does the Home Office, the Ministry of Justice also has a number of linked 'arms length' agencies, including the Prisons and Probation Inspectorates and the Parole Board.

Office of the Attorney General

The Attorney General is responsible to Parliament for the Crown Prosecution Service (CPS), the Serious Fraud Office (SFO), and a series of other bodies including the Prosecutions Office of the Department of Revenue and Customs and the Treasury Solicitor's Department. The Attorney General also has a number of public interest functions, including responsibility for taking action in relation to 'unduly lenient sentences'. The Attorney General (and the Solicitor General) also deals with questions of law arising on government bills and with issues of legal policy. A recent well-known and controversial example of such legal advice concerned the Attorney General's opinion on the legality of the Iraq War.

Figure 23.1	Primary governmental responsibilities in the criminal justice system (England and Wales)		
Ministry of Justice	**Home Office**	**Office of the Attorney General**
Criminal law	Security and counter-terrorism	Director of Public Prosecutions
NOMS	Policing in England and Wales	Crown Prosecution Service
Criminal courts	Immigration and asylum	Serious Fraud Office
Sentencing	Criminal justice inspectorates and Ombudsmen	Revenue and Customs prosecutions
Youth justice	Crime reduction and community safety	
Judicial appointments	Identity and citizenship	
Human rights		
Prisons, probation and sentencing policy		

Source: Hough and Roberts (2004).

The criminal justice system

Having briefly outlined the general division of responsibilities within government for criminal justice, let us turn our attention to the criminal justice system itself. The first thing to note is that there is no single system of criminal justice in the United Kingdom. There are three distinctive systems: in England and Wales, Scotland, and in Northern Ireland. The focus in this book is primarily upon England and Wales though, where particularly important – such as in juvenile justice and policing (see Chapters 25 and 29) – particular attention will be paid to the Scottish and Northern Irish cases. The criminal justice system is made up of a number of major agencies, organisations and actors.

Major agencies, organisations and actors

The police

There are currently 43 constabularies in England and Wales, a further eight regional forces in Scotland, together with a single Police Service of Northern Ireland. In addition to local forces (see Chapter 25), there is also the Serious and Organised Crime Agency responsible for criminal investigation of cases of organised and international crime (see Chapter 19) and a relatively newly-established body – the National Policing Improvement Agency – with responsibility for improvements in police technology, recruitment and training.

Crown Prosecution Service

Established in 1985 and currently administered in 42 areas, contiguous with police force areas. The CPS is the principal prosecuting authority in England and Wales and is responsible for:

- Advising the police on cases for possible prosecution.
- Reviewing cases submitted by the police.
- Where the decision is to prosecute, determining the charge in all but minor cases.
- Preparing cases for court.
- Presentation of cases at court.

Probation Service

Now a national service in England and Wales, though prior to 2000 it had been divided up into local areas (like police, CPS and other agencies). Now the National Probation Service is being incorporated into the National Offender Management Service (NOMS) (see Chapter 27). The NPS is responsible for supervision of offenders in the community (about 175,000 new cases each year), providing information to sentencers in court, and working on secondment within youth offending teams.

Youth Offending Teams

Formerly known as Juvenile Justice Teams, these are multi-agency bodies responsible for the supervision of young offenders serving community sentences. In Scotland, probation was merged with other welfare services in the 1960s and probation officers are known as criminal justice social workers. In Northern Ireland, a non-departmental public body, the Probation Board for Northern Ireland is responsible for the provision of community supervision.

Prisons

There are currently 139 prisons run by the Prison Service (including Young Offender Institutions) which is an executive agency linked to the Ministry of Justice (though day-to-day operation of 11 prisons is the responsibility of private companies – see Chapter 28). Subject to no little controversy, the Prison Service is in the process of being incorporated into a new body – NOMS – with the Probation Service. In Scotland there are a further 16 prisons run by the Scottish Prisons Service. The Northern Ireland Prison Service administers three prisons of differing levels of security.

Legal Services Commission (LSC)

The Legal Services Commission looks after the system of Legal Aid in England and Wales. It is a non-departmental public body sponsored by the Department for Constitutional Affairs. The Criminal Defence Service is responsible for providing legal support for those accused of crimes in criminal courts and is run by the LSC in partnership with criminal defence lawyers and representatives. The Scottish Legal Aid Board and the Northern Ireland Legal Services Commission provide similar services in other parts of the UK.

Criminal courts

In England and Wales there are three legal categories of offence: summary, indictable and those triable either way:

- Summary offences are those that are generally less 'serious'. They include the bulk of motoring offences and are heard in magistrates' courts.

- Indictable offences are more serious and range from most types of assault, sexual offences to murder. Indictable offences are heard in the Crown Court.
- Offences that are triable either way can, as their name implies, be dealt with in magistrates' or Crown Court.

The Judiciary is headed by the Lord Chief Justice. Cases in the Crown Court will be heard by circuit judges, though less serious or complex cases may be heard by recorders (who are experienced barristers or solicitors who may go on to become circuit judges). There are, in addition, high court judges who hear the most serious and complex cases. Contested cases in the Crown Court are heard in front of judge and jury (in fact the majority are guilty plea cases which therefore don't require a jury). Jurors are chosen at random from people aged 18 to 70 whose names appear on the electoral register. Up until the Criminal Justice Act 2003 there were a number of exemptions from jury service for people in particular occupations. Almost all of these have now been removed, the aim being to increase the spectrum of public participation in the justice system.

Although some cases within magistrates' courts will be heard by a district judge, the majority will be heard by a panel of three magistrates. Magistrates are members of the public aged between 18–65, and they must sit for a minimum of 26 half-day sessions per year. No legal qualifications are required, but training is provided. Almost all ten to 17 year-olds will have their case dealt with in the youth court – essentially a specialised form of magistrates' court. As in the magistrates' court, the case will be heard by magistrates or by a district judge (formerly known as a stipendiary magistrate). The courts system in Northern Ireland is similar in its operation to that in England and Wales. The most significant exception is the existence of emergency legislation allowing for trial without jury in cases involving charges relating to terrorism. Scotland has a three-tier criminal court system: the high court, the sheriff courts and the district courts (see box on next page).

Finally, there are coroners' courts in which cases involving violent, unnatural or unexplained deaths are heard. Coroners are judicial officials responsible for presiding in *inquests* – the name for such hearings – and, occasionally with a jury, for reaching a judgement as to the cause of death.

Criminal Cases Review Commission (CCRC)

This is an independent body which reviews possible miscarriages of justice in the criminal courts in England, Wales and Northern Ireland. It has responsibility for reviewing convictions and sentences handed down by both the magistrates' courts and the Crown Court once normal appeal procedures have been exhausted. In its reviews it considers two main aspects of cases. First, whether convictions can be considered to be 'safe', and therefore can be upheld. Second, the CCRC can also consider whether the sentence imposed was appropriate or whether, for example, any evidence that had been withheld would have affected the sentence given had it been available. The CCRC cannot overturn convictions or reduce sentences, but merely refer cases to the appropriate appeal court.

Crime and Disorder Reduction Partnerships (CDRP)

CDRPs (or Community Safety Partnerships, in Wales) were established by the Crime and Disorder Act 1998. They are multi-agency partnerships involving representation from police, local authorities, probation, health, and some other bodies, and are tasked with monitoring local crime problems, and publishing and overseeing plans for local crime reduction. Similarly, both Scotland and Northern Ireland have Community Safety Partnerships based on local council areas.

Criminal Injuries Compensation Authority (CICA)

The CICA administers the criminal injuries compensation scheme throughout England, Scotland and Wales. It pays compensation to people who have been the victim of a violent crime. The first scheme was set up in 1964 (see Chapter 17), and from that point until 1996 awards were set according to what the victim would have received in a successful civil action against the offender. The level of compensation has subsequently been determined according to a scale, or tariff, set by parliament. The tariff includes descriptions of over 400 injuries, with each attached to one of 25 levels of compensation between £1,000 and £250,000.

Forensic Science Service (FSS)

The FSS is a trading name of Forensic Science Service Ltd, a UK government-owned company which provides services to police forces in England and Wales, as well as training, consultancy and scientific support services for private and overseas customers. It provides services at the scenes of crimes, in support of investigations into violent, property and financial crimes, and as expert witnesses in court.

Parole Board

The Parole Board for England and Wales is an independent body which makes assessments about whether prisoners may be released from prison or returned to custody. It was established in 1968 and became a non-departmental public body in 1996. The majority of decisions are 'paper decisions', taken on the basis of written details of the prisoner's case and assessed by three members of the Parole Board. A smaller number of cases, often concerning prisoners on life or extended sentences, involve oral hearings.

Volunteers in the criminal justice system

We have already briefly discussed the magistracy, a body of voluntary lay members of the public who, after training, hear cases in magistrates' courts and the youth court. In addition to the magistracy, there are a large number of volunteers working within the criminal justice system:

- *Policing*
  - Independent custody visitors (lay visitors) who visit police custody suites to check conditions.
  - Special constables – volunteer police officers (see Chapter 25).
  - Neighbourhood watch schemes (see Chapter 24).
  - Police authority lay members – overseeing the work of the police service.
- *Probation*
  - There is a wide range of activity provided via the voluntary sector, including education initiatives, mentoring and the like.
  - Probation boards – overseeing the work of the probation service.
- *Prisons*
  - Member of an independent prison monitoring board – overseeing the work of prisons/YOIs.
  - Prison visitor – offering advice and friendship to prisoners.

Criminal justice in Scotland

There are some important differences between the criminal justice systems of England and Wales and that of Scotland. First of all, Scots criminal law is based on a common law tradition. This means that much greater emphasis is placed upon *precedent* (earlier decisions by the higher criminal courts) or from 'institutional writers' – legal authorities whose views have become received understanding.

Although there is an important statutory element in Scots law, with some offences being UK-wide, many serious offences such as rape, robbery and assault are common law crimes. There are a few matters to do with things like drugs and international co-operation in criminal justice that are governed from Westminster, otherwise most criminal legislation affecting Scotland is passed by the Scottish parliament.

Overall responsibility for criminal justice policy in Scotland lies with the Minister of Justice and their Deputy. The department responsible is called the Scottish Executive Justice Department and it has responsibility for the police, the district courts, the children's hearings system (see Chapter 29) and the legal aid system. An executive agency of the department, the Scottish Courts Service, has responsibility for the administration and staffing of the high court and sheriff courts, and another agency, the Scottish Prison Service, runs the prisons system.

Scotland has a three-tier criminal court system: the high court, the sheriff courts and the district courts. Three verdicts are available: guilty; not guilty; and not proven. A 'not proven' verdict is effectively the same as a 'not guilty' verdict in that the accused is acquitted and is free from further prosecution on the particular matter (though in England it is now possible for an accused to be retried for the same offence). The majority of cases are heard in sheriff courts, and in these cases it is generally the Procurator Fiscal who presents the prosecution case.

In Scotland the prosecution system is managed by the Crown Office and Procurator Fiscal Service. Once the police have investigated a crime they submit a report to the Procurator Fiscal. It is the Procurator who considers whether criminal proceedings should take place and, as with the CPS in England and Wales, this decision is based on the *public interest*. In cases which will go before a jury, the Procurator Fiscal interviews witnesses and gathers and reviews forensic and other evidence prior to taking the decision about prosecution. Where the Procurator Fiscal decides not to pursue a prosecution there is a variety of alternatives that they can pursue including warnings and fixed penalty fines.

- *Youth Justice*
  - Youth offender panel members (see Chapter 29).
  - Mentors – providing advice and guidance to young people in trouble.
  - Appropriate adults – attending police stations when young people are being interviewed by the police under caution.
- *Victims*
  - Victim support volunteer – offering support to crime victims (see Chapter 17).

Is it really a system?

To what extent is it accurate to talk of this conglomeration of agencies and institutions as if they were a *system*? One way in which we might think about this is to ask two related questions: to what extent do the main agencies in the criminal justice system work co-operatively; and, to what extent do they share similar or the same aims and objectives? In answer, quite a lot of evidence can be amassed to show how criminal justice agencies work in partnership and to similar goals. However, there are also many examples of poor, or even non-existent, partnership-working as well as an absence of shared aims – or even occasionally the existence of competing aims (Hughes, 2007).

There are a number of well-rehearsed examples. Within youth justice, for example, the Audit Commission (1996) in the mid-1990s observed that the major agencies involved often failed to work to joint objectives (see Chapter 29). Worse still, it suggested, their activities often cut across each other. As a consequence, the subsequent Labour government introduced a variety of measures to attempt to overcome such problems, including the imposition of an overarching aim for youth justice, the creation of the Youth Justice Board to oversee practice, and the establishment of multi-agency Youth Offending Teams to deliver services.

Similar observations had been made for a number of years in relation to crime prevention and community safety (see Chapter 24). The 1998 Crime and Disorder Act also sought to bring about greater planning and co-operation through the creation of local crime and disorder (now crime and disorder reduction) partnerships in which the police and local authorities would have joint responsibility for assessing and auditing local problems and implementing initiatives. In announcing a review of CDRPs in 2004, the government commented that 'a significant number of partnerships struggle to maintain a full contribution from key agencies and even successful ones are not sufficiently visible, nor we think accountable, to the public as they should be' (quoted in Crawford, 2007: 897). Many of the same problems – and diagnoses – can be seen behind the creation initially of the National Probation Service and the subsequent desire to merge both Probation and Prison Service into NOMS. However, the attempted creation of NOMS is, perhaps, also an illustration of the profound difficulties that can ensue if fundamental structural reorientation is undertaken without thinking through the cultural and practical implications of the changes (Rumgay, 2007).

The government's Strategic Plan for criminal justice, covering the period 2004–08, devoted considerable space to problems of co-ordination, joint working and consistency within criminal justice. In particular, it highlighted continuing difficulties in terms of differing geographical boundaries between agencies, and ongoing difficulties in relation to joint working between agencies. Nevertheless, it also drew attention to what it took to be a number of improvements including the reforms within youth justice, and the creation of a National Criminal Justice Board and local boards to co-ordinate activity. The aim, according to government, is to produce more 'joined up' criminal justice. Critics, however, point to a range of difficulties and limitations in this connection:

- The increasing role given to the private sector and, more particularly, the growing emphasis on the role of the market in criminal justice, isn't necessarily compatible with what is thought of as 'partnership working' – leading to less, rather than greater, co-operation (Raynor, 2007; Rumgay, 2007).
- Related to the previous point, there is also the concern that increased competition, through ideas like 'contestability' (introduced by the Carter Review, 2003) will lead to fragmentation of provision (Bailey *et al.*, 2007).
- Despite the fact that partnership working between agencies requires considerable autonomy at a local level, in practice government has dramatically increased centralised control (Crawford, 2001).
- Increased central government control has drastically narrowed the focus of criminal justice to the extent that it feels as if it is only crime reduction or prevention that counts; this, it is

argued, undermines the activities of criminal justice agencies which historically have seen themselves as working to a much broader agenda (including, for example, the rehabilitation of offenders or the protection of defendant's rights) (Sanders and Young, 2007).

- Finally, long-term goals such as those implied in the idea of joined-up criminal justice are argued increasingly to be undermined by penal populism – short-term appeals to the electorate (Pratt, 2007).

Review questions

1 Which are the main government departments with responsibilities for criminal justice?

2 What are the major responsibilities of each?

3 In what ways might the term 'system' in criminal justice system be considered problematic?

The criminal justice process

We have briefly surveyed the contours of the criminal justice system, including the major government departments and criminal justice agencies. The next question for us is how the system works in practice. We will consider the various constituent parts in greater detail in subsequent chapters. Here we simply look briefly at the major decision-making points and the general relationship between the various elements of the criminal justice system.

First, a reminder. In Chapter 3 we looked at the various sources of information available to us as the basis for studying crime. A comparison of the two main sources – the British Crime Survey and police recorded crime statistics – shows that only a small proportion of crimes end up being processed in the criminal justice system and only a fraction end with a conviction in a criminal court. Thus, when thinking about the criminal justice system, it is important to remember that less than half of all offences ever come to the attention of the police, and only a very small proportion of the overall total ever end up in a criminal court. This should give pause for thought to anyone who thinks that increasing the resourcing or the general effectiveness of criminal justice agencies is somehow a solution to the problems presented by crime and disorder.

The criminal justice process is relatively complex. Its major elements are as follows:

- The beginning of the formal criminal justice process occurs when an offence comes to the attention of the police. This can either be because an offence is reported to them, or because it comes to their attention during the course of police work.

- In the majority of cases, where a crime is recorded, no suspect will be detected (up to three-quarters of cases).

- Where a suspect is detected the police have a number of options/decisions to make:
  - They may issue a summons requiring the suspect to attend court.
  - They may make an arrest and take the suspect to a police station for interviewing;

- After arrest and interview, there are various courses of action open to the police and Crown Prosecution Service. They can:
  - *Release the suspect without charge/take no further action* – No action occurs either because the police consider there to be insufficient evidence to prosecute, or that an informal warning is sufficient (or because it is otherwise expedient in their eyes to take no action).
  - *Caution the offender* – Cautions can be given when there is sufficient evidence for a conviction, but where it is felt not to be in the public interest to prosecute. For a caution to be administered the offender must admit guilt and consent to the caution. For young offenders, the system has been replaced by one of *reprimands* and *final warnings* (see Chapter 29).
  - *Charge the suspect and release them on bail* – Charging decisions are made in conjunction with the CPS.
  - *Charge the suspect and remand them in custody* – The suspect must then be brought before a court as soon as possible where the decision will be taken about whether the remand in custody will continue.

- If a suspect is charged, the file is then passed to the CPS, which decides whether to continue with the case or whether it should be discontinued.

- If the case proceeds it will go to a magistrates' court if the offence charged is a summary one or if it is triable either way.

- If triable either way and the suspect indicates that they intend to plead guilty then sentence will be passed in the magistrates' court unless the magistrates consider their sentencing powers insufficient, in which case it will be sent to the Crown Court.

- If triable either way and the suspect indicates they intend to plead not guilty, then three main possibilities arise:
  - The magistrates may decide to send the case to the Crown Court.
  - They may decide to hear the case themselves.
  - If the latter, the defendant may elect for trial in the Crown Court.
- If the case involves an indictable offence, or if it was an either way offence and the defendant elected for trial, then the case will be heard in the Crown Court.

A summary of the court process (for indictable and either way offences) is provided below in Figure 23.2.

Although this provides the basic outline of the criminal process there are a number of other factors which may affect how cases are dealt with. Thus, there are special provisions for mentally disordered suspects/defendants, additional safeguards where young offenders are concerned, and different timescales for detention where terrorist cases are involved.

Furthermore, although the CPS brings about three-quarters of prosecutions to magistrates' courts and 95 per cent of prosecutions in the Crown Court, there are various other bodies that may also do so. The main organisations include:

- Revenue and Customs (formerly the Inland Revenue and Customs and Excise).
- The TV Licensing Records Office.
- The Serious Fraud Office.
- The Department of Trade and Industry.
- The Driver and Vehicle Licensing Authority (DVLA).
- The Department of Work and Pensions.
- The Health and Safety Executive.
- Local Authorities.
- The National Society for the Prevention of Cruelty to Children.
- The Royal Society for the Prevention of Cruelty to Animals.

Fixed-penalty notices

Finally, governments have recently increased the use of Fixed Penalty Notices (FPNs). Historically, they have been used in the main to deal with environmental offences such as litter, graffiti and dog fouling. They are generally issued by local authority officers and, more recently by police community support officers (PCSOs) and other wardens. They can be issued to anyone over the age of ten and are generally for the sum of £50. The typical offences covered by FPNs include: minor graffiti offences; fly posting; dog fouling; dropping litter; and causing excessive noise.

Fixed Penalty Notices and Penalty Notices for Disorder have become important in the government's anti-social behaviour strategy. Here an officer from the Metropolitan Police displays a new 'on the spot' fine ticket when it was trialled in Croydon.

More recently, an equivalent form of penalty has been introduced for other forms of nuisance behaviour. These Penalty Notices for Disorder (PNDs) can be issued by the police and, in limited circumstances by PCSOs and other wardens. PNDs are generally for £50 or £80 and can only be issued to someone over 16. PNDs were introduced as part of the government's anti-social behaviour strategy (see Chapters 24 and 29) and cover such offences as: harassment; drunk and disorderly behaviour; minor criminal damage; retail theft; and sale of alcohol to a person under 18 years of age. Again, receipt of a penalty notice does not count as getting a conviction. However, failure to pay can lead to a criminal conviction and even imprisonment.

Expenditure and employment

The amount of money spent on criminal justice is very substantial indeed and has been growing markedly in recent times. According to an independent audit, UK spending on criminal justice increased on average by 4.1 per cent per annum between 1979 and 1997 in real terms and was the fastest-growing area of public expenditure in that period (Solomon *et al.*, 2007). This trend has continued since then, although other areas of public expenditure growth have been greater in the last few years.

Figure 23.2 Flows through the criminal justice system, 2005

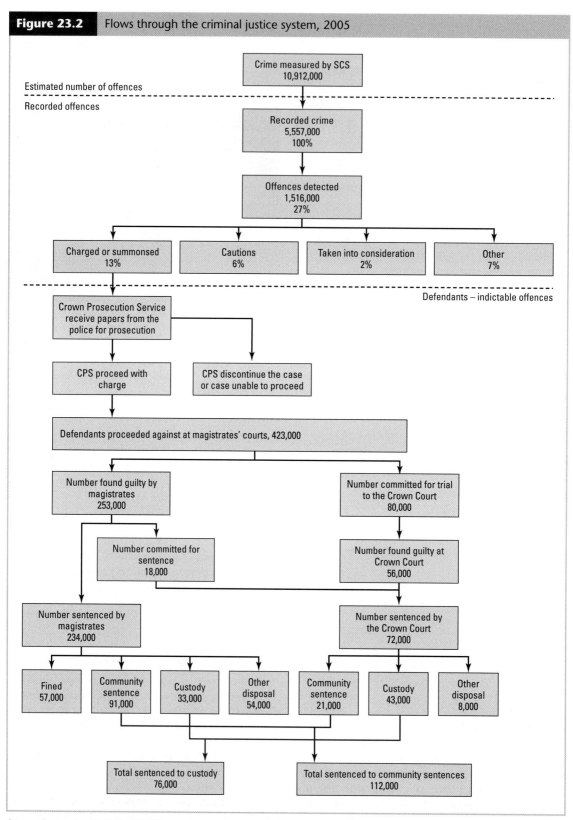

Source: Sentencing Statistics (2006).

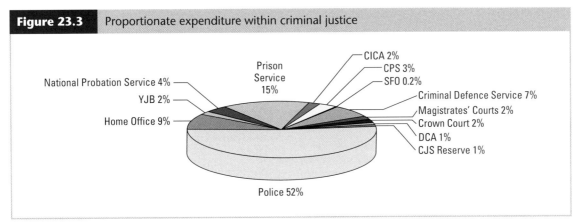

| **Figure 23.3** | Proportionate expenditure within criminal justice |

Source: Home Office online report 19/05.

Expenditure on criminal justice was anticipated to be well over £20 billion by 2007–08, up one-third over the course of a decade. A breakdown of the major areas of expenditure is shown in Figure 23.3. As can be seen, the police service accounts for more than half of the total expenditure on criminal justice in England and Wales. Staff costs account for a substantial part of criminal justice expenditure.

Management and oversight in criminal justice

From the mid-1980s onward, a policy of 'tight resourcing' was applied across much of criminal justice. The 3-Es of economy, efficiency and effectiveness became watchwords by which all public services, including police, probation, courts, and others, were to be managed. Public services, including criminal justice agencies, were encouraged to change their management styles and, increasingly, bodies such as the Audit Commission and the National Audit Office exercised greater scrutiny over performance and expenditure.

New public management

As the 1990s wore on, one of the solutions that government pursued in relation to the problems it faced in the criminal justice arena was increasingly to seek to make institutions and agencies more businesslike. Initially identified by Bottoms (1995) as a form of 'systemic managerialism', the aim has increasingly been to apply the 'perceived attributes of the well-run private sector company (of high

efficiency, of explicit accountabilities, of clear objectives, and of measured performance)' (Raine and Willson, 1993: 23). What has become known as 'new public management' (NPM) has had a marked impact across the criminal justice system (see Hough *et al.*, 2006; Jones, 2003). The attributes of NPM vary, but in criminal justice they would appear to include (McLaughlin *et al.*, 2001):

● Increased emphasis on achieving results rather than administering processes.

● The publication of league tables illustrating comparative performance.

● The identification of core competencies.

● The costing and market-testing of all activities to ensure value for money.

● The externalisation of non-essential responsibilities.

● The establishment of a purchaser–provider split.

● The encouragement of inter-agency co-operation.

● The redesignation of clients as 'customers'.

● The setting of explicit targets and performance indicators to enable the auditing of efficiency and effectiveness.

Part of this new management creed is held to involve a devolution of decision-making and of budgetary control and, indeed, there have been moves within the prison and police services to provide local managers with considerably enhanced powers. All too often, however, it appears that lip-service has been paid to such devolution of responsibility, rather than there being any significant reorientation of power and influence. More than anything else, the reason for this has been a continual, and by no means always gradual, accretion of power to central government. Here lies one of the fundamental and continuing tensions in contemporary criminal justice. Garland (2001: 19) describes it as:

> ... a new and all-pervasive managerialism that affects every aspect of criminal justice. Within specific agencies and organizations, performance indicators and management measures have narrowed professional discretion and tightly regulated working practice. Across the system as a whole, new forms of system-monitoring, information technology and financial auditing have extended centralized control over a process that was previously less well co-ordinated and highly resistant to policy management. This emphasis upon the cost-effective management of risks and resources has produced a system that is increasingly selective in its responses to crime and offending.

The impact of NPM has been highly controversial and can be seen across the criminal justice system, such as in the use of league tables for police forces, the introduction of national objectives, and through the creation of a host of bodies whose responsibility it is to inspect, assess, audit and, where necessary, impose sanctions upon the work of criminal justice agencies. It is, as McLaughlin *et al.* (2007) argue, becoming progressively institutionalised within criminal justice. One of the clearest examples of this trend is to be found within the youth justice arena with the creation of the Youth Justice Board.

Youth Justice Board

Established by the Crime and Disorder Act 1998, the Youth Justice Board (YJB) oversees the youth justice system in England and Wales. The YJB advises the Ministry of Justice on the operation of the youth justice system, sets standards and monitors performance in youth justice, and has responsibility for purchasing all the places within what is now generally referred to as the *secure estate* for children and young people. The YJB spends around 70 per cent of its budget on providing custodial places. The secure estate comprises three main types of institution:

● *Secure children's homes* – These institutions tend to be small and are run by local authority social services departments and overseen by the Department of Health and the Department for Education and Skills.

● *Secure Training Centres (STCs)* – These are custodial institutions for vulnerable young people. There are currently four STCs, all run by the private sector. They have a higher staff–young offender ratio than YOIs.

● *Young offender institutions (YOIs)* – YOIs are run by both the Prison Service and the private sector and accommodate both juveniles (under 18s) and young adult offenders (18–21 year-olds). They tend to be larger than both STCs and secure children's homes.

In addition to establishing the YJB, the Crime and Disorder Act 1998 established for the first time an overarching aim for the youth justice system. This is to prevent offending by children and young people. As part of its work the YJB oversees and monitors the work of local Youth Offending Teams and assesses their work against national standards. The intention is that such National Standards will help to ensure that youth justice agencies fulfil the overarching aim by:

● preventing crime and the fear of crime by ensuring that services are targeted at children and young people at high risk of offending, and meet the needs of victims and communities;

● ensuring that young people who do offend are identified and dealt with without delay, with punishment proportionate to the seriousness and frequency of offending; and

● promoting interventions with young offenders that reduce the risk factors associated with offending, increase the protective factors and reinforce the responsibilities of parents.

The danger, as in other areas of criminal justice, is that such micro-management will undermine the creative potential that professionals bring to their work with offenders and, through the imposition of a broad range of performance and outcome indicators, shift resources towards those aspects of work which are measured and away from those that are not. On a general level in youth justice – as in so much criminal justice – managerialism has given a very particular inflection to the nature of work undertaken by Youth Offending Teams with every aspect now dominated by a concern with crime prevention. Indeed, as Pitts (2000: 31) summarises it:

> In no small measure social work professionalism is being replaced by a series of organisations whose performance is amendable to measureable/quantifiable outcomes. The practice of youth justice is being transformed into a technical

process in which the 'less than heroic' objectives of reducing risk and expenditure have replaced any notion of winning the 'war on crime'.

Inspectorates

There are currently separate inspectorates for the police, the Crown Prosecution Service, court administration, prisons and the National Probation Service. In March 2005 the government announced its intention to reduce the number of public sector inspectorates from 11 to four, and as part of this to create a single inspectorate for justice, community safety and custody.

Her Majesty's Inspectorate of Constabulary for England, Wales and Northern Ireland (HMIC)

Established by the County and Borough Police Act 1856, HMIC is responsible for examining and improving the efficiency of the Police Service in England and Wales (and more recently Northern Ireland). HM Chief Inspector of Constabulary is independent both of the Home Office and of the Police Service. Since October 1993 HMIC has had two inspectors from non-police backgrounds. The inspectorate has three main areas of responsibility:

- The formal inspection and assessment of the 43 police forces in England and Wales, the Police Service of Northern Ireland (supporting the Chief Inspector of Criminal Justice in Northern Ireland) and a variety of other policing bodies.

- Acting as the Home Secretary's principal professional police adviser and as independent advisory body to police forces and police authorities.

- Advising the Home Secretary on senior appointments in the police service.

Her Majesty's Inspectorate of Court Administration (HMICA)

HMICA's role is to inspect the systems that support the Crown, county and magistrates' courts in England and Wales (as a result of the Courts Act 2003). In addition it also inspects CAFCASS (the Children and Family Court Advisory and Support Service) in England. By invitation, HMICA may inspect the courts in Northern Ireland and CAFCASS in Wales. According to HMICA, its priority is to examine the quality of service provided to court users, particularly victims and witnesses, as well as defendants and jurors.

Her Majesty's Crown Prosecution Service Inspectorate (HMCPSI)

HMCPSI is the independent Inspectorate for the Crown Prosecution Service (CPS), the principal prosecuting authority for criminal cases in England and Wales. The inspectorate's remit was extended to include the Revenue and Customs Prosecution Office in April 2005, and the Chief Inspector of Criminal Justice in Northern Ireland has invited HMCPSI to conduct statutory inspection work in relation to the Public Prosecution Service which was established there in 2005. The Chief Inspector of HMCPSI is appointed by and reports to the Attorney General.

Her Majesty's Inspectorate of Prisons for England and Wales (HMIP)

HMIP is an independent inspectorate which reports on conditions for and treatment of those in prison, young offender institutions and immigration removal centres. The Chief Inspector of Prisons is appointed by the Home Secretary for a term of five years. The Chief Inspector reports directly to the Home Secretary on the treatment and conditions for prisoners in England and Wales and other matters. HMIP also has statutory responsibility to inspect all immigration removal centres and holding facilities on behalf of the Immigration and Nationality Directorate, and inspections have also been carried out at the Military Corrective Training Centre in Colchester, prisons in Northern Ireland, the Channel Islands, the Isle of Man and some commonwealth dependent territories.

Her Majesty's Inspectorate of Probation for England and Wales (HMI Probation)

HM Inspectorate of Probation is an independent inspectorate, funded by the Home Office and reporting directly to the Home Secretary. In its statement of purpose it states that it has responsibility to:

- Report to the Home Secretary on the work and performance of National Probation Service (NPS) and of Youth Offending Teams (YOTs), particularly on the effectiveness of work with individual offenders, children and young people aimed at reducing re-offending and protecting the public.

- In this connection, and in association with HM Inspectorate of Prisons, to report on the effectiveness of offender management under the auspices of the National Offender Management Service (NOMS) as it develops.

- Contribute to improved performance in the NPS, NOMS and YOTs.

Prisons and Probation Ombudsman

Inspections of the activities of criminal justice agencies are also performed by a series of other bodies. In particular, there are a number of agencies that have responsibility for the handling of complaints within the criminal justice system. The Prisons and Probation Ombudsman, for example, is responsible for the investigation of complaints from prisoners and those subject to probation supervision, or those upon whom reports have been written. The Ombudsman is completely independent of both the Prison Service and the National Probation Service (NPS).

The Ombudsman can investigate all decisions taken by Prison Service staff, and others working on behalf of the Prison Service, that relate to individual prisoners. This includes privately run prisons, but does not cover clinical decisions made by doctors. The Ombudsman now also has responsibility for investigating deaths in custody (Harding, 2007). The Ombudsman can investigate decisions taken by staff of the National Probation Service or others working on their behalf. Areas not covered by the Ombudsman include policy decisions taken by ministers, the exercise of ministerial powers in relation to the setting and review of tariffs for particular prisoners, or the release from prison of those serving mandatory life sentences.

Independent Police Complaints Commission (IPCC)

The IPCC is an independent body responsible for the investigation of certain classes of complaint against the police. In the aftermath of a series of corruption scandals in the 1970s, a part-time body, the Police Complaints Board was established. It was fairly swiftly replaced by the Police Complaints Authority, which was a full-time body and had greater powers to supervise the investigation of complaints. Despite this, the PCA was seen by some critics as being insufficiently independent of the police and subsequently the Police Reform Act 2002 introduced the IPCC. Operational from 2004, the IPCC has a range of strengthened powers which allow it to choose to manage or supervise the police investigation into a case and, independently, to investigate the most serious cases.

The IPCC has a series of teams of investigators in each of its regions, which assist with supervision and management of some police investigations, and carry out independent investigations into serious incidents or allegations of misconduct by persons serving with the police. According to the IPCC, serious incidents are those involving death or serious injury. Serious allegations include allegations:

- of serious or organised corruption;
- against senior officers;
- involving racism;
- of perverting the course of justice.

(http://www.ipcc.gov.uk/index/about_ipcc/investigations.htm)

Politics and criminal justice reform

Crime is now a staple of political discourse and of electoral politics. Whilst this may not feel surprising it is, in fact, a relatively new political phenomenon. Until the early 1970s in the UK, for example, criminal justice policy barely featured in major elections and certainly was far from the 'wedge issue' it became in the 1980s. We return to the issue of the politics of crime and its control in a large number of chapters in this book. We raise it here specifically in relation to one hugely important feature of contemporary criminal justice – the sheer quantity of legislation and the amount of change that characterises the system.

In the criminal justice arena, politicians' concern with how they are likely to be perceived has had a profound effect on policy-making in recent times. Crucially, as numerous commentators have noted, by the 1990s the old divisions between 'conservative' and 'liberal' political positions on crime had disappeared, and had been replaced by what appeared to be a straightforward 'tough on crime' message. The past two decades have seen a progressively intensifying battle by the major political parties to be seen as the party of law and order. A 'tough on crime' stance has come to be associated with electoral success and its opposite, being 'soft on crime', with electoral failure.

The lengthy political dominance of Conservatism during the 1980s in the UK led to vociferous debates within the Labour Party over the possible sources of electoral success in what were clearly changed times. The Labour Party sought to dump its various 'hostages to fortune' (Downes and Morgan, 1997) not least of which was its previously more liberal policies on crime control. 'New Labour' in the UK embraced so-called 'third way' politics. In the criminal justice arena this meant attempting to modify the old-fashioned liberal penal welfarism that the party had largely clung to throughout the 1980s and into the 1990s by adding into the mix what was by now considered the *sine qua non* of successful electoral politics: a healthy dose of punitive rhetoric and the promise of similarly punitive policies. This mixture has never been more successfully captured than in Tony Blair's 1993 soundbite, 'tough on crime and tough on the causes of crime'.

The outcome of such shifts has been that crime once again has largely ceased to be a wedge issue – something that parties use to signal significant differences between them. In Britain, a new political consensus has emerged around crime. In this consensus, tough rhetoric, and often tough action, have become the political bottom-line for any politician concerned with electoral success. There has been a profound shift away from discourses and practices which highlighted welfare and rehabilitation as central objectives of the system of punishment (see Chapters 27 and 28).

Governments, keen to display their 'toughness', have done so in a number of ways. There has been increased emphasis on punishment, assertions that 'prison works' and a general disparaging of welfare-oriented policies and practices of rehabilitation. There has been the increased emphasis on tackling disorder and anti-social behaviour (see Chapters 24 and 29) and increased powers given to the police and others (see Chapter 25). Overall, there has been a vast expansion in 'criminalisation', underpinned by a quite extraordinary torrent of legislation. This can be seen in the sheer weight of criminal justice legislation in the decade since 1997. Ignoring laws that have been passed containing crime-related provisions, but which are primarily aimed at other matters, there were still well over 40 major Acts of Parliament in the area of criminal justice and penal policy between 1997 and 2006. It has been estimated that more than 3,000 new criminal offences have been created since 1997, one for every day the Blair government was in power (Nigel Morris, 'Blair's "Frenzied Law-Making"', *The Independent*, 16 August 2006).

In addition, as we have seen, there has also been the huge weight of reform that has taken place in criminal justice in the last decade. To reiterate, this has included (among many others):

- The reform of the Home Office and the creation of the Ministry of Justice.
- The amalgamation of the Prison and Probation Services into NOMS.
- The overhaul of the youth justice system.

- Successive changes to the system of sentencing and reorganisation of the penalties available to the courts.
- The introduction and then reform of local CDRPs.

The politics of crime control have had a dramatic impact on the nature and scale of punishment. Equally, it has undoubtedly been politics that has been the primary driving force behind the almost constant flow of new legislation and of organisational reform in criminal justice. Few changes – either to the law or to criminal justice institutions – are allowed to bed down before new ones are introduced. The consequence is that criminal justice professionals work in a system that is in an almost constant state of flux – a situation quite different from that which prevailed as recently as 20 years ago. This forms an important backdrop to the more detailed discussion of various aspects of the criminal justice system and process that follows in subsequent chapters.

Review questions

1 What are the two main criminal courts in England and Wales and what are the main differences between them?

2 Think of three reasons why criminal justice agencies might find it difficult to work with each other.

3 What is meant by 'managerialism' or 'new public management'? (Give examples.)

Understanding criminal justice

In Chapter 2 we looked at the history of the emergence of the modern criminal justice system. Here we turn our attention to how to characterise our contemporary system. To do so, we take two well-established distinctions used in portraying criminal justice and examine their application to domestic criminal justice.

Adversarial versus inquisitorial systems

The British system of justice is generally described as adversarial. At its heart is a contest between accuser and accused. The contest is about amassing sufficient evidence to establish guilt (or failing to do so); it is not primarily about establishing *the truth*. Collecting information and evidence in order that all parties may come to understand what happened in the course of a particular incident is not what happens as a result of a criminal investigation. To the extent that this is the impression given by film and television drama, it is largely misleading. There are other forums – such as public inquiries – which do play such a role (or, at least, come much closer to doing so).

In a court of law the standard required to establish 'guilt' is to convince either the magistrates, or the jury if a Crown Court trial, that the prosecution's case is supported by evidence and that guilt is determined 'beyond reasonable doubt'. This is generally considered to be a fairly high standard of 'proof' and lower standards are used in other proceedings such as in complaints and disciplinary cases involving police officers where the standard of proof is 'the balance of probabilities'.

The ideal typical form of adversarial justice – and certainly the one that dominates all media representations – is the Crown Court, involving smart surroundings with judge presiding, lawyers in robes and wigs, and a jury of twelve listening intently to the case. Again, this is highly misleading. The vast majority of criminal cases are heard in magistrates' courts or the youth court. In all, only about three to four per cent of criminal cases reach the Crown Court. Moreover, justice in the magistrates' courts is a very different process. Indeed, if you have never done so then you should visit your local courts and watch the justice system in action. You will probably find crowded buildings, lots of people milling around, and cases presented and completed in a relatively short period of time, often without the defendant saying anything other than confirming their name and entering a plea.

By contrast with our adversarial system of justice there are other jurisdictions which place greater emphasis upon some form of search for the truth. These systems, such as that in France, are more usually described as *inquisitorial*. In the French system there is judicial supervision of the criminal investigation from the outset to the completion of the case. A dossier prepared by the *juge d'instruction* is provided for trial judge and will include witness statements and any statements made by the defendant (Hodgson, 2005). The judge is then in a position to make decisions such as which witnesses will be called and also plays a primary role in cross-examination (supported by defence and prosecution

lawyers). Again, as with the adversarial model, it is important not to exaggerate the extent to which systems such as that in France actually operate inquisitorially in practice. Recent research (Hodgson, 2004) suggests, for example, that the police occupy a fairly dominant position in relation to much French criminal justice.

The shortcoming of the inquisitorial approach, it is argued, is that the judge may come to favour one party, being influenced by his or her particular reading of the case. By contrast, the theory in the adversarial system is that the judge remains impartial, in effect working to enable both parties to advance their case. Both systems, for different reasons, can argue that they are more effective at getting at 'the truth'. The inquisitorial system – in its ideal form – is focused on such a search. From the outset the aim is to gather information and construct a case, guided by the *juge d'instruction* or similar, in such a way as to uncover the facts of the case. The danger in such a system is, as already argued, that the powerful position of the judge can lead to a skewed investigation and outcome.

By contrast, in the adversarial system, police investigation and subsequent trial are not based on the search for the truth *per se*, but on a contest between competing claims about what occurred. The advantage, it can be argued, is that the contest, supervised by a neutral arbiter, allows for careful and thorough scrutiny of whether any particular case can be proven. Alternatively, critics may claim that in the adversarial system the emphasis on the contest means that all sorts of tactics may be employed – suppression of evidence, aggressive cross-examination of witnesses – to bring advantage to one side or the other, with the result that the outcome is likely to reflect the impact of such tactics, or other questions of resources, rather than 'the truth' (Pollard, 1996).

In addition to differing approaches to investigation and inquiry, the differences between adversarial and inquisitorial systems of justice 'also express different conceptions of how power should be allocated in society' (Sanders and Young, 2007: 14). What they mean by this is that the two systems place differing emphases upon the need for safeguards to protect the citizen against the power of the state. The adversarial system is based on a contest between state and citizen (legal cases are presented as *Regina vs Bloggs*). This is an unequal contest and it is assumed that safeguards are necessary to protect the accused. These safeguards cover such matters as the process by which evidence can be collected, how long a suspect may be detained by the police, and what may be presented and said in court.

By contrast, in inquisitorial systems where the overriding aim is held to be the search for the truth, and the process is therefore considered to be more neutral than the adversarial contest, there is less concern about the abuse of state power. As a consequence, in some inquisitorial systems there is a tendency for suspects to be detained for far longer than would be allowed under Police and Criminal Evidence Act 1984 (PACE) provisions, for example (see Chapter 25). What it is important to take from this discussion concerns justice in theory and practice, more than the issue of which systems of justice are the more reliable. Adversarial and inquisitorial approaches are underpinned by a series of theoretical and philosophical assumptions about how they *should* work. How they *actually* work may differ, more or less markedly, from the theory. This may give rise to a further series of questions about criminal process and whether, depending on the aims of the justice system, the safeguards that exist are considered to be insufficient (providing too little of a brake on the power of the state) or excessive (hampering the work of police and prosecution).

Due process versus crime control

One of the most influential analyses of criminal justice, by Herbert Packer (1968), distinguishes between two ideal typical models: *due process* and *crime control*. The essential elements of these two ideal types are as follows

Due process	Crime control
(The obstacle course)	(The conveyor belt)
Presumption of innocence	Guilt implied
Right to a fair trial	Legal controls minimal
Equality before the law	System designed to aid police
Defendants' rights	Crime fighting is key

Remember, ideal types are not descriptions of things *as they are*. They are abstract models designed to help us identify the characteristics or elements of particular phenomena. Thus, nowhere would it be argued that any system of justice could be described as a straightforward illustration of *either* due process *or* crime control values. As Packer (1968: 153) noted:

These models are not labelled Is and Ought, nor are they to be taken in that sense. Rather, they represent an attempt to abstract two separate value systems that compete for priority in the operation of the criminal process. Neither is presented as either corresponding to reality or representing the ideal to the exclusion of the other.

Rather, the purpose of the contrast between the ideal types is to help us identify where the balance of a particular system of justice lies: as well as the relative weighting of due process and crime control values.

In the crime control model, the prevention or reduction of crime is the overriding aim. In the absence of such an objective, public regard for the criminal law and the system of justice would decline. Much emphasis is therefore placed on facilitating criminal investigation, interrogation and the pursuit of offenders. Consequently, less emphasis is placed upon suspects' rights, and there is an assumption that bureaucratic protections would only serve to hamper police work. Much trust is therefore placed in the hands of the police and other authorities in the investigation of crime and the management of the justice system. While accepting that mistakes will happen, the crime control model tends to assume that this is the acceptable collateral damage of the bigger task of controlling crime.

By contrast, as it sounds, the due process model places much less faith in the reliability of the police and others in bringing offenders to justice. Genuine mistakes can occur at all stages of the criminal justice process and, moreover, people may act corruptly or dishonestly. Thus, the due process model lays emphasis on the protection of rights and seeks to ensure that there exists a system of safeguards which places limits on the coercive powers of the police and others, and underpins the basic values of criminal justice: a presumption of innocence and the right to a fair trial. The due process model also places great emphasis on the importance of equality: all are equal before the law and therefore should be provided with access to legal advice where necessary, together with other forms of protection. Sanders and Young (2007: 22) very helpfully summarise the contrast as follows:

Crime control values prioritise the conviction of the guilty, even at the risk of the conviction of some (fewer) innocents, and the cost of infringing the liberties of suspects to achieve its goals; while due process values prioritise the acquittal of the innocent, even if risking the frequent acquittal of the guilty, and giving high priority to the protection of civil liberties as an end in itself.

It is around such contrasts that many debates about the nature of criminal justice revolve. How might one characterise criminal justice in England and Wales using such models? Answering such a question involves examining both the principles that underpin the criminal justice system – the legal protections afforded suspects, and so on – and how these are put into practice. One way of concluding this discussion for the time being is to look at how debates around these issues are far from straightforward. To do so we look at an exchange between the authors of a book called *The Case for the Prosecution* and one of their critics.

Are 'due process' and 'crime control' models helpful in understanding the working of criminal justice in the UK? This book generated an illuminating debate.

The Case for the Prosecution by McConville, Sanders and Leng was published in 1991. The book, based on empirical research, examines the treatment of suspects in police custody and uses Packer's two models to frame arguments about how we should understand such treatment. In particular, they looked at what they refer to as 'case construction' and the ways in which safeguards are ignored, subverted or negotiated by the police so as to enable them to secure the goals they seek: the creation of successful prosecution cases. As such, they argue

that in practice this aspect of the criminal justice system comes closer to Packer's crime control model in that regard for due process is much less strong than is often argued.

In a response to this argument, Smith (1997) is critical of the approach taken and the conclusions reached. He argues, rather, that 'crime control is necessarily the goal of criminal process, and the criminal justice system can neither be understood nor justified except by reference to that objective'. In this vein he argues – as he suggests Packer himself did – that due process and crime control are in fact twin aims of the criminal justice system. His second line of criticism is that the 'case construction' argument overstates and misrepresents the role of the police who have a host of responsibilities and objectives which include, but go far beyond, those of crime control. In essence his suggestion is that McConville *et al.* tend to rely on a contrast between due process and crime control, assessing police activity as if it could be characterised one way or the other. In the concluding sentence of his critique, Smith (1997: 344) summarises the essence of this argument when he says, 'Due process values can only be sustained if it is recognized that crime control is a "high purpose" and that the police have a legitimate job to do'.

McConville *et al.*'s response (1997) to Smith's critique of their use of Packer's model is to argue that he misrepresents their position. They did not argue, they say, that the overriding goal of the justice system should be due process and, indeed, they accept that crime control is, and must be, a fundamental aim – though Smith (1998) later argues that such a recognition didn't appear in the original book. However, 'to accept this is not necessarily to accept the values of the Crime Control Model' (1997: 356). By this they mean that whilst attempting to control crime is a perfectly legitimate goal of the criminal justice system, that aim should not, in their view, override a commitment to due process values. Acceptable means must be found for identifying and convicting those who have committed crimes.

Smith (1998) in a further response remains unconvinced. He suggests that McConville *et al.*'s conclusion that the criminal justice system 'is not, on the whole, due process-based, despite much rhetoric and many rules to the contrary' (1997: 356) reveals their true intention. This, he says, 'is to imply that the appropriate yardstick for the whole of the criminal justice system is the values of Packer's due process model; that these values are apparently inherent in both the rhetoric and rules of the present system; and that the system fails to the extent that it does not express these values fully, unequivocally, and to the exclusion of others' (1998: 615). Due process, however, can never be the ultimate yardstick because criminal justice must always be a compromise between due process *and* crime control.

In an attempt to bring the two sides in the debate together, Peter Duff (1998) suggests that at least some of the differences between the two camps are a result of terminological confusion. The confusion arises because the term *crime control* is used in two quite different ways. First, it is used to capture the overall goal of criminal justice – the repression of criminal conduct. Second, it is also used to label a set of values which influence the practice of criminal justice – those values that contrast with the values of due process. This is the distinction that McConville *et al.* referred to above as that between crime control and the Crime Control Model. In these terms it appears that the two sides in the debate may generally agree in relation to the importance of crime control, but may have different views as to the relative weight to be given to the Crime Control Model or crime control values in a practical system of justice. There is clearly no easy resolution to this argument. Indeed, elements of it are reproduced here precisely in order to illustrate the complexities involved in attempting to capture the nature and practice of criminal justice.

There are a number of ways in which the criminal justice process can be analysed. Sanders and Young (2007), for example, also utilise Packer's two contrasting models as their preferred means of doing so. The analytical process of attempting to identify 'where on the spectrum between crime control and due process English criminal justice is today to be located must ... take account of both the formal law as laid down in statutes and case law, and the actual operation of the system by officials operating within that legal framework' (2007: 26). An alternative is to adopt a rights-based approach – such as those set out in major human rights frameworks (see Chapter 34) – and to explore to what extent these rights are upheld or protected by the operation of the criminal justice system (see Ashworth and Redmayne, 2005). Whichever the preferred method, the objective is to develop some measure or model against which to assess criminal justice. As has been alluded to at several points in this chapter, and as will become clearer in subsequent chapters, the criminal justice system and process in England and Wales has undergone fairly unrelenting, often very substantial, reform in the last decade or more. Beyond the analytical question of what form these changes take there lies the important normative question of whether these changes should be viewed positively or negatively, and why.

Review questions

1 What are the main differences between an adversarial and an inquisitorial system of justice?

2 What are the major differences between Packer's models of 'due process' and 'crime control'?

3 What are the two ways in which the term 'crime control' is used in Packer's model?

Questions for further discussion

1 What might be the consequences of splitting the Home Office and creating a Ministry of Justice?

2 What are the pros and cons of managerialism?

3 In what ways has criminal justice politics changed in recent years?

4 Which do you think is the more effective – an adversarial or an inquisitorial system of justice – and why?

5 If you wanted to maximise either 'crime control' or 'due process' values in the criminal justice system, what might you do?

Further reading

There are a number of excellent textbooks on the subject of criminal justice. The ones I have generally found most useful are:

Ashworth, A. and Redmayne, M. (2005) *The Criminal Process*, 3rd edn, Oxford: Oxford University Press

Davies, M. *et al.* (2005) *Criminal Justice*, 3rd edn, Harlow: Longman

Sanders, A. and Young, R. (2007) *Criminal Justice*, 3rd edn, Oxford: Oxford University Press

Uglow, S. (2002) *Criminal Justice*, 2nd edn, London: Sweet and Maxwell

The debate between McConville, Sanders and Leng and Smith is both important and entertaining. The relevant references are:

McConville, M. *et al.* (1991) *The Case for the Prosecution*, London: Routledge

Smith, D.J. (1997) Case construction and the goals of criminal process, *British Journal of Criminology*, 37, 3, 319–346, Oxford: Oxford Journals

McConville, M. *et al.* (1997) Descriptive or critical sociology: The choice is yours, *British Journal of Criminology*, 37, 3, 347–458, Oxford: Oxford Journals

Smith, D.J. (1998) Reform or moral outrage: The choice is yours, *British Journal of Criminology*, 38, 4, 614–622, Oxford: Oxford Journals

Websites

Criminal Justice Online is a terrific repository of information: http: //www.cjsonline.gov.uk/

Government department websites contain a lot of information about the criminal justice system and process. Well worth a look are:

Home Office: www.homeoffice.gov.uk

Ministry of Justice: http: //www.justice.gov.uk/

Law Officers' Departments: www.lslo.gov.uk

NACRO, the crime reduction charity, has much information about its own work and also more generally about criminal justice: http: //www.nacro.org.uk/

Chapter outline

Defining crime prevention 566

Crime prevention as a policy issue 566
'Five Towns' and 'Safer Cities' 568
Neighbourhood Watch 568
From crime prevention to community safety 569
Crime and Disorder Act 1998 570
From community safety to crime reduction 570
Reviewing the Crime and Disorder Act 573

Anti-social behaviour 574
Broken Windows 575
The anti-social behaviour and respect agendas 576

Crime prevention in practice 577

Situational crime prevention 578
Displacement 582

Social and community crime prevention 583
Criminality prevention 583
Risk-focused prevention 584
The Perry Pre-School Project 584
Cognitive-behavioural interventions with
young people 585
Community approaches and prevention 585
Operation ceasefire 585
Mentoring 587

Analysis for crime prevention 588
Hot spots 589
Repeat victimization 589
Kirkholt Burglary Prevention Project 591

Questions for further discussion 593
Further reading 594
Websites 594

24

Crime prevention and community safety

CHAPTER SUMMARY

Recent decades have witnessed the progressive rise of crime prevention up the political and academic agenda. Rising crime rates after the Second World War and disappointing research evidence on the impact of criminal agencies in controlling crime led to increased emphasis on the responsibility both of non-criminal justice agencies and individual citizens in preventing crime. In parallel, the academic world saw the emergence of a set of neo-classical approaches (see also Chapter 14) which emphasised rationality and opportunity in understanding criminality.

In this chapter we look at:

● the politics of crime prevention and how this has changed in emphasis and orientation;

● examples of crime prevention activity in practice.

Defining crime prevention

There are, arguably, two main ways of classifying crime prevention initiatives or approaches. The first distinguishes primary, secondary and tertiary activities. Primary prevention generally refers to action that is targeted at a general population and which aims to prevent (crime) before it occurs. Secondary prevention is action targeted at a more specific 'at risk' population. Finally, tertiary prevention tends to be targeted at known offenders in order to reduce offending and/or the harms associated with offending (Brantingham and Faust, 1976). The second, best known and most widely used of all the means of distinguishing models of crime prevention, is that between 'situational' and 'social' approaches. 'Situational' crime prevention has been described as:

> ... a pre-emptive approach that relies, not on improving society or its institutions, but simply on reducing opportunities for crime ... Situational prevention comprises opportunity-reducing measures that are (1) directed at highly specific forms of crime, (2) that involve the management, design or manipulation of the immediate environment in as specific and per-manent way as possible (3) so as to increase the effort and risks of crime and reduce the rewards as perceived by a wide range of offenders.
>
> (Clarke, 1992: 4)

Early, and influential, work on crime prevention and the environment includes Oscar Newman's theory of defensible space (Newman, 1972) and the notion of crime prevention through environ-mental design (Jeffrey, 1971), (see Chapter 14). Critics of situational prevention tend to view it as a superficial response to what they regard as the more 'fundamental' causes of crime such as poverty, poor housing, unemployment and inade-quate education and parenting. As Weatheritt has put it, 'on this view, it is not the physical environ-ment which needs to be manipulated, but rather the social conditions and psychological disposi-tions that create offenders in the first place ... What is needed, therefore, is programmes of action which will help change people's attitudes to offending, encourage respect for law and reduce the wish to commit crimes' (1986: 57). By contrast, then, 'social' crime prevention can be linked to control theory which focuses on the informal con-trols that are held to inhibit offending behaviour most of the time.

Crime prevention as a policy issue

Crime prevention – broadly conceived – has long historical antecedents, though for the bulk of the nineteenth and twentieth centuries there was relatively little official interest in harnessing and managing crime prevention activities in the community. The increasingly visible shortcomings of the criminal justice system as a means of pre-venting crime led to the growing emphasis on crime prevention. The limitations of criminal jus-tice responses were numerous. The widely-held assumption that improving social and economic conditions in post-war society would lead to diminishing levels of crime was increasingly hard to sustain by the late 1970s. Moreover, the belief that the criminal justice system could be relied upon to control crime if only the right methods and level of resources were provided was also shown to be unfounded. By this time belief in the rehabilitative qualities of custodial punishment had largely disappeared. The 'optimism of the late-1950s, that the system could be adapted to control crime, initially gave way to crisis management, as measures such as the suspended sentence, parole and community service were designed to take some pressure off our bulging prisons, and latterly melted into a pessimism that "nothing works"' (Gilling, 1997: 75).

It was against this background that crime prevention began to gain ground. In 1960, the then Home Secretary, R.A. Butler, established the Cornish Committee on the Prevention and Detection of Crime, and, in 1963, the Home Office established the National Crime Prevention Centre at Stafford for training specialist police officers. The Cornish Committee reported in 1965 and in its report acknowledged the potential role of the wider community in the prevention of crime. In relation to the formal criminal justice system it recommended the appointment of specialist crime prevention officers – indeed departments – within police forces. It also recommended the establishment of crime prevention panels as a means of building relationships between the police and other organisations with a role to play in the prevention of crime. Throughout the 1970s and into the 1980s, official research conducted by the Home Office pointed to the limitations of the criminal justice system generally, and the police in particular, in the prevention of crime. Partly as a consequence, interest grew in the prevention of *offences*. Further Home Office research, informed by rational choice theory (see Chapter 14), sought to reduce opportunities for crime by analysing the circumstances of particular offences, and then implementing and testing particular approaches.

During the 1980s the focus of attention began to move, slowly, from purely situational approaches to a combination of situational and social crime prevention initiatives. The report of a Home Office Working Group on co-ordinating crime prevention efforts, published in 1980, outlined a four-stage methodology for crime prevention which, though amended, has been the dominant method ever since. The four stages are summarised by Crawford (1998: 36) as:

- A thorough analysis of the crime problem, 'high crime' area, or situation in which the offence occurs, in order to establish the conditions that need to be met for the offence(s) to be committed.

- The identification of measures which would make it more difficult or impossible to fulfil these conditions.

- The assessment of the practicability, likely effectiveness, and cost of each measure.

- The selection of the most promising measures.

In practice two further stages have been added:

- An implementation process.

- The subsequent monitoring and evaluation of the initiatives undertaken.

In addition to these factors, the police gradually became more sympathetic to the idea of collaboration in crime prevention. In part, this was the result of spectacular 'failures' such as Swamp 81 in Brixton (see Chapters 2 and 25), and the more general perceived failure to impact on crime despite the heavy investment in resource terms made by government in the early 1980s. A Home Office circular released in 1984 was highly influential and was described some years later by one leading commentator as 'the most comprehensive statement of British policy on crime prevention' (Waller, 1989: 25). It stated that:

> Whilst there is a need to address the social factors associated with criminal behaviour, and policies are continually being devised to tackle this aspect of the problem, these are essentially long-term measures. For the short-term, the best way forward is to reduce through management, design or changes in the environment, the opportunities that exist for crime to occur.

The circular emphasised the traditional role of the police in the prevention of crime, and then went on to outline the potential contribution of other agencies: 'since some of the factors affecting crime lie outside the control or direct influence of the police, crime prevention cannot be left to them alone. Every individual citizen and all those agencies whose policies and practices can influence the extent of crime should make their contribution. *Preventing crime is a task for the whole community*' (Home Office, 1984: 1, emphasis added).

'Five Towns' and 'Safer Cities'

The next significant development was the establishment of what was known as the Five Towns Initiative in 1986: five local areas were provided with funding for a 'co-ordinator' whose responsibility was to service a multi-agency committee. The function of this committee was to oversee local crime prevention activity. This approach was extended in the Safer Cities project which started in 1988 and involved 20 local projects with the aim of reducing crime, lessening fear of crime and creating 'safer cities where economic enterprise and community life can flourish'. A second phase of the Safer Cities Programme was announced in 1992, with projects starting in 1994. Responsibility for the programme was transferred from the Home Office to the Department of the Environment as part of the Single Regeneration Budget (SRB) and covered 32 towns and cities.

The Safer Cities programme was criticised on several grounds. Some critics felt that it was insufficiently embedded in existing local authority structures, particularly structures for ensuring accountability. To this end it was argued that Safer Cities suffered a 'democratic deficit' (Crawford, 1998). Second, Safer Cities was criticised for being a vehicle for the dissemination of government ideology (King, 1991, though see Crawford, 1998). Third, some accused it of having a fundamentally short-term orientation. According to Crawford (1997: 33) Safer Cities 'represents a classic "trickle down" process whereby central government has sought to implant a particular model of policy formation and implementation, and to stimulate its spread through "seed-corn" funding. Despite its problematic structure and short-term project orientation, it has impacted on grass roots projects, as well as voluntary and statutory organisations and business, raising the profile of crime prevention and inter-agency partnerships.'

Neighbourhood Watch

Without doubt the best known and widely adopted crime prevention programme in Britain has been Neighbourhood Watch (NW). NW appeared first in Britain in the early 1980s (the first scheme was established in Mollington, Cheshire in 1982) and was promoted force-wide by the Metropolitan Police in 1983. Neighbourhood groups would be formed to carry out informal surveillance, thereby

deterring thieves through 'opportunity reduction' and providing an early warning system for the police. The spread of NW was remarkable. Within a decade of its establishment, over five million households were covered by one of over 100,000 schemes in England and Wales (Central Statistical Office, 1994).

A familiar Neighbourhood Watch notice. The Neighbourhood Watch movement now claims to cover six million households in the UK, with over 170,000 neighbourhood groups in existence.

Despite the substantial take-up and spread of NW, subsequent evaluations have indicated that in relation to its primary objective of reducing crime it has been of mixed success (Rosenbaum, 1988; Bennett, 1989), and that a significant part of the reason for this lies in 'programme failure': failure by both the police and the public to implement programmes fully. The police have been central to the setting up of NW all around the country, yet generally they are not in a position to deploy sufficient resources to sustain the schemes which, without their input, quickly fall into disuse (McConville and Shepherd, 1992). Moreover, schemes tend to flourish in parts of the country which have relatively low crime rates. Consequently, police resources that are devoted to crime prevention are diverted away from those areas where they are most needed (Laycock and Tilley, 1995).

From crime prevention to community safety

The main issue affecting and, arguably, inhibiting, the development of crime prevention in the 1980s and into the 1990s was the unwillingness of government to task any one agency with taking lead responsibility for such measures. The issue of lead responsibility for crime prevention was put back on the agenda as a result of the report of the Morgan Committee – an inquiry established by the Standing Conference on Crime Prevention – whose terms of reference were to: 'consider and monitor the progress made in the local delivery of crime prevention through the multi-agency or partnership approach, in the light of the guidance in the booklet "Partnership in Crime Prevention" and to make recommendations for the future'. The Morgan Committee's final report (Standing Conference on Crime Prevention, 1991) observed that 'At present, crime prevention is a peripheral concern of all the agencies involved and a truly core activity for none of them' (1991, para. 3.15). The report contained 19 major recommendations which included:

- The introduction of a statutory responsibility on local authorities (alongside the police) for the 'stimulation of community safety and crime prevention programmes, and for progressing at a local level a multi-agency approach to community safety'.

- The establishment of a local authority co-ordinator with administrative support wherever possible.

- More specific attention at a local level to involving businesses as partners 'instead of regarding [them] solely as a possible source of funds'.

- Ensuring that police and other agencies' information systems are compatible, to aid data exchange.

- The local crime partnership should exploit the 'important resource represented by the voluntary effort'.

- The establishment of an independent standing conference with co-ordinating responsibilities.

- Government should examine how the strong focus needed at the centre could be provided by strengthening existing organisations or creating new ones.

The Morgan Committee declared their preference for the term 'community safety' over 'crime prevention'. The latter, they suggested 'is often narrowly interpreted and this reinforces the view that it is solely the responsibility of the police', whereas the former 'is open to wider interpretation and could encourage greater participation from all sections of the community in the fight against crime' (1991: 13). The Morgan Committee were critical of what they saw as confusion at a local level, with numerous, centrally-funded crime prevention schemes running undue risks of overlapping with each other and consequently duplicating efforts: 'What is clearly perceived at a local level is a tendency for government departments to promote *ad hoc* initiatives, often implemented without proper consultation either with other government departments or with the local authorities' (1991: 26).

Although a decade or so earlier there had been little acceptance within local government of responsibility for crime prevention (Crawford, 1997) by the time of the Morgan Report, Community Safety Departments and Officers had become relatively commonplace within local government – at least in metropolitan areas. However, in the run-up to the 1992 general election the existing Conservative government was concerned about too great an emphasis on the socio-economic bases of crime, and was heavily engaged in attempting to decrease – not increase – the powers and responsibilities of local authorities. As such, the Morgan Committee's main recommendations were not implemented.

The 1990s quickly became a period in which the Home Secretary and his shadow appeared to be engaged in competition to 'out-tough' each other in relation to crime and penal policy (see Chapter 1). The criminal justice agenda once more became dominated by punitive rhetoric and a practical emphasis on crime control, neither of which, on the surface, would appear to be compatible with continuing interest in crime prevention, particularly social or community crime prevention. Nevertheless, crime prevention continued to be a central element within contemporary crime control strategies, with the Local Government Association lobbying for the full implementation of the Morgan Report. Therefore, prior to the 1997 General Election, the Labour Party made a manifesto commitment to implement the major recommendations of the Morgan Committee and, soon after the election, published precise details of their plans in a consultation document, *Getting to Grips with Crime*. The document opened with a discussion of the Morgan Report and, in particular, the key strategic role of local authorities. The document stated:

Even though the previous administration chose not to implement the Report, many of Morgan's key findings have in fact been taken on board spontaneously by partnerships all over the country, to their benefit and – most importantly – that of local communities ... The years which have elapsed since Morgan have seen a complete acceptance of the partnership concept at all levels of the *police service*. The service now explicitly recognises that it cannot cope with crime and disorder issues on its own ... The Government accepts the principle set out in Morgan that the extent, effectiveness and focus of existing local activity would be greatly improved by clear statements in law as to where responsibility for this work lies. (Home Office, 1997b: 3–5)

The government said that it was not persuaded that the Morgan view that giving local authorities lead responsibility would be workable in practice. Its views, rather, were that the 'principles of partnership' required joint working and collective responsibility. The new structures and requirements were set out in detail in the Crime and Disorder Act 1998.

Crime and Disorder Act 1998

The Act placed a statutory duty on chief police officers and local authorities, in co-operation with police authorities, probation committees and health authorities to formulate and implement a 'strategy for the reduction of crime and disorder in the area'. The Police Reform Act 2002 subsequently amended the Act to place the responsibility on chief police officers, local authorities and Primary Care Trusts (this was implemented in April 2004). In undertaking this responsibility the lead agencies are required by the Act to:

- Carry out a review of the levels and patterns of crime and disorder in the area.

- Prepare an analysis of the results of that review.

- Publish in the area a report of that analysis.

- Obtain the views on that report of persons or bodies in the area (including police authorities, probation and health and any others required by the Home Secretary) whether by holding public meetings or otherwise.

Once a strategy has been formulated, it is to be published by the responsible authorities. The publication should include details of:

- the bodies involved in the strategy;

- the results of the local audit;

- the objectives and performance targets.

In this way it parallels in many respects the nature of local policing plans, published annually by local police authorities.

In terms of the early activities of crime and disorder partnerships, perhaps predictably, the signs were mixed. Research undertaken by the Home Office (Phillips, 2002) suggested that whilst crime and disorder partnerships continued to experience many of the difficulties that had previously been identified in multi-agency activity (leadership, accountability, strategic focus), there were also a number of very positive signs in the working practices of the 376 newly-established partnerships. Based on an in-depth study of three partnerships, the study found little evidence, for example, of the conspiratorial model of multi-agency working referred to by previous researchers as the 'police take-over' (Sampson *et al.*, 1988). Rather, partnerships did not appear to be dominated by any one agency. However, Phillips (2002) went on to suggest that this was perhaps a 'honeymoon' period, and identified three areas where there was potential for conflict: in identifying, prioritising and solving the crime issue.

In addition, Phillips (2002) suggested that it was expected that the statutory authorities would do the 'lion's share' of the work, thus making the notion of partnership a problematic one. In consequence, a number of commentators noted the absence of certain agencies, in particular the Health Authorities (Audit Commission, 1999; HMIC, 2000). Indeed, it is the case that some agencies have been difficult to engage in the community safety agenda and, therefore, their ability to participate in and contribute to the work of community safety has been limited.

From community safety to crime reduction

As we have seen, during the 1990s 'crime prevention' as an organising idea was gradually superseded by the term 'community safety'. The primary intention was to signal the fact that the strategies involved in such a project could not be reduced to policing, or even criminal justice, but of necessity had to involve a range of agencies. However, by the time of the 1998 Crime and Disorder Act, community safety was itself being replaced as the master

Key developments in crime prevention in the UK, 1975–2007

The Effectiveness of Sentencing: A review of the literature	1976
Crime as Opportunity	1976
Designing Out Crime	1980
Co-ordinating Crime Prevention Efforts	1980
Situational Crime Prevention	1980
First British Crime Survey Report	1983
Crime Prevention Unit set up	1983
Home Office Standing Conference	1983
Home Office Circular 8/84, *Crime Prevention*	1984
First Crime Prevention Unit Paper	1985
Five Towns Initiative	1986
Gas and suicide	1988
Getting the Best Out of Crime Analysis	1988
Safer Cities	1988
Crime Concern 1988	1988
First Kirkholt report, beginning of repeat victimization focus	1988
Crash helmets and motor-bike theft	1989
Home Office Circular 44/90	1990
Morgan Report	1991
Police Research Group established	1992
Single Regeneration Budget	1993
First CCTV challenge	1995
Repeat Victimization Task Force set up	1996
First issue of *International Journal of Risk, Security and Crime Prevention*	1996
National Training Organisation	1998
Home Office Research Study 187	1998
Policing and Reducing Crime Unit established	1998
Crime and Disorder Act 1998, and guidance	1998
Beating Crime	1998
Crime Reduction Programme	1999
Safety in Numbers	1999
Crime Targets Task Force	1999
Foresight Programme	1999
Calling Time on Crime	2000
The Home Office Policing and Crime Reduction Directorate	2000
Appointment of Regional Crime Directors	2000
Preparation and publication of 'toolkits' to deal with specified problems	2001
Formal establishment of Jill Dando Institute for Crime Science at UCL	2001
Police Reform Act	2002
'Respect' White Paper Anti-Social Behaviour Act 2003	2003
Building Communities, Beating Crime	2004
National Community Safety Plan	2005
Review of the provisions of the Crime and Disorder Act	2006
Police and Justice Act	2006

Source: Updated from Tilley (2002).

term by the phrase 'crime reduction'. Crime reduction – or crime and disorder reduction as it became – had a somewhat narrower, enforcement-oriented agenda than had the Morgan Report-influenced notion of community safety.

In November 1999 the Labour government published its Crime Reduction Strategy. The Strategy announcement began by reiterating some of the tough rhetoric so beloved by the Home Secretary and Prime Minister at that time:

> The government is embarked on a crusade against crime ... We must, in other words, be tough on crime and tough on the causes of crime ... It means tough and consistent prison sentences for serious criminals, far more rigorous enforcement of community sentences and zero tolerance of anti-social behaviour. (http://crimereduction.gov.uk/crsdoc1.htm)

The Comprehensive Spending Review provided £400 million for the Crime Reduction Programme. The money was to be spent on a variety of crime reduction initiatives and, crucially, on the evaluation of those initiatives (much influenced by the review contained in Goldblatt and Lewis, 1998). The government was committed, it announced, to using 'hard evidence' as the basis for the approach to reducing crime. All police authorities and crime and disorder partnerships were required to set five-year targets, and annual milestones, for the reduction of vehicle crime, of burglary and of robbery. From 2000, information has been published not just by police force area, but also by Basic Command Units. In some respects the Crime Reduction Programme was a brave and rather optimistic strategy. Indeed, the promise that crime policy would in future be evidence-based bordered on the naïve. And so it has proved.

In the event, the Crime Reduction Programme (CRP) only ran for approximately three years – from 1999 to 2002. A total of £400 million was made available by the Treasury for the CRP in what has been described as 'the most comprehensive, systematic and far-sighted initiative ever undertaken by a British government to develop strategies for tackling crime' (Maguire, 2004: 214). The emergence of the CRP was, in part, a consequence of a rediscovery of faith in the idea of using scientific knowledge to reduce crime. From the 1970s, a generalised penal pessimism had taken hold, captured by the phrase 'nothing works'.

The rise of routine activities theory, situational crime prevention and related techniques (see Chapter 14) marked a shift in which government once again – albeit in a different, arguably narrowly technical form – began to explore how existing and new evidence might be utilised to reduce offending behaviour. Despite the shift in penal policy in this period, work exploring interventions with offenders had continued throughout the 1980s and began to garner interest and attention in the Home Office and elsewhere. These interventions included such things as basic skills programmes (focusing on literacy and numeracy), resettlement projects for prolific offenders and offending behaviour programmes, including a particular emphasis on cognitive-behavioural therapy (Raynor, 2004).

According to Maguire (2004) the CRP was different from previous initiatives – such as Safer Cities – in at least five important ways:

1 The size of the funding was very substantially larger than any previous initiative in this area.

2 It incorporated an especially broad range of interventions and these were 'based on an eclectic mix of crime prevention theories and delivered in many different settings by many different agencies' (2004: 216).

3 Evaluation and research evidence occupied a much more central role than in previous initiatives. There was a clear commitment to 'evidence-based policy' and encouragement given to the collection of scientific knowledge aimed at answering the question 'what works?'.

4 It was initially planned to be a long-term initiative of up to ten years.

5 'It offered, for the first time, a prospect of genuine and sustained multi-agency work in the crime reduction field, underpinned by the statutory duty of all local authorities and police forces, under the Crime and Disorder Act, to set up formal partnerships (including other key agencies) to analyse and respond to local crime problems. These partnerships were to be centrally involved in the CRP through the design of local interventions, bidding for funds, and project management and delivery.' (2004: 217)

The projects implemented and evaluated as part of the CRP included such diverse areas as burglary reduction programmes, offending behaviour programmes, and experiments involving police innovation. High hopes, however, were fairly quickly dashed. Why? Maguire lists four major problems.

- First, there were widespread implementation problems. Many practical projects simply failed to get off the ground in the way that had been anticipated or hoped.

- Second, co-operation between criminal justice agencies was sometimes problematic and this made it difficult to get multi-agency programmes up and running smoothly. Although the Crime and Disorder Act placed joint partnership working between local authorities, police and other bodies on a statutory footing, it often proved tricky to get organisations for which crime was not perceived as a primary responsibility, fully involved in new programmes.

- Third, the political climate changed. Ministers started to press for quicker results and their tolerance of the difficulties that emerged rapidly dwindled. Targets for the CRP quickly became unrealistic, fuelling dissatisfaction and disillusionment among practitioners.

- Finally, the positive relationship between government and academic criminological research quickly soured as it became clear that the research was not delivering positive messages to government and was unlikely to provide the basis for 'evidence-led' crime reduction that had initially been hoped for. In the event then, the plug was pulled relatively quickly and government backtracked away from the idea of evidence-led policy-making in relation to criminal and penal policy.

Reviewing the Crime and Disorder Act

A review of Crime and Disorder Reduction Partnerships (CDRPs, or Community Safety Partnerships) was undertaken in the aftermath of the publication of the *Building Communities, Beating Crime* White Paper (2004). The review, which concluded in 2006, uncovered a number of ongoing problems in relation to the capacity of CDRPs. Despite almost a decade of activity, partnerships were found still to be having problems with strategic direction, accountability, information-sharing and local forms of consultation with the community. The report (Home Office, 2006a) acknowledged that these ongoing difficulties were in part due to the almost continuous change that had been a feature of CDRPs since their inception –

what McLaughlin (2001) calls the 'permanent campaign'. In response, government proposed a variety of changes, the majority of which it incorporated into the Police and Justice Act 2006. These will begin to have an impact between late summer 2007 and spring 2008. The major changes include:

- Removal of the requirement to audit communities every three years.

- Community consultation and information-gathering will be conducted through both formal and informal feedback, and will be updated every six months using the National Intelligence Model (see Chapter 25).

- Local three-year community safety plans (rather than strategies) will be refreshed every year.

- Plans will be integrated with other local strategies and plans using Local Area Agreements.

- The section 17 duty on local authorities to consider the crime and disorder implications in all their decisions will be extended to include anti-social behaviour, substance misuse and behaviour which adversely affects the environment.

- The power to share information under s.115 of the Crime and Disorder Act will become a duty among the three statutory agencies (and probation).

- A set of national standards will be introduced and will include: leadership; intelligence-led decision-making; and community engagement and accountability.

- There will be a split between strategic and operational decision-making and guidance on what this will look like.

- Scrutiny committees within local authorities will have responsibility for 'overseeing' the work of CDRPs.

The thrust of these changes on the one hand is to highlight the shift that is also taking place in policing toward a greater focus on the collection of intelligence and the proactive organisation and planning of activities (see Chapter 25) and, on the other, involves an attempt to co-ordinate local activities using new National Frameworks and Local Strategic Agreements (to integrate policing and community safety plans). In addition to the continuing government preoccupation with crime reduction, the other addition is the increased emphasis being placed on disorder and anti-social behaviour.

Anti-social behaviour

The Crime and Disorder Act 1998 introduced a range of new court orders – the bulk of which are discussed in Chapter 29. One of the most intriguing of the new orders was the 'Anti-Social Behaviour Order' (ASBO). Prior to the publication of the Bill, this proposed new order was referred to as a 'community safety order' (Home Office, 1997a). Outlining its rationale for the new order, the Government said:

> Anti-social behaviour causes distress and misery to innocent, law-abiding people – and undermines the communities in which they live. Neighbourhood harassment by individuals or groups, often under the influence of alcohol or drugs, has often reached unacceptable levels, and revealed a serious gap in the ability of the authorities to tackle this social menace.

The solution proposed by the government was a court order which could be applied for by a local authority or the police, which would apply to named individuals aged over ten who had acted 'in an anti-social manner, that is to say, in a manner that caused or was likely to cause harassment, alarm or distress to one or more persons not of the same household as himself'. Originally designed as a response to the perceived problem of 'noisy neighbours' the order involved a combination of civil and criminal proceedings. The orders were granted in a magistrates' court, but required only the civil burden of proof. The definition of anti-social behaviour has a remarkably wide potential range which, according to one group of distinguished commentators, would be 'bad enough if the order were of a genuinely civil nature but doubly disturbing if, as we believe, the order is a criminal disposal in substance' (Gardner *et al.*, 1998: 26).

What was interesting about the order at the time of its introduction – particularly given its original title – is how uneasily it appeared to sit with the rest of the government's policies on community safety which were more preventative and less punitive in character. Running through the Crime and Disorder Act there is an amalgam of preventative, ameliorative and punitive elements. As Faulkner (1998: 8) described it: 'the new government's approach to the problems of crime and justice ... is based on prevention and support for people in difficulty, combined with the coercion of those who do not comply'. Thus, the Act introduces child curfews and

anti-social behaviour orders as well as removing the principle of *doli incapax* (see Chapter 29). Even the more preventative orders such as the parenting order and the drug treatment and testing orders were to be enforced by severe penal sanctions in cases where other conditions have not worked.

None of this is at all surprising. The mixture of prevention, populism and punishment characterised many of the new Home Secretary's speeches during the first New Labour administration. This is perhaps best illustrated by the speech Jack Straw gave at the launch of the London Borough of Lewisham Community Safety Strategy in September 1995. This was the speech in which he railed against the 'aggressive begging of winos and addicts' and the 'squeegee merchants who wait at large road junctions to force on reticent motorists their windscreen cleaning service ... Even where graffiti is not comprehensible or racialist in message' he went on, 'it is often violent and uncontrolled in its violent image, and correctly gives the impression of a lack of law and order on the streets' (Anderson and Mann, 1997). The speech not only reflected much progressive thinking about community safety and the need for local leadership and partnerships, but also elements of Wilson and Kelling's 'Broken Windows' thesis (Wilson and Kelling, 1982). Though there was some fairly quick backtracking from elements of the speech in the days that followed, the 'populist punitiveness' (Bottoms, 1995) that inspired it was clearly visible in elements of the Crime and Disorder Act and, arguably, has become ever more visible in government policy since that time.

Squeegee merchants – amongst the targets of the new Labour government in the 1990s as it sought to get 'tough on crime'.

Broken Windows

Originally published in 1982 in a magazine, *Atlantic Monthly*, the article by James Q. Wilson and George Kelling, entitled 'Broken Windows: the police and neighbourhood safety', has become one of the most widely-quoted and influential articles within contemporary criminology. 'Broken Windows' looks at the relationship between crime and disorder. Wilson and Kelling argue that local citizens are particularly concerned about public order and that, moreover, disorder and crime are linked. In explaining this they make reference to a famous experiment conducted by an American psychologist, Philip Zimbardo.

In this experiment Zimbardo arranged to have two cars without licence plates parked with their bonnets up, one on a street in the Bronx in New York, the other in Palo Alto, California. They reported that the car in the Bronx was attacked within ten minutes. First, the radio and battery were removed, subsequently almost everything else that could be removed was also taken. Then, they say, random destruction began, windows were smashed, parts torn off, and so on. By contrast, the vehicle in Palo Alto remained untouched for about a week. At that stage Zimbardo broke one of its windows with a sledgehammer. Almost immediately passers-by joined in. Within hours the car had been overturned and all but destroyed. How to explain this? According to Wilson and Kelling:

> Untended property becomes fair game for people out for fun or plunder and even for people who ordinarily would not dream of doing such things and who probably consider themselves law-abiding. Because of the nature of community life in the Bronx – its anonymity, the frequency with which cars are abandoned and things are stolen or broken, the past experience of 'no one caring' – vandalism begins much more quickly than it does in staid Palo Alto, where people have come to believe that private possessions are cared for, and that mischievous behaviour is costly. But vandalism can occur anywhere once communal barriers – the sense of mutual regard and the obligations of civility – are lowered by actions that seem to signal that 'no one cares'.

Wilson and Kelling used the broken windows of Zimbardo's cars as a metaphor for the ways in which what they refer to as 'untended' behaviour leads to the breakdown of community controls. Visible signs of disorder which go unchallenged are likely to breed further disorder and possibly lead to more serious offending. Their argument is that 'serious street crime flourishes in areas in which disorderly behaviour goes unchecked'. The policy implication is that it is important to do something about the 'broken windows' – whatever these may be (for critical assessments of this argument see Harcourt, 2001; Karmen, 2001). This argument, that cracking down on low-level disorderliness is an important strategy for the police service in the maintenance of order, had a particular impact in New York City in the 1990s. At that time Kelling, one of the authors of the article, was working as a consultant, initially with the New York Transit Police (responsible for the city's subways) and subsequently with the New York Police Department. In both cases a series of strategies was developed, building on elements of the broken windows thesis, aimed at increasing order and reducing crime – in the subways and on the streets.

Graffiti on a New York subway carriage, 1980. The successful 'Clean Car Program' provided a model for other initiatives in the US and elsewhere – and the impetus to 'zero tolerance policing'.

One of the problems on the subway was graffiti. Numerous city administrations had attempted to remove the graffiti, but none hitherto had any lasting success. In the 1980s a new programme was instituted. Called the 'Clean Car Program' it involved taking trains out of service if they had graffiti on them, and only returning them to service if they were clean. The primary motive for 'graffiti artists', they reasoned, was the desire to have their work seen. In a period of five years, graffiti was largely removed from the subway system (Kelling and Coles, 1996). The programme was followed by others focusing on homelessness, begging, fare-dodging, and drug dealing.

The successes of the strategies employed in the subway were later utilised and expanded in New York City itself. A series of programmes aimed at what became known as 'quality of life', or to some as 'zero-tolerance policing' (see Chapter 25) were used to crack down on a variety of what Wilson and Kelling would have thought of as 'broken windows'. One of these was what became known as 'squeegeemen' – people at road junctions and traffic lights who would 'clean' windscreens and then ask, or demand, money in return. In New York in the early 1990s they were perceived by many to be a real problem, working at all the major routes into the City and often becoming very threatening. The difficulty the Police Department felt it faced was that in the absence of actual physical threat to drivers no crime was being committed. The solution adopted was to prosecute everyone engaging in this activity for 'jaywalking'. The then mayor, Rudy Giuliani, describes what happened then (2002: 43):

> So we started writing summonses for these guys, and found that a certain percentage already had warrants for violent and property crimes. In under a month, we were able to reduce the problem dramatically. Things had visibly improved. New Yorkers loved it, and so did all the visitors, who brought money into the city and provided jobs for its inhabitants. That was our first success.

Tourists were not the only visitors. Innumerable British politicians also visited New York to see for themselves why the city's crime rate was apparently dropping so dramatically. Many – such as Jack Straw quoted earlier – returned to talk with great enthusiasm about 'zero-tolerance policing' and to promote similar tactics. Whilst, in practice few NYPD-style strategies were ever adopted by British police forces, the one area in which an American influence is visible is the impact that the 'broken windows'

theory had on the Labour government's anti-social behaviour strategy (for further detail see Jones and Newburn, 2007; Newburn and Jones, 2007).

The anti-social behaviour and respect agendas

Although ASBOs were made available by the Crime and Disorder Act from early 1999, they were slow to take off. There appeared to be some reluctance among local authorities to take advantage of the new power. Indeed, in many areas there was considerable disquiet about what was seen to be a potentially heavy-handed approach to particular problems. A Home Office report (Campbell, 2002) illustrated the existence of a number of factors inhibiting the take-up of ASBOs in local areas. The report noted that there had been a total of 484 ASBOs made in the first two years of their availability. Of these 84% had been made on males and 58% on under-18s. In terms of which agency made the application for the order, there was an almost even split between the police and local authorities. In terms of the forms of behaviour cited in the application, the three most common were verbal abuse (59%), harassment (55%) and threats (46%).

The research reported that a number of areas had become somewhat disillusioned by the process of applying for ASBOs and no longer thought that they would work. The most common reasons given for this were the length of time applications have taken, and dissatisfaction with the courts' treatment of ASBO applications, appeals and breaches, and possibly also poor communication between partner agencies, resulting in ineffective orders. This lack of effective partnership working was also picked up by the government's Social Exclusion Unit (2000) and, in response, the Home Office introduced a new anti-social behaviour action plan. Since that time, successive Home Secretaries have introduced measures to stiffen ASBOs and to increase their usage.

Central to this resolve have been the Police Reform Act 2002, the Anti-Social Behaviour Act 2003 (see also Chapter 29) and the Police and Justice Act 2006. The 2002 Act extended the means by which ASBOs could be obtained, and also enabled the Orders to be imposed in conjunction with a criminal sentence if evidence of past anti-social behaviour was presented in court. The 2003 Act made a number of changes, including increasing powers available locally to close crack houses, to take measures against social tenants and increasing the range of interventions available to authorities dealing with parents of children who are truanting or behaving 'anti-socially'. In addition, the Act increased police powers, in particular to disperse groups (where a 'group' could comprise as few as two people) in areas where there was a particular problem of anti-social behaviour and also to impose curfews on under-16s. The 2006 Act situated anti-social behaviour firmly within the remit of CDRPs and local authority decision-making.

At the same time, an Anti-Social Behaviour Unit was set up in the Home Office headed by the government's former 'homelessness tsar', Louise Casey. A controversial figure, Casey has developed a very high profile in recent years as the public face of the government's anti-social behaviour and 'Respect agenda' (Morgan, 2006).

The campaign subsequently has tended to emphasise enforcement over community support, with the consequence that there has been a substantial increase in the use of ASBOs in many local areas. A total of 7,356 ASBOs had been made between their introduction in 1999 and September 2005. For the first four years there were approximately 100 ASBOs per quarter. By the third quarter of 2005 this had risen to over 800 and the government has continued to press for further use of these powers. Thus, commenting on the release of the figures, Home Office Minister Hazel Blears said: 'I am extremely encouraged that they continue to be used. Over the past 12 months we have seen enthusiastic take-up of ASBOs, which sends out a clear message to those people who persist in this behaviour that action will be taken against them' (http://press.homeoffice.gov.uk/press-releases/clamp-down-anti-social-behaviour).

As yet, the impact of this is unknown. Are people who otherwise wouldn't have any significant contact with the criminal justice system being pulled into its orbit? Is the anti-social behaviour campaign resulting in greater numbers ending up in prison? According to Morgan (2006: 107–8) the 'limited data collected by the [Youth Justice Board] so far suggest that most juveniles received into custody where the primary offence is breach of an ASBO have committed many previous and relatively serious offences ... The most that can be said, therefore, is that the ASBO and ASBO-breach route is possibly being used by the police to fast-track young offenders into custody.' This is relatively straightforward as ASBOs tend to be made for several years, and tend to have multiple conditions (not doing certain things, in the main) and breach proceedings are, therefore, often easier to bring than are proceedings for a new criminal offence. What is clear is that the early years of the twenty-first century have seen a shift in the narratives and rhetoric in the 'crime reduction' arena which has highlighted the 'tough' elements of the government's agenda. Crime and disorder reduction partnerships have found themselves at the forefront of the new drive against anti-social behaviour. Some, like Greater Manchester, have appeared only too happy to embrace this agenda, whereas others continue to be more reticent. It seems unlikely that the government's agenda, especially its desire to increase the use of ASBOs and related measures such as Acceptable Behaviour Contracts (ABCs), on-the-spot fines and compensation payable by parents of children under ten who are involved in anti-social behaviour, will change markedly in the near future.

Review questions

1 What are the main differences between 'primary', 'secondary' and 'tertiary' crime prevention?

2 What did the shift in terminology from 'crime prevention' to 'community safety' signal?

3 What did the shift in terminology from 'community safety' to 'crime and disorder reduction' signal?

4 What is the basic argument in Wilson and Kelling's 'Broken Windows' article?

Crime prevention in practice

At the beginning of this chapter we looked at a number of ways of classifying crime prevention activities. Distinctions can be drawn, for example, between 'primary', 'secondary' and 'tertiary' crime prevention activities. For the purposes of the discussion here, however, we will focus on the simpler distinction between *situational* and *social crime prevention*. The former, broadly speaking, focuses on programmes which seek to affect crime opportunities, whereas the latter are more broadly focused on both the causes of certain types of criminal or deviant behaviour and the controls necessary for prevention.

Examples of 'target hardening' measures – an alley-gate restricting access to housing ('deflect offenders'), red traffic light camera ('strengthen formal surveillance'), roadside speed checker ('alert conscience').

Situational crime prevention

The approaches generally located under this heading are all underpinned by some form of 'opportunity theory' of crime. These theories, such as rational choice and routine activities, have been referred to by Garland (2001) as the 'new criminologies of everyday life'. In this volume they have generally been referred to as varieties of 'contemporary classicism' (see Chapter 14 for a full discussion). Opportunity theories stress the importance of immediate, contingent and what are often malleable factors in relation to crime. At heart, this is a set of practical approaches that argue that there are elements in the environment of crime that can be manipulated in order to reduce or otherwise change opportunities.

The best known approach to manipulating opportunities involves changing the physical environment in some way – often referred to as 'target hardening'. At its simplest this might simply mean making sure a car or a house is locked. The 'target' – the car or house – is, by its nature, obviously more difficult to break into if it is locked. As Table 24.1 illustrates, there are a great many other ways of affecting opportunities for crime:

Opportunity, Clarke (2005: 42) argues, is important in four main ways:

1 Criminally disposed individuals will commit a greater number of crimes if they encounter more criminal opportunities.

2 Regularly encountering such opportunities could lead these individuals to seek even more opportunities.

3 Individuals without pre-existing dispositions can be drawn into criminal behaviour by a proliferation of criminal opportunities and temptations.

4 More particularly, individuals who are generally law-abiding can be drawn into committing specific forms of crime if they regularly encounter easy opportunities for these crimes.

At the heart of much situational prevention is a particular methodology which utilises a form of action research which can also be found in other fields of activity such as problem-oriented policing. According to Clarke (1997), this methodology has five main stages:

1 Collection of data about the nature and dimensions of the specific crime problem.

2 Analysis of the situational conditions that permit or facilitate the commission of the crimes in question.

3 Systematic study of possible means of blocking opportunities for these particular crimes, including analysis of costs.

4 Implementation of the most promising, feasible and economic measures.

5 Monitoring of results and dissemination of experience.

A few practical examples will help illustrate the variety of situational approaches to crime prevention. Marcus Felson reports on a series of changes made to the physical environment and layout of the Port Authority Bus Terminal in New York City, described

Table 24.1	Twenty-five techniques of situational prevention			
Increase the effort	**Increase the risks**	**Reduce the rewards**	**Reduce provocations**	**Remove excuses**
1. *Target harden* • Steering column locks and immobilisers • Anti-robbery screens • Tamper-proof packaging	6. *Extend guardianship* • Go out in group at night • Leave signs of occupancy • Carry mobile phone	11. *Conceal targets* • Off-street parking • Gender neutral telephone directories • Unmarked armoured trucks	16. *Reduce frustrations and stress* • Efficient lines • Polite service • Expanding seating • Soothing music/ muted lighting	21. *Set rules* • Rental agreements • Harassment codes • Hotel registration
2. *Control access to facilities* • Entry phones • Electronic card access • Baggage screening	7. *Assist natural surveillance* • Improved street lighting • Defensible space design • Support whistle blowers	12. *Remove targets* • Removable car radio • Women's shelters • Pre-paid cards for pay phones	17. *Avoid disputes* • Separate seating for rival soccer fans • Reduce crowding in bars • Fixed cab fares	22. *Post instructions* • 'No parking' • 'Private property' • 'Extinguish camp fires'
3. *Screen exits* • Ticket needed for exit • Export documents • Electronic merchandise tags	8. *Reduce anonymity* • Taxi driver IDs • 'How's my driving?' deals • School uniforms	13. *Identify property* • Property marking • Vehicle licensing and parts marking • Cattle branding	18. *Reduce temptation and arousal* • Controls on violent pornography • Enforce good behaviour on soccer field • Prohibit racial slurs	23. *Alert conscience* • Roadside speed display boards • Signatures for customs declarations • 'Shoplifting is stealing'
4. *Deflect offenders* • Street closures • Separate bathrooms for women • Disperse pubs	9. *Use place managers* • CCTV for double-decker buses • Two clerks for convenience stores • Reward vigilance	14. *Disrupt markets* • Monitor pawn shops • Controls on classified ads • Licensed street vendors	19. *Neutralise peer pressure* • 'Idiots drink and drive' • 'It's OK to say No' • Disperse trouble-makers at school	24. *Assist compliance* • Easy library checkout • Public lavatories • Litter receptacles
5. *Control tools/ weapons* • 'Smart' guns • Disabling stolen mobile phones • Restrict spray paint sales to juveniles	10. *Strengthen formal surveillance* • Red-light cameras • Burglar alarms • Security guards	15. *Deny benefits* • Ink merchandise tags • Graffiti cleaning • Disabling stolen mobile phones	20. *Discourage imitation* • Rapid repair of vandalism • V-chips in TVs • Censor details of *modus operandi*	25. *Control drugs and alcohol* • Breathalysers in bars • Server intervention programmes • Alcohol-free events

Source: Clarke (2005).

as the busiest and biggest bus terminal in the world. A series of physical changes were made, including:

- Redesigning entrances and escalators to enable a better flow of people and moving crowds and passengers through more quickly.
- Removing niches and corners; closing off empty spaces; narrowed or connected columns so as to 'deny illicit activities a place to hide or linger'.
- Controlling emergency staircases and fire doors to deny places for sleeping, injecting drugs or other violations.
- Removing seats and benches, making long-term stay uncomfortable.
- Changed sanitation and lighting.

According to Felson (1998), the lavatories in the bus station were a particular problem, being 'sites for homosexual liaisons, thefts of luggage and wallets, and drug taking. Homeless people removed ceiling tiles and moved into the ceiling area' (1998: 161). The changes made to the lavatories are summarised in Table 24.2

Most of the changes were relatively minor and only the addition of attendants required any increase in long-term labour costs. Changes made a significant difference, however, increasing security and reducing crime. The smaller sinks stopped the previous practice in which homeless people used them for bathing in. The location of shops near the lavatories provided natural surveillance, and the other improvements made the environment look better and feel safer.

The second example concerns the theft from shopping bags in Birmingham city centre (Poyner and Webb, 1997). The thefts occurred mainly in what was known as the 'Bull Ring', where there was a large retail market of over 1,000 stalls. Occurring in a market area, the researchers hypothesised that offenders were following their targets – often older women – around the market until a moment when they were preoccupied, and then taking their purse from their shopping bag. Two elements of the crimes were identified as having crime prevention potential:

1 The offences occurred in a specific location and at specific times (the three busiest market days – Tuesday, Friday and Saturday – and between midday and 2pm on Tuesdays and 1–4pm on Fridays and Saturdays. This suggested that intensive policing at particular times might have a dramatic effect.

Table 24.2	Making washrooms that discourage crime, Port Authority Bus Terminal, New York City	
Washroom (Toilet) characteristics	**Before changes**	**After changes**
1. Ceiling panels	Removable	Secure
2. Stall doors	Tall, low to ground	Less so
3. Stall walls	Easy to write on	Resistant to writing
4. Ventilation	Poor	Good
5. Corner mirrors	Absent	Present
6. Sink size	Six users	One user each
7. Fixture controls	By hand	Automatic
8. Lighting	Poor	Good, secure
9. Tile	Small squares, dark	Big bright tiles
10. Walls	Angled	Straight
11. Nooks	Present	Absent
12. Stores	Far from entry	Near entry
13. Size	Small	Large
14. Attendants	Absent	Present

Source: Felson (1998).

2 Much of the crime occurred in two of the four markets, and these were the ones with the more densely packed stalls. This suggested that altering the layout of the stalls might affect the opportunity for such crime.

Both strategies were employed: one of the markets was being redesigned anyway and the stalls were placed three metres apart instead of two metres as previously. The police undertook a specific surveillance operation including a covert operation using plain-clothes officers. Data subsequently collected from police files suggested that there was a substantial reduction in this particular type of theft in the order of 40% in the first year and nearer 70% over a two-year period. Interestingly, the evaluators cast doubt on the role of policing in these reductions, suggesting that police action appeared to have redistributed much of the crime rather than preventing it. In part, it seems that during the period under consideration there was an overall decline in the amount of trade done in the markets and this may have accounted for some of the decline in theft. In practice, it appears that the design changes may well have had the greatest impact – with the new layout with wider aisles in one of the markets, and improved lighting in another, being especially important.

Finally, one of the most famous illustrations of the application of the preventative approach concerns a study of British gas suicide by Clarke and Mayhew (1988). At the heart of the story is a sudden and largely unexpected decline in the number of suicides in England and Wales between 1963 and 1975 from 5,714 to 3,693 (a decline of 35%). Changes between 1960 and 1980 are illustrated in Figure 24.1.

As Figure 24.1 illustrates, in the early 1960s almost half of all male suicides and slightly over half of all female suicides were committed using domestic gas. A gradual process of detoxification, replacing gas supplies which previously had high levels of carbon monoxide with natural gas that was not poisonous, culminated in 1997 by which time suicide by this method had all but been eliminated. The gradual decline of suicide using domestic gas supplies matches very closely the switch in the type of gas available in the home. One of the most interesting findings from the study of this transformation is that suicide overall declined, and it appears that the changing nature of domestic gas supply accounts for the vast majority of the decline. Intriguingly, therefore, it appears that people who might otherwise have attempted and succeeded in killing themselves no longer did so – that is to say, they didn't switch to another method.

Why is this of relevance to criminologists? Clarke and Mayhew suggest two main reasons. First, they argue that it illustrates the importance of promoting opportunity-reducing measures for crime – what we have been referring to here as

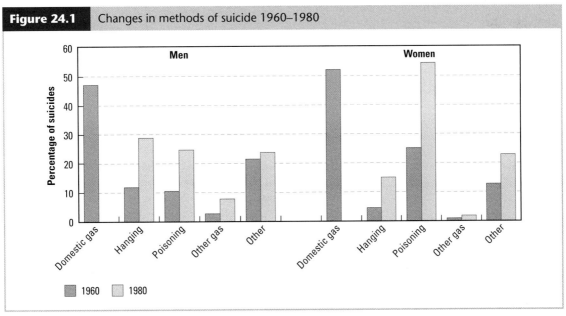

Figure 24.1   Changes in methods of suicide 1960–1980

Source: Clarke and Mayhew (1988).

'situational prevention'. Second, they suggest that it also illustrates the value of 'choice' or 'decision' models of crime. Crucially, it also contains lessons relating to 'displacement' – the fact that the declining ability to use one method of suicide was not replaced by another suggests, they argue, that it should be up to the critic of situational measures to prove that there has been displacement of crime, rather than being the responsibility of those involved in situational experiments to prove that there has not.

Displacement

One of the most frequently-voiced criticisms of situational crime prevention measures concerns *displacement*: the idea that the impact of such measures tends to be geographically limited and simply to mean that crimes that would have been committed are now more likely to be committed elsewhere. According to this line of criticism, situational measures don't *prevent* crime they merely *displace* it from one place to another. So serious is this criticism that Clarke (1997) has referred to it as the 'Achilles heel' of situational prevention. Thus, as Heal and Laycock (1986: 123) argued:

> There is little point in the policy-maker investing resources and effort into situational prevention if by doing so he merely shuffles crime from one area to the next but never reduces it. For this reason, the possibility of displacing crime by preventive intervention is a crucial issue for the policy-maker.

There are a number of different forms of possible displacement (Hakim and Rengert, 1981):

- *Temporal* – committing the intended crime at a different time.
- *Spatial* – committing the intended crime in a different place.
- *Target* – switching the crime focus from one target to another.
- *Tactical* – committing the intended crime using a different method.
- *Functional* – committing a different type of crime from the type initially intended.

There are numerous studies apparently providing examples of differing forms of displacement of criminal activity. Thus, the introduction of steering column locks for new cars in the UK displaced car

theft to older, less well-protected vehicles (Mayhew *et al.*, 1976), and early research on police 'crackdowns' on the New York subway suggested that robberies had been displaced to the street (Chaiken *et al.*, 1974). Similarly, a study by Allatt (1984) of crime prevention activities on a British housing estate found that there was a substantial decrease in burglary on the estate subject to target-hardening measures, but this was largely offset by substantial increases in property crimes on a neighbouring estate. However, Pease (1997) amongst others, cautions against the easy assumption that somehow displacement undermines the claims of situational prevention. First, identifying displacement, or its absence, is extremely difficult. Thus, according to Barr and Pease (1990: 293):

> If, in truth, displacement is complete, some displaced crime will probably fall outside the areas and types of crime being studied or be so dispersed as to be masked by background variation. In such an event, the optimist would speculate about why the unmeasured areas or types of crime probably escaped displaced crime, while the pessimist would speculate why they did not. No research study, however massive, is likely to resolve the issue. The wider the scope of the study in terms of types of crimes and places, the thinner the patina of displaced crime could be spread across them; thus disappearing into the realm of measurement error.

Second, all examples of 'displacement' are not necessarily evidence of failure. Thus, there may be occasions when, as a result of preventive efforts, there is some change in the criminal activities which makes them less harmful (moving the site of a drugs market or a red light area, for example). This, Pease (1997) calls crime *deflection* rather than crime displacement.

Whether or not displacement is likely depends on a number of factors. One of these is what Cornish and Clarke (1987) refer to as 'choice structuring properties' – in effect the differential nature of the choices faced by offenders under differing circumstances. A study by Mayhew *et al.* (1989) examined motor-cycle thefts in West Germany between 1980 and 1986. They found that, during this period, one of the consequences of the enforcement legislation making motor-cycle helmets compulsory was that theft of motorbikes reduced by 100,000. The reason was that offenders who were unable to steal a helmet at the same time they stole a bike were taking significantly increased risks in going ahead with the theft because they were much more likely to be stopped by the police. The researchers hypothesised that many such thefts were most likely undertaken in order to joyride or for some other temporary use, such as getting home late at night. If this was the case then it was likely that there would be some increase in the theft of cars and bicycles to offset the decline in theft of motor cycles. However, although there was an increase in bicycle thefts, this was both small and temporary (most likely because bicycles neither provide the thrill nor, necessarily, a real practical alternative to a motor cycle). The difference choices available affect the outcomes and these are 'choice structuring properties'.

A final reason for taking a more thoughtful approach toward the impact of preventive efforts is that just as it is possible that they may displace criminal activity from one place to another, it is also possible that they may have positive consequences in places that were not initially targeted. Thus, one of the positive outcomes of situational prevention – in some ways the reverse of displacement – is what has been referred to as the *diffusion of benefits*. Clarke (2005: 52) provides the following examples of this phenomenon:

- Security added to houses that had been repeatedly burgled in Kirkholt reduced burglaries for the whole of the estate, not just for those houses given additional protection (Pease, 1991).

- When street lighting was improved in a large housing estate in Dudley, crime declined in both that estate and a nearby one where the lighting was not changed (Painter and Farrington, 1997).

- When 'red light' cameras were installed at some traffic lights in Strathclyde not only did fewer people 'run the lights' at these locations, but also at other traffic lights nearby.

- CCTV cameras installed to monitor car parks at the University of Surrey reduced car crime as much in one car park not covered by the cameras as in the three that were covered (Poyner, 1991).

- As expected, electronic tagging of books in a University of Wisconsin library resulted in reduced book thefts. However, thefts also declined of videocassettes and other materials that had not been tagged (Scherdin 1986).

Finally, Clarke also discusses what have come to be called the 'anticipatory benefits' of situational prevention. These occur when offenders believe that crime prevention measures have been brought in before they are actually instituted. One review (Smith *et al.*, 2002) suggested that 40% of crime prevention studies showed some element of anticipatory benefit.

Social and community crime prevention

According to Crawford (1997: 104), social crime prevention 'embodies predispositional assumptions about what causes an individual to offend. It is concerned with preventing criminality or criminal propensities from developing within a person or group, rather than with preventing the opportunites for crime itself.' Community crime prevention 'refers to actions intended to change the social conditions that are believed to sustain crime in residential communities' (Hope, 1995: 21). We begin by looking at what is sometimes referred to as 'criminality prevention' – interventions generally aimed at reducing or preventing crime by young people – and then move on to consider broader community-based prevention strategies.

Criminality prevention

Much recent activity in relation to youth crime has focused on increasing opportunities for intervention in the lives of young offenders, and also with those deemed to be 'at risk' of offending (see Chapters 16 and 33). The rise of criminality prevention represents something of a shift in thinking in relation to youthful offending which can be seen most particularly in the declining influence of the idea of *diversion* from the criminal justice system (Newburn and Souhami, 2005). Whereas the 1980s were dominated by a professional ethic which emphasised the potentially criminogenic consequences of contact with the formal criminal justice system, the 1990s and the years since have seen a significant move toward seeing failure to intervene as a problem. The shift is part of the rise of the 'what works' paradigm (see also Chapter 27) and brings with it a much greater emphasis on measurement of outcomes.

Risk-focused prevention

Much work in this area in currently couched in the language of 'risk'; often also referred to as 'developmental crime prevention' (Homel, 2005). In particular, longitudinal research has been used to identify those factors – demographic and social – that appear to be linked with a heightened likelihood of involvement in offending. These are generally referred to as 'risk factors'. Some of the main risk factors that have been found to be related to youthful offending include:

- low income and poor housing;
- living in dilapidated inner city areas;
- a high degree of impulsiveness and hyperactivity;
- low intelligence and low school attainment;
- poor parental supervision and harsh and erratic discipline;
- parental conflict and broken families.

The basis of this approach involves seeking to identify the most important risk factors in relation to particular offenders or groups of offenders and then implement measures that are best designed to counteract them. The idea draws somewhat on preventive health models which seek to encourage healthy eating and lifestyles. Although the approach seems superficially straightforward, in practice it is extremely complex and brings with it a number of problems:

- The risk factors are often very similar for very different types of conduct. Thus, for example, there is considerable overlap in the risk factors for such behaviours as violent offending, mental health problems and educational failure (Farrington and Welsh, 2007).
- Identifying something as a risk factor is not the same as identifying a 'cause'. Consequently, altering a risk factor will not necessarily have an appreciable impact on the behaviour being targeted.
- The power of risk factors lies in their combination. That is to say, it is the presence of multiple risk factors that offers the best predictive value in relation to offending. Again, affecting one or two of these will not necessarily have an impact on the offending.

Homel's (2005: 97–8) conclusion in relation to the risk-factor paradigm, whilst far from perfect (and certainly not as all-convincing as some of its most vocal proponents would suggest) is that it:

… has at least provided a bridge between longitudinal and prevention research that has helped move prevention policies from the realm of good ideas to evidence-based practice. Reference to risk factors should help to ensure that interventions deal effectively with some of the baggage that people carry and the barriers they face, so increasing the odds that some developmental pathways will take a more positive direction.

The Perry Pre-School Project

One of the best-known prevention programmes is a pre-school intellectual enrichment project carried out in Ypsilanti, Michigan in the USA. It was very similar to a Head Start programme, and was focused on disadvantaged African-American children. The programme began with a relatively small number of children who were divided into a group for whom a variety of interventions would be provided and a control group. Those in the experimental group attended a pre-school programme and their family also received weekly home visits. This lasted for approximately two years whilst the children were aged three to four.

An initial evaluation examined the outcomes for the children in both the experimental and control groups over the long-term – until the children were in their mid- to late-twenties. Some of the results are dramatic. By age 27, the experimental group had only half as many arrests as the controls (averaging 2.3 compared with 4.6). They were also more likely to have graduated from High School, to have significantly higher earnings, and more likely to be homeowners. A higher proportion of the women in the experimental group were married and fewer had children born outside marriage. One of the most publicised findings from the evaluation came from a cost-benefit analysis which suggested that for every dollar spent on the programme at least seven dollars were saved in the longer run (Barnett 1996).

A later follow-up, undertaken when the children had reached 40, found that the experimental group had fewer lifetime arrests for violent crimes (32% *vs.* 48%), property crimes (36% *vs.* 58%) and drugs offences (14% *vs.* 34%). They were also more successful educationally (77% had graduated from High School compared with 60% of controls) and had better work records (76% were in work compared with 62% of controls). The later cost-benefit analysis suggested that for every dollar spent approximately $17 were saved. The researchers estimated that of this saving about one-quarter went to the programme participant and three-quarters back to the taxpayer (Farrington and Welsh, 2007).

Cognitive-behavioural interventions with young people

The rise of the 'what works' movement has meant considerable investment in programmes influenced by cognitive behaviourism. In the UK, cognitive skills programmes were introduced in the early 1990s (Porporino and Fabiano, 2000) with the aim of affecting the ability of offenders to engage in appropriate thinking (about the likely consequences of their actions) in order to avoid those strategies that lead toward offending and enhance those that direct them elsewhere. Although most work in this area has been undertaken with adult offenders, there is some evidence that suggests that such programmes may be more effective with young offenders than interventions that do not include a cognitive-behavioural element (Lipsey, 1992). Existing UK evidence is only available for prison-based programmes, though such evidence may provide some insight for future community-based interventions.

A Home Office study (Cann *et al.*, 2003) in the UK examined the impact on a sample of 1,534 young offenders (aged 21 or less) who had participated in one of two cognitive-behavioural programmes between 1998 and 2000: the Enhanced Thinking Skills and the Reasoning and Rehabilitation Programmes. Matched against a comparison group, the young offenders on the programmes were subject to both one year and two year reconviction studies. The study found a statistically significant difference in reconviction between those who had completed the programme and the comparison group. However, there were relatively high non-completion rates in the programmes and when all 'starters' were included in the analysis, no significant differences in outcome were found. Moreover, the positive results found for programme completers after one year were not maintained after two. This led the researchers to conclude that such programmes can have an impact – so long as young offenders can be persuaded to complete the course – and that post-release 'booster programmes' might also be beneficial.

A similarly inconclusive picture is painted by cognitive programmes run by the Youth Justice Board. Costing £3.9 million, 23 projects focused on moral reasoning, problem-solving and self-management, with the aim of 'encouraging offenders to understand the impact of their offending and to equip them with the skills and knowledge they need to go on to lead law-abiding lives'. The projects were very varied in their focus and completion rates varied from 47% to 86% and were particularly low for the persistent offender projects (where the greatest impact might have been expected). The overall reconviction rate was a little over 60%, though it was nearer 80% for those persistent offenders for whom information was available. As with some other elements of the 'what works' field there is still some distance to go before we gain any clear picture of effective interventions.

Community approaches to prevention

In a review of community crime prevention, Hope (1995) notes the apparent paradox that much criminological research seems to show that the nature of local communities has an important influence on crime, yet much of the effort that has gone into attempting to change the nature of local communities in order to reduce crime has had relatively little impact. One potential explanation for this is *implementation failure*: the fact that practical initiatives are often not implemented in such a way as to allow for a proper evaluation of a crime prevention theory. This is related to the complexity of many of the programmes that are attempted for, even though many may be ostensibly simple in design, they are usually extremely difficult to undertake in practice. They involve partnerships between agencies that may not be used to working with each other, may have very different goals, and they operate in environments where things change on an almost daily basis and where funding is insecure (see Hope and Foster, 1992).

Operation ceasefire

This was another name for the Boston Gun Project, a problem-oriented policing initiative which focused on homicide victimization among young people in Boston, USA. Implementation began in early 1996. It had two main elements:

1 A direct law enforcement initiative against firearms trafficking.

2 An attempt to generate a strong deterrent to gang violence.

The firearms trafficking strategy included focusing attention on traffickers of guns used by the city's most violent gangs and restoring the serial numbers of confiscated guns and then tracking those guns. The second strategic element, known as the 'pulling levers' strategy sought to deter violent behaviour (especially gun violence) by:

● Targeting gangs engaged in violent behaviour.

● Reaching out directly to members of the targeted gangs.

● Delivering an explicit message that violence would not be tolerated.

● Backing up that message by 'pulling every lever' legally available when violence occurred. (Kennedy *et al.*, 2001)

In addition to these measures, what were referred to as the 'Streetworkers' (a coalition of Boston social workers), probation and parole officers, and, later, churches and other community groups offered a variety of services to gang members. At the heart of the programme was a strong message to gang members – made directly to formal and informal meetings with gangs, via meetings with inmates in secure juvenile facilities, and through gang outreach workers – that 'violent behaviour (especially gun violence) would evoke an immediate and intense response' (Kennedy *et al.*, 2001).

The researchers evaluating the programme suggest that operation was associated with a decrease of:

● 63% in youth homicides per month.

● 32% in shots-fired calls for service per month.

● 25% in gun assaults per month.

● 44% decrease in the number of youth gun assaults per month in the highest risk district.

Why did the homicide rate drop, and do so markedly? The researchers' conclusion is interesting as it distinguishes this particular programme from much else that occurs in this field:

> Neither Operation Ceasefire nor the Wendover Street operation before it are enforcement operations in the usual sense of the term: they are not aimed at taking offenders off the streets, eliminating gangs, zero tolerance, or raising the probability that violent offences will be met with stiff prison terms. Nor, however, are they composed of classic prevention elements. Fundamentally, they are not about the provision of facilitative services and they do not provide much in the way of additional resources, rely on changing offenders' character, or aim to change root cause elements of the environment. In essence, the Boston Gun Project was an exercise in deterrence and getting deterrence right. (Kennedy *et al.*, 2001: 48)

What the authors appear to mean by 'getting deterrence right' is using the authority of the police and other agencies to provide both guidance and support to gang members in the context of a much more certain knowledge that offences, if committed,

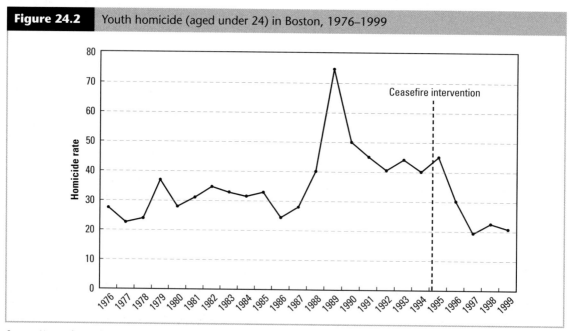

Figure 24.2   Youth homicide (aged under 24) in Boston, 1976–1999

Source: Kennedy *et al.* (2001).

would be dealt with severely. In many ways, there-fore, as a prevention project its character is rather different from many others discussed here.

Mentoring

Mentoring as a formalised response to a variety of social problems – ranging from offending to social exclusion and social welfare issues – has its origins in the USA. In the main, though programmes vary considerably, mentoring refers to an act of guardianship and guidance in which a relationship is established 'between two strangers, instigated by a third party, who intentionally matches the men-tor and mentee according to the needs of the younger person as part of a planned intervention programme' (Freedman, 1993).

Although Sherman *et al.* (1999) note that men-toring provides the highest 'dosage' of adult–child interaction of all formal community-based pro-grammes, the results from extant research are far from unequivocally positive. As in other areas the greatest problem is the paucity of rigorous research. Though they were undoubtedly right in that assess-ment, the application of the particular scale they used to assess research continues to be the subject of considerable controversy (see, for example, Hope, 2005; Pawson, 2006 and discussion in Chapter 35). Sherman *et al.* assessed seven evalua-tions of mentoring programmes (see Table 24.3).

The most positive results were drawn from a con-trolled experiment evaluating the Big Brothers/Big Sisters Programme in eight cities (Tierney and Grossman, 1995). The study, described as 'tightly randomized', found that although it was unclear as to whether BBBS reduces criminality in later life, it was positively associated with substantial benefits for young people after one year:

> After spending around 12 hours monthly with their volunteer adult mentors, the treatment group children had 45% less reported onset of drug abuse than the control group children, who had been put on the waiting list. They also had 27% less onset of alcohol use, and 32% less frequency of hitting someone. The program also reduced truancy: treatment group children skipped 52% fewer days of school and 37% fewer classes on days they were in school. (http://www.ncjrs.org/works/chapter3.htm)

Moreover, the programme appeared to be highly cost-effective. The fact that it used volunteer men-tors kept the costs down (though some cost-benefit calculations would include an opportunity cost for volunteers' time), the major financial burden being the process of matching mentors and young peo-ple. Though the potential long-term savings have not been calculated, according to Sherman and colleagues even the short-term benefits might jus-tify government support for the programme. Crucially, however, four of the seven projects reviewed by Sherman failed to show any evidence of success and of those that did show 'promise', most were successful at curbing the propensity for drug use, and not delinquency or offending, in the 10–14 age group only. Moreover, success was linked to the level of 'dosage' that the young per-son received from their mentor. Thus, even in the United States, where there has been greater invest-ment in experimental and quasi-experimental social science research in the last two to three decades, the research evidence on the potential of mentoring remains remarkably slim.

The UK lags even further behind and the avail-able empirical evidence is largely restricted to two main programmes: the Dalston Youth Project (DYP) and Mentoring Plus. Working with young disaffected youths from one of the most deprived boroughs in England and Wales, DYP has run pro-grammes for 11–14 year-olds and 15–18 year-olds. Both sets of programmes have been the subject of small-scale evaluative research. Research on the older age group suggests some possible impact on self-reported offending and truancy – though not drug use – but, unfortunately, the numbers involved in the study are far too small to allow for the results to be treated with anything other than considerable caution.

A recent study of Mentoring Plus produced mixed results in relation to offending. Fairly size-able reductions in offending were measured both during the course of the one-year mentoring pro-grammes and they were maintained during the six-month follow-up period (Newburn and Shiner, 2005). However, substantial and in some cases more marked reductions in offending were reported by non-participants in the programme, with the consequence that the changes apparent among those young people involved in mentoring could not with any confidence be attributed to the pro-gramme. The research also found little evidence of impact on participants' use of illicit drugs. At the start of the programme drug use was more wide-spread among participants than non-participants and these differences continued to be evident dur-ing the period covered by the programme as overall levels of use remained very stable among both par-ticipants and non-participants.

Table 24.3	Selected community-based mentoring evaluations (US)		
Primary source (secondary)	**Scientific methods Score**	**Program content**	**Program effects**
McCord 1978, 1992 Powers and Witmer 1972	5	2 visits monthly by paid male counsellors for 5.5 years with 253 at-risk boys under 12 in 1937–42; WW2 end	No effect on criminal record; treatment group did worse on diagnosed mental health
Tierney et al., 1995	5	Big Brothers and Sisters, 1 year for 10–14 yr-olds, 60% minority and 27% abused; 3 hrs wkly	46% reduction in drug use onset, 32% reduction in hitting people, relative to controls
Green 1980 (Howell 1995)	4	Big Brothers for fatherless white boys 1/2 day weekly for 6 months	No effects on disruptive class behaviour; no measures of drug use
Goodman 1972 (Howell 1995)	2	College student mentors of 10–11 yr-old boys 6 hrs wkly over 2 years	High control group attrition; program effects on crime unknown
Dicken, Bryson and Kass 1977 (Howell 1995)	3	College student mentors for 6–13 yr-olds, 6 hrs wkly, 4 months	No difference in teacher-rated behaviour of mentees
Fo and O'Donnell 1974 (Howell 1995)	5	12 weeks of paid community mentors with at-risk 11–17 yr-olds; N = 26	Truancy reduced significantly under some conditions
Fo and O'Donnell 1975 (Howell 1995)	5	1 year of paid community mentors meeting weekly with at-risk 10–17 yr-olds	Lower recidivism for treatment groups with priors, higher without

Key (scientific methods score)
5-point scale:
1 = No reliance or confidence should be placed on the results of this evaluation because of the number and type of serious shortcomings(s) in the methodology employed
3 = Methodology rigorous in some respects, weak in others
5 = Methodology rigorous in almost all respects

Source: Sherman *et al.* (1999).

The mixed, indeed arguably largely disappointing, results from studies of mentoring are not untypical of evaluation outcomes from risk-oriented interventions more generally. This may reflect a number of things. Straightforwardly, it may indicate that the interventions being evaluated are simply not working very well. Alternatively, it may reflect the quality or nature of the research being undertaken. It is undoubtedly the case that there has been under-investment in the type of experimental research, or quasi-experimental research that is, arguably, best suited to understanding outcomes of this sort. It may also reflect the difficulty of undertaking this type of work in a political and funding environment that is unpredictable and often unstable.

Analysis for crime prevention

As we have seen, much crime prevention activity involves a methodology that begins with the analysis of a particular crime problem. In order to understand how best to intervene to prevent or reduce crime, it is necessary to understand the problem and, more particularly, to look for patterns in offending, such as patterns in the location of crime, in the timing of particular activities, in the nature of the victims or offenders, and so on. Analytical approaches reflect elements of the criminological theories that underpin them. Cope (2003) provides a useful summary guide to the links between theory and crime analysis (see Table 24.4).

Hot spots

One thing that is now well established is that crime is not evenly distributed geographically. Some communities experience significantly higher levels of crime than others. Moreover, taking even small areas of our society, it is clear that there are clusters of crime in particular locations. Nowadays these are generally referred to as 'hot spots'. Even within the highest crime neighbourhoods there will be areas, often quite large areas, where there is relatively little crime and other spaces where there is a very particular concentration of crime. It is relatively easy to understand why this might be important to those who seek to reduce crime – not least the police: if it is possible to identify and tackle crime in the very worst locations, then the potential impact on overall crime levels could be dramatic.

Tactics in 'hot spots policing' vary from traditional enforcement methods – such as extra patrols, surveillance, use of stop and search – through to crackdowns and the use of a variety of situational methods. A review of five major experimental attempts at evaluating hot spots policing (Weisburd and Braga, 2006) found positive results in four cases. In one case, a problem-oriented policing experiment in Jersey City, the strategy resulted in reductions in overall crime and in calls for service (emergency calls to the police), as well as reductions in all major crime types. Although the research tends to support the principle that targeted policing in hot spot areas yields positive results, it was not clear which policing tactics were the most beneficial.

Repeat victimization

In Chapter 3 we came across the distinction between crime *incidence* and *prevalence*. Incidence refers to the average number of cases of victimization per head of population whereas prevalence refers to the proportion of the population who are victims within a given time period. There is a third measure called *concentration* which refers to the average number of victimizations per victim. The notion of 'repeat victimization' builds on this idea of concentration and examines the way in which the distribution of crime victimization is skewed, i.e. not evenly distributed. This differential impact can be illustrated in the following way (see Figure 24.3).

| **Figure 24.3** | Distribution of victimization for all offences, BCS 1992 |

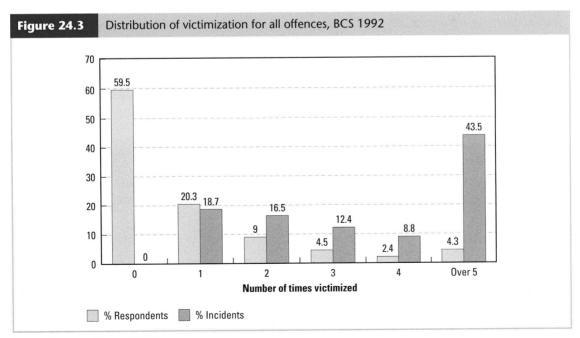

Source: Farrell and Pease (1993)

Table 24.4	A summary integrating theory into volume crime analysis	
Theory	**Definition**	**Analysis**
Routine activities theory	Opportunities for crime are associated with the routine activities of everyday life. Three conditions are needed for crime to occur: a likely offender, a suitable target and the absence of a capable guardian. The acronym VIVA (Value, Inertia, Visibility, Access) is used to assess the suitability of targets.	Focuses on the offender, offence and situation of crime. Provides an insight into opportunities for crime and how they might relate to offenders' lifestyles and daily activities. This may further explain crime patterns, increase the understanding of hot spots (where the three factors regularly coincide) and enable the identification of potential 'hot products' that are desirable to steal.
Rational choice theory	Offenders seek advantages through crime and make decisions about offending that are rational within the constraints of time and ability.	Focuses on the offender and offence. Supports the analysis of approaches to crime and *modus operandi*. Interpreting decision-making processes from crime patterns and targets in detailed profiles of offenders may offer an insight into potential crimes that have been committed by the same person, or enable predictive crime patterns to be hypothesised.
Crime pattern approaches	A general term applied to the study of interaction between the offender and his or her environment.	Focuses on spatial and situational aspects of crime. Facilitates the interpretation of crime patterns by exploring the relationship between opportunity for crimes and offenders' awareness spaces. Also supports criminal investigations.
Repeat victimization	When the same location, person, business, organisation, household or vehicle experiences more than one crime within a specified time frame.	Offers an insight into patterns of victimization. Understanding the temporal and spatial distribution of repeat victimization may provide the means to 'predict' patterns of victimization.
Situational crime prevention	A process that aims to reduce crime by intervening in the proximal causes of offences.	Focuses on the situation of crime. A useful analytical recommendation that follows from understanding the opportunities and circum-stances of offences.
Displacement	The process by which offenders seek alternative methods of offending when opportunities to commit crime are blocked. Displacement can be temporal, spatial, involve different tactics or be directed towards different targets.	Helpful for evaluation (results analysis). Important to consider the intended and 'unintended', positive and negative consequences of police interventions.

Source: Cope (2003).

Figure 24.3 shows how criminal victimization is distributed as measured by the British Crime Survey. Dividing respondents into groups according to the number of cases of victimization they report, the chart then shows the proportion of respondents falling into each group and the proportion of incidents of victimization that they account for. Thus, from left to right one can see that almost 60% of respondents had not experienced any victimization in the past 12 months. Approximately 20% of respondents reported one incident and these respondents accounted for a little under 20% of reported incidents. At the right hand side of the chart however are those 4% of respondents who reported five or more experiences of victimization in the past year. They account for over 40% of all incidents of criminal victimization.

One key criminological research finding, therefore, is that criminal victimization is a very good predictor of criminal victimization. If you have been a victim of crime you are quite likely to be so again. Moreover, research in the area suggests that the time of greatest risk is immediately after victimization. Such findings have been shown to apply to crimes as varied as residential burglary and domestic violence. This had led researchers to argue for two significant policy implications:

1 Crime prevention measures need to be in place soon after victimization.

2 Temporary prevention measures which provide cover during the high risk period after victimization might be an effective means of preventing crime. (Farrell and Pease, 1993)

Before we move on, however, it is important to note that it is not just individual citizens who can be the focus of attention in understanding repeat victimization. In one sense, 'hot spots' are a form of repeat victimization – on this occasion it is the place, rather than the person that is victimized repeatedly. Farrell's (2005: 147) typology of repeat victimization is shown in Table 24.5.

Kirkholt Burglary Prevention Project

One of the best-known practical applications using the idea of repeat victimization is what has become known as the Kirkholt Burglary Prevention Project (Forrester *et al.*, 1988; Forrester *et al.*, 1990). Kirkholt is a local authority estate two miles south of Rochdale town centre. It had a particularly high level of domestic burglary – double the rate for 'high risk' areas as measured by the BCS – even though by housing type it is not an obviously high-risk area.

Table 24.5	A typology of repeat victimization	
Repeat type	**Characteristics**	**Example(s)**
Target	Crime against the same target.	Crime against the same person, building, household, vehicle or other target, however defined.
Tactical (virtual)	Crimes requiring the same skill, or *modus operandi*, to commit. Often the same type of target.	Particular type of locks picked (on different types of property); websites with particular types of security are repeatedly targeted; theft of same model of car; burglary of property with same layout.
Temporal	An offending spree – temporal proximity is the defining characteristic.	Multiple burglaries of different properties in the same night; theft of car, then robbery and getaway.
Spatial (near)	Crime in nearby location due to proximity and characteristics.	High crime areas; hotspots.
Crime type	The same target victimized by different types of crime.	The same person is burgled, assaulted, robbed at different times.
Offender	Victimization of same target by different offenders.	A property appears attractive to different offenders; an easy or rewarding target.

The Kirkholt estate, Rochdale. Replacing coin-fed meters by token meters had an immediate impact in reducing burglary during the Kirkholt Burglary Prevention Project – would you expect this to be displaced elsewhere?

A burglary prevention initiative was established and a decision was taken to focus efforts on the problem of repeat victimization. The burglary profile of the estate had a number of important features, notably the taking of money from electricity and gas pre-payment meters. One objective was, therefore, to replace such meters by token meters or other forms of payment. In addition, much of the entering of homes occurred in the first place the burglar attempted to enter, suggesting that many homes were far from secure. Again, the response was to upgrade security. Finally, a system of 'cocoon neighbourhood watch' was established, whereby groups of approximately six houses or flats contiguous with a place that had been burgled, took on responsibility for informal surveillance. In this, the first phase of the project, burglary fell by 40% within five months of the start. Repeat victimizations fell to zero over the same period and never exceeded two thereafter. The trends in nearby areas were quite different, though the evaluators argued that there was no evidence that crime was displaced from Kirkholt to the others.

In its second phase, the project added a probation focus to its strategy. Many of the elements of the first phase continued – with security advice, victim support, target-hardening and a home watch scheme – but added into the mix was a greater social crime prevention element involving offenders in group work and other activities. Put crudely, where the first phase had focused on the target areas, the second phase expanded to include offenders also. An analysis of social inquiry reports (reports on offenders produced by the probation service for the courts) found that 70% of those convicted of burglary had 'addictive problems', and two-thirds, found guilty of handling offences, appeared to be having difficulty in relation to employment (Forrester *et al.*, 1990). As a consequence, resources were directed toward dealing with drug and alcohol abuse, unemployment and also debt, which had been identified as a problem among many of those convicted. Burglary continued to decline and by 1989/90 was one-quarter the level it had been in 1986/87. Separating out which elements of the project had the most significant effect is all but impossible. However, one thing about which the evaluators were confident was the importance of the focus upon repeat victimization:

> To acknowledge that the best predictor of the next victimization is the last victimization is to acknowledge that victim support and crime prevention are two sides of the same coin. Since repeat victimization is most pronounced in those areas which suffer most from crime, a prevention strategy based on the prevention of repeat victimization has most to offer to those areas which suffer most. Since those areas which suffer most crime suffer disproportionately

serious crime, the same strategy is potentially even more powerful in alleviating suffering from crime. Thus, the prevention of repeat victimization will, almost automatically, direct crime prevention activity to places and people in most need of it. (Forrester *et al.*, 1990: 45)

On this basis, Pease and others have argued that repeat victimization could form the basis of a broad crime prevention strategy. Doing so, they argue, has a number of advantages:

- Attention to dwellings or people already victimized has a higher 'hit rate' of those likely to be victimized in the future.

- Preventing repeat victimization protects the most vulnerable social groups, without having to identify those groups as such, which can be socially divisive. Having been victimized already probably represents the least contentious basis for a claim to be given crime prevention attention.

- Repeat victimization is highest, both absolutely and proportionately, in the most crime-ridden areas, which are also the areas that suffer the most serious crime. The prevention of repeat victimization is thus commensurately more important the greater the area's crime problem.

- The rate of victimization offers a realistic schedule for crime prevention activity. Preventing repeat victimization is a way of 'drip-feeding' crime prevention.

- Even from the unrealistic view that crime is only displaced, avoiding repeat victimization at least shares the agony around. (in Farrell, 1995: 495)

Review questions

1 What different types of crime displacement are there?

2 What is meant by 'hot spots' and 'repeat victimization'?

3 What are the major types of 'repeat victimization'?

4 What are the shortcomings of situational and community crime prevention?

Questions for further discussion

1 What does the shift from crime prevention to crime and disorder reduction tell us about the politics of crime control?

2 When we use terms like community safety, what do we mean by 'community'?

3 What are the main crime prevention measures used in the place where you are a student?

4 What are the main dangers and benefits of an increasing focus on anti-social behaviour?

5 Is repeat victimization a viable basis for a broad crime prevention strategy?

Further reading

A very helpful overview of a great many of the issues, ideas and debates in this area can be found in:

Tilley, N. (ed.) (2006) *Handbook of Crime Prevention and Community Safety*, Cullompton: Willan

In addition, wherever possible students should read Clarke and Mayhew's classic (1988) essay: 'The British Gas Suicide Story and its Criminological Implications, in Morris, N. and Tonry, M. (eds) *Crime and Justice*, vol. 10, Chicago: University of Chicago Press, pp. 79–116.

There is a very good collection of critical essays on the government's Crime Reduction Programme in

Criminology and Criminal Justice, vol. 4. no. 3, 2004, London: Sage

The politics of community safety and crime reduction are captured in rather different ways in:

Crawford, Λ. (1998) *Crime Prevention and Community Safety*, Harlow: Longman

Gilling, D. (2007) *Crime Reduction and Community Safety: Labour and the politics of crime control*, Cullompton: Willan

Hughes, G. (2007) *The Politics of Crime and Community*, Basingstoke: Palgrave

Hughes, G. *et al.* (eds) (2002) *Crime Prevention and Community Safety*, London: Sage

An interesting, though variable, collection of essays on developmental prevention is contained in: France, A. and Homel, R. (eds) (2007) *Pathways and Crime Prevention: Theory, policy and practice*, Cullompton: Willan

There are a number of interesting and recently published books on anti-social behaviour including:

Burney, E. (2005) *Making People Behave: Anti-social behaviour, politics and policy*, Cullompton: Willan

Simester, A. and von Hirsch, A. (eds) (2006) *Incivilities: Regulating offensive behaviour*, Oxford: Hart

A great many practical examples of crime prevention can be found in a series entitled *Crime Prevention Studies*, published by Criminal Justice Press, Monsey: New York and Willan in the UK (the series now runs to over 20 volumes, some of which can be found online).

Websites

There are a number of useful websites providing crime prevention advice and information. Two of the best are the crime reduction website and the problem-oriented policing website. The latter in particular contains a very good library of downloadable material.
http://www.crimereduction.gov.uk/cpindex.htm
http://www.popcenter.org/

The American National Crime Prevention Council maintains a website with some useful material:
http://www.ncpc.org/
The 'what works' review conducted by Sherman and colleagues is available online at:
http://www.ncjrs.gov/works/

Chapter outline

The organisation of policing   598

Understanding policing   602
  What do the police do?   602
  Criminal investigation   603
  National Intelligence Model (NIM)   604
  Investigation and forensics   605

Police powers   606
  Stop and search   607
  Arrest   607
  Detention at the police station   608
  Right to silence   610

Models of policing   611
  Community policing   612
  Problem-oriented policing   612
  Intelligence-led policing   612

A brief history of policing   613
  Emergence of the 'new police'   613
  The Royal Commission on the Police   614
  Problems of legitimacy   615
  Centralisation   616

Key themes in policing   617
  Police culture   617
  Zero-tolerance policing   619
  Police corruption   622
    The causes of police corruption   623
  Police governance   626
  Plural policing   629
  A revolution in policing?   632

Questions for further discussion   634
Further reading   634
Websites   634

25

Policing

The police are one of the most visible and recognisable institutions in modern society. They are a staple in television and cinema and most citizens will have had some contact with the police at some stage – if only to ask directions. The police are also a source of debate and controversy. Most people will have a view about what the police should and should not do. In the past 20 years or so, the study of the police and policing has been arguably one of the biggest growth areas in British criminology and, perhaps, criminology in general. In this chapter we consider:

● the organisation of policing in Britain;

● what it is that the police do;

● the recent history of policing;

● some of the key issues in the study of policing: corruption, police culture, governance and accountability;

● the rise of 'plural policing'.

The organisation of policing

There are currently 43 police forces in England and Wales. These comprise the 41 provincial forces and the Metropolitan and City of London Police. There are eight regional police forces in Scotland and a single force in Northern Ireland – the Police Service of Northern Ireland (PSNI), previously (prior to 2001) the Royal Ulster Constabulary (RUC). These are the main 'public' constabularies, or 'Home Office forces' in the UK. However, there are a num-ber of other 'public' forces with more limited remits (either functional or geographical) including the British Transport Police, the UK Atomic Energy Authority Police, and the Ministry of Defence Police. The 43 main police forces vary significantly in size. The largest, by far, is the Metropolitan Police with almost 31,000 officers and a further 14,000 civilian staff. The smaller forces, by contrast, such as Bedfordshire, Cumbria and Suffolk have few more than 1,000 officers each. In recent times overall police officer numbers have increased markedly (see Table 25.1).

Table 25.1	Total police officer strength in England and Wales, March 1994 – March 2006										
	ACPO ranks	(Chief) Superint-endents	Chief Inspectors	Inspectors	Sergeants	Constables	Total police strength	Specials	Police civilian staff	PCSOs	Traffic wardens
1994	204	1,668	1,990	6,652	19,377	95,915	**127,897**				4,968
1995	206	1,414	1,842	6,559	19,132	96,027	**127,222**		51,095		4,691
1996	195	1,318	1,706	6,272	18,832	96,521	**126,901**	19,775	52,933		4,385
1997	193	1,290	1,679	6,164	18,811	96,914	**127,158**	19,874	53,011		4,180
1998	192	1,230	1,609	6,050	18,603	97,072	**126,814**	18,256	52,975		3,788
1999	200	1,213	1,604	5,936	18,738	96,150	**126,096**	16,484	53,031		3,342
2000	196	1,226	1,574	5,941	18,500	94,518	**124,170**	14,347	53,227		2,855
2001	195	1,218	1,552	6,012	18,501	95,898	**125,682**	12,738	54,588		2,516
2002	204	1,256	1,550	6,159	18,574	99,467	**129,603**	11,598	58,909		2,233
2003	195	1,256	1,659	6,269	18,612	103,435	**133,366**	11,037	62,172	1,176	2,067
2004	208	1,380	1,755	6,411	18,828	108,524	**139,200**	10,998	67,597	3,417	1,652
2005	214	1,456	1,841	6,760	20.183	109,037	**141,230**	11,918	70,869	6,201	1,252
2006	216	1,467	1,847	6,923	20,889	108,279	**141,381**	13,179	73,243	6,737	1,036

Source: Clegg and Kirwan (2006).

Figure 25.1	The rank structure in British policing		
Represented by	**Provincial forces**	**Metropolitan Police**	**City of London Police**
Police Federation	Constable Sergeant Inspector Chief Inspector	Constable Sergeant Inspector Chief Inspector	Constable Sergeant Inspector Chief Inspector
Superintendents' Association	Superintendent Chief Superintendent	Superintendent Chief Superintendent	Superintendent Chief Superintendent
ACPO	Asst Chief Constable Deputy Chief Constable Chief Constable	Commander Deputy Asst Commissioner Assistant Commissioner Deputy Commissioner Commissioner	Commander Asst Commissioner Commissioner

Source: Mawby and Wright (2003).

With the exception of the Metropolitan and City of London Police Forces, all police forces share a general rank structure and organisational structure. The Metropolitan Police differs from others because of its size; the City of London force is an historical anomaly and adheres to few of the major characteristics of the other forces. All officers enter the police service as constables and then proceed through the ranks as set out above in Figure 25.1.

In addition to uniformed officers there is a significant, and growing, number of civilians or 'police service staff' within policing. For much of the history of policing, civilian staff have acted simply in administrative support capacities and have been relatively invisible within forces. From the 1980s onward, however, when the Thatcher governments first began to explore *economy, efficiency and effectiveness* in all public services, the issue of increased civilianisation began to rise up the agenda. Since that time, forces have been encouraged – and many have sought – to *civilianise* numerous functions previously carried out by police officers. Civilians are now to be found in a wide variety of posts and at all levels, up to and including senior ranks in, for example, heads of force financial and corporate communications functions.

Forces also have two other cadres of 'officer': the (Police) Community Support Officer (PCSO) and the special constable. PCSOs were introduced in 2002 and are essentially a tier of patrol officer, employed by police forces, but who have neither undergone full police training nor have full police powers. We discuss PCSOs in greater detail later in the chapter. Special constables are volunteers who work a minimum of four hours per week alongside or in support of police officers. They wear uniforms that are almost identical to police constables and, perhaps most importantly, they have the same powers as fully sworn police officers. There are approximately 13,000 members of the special constabulary currently in England and Wales and the numbers have recently been on the increase. Over the past decade or more there have been numerous attempts to increase both the representation of women and minority ethnic groups within the police service. The proportion of female officers has been increasing, with women now comprising 22 per cent of police service strength. However, only 12 per cent of ACPO rank officers are female and the first female chief constable wasn't appointed until 1995 (see Chapter 32). Similarly, in the area of minority representation, efforts to boost recruitment have generally met with mixed success, although there has been an increase in the last decade (see Figure 25.2). Currently minority ethnic officers make up less than four per cent of overall police numbers, and even the Metropolitan Police Service has only just over seven per cent minority ethnic officers.

In Figure 25.1 above in which the rank structure of the police is outlined there is also, on the left-hand side, a listing of the main police representative bodies: the Police Federation, the Superintendents' Association, and the Association of Chief Police Officers (ACPO). As the figure indicates, these three bodies represent the senior managers, middle managers and the 'federated

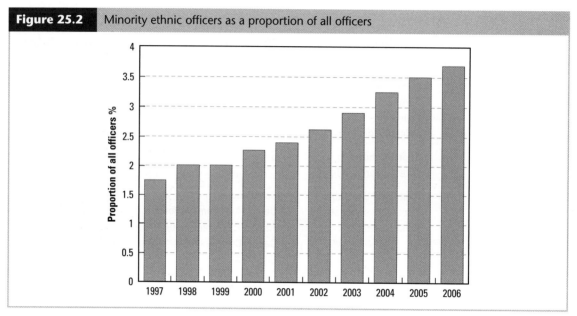

Figure 25.2   Minority ethnic officers as a proportion of all officers

Source: Clegg and Kirwan (2006).

ranks' of the service. By far the largest of the three, therefore, is the Police Federation. Established just after the First World War in 1919 it has generally been the most 'union-like' of the representative bodies; hardly surprising perhaps given it represents the bulk of officers and, by definition, the least powerful and least well paid. The Police Federation became somewhat more prominent in the 1980s and 1990s as it sought to resist what it perceived to be various threats to its members' interests. This culminated in a meeting held at Wembley conference arena in 1993 when it is estimated that over 20,000 police officers gathered to protest about changes to policing that the then Conservative government were believed to be planning as a result of recommendations made by the Sheehy Inquiry (Leishman *et al.*, 1995).

The Superintendents' Association, established by the Police Act 1964, is also both a representative body and a pressure group, but its odd position as a relatively small body representing the middle ranks of the police service in some ways makes it less effective than the Police Federation (which is much larger) and ACPO (which represents the bosses). Nevertheless there have been times, particularly when it has been headed by a media-friendly chairman, that it has gained a certain public profile. In the debates over force amalgamations during 2005–06, for example, the Superintendents' Association set itself apart by being the only body to recommend the establishment of a national police force. In recent times, however, it has been ACPO

that has become the most effective police lobbying body. Rather like the Federation, but to greater effect, ACPO was 'politicised' in the 1980s and 1990s, becoming an organising and representative body not only publicly, but also, crucially, behind the scenes in Whitehall (Reiner, 1991; Wall, 1998).

Before we move on there are a few further policing organisations we should mention. We have focused thus far on local forces. However, there are a number of police bodies at a national level that have particular functions and areas of responsibility. With growing evidence of organised crime crossing both local and national boundaries, so new policing structures have been designed to respond to the perceived threat such activities pose. Regional Crime Squads (RCSs) were established in England and Wales in 1965 and they expanded significantly throughout the 1970s and 1980s, although the number of squads was reduced from nine to six in the early 1990s.

Other developments included the Home Office appointment of a National Coordinator for Drugs Intelligence to oversee the creation of the National Drugs Intelligence Unit (NDIU) and the establishment of the National Football Intelligence Unit (NFIU) in 1989. By 1992 the NFIU, the NDIU, the regional criminal intelligence offices as well as a variety of other bodies were incorporated into the newly established National Criminal Intelligence Service (NCIS). Shortly after, plans were revealed to create an operational unit to tackle serious and organised crime on a national level. This was

Figure 25.3   Police forces in England, Wales, Scotland and Northern Ireland

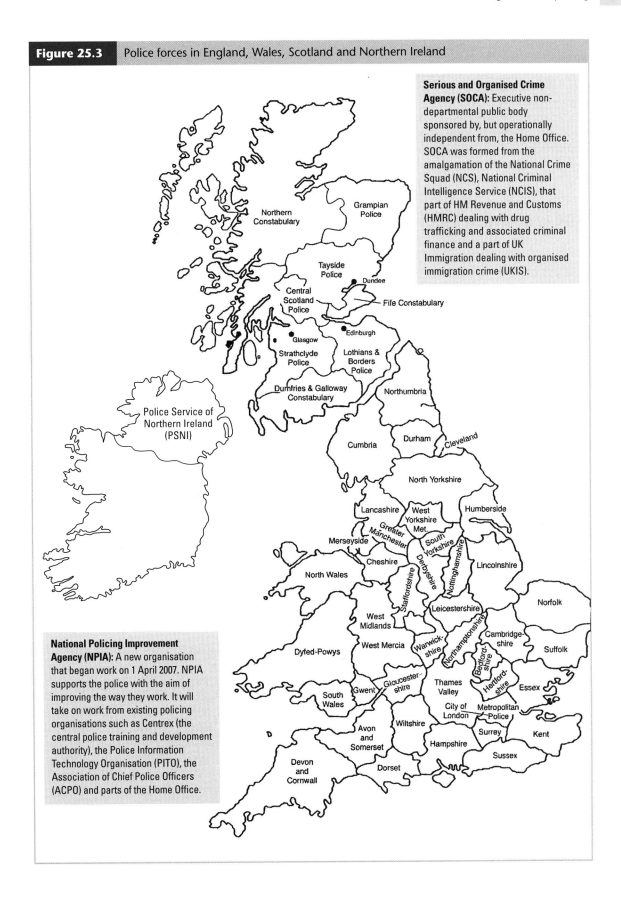

Serious and Organised Crime Agency (SOCA): Executive non-departmental public body sponsored by, but operationally independent from, the Home Office. SOCA was formed from the amalgamation of the National Crime Squad (NCS), National Criminal Intelligence Service (NCIS), that part of HM Revenue and Customs (HMRC) dealing with drug trafficking and associated criminal finance and a part of UK Immigration dealing with organised immigration crime (UKIS).

National Policing Improvement Agency (NPIA): A new organisation that began work on 1 April 2007. NPIA supports the police with the aim of improving the way they work. It will take on work from existing policing organisations such as Centrex (the central police training and development authority), the Police Information Technology Organisation (PITO), the Association of Chief Police Officers (ACPO) and parts of the Home Office.

realised with the creation of the National Crime Squad in 1998 under the auspices of the Police Act 1997 (which also placed NCIS on a statutory footing). Less than six years later, in February 2004, the Government announced plans for the establishment of the Serious and Organised Crime Agency (SOCA), which involves the amalgamation of NCIS and NCS, and their partner agencies, into a single agency with national and trans-national jurisdiction.

Understanding policing

The sociological and criminological study of policing really began to take off in the 1960s. The work of Michael Banton in the UK, and pioneering police scholars like William Westley and others in the States, provided the basis on which a huge body of work has developed in recent decades. Banton originally drew a distinction between sociology *for* the police (work aimed at improving efficiency, effectiveness, etc.) and sociology *on* the police (critical work aimed at understanding the nature and impact of policing). Work in both these traditions has expanded markedly and now constitutes a field of study in itself.

Much early work focused on the nature of the police role and of police 'culture'. Banton's work, followed by that of Cain, Reiner, Chatterton and Holdaway in the 1970s and Smith and Gray in the 1980s, set the parameters for much that followed. Banton's observation that the police officer is primarily a 'peace officer', rather than a 'law officer', spending relatively little time enforcing the law compared with 'keeping the peace', had a profound influence on criminological work in this area. Much of the work that followed in its wake also focused primarily on largely functional definitions of police work with Cain, for example, arguing that the police ought to be defined in terms of their main practice – the maintenance of order.

In contrast, emerging work by American scholars, notably Egon Bittner, focused on the legal capacity brought by the police to their activities. His argument was that it is the police's position as the sole agency with access to the state's monopoly of the legitimate use of force which makes them distinctive:

> The police are empowered and required to impose or, as the case may be, coerce a provisional solution upon emergent problems without having to brook or defer to opposition of any kind of emergency, without any exceptions whatever. This and this alone is what the existence of the police uniquely provides, and it is on this basis that they may be required to do the work of thief-catchers and of nurses, depending on the occasion. (Bittner, 1980)

So what is it, precisely, that policing involves?

What do the police do?

The Metropolitan Police's first instruction book indicated that 'every effort of the police' was to be directed at the prevention of crime. It went on:

> The security of person and property, the preservation of the public tranquillity, and all other objects of a police establishment will thus be better effected than by the detection and punishment of the offender after he has succeeded in committing the crime. This should be constantly kept in mind by every member of the police force, as the guide for his own conduct. Officers and police constables should endeavour to distinguish themselves by such vigilance and activity as may render it impossible for any one to commit a crime within that portion of the town under their charge.

This short, early description of policing covers a wide range of responsibilities: the prevention of crime, the maintenance of order, and detection of crime and punishment of the offender. Popular representations of policing invariably focus on crime, frequently making police work appear to be utterly dominated either by very serious criminal activity or by a constant need to respond to incessant public calls for assistance (again usually calls prompted by crime). However, policing involves much more than crime work. The police are frequently the only 24-hour service agency available to respond to those in need. The result is that they deal with everything from unexpected childbirths, drunks, emergency psychiatric cases, family disputes, missing persons and traffic violations to occasional incidents of crime. This range of examples is deliberate for much research suggests that relatively little police time is spent on actual criminal cases.

Data from an early British Crime Survey (Skogan, 1990) found that only about 18 per cent of contacts between police and public involved specific crime

incidents and a further 12 per cent involved disturbances of some kind. Far more contacts involve an
exchange of information, frequently of a non-crime
and non-emergency nature. It is clear, therefore, that
police work cannot accurately be encompassed by
terms such as 'law enforcement' or 'crime control'.
Now it is important not to overstate this case. Even
though, as some have argued, much police work is
not spent on tasks that are 'crime-related', it is not
entirely clear how such work should be classified.

Moreover, there is considerable research evidence
that suggests that within mainstream police culture
much work of this kind is considered to be 'bullshit'
and that it is crime-related activity that is considered
to be 'real' police work. Moreover, there is no simple
distinction between 'crime-related' activity and
other service work, for when a call is received from
the public it is often difficult to determine immediately whether the call concerns a 'crime'. In
categorising police time, therefore, it is probably
more accurate to think of much of the work as
'potential crime', incidents that *might* involve or
lead to a crime being committed. Research by
Shapland and Vagg classified messages received by
the police in precisely this way (see Figure 25.4).

Research around the world has shown that peacekeeping is the primary police function, even in
societies where the police are routinely armed, such
as the United States, or where the society is divided,
as Northern Ireland was during the Troubles.

At the heart of our picture of policing is the
patrol officer – either on foot or in a car. What does
their job consist of? One of the very best descriptions of routine police work was provided by David
Bayley (1994) when he said:

> The police 'sort out' situations by listening
> patiently to endless stories about fancied slights,

old grievances, new insults, mismatched
expectations, indifference, infidelity, dishonesty
and abuse. They hear about all the petty, mundane, tedious, hapless, sordid details of
individual lives. None of it is earthshaking, or
worthy of a line in a newspaper – not the stuff
that government policy can address, not even
especially spicy; just the begrimed reality of the
lives of people who have no one else to take
their problems to. Patient listening and gentle
counselling are undoubtedly what patrol officers
do most of their time.

Of course the police, including patrol officers, also
engage in proactive activities – the gathering of
intelligence, surveillance, and so on. But these
activities are not the norm, particularly for those
uniformed officers, the majority, engaged in what
is called 'relief' policing – basic policing organised
into shift teams, covering 24 hours, and responding to whatever may arise during the shift. A great
deal of police work is instigated by the public. Calls
are generally received either via the 999 system
(less than 30 per cent of calls) or through the general network. Fewer than half of the calls receive an
immediate response. Although much relief work is
considered to be boring by officers, reacting to calls
and looking for excitement (and *real* police work)
have tended to be the dominant approach among
uniform reliefs.

The next major segment of police work is criminal investigation. Dedicated detectives account for
roughly 15 per cent of police resources. Just as patrol
activity is largely reactive, so the same has generally
been true of criminal investigation. There are considerable attempts to change this now, not least with
the introduction of what is called the 'National
Intelligence Model'. This, like other attempts at
reforming policing, is an attempt to make policing
much more constructive in its use of data and 'intelligence', and proactive in its use of resources and in
its general approach to crime reduction. We consider
some of these models later in the chapter.

Criminal investigation

As we have seen, the police have many functions
and responsibilities, and understanding the balance between them has generated much academic
debate. This is not a static debate as the nature and
practice of policing changes over time. In particular
there has been a gradual shift in recent times in
which increasing emphasis has been placed on

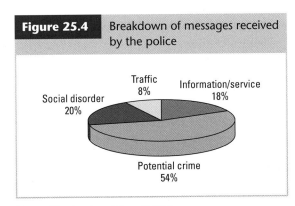

| Figure 25.4 | Breakdown of messages received by the police |

Traffic 8%
Information/service 18%
Social disorder 20%
Potential crime 54%

Source: Shapland and Vagg (1990).

crime control. Over time, as politicians have appeared to become less and less impressed with the efficiency and effectiveness of the British police service, and as law and order has become progressively politicised, so governments have begun to identify crime control as the key task in policing.

Over the past 15 years, significant effort has been devoted to exploring organisational and technological means for improving police performance in this area. All aspects of policing, including investigatory capacities and techniques, have been affected by this shift with significant government investment in forensics, such as DNA testing and improving the connectivity of information and communication technology, between forces and agencies.

Over time, a stereotypical picture of police detective work has built up. Maguire (2003: 367) suggests that the typical popular portrayal of such work contains the following six assumptions:

- That it is 'reactive' (i.e. that the police respond to a crime complaint from the public rather than generate the investigation themselves).

- That it is focused on an offence which has already taken place.

- That the offence which is being investigated is clear from the outset.

- That the inquiries are geared to uncovering the 'truth' about what has happened.

- That it is carried out by detective (CID) officers.

- That the main investigative skills lie in discovering and interpreting 'clues' to find out 'who did it'.

He then goes on to note that while it is perfectly possible to find cases that adhere to this general pattern, in practice day-to-day investigative work is very different. It is different for some of the following reasons:

- The vast majority of investigative work is 'suspect centred'. It involves the surveillance of, and collection of intelligence on, what are sometimes euphemistically referred to as the 'usual suspects' and then working to link them to existing criminal activity.

- There is a critical standpoint which views with great scepticism the claim that investigative work is focused on the search for the 'truth' and, by contrast, argues that it is more about constructing successful cases against known offenders leading to convictions (Sanders and Young, 2007; and see Chapter 23).

- Increasingly, there is a strand of investigative activity that is better thought of as *proactive* than *reactive*. There is growing emphasis upon the use of covert surveillance, informants and the like in contemporary investigative practice.

Historically, criminal investigation has been organised in three main ways:

- into specific criminal investigation departments;

- into specialist squads such as robbery teams or squads focusing on particular problems like organised crime;

- into major inquiry teams set up in response to particularly significant events. Though there have been many notable successes, the history of criminal investigation in British policing has also come in for some extremely serious criticism. Indeed, and particularly since the 1970s, it has been regularly beset by scandal. Such scandals, together with a more pervasive sense that policing generally, and criminal investigation more particularly, was not especially efficient, have led to growing calls for reform.

National Intelligence Model (NIM)

The long-term outcome of the general pressure to increase efficiency and work more strategically has been the emergence, via the idea of intelligence-led policing, of what has come to be known as the *National Intelligence Model* (NIM). Launched by ACPO in 2000, NIM was endorsed by government and, according to the National Policing Plan, was to be 'adopted by ALL forces to commonly accepted standards'.

NIM is expected to work at three levels:

- basic command unit;

- force/regional;

- national/international in relation to serious and organised crime.

It is described by at least some of its proponents as a 'business model', designed to enable police managers to allocate resources and, at its heart, is the aim of gathering and using 'intelligence' in a structured manner in relation to strategies, tactics, problems and targets. The driver at each level of policing is what is called 'the Tasking and Co-ordinating Group', a body which includes managers with responsibility for controlling the necessary resources (a superintendent at BCU level for example). According to Maguire and John (2007: 214)

Forensic officers after completing the search of a house following one of the Ipswich murders in 2006. Images of this kind have reinforced popular fascination with crime scene investigations, and the role of forensic science in solving crime, but forensic evidence has not always proved to be failsafe in court.

'the model splits policing into the two overarching fields of core policing "business" and its required "outcomes". The link between them is the tasking and co-ordinating process.'

It remains early days for NIM and while there appears to be considerable commitment to the model, there is a very long way to go before it can be claimed that it has been embedded successfully within the police service.

Investigation and forensics

Criminal investigation has long been a staple of popular culture (see Chapter 4). Indeed, it appears that modern television is all but obsessed with forensic science. From *Cracker* to *Crime Scene Investigation* and its multiple spin-offs, the schedules are now full of images of highly skilled experts and technicians 'cracking' crime through the appliance of science. Now, the success of such dramas is in part that they play to our long-held desire for security and to our belief in the efficacy of scientific knowledge in making the world a better and safer place. Of course, forensic sciences don't lead straightforwardly to a massive hike in clear-up rates or, necessarily, to solutions to the most complex criminal investigations. And, yet, clearly they have huge potential and represent a significant advance. But what are forensic techniques, what do they involve and what are their promises and limitations?

Much forensic science focuses upon the collection of material traces at the scenes of crime or other locations. Material traces are either physical or biological evidence. Physical evidence includes such things as glass, fibres and paint, but also what is often referred to as 'impression evidence' such as handwriting, shoeprints and fingerprints. Biological evidence includes organic matter such as blood, semen, saliva, urine and hair, as well as plants, pollen and insects.

According to Broeders (2007) the forensic identification discipline that earned the greatest reputation for reliability over the past century is *dactyloscopy*: the comparative examination of fingerprints. According to Tilley and Ford (1996) scenes of crime officers spend around 70 per cent of their time looking for fingerprints with the remainder being spent looking for other forensic evidence. There are a number of different types of 'fingerprint':

- *Plastic fingerprints* – impressions left by fingers in soap, dust, putty or other soft materials.
- *Visible fingerprints* – marks left by the fingers, but coated with grease, blood, paint or ink.
- *Latent fingerprints* – secretions from the skin that are made visible by some form of technological enhancement. (Williams and Johnson, 2007)

A more recent, but now considered highly effective, technique is DNA analysis. Because DNA is found in most cells in the body there is a broad range of source materials that can be tested. These include blood, saliva, hair, nasal secretions and semen. Material to be used for DNA analysis is generally collected in one of four ways:

- By recovering an item anticipated to contain DNA;
- Through 'swabbing' of a visible stain;
- By scraping a dried stain;
- By cutting away part of a fixed item which is stained with something likely to contain DNA. (Williams and Johnson, 2007)

New technologies have not only enabled such techniques to develop, but also have made possible the creation of huge biometric databases containing DNA profiles and scans of fingerprints and irises. Such databases raise serious issues around freedom, surveillance and human rights, and this has become a particularly controversial issue since 2001 and the emergence of the 'War on Terror'. One response to the airing of such concerns is sometimes to argue that the accuracy of the information that is collected and stored in these databases is such that the 'innocent have nothing to fear'. This returns us to one of the key messages of much popular drama involving crime scene investigation – the idea that these are essentially reliable, failsafe methods by which the guilty can be identified and innocent protected. However, cases such as those of Sally Clark and Angela Cannings, both wrongly convicted of the killings of their children on the basis of deeply flawed forensic evidence, have cast serious doubt on the appropriateness of relying upon such evidence in criminal cases. Indeed, even those forms of trace materials we have historically felt we can rely upon have significant limitations. As Broeders (2007: 303–4) notes:

> Traditionally, fingerprint examiners have used categorical conclusions ['yes' or 'no'] with a pos-itive identification carrying the implication that a crime-scene finger mark originates with absolute certainty from a particular finger. However … unique source attribution … is not logically possible, barring forensically rather exceptional circumstances. Indeed, it appears that the less far-reaching – usually verbal – probabilistic conclusions that tend to be widely used in other traditional forensic identification disciplines, as in handwriting, paint, or firearms examination, are also somewhat problematic.

The danger, as in the Clark and Cannings cases as well as many others, is that the strength of forensic evidence can be overestimated and over-stated, consequently lending 'an aura of scientific respectability to the legal decision-making process which is not only frequently unjustified but is also at all times undesirable' (Broeders, 2007: 332). The solution, Broeders argues, is always to couch the forensic evidence in probabilistic terms, allowing magistrate, judge or jury to reach a decision on the basis of all the evidence in front of them.

Review questions

1 What are the main representative bodies in policing?

2 What proportion of current police service strength is made of minority ethnic officers?

3 What are the main functions of the police?

4 What are the main material traces collected at scenes of crimes?

Police powers

There is not the space here to consider all police powers in detail. Rather, we will look at the major powers, particularly as they affect the rest of the criminal prosecution process: stop and search, arrest, detention and questioning. What can the police reasonably do in investigating crime? What rights do we have as citizens against unwarranted intrusion by state agencies? In many respects such questions go to the heart of the criminal justice process: what is the balance between the need to control crime on the one hand and the protection of individual liberties on the other? Many critics suggest that in recent decades we have witnessed a gradual shift toward the lessening of basic freedoms as the power of the police and other agencies with a crime control mandate has increased. Thus, Sanders and Young (2007: 123) argue, 'the police themselves generally decide what powers they will exercise and when. This is a crime control approach.'

Stop and search

We discussed earlier the Brixton riots of the early 1980s and the Inquiry which followed led by Lord Justice Scarman. One of the precipitating factors of the disturbances was what was perceived locally to be the heavy-handed and indiscriminate use of stop and search powers. Although police officers were supposed only to use such powers when they had 'reasonable suspicion' that the person concerned had been involved in a particular offence. However, by the early 1980s such practices – widely referred to as 'Sus' laws – had fallen into considerable disrepute.

The Royal Commission on Criminal Procedure (1981) argued for the introduction of both safeguards and standardised practices in relation to stop and search and, subsequently, both were enacted as part of PACE. The basic powers of stop and search are as follows:

- S.1(2) (b) allows a police officer to 'detain a person or vehicle for the purpose of a search'.

- S.1(3) of PACE allows an officer to stop and search if he has reasonable grounds for suspecting that he will find stolen or prohibited articles or any article to which subsection 8A applies.

- S.163 of the Road Traffic Act 1988 provides a general power under which police officers may stop vehicles. There is no requirement of reasonable suspicion.

- S.60 of the Criminal Justice and Public Order Act 1994 introduces further powers to stop and search vehicles for guns, knives or other weapons but where there is no requirement that there be reasonable suspicion relating to any individual vehicle.

- Ss.44–47 of the Terrorism Act 2000 and the Anti-Terrorism, Crime and Security Act 2001 provide powers for police officers and PCSOs to stop any vehicle in order to search for articles that could be used in connection with terrorism.

Stops and searches can only take place when an officer has 'reasonable grounds for suspecting' that evidence of particular offences will be found and, similarly, seizure of particularly items can only take place when there is 'reasonable suspicion' that they are relevant to the inquiry. The relevant PACE Code of Practice says:

> Reasonable grounds for suspicion depend on the circumstances in each case. There must be an objective basis for that suspicion based on facts, information and/or intelligence which are relevant to the likelihood of finding an article of a certain kind … Reasonable suspicion can never be supported on the basis of personal factors alone without reliable supporting intelligence or information or some specific behaviour by the person concerned. For example, a person's race, age, appearance, or the fact that the person is known to have a previous conviction, cannot be used alone or in combination with each other as the reason for searching that person.

Although the intent in the Code is clear, in practice officers continue to have significant discretion in the use of their powers to stop and search. This has led to particular concern in relation to questions of discrimination (see Chapter 31). Here we will simply note that this remains an area of considerable controversy and whether the use of these powers is actually evidence of discriminatory practice by the police or not is almost beside the point. The fact is that this is how it is experienced by those on the receiving end of such powers.

Arrest

The place of arrest has changed quite markedly in the criminal justice process. Historically, arrest was generally used as a means of bringing people to court. Under such circumstances, suspects for a crime were interviewed and when the police were satisfied they had enough evidence to proceed, a warrant for the arrest of a suspect was issued, the person concerned was then arrested to appear in court on particular charges. It was for this reason that being interviewed by the police was often referred to using the euphemism 'helping the police with their inquiries'.

Over time – through practice and as a result of legislation – this has changed to the position we now occupy where arrest is often the beginning of the investigative process; the means by which suspects are brought in for questioning. 'Helping the police with their inquiries' was always something of a fiction, and this fiction has gradually been replaced by the more formal mechanism of arrest.

Three pieces of legislation have formalised the process:

- The Criminal Law Act 1967 created a range of what it referred to as 'arrestable offences': offences for which the police could make an arrest without first having obtained a warrant from local magistrates.

- This ability was widened under PACE which allowed the police, under certain limited circumstances such as a refusal to provide name and address, to arrest people for non-arrestable offences.

- The process was effectively completed by the Serious and Organised Crime and Policing Act 2005 which made all offences arrestable so long as the police believe it necessary to enable prompt questioning of the person concerned.

The grounds for arrest have also changed substantially over time. Under PACE 1984 there was a distinction made between serious offences – any offence punishable by five years' imprisonment or more, plus one or two other specified offences – and less serious offences. The former, being 'arrestable', required no particular justification other than the need to question the person concerned. For an arrest of someone for a less serious (i.e. non-arrestable) offence, the police were required to have reasonable grounds for suspecting that an offence had been, was being, or was likely to be committed and that a summons was likely to be insufficient.

As already mentioned, the distinction between arrestable and non-arrestable offences no longer exists. Rather, PACE has been amended and its new s.24 allows the police to arrest someone without a warrant whom they know to be, or they have reasonable suspicion is, about to commit an offence, or is in the process of committing an offence, or who is guilty of already having committed an offence. According to Sanders and Young (2007: 124) this change 'simply prioritises considerations of police efficiency over the interests of suspects'.

What critics find particularly problematic about the current situation is that it enables the police to arrest and question a great number of innocent people without any great concern that there will be any real comeback. As we will see in subsequent chapters, some scholars argue strongly that wherever possible there should be protections against prosecutions being brought against the innocent. They also tend to argue that the same principle should apply to the deprivation of liberty that is involved in arrest. Thus, as Ashworth and Redmayne (2005: 86) put it, 'It is difficult to see why a person suspected of a minor offence, such as common assault or careless driving, should be subjected to the coercive power of arrest just to enable questioning by the police'.

Detention at the police station

In Chapter 23 we considered the debate between McConville *et al.* and Smith in relation to the idea of case construction and the application of Packer's ideal types of due process and crime control. That debate focused largely around police powers and, in particular, the treatment of suspects whilst detained at the police station. As we have seen it is now not unusual for arrests to be made prior to a suspect being taken to a police station for questioning. There is, however, as a result of PACE 1984, a series of safeguards that are supposed to protect the rights of suspects held in police custody.

Prior to PACE, suspects were protected by what were known as Judges' Rules. These rules, which laid down procedures for the questioning of suspects, were replaced initially by four codes of practice. These covered police statutory powers to stop and search, the search of premises and seizure of property, the detention, treatment and questioning of people by the police, and identification procedures. A fifth code covering tape-recording of interviews with suspects was introduced subsequently, and in 1991 revised codes of practice, directed primarily at reinforcing the suspect's right to legal advice, came into operation. The PACE codes of practice have been further revised in 2006, in particular adding Code G covering the new powers of arrest introduced by the Serious and Organised Crime and Policing Act 2005.

Once arrested and taken to a police station, a suspect is then taken before what is known as a 'custody officer'. If you watch police dramas – *The Bill*, for example – the police officer 'booking in' suspects who have been arrested is the custody officer. The custody officer plays an important role within the police station, being responsible for overseeing police behaviour and ensuring it complies with PACE and its related codes of practice. This includes assessing whether there is sufficient evidence to charge the suspect, decisions about whether to sanction their detention in custody pending further questioning, and then monitoring conditions in what is now generally and euphemistically referred to as the 'custody suite'

The booking-in desk at Southampton Central Police Station following an arrest. It is the responsibility of the custody officer to ensure that procedures and treatment of suspects comply with PACE (Police and Criminal Evidence Act 1984), and that suspects are made aware of their rights, including the right to free legal advice and the right to silence.

(the cell area) in the station. Arguably one of the most important roles within public policing, the 1995 Masefield Report said the custody sergeant is:

> [T]he guarantor of the suspect's rights and takes the important decisions whether to endorse the arrest and whether there is sufficient evidence of a particular offence to bring a charge. He also makes decisions on bail. These are important not just for the suspect but for the criminal justice system as a whole. The custody officer is a major guardian of the standards of the whole system.

Monitoring the treatment of suspects includes such matters as:

- how frequently and for what periods of time the suspect is questioned;
- whether suspects receive medical attention;
- that suspects are adequately fed and otherwise looked after;
- if necessary, that suspects are continuously monitored if there is any concern about suicide risk.

The treatment of the suspect is not only monitored in this way, but is now often accompanied by CCTV surveillance of at least the public areas of the custody suite, and a paper record – the custody record – is maintained by the custody officer.

Suspects' rights are encapsulated in Code of Practice C of PACE. First of all, custody officers are bound to inform suspects of their rights orally and also give them details of their rights in writing. These rights, which are available to all suspects, though some of them may be delayed in the case of terrorist suspects, include:

- The right, if they request it, to consult a lawyer privately. Legal advice is provided free of charge by a duty solicitor in the police station, if required. Research suggests that around one third of suspects are not told that legal advice is free, and indeed, legal representation is requested in only about one third of cases (Brown *et al.*, 1992; Bucke and Brown, 1997). Initial contact with a lawyer is increasingly made by telephone and around one fifth of suspects that receive legal advice do so only by telephone (Phillips and Brown, 1998).

- The right to consult a copy of Code of Practice C.
- The right to have someone informed of their arrest.
- The right to be able to make a telephone call to a person of their choice.
- The right to receive visits 'at the custody officer's discretion'.

Particular arrangements are to be made for certain classes of 'vulnerable' suspect. As with the criminal justice process generally, the fact of being a juvenile means that special protections are required. In addition, any suspect who is hearing impaired, mentally handicapped or mentally disordered has special protections whilst in the police station. Vulnerable suspects should not be interviewed without the presence of an appropriate adult. Appropriate adults are generally social workers – or in the case of juveniles, parents or guardians – and they are there to see that the suspects' rights are protected. They are there to offer advice, to ensure that a solicitor is present and to attend interviews themselves.

As many as one-quarter of suspects may be juveniles and so, consequently, special protections should be a routine matter within the police station. Home Office research (Bucke and Brown, 1997) found that over 90 per cent of juveniles had an appropriate adult with them during interview, but the proportion was much lower for other types of vulnerable suspect. How successful the appropriate adult is in their role as protector of the suspect's rights quite possibly depends on the nature of the appropriate adult: there is considerable evidence of parents acting in concert with the police to secure confessions from children, whereas experienced social workers may well be more willing and better able to withstand such pressures.

There are time limits on the period during which suspects can be detained in custody. Originally there was a distinction between normal offences for which the time limit was 24 hours and serious arrestable offences for which an extended period of 36 hours was available. The Serious and Organised Crime and Policing Act now allows for 36 hour detention for all arrestable offences. This period of detention has to be reviewed by the custody officer (or a more senior officer) at intervals of approximately nine hours. Applications to a local magistrates' court can be made for extended periods of detention up to a maximum of 60 hours beyond the original 36 hours.

The time limits in terrorist cases are far more extensive. The Terrorism Act 2000 allowed the police to detain suspects for up to 14 days (with judicial approval) and this was subsequently doubled to 28 days by the Terrorism Act 2006, though the government's original intention had been to allow for detention of up to a period of three months. Such detention without trial runs counter to international human rights law and, indeed, required 'derogation' (the partial revocation of a law) from the European Convention to enable it to happen. There is every prospect that there will be attempts to extend these time limits in the months and years to come.

Finally in relation to detention, mention must be made of 'control orders'. Control orders are effectively a form of 'house arrest' that can be put in place for renewable periods of six or 12 months and contain a series of restrictions (on movement, on contact with others and even use of the internet), breach of which is a serious criminal offence. Control orders were introduced when controversial provisions in the Anti-Terrorism, Crime and Security Act 2001, which allowed for the indefinite detention of foreign nationals suspected of terrorism, were abolished as a result of successful human rights challenges.

Right to silence

One of the traditional protections afforded citizens subject to police interrogation is the right to refuse to answer questions. On the assumption that the accused is innocent until proven guilty, and that the onus is on the state to prove guilt, the right to silence has long been considered a fundamental part of fairness in the criminal process. Until 1994, the right to silence consisted of a number of elements:

- Subsequent to any arrest, a suspect had to be cautioned and informed that they could refuse to answer questions. The old caution went as follows: 'You do not have to say anything unless you wish to do so but what you say may be given in evidence'. The suspect had to be reminded of the caution if they were interviewed in the police station, and after every break in the interview.

- Except in very limited circumstances it was not permitted for the prosecution to comment upon, or draw any inferences from, a defendant's refusal to answer questions.

- Similarly, any comment made by the judge on the refusal to testify in court was limited in extent and always accompanied by a reminder to the jury that they must not assume guilt from such silence.

Table 25.2	Suspects' use of the right of silence during police interviews			
	Refused all questions %	**Refused some questions** %	**Answered all questions** %	**Total** %
Pre-reform	10	13	77	100
Post-reform	6	10	84	100

Source: Bucke *et al.* (2000).

During the 1980s critics increasingly argued that the restrictions were hampering the crime control efforts of the police and other criminal justice institutions and that they should be reformed. The Royal Commission on Criminal Justice reviewed the use of the right to silence and concluded that it should be retained. The Royal Commission was particularly concerned that any increase in the pressure on suspects to answer questions during interrogation might 'increase the risk of innocent people, particularly those under suspicion for the first time, making damaging statements' (RCCJ 1993, para 23).

Subsequently, however, the Criminal Justice and Public Order Act 1994 substantially revised the right to silence. The revised caution is:

'You do not have to say anything. But it may harm your defence if you do not mention when questioned something which you later rely on in court. Anything you do say may be given in evidence.'

This is a fairly complex warning and some commentators have raised doubts as to whether it can reasonably be assumed that it will be understood by all suspects (Ashworth and Redmayne, 2005).

At heart, the changes in the Act allow the courts to draw adverse inferences from a defendant's silence when, for example, they rely on facts in court that they failed to mention when questioned by the police, when they fail to provide an explanation for incriminating objects or marks, or for their presence near the scene of a crime, or simply when they refuse to testify in their own defence in court. These changes have led to a decline in the number of suspects refusing to answer questions, but not to any increase in the number of confessions produced. Table 25.2 above shows the results of Home Office research comparing the situation before and after the changes to the right to silence and indicates a drop in the proportion of suspects refusing to answer some or all questions.

The Home Office researchers argued that the changes may have brought with them a number of efficiencies in the investigative process: police officers being more likely to disclose evidence prior to first interview, enabling legal advisors to provide better advice to suspects about whether refusal to answer questions is a sensible course of action; and the reduced use of silence providing greater opportunity for police to check statements and improve the quality of the cases. However, changes to the right to silence are highlighted by critics as clear evidence of what they perceive to be the drift away from due process concerns in the criminal process and the gradual privileging of crime control priorities.

Review questions

1 How has the police use of the power of arrest changed in recent times?

2 What are the main safeguards provided by PACE?

3 What are the primary responsibilities of the custody officer?

4 What are the main types of 'vulnerable suspect'?

5 How has the right to silence been reformed?

Models of policing

The attentive reader will have noticed that sometimes we talk of police *forces* and on other occasions of police *services*. For much of the twentieth century constabularies were most usually referred to as police forces. In the aftermath of the riots of the early 1980s, and the Scarman Report which followed, significant changes occurred in the public presentation of the nature and limitations of policing. The process was initiated by Sir Kenneth Newman, then Commissioner of the Metropolitan Police, who stressed that crime could not be controlled by the police alone, and that significant levels of public co-operation were needed if inroads were to be made. His successor as Commissioner, Sir Peter Imbert, continued this process of reorientation with his 'Plus Programme' in London.

To the extent that the police could realistically ever have been described as primarily a law enforcement or crime-control agency, the 1980s and early 1990s witnessed, in changing the 'public face' of policing, a significant movement away from this role. Symbolically, the police started to refer to themselves as *services*. The intention, clearly, was to de-emphasise the confrontational, conflictual aspects of policing and, rather, to attempt to highlight the more community-oriented, service-oriented aspects of police work. During roughly the same period there were calls from within and outside policing to increase and improve relationships with local communities. *Community policing* originally emerged in the United States, but had considerable influence on British policing during the 1980s.

Community policing

Originally associated with John Alderson, the chief constable of Devon and Cornwall, community policing was never very clearly defined, but emphasised the importance of developing close relationships between police and community and, more particularly, seeking to orient policing in such a way as to be responsive to community demands, rather than simply imposing policing priorities on local neighbourhoods. According to Tilley (2003) the most important elements of community involvement in policing in such a model include:

- Defining what constitute problems or policing needs;
- Shaping forms of local policing by the police service;
- Examining identified local problems alongside the police service;
- Determining responses to identified issues;
- Implementing responses to issues as participants in community policing;
- Working with the police to address community-defined problems;
- Informing or supplementing the operational work of police officers.

Though in many respects the community policing model is better regarded as something the police aspire to than an accurate description of policing practice, these ideals or aspirations came to dominate the philosophies held by chief officers in British policing from the mid-1980s onward. The most recent variant in the UK is called 'neighbourhood policing', a very substantial attempt by government to create closer links between the police and local communities (see http://www.neighbourhood policing.co.uk/). As pressure has mounted on police forces – from governments demanding 'value for money' and increased effectiveness (however that is measured) and from contextual factors such as the increasing calls on police time by the public – so another policing model – *problem-oriented policing* (POP) – has gained greater visibility.

Problem-oriented policing

Associated with the American policing scholar, Herman Goldstein, POP shares a number of characteristics with community policing. At its heart lies the idea that considerable thought should be given by police forces to analysing or researching the problems that confront them – problems often identified and defined by the community – and then applying police resources and strategies to these problems in a way that is believed might best solve or reduce them. Crucial to this is shifting the police away from a reactive model that focuses on individual events toward a proactive mentality that looks for patterns and commonalities in the matters that come to their attention. Such patterns may include (Tilley, 2003):

- *Repeat victimisation* – the heightened risk experienced by those who have already been victimised.
- *Hotspots* – the concentration of incidents in particular places.
- *Prolific offenders* – the evidence that a minority of offenders are responsible for a disproportionate proportion of offences.
- *Hot products* – some items are particular attractive to offenders/particularly likely to be stolen.
- *Hot classes of victim* – some victims are particularly vulnerable to certain types of crime.

Intelligence-led policing

More recently still, senior British police officers have begun to talk of *intelligence-led policing*. Rather like POP it involves the collection and analysis of data about crime and disorder, followed by allocating police resources in a manner best suited to responding to the matters identified. Intelligence-led policing, and its formal embodiment in British policing, the *National Intelligence Model,* is very much in its infancy. Early research on its implementation suggests that traditional responsive policing styles continue to restrict the development of proactive models and that a number of cultural barriers to proactive policing still exist within contemporary policing.

In an attempt to illustrate how various innovative policing strategies relate to one another, Weisburd and Eck (2004) distinguish policing strategies along two dimensions: the *diversity of approaches* involved and the *level of focus.* Traditional law enforcement approaches, involving a fairly standardised set of tactics, score fairly low on the *diversity* dimension. Similarly, strategies that are applied relatively uniformly across circumstances, times and places by policing agencies score relatively low on the *level of focus* dimension. They argue that traditional policing methods – what they call the *standard model* – have rarely been characterised by a diversity of approaches or been particularly targeted or focused. By contrast, innovations in policing over the last decade or so have tended to move outward along one or both of the dimensions. They illustrate this in the following way:

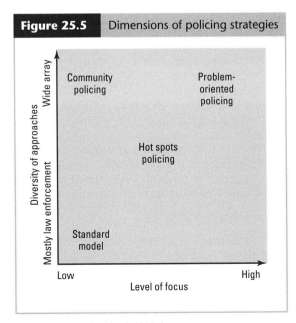

| **Figure 25.5** | Dimensions of policing strategies |

Source: Weisburd and Eck (2004).

Review questions

1 What are the main characteristics of community policing, problem-oriented policing and intelligence-led policing?

2 What are the main differences between the three models?

3 Are the police a force or a service?

A brief history of policing

As we saw in Chapter 2, in an attempt to establish order over an unruly realm, in the twelfth century Henry II established the basis of a system of criminal justice, including a trial and jury system. Nevertheless, for some centuries order was generally maintained through a system of local community-based peacekeeping. Responsibility for keeping the peace rested on local householders, and a duty to help via the raising of the 'hue and cry' formed the basis of much local 'policing'. The Anglo-Saxon principle of Frankpledge underpinned the system of mutual responsibility that existed to maintain, or to attempt to maintain, order during this period. Reforms in the thirteenth century aimed to fortify towns and introduced watchmen to patrol between sunset and sunrise.

Emergence of the 'new police'

Formalised policing only begins to emerge in the eighteenth century and what we would recognise as modern police forces were not introduced until the beginning of the nineteenth century – the City of Glasgow Police in 1800, the Royal Irish Constabulary in 1822 and the Metropolitan Police in 1829. There was considerable resistance to the introduction of the 'new police' and great efforts were made to distinguish the police from the military. It was not until the second half of the nineteenth century that police forces covered the whole of Britain.

During this time the police gradually acquired a broad range of responsibilities – including matters way beyond those of crime and order. Much activity in the nineteenth century was directed toward standardising policing, partly through reducing the number of forces and using the Inspectorate of Constabulary to rationalise policing practices. The two World Wars and the industrial unrest in the first half of the twentieth century further separated police forces from their local authorities, giving

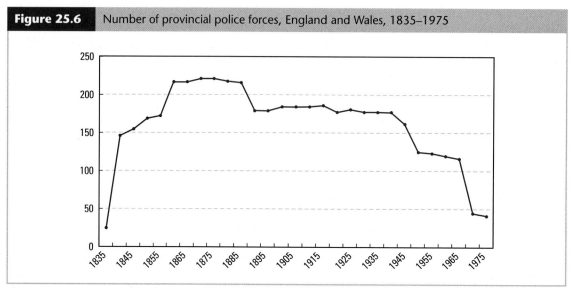

Figure 25.6   Number of provincial police forces, England and Wales, 1835–1975

Source: Wall (1998).

forces greater independence and gradually reducing the power of local authorities.

Though the problems of pay and working conditions were not as bad at the end of the Second World War as they had been at the end of the First, gradually reforms took hold which signalled the beginnings of a shift away from traditional beat work, and towards a new world dominated by radios and cars. By this point public trust in policing was extremely high, and the century or so that had passed since the introduction of the new police had witnessed a remarkable transformation in the status and public acceptability of the police. As numerous academic commentators have noted, this high point in police legitimacy is perhaps best captured in the form of PC George Dixon, initially in the Ealing film, *The Blue Lamp,* and subsequently in the BBC television series, *Dixon of Dock Green.* Nevertheless, even at this point in their history, the police were by no means free from scandal, and a number of high profile cases in the 1950s eventually led to the establishment of a Royal Commission on the Police, which reported in 1962 and led directly to the Police Act 1964. This remains the landmark piece of legislation in British policing.

The Royal Commission on the Police

The Royal Commission took the view that policing should remain largely local in nature, though a minority opinion from one member of the Commission, Dr A.L.Goodhart, argued in favour of a national police force – something that simply could not have been countenanced in Peel's time and, indeed, was still broadly viewed as untenable in the 1960s. Fifty years later, as we will see, we are edging closer and closer to Goodhart's model, with the number of forces having shrunk now to 43 from over 200 in the late nineteenth century (see Figure 25.6) in England and Wales and with proposals for further reductions appearing regularly.

Key dates

1835	Municipal Corporations Act	} required local areas to employ constables
1839	County Police Act	
1856	County and Borough Police Act	– made police forces compulsory
1888	Local Government Act	– required amalgamations of very small forces
1964	Police Act	– eventually reduced force numbers to 49 (from 117)
1972	Local Government Act	– reduced number of provincial forces to 41

Most importantly of all, the Royal Commission recommended, and the 1964 Act established, a reformed system for police governance – we discuss that subject in greater detail in the final section. In the post-war years, and up until roughly the time of the 1964 Act, policing remained organised on a beat system. With officers in rural areas responsible for the policing of an entire area and their urban counterparts providing 24-hour cover via shift work, walking a fixed or variable beat remained at the heart of policing. Whilst the phrase 'bobby on the beat' still has considerable resonance, the time when Dr Martens treading on paving stones was a quintessential part of policing has long since passed. By the late 1960s the Home Office was encouraging officers into cars in the – quite possibly misguided – belief that it would both make them more effective and bring them into closer contact with their communities. In retrospect it seems, on the contrary, to have aided and abetted the transformation of policing in something akin to a 'fire brigade' service. Though the British bobby was still portrayed as an honest crime-buster, even this image was about to come under severe strain.

Problems of legitimacy

Initially, a series of corruption scandals involving the Drugs Squad and the Obscene Publications Squad of the Metropolitan Police provided a stiff challenge to those that sought to portray 1970s policing as being little different from that seen in *Dixon of Dock Green*. Later in the decade a series of very public miscarriages of justice, many of them involving people falsely convicted of offences connected with Northern Irish terrorism, further complicated the public image of policing. On the surface, much of the successful policing legitimisation project that had been undertaken throughout the nineteenth century and up to the middle of the twentieth, was being swiftly undone.

The early 1980s then saw a series of urban disorders, notably in Brixton, and a major industrial dispute involving striking miners, neither of which could be said to have produced positive news stories for the police service. Lord Scarman's Inquiry, referred to above, was scathing of the Metropolitan Police's communication failures with the Brixton community. Images of inner-city communities in London, Bristol, Birmingham, Liverpool and elsewhere, aflame after confrontations with the police, were then joined shortly after by pictures from South Wales, Derbyshire, Nottinghamshire and Yorkshire showing police officers on horseback charging into local protesters as officers in riot gear used their newly-acquired riot equipment to

Police officers on the streets of Brixton as the disturbances break out in April 1981. Lord Scarman's subsequent Inquiry was highly critical of the Metropolitan Police's communication failures with the Brixton community, and its recommendations led to significant reforms in approaches to policing.

'police' the dispute. The tactics adopted, as Waddington (1991) put it, 'did immense damage to the police reputation for restraint'.

During this period, and perhaps not surprisingly given the picture painted here, public confidence in policing began to decline, and in some respects to decline quite markedly. However, it was declining from a high level – the era associated with Dixon does appear to have been characterised by high levels of public trust – and thus the deteriorating public rating of policing still left the police enjoying levels of public confidence most other professions and occupations could only dream about. Below the general picture, however, the reality was more complex and less comfortable.

In particular, as the experience of Brixton in London, Handsworth in Birmingham, St Paul's in Bristol and Toxteth in Liverpool had graphically illustrated, police relations with minority ethnic communities was often far from positive. Lord Scarman recommended that much greater attention be paid to recruitment from minority communities and to consultation with such communities. However, he specifically rejected 'institutional racism' as an explanation for the problems that had precipitated the Inquiry. Nevertheless, it was the trigger for much reform in policing, and Scarmanesque ideas – not least that the maintenance of order should, where necessary, take precedence over crime control – had become the dominant philosophy in policing by the end of the 1980s.

Just as Scarman had a lasting impact on the landscape of British policing so, more than a decade on, did another inquiry which again focused on relationships between the Metropolitan Police and minority ethnic Londoners. The precipitating event was the murder, on 22 April 1993, of 18 year-old Stephen Lawrence in Eltham, South London. The reason for the inquiry was the marked failure by the Metropolitan Police successfully to investigate the unprovoked and racist attack on the black teenager, Stephen Lawrence, by a group of five white youths whilst he was waiting at a bus stop (see Chapter 31). Established by the incoming Labour government in 1997, the Lawrence Inquiry concluded memorably, and in contrast with Scarman, that:

> There is no doubt but that there were funda-mental errors. The investigation was marred by a combination of professional incompetence, *institutional racism,* and a failure of leadership by senior officers. (1999, para 46.1, *emphasis added*)

The inquiry made 70 recommendations covering such varied aspects of policing as the monitoring and assessment of performance, the reporting and recording of racist incidents and crimes, family liaison, first-aid training, stop and search, and recruitment and retention. The Lawrence Inquiry, as Reiner has argued, 'transformed the terms of the political debate about black people and criminal justice … what had not [previously] featured in public awareness and political debate was the disproportionate rate at which black people suffered as victims of crime'. We return to this theme later in the chapter. For the time being we leave the Lawrence Inquiry noting simply that the issue of relationships with Britain's minority communities – which are proliferating and changing – is undoubtedly set to remain one of the central sources of debate, and quite likely controversy, in policing.

Centralisation

A number of other important developments can be identified in policing in the last 50 years. These include significant centralisation as well as what might be termed 'pluralisation'. The latter concerns the proliferation of policing bodies that have become visible in recent decades – not least the apparently significant expansion of the private security sector. We discuss this in detail below. For now, we draw our brief history of policing to a close by considering the progressive centralisation of policing.

Centralisation is visible in at least five major ways:

1 The progressive reduction in the number of police forces in England and Wales (see Figure 25.6).

2 The increasing ability of forces to co-ordinate their activities across force boundaries.

3 The creation of regional and national policing bodies.

4 The formalisation of the activities of police representative bodies – particularly the Association of Chief Police Officers (ACPO).

5 The increasing government oversight of, and influence over, policing through new legislation and managerial reforms.

We have already seen how since the introduction of the new police in the early nineteenth century the number of forces has progressively been reduced. Most recently (2005–06) the government floated proposals for the possible reduction of the number of provincial police forces down to as few as 15 or 18. In the event, a dispute over financing such changes, together with other pressures on the Home Office, meant that the idea was shelved. This is likely to be temporary, however, and the eventual further reduction of the number of provincial forces seems inevitable.

The second aspect of centralisation is the growing ability of forces to work across their geographical boundaries. The policing of the miners' strike in 1984 focused attention on the increasingly 'national' nature of policing in Britain. In 1972, the National Reporting Centre (NRC) was established as a system for co-ordinating and managing mutual aid between forces in times of emergency. It had been used on a relatively small number of occasions prior to the miners' dispute, but was utilised on a unprecedented scale during the strike and was, at that point at least, the 'high point in the national co-ordination of policing public order'.

A perhaps more significant indicator of progressive centralisation has been the emergence of a growing number of regional, and later national, policing bodies. The 1964 Act created Regional Crime Squads and, having grown substantially during the 1970s and 1980s, they were reduced in number in the early 1990s, and then eventually superseded by the National Criminal Intelligence Service and the National Crime Squad. Indeed, for much of the 1990s there was talk of the creation of a 'British FBI', although for much of this time such an idea looked very unlikely. In 2004, however, proposals for just such a development were published, and put into force through the Serious and Organised Crime and Policing Act 2005. The Serious and Organised Crime Agency (SOCA) came into being on 1 April 2006.

The fourth facet of centralisation has been the increasing degree of co-ordination brought to policing by the association representing all those in senior ranks in the police service: ACPO. Established in 1948, it was initially more of a gentleman's club than a lobbying body. Since the early 1990s, when a series of challenges to the police service were laid down by the Conservative government of the day – not least privatisation of elements of police work – ACPO has gradually become a significantly more effective body at representing the interests of its members. The Head of the Audit Commission in the early 1990s noted that the police service was the least affected of all public services by the 'Thatcher revolution'. If he was right, and certainly in some respects he may well have been, it was not because governments thought differently, but was more a consequence of the ability of ACPO to intimidate successive Home Secretaries.

Despite the power and influence exercised by ACPO, and by individual chief constables locally, the clearest element of long-term centralisation of British policing has been the gradually increasing power of central government in this arena. This is visible in two main ways. First, through the successive reforms of police governance (discussed in greater detail below) which have gradually altered the power of local authorities and, more recently, of chief officers and enhanced the ability of government to set policing priorities. The second is the spread of 'managerialism'. All of this has substantially increased government 'steering' of policing.

The most vivid illustration of the current trend toward government 'micro-management' of policing was provided by the 'Street Crimes Initiative' in 2002. As a result of growing concern in government about levels of recorded street crime, and the perceived failure by the police service to respond adequately, a decision was taken by the Prime Minister to provide extra resources to the ten forces with the worst recorded levels of street crime to support extra police activity aimed at tackling the problem. The unusual aspect of the initiative was that it involved the chief officers of each of these ten forces reporting, on a weekly basis, directly to a nominated cabinet minister. This level of oversight – what might be seen in some ways as 'interference' – in local policing matters by national politicians was extraordinary, but may well be a sign of things to come.

Key themes in policing

Police culture

Police culture has long been considered an important topic, in part because of the difficulties associated with reforming the police service. Accurately or otherwise, the police service has been perceived as being resistant to change and, in this regard, it has often been assumed that it is the entrenched beliefs and attitudes of those employed within the police service that present one of the greatest barriers.

Defined by Reiner (2000) as 'how police officers see the social world and their role in it', or 'the values, norms, perspectives and craft rules' that inform officers' conduct, 'cop culture' has formed the basis for a considerable criminological literature. He draws a distinction between 'cop culture', the attitudes, views, behaviour and orientation of officers expressed during the course of their work, and 'canteen culture', the beliefs and values more typical of the off-duty officer. There has been something of a tendency in some writing on policing to assume that what officers say in off-duty banter in the police canteen or pub is not only indicative of how officers think, but also of how they behave when on duty. This, as Waddington (1999) has argued, is not only potentially misleading, but also quite probably wrong. Much of what officers do when off-duty, he argues, is better seen as a safety-valve, a way of releasing the tension and pressure of the realities of life as a police officer.

This leads us to a second observation about police *culture*, namely the potentially misleading assumption that sometimes comes through in writing about the police, that the police service has a single, monolithic culture. In fact, as a sizeable body of work now illustrates, it is better to think either of police *cultures,* or *culture and subcultures*: there may be considerable cultural variation between and within police forces. One important distinction is that drawn by Ianni and Ianni (1983), who talk about 'street cops' and 'management cops' as representing two distinct, ideal-typical, types of

Excitement and the thrill of the chase – often referred to as 'blue-light syndrome' – are often cited as important elements of the job for police officers.

police culture. Reiner in his analysis of 'cop culture' identifies seven core characteristics of what in this regard we might think of as 'street cop' culture:

1 *Mission (Action-cynicism-pessimism)* – The view that it is not simply a job but has a wider purpose – a mission – linked with the preservation of order and, possibly, a particular type of order. This is also what tends to make it a *conservative* culture. It is also a potentially exciting mission, and it is often the exciting elements of the job that are highly prized by officers. The nature of the police routine also breeds cynicism and pessimism and a feeling of being part of a minority – a 'thin blue line' – standing in the way of moral and social decline.

2 *Suspicion* – Perhaps not surprisingly this is a job that requires suspiciousness. It is necessary to the job, and therefore tends to be reinforced by everyday working experiences, but is built in to police training.

3 *Isolation/solidarity* – For a number of reasons police culture tends to be characterised by a high degree of solidarity. In part the nature of the job, including the suspiciousness of others mentioned above, as well as the hours of work, the intensity of some of the work, and also the feeling of being part of a 'thin blue line', encourages officers to bond strongly. This is not to say that conflict is not present in police organisations – there is often considerable conflict – simply that officers come to rely on one another and to develop something of an 'us' and 'them' attitude.

4 *Conservatism* – For the reasons described above, police officers tend to inhabit a morally conservative world – much of what they do is, necessarily, focused on maintaining things as they are. There is also quite strong evidence that officers also tend toward political conservatism.

5 *Machismo* – The police world, as Reiner puts it, 'is one of old-fashioned machismo'. There are many characteristics which are highly valued within police culture and these will often include physical resilience, bravery and (male) sexual promiscuity. Police organisations are notoriously sexist and male-dominated. The first woman chief constable, Pauline Clare, was appointed to run Lancashire Constabulary in 1995 (166 years after the establishment of the new police).

6 *Racial prejudice* – A number of studies of police officers and policing have also shown clear evidence of racial prejudice. Despite considerable efforts in Britain to change recruitment patterns to the police service, minority ethnic recruitment remains low (see Chapter 31). In the aftermath of both the Scarman and the Lawrence Inquiries, reform of policing sought to reduce prejudice and encourage more constructive relationships between the police service and Britain's black and minority ethnic communities. There is evidence of change, but there are still clearly continuing problems in police community relations with ethnic minorities.

7 *Pragmatism* – Perhaps predictably, given what has been said about a culture that is action-oriented, conservative, and macho, police culture also tends to be quite pragmatic and down-to-earth. Though in recent years those in senior ranks have become rather more progressive and intellectual, the police service tends to be characterised by a 'can-do', achievement-orientated, frame of mind.

In addition to street cop culture Ianni and Ianni talked about 'management cops' whose general ethos was distinguishable from that of officers on the front line. This management cop culture, they argue, 'seeks to maximise those bureaucratic benefits that come from efficient organisation, rational decision-making, cost-effective procedures, and objective accountability at all levels of the organisation' (2004: 301). Both street cops and management cops traditionally share general organisation goals, they suggest, but differ in the ways in which they believe this is to be delivered. Over time, however, so embedded have these different cultures become that they no longer share a common vocabulary, a common set of work experiences or, some of the time, general work objectives. This in part explains, they suggest, the 'growing alienation' of the street cop, who is less and less likely to see those in positions of authority in the organisation as fellow professionals, and are more likely to see them as functionaries or bureaucrats. This, in turn, is likely to affect clients' experiences of police services.

Janet Chan (1997) offers four major criticisms of existing work on police culture:

1 Too often it is presented as if it were monolithic and universal.

2 It pays insufficient attention to individual agencies in the process of creating and learning

norms and rules; they tend to be treated as 'cultural dopes'.

3 Existing work underplays the importance of the social, political, legal and organisational context of policing.

4 Current theorisations of policing culture leave little room for the possibility of change.

So, how is it possible to change police culture? Chan's (1997) argument is that we can conceptualise the processes more clearly if we adopt and adapt the French sociologist Pierre Bordieu's terminology of *field* and *habitus*. 'Field' refers to the structural location of police work – the power relationships that structure the world within which policing operates, whereas '*habitus*' refers to 'cultural dispositions' – those perceptions, understandings, and forms of knowledge which guide action. She points to four dimensions of cultural knowledge:

1 Dictionary knowledge (establishes a categorisation of people that officers come into contact with).

2 Directory knowledge (informs officers about how to get their work done).

3 Recipe knowledge (prescribes acceptable and unacceptable practices).

4 Axiomatic knowledge (the basic rationale of policing).

In short, Chan's argument is that this elaboration of forms of cultural knowledge enables us better to understand how field and *habitus* interact and reinforce each other (or not as the case may be) in processes of change. She uses a sporting metaphor to explain this. If the rules of the game, or the physical space in which the game is played, is changed it will not, of necessity, lead the players to change their behaviour in a particular direction. Similarly, changing the objectives of the game may also affect behaviour, but unless these changes are reinforced by changes in the field, it is quite likely that behaviour may revert to its earlier patterns. In relation to policing, she argues therefore, old arguments about whether it is the rules governing policing or police culture itself that need to be changed are each shown to be insufficient.

Zero-tolerance policing

The background to the emergence of the term 'Zero-tolerance Policing' (ZTP) over the past decade has been both the reality and the politics of crime control in New York City. By the late 1980s New York City was in deep trouble. It was suffering severe economic depression following the stock market crash of 1987. The crack epidemic was at its height and levels of crime, especially serious violent crime and homicide, were at all time highs. In 1990, not long after his election as mayor of New York City, David Dinkins was attacked for lack of action against what was perceived to be the crisis-level scale of crime and violence in the city. The *New York Post* headlined its front page 'Dave, Do Something!', and *Time* magazine talked of the 'rotting of the big apple'.

One of Dinkins' responses to the crisis was the passage of the 'safe streets' legislation and the imposition of a new revenue tax, the 'Safe Streets Tax', across the city to pay for massive police recruitment. President Clinton had also made a promise to increase the number of police officers in the United States by 100,000 a key part of his 1992 presidential election campaign. Once elected, he set about fulfilling the promise and in 1994 enacted the Violent Crime Control and Law Enforcement Act. As a result of Dinkins' expansion plans, Clinton's COPS (community police officers) programme, and the absorption of the Transit Police (responsible for policing the subways), the New York City Police Department (NYPD) increased from 36,000 officers in 1990 to 47,000 in 1995. Despite the increases in police numbers, and the fact that crime was already beginning to fall, Dinkins lost the 1993 Mayoral election to an ex-federal prosecutor, Rudolph W. Giuliani.

Giuliani was elected on a quality of life and crime 'ticket', and one of his first acts was to look for a new chief of the NYPD. In due course, he appointed Bill Bratton, ex-chief in Boston and of New York's transit police. Whilst in charge of the transit police, Bratton had worked with George Kelling, one of the authors, with James Q. Wilson, of the famous 'Broken Windows' article in *Atlantic Monthly* (see Chapter 20). The fifth of the eight policing strategies adopted by the NYPD under Bratton was called 'Reclaiming the Public Spaces of New York'. It was, according to Bratton (1998: 228) the 'lynchpin' strategy:

> Boom boxes, squeegee people, street prostitutes, public drunks, panhandlers, reckless bicyclists, illegal after-hours joints, graffiti – New York was overrun … We could solve all the murders we liked, but if the average citizen was running a gauntlet of panhandlers every day on his way to and from work, he would want that issue solved.

Though Bratton avoided the term 'zero tolerance', his description of the NYPD's approach to

The face of zero-tolerance policing: Bill Bratton, chief of police in New York during its so-called 'zero-tolerance' days in the mid-1990s, now chief of the Los Angeles Police Department.

quality of life policing illustrates how the term might become associated with such a phrase:

> Previous police administrations had been handcuffed by restrictions. We took the handcuffs off. Department attorneys worked with precinct commanders to address the problems. We used civil law to enforce existing regulations against harassment, assault, menacing, disorderly conduct and damaging property. We stepped up enforcement of the laws against public drunkenness and public urination and arrested repeat violators, including those who threw empty bottles in the street or were involved in even relatively minor damage to property … If you peed in the street, you were going to jail. We were going to fix the broken windows and prevent anyone from breaking them again. (1998: 229)

The reason that the strategies adopted in New York have become so well-known – aside from the fact that they have been well-publicised – is that they have become associated with a quite remarkable drop in crime in the city. Although crime was dropping in the majority of major American cities during the 1990s, the extent and rate of decline was greater in New York than most – though not all. Thus, for example, between 1990 and 1998 homicide was down 72%, motor vehicle theft 70%, burglary 61%, robbery also 61%, larceny 49%, aggravated assault 36%, and forcible rape 35%. So significant were the drops in crime that what had occurred in New York was widely referred to as a 'miracle'. It is this drop in crime that has become associated, in Britain and elsewhere, with *zero-tolerance policing*.

In fact, it is difficult to identify the concrete elements of zero-tolerance policing because, in many respects, it was a media invention. Nevertheless, the key elements of what was called 'quality of life policing' in New York City were:

- vigorous law-enforcement responses to minor crime and disorder;
- the use of civil remedies against those perceived to be involved in criminal activities;
- enhanced accountability, using COMPSTAT (see box opposite), of local police managers for crime and disorder in their areas;
- public target-setting in relation to crime reduction;
- conspicuous use of the media as a public relations tool on behalf of the police and policing strategies;
- aggressive action against street crimes.

Although there has been a lot of talk in Britain about zero-tolerance policing, in fact British policing has remained largely resistant to many aspects of such an approach. In the few areas in the UK that did introduce policing initiatives that became associated with zero tolerance, they tended to adopt some of the elements of New York's 'quality of life' policing – most particularly the focus on enforcement strategies targeting low level crime and disorder (begging, squeegeeing, public drinking and the like), and the use of media and public target-setting as a means of highlighting the new strategic approach. In this way the UK policing initiatives that became associated with ZTP to differing degrees all involved enhanced levels of uniform patrol, a more vigorous approach to enforcing the law against minor offences and disorder, a heightened use of 'stop and search', the use of high profile 'crackdowns' against particular kinds of street offences, all packaged together in a rhetoric that promoted the 'reclaiming' of public spaces for 'decent' and 'law-abiding' people (Dennis and Mallon, 1997).

Nevertheless, it remains the case that most British police forces have been reluctant to adopt anything

Jack Maple on COMPSTAT

Jack Maple was Bill Bratton's second-in-command at the NYPD in the mid-1990s and was responsible for developing COMPSTAT, a method of collecting, mapping and disseminating crime records, and using these operationally.

Before long, I had reduced those ideas to four principles, which were to become our guideposts as we went about redefining the objectives, methods, and outcomes of the New York Police Department and, in turn, police organizations everywhere:

1 Accurate, timely intelligence
2 Rapid deployment
3 Effective tactics
4 Relentless follow-up and assessment

Relentless follow-up and assessment may have been the most important principle of the four, because it gave birth to weekly meetings at which [we] debriefed precinct, narcotics, and squad commanders about crime maps for their areas and gauged their ongoing compliance with the four fundamental principles:

1 Was the precinct or division's crime information timely and accurate?
2 Was deployment rapid, synchronized, and focused?
3 Were the tactics they used effective?
4 Were the commanders relentless about follow-up and assessment?

Nobody ever got in trouble because crime numbers on their watch went up ... Trouble arose only if the commanders didn't know why the numbers were up or didn't have a plan to address the problems.

The entire process, with meetings as its centerpiece, soon came to be known as 'Compstat'. (Maple, 1991)

that might smack of 'zero tolerance'. Why? To understand the reluctance of many senior officers to embrace such ideas one needs to go back as far as the early 1980s. The experience of the Brixton riots in 1981 and the urban disorders in other cities convinced Lord Scarman – who had been appointed by the government to conduct an inquiry into the Brixton disturbances (see box on next page) – and in turn convinced a lot of chief constables that many of the problems that had been experienced stemmed from the heavy-handed tactics adopted, as well as from the failure properly to consult the community.

The Scarman Inquiry

During the 1980s the Conservative Government introduced what has been described by one commentator as the 'single most significant landmark in the modern development of police powers': the Police and Criminal Evidence Act 1984 (PACE). The following year it also removed the police's prosecutorial role with the introduction of the Crown Prosecution Service (CPS), and in 1986 passed legislation to alter significantly the public order laws (via the Public Order Act 1986). All of these developments can, at least in part, be traced back to the urban unrest of 1981.

On 10 April 1981, an hour-long riot occurred in Brixton. This was the prelude to a full weekend of disorder in which over 400 police officers were reported injured, over 250 people arrested, and over 7,000 police officers were involved in attempting to restore order. Further serious disorder occurred in Liverpool, and later in the cities of Birmingham, Sheffield, Nottingham and Hull among others. Following a police raid on houses in Railton Road, rioting again broke out in Brixton in July, and then, briefly, again in Liverpool.

In the aftermath of the 1981 riots, Lord Scarman was appointed to inquire into the causes of the unrest in Brixton in April and to make recommendations. From the inception of the 'new police' onwards, there has been disagreement about the main or central functions of the police, and this was an issue that Scarman also tackled and which has continued to be the subject of vigorous debate since. Following Sir Robert Peel's formulation he highlighted 'the prevention of crime ... the protection of life and property, the preservation of public tranquillity' as the core policing duties, though in the event of a conflict of aims, he felt that the maintenance of public tranquillity was the primary responsibility – i.e. he recognised that there would inevitably be situations in which the enforcement of the law would have to come second to the maintenance of the public peace.

Lord Scarman presents his report into the 1981 Brixton riots in South London.

Scarman was critical of the policing of Brixton and especially the heavy-handed 'Swamp 81' operation. In response to high levels of street crime, a saturation exercise had been planned in which large numbers of police officers patrolling the streets and using 'stop and search' powers would attempt to 'detect and arrest burglars and robbers' (Scarman, 4.39). Scarman concluded that the lack of consultation with community representatives prior to 'Swamp 81' was 'an error of judgement' (Scarman Report, 4.73), that the whole operation 'was a serious mistake, given the tension which existed between the police and local community' (*ibid*, 4.76) and that 'had policing attitudes and methods been adjusted to deal fully with the problems of a multi-racial society, there would have been a review in depth of the public order implications of the operation, which would have included local consultation. And, had this taken place, I believe ... that a street "saturation" operation would not have been launched when it was' (*ibid*, 4.77).

In the aftermath of the Scarman Inquiry, as Reiner's (1991) research documented, there emerged a general consensus within British policing that viewed the type of tactics later associated with zero-tolerance policing as being counter-productive.

Police corruption

From the earliest days of the Bow Street Runners, through the formation of the new police in the 1820s, to the scandals in the 1960s and 1970s, policing in the UK has been punctuated with examples of malpractice and misconduct. The range of corrupt activities uncovered included the concealment of serious crimes, bribery, and the fabrication and planting of evidence. Modern day scandals of the sort characterised by the treatment of the *Birmingham Six*, the *Guildford Four*, to those involved in the Carl Bridgewater affair, have involved the suppression of evidence, the beating of suspects, tampering with confessional evidence and perjury.

The experience of the police service in the UK is in no way unique. The history of policing in other jurisdictions in places such as the United States and

Australia is similarly marked with examples of police malpractice and misconduct. The Knapp Commission which investigated the NYPD suggested that it suffered from corruption from the outset: systematic payoffs from brothels and gambling dens and shakedowns of small businesses were documented from the end of the nineteenth century through to the 1950s. During the 1970s widespread 'graft' and bribery covering drugs, vice, gambling enforcement and criminal investigation more generally were uncovered.

There has been no shortage of examples of misconduct and corruption in the history of policing. Indeed, it remains a real and live issue for the police service, and all major police forces or departments have large internal affairs departments whose work concentrates of tackling just such problems. Clearly, however, the range of activities that such departments must focus upon is hugely varied. Attempting to define corruption is therefore far from straightforward though it is generally agreed that it necessarily involves an abuse of position. In Kleinig's view, 'Police officers act corruptly when, in exercising or failing to exercise their authority, they act with the primary intention of furthering private or departmental/divisional advantage'. A typology of corrupt acts is set out below in Figure 25.7.

There have been a number of interesting treatments of the corruption problem in policing. Much of the literature focuses on the more serious end of corrupt activities – things where there is little doubt about their corrupt nature – and we will consider some of this a little later. However, there is also much to be gained by focusing on the ethical issues raised by much less straightforwardly *corrupt* activities. In particular, an interesting debate has emerged in relation to the question of whether, and under what circumstances, it is appropriate for police officers to accept 'gratuities': small favours like a free cup of coffee or free meal. The reason that this is important is that it raises the question of ethics, and there is much to be said for the view that police corruption and misconduct is fundamentally a question of ethics. As to the question of accepting gratuities, like so many ethical questions, the answers are far from straightforward. You might like to think about your own views before looking at the list of pros and cons below in Figure 25.8.

The causes of police corruption

When confronted with allegations of corruption for which there is supporting evidence, police agencies will frequently claim that the problem

Figure 25.7	Types and dimensions of police corruption
Type	**Dimensions**
Corruption of authority	When an officer receives some form of material gain by virtue of their position as a police officer without violating the law *per se* (e.g. free drinks, meals, services, etc.)
'Kickbacks'	Receipt of goods, services or money for referring business to particular individuals or companies
Opportunistic theft	Stealing from arrestees (sometimes referred to as 'rolling'), from traffic accident victims, crime victims and the bodies or property of dead citizens
'Shakedowns'	Acceptance of a bribe for not following through a criminal violation, e.g. not making an arrest, filing a complaint or impounding property
Protection of illegal activities	Police protection of those engaged in illegal activities (prostitution, drugs, pornography) enabling the business to continue operating
'The fix'	Undermining of criminal investigations or proceedings, or the 'loss' of traffic tickets
Direct criminal activities	A police officer commits a crime against a person or property for personal gain 'in clear violation of both departmental and criminal norms'
Internal payoffs	Privileges available to police officers (holidays, shift allocations, promotion) are bought, bartered and sold
'Flaking' or 'padding'	Planting or adding to evidence (argued by Punch [1985] to be particularly evident in drugs cases)

Figure 25.8	Arguments supporting and opposing the acceptance of gratuities
Arguments in support of acceptance	
Appreciation	Natural and reasonable to show appreciation to those providing a public service. Rude to refuse
Not significant	Gratuities are not significant enough to buy or cultivate favour
Officially offered	When offered officially by a company or corporation (e.g. the discounted 'Big-Mac' that McDonalds® have offered in some jurisdictions to police officers) involves no personal sense of obligation
Links with the community	Part and parcel of fostering close links with the community, including business people. In turn, a fundamental of 'good policing'
Police culture	An entrenched part of police culture. Any attempt to end it will result in displeasure and cynicism
Trust and discretion	Attempts to prohibit acceptance imply that officers cannot be trusted to exercise discretion and are incapable of making sensible moral judgements to guide their behaviour
Arguments in opposition to acceptance	
Sense of obligation	Even the smallest gift inevitably creates a sense of obligation if it becomes regularised
'Slippery slope'	Gratuities lead to a 'slippery slope' where the temptations become imperceptibly greater and refusal increasingly difficult
Remove temptation	Not all officers can exercise proper judgement on what is reasonable to accept. More sensible for the organisation to remove temptation altogether
Purchase preferential treatment	Businesses which offer gratuities are, in essence, seeking to purchase preferential treatment (e.g. encourage greater police presence in the vicinity of their business)

identified is limited to a small number of corrupt officers who are quite unrepresentative of the wider standards exhibited by the organisation. Thus, during the Knapp Commission hearing, representatives of the NYPD argued that the corruption uncovered by Officer Serpico and others was confined to a few 'rotten apples'. The Commission's view, however, was different:

> According to this theory, which bordered on official Department doctrine, any policeman found to be corrupt must promptly be denounced as a rotten apple in an otherwise clean barrel. It must never be admitted that his individual corruption may be symptomatic of underlying disease ... A high command unwilling to acknowledge that the problem of

corruption is extensive cannot very well argue that drastic changes are necessary to deal with the problem.

The Knapp Commission concluded that corrupt 'pads' existed in every plain clothes gambling-enforcement squad in New York, and that corruption could be found, indeed, was often extensively found, in drugs enforcement, criminal investigation and in uniformed patrol. A system of internal corruption, where managerial discretion and favour were bought and sold in a marketplace of payoffs, was also uncovered. Corrupt practices were highly and often sophisticatedly organised, and were protected and reinforced by tolerance of or selective blindness towards it by non-participating officers. This led the famously reformist

Frank Serpico, a NYPD detective in the 1960s, famously sought to report corruption within the police department, eventually taking his story to the *New York Times*. His experiences, including being shot in an attempt to prevent him testifying against fellow officers, formed the subject of a subsequent film starring Al Pacino. *Above Left:* the real Frank Serpico in 1971. *Above right:* Al Pacino as Serpico in a still from the film.

Commissioner of the NYPD, Patrick V. Murphy, to conclude:

> The 'rotten apple' theory won't work any longer. Corrupt police officers are not natural-born criminals, nor morally wicked men, constitutionally different from their honest colleagues. The task of corruption control is to examine the barrel, not just the apples – the organisation, not just the individuals in it – because corrupt police are made, not born.

The reasons for corruption are to be found in the nature of the police organisation and the way it is sometimes run, as well as in the wider context in which police officers operate. The varying causal factors are summarised in Figure 25.9.

A review of research literature in the field of corruption (Newburn, 1999) concluded that the 'bad apple' theory of corruption has been all but fully discredited. Successive major commissions of inquiry have catalogued the ways in which corruption is frequently highly organised and systematic. It is possible to make a number of general observations about police corruption:

- Police corruption is pervasive, continuing and not bounded by rank.

- The boundary between 'corrupt' and 'non-corrupt' activities is difficult to define, primarily because this is an ethical problem.

- The 'causes' of corruption include factors that are intrinsic to policing as a job, the nature of police organisations and 'culture' and the opportunities open to police officers.

- Some areas ('vice', drugs, gambling) of policing are more prone to corruption than others.

- Corrupt police departments/forces can be successfully reformed.

- Reform, however, tends not to be durable and constant vigilance is necessary.

Figure 25.9	Causal factors affecting the development of corrupt practices

A. Constant factors

Discretion	The exercise of discretion is argued to have both legitimate and illegitimate bases
Low managerial visibility	A police officer's actions are often low in visibility as far as line management is concerned
Low public visibility	Much of what police officers do is not witnessed by members of the public
Peer group secrecy	'Police culture' is characterised by a high degree of internal solidarity and secrecy
Managerial secrecy	Police managers have generally worked themselves up from the 'beat' and share many of the values held by those they manage
Status problems	Police officers are sometimes said to be poorly paid relative to their powers
Association with law-breakers/ contact with temptation	Police officers inevitably come into contact with a wide variety of people who have an interest in police not doing what they have a duty to do. Such people may have access to considerable resources

B. Variable factors

Community structure	Refers to the extent of conflict within the community, the level of corruption in public life, and other indicators of 'health' in public life
Organisational characteristics	Levels of bureaucracy, integrity of leadership, solidarity of work subcultures, moral career stages of police officers, and the perception of legitimate opportunities
Legal opportunities for corruption	Moral: so-called 'victimless crimes' associated with the policing of 'vice'. Regulative: the exploitation of minor or trivial regulations such as those associated with construction, traffic and licensing
Corruption controls	How the guardians are themselves 'guarded'
Social organisation of corruption	Two basic forms: 'arrangements' (where corruption is regularised) and 'events' (which are more 'one-off' activities). The former are easier to detect
'Moral cynicism'	Association with lawbreakers and contact with temptation is inevitable in police work, inclining officers towards moral cynicism

Police governance

Prior to the 1964 Police Act two systems of governance existed outside London. In urban areas there were Watch Committees, made up entirely of local councillors, who were frequently active in the management and oversight of their local police forces. The early chief officer of borough police forces was merely 'the superintending or executive officer of the watch committee'. In rural areas, and very much in contrast, there were joint standing committees in which non-elected magistrates played an important role and where the chief officers were much less tightly controlled.

The 1964 Police Act smoothed out these differences and created a unified system of police governance. It created what has become known as the tripartite structure for police governance. *Tripartite* because it has three parts, the three being what might these days be called the main stakeholders in policing: the Home Secretary, the chief constable, and the local police authority. Crucially, the Police Act placed forces under the 'direction and control' of its chief constable. The Act represented another important step in reducing the power and influence of local authorities and although there have been brief moments – not least in the 1970s – when local councils have attempted to exert what

Figure 25.10 The tripartite structure

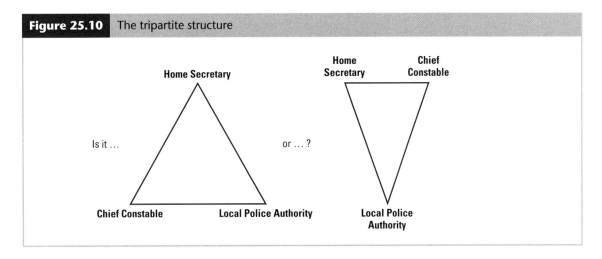

authority they have, this is a process that continued for much of the rest of the century.

As a consequence, although the ideal behind the tripartite structure is often represented as an equilateral triangle, indicating that the three main parties are in some form of roughly equal balance, many commentators have argued that an isosceles triangle – with Home Secretary and Chief Constable being the most powerful players in the relationship – better represents the reality of policing in recent decades (see Figure 25.10).

The exceptions to this new system of governance were the Metropolitan and the City of London Police forces which continued to be responsible to the Home Secretary and the City of London Authority respectively. For the 41 police forces outside London, the Act specified the duties and responsibilities of each of the members of the tripartite structure.

In making sense and bringing some order to discussions of police accountability there is a very useful distinction drawn by Geoffrey Marshall between two ideal typical models of governance. These he called the 'explanatory and co-operative' and the 'subordinate and obedient'. To these a third has been added by Robert Reiner which he called 'calculative and contractual'. Marshall's argument was that despite the fact that many had hoped that the 1964 Act would produce a form of stringent oversight along the lines he characterised as 'subordinate and obedient', in practice, either by accident or design, very considerable powers had been left in the hands of chief constables and therefore the system of governance would more realistically be characterised as 'explanatory and co-operative'.

As we shall see, developments since the Police Act have further reduced the powers of local police

authorities and, in many respects, enhanced the power of government. In surveying the field in the early 1990s, Reiner noted the shift there had been towards a more financially-oriented set of concerns about policing. Increasingly, government was using financial and performance management and audit techniques to steer local police services. This new mode of governance he called 'calculative and contractual'. The key attributes of each of these three types are set out below in Figure 25.11.

Significant reform of police governance was brought about by the Police and Magistrates' Courts Act 1994. Passed by a Conservative government, the Act changed the composition of police authorities – specifically by introducing what became known as 'independent members' to these committees, and reducing the number of elected councillors and magistrates. Henceforward, the

Figure 25.11 Three ideal-types of police accountability

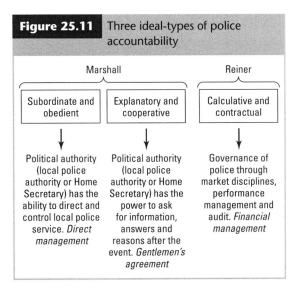

majority of police authorities were to be made up of 17 members (nine councillors, five independent members and three magistrates).

Equally importantly, the police authorities themselves became independent of local authority structures, and their duty became that of providing an 'efficient and effective' police force (under the 1964 Act it had been to provide an 'adequate and efficient' force). The other significant reform was to introduce a requirement that in future police authorities would produce an annual policing plan, containing local police objectives and related performance targets. It was these changes, among others, that led Reiner to describe this mode of governance as 'calculative and contractual'.

In fact, the shift was signalled in the early 1980s when, as part of their more general Financial Management Initiative, the then Conservative government began to emphasise the importance of what it termed the 3Es – *economy, efficiency* and *effectiveness* – in the ordering of public services. Gradually the calculative and contractual mode of governance took hold and by the early 1990s it underpinned the majority of government attempts at reform of police organisation and practice. A number of inquiries set in train at this time – including the Sheehy Inquiry and the Review of Core and Ancilliary Tasks – were all influenced by private sector ideas and ideals and all sought to make the police more competitive. By the late 1990s, many of the accoutrements of private sector management – fixed term contracts, performance-related pay, competitive tendering, league tables and (key) performance indicators – had become part of the everyday reality of policing.

The election of a Labour government in 1997 also heralded some changes in police governance. Initially, these concerned the role of the police in what by now was being called 'community safety'. In particular, the Crime and Disorder Act 1998 (see Chapter 24) placed a statutory responsibility upon police forces, in partnership with local authorities, to audit local crime problems and produce a local community safety plan – now known as a crime and disorder reduction plan.

Successive governments in the 1980s and 1990s had talked about reform of policing, but the majority had shied away from the battles that would inevitably be involved. In their second administration, however, it appeared that the Labour government had slightly more appetite for the fight. Particularly under David Blunkett as Home Secretary, there were successive reforms that began to have a quite significant effect on the landscape of British policing. The Police Reform Act 2002, for example, introduced a highly centralising measure, the Annual Policing Plan, in which governmental priorities were to be set out and against which police performance was to be assessed. The Act also gave the Home Secretary powers to intervene in forces where its performance had been judged to be inefficient or ineffective.

In recent times, further reform has been proposed. Many in government and the police service

Key developments in police accountability

Police Act 1964

Established the 'tripartite structure', setting out the roles and responsibilities of the three main elements in the direction and control of policing: chief constable, Home Secretary, and local police authority. Introduced formal police complaints system.

Police and Criminal Evidence Act 1984

Sought to establish a balance between police powers – of stop and search, arrest, detention and interrogation – and suspects' rights. Established the Police Complaints Authority (with greater independence from the police).

Police and Magistrates' Courts Act 1994

Reformed local police authorities: reduced number of elected representatives and introduced 'independent' members. Made police authorities more 'businesslike'. Introduced local policing plans.

Crime and Disorder Act 1998

Introduced Crime and Disorder Partnerships (now Crime and Disorder Reduction Partnerships) in which police and local authorities have joint responsibility for producing a local crime audit and for publishing and implementing plans to reduce crime and disorder locally.

Police Reform Act 2002

Gave Home Secretary power to publish an annual policing plan which would contain objectives for all police forces. Increased government's powers to intervene to take over the running of 'failing forces'.

have taken the view that there is no longer any justification for preserving the contemporary structure of 43 constabularies. Although financial and political considerations appear to have put reform on hold, as argued earlier it appears only a matter of time before a reduction to approximately 20 forces or fewer will be announced. This will, of course, have very significant implications for police governance. Police authorities will have to be reformed.

In many cases, force sizes will mean that an authority at force level will inevitably be rather detached from local concerns and needs. The implication, therefore, is that consideration will eventually have to be given to the establishment of some form of local policing forum at local divisional or what is known as Basic Command Unit (BCU) level. Overall, then, policing is being pulled in different directions. One set of pressures is progressively creating bigger and bigger police forces and possibly eventually a national police force (and at the same time *trans-national* policing bodies are also appearing – see Chapter 19), whilst simultaneously other influences endeavour to make policing locally focused and accountable. Not only is the shape of public policing changing, but the range of bodies involved in policing activity appears to continue to grow, and it is to this we turn next.

Plural policing

Michael Banton opened his classic study of British policing with the observation that:

> A cardinal principle for the understanding of police organisation and activity is that the police are only one among many agencies of social control.

Despite this, the bulk of sociological or criminological writing on the subject of policing has focused on *the police,* that body of largely uniformed representatives of the state, exercising powers to use force that are generally unavailable to others. So far, this chapter has been no exception, beginning with a history of public policing, looking at police powers, the governance of the police, and considering how we might characterise police culture and understand police corruption. However, as has become increasingly visible in recent decades, there are many aspects of policing beyond the police. There appears, for example, to have been a very significant expansion in private security in recent times. Closed-circuit television cameras now survey every city centre, walled and gated communities are beginning to spring up and a growing array of uniformed guards, wardens and others are to be found patrolling streets and local communities.

The rise of private security – 'policing beyond the police'. *Left*: A security guard at work in a modern shopping centre. *Right*: An increasingly common notice warning of 24-hour surveillance.

Police community support officers (PCSOs) on patrol in London. An example of the increased pluralisation of policing, PCSOs 'support the work of your local police and provide a visible and reassuring presence on the streets' (Home Office websites).

the state, civil society and the market have been restructured.

7 Government policy has gradually extended beyond crime to take in fear of crime, disorderliness and anti-social behaviour.

8 The period since the Second World War has seen the gradual decline and, in some cases, disappearance of 'secondary social control occupations' (such as park keepers, and train guards and bus conductors).

Having considered some of the broad changes underpinning the growing pluralisation of policing, let's now examine some of the features of the contemporary landscape of policing. One of these concerns the emergence of what is currently referred to as the 'extended policing family'. This odd term refers to the broadening array of organisations and agencies that now tend to be found working in partnership with the police in the provision of services. One of the areas where significant changes have been seen is in that symbolically most important area of police activity: patrol.

In 2001 a Home Office White Paper (*Policing a New Century*) proposed that agents and agencies such as neighbourhood and street wardens, security guards in shopping centres, park keepers and

Crawford (2003) identifies eight trends that set the context for understanding the growing pluralisation of policing:

1 Crime and fear of crime have become increasingly important and visible parts of social life in the last 30–40 years. Related to this, the demand for security has also become a central feature of contemporary life.

2 Recognition of the limits of the formal criminal justice generally, and the police more particularly, has been growing.

3 The idea of the state's monopoly over crime control and security has become increasingly hard to sustain.

4 Financial constraints have progressively limited what public bodies such as the police can be asked to perform.

5 As state agencies and the formal justice system have come under increasing pressure, so crime prevention has grown in importance and emphasis.

6 There has been a trend toward the increasing dispersal of responsibility for crime control beyond the state as the relationships between

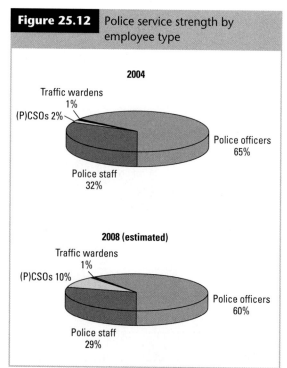

Figure 25.12 Police service strength by employee type

2004

Traffic wardens 1%
(P)CSOs 2%
Police officers 65%
Police staff 32%

2008 (estimated)

Traffic wardens 1%
(P)CSOs 10%
Police officers 60%
Police staff 29%

Sources: Christopherson and Cotton (2004: 2); Crawford *et al.* (2005: 12).

other 'authority figures' could be accredited by, and work alongside, the police in a formal capacity. More controversially, the government also proposed a power to enable chief constables to appoint support staff to provide a visible presence (to patrol) in the community.

These '(police) community support officers' that were eventually introduced by the Police Reform Act 2002 are under the control of the chief constable and have limited powers to detain suspects, to stop vehicles and to issue fixed-penalty notices. The first PCSOs started patrolling and their numbers have expanded markedly in the years since, now numbering well over 6,000. The Home Office targets are for them to reach 25,000 in the next few years. PCSOs currently account for approximately two per cent of police service strength and are set to expand to at least ten per cent (see Figure 25.12).

Besides the main constabularies, what are the other main organisations and agencies involved in policing? The box below provides an overview of the five main categories of policing bodies. We have already considered 'Home Office forces' in some detail. In addition there are numerous *specialist policing bodies*. Some of the longest standing, though least known, are the security services. The UK has two primary security services: MI5 (responsible for internal or domestic security) and MI6

(responsible for the gathering of intelligence from overseas). The reason for including the security services in a discussion of policing is that such bodies, though not terribly visible, are heavily involved in policing activities – not least in relation to anti-terrorist activity. Other specialist bodies include the British Transport Police – a force with responsibility for policing the main railway and other public transport facilities – and investigators and others employed by other government departments such as the Department of Social Security and the Inland Revenue.

Municipal policing is one of the areas that has expanded markedly in the last decade. Some local authorities have a long history of employing their own patrol services. Wandsworth in London, for example, has had a Parks Police for over 20 years. The officers, who are sworn constables, are responsible for maintaining order in the parks and open spaces in the borough and, where necessary, make arrests and do many of the other things one would expect a police service to undertake. With the growth of the anti-social behaviour agenda since the mid-1990s there has been a significant expansion of local authority involvement in the application of, and *policing* of, ASBOs (see Chapter 24). Another relatively recent development has been the growth of 'public auxiliaries' such as wardens. Since the

The main policing bodies in England and Wales

Home Office police forces
- 43 police forces in England and Wales
- Central agencies – Serious and Organised Crime Agency

Specialist policing bodies
- State security services (MI5/MI6)
- Customs and Excise
- British Transport Police
- State department investigators – DSS, Inland Revenue
- Regulatory authorities – Health and Safety Executive
- Trading Standards Officers

Municipal policing
- Environmental health officers
- Public auxiliaries

- Traffic wardens
- Community safety partnerships
- Anti-social behaviour teams
- Policing through housing and education

Civilian policing
- Special constabulary
- Neighbourhood watch
- Citizens' patrols
- Vigilantism

Commercial policing
- Staffed services – security guards, etc.
- Private investigation services
- Installation and monitoring of security equipment

Source: Based on Fig.7.1 in Crawford (2003).

government's Social Exclusion Unit recommended the introduction of neighbourhood wardens in the late 1990s, there has been considerable expenditure by local authorities in this area.

Finally, we have *commercial policing*. This is what otherwise might generally be referred to as private security. It comprises a uniform sector – private security guarding – together with private investigatory services and all those involved in the installation and monitoring of security equipment: CCTV, alarms and the like. Although it appears that the commercial policing sector has expanded markedly in recent times, now outstripping the number of police officers, it is easy to exaggerate the novelty in this. In fact, research using data from the UK census suggests that the number of private security guards was greater than the number of police officers as early as 1961 (see Table 25.3).

Though long-standing then, it is undoubtedly the case that the last two decades or so have seen a number of important changes in the general shape of policing, not least the increasingly visibility of a mixed economy of provision. So complex has this become, and so profoundly do some feel this has changed the role of policing, that there are commentators – such as Shearing and Johnston – who argue that rather than using the term *policing* it is now more accurate to think of this array of activities and providers as being involved in the *governance of security*.

A revolution in policing?

Clearly there have been some very spectacular changes in policing in recent times – not least in the spread and growth of privatised security. The question of how significant a change this represents has been the cause of a certain amount of debate within criminology. Writing in the mid-1990s, two eminent criminologists, David Bayley and Clifford Shearing, argued that modern societies 'have reached a watershed in the evolution of their systems of crime control and law enforcement' and that 'future generations will look back on our era as a time when one system of policing ended and another took its place' (1996: 585).

At the heart of Bayley and Shearing's argument is the suggestion that recent decades have witnessed the ending of the public monopoly in policing. By this they mean that where once the bulk of policing was undertaken by the public police, it is now increasingly undertaken by a range of public and private bodies. In particular, they argue, the fact that private security guards now outnumber police officers in many countries is clear evidence of the end of the public monopoly. Second, they argue that the public police have been conducting a 'search for identity' – the public police have increasingly come to question their role, they suggest. This can be seen in a number of ways:

- The 'visible deterrent' of patrol has declined as the police have been submerged by increases in emergency calls from the public.
- Clear-up rates are low, and in many cases, declining.
- There has been a continuous search for new approaches (such as community policing and problem-oriented policing).
- There is increasingly rigorous supervision of policing by government.

This portrayal of contemporary policing has been questioned, most notably in a response by Jones and Newburn (2002). They argue that to talk of a 'public monopoly' in policing is misleading for such a thing has never existed. In fact, the notion of a public monopoly was a myth created to sustain and legitimise public policing. The extent to which it has taken hold as an idea reflects the relative success of that legitimisation project. This is not to deny the reality of some very significant changes in policing in recent decades – not least the process of pluralisation outlined earlier. However, Jones and Newburn go on to argue that the growth of private security, for example, is not as recent or quite as dramatic as the 'transformation thesis' would imply. Thus, there is ample evidence to suggest that there were more private security guards than police officers in the early 1960s and that at the height of the era when a supposed 'public monopoly' existed – the 1940–50s – there was already a very sizeable private security industry (see Table 25.3).

Table 25.3	Changes in commercial and public policing employment 1951–2001			
	1951	**1971**	**1991**	**2001**
Police officers	84,585	115,170	149,964	166,407
Security guards	66,950	129,670	159,704	161,013

Source: Jones and Newburn (2006: 42).

Jones and Newburn argue that the real 'transformation' that is taking place concerns something considerably broader than simply 'policing'. They argue that what we have been witnessing over the past half-century or longer is the gradual and sustained formalisation of social control. To illustrate this they distinguish between 'primary' and 'secondary' social control activities. *Primary social control* activities or occupations they define as those forms of crime control, order maintenance and so on that are undertaken as a core part of an occupational role, e.g. police forces, regulatory bodies and private security.

Secondary social control activities are forms of order maintenance, crime control and so on that are undertaken, but not as a primary or defining part of the job, e.g. park-keepers, railway guards, bus conductors, etc. Using data from the census they are able to show that the last half-century has seen a dramatic decline in secondary social control occupations, just as primary social control occupations have expanded substantially (see Table 25.4).

More recently, Lucia Zedner (2005) has offered a critique of both Bayley and Shearing and Jones and Newburn. In an historical overview she explores the emergence and development of policing in Britain and argues that rather than seeing the current trends as indicating that a new system of

policing is emerging, it is more accurate to see them displaying significant links with the period before the new police emerged. That is to say, in the eighteenth century, for example, much crime control activity remained the responsibility of individuals, communal self-help and private provision. Crime control was gradually taken over by state provision – in the shape of the police – but is now in flux with community-based and private forms of provision coming to the fore. Whether one sides with Bayley and Shearing, Jones and Newburn, or Zedner in this debate, what is clear is that important shifts have been taking place, and that the policing arrangements associated with Dixon of Dock Green (see Chapter 4) are long gone.

Review questions

1 What are the main characteristics of police culture?

2 What are the main causes of police corruption?

3 What do we mean by zero-tolerance policing?

4 Distinguish between the three main models of police governance.

Table 25.4	Primary and secondary social control occupations in Britain		
	1951	**1971**	**1991**
Police officers	84,585	115,170	149,964
Security guards and related	66,950	129,670	159,704
'Roundsmen/roundswomen'*	98,143	48,360	49,182
Bus (and tram) conductors	96,558	57,550	2,471
Rail ticket inspectors/guards	35,715	46,800	15,642

* people delivering door-to-door

Source: Jones and Newburn (2002:141).

Questions for further discussion

1 How useful is the term 'police culture'?

2 Is police corruption generally a question of a 'few bad apples'?

3 Are we witnessing a revolution in policing?

4 How important are the police in policing?

5 Is police governance now largely about financial management?

Further reading

Robert Reiner's (2000) *The Politics of the Police*, Oxford: Oxford University Press remains the single most important overview of the sociology of policing in Britain.

The most comprehensive and up-to-date review of most aspects of contemporary policing by the leading authors in the field can be found in Newburn, T. (ed.) (2003) *Handbook of Policing*, Cullompton: Willan

A broad selection of classic and contemporary articles and readings can be found in Newburn, T. (ed.) (2004) *Policing: Key Readings*, Cullompton: Willan

Other texts that provide useful material include:

Henry, A. and Smith, D. (eds) (2007) *Transformations of Policing*, Aldershot: Ashgate

McLaughlin, E. (2006) *The New Policing*, London: Sage

Rowe, M. (ed.) (2007) *Policing Beyond Macpherson*, Cullompton: Willan.

Websites

The main official site for information on the police is: http://www.police.uk/

Local forces will have their own websites and you can find these easily via Google.

The Home Office has several sites (Research and Statistics, Policing) that contain useful data on research and on reform. See, for example:

http://police.homeoffice.gov.uk/
http://www.homeoffice.gov.uk/rds/policerspubs1.html

The Centre for Problem-oriented Policing has a mass of useful crime prevention-related material: http://www.popcenter.org/

Chapter outline

Introduction	638
The Crown Prosecution Service (CPS)	638
Sufficient evidence	639
The public interest	640
Downgrading of charges	641
Discontinuance	641
Magistrates' courts	641
The magistracy	642
The Crown Court	643
The judiciary	643
Juries	644
Pre-trial decisions	645
Bail and remand	645
Bail	646
Remand	647
Offending while on bail	648
Mode of trial decision	649
Defendants' rights	650
Pleas and bargaining	651
Charge bargaining	651
Plea bargaining	652
Evidence	653
Disclosure	653
Exclusion	654
Appeals	654
Miscarriages of justice	655
Criminal Cases Review Commission (CCRC)	656
Questions for further discussion	657
Further reading	657
Websites	657

26

Criminal courts and the court process

The criminal process generally begins when someone is arrested. Given that, as we have already seen in previous chapters, only a proportion of such cases eventually end up in a criminal court, the first question is whether charges will be brought against a suspect.

In this chapter we look at:

- the procedures involved and the reasons why criminal charges may not be brought;

- what happens to cases thereafter;

- the prosecution process, beginning by looking at the two main parts of the court system in England and Wales: magistrates' courts and the Crown Court.

There are a number of important elements of criminal procedure that govern the way in which cases proceed through the criminal justice system, and we look at;

- how decisions are made about whether defendants will be bailed or will be remanded in custody;

- the bargaining that occurs around both charges and pleas;

- the nature of evidence;

- mode of trial decisions;

- the appeal system.

Introduction

In the previous chapter we considered the powers of stop and search, arrest and detention available to the police, together with some of the issues that arise in relation to police questioning of suspects in the police station. Once questioning has ended, a number of choices face the police. They can release the person concerned – possibly for further inquiries to be made prior to further questioning taking place, or simply make an end to this inquiry. The alternative is to bring charges. This, however, is no longer a police responsibility, but is undertaken by an independent body – the Crown Prosecution Service.

The Crown Prosecution Service (CPS)

When crime control was a largely community-based activity, rather than something organised by the state, prosecutions largely relied upon the victim bringing a case against an offender. The development of formalised and bureaucratic police forces from the early nineteenth century gradually shifted this responsibility, with the police acquiring greater and greater power to bring prosecutions. The police remained the main prosecuting authority in criminal cases until the mid-1980s – though prosecutions were also brought by the Director of Public Prosecutions (in murder and a limited number of other highly serious cases) and by other regulatory bodies such as Customs and Excise, the Inland Revenue and local authorities.

There were increasing concerns about the police role in prosecution, stimulated amongst other things by the *Confait case* (see box below), which led to the establishment of a Royal Commission on Criminal Procedure which reported in 1981.

The Royal Commission favoured the establishment of an independent prosecution system and, in due course, the Crown Prosecution Service (CPS) was established as a result of the Prosecution of Offences Act 1985. The Act requires the CPS to publish a Code for Crown Prosecutors which sets out its operating principles and practices, and it has done so and revised the Code several times since.

The CPS is organised into 42 local branches and a headquarters. It is headed by the Director of Public

The Confait case

Concerning the case of Maxwell Confait, a young man murdered in April 1972.

After a short period, three young men were arrested. The oldest, though aged 18, had a mental age of eight. The other two arrested were aged 15 and 14. Although all three had alibis for the time the police surgeon originally estimated death to have occurred, two confessed to the murder and one to witnessing it and to setting fire to the house in which the murder took place.

Of the three, one was convicted of manslaughter on the grounds of diminished responsibility and the other two of arson and burglary. Their initial appeals, alleging they had been beaten by the police, were unsuccessful. After much public concern and political debate, the convictions were eventually overturned in the Court of Appeal in 1975. Evidence which emerged some years later completely exonerated the three young men.

An official inquiry led by Sir Henry Fisher, which reported in 1977, was highly critical of the treatment of the suspects by the police: they were interviewed without an adult present, were not informed of their rights, and were subjected to highly oppressive questioning. His call for the reform of the Judges' Rules led to the subsequent establishment of the Royal Commission on Criminal Procedure.

Prosecutions who is accountable to the Attorney General. The Attorney General answers to parliament on matters of policy in relation to the work of the CPS, but not in relation to individual cases.

The role of the CPS has changed somewhat over the past two decades or so of operation. In the aftermath of the Glidewell Review in 1998 there has been a greater use of trained but not legally qualified staff by the CPS to undertake the preparation of cases and even the presentation of some cases in the magistrates' courts (Glidewell, 1998). As a result of the Glidewell Review, the CPS increasingly viewed itself as independent of, but not entirely separate from, the police. CPS lawyers were placed within criminal justice units at police stations and this further reduced the administrative distance and increased the degree of collaboration between the two organisations.

More far-reaching changes were recommended by the review of criminal courts conducted by Lord Justice Auld. The Auld Review (2001: 399) called for an expanded role for the CPS:

The prosecutor should take control of cases at the charge or, where appropriate, pre-charge, stage, fix on the right charges from the start and keep to them, assume a more direct role than at present on disclosure and develop a more proactive role in shaping the case for trial, communicating appropriately and promptly with all those concerned. For all this the Service needs greater legal powers, in particular the power to determine the initial charge.

The subsequent Criminal Justice Act 2003 extended the remit of the CPS along these lines, giving them greater flexibility to take decisions and introducing what has become known as a 'statutory charging scheme' under which the bulk of charging decisions, excepting minor cases, are made by the CPS rather than the police. There had anyway been greater joint working between CPS and police in recent times, partly in an attempt to reduce misunderstandings, conflicts and disputes between the two agencies.

Sufficient evidence

In relation to prosecution, Ashworth and Redmayne (2005) argue that one of the basic principles of criminal justice should be that there should be strict safeguards against the bringing of proceedings in court unless there is sufficient evidence to do so. Or, as they put it, not only should innocent people not be convicted, but they should not be prosecuted. There are two reasons for this:

● Such a barrier is a further protection against the possibility that an innocent person might be convicted.

● The process of prosecution is a major imposition, involving time, stress and possible social stigma. Indeed, it may be experienced as a punishment in itself and, therefore, wherever possible ought not to be imposed on the innocent.

Now, it cannot be known who is innocent in all cases, with certainty, in advance of bringing a prosecution. The test becomes whether there is deemed to be sufficient evidence. How is *sufficiency* to be assessed? Historically, the *'prima facie* test' was used by the police. This sought to assess whether the available evidence would, if accepted, result in a conviction by a reasonable jury or magistrates' court. The Code for Crown Prosecutors has subsequently used a test in which the available evidence is felt to provide a 'realistic prospect of conviction'.

In applying such a test the prosecutor must take into account the credibility of the evidence and the likely lines of defence that will be used in court.

The public interest

In 1951, the Attorney General, argued that 'It has never been the rule in this country – I hope it never will be – that suspected criminal offences must automatically be the subject of prosecution' (*Hansard,* HC vol. 483, col. 681, 29). This principle means that it is not only a question of having sufficient evidence which affects the decision whether a prosecution will be brought, but also whether it is in the public interest. In this manner, the 2004 Code for Crown Prosecutors states (http://www.cps.gov.uk/victims_witnesses/code.html):

> A prosecution will usually take place unless there are public interest factors tending against prosecution which clearly outweigh those tending in favour, or it appears more appropriate in all the circumstances of the case to divert the person from prosecution.

The factors considered to favour prosecution include:

- A conviction is likely to result in a significant sentence, in a confiscation or any other order.
- A weapon was used or violence was threatened during the commission of the offence.
- The offence was committed against a person serving the public (for example, a police or prison officer, or a nurse).
- The defendant was in a position of authority or trust.
- The evidence shows that the defendant was a ringleader or an organiser of the offence.
- There is evidence that the offence was premeditated.
- There is evidence that the offence was carried out by a group.
- The victim of the offence was vulnerable, has been put in considerable fear, or suffered personal attack, damage or disturbance.
- The offence was committed in the presence of, or in close proximity to, a child.
- The offence was motivated by any form of discrimination against the victim's ethnic or national origin, disability, sex, religious beliefs, political views or sexual orientation, or the suspect demonstrated hostility towards the victim based on any of those characteristics.

- The defendant's previous convictions or cautions are relevant to the present offence.
- The defendant is alleged to have committed the offence while under an order of the court.
- There are grounds for believing that the offence is likely to be continued or repeated, for example, by a history of recurring conduct.

The main public interest factors that are likely to prevent prosecution include:

- The court is likely to impose a nominal penalty.
- The defendant has already been made the subject of a sentence and any further conviction would be unlikely to result in the imposition of an additional sentence or order.
- The offence was committed as a result of a genuine mistake or misunderstanding (these factors must be balanced against the seriousness of the offence).
- The loss or harm can be described as minor and was the result of a single incident, particularly if it was caused by a misjudgement.
- There has been a long delay between the offence taking place and the date of the trial, unless:
  - the offence is serious;
  - the delay has been caused in part by the defendant;
  - the offence has only recently come to light; or
  - the complexity of the offence has meant that there has been a long investigation.
- A prosecution is likely to have a bad effect on the victim's physical or mental health, always bearing in mind the seriousness of the offence.
- The defendant is elderly or is, or was at the time of the offence, suffering from significant mental or physical ill health.
- The defendant has put right the loss or harm that was caused (but defendants must not avoid prosecution or diversion solely because they pay compensation).
- Details may be made public that could harm sources of information, international relations or national security.

Because of their position, it is possible that, in making such an assessment, the CPS may be more aware of factors favouring prosecution than they will be of any that may favour the defendant: they are more closely in touch with the police, for example, and less likely to know about the personal and social circumstances of the defendant. One caveat is that a primary criterion for diversion is the relative non-seriousness of the case – and this is something about which the CPS will routinely be aware.

Downgrading of charges

The Code for Crown Prosecutors states that Crown Prosecutors should select charges which:

- reflect the seriousness and extent of the offending;
- give the court adequate powers to sentence and impose appropriate post-conviction orders;
- enable the case to be presented in a clear and simple way.

The consequence, it is argued, is that 'Crown Prosecutors may not always choose or continue with the most serious charge where there is a choice'. One of the issues that has been raised in relation to the work of the CPS concerns its practice in relation to possible 'downgrading' of charges. This can happen in two ways: either by reducing charges to a level lower than that originally intended, or by accepting a plea of guilty to a lesser offence.

There is some research evidence which appears to suggest that downgrading takes place in cases of violence (Hedderman and Moxon, 1992; Cretney and Davis, 1995) and also that the 'racially aggravated' element in offences can sometimes be dropped (Burney and Rose, 2002). Ashworth and Redmayne (2005) suggest that evidence about the acceptance of guilty pleas for lesser offences is more difficult to come by.

It is difficult to assess such shifts in charging levels, certainly prior to the increased charging powers available early on to the CPS, as it is perfectly possible that the police may have been 'over-charging' in particular cases, leading the CPS to readjust later in the case. One of the anticipated benefits of closer involvement of the CPS early in cases will be some diminution in the disparity between initial charges and those eventually presented in court.

Discontinuance

A further criticism that has been levelled at the CPS concerns what are known as 'discontinuance rates'. The CPS has the power to *discontinue* charges brought in magistrates' courts – effectively drop the case. Somewhere between 13–17 per cent of cases have been discontinued by the CPS in recent years (CPS Annual Report, 2006). The CPS may discontinue cases for a number of reasons, including circumstances where it is felt that there is insufficient evidence to bring a prosecution, or that there are public interest considerations.

A survey by the CPS in 1994 (National Audit Office, 1997) found that there was insufficient evidence to proceed in 43 per cent of cases, in a further 28 per cent of cases a prosecution was deemed not to be in the public interest, and in 19 per cent the prosecution couldn't go ahead because witnesses failed to appear, or there was some similar practical reason. Research by Phillips and Brown (1998) found that cases were terminated because of lack of supporting evidence (33%), there was no evidence in support of some key element in the case (24%), there was anticipated witness failure (20%) or actual refusal by a witness (19%). Around one-third of all cases that are discontinued are so treated in the public interest; these are largely made up of cases in which nominal penalties are considered likely, or cases in which cautions are felt more appropriate.

One aspect of the criticism of the CPS's policies that is hard to accept, Ashworth and Redmayne (2005) argue, relates to discontinuation on evidential grounds. Here, they suggest, the CPS is on solid ground as 'to prosecute when the evidence is insufficient inflicts unjustified anxiety on the defendant and wastes public resources' (2005: 195). How will the new charging arrangements affect practice in this area? On the one hand, it is clearly intended to reduce discrepancies between the police and the CPS and reduce discontinuance rates by bringing appropriate charges in the first instance. On the other hand, some critics are concerned about the likely influence that the police will bring to bear on the CPS and how independent the prosecution service remains.

Magistrates' courts

Magistrates' courts are the lower criminal courts. There are approximately 460 magistrates' courts in England and Wales hearing about two million cases each year. As we have discussed, these courts hear summary offences and those triable either way cases, that are not referred or otherwise redirected to the Crown Court. The vast majority of criminal cases are heard in the magistrates' courts.

It is relatively rare for cases to be heard the first time they are scheduled in a magistrates' court. There are a number of reasons why they are likely to be postponed, including the need to wait for pre-sentence reports (from the probation service, for example) or because one of the parties fails to appear. This has led to considerable criticism of the justice process, and a number of initiatives have been introduced to attempt to speed up or streamline procedures. Cases are heard by a bench of three lay magistrates (volunteer members of the public who have received some training rather than professional lawyers) or by a district judge (formerly stipendiary magistrates).

There are approximately 100 district judges in England and Wales, now hearing a very substantial proportion of cases in magistrates' courts – especially in London. They tend to hear the more serious – either way – cases, and also tend to sit more frequently than their lay colleagues. Research tends to show that they show greater command over proceedings and, not surprisingly perhaps, over the law (Morgan and Russell, 2000).

The vast majority (90–95%) of defendants plead guilty in magistrates' courts and there is therefore no trial (see Table 26.1). The magistrates or district judge are responsible for judging the case in summary trials and for determining sentences where there is a finding of guilt or a guilty plea. There is a range of other tasks for magistrates:

- Remanding people into custody.
- Issuing warrants.
- Deciding upon bail.
- Requesting reports.
- Referring cases to other courts.
- Enforcing fines.
- Dealing with breaches of existing sentences.

Lay magistrates are less likely to refuse bail and to use imprisonment as a sentence than are district judges. Court users, however, have greater confidence in district judges than lay magistrates (Morgan and Russell, 2000).

The magistracy

Magistrates are volunteers. They are unpaid for their work, work upwards of the equivalent of half a day per week on average and, as non-professionals, are advised on points of law and procedure by a court clerk. Morgan and Russell (2000: 13) describe the work of lay magistrates as follows:

Though sitting in court is the activity for which lay magistrates are appointed, it is by no means their only activity. They receive training both initially and continuously to perform specialist functions and keep up-to-date. They mentor and appraise each other. If they wish to chair panels they must be willing to train for the task. They are encouraged to play a part in the life and administration of the court – attend bench meetings, sit on liaison and administrative committees and represent the bench on local fora. Many benches take a pride in the fact that their members undertake various activities to educate the community at large about the role of the magistracy and the work of magistrates' courts. Finally, there are some duties which are performed outside the court setting: hearing applications from the police for search warrants; witnessing statutory declarations; visiting licensed premises preparatory to hearing licence renewals; reading case papers in advance of hearings, and so on. Once a person has been appointed a lay magistrate, he or she exercises a wide discretion as to how many of these activities to get involved in and to what degree.

One of the main sources of concern in relation to the magistracy has centred on the fact that they are widely assumed to be unrepresentative of the wider population. At the time of Morgan and Russell's (2000) research the picture was complex:

- 49 per cent of magistrates were women.
- Only four per cent were aged under 40, whereas almost one-third (32%) were aged 60 or over.
- Although the ethnic origin of magistrates is approaching national representativeness, the make-up of benches varies markedly region by region.

In their survey, two-fifths (40%) of magistrates said that they were retired and 69 per cent give their current or former occupation as being professional or managerial, with 12 per cent saying that they had clerical or other non-manual jobs, three per cent skilled manual and five per cent unemployed. Professional and managerial occupations are therefore heavily over-represented.

One of Lord Justice Auld's comments in his review of criminal courts (Auld, 2001) was that too little effort was expended in recruiting magistrates, and he observed that whilst £4.7 million was spent on recruitment to the Territorial Army, only £35,000 was spent on recruiting magistrates (Darbyshire, 2002).

What then of district judges? They are generally appointed when in their 40s, and must be barristers or solicitors. Approximately two-thirds (64%) of district judges are solicitors and a quarter have previously been clerks in magistrates' courts. Full-time district judges are overwhelmingly male (84%) and only two of the 96 working at the time of Morgan and Russell's (2000) research were from ethnic minorities.

The Crown Court

The Crown Court is where indictable offences and a proportion of triable either way cases are heard. Cases are presided over by a judge – generally what are called circuit judges, though more serious cases will be heard by a high court judge. It is referred to as the *Crown Court* as technically it is a single court that holds hearings in a number of centres around the country. Cases arrive at the Crown Court either because they have been sent there for trial by a magistrates' court, have been sent by a magistrates' court for sentencing, or they are appeals against the decision of guilt or the sentence handed down by the magistrates' court.

Table 26.1 provides a breakdown of cases reaching the magistrates and the Crown Court in England and Wales between 1995 and 2005–06.

Table 26.1 Defendants proceeded against, convicted, cautioned and sentenced 1995–2005						
	1995	**1997**	**1999**	**2001**	**2003**	**2005**
Penalty notices for disorder (PND)	–	–	–	-	–	146,481
Total proceeded against	1,836,307	1,855,333	1,881,765	1,837,733	2,000,822	1,895,002
Total found guilty or cautioned	1,645,831	1,667,915	1,674,593	1,579,533	1,733,016	1,783,369
Total cautioned	291,247	282,093	266,132	229,860	241,806	298,945
Total sentenced	1,354,294	1,384,678	1,407,998	1,348,494	1,489,827	1,482,453
Indictable only	12,354	13,307	13,219	14,574	15,478	16,053
Triable either way	289,505	305,542	328,445	308,629	318,452	290,545
Summary non-motoring	409,982	416,515	433,475	441,946	493,286	508,729
Summary motoring	642,453	649,314	632,859	583,345	662,611	667,126
Total sentenced at magistrates' courts	1,280,038	1,305,176	1,330,828	1,276,426	1,413,764	1,406,712
Total committed for trial to the Crown Court	79,021	87,679	72,290	79,169	81,595	80,874
Total committed for sentence to the Crown Court	4,180	7,303	20,417	16,882	17,756	19,424
Total sentenced at the Crown Court	74,256	79,502	77,170	72,068	76,063	75,741

Source: Sentencing Statistics (2005).

The judiciary

There has long been concern about the narrow social background from which judges are drawn: historically the judiciary has been overwhelmingly male, white and Oxbridge-educated. By the mid-1990s only one member of the Court of Appeal and seven of the 96 high court judges were women. Similarly, only five of 517 circuit court judges, 12 out of 891 recorders and five of the 354 assistant recorders were drawn from ethnic minorities (Home Affairs Committee, 1996). There have been a number of initiatives since then to improve the diversity of the judiciary and there are signs that new appointments are indeed slowly being drawn from a broader social background (see Figure 26.1).

The Commission for Judicial Appointments was established in 2001 to oversee the appointments of judges and Queen's Counsel (a legal elite drawn predominantly from barristers, but also from senior members of the solicitors' profession), and to investigate complaints. It was replaced by the Judicial Appointments Commission in 2006. This took the appointment of judges out of the hands of the

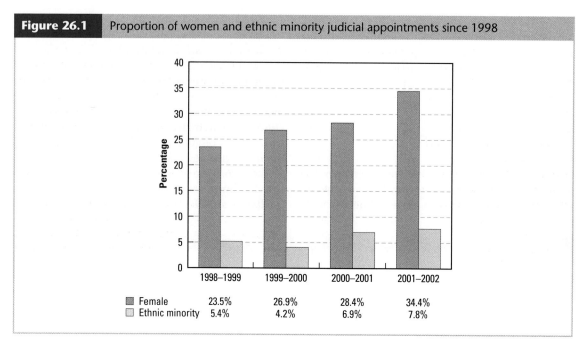

Figure 26.1   Proportion of women and ethnic minority judicial appointments since 1998

	1998–1999	1999–2000	2000–2001	2001–2002
■ Female	23.5%	26.9%	28.4%	34.4%
▢ Ethnic minority	5.4%	4.2%	6.9%	7.8%

Source: Department for Constitutional Affairs (http://www.dca.gov.uk/dept/report2003/06.htm).

government – previously it was the responsibility of the Department for Constitutional Affairs – and created an independent body of 15 members to manage the process. There are now targets for recruitment published by the Department for Constitutional Affairs which seek to increase the proportion of judges and other senior lawyers who are female and from ethnic minority communities, and in future the Judicial Appointments Commission will collect and publish statistics on the ethnic origin, gender, disability status and professional background of:

● those eligible to apply for judicial office;

● applications received;

● those appointed;

● those in post.

Juries

When one thinks of a criminal trial, particularly as depicted in cinema or television, at the heart of the process one thinks of there being a jury: twelve men and women (or simply twelve angry men, if you're a Henry Fonda fan) charged with weighing the evidence and determining whether guilt has been established 'beyond reasonable doubt'. To be a member of a jury one must be aged between 18 and 70, resident in the UK, not suffer from a mental disorder or be otherwise disqualified. The Auld Review conducted in 2001 sought to broaden the base from which jury members were drawn or, more accurately, sought to narrow the circumstances under which people could avoid this particular duty. Subsequently, the Criminal Justice Act 2003 has ended excusals as of right from jury duty with the exception of serving military personnel.

Lists of jurors are then randomly generated from the register and are summoned to attend court on particular dates. Although, as mentioned, the rules excusing people from jury service have been tightened considerably in recent years, there remain circumstances under which jury duty can potentially be postponed – such as especially urgent or pressing work or family commitments. In addition, even when called, it is possible for an objection to be raised by either defence or prosecution on the grounds that jurors may in some way be prejudiced against the defendant.

Despite its position in popular consciousness, the jury trial plays an important but, arguably, very minor role in the criminal justice process. As we have already seen, somewhere in the region of 95 per cent of criminal cases are heard in the magistrates' courts. Consequently, only around five per cent of cases might actually involve consideration by a jury. In practice, the figure is much lower as the majority of Crown Court cases involve a plea of guilty and there is, therefore, no necessity for a jury to be sworn in.

Relatively little is known about how juries work as, currently at least, research on this subject is prohibited by the Contempt of Court Act 1981. Both the Royal Commission on Criminal Justice in 1983 and the Auld Review in 2001 sought to have this rule overturned but, as yet, this has not occurred. The government conducted a further consultation exercise in 2004–05, and the responses largely favoured allowing such research.

In most cases juries have to attempt to reach a unanimous verdict. Since 1967, majority verdicts (11:1 or 10:2) have been allowed, and they form almost one-quarter of all guilty verdicts. Where juries cannot reach agreement, they will be discharged by the judge and in most cases the trial will have to restart with a new jury at a later date.

The primary reason given for introducing majority verdicts was to avoid the problem associated with trials being undermined by a single 'rogue juror' and to limit the ability of a defendant 'nobbling' the jury by intimidating a single member. However, Sanders and Young (2007: 511) argue that their introduction is a clear move in a 'crime control' direction, such arguments giving greater weight to the conviction of the guilty than to the acquittal of the innocent.

There is some controversy over the advantages and disadvantages of the jury system. For many it is perceived as the symbolic core of the British justice system. However, there have been many occasions where commentators of various sorts, politicians not least, have argued in favour of restrictions on the right to jury trial. What are the pros and cons?

Arguments in favour of juries	Arguments against juries
They are democratic, ensuring trial by one's peers	Juries are unrepresentative
They allow for public participation	Juries cannot cope with highly complex cases (e.g. complex fraud)
Jury members are not swayed by professional prejudice	Juries can be swayed by prejudice
Juries are a barrier to the enforcement of unpopular laws	Juries are too easily persuaded by rhetoric rather than fact
Juries confer legitimacy on the criminal justice process	Juries may be dominated by a few individuals
	Juries are insufficiently knowledgeable about the law

The table above lists as one of the 'arguments against', the notion that juries may find certain types of case too complex. This argument has been used in recent years as the basis for allowing certain types of case – most obviously complex fraud cases – to be heard by a judge only. The Criminal Justice Act 2003 allows for Crown Court trials without juries in cases which are deemed so long or so complex that they would be overly burdensome. This remains a somewhat controversial position with relatively little evidence available to support the idea that juries cannot understand such cases if they are properly explained (Myers *et al.*, 1999).

Pre-trial decisions

If we turn now to the court process itself, there are a number of considerations that must take place before the trial (if indeed there is a trial). These include the entering of a plea by the defendant, and any discussions that may revolve around that decision, the question in some cases about which court will hear the case and, crucially, whether or not a defendant will be released on bail.

Bail and remand

People arrive in court in a number of different ways:

- They may receive a summons through the post requiring them to attend court on a particular date.
- If arrested, they may be released on bail by the police to attend court.
- They may be kept in police custody overnight and from there taken to court.
- They may be remanded in prison and be taken to court from there.

About 80 per cent of summary cases and 40 per cent of indictable offences are dealt with on the first occasion, whereas most serious cases are not dealt with the first time someone appears in court. Time is required in a proportion of cases for the defence or the prosecution to prepare their cases, and proceedings will be adjourned to allow that to happen. In addition, magistrates may also require reports to be written prior to sentencing and, again, proceedings will be adjourned. At this stage there are a number of options that the police and magistrates may consider: defendants may be released with or without bail, or they may be remanded into custody for a fixed length of time to await trial.

Defendants who have not been convicted may be held in custody for up to eight days, or 28 days if they have previously been remanded in custody for the same offence. Those who have been convicted may be remanded for up to three weeks for reports. There are also a limited number of circumstances in which suspects may be detained without having been charged. Control orders, introduced by the Prevention of Terrorism Act 2005, and which are used in cases where people are believed to represent a threat to national security, currently:

- allow the imposition of curfew restrictions (the length of which have been subject to legal debate);
- restrict the suspect to living at one address;
- allow for the suspect to be electronically tagged;
- allow for the suspect to be subject to restrictions on who visits them, on whether they can access the internet, and where they can worship.

The efficacy of such measures was brought into sharp relief in mid-2007 when three of the 17 people subject to control orders absconded and could not be found by the police.

Bail

The Bail Act 1976 provides the criteria under which people accused, arrested or convicted of an offence may be released to attend court at a later date. Courts have four main alternatives:

- Unconditional bail.
- Conditional bail – generally living at a particular address; limitations placed on contacting certain people or going to certain places; and reporting to a police station.
- Release subject to a surety or security (financial deposit, a sum guaranteed by a third party or the surrender of a passport, and a fine or a short prison term may be imposed if the court date is ignored).
- Remand in custody.

There are several different points in the criminal justice process where the question of bail may arise:

- So-called 'street bail' (Hucklesby, 2002), granted by the police who, after making an arrest, bail the suspect with the requirement that they report to a police station at a specified date.
- Police bail, granted by the police at a police station, the arrestee being bailed to appear at a specified date in court.
- Court bail/remand decisions occur at some stage between the first and the last court appearance.
- Potential bail/remand decision after conviction, but before sentence has been passed.
- Remand pending appeal against sentence.

It is generally assumed that people will be granted bail. A fundamental assumption of our system of justice is that the police and courts should not be able to imprison people without good cause. In most cases we assume that detention without trial is wrong. This practice, according to Ashworth and Redmayne (2005), is based primarily on three principles:

- A presumption of both liberty and innocence on the part of the defendant.
- Each case should be treated on its merits.
- Courts should wherever possible impose the least restrictive conditions on a defendant awaiting trial.

Nevertheless, there are occasions when these principles may be overridden and a suspect may be imprisoned whilst awaiting trial. Thus, bail may be refused those charged with imprisonable offences if the police or the court thinks that there are substantial grounds for believing that the defendant:

- will fail to return to court;
- will commit an offence;
- will interfere with witnesses.

In addition, bail may also be refused if:

- the defendant is already on bail;
- the defendant is already in custody on other charges;
- the defendant has already absconded in the present proceedings;
- it has proved impractical to obtain information in order to make a bail decision.

In considering whether to refuse bail or impose restrictions, the courts and the police may consider:

- the nature and seriousness of the offence, and the likely sentence;
- the previous convictions of the defendant;
- the family and other circumstances of the defendant;
- any previous bail record such as failures to appear in court.

A number of important questions arise in relation to the main criteria for refusing bail. First, whilst on the surface the reasoning behind the desire to prevent future offending taking place seems clear, it still leaves unanswered the question of what type and/or seriousness of offence is necessary to bring such considerations into play. Moreover, it sits somewhat uncomfortably with the presumption of innocence. It is, after all, a form of preventive detention (the use of the prison to stop things happening, rather than to punish for things that have happened). Indeed, decision-making in relation to the refusal of bail always turns on the question of risk – how likely is it that the defendant will commit further offences, interfere with witnesses, abscond and so on (for a discussion of risk see Chapter 16)? Such prediction is fraught with difficulty and far from certain. Given that questions of individual liberty depend on such methods, great caution is necessary, and this leads a number of commentators to argue that the use of custodial remands for non-serious offences should simply be ruled out (Ashworth and Redmayne, 2005).

Remand

The notion of remand originally emerged as a response to difficulties associated with non-attendance in court. It is only more recently – the last half century or so – that it has also become a source of protection against future offending. At any point a very significant minority of people in prison are there on remand. That is to say, in plain English, they have not (yet) been convicted of an offence. For the most recent year that figures are available, 2005, the proportion of the prison population that was unsentenced was approximately 17 per cent, down from almost 22 per cent in 1995 (RDS NOMS, 2006).

Now, you may feel that this is not a particular problem, especially if you are aware that time spent in prison on remand is eventually deducted from any prison sentence imposed later by a court. However, Ashworth and Redmayne (2005: 207)

argue that the 'bail/custody decision raises some of the most acute conflicts in the whole criminal process'. This is the case because there are clear public concerns to ensure that successful prosecutions are brought in the interests of safety and security from crime. Equally, however, there are important legal principles that protect citizens against inappropriate imprisonment, not least Article 5 of the European Convention on Human Rights which safeguards the citizen's right to liberty.

There are a number of very important reasons why there is considerable concern about the use of remand. First, a small but still significant minority – between 15–20 per cent – of prisoners held on remand either will be acquitted in court or may not even be proceeded against. In addition, an even more sizeable portion of remand prisoners (approximately one-quarter of men on remand and one-third of women), though eventually convicted, will not receive a custodial sentence. Is it right to think they should not have been kept in custody? Ashworth and Redmayne (2005) suggest that there are a number of reasons why remand decisions are made, at least two of which cast some doubt on such an assumption:

- The fact that a non-custodial sentence has been passed may reflect the fact that time in custody has already been served.
- The criteria used for determining bail are different from those used in determining whether or not to impose a custodial sentence (thus refusal of bail may have been on the basis that there was perceived to be a significant risk that the defendant would fail to attend court, rather than on the basis of offence seriousness).

A second reason for concern about the use of remand is that the conditions in prison for those on remand are often notoriously bad. Remand prisoners tend to be placed in local prisons which are frequently the most crowded. They are often locked in their cells for most of the day, with no regular access to showers and with little exercise. They frequently share cells with convicted prisoners (even though they are meant to be segregated) and, campaign groups argue, often have limited access to legal information to prepare for their trial. A review by HM Inspector of Prisons (2000: 119) concluded that:

> One of the most significant findings is the gap between official provision for remand prisoners and their legitimate needs. The latter include

not only satisfactory access to due process but also reasonable opportunities to sustain mental and physical health whilst awaiting the decision of the courts ... [T]he overall picture across the Prison Service is one of inconsistency and lack of coherence in the proper treatment of this significant part of the prison population. This is not acceptable.

There are a number of further procedural issues relating to remand decisions. One concerns access to legal advice where research shows that young offenders in particular often encounter difficulties in contacting lawyers, and in being visited by legal advisers whilst in prison. Second, there have long been concerns that courts faced with insufficient information about an offender's circumstances will tend to make more conservative decisions. As a consequence 'bail information schemes' have developed which seek to provide information to decision-makers so as to maximise the likelihood of appropriate decisions. Although the vast majority of prisons now have such schemes, there remain a large number of magistrates' courts that have no such provision (Dhami, 2001).

Bail and remand decisions may be influenced by the speed with which such decisions are taken – both in terms of the speed with which cases may appear in court (with the CPS having little time to prepare) and the relatively short time allowed for such hearings in court. One study in the 1980s found that almost nine-tenths of cases resulting in custodial remand took less than ten minutes to conclude.

Finally, there is some evidence which suggests the possibility of discrimination in remand decision-making. Research by Hood (1992) found that a higher proportion of African-Caribbean than white defendants were remanded in custody pending trial, and this disproportion remained even when other factors were taken into account. Subsequent research by Hood and Feilzer (2004) found a similar pattern for young offenders, and a more recent review of CPS decision-making also found that bail was opposed more frequently for African-Caribbean defendants. Concerns about such differences are reinforced by the fact that the proportion of custodial remands which do not result in a conviction are higher for African-Caribbean defendants than for those of other ethnic origins.

Offending while on bail

One of the concerns about bail focuses on that minority of defendants who fail to appear on the due date at either the magistrates' or the Crown Court. Rather like remand decisions that end without conviction or with a community penalty, it is possible to ask whether these decisions represent poor decision-making by the police or courts. Whilst it is possible they may, it is also possible that there was simply no indication that such an outcome was likely at the time the decision was taken or, even if there was, that the risks were sufficient to justify custodial remand. Ashworth and Redmayne (2005: 232) conclude that this is 'par excellence, a sphere in which non-custodial methods of securing attendance should be developed, particularly bail hostels and electronic tagging'.

Greater concern is undoubtedly caused by those defendants who are bailed and go on to offend before they reappear in court. Morgan and Henderson (1998) studied over 2,000 bail cases. They found slightly under one-fifth (17%) were convicted of an offence committed whilst on bail. The chances of this occurring were greatest when there was an extended wait before the trial, where the defendant had originally been charged with car crime, burglary or robbery, and where there had been a previous custodial sentence or a previous breach of custody.

It is important not simply to assume that offending whilst on bail be taken as an indicator of a failure to recognise cases where custodial remand would have been appropriate. Depriving someone of their liberty requires strong justification, Ashworth and Redmayne (2005: 226) argue: 'Protecting a person against threats of violence may ... be a sufficient reason for custodial remand. But we should ask whether protecting the public against theft or car crime is sufficient to outweigh this fundamental right.' They conclude by arguing that:

- Remand decisions are largely based on prediction, the accuracy of which is often poor.
- Rather than talking of 'balancing' offenders' rights against other considerations, the starting point ought to be the right to liberty established in Article 5 of the European Convention.
- CPS, magistrates and judges should all be encouraged to question decisions made by those earlier in the criminal justice process (i.e. CPS should be more questioning of police decisions, and magistrates and judges should be more questioning of CPS decisions).
- The freedom given to the police to make bail/remand decisions early in the criminal process should be reviewed and probably limited.

- Courts should adopt a more legalistic and rights-based approach to such decisions, rather than straightforwardly risk-oriented decisions.

Review questions

1 What is the relevance of Article 5 of the European Convention to questions of bail/remand?

2 What are the four main options open to courts in relation to the bail/remand decision?

3 What are the three main grounds for refusing bail?

Mode of trial decision

As we have seen, summary cases are always heard in magistrates' courts and indictable only offences in the Crown Court. However, there are a large number of cases 'triable either way'. These may, in principle, be heard in either court. The process by which this decision is taken is, however, complex and was addressed in Chapter 23. In summary, a mode of trial hearing is held at which magistrates decide whether to try the case themselves. If it is particularly complex or serious then they are likely to let it be dealt with in the Crown Court. Once they have made their decision to retain a case in the magistrates' court it is then up to the defendant to decide whether they wish to opt for a jury trial. Again, if they do so, then the case moves to the Crown Court. One final complication is that even in either way cases that are heard in the magistrates' court, it is still possible for them to be committed to the Crown Court for sentencing.

Why do defendants make the decisions they do about mode of trial? Research conducted in the early 1990s by the Home Office (Hedderman and Moxon, 1992), based on interviews with just under 300 defendants and approximately 100 solicitors, indicated that the most frequently-cited reason for opting for a Crown Court trial was a belief that this would increase the chance of acquittal (see Table 26.2).

Table 26.2	Reasons defendants and solicitors gave for preferring Crown Court trial		
Reasons		**Defendants %**	**Solicitors %**
Better chance of acquittal		69	81
Magistrates on the side of the police		62	70
Lighter sentence		59	38
To get more information about prosecution case		48	45
Would be sent to Crown Court for sentence		42	40
More likely to get bail		36	11
Crown Court would be quicker		34	6
Would delay start of trial		28	19
Co-defendant wanted case to go to Crown Court		26	19
To serve part of sentence on remand		24	(not asked)
Easier to get legal aid		19	4

Source: Hedderman and Moxon (1992).

There are a number of problems in this particular part of the criminal justice process. A straightforward one is delays. The Home Office examined in detail the delays inherent in the system. The evidence presented in what has become known as the Narey Report (Narey, 1997) suggested that between 1985 and 1995 – a period in which recorded crime rose by more than two-fifths – the number of prosecutions at magistrates' courts for indictable (including triable either way) offences fell by 11 per cent. Even though there was a falling caseload, delays appeared to be increasing:

● The average time taken to complete indictable and triable either way cases, from the date of the offence, deteriorated from 98 days to 132 days or by more than a third.

● The average time taken by the police to charge or summon a defendant (from the date of offence) deteriorated from 38 to 45 days.

● The average time between charge or summons and the first listing of the case at magistrates' courts deteriorated from 18 to 28 days.

● The average time between the first listing and the completion of the case at magistrates' courts deteriorated from 41 to 60 days.

The Crime and Disorder Act 1998 introduced a number of reforms, including what are known as 'Narey hearings', in an attempt to speed up the court process. These were effectively a means of getting many of the less serious cases, in which a guilty plea was expected, into court quickly.

Another significant difficulty concerns the number of what are termed 'cracked cases'. These are contested cases which are scheduled to be heard in the Crown Court. The arrangements are made for the case, including preparing the case, calling witnesses and so on, only for the defendant to change their plea to 'guilty' at the last minute, thereby doing away with any need for a trial. Not only is this very time-consuming but it is, of course, extraordinarily expensive. Consequently, a lot of effort has gone into improving what is referred to as 'case management'.

Cases in the Crown Court take much longer, and cost much more, than cases in magistrates' courts. As a consequence of the increasing burdens on the courts and, possibly, also a desire to take advantage of the much lower rate of acquittals in magistrates' courts, there has been a concerted move in recent years to increase the proportion of triable either way cases that are dealt with in the lower courts. There are a number of reasons advanced for resisting such pressure, not least the rather cursory form of hearing that is often argued to be characteristic of magistrates' courts. There is also an equality element to this issue. There is research evidence (e.g. Phillips and Brown, 1998) that cases against black defendants tend to be

The statue of Lady Justice at the top of the Central Criminal Court (the Old Bailey) in London – perhaps the most familiar symbol of the English legal system. In one hand Lady Justice holds a sword representing the power to punish, in the other the scales of justice symbolising fairness and equality. How far does this characterise the work of the courts in practice?

weaker than those against white defendants and are often charged at a higher level. The option of a Crown Court trial therefore becomes an important potential defence against such practices and, indeed, black defendants tend to opt for Crown Court trial more frequently than others. Removal of this option would, arguably, reduce one important protection against discrimination (Ashworth and Redmayne, 2005).

Defendants' rights

Defendants have a number of rights, not least the right to a fair trial as outlined in the Human Rights Act. Prior to a case coming to court, the defendant has the right:

- to know the nature and details of any charges;
- to legal representation;
- to bail, unless there are specific reasons for not granting it;
- to jury trial if the case is triable either way;
- to advance disclosure in such cases.

During a trial, the defendant also has the right:

- to legal representation and, under some circumstances, legal aid;
- to challenge jurors;
- to call evidence;
- not to give evidence;
- to cross-examine witnesses.

Pleas and bargaining

Although there are options such as 'not guilty by reason of insanity', in the main defendants in criminal cases have a straight choice between *guilty* and *not guilty*. Whilst this may seem an uncontroversial idea, a guilty plea has only become a standard feature of our criminal justice process in the last two centuries. Moreover, historically in many jurisdictions the idea of a guilty plea has been anathema. Rather, in countries such as France and Germany the idea of guilt has been something that the state has to satisfy itself of rather than something it is for those accused to admit. Increasingly in these jurisdictions, however, the idea of an admission of guilt, often in connection with a reduction in sentence, has been becoming more acceptable.

In England and Wales there are major incentives provided to get defendants to plead guilty. Indeed, Sanders and Young (2007) refer to this element of the justice process as the 'mass production of guilty pleas'. Over nine-tenths of magistrates' courts cases involve guilty pleas, and only one-quarter of cases in the Crown Court are contested. Why is this so? Undoubtedly, in part it is because many of those accused of offences are actually guilty. However, they could still opt for a trial. As indicated, there are a number of incentives which make pleading guilty a more attractive option for some than opting for trial. Thus, s.144 of the Criminal Justice Act 2003 says:

> In determining what sentence to pass on an offender who has pleaded guilty to an offence

before that or another court, a court must take into account:

> (a) the stage in the proceedings for the offence at which the offender indicated his intention to plead guilty; and
>
> (b) the circumstances in which this indication was given.

In effect, a sentence discount is available to defendants who plead guilty, particularly where this is done early on. The discount can be anything up to one-third of the sentence. In addition to this general incentive provided to all defendants, there are two other processes which have a bearing on pleas: these are generally referred to as *charge bargaining* and *plea bargaining*.

Charge bargaining

This has two basic forms:

- *Cases where a defendant faces a range of charges varying in seriousness and conveys an intention to plead not guilty* – The prosecution may drop one or more of the charges in exchange for plea of guilty to one or more of the others.
- *Cases in which a defendant is faced with a serious charge* – Again, the defendant signals an intention to plead not guilty. In discussion with the prosecution they agree to plead guilty to a lesser charge and the more serious one is withdrawn. Such processes are particularly visible in cases of violence where murder may be downgraded to manslaughter, affray to grievous bodily harm (GBH), GBH to actual bodily harm (ABH), and so on.

Research by Mulcahy (1994) found considerable evidence of such practices in magistrates' courts, encouraged by both defence and prosecution (see also Hedderman and Moxon, 1992). Mulcahy argues that there are three main reasons why legal practitioners justify such negotiated settlements:

- Defence lawyers in particular are acutely aware of the potential costs and disadvantages of trials, and look to avoid them wherever possible.
- Lawyers seek to achieve substantive justice by resolving cases through the entry of 'appropriate' pleas to 'appropriate' charges.
- Legal practitioners largely view defendants as both morally culpable and substantively guilty, and therefore tend often to see trials as unnecessary.

Such findings, Mulcahy argues, are indicative of a 'crime control' (Packer, 1968) approach to the justice process (see Chapter 23), in which legal practitioners are more concerned with punishing the guilty than with safeguarding defendants' rights.

According to Ashworth and Redmayne (2005), the Code for Crown Prosecutors implies that accepting guilty pleas to lesser offences is acceptable so long as the maximum sentence for the new (lesser) offence is not too low, given the seriousness of what the offender did. There are clearly a number of administrative advantages to charge bargaining. First and foremost it produces an increased number of guilty pleas, thus saving court time and public money. It also, if taken at face value, possibly increases the number of offenders being convicted for the offences they have committed.

For some defendants there are also some potential advantages. Assuming they have committed the offence, the bargaining process offers them the prospect of a lower sentence (unless they were 'overcharged' in the first place). For the defendant who has not committed the offence charged, the process may be altogether more problematic. It is perfectly possible to envisage situations in which defendants who have not committed the offence, but who are under the impression that the prosecution feels it has a strong case against them, being advised by a persuasive lawyer that their best bet might be to plead guilty to a relatively minor charge (carrying, say, the prospect of a community sentence) than risk a trial and a possible prison sentence.

Plea bargaining

Although plea bargaining is a well-established feature of the American justice system, as anyone familiar with US cop and courtroom dramas will be well aware, it is arguably a less well-publicised part of the English justice process. There is a range of ways in which plea bargaining may occur:

- *Sentence discounting* – This we have already briefly visited in the shape of s.144 of the 2003 Criminal Justice Act. In practice, sentence discounts appear quite substantial. Ashworth and Redmayne (2005) report that, in 2002, 76 per cent of adult males pleading not guilty and convicted in the Crown Court received a custodial sentence compared with 62 per cent of those who pleaded guilty. Moreover, the former also received substantially longer prison terms.
- *'Plea before venue'* – In practice the earlier a guilty plea is lodged, the greater the sentence discount

is anticipated to be. Since 1997, defendants charged with triable either way offences appear in magistrates' court and are asked whether they intend to plead guilty. In relation to those who intend to plead guilty a major question concerns whether they are likely to be sentenced in the magistrates' or Crown Court. Because defendants cannot know this at the point they are required to indicate their intended plea, it is now established that it is appropriate for an enhanced sentence discount to be applied (i.e. above the one-third maximum).

- *Indication of sentence* – The Criminal Justice Act 2003 enables a defendant charged with a triable either way offence to request an indication of whether a custodial or non-custodial sentence is likely if he were to plead guilty. New guidance was provided in 2005 by the Lord Chief Justice (in Goodyear [2005] EWCA Crim, 888) on how an advance indication of sentence might be sought from a trial judge. The guidance reaffirmed the principle that a defendant's plea must be his or her own, 'entered voluntarily and without pressure, and that there must be no bargaining with or by the Judge. Any request for an indication must be initiated by the defendant and will be confined to the sentence which would be imposed on a plea of guilty at the stage in the proceedings at which the indication was sought' (Court of Appeal, 2005).

The magistrates' court need not comply with this request in all circumstances, but if it does indicate the likely sentence it is then bound by that decision.

- *Pre-trial hearings* – Such hearings in magistrates' courts are used as the basis for the swapping of information between defence and prosecution. The assumption is that this may save time, and may also increase guilty pleas. In the Crown Court there is a range of pre-trial meetings including the non-statutory 'plea and directions' hearing at which non-binding rulings can be made.
- *On the advice of lawyers* – Although there are supposed to be strict limits on the extent and nature of contact between defence counsel and the judge, it appears that it remains far from uncommon for discussion of plea to take place prior to the trial and for this to have a direct impact on defendants' later pleas.

The final example of bargaining in court processes concern cases where deals are reached over precisely which facts will be presented in court –

sometimes referred to as *fact bargains* (Ashworth and Redmayne, 2005). There may be cases, it is suggested, in which a guilty plea may be entered in exchange for certain facts not being presented in court – perhaps aggravating factors or the role played by a friend or accomplice.

Like charge bargaining, it may be argued that plea bargaining brings a number of administrative and financial advantages – speeding up court processes and reducing the cost to the Exchequer. There may be benefit to victims in removing some of the less pleasant aspects of giving evidence in contested cases – though some victims may wish, as it were, 'to have their day in court'. It is also possible to argue that defendants may gain in terms of reduced sentence. As argued earlier in relation to charge bargaining, this only applies to the guilty defendant. It is possible, by contrast, that some innocent defendants may find the pressure to plead guilty difficult to resist, and there is some research evidence to suggest that as many as one in ten of all those pleading guilty in the Crown Court actually claim to be innocent (Zander and Henderson, 1993). Having reviewed existing practices in relation to both charge and plea bargaining, Ashworth and Redmayne's (2005: 285) rather damning conclusion is that in effect, 'there is an element of gambling in the defendant's decision-making here: the roulette wheel has taken the place of the rule of law'. Indeed, they go on to argue that sentence discounts for guilty pleas run counter to human rights law in at least four respects:

- The right to be presumed innocent until proven guilty may be undermined by the sheer extent of the inducement to plead guilty.

- The right to a fair trial includes both privilege against self-incrimination which, again, they argue could be viewed as being undermined.

- Defendants of African-Caribbean and Asian origin plead not guilty at a higher rate than do white defendants (they are also more likely to be acquitted, which might be taken as an indicator that the higher rate of not guilty pleas has some substance). The guilty plea discount therefore disproportionately favours white defendants and might be considered a form of indirect discrimination.

- The scale of guilty pleas – their 'mass production' (Sanders and Young, 2007) runs counter to the right to a 'fair and public' hearing.

Evidence

Evidence, which may take many forms, is the basis upon which argument around innocence and guilt is constructed in a criminal trial. Evidence may be presented as:

- Oral testimony on the witness stand.
- Documentary evidence such as witness statements.
- Exhibits, such as weapons and clothing.
- Audio and photographic materials, such as CCTV footage.
- Eye-witness testimony.
- Confession.
- Expert testimony by psychiatrists, doctors, etc.

Disclosure

One of the more important pre-trial issues concerns *disclosure* of evidence. The prosecution is required to disclose its case to the defence in cases that go to the Crown Court, and are also required to provide to the defence all evidence upon which the Crown proposes to rely in a summary trial in a magistrates' court. There is also an obligation on the prosecution in the more serious cases to bring to the attention of the defence major items of evidence that are not to be used in court (these may potentially contain information of value to the defence, hence the requirement to disclose it). Clearly, this is an area where there is considerable potential for dispute to arise and research evidence suggests that there is relatively little confidence among lawyers in this aspect of the law (Plotnikoff and Woolfson, 2001).

There are slightly different procedures in relation to the disclosure of evidence by the defence. The Criminal Justice Act 2003 requires the defence to provide a summary statement in which it outlines its case and provides a list of witnesses whom it intends to call and experts it has consulted. Adverse inferences may be drawn from a failure to adhere to these obligations. That is to say that the prosecution may suggest in court that a failure to disclose casts doubt on the defence's case. Despite this, it appears that there is a widespread lack of compliance with the 2003 Act (Redmayne, 2004).

Finally, and controversially, in this regard there is what is known as *public interest immunity*. Where there is sensitive material that would cause difficulties if disclosed – details of an informant, for example – the prosecution may apply for public interest immunity which allows that this material not be disclosed. Although the defence may be informed that such immunity has been sought or given, this is not always the case, and there are occasions when the defence is not informed at all about such an application.

Exclusion

Earlier we briefly examined some of the key elements of the idea of a 'fair trial'. In addition to advance notice of the evidence against them, and the right both to call witnesses and cross-examine prosecution witnesses, defendants are also meant to be protected against the use of evidence against them which has been obtained inappropriately. The most obvious examples here are the restrictions placed on the way in which suspects can be interrogated. Evidence, such as confessions gained as a result of threats or actual violence, is inadmissible in court. Police powers in this regard were outlined in Chapter 25. Here, we consider practices in criminal trials in relation to unfairly- or illegally-obtained evidence.

There are essentially four different approaches courts may take in relation to the exclusion of evidence (Ashworth and Redmayne, 2005):

- *Disciplinary approach* – Here illegally- or unfairly-obtained evidence is excluded in order to deter the police from behaving in a similar manner in the future. As with deterrence theory more generally, this relies upon two assumptions – that officers in other cases will know that this has happened and, second, that they will be sufficiently concerned about being caught to modify their own behaviour – for which there is little empirical support.

- *Remedial approach* – The remedy spoken of here is aimed at the defendant and, through the exclusion of evidence, creating a situation like that had their rights not been breached. Again, this involves a sizeable assumption: that evidence, such as a confession, would not have been secured without the breach of the defendant's rights.

- *Moral legitimacy approach* – The exclusion of evidence in this case is undertaken in order symbolically to protect the integrity of the system in the eyes of the public.

- *External approach* – In which it would be argued that the issue of improperly obtained evidence

should not be dealt with within the confines of the court case itself, but in some other forum. Thus, unfairly- or illegally-obtained evidence would still be used, but disciplinary or other procedures would be used to sanction those responsible for the breach of rights.

In practice in England and Wales, prior to PACE there were far fewer restrictions on the nature of evidence that could be placed before the courts. However, PACE states that:

> In any proceedings the court may refuse to allow evidence on which the prosecution proposes to rely to be given if it appears to the court that, having regard to all the circumstances, including the circumstances in which the evidence was obtained, the admission of evidence would have such an adverse effect on the fairness of the proceedings that the court ought not to admit it.

Although practice varies, it is now the case that evidence which appears to have involved a breach of PACE provisions for safeguarding the rights of suspects is now regularly excluded from court. According to Ashworth and Redmayne (2005), the rationale behind the exclusion of evidence involving breaches of PACE rules would appear to be remedial, rather than that of disciplining the police.

Appeals

Appeals are an important part of the criminal process and are available to both prosecution and defence. There are effectively five main forms of appeal procedure:

- In relation to cases from the magistrates' courts, the defence may lodge an appeal on matters of fact in cases where there was a not guilty plea. Such cases are heard in the Crown Court by a judge sitting with two magistrates, with the case, in effect, being heard again. Such appeals must commence within 21 days of the conclusion of magistrates' court proceedings. During 2005, a total of 12,843 appeals were made to the Crown Court. Of those dealt with 5,537 (43%) had their appeals allowed or their sentence varied. Of the remainder, 3,791 (30%) were dismissed and 3,477 (27%) were abandoned or otherwise disposed (Judicial Statistics, 2005).

- Prosecution and defence may appeal from the magistrates' court on questions of law. Such cases are heard in the divisional court with the magistrates' court clerk supplying a summary of the case and their ruling.

- Prosecution and defence may mount a challenge to the magistrates' decision by way of judicial review. Again this will be heard by the divisional court, though the appeal may go on to higher courts. As with other appeals to the divisional court, such cases concern errors of law. Judicial review is the more likely avenue in cases where it is felt, for example, that there wasn't fair opportunity for the defence to present its case, or where there were other irregularities in the trial.

- From the Crown Court the defendant can appeal on factual or legal grounds. The case will be heard by the Court of Appeal and, again, can go on to the House of Lords. Leave to appeal must be sought within 28 days of conviction. If the Court of Appeal grants leave, the full appeal will be heard. During 2005, a total of 7,023 applications for leave to appeal were received, of which 1,661 were against conviction in the Crown Court and 5,178 against the sentence imposed. During 2005, a total of 6,104 appeals were considered by a single judge in the Court of Appeal, of which 1,471 were against conviction in the Crown Court and 4,633 were against the sentence imposed. Of these 24 per cent (360) of those seeking to appeal against conviction were granted, as were 33 per cent (1,541) against sentence. During 2005, a total of 255 appeals were disposed of in the House of Lords, of which 79 were allowed (Judicial Statistics, 2005).

- From the Crown Court, the prosecution can appeal against a number of pre-trial decisions and some of the rulings made by the judge during the course of the trial.

How are the statistics on appeals to be interpreted? In relation to appeals against conviction in the Crown Court the success rate in recent years (the proportion seeking leave to appeal who eventually have their appeal heard and allowed) has been of the order of ten per cent. Is this success or failure? Malleson (1991) has argued that the appeals procedure is like an obstacle race in which only the most determined are likely to succeed, and Sanders and Young (2007: 567) suggest that the 'true function of the various filters within the appeal system is not so much to weed out weak appeals as to deter all but the most committed from challenging their conviction'.

Miscarriages of justice

In recent decades there have been a substantial number of high profile miscarriages of justice – essentially cases in which people have been convicted of crimes that they did not commit, and in many cases where there was evidence available to suggest their innocence. In the 1970s, the convictions in the aftermath of a series of bombings in England by the IRA were widely criticised and led to public campaigns in defence of those who had been found guilty. The 'Guildford Four' were jailed for life in 1975 and their convictions overturned in 1989; the 'Birmingham Six', also convicted in 1975, had to wait until 1991 for the Court of Appeal to accept that the verdicts were unsafe. In both cases, improper means had been used by the police, including the fabrication of evidence (Nobles and Schiff, 2000; Savage and Milne, 2007).

More recently – since the advent of PACE – the case of the 'Cardiff Three' has reignited concerns about the justice system. The case involved the conviction of three men – Stephen Miller, Tony Paris and Yusuf Abdullahi – for the murder of 21 year-old Lynette White in 1988. The three men were jailed for life for the violent murder in which the young woman had been stabbed 50 times. The convictions were eventually overturned in 1992. The police were found to have bullied the three defendants, intimidating one of them into confessing and thereby contributing to the convictions of the other two. One of the suspects, described as having an IQ of 75, had denied involvement to the police over 300 times. Commenting on the police interrogation, the Lord Chief Justice said that it was 'hard to conceive of a more hostile or intimidating approach by officers to a suspect ... It is impossible to convey on the printed page the pace, force and menace of the officer's delivery' (the *Guardian*, 17 December, 1992). In 2003, and using new DNA evidence, the police arrested someone for Lynette White's murder.

Cases such as these highlight a number of ways in which miscarriages of justice may occur: through the intimidation of suspects, the use of uncorroborated or even fabricated evidence. Other victims of miscarriages of justice have argued that failures by legal representatives have contributed to the outcome of the trial: either because of the shortcomings of defence lawyers or failures by the prosecution to disclose evidence likely to be of benefit to the defence.

The 'Birmingham Six' (with Chris Mullen, MP, centre) outside the Old Bailey in London after their convictions were quashed in 1991 on their third appeal. They were originally found guilty of murder and conspiracy after 21 people were killed in two pub bombings in central Birmingham in 1974.

Criminal Cases Review Commission (CCRC)

Established by the Criminal Appeal Act 1995, the CCRC was created to consider cases thought to be potential miscarriages of justice. The Royal Commission on Criminal Justice (the Runciman Commission) was established earlier in the decade in the aftermath of a series of high profile miscarriages of justice, several of which had involved people accused of terrorist offences. The Runciman Commission proposed the establishment of a new independent body to consider such cases (RCCJ, 1993), and the CCRC began its work in 1997.

The CCRC reviews possible miscarriages of justice and decides if they should be referred to an appeal court. Its formal responsibilities include:

- Reviewing suspected miscarriages of justice and referring a conviction, verdict or finding or sentence to an appropriate court of appeal where it is felt that there is a 'real possibility' that it would not be upheld.

- To investigate and report to the Court of Appeal on any matter referred to the Commission.

- To consider and report to the Secretary of State on any conviction referred to the Commission

for consideration of the exercise of Her Majesty's prerogative of mercy.

The Commission has jurisdiction over criminal cases at any magistrates' or Crown Court in England, Wales and Northern Ireland and reviews the cases of those who feel they have been wrongly convicted of criminal offences, or unfairly sentenced. The CCRC does not consider innocence or guilt, but whether there is new evidence or argument that may cast doubt on the safety of an original decision. The CCRC has wide-ranging investigative powers and can obtain and preserve documentation held by any public body. It can also appoint an investigating officer from another public body to carry out inquiries on its behalf. Once its investigations are complete it can refer a case back to the appropriate appeal court for reconsideration. The CCRC has reviewed well over 9,000 cases since it was created and approximately four per cent of its caseload has been referred to the appeal courts (see Table 26.3).

In 2005–06 the appeal courts decided the cases of 49 individuals referred by the Commission. Of these, five related to sentence only and the remainder were cases in which the CCRC raised concerns about the conviction itself. Of the latter 44 cases, 14 involved

Table 26.3	The work of the Criminal Cases Review Commission 1997–(Jan) 2007
Total applications	9388
No. of referrals	351
Completed	308
of which	90 were upheld
	216 were quashed
	2 reserved

dishonesty offences, 11 murder or attempted murder, ten sexual offences, three involved non-fatal violence and three involved drugs offences. The remaining three involved criminal damage, belonging to a proscribed organisation, and making an explosive device. In 31 of the 44 convictions referred by the Commission, the appeal courts ruled they were unsafe, and of the five sentences referred, four were reduced.

Miscarriages of justice remind us that for all the emphasis that government currently places on crime reduction and prevention as core goals of the criminal justice system, there are a number of other very important – perhaps even more important – goals of the justice system, and that these involve the protection of freedoms and rights. If, as recent research suggests (Tyler, 1990; Tyler and Huo, 2002), people tend to comply with the law when they perceive the regulatory order as procedurally just, then it becomes of quite fundamental importance to ensure that due process is observed and that the balance with crime control is maintained.

Review questions

1 What are the main considerations in the mode of trial decision?

2 What is the difference between charge bargaining and plea bargaining?

3 What are the main avenues of appeal in criminal cases?

4 What are the main sources of miscarriages of justice?

Questions for further discussion

1 Is it ever in the public interest not to prosecute an offender where there is sufficient evidence to do so?

2 Are jury trials a good thing?

3 Should we be restricting the right to trial by jury?

4 Should custodial remands for non-serious offences be ruled out?

5 What are the advantages and disadvantages of charge and plea bargaining?

Further reading

The best guide to the criminal justice and prosecution process is undoubtedly Ashworth, A. and Redmayne, M. (2005) *The Criminal Process*, 3rd edn, Oxford: Oxford University Press. Another very valuable volume, adopting a more overtly critical approach, is Sanders, A. and Young, R. (2007) *Criminal Justice*, 3rd edn, Oxford: Oxford University Press. The two can profitably be read together as the contrast is valuable.

Other very useful and generally comprehensive guides include:

Davies, M. *et al.* (2005) *Criminal Justice*, 3rd edn, Harlow: Longman

Joyce, P. (2006) *Criminal Justice*, Cullompton: Willan

Uglow, S. (2002) *Criminal Justice*, 2nd edn, London: Sweet and Maxwell

Websites

The Crown Prosecution Service website contains annual reports and a small number of useful publications: www.cps.gov.uk

Details of the courts system can be found at the website of the Ministry of Justice: http://www.justice.gov.uk/ and at that of HM Courts Service: www.hmcourts-service.gov.uk/

Much information about the work of the Criminal Cases Review Commission, including details of cases and the judgements made by the appeal courts, is available on their website: www.ccrc.gov.uk

A lot of campaigning material and critical commentary on the criminal justice system and process can be found at the website of the Legal Action Group: www.lag.org.uk

Chapter outline

Introduction 660

Types of sentence 660
  Discharges 661
  Fines and other financial penalties 661
  Community punishment 661
    The Community Rehabilitation Order 661
    The Community Punishment Order 661
    The Community Order 662
  The suspended sentence of imprisonment 662

Sentencing policy 663
  The Criminal Justice Act 1991 664
  Sentencing reform after the 1991 Act 666
    The Crime (Sentences) Act 1997 667
  Sentencing reform under New Labour 667
    The Auld Review of Criminal Courts 668
    The Halliday Review 668
    Justice for All 669
    Criminal Justice Act 2003 669

Trends in non-custodial sentencing 670

Probation 673
  Punishment in the community 674
  Crime, Justice and Protecting the Public 675
  New Labour and probation 676
    The probation service and 'what works' 676
    A national probation service 677
    The Carter Review and the emergence of NOMS 678

Conclusion 680
Questions for further discussion 680
Further reading 681
Websites 681

27

Sentencing and non-custodial penalties

CHAPTER SUMMARY

In previous chapters we looked at the police and police powers, the prosecution and courts process. We now turn our attention to sentencing and to non-custodial penalties.

This chapter considers:

- the sentences that are available to the courts;

- how sentencing policy has changed in recent years.

As we will see, there has been a series of shifts in which just deserts concerns briefly came to the fore, only quickly to be diluted as populist punitive influences emerged in the mid-1990s. In parallel with trends in imprisonment, it appears community penalties are being used with increasing frequency – where previously fines and discharges might have sufficed.

We conclude this chapter by examining the history and development of what is arguably the best-known element of community-based work with offenders: probation.

Introduction

At the heart of the justice process, in cases where guilt is established, there is a system of imposing punishments. This is the sentencing system, and despite this deceptively simple description it plays a number of not always compatible roles: punishment, rehabilitation, retribution and deterrence among others. We dealt with these differing theories of punishment in some detail in Chapter 22. Here we focus more particularly on the sentencing process in England and Wales, and how sentencing policy and practice has been changing in recent decades.

Types of sentence

There is now a complex range of penalties available to the courts. This has not always been the case. In pre-modern times, felonies were punishable by death, misdemeanours by either unlimited imprisonment or unlimited fines. There were various other alternatives ranging from the use of the stocks to transportation. In the main, however, the system of punishment was relatively simple (Thomas, 2002).

As we saw in Chapter 2, the widespread use of the death penalty largely came to an end in the nineteenth century and once transportation also ceased, the prison emerged as a standard response to serious (and often not so serious) offending. The last century or so has seen the introduction of a huge number of community-based forms of punishment from the probation order in 1907 and community service orders in 1972 to more recent innovations such as drug treatment and testing orders (see Chapter 21) and referral orders (see Chapter 29).

From the 1970s to the early 1990s one of the overriding concerns in penal policy was the aim of reducing the prison population. The key method used was the introduction of an array of alternatives to custody, the assumption generally being that their existence would enable courts to use imprisonment more sparingly. As we shall see, this 'policy of proliferation' (Ashworth, 1992: 242) has not had the consequences initially anticipated. There are a number of reasons for this. Initially at least there was something of a 'taboo' concerning discussion of sentencing policy by politicians (Stern, 1989). The separation between the executive and the judiciary made commenting on sentencing highly contentious. Sentencing has also traditionally been a somewhat individualistic practice. There has long been resistance to the idea of providing guidelines for sentencing practice. Even where there have been guidelines, there have rarely been mechanisms for translating these into practice. Much of this has changed in recent years – indeed, arguably this is *the* major change in the field of sentencing in the last decade or decade and a half. Politicians now regularly involve themselves in sentencing policy and there is much less reticence about constructing guidelines for sentencing practice and mechanisms for operationalising these. The whole area has become deeply politicised. As part of this, reducing the use of imprisonment is no longer a political imperative – indeed quite the reverse. As a consequence, increasing use of non-custodial penalties has been accompanied by a continued expansion in the use of imprisonment. Before looking at sentencing policy in more detail we must first look at the major non-custodial penalties that are available to the courts.

Discharges

There are two main forms. The *absolute discharge* means that the person is released without further punishment being imposed. By contrast, the *conditional discharge* also frees the defendant without penalty, though it requires them to avoid future offending. Thus, under a conditional discharge if, during a specified period up to a maximum of three years, the person is not found guilty of another offence then the matter will be regarded as closed. However, if they are convicted during that period then they can be sentenced in court not only for the new offence but also for the old one.

Fines and other financial penalties

The most long-standing of the non-custodial penalties which currently exist is the fine. Convictions for summary offences are highly likely to result in the imposition of a fine.

The level of the fine will generally reflect the seriousness of the offence. Initially, courts required that fines be paid in full, and it was not until 1914 that paying by instalments became possible. The major increase in the use of fines took place after the Second World War. By the 1970s over half of adult offenders convicted of indictable offences were fined. The increasing popularity of the fine as punishment seemed to tail off in the 1980s, a time when the use of other non-custodial penalties and custody both rose.

Since the Criminal Justice Act 1972, courts have had widespread powers to order compensation against offenders. Compensation orders are made against defendants in cases where there is an identifiable victim and where the offence involves personal injury or property damage. As modified by Criminal Justice Acts in 1982 and 1988, the ordering of compensation has dramatically increased in magistrates' courts, though it is still rarely used as a sole penalty (see Chapter 17). Finally, courts may also order costs against defendants.

Community punishment

Historically, a range of different community-based penalties have been available to the courts – though they have grown substantially in number over the past 30 years or so (Bottoms, 1983). These have now all been replaced by a single community order with a variety of sentencing options as a result of the Criminal Justice Act 2003. Before returning to this legislation, it is worth briefly reviewing the basic outline of community penalties prior to the passage of the Act.

The Community Rehabilitation Order

For most of its history this penalty was known as the probation order. Introduced in the early twentieth century, the probation order was used increasingly up until the 1960s. From the mid-1960s, and through the 1970s, there was an almost continual decline in the use of the probation order (Haxby, 1978). Whilst there is no simple explanation for this decline, the introduction of the suspended sentence of imprisonment and of community service orders clearly played a part. The low point for the probation order came in 1978 when only five per cent of people aged 21 and over, sentenced for indictable offences, received probation (McWilliams, 1987).

The trend in the period immediately before the Criminal Justice Act 1991 was towards greater use of probation. Prior to the Act, a probation order was made instead of sentencing the offender. After 1991 probation became a sentence of the court, i.e. a *punishment*. The Act stated that the court may not impose a community sentence such as probation unless the offence 'was serious enough to warrant such a sentence'. Consequently, therefore, the court must be satisfied that the offence was too serious to warrant, say, a fine or a discharge. The Probation Order was renamed the Community Rehabilitation Order under the Criminal Justice and Court Services Act 2000.

The Community Punishment Orders

Community Service Orders (CSOs) were introduced by the Criminal Justice Act 1972, but were not in operation nationwide until the mid-1970s. Under a CSO an offender was required by a court, assuming that the offender consented, to undertake between 40 and 240 hours unpaid work organised and supervised by the probation service. The CSO became an established sentence fairly rapidly (McIvor, 1992). Approximately one in six young adult offenders were dealt with in this way and it was always a sentence that was used disproportionately with this age group. Again, the order was renamed by the Criminal Justice and Court Services Act 2000 and became the Community Punishment Order.

The Community Order

There is now a single Community Order which, in effect, incorporates the Community Rehabilitation Order and the Community Punishment Order as well as a range of other previously-existing community penalties. The Community Order may be imposed on offenders aged 18 and over (its use for 16 and 17 year-olds awaits youth justice legislation) and comes with a list of potential 'requirements' that sentencers can select from. In principle the order may last for as short as a few hours and for as long as three years.

In all there are 12 requirements that sentencers can select. These are:

- Unpaid work (40–300 hours).
- Supervision (up to 36 months; 24 months maximum for a Suspended Sentence Order (SSO)).
- Accredited programme (length to be expressed as the number of sessions; must be combined with a supervision requirement).
- Drug rehabilitation (6–36 months; 24 months maximum for SSO; offender's consent is required).
- Alcohol treatment (6–36 months; 24 months maximum for SSO; offender's consent is required).

- Mental health treatment (up to 36 months; 24 months maximum for SSO; offender's consent is required).
- Residence (up to 36 months; 24 months maximum for SSO).
- Specified activity (up to 60 days).
- Prohibited activity (up to 36 months; 24 months maximum for SSO).
- Exclusion (up to 24 months).
- Curfew (up to 6 months and for between 2–12 hours in any one day; if a stand-alone curfew order is made, there is no probation involvement).
- Attendance centre (12–36 hours with a maximum of three hours per attendance).

Home Office (2005d) guidance on the use of the Community Order urges probation officers to avoid the overuse of requirements and suggests that between one and three would represent the normal range for most Community Orders. Research on the early implementation of the Community Order showed little innovation, with the Order seemingly mirroring the old community sentences (Mair *et al.*, 2007).

The suspended sentence of imprisonment

The suspended sentence of imprisonment was introduced at the same time as parole, by the 1967 Criminal Justice Act. Such a sentence had been

Cleaning up the environment provides a focus for offenders sentenced to unpaid work as part of a Community Order – one of a number of options open to the courts in seeking an appropriate form of 'punishment in the community'.

considered twice, and rejected in the 1950s. Its popularity in the late 1960s was linked with a political desire to find ways of reducing the number of people in prison. Up until 1972 courts were required to suspend the majority of prison sentences of less than six months. The situation now, since the Criminal Justice Act 2003, is that a court which passes a prison sentence of less than 12 months is able to suspend that sentence for a period of between six months and two years while ordering the offender to undertake certain requirements in the community. The custodial part of the sentence will not take effect unless the offender fails to comply with those requirements or commits another offence within the period of suspension. The problem historically with the suspended sentence is that it has not generally been limited to cases where the offender would otherwise have been sent to prison. Though estimates vary, it is suggested that up to half of those given suspended sentences would not have been sentenced to immediate custody had the suspended sentence not existed (Bottoms, 1987).

Sentencing policy

Recent history in sentencing practice can be divided into a number of periods. Ashworth (1983) distinguished between the periods 1967–1972 and 1973–1981, and to this may be added the period up to and just beyond the Criminal Justice Act 1991 and, finally, the period since 1992. Ashworth has argued that the main characteristic of penal change between 1967 and 1972 was the introduction of a series of new penalties for the courts to use in the sentencing of offenders. In the period following this up until the early 1980s it 'was the orchestration of changes in the sentencing practices of the courts' (1983: 132).

There was significant statutory change in the late 1960s and early 1970s and, even though there was very little legislative change between 1973 and 1981, there was, nevertheless, quite considerable change in sentencing practice. Thus, in the mid-1970s the use of immediate and suspended imprisonment was at its lowest proportionate level and the fine was at its highest. From that point onwards, the fine and probation have taken a smaller share, whereas the use of immediate imprisonment and community service have increased.

The policy advocated by government ministers in the 1970s and especially the 1980s was one of 'bifurcation', wherein long custodial sentences would be reserved for the violent, the dangerous and those from whom the public need protection; and shorter sentences or non-custodial sentences would be increasingly used for the more run-of-the-mill offenders. In addition, one of the responses to the feeling that the increasing expenditure on criminal justice, and the increasing array of sanctions available to the courts, was having precious little effect on levels of crime was to move away from formal processes for dealing with offenders. Particularly in relation to youth justice policy (see Chapter 29) a policy of 'diversion' was increasingly advocated. By this was meant, at its most minimal, diversion from custody and, at its most far-reaching, diversion from formal criminal justice processes (Newburn and Souhami, 2005).

This might mean, amongst other things, the *de facto* decriminalisation of certain offences; informal cautioning rather than charging, or referral to mediation schemes rather than charging and prosecuting. During the 1980s, however, there developed a fairly full-blown critique of the proliferation of diversion schemes and alternative forms of dispute resolution. The majority of the arguments gelled around Cohen's (1985) 'dispersal of discipline' thesis (see Chapter 16). In summary, Cohen's argument was that there had been a dispersal of discipline and social control via the increasing use of community-based penalties. One of the unintended consequences of informalism was to draw into the criminal justice system people who would not otherwise have been dealt with under formal procedures. In addition, 'diversion schemes also formalised the informal by giving quasi-official powers to new people – parents, social workers, colleagues became parties to contracts, treatment, reporting' (Hudson, 1993: 40).

In his critique of Cohen, Bottoms (1983) suggests that an analysis of the period since the war shows that both imprisonment and probation declined as a proportion of all offences and that, in fact, it was the penalties not involving supervision – such as the fine and the suspended sentence – which flourished. This was reversed in the 1980s with a significant decline in the proportionate use of the fine, and a commensurate increase in the use of probation, community service and imprisonment.

One of the consequences of the critique of informalism was the development of the contradictory trend towards formalism. Formalism involved a desire to return to a type of classical or formal justice model. The most influential of these were based on the 'just deserts' principle which would link sentencing to the seriousness or gravity of the offence under consideration. At its core, however, Hudson (1993) suggests that this model contained a desire to curb professional discretion through sentencing guidelines (generally via the Court of Appeal).

Much of what happened in the 1980s appears to have occurred despite the absence of a well developed or articulated penal policy. Nevertheless, the primary driving force remained the crisis in the prisons. Despite the proliferation of alternatives to custody in the 1960s and 1970s, the policies of bifurcation and informalism and, crucially, increasing attempts to limit judicial discretion throughout the 1980s, the prison population continued to rise. This, together with the collapse of faith in rehabilitation, led to pressure for reform of sentencing policy. Wasik (1992: 127) argues that 'the apparent ineffectiveness of the Court of Appeal in persuading sentencers to send fewer offenders to custody, and for shorter periods of time ... persuaded the legislature that this objective ha[d] to be achieved by legislative reform to fetter the discretion of sentencers'. The result was the Criminal Justice Act 1991.

The Criminal Justice Act 1991

Out of the variety of competing sentencing principles still around during the 1970s and 1980s, it was desert theory (see Chapter 22) that by the end of the decade had won the day. In an observation that now truly feels that it belongs to a different era, the 1990 White Paper, *Crime Justice and Protecting the Public*, observed that:

> Deterrence is a principle with much immediate appeal ... But much crime is committed on impulse, given the opportunity presented by an open window or unlocked door, and it is committed by offenders who live from moment to moment; their crimes are as impulsive as the rest of their feckless, sad or pathetic lives. It is unrealistic to construct sentencing arrangements on the assumption that most offenders will weigh up the possibilities in advance and base their conduct on rational calculation. Often they do not. (Home Office, 1990, para 2.8)

The Green Paper preceding the White Paper and Act, published in 1988, was similarly blunt in relation to incarceration:

> Imprisonment is not the most effective punishment for most crime. Custody should be reserved as punishment for very serious offences, especially when the offender is violent and a continuing risk to the public. But not every sentencer or member of the public has full confidence in the present orders which leave offenders in the community. [Hence] ... the Government's proposals, which aim to increase the courts' and the public's confidence in keeping offenders in the community. (Home Office, 1988: 1–2)

The White Paper formed the basis for the Criminal Justice Act 1991, an Act that lay down a set of general guidelines for sentencing – not an American-style sentencing grid, but rather a set of general principles. At its heart was the assumption that penal severity should be proportionate to offence seriousness (and should not be overridden by other factors), otherwise known as 'just deserts'. Importantly, the Act prevented the use of custody unless the court was satisfied that the offence was 'so serious that only a custodial sentence could be justified' (though there were exceptions). Perhaps equally importantly, the Act's guidelines also applied to non-custodial penalties.

The Act stated that a court shall not pass a community sentence 'unless it is of the opinion that the offence, or the combination of the offence and one other offence associated with it, was serious enough to warrant such a sentence'. Thus, the only justification for imposing a community sentence under the Act was offence seriousness and, crucially therefore, community sentences were not to be considered to be 'alternatives to custody', but as distinctive penalties in their own right. It was at this point that the probation order became a sentence in its own right rather than an order made in place of a sentence.

The Act then represented a significant departure, not only from previous legislation, but also from the previous style of policy-making. As one senior Home Office official commented:

> The Act can be seen as a first attempt to construct a truly comprehensive piece of legislation governing sentencing. It covers the whole process: virtually the whole range of disposals available; the reasoning to be applied when reaching decisions; the methods by which sentences can be calculated and implemented; and, in the case of custody, the whole process from reception, right through to the expiry of the term imposed. The sheer scale of the attempt,

| Figure 27.1 | The sentencing framework in the Criminal Justice Act 1991 |

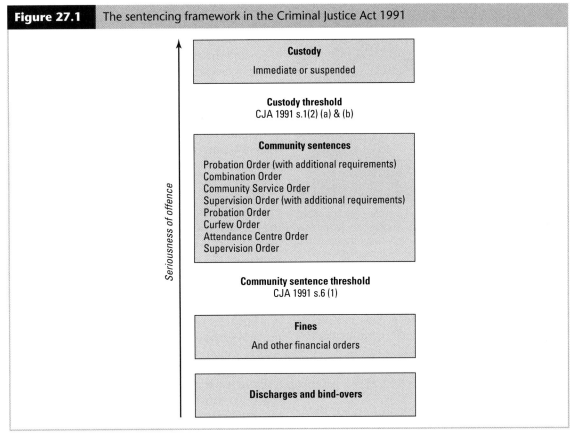

Source: Brownlee (1998).

taken as a whole, is probably unprecedented. Previous reforms have been more piecemeal ... The Act breaks new ground in another way. This Act – as distinct from any others on the subject – seeks to incorporate a clearly stated set of principles about sentencing – a sentencing philosophy if you like ... Governments habitually explain their policies in White Papers – in this case, the White Paper 'Crime, Justice and Protecting the Public'. If this is the case, the Act seeks to incorporate the policies in statutory form. (quoted in Gibson *et al.*, 1994: 33)

One of the key changes introduced by the 1991 Act was the amendment of the system of fines. Largely in response to perceived difficulties and inequities in the operation of the system of financial penalties, the 1991 Act contained provision for the introduction of what has been called the 'unit fine'. In essence, and using a set of guidelines, offences before the court were to be assessed in terms of their number of units of 'seriousness'. This could range from 1–50 units. Once the seriousness of the offence had been determined in this manner, the

offender would be required to complete a means test which would assess their weekly disposable income. This would determine the amount to be paid per individual unit, subject to the statutory minima and maxima of £4 and £100.

In principle, the intention was that fines should be equalised in terms of their impact upon offenders committing similar offences, but who were of vastly differing means. A lot of effort went into piloting the new system. In the four Crown Court centres in which the research was conducted, fines were paid more quickly, there were fewer committals to prison for default, the poorest defendants were fined the least, and there was no extension in the use of fines (Moxon *et al.*, 1990). However, unit fines, once formally introduced, were widely criticised almost from the outset. Raine and Willson (1993: 38) suggest that 'the "professionals" were wary about their discretion being eroded and many were opposed to the scheme, especially when a serious offence by a low-income defendant attracted a smaller fine than a minor one by a comparatively wealthy defendant'.

Electronic tagging has become an increasingly important method of monitoring offenders sentenced to curfew orders – though many questions have been raised about the reliability of the technology and its appropriateness for use with particular kinds of offenders.

The Act also introduced a new, tough community penalty: the 'combination order'. This was probation and community service combined; the minimum period of supervision being 12 months, the maximum three years. Section 12 of the 1991 Act created a new order, the curfew order. In addition, there was also provision for electronic monitoring to take place, though a curfew order could be made in combination with such 'tagging'. These orders could be made on anyone over the age of 16 and they required the offender to be in a specified place at a specified time.

Sentencing reform after the 1991 Act

Despite the extensive process of consultation that had preceded the White Paper, the broad degree of support for the intentions behind the legislation that there appeared to be amongst criminal justice professionals and practitioners, and some of the early positive signs visible in sentencing, there was swift governmental retreat from the 1991 Act. It started with the arrival of Kenneth Baker as Home Secretary and the reintroduction of penal populism in the form of campaigns against 'bail bandits' and 'joyriding' – the latter ending with the hasty passage of new legislation: the Aggravated Vehicle Taking Act 1991. The appointment of Kenneth Clarke as Home Secretary signalled a more radical change in the criminal justice policy agenda, a process which gathered speed under his successor, Michael Howard, appointed in May 1993.

In the country at large, public worries about crime were heightened by the brutal and shocking murder of two year-old James Bulger in February 1993, and the very high profile trial of the two ten year-old defendants later in the year (see Chapter 29). At the 1993 Conservative Party conference the Home Secretary, in outlining his criminal justice policy – a policy which he recognised would lead to an increase in the use of custodial sentences – said: 'I do not flinch from that. We shall no longer judge the success of our system of justice by a fall in our prison population ... Let us be clear. Prison works.'

The process culminated in the passage of the Criminal Justice Act 1993 which reversed some of the key elements of the earlier legislation, in particular the criteria justifying the use of custodial sentences; the role of an offender's previous record in sentencing; and the newly established unit fine system. One former senior Home Office administrator said: 'The Government's change of direction in its policies on crime and criminal justice [at this time] is probably the most sudden and the most radical which has ever taken place in this area of public policy' (quoted in Gibson *et al.*, 1994: 84).

From early 1993 onward sentencing trends began to change. First of all there was a very sharp increase in the prison population, though this was partly a consequence of an increase in the number of prisoners on remand. There was some indication that commencements of both probation orders and community service orders rose, though there also appeared to be a trend towards longer orders.

Despite the breadth and the speed of change in penal policy, the legislative programme was, however, still not complete. In addition to reaffirming his belief in the efficacy of imprisonment, Michael Howard announced at the 1993 Conservative Party conference a 27-point package of 'emergency action to tackle the crime wave'. This included restricting the right to silence, reducing the use of cautioning and tightening bail provisions, and the introduction of secure training centres for persistent juvenile offenders. Later in the year the Criminal Justice and Public Order Bill was introduced, and it included, in some form, all the above-mentioned measures, together with provisions for new custodial sentences for 12–14 year-olds; increased the grounds for refusing bail; allowed inferences to be drawn from the use of the right of silence; and a new offence of aggravated trespass.

The Crime (Sentences) Act 1997

At the 1995 Conservative Party conference Michael Howard, an avowed Americanophile, promoted three sets of changes based in part on US policy: increased honesty in sentencing ('no more half-sentences for full-time crimes'); mandatory minimum sentences ('if you don't want to do the time, don't do the crime'); and, a variant on three strikes ('anyone convicted for a second time of a serious violent or sexual offence should receive an automatic sentence of life imprisonment'). The subsequent Crime (Sentences) Act 1997 introduced three sets of 'three strikes' mandatory sentences: an automatic life sentence for a second serious sexual or violent offence; a minimum seven year prison sentence for third time 'trafficking' in class A drugs; and, a minimum three-year sentence for third-time domestic burglary.

During the passage of the Bill, the then Shadow Home Secretary had been careful not to appear to be especially hostile to the Bill. Nevertheless, in some circles it was anticipated that once in power Jack Straw would not implement the three strikes provisions. Any such hopes were quickly dashed. In an early statement as Home Secretary in July 1997 he committed the government to implementing the automatic life sentences without delay. He then, claiming that the other mandatory minimum provisions had been 'significantly improved by Labour amendments' (HC 299, 242, 30 July 1997), said that the seven-year sentence for third-time drug traffickers would be implemented later in the year. Although it took a little longer, the three strikes provision for burglary was eventually implemented in 1999.

Sentencing reform under New Labour

Considerable attention during the 1990s was paid to the aim of ensuring greater consistency in sentencing. In their election manifesto, the Labour Party (1997) proposed to:

> ... implement an effective sentencing system for all the main offences to ensure greater consistency and stricter punishment for serious repeat offenders. The courts will have to spell out what each sentence really means in practice. The Court of Appeal will have a duty to lay down sentencing guidelines for all the main offences. The attorney general's power to appeal unduly lenient sentences will be extended.

The 1991 Act had sought to impose new restrictions and politicians had for much of the rest of the decade attempted to limit judicial discretion. For this and other reasons the 1991 Act is rightly considered to constitute 'a landmark in the development of English sentencing law' (Ashworth, 2000: 357). However, what the Act did not do, Ashworth argues, is make any substantial changes to the 'transmission mechanism' whereby general rules and principles contained in statute are translated into consistent and coherent practice in court. In many areas there has been a substantial gap between sentencing policy and sentencing practice, and there continues to be wide variation in sentencing between courts (and sometimes among different sentencers in the same court).

In response, the Crime and Disorder Act 1998 both introduced a Sentencing Advisory Panel and placed the provision of guideline judgments by the Court of Appeal on a statutory footing. The Sentencing Advisory Panel began operation in July 1999, its role being to encourage consistency in sentencing. Under the Act, the Court of Appeal had to attend to the advice of the Panel before issuing new sentencing guidelines for groups of offences. The Panel itself had the autonomy to propose that the Court should issue or revise guidelines. The panel was arguably therefore more 'advisory' and less 'directive' than Andrew Ashworth's original (1995: 343) proposals that such a body should have the 'task of developing and keeping under review a corpus of coherent sentencing guidance for the Crown Courts and magistrates' courts'.

The aim of developing a more consistent and coherent sentencing system was also contained in the Powers of Criminal Courts (Sentencing) Act 2000 – which consolidated previous sentencing legislation and sought, if not to codify, then at least to clarify it – and the Criminal Justice and Court Services Act 2000 which, though primarily concerned with the reform of the probation service, stated that its initial purpose was to provide for 'courts to be given assistance in determining the appropriate sentences to pass, and making other decisions, in respect of persons charged with or convicted of offences'.

One of the potentially most significant changes to sentencing policy and practice in the UK in recent years has been the 'incorporation' into law of the European Convention on Human Rights via the Human Rights Act 1998 (see also Chapter 34). In fact, in a strict sense, the Act does not incorporate the Convention, or the rights secured by its

Articles (Cheney *et al.*, 2001). Rather, it declares that certain Articles are 'to have effect for the purposes of the Act', with the result that primary and subordinate legislation should be compatible with those Articles so far as possible, and that public authorities must not act in a way which is incompatible with a Convention Right. Consequently – and in order to protect parliamentary sovereignty – the judiciary has no power to strike down or amend primary legislation. However, a 'declaration of incompatibility' would be expected to 'trigger a very speedy amendment of the primary legislation by statutory instrument' (Cheney *et al.*, 2001: 16).

New Labour Home Secretaries have been operating within difficult territory so far as sentencing and the courts are concerned. The modernising agenda has led in the direction of significant reform of both the organisation of the courts and the framework of sentencing. Populist pressures, however, have meant that any reform seemingly has to be located, at least in part, within a punitive rhetoric. In order to stimulate fresh thinking, and possibly to distance himself from politically difficult ideas, Jack Straw set up two Reviews: the Review of Criminal Courts in England and Wales under Lord Justice Auld (Auld, 2001); and the Review of the Sentencing Framework under John Halliday (Home Office, 2001a).

The Auld Review of Criminal Courts

The major recommendations of the Auld Review included:

- The establishment of a national Criminal Justice Board to replace bodies like the Trial Issues Group, as well as local Criminal Justice Boards for giving effect to the national body's directions.

- A unified criminal court which would replace the Crown Court and the magistrates' courts with three divisions.

  - The Crown division, like the Crown Court, with jurisdiction over all indictable-only offences and the more serious either way offences.

  - The District division, constituted by a judge or recorder and at least two magistrates, to exercise jurisdiction over a 'mid-range' of either way cases (that is those most likely to incur penalties of more than six months and no more than two years imprisonment).

  - The magistrates' division, like the magistrates' courts, with jurisdiction over all summary cases and the less serious either way cases.

- The encouragement of greater participation in the jury system through the removal of the right to ineligibility or excusability.

However, two leading commentators argued that in terms of lasting influence it would be the Halliday Report that would be 'the starting point for consideration of changes to English sentencing and sanctions' (Tonry and Rex, 2002: 2).

The Halliday Report

The review of the sentencing framework was established in 2000 and it was in part stimulated by what was perceived to be something of a muddle in sentencing that had emerged in the aftermath of the various reforms to the 1991 Act. The announcement of the Halliday Review made clear the reasons for its establishment:

> Public confidence in our system of justice is too low. There is a feeling that our sentencing framework does not work as well as it should and that it pays insufficient weight to the needs of victims … There is insufficient consistency or progression in sentencing and sentencers receive insufficient information about whether their sentencing decisions have worked.

The Report's recommendations were extensive and added up, if implemented, to what would have been a fairly radical overhaul of the existing system. The Report examined the apparent problems with the extant system, outlined its vision of the appropriate philosophical basis for the sentencing system, recommended a number of reforms to the system, covering sentence design, the prison estate, sentencing decision-making and enforcement and the governance of discretion. The Report's criticisms of the existing system were themselves far-reaching, including the alleged failure of the current system to focus on crime reduction and reparation, its failure to deal satisfactorily with previous convictions, its ineffective use of short prison sentences and, indeed, elements of longer sentences, together with the system's general absence of consistency, transparency and clarity.

Philosophically, the Report offered a modification of the 'just deserts' approach, or what is referred to as 'limited retributivism' (see Chapter 22). The modification of just deserts is undertaken primarily in order to take account of the fact that 'sentence severity should increase as a consequence of sufficiently recent and relevant previous convictions' (Home Office, 2001a: para 2.7). The result would be a 'punitive envelope' indicating the possible range of sentence. The primary influence on the content of the envelope would be utilitarian – selecting the option that would best serve the purposes of crime reduction and reparation. Baker and Clarkson (2002) in their evaluation of the Report's recommendations argue that such proposals might lead to substantial disparities in the sentences received by offenders who commit similar crimes and have similar records. Indeed, they conclude that despite 'the Report's proposed codified guidelines and the limitation that the actual sentence imposed be within the bands set by the punitive envelope, the reality is the abandonment of the proportionality principle and a return to the "bad old days"' (2002: 93).

The Report made great play of the need for 'seamlessness' both of the management of offenders in custody and the community, and in terms of the relationship between the courts, partner agencies and the public. As intimated earlier, the impression that public confidence in the justice system was low was a primary driving force behind the review, and restoring and maintaining public confidence is effectively presented by the Report as a goal of sentencing policy. Thus, in discussing the body responsible for issuing sentencing guidelines, the report recommended that it should 'also be responsible for monitoring their application, keeping them up-to-date and otherwise revising them as necessary' (2001: ix).

Justice for All

The eventual outcome of both reviews was a White Paper, *Justice for All* (Home Office, 2002), which recommended a broad range of reform measures, again using the language of modernisation. Most notably, these included the scrapping of the double jeopardy rule (recommended by the Stephen Lawrence Inquiry – see Chapter 25), unifying the administration of the magistrates' and Crown Court, increasing magistrates' sentencing powers from six to 12 months, creating 'intermittent' prison sentences, 'custody plus' (in which offenders serve a short prison sentence of between two weeks and three months followed by at least six months' community work) and 'custody minus' (the new suspended sentence). The overall aim of the reform process was said to be to 'rebalance' the criminal justice system in favour of victims and witnesses at the expense of defendants (see Chapter 17). Its approach, thereafter, was pragmatic rather than philosophical, attempting to reduce delays, increase detection rates and increase conviction rates (referred to as 'closing the justice gap').

Criminal Justice Act 2003

The subsequent Criminal Justice Act 2003 brought together many of the proposals contained in the Halliday and Auld reviews including:

- *Custody Plus* – Custodial sentences of less than 12 months combine custodial terms of between two weeks and three months with a 'licence period' of at least six months (though, by mid-2007, this had still not been implemented).

- *Intermittent custody* – Custodial sentences that may be served in short blocks, thereby allowing offenders to continue in work (introduced in early 2007).

- *Custody Minus* – A suspended sentence with a presumption that it will be activated if the community-based element of the sentence is breached (this is now referred to as the Suspended Sentence Order (SSO) (see Mair *et al.*, 2007).

- A new mandatory minimum sentence (five years) for unauthorised possession of a prohibited firearm.

The Criminal Justice Act 2003 was the first piece of legislation to spell out fully the varied aims of the sentencing system. These, it said, were:

- The punishment of offenders.
- The reduction of crime (including its reduction by deterrence).
- The reform and rehabilitation of offenders.
- The protection of the public.
- The making of reparation by offenders to persons affected by their offences.

In addition, the Act introduced a structured sentencing framework via Sentencing Guidelines. A newly established body, to work with the Sentencing Advisory Panel, the Sentencing Guidelines Council is the lead body for the framework, and it has introduced a series of new guidelines in which the harm caused by the offence and offender culpability are to be the primary considerations in determining sentences.

Trends in non-custodial sentencing

As was indicated earlier in the chapter, although successive governments made either reducing the prison population, or at least attempting to halt its increase, a central element of penal policy, all this stopped in the early 1990s. From that point onward the prison population has increased, and has done so markedly (see Chapter 28). As we will see, community penalties also appear to have been subject to similar influences. An increasing proportion of offences are subject to community penalties rather than fines or discharges, and the absence of previous convictions appears to be having a diminishing effect on the likely imposition of community penalties (Newburn, 2007).

As we have seen there are a number of non-custodial disposals available to the courts. The two that have generally been used most frequently are the fine and the absolute or conditional discharge. In addition there is a range of community punishments, generally involving community supervision by the probation service (or by a Youth Offending Team for young offenders). Until recently, when they were replaced by a generic Community Order, the main forms of supervision available for those aged 16 and over were:

- *Community Rehabilitation Order (CRO)* – Formerly the Probation Order, can be between six months and three years in length and have additional requirements such as residence requirements and drug treatment.

- *Community Punishment Order (CPO)* – Formerly the Community Service Order, consists of unpaid work of 40–240 hours.

- *Community Punishment and Rehabilitation Order (CPRO)* – Formerly the Combination Order, combines probation supervision of between one and three years and 40–100 hours of community service.

- *Drug Treatment and Testing Order (DTTO)* – Introduced in 2000, the order lasts between six months and three years.

In the main, it is too early to examine trends in the new Community Order (though for details of initial trends see Mair *et al.*, 2007). In relation to community penalties more generally, the number of offenders starting community sentences under the supervision of the probation service increased by 30 per cent between 1993 and 2003. CROs accounted for just under half (46%) of such sentences and CPOs a further 40 per cent. Though orders of all lengths increased during the decade from 1993, proportionately it was the longest orders that increased the most – though these remain relatively infrequently used compared with the shorter orders. Summary motoring offences are the largest offence group among those beginning CROs, CPOs and CPROs. In relation to CROs 'theft and handling' and 'other summary offences' are the next largest categories. An increase in the number of summary motoring offences resulting in CROs accounted for the bulk of the increase in the use of the order between 1998–2003.

As with the use of custody during this period, a general process of 'racheting up' has also occurred in relation to community penalties. Thus, whereas in 1991, 22 per cent of convictions for an indictable offence resulted in a community sentence, by 2001 this had risen to 32 per cent. The most significant element in explaining this trend is the progressive falling-out-of-favour of the fine as a penalty. During the same period, there was a 25 per cent fall in the use of fines and there was also a substantial, though less dramatic, drop in the use of absolute or conditional discharges in the sentencing of indictable offences (Figure 27.2). Again there is no evidence that these trends reflect changes in the seriousness of the offences, or in the nature of the offenders coming before the courts. Thus, two-thirds of the increase in the number of offenders receiving a community sentence had no previous convictions (Carter, 2003).

There are a number of reasons why the fine has become a progressively less popular sentencing option (Mair, 2004). The decline began in the 1980s, a period in which poor economic conditions and high levels of unemployment, arguably, made financial penalties a less plausible option than they had previously been. However, the available alternatives were generally higher up the tariff. As the decade proceeded, the climate became progressively more punitive – at the very least reinforcing any trend that existed toward increasingly tough sentencing. The bottom line is that, for a combination of reasons, the fine increasingly lost credibility as a sanction and, from a position where it accounted for almost half of all sentences for indictable offences, it has now fallen to below one-quarter and has been replaced by custody as the most popular sanction for such offences (see Figure 27.2).

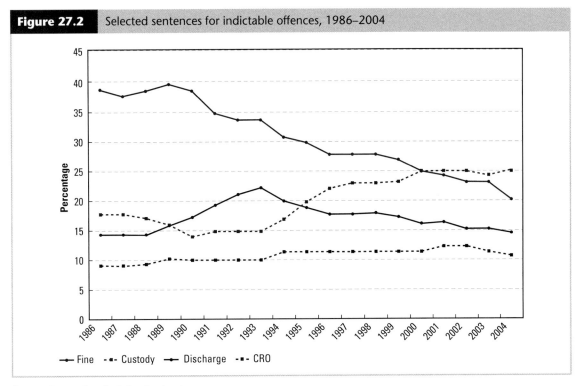

Figure 27.2 Selected sentences for indictable offences, 1986–2004

—◆— Fine   –■– Custody   —●— Discharge   –■– CRO

Source: Sentencing Statistics (various).

Unlikely offender? In 2006 the Lord Chief Justice, Lord Phillips, passed himself off as a convicted drink-driver and served part of a community order cleaning up a council estate – hoping to persuade people that community service sentences were not a soft option.

Concerns about the general effectiveness of community penalties, and about public perceptions of their 'toughness', led to increased attempts to ensure compliance – and punish non-compliance – with such orders. One of the significant changes over the past decade has been the consequent increase in the proportion of community orders that are terminated because of further offending, non-compliance or some related negative reason. Non-compliance is generally referred to as a 'breach' of the order. Where an offender breaches their order they are returned to court to be re-sentenced. Breach of a court order is an offence in itself and an offender can receive a separate sentence for it, including being re-sentenced for the original offence, which may mean the imposition of a prison sentence.

Although the majority of orders cease for positive reasons, this proportion has declined markedly in recent years. In 1993, for example, 11 per cent of CROs resulted in a breach compared with 29 per cent in 2003 (see Table 27.1). Similar trends can be seen in relation to the CPO where the proportion resulting in a breach rose from just under a quarter

(24%) in 1993 to over a third (34%) by 2003. Moreover, DTTOs, which have only recently been introduced, have had a stubbornly low completion rate – at 27 per cent, for example, in 2003 – with almost half of orders being breached.

Despite the fact that the proportion of breached orders resulting in imprisonment has generally declined in the past decade (from 38% to 18% of CROs between 1993–2004 and from 21% to 12% of CPOs) the overall increase in the proportion of community penalties being breached has meant that the total number of custodial sentences being imposed as a result of unsuccessful completion of orders has generally been rising (see Table 27.2).

A total of 8,610 custodial sentences were made as a result of breach of community sentences in 1998. By 2004 this had risen to 12,453, an increase of 45 per cent. Breaches of DTTOs – introduced fully in 2000 – accounted for over two-fifths (44%) of this increase. The expanding use of community penalties, in an environment in managerialist and risk-oriented times where there is a decreased tolerance of the violation of conditions attached to

particular orders, has led to a very significant rise in breach rates and to further increases in custodial sentencing. We look in more detail at trends in imprisonment in the next chapter. For the remainder of this chapter we will examine the history and practice of the main constituent of community-based punishment, probation.

Review questions

1 What are the main non-custodial sentences available to the criminal courts?

2 What have been the major trends in the use of non-custodial penalties in the last 20 years?

3 What were the major reasons for the swift retreat from the 1991 Criminal Justice Act?

4 What was the purpose of renaming probation and community service orders?

5 What is meant by 'limited retributivism'?

Table 27.1	Proportion of offenders breaching CPOs, CROs, CPROs and DTTOs										
	1994	**1995**	**1996**	**1997**	**1998**	**1999**	**2000**	**2001**	**2002**	**2003**	**2004**
All	18	20	22	23	21	24	30	29	31	35	37
CRO	10	11	12	1	14	18	23	23	25	29	31
CPO	24	26	28	28	29	30	35	32	32	34	37
CPRO	26	34	36	40	25	29	35	4	50	56	60
DTTO	–	–	–	–	–	–	–	32	44	48	49

Source: Offender Management Caseload Statistics 2003, December 2004, and RDS NOMS (2005).

Table 27.2	Number of offenders breaching community supervision entering custody							
	1993	**1998**	**1999**	**2000**	**2001**	**2002**	**2003**	**2004**
CRO	1,828	2,290	2,874	3,246	3,109	3,462	3,670	3,448
CPO	2,057	2,481	2,668	2,764	2,441	2,369	2,118	2,278
CPRO	421	1,444	1,798	1,884	1,560	1,421	1,489	1,530
DTTO	–	–	–	–	18	399	1,105	1,459

Source: Sentencing Statistics (2003).

Probation

The idea of probation is a century old and has gone through various phases in which the dominant working philosophy has changed. Whitehead and Statham (2006) summarise these changes in the following way:

1876–1930s – Saving offenders' souls by divine grace

1930s–1970s – Casework, diagnosis, rehabilitation and positivism

1970s – Alternatives to custody

1980s – Punishment in the community; penal pessimism

1997 onward – Punishment; renaissance of rehabilitation; evidence-based practice

As we saw in Chapter 2, the probation service as we know it today has its origins in the Victorian temperance movement and the police court missionaries who began work in the 1870s and 1880s. Although the legal basis for alternatives to imprisonment increased during the course of the nineteenth century, it was not until the first decade of the twentieth century that probation was put on a statutory footing. The nature and scale of the work undertaken by probation officers has changed markedly during the last 90 years, with the pace of change increasing sharply in the past 25 years.

Section 2 of the Probation of Offenders Act 1907 says that where an offender has been released on condition of their recognisance, they should: 'be under the supervision of such person as may be named in the order during the period specified in the order'. Such an order was in future to be referred to as a probation order. Conditions could be attached prohibiting the offender from mixing with undesirable persons or visiting undesirable places and requiring abstention from alcohol. Local areas were given the power, but not compelled, to appoint probation officers for their area. The duties of such officers were:

To visit or receive reports from the person under supervision at such reasonable intervals as the probation officer may think fit;

To see that he observes the condition of his recognizance;

To report to the court on his behaviour;

To *advise, assist and befriend* him and, when necessary, to endeavour to find him suitable employment (*emphasis added*)

It was in the mid-1920s that the basis of a national, bureaucratic probation machinery, including probation committees for overseeing the work, was established. From approximately this period there began a gradual movement away from the 'missionary ideal' towards what McWilliams (1986) and others have referred to as a more therapeutic or diagnostic approach to work with offenders. The change – and this, of course, was very gradual – was from a system dominated by missionaries whose task it was to reform the wicked, to one run by professionals who wanted to 'heal the sick' (May, 1994). From its somewhat precarious beginnings, probation had by this stage become quite firmly established. From under 10,000 people placed on probation in 1919, there were 25,000 in 1936, and 35,000 by 1943 (with 50,000 in total under supervision).

Probation continued to expand in the post-war period. Probation officers were also given responsibility for all after-care in the community from 1963, for the after-care of detention centre trainees in 1964, for borstal trainees and young prisoners in 1967, and for those sentenced to life imprisonment from 1968. In the 1970s, government began to identify the probation service as a vehicle for the management of more serious offenders in the community, including increasing numbers on post-custodial and parole licence. The numbers under supervision increased from 55,000 in the mid-1950s to over 150,000 in the early-1980s, with community service becoming a central part of the work of the probation service since this point (McWilliams, 1981).

Crucially, initiatives were also introduced by government which, some believed, compromised the traditional welfare philosophy of probation. Thus, for example, whilst parole 'was intended not only to reduce the prison population, but to assist in the process of resettlement of the offenders in the community ... it also incorporated elements of "public protection" in the community, through the monitoring of the parolee's progress by a probation officer' (May, 1994: 864). Day training centres and bail hostels were also introduced with the intention of stiffening up the public image of community-based sanctions by adding conditions to probation orders. There was, in short, declining confidence in the potential of the standard probation order.

For much of the period after the Second World War, 'probation existed in a relatively benign political world ... and ... the centre, in the form of the Home Office, provided a light touch in local probation areas' (Whitehead and Statham, 2006: 21). That said, it came under increasing pressure as a number of empirical research studies appeared to question its effectiveness. A study by Leslie Wilkins, undertaken in the late 1950s (Wilkins, 1960), found little difference in the reconviction rates of matched samples of offenders on probation and other orders. Subsequent research by the Home Office in the 1960s and the IMPACT study (Folkard *et al.*, 1974) also cast doubt on the extent to which probation reduced recidivism. Finally, Robert Martinson's famous essay on 'What Works' (1974) eventually ushered a new era of general pessimism about the effectiveness of the bulk of interventions with offenders.

Punishment in the community

At around this time there emerged the 'new criminology': at its heart a sociology of deviance that questioned the functions of the criminal justice system, including the 'nature' of probation (see Chapter 12). Could it be, as Harris puts it, 'that the service, far from acting in a humane manner, was a repressive arm of the state?' (1994: 935–6). Insights derived from this sociology of deviance led to a questioning of the role of the 'neutral' professional and, as one consequence, to the development of radical social work practices and groupings. The third challenge was to the very idea that intervention by probation officers might have some effect on the individual's propensity to offend.

The dominant position occupied by the 'rehabilitative ideal' which had formed the basis for the introduction of many non-custodial initiatives, was no more, and a form of penal pessimism developed. As Bottoms and McWilliams (1979: 159) put it:

> The reformation of the criminal ... has been central to the English approach to criminal justice since the end of the nineteenth century ... But penological research carried out in the course of the last twenty years or so suggests that penal 'treatments', as we significantly describe them, do not have any reformative effect, whatever other effects they may have. The dilemma is that a considerable investment has been made in various measures and services, of which the most obvious examples are custodial institutions

for young adult offenders and probation and after-care services in the community. *Are these services simply to be abandoned on the basis of the accumulated research evidence?* Put thus starkly, this is an unlikely proposition but one which, by being posed at all, has implications for the rehabilitative services concerned. *Will this challenge evoke a response by ... probation officers* by the invention of new approaches and methods? (*emphasis in original*)

Probation officer giving advice to an offender. Some professionals have been concerned at the move from the traditional probation role 'to advise, assist and befriend' to a more punitive approach with 'protecting the public' as the priority.

Part of the answer to this is that a significant proportion of the energies of the probation service have gone into adapting to the increasing responsibilities and changing circumstances in which they have been operating in the past 30 years. During this period, the service itself has had less and less control over its working environment as central government has progressively intervened. The traditional function as set out in the 1907 Act, 'to advise, assist and befriend', was increasingly being challenged by the requirement on probation officers that they administer what they perceived to be ever more punitive community-based sanctions, thus turning them into 'screws on wheels' (Haxby, 1978: 162). Toughening-up the form and the content of community sanctions has been, perhaps, the major characteristic of policy in this area since the early to mid 1970s.

In parallel with the development of policy in relation to policing (Chapter 25) a key element of policy in this area for the past 20 years or more has been the increasing involvement of and direction from the central government. In 1984, for example, the Home Office published its *Statement of National Objectives and Priorities* (SNOP) for the probation service (Home Office, 1984). SNOP outlined how the resources available to the service might be 'effectively and efficiently' used, and suggested that this was the responsibility of both the local probation committee and the Chief Probation Officer (Mair, 1995). A further Home Office report (the Grimsey Report) on the Probation Inspectorate recommended 'efficiency and effectiveness' inspections (Home Office, 1987), and in 1989 the Audit Commission issued a report entitled *The Probation Service: Promoting Value for Money*.

The culmination of all the Conservative government's initiatives in relation to the probation service and community sanctions throughout the decade was its 1988 Green Paper: *Punishment, Custody and the Community* (Home Office, 1998). It suggested that custody was most likely the right punishment for the majority of violent offenders, but pointed out that 95 per cent of recorded crime was non-violent. For less serious offenders, custody might not be the appropriate option:

> Imprisonment restricts offenders' liberty, but it also reduces their responsibility; they are not required to face up to what they have done and to the effect on their victim or to make any recompense to the victim or the public. If offenders are not imprisoned, they are more likely to able to pay compensation to their victims and to make some reparation to the community through useful work. Their liberty can be restricted without putting them behind prison walls. Moreover, if they are removed in prison from the responsibilities, problems and temptations of everyday life, they are less likely to acquire the self-discipline and self-reliance which will prevent reoffending in future. *Punishment in the community would encourage offenders to grow out of crime and to develop into responsible and law abiding citizens.* (Para 1.1, emphasis added)

Community-based sanctions were to be thought of as punishments which restricted liberty, but which enabled offenders to face up to the effects of their crimes, thus potentially being of benefit to the victim, and economical for the tax-payer.

As far as proposals for the future were concerned, the Green Paper began by setting out the three principles underpinning alternatives to custody where a fine alone, given the seriousness of the offence, would be inadequate. First, that it should restrict freedom of action – as a punishment; second, that it should involve action to reduce the risk of further reoffending; and third, that it should involve 'reparation to the community and, where possible, compensation to the victim'.

The Green Paper set out a number of possibilities in relation to restricting the liberty of offenders. These included:

- Introducing curfew powers for the courts to require offenders to stay at home at specified times.

- Extending and formalising the existing experiments in 'tracking' – where probation staff were used to maintain frequent contact with the offender.

- The introduction of electronic monitoring – which could be used as a method of enforcing curfews or supplementing the process of tracking – though the Green Paper suggested that it could most appropriately be used to keep offenders out of custody.

Crime, Justice and Protecting the Public

Following on less than two years after the Green Paper, a White Paper containing the government's proposals for legislation was published (Home Office, 1990). One of the most interesting aspects of the White Paper is that it set out the grounds of the government's interest in sentencing policy. Though reaffirming the independence of the judiciary – 'no government should try to influence the decisions of the courts in individual cases' – it nevertheless declared that 'sentencing principles and sentencing practice are matters of legitimate concern to Government' (para. 2.1). As we saw earlier in the chapter, the White Paper was underpinned by the principle of 'proportionality' or 'just deserts'.

The legislative outcome of *Punishment, Custody and the Community* and *Crime, Justice and Protecting the Public* was, of course, the 1991 Criminal Justice Act. The Act encouraged greater use of community sanctions within a sentencing framework informed by just deserts, but not completely constrained by it. The probation order became a sentence of the court thereby emphasising its role in punishment rather than its welfare and rehabilitative functions – a change of significant symbolic importance for the service. Perhaps most far-reaching for the probation service was the introduction of what then became known as the 'combination order': the power of the court to sentence an offender to probation (with requirements if considered appropriate) and community service for the same offence. The intention, clearly, was to give the courts confidence that there were sentences at their disposal which were appropriate for use in relation to offenders who might otherwise have been incarcerated, i.e. that were sufficiently punitive. In this spirit, the Act also introduced a new Curfew Order, to be monitored using electronic tags.

The emergence of a more punitive approach to criminal justice policy-making in the 1990s has been noted in several of the previous chapters. Needless to say, the probation service was affected quite significantly by this change of climate. One fairly immediate consequence of the return to 'populist punitiveness' was that punishment became the highlighted element of community penalties. In early 1995 another Green Paper was issued, the title of which – *Strengthening Punishment in the Community* – illustrated its intentions (Home Office, 1995b). In it, the government made clear its intention to tackle the fact that too often probation 'supervision is still widely regarded as a soft option'. Brownlee (1998: 28) suggests that it was abundantly clear that the 'principal aim of the proposed changes was to secure a further shift in responsibility for the implementation of community sentences towards the courts' and away from probation officers and other 'caring professionals'. The proposal for an integrated sentence was widely criticised, but the general anti-social work thrust of the Paper was, as we have seen, pursued with vigour.

New Labour and probation

Though no reference was made to reform of probation in the Labour Party's 1997 election manifesto, the first 18 months of the new Labour government saw a series of leaks outlining potential shake-ups of the service. These included merging it with the prison service to create a national 'corrections service', and changing the name of the probation service to reflect the changed climate within which it was working. A number of options were floated, including the Public Protection Service, the Offender Risk Management Service, the Community Justice Enforcement Agency and even the Community Rehabilitation and Punishment Service, though the acronym that would have resulted probably sank that one.

The probation service and 'what works'

At the heart of the New Labour modernisation agenda there has been an emphasis on 'what works' and 'cost-effectiveness' (see Home Office, 1999). The 'what works' paradigm has led to an apparent government desire to prioritise evidence-based policy and practice, to invest massively in research and evaluation and to promote accreditation programmes (Raynor, 2004). Not only is there an inherent centralising momentum in the 'what works' paradigm, but there is also a tension between what one might characterise as *effective* interventions ('what works') and *efficient* interventions (what it costs and how long it takes). Across government the Treasury has become increasingly important. Just as the comprehensive spending review gave impetus to the adoption of the 'what works' paradigm so, via the Treasury-led emphasis on cost-effectiveness, the linking of costs to outcomes and the measurement of the financial impact of interventions has determined much of the shape of the government's crime control agenda. Nowhere has this been more visible than in relation to the community penalties and the probation service.

Part of the attraction of the 'third way' in criminal justice was the promise it held in steering a course between Old Labour welfarism and New Labour punitiveness (Crawford, 2001). At the heart of this programme was the explicit distancing of government from old-fashioned 'nothing works' pessimism and the rise of the 'what works' agenda. This has had its most profound effect on the probation service and the system of community penalties in England and Wales. Influenced in particular by cognitive-behavioural approaches developed in Canada and by research, especially meta-analytical research (Andrews *et al.*, 1990; Lipsey, 1992), which claimed to show significant impacts with some offenders under some circumstances, the 'what works' agenda revived, albeit in a more limited fashion, faith in the idea of rehabilitation (Raynor and Vanstone, 2002). In 1999 the Home Office issued its Correctional Policy Framework (which forms the basis of its 'what works' approach):

Correctional policy is driven by What Works principles. This means that offending behaviour programmes should involve planned interventions over a specified period of time, which can be shown to change positively attitudes, beliefs, behaviour and social circumstances. Usually, they will be characterized by a sequence of activities designed to achieve clearly defined objectives based on a theoretical model or empirical evidence. There should also be a capacity to replicate the programme with different offenders to achieve the same results. (Home Office, 1999)

In 1999, a Joint Prisons and Probation Accreditation Panel (JPPAP) was established (it was later renamed the Correctional Services Accreditation Panel). Like the Youth Justice Board (YJB), the JPPAP was a non-departmental public body. Comprising a range of academics and criminal justice professionals, the Panel's central function was to accredit programmes that, on the basis of rigorous research, are believed to reduce reoffending. According to the Panel (JPPAP, 2001) the principles associated with effective interventions include:

- Effective risk management.
- Targeting offending behaviour.
- Addressing the specific factors linked with offenders' offending.
- Relevance to offenders' learning style.
- Promoting community reintegration.
- Maintaining quality and integrity of programme delivery.

The 'what works' approach has not been without its critics. Peter Raynor, one of the panel members, has noted that, whilst 'it is true that the evidence base in Britain is still fairly small, and although existing research projects will enable it to grow rapidly, not all of it will necessarily support the management decisions which have already been taken. Some of these may have to be changed if the commitment to evidence-based policy is to be maintained' (Raynor and Vanstone, 2002: 105). The probation service, in the form of its main union NAPO, has been critical of the impact of the approach on the ability of its members to use their own skills and judgement when working with offenders. Others have been sceptical about the research evidence itself, querying whether the evidence for some programmes was as firm as it was being presented as being (Merrington and Stanley, 2000) or questioning the apparent adherence to a narrow cognitive-behavioural dominated model of working with offenders (Mair, 2000).

A national probation service

In a classic piece of New Labour managerialism, an entirely new vehicle was created for the implementation of a 'what works'-led agenda in relation to non-custodial penalties. With relatively little public discussion, and no visible professional dissent, after almost a century, the 54 local probation services in England and Wales were disbanded and replaced by the National Probation Service for England and Wales in April 2001. The aim was that this new service would be more effectively controlled from the centre and that the raft of new programmes, influenced by the 'what works' agenda, could be rolled out quickly and as uniformly as possible (Mair, 2004).

The Criminal Justice and Court Services Act 2000 created the new National Probation Service for England and Wales, thereby radically restructuring a service that had been in existence for almost a century. The new structure comprised 42 local areas, each contiguous with local police force boundaries, each of which has a local probation board. The latter replace the previously existing 54 Probation Committees. From 2001 the new national service was directly accountable to the Home Secretary. Where previously funding had come jointly from the Home Office and local authorities (though in a ratio of approximately 80:20) the new service was directly and, in effect, completely funded by the Home Office.

The Act defined the purpose of the service as 'assisting courts in sentencing decisions and providing for the supervision and rehabilitation of persons charged with, or convicted of, offences' (*Probation Circular 25/2001*). The aims of the service were to:

i) protect the public;

ii) reduce offending;

iii) provide for the proper punishment of offenders;

iv) ensure that offenders are aware of the effects of their crimes on their victims and on the public;

v) rehabilitate offenders.

More generally, the Act allowed for 'national priorities to be interpreted in the light of local circumstances and local needs' (*Probation Circular 52/2001*) and it is this provision that provided the space within which the nature of the emergent 'tripartite relationship' between the service, probation boards and the Home Secretary could develop.

Nonetheless, when compared even with the reformed police authorities (see Chapter 25), the new system of governance for the probation service is highly centralised.

One of the controversial aspects of the new legislation concerned the changes made to the names of community penalties. The 'tough on crime' rhetoric and practice of successive governments had seen the probation service under considerable pressure – indeed sometimes hostile attack. As was noted above, during the 1990s, it was mooted on more than one occasion that the probation service should be renamed and/or merged with the prison service. Under New Labour both of these suggestions received new impetus. The desire to toughen the appearance of community punishment was acted upon, with the major and long-standing orders all being renamed. As we have seen, the 2000 Act renamed the probation order and other long-standing community orders.

The Carter Review and the emergence of NOMS

Raynor and Vanstone (2007) argue that if 1999–2000 was the high point of optimism in the 'what works' movement in England, then 2003–04 will almost certainly come to be seen as its low point. In particular, this was the period that the idea of integrating prisons and probation – on the agenda for some years previously – was finally formalised. The turning point is to be found in the publication of a report entitled *Managing Offenders, Reducing Crime* (Carter, 2003). The report arose from a review of correctional services undertaken by a businessman, Patrick Carter. The Carter Review highlighted a number of problems in the penal system, including the progressive use of harsher custodial and non-custodial sentences with less serious offenders, the declining use of the fine and the relationship between public opinion, politics and increasing punitiveness.

His major recommendation was the merging of probation and prison into a single National Offender Management Service (NOMS). He proposed what he called 'end-to-end offender management' in which the two hitherto separate agencies would provide a seamless service of management and supervision of offenders. The new agency was to have a Chief Executive, a National Offender Manager responsible for the Agency's overall crime reduction targets, and ten Regional Offender Managers (ROMs) responsible for organising provision. More radically still, Carter's suggestion was that these ROMs should commis-

sion services from among a variety of providers. That is to say, not only was the probation service to be merged with the prison service, but many of the things that it had hitherto provided would now be delivered by either the private or the voluntary sector (Hough *et al.*, 2006).

The Carter Review also recommended the introduction of a purchaser/provider split, with ROMs contracting rather than managing services on an equal basis from the public, private and voluntary sectors. The process of deciding which provider to use was called *contestability*. This idea has been much debated and criticised. It remains somewhat unclear what it means. Nellis (2006) describes it as follows:

> At its mildest, contestability seems merely to be a synonym for the process of market testing rather than for the specific outcome of privatisation or contracting out. This is how the Home Office now tends to project it. At its strongest, it seems to be about the engineering of a mixed economy of provision, which intentionally and systematically destroys the near-monopoly of the public sector, in order to institutionalise a permanently competitive – and in the government's terms more desirable – environment. This is what current stakeholders in corrections – the Probation Boards' Association (PBA), National Association of Probation Officers (NAPO), and the Prison Officers Association (POA) – fear is the real agenda, regardless of what is being said officially, even by the HM Inspectorate of Probation, which ostensibly endorses the mild view.

Government conducted a very brief consultation exercise on its new proposals. Press reports suggest that somewhere in the region of 740 of the 748 responses that were received were negative ('Home Office retreats on probation reform', the *Guardian*, 3 April 2006). Nevertheless, the government very quickly announced that it intended to implement the major recommendations of the Carter Review and indeed it has attempted to press ahead without delay. The government set out its plans for the National Offender Management Service (NOMS) in *Reducing Crime – Changing Lives*. NOMS was to have an overall remit to reduce reoffending and was also to be responsible for:

● Improving the enforcement and credibility of community punishments so that prison is not the first resort for less serious offenders.

- Ensuring that both custodial and community punishments make offenders address their behaviour and offer a path away from crime.
- Raising educational standards among offenders in order to break the link between low educational attainment and criminality.

However, the creation of NOMS, which formally came into existence in June 2005, has been fraught with difficulty and it is still some way from being fully realised (Gelsthorpe and Morgan, 2007). ROMs were appointed and began commissioning services in April 2006. The probation service has begun to contract out more of its services, but government considered that legislation was still necessary. The Offender Management Bill is due to become law during 2007 and it will establish the basis for operation and governance of NOMS.

The restructuring of the probation service remains a source of considerable concern in some quarters. Harry Fletcher, the Assistant General Secretary of NAPO, warned that:

> This Bill will, if implemented, lead to the abolition of the National Probation Service and its replacement with a competitive market. Local accountability would be lost, information sharing between agencies will be diminished by competition, and public protection compromised. The Bill is not about improving standards, it is about privatisation, yet to date no business case has been produced by the Government to show how the replacement of Probation by a market will actually work and improve the delivery of service. Whole probation Areas could be sold off under the arrangements, including the supervision of high risk offenders. The experience of privatisation in probation work so far has been a disaster... The way forward is through partnership with the voluntary and private sector not competition. The Government should look to arrangements in Scotland for offender management where there is a statutory duty on agencies to cooperate with each other to reduce reoffending.
>
> (http://www.napo2.org.uk/noms/archives/2006/11/offender_manage.html)

The reference above to Scotland concerns the *Management of Offenders (Scotland) Act* which was passed by the Scottish Parliament in late 2005. The Act establishes new Community Justice Authorities which will have the responsibility of co-ordinating

The creation of the National Offender Management Service (NOMS) has aroused considerable anxiety in some quarters – not least on the part of the National Association of Probation Officers (NAPO) – especially the increased emphasis given to privatisation.

and improving the delivery of services for offenders, and be responsible for monitoring and reporting on the effectiveness of joint working between local agencies to tackle reoffending. The eight regional Community Justice Authorities will oversee strategic planning and endeavour to ensure that there is successful partnership working across agencies. Comparing this with developments south of the border, McIvor and McNeill (2007) note that 'while recent policy developments signal a closer role for central government and other agencies in determining the strategic direction of offender management in Scotland, Scottish policy has, in the face of strongly voiced opposition, stopped short of the organizational changes brought about through the creation of the National Offender Management Service in England and Wales'.

In addition to progressive privatisation, the eventual Offender Management Act will also continue a swift and thoroughgoing process of centralisation. It will, for example, give the Home Secretary the power to establish Probation Trusts. These will replace the previously existing local Probation Boards. It is expected that they will continue to have local ties, but will not necessarily limit their activities to that area, and might for example develop particular areas of expertise and deliver those services in another area as well as locally. The ending of local Probation Boards, together with the creation of a National Probation Service and NOMS, adds up to a massive centralising shift in the provision of probation and related services. Rather like many of the changes that are detectable in policing (see Chapter 25), these represent a substantial increase in central government direction in criminal justice practice.

Review questions

1 What are the main aims of the modern probation service?

2 How do these differ from probation service aims earlier in the twentieth century?

3 What are the main changes in the governance of the probation service in the past decade?

Conclusion

The history of non-custodial penalties has been a turbulent one (Bottoms *et al.*, 2004a). A number of different 'eras' are identifiable (Bottoms *et al.*, 2004b). Beginning with the extended period in the first half of the twentieth century, characterised by Garland (1985) as 'penal welfarism', there then emerged a period in which there was a proliferation of non-custodial orders – generally presented as 'alternatives to custody'. However, as faith in rehabilitation declined, the emphasis on punishment grew – probation and other alternatives to custody being replaced by 'punishment in the community'. However, even this was not enough to slake the thirst of those promoting the new punitiveness (Pratt *et al.*, 2005). Although the last decade and more has seen considerable growth of

interest in restorative justice (see Chapter 30), the overwhelming trends have involved progressive managerialism, increasing centralisation and a ratcheting up of the use of punishment. Not only are substantially more people being sent to prison, but there are now far more being sentenced to community-based punishment. And, lest we make the mistake that this is being driven by crime, the available evidence suggests that this increase in the use of non-custodial penalties is occurring in cases which previously would have been dealt with through the use of fines or other means.

Penal populism, then, has been a significant driving force behind many of the changes we have discussed in this chapter. It would be wrong, however, simply to assume that this is somehow simply a reflection of changing public attitudes. Despite the fact that the new punitiveness expressed and acted upon by politicians is often justified by reference to public opinion and public demands, there is little evidence that the public is actually especially punitive (Roberts, 2002) or, certainly, as punitive as is often believed (Stalans, 2002). Indeed, to some degree, research suggests that elements of public punitiveness are a product of generalised ignorance about criminal justice and that exercises aimed at improving public understanding of sentencing have an impact on public confidence in the penalties the courts hand out (Hough, 1996). Indeed, rather than politics *following* public opinion, work by Beckett and Sasson (2003) suggests that the relationship may well be largely the other way around. Recent shifts in penal policy undoubtedly reflect broader social and cultural changes taking place. However, politics is an important part of this and should not be ignored. In the area of sentencing and non-custodial penalties, the consequence of penal populism is policy that has been 'contingent, opportunistic and *ad hoc* [rather] than logical and consistent' (Pratt, 2007: 123).

Questions for further discussion

1 Has the fine outlived its usefulness as a form of punishment?

2 To what extent is a 'just deserts' philosophy still visible in current sentencing policy?

3 What do you think are the advantages and disadvantages of an increasingly structured approach to sentencing?

4 Does the rise of 'offender management' spell the end for probation?

5 What are the advantages and disadvantages of placing prisons and probation within a single organisation?

Further reading

In relation to sentencing policy, the volume to consult is Andrew Ashworth's (2005) *Sentencing and Criminal Justice*, Cambridge: Cambridge University Press. Also very useful in the whole area covered by this chapter is Cavadino, M. and Dignan, J. (2005) *The Penal System*, 3rd edn, London: Sage. On probation, there are a number of good texts, but you can probably find the bulk of what you need in Gelsthorpe, L. and Morgan, R. (eds) (2007) *Handbook of Probation*, Cullompton: Willan.

For those interested in the history of probation, the series of articles written by Bill McWilliams between 1981 and 1987 are an excellent starting point:

McWilliams, B. (1981) The probation officer at court: From friend to acquaintance, *Howard Journal of Criminal Justice*, 20, 97–116, Oxford: Blackwell Publishing

McWilliams, B. (1983) The mission to the English Police Courts 1876–1936, *Howard Journal of Criminal Justice*, 22, 129–147, Oxford: Blackwell Publishing

McWilliams, B. (1985) The mission transformed: professionalisation of probation between the wars, *Howard Journal of Criminal Justice*, 24, 4, 257–74, Oxford: Blackwell Publishing

McWilliams, B. (1986) The English probation system and the diagnostic ideal, *Howard Journal of Criminal Justice*, 25, 4, 241–260, Oxford: Blackwell Publishing

McWilliams, B. (1987) Probation, pragmatism and policy, *Howard Journal of Criminal Justice*, 26, 2, 97–121, Oxford: Blackwell Publishing

On NOMS, a useful start can be found in: Hough, M. *et al.* (eds) (2006) *Reshaping Probation and Prisons: The new offender management framework*. Researching Criminal Justice Series Paper No. 6., Bristol: Policy Press.

An extremely helpful of collection of essays can be found in: Bottoms, A.E. *et al.* (eds) (2004) *Alternatives to Prison: Options for an insecure society*, Cullompton: Willan

On the controversies surrounding what works, there is a fine collection of essays in Mair, G. (ed.) (2004) *What Matters in Probation*, Cullompton: Willan

There is a lot of useful research and statistical information on the Home Office website, all of which can be downloaded. In relation to 'what works' and non-custodial interventions you might want to start with: Harper G. and Chitty, C. (2005) *The Impact of Corrections on Offending*, Home Office Research Study No. 291, available at: http://www.homeoffice.gov.uk/rds/horspubs1.html

Websites

The Sentencing Guidelines website contains a lot of useful information, including details of cases and decisions: http://www.sentencing-guidelines.gov.uk/

Unless something changes remarkably quickly it is highly likely that the whole area of 'offender management' will remain extraordinarily complex. A regular visit to the NOMS website is therefore recommended: http://www.noms.homeoffice.gov.uk/

The National Association of Probation Officers is regularly involved in campaigning in this area and has useful research and other material: http://www.napo.org.uk/

Chapter outline

The rise of the prison	684
Imprisonment in Britain	685
Prison security	686
Strangeways and Woolf	689
Trends in imprisonment	690
Imprisonment and penal politics	694
International trends	695
Capital punishment	698
The prison system	700
Types of prison	700
Private prisons	701
Life on the inside	702
Prisoners	703
Incarceration and social exclusion	705
Violence in prison	705
Prison officers	707
Release from prison	709
Governance, accountability and human rights	709
Independent inspection	710
Grievance or complaints procedures	710
Human rights and imprisonment	711
Questions for further discussion	713
Further reading	713
Websites	713

28

Prisons and imprisonment

CHAPTER SUMMARY

In Britain, we now have record numbers in our jails, and the same is true in many other nations. There are currently over nine million people in prison around the world. Of these, over two million are in prison in the USA, one and a half million in China, and close on one million in the Russian Federation.

In this chapter we look at:

- the emergence of the prison as a core part of the modern system of punishment;
- how prison policy has changed in recent decades.

As the prison has developed as one of our key responses to crime, the death penalty has been diminishing in use.

We consider:

- the current use of capital punishment and consider the issue of abolition;
- life 'inside';
- who is incarcerated in our prison system;
- what prisons are like for inmates and staff.

The rise of the prison

As we saw in Chapter 2, something akin to imprisonment can be found as far back as the thirteenth century. However, according to many historians, prison as we now understand it has only been around for something like three centuries (during which time it has changed markedly in its style and function). From the early 1700s a system of houses of correction or bridewells existed (McGowen, 1995) being used primarily for vagrants and drunks. However, for much of the eighteenth century, and well into the nineteenth, there remained considerable resistance to the idea of imprisonment as a standard, frequently used form of punishment.

Rather, the death penalty continued to be used as a symbolic means of conveying the power of the state. Transportation to the colonies – to America originally, and then to Australia after the American Revolution – became the everyday means of dealing with a very wide range of offenders and offences. In the mid-nineteenth century the distinction between transportation and penal servitude was abolished and in 1867 transportation ceased altogether.

As we saw when we looked at the history of policing (see Chapters 2 and 25) it is possible to construct somewhat contrasting histories of our major criminal justice institutions. In the case of the police we discuss what have been referred to as

'whig' and 'radical' histories. Something similar can be detected in histories of imprisonment (see Weiss, 1987). In an example of a recent rather Whiggish history, Coyle (2005) argues that the development of the modern prison can be traced to two sources: firstly the work of reformers such as John Howard, Elizabeth Fry and Thomas Buxton in the eighteenth and early nineteenth centuries and, secondly, and related to this, the gradually changing status of prison work into an increasingly respectable occupation.

Coyle's history of imprisonment then focuses on what he describes as the gradual liberalisation of the treatment of prisoners which characterised the first half of the twentieth century. Thus, close cropping of prisoners' hair was abolished in the 1920s (though it remained the case that long hair was still shorn up until the early 1970s and, famously, the defendants in the obscenity trial of *Oz* underground magazine had their hair cut short before their trial at the Old Bailey). In the 1930s the Prison Rules abolished the use of solitary confinement at the beginning of long sentences.

By contrast, there is a range of more radical interpretations of history which, in different ways, present the rise and spread of the prison as representing the development of a more insidious and subtle form of social control. Here the works of Foucault (1979), Ignatieff (1978) and Melossi and Pavarini (1981) have perhaps been the most important. Most influentially (see Chapters 16 and 22), Foucault's *Discipline and Punish* contained a counter-thesis which saw the 'birth of the prison' as indicative of a shift in the governance of conduct in which, progressively, citizens would be set to work and subject to forms of surveillance and control that sought to make them more useful (see Chapter 2).

Imprisonment in Britain

In the mid-1800s proposals were developed for a penitentiary system. Officials had been to America to look at two models there: one organised around solitary confinement based in the Eastern State Penitentiary in Philadelphia, the other a silent regime used in Auburn and Sing Sing (on the Hudson River north of New York City). It was a prison along the lines of the Philadelphia model that was pressed for, it being believed at the time that separation was 'not only morally beneficial, by preventing contamination and providing an opportunity for reflection and self-examination, but greatly facilitated the task of security and control' (Home Office, 1979, para 2.6).

A view of a hallway (as it is today) in the Eastern State Penitentiary in Philadelphia, USA, where prisoners were kept in solitary confinement. It was opened in 1829. Charles Dickens, who visited the prison in 1842, wrote, 'The system here is rigid, strict and hopeless solitary confinement. I believe it, in its effects, to be cruel and wrong.'

The Convict Service was established in 1850 and this formalised central control of prisons. The ending of transportation gave further impetus to the increasing use of imprisonment for serious crimes, and not merely the summary offences and petty felonies which had been its primary focus in the previous period. The consequence was an increasing emphasis on long sentences of imprisonment. Those who would otherwise have been transported spent a period in solitary confinement and were then transferred to one of a number of centrally-run public works or 'invalid' prisons where they engaged in 'hard labour' – usually quarrying.

The prison population in England and Wales dropped from a high of over 30,000 in 1877 – when the Prison Act was passed – to a low point of a little over 9,000 at the end of the First World War. Thereafter, the population rose slightly, but generally hovered between 10,000–12,000 in the years up to the Second World War. The story since then has been one of expansion. The trend has not been uni-linear and there are important lessons to be learnt from the falls as well as the rises. Nevertheless, it is the growth in the prison population, indeed what has been referred to elsewhere as the 'crisis in prison numbers' (Cavadino and Dignan, 1992), that has set the tone for much that has happened in criminal justice policy-making since 1945.

The oft-quoted conclusion of the Gladstone Report (1895) was that 'We start from the principle that prison treatment should have as its primary and concurrent objects deterrence and reformation'. The Report led within a short time to the 1898 Prison Act which unified the local and convict prison systems, introduced remission of sentence and restricted the use of corporal punishment. An emphasis on rehabilitation was a consistent part of prisons policy – alongside other objectives – for the next 70 years or so.

In the immediate post-Second World War period, significant and sustained rises in recorded crime led to a rise in the average size of the prison population. Pressure on the system was exacerbated by the escalation of long-standing industrial relations problems. In response to mounting public concern about levels of crime, especially among young people, a White Paper – *Penal Practice in a Changing Society* – was published in 1959. A great deal was said about the size of the prison population, and particularly about the degree of overcrowding in detention centres.

Details of a prison-building programme were outlined and, despite the increasing evidence that was available about the relative ineffectiveness of custodial sentences as a method of rehabilitating offenders, the White Paper affirmed the government's commitment to the use of prison. This was the point at which the diagnosticians held sway within the probation service, and a similar medical model underpinned official faith in the prison system. The White Paper included, for example, the announcement that work was to begin on the first purpose-built psychiatric prison at Grendon Underwood. Thus, at the end of the 1950s, tough talking on crime and punishment was combined with a faith in rehabilitation that was largely undiminished.

This was also the period in which serious discussion of the possible abolition of the death penalty began in earnest. If anything changed the mood during the course of the 1950s it was a series of cases in which either the guilt of the offender or the appropriateness of the death penalty was called into question. The cases of Derek Bentley (see box), Timothy Evans, James Hanratty and Ruth Ellis reinforced the abolitionists' case, though the Conservative government remained resistant to the idea of changing the law during most of the 1950s. Although various attempts

at reform were made, it wasn't until the election of a Labour government in 1964 that abolition appeared a realistic possibility.

Prison security

In the 1960s there were a number of quite significant crises that gripped the prison system from time to time, not least in relation to matters of 'security'. Up until the early 1960s issues of prison security had not been considered to be especially important, though the increasing numbers of prisoners convicted of the most serious crimes and sentenced to very long terms of imprisonment was beginning to put the issue on the agenda. In addition, there was an increase both in the number of prison escapes in the period, and in the number of 'high profile' escapees. In August 1964 accomplices of one of the 'Great Train Robbers', Charles Wilson, broke into Birmingham prison and helped him escape. He had served only four months of his 30-year sentence. In July 1965, another of the gang, Ronald Biggs also serving 30 years, escaped from the exercise yard at Wandsworth prison.

Derek Bentley

On 28th January 1953, Derek Bentley was hanged at Wandsworth Prison for the murder of PC Sidney Miles. Aged 19, Bentley had received the death sentence for his part in a break-in during which the police officer was shot by Bentley's accomplice, Christopher Craig. However, at the time of the shooting Craig was a juvenile and was therefore spared the death penalty. The case became something of a *cause célèbre* in which the Home Secretary was petitioned by a large number of MPs and a vigil was held outside the prison. Their argument was that Craig was the ringleader and that Bentley, though an adult, had a mental capacity that cast doubt on the appropriateness of treating him in this way. Crucial to his conviction was police evidence alleging that Bentley had encouraged Craig by shouting 'Let him have it'. By contrast, his defence argued that he had already been arrested before Craig fired the shots that killed PC Miles and that he was simply urging Craig to hand over his gun. In 1993 Bentley was granted a partial pardon by the then Home Secretary Michael Howard, and in 1998 the Appeal Court quashed Bentley's conviction on the grounds that the original trial judge was biased against the defendants and misdirected the jury on points of

law. Scientific evidence was also revealed which suggested that the police officers who testified against Bentley had lied.

The 'Great Train Robber' and the spy: the prison escapes of Ronnie Biggs *(left)* and George Blake *(right)* greatly embarrassed the prison service and government of the day and led to the introduction of a new security classification system.

Perhaps most embarrassingly of all, and certainly the final straw as far as the government was concerned (Stern, 1989) was the escape one year later of the spy, George Blake, from Wormwood Scrubs. In response, the government established the Mountbatten Committee, which reported that the central problem lay with the insufficiently secure accommodation for the small number of very high risk prisoners, together with overly-secure regimes for the rest. The major recommendation made by the Mountbatten Committee were that a system for categorising inmates should be introduced.

The Mountbatten Committee also proposed that those in the top security category should be housed together in a new purpose-built, top-security prison. This was given the name 'Vectis' and was to be located on the Isle of Wight, rather than in the currently existing maximum-security blocks. However, this policy of 'concentration' was not implemented, and Category A prisoners were housed in 'dispersal' prisons rather than being all housed in a single very high-security institution.

The May Committee a decade later suggested that there had been an increase in levels of security across prisons generally, and a number of critics argued that the consequence of adopting the policy of dispersal was to subject a very large number of prisoners to a degree of security deemed to be necessary, in fact, for very few. Stern (1989), for example, estimated that in 1988, 390 convicted prisoners deemed to be Category A were housed in prisons with room for 2,968. The control of Category A prisoners never really ceased to be a problem. In 1969, one of the dispersal prisons,

Security categories

In England and Wales prisoners are allocated to four security categories:

- *Category A* – Those whose escape would be highly dangerous to the public or the police or to the security of the State.

- *Category B* – Those for whom the very highest conditions of security are not necessary, but for whom escape must be made very difficult, and who ought to be kept in very secure conditions.

- *Category C* – Those who cannot be trusted in open conditions, but who do not have the ability or resources to make a determined escape attempt. For them there should be prisons with sufficient defences to make escape difficult (Cat C is subdivided to include a category for young offenders involved in gangs).

- *Category D* – Those who can reasonably be entrusted to serve their sentences in open conditions.

(*Mountbatten Report*, 1966, paras 15 and 217.)

Parkhurst, saw the worst prison riot for nearly 40 years in which 28 prisoners and 35 prison officers were injured (Ryan, 1983).

The other significant illustration of the impact of rising prison numbers lies in the introduction of parole in 1967. Its introduction was defended on rehabilitative grounds (Home Office, 1965; Morgan, 1983). The White Paper, for example, argued that 'a considerable number of long-term prisoners reach a recognisable peak in their training at which they may respond to generous treatment, but after which if kept in prison they may go downhill'. (para. 5), though this was heavily criticised by leading academic commentators such as Roger Hood (see Maguire, 1992). Nevertheless, it is clear that the introduction of parole was also a pragmatic response to prison crowding (Bottomley, 1984). Although the Act led briefly to a decline in prison numbers, they began to rise again in the 1970s. The prison system was also undergoing a process of radicalisation, with, on the one hand, the Prison Officers Association becoming increasingly militant and, on the other, the prisoners' rights movement beginning to take off.

There was a disturbance at Brixton prison in 1972 and this was followed later that year by further disturbances at Gartree and at Albany, though the most serious riot in the period happened four years later at Hull. Hull, originally a local prison, was reclassified as a training prison in 1966 and as a dispersal prison in 1969. The riot, which lasted for four days, resulted in damage to the prison estimated then at £725,000 (Thomas and Pooley, 1980), a large number of injuries to prisoners as order was restored, and prosecutions of prison officers for assault. Similar brutality, it was claimed, was used in quelling another disturbance at Gartree in 1978, and the following year saw the introduction (its existence had never before been officially mentioned) of the paramilitary Minimum Use of Force Tactical Intervention squad (MUFTI) to bring a disturbance at Wormwood Scrubs to an end.

At the end of the 1970s, a committee of inquiry, under the chairmanship of a High Court judge, Mr Justice May, was instructed by the then Home Secretary, Merlyn Rees, to inquire into the state of the prison services in the UK, and to have regard to: the size of the prison population; the capacity of the prison service to accommodate it; the responsibility of the prison service for control, security and treatment of inmates; and the pay and conditions for staff. The Committee took the view that imprisonment should be used as little as possible and backed policies to reduce the prison population, even though it felt that there was little chance of their being successful. As a consequence it therefore recommended a massive building and refurbishment programme to end enforced cell-sharing and end slopping out, and this was acted upon without delay (King and McDermott, 1989). In 1982 the biggest prison-building programme

undertaken in the twentieth century began, in which 25 new prisons were to be built at an estimated capital cost of over £1.3 billion (Cavadino and Dignan, 1992).

However, the May Committee's notion of 'positive custody' never garnered much support and during the 1980s considerable emphasis continued to be placed by campaigners on prisoners' rights and on timetables for the introduction of minimum standards and conditions without, it must be said, a great deal of success (Morgan, 1994b). It was abundantly clear by the early 1980s that the dispersal policy in relation to the long-term prison population was not succeeding in terms of control. Disturbances continued and only two of the eight dispersal prisons had not been the site of a major disturbance by 1983 (Bottoms and Light, 1987). In the mid-1980s there were a number of disturbances of a quite serious nature in prisons in England. Among the dispersal prisons, Gartree and Parkhurst experienced protests in 1985 and then in the full range of institutions there were, from 1986 to 1988, 22 separate disturbances, 42 acts of concerted indiscipline, 25 roof-climbing incidents and 245 escapes (Scraton et al., 1991).

In addition to these disturbances, once again there were a significant number of disputes involving prison staff. A study undertaken by the Prison Department and a team of management consultants in 1986 presented, according to the Home Secretary, Douglas Hurd, 'a telling indictment of the complementing and shift systems and the working practices that surround them' (McDermott and King, 1989: 161). In a bid to resolve some of the problems related to staffing and working practices, the Home Office introduced what it called the 'Fresh Start' package, which sought to buy out overtime working, albeit at the cost of still further increases in staffing. The basic idea was that the improved working practices that were proposed would produce cost savings, and a proportion of these savings would be reinvested to enhance regimes. Fresh Start abolished overtime, it reduced prison officers' working hours and, according to one observer, through its creation of a modern management structure, 'has moved the Prison Service from the 1950s to the 1980s organisationally' (Stern, 1989: 158), though research conducted in five prisons in the immediate aftermath of the introduction of Fresh Start painted a rather more gloomy picture (McDermott and King, 1989). Not long after, one of the most startling occurrences in recent British prison history occurred – the Strangeways riot.

Strangeways and Woolf

The disturbance that occurred at Strangeways in April 1990 was not only the most serious of all the disturbances that year, but was the longest and most serious riot in British penal history. It began on 1 April and continued until the 25 April. At the time Strangeways was the largest prison in England and Wales and, indeed, one of the largest in Europe. It was extremely overcrowded, holding 1,647 prisoners when its certified normal accommodation was 970. Almost three-fifths of the prisoners held there were on remand.

An immediate departmental inquiry was set up, and was to be conducted by Lord Justice Woolf. The eventual terms of reference were: 'To inquire into the events leading up to the serious disturbance in Her Majesty's Prison Manchester which began on 1 April 1990 and the action taken to bring it to a conclusion, having regard also to the serious disturbances which occurred shortly thereafter in other prison establishments in England and Wales.'

Central to Woolf's understanding of the disturbances was the identification of three requirements which must be met if the prison system is to be stable. These were *security*, *control* and *justice*.

- *Security* – refers to the obligation of the Prison Service to prevent inmates escaping.
- *Control* – is the obligation to prevent prisoners being disruptive.

- *Justice* – is the obligation to treat prisoners with humanity and 'to prepare them for their return to the community in a way which makes it less likely that they will reoffend'. (Woolf, 1991, para. 9.20)

Woolf argued that sufficient attention must be paid to all three of the requirements and that the three must be kept in balance and, as Morgan (1992a: 233) notes, 'It is apparent that, in Woolf's view, the Prison Department has overemphasised security, given insufficient weight to justice and often adopted inappropriate control measures.' Woolf's recommendations covered greater co-ordination in the criminal justice system, more visible leadership of the Prison Service, the setting of standards for prison conditions, and a variety of changes to the nature of regimes, including grievance procedures.

One of the aspects of imprisonment highlighted by the Woolf Report for change was the practice of 'slopping out' – the fact that, at this stage, cells had no internal sanitation meant that prisoners had to defecate and urinate into a plastic chamber pot:

> When courts send prisoners to prison, they are entitled to expect that prisoners will be treated in accordance with the Prison Service duty to look after them with humanity ... However, to lock up prisoners for long periods at a time with no alternative but to use a bucket for their basic needs, which then has to remain in the cell, sometimes for many hours, is manifestly inconsistent and makes a mockery of that duty ... It is not just.

The Strangeways riot

The disturbance began during a service in the prison chapel, the officers who were present quickly having to withdraw. During the ensuing disturbance and siege the inside of the prison was gutted, a total of 147 officers and 47 prisoners received injuries (including those affected by smoke or fumes) and one prisoner received injuries which it was thought may have contributed to his death. At the end of the disturbance the prison was entirely uninhabitable and the estimated cost of repair and refurbishment (though much of the refurbishment, it might be argued, was necessary anyway) was £60 million. What happened in Manchester led, by one means or another, to protests and disturbances in other parts of the country including at Dartmoor prison, at Pucklechurch youth remand centre, at Glen Parva YOI, and at Bristol and Cardiff prisons.

Prisoners on the roof at Strangeways Prison.

The commitment we have proposed (eliminating slopping out by 1996) would remove a practice which is a blot on our prison system and which undermines the justice of the sentence which the prisoners are serving. (paras. 11–101)

There followed a brief moment of optimism after the publication of the Woolf Report. There have undoubtedly been some important changes within prisons in the period since, not least in the general sanitary conditions and in the overhaul of complaints and grievance procedures which we will consider later. In many other respects, however, the last decade has seen most positive developments severely hampered by a continuous growth in prison numbers. In a speech in 2002, Lord Woolf, by then the Lord Chief Justice, observed that:

The problem of overcrowding is a cancer eating at the ability of the Prison Service to deliver. Many inmates should not be in jail, the most significant group being those jailed for less than 12 months ... There is an opportunity now for a different approach, a holistic approach, which recognises that all parts of the justice system need to pull together. (Lord Woolf, 30 October 2002)

An opportunity there may have been, but as we will see it was not grasped, and prison numbers have continued to grow, and to grow remarkably quickly in recent years. In the aftermath of Strangeways and the Woolf Inquiry there were a number of other incidents which, once again, drew attention to the issues of security and control. First was an attempted escape from Whitemoor prison in 1994 and subsequently a briefly successful escape from Parkhurst on the Isle of Wight. In response, two inquiries were established – the Woodcock Inquiry into the Whitemoor case and the Learmont Inquiry into the Parkhurst escape – and the Director-General of the Prison Service, Derek Lewis, was sacked by Michael Howard, the then Home Secretary. The Learmont Inquiry recommended the building of an American-style 'supermax' prison to house all prisoners deemed to be exceptional and high-risk Category A (King, 2007). However, rather than the introduction of a British supermax, in 1998 the Prison Service introduced what are known as Close Supervision Centres (CSCs) (Clare and Bottomley, 2001) which remove the most seriously disruptive prisoners from mainstream dispersal or training prisons and contain them in small, highly-supervised units.

Although overcrowding may not be the central problem in formenting disorder within prisons, it is undeniably an important indirect influence (King, 2007). At the time of the publication of the Woolf Inquiry, the prison population in England and Wales was around 42,000. It has grown almost continuously since then and this undoubtedly means that the prison system remains under very significant pressure.

Trends in imprisonment

There have been some significant changes in trends in punishment over the course of the last century and, more particularly, in recent decades. This is clearest in relation to the use of imprisonment. Figure 28.1 shows the prison population in England and Wales for the past century or so. Standing at approximately 20,000 at the turn of the twentieth century, the prison population declined roughly from the First World War through to the Second World War and then began to rise. It reached its turn of the century levels again by the late 1950s and by the early 1980s reached an historic high in the low 40,000s. The population was reaching 50,000 by the end of the decade, at which point various strategies were employed, successfully, to begin to reduce the numbers in prison. Intriguingly, at roughly the point that crime reached its peak in England and Wales the prison population once again began to rise, and did so markedly more quickly than at any point since the Second World War.

If the period from the Second World War until the early 1970s represents the time in which the 'rehabilitative ideal' (Allen, 1981) was at its height, then the last 30 years, and the last ten in particular, have seen a fairly rapid shift in a more punitive direction (see also Chapters 1 and 27). There was anticipation in some quarters that the prison population might fall during the 1980s. Not only did this not occur, but the numbers steadily increased – from 42,000 at the beginning of the decade to over 48,800 by its end.

The Conservative government was not especially happy about the prospect of increased overcrowding and pursued a number of means of limiting the prison population, including the introduction of bail information schemes, time limits for bringing cases to trial, and issuing advice to sentencers on restricting remands in custody. There is some evidence that these measures had a levelling effect from about 1987 onwards up until 1991 whereupon the level once again rose. However, what has happened to the prison population in the past 10 years is dramatic by the standards of the preceding decades.

Figure 28.1   Prison population England and Wales, 1900–2005

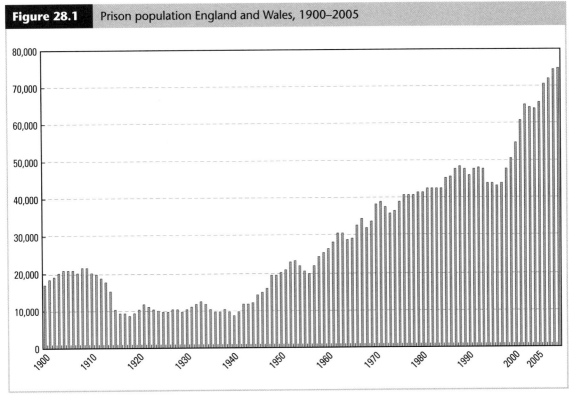

Source: *Prison Statistics England and Wales* (various).

Around 1993/94 any official attempt to reduce, or even to maintain a stable prison population was abandoned. The result has been that the prison population increased by over two-thirds (69%) between 1993 and 2005 and by early 2007 it had reached over 80,000. The one obvious exception has been the increasing use of what is known as the early release 'safety valve'. The electronically-monitored Home Detention Curfew (HDC) was introduced as part of the Crime and Disorder Act 1998. According to the then Home Secretary, Jack Straw:

> The case for introducing an element of tagging into the last part of a short-term prison sentence is very strong ... but it has been reinforced by the recent rise in the prison population. No-one wants to see an unnecessarily overcrowded prison system, and it would be the height of irresponsibility not to take advantage of modern technology to help prevent that. The alternatives are bound to be at the expense of constructive prison regimes, and at the expense of improving the prisoner's prospects for resettlement – in other words, at the expense of the law-abiding public. (quoted in Leng *et al.*, 1998: 126)

In October 2002, Straw's replacement as Home Secretary, David Blunkett, announced that the maximum curfew period would be extended from the existing 60 days to 90 days. Though there had been some controversy over the numbers re-offending whilst on curfew, of the 59,000 prisoners released under the HDC by the end of 2002 fewer than 3% offended while on curfew. Despite the apparently impressive numbers, the HDC has only a marginal effect, albeit a potentially important one, on overall prison numbers.

Nevertheless, as we have seen, the increase in overall prison numbers has led to problems of overcrowding and considerable concern from the Prison Service itself about the ability of the system to provide an appropriate setting in which interventions aimed at reducing re-offending might have a realistic chance of success (HM Chief Inspector of Prisons, 2005). The increasing use of custody is more usually illustrated using the incarceration rate. Again, this shows very clearly the substantial growth in the use of custody over the past decade or so. Thus, the incarceration rate in England and Wales in 1993 was under 90 per

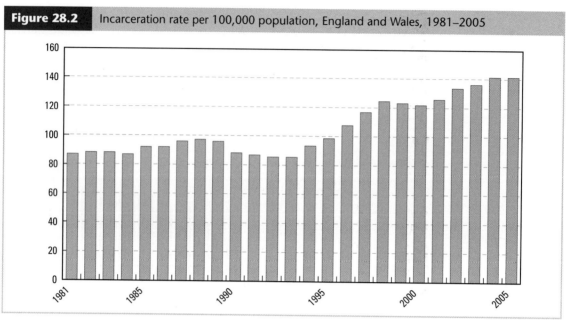

| **Figure 28.2** | Incarceration rate per 100,000 population, England and Wales, 1981–2005 |

Source: Prison Statistics England and Wales (various).

100,000. By 2005 it had reached 142 per 100,000 (see Figure 28.2) making England and Wales the highest incarcerator in Western Europe.

The reasons for the expanding prison population are undoubtedly complex. In straightforward practical terms there are three main possibilities:

- An increase in the numbers being caught and sentenced.

- An increase in the seriousness of the crimes being prosecuted.

- An increase in sentence severity.

According to the 2003 *Correctional Services Review* (otherwise known as the Carter Report, 2003) there is no evidence that the changes reflect an increase in the numbers of offenders being caught or convicted – these have remained relatively stable. Moreover, there does not appear to have been any substantial increase in the seriousness overall of the offences before the courts (Hough *et al.*, 2003). Rather, the available evidence suggests that the sanctions imposed by the courts have been becoming increasingly severe over the past decade or so. Thus, the proportion of offenders found guilty of an indictable offence receiving a custodial sentence rose from 15% in 1991 to 25% in 2001 (Carter, 2003).

Similarly, whereas a first-time domestic burglar had a 27% chance of receiving a custodial sentence

in 1995, this had risen to 48% by 2000. In addition, average sentence lengths for such offenders had risen from 16 to 18 months. An indication that there was a progressive ratcheting-up of court imposed punishments is illustrated by the fact that over half of the increase in offenders convicted of indictable offences receiving a custodial sentence between 1996 and 2003 was accounted for by people with no previous convictions. Indeed, the trend has affected less serious offences also. The proportion of offenders sentenced to immediate custody for an indictable offence in magistrates' courts rose from 7.1% in 1994 to 14.7% in 2004 (Nicholas *et al.*, 2005).

Over the past decade or so there has also been a general increase in sentence lengths. Figure 28.3, which is based on prison admissions data, shows a substantial increase in the numbers of offenders sentenced to up to one year in prison. The increases in the number sentenced to more than a year is less steep, but nevertheless increasing.

If we shift our focus from prison receptions to the 'average daily population' the increase in sentencing, or in time served, becomes starker. Between 1994 and 2004, the number of male prisoners serving longer-term, determinate sentences of four or more years more than doubled (107%). The number serving sentences of 12 months up to four years increased by almost three-fifths (57%) and the number under short-term sentences (under a year) increased by almost half (48%). The number

Figure 28.3 Adult male receptions into custody by sentence length 1992–2002

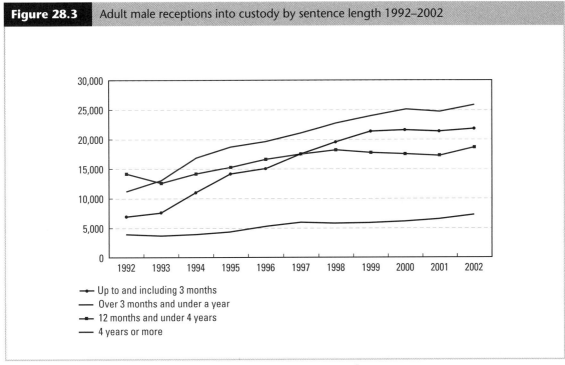

— Up to and including 3 months
— Over 3 months and under a year
— 12 months and under 4 years
— 4 years or more

Source: Carter (2003).

Table 28.1 Prison population by sentence length, 1994–2004

Sentence Length	1994	1995	1996	1997	1998	1999	2000	2001	2002	2003	2004
Remand	12,533	11,056	11,568	12,105	12,903	12,589	11,433	11,061	13,081	13,037	12,495
≤ 6 months	3,891	4,339	4,582	4,929	5,099	5,190	6,389	6,202	5,447	5,971	5,751
≥ 6 ≤ 12 months	2,060	2,210	2,376	2,475	2,511	2,190	6,389	6,202	5,447	5,971	5,751
12 months to less than 4 years	13,621	15,203	17,112	19,796	21,130	19,741	19,633	20,053	21,858	21,378	21,436
4 years to life	12,472	13,822	15,355	17,753	19,485	19,966	20,071	20,764	22,471	24,416	25,837
Life	3,192	3,289	3,489	3,721	3,934	4,206	4,593	4,810	5,147	5,419	5,594

Source: RDS NOMS (2005), *Offender Caseload Management Statistics 2004*.

of life sentence prisoners also increased 75% between 1994 and 2004 (see Table 28.1). Of the total increase in the prison population during this period, approximately two-fifths was accounted for by a rise in the number of prisoners serving four years or more and a further quarter was accounted for by an increase in those serving medium term sentences (one to four years).

In terms of offence types, the largest increase between 1993 and 2003 was drug offences, which

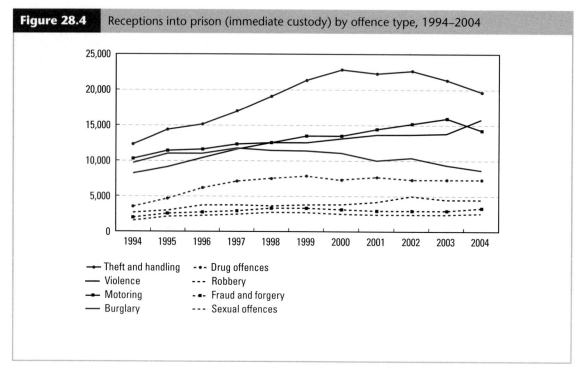

Figure 28.4 Receptions into prison (immediate custody) by offence type, 1994–2004

Legend:
- Theft and handling
- Violence
- Motoring
- Burglary
- Drug offences
- Robbery
- Fraud and forgery
- Sexual offences

Source: RDS NOMS *Offender Caseload Management Statistics* 2004 (2005).

increased by 222% during the decade, though there also appears to have been a substantial increase in the number of immediate custodial sentences resulting from violent offences (see Figure 28.4).

Imprisonment and penal politics

Though the reasons for the rise of the prison population are undoubtedly complex, it is clear that there has been a substantial increase in sentence severity. More people are being sent to prison, and the sentences are longer. There is little or no evidence that the offending for which people receive custodial sentences is getting significantly more serious. So, why the changes in sentencing practice? As we noted in the previous chapter in relation to community sanctions, in searching for a reason it is hard to look far beyond contemporary penal politics. Crime has become a staple of political discourse and of electoral politics. Though it may not feel surprising, it is a relatively new political phenomenon.

For a fuller discussion of the politicians' concerns regarding criminal justice, see Chapter 23.

Michael Howard, Conservative Home Secretary 1993–1997, gave a speech to the 1993 party conference at which he famously announced his belief that *prison works*.

International trends

Coyle (2005) suggests that, in terms of the use of imprisonment, it is possible to divide the countries of the world into five main groups:

1 A significant number of developing countries, including some former colonies, where prisons were introduced by former imperial powers. These include various countries in sub-Saharan and East Africa, South Asia, the Caribbean, India and parts of the Middle East.
2 Countries where there appears to have been a complete breakdown of order in the prison system. Many Latin American prison systems fall into this category.
3 Many of the states of the former Soviet Union have prison systems characterised by extreme overcrowding and poor health.
4 Countries which historically have regarded prison as something generally to be avoided or used minimally. Many Western European countries fall into this category.
5 Countries which make extensive use of imprisonment as a plank of public policy. The leader here, as we have seen is the US, together with Russia and South Africa.

Incarceration rates – which are usually calculated as the number of people per 100,000 population – vary markedly country to country (and within federal systems like the United States, markedly within the country). The United States currently has the highest incarceration rate in the world (see Table 28.2)

What are we to make of the differing levels of incarceration around the world? First, we must note that beneath what appears a general trend in the direction of increased punitiveness and exclusionary practices in crime control, there remain some considerable and apparently quite deeply-embedded national differences in criminal justice and penal policies (Newburn and Sparks, 2004). Indeed, there exist many variations within some jurisdictions. Thus, the USA is made up of many criminal justice systems and there exist extensive variations between these. As one example, taking incarceration rates in the 30 years 1970–2000, Hinds (2005) has shown that custody rates were consistently higher in this period in the Southern States and lower in the Northeast and Midwest

Table 28.2	Incarceration rates per 100,000 population, selected countries, 2005
United States	714
Russian Federation	532
South Africa	413
Thailand	264
Chile	212
Poland	209
Israel	209
Czech Republic	184
Brazil	183
New Zealand	168
England and Wales	142
Spain	140
Scotland	132
Netherlands	123
Australia	117
Canada	116
Italy	96
Germany	96
France	91
Northern Ireland	83
Sweden	76
Finland	71
Denmark	70
Norway	65

Source: www.kcl.ac.uk/depsta/rel/icps/**world-prison-population**-list-2005.pdf

compared with other regions (see Figure 28.5). In 2000 the custody rate in the Southern States was double that of the Northeastern States. Whilst identifying general trends continues to be important, it is equally vital not to lose sight of the nature and sources of continuing variation.

Figure 28.5 Incarceration rates per 100,000 population, USA by state and region, 2004

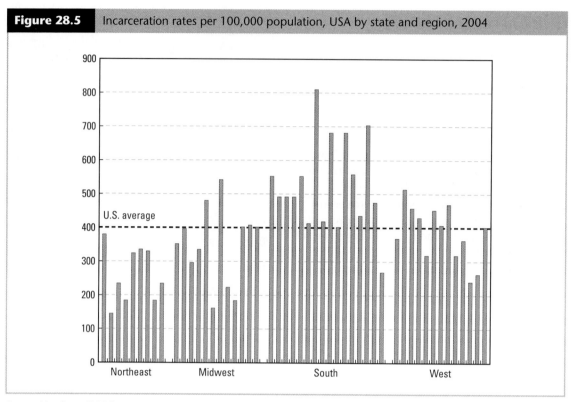

Source: Newburn (2006).

One way of illustrating international variation is to look at recent experience in Europe (Figure 28.6). Thus, in Scandinavia for example, despite generally rising crime rates over the past 40–50 years, prison populations have remained relatively stable (Denmark, Norway and Sweden) or reduced from a previously enormously high level to something akin to other Scandinavian countries (Finland). Finland had the highest rate of imprisonment in Western Europe in the 1950s – at its highest it reached 187 per 100,000. However, it has fallen fairly consistently since that period: to 154 in 1960, to 113 by 1970, 106 in 1980 and by 2000 it had reached 55 (significantly lower than England which was going in the other direction). As Coyle (2005: 21) notes, 'This did not happen by accident. Rather, the decrease was the result of deliberate, long-term and systematic policy choices.'

It is important to note, however, that there appear to have been some increases in incarceration rates in recent years (von Hofer, 2004), possibly related to extended sentence lengths, particularly for drug-related crimes (Bondeson, 2005). How might one explain the existence of generally milder penal policy in Scandinavia? Bondeson sug-

gests that there is some evidence, though far from unequivocal, that attitudes to punishment are less punitive in Scandinavia and that fear of crime is also lower. Moreover, it seems possible that the media are also more constrained, and thoughtful, in their treatment of crime and justice issues.

A number of broader socio-cultural explanations also seem plausible. On a general level it appears to be the case that there remains greater support for a broadly welfarist approach to public policy, including penal policy, in Scandinavia than in some other parts of Europe and certainly than in the US. The Nordic countries have more homogenous populations than, say, the UK and the US, which may have served to protect against the emergence of those forms of populism that are increasingly visible elsewhere (Downes and Hansen, 2006; Cavadino and Dignan, 2006).

The number of people in prison in Italy has been rising slowly, but the incarceration rate remains close to the European average of 100 per 100,000 population (Solivetti, 2004). Italy does differ somewhat from much of the rest of Europe, however, in the way it reaches its average. The prison population in Italy has both a higher

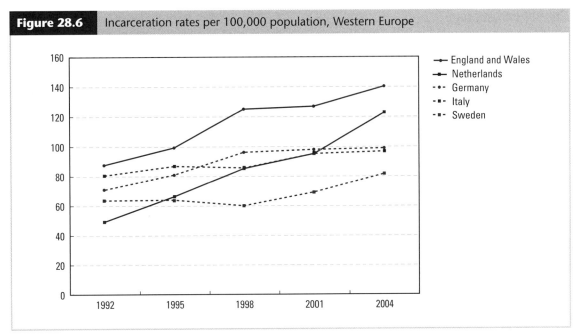

Figure 28.6 Incarceration rates per 100,000 population, Western Europe

Source: World Prison Brief (http://www.kcl.ac.uk/depsta/rel/icps/worldbrief/world_brief.html).

proportion of very long prison sentences compared with, say, the Scandinavian countries, and also a significant proportion of those in prison are detained awaiting final sentence (Nelken, 2005). In explaining the relatively lenient criminal justice responses found in Italy, particularly in relation to dealing with youthful criminality, Nelken (2005) points to a number of important socio-cultural factors, including the relative absence of ghetto housing estates, the strength and surveillance capacities of the family, and the lack of a youthful drinking culture (at least when compared with Northern Europe).

One of the most interesting and intriguing contrasts with the USA is Canada. Mulroney's Progressive Conservative government of the late 1980s largely continued the approaches established by its Liberal predecessor (Hatt *et al.*, 1992) and during the 1990s the new Liberal federal government set about establishing a distinct 'Canadian way' for dealing with social problems, including crime (Meyer and O'Malley, 2005). This distinctive way was explicitly designed to differ from the example being set by the nation's nearest neighbour: '[W]e have two choices – go the way of the US and build more prisons, or develop meaningful, lasting alternatives to incarceration for low-risk

offenders who can be better managed in the community'. (Canada, 2001, quoted in Meyer and O'Malley, 2005). In summary, such an approach to criminal justice policy has led to a federal prison system with a comprehensive programme of health, educational and training programmes for inmates, incarceration rates that are both low and declining, together with the removal of the death penalty. That said, as Moore and Hannah-Moffatt (2005: 97) conclude in their recent review, '[A]ppearances can be deceiving. The liberalism of Canadian punishment is a veil underneath which remains an extremely punitive system', albeit of a distinctive form in which therapeutic initiatives are central to the system of punishment.

The varied cultures of control in contemporary advanced economies clearly have many commonalities. Moreover, such shared characteristics are undoubtedly the product of broad social, cultural, political and economic pressures. However, it is also clear that particular socioeconomic, cultural and political contexts frame and shape *local* cultures of control in quite different ways. Understanding similarities and differences in the pattern of contemporary systems of crime control is arguably, therefore, one of the most pressing tasks currently facing criminologists (see Tonry, 2007).

Capital punishment

In August 1964, a matter of days after the escape from prison of one of the Great Train Robbers, Charles Wilson, two men were hanged, one in Strangeways prison in Manchester, the other in Walton in Liverpool. Peter Allen and Gwynne Evans had been convicted of the murder of another man in an argument about money. The case was in many ways unexceptional. It is noteworthy largely for the fact that they were the last two men to be executed in England (Block and Hostettler, 1997).

Capital punishment had been relatively common in the Middle Ages and for some time beyond but, as we have seen, was gradually replaced by the greater use of imprisonment in the eighteenth and nineteenth centuries. By the twentieth century capital punishment in Britain was declining in use, with years in which there were more than a dozen cases being relatively rare. This rate of executions remained until the late 1950s by which time political opposition to capital punishment was growing.

Numbers dwindled further in the 1960s, and Allen and Evans were the only two executed in 1964. In the event it was only a Private Members Bill (not government legislation) which brought a temporary end to capital punishment in 1965. The Murder (Abolition of the Death Penalty) Act 1965 suspended capital punishment for a period of five years. A free vote in parliament in 1969 confirmed the ending of capital punishment. Although there has been debate about the potential reintroduction of hanging since that time – particularly in the aftermath of especially unpleasant crimes – there has not in that time been any serious suggestion that parliament would consider bringing back the death penalty.

In this, Britain is in step with much of the rest of the world. The death penalty was abolished in Italy after the fall of Mussolini in 1944, in Spain in the aftermath of Franco's defeat and in France in 1981 after the election of a socialist government. Capital punishment has not been used at any point since 1997 in any part of the geographical area made up by the 47 member countries of the Council of Europe and, indeed, abolition of the death penalty is assumed as a natural condition of membership in both the Council of Europe and the European Union. Thus, any country wishing to join such bodies must declare a moratorium on the death penalty, and any member wishing to reintroduce the death penalty would need to withdraw.

In an era in which human rights discourses are becoming more and more visible (see Chapter 34) the death penalty is seen as increasingly anachronistic. According to Amnesty International, a total of 128 countries have abolished the death penalty in law or practice:

- 89 countries and territories have abolished the death penalty for all crimes.
- 10 countries have abolished the death penalty for all but exceptional crimes such as wartime crimes.
- 29 countries can be considered abolitionist in practice: they retain the death penalty in law, but have not carried out any executions for the past ten years or more and are believed to have a policy or established practice of not carrying out executions.

This means that 69 countries and territories retain and use the death penalty, although the number of countries which actually executes prisoners in any one year is much smaller. Amnesty estimated that in 2005 at least 5,186 people were sentenced to death in 53 countries. Of these, at least 2,148 were executed in 22 countries. China is believed to have executed at least 1,770 people in 2005, therefore being responsible for four-fifths of the judicial executions in the world. In 2005, at least 94 people were executed in Iran, at least a further 86 in Saudi Arabia, and a total of 60 in the United States. Over 94% of all known executions took place in these four nations. In addition, there are estimated to be at least 20,000 in prison awaiting execution.

Not only is the United States the highest incarcerator in the world, but it is also distinguished from the majority of other developed societies by the fact that it retains the death penalty. Interestingly, at the time that many other countries were abandoning the use of capital punishment the United States also did so, temporarily, in 1967. A moratorium was placed on its use which remained in place for a decade, only being overturned in 1977. Since then more than 1,000 people have been executed in the US. By July 2006 there were 3,366 prisoners on 'death row' in American prisons (Death Penalty Information Center, 2006).

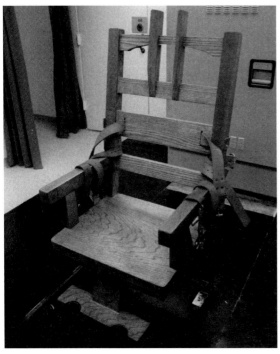

Electric chair used in the state of Florida, USA, where prisoners condemned to death have the choice of the electric chair or lethal injection. Originally devised in the late nineteenth century as a more humane alternative to hanging, it has become a symbol of the inhumanity of the death penalty.

And, yet, we must be careful when describing the death penalty as an *American* phenomenon, for only some American states use capital punishment. In practice, 12 of the 50 US states don't have the death penalty at all, and of those that do a great many do not use it. The vast majority of executions take place in the Southern states of Texas, Virginia and Oklahoma. Of the 1,004 executions that took place in the US between 1977 and 2005, over four fifths (82%) were in the Southern states, and one third of all executions in that time took place in a single state: Texas. Of the 53 executions in America in 2006, 24 took place in Texas. Half of all death row prisoners in the US are in prison in only four of the 50 states: California, Florida, Texas and Pennsylvania. Moreover, in the United States the death penalty appears to be in decline.

The pattern and use of the death penalty in America has led to an interesting criminological debate about how it should be understood. On the one hand, Zimring (2003) has argued that the patterning of executions in the United States reflects long-standing cultural traits associated particularly with the legacy of lynching. Indeed, using a wealth of data, he is able to show how the contemporary spread of the death penalty in the US is much closer to the pattern of lynching in the early part of the twentieth century than it is to the pattern of capital

| **Figure 28.7** | Executions in the United States, 1976–2006 |

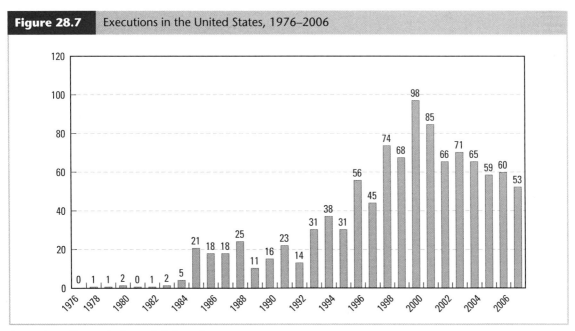

Source: http://www.deathpenaltyinfo.org/

punishment in that era. By contrast, Garland (2005) is critical of what he sees as an argument based on a notion of 'American exceptionalism' – that somehow America is different from other nations in this regard. In fact, he suggests, America is simply slightly out of sync, and it is only a matter of time before it completes the process of abolition. The fact that the death penalty remains is a reflection more of contemporary politics than long-standing cultural values.

Review questions

1 What did Woolf consider the three main elements contributing to a stable prison system?

2 What is meant by 'incarceration rate'?

3 What have been the main contributory factors to the increasing use of the prison in England and Wales?

4 How would you describe the current pattern of the use of the death penalty around the world?

The prison system

At the time of writing, mid-2007, there are currently 139 prisons in England and Wales holding just over 80,000 prisoners. Many were built in the Victorian era and, as we saw earlier, only had such facilities as internal sanitation installed in cells in the last 10–15 years. The majority are 'public' prisons run by the Prison Service, but there are a small number of 'private prisons' which are operated by commercial organisations (see below).

Types of prison

Prisons are classified and described in a number of different ways – both by *function* and by *security* classification.

- *Local prisons* – take men and young offenders direct from court on remand before trial or after conviction and sentence. Such institutions are responsible for initial assessment and classification of convicted prisoners before allocation to other prisons or to a young offender institution (except for Category A prisoners who are classified at Prison Service headquarters). All local prisons are 'closed'.

HMP Leicester, opened in 1828 – one of a number of local prisons built in the Victorian period, many of them looking like medieval castles or fortresses.

- *Training prisons* – which may be 'open' or 'closed' institutions depending on their security level, provide training facilities and vocational courses for inmates.

- *Young offender institutions* – are for young offenders aged between 15 and 21 years of age. In terms of their security, prisons, like prisoners, are separated into four different categories.

- *Secure Training Centres* (STCs) – privately run, education-focused centres for offenders up to the age of 17.

- *Local Authority Secure Children's Homes* (LASCHs) – run by social services and focused on the physical, emotional and behavioural needs of vulnerable young people.

Prisons are also classified according to their security rating:

- *Open prisons* – Have no perimeter fence or wall. Doors will often be locked, especially at night, but that is generally the limit of the security. Many prisoners will leave the prison during the day, often to work. All prisoners will be in Category D. (Open prisons include Askham Grange, Kirklevington Grange.)

- *Category C prisons* – Have somewhat higher security – a perimeter fence or wall – but with a certain amount of freedom within the prison itself. Prisoners will generally be in Category C or D and many will be awaiting transfer to an open prison. (These include Dartmoor and Risley.)

- *Category B prisons* – These hold Category B prisoners, together with prisoners with Categories C and D. These have significantly higher perimeter security and internal freedoms are considerably restricted. (Gartree, Leeds, Wandsworth)

- *High security prisons* – These prisons hold Category A prisoners, together with some Category B prisoners. (Long Lartin, Wakefield and Whitemoor are examples.)

For full, up-to-date information on the location and types of prisons in the UK refer to http://www.hmprisonservice.gov.uk/resourcecentre/estate_map/

Private prisons

Private prisons in the UK have a long history. From the Middle Ages onwards, gaols were run as private businesses, and during the 18th and 19th centuries, private entrepreneurs made sizeable profits transporting prisoners to the colonies (see Chapter 2). The recent re-emergence of private prisons in Britain initially began in the immigration detention sector. In the early 1970s, the Home Office contracted the private security firm, Securicor, to run detention centres for suspected illegal immigrants at the four principal airports in England (Ryan and Ward, 1989).

Although a number of influential think tanks proposed the idea of privatising aspects of imprisonment, it was not until the early 1990s that it became a reality. The Criminal Justice Act 1991 included a provision to allow for the contracting-out of prisons, and covered sentenced prisoners, and existing prisons and remand centres. During 1991, contract details were announced for two privately-contracted penal establishments – the first was the Wolds won by the security company Group 4, and the first prisoners were received in Spring 1992 (James *et al.*, 1997).

Despite vociferous criticism from opposition MPs, privatisation continued to gather momentum. The contract for a second privately-managed prison (Blakenhurst) was signed with UK Detention Services in December 1992. In September 1993, Home Secretary Michael Howard announced that the government planned to privatise about 10% of the prison system in England and Wales. The contract for the third private prison, Doncaster, was signed with Premier Prison Services (jointly owned by the American Wackenhut Corrections Corporation and a British firm, Serco Ltd.) in February 1994.

In August 1994, it was announced that a shortlist of 20 prisons were to be 'market tested' to see whether the Prison Service or the private sector was likely to be the most efficient operator and, later that year another privately-run prison, Buckley Hall, would be managed by Group 4. In June 1995, a consortium including Tarmac and Group 4 won the contract to build and manage a 600-cell Category B prison at Fazakerley, Liverpool. Another group, including Costain and Securicor were contracted to construct and run an 880-place Category B prison at Bridgend in South Wales (Harding, 1997). These were the first of six new penal institutions planned under the government's Private Finance Initiative (PFI). In 1996, the government published a White Paper proposing to privately finance, design and build a further 12 prisons to come on stream at a rate of one or two a year from 2001–02 onwards, providing 9,600 new prisoner places (*Prison Privatization Report International no. 1*).

May 1997 saw the election of a Labour government that had been unequivocally opposed to the contracting-out of prisons whilst in opposition. In March 1995 Jack Straw, then Shadow Home Secretary, said:

> It is not appropriate for people to profit out of incarceration. This is surely one area where a free market certainly does not exist … at the expiry of their contracts a Labour government will bring these prisons into proper public control and run them directly as public services. (*The Times*, 8 March 1995)

However, not long after the election, there were signs that the Labour Party was to reverse its previous position. In June 1997, Jack Straw, by now Home Secretary, announced that he had renewed UK Detention Services management contract for Blakenhurst and agreed to two new privately-financed, designed, built and run prisons. The following year, Straw confirmed the U-turn in a speech to the Prison Officers Association (POA) when he stated that in future all new prisons in England and Wales would be privately constructed and run (although the Prison Service was now also to be allowed to tender for the contracts when current contracts expired). The threat of privatisation was also to be used to promote reform in 'underperforming' public prisons.

Lowdham Grange private prison in Nottingham. Opened in 1998 it is a Category B closed training prison for adult males, one of four private prisons in the UK managed by Serco.

By early 2007 there were a total of 11 privately operated prison service establishments in England and Wales, though it is likely that as the prison system expands there will be further contracts in the pipeline. That said, the shifting governance of prisons has not been only one way – on two occasions private contractors have lost the contract for running particular prisons, both being returned to Prison Service management. Though privatisation has not spread as far as some critics initially feared, there is now considerable political support for such provision (see Carter, 2003) and it seems that this part of the penal system will remain a mixed economy for the foreseeable future.

Life on the inside

Before we look at who is to be found in our prisons, let us begin by exploring the nature of prison life a little. We do this by looking at two classic pieces of work: Gresham Sykes' study of the impact of life in a maximum security prison, *The Society of Captives*, and Erving Goffman's study of the impact of what he called 'total institutions': *Asylums*.

Sykes describes five forms of deprivation experienced by inmates of the maximum security prison. Each of these challenges the prisoner's sense of self,

the foundations of their personality and being. The five are:

- *The deprivation of liberty* – This is the first and most obvious form of deprivation experienced by captives. As Sykes (1971: 65) puts it, 'the prisoner's loss of liberty is a double one – first, by confinement to the institution and second, by confinement within the institution. That is to say, the inmate cannot leave the prison and is hugely restricted in what he is able to do at any time within the prison.'

- *The deprivation of goods and services* – We live in a consumer-oriented age surrounded by material possessions. What inmates are able to 'own' in prison is strictly regulated as is their access to services that might be considered 'normal' (access to leisure activities, for example, is limited).

- *The deprivation of heterosexual relationships* – As Sykes (1971: 70) graphically puts it, 'If the inmate … is rejected and impoverished by the facts of his imprisonment, he is also figuratively castrated by his involuntary celibacy.'

- *The deprivation of autonomy* – A good illustration of the denial of autonomy is to be found in Léon Faucher's timetable 'for the House of young prisoners in Paris' found in Foucault's *Discipline and Punish* (see excerpt in Chapter 22). Here, described in minute detail, is a daily regime to which inmates are expected to adhere. In many, if not most things, there is no choice for the inmate.

- *The deprivation of security* – Again, Sykes' own words put this at its clearest: 'However strange it may appear that society has chosen to reduce the criminality of the offender by forcing him to associate with more than a thousand other criminals for years on end, there is one meaning of the involuntary union which is obvious – the individual prisoner is thrown into prolonged intimacy with other men who in many cases have a long history of violent, aggressive behaviour' (1971: 77). Read any personal account of life in prison and you will find some expression of the insecurity found in this secure setting.

In *Asylums* Goffman (1961) picks up this theme and explores how entry into a total institution – an asylum, a prison, the army – involves a series of adaptive processes that involve what he calls the 'mortification of the self' – a series of ritual humiliations and degradations that have an impact on the individual's sense of self and mark out the inmate's 'moral career' in the institution.

'The Inmate World' (Goffman)

The recruit comes into the establishment with a conception of himself made possible by certain stable social arrangements in his home world. Upon entrance, he is immediately stripped of the support provided by these arrangements ...

The processes by which a person's self is mortified are fairly standard in total institutions; analysis of these processes can help us to see the arrangements that ordinary establishments must guarantee if members are to preserve their civilian selves ...

The process of entrance typically brings with it other kinds of loss and mortification ... We very generally find staff employing what are called admission procedures, such as taking a life history, photographing, weighing, fingerprinting, assigning numbers, searching, listing personal possessions for storage, undressing, bathing, disinfecting, haircutting, issuing institutional clothing, instructing as to rules, and assigning to quarters ...

As part of this rite of passage he may be called by a term such as 'fish' or 'swab', which tells him that he is merely an inmate, and, what is more, that he has a special low status even in this low group ...

Once the inmate is stripped of his possessions, at least some replacements must be made by the establishment, but these take the form of standard issue, uniform in character and uniformly distributed ...

Just as the individual can be required to hold his body in a humiliating pose, so he may have to provide humiliating verbal responses. An important instance of this is the forced deference pattern of total institutions; inmates are often required to punctuate their social interaction with staff by verbal acts of deference ...

On the outside, the individual can hold objects of self-feeling – such as his body, his immediate actions, his thoughts and some of his possessions – clear of contact with alien and contaminating things. But, in total institutions these territories of the self are violated ... New audiences not only learn discreditable facts about oneself that are ordinarily concealed but are also in a position to perceive some of these facts directly. Prisoners and mental patients cannot prevent their visitors from seeing them in humiliating circumstances ...

Finally, in some total institutions the inmate is obliged to take oral or intravenous medications, whether desired or not, and to eat his food, however unpalatable.

Source: Goffman (1961: 24–35).

Prisoners

There are currently over 80,000 people in Britain's prisons. This is a record. What do we know about who is currently held in our jails? Table 28.3 provides a summary overview of the prison population for 2005 when the overall number in prison was around 75,000. As the table illustrates, approximately 95% of the prison population is male and around 16% of those in prison have not been convicted and are held there on remand.

The first point to note is that women represent a relatively small, though growing, part of the overall prison population. The fact that numbers are small, and that the prison system has been designed largely with the needs of male prisoners in mind, makes life in prison particularly problematic for women (for further discussion and detail see Chapter 32). Table 28.3 also shows that at any time a substantial minority of prisoners are on remand. That is to say, they are in prison pending trial having not yet been convicted. Beyond the sheer fact of being deprived of liberty without having been convicted of a crime, remand prisoners face a number of problems. The remand sector of the prison system tends to have some of the worst overcrowding and poorest conditions. Often housed in some of the oldest prisons, those on remand often have very restricted access to training and other facilities and prison inspections have regularly found remand prisoners to be spending particularly long periods locked up (HM Chief Inspector of Prisons, 2000). A further particular concern was that remand prisoners were found often to have limited access to legal advisers with the possibility, therefore, that their defence would be compromised.

People from black and minority ethnic communities are significantly over-represented in the prison system. Again, taking the prison population at the end of 2005 shows that white prisoners make up slightly under three-quarters of inmates despite accounting for over 90% of the population in England and Wales (see Table 28.4)

Table 28.3	Population in custody at the end of each quarter, England and Wales, 2005			
	Q1 2005	**Q2 2005**	**Q3 2005**	**Q4 2005**
Total population in custody	**75,428**	**76,675**	**77,807**	**74,626**
Pop. in prison	74,962	76,190	77,307	74,194
Pop. in police cells	0	0	0	0
Pop. in local authority secure accom.	232	237	249	216
Pop. in secure training centres	234	248	251	216
Population in custody				
Males and females	**75,428**	**76,675**	**77,807**	**74,626**
Remand	12,446	12,965	13,645	12,627
Immediate custodial sentence	61,855	62,563	62,962	60,814
Fine defaulters	52	78	96	40
Non-criminal	1,075	1,069	1,104	1,145
Males	**70,927**	**72,017**	**73,039**	**70,261**
Remand	11,496	11,944	12,599	11,765
Immediate custodial sentence	58,355	58,963	59,306	57,363
Fine defaulters	48	77	90	39
Non-criminal	1,028	1,033	1,044	1,094
Females	**4,501**	**4,658**	**4,768**	**4,365**
Remand	950	1,021	1,046	862
Immediate custodial sentence	3,500	3,600	3,656	3,451
Fine defaulters	4	1	6	1

Source: *Offender Management Caseload Statistics* (http://www.homeoffice.gov.uk/rds/omcs.html).

Table 28.4	Prison population by ethnicity, 2005	
	Number	%
All	**74,195**	
White	54,645	73.6
Mixed	2,113	2.8
Asian or Asian British	4,797	6.5
Black or Black British	11,207	15.1
Other	1,433	1.9

Source: *Offender Management Caseload Statistics* (http://www.homeoffice.gov.uk/rds/omcs.html)

An expanding part of the prison population is made up of foreign nationals. Whereas there were 4,259 foreign nationals in prison in England and Wales in 1996, this had risen to over 10,200 by 2005, accounting for almost 14% of the overall population. These prisoners potentially have an additional set of needs from those prisoners would normally have. These include problems with language and communication, cultural concerns to do with diet, and concerns about resettlement.

Research by the Prison Reform Trust (PRT) (Ruthven and Seward, 2002) found that foreign national prisoners awaiting trial experience particular problems accessing basic information about the legal system. Many have little understanding of the nature and workings of the criminal justice and penal system and have real difficulties understanding prison procedures and rules. Moreover, the PRT found there to be a specific problem in relation to prisoners who have been recommended for deportation or have other issues to do with immigration. Such prisoners have very particular information needs but frequently find that access to legal and immigration advice is limited.

Incarceration and social exclusion

There is substantial evidence indicating enormously high levels of disadvantage among those to be found in prison. This is not simply that those who receive custodial sentences are predominantly drawn from the poorer and more marginal sections of our society – though this is very much the case – but research evidence points to a problem of multiple disadvantage among those in our jails. A report by the government's Social Exclusion Unit (SEU) (2002) on the subject of prisoner resettlement reported that compared with the population as a whole, prisoners are:

- 13 times more likely to have been in care as a child;
- 10 times as likely to have been a regular truant from school;
- 13 times more likely to have been unemployed;
- 2.5 times more likely to have a family member who has been convicted of a criminal offence;
- 6 times more likely to have been a young father.

In addition, the basic skills and educational achievements of people in prison are starkly different from the population as a whole:

- 80% of prisoners have the writing skills of an 11 year-old.
- 65% of prisoners have the numeracy skills of an 11 year-old; and
- 50% of prisoners have the reading skills of an 11 year-old.

Linked with the SEU's findings in relation to social exclusion, a study by the Office for National Statistics (ONS, 1998) found that over three-quarters (78%) of male prisoners on remand, two-thirds (64%) of male sentenced prisoners and half of female prisoners had some form of personality disorder. Approximately two-thirds of prisoners had used illicit drugs in the year before imprisonment and close to three-fifths of male prisoners and two-

fifths of female prisoners drank to a hazardous degree prior to their incarceration (SEU, 2002). This picture was reinforced by the NOMS National Strategy document (NOMS, 2005) which suggested that up to one-third of all problematic drug users in the UK were in prison or serving a community sentence. Home Office data (2003, *Prison Statistics)* suggests 73% of sentenced prisoners had used drugs in the year prior to imprisonment, and the Prison Service estimates that half of all men, and three-fifths of all women received into prison have a chronic substance abuse problem (Coyle, 2005).

One part of the prison population that has very particular circumstances and needs is women in prison. As noted earlier, we deal with this matter in greater detail in Chapter 32, but quotes from two respected bodies – the Chief Inspector of Prisons and the Fawcett Society – illustrate some of the issues raised by women's imprisonment.

> Overall, our reports record the extent of the distress and vulnerability in the women's prison population. This is most evident in the local prisons that receive women directly from court; but managing severely damaged and self-harming women is part of the core business of all the closed prisons we inspected. It is hard to meet that level of need – as the number of self-inflicted deaths among women testifies. It is equally hard to provide a positive, interactive regime for less damaged women who nevertheless need support to overcome their difficulties. (HM Chief Inspector of Prisons, 2005: 52)

> Female prisoners are a disproportionately disadvantaged population with high levels of poverty, low levels of educational attainment, and poor employment histories ... Women with histories of abuse and violence are over-represented in the prison population ... Women prisoners suffer from particularly poor physical and mental health ... Furthermore, 37% of women in prison have previously attempted suicide, a much higher figure than for both male prisoners and the general female population. (Fawcett Society, 2004: 43)

Violence in prison

As we saw earlier when discussing the history of imprisonment, one of the long-standing concerns about prison life concerns security and order. The available evidence on British prisons suggests that, on the one hand, there is a considerable amount of violence within prisons and yet, on the other, the majority of prisoners feel safe most of the time (Bottoms, 1999). Joe Sim (1994: 104) argues that violence within male prisons is a normal expression of a particular form of masculinity:

> Violence and domination in prison can therefore be understood not as a pathological manifestation of abnormal otherness but as part of the normal routine which is sustained and legitimated by the wider culture of masculinity: that culture condemns some acts of male violence but condones the majority of others.

Recent research by Edgar *et al.* (2003) used a victimization survey to explore experience of violence in four institutions: two adult prisons (Wellingborough and Bullingdon) and two Young Offender Institutions (Huntercombe and Feltham). A total of 1,566 inmates took part in the study. Table 28.5 summarises the main findings and illustrates the relatively high levels of both assault and threats.

These data suggest that nearly one-third of young offenders and one-fifth of adult prisoners have experienced assault in the last month and that one quarter and one-third respectively have had property stolen over the same period. On this basis, the researchers calculate that a prison of 500 inmates would have at least 150 assaults in an average month. As they note, although 'many of these incidents were undoubtedly minor, the rates of assault demonstrate a level of harmful activity which is frustrating for staff, frightening for many inmates and potentially destabilizing for regimes' (2003: 30).

For young prisoners in particular, the relatively violent and intimidating nature of prison culture can be one of the main reasons that they find it difficult to adapt to incarceration. Another type of violence in prison, and one almost certainly related

to difficulties in coping with prison life, is violence directed at oneself (we consider the issue of suicide in Young Offender Institutions in greater detail in Chapter 29). Research by Harvey (2007), which involved interviews with 25 young offenders who had recently self-harmed, found there to be a wide variety of reasons attached to such behaviour including: conflict with staff or other prisoners; guilt; self-disgust; inability to cope with prison life; uncertainty over bail or sentence; relationship problems outside, including lack of support; and various psychological problems. More than half of the prisoners interviewed had received psychiatric treatment in the past and were reported as suffering from depression, borderline personality disorder and psychosis.

Finally in this regard, there is very substantial concern within the prison system about the problem of suicide, which tends to be substantially higher than in society generally. Thus, in 2005 there were 78 suicides in prisons – a rate of over 100 per 100,000 prisoners. By contrast, the suicide rate for adults aged between 25–34 in England and Wales is about 18 per 100,000 (Liebling, 2007). Of the 78 deaths in 2005, 63 were male adult prisoners, three were female adult prisoners, ten were young adults and two were juveniles. Why are suicide rates so high? In part, it is likely that this reflects the particular vulnerability of many who are imprisoned. Thus, for example, there are high rates of psychiatric and personality disorders within the prison population and, as we have seen, high rates of drug and alcohol problems, all of which may be exacerbated by the circumstances of prison life: social isolation, psychological pressure, the threat of violent victimization, and sometimes poor relationships between prisoners and staff.

Table 28.5	Proportion of prisoners that had been victimized at least once in the previous month (%)					
	Feltham	**Huntercombe**	**All young offenders**	**Bullingdon**	**Wellingborough**	**All adults**
Assault	32	26	30	20	17	19
Threats	46	40	44	27	25	26
Robbery	11	8	10	5	2	4
Cell theft	28	26	27	30	42	34
Hurtful verbal abuse	58	51	56	26	26	26
Exclusion	20	12	18	7	7	7

Source: Edgar *et al.* (2003: 30).

Prison officers

There has been surprisingly little research undertaken on prison officers – certainly when compared with the amount of attention paid by criminologists to police officers and their work. Research by Kauffman (1988) and more recently by Liebling and Price (2001) and Crawley (2004) has begun to correct this, however. At the time of Liebling and Price's study there were just under 44,000 working for the Prison Service, of whom approximately 24,000 were prison officers and a further 1,000 were governors. The remainder were chaplains, psychologists, medical staff, operational support personnel and the like. A breakdown of Prison Service staff in 2003/04 is given in Figure 28.8. Given their number, therefore, prison officers 'have the most significant influence on prison life for prisoners' (2001: 15), making it especially important that we understand a little more about them.

Approximately 17% of prison officers (or 3,300 in total) are female, and women are disproportionately represented in the lower officer grades (see also Chapter 32). Female officers and governors work predominantly in female prisons. There is also under-representation of ethnic minorities among prison staff (see Figure 28.9).

Ethnic minority officers are also under-represented in the higher officer grades and governor grades of the Prison Service. As with the police service, there are now targets set by government for recruitment from minority ethnic communities, and in both organisations, the perception that the institutions are racist appears to be one of the major barriers to success in this area. One of the areas in which there has been substantial change in recent years is in the age of prison officers. Thus, whereas officers under the age of 30 made up 17% of staff in 1988, the proportion had increased to 28% by 1993. This was a result of changes introduced by the Fresh Start initiative discussed earlier. Those new officers recruited in the early 1990s have tended to stay with the Prison Service and so, once again, the officer profile is aging somewhat. Thus, according to Liebling and Price (2001: 22–23):

> the typical prison officer is male; is white; is aged between 30 and 40; and has around 10 years of experience. This means that he joined the Prison Service in around 1990, at about the

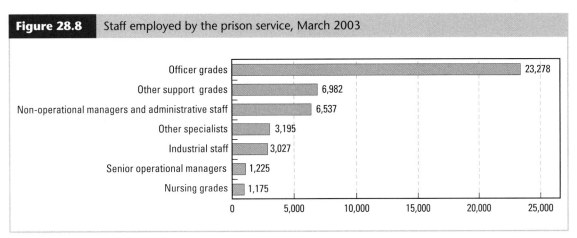

| Figure 28.8 | Staff employed by the prison service, March 2003 |

Officer grades — 23,278
Other support grades — 6,982
Non-operational managers and administrative staff — 6,537
Other specialists — 3,195
Industrial staff — 3,027
Senior operational managers — 1,225
Nursing grades — 1,175

Source: National Audit Office (2004).

| Figure 28.9 | Ethnic background of prison officers and selected populations (%) |

	White	Asian	Black	Other	No data	TOTAL
Prison officers	95.0	0.8	1.7	0.4	2.2	100
England and Wales population	93.0	4.0	2.2	0.8	0	100
Prison population	81.5	3.0	12.4	3.0	0	100

Source: Liebling and Price (2001: 18).

time of the disturbances at Manchester prison. He will have seen the optimistic and reforming Woolf Report give way to the critical Woodcock and Learmont Reports and the highly-security conscious era that followed. He will have seen the prison population rise ... will also have witnessed the introduction of many new policies ... [and] will have watched imprisonment become much more politicised.

Prison officers are generally contracted a 39-hour week and the majority work every other weekend. They work a shift pattern – in order to cover the 24-hour nature of the job – and therefore have a fairly complex working arrangement. Officers have a wide range of different roles including supervision, discipline, control, and administration. It is all but impossible, therefore, to describe a 'typical day'. Liebling and Price get around this problem by looking at the work of the 'landing officer' – arguably one of the core prison-officer roles – and describe what their day might look like to an outsider.

A prison officer chatting to an inmate at Brockhill women's prison in Redditch. Not that things are always so relaxed – research evidence has shown high levels of stress among prison officers.

It is their responsibility to unlock the landing in the morning and, in the main, to remain on the wing during the breakfast period. They have responsibility, therefore, for ensuring that this is conducted in an orderly fashion and then ensuring that those prisoners who are going to work do so and checking why others are not. While prisoners work there are normal landing duties such as

checking locks, bolts and bars and possibly conducting searches. Afternoons may involve work, training or education and are a time when some of the more relaxed interaction may occur. Evening association, Liebling and Price suggest, is more likely to be seen as 'prisoner time' and officers most likely interact less with inmates during this period.

There is now a fair amount of research evidence indicating relatively high levels of stress among prison officers. Interestingly, some of this research indicates that it is organisational strains and conflicts which are often the source of such stress, rather than problems with prisoners. Thus, one relatively recent study (Cox *et al.*, 1997) found that the main areas of officer dissatisfaction were: lack of management recognition for the work they did; insufficient support from headquarters; and pressures of time. Liebling and Price's (2001) research similarly found that 95% of officers they interviewed felt that 'the nature of the job' was the main cause of stress.

How safe is the work? According to a National Audit Office (2004) study, the number of recorded assaults on staff that resulted in sickness absence increased from 397 in 1999–2000 to 693 in 2002–03, though the average number of days lost decreased. Home Office research on violence against officers found that the most significant factor influencing the likelihood of assault was the age and experience of the prison officer (Ditchfield, 1997), the argument being that maturity and experience tended to reduce officer aggressiveness and provide the social skills to manage difficult situations within the prison.

There is something of a contrast within criminology in the amount of critical attention that has been paid to police officers compared with prison officers. There is a very sizeable literature, for example, exploring police culture, the use of force and, indeed, violence by police officers, and also a very considerable and important body of work on police corruption (see Chapter 25). The same cannot be said of prison officers, and it is only relatively recently in the UK that a more critical literature has started to emerge (Scott, 2006; Sim, 2007). The focus of elements of this work is upon the myriad ways in which prison officers' powers are used – and, on occasion, misused – in order to maintain the prison system *status quo* and their own authority. Relatedly, joint investigative work by the Metropolitan Police and the Prison Service (HMP and MPS, 2006) on officer corruption suggested that it had intelligence that over 1,000 members of Prison Service staff had been involved in misconduct. This is undoubtedly an area in which increased criminological attention is required.

Release from prison

Prisoners who have been sentenced to life imprisonment or detention without limit of time have the punishment part of their sentence set in open court by a sentencing judge. Once the punishment part of the sentence has been served the parole board will decide if the prisoner should be released on life licence. There are conditions to the licence and if the conditions are broken prisoners may be returned to prison immediately. Where shorter sentences are concerned, prisoners will be discharged from prison either at the end of their sentence or via one of the three main grounds for early release. These are:

- *Automatic release (remission)* – The idea of remission goes back to the idea of a ticket of leave for convicts that were subject to transportation. At this stage and afterward, remission was something that was earned. Gradually, there was a shift toward the idea of more automatic release. Starting with one-sixth of the sentence, remission gradually increased to one half of the sentence. The term *remission* was abolished by the 1991 Criminal Justice Act. It was replaced by the term 'added days' in an effort to replace the idea of remission as a privilege, but rather something that was a right, but could be forfeited as a result of ill-discipline.

- *Discretionary release (parole)* – Release under a supervision licence was introduced by the 1967 Criminal Justice Act, in part as a means of regulating the size of the prison population. Parole came into operation in 1968 and has been reformed several times since (see Chapter 23).

- *Home detention curfew (HDC)* – Introduced as part of the Crime and Disorder Act 1998, HDC allows prisoners serving between 3 months and 4 years to be released up to 90 days early, either conditionally or unconditionally, subject to a curfew which is enforced by electronic tagging.

As we saw in the previous chapter, the *Review of Correctional Services* (Carter, 2003) was critical of the apparent gap between the services provided in prison and the supervision of offenders once they had been released. The Carter Report recommended

much closer and continuous forms of supervision and, moreover, that this should be underpinned by the creation of a seamless correctional service – the National Offender Management Service (NOMS) – rather than separate prison and probation services. NOMS is still coming into existence and its precise nature is not yet well established (see Chapter 27).

Problems with employment, accommodation and finance are fairly common on release from prison. A survey of prisoners in the last weeks of their sentence prior to release found that approximately 30% had some form of employment, education or training lined up for after their release – meaning, of course that 70% of prisoners did not (Niven and Stewart, 2005). Roughly 70% of respondents said that they had accommodation to go to on release from custody, and the research suggests that strong family and other social ties are a crucially important factor in successful resettlement after prison.

One consistent problem faced by people released from prison concerns finance. Prisoners serving more than 14 days are entitled to a discharge grant. Equivalent to approximately one week's benefit payment, in early 2007 the discharge grant was £46.75. As we have seen, only a small proportion of people released from prison have jobs to go to. The majority are therefore dependent on benefits. These, however, are paid fortnightly in arrears and often take considerably longer than two weeks to arrange. Consequently, very large numbers of recently-released prisoners face their first few weeks on the outside short of money – a situation many have described as hardly being compatible with successful resettlement (Rowlingson *et al.*, 1997).

Governance, accountability and human rights

Public institutions generally have systems in place so that 'customers' or others who use them can make complaints or have grievances heard. Prisons are unusual places where, as we have seen, the basic conditions of existence require that some of the normal assumptions of everyday life are stripped away. The removal of certain freedoms is the essence of imprisonment. That is not to say, however, that prisoners have *no* rights. The Woolf Report (1991) drew an important distinction when it observed that offenders were sent to prison *as* punishment rather than *for* punishment. Woolf argued for the importance of an effective and fair means of hearing and addressing the complaints of prisoners on both moral and practical grounds:

- *Moral*, because the uneven power relationship between the inmate and the guard imposes a duty on the latter to behave appropriately and justly.

- *Practical*, because order is much more likely to be maintained if inmates feel that they are being dealt with in a manner that is fair.

In what follows we look briefly at three aspects of the governance of the prison system: independent inspection of prisons; complaints procedures; and, the application of human rights legislation.

Independent inspection

Prisons inspection has a long history stretching back to the work of John Howard. His oft-quoted observation about prisons in the late eighteenth century was:

> The care of a prison is too important to be left to a gaoler; paid indeed for his attendance, but often tempted by his passions, or interests, to fail in his duty. To every prison there should be an inspector appointed ... Sheriffs have this power already ... But some excuse themselves from attention to this part of their duty, on account of the short duration, expense and trouble of their office, and these gentlemen have no doubt been fearful of the consequences of looking into prisons. (quoted in Ramsbotham, 2005: 51)

Inspection continued under the Prison Commission until the 1960s, itself replaced by the Home Office Prison Department from 1962. Independent inspection of prisons was introduced in 1981 after the recommendation of the May Report (1979). May recommended strongly that the Chief Inspector of Prisons should not be drawn from the Prison Service itself and this has been the case since that time – the Inspectors being: Bill Pierce (formerly Chief Probation Officer for London); Sir James Hennessy (a retired diplomat); Stephen Tumin (a Judge); David Ramsbotham (a retired military officer); and Anne Owers (a human rights campaigner).

In addition to HMIP, there are two other bodies that are responsible for inspecting prisons. First, there is what used to be called Prisons Boards of Visitors, but which, since 2003, have become Independent Monitoring Boards. These boards are made up of lay members of the public who, acting in an independent and unpaid inspectorate, monitor the day-to-day life in their local prison or immigration removal centre in order to ensure that proper standards of care and decency are maintained. UK prisons are also inspected by the Council of Europe – specifically the European Committee for the Prevention of Torture and Inhuman or Degrading Treatment or Punishment (CPT). It has been critical of the prison system on a number of occasions and after its visit in 2001, the CPT concluded that 'much remains to be done to achieve the prison service's objective of holding all prisoners in a safe, decent and healthy environment' (quoted in Coyle, 2005). The HM Inspectorate of Prisons, as well as other bodies, inspect prisons and report on the conditions in which prisoners live and the treatment they receive. Prisoners' grievances and complaints are dealt with separately.

Grievance or complaints procedures

A Home Office working party in the late 1980s described the prisons grievance procedures as 'piecemeal'. There existed a wide range of procedures including applications to a wing manager or duty governor, applications to members of what were then Boards of Visitors or even a petition to the Home Secretary. New procedures were introduced in 1990 to ensure that complaints were generally dealt with at a higher level of the prison system, and to allow for confidential complaints to be made. Concerns about the system continued, however, and in 1994, following the Woolf Report, the role of independent Prisons Ombudsman was created.

The Prisons Ombudsman investigates complaints submitted by individual prisoners who have failed to obtain satisfaction from the Prison Service complaints system. The Ombudsman is able to consider the merits of matters complained of, as well as the procedures involved. The Ombudsman's first Annual Report showed that the new office dealt with over 2,000 complaints during its first 14 months. This resulted in 424 full investigations, of which just under half (44%) were upheld. The Prison Service accepted 90% of the recommendations made to them. The most recent Annual Report reports that a total of 4,159 complaints were received in 2005–06 and, of these, a total of 1,469 were investigated. A summary of the types of complaints made is illustrated in Figure 28.10.

Figure 28.10 Complaints received from prisons by category, 2005–06

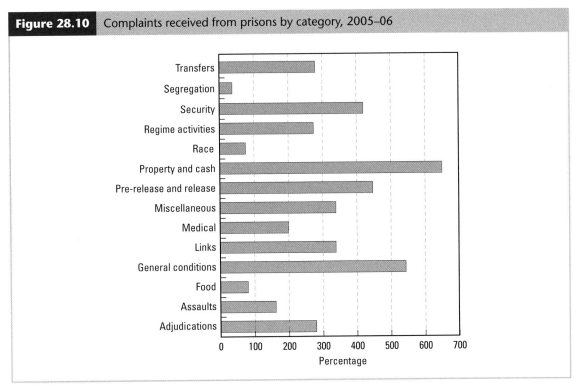

Source: Prisons and Probation Ombudsman *Annual Report 2005–06*.

Human rights and imprisonment

A recent report outlining a human rights approach to the management of prisons (Coyle, 2002) noted that:

> People who are detained or imprisoned do not cease to be human beings, no matter how serious the crime of which they have been accused or convicted. The court of law or other judicial agency that dealt with their case decreed that they should be deprived of their liberty, not that they should forfeit their humanity.

There are a number of important international standards and human rights treaties affecting domestic imprisonment and standards of incarceration. These include:

- Universal Declaration of Human Rights (1948).
- Convention Against Torture and Other Cruel, Inhuman or Degrading Treatment or Punishment (1984).
- Conventions on the Elimination of all Forms of Racial Discrimination (1966).

- Elimination of All Forms of Discrimination against Women (1979).
- International Covenant on the Rights of the Child (has been ratified by the UK and, therefore, binding).

A range of bodies is now actively engaged in attempting to monitor standards in prisons systems around the world in relation to adherence to fundamental human rights standards including, as we have seen, the European Committee for the Prevention of Torture (Morgan and Evans, 1999). Human rights concerns cover such matters as the conditions in which prisoners are kept, their access to health care, the nature of disciplinary and grievance procedures, and contact with the outside world. In recent times, the most highly publicised human rights-related concerns have been those connected with the war in Iraq and, in particular, with the treatment of people arrested and detained in prisons such as Abu Ghraib and the American detention facility at Guantánamo Bay in Cuba.

Conditions at Guantánamo Bay

Camp Delta's perimeter fence is covered by thick, green tarpaulins so that inside, the one relief from Gitmo's pervading heat and dust, the sparkling blue ocean, is invisible. Even without the tarps, however, most of the detainees – the 550 in 'maximum security' conditions – would get few opportunities to look at the view. The best they can hope for, in return for behaving compliantly and 'cooperating' with their interrogators, is to be led in handcuffs and leg irons from their cells to a small, covered yard for twenty minutes of exercise in the company of one other detainee, followed by a shower and change of clothes, five days a week. Less amenable detainees will enjoy this privilege only twice in the same period.

[...]

Kellogg, Brown and Root's standard issue Gitmo cell is a pre-fabricated metal box, painted a faded green, a little larger than a king-sized bed: 56 square feet (5.2 square metres). Next to the hard steel wall-mounted bed, two and a half-feet wide, is an Asian-style toilet, a hole in the floor, facing the open grille of the door. The guards, some of them women, are supposed to pass by the cell every 30 seconds. Next to the toilet is a small sink and a single tap, so low that the only way to use it is to kneel.

[...]

Cells of this size are not uncommon in maximum security American prisons, although in many states, inmates – even on death row – may spend hours each day in less confined conditions, associating with other prisoners or at work. They will also normally have unrestricted access to television, books, music, letter-writing materials, and frequent visits.

Of course, at Gitmo, none of the detainees has been convicted of a crime, but there, at the highest security level, the occupants are not allowed to keep even a cup. If they wish to drink, they must either bend and drink from the tap, or attract the attention of a guard. They are also given the following items: a thin mattress and a blanket; one set of orange clothing, consisting of a T-shirt, boxer shorts and trousers; a toothbrush, soap and shampoo; and a prayer cap, mat and copy of the Koran. There is no air-conditioning in the cell blocks. When the temperature inside reaches 86°F (30°C), the guards are permitted to switch on ceiling fans – not in the cells, but the corridor. The lights stay on all night.

A detainee resting in his cell at Camp Delta, Guantánamo Bay.

Source: Rose (2004: 59–60).

Lest we imagine, however, that abuses of basic rights are confined to other jurisdictions, it is as well to conclude by reminding ourselves of the situation in the UK. A Law Lords judgment in 1983 concluded that 'Under English law a convicted prisoner retains all civil rights which are not taken away expressly or by necessary implication' (quoted in Coyle, 2005). One such right is to make applications to the European Court of Human Rights in Strasbourg and this had led to a number of important judgments in recent years:

- In 1998 the UK was found to be in breach of Article 6 (the right to a fair trial) when the prison disciplinary system was judged to be unfair. As a consequence the system was changed, with serious charges now being heard by an independent adjudicator rather than a prison governor.

- In the case of Mark Keenan in Exeter prison, in 2001 the UK was found to have violated Article 3, prohibiting torture and inhuman or degrading treatment as a result of a failure to provide appropriate monitoring and segregation for a mentally-ill prisoner.

- In 2002 the UK was adjudged to have violated Article 2 (the right to life). A pre-trial prisoner, Christopher Edwards had been murdered by a cell mate in Chelmsford prison.

- In 2002, the UK was found to have violated Article 3 in a case in which a prisoner with no arms or legs was imprisoned in conditions which took no account of her disabilities (see *Price* v *United Kingdom Application* 33394/96).

The prison system is coming under increasing pressure as the numbers of people incarcerated grows. Under such circumstances Woolf's (1991) observation that people are sent to prison *as* punishment not *for* punishment becomes ever more important, as does his assertion that the three goals of security, control and justice should always be kept in balance.

Review questions

1 In the context of imprisonment, what does Goffman mean by the 'mortification of the self'? Give examples.

2 What is the importance of the distinction between being sent to prison *as* punishment rather than *for* punishment?

3 What are the three main forms of early release from prison?

4 What are the main human rights protocols relating to the treatment of people in prison?

Questions for further discussion

1 What has been the main impact of the Woolf Inquiry?

2 Is it more valuable to look at similarities in patterns of imprisonment around the world or differences?

3 Is America an example of the gradual ending of capital punishment or of its rebirth?

4 In what ways, if at all, is it important to treat prisoners' complaints seriously?

5 What are the main human rights concerns raised in relation to contemporary imprisonment (a) in Britain, and (b) elsewhere?

Further reading

As an introduction to the sociology of imprisonment I think it is still hard to beat Roger Matthews (1999) *Doing Time*, Basingstoke: Macmillan

The best source of information on prison officers is: Liebling, A. and Price, D. (2001) *The Prison Officer*, Winchester: Waterside Press/Prison Service Journal (soon to appear in a new edition)

A comprehensive and impressive selection of essays on a very broad range of subjects related to prisons and imprisonment can be found in: Jewkes, Y. (ed.) (2007) *Handbook on Prisons*, Cullompton: Willan

A fine collection of excerpts from original source materials can be found in:

Jewkes, Y. and Johnston, H. (eds) (2006) *Prison Readings: A critical introduction to prisons and imprisonment*, Cullompton: Willan

Placing imprisonment in its broader context, perhaps the most useful text is Cavadino, M. and Dignan, J. (2002) *The Penal System*, 3rd edn, London: Sage, though if you want to locate it in its international context, then the book to consult is: Cavadino, M. and Dignan, J. (eds) (2006) *Penal Systems*, London: Sage

Websites

On prisons systems generally, and useful data on the numbers in prison, the International Centre for Prison Studies hosts a very useful website: http://www.kcl.ac.uk/depsta/rel/icps/

Reports from the Inspectorate of Prisons can often be very useful and illuminating. They are all available at: http://inspectorates.homeoffice.gov.uk/hmiprisons/inspect_reports/

On the death penalty, there are a number of helpful sites. For the US there is the death penalty information center: http://www.deathpenaltyinfo.org and more generally it is worth looking at Amnesty International's site: http://web.amnesty.org/pages/deathpenalty-index-eng

The *Guardian* newspaper runs a special feature on prisons: www.guardian.co.uk/prisons

Chapter outline

Youth crime   717
   Persistent young offenders   718
   Trends in youth crime   720
   Ethnic minority youth and crime   720
   Drug use and crime   721
   Victimization   724

Youth justice   725
   Childhood and punishment   725
   Emergence of a juvenile justice system   726
   The tide turns   727
   The punitive shift   728
   The rise of managerialism   730
   A new youth justice?   731
   Youth Offending Teams (YOTs)   731
   Non-custodial penalties   731
   Anti-social behaviour   732
   Referral orders   733
   Youth Offender Panels (YOPs)   734

Contemporary youth justice   734
   Anti-social behaviour   735
     Criticisms of the anti-social behaviour agenda   735
   Young people and imprisonment   737
   Community alternatives   739
   Referral orders and restorative youth justice   739
   Young people, crime and justice   740

Questions for further discussion   741
Further reading   741
Websites   741

29

Youth crime and youth justice

CHAPTER SUMMARY

Young people are a fairly consistent source of adult concern. In an important book called *Hooligan*, Geoffrey Pearson examines what he refers to as 'respectable fears'. In the book he illustrates how adult anxieties about younger generations have been a more or less constant feature of British social life for at least two centuries. Successive generations find something in 'the young people of today' that makes them feel that somehow things are deteriorating: that adolescents are less well-behaved, responsible and respectful than they were when they were young. Although concerns about youthful misbehaviour may have a long history, we have only had a separate formal system for juvenile offenders for a century. In this chapter we look at:

- the extent of young people's involvement in crime and their experience of victimization;
- the nature of young people's drug use;
- the history of responses to youth crime;
- recent developments in youth justice and whether we are seeing the emergence of a 'new youth justice';
- the issue of anti-social behaviour and official responses to it;
- the growing importance of restorative justice initiatives within youth justice.

We worry a lot about young people. They are a major source of both adult anxiety and adult moralising. Such concerns are illustrated in a recent survey of attitudes toward young people and youth justice. A nationally-representative sample of people was asked whether they thought 'teenagers today ... are more respectful of authority than teenagers of 20 years ago, less respectful or about the same?'. The responses are detailed in Table 29.1.

Well over four-fifths of people surveyed think young people today are less respectful than the young people of a generation ago. What is almost certain is that adults asked the same question 20 years ago would also have felt something similar (though not necessarily to the same degree). As Pearson (1983: 209–10) notes, 'each era has been sure of the truthfulness of its claim that things were getting steadily worse, and equally confident in the tranquillity of the past'. At the very least, therefore, when looking at contemporary youth crime and youth justice it is important to place our current concerns in their longer term historical context.

Table 29.1	Perceptions of teenagers today, compared with 20 years ago, by age of respondent (%)			
Teenagers today are ...	Aged 16–29	Aged 30–59	Aged 60+	Total
More respectful	–	1	1	1
About the same	9	12	9	11
Less respectful	84	84	88	84
Don't know/too young to say	7	3	2	4
Total	100	100	100	100

Source: Hough and Roberts (2004).

Hoodies – the latest in a long line of 'folk devils'? This photo was taken in Bristol in 2007. Bristol City Council is one of 40 local authorities in England and Wales to be declared a 'Respect zone' on the basis of indices such as deprivation, high levels of anti-social behaviour, truancy and school exclusion levels.

Youth crime

So significant is the link between age and crime that two well-known American criminologists, Hirschi and Gottfredson (1983: 552), have argued that the age–crime distribution 'represents one of the brute facts of criminology'. Of course, young people are also the focus of considerable adult concern – concern which has focused on terms like *delinquency* and more recently *anti-social behaviour*. Our focus in the first section of this chapter is on what various sources of data have to tell us about the nature of youth crime, before then moving on to look at the history of youth justice.

Official statistics suggest that at least one-fifth of all those cautioned or convicted in any one year are aged between ten and 17 and well over one-third (37%) are aged under 21. Self-report studies which ask respondents to talk about how many offences they have committed, if any, in the past year or during the course of their lives, confirm that offending in the teenage years is relatively common. Research conducted by the Home Office in the mid-1990s found that over half of males and almost one-third of females aged between 14 and 25 admitted to committing at least one criminal offence (Home Office, 1995a). A more recent self-report study found that ten to 17 year-olds were responsible for over one-third of the incidents measured, even though they comprised one-seventh of the sample (Budd *et al.*, 2005). The same study found that that approximately one-third of young males and just under one-fifth of young females aged between ten and 25 reported having committed at least one offence in the past year (see Figure 29.1).

Estimates of the peak age of offending vary, but generally place it somewhere between 15 (MORI, 2004) and 18 and show it to be higher for males than it is for females. The first Youth Lifestyles Survey (YLS) showed the peak age of offending for males to be 14 for 'expressive property offences', 16 for violent offences, 17 for serious offences, and 20 for drug offences (Graham and Bowling, 1995). Among females, the peak age of offending was 15 for expressive property and serious offences, 16 for violent offences, and 17 for drug offences.

| Figure 29.1 | 10–25 year-olds committing offences in last 12 months, by sex (%) |

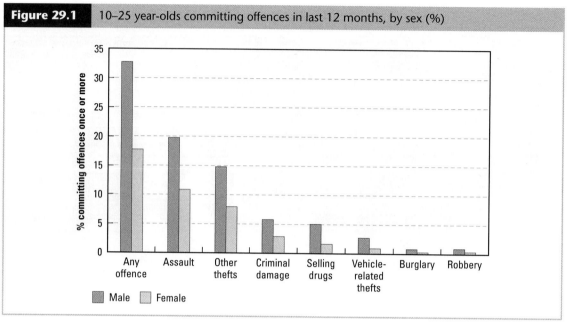

Source: Budd *et al.* (2005).

Looking, however, at the proportions of males at different ages who admitted to having committed various offences within a one-year period, Graham and Bowling found that 22–25 year-olds had the highest rate of property-related offending (if fraud and theft from work were included). This led them to conclude that the nature of offending changes significantly between the ages of 14 and 25. In particular, young men do not appear to desist from property offences in their early twenties in the way they do for other forms of crime.

In terms of patterns of offending, it is also important to note that there is considerable evidence to show that working-class males are disproportionately involved compared with other social groups. Work in the mid-1990s on persistent young offenders found under one-tenth came from households whose head was in non-manual employment (Hagell and Newburn, 1994). Although self-report studies tend to show less of a gap in levels of offending by social class (Graham and Bowling, 1995), the 1998/99 YLS found that young males in lower social classes were more likely to be 'persistent offenders' compared with those from higher social classes (Flood-Page *et al.*, 2000).

Persistent young offenders

We know that of those who commit criminal offences, some commit many more than others. To what extent it is possible to identify that minority of offenders who are most heavily involved in crime and, more particularly, to what extent it is possible to predict who these people are likely to be, has become a key policy issue in recent years. Put crudely, the objective for policy-makers is to identify and focus attention on what is assumed to be that small minority of offenders who are disproportionately responsible for a substantial proportion of overall crime. If much of this offending can be prevented (by locking them up, if needs be) then it is assumed that this will have a reasonably substantial impact on crime rates. This seems like a sensible idea in the abstract. The problem is that in practice it is far less easy to implement than it sounds.

The first issue is how to identify these 'persistent' or 'prolific' offenders. Early research by Marvin Wolfgang and colleagues (1972) used *number of arrests* as the method of distinguishing what they referred to as 'chronic offenders'. In their study, a follow-up of nearly 10,000 boys, they suggested that the chronic offenders (those with five or more arrests each) represented 6.3 per cent of the cohort and accounted for over half of the total number of arrests for the whole group. A similar finding was reported by West and Farrington (1977), though their threshold was six or more convictions. More recent self-report data from the Youth Lifestyles Survey also illustrates the uneven distribution of offending (see Table 29.2).

Table 29.2	The distribution of crime by offenders (1998/99 YLS)			
	Male		**Female**	
No. of offences	% sample	% all crime	% sample	% all crime
0	74	–	89	–
1	5	5	3	7
2	5	10	3	15
3–5	6	21	2	24
6–9	2	17	0.4	10
10 or over	2	48	0.8	43

Source: East and Campbell (1999).

Similarly, the 2004 Home Office Crime and Justice Survey uses self-report data to distinguish between what it refers to as *prolific* and *serious* offending. *Prolific* offending was defined as having committed six or more offences in the previous year, whereas *serious* offending was defined as having committed any of the following offences in the previous year: theft of a vehicle; burglary; robbery; theft from the person; assault resulting in injury; and selling Class A drugs. Figure 29.2 breaks down the 2004 CJS juvenile cohort into those who have and those who have not offended in the previous year, and then sub-divides the offenders into *prolific, serious* and *prolific and serious* offenders.

According to the survey approximately one-quarter of juveniles that had offended in the previous year would be defined as being serious *and* prolific and six in ten would be defined as either serious *or* prolific. On this basis the researchers estimate that there were approximately 420,000 *serious* or *prolific* juvenile offenders in England and Wales, rather reinforcing the difficulties highlighted by previous research in identifying what is often thought to be a *small* group responsible for a disproportionate amount of crime (see Hagell and Newburn, 1994).

Research conducted for the Home Office in the early 1990s, when there was particular political

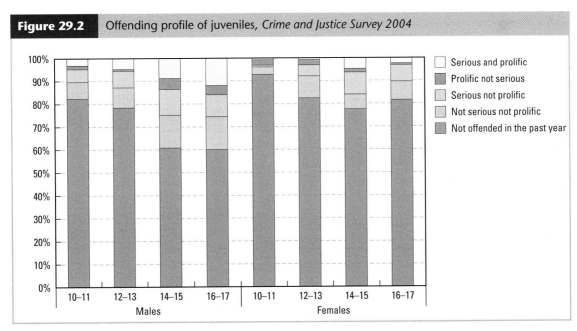

| Figure 29.2 | Offending profile of juveniles, *Crime and Justice Survey 2004* |

Source: Budd *et al.* (2005).

concern about persistent offending, also identified a number of other problems in relation to identifying persistent offenders. First, different definitions or thresholds identify different individuals – there is no easily identifiable, and consistent, body of young people who are *persistently* offending (Hagell and Newburn, 1994). Second, much of the offending by those who either admit to more offences, or who are more regularly arrested by the police, is fairly transient in nature. Offending tends to be concentrated over relatively short bursts of time. Consequently, by the time such individuals have been identified, they may well have ceased their offending (at least temporarily) and will have been 'replaced' on the streets by other prolific offenders.

Third, attempts at early identification – i.e. before an extensive criminal career is under way – tend to be highly inaccurate. Such predictive work tends to result in the identification of what are called 'false positives' (young people identified as likely to go on to have an extended criminal career who actually don't do so) and 'false negatives' (young people who are not identified as being likely to become offenders who do go on to offend fairly extensively). Such activity therefore raises a whole host of ethical, moral and practical dilemmas. Policy interest in this area hasn't declined, however, and we return to this below.

Trends in youth crime

It is difficult to estimate levels of youth crime, in large part because one is rather dependent on official criminal statistics. These, of course, only capture what is reported to and recorded by the police (see Chapter 3). They provide an indication of trends, but are best treated with a fairly high degree of caution. Two measures of juvenile crime can be drawn from official statistics. First, we can look at the overall number of offences committed by ten to 17 year-olds. This shows the number of known male offenders to have decreased from 230,700 in 1981 to 145,700 in 1999 – a drop overall of almost two-fifths (37%). The figure for females went from 42,200 in 1981 to 35,900 in 1999 – a decrease of 15%.

However, this can be slightly misleading because it doesn't take account of any possible changes to the number of ten to 17 year-olds in the population between these dates (i.e. if there had been a substantial drop in the number of ten to 17 year-olds in the population this would account for the drop in the number of recorded crimes). Consequently, it is more sensible to look at the overall offending rate per 100,000 of the population over time. This shows the offending rate to have dropped from 7,000 in 1981 to 5,400 in 1999 for males and to have increased from 1,300 to 1,400 for females. Thus, both sources of data indicate a likely decline in male offending over the period, but there would appear to be some possibility that the female offending rate has increased (though the overall numbers are relatively small).

A third method of looking at trends in juvenile offending, and a means of checking the data already considered, is to look at the results of self-report studies. Studies such as the Youth Lifestyles Survey, which ask the same questions of young people, and which are repeated at different times, can be used to see whether the proportion of young people 'reporting' that they have committed criminal acts changes over time. Thus, the YLS, which was conducted in 1992/93 and 1998/99, suggests that there was no overall change in the proportion of males and females aged 14–25 admitting offending in the last year. There were some differences between age groups. Thus, there was a 14 per cent increase in the proportion of 14–17 year-old males admitting an offence and a six per cent decrease in the proportion of 18–25 year-old men doing so. The proportion of all 14–25 year-old females admitting offending was unchanged during the same period (see Figure 29.3).

Ethnic minority youth and crime

If young people generally have been a source of considerable adult anxiety about crime then, in

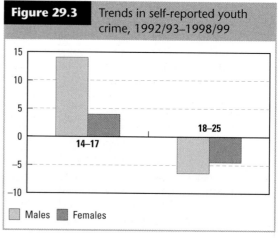

Figure 29.3 Trends in self-reported youth crime, 1992/93–1998/99

Source: East and Campbell (1999).

Policing the Crisis

On 15 August 1972 an elderly widower, Mr Arthur Hills, was stabbed to death near Waterloo Station as he was returning home from a visit to the theatre. The motive was, apparently, robbery ... [The national press] labelled it – borrowing a description proffered by a police officer – 'a mugging gone wrong'.

... During the thirteen months between August 1972 and the end of August 1973, 'mugging' received a great deal of coverage in the press in the form of crime reports, features, editorials, statements by representatives of the police, judges, the Home Secretary, politicians and various prominent public spokesmen ... In short, the judiciary declared 'war' on the muggers. Editorials quickly followed.

... In this study we argue that there was a *moral panic* about 'mugging' in 1972–73 ... this is not to deny that, on occasions during the past few years (but also, almost certainly, for at least a century), individual men and women have been suddenly attacked, rough-handled and robbed in the street. We think, however, that it requires explanation how and why a version of this rather traditional street crime was perceived, at a certain point in the early 1970s, as a 'new strain of crime' ... [W]e think it requires to be explained why and how the weak and confused statistical evidence came to be converted into such hard and massively publicised facts and figures ...

The impression that 'violent crime', particularly 'mugging', was increasing produced a massive and intense coverage by the press, official and semi-official spokesmen, and sentences of an increasing severity in court.

... Our narrative began with the 'first' British mugging. But it has ended with a different, and perhaps rather unexpected theme: the confrontation in our cities between 'police power and black people'. Although by no means all 'muggers' charged in this period were black, the situation and experience of black youths has, we believe, a *paradigmatic relation* to the whole 'mugging' phenomenon ... The intersection between the courts, the media and 'mugging' in this period are not hard to discover ... But in contrast with the courts and the media, the role of the police seemed to us peculiarly, though perhaps not surprisingly, 'invisible'.

... In looking at the police, then, we are pushed back, behind the headlines and the judges' homilies, to an earlier, 'pre-mugging', period ... On the margins of the 'mugging' epidemic, then, there arises its *pre-history*: the longer and more complex story of the striking deterioration in police–black relations, especially between the police in certain areas of big cities and sections of black youth. It is only in this context that the *innovatory* role of the police, in the generation of a moral panic, can be properly assessed and understood.

Source: Hall, S. *et al.* (1978: 3–52).

recent decades, much attention has been focused on minority ethnic youth in particular. Increased concern arose during the 1970s, partly as a result of a 'mugging panic' early in the decade, and also in relation to other signs of poor or deteriorating relationships between the police and black youth (see box).

Concerns about black criminality were reinforced by the release of statistics by the Metropolitan Police suggesting that crime rates were particularly high among African-Caribbean youth in the capital. In terms of available research data, the results of the YLS many years later were striking, for they suggested that, in general, white and African-Caribbean youth have similar rates of participation in offending, though these are significantly higher than self-reported participation by South Asian youth (Graham and Bowling, 1995). Data from the more recent self-report Offending, Crime and Justice Survey (OCJS) (Sharp and Budd, 2005) show slightly

higher levels of self-reported offending among black or black British respondents (the terminology used by the authors) compared with white respondents (see Figure 29.4).

The OCJS also included a series of questions about anti-social and other 'problem' behaviours. The results show slightly higher overall levels of anti-social behaviour among white young people aged ten to 15, but these differences were not significant. The more sizeable differences appeared to be in relation to treatment within the criminal justice system which, in some instances at least, were 'consistent with discriminatory treatment' (Sharp and Budd, 2005).

Drug use and crime

Prior to the late 1970s drugs were not a particular source of anxiety so far as youthful behaviour was concerned. After that point 'the heroin habit'

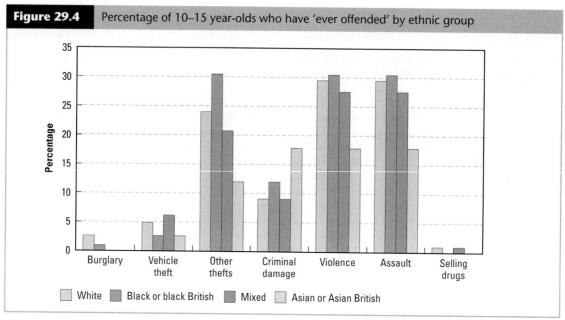

Figure 29.4 Percentage of 10–15 year-olds who have 'ever offended' by ethnic group

Source: Sharp and Budd (2005).

really began to take off and for the first time its use became associated with the young unemployed (Pearson, 1987). The number of known addicts trebled between 1979 and 1983, and research in the late 1980s confirmed the impression of a significant spread of heroin use (Parker *et al.*, 1988). Public concern about increasing heroin use was followed by fears of a possible 'crack' epidemic, though, in the main, the worst of these fears have not been realised. Research in the 1990s suggested that 'the picture now is one of continuing widespread availability of a great variety of drugs, use being shaped by familiar factors such as local supply, contexts of use, preferred styles of consumption and purpose or intent' (South, 1994: 399).

Data on the incidence and prevalence of drug use among young people are now available as a result of a number of important surveys (see for example Measham *et al.*, 1994; Miller and Plant, 1996; Ramsay *et al.*, 2001; Goulden and Sondhi, 2001). Prevalence for 15–20 year-olds varies between approximately 10–35 per cent in national surveys and 5–50 per cent in local surveys. All research on prevalence shows cannabis to be the most frequently-used drug, though use of LSD, amphetamines, and ecstasy has increased since the late 1980s (Parker *et al.*, 1995). Figure 29.5 shows the prevalence of drug use by males and females aged ten to 25 during the preceding year.

Drug use and age are clearly linked. Use of illicit drugs is rare in early teenage years, increases sharply in the mid-teens, and is generally shown to peak in the late teens or early twenties. It has been the annual surveys conducted by Howard Parker and colleagues since the early 1990s that have probably been most influential in framing contemporary understandings of youthful drug use (Measham *et al.*, 1994; Parker and Measham, 1994; Parker *et al.*, 1995; Parker *et al.*, 1988, 2000). Conducted in schools in the north-west of England, the surveys provide data on use of illicit drugs among samples of children aged approximately 14 in the first survey through to the age of 18. The surveys indicate relatively high prevalence rates of 'lifetime use' reported by over a third (36%) of 14 year-olds to almost two-thirds (64%) of 18 year-olds (Parker *et al.*, 1998).

Both national and local surveys indicate that, at least until recently, drug use by young people appears to have been on the increase. Mott and Mirrlees-Black (1993), for instance, noted that the percentage of 16–19 year-olds reporting cannabis use more than doubled between 1983 and 1991. The late 1980s and early 1990s witnessed an increase in the use of dance drugs. Though this increase started from a relatively low baseline, by the mid-1990s dance drugs had become an important part of the youth drug scene (Measham *et al.*, 1993). Moreover, according to Parker *et al.* (1995),

Research evidence suggests that the prevalence of youthful drug use has increased substantially in the last two decades. Cannabis remains the most commonly used drug.

unlike the situation a decade previously, there were no longer any significant differences in the prevalence of illicit drug use by young men and women, though the authors recognise that in terms of the quantities, the frequency, and the repertoire of drug use, gender differences may still remain. Parker *et al.* (1995) conclude that the ways in which young people perceive and relate to illicit drugs is changing quite dramatically, and that adolescents now live in a world in which the availability of drugs is unexceptional, even 'a *normal* part of the leisure–pleasure landscape' (1995: 25; though for a critical review see Shiner and Newburn, 1997, 1999, and see Chapter 21). The most recent national surveys of youthful drug use suggest that there has been some stabilising of prevalence rates, though there appears to have been a significant increase in cocaine use since the mid-1990s.

Recent years have seen growing attention, both at an official level and academically, paid to levels and types of drug use among 'vulnerable groups' (Lloyd, 1998). A growing body of research has highlighted the particularly 'vulnerable' position of young offenders (see for example, Wincup *et al.*, 2003). The second YLS found that three-quarters (74%) of 'persistent offenders' reported lifetime use of drugs, and almost three-fifths (57%) reported having used drugs in the past year (Goulden and Sondhi, 2001) and, more particularly, found that

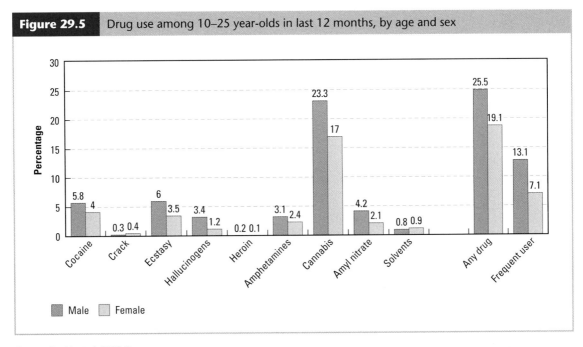

Figure 29.5   Drug use among 10–25 year-olds in last 12 months, by age and sex

Source: Budd *et al.* (2004).

the rates of use of drugs such as crack and heroin were significantly higher among young serious and/or persistent offenders than they are in the general population (see also Bennett, 2000).

More recent work on young offenders largely confirms this general picture (Hammersley *et al.*, 2003). Similarly, the 2004 OCJS shows higher rates of offending among drug users when compared with non-users, and higher levels still among Class A drug users and frequent users (see Figure 29.6).

Victimization

Young people are frequently victims of crime. However, leaving aside studies of child abuse and domestic violence, most criminological studies, with some important exceptions, pay scant attention to young people's experiences as victims of crime. The BCS usually limits its sample to those aged 16 or older (see Chapter 3). However, the fourth BCS included questions for 12–15 year-olds with illuminating results. It found that 12–15 year-old boys and girls are at least as much at risk of victimization as adults and, for some types of crime, more at risk than adults and older teenagers (Aye Maung, 1995). More recently the Crime and Justice Survey (CJS) found that young people are more likely to be the victim of personal crimes (assault, robbery, theft from the person and other personal theft) than those in older age groups (Wood, 2005) (see Figure 29.7).

According to the CJS over one-fifth (22%) of ten to 15 year-olds report having experienced some form of violence in the past year and over a third (35%) report some form of personal crime. Unusually, in addition to criminal victimization, the CJS also sought information on 'bullying'. Almost one-fifth of ten to 17 year-olds (19%) said that they had been 'bullied in a way that frightened or upset them'. Those most at risk were ten to 11 year-olds, of whom 27 per cent said they had been bullied. In over half the cases, bullying involved face-to-face abuse or 'verbal offensiveness' and in a third of cases it involved physical assault.

Not only were young people more likely to be victimized than older age groups, they were also more likely to experience repeat victimization. Thus, 60 per cent of ten to 15 year-olds that had experienced violence in the previous year did so more than once compared with 51 per cent of 16–25 year-olds and 44 per cent of 26–65 year-olds (Wood, 2005). Although the survey does not break down such experience by ethnic origin, data from the BCS suggest that African-Caribbeans generally face higher risks than young people from other ethnic groups (see Chapter 31).

The BCS found that only about one in ten incidents were brought to the attention of the police, though the proportion rose to one in five of the more serious cases experienced. In contrast, one in three members of the sample said that they had had

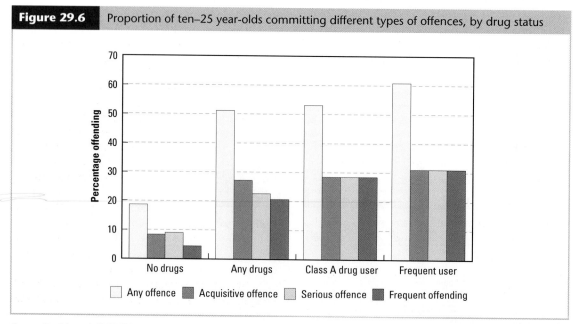

Figure 29.6   Proportion of ten–25 year-olds committing different types of offences, by drug status

Source: Budd *et al.* (2005b).

Figure 29.7   Percentage of age groups victimized once or more in last 12 months

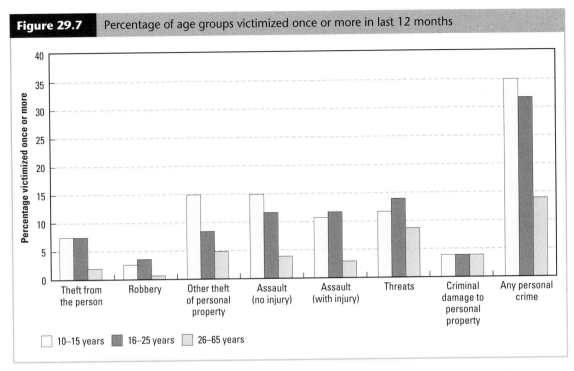

Source: Wood (2005).

some form of contact with the police in the previous six to eight months. About one-fifth had been stopped and eight per cent said they had been searched, a higher rate than is the case for older age groups (Aye Maung, 1995). Juveniles were also less likely to be told why they were being stopped than were their elders. It is this combination of being vulnerable, but also being more likely to be stopped or 'moved on', that leads a large proportion of young people to feel both over-controlled and under-protected by the police (Loader, 1996).

Review questions

1 What did Hirschi and Gottfredson mean when they said the age–crime curve is one of the 'brute facts of criminology'?

2 What is meant by the 'peak age of offending'?

3 What do self-report studies have to tell us about patterns of youthful offending among different ethnic groups?

4 Why might young people feel over-controlled and under-protected?

Youth justice

Childhood and punishment

In England and Wales no child may be guilty of a criminal offence below the age of ten. Between the ages of ten and 18, young offenders are dealt with in what is now referred to as the 'youth court', distinguishable in style and approach from the adult magistrates' courts which, together with the Crown Court, deal with offenders aged 18 or above. This system reflects, in crude terms, the distinctions made between three life stages: childhood, adolescence, and adulthood. These categories are historically contingent and, just as a separate justice system for juveniles is a relatively recent invention, so the categories of childhood and adolescence have not always been recognised in the way they are today.

According to the French historian, Philippe Aries, in the Middle Ages childhood was a considerably foreshortened period: 'Children were mixed with adults as soon as they were considered capable of doing without their mothers or nannies, not long after a tardy weaning (in other words at about the age of seven)' (Aries, 1973: 395). Society was divided by status and was not generally stratified by age (Stone, 1979). However, from the seventeenth century onward, childhood was progressively extended and increasingly separated from adulthood. In Aries' view, it is only since that time that we have become preoccupied with the physical, moral, and sexual development of young people. As childhood as a separate category evolved, so there developed with it the idea that children were a responsibility – that they required protection – and, moreover, that children were creatures with the potential for good and evil, discipline being required to ensure that the former predominated over the latter.

Furthermore, as these two phases in the life-cycle were progressively separated and, through restrictions on work and the formalisation of education, the transition between the two was extended, so the opportunity for the development of a further, intermediary phase increased. This we have come to refer to as 'adolescence'. It was in the nineteenth century that the distinctively modern adolescent started to appear. Institutions were developed for delinquents and for those *at risk* of delinquency – the 'perishing classes' (those that

hadn't yet fallen into crime, but were considered likely to do so) – and it was out of these that the modern juvenile justice system grew. By the turn of the century, young people in the new cities and manufacturing towns were experiencing considerable economic independence, and leisure time was expanding. It was at this time that heightened concerns about delinquency and hooliganism emerged (Rook, 1899; Booth, 1902).

Emergence of a juvenile justice system

The modern juvenile justice system emerged in roughly the same period as 'adolescence' and 'delinquency' were 'discovered'. Many of the social reformers in the nineteenth century who campaigned to protect children from danger and exploitation demanded that they should be removed from the 'adult' prison system and placed in privately managed, state-funded institutions. The Youthful Offenders Act 1854 provided the basis for reformatories for the 'dangerous classes', and legislation three years later established the industrial schools for the 'perishing classes'. Although such institutions were part of the educational system

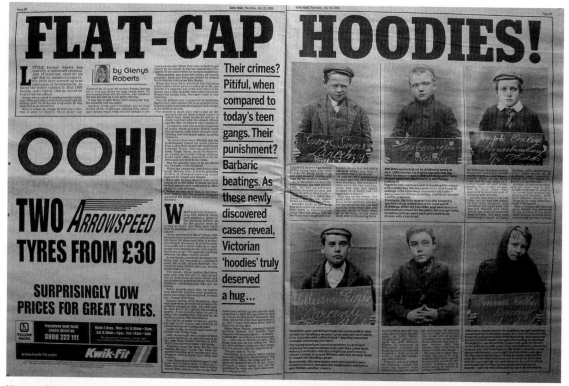

Young offenders from the late nineteenth century. These pictures were reprinted in the *Daily Mail* in July 2006 under the headline 'Flat Cap Hoodies'.

rather than the penal system, they housed children aged between seven and 14 who had been convicted of vagrancy. Juvenile courts began to emerge around the turn of the century and were formalised by the Children Act 1908, an Act which also barred under-14s from prison and restricted the imprisonment of 14–15 year-olds.

The juvenile courts – special sittings of the magistrates' courts in the early years – were empowered to act in criminal cases and in cases of begging and vagrancy, though they remained, in essence, criminal courts. Nonetheless, reflecting the changes that had taken place in the nineteenth century, the new arrangements endorsed 'the conception of the child or juvenile as a special category' (Garland, 1985: 222). Also in 1908, 'borstals' were created to cater for 16–21 year-olds (the 'juvenile-adult category') who 'by reason of his criminal habits and tendencies or associations with persons of such character, it is expedient that he should be subject to detention for such a term and such instruction and discipline as appears most conducive to his reformation and the repression of crime' (quoted in Garland, 1985). Welfare concerns were given further prominence by the Children and Young Persons Act 1933. This Act prohibited capital punishment for those under the age of 18, and reorganised the reformatory and industrial schools, bringing about the creation of 'approved schools' which provided juvenile offenders with education and training, and remand homes which kept remanded juveniles apart from adult prisoners.

Further restrictions on the use of imprisonment of juveniles were imposed in the 1940s and this marked the beginning of a lengthy trend of attempting to restrict the use of custody for juvenile offenders. However, levels of recorded crime rose in a generally sustained and sharp way from the mid-1950s on as, by and large, did recorded juvenile crime until the 1980s. At the end of the 1950s the Ingleby Committee focused on the conflict that it felt existed between the *judicial* and *welfare* functions of the juvenile court. Although its proposals to raise the age of criminal responsibility to 14 did not become law, the Children and Young Persons Act 1963 subsequently raised the age of criminal responsibility to ten.

At the end of the decade a highly welfare-oriented piece of legislation, the Children and Young Persons Act 1969, abolished the system of approved schools, and the remand homes or remand centres for juveniles which existed alongside them, and replaced them with community homes with residential and educational facilities. Although it retained the juvenile court, it sought to make care more important than criminal proceedings. The intention was that the juvenile court should become a welfare-providing agency and 'an agency of last resort' (Rutter and Giller, 1983), referral happening only in those cases in which informal and voluntary agreement had not been reached between the local authority, the juvenile, and parents (Morris and McIsaac, 1978). It was also intended that detention centres and borstals for juveniles be phased out and replaced by a new form of intervention – intermediate treatment.

What would full implementation of the 1969 Act have meant? First, it would have abolished prosecution of any child under 14 for a criminal offence, with the exception of homicide. Secondly, it would have restricted civil care measures for that group as well. Thirdly, wherever possible, the assumption would have been that children would be dealt with outside court. Though 14–16 year-olds could have been prosecuted, non-criminal care proceedings would be available and would be the preferred option in most cases. For those prosecuted, there would have been two main disposals available – the care order and the supervision order – both of which would be supervised by social workers given considerable discretion (Bottoms, 1974). The intention was that the use of penal custody for offenders aged 14–16 should be phased out (Nellis, 1991). This added up to 'the most developed application of welfare principles to criminal justice ever seen in an English statute' (Bottoms and Stevenson, 1992: 36).

The tide turns

The politics of youth crime were beginning to change however, and the 1970 General Election put paid to any possibility of full implementation of the 1969 Act, with the consequence that juvenile courts continued to function largely as they had before. Most significantly, although care proceedings on the commission of an offence were made possible, such powers were used exceedingly sparingly, and the number of custodial sentences rose from 3,000 in 1970 to over 7,000 in 1978 (Rutter and Giller, 1983; Cavadino and Dignan, 1992). Partial implementation, and the consequences which flowed from that, led one group of commentators at the end of the decade to argue that the 'tragedy' of the 1969 Act was that people had 'been persistently led to believe that the juvenile criminal justice system has become softer and softer, while the reality has been that it has become harder and harder' (Thorpe *et al.*, 1980, quoted in Muncie, 1984).

According to two informed commentators, youth justice policy at the end of the 1970s 'bore little resemblance to that proposed in the 1969 Act' (Morris and Giller, 1987). A new Conservative government, led by Margaret Thatcher, was elected in 1979 on an explicitly 'law and order' manifesto, and set about introducing a series of measures that would illustrate their tough approach. One of the more newsworthy was the proposal to reintroduce a limited number of detention centres with 'tougher' regimes – the so-called 'short, sharp shock' treatment proposed by the Home Secretary, William Whitelaw, who announced that life at the centres would 'be conducted at a brisk tempo. Much greater emphasis will be put on hard and constructive activities, on discipline and tidiness, on self-respect and respect for those in authority ... These will be no holiday camps and those who attend them will not ever want to go back' (quoted in Home Office, 1984b). Although the experiments were quickly found to fail they were extended by Whitelaw's successor, Leon Brittan.

Whilst the Thatcherite rhetoric remained tough, the paradox is that 'the decade of "law and order" was also the decade of what has been called "the successful revolution" in juvenile justice' (Rutherford, 1992). The 1980s saw something of a brief revolution in juvenile justice in England and Wales. Most notably, there was a significant decline in the use of imprisonment for juveniles between 1981 and 1988, and the decline was particularly strong after 1984. Though a number of factors contributed to this reduction, such as a decline in the number of juveniles in the population as a whole, together with some legislative changes that sought to encourage the use of intensive community-based punishments (generally referred to as *intermediate treatment*), the major reason for the declining use of custody was to be found in juvenile justice practice. Increasingly during the 1980s there developed a sense, particularly in relation to juveniles, that prison was a relatively ineffective, as well as expensive, measure. Using language that would be unthinkable for either of the major political parties today, the 1988 Green Paper published by the Home Office, *Punishment, Custody and the Community*, stated that:

> ... most young offenders grow out of crime as they become more mature and responsible. They need encouragement and help to become

law abiding. Even a short period of custody is quite likely to confirm them as criminals, particularly as they acquire new criminal skills from the more sophisticated offenders. They see themselves labelled as criminals and behave accordingly.

This statement, offering a fairly standard version of labelling theory (see Chapter 10), also underpinned the everyday working philosophy of many working in juvenile justice. Consequently, what became known as *diversion* – from custody and from court – became a core objective for juvenile justice teams; wherever possible social workers sought to encourage cautioning rather than charging, and community rather custodial penalties.

The punitive shift

The tenor of public statements and public policy in relation to juvenile offending changed markedly in the early 1990s. Two sets of events stimulated concern initially. These were the urban disturbances of 1991 (Campbell, 1993) and a developing moral panic about so-called 'persistent young offenders' around the same time. In 1991 a number of small English towns and cities (the most highly publicised disturbances were at Blackbird Leys in Oxford, Ely in Cardiff and Meadowell in Tyneside) experienced outbreaks of disorder, and there seemed to be a particular problem associated with 'joyriding' – certainly the press was full of stories of young people stealing cars and then using them for spectacular, and highly public, shows of bravado. Blackbird Leys, for example, was home to frequent, and popular, public displays of 'hotting' high performance cars. Although this had apparently being going on for some time, in August 1991 the police decided to put an end to it. This was easier said than done and the next few weeks saw highly public (spectators allegedly brought deckchairs with them) police attempts to outmanoeuvre and outdrive the local hotting stars. The end result was a series of large-scale public order disturbances, scores of arrests, some exciting television, and the venting of moral outrage in the press.

Such tales were joined by what was to become another regular storyline throughout 1992, that of the young and highly *persistent* young offender. These youngsters, it was alleged, were so involved in crime that they accounted for a significant proportion of juvenile crime in the areas in which they lived. Furthermore, it was suggested that the police and courts were powerless to deal with them. The Home Secretary, for example, said a small number of children 'are committing a large number of crimes. There is a case for increasing court powers to lock up, educate and train them for their own and everyone else's interest.' It was open season in the press. On 10 September 1992, the *Daily Mail,* under the headline 'One-boy crime wave', began: 'He was only 11 when his life of crime began with the theft of chocolate bars from a corner shop ... within two years he had become a one-boy crime wave'. The previous day the *Sun* had reported the case of a young boy of 13 it claimed had committed 225 thefts and had been arrested 14 times. And so it went on.

Public concern might not have reached the pitch it eventually did were it not for the tragic events of 12 February 1993 and their highly publicised aftermath. It was at approximately 3.30 that afternoon that two year-old James Bulger was abducted from the Strand shopping centre in Bootle, Liverpool. As time passed, and the young boy remained missing, the search spread and intensified. Enhanced still photographic images from the closed-circuit televi-

CCTV pictures of James Bulger were broadcast across the nation in the aftermath of his abduction. This image shows him being led out of a shopping centre in Liverpool on 12 February 1993.

sion cameras at the shopping centre were broadcast on national television. These showed James walking with, or being led by, one of two young people with whom witnesses had seen him leaving the shopping centre; pictures which appeared to convey both innocence and, because of what was then already suspected and later confirmed, something much more sinister.

Eventually, two days later, James Bulger's battered body was found near a railway line in Liverpool, some two miles from the shopping centre. The abduction and murder of such a young child would always have had a significant public impact. The Bulger case acted as a 'focusing event' (Birkland, 1997) – a dramatic, sudden, and indicative illustration of policy failure. The arrest and charging of two ten year-old boys 'inspired a kind of national collective agony' (Young, 1996: 113), and provided the strongest possible evidence to an already worried public that something new and particularly malevolent was afoot.

The politicians responded quickly. Tony Blair, then Shadow Home Secretary, delivered what one biographer (Sopel, 1995: 155) described as a powerful 'speech-cum-sermon':

The news bulletins of the last week have been like hammer blows struck against the sleeping conscience of the country, urging us to wake up and look unflinchingly at what we see. We hear of crimes so horrific they provoke anger and disbelief in equal proportions ... These are the ugly manifestations of a society that is becoming unworthy of that name. A solution to this disintegration doesn't simply lie in legislation. It must come from the rediscovery of a sense of direction as a country and most of all from being unafraid to start talking again about the values and principles we believe in and what they mean for us, not just as individuals but as a community. We cannot exist in a moral vacuum. If we do not learn and then teach the value of what is right and what is wrong, then the result is simply moral chaos which engulfs us all.

The Conservative Home Secretary at the time, Kenneth Clarke, announced that the government proposed to introduce legislation that would make a new disposal available to the courts. These 'secure training orders' were to be aimed at 'that comparatively small group of very persistent juvenile offenders whose repeated offending makes them a menace to the community' (*Hansard*, 2 March 1993, col. 139). The new order would apply to 12–15 year-olds (though this was later amended to 12–14 year-olds) who had been convicted of three imprisonable offences, and who had proved 'unwilling or unable to comply with the requirements of supervision in the community while on remand or under sentence'.

His successor, Michael Howard, who became Home Secretary in May 1993, was even more vigorous in embracing 'populist punitiveness' (Bottoms, 1995). He quickly announced a package of measures that involved a reassertion of the central position of custody in a range of sanctions whose primary aim was deterrence. Most famously, he announced that previous approaches, which involved attempts to limit prison numbers, were henceforward to be abandoned. The new package of measures would be likely to result in an increase in prison numbers, an increase which he appeared to welcome:

> I do not flinch from that. We shall no longer judge the success of our system of justice by a fall in our prison population … Let us be clear. *Prison works.* It ensures that we are protected from murderers, muggers and rapists – and it makes many who are tempted to commit crime think twice. (*emphasis added*)

The public and political mood was reinforced by the reporting of the trial of the two youngsters accused of James Bulger's murder, which took place at Preston Crown Court in November 1993. On the day after the verdict, the *Daily Mail* carried 24 stories about the case, and a total of almost 40 stories in the three days after the trial. The broadsheets gave it similar space: the *Guardian* including 22 articles, and the *Daily Telegraph* 23 articles and two editorials (Franklin and Petley, 1996). The tone of most of the coverage – despite the age of the offenders – was extremely hostile.

It was in the context of this rather charged atmosphere, and under threat from the Labour Party that was embracing 'law and order' policies itself, that Michael Howard's new measures were introduced. The legislation that followed, the Criminal Justice and Public Order Act 1994, was controversial in a number of ways. It doubled the maximum sentence in a Young Offenders Institution for 15–17 year-olds to two years. It introduced the possibility that parents of young offenders could be bound over to ensure that their children carried out their community sentences, and provided for the introduction of 'secure training orders' for 12–14 year-olds. Five new secure training centres (STCs) were to be built, each housing approximately 40 inmates. The new sentences would be determinate, of a maximum of two years,

The front page of the *Daily Mail* the day after the end of the trial of the two boys accused of Jamie Bulger's murder. Coverage of this kind eased the passage of tough new legislation the following year.

half of which would be served in custody and half under supervision in the community.

Outside parliament, there was widespread criticism of the new provisions and Home Office-funded research cast doubt on the likely efficacy of such a policy (Hagell and Newburn, 1994). By and large, the secure training order met with relatively little political hostility with New Labour seeking to outflank the Conservatives over 'law and order' (see Chapter 1). The predictable consequence was a rise in the use of youth custody. The number of 15–17 year-olds given custodial sentences rose by almost four-fifths (79%) between 1992 and 1998. The number of young people serving custodial sentences more than doubled (122%) between 1993 and 1999.

The rise of managerialism

The next important event was a report published by the Audit Commission entitled *Misspent Youth*. It was hugely influential, largely because much of what it had to say about youth justice, and many of the recommendations it made, struck an immediate chord with the Labour opposition which was soon to be the Labour government. Both published in 1996, the parallels between the Labour Party's pre-election consultation document, *Tackling Youth Crime and Reforming Youth Justice* (Labour Party, 1996), and the Audit Commission's hugely influential report, *Misspent Youth* (Audit Commission, 1996), are striking. The Audit Commission had little of a positive nature to say about the youth justice system and a number of biting criticisms. Its view was that the system in England and Wales was uneconomic, inefficient, and ineffective. The solutions it proposed involved much greater central government management and direction of youth justice.

A new youth justice?

Labour's first six months were a frenzy of activity. Six consultation documents on youth crime were published and then a major piece of legislation was passed: the Crime and Disorder Act 1998. This Act, though followed by others, contains the key elements of Labour's 'new youth justice':

- the establishment of the Youth Justice Board (YJB);
- the creation of Youth Offending Teams (YOTs);
- the restructuring of the non-custodial penalties available to the youth court.

In its White Paper, *No More Excuses* (Home Office, 1997), the government had said that there was:

> Confusion about the purpose of the youth justice system and principles that should govern the way in which young people are dealt with by youth justice agencies. Concerns about the welfare of young people have too often been seen as in conflict with the aims of protecting the public, punishing offences and preventing offending.

In an attempt to ameliorate such confusion the reforms contained, for the first time, an overarching mission for the whole youth justice system: '... to prevent offending by children and young persons'. It then established a non-departmental public body – the Youth Justice Board – whose principal function was to monitor the operation of the youth justice system and the provision of youth justice services, together with monitoring national standards and establishing appropriate performance measures. Subsequently it has also become the commissioning body for all placements of under-18s in secure establishments on remand or sentence from a criminal court. The other major change brought about by the Crime and Disorder Act was the creation of Youth Offending Teams (YOTs).

Youth Offending Teams (YOTs)

Prior to the 1998 Act, youth justice teams, comprising mainly social workers, had had primary responsibility for working with young offenders subject to non-custodial penalties, and for liaising with other criminal justice and treatment agencies in connection with that work. Stimulated by a concern with efficiency and consistency on the one hand, and by a pragmatic belief in multi-agency working on the other, New Labour's new model YOTs had to include a probation officer, a local authority social worker, a police officer, a representative of the local health authority, and someone nominated by the chief education officer. YOTs have been in operation in all local authority areas since April 2000.

Non-custodial penalties

In addition, New Labour also promised increased, and earlier, interventions in the lives of young offenders (and those 'at risk' of becoming young offenders). The Crime and Disorder Act scrapped the caution (informal and formal) and replaced it with a reprimand (for less serious offences) and a final warning. As the name implies, one of the crucial characteristics of the final warning is that, except in unusual circumstances, it may be used only once. In addition to the change of name, and the more sparing manner of usage, the new system of reprimands and final warnings also set in motion a set of other 'rehabilitative' activities.

The Criminal Justice and Court Services Act 2000 removed the requirement that a police reprimand or final warning be given to a young offender only at a police station. This introduced the possibility of 'conferences' at which parents, victims, and other adults could be present – what has sometimes been referred to as 'restorative cautioning' (Young and Goold, 1999). Though one of the intentions behind the new warnings system may have been to encourage more restorative practices with young offenders, to date there is little evidence that the new system is experienced as a more participative one by young people.

Anti-social behaviour

The Labour Party in opposition had been much influenced by the 'Broken Windows' thesis (Wilson and Kelling, 1982) and sought to introduce a range of measures that would enable local agencies to tackle 'low-level disorder' or 'anti-social behaviour'. This idea that tackling low-level crime, or behaviour that is offensive even if not criminal, is important in reducing crime is something that has shaped a very considerable element of New Labour's criminal justice and social policy. The opening sentences of the Labour Party's 1996 discussion document, *Tackling the Causes of Crime* (Labour Party, 1996), begin:

> The rising tide of disorder is blighting our streets, neighbourhoods, parks, town and city centres. Incivility and harassment, public drunkenness, graffiti and vandalism all affect our ability to use open spaces and enjoy a quiet life in our own homes. Moreover, crime and disorder are linked. Disorder can lead to a vicious circle of community decline in which those who are able to move away do so, whilst those who remain learn to avoid certain streets and parks. This leads to a breakdown in community ties and a reduction in natural social controls tipping an area further into decline, economic dislocation and crime.

It was this, eventually, that developed into New Labour's 'anti-social behaviour agenda'. Though anti-social behaviour was discussed in the very early Labour documents in the lead-up to the 1997 general election, the focus at that stage was still primarily on the criminal justice system, and criminal sanctions, as a means of tackling crime. Thus, the 1998 Crime and Disorder Act not only overhauled the youth justice system, but also introduced a raft of new criminal measures including parenting orders, child safety orders and curfew orders. Most controversially, the Act also introduced Anti-Social Behaviour Orders (ASBOs). At the consultation stage these had been referred to as 'community safety orders' and were designed to tackle 'anti-social behaviour [which] causes distress and misery to innocent, law-abiding people – and undermines the communities in which they live'.

Prior to the Crime and Disorder Act, much behaviour of this kind had been dealt with, if at all, under the provisions of the Housing Act 1996, the Noise Act 1996, the Environmental Protection Act 1990, or the Protection from Harassment Act 1997. However, proceedings against juveniles were often problematic under such legislation (Nixon *et al.*, 1999). By contrast, anti-social behaviour orders (ASBOs) were clearly designed with juvenile 'anti-social behaviour' in mind. The orders are formally civil, requiring a civil burden of proof. Orders consist of prohibitions deemed necessary to protect people – within the relevant local authority area – from further anti-social conduct.

What is most controversial about the order, however, is that non-compliance is a criminal matter, triable in either a magistrates' court or the Crown Court and carrying a maximum sentence in the magistrates' court of six months' imprisonment, or five years' imprisonment plus a fine in the Crown Court. This led some of the most distinguished critics of the new order (Gardner *et al.*, 1998) to observe that it was strange 'that a government which purports to be interested in tackling social exclusion at the same time promotes a legislative measure destined to create a whole new breed of outcasts'.

Concerns similar to those voiced about the ASBO were also aimed at the provisions in the Act that allowed local authorities to introduce 'local child curfew schemes'. The provisions in the Crime and Disorder Act enabled local authorities, after consultation with the police and with support of the Home Secretary, to introduce a ban on children of specified ages (though under ten) in specified places for a period of up to 90 days. Children breaking the curfew were to be taken home by the police, and breach of the curfew would constitute sufficient grounds for the imposition of a child safety order. In practice, there has been remarkable reluctance to use such powers, and no child curfew orders have yet been made.

Despite such reluctance, and sustained criticism of curfews from some quarters, the government has remained keen on the idea of curfews. Armed with what appeared to be some positive results from an evaluation of a scheme in Hamilton in Scotland (McGallagly *et al.*, 1998), new legislation was introduced to extend the reach of curfew powers. The Criminal Justice and Police Act 2001 extends the maximum age at which children can be subject to a curfew, up from ten to 'under 16', and also makes provision for a local authority or the police to make a curfew on an area and not just an individual.

The final element of the Act that drew sustained criticism (*inter alia* Wilkinson, 1995) was the abolition of the presumption – that could be rebutted in court – that a child aged between ten and 13 is incapable of committing a criminal offence (generally known as *doli incapax*). While the UK has long been out of step with much of the rest of Western

The main forms of anti-social behaviour

Interpersonal/malicious ASB is behaviour directed against specific individuals or groups, e.g:

- intimidation/threats by neighbours
- minor violence
- hoax calls
- vandalism directed at individuals or groups
- serious verbal abuse (e.g. directed at public sector workers)

Environmental ASB is behaviour that, deliberately or through carelessness, degrades the local environment, such as:

- dog fouling
- setting fire to rubbish
- noise nuisance
- graffiti (e.g. on the transport network)
- abandoned vehicles
- littering/fly-tipping

ASB restricting use of shared space refers to threatening or physically obstructive behaviours that stop people using shared spaces, such as:

- intimidating behaviour by groups of youths
- drug use in public places
- street drinking/drunkenness
- soliciting and kerb-crawling
- obstructive/inconsiderate use of vehicles

Source: Millie *et al.* (2005).

Europe with its significantly lower age of criminal responsibility, the principle of *doli incapax* has traditionally protected at least a proportion of children under the age of 14 from the full weight of the criminal law. However, during the course of the 1990s, spurred in part by the Bulger case, pressure had built up to abolish the principle, and politicians from both major parties were vocal in their criticism of it. Jack Straw, in 1998 when Home Secretary, said for example: 'The presumption that children aged ten to 13 do not know the difference between serious wrongdoing and simple naughtiness flies in the face of common-sense and is long overdue for reform'.

Those concerned about the trajectory of New Labour's youth justice have also pointed to its perceived failure to tackle the problem of increasing use of custodial sentences for young offenders. Indeed, in its first term, Labour continued with the previous administration's secure training centre building programme – even arguing that they might be expanded – and introduced a new, generic custodial sentence: the Detention and Training Order (DTO). Available to the courts from April 2000, in a DTO half of the sentence is served in custody and half in the community. The DTO is a single sentence replacing the secure training order (available for 12–14 year-olds) and detention in a Young Offenders' Institute (YOI) (available for 15–17 year-olds). Long-term detention under s53 of the Children and Young

Persons Act 1933 for 'grave offences' remains an available sentence in the Crown Court.

The final major change in youth justice under New Labour has been the introduction of a number of measures apparently influenced by restorative justice principles (see Chapter 30). Elements of the Crime and Disorder Act, including the reformed cautioning system, action plan orders, and reparation orders all sought to promote the idea of reparation and, wherever possible, to seek victims' views. However, arguably, the most significant development has been the creation of referral orders as part of the Youth Justice and Criminal Evidence Act 1999.

Referral orders

The referral order is available in the youth court and adult magistrates' courts, and may be made for a minimum of three and a maximum of 12 months depending on the seriousness of the crime (as determined by the court). The order is mandatory for ten to 17 year-olds pleading guilty and convicted for the first time by the courts, unless the crime is serious enough to warrant custody, or the court orders an absolute discharge. The disposal involves referring the young offender to a Youth Offender Panel (YOP). The intention is that the panel will provide a forum away from the formality of the court. As Crawford (2002) argues, the panels draw on a range of sources:

- the Scottish children's hearings system (Whyte, 2000);
- the experience of family group conferencing (Morris and Maxwell, 2000);
- the history of victim–offender mediation in England and Wales (Marshall and Merry, 1990), and
- restorative cautioning (Young, 2000).

Youth Offender Panels (YOPs)

Youth Offender Panels consist of one YOT member and (at least) two community panel members, one of whom leads the panel. One or both parents of a young offender aged under 16 are expected to attend all panel meetings in all but exceptional cases. The offender can also nominate an adult to support him or her. It is not intended that legal representatives acting in a professional capacity be included in panel meetings either directly or as an offender's supporter. To encourage the restorative nature of the process a variety of other people may be invited to attend given panel meetings (any participation is strictly voluntary).

Those who may attend include:

- the victim or a representative of the community at large;
- a victim supporter;
- a supporter of the young person and/or anyone else who the panel considers to be capable of having a 'good influence' on the offender;
- signers and interpreters for any of the participants in the process who require them.

The aim of the initial panel meeting is to devise a 'contract' and, where the victim chooses to attend, for them to meet and talk about the offence with the offender. It is intended that negotiations between the panel and the offender about the content of the contract should be led by the community panel members. The contract should always include reparation to the victim or wider community, and a programme of activity designed primarily to prevent further offending.

Contemporary youth justice

There is a strong view in government that the youth justice reforms since the late 1990s have been a success (though there have been continuing criticisms, too). In particular, reviews by the Audit Commission (2004) and the National Audit Office (2004) have generally been highly favourable. The Audit Commission, for example, suggested that:

- The new arrangements were a significant improvement and represented a good model for delivering public services.
- Juvenile offenders were now more likely to receive an intervention, were dealt with more quickly and were more likely to make amends for their wrong-doing.
- Magistrates were generally very satisfied with the service received from YOTs.
- Reconviction rates for young offenders had fallen.

Nevertheless, the evidence is, in some ways, mixed and, in relation to some specific areas of government policy, there has been some strong criticism of elements of the new provisions. The Audit Commission, for example, found that too many minor offenders are appearing before the courts; the amount of contact time with offenders subject to supervision orders has not increased; public confidence in the youth justice system remains low, and black, minority ethnic and mixed race offenders remain substantially over-represented among the stubbornly high custodial population. One academic commentator suggested that:

Despite the vast array of youth justice reforms since 1997, there is little evidence of any significant impact on young people, on the outcomes administered by the courts, or on other key stakeholders such as victims ... In some quarters, it might be felt that a greater level of activity and a greater intensity of intervention ... [are] indicative of a more responsive and committed approach to youth justice ... On the other hand, serious questions must be asked about the consequences of this commitment ... there is clearly a diminution of the rights of children ... with collateral impacts such as increasing evidence of harmful treatment in custody. (Smith, 2003: 138)

The most vociferous criticism, however, has been aimed at the government's anti-social behaviour agenda. Flagged up in its discussion documents prior to the 1997 general election, this strand of New Labour's social policy has become more and more central in its approach to governing in recent years.

Anti-social behaviour

As we saw above, one of the most controversial elements of New Labour's youth justice-related reforms has concerned what has come to be known as its 'anti-social behaviour agenda'. It is the ASBO that has been centre-stage. Moreover, since it was introduced in 1998 the ASBO has changed in a number of important ways. For example, applications for orders can be made by social landlords as well as by the police and local authorities. Although orders are formally civil, and require a civil burden of proof, following the Police Reform Act 2002 they can also be made as the result of a conviction. Despite initial reluctance, ASBOs are now being sought regularly. Crucially, both the Prime Minister and successive Home Secretaries have sought to highlight what they see as the importance of the ASB agenda, and ASBOs in particular, with a series of major speeches, including proposing the idea of extending such order to the under-tens (so-called 'baby ASBOs').

In 2003 the Anti-Social Behaviour Unit (ASBU) was created within the Home Office to promote local activism, and further legislation (the Criminal Justice and Court Services Act 2000, the Criminal Justice and Police Act 2001, the Police Reform Act 2002 and, in particular, the Anti-Social Behaviour Act 2003) added a raft of additional powers which the courts, police and local authorities were encouraged vigorously to use. From a

Public notices concerning anti-social behaviour have become a common sight on Britain's streets. This order was imposed in Hackney, London, in 2004.

point a few years ago where anti-social behaviour was rarely talked about politically, it has become a staple in recent times, and the acronym, ASBO, has become an everyday term. The number of orders imposed nationally ran at around 100 per quarter until the end of 2002, but by the end of 2004 the rate was over 500 rising to 600 per quarter in 2005, juveniles being the subjects of 45 per cent of them. Great pressure from above was exerted on decision-makers in areas without ASBOs in place. Most police force plans now include targets for either the number of ASBOs to be sought or aim generally to increase their number (Morgan, 2006).

Criticisms of the anti-social behaviour agenda

The ASB policy has been the subject of criticism from a number of quarters. Perhaps most embarrassingly for the government, the Commissioner for Human Rights observed:

The ease of obtaining such orders, the broad range of prohibited behaviour, the publicity surrounding their imposition and the serious consequences of breach all give rise to concerns ... What is so striking ... about the multiplication of civil orders in the United Kingdom, is the fact that the orders are intended to protect not just specific individuals, but entire communities. This inevitably results in a very broad, and occasionally, excessive range of behaviour falling within their scope as the determination of what constitutes anti-social behaviour becomes conditional on the subjective views of any given collective .... such orders look rather like personalised penal codes, where non-criminal behaviour becomes criminal for individuals who have incurred the wrath of the community ... I question the appropriateness of empowering local residents to take such matters into their own hands. This feature would, however, appear to be the main selling point of ASBOs in the eyes of the executive. One cannot help but wonder ... whether their purpose is not more to reassure the public that something is being done – and, better still, by residents themselves – than the actual prevention of anti-social behaviour itself. (Council of Europe, 2005, paras 109–111)

A number of other criticisms of the ASB agenda, and of ASBOs, have been made:

- That the government's ASB campaign has tended to reinforce a 'declining standards' narrative negatively focused on young people (Millie *et al.*, 2005).

- That the minimum ASBO was so long, and the number of prohibitions imposed so often excessive, that breach was made likely.

- Despite guidance being issued emphasising the need for full consultation with the relevant YOT prior to an order being sought (YJB *et al.*, 2005) there is evidence that this is being circumvented with applications being made in adult courts not covered by YOT representatives.

- That in some areas ASBOs have been sought and granted without the recommended lower tier measures (home visits, warnings letters and Acceptable Behaviour Contracts [ABCs]) first being tried (Morgan and Newburn, 2007).

- That ASBOs, following breach, have been dragging into custody young people who would not previously have got there.

- That ASBOs have provided an evidential short-cut for the police to fast track persistent young offenders into custody (see the evidence to and report of the Home Affairs Committee, 2005).

- Groups such as ASBOwatch have documented a series of cases in which the conditions of the

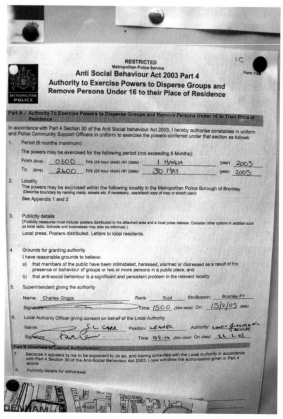

A notice giving the terms of a 'dispersal order' – placing restrictions on the number of young people who can gather in public; Penge, south-east London, 2005.

orders have been either excessive and/or absurd. For example:

Nicky East – A 14 year-old prohibited from wearing hooded tops with the hood up, or items which conceal his face, apart from when the weather is bad. No definition of what constitutes 'bad weather' is provided (July 2005).

Joseph Newcombe – A four year-old boy was threatened with an order after he threw his toy at the car of a council worker who was visiting his family's home. His mother claims that two days later the official returned and announced she wanted to give the child an ASBO.

Amasiah and Tobijah Thompson – 15 and 14 year-old brothers served an interim order banning them from entering a half-mile exclusion zone around Villa Park football stadium in Birmingham two hours before kickoff in response to their attempts at 'car minding' (February 2005).

Ryan Wilkinson – A ten year-old boy banned from four areas of Leeds and having any contact with 17 named youths for the next five years. He is also subject to a 7pm to 7.30am curfew unless accompanied by family members (February 2005).

Kyle Major – A 16 year-old who suffers from a severe form of attention deficit hyperactivity disorder served an order (January 2005).

Luke Davies – A 17 year-old forbidden from using the front door of his home until the age of 21 (January 2005).

(*Source*: http://www.statewatch.org/asbo/ASBOwatch.html)

Young people and imprisonment

The population of young people housed in prisons and other secure accommodation is exceedingly needy. Histories of self-harm are relatively common. Almost one-third of young offenders in custody have identifiable mental health problems and over half have significant or borderline learning difficulties (Harrington and Bailey, 2005). It is difficult to say to what extent the latter finding reflects intrinsic learning difficulties or an absence of intellectual stimulation. Two thirds of DTO detainees have been excluded from education, 40

per cent have at some stage been in the care of a local authority and 17 per cent have been on a child protection register (Hazel *et al.*, 2002; see also HMIP, 2005).

The result is that children in custody typically have literacy and numeracy ages some four to five years below their chronological ages. These problems are often compounded by substance abuse with around one-third reporting that they take drugs not to get high but just to 'feel normal', or to 'forget everything' or 'blot everything out' (Galahad SMS Ltd, 2004). Which is to say that they have taken drugs as a form of self-medication. Fourteen children and young persons died in youth custody between 1997 and 2005 (see box below), 13 by suicide and one while being restrained, two in STCs and 12 in YOIs (see Goldson and Coles, 2005). The YJB estimates that some 200–300 older boys 'require more intensive support than can currently be provided in YOIs' (YJB 2005, para 16) and, consequently, it is clear that the more overcrowded the system, the more likely it is that further such tragedies will occur.

There is further evidence of the particular vulnerability of young people held in custody from a Department of Health Psychiatric Morbidity survey (Lader *et al.*, 1997). The survey found that in the

---

Deaths in custody

Philip Knight, 15

Taken into care at the age of 15, Philip was arrested having stolen a handbag from a table in a café. Because it contained a lot of money, the crime was treated as being particularly serious. After appearing in court Philip slashed his wrists. He was moved by social services and when his behaviour deteriorated further, he was moved to prison in Swansea. After an altercation with a cell mate he was placed in solitary confinement where he again slashed one of his wrists. Transferred to the prison hospital he told a prison officer he wanted to die. After his eventual court appearance on the theft charge he was returned to Swansea Prison rather than a juvenile secure unit. The same day he was returned to prison he hanged himself.

Jeffrey Horler, 15

From a disrupted background, Jeffrey had been 'looked after' by social services on a number of occasions. He had also been in trouble several times and eventually

received a four-month prison sentence. Although he lived in Norfolk, the lack of appropriate places meant he was sent to Feltham in West London to serve his sentence. During his first month there his grandmother died. Very distressed, he was given permission by Feltham to attend the funeral. Social services in Norfolk, however, decided this was inappropriate (without discussing it with him). Three weeks later Jeffrey hanged himself.

Anthony Redding, 16

Sentenced to four months for car-related offences Anthony was sent to HMYOI Brinsford near Wolverhampton. Bullied at school, he was also bullied whilst in custody. He was placed on 'suicide watch' (checked every 15 minutes). Once moved to a shared prison cell he attempted to hang himself. He was moved back to the Health Care Centre as a consequence, but kept there less than a week and then returned to a cell. Again, he was to be checked at regular intervals but, despite this, within days Anthony hanged himself.

Source: Goldson and Coles (2005).

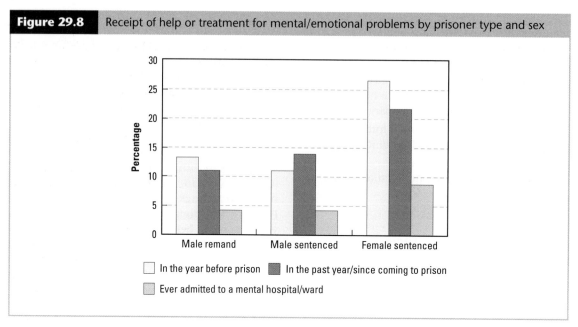

Figure 29.8 Receipt of help or treatment for mental/emotional problems by prisoner type and sex

Source: Lader *et al.* (1997).

12 months before entering prison, 13 per cent of male young offenders on remand and 11 per cent of those sentenced to custody had received help or treatment for a mental or emotional problem. The proportion among female young offenders was approximately double the total for males at 27 per cent (see Figure 29.8) – reflecting a similar pattern of particular vulnerability for adult female prisoners (see Chapter 32).

Perhaps most worryingly the research found that the number of young offenders – male and female – who had had requests for help or support turned down during their time in prison was twice that of those who had similar experiences prior to being imprisoned.

The general marginalisation of this group of young people, and the range of 'risk factors' in their background that make them especially vulnerable to mental illness/disorder, can be seen in the following findings reported by Lader and colleagues (1997):

- The proportion of people in each sample group who had been taken into local authority care as a child was 29% of the male sentenced group, 35% of the women and 42% of the male remand group.

- Of the sample, 60% reported leaving school before their 16th birthday and about 10% of the respondents had left school aged 13 or younger.

- More than 70% of the men in the sample, both remand and sentenced, said they had a previous conviction for a criminal offence. The proportion of women with a previous conviction was somewhat smaller, being only 40%.

- The vast majority, over 96% in all groups, had experienced at least one stressful life event and about 40% had experienced five or more. The most commonly-reported stressful events for all groups were being expelled from school and running away from home – these were reported by over half of all sample groups.

- Women were far more likely than men to report having suffered as a result of violence at home and sexual abuse. About 40% of the women and about 25% of the men interviewed reported having suffered from violence at home, while about 33% of the women reported having suffered sexual abuse compared with just under 5% of the men.

- During their current prison term, about 50% of young offenders reported experiencing some form of victimization.

- Hazardous drinking in the year before coming to prison was associated with the type of household people were living in, their ethnic group, previous convictions and some stressful events such as being sacked or made redundant, and running away from home.

- The odds of being dependent on drugs in the year before coming to prison were nearly five times greater for those who were living off crime than for those who were working before coming to prison. Other factors associated with drug dependence before prison were: ethnic group; having suffered the death of a close friend or relative; homelessness and serious money problems.

Community alternatives

One of the Youth Justice Board's aims has been to reduce the use of custody by increasing sentencers' confidence in community alternatives, in particular the Intensive Supervision and Support Programme (ISSP). ISSP can be used as a condition of bail, or as an adjunct to a community or custodial sentence, for serious offenders or persistent young offenders who, at the time of appearing in court, have previously been charged, warned or convicted on four or more separate occasions in the preceding 12 months and have previously received at least one community or custodial sentence. An ISSP runs for a maximum of six months with intensive supervision (including electronic tagging or tracking) and engagement (education or vocational training, offending behaviour programmes, recreational activities, etc.) for 25 hours a week for three months.

The research shows that the ISSP is being targeted at relatively serious and persistent offenders (burglary and robbery being the most common index offences, with, on average, 12 offences in the preceding two years), a high proportion of whom would most likely have received a custodial sentence had an ISSP not been an option, though it is conceded that there has been some net-widening effect. Further, though the headline reconviction rate within a follow-up period of two years is, at 91 per cent, very high, the rate for offenders with as many reconvictions released from custodial sentences is higher. Nevertheless, a recent evaluation of the ISSP concluded that such an intervention 'should be effective in reducing the offending levels of high-risk young offenders' (Moore *et al.*, 2006: 168). At the other end of the sentencing continuum from the ISSP is the referral order, argued by two commentators to be possibly 'the emerging jewel in the crown of the reformed system' (Morgan and Newburn, 2007).

Referral orders and restorative youth justice

Approximately one-quarter of all appearances before the youth court now result in a referral order. Early reports from the evaluation of the referral order pilots indicated mixed success. On the positive side, the youth offender panels were described as having established themselves within a year of operation as deliberative and participatory forums in which a young person's offending behaviour could be addressed (Newburn *et al.*, 2001b). The informal setting of youth offender panels appeared to allow young people, their parents/carers, community panel members, and YOT advisers opportunities to discuss the nature and consequences of a young person's offending, as well as how to respond to this in ways which might repair the harm done and to address the causes of the young person's offending behaviour. In addition, the evaluators argued that the successful integration of a large number of volunteers within the youth justice process provides an opportunity for a potentially powerful new exterior voice to participate and influence this arena.

Overall, however, research on the introduction of referral orders (Crawford and Newburn, 2003) contained mixed findings:

- Young people were generally happy with their experience of attending panel meetings.
- Over four-fifths (84%) of young people felt they were treated with respect.
- Compared with their experience of the youth court, parents understood the referral order process better, felt it easier to participate and perceived it to be fairer.
- Over 75% of victims who did attend a panel meeting said that the opportunity to express their feelings and speak directly to the offender had been very important in their decision.
- The most common compulsory element in all contracts was some form of reparative activity (40%). This was followed by offending behaviour work (9%) and supervision/assessment sessions with a YOT worker.
- Victims attended in only 13% of cases where at least an initial panel was held.

As the final bullet point indicates, one of the major difficulties encountered so far, as in other restorative justice developments (Dignan, 2000; Miers *et al.*, 2001), concerns the involvement of victims (Newburn *et al.*, 2001a, 2001b). During the period of the referral order pilots, the level of victim involvement in panels was very low. There were a number of reasons for this. They appeared to concern issues of implementation rather than problems with the general principles underlying referral orders. The response of all the major participants in the process to date has been largely supportive of the general principles underlying such orders.

The introduction of referral orders and youth offender panels and, more especially, the involvement of community panel members, represents a fairly radical departure in youth justice in England and Wales (Crawford and Newburn, 2002). However, as a number of authors have noted (Crawford, 2002), there are some important tensions between attempts to extend the reach of restorative justice and other aspects of New Labour's approach to youth justice. Firstly, as we have seen, apparent promotion of restorative justice exists alongside the increasing use of custody for young offenders. Secondly, despite the more inclusive tone associated with restorative justice, much contemporary youth justice discourse remains profoundly punitive.

Thirdly, there is a tension between the managerialism at the heart of New Labour's reforms – and its concern with speed, efficiency, cost reductions, and performance measurement – and the core of restorative justice in which there is an expectation that local people will play a central role in the handling of cases in their own local area (Crawford and Newburn, 2002). Thus, the growing emphasis on output and outcome measurement puts at risk restorative justice processes, which place greater emphasis on providing a secure forum in which there is room for emotions to be expressed, and for sometimes complex negotiations to take place. Most fundamentally, the greatest danger, perhaps as a result of a combination of the above, is that the very idea of restorative justice, 'and the mainly positive image which it has enjoyed thus far, might become subordinated to the more traditional and punitive approaches of the past' (Dignan, 1999: 54).

Review questions

1 What have been the main criticisms levelled at the government's anti-social behaviour agenda?

2 What evidence is there that young people in custody are particularly vulnerable?

3 What evidence is there of success in the use of referral orders in youth justice – and what problems are there?

Young people, crime and justice

We haven't always treated 'children' and 'adolescents' all that differently from adults. It is only in recent centuries that we have recognised, or created, such categories. Adolescence is the period in which young people appear to engage disproportionately in anti-social activities, including crime. For the majority, there is a marked fall in criminal behaviour during early adult life, though a minority continues to persist in their offending 'careers'. In many ways, therefore, in relation to controlling crime, the aim has been the management of this 'problem population'. For the whole of the last century and into this, young offenders have also been seen as a group necessitating an approach different from that employed with adults.

For much of the twentieth century an uneasy tension existed between approaches that were broadly 'welfarist' in conception and intention, and a more punitive model which, in its 1970s incarnation, placed greater emphasis on individual responsibility, due process, and punishment. More recently, we have witnessed another significant shift in both the rhetoric and reality of youth justice. In the early 1990s the developing managerialist discourses of the previous decade were joined by the embracing of 'populist punitiveness' by politicians of all hues (see Chapter 1). The shape of New Labour's policies was influenced by one further factor: the perception that it was not simply crime but anti-social behaviour that should be the focus of intervention. The consequence is a somewhat odd mixture of policies and practices.

One can see clear continuities and some differences between New Labour and previous administrations. Much of the punitive rhetoric is largely similar, and their 'managerialism' is in many respects an enhanced version of what was launched in the early 1990s, albeit that it has led to the creation of a youth justice system that is significantly better funded, and arguably more effective, than the system it replaced. On the other hand, the restorative justice-influenced reforms offer the prospect of a more participatory and deliberative form of youth justice, though this is more than offset by the continued high levels of youth custody in the current system. New Labour's modernisation of youth justice is an uneasy mix in which the desire to produce technically competent, well-resourced, and publicly-responsive local systems has continually been in tension with a strong desire to manage and control from the centre. And, moreover, the controlling centre has continually been shaped by its desire to capture headlines and compete to be seen as 'tough on crime'.

Questions for further discussion

1 Why might the age-crime curve be the shape it is?

2 Should criminal justice interventions be primarily focused on 'persistent' young offenders?

3 How would you characterise the main changes in the philosophies underpinning juvenile/youth justice?

4 Are we witnessing the emergence of a distinctive 'new youth justice'?

5 Are new anti-social behaviour initiatives just the latest in a long line of mistaken attempts to control young people?

Further reading

Geoffrey Pearson's (1983) *Hooligan: A history of respectable fears*, Basingstoke: Macmillan: a wonderfully enjoyable study of adult anxiety and moral panic.

The best general text is John Muncie's (2003) *Youth and Crime*, 2nd edn, London: Sage

Recent valuable texts on contemporary youth justice include:

Smith, R. (2007) *Youth and Crime*, 2nd edn, Cullompton: Willan

Goldson, B. (ed.) (2000) *The New Youth Justice*, Lyme Regis: Russell House

Goldson, B. and Muncie, J. (eds) (2006) *Youth Justice*, London: Sage

Muncie, J. and Goldson, B. (eds) (2006) *Comparative Youth Justice*, London: Sage

There is also a specialist journal, *Youth Justice*, published by Sage which contains up-to-date articles on all aspects of youth crime and justice.

Websites

The Youth Justice Board contains quite a lot of research material (of variable quality) and is well worth checking: www.yjb.gov.uk

The crime prevention charity NACRO produces regular bulletins on youth crime, many of which can be found on their website: http://www.nacro.org.uk/

Chapter outline

Introduction   744
   Conflicts as property   744

Criminal justice and restorative justice   746

Defining restorative justice   747

The objectives of restorative justice   748
   Victim involvement   748
   Community involvement   749
   Offender reintegration   750

Types of restorative justice   751
   Court-based restitutive and reparative measures   751
   Victim–offender mediation (VOM)   752
   Family group conferencing   753
   Healing and sentencing circles   756
      Healing circles   756
      Sentencing circles   756
   Citizens' panels and community boards   757

Assessing restorativeness   758

The limits of restorative justice?   760
   Restorative justice and corporate crime   760
   Restorative justice and domestic violence   761

Assessing restorative justice   763

Questions for further discussion   767
Further reading   767
Websites   767

30

Restorative justice

Introduction

It is probably realistic to say that *restorative justice* 'has possibly been the most influential development in "crime control" in the past decade' (Crawford and Newburn, 2003: 38). Rather than traditional forums which rely on judges to sentence offenders and, where appropriate, punishment is imposed by the state, restorative justice seeks to place greater emphasis upon, and give a role to, the victim of crime, and the wider community. In addition, restorative justice also emphasises the importance of repair or reparation by the offender to the victim or, more broadly, to the community. As such, restorative justice harks back to earlier times when responding to crime was much more a community-based responsibility.

Indeed, much modern restorative justice has been inspired by indigenous practices originating in New Zealand, Australia and North America. In many cases such native practices were revitalised during modern struggles against colonialism. Johnstone (2002) gives the example of the revitalisation of Maori forms of justice and punishment. Initially, Maori practices were restricted and later they were largely 'silenced' by colonial settlers. By the 1980s, however, with rising rates of Maori offending and with a more general disenchantment with traditional justice systems, interest grew in indigenous practices. By the end of the decade family group conferencing, which drew on such approaches, had emerged.

In charting the rise of restorative justice, Dignan (2005) outlines three philosophical strands that may be distinguished. These he calls:

- *The civilisation thesis* – This set of arguments is associated with reform movements that sought to civilise the justice process, attempting to make it more humane and less preoccupied with punishment and the infliction of harm.

- *The communitarian thesis* – This focuses its attention on the fact that traditional criminal justice privileges the state and consequently disenfranchises the main parties to a conflict.

- *The moral discourse thesis* – This approach seeks to emphasise the importance of engaging in a moralising dialogue with the offender, rather than simply imposing sanctions against the offender.

One of the most influential early articles arguing for a radical shift in the way in which criminal conflicts are resolved, and in which elements of all three strands are visible, was published in the late 1970s by the Norwegian criminologist Nils Christie.

Conflicts as property

In much restorative justice literature an historical picture is drawn which suggests that restorative practices were fairly normal responses to crime and deviance until the early Middle Ages. Since that time, slowly, such practices have been suppressed and replaced progressively by a centralised state power that manages the system of punishment. In a famous essay Nils Christie argued that this long-term historical process resulted in conflicts in effect being *stolen* from those that are involved. Christie argues that conflicts between community members should be seen as 'something of value, a commodity not to be wasted' (1977: 1).

With an echo of Emile Durkheim, Christie argues that conflicts provide an opportunity to clarify norms and standards. But to take advantage of this

Conflicts as Property

Christie's article, now widely quoted and reproduced, was first published in the *British Journal of Criminology* in 1977. In typical style (as you will find if you read his work) Christie opens the piece provocatively by saying: 'Maybe we should not have any criminology ... Maybe the social consequences of criminology are more dubious than we like to think.' He goes on to argue that in his view criminology has played its own part in the long-term process by which conflicts have progressively been taken away from the parties involved and have been appropriated by others. In particular, he says, 'criminal conflicts have either become *other people's property* – primarily the property of lawyers – or it has been in other people's interests to *define conflicts away*'.

It is the victim of crime, Christie argues, who is the particular loser as a result of such arrangements. Not only have they suffered in some way – having been injured or having had property stolen or damaged – but often there is little or no compensation for their loss and, more importantly, they play little part in whatever proceedings follow.

Most importantly, he says, we are all the loser: 'This loss is first and foremost a loss in *opportunities for norm-clarification*'. By this he means that what has disappeared is a public process in which citizens participate in discussing right and wrong, to understand the conflict and to decide upon what should be done.

Nils Christie, Norwegian criminologist and author of 'Conflicts as Property' and *Crime Control as Industry*.

opportunity citizens, rather than lawyers and other experts such as treatment professionals, should decide what is relevant in a case and should be able to discuss issues of responsibility and blame. The absence of such opportunities – in which the offender might offer some form of explanation or account of the offence – increases the likelihood that the victim will end up feeling more frightened and more anxious. The victim, Christie argues, 'has a need for understanding, but is instead a non-person in a Kafka play' (a reference to the work of Franz Kafka in which the themes of alienation and overpowering bureaucracy are often present).

Involving the victim, by contrast, potentially brings all sorts of benefits. Their involvement means that their losses must be considered and therefore naturally leads to some form of discussion of restitution. Moreover, such involvement might not only reduce victim anxiety, but it might also have a positive impact on the offender. Under

current circumstances the offender doesn't have the opportunity of such personal confrontation. Crucially, the offender 'has lost the opportunity to receive a type of blame that it would be very difficult to neutralise'. This argument, as we will see later on, is resonant of one later advanced by John Braithwaite in his theory of 'reintegrative shaming' (Braithwaite, 1989).

Christie's conclusion, therefore, is that we should rid ourselves of the assumption, he says, that conflicts are pathological and therefore need to be solved as quickly as possibly or, indeed, *solved*. Rather, he suggests that living with conflicts may show that 'participation is more important than solutions' (1982: 93). As we will see, these themes recur regularly throughout the literature on the theory and practice of restorative justice. Before moving further, however, we need to step back and ask what is meant by *restorative justice*?

Criminal justice and restorative justice

Restorative justice is generally presented as an alternative to punitive and therapeutic approaches to crime. Though, as we will see, the term restorative justice is now used to cover a broad range of processes and practices, it is generally distinguished by its advocates from contemporary criminal justice practices. Put slightly differently, it is the case that restorative justice is defined both negatively (what it is not or what it is to be compared with) and positively (how it is to be identified and understood). Many descriptions of what restorative justice is not are somewhat confusing – it is not always clear what restorative justice is being contrasted with.

In early work, Zehr (1990: 81) compared restorative justice with what he then characterised as 'retributive justice' but has subsequently simply come to call contemporary criminal justice. He suggests that this latter approach to justice has six main characteristics:

1 crime is essentially *lawbreaking;*

2 when a law is broken, justice involves establishing *guilt;*

3 so that just deserts can be meted out;

4 by inflicting *pain;*

5 through a *conflict* in which *rules* and intentions are placed above outcomes;

6 ... the state, not the individual, is defined as the victim.

Paradigms of justice – old and new (Zehr, 1985)

Old paradigm	New paradigm – Restorative justice
1 Crime defined as violation of the state	1 Crime defined as violation of one person by another
2 Focus on establishing blame, on guilt, on past (did he/she do it?)	2 Focus on problem-solving, on liabilities and obligations, on future (what should be done?)
3 Adversarial relationships and process normative	3 Dialogue and negotiation normative
4 Imposition of pain to punish and deter/prevent	4 Restitution as a means of restoring both parties; reconciliation/restoration as goal
5 Justice defined by intent and by process: right rules	5 Justice defined as right relationships: judged by outcome
6 Interpersonal, conflictual nature crime obscured, repressed: conflict seen as individual *vs.* state	6 Crime recognised as interpersonal conflict: value of conflict recognised
7 One social injury replaced by another	7 Focus on repair of social injury
8 Community on sideline, represented abstractly by the state	8 Community as facilitator in restorative process
9 Encouragement of competitive, individualistic values	9 Encouragement of mutuality
10 Action from state to offender: – victim ignored – offender passive	10 Victim's and offender's roles recognised in both problem and solution: – victim rights/needs recognised – offender encouraged to take responsibility
11 Offender accountability defined as taking punishment	11 Offender accountability defined as understanding impact of action and helping decide how to make things right
12 Offence defined in purely legal terms, devoid of moral, social, economic dimensions	12 Offence understood in whole – moral, social, economic, political
13 'Debt' owed to state and society in the abstract	13 Debt/liability to victim recognised
14 Response focused on offender's past behaviour	14 Response focused on harmful consequences of offender's behaviour
15 Stigma of crime un-removable	15 Stigma of crime removable through restorative action
16 No encouragement for repentance and forgiveness	16 Possibilities for repentance and forgiveness
17 Dependence on proxy professionals	17 Direct involvement by participants

From this perspective the promotion of restorative justice is, in part, built upon a critique of criminal justice. This critique includes (Crawford and Newburn, 2003: 21):

- Its ineffectiveness and failure to deliver on its promise of offender reform and crime prevention.
- Its marginal role in responding to crime – only a small minority of cases are formally processed in the criminal justice system (see Chapters 3 and 26).
- Its 'theft' of conflict from the main parties to a dispute, particularly the victim.
- Its failure to hold offenders meaningfully to account.
- Its over-reliance on punishment.
- Its remoteness from the crime and harm that formed the basis of the case.
- Its reliance on formal social control rather than informal, community-based controls.
- Its insensitivity to cultural and ethnic diversity.
- Its inefficiency.
- Its social and financial cost.

Defining restorative justice

The earlier discussion outlines in some detail what restorative justice sets itself against; it illustrates what restorative justice *is not*. But what is it? Is it, as some that promote it argue, a new paradigm of criminal justice – a new way of understanding and doing *justice* – or is it a set of practices that can be utilised outside or within criminal justice, but are not a replacement for formal justice systems as we currently understand them? Despite its growing popularity there are, as Johnstone (2002) notes, a number of misconceptions about restorative justice:

- Some commentators appear to view it as 'rehabilitation repackaged'.
- It is sometimes seen as part of the victims' rights movement (see Chapter 17).
- There is often great emphasis placed on restorative justice *techniques* at the expense of restorative justice *values*.

As we will see, there is huge variety in restorative justice practice and, therefore, seeking an agreed-upon definition is highly problematic. The most commonly repeated definition is that offered by Tony Marshall (1996: 37):

> Restorative justice is a process whereby parties with a stake in a particular offence come together to resolve collectively how to deal with the aftermath of the offence and its implications for the future.

Three core elements of restorative justice are identified in the definition: the idea of parties with a stake in the offence; the importance of participation, deliberation and communication in seeking resolution; the highlighting of potential outcomes or forms of resolution such as the repair of harm. Dignan (2005), however, suggests that the definition is of relatively little value as:

- it restricts the scope of restorative justice to criminal justice and, consequently, overlooks less formal procedures and contexts;
- it characterises restorative justice as a particular type of *process* which, though flexible, fails to focus on *outcomes* and in so doing raises the possibility that undue attention will be paid to questions of equity and fairness;
- by failing to consider outcomes it diverts attention away from those cases where restorative justice processes may be inappropriate, but where its values and aims may still apply;
- it overlooks potential conflict as to who the 'stakeholders' in offence might be;
- it not only fails to specify who the crucial stakeholders are but it offers no account of the form their participation might take; and
- it has nothing to say about the aim of the process. Is it, asks Dignan (2005: 5) 'an end in itself, irrespective of any outcome … or is it a means to some other end'?

Dignan goes on to argue that, at heart, restorative justice has generally been applied to a range of practices that share three principal features. These are, first, that that they have the goal of endeavouring to put right the harms caused by the offence itself. Second, that such processes seek to balance the accountability of the offender with the needs of those harmed by the offence. Finally, the nature of the decision-making process involved encourages involvement by the main participants in determining responses to the offence. A variant of this can be found in the UK government's more recent attempt to summarise its approach to restorative justice (Home Office, 1997) in the so-called '3-Rs':

- *Restoration* – Offenders apologising to their victims and making amends for the harm done.
- *Reintegration* – Offenders paying their debt to society and then rejoining the law-abiding community.
- *Responsibility* – Offenders, and their parents, facing the consequences of their offending and taking responsibility for the cessation of such behaviour.

The objectives of restorative justice

According to Dignan (2005), three broad policy strands can be identified in the precursors to restorative justice. These he refers to as *abolitionism, separatism,* and *reformism.* Abolitionism is a radical stance in which conventional justice is subjected to a thorough critique and its dismantlement is urged. Advocates aligning themselves with abolitionism view restorative justice as an alternative system or paradigm. Separatists agree that restorative justice and criminal justice are incompatible, but accept that it is simply not realistic to think that the latter will be abolished, and argue therefore that the two should be seen as alternatives to each other, and that they should be kept separate. Finally, reformists urge no such separation and argue that criminal jus-

tice can be modified in order to bring it closer to the principles and values of restorative justice.

According to John Braithwaite (1996: 13) restorative justice 'means *restoring victims,* a more victim-centred criminal justice system, as well as *restoring offenders* and *restoring community'* (*emphasis added*). Tony Marshall (1998) illustrates these relationships between the three elements in Figure 30.1.

Later in the chapter we will look at restorative justice in practice. Before doing so, however, we must look in slightly greater detail at these three major elements of restorative justice: victim involvement and restoration; community involvement and restoration; and the reintegration of offenders.

Victim involvement

Much of what restorative justice is concerned with is meeting the *needs* of victims. But what are they? At the heart of much of this approach lies the view that crime is experienced very personally by victims of crime. They are experienced as attacks on the person:

> Crime is in essence a violation: a violation of the self, a desecration of who we are, of what we believe, of our private space. Crime is devastating because it upsets two fundamental assumptions on which we base our lives: our belief that the world is an orderly, meaningful place, and our belief in personal autonomy. Both assumptions are essential for wholeness. (Zehr, 1990: 24, quoted in Johnstone, 2002: 65)

The needs that arise from such an experience include compensation or reparation, to have questions answered, to have their experiences and emotions heard and understood and to be empowered. According to Braithwaite (1996: 13), the process of 'restoring victims' may cover:

- restoring property loss;
- restoring injury;
- restoring a sense of security;
- restoring dignity;
- restoring a sense of empowerment;
- restoring deliberative democracy;
- restoring harmony based on a feeling that justice has been done;
- restoring social support. (in Johnstone, 2003: 86)

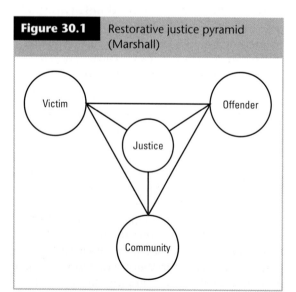

Figure 30.1 Restorative justice pyramid (Marshall)

These, it is argued, cannot easily be met by traditional criminal justice approaches. In particular, restorative justice advocates argue that retributive forms of justice are overly preoccupied with affixing blame and establishing guilt, rather than exploring how harms can be made good and future problems avoided. Much writing on restorative justice focuses on the negative consequences of stigmatisation (Braithwaite, 1989).

Akin to labelling theory, it is argued that the process of defining someone as an offender in retributive justice systems allows little room for that person to shed the label. The level of stigmatisation involved in retributive justice, therefore, encourages people to avoid admitting guilt – the personal cost is simply too great. Linked with this is the argument that such systems tend to focus their entire attention on the offender as a free-floating rational actor, rather than someone bound up in a complex web of relationships and influences. Restorative justice, by contrast, can enable those around the offender to share elements of responsibility – in particular for change. In this respect it proposes a more collective conception of *responsibility*. Finally, rather than being preoccupied with the infliction of pain through punishment as happens in retributive justice, restorative techniques are much more concerned with reform and reintegration.

Community involvement

There are a number of reasons why community involvement is considered important to restorative justice. On the one hand it is felt that the community can bring significant influence to bear on the offender, both in terms of reparation and also in rehabilitation. On the other hand it is also argued to be important as a means of empowering communities and increasing their capacity for informal social control. Indeed, as we will see later in the chapter, there are strong links between much of the thinking underpinning restorative justice and some recent developments in what is increasingly referred to as *community justice* initiatives. Of course, such discussions must inevitably bring forth the question of what is meant by *community* in this regard (observing that the meaning of the term is problematic has become something of a criminological cliché). Thus, Tony Marshall (1998: 30) in his overview of restorative justice observes:

> As with any initiative that invokes 'community' it is necessary to think about what this may actually

involve. Neighbourhoods differ in their capacities to support potential offenders in their midst. Programmes that seek to tap into community support may therefore be tapping into something that hardly exists. In the more broken communities, resources and education may be needed to be committed for restorative justice programmes to work. Otherwise there is the danger that such programmes will increase the burden of expectation and involvement of local people and groups to a level they cannot sustain. Initiatives like conferencing, therefore, may need to be introduced gradually and in parallel with the development of other community programmes.

Dignan (2005) identifies a further seven questions in connection with ideas of community that are raised, but not necessarily addressed, in the restorative justice literature:

1 Assuming it can be defined satisfactorily, how is it to be operationalised; that is, who from a *community* should participate in restorative justice?

2 In what capacity are communities, or community representatives, to participate?

3 If a community participates as a victim, what forms of redress might be appropriate?

4 Should the role accorded the community be affected by the capacity in which it participates in the process?

5 When the wishes of the victim and community are different, how should this be resolved?

6 When designing restorative justice initiatives, what assumptions are made about the nature of community – and are these accurate?

7 What safeguards are required to ensure that the interests of victims and offenders are not affected by misconceptions about the nature of the community?

For Braithwaite (1996) there are three levels at which it is possible to conceptualise the process of 'restoring community' through restorative justice practices:

- At the *micro* level, restorative justice involves people close to both victim and offender and, in this way, is a bottom-up method of reinforcing community ties and the purpose of community.

- At the *meso* level, restorative justice helps to foster a sense of community within institutions such as schools, churches, professions, neighbourhoods, and so on. Alternative methods of resolving disputes within such institutions can strengthen social bonds, the institution itself and therefore a broader sense of community.

● Finally, at the *macro* level it helps to focus attention upon the importance of designing institutions of deliberative democracy (ideas in political theory that stress the importance of decision-making through participation and debate rather than simply voting) that enable crucial social issues concerning local injustices to be communicated nationally. As he argues, 'to the extent that restorative justice deliberation does lead ordinary citizens into serious democratic discussion about racism, unemployment, masculinist cultures in local schools and police accountability, it is not an unimportant element of a deliberatively rich democracy' (in Johnstone 2003: 88).

Offender reintegration

The key to crime control is cultural commitments to shaming in ways that I call reintegrative. Societies with low crime rates are those that shame potently and judiciously; individuals who resort to crime are those insulated from shame over their wrongdoing. (Braithwaite, 1989: 1)

Public shaming, of course, was once a staple of punishment systems (Thompson, 1994). The pillory, the stocks, even the infamous 'scarlet letter' which adulterers were once forced to wear, are all testimony to the fact that punishment was once organised around public rituals of shaming. Over the past two centuries such ceremonies have gradually disappeared as punishment has become an increasingly private, and also generally less brutal, affair.

As we saw in Chapter 2, prior to the modern era 'shaming' was a central element in punishment. As state punishment became more formalised, and in Foucault's terms diffused, it lost much of its shaming element. In recent times shaming has made something of a comeback with so-called 'naming and shaming' initiatives in which offenders are publicly identified and their offences advertised. Some of the more extreme examples – usually from America – have involved offenders being required to wear placards (Whitman, 1998) with messages on them such as 'I STOLE FROM THIS STORE', or in the case of sex offenders to have notices posted outside their houses. Less extreme, but still overt, are the sex offender registration and notification schemes that have emerged over the past decade in

Breanna Klewitz, 23, of Albany, Georgia in the USA. She had been sentenced to walk a city centre pavement with this sandwich board as a condition of her probation for burglary.

the USA. In such schemes, sex offenders are required to register their personal details, including their home addresses, and these details are then published on a website.

Critical theories, including labelling theory, have pointed to the negative consequences of criminal justice stigmatisation. Accordingly, for many criminologists the idea of shaming has often been viewed as characteristic of outmoded and inappropriately punitive systems of crime control, though the arguments are complex (see Kahan, 2006). However, according to one influential school of thought, there is a role for shaming in contemporary criminal justice.

In *Crime, Shame and Reintegration,* John Braithwaite (1989) argues that systems of punishment that emulate family functioning will be more effective in managing and controlling bad behaviour than straightforwardly punitive systems. More particularly, he argues that punishment is only effective when it is delivered in circumstances where authorities are perceived to be legitimate, respected and respectful, and where offenders have some form of stake in society and are concerned about how they are viewed by others. Braithwaite argues that formal systems of justice tend to involve two types of shaming:

> The crucial distinction is between shaming that is reintegrative and shaming that is disintegrative (stigmatisation). Reintegrative shaming means the expressions of community disapproval ... are followed by gestures of reacceptance into the community of law-abiding citizens ... Disintegrative shaming (stigmatisation), in contrast, divides the community by creating a class of outcasts. (Braithwaite, 1989: 55)

- *Disintegrative shaming* – This form of shaming – which generally comes from strangers – involves the isolation or humiliation of the offender. The likelihood is that the offender's response will be defiant rather than compliant.

- *Reintegrative shaming* – This is where the disapproval conveyed through shaming – usually from intimates – is accompanied by forgiveness (as happens when families function effectively). This increases the likelihood that the offender will respond positively; feelings of guilt and embarrassment deterring future offending.

In a similar vein, Martha Nussbaum (2004) has distinguished between 'constructive' and 'stigmatising' shaming. Many of the modern 'naming and shaming' practices, such as those mentioned earlier aimed at sex offenders, and those associated with publicising Anti-Social Behaviour Orders (see Chapter 29), come closer to Braithwaite's model of 'disintegrative shaming' in which humiliation and stigmatisation are central.

By contrast, it is *reintegrative shaming* that he suggests is central to restorative justice practices. Elements of social control theory can be found in this approach. Braithwaite's theory suggests that those who are embedded in interpersonal relationships – that is they depend on others and others depend on them – will care more about what people think of them and are therefore more susceptible to shame (see Chapter 11).

Braithwaite's theory of reintegrative shaming is by no means accepted uncritically by proponents of restorative justice. For example, Marshall argues that 'Braithwaite's theory is only one of crime control and prevention, and does not encompass the victim-interests and justice issues that are primary components of restorative justice as a whole'. Nevertheless, what the majority of restorative justice initiatives share is an assumption that offender reintegration is an overriding aim and that this is unlikely to be achieved through mechanisms which degrade and which weaken offenders' links with the local community.

> **Review questions**
>
> 1 What are the main differences between mainstream criminal justice and restorative justice?
>
> 2 What did Christie mean when he said conflicts had been stolen?
>
> 3 What are generally held to be the main objectives of restorative justice?
>
> 4 How do disintegrative and reintegrative shaming differ?

Types of restorative justice

Crawford and Newburn (2003) argue that there are essentially four forms of restorative justice practice that we may identify:

- victim–offender mediation;
- conferencing;
- sentencing circles;
- citizens' panels and community boards.

To this list, Dignan (2005) adds a fifth: court-based restitutive and reparative measures. A brief examination of each of these main forms of restorative justice will serve to illustrate the wide variety of programmes that find themselves located under this rubric.

Court-based restitutive and reparative measures

Such measures include a variety of measures from community service to court-based compensation and reparation schemes. In Chapter 17 we briefly considered the history of court-ordered compensation and the introduction and reform of the state-based criminal injuries compensation scheme. In doing so we saw some of their strengths (acknowledging victimization in circumstances where it had previously been ignored) and weaknesses (a limited conception of victimization and a limited 'reach' in terms of the proportion of victims helped by such schemes). Dignan also suggests that community service should be considered under this heading too, for it potentially involves some form of reparation to the benefit of the community – though there is little guarantee of much direct connection between the 'community' that benefits from such activity and the one affected by the original offence.

In addition to these two sets of initiatives, the last decade has seen a number of reforms that have sought to introduce measures within the formal court system that are influenced by restorative justice practices and values. The initial changes brought about as part of the 1998 Crime and Disorder Act included *reparation orders*, a low-level sentence largely replacing the conditional discharge and intended to include some form of community-based reparation, reform of the cautioning system to allow for greater element of reparation and an *action plan order*, which involved a short sentence of community-based reparative activity.

A more significant set of changes were introduced as part of the Youth Justice and Criminal Justice Act 1999. This included a new mandatory sentence for young offenders appearing in court for the first time and pleading guilty: the *referral order*. This involved a panel meeting and thus is discussed below in relation to conferencing initiatives which it more closely resembles. However, given that it is a court-ordered disposal and contains a requirement to consider making reparation, it also shares characteristics with other court-ordered reparative initiatives.

Victim–offender mediation (VOM)

The first recognised victim-offender mediation programme was established in Canada in Kitchener, Ontario. It was established in the 1970s by the Mennonites – a Christian sect of Anabaptists (rebaptisers) – and from there it spread to the USA, the UK and beyond. In fact the Kitchener programme was called a Victim–Offender Reconciliation Project (VORP) – reconciliation between victim and offender being a central goal.

Central to the spread of such initiatives has been the work of a North American Mennonite, Howard Zehr, and VOM programmes are said to account for over half of all restorative programmes in the USA.

This approach brings together the offender with their victim in a meeting facilitated by a mediator. The aim of the meeting is that victim and offender should discuss the offence and the harm that was caused. The objective is that such meetings be face-to-face but, on occasion, the mediator acts as an intermediary between the two parties – a kind of shuttle diplomat. Dignan (2005: 112) identifies five main objectives of VOM programmes:

1 To support the healing process for victims by providing a voluntary opportunity to meet and speak with the offender and participate in discussions about the way the offence should be resolved.

2 To encourage offenders to take direct responsibility for their actions by requiring

Howard Zehr

Howard Zehr is a pioneer of restorative justice and his book, *Changing Lenses: A New Focus for Crime and Justice*, is an important influence in the restorative justice movement.

First published in 1990, *Changing Lenses* set out many of the principles of the restorative justice movement. Zehr believed it was essential to enter into 'the actual experience of crime and justice as deeply as we can', and that this provided an essential basis for 'understanding what we do, why we do it, and – hopefully – what we might do differently'.

Zehr was director of the Mennonite Central Committee US Office on Crime and Justice and was founder and Director of the first US Victim–Offender Reconciliation Program. He is currently Professor of Sociology and Restorative Justice in Eastern Mennonite University's graduate Conflict Transformation Program.

them to hear about the impact of their offence on the victim, and by providing an opportunity for them to participate in discussions about the way the offence should be resolved.

3 To facilitate and encourage a process that is empowering and emotionally satisfying for both parties.

4 To 'redress the balance' by switching the emphasis from the 'public interest' to the interpersonal interests of those most directly affected by an offence.

5 Where desired, to enable the parties to agree on an outcome that addresses the harm caused by an offence in an appropriate and mutually acceptable manner.

There have been a number of examples of VOM in the UK beginning with a project run by Exeter Youth Support team in 1979 in which such meetings were attempted as an addition to cautioning a young offender, but where a caution was considered an insufficient response. Such initiatives have developed in a somewhat *ad hoc* fashion and the next development was a series of projects that were established in 1985 by the Home Office research unit; these schemes, in Coventry, Wolverhampton, Leeds and Cumbria, worked at various levels and stages of the criminal justice process – the Leeds scheme, for example, took cases from the Crown Court. Though established on a wave of enthusiasm, the projects suffered from declining political support within the Home Office and any hopes of ongoing funding and support were fairly quickly dashed. Although a number of VOM projects have continued to operate, some have re-badged themselves as restorative justice initiatives and, in the main, this approach 'has been eclipsed by the growth of conferencing as an alternative approach to dispute processing' (Crawford and Newburn, 2003: 27).

Family group conferencing

Possibly the most significant developments in the field in recent times, Family Group Conferences (FGCs) first emerged formally in New Zealand as a result of the Children, Young Persons and their Families Act 1989. Since that time this approach has been at the forefront of the theory and practice of restorative justice – even though they were not originally framed in this way in New Zealand. Dignan (2005) identifies three main factors in the rise of conferencing in New Zealand:

- The perceived limitations of the formal criminal justice system's dealings with both the Maori population and also Pacific Island Polynesians.

- A 'welfare-based' commitment to empowering both families and young people.

- The growing influence of the victims movement, which had been particularly influential in reforms of the youth justice system.

Conferencing varies considerably from jurisdiction to jurisdiction in terms of:

- the forms of referral (caution, diversion from court, pre-sentence or part of sentence);

- the seriousness of the offences concerned;

- the form and nature of facilitation;

- the power given to key stakeholders, such as victims, over the outcome; and

- whether the programme is statutory or non-statutory.

The 1989 Young Persons and their Families Act introduced a statutory framework for the referral of offenders aged 14–17 to a pre-trial conference. The conference is convened and facilitated by a co-ordinator whose role it is to act as mediator and to deal with any conflict involving the participants (victim, offenders, family, supporters, police and other professionals). The meetings are generally informal and flexible and their aim is to encourage acceptance of responsibility and the making of amends. Planning the latter may involve the offender and family taking some time out of the conference to consider how reparation might be made. What is perhaps most interesting about the New Zealand model of conferencing is that, by and large, it is not used for minor offences or as part of, or an alternative to, cautioning, but is generally reserved for use in medium and the more serious offences (excluding murder and manslaughter).

In all but two states, conferencing has some statutory basis in Australia and in three states (New South Wales, South Australia and Western Australia) a high proportion of young offenders are subject to conferences. The states vary markedly in the type of conferencing practised. Perhaps the best known of Australian conferencing initiatives is that developed at Wagga Wagga from 1991 onwards. It has a number of key characteristics which distinguish it from the New Zealand model:

- Cases are diverted by the police as a form of 'effective cautioning' (meaning that they are

An example of a family group conferencing session

A family conferencing group convened in a local school to consider a case in which a student had injured a teacher and broken the teacher's glasses in an altercation. Group members included the offender, his mother and grandfather, the victim, the police officer who made the arrest, and about ten other interested parties (including two of the offender's teachers and two friends of the victim).

The conferencing process began with comments by the offender, his mother and grandfather, the victim and the arresting officer. Each spoke about the offence and its impact. The youth justice co-ordinator next asked for input from the other group members and then asked all participants what they thought the offender should do to pay back the victim and the community for the damage caused by his crime.

In the remaining 30 minutes of the hour-long conference, the group suggested that the offender should make restitution to the victim for his medical expenses and the cost of new glasses and that the offender should also perform community service work on the school grounds.

Source: Bazemore and Umbreit (2001)

generally less serious than those forming the basis of conferencing in New Zealand).

- They are police-led (facilitators are generally police officers).
- Conferences are quite formalised, often following a 'scripted' format.
- This script is heavily influenced by Braithwaite's theory of 'reintegrative shaming' (see below).
- The victim is only one of many parties to the process, whereas the victim and offender are central to the decision-making in family group conferencing.
- This model places less emphasis on pre-conference preparation of the main parties.
- Family group conferences often include an extra phase referred to as the 'action planning stage'.

This model has also been used, and evaluated, in Canberra. The RISE program (Reintegrative Shaming Experiment) as it is known found that conferences increase offenders' respect for the law and have a higher degree of procedural fairness than formal court processes. The researchers also found relatively high levels of victim satisfaction. The Wagga Wagga model has also had influence beyond Australia. Experiments with *restorative cautioning,* for example, in Thames Valley in England were heavily influenced by this form of Australian conferencing. For almost ten years now, Thames Valley Police have used conferencing as an alternative to the normal cautioning procedure. Restorative cautioning involves a structured discussion about the offence, wherever possible with the victim present. Where the victim is absent arrangements are generally made for their views to be conveyed at the meeting. The aims of the conference are:

- to get offenders to recognise the consequences of their behaviour;
- to have them think what in their lives/lifestyle contributes to such behaviour;
- to get them to commit to changing their behaviour;
- to offer an apology to the victim and to agree to reparation;
- to offer an opportunity to victims to meet the offender and to talk about their experiences;
- to create the possibility that some form of forgiveness may be (eventually) extended to the offender.

In evaluating the impact of the approach Young and Goold (1999: 136) caution against the unrealistic expectations that are often attached to restorative justice initiatives:

> We believe that it would be wise, however, to place less stress in future on the possible impact of restorative cautioning on reducing re-offending. In our view, the cautioning session should be regarded primarily as an opportunity to allow all those affected by an offence to express their own sense of harm and need for repair in a safe environment, and also as a more accountable, open and discursive form of criminal justice than old-style cautioning.

One of the largest experiments with restorative justice-based processes in British criminal justice is the introduction of referral orders and youth offender panels. This initiative contains a variety of restorative justice influences, including community boards, victim–offender mediation and conferencing. Introduced by the Youth Justice and Criminal

Evidence Act 1999, the referral order is available in the youth court and may be made for a minimum of three and a maximum of 12 months depending on the seriousness of the crime (as determined by the court). The order is mandatory for ten to 17 year-olds pleading guilty to an imprisonable offence and convicted for the first time by the courts, unless the crime is serious enough to warrant custody, or the court orders an absolute discharge.

The disposal involves referring the young offender to a youth offender panel (YOP). The intention is that the panel provide a forum away from the formality of the court. The order constitutes the entire sentence for the offence (though it can be combined with certain ancillary orders, including those for costs) and, as such, substitutes for action plan orders, reparation orders and super-

vision orders. Panels comprise one YOT member and at least two community panel members, one of whom leads the panel.

Parents of all offenders aged under 16 are expected to attend all panel meetings. The offender can also nominate an adult to support them, but it is not intended that legal representatives participate. To encourage the restorative nature of the process a variety of other people, particularly victims, may be encouraged voluntarily to attend given panel meetings. The aim of the initial panel meeting is to devise a 'contract' and, where the victim chooses to attend, for them to meet and talk about the offence with the offender. The contract should always include reparation to the victim or wider community and a programme of activity designed primarily to prevent further offending.

The general atmosphere of youth offender panels

A total of 92 panels were observed during the course of the research. There were no threats of violence during any of the panel meetings. In general, initial panels were largely successful at achieving a potentially 'restorative atmosphere'. All panel members were predominantly considered to be non-judgemental by observers. As would be expected of someone in their role, panel chairs emerged as the most directive, though as volunteers chairing a meeting containing professional 'experts' this can perhaps be taken as an indication of the success of the youth offender panel model. What, though, of the impact of panels? The observation process during the research included estimates of changes of atmosphere in the panels.

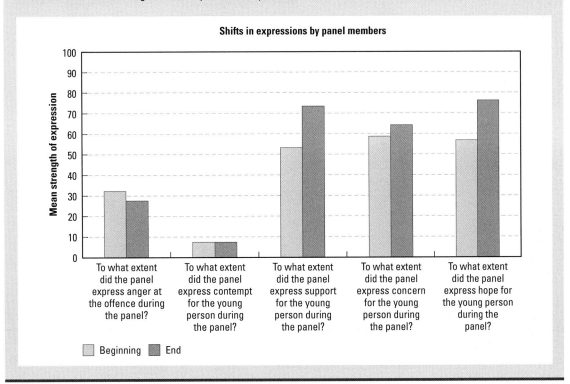

Shifts in expressions by panel members

Source: Crawford and Newburn (2003: 128)

Healing and sentencing circles

Circles originate in the practices of First Nation people in Canada and their growth has been stimulated by the re-emergence of tribal sovereignty on North American reservations. They are like conferences in that they seek to involve participants beyond the victim and offender. In particular, they tend to share the aim of involving families and community members in the process of finding solutions. The circle has a facilitator ('the keeper of the circle') and often use a 'talking piece' (a feather or other symbol) which is passed between members of the circle allowing them to speak when in possession of it. Circles often involve more than one meeting and are centrally about community enhancement and reinforcement. They have two main forms: *healing circles* and *sentencing circles*.

Healing circles

Healing circles have tended to focus on particular problems with indigenous communities – such as sexual assault, domestic violence and incest. The circle seeks to focus on the cause of the problem and address not only the harm caused but, wherever possible, its social and cultural basis as well. Offenders are encouraged to take responsibility and to seek support, and communities are encouraged to share responsibility in attempting to ensure that similar problems do not recur.

Sentencing circles

By contrast, sentencing circles are part of the formal justice system and replace other forms of sentencing. They may result in a conviction and criminal record and, although they have no statutory basis, they rely on judicial discretion. Although they work in partnership with the criminal justice system, sentencing circles use community direction as a basis for reaching consensus about the sentencing plans which are developed for responding to the problem at hand. They are often lengthy processes, taking many hours and sometimes spread over more than one day. Though victims may be involved they are not essential as the circle is concerned with sentencing: the focus is upon the offender. The judge imposes the agreed sentence, but is only one party in the determination of that sentence.

A sentencing circle. Part of the formal criminal justice system, sentencing is determined by a judge in discussion with others, including on occasion the victim.

An example of a circle sentencing session

The victim was a middle-aged man whose parked car had been badly damaged when the offender, a 16 year-old, crashed into it while joyriding in another vehicle. The offender had also damaged a police vehicle.

In the circle, the victim talked about the emotional shock of seeing what had happened to his car and his costs to repair it (he was uninsured). Then, an elder leader of the First Nations community where the circle sentencing session was being held (and an uncle of the offender) expressed his disappointment and anger with the boy. The elder observed that this incident, along with several prior offences by the boy, had brought shame to his family. The elder also noted that in the old days, the boy would have been required to pay the victim's family substantial compensation as a result of such behaviour. After the elder finished, a feather (the 'talking piece') was passed to the next person in the circle, a young man who spoke about the contributions the offender had made to the community, the kindness

he had shown towards elders, and his willingness to help others with home repairs.

Having heard all this, the judge asked the Crown Council (Canadian prosecutor) and the public defender, who were also sitting in the circle, to make statements and then asked if anyone else in the circle wanted to speak. The Royal Canadian Mounted Police officer, whose vehicle had also been damaged, then took the feather and spoke on the offender's behalf. The officer proposed to the judge that in lieu of statutorily required jail time for the offence, the offender be allowed to meet him on a regular basis for counselling and community service. After asking the victim and the prosecutor if either had any objections, the judge accepted this proposal. The judge also ordered restitution to the victim and asked the young adult who had spoken on the offender's behalf to serve as a mentor for the offender.

After a prayer in which the entire group held hands, the circle disbanded and everyone retreated to the kitchen area of the community centre for refreshments.

Source: Bazemore and Umbreit (2001)

In summary, sentencing and healing circles may involve a number of interrelated processes, including (Dignan, 2005: 125):

1 A circle to consider an application by an offender to invoke the circle process.

2 A healing circle specifically for the victim.

3 A healing circle specifically for the offender.

4 A sentencing circle to formulate a consensus as to what happened, to identify the harm caused by an offence and to devise an appropriate sentencing plan.

5 One or more follow-up circles to monitor the agreement and support the offender's compliance.

Citizens' panels and community boards

There are a number of examples of such forums including community peace committees that have operated in South Africa, reparative boards in the American state of Vermont and community boards in San Francisco. The South African peace committees have operated in Zwelethemba near Cape Town since 1997. Their two main characteristics are first that they are problem-solving – with an emphasis on peace-making and building – and, second, that they seek to maintain such peace-making strategies over time.

Committees are usually convened at the request of a victim and voluntary members act as facilitators

An example of a community reparative board session

The reparative board convened to consider the case of a 17 year-old who had been caught driving with an open can of beer in his father's pickup truck. The youth had been sentenced by a judge to reparative probation, and it was the board's responsibility to decide what form the probation should take. For about 30 minutes, the citizen members of the board asked the youth several simple, straightforward questions. The board members then went to another room to deliberate on an appropriate sanction for the youth. The youth awaited the board's decision

nervously, because he did not know whether to expect something tougher or much easier than regular probation.

When the board returned, the chairperson explained the four conditions of the offender's probation contract: (1) begin work to pay off his traffic tickets, (2) complete a state police defensive driving course, (3) undergo an alcohol assessment, and (4) write a three-page paper on how alcohol had negatively affected his life. The youth signed the contract, and the chairperson adjourned the meeting.

Source: http://www.ncjrs.gov/html/ojjdp/2001_2_1/page2.html – accessed 14.2.07

– albeit without any particular authority. Vermont's community boards, similarly, involve local people in problem-solving. Their focus is on enhancing social control at the local level and cases are referred to them by judges after the conviction of an offender – usually for offences that would otherwise have resulted in probation or a short custodial sentence. Boards negotiate a contract with the offender which is subsequently ratified by the court. Board members have four main aims:

- Engage the offender in ways that will help him or her better understand the harmful consequences of the offence on the victim and wider community.

- Identify ways that the offender can repair the harm to victims.

- Engage the offender in making amends to the community.

- Work with the offender to find a strategy to reduce the likelihood of re-offending (quoted in Crawford and Newburn, 2003).

Research on the boards has shown mixed results. On the one hand fairly sizeable proportions of offenders appear to complete the terms of their probation yet, on the other hand, there appears to be considerable variation between boards in terms of both the process and outcomes, with one set of evaluators concluding that 'community volunteers involved in the boards often appear amateurish, undiplomatic, and less knowledgeable about restorative principles than trained mediators' (Karp and Walther, 2001: 215).

A similar approach has been used in 'Circles of Support and Accountability' which, having been operating in Canada for a decade or more, have recently been established in various parts of the UK. Such circles, which consist of about six people from the local community, work with convicted sex offenders on release from prison. These circles work closely with the police and other agencies involved in multi-agency public protection activity (Quaker Peace and Social Witness, 2005) and are designed to be both a support and a safety mechanism, befriending the offender whilst holding him accountable for his actions.

Assessing restorativeness

In the previous two sections we looked at the general objectives of restorative justice and then examined the broad array of initiatives that can be found under the general heading of *restorative jus-*

tice. A number of questions arise. First, what is it that unites these programmes over and above a critique of retributive justice systems? In this regard, Johnstone (2002) identifies seven potentially distinctive features of restorative processes:

- The role of the third party in disputes (i.e. the mediator or facilitator) is simply as the facilitator of any resolution, rather than someone exercising the power to impose a resolution. The other parties/stakeholders (the victim and offender) are the primary decision-makers in the process.

- 'Sentencing' decisions are not made according to legal rules, but rather are governed by what the parties to the decision consider to be reasonable and appropriate.

- The main stakeholders represent themselves rather than having legal representatives to speak for them.

- Restorative justice processes take place in informal settings rather than courthouses or similar.

- Similarly, restorative justice is largely informal in its proceedings as well as its surroundings.

- There is an absence of technical and legal language in restorative justice.

- Whereas conventional criminal justice seeks to keep offender and victim apart and to curb the expression of emotions, restorative justice encourages direct communication between victim and offender and is often characterised by emotional communication.

More particularly, the second question that arises is what does *restorativeness* mean? What is this attribute that such programmes are believed, or hoped, or argued, to share? Van Ness and Strong (2006) outline four core elements of restorative justice that they argue can be empirically investigated:

- *Encounter* – Entailing some form of meeting or meetings, usually face-to-face between the main parties. This meeting will usually allow the parties to tell their own story and it is expected that some understanding of each other's position will develop.

- *Reparation* – A process in which the offender or responsible party makes amends, directly or otherwise, for any harm caused.

- *Reintegration* – The re-entry of each party, but particularly the offender/responsible party, into the community as contributing full members. Such reintegration requires action not just by

Figure 30.2   McCold's restorative practices typology

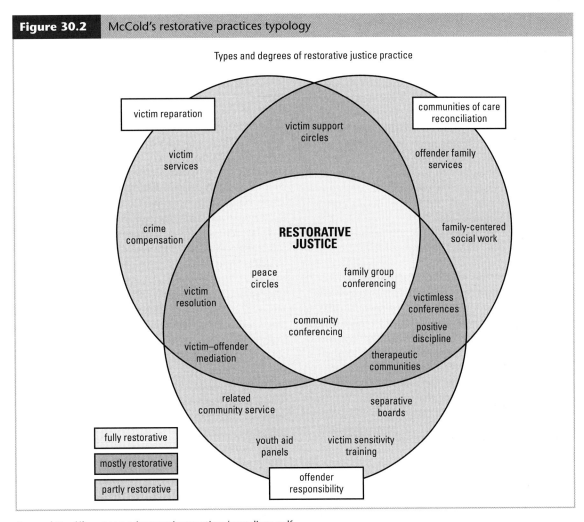

Types and degrees of restorative justice practice

Source: http://fp.enter.net/restorativepractices/paradigm.pdf

the offender and/or victim, but also by the community.

● *Participation* –The opportunity for full and direct involvement of all parties in the three other aspects: encounter, reparation and reintegration.

According to such a breakdown, initiatives may be *more or less restorative* depending upon how they are organised. The third question that arises, therefore, is how restorative are the different programmes outlined earlier and how do we assess this?

In this vein, McCold classified a variety of restorative justice approaches according to the degree of involvement of the three main stakeholders: the offender; the victim; and the community (of care) (see Figure 30.2). In his view it is only when all three are fully and actively involved that an initiative can be considered 'fully restorative'. Where one of the

three stakeholders is less involved/missing the initiative can only be said to be 'mostly restorative' and where only one stakeholder is fully involved such an initiative would be considered at best to be 'partly restorative'.

Review questions

1   What are the five main types of restorative justice programme?

2   What are the main differences between victim–offender mediation and conferencing?

3   What are the main differences between healing and sentencing circles?

4   What are the three main stakeholders in restorative justice identified by McCold?

The limits of restorative justice?

So far we have talked about restorative justice in theory (as an alternative philosophical approach to 'doing justice') and in practice (what types of schemes and programmes exist that can lay some claim to basing their approach in whole or part on restorative justice?) Before we come to the crucial question of the impact of restorative justice, there remains the question of whether there are limits to the types of crimes that can be the focus of restorative justice-type interventions.

In practice many programmes cater for juvenile rather than adult offenders, and yet there also exist numerous examples of adult programmes. Similarly, and linked with this, much restorative justice activity occurs in the aftermath of less, rather than more, serious offences. And yet there are also examples of successful restorative justice practice in more serious cases. So, where do the limits lie? Is restorative justice appropriate for minor offences? Can it be used effectively with adults as well as juveniles? What of cases where either the victim or the offender does not wish to participate? In exploring this we consider two types of offence that are often thought to be among the least appropriate for restorative justice intervention: corporate crime and domestic violence.

Restorative justice and corporate crime

It is sometimes suggested, or perceived, that corporate crime is not amenable to restorative justice practices. Young (2002) outlines five major reasons offered in support of such a position:

1 Much restorative justice literature is based – explicitly or implicitly – on the idea of an individual, personal victim of crime (and often an individual, personal offender as well).

2 Restorative justice advocates place great emphasis on the psychological and emotional benefits of the process; 'healing' is a more difficult idea in relation to corporations.

3 An encounter in which either the victim or the offender is a corporation is very different from one in which both parties are individuals, not least in the extent to which the encounter is felt to be meaningful.

4 The power imbalance between a corporate offender and an individual victim may seem too great.

5 Problems of representation may arise – who is most appropriate to represent the corporate victim/offender?

Despite this there are a number of reasons why it is, arguably, important that restorative justice should seek to include cases involving corporate victims. First, as Young (2002) argues, excluding such cases places considerable limits, and, perhaps, *too* considerable limits, on restorative justice as an important set of practices. Second, Dignan (2005) suggests that there is no principled reason why restorative justice should be considered ill-suited to cases involving corporate victims. There is no reason to believe, he says, that the supposed benefits of restorative justice, such as reparation and dialogue with the offender, are not important to corporate victims.

Perhaps the strongest case for the argument that restorative justice is perfectly well suited to corporate regulation and corporate crime has been made by John Braithwaite. Indeed, he argues (2003: 161) that 'some of the most moving and effective restorative justice conferences I have seen have been business regulatory conferences'. Using an example from research on the regulation of nursing homes, Braithwaite suggests that inspectors whose approach is stigmatising cause compliance to deteriorate in the two years after inspection (see Figure 30.3). Similarly, encounters involving inspectors who are tolerant and understanding toward elder abuse also result in deteriorating levels of compliance. By contrast, the inspectors who were able to demonstrate improvement in compliance rates were those that had 'a philosophy of communicating clear disapproval of instances of neglect, while at the same time expressing confidence in the integrity of nursing home staff and management' (2003: 163).

In explaining this finding Braithwaite (2003: 163–4) says that the 'assumption of the sophisticated inspector is that we all have multiple selves – greedy egoistic selves, incompetent selves and socially responsible, caring selves. A sophisticated regulatory strategy can entice the worst of us to put our best self forward.' What happens if it fails to do so, as Braithwaite admits is likely often to be the case? Under such circumstances it is likely to be necessary to escalate up what he calls the 'enforcement pyramid' (Ayres and Braithwaite, 1992) toward strategies that are based on deterrence or, if that also fails, incapacitation (which in corporate regulation is likely to mean the removal of licences to practise or trade).

The underlying assumption in such an approach is that punishment works some of the time, but far from all the time. In the responsive regulation pyramid model (see Figure 30.4) the intention is that the cheaper and more respectful options should be tried first (which works in a great many cases). More costly punitive measures are used later usually, Braithwaite

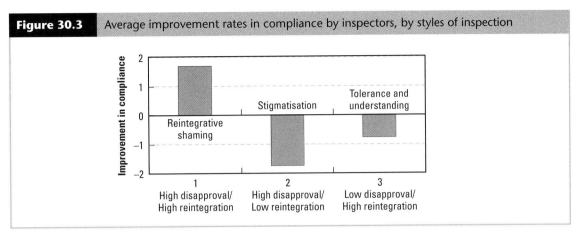

Figure 30.3 Average improvement rates in compliance by inspectors, by styles of inspection

Source: Braithwaite (2003).

says, in cases where businesses have made a rational calculation that it makes no economic sense to comply earlier. This also has the consequence, he argues, of increasing the legitimacy of these forms of regulation as other options have been attempted first.

Restorative justice and domestic violence

In a similar manner to the case of business regulation outlined above, Braithwaite and Daly (1994) apply the idea of an enforcement pyramid to the area of men's violence against women. The basis of the case they make is that traditional justice system interventions appear to work poorly in this area (see also Hudson, 1998):

- Most men are not made accountable for acts of rape or violence against intimates.

- The men who are arrested and prosecuted for violence against women are likely to have 'got away with it' before and may have entrenched patterns of raping and assaulting women.

- Women victimized by men's violence are re-victimized by engaging in the criminal process.

Building on the Wagga Wagga approach to conferencing – which they describe as 'citizenship ceremonies of reintegrative shaming' (1994: 193) – Braithwaite and Daly argue that there are two potential advantages to such interventions. First, they give a voice to the victim and to victims' relatives and other supporters. Second, the presence of the offender and their supporters in the process builds in the possibility of reintegration.

Once again, they propose an enforcement pyramid (see Figure 30.5). This is controversial for it implies that imprisonment is not necessarily the most appropriate response to men's violence against women. That said, they argue that if non-custodial approaches fail and if it appears that imprisonment will offer greater protection, then imprisonment is the appropriate response.

At the base of the pyramid the assumption is that violence within families is least likely to occur where there is strong disapproval of violence and that this has been internalised by family members. Most social control at this level consists of self-sanctioning and the impact of conscience. If this fails then community sanctioning is the next stage

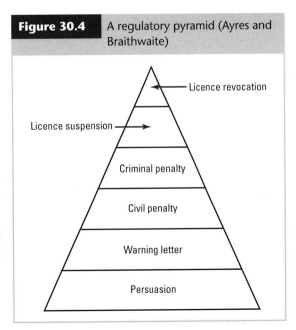

Figure 30.4 A regulatory pyramid (Ayres and Braithwaite)

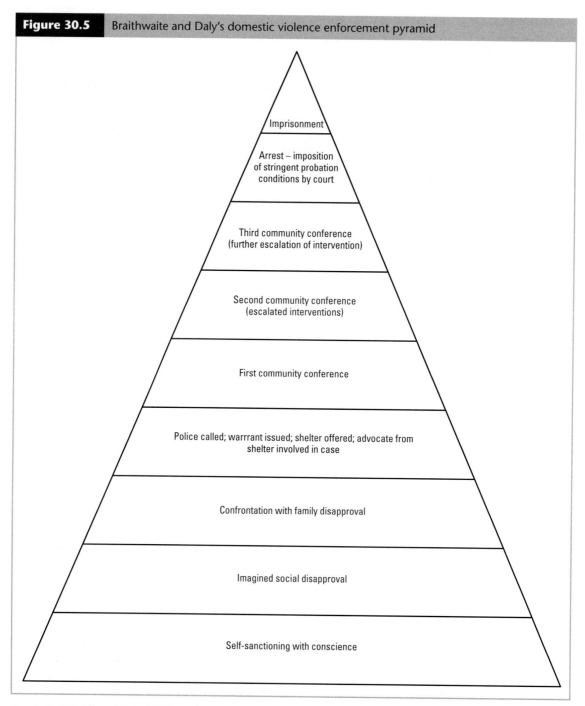

Figure 30.5 Braithwaite and Daly's domestic violence enforcement pyramid

Imprisonment

Arrest – imposition of stringent probation conditions by court

Third community conference (further escalation of intervention)

Second community conference (escalated interventions)

First community conference

Police called; warrrant issued; shelter offered; advocate from shelter involved in case

Confrontation with family disapproval

Imagined social disapproval

Self-sanctioning with conscience

Source: Braithwaite and Daly (1994).

– where local disapproval expressed through gossip and other means is often enough to instil control.

If such social sanctioning fails, then outside intervention – by the police – is required. Braithwaite and Daly propose the use of warrants rather than mandatory arrest because of their overriding principle of avoiding automatic puni-

tiveness. Beyond this is the stage at which conferences are held to deal with the behaviour and, as the pyramid implies, several conferences might be held before an arrest warrant was acted upon. At the apex of the pyramid is imprisonment, for 'men who repeatedly batter may ultimately have to be removed from their homes or imprisoned'. They go on, 'But to repeat perfunctory arrests while waiting for the victim's luck to run out, waiting for the day when her arrival in the hospital emergency room or the morgue will justify locking him up, is a deplorable policy. Equally, locking up all assailants is unworkable: there are too many for our prisons to accommodate. A policy based on the enforcement pyramid is more practical and more decent.' (1994: 201)

John Braithwaite, based at the Australian National University in Canberra, is one of the most prolific and important scholars on the subject of restorative justice.

What objections might be raised to such an approach? At least three major issues are raised by the idea of applying restorative justice techniques in relation to domestic violence:

● The parties to the conflict will generally differ markedly in terms of their power and, often, resources – violence against women is anyway a crime of domination – and therefore they are likely to have unequal bargaining power.

● There is no guarantee that communities will be particularly condemnatory of the behaviour involved. As Braithwaite and Daly (1994: 208) put it, 'can we expect "communities of concern" to be any less sexist and misogynist than traditional justice system responses or state intervention?'

● The absence of procedural safeguards may mean that 'justice' is not done.

Similar issues and questions raised in relation to violence against women also arise in connection with the potential use of restorative justice approaches in responding to racial violence (Hudson, 1998).

Assessing restorative justice

What are the main claims of restorative justice? According to Johnstone (2002) there are four:

● *Preventing offending* – The argument that offenders who experience restorative justice interventions are less likely to commit further offences than similar offenders who are subject to other, more conventional interventions.

● *Satisfying victims* – A central claim made by proponents of restorative justice is that it is much better than traditional approaches at involving and providing a satisfactory experience to victims of crime.

● *Benefiting criminal justice agencies* – Through involvement in more effective processes in which harms are repaired and in which victims and community members feel that they have a greater stake

● *Monetary savings* – Being community based, often involving volunteers and without all the accoutrements of the formal criminal justice system, it is often suggested that restorative justice is cheaper and more efficient than criminal justice.

To what extent does it appear that restorative justice initiatives meet these objectives? In his 'optimistic account' of restorative justice, John Braithwaite lists 15 theoretically informed reasons why restorative justice might outperform traditional forms of criminal justice. By way of balance, he also lists 13 reasons (see box on next page) why one might be more sceptical of the claims of restorative justice.

Braithwaite then examines the existing research evidence on the impact of restorative justice practices. As we saw earlier, Braithwaite takes restoring victims, restoring communities and reintegrating offenders as being the most important aims. In relation to the first of these, restoring victims, he reports that a large number of research studies show high levels of victim satisfaction, although one of the consistent problems with many programmes has been low levels of victim participation.

In relation to the second of his criteria, he concludes that 'the evidence of restorative justice restoring communities is of very small

Braithwaite's optimistic and pessimistic accounts of restorative justice (RJ)

The optimistic account

A. RJ practices restore and satisfy victims better than existing criminal justice (CJ) practices

B. RJ practices restore and satisfy offenders better than existing CJ practices

C. RJ practices restore and satisfy communities better than existing CJ practices

D. Reintegrative shaming theory predicts that RJ practices reduce crime more than existing CJ practices

E. Procedural justice theory predicts that RJ practices reduce crime more than existing CJ practices

F. The theory of bypassed shame predicts that RJ practices reduce crime more than existing CJ practices

G. Defiance theory predicts that RJ practices reduce crime more than existing CJ practices

H. Self-categorisation theory predicts that RJ practices reduce crime more than existing CJ practices

I. Crime prevention theory predicts that RJ practices reduce crime more than existing CJ practices

J. RJ practices deter crime better than practices grounded in deterrence theories

K. RJ practices incapacitate crime better than CJ practices grounded in theory of selective incapacitation

L. RJ practices rehabilitate crime better than CJ practices grounded in the welfare model

M. RJ practices are more cost-effective than CJ practices grounded in the economic analysis of crime

N. RJ practices secure justice better than CJ practices grounded in 'justice' or just desert theories

O. RJ practices can enrich freedom and democracy

The pessimistic account

A. RJ practices might provide no benefits whatsoever to 90% of victims

B. RJ practices have no significant impact on the crime rate

C. RJ practices can increase victim fears of re-victimization

D. RJ practices can make victims little more than props for attempts to rehabilitate offenders

E. RJ practices can be a 'shaming machine' that worsens the stigmatisation of offenders

F. RJ practices rely on a kind of community that is culturally inappropriate to industrialised societies

G. RJ practices can oppress offenders with a tyranny of the majority, even a tyranny of the lynch mob

H. RJ practices can widen nets of social control

I. RJ practices fail to redress structural problems inherent in liberalism, like unemployment and poverty

J. RJ practices can disadvantage women, children, and oppressed racial minorities

K. RJ practices are prone to capture by the dominant group in the RJ process

L. RJ processes can extend unaccountable police power, even compromise the separation of powers among legislative, executive, and judicial branches of government

M. RJ practices can trample rights because of impoverished articulation of procedural safeguards

Source: Braithwaite (1999: 18–19).

accomplishments of micro-community building and of modest numbers of community members going away overwhelmingly satisfied with the justice in which they have participated' (1999: 38). Finally, he suggests that offender satisfaction has generally been extremely high, with no study showing that restorative justice makes things worse. In relation to re-offending the research evidence remains somewhat slim, with most studies having either small samples and/or no control groups and exhibiting other methodological limitations. The most substantial effects have been found in the following studies:

- In the RISE programme the frequency of arrest among white people under 30 years of age who were assigned to RJ dropped by 84 per 100 offenders *more* than in the control group (the same

effects were not found for aboriginal people).

- In a study of restorative cautioning in Northumbria females under 18 who were assigned to a 'conference' rather than a standard final warning for assault had twice as great a reduction in arrests per 100 offenders.

- Similar reductions in arrest rates were found for young males assigned to a 'conference' rather than a final warning for property offences in the Northumbria study (Sherman and Strang, 2007).

There remain a number of doubts about restorative justice and a number of criticisms have been made of the approach. The first concerns the contrast that is often drawn between restorative justice and other, mainly retributive, approaches to criminal justice. It is argued that advocates of restorative justice are sometimes overly critical of traditional, judicial forms of punishment (as if they have nothing to recommend them) and, consequently, or relatedly, are uncritical and short-sighted when it comes to any limitations or shortcomings of restorative justice.

Thus, it might be argued that the picture painted of retributive justice by proponents of restorative justice is overly negative, indeed one-sided. It is possible, some argue, that the imposition of pain through punishment – generally signalled to be one of the least positive elements of retributive justice – can actually be beneficial, so long as it is appropriately administered and is proportionate. Thus, Anthony Duff (1999:51–2) has argued that punishment, though not an end in itself, should rather be considered part of a constructive response to offending which aims to:

... bring the criminal to understand, and to repent, the wrong he has done: it tries to direct (to force) his attention onto his crime, aiming thereby to bring him to understand that crime's character and implications as a wrong, and to persuade him to accept as deserved the censure which punishment communicates – an acceptance which must involve repentance ... by undergoing such penitential punishment the wrongdoer can reconcile himself with his fellow citizens, and restore himself to full membership of the community from which his wrongdoing threatened to exclude him.

Linked with this, some commentators have been particularly sceptical of the claims of advocates that restorative justice was the dominant form of justice in earlier historical times. In this manner Braithwaite (1999: 2) says that 'restorative justice has been the dominant model of criminal justice throughout most of human history for all the world's peoples'. Reviewing the evidence for such a claim, Bottoms (1999) concludes that dispute resolution in pre-modern societies was considerably more varied than many restorative justice advocates suggest, and that whilst many such procedures were genuinely reconciliatory they also often involved a high level of coercion and threat of sanctions. Moreover, where such practices did exist they were often connected to features of those societies that are either not to be found, or are not very prominent, in modern industrial societies.

Linked to this, some critics have argued that the nature of contemporary industrial society, particularly its individualised and privatised nature, makes it unlikely that interventions that rely upon community-based responses will be likely to be sustainable. Braithwaite's (1993) response to such criticism is that

we consistently underestimate the extent and variety of interdependencies in modern society. They exist, but are organised often on a non-geographical basis:

Admittedly, it is easier to cut oneself off from disapproval by some of these non-geographical communities of modernity (by simply withdrawing from them) than it is to cut oneself off from the disapproval of fellow villagers. But the reverse is also sometimes true. One cannot withdraw from the disapproval of one's international professional community by moving house; to do that one must learn a new career. (1993: 14)

A related criticism, by criminologists such as Blagg (1997), is that there is a process of 're-colonising' taking place in which exploitation of indigenous practices is occurring once again. As Kathy Daly (2000: 12) has argued:

If the first form of human justice was 'restorative justice', then advocates can claim a need to recover it from a history of 'takeover' by state-sponsored 'retributive justice'. *And*, by identifying current indigenous practices as 'restorative justice', advocates can claim a need to recover these practices from a history of 'takeover' by white colonial powers who instituted retributive justice. (quoted in Johnstone, 2002: 48)

Moving to restorative justice in practice, some critics have argued that many such initiatives, rather than empowering stakeholders, may actually make those who are relatively powerless weaker. Pressure may be brought to bear to divert cases away from formal justice systems, resulting in a failure properly to punish (perhaps against the wishes of the victim).

In this manner, restorative justice has been accused of undermining the right of victims and offenders. It has sometimes been suggested that restorative justice practitioners may be less, and arguably insufficiently, concerned about procedural safeguards (what elsewhere we have referred to as 'due process') – ensuring that all parties are treated fairly and according to strict rules. Under such circumstances what might ordinarily be thought of as the rights of the accused may be affected. Although it could be argued that the safeguards associated with criminal justice are not appropriate to the more informal setting of restorative justice, Johnstone (2002: 31) argues that this 'is unconvincing and dangerous'.

Similarly, Ashworth (2002: 592) raises a host of due process questions. Referring to Ayres and Braithwaite's 'enforcement pyramid', for example, he asks what types of deterrent strategies are allowed by such a scheme? What forms of incapacitation are allowed? Can people be sentenced on the basis of their previous record as well as the current offence? Restorative justice, it is suggested, may pose a threat to attempts to develop 'principled sentencing' wherein punishment should be proportionate to offence. A frequent criticism of restorative justice programmes is that they invite disproportionate interventions. As Ashworth therefore observes, 'The answers to these questions about restorative justice and recalcitrant offenders remain unclear, but the need for firm safeguards against undue severity does not disappear if a system is labelled "restorative". Penal history yields plenty of examples of apparently benign policies resulting in repressive controls.' Similarly, a number of commentators have raised the potential problem of 'net-widening' as a consequence of restorative justice interventions (Hudson and Galaway, 1996).

There are a number of issues relating to the role of victims in restorative justice. One of the significant limitations of some restorative justice initiatives concerns the tendency for only limited numbers of victims to take part. This is a rather substantial problem for an approach that relies upon victim–offender contact for much of its power. Moreover, there is a tendency in some of the restorative justice literature to portray victims in a rather uncomplicated and unproblematic manner. The reality is often much messier and more complicated. Dignan (2005) offers a number of examples of potentially problematic circumstances:

- Cases in which victims are not 'strangers', most problematically perhaps in cases of domestic violence.

- Cases involving 'representative' or 'generic' victims, such as victims of hate crimes.

- Secondary or indirect victims.

- Cases involving victims of 'non-standard' offenders, such as cases involving victimization by corporations or by the state.

- Cases where offenders have the good fortune to face a forgiving victim and others the misfortune to face a vengeful victim.

- Cases where the victim is in some way involved or culpable.

- Cases involving impersonal victims such as corporations, businesses, etc.

As we have seen, restorative justice proponents hold that such an approach can accommodate such circumstances and work well. Others remain more sceptical. As things stand there remains something of a gap between some of the rhetoric of supporters of restorative justice – who occasionally

appear rather evangelical – and some of the evidence of restorative approaches in practice. It is possible that this reflects the relative novelty of such approaches. As Daly (2003: 234–5) observes:

> There are limits to the idea of restorative justice, which stem in part from organisational constraints on what can be achieved, and in part, from popular understandings of what 'getting justice' means to people. It will take time for people to imagine that they can have their day in conference rather than in court. It will take time, perhaps a very long time, for people to become familiar with new justice scripts and social relations in responding to crime.

Finally, although this chapter has focused upon the possible application of restorative justice in relation to criminal activity, we should acknowledge that it is used, and has potential, way beyond this arena. Thus, the vast majority of disputes are resolved or dealt with without recourse to courtrooms. A huge field – often known as 'Alternative Dispute Resolution' (ADR) – has developed in which civil disputes are subjected to mediation and brought to a conclusion without the need for litigation. Second, as Roche (2006: 227) notes, 'the dominant mode of corporate regulation is arguably restorative justice, even if it is rarely described as such' and there is much research evidence showing that formal prosecution is generally used as a last resort in this area (Grabosky and Braithwaite, 1986; Hawkins, 2002). Lastly, the rise of 'truth commissions' in states that have experienced massive internal conflict such as South Africa under apartheid, and Sierra Leone and East Timor after civil war (see Chapter 34), is another example of the positive use of restorative techniques such as victim involvement, the search for the truth rather than the establishment of guilt, and the centrality of reconciliation. As such, it is perhaps best to think of restorative justice as a set of principles that have application in a variety of settings, of which criminal justice is only one, and then not necessarily the most important.

Review questions

1 What are the main claims of restorative justice?

2 What are the main features of Ayres and Braithwaite's 'enforcement pyramid'?

3 What is being suggested when critics talk of restorative justice *re-colonising* indigenous practices?

Questions for further discussion

1 Are retribution and restoration entirely incompatible aims for criminal justice?

2 How do the main approaches to restorative justice compare?

3 Are there particular types of conflict that are particularly suited to restorative justice interventions? And particular types that are less well suited?

4 What are the main dangers of restorative justice approaches?

5 What is meant by 'restorativeness'?

Further reading

There are two compendiums that provide a comprehensive introduction to restorative justice debates:

Johnstone, G. and Van Ness, D. (eds) (2006) *Handbook of Restorative Justice,* Cullompton: Willan (in particular see chapters by Gerry Johnstone and Daniel Van Ness, Declan Roche, David Miers, Lode Walgrave, Gerry Johnstone, and, 'Regional reviews' [ch. 24 and 25]

Johnstone, G. (ed.) (2003) *A Restorative Justice Reader,* Cullompton: Willan (in particular, see extracts from the work of Tony Marshall, Nils Christie, John Braithwaite, Barbara Hudson, Allison Morris and Gabrielle Maxwell, and Kathleen Daly)

Other extremely useful texts include:

Dignan, J. (2005) *Understanding Victims and Restorative Justice,* Buckingham: Open University Press

Johnstone, G. (2002) *Restorative Justice: Ideas, values, debates,* Cullompton: Willan

McLaughlin, E. *et al.* (eds) (2003) *Restorative Justice: Critical issues,* London: Sage

Von Hirsh, A. *et al.* (eds) (2003) *Restorative Justice and Criminal Justice: Competing or reconcilable paradigms?* Oxford: Hart

Zehr, H. (2005) *Changing Lenses: A new focus for crime and justice,* 3rd edn, Scottdale, PA: Herald Press

A good recent review of research evidence is:

Sherman, L. and Strang, H. (2007) *Restorative Justice: The evidence,* London: The Smith Institute (also available at: http://www.smith-institute.org.uk/publications.htm)

Finally, most students may find it difficult to access a copy, but if it is available in the university library it is well worth while reading John Braithwaite's (1999) essay: 'Restorative justice: Assessing optimistic and pessimistic accounts', in Tonry, M. and Morris, N. (eds) *Crime and Justice, vol.25,* Chicago: Chicago University Press. It is also reprinted in Braithwaite, J. (2002) *Restorative Justice and Responsive Regulation,* Oxford: Oxford University Press.

Websites

Restorative Justice Online contains a lot of resources, especially North American: http://www.restorative-justice.org/

Similarly, the *Real Justice* website contains a lot of information on conferencing: http://www.real justice.org/index.html

There are lots of restorative justice organisations, many of which maintain websites. These include:

The Restorative Justice Consortium: http://www.restorativejustice.org.uk/

Restorative Justice Ireland: http://www.extern.org/restorative/

National Centre for Restorative Justice in Education: http://www.transformingconflict.org/

Part 5
Critical Issues in Criminology

31 Race, crime and justice

32 Gender, crime and justice

33 Criminal and forensic psychology

34 Globalisation, terrorism and human rights

Chapter outline

Introduction   772

Sources of data   772

Ethnicity and victimization   773
   Victimization and risk   773
   Fear of crime   774
   Racist hate crimes   774
      Racist offenders   778
   Community, conflict and cohesion   779

Ethnicity and offending   780
   Self-reported offending   781
   Anti-social behaviour   783
   Drug use   784

Experience of the criminal justice system   785
   Stop and search   785
      Racism and stop and search   787
   Ethnicity and policing   788
      From Scarman to Lawrence   789
   Cautioning, arrest and sentencing   791
   Ethnicity and imprisonment   793
      Treatment in custody   794
      Deaths in custody   795
   Views of the criminal justice system   796

Minority representation in the criminal justice system   798

Questions for further discussion   801
Further reading   801
Websites   802

31

Race, crime and criminal justice

Equal in the eyes of the law? To what extent can we say that our criminal justice system treats people fairly? One of the consistently discussed problems of criminal justice in recent decades has been the particular difficulties faced by minority ethnic communities. In particular it is argued that racist attitudes and behaviour of professionals mean that minorities are poorly treated and end up over-represented in the criminal justice system.

In this chapter we consider:

- the experience of minority ethnic communities both in terms of offending and victimization;

- the question of racism and the apparent over-representation of minorities at all stages of the criminal justice process from arrest through to imprisonment;

- a number of key contemporary issues, including hate crimes and community cohesion.

Introduction

In this chapter you will find that the term 'ethnicity' tends to be used, rather than 'race'. In crude terms the distinction here is between one category (race) which is biological, and another (ethnicity) which is social. 'Ethnicity' is used, therefore, to describe social groups believed or perceived to differ from other social groups in terms of various possible characteristics including geographical origin, language, cultural traditions and religion, among many other things. However, much of the time some fairly broad categories are used ('white', 'black', 'Asian', 'mixed', 'other'), not because they are taken to be the best way of understanding ethnicity, but because they tend to be the categories used in many of the main research studies reported here. Often this is the case because the numbers of minority ethnic respondents are insufficiently large to support finer-grained categories. The data, as we will discover, reveal some interesting, and for many perhaps worrying, trends, but by their very nature operate at a considerable level of generality. The crucial point is to be aware that the categories used, though widely accepted, are far from unproblematic, and you should bear this in mind as you work your way through the chapter. The term 'racism' is used in a fairly broad manner in this chapter to refer to attitudes, opinions and practices that have the consequence of treating people in a discriminatory manner on the basis of their perceived ethnic origin.

Sources of data

When discussing various aspects of crime and justice in other parts of this book we have relied on information drawn from a wide variety of empirical research studies. In addition, when talking about broad trends we have used the two main sources of 'official' data: recorded police statistics and the British Crime Survey (their strengths and limitations are explored in Chapter 3). Again, in this chapter we will draw on all these different sources. In addition, however, there is a further source of information that will play an important role in our consideration of racism, crime and justice. Under the Criminal Justice Act 1991 (s.95) the Home Secretary is required to publish statistics which will enable those involved in the criminal justice system to avoid discrimination on grounds of race, sex or any other improper grounds. Since 1992 the Home Office has published documents on race and criminal justice which bring together statistical data on the representation of black and minority ethnic groups as suspects, offenders and victims with the criminal justice system and as employees within criminal justice agencies. These documents, generally published annually, are a rich source of data and can be downloaded from the Home Office Research, Development and Statistics website: http://www.homeoffice.gov.uk/rds/pubsstatistical.html

Ethnicity and victimization

We begin with victimization partly as a corrective to the tendency in some popular discourse to link crime to minority ethnic communities. As we saw, for example in Chapter 4, moral panics from the 1980s onward have tended to associate street crime ('mugging') with young African-Caribbean men. And, although there are some differences in the apparent patterns of offending between ethnic groups, self-report data, as we will see, tend to undermine any suggestion that people from minority ethnic communities are disproportionately responsible for crime. What about the experience of criminal victimization? How is that distributed according to ethnicity?

Victimization and risk

The British Crime Survey is the most comprehensive and reliable source of information about victims of crime. It was the 1988 survey which first had a sizeable 'booster sample' of minority ethnic respondents and was able to show significant differences in the risk of victimization between different ethnic groups, particularly in relation to violence. Subsequent BCSs continued to show greater risks faced by all minority groups compared with whites. However, more recent analyses, using broad offence categories, have suggested that whilst, overall, Asian

people are at slightly greater risk of crime than others, the risks faced by blacks and whites are roughly similar (see Figure 31.1). In fact, most of the differences in victimization between white and minority ethnic groups are argued to be the result of differences between the groups in terms of the places that people live, different age and social class distributions and income differences.

Of course, that is a very general picture and beneath the general trend there are some important differences in both patterns of victimization, and also the experience of victimization. Thus, if crime is divided into *household* and *personal* crime the data show minority ethnic groups to be at greater risk of personal crime, but not household crime compared with white people. Across the board, however, the exception to the general pattern concerns people of mixed ethnic origin who have a markedly higher risk of victimization than all other groups, even after factors like age (and this is a younger group generally) have been taken into account. In addition, as Bowling (1993) has argued, although some reported victimization may appear relatively minor when considered in isolation, when experienced repeatedly over time victimization tends to have much more acute consequences for the victim. It is important, therefore, that criminal justice agencies (and criminologists) appreciate the cumulative impact of much racist victimization.

There are also very sizeable differences in the risks faced by different ethnic groups in relation to

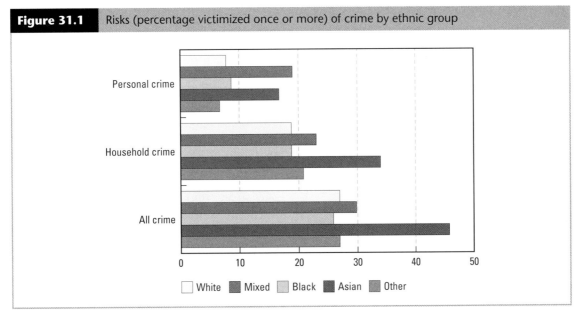

| Figure 31.1 | Risks (percentage victimized once or more) of crime by ethnic group |

Source: Hearnden and Hough (2004).

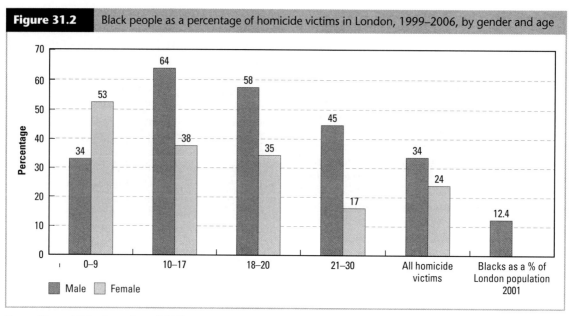

Figure 31.2 Black people as a percentage of homicide victims in London, 1999–2006, by gender and age

Source: Home Affairs Committee (2007).

the most serious crimes. Data on homicide for the combined years 2000/01 and 2002/03 show that the risk of becoming a victim faced by black people is six times that of white people. Recent information produced for the Home Affairs Committee on homicide in London (where the vast majority of homicide takes place) shows the very disproportionate risks faced by black young people (see Figure 31.2).

Moreover, and predictably, there are considerable differences between ethnic groups in the frequency with which they estimate that incidents are racially motivated. According to the 2002/03 BCS, four per cent of those of mixed ethnic origin were victims of racially motivated offences, compared with three per cent of Asian people, two per cent of black people, and less than one per cent of white people. We return to the subject of hate crimes later in the chapter.

Fear of crime

In addition to looking at victimization itself, the BCS also asks respondents about:

- concerns about crime;
- perceptions of criminal justice agencies.

The available data suggest that a higher proportion of ethnic minority than white respondents report being worried about burglary, car crime and violent crime. Of course, a higher proportion of minority ethnic groups live in inner-city areas, where both crime and worry about crime are higher. However, even controlling for the type of area in which people live, all minority ethnic groups report higher levels of worry than do white respondents (see Figure 31.3).

Racist hate crimes

Peter Fryer (1984) in his history of black people in Britain shows that harassment and, indeed, violent attack are by no means confined to recent times. It is possible that these problems have become more extensive, though it is difficult for us to know. What is certain is that racist hate crime has relatively recently become a politicised matter. In this, 1981 was an important year, in part because of the urban riots and the Scarman Inquiry which followed. But, it was also the year of the New Cross Fire in which 13 young black people died in circumstances many believed to be the result of a racist attack. 1981 was also the year that violence specifically targeted at minority ethnic communities was recognised for the first time in an official Home Office report (Bowling and Phillips, 2002). In subsequent years, evidence on the nature and extent of violence and intimidation against people from minorities has grown vastly. Central to this was the Macpherson Inquiry into the police investigation of the murder of Stephen Lawrence which

Figure 31.3   Worry about crime by ethnic group (2002/03) – percentage 'very worried'

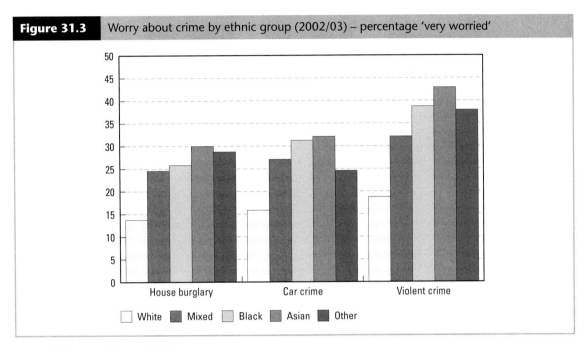

Source: Salisbury and Upson (2004).

'succeeded in bringing the issue of racist violence from the periphery to the centre of law and order policy in Britain' (Webster 2007: 68).

In the aftermath of the murder of Stephen Lawrence in 1993 the then Home Secretary, Michael Howard, had rejected calls to introduce a new criminal offence of 'racial violence' arguing that 'all violent crimes, regardless of motivation, can already be dealt with properly under existing legislation' (*Hansard*, HC Deb vol 235 col 32, 11 January 1994). The Labour Party took a different view and in their 1997 General Election manifesto (Labour Party, 1997) committed themselves to introducing a new offence of racial harassment and a new crime of racially motivated violence. In the event the Crime and Disorder Act 1998 introduced 'racially aggravated offences'. Racial aggravation is defined as occurring when 'at the time of committing the offence, or immediately before or after doing so, the offender demonstrates towards the victim of the offence hostility based on the victim's membership (or presumed membership) of a racial group' or where 'the offence is motivated (wholly or partly) by hostility towards members of a racial group based on their membership of that group'.

All police forces collect data on 'racist incidents'. From 1986 until 1999 the definition used was:

Any incident in which it appears to the reporting or investigating officer that the complaint involves an element of racial motivation; or any incident which includes an allegation of racial motivation made by any person.

The difficulty with such a definition is that it puts all the responsibility, and power, into the hands of the police officer. As a consequence, the Stephen Lawrence Inquiry proposed a significant change and, since 1999 the police have operated on the basis that:

A racist incident is any incident which is perceived to be racist by the victim or any other person.

This prioritises victims' experiences and also allows for the inclusion of incidents beyond what would normally be defined as 'crimes'. The number of racist incidents recorded by the police rose from approximately 13,000 in 1996/97 to almost 58,000 by 2004/05 (Home Office, 2006). Some of this increase may reflect increased confidence in the reporting procedures, particularly given that BCS estimates of racist offences declined over the same period. The police recorded 37,000 racially or religiously aggravated offences in 2004/05, which represented an increase of six per cent on the previous year. Of these, 61% were harassment, 15% criminal damage, 14% less serious wounding and ten per cent common assault.

In addition to racist incidents, the Crime and Disorder Act 1998 introduced the concept of racially

Table 31.1	Racially or religiously aggravated offences, 2003/04 and 2004/05									
	Harassment		Less serious wounding		Criminal damage		Common assault		Total	
	2003/04	2004/05	2003/04	2004/05	2003/04	2004/05	2003/04	2004/05	2003/04	2004/05
Total	20,560	22,623	4,840	5,315	5,581	5,417	4,015	3,673	34,996	37,028
% racially aggravated	11.9	10.4	1.1	1.1	0.5	0.5	1.7	1.7	1.8	1.8

Source: Home Office (2006).

aggravated offences – which was subsequently extended to include religiously aggravated offences by the Anti-Terrorism, Crime and Security Act 2001. Parliament approved a bill on 31 January 2006 that made it a criminal offence to use threatening words or behaviour with the intention of stirring up hatred against any group of people defined by their religious beliefs or lack of religious beliefs. An offence is racially or religiously aggravated if:

At the time of committing the offence, or immediately before or after doing so, the offender demonstrates towards the victim of the offence hostility based on the victim's membership (or presumed membership) of a racial or religious group; or

The offence is motivated (wholly or partly) by hostility towards members of a racial or religious group based on their membership of that group.

'Membership', in relation to racial or religious group, includes association with members of that group. 'Presumed' means presumed by the offender.

A total of just over 37,000 such offences were recorded in 2004/05, a rise of six per cent on 2003/04. The vast majority of such offences are classified as 'harassment', with the remainder being divided between criminal damage, less serious wounding and common assault (see Table 31.1).

Such statistics, it is acknowledged, massively underestimate the extent of racist crime. Beyond the under-reporting of such offences and, in all likelihood, the under-recording too, there is the fact that much racist offending and harassment is relatively low-level and fairly continuous. Thus, rather than being made up of a series of discrete events, as the statistics imply, racist harassment and other offences are often experienced as something more akin to a campaign of intimidation. An extreme illustration of this concerns the infamous case of Mal Hussein in Lancaster (see box opposite).

The introduction of notions like 'racial aggravation' and the identification of 'hate crimes' as the basis for the potential imposition of enhanced penalties have not gone without criticism. Jacobs and Potter (1998), for example, have argued that the use of relatively wide provisions such as these may have the unintended consequence of 'sweeping up' many relatively minor offences whilst more entrenched forms of racism escape. They doubt the assumed deterrent effect of such legislation. Take 'racially aggravated assault' for example. Jacobs and Potter's argument is, given that assault is already illegal and the offender has clearly already ignored any sanctions that apply to this particular crime, why should we believe that an increase in the sanction will make any difference, particularly if we assume that the racial or other form of prejudice that underpins the crime is a fairly deeply held belief?

A second danger, they suggest, is that hate crimes legislation will increase social divisions rather than help diminish them. In essence their argument is that hate crime laws treat crimes as being unequal and, consequently, treat victims as unequal, too. Many might believe, they argue, 'that all perpetrators of serious crimes are equally deserving of condemnation and all victims are equally deserving of sympathy' (1998: 132–3). It is highly likely therefore, they suggest, that those individuals whose victimization doesn't come under the protection of such laws will feel aggrieved. The danger lies in the potential within such laws for social conflict.

Finally, there is also the danger that such legislation will be used by the police as a means of

Shot at, bombed, abused: life for one couple in racist Britain

Michael Gillard and Melissa Jones, *The Guardian* 2 March 1999.

The bullet hole is still in the window after the last shooting. Mal Hussein and Linda Livingstone have suffered more than 2,000 racist attacks at their Lancaster corner shop. Now, an inquiry has begun into how police dealt with an eight-year race-hate campaign...

The couple have been the victims of more than 2,000 racist attacks, many orchestrated by five core criminal families well known to the police and Labour-run local council. These attacks include two shooting incidents by an unknown gunman, stonings and death threats. But the most deplorable assaults have been the six fire-bombings of their property while the couple were inside.

The place is Ryelands Estate in the historic city of Lancaster. Here all the recommendations in the damning Macpherson report are relevant and many of the mistakes in the bungled Lawrence murder inquiry apparent.

Mal Hussein and Linda Livingstone invested their joint savings in 1991 into a small grocery store with an upstairs flat located in the heart of the estate. Since then the dehumanisation of daily racist abuse have turned them into psychologically scarred prisoners of an intolerable situation and broken relationship ...

The chief constable of Lancashire police, Pauline Clare, yesterday ordered an internal inquiry into allegations that officers have failed to properly investigate the eight-year race hate campaign ...

Trouble began for Mal and Linda within a week of arrival. Two residents, one of whom identified himself as the King of Ryelands while the other played with a knife, demanded extortion money. Mal refused and reported the incident to the police who, he says, took no action because there were no witnesses.

Their property was vandalised day and night for the next two weeks. 'We would wake up to see the whole place daubed with racist graffiti,' said Mal. `Things like 'Burn the Paki!' 'Black grass!' 'Burn Saddam Hussein!' 'Mal is a black bastard!' The police were called on each occasion but they took no statement from us, they left without taking any further action. We were also subject to a torrent of racist abuse on a daily basis.'

This was nothing compared with a yearly event celebrated on Ryelands on November 4 called Mischief Night. Traditionally it was an excuse for tenants to riot and crowds of drunken youths and their parents to burn settees and mattresses in the street. Their target in 1991, however, and for the next five years, was Mal and Linda's home. Fireworks were thrown into the shop and a petrol-soaked mattress blocked the shop door. The couple called the police in panic. They were later warned by one customer that they would also be petrol bombed.

The police came and went but that did not stop the attack. `We were very scared and locked ourselves in the shop. The crowds continued shouting abuse and making threats late into the night. Despite this the police took no further actions,' said Mal ...

Even though one of the attackers threatened to kill Mal in front of an attending police officer, the shopkeeper was charged with intent to cause grievous bodily harm. Part of his bail conditions were that he was banned from his home and Lancaster until his trial a year later.

During his exile Linda ran the shop with her elderly parents. The attacks did not let up. In fact the same assailant was arrested inside their flat ... In 1992 Mal was acquitted of all charges. He believes he should not have been prosecuted because he was only standing up for his rights and demanding police protection.

These appalling incidents and the sparsity of prosecutions shaped the couple's view of the police more as 'spectators.' ... There have been hundreds of incidents every year which Mal and Linda report to the police and log in diaries made available to the council. The couple have played a key role in more than 40 successful prosecutions of racist residents and tenants. The fire-bombings of their property in 1995 and 1996 were filmed by two television crews and in the latter case resulted in the jailing of three adults and five children for a total of 24 years ...

The future is uncertain for the couple. After Mischief Night in 1996 they vowed to get off Ryelands and now a novel scheme has been launched to help them. Kushminder Chahal, who has conducted an 18-month study on how victims of race crime in Britain internalise routine abuse, has formed a charitable company called Share In Anti Racism to receive donations to buy the couple's business. The shop will employ white staff and the profits ploughed into supporting other isolated victims of race hate campaigns.

(http://www.guardian.co.uk/racism/Story/0,,209466,00.html)

punishing individuals they consider to be particularly problematic. Thus Dixon and Gadd (2006: 217) found that 'the anti-hate crime provisions of the [Crime and Disorder Act 1998] may be used against (often multiply) disadvantaged people, including individuals from minority ethnic backgrounds. Indeed, on occasions ... charges of racial aggravation may be used as a resource by the police in dealing with particularly troublesome individuals who, for various reasons, fall into the category of "police property"'.

Racist offenders

What do we know about racist offenders? Early research by Webster (1995, 1996) in the north of England examined the broader community cultural context which gave a degree of legitimacy to those involved in racist attacks and distinguished between 'normal', 'aggressive' and 'violent' racists. Research by Hewitt (1992) in the London Borough of Greenwich, where Stephen Lawrence was murdered, identified a number of factors which he argued combined to create the conditions within which racist attacks may occur. These conditions included:

- entrenched local racism;
- local social and economic deprivation;
- *passive* engagement in leisure activities;
- few affordable youth facilities;
- high levels of (adult) criminality linked with wider criminal networks;
- a violent youth subculture.

He went on to argue that perpetrators' views of minorities were in part a reflection of problems with their own identity. In the context in which their sense of self is problematic, racist attitudes and language come to play an important part in their self-definition. Subsequent research by Sibbitt (1997) similarly found that the views expressed by perpetrators tended to be widespread in the communities in which they lived and that these were used by aggressors to defend their actions (essentially a form of neutralisation technique – see Chapter 8). Sibbett (1997: 101–2) argued that within 'the perpetrator community, there are many different types of perpetrators. Some are already heavily engaged in crime and/or violent and other anti-social behaviour. They terrorise not only members of ethnic minorities but others in the community more generally. These may include the owners of local businesses, members of other groups they see as different and threatening (e.g.

homosexuals, fans of opposing football teams), other neighbours and even members of their own families.' She offered a typology of perpetrators differentiated broadly according to age:

- *The pensioners* – Tend to have lived in the area a long time, have been the victims of various forms of threatening behaviour and see black people as a convenient scapegoat for their problems.

- *The people next door* – The people next door are adults who have grown up hearing their parents blame black people for their family's, and the country's, ills. The adult male may often be involved in other criminal activity, and violence may be a routine part of his lifestyle.

- *The problem family* – The adults in this family have their own problems such as poor physical or mental health and feel persecuted by the authorities. They behave abusively towards their children and towards others in general.

- *15–18 year-olds* – They have grown up in a family where racist attitudes are prevalent. After school they will hang around with friends with particularly virulent racist views. They engage in anti-social behaviour, often in groups.

- *Ten to 14 year-olds* – Low achievers, with little input or guidance from parents, they have low self-esteem and tend to bully those they see as weaker than themselves. They are particularly likely to pick on minority ethnic children in areas where racism is common.

- *Four to ten year-olds* – Racism is part of their environment – something regularly expressed by relatives of all ages. They see it as normal to speak of non-whites as 'people who do not belong here' and 'should go back to their own country'.

A study by Ray and Smith (2001; also Ray *et al.*, 2004) focusing on 64 racist offenders, produced a number of interesting findings.

- First, they found almost no cases in which perpetrators attacked strangers simply on the basis of their membership of a particular group. Rather, in the vast majority of cases the victim was known to the perpetrator, albeit not well.

- Second, the offenders were not 'specialists' in racist violence – which might be expected to be the case if their offending were politically motivated. In many cases violence was a regular means of solving disputes.

- Third, although the study was based in Manchester, few of the offenders came from the cosmopolitan centre of the city itself but, rather, lived in areas to the north and west where communities are more segregated. By and large most lived on working-class estates which were almost homogenously white.

This leads Ray and Smith to argue that in the vast majority of cases they studied racist violence didn't match up to the classic image of 'hate crime'. Moreover, they suggest, in important respects such violence was driven by deep-seated feelings of alienation, shame and rage characteristic of males trapped in deprived and run-down estates with little positive contact with people of different ethnic origins. Consequently, reduced racial segregation, they argued, would in all likelihood be a positive development and likely lead to reduced racist violence.

Community, conflict and cohesion

The discussion of racist hate crime provides one illustration of the problems and dangers facing many people from minority ethnic communities. Some relatively recent developments also illustrate the broader cultural and community-focused conflicts that can also arise. In mid-2001, several towns in the north of England experienced considerable unrest. The riots were notable for the fact that they were the most significant public disturbances for some years but, crucially, with the possible exception of the Southall riot in 1981, for the first time they very conspicuously involved young Muslims.

The largest disturbances occurred in Oldham in May, in Burnley in June and Bradford in July. The riot in Oldham lasted for a weekend, during the course of which a great number of shops, other premises and cars were fire-bombed, and there were significant confrontations between the police and local minority ethnic youth. A week after the riot the house of the Asian deputy-Mayor of Oldham was fire-bombed. A review conducted by an independent team led by a senior civil servant suggested that significant factors included many

An Asian youth throwing a stick at the police during the disturbances in Bradford in July 2001. Subsequent inquiries into the causes of the disturbances pointed to the activities of the National Front as a precipitating factor, and the longer-term impact of segregation across ethnic lines and the marginalisation of minority ethnic communities.

years of 'deep-rooted' segregation between communities, together with the failure of the local authorities to address causes of racial division (Cantle, 2001).

Seemingly, there had been some specific conflicts between local Asian and white youths in the run-up to the Oldham riots and, similarly, the disturbances in Burnley were also sparked off by violence between local Pakistani and white youths outside a nightclub. The conflict continued with a number of isolated attacks on individuals together with larger-scale disturbances, including an attack on a pub by a group of Pakistani youths and the fire-bombing of a number of Asian businesses in the town.

Two weeks later, rioting broke out in Bradford. Plans announced by the National Front to hold a march in the city, and a potential counter-demonstration by the Anti-Nazi League, led eventually to confrontations, some involving local Pakistani youth and white extremists some of whom, it was alleged, had travelled some distance in anticipation of trouble. Police intervention pushed various groups toward the Manningham area of the town where rioting ensued on a scale which required police reinforcements to be drafted in from Manchester and Humberside among other areas. Of the 270 people arrested, some 90 per cent were Asian-Muslim, and 145 were eventually charged with riot. In response to a campaign established to protest against the severe sentences handed down to many of those convicted, the then Home Secretary, David Blunkett, said: 'For every sentence, for every tough new law, for every sensible measure, there's some bleeding heart liberals who are there wanting to get them off, get them out and reduce their sentence' (quoted in Allen, 2005).

A number of factors were highlighted in the various reports written in the aftermath of the 2001 riots. One of these was the precipitating role of extremist far-right political parties in each of the disturbances. More fundamental was the common conclusion that long-term marginalisation of minority ethnic communities, segregation across ethnic lines and, as the Final Cantle Report on the Oldham riot (Institute of Community Cohesion, 2006) put it, the problems emanating from communities leading 'parallel lives'. Finally, there was the role of the police and the perception among minority communities that, once again, they were being policed rather than protected. As one response to the Bradford disturbances noted:

For many years the predominantly Pakistani community has been complaining of targeted

policing and racism on the part of police officers. Instead of keeping out National Front activists bent on stirring up racial violence, the police instead engaged in heavy-handed tactics against the community. This inevitably built up resentment and anger on the part of the local community. (quoted in McGhee, 2005)

Not to be underestimated also, Webster (2003) argues, are the housing and social policies that maintain relatively high degrees of segregation. Although some official reports (Denham, 2002) suggested that much of this was a consequence of self-segregation, Webster suggests that this is a mistaken view. Rather in places like Bradford, Oldham and Burnley Asian populations have been growing faster in traditional areas of Asian settlement as a consequence of the youthfulness of the population. Nevertheless, 'the evidence is that Asians, like other groups, including the white majority, wish to live in affluent areas whatever the ethnic make-up of those areas, but are prevented from doing so because they cannot afford it and/or are discriminated against in the housing and labour markets. These factors are ignored in the reports on the disorders' (Webster, 2007: 106).

Relatedly, Chakraborti (2007) argues that although the *idea* of community cohesion is an appealing one, aspects of the term have actually served to antagonise Muslim communities. In part, this is because it serves to sideline other important contributory factors such as discriminatory policing, far-right political fear-mongering and residential segregation. Additionally, he argues, 'in overlooking such factors, this "solution" was seen as overly simplistic by seemingly condoning the violence of white communities as representative of frustration and instability, but condemning the violence of Muslims as representative of their unwillingness to accept the norms of national identity.'

Ethnicity and offending

A long-standing and contentious area in criminology concerns the nature of offending by people of different ethnic origins. Are white people more likely to commit certain types of crime than people of other ethnic origins? Are people of particular origins *associated* with particular types of crime? If so, why? Is there any basis in reality for our assumptions in this area, and what do assumptions, common portrayals or understandings tell us about ethnic relations and criminal justice? Bowling and Phillips (2002: 78) quote a government report from 1972 which expressed the official view at the time. It stated, 'coloured immigrants are no more involved in crime than others; nor are they generally more concerned in violence, prostitution and drugs. The West Indian crime rate is much the same as that of the indigenous population. The Asian crime rate is very much lower.' However, within a relatively short period, some important opinions, not least those of the police, appeared to take a very different view and public concerns about crime associated with minorities seemed to grow relatively quickly. Bowling and Phillips identify three main reasons for this:

● There was growing conflict between the police and black communities.

● The police started to collect, and in due course publish, statistical material on the involvement of black people in crime, including particular offences such as robbery ('mugging').

● New media representations of criminality had the effect of creating strong links between images of blackness and criminality.

The effect of such changes ultimately undermined the view that levels of offending by African-Caribbeans were little different from the white majority and instead gradually created the view that black youths in particular were a potent source of danger. In the next section we look at what the available statistics are able to tell us about levels of crime among different ethnic groups. As ever, before doing so we must remind ourselves that the data need to be treated with a significant degree of caution. This, as we have seen, is the case in relation to crime generally (see Chapter 3). In this area extra caution is required as not only is 'crime' a malleable and moveable notion, but 'ethnicity' is highly variable too.

Self-reported offending

In terms of understanding levels of crime among different ethnic groups, official criminal statistics are not entirely helpful. The proportion of offences that are never reported to the police, and the sizeable number that, once reported, never result in the identification of an offender, place profound limits on the reliability of such information. Moreover, research over many years has documented the difficulties that victims have in accurately remembering the details of the offender in personal crimes, and

this tends also to limit what can be learned from reports to the police about the nature of perpetrators. None of this should be taken to suggest that police-recorded crime statistics are without their uses. As we shall see below, for example, they can be used to investigate questions relating to the treatment of different ethnic groups by the criminal justice system.

In terms of patterns of offending, therefore, we will rely primarily on self-report studies. Though self-report data are not without their limitations (see Chapter 3) they provide the best source for these purposes. The first major British self-report survey to contain sufficient numbers from minority ethnic groups to make comparisons possible was the first Home Office Youth Lifestyles Survey (YLS) (Graham and Bowling, 1995). The headline finding from the YLS was that white and black rates of offending were very similar, whereas those reported by Asian respondents were substantially lower. A second YLS was subsequently undertaken in the late 1990s (Flood-Page et al., 2000).

The YLS has since been replaced by a larger-scale exercise called the Offending, Crime and Justice Survey (OCJS) (Sharp and Budd, 2005). This is a large survey of over 10,000 respondents aged ten to 65, with booster samples of young people and of minority ethnic respondents. In assessing offending, the OCJS focused on 20 'core' offences falling into seven broad categories:

● burglary;

● vehicle-related thefts;

● other thefts;

● criminal damage;

● robbery;

● assault;

● selling drugs.

As is standard practice in self-report studies, the OCJS distinguishes between offending during the lifetime and during the past year.

In line with other research, the OCJS found considerable variation among ethnic groups in reported lifetime offending levels. The highest overall prevalence rates were reported by white respondents, with over two-fifths (42%) reporting at least one offence during their lifetime. This was only marginally higher than those of mixed ethnic origin (39%), but significantly higher than Asian (21%), black (28%) and other (23%) respondents (see Figure 31.4). The OCJS also sought to identify the commission of 'serious' offences, which it limited to: theft of a vehicle, burglary, robbery, theft from the person, assault resulting in injury, and selling Class A drugs. Again,

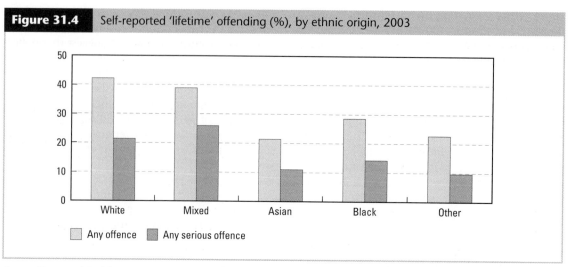

Figure 31.4 Self-reported 'lifetime' offending (%), by ethnic origin, 2003

Source: Sharp and Budd (2005).

lifetime prevalence rates were higher for white respondents, with the exception in this case of respondents of mixed ethnicity.

The general pattern visible in Figure 31.4 is fairly consistent across offence types. That is to say, white respondents, and in relation to some offences those of mixed ethnic origin, had the highest reported levels of offending, and Asian respondents consistently had the lowest levels. Thus, just comparing white with black respondents, the self-reported lifetime involvement in vehicle theft, other theft, criminal damage, and assault were all significantly higher

among the former, as was selling drugs, though this difference was not statistically significant.

The only difference was in relation to robbery where two per cent of black respondents reported having committed such an offence during their lifetime compared with less than half a per cent of white respondents (a statistically significant difference). The issue of robbery is a particularly emotive one as, of all offences, it is arguably street robbery that has become most closely bound up with public debates and media representations of 'black criminality'. It remains a hugely contentious, and in many respects,

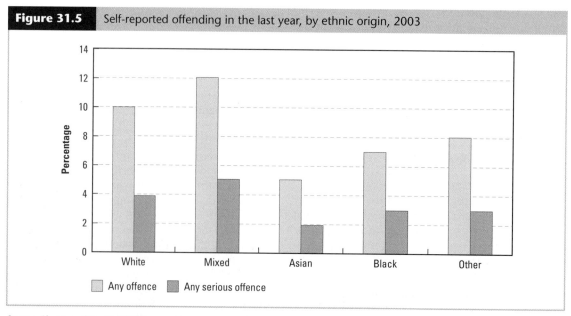

Figure 31.5 Self-reported offending in the last year, by ethnic origin, 2003

Source: Sharp and Budd (2005).

not very well understood area. Bowling and Phillips (2002) offer a range of possible hypotheses that might be used to explain black over-representation in robbery, including:

- robbery is related to poverty and social exclusion; factors which disproportionately affect black communities;
- many offences classified as 'robbery' are minor and could easily be classified in other ways;
- robbery is associated with gaining status and a name; black youth may particularly seek status and self-esteem through such means;
- some robbery may be a manifestation or expression of 'black power' in general circumstances characterised by powerlessness;
- young black people, subject to regular stop/searches, may feel 'labelled' and respond accordingly.

The patterns revealed in relation to offending in the last year are largely similar to lifetime offending. The highest prevalence rates are among 14–17 year-olds, with a third having committed an offence in the previous 12 months compared with approximately ten per cent of ten to 65 year-olds. Overall, 12 per cent of respondents of mixed ethnic origin and ten per cent of white respondents reported having committed an offence in the last year, compared with five per cent of Asian and seven per cent of black respondents. A similar pattern held in relation to serious offending,

with Asian respondents having the lowest prevalence levels, and mixed ethnic origin and white respondents the highest (see Figure 31.5).

Anti-social behaviour

In addition to looking at self-reported offending, the OCJS also considers anti-social and other behaviours perceived officially as 'problematic'. To do so, respondents to the survey aged ten to 25 were asked if they had been involved in the following six forms of behaviour:

- being noisy or rude in a public place;
- behaviour leading to a neighbour complaining;
- graffiti-writing;
- joy-riding;
- carrying some form of weapon;
- racial harassment (attacked, threatened/rude).

Though defined for the purposes of the survey as anti-social, clearly some of these behaviours can easily fall into the category of crime and should certainly not be interpreted as being straightforwardly less 'serious' than some of the forms of criminal conduct discussed earlier.

Overall, the survey found that 29 per cent of ten to 25 year-olds reported having engaged in one of the behaviours in the list. The differences between most ethnic groups are relatively small, though

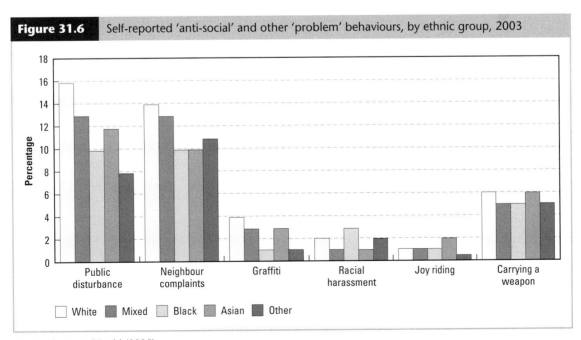

Figure 31.6   Self-reported 'anti-social' and other 'problem' behaviours, by ethnic group, 2003

Source: Sharp and Budd (2005).

Asian respondents consistently reported lower levels of engagement in such behaviours and respondents of white or mixed ethnic origin the highest (see Figure 31.6).

Some of the differences in overall reported rates diminish to an extent if account is taken of the varying age structures of the different ethnic groups, though – even controlling for this factor – white respondents have an above-average rate in relation to public disturbances, neighbour complaints and graffiti.

Drug use

The final area of criminal or potential criminal conduct that we will consider in this context is drug use. Again, like some other areas of offending, public attitudes and perceptions sometimes involve a fairly strong link between ethnicity and various forms of drug use and, as we will see, these are in most respects a very poor guide to actual behaviour. As with offending and 'anti-social behaviour', the OCJS contained questions relating to drug use over the lifetime and during the last year. Overall, the OCJS found that 13 per cent of ten to 65 year-olds reported having used at least one illicit drug in the past year and four per cent had used a Class A drug. The highest rates of usage were reported by people

of mixed and white ethnic origin and the lowest by Asian respondents (see Figure 31.7).

In understanding patterns of drug use it is particularly important to control for differences in age and gender in the structure of particular ethnic groups. Having done so, the authors of the OCJS found that:

- Males of mixed ethnic origin were most likely to have used any drug (27% compared with 16% of white and black respondents).

- Class A drug use was similar for males of white, mixed and other ethnic origins, but much lower for Asian and black respondents.

- Female drug use, and use of Class A drugs, is also higher for those of white and mixed ethnic origin, and lower for those in black and Asian groups.

Given such findings, a number of important questions arise in relation to the over-representation of black men in the criminal justice process. As one example, despite the evidence of relatively high levels of drug use among young white males, it remains the case that a black person is much more likely to be stopped by the police on suspicion of possessing drugs. Indeed, as we will see below, the use of stop and search powers remains one of the most controversial aspects of the criminal justice process.

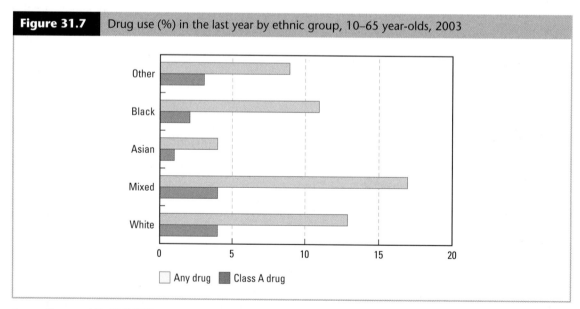

Figure 31.7   Drug use (%) in the last year by ethnic group, 10–65 year-olds, 2003

Source: Sharp and Budd (2005).

Experience of the criminal justice system

To operate successfully, any criminal justice system needs to be perceived as legitimate in the eyes of the public. There are, however, many 'publics' (men/women; people of different ages and ethnic origins and so on) and criminal justice impinges on them in different ways. Research over many years has indicated that people have widely differing experiences of many aspects of criminal justice – from policing through to treatment in court. Moreover, British society has become increasingly socially and culturally diverse. Where once the key sources of social and political identity in British society were based around economic and class divisions, it is argued that these are of declining significance as other forms of differentiation come to the fore, including religion, age, gender, race, region, nationality, ethnicity, and sexuality. Our concern here is with how perceptions and experiences of criminal justice differ across the population according to ethnicity.

Table 31.2 provides a basic breakdown of people at differing stages of the criminal justice process. On a crude level this gives a sense of whether particular groups are over- or under-represented, say, among arrest figures or in the prison population. What becomes immediately obvious is that black and Asian people figure in greater proportions at most stages of the criminal justice process than they do in the population generally. This is particularly true for blacks who, making up approximately two per cent of the overall population, make up one in seven of those stopped and searched and one in ten of the prison population. It is important, however, not to make too many assumptions about what these figures mean. First, we need to look at the various stages of the criminal justice process in a little more detail.

Stop and search

Policing by public consent has long been a central theme in discussions of British policing. Much policing is inherently conflictual or adversarial and, almost inevitably, adversarial police contacts are more likely to be experienced by economically disadvantaged groups in society. There is now a considerable body of research which shows that members of such groups – the unemployed, those living in the most deprived areas, and minority ethnic groups, in particular – have highly differing experiences of, and views about, the police from other groups in the populations (see, for example, Fitzgerald et al., 2003; Skogan, 2006).

One of the long-standing sources of contention in relation to criminal justice has concerned the use of

Table 31.2	Representation of ethnic groups at different stages of the criminal justice process, 2004/05			
	White	Black	Asian	Other
Population (aged 10 and over)	91.3	2.8	4.7	1.2
Stops and searches	74.7	14.1	7.2	1.5
Arrests	84.4	8.8	4.9	1.4
Cautions	83.8	6.4	4.4	1.2
Young offences	84.7	6.0	3.0	3.3
Prison receptions	76.8	13.5	5.4	0.7
Prison population	80.7	10.2	5.4	0.5

Source: Home Office (2006).

stop and search powers by the police. The apparently disproportionate application of this power against young black men has been described as 'the most glaring example of an abuse of police powers' (Bowling and Phillips, 2002) and, according to the late Bernie Grant MP, 'nothing has been more damaging to the relationship between the police and black community than the ill-judged use of stop and search powers' (quoted in Bowling and Phillips, *ibid*). Research by the Home Office (Miller *et al.*, 2000) has found experience of being stopped and searched is associated with reduced confidence in the police, and that the use of such powers against people from minority ethnic communities contributes directly to poorer relationships between them and the police. The lack of trust and confidence in the police among minority ethnic communities was highlighted in both the Scarman (Scarman, 1982) and the Lawrence (Macpherson, 1999) Inquiries (see Chapter 25).

The main legislative sources of the power to stop and search are contained in:

● section 1 of the Police and Criminal Evidence Act 1984 (PACE) which allows an officer who has reasonable grounds for suspicion to stop and search a person or vehicle to look for stolen or prohibited items;

● section 60 of the Criminal Justice and Public Order Act 1994 which allows a senior officer to authorise the stop and search of persons and vehicles where there is good reason to believe that to do so would help to prevent incidents involving serious violence, or that persons are carrying dangerous instruments or offensive weapons;

● section 44 of the Terrorism Act 2000 which allows an officer to stop and search persons and vehicles – at a time and place where an appropriate authorisation exists – to look for articles that could be used in connection with terrorism whether or not there are reasonable grounds to suspect the presence of such articles.

The figures below illustrate the most frequently presented finding in relation to stop and search: that black people and those of mixed origin are much more likely to be stopped by police than white people. Asian people are more likely to be stopped than white people when in a car, but not on foot.

Figure 31.9 opposite presents data on stop and search for different ethnic groups as a rate per 100,000 population. It indicates somewhat more starkly the relative risks faced by different groups. Very approximately, it suggests that the number of searches of black suspects was six times that of white suspects in 2002/03, with Asian suspects also having a higher rate than whites. Hearnden and Hough (2004) go on to argue that, in addition, existing evidence suggests that a higher proportion of stops of black than white people result in searches, though it is possible that searches of black people may be concentrated among a relatively small group in the population.

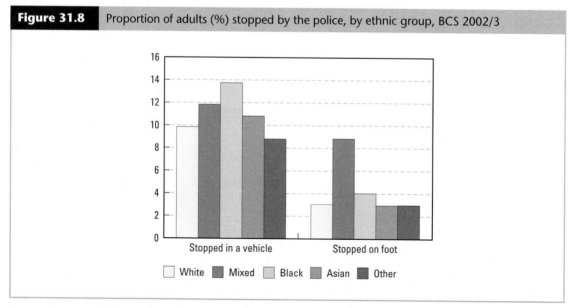

Figure 31.8   Proportion of adults (%) stopped by the police, by ethnic group, BCS 2002/3

Source: Hearnden and Hough (2004).

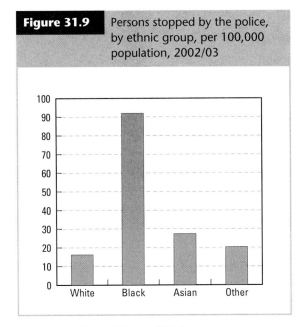

Figure 31.9   Persons stopped by the police, by ethnic group, per 100,000 population, 2002/03

Source: Hearnden and Hough (2004).

The data above relate to stops made under PACE. Evidence in relation to stops made under other legislation paints a similar picture. Thus, section 60 searches of black people under the Criminal Justice and Public Order Act 1984 are 13 times those of white people, and the Asian rate is also five times higher. Similarly, searches under s.44 of the Terrorism Act 2000 also differ markedly, the rate per 10,000 population being three for whites, 14 for black and Asian people, and 24 for those of 'other' ethnic origin.

Racism and stop and search

Although stop and search figures have often been interpreted relatively straightforwardly as an indicator of police racism, some recent research has drawn attention to some of the shortcomings of using the data in this rather uncritical manner. Home Office research attempted to move beyond local population statistics to estimate the 'available population' for stop and search, i.e. those actually using the streets being patrolled by the police at times when stops and searches are carried out.

Such research has found that the 'available population' tended to be very different in profile from the resident population and, crucially, the studies concluded that there was, in fact, no general pattern of bias against people from minority ethnic groups (MVA and Miller, 2000), a finding supported by more recent research in Reading and Slough

(Waddington *et al.*, 2004). That is to say, such research argued that, although compared with their proportion in the general population, young black males were much more likely to be stopped by the police than were whites, this difference disappeared if one compared stop rates with who was likely to be on the streets that were being policed at the times they were being policed. Now, one response to such a finding might be that it is police decision-making about which streets to police, and when to police them – i.e. to focus on communities with high minority ethnic youth populations – that leads inevitably to a large number of young black males being stopped.

One small-scale study, which looked at police use of a different power, possibly sheds some light on the issue of the discriminatory use of powers. The study, conducted in one police station in London, examined police use of their powers to strip-search suspects in custody. The study showed that even when other factors were controlled for – such as the type of offence – there was a striking disproportion in the use of strip-search powers against African-Caribbean arrestees in the police station. Moreover, as the study was based on studying the records relating to *every* prisoner over an 18 month period, the figures were not subject to the same shortcomings as stop and search figures. Crucially, those passing through the custody suite of a police station represented the entire 'available population' for strip-search. Consequently, any disproportionality in the use of powers was just that – it was not a reflection of who happened to be in custody. On the contrary, the data raise the very real possibility that police racism plays a part in the use of such powers (Newburn *et al.*, 2004). Of course, even if true, this does not necessarily mean that the same assumptions can be applied to the use of stop and search powers.

Drawing such research together is difficult, therefore. It is clear that blacks are significantly more likely to be stopped than whites based on their numbers in the general population. However, studies of the 'available population' suggest that police activity may reflect who happens to be on the particular streets that they patrol. These broader decisions about where to direct patrols may themselves have discriminatory outcomes. Although not directly comparable, the study of police use of strip-search powers indicates that they tend to be disproportionately targeted at minorities, reinforcing long-standing concerns and arguments about police discrimination. Nevertheless, one conclusion that can be drawn is that irrespective of whether or not police stop and search powers are actually being used in a discriminatory fashion, it seems undeniable that this is how they are experienced by minority ethnic communities. As such, this continues to constitute an important area for the future of police–minority community relations.

Ethnicity and policing

The nature of police relationships with, and the policing of, minority ethnic communities has been the subject of considerable attention, and no little controversy, over the past 30 years. Concerns about over-policing (being subject disproportionately to stop and search, surveillance, arrest and so on) and under-protection (not having victimization treated seriously or responded to appropriately) have been regular features of both individual and collective complaint. Important research in the 1980s by the Policy Studies Institute found widespread evidence of discriminatory behaviour by police officers and compared police culture to that of a 'rugby club'. Newspaper headlines that followed the publication of the report in 1983 included:

DRUNKS AND BULLIES IN THE MET POLICE

(19 November, *Birmingham Post*)

DRUNK, DISHONEST, PREJUDICED AND BULLIES

(19 November, *The Daily Record*)

RACISTS IN BLUE

(19 November, *The Sun*)

SHAMING OF LONDON POLICE … RACIALIST, SEXIST, DRUNKEN AND BULLYING SAYS THEIR OWN REPORT

(18 November, *The Standard*)

GUILTY: RACIALISM, CORRUPTION, BRUTALITY AND ABUSE

(25 November, *Caribbean Times*)

LONDON'S RACIST POLICE

(26 November, *The Voice*) (quoted in Henry, 2007: 13)

A number of high profile cases in which police officers were alleged either to have used excessive force or, alternatively, to have failed to provide adequate protection, or to have failed to respond appropriately to requests for help, appeared in the 1970s and 1980s and have continued since. During this period, general public confidence in the police has declined. What, then, of the views of minority ethnic communities? The Home Office Citizenship Survey, conducted in 2001, asked respondents a series of questions about trust in criminal justice. Between 70–80 per cent of all ethnic minority groups reported trusting the police 'a lot' or 'a fair amount' with the exception of black respondents of whom only 59 per cent replied in this way. The survey also asked respondents whether they expected to be treated worse than other ethnic groups when using various criminal justice services. Again, the police service fares relatively poorly, with black respondents six times more likely than white respondents to say they expected to be treated worse – though the prison service was also rated very similarly (see Figure 31.10).

In addition to such 'snap-shot' data, the availability of research in the 1980s (*Police and People in London* – PPL, Smith *et al.*, 1983) and more recently in 2000 (*Policing for London* – PFL, Fitzgerald *et al.*, 2002) allows for some assessment of change over the last 20 years to be made. The PFL survey included a series of questions which replicated those asked in PPL. They covered the issue of police integrity and included views about police use of unnecessary force, the use of violence in police stations, planting of evidence, taking bribes and extracting favours.

Hough (2007) reports what he describes as two conflicting trends. On the negative side, the proportion of people believing that the police never act illegally has dropped markedly. Thus, for example in the PPL survey in the early 1980s, 63 per cent of respondents said that they believed the police never used excessive force at arrest and 40 per cent said they believed the police never fabricated evidence. By the time of the PFL survey in 2000 the proportions had dropped to 45 per cent and 29 per cent respectively. On the positive side, the proportion believing that illegal behaviour by the police is common has remained relatively stable.

The two surveys also asked questions about discrimination. Respondents were asked to what extent they felt the police treated particular groups unfairly. Crucially for our purposes here respondents were asked about police treatment of ethnic minorities. Whereas in the PPL survey in 1981 just over a fifth (22%) said they thought the police

Figure 31.10   Respondents (%) expecting to be treated worse than people of different ethnic origin by different criminal justice agencies, by ethnic group, 2001

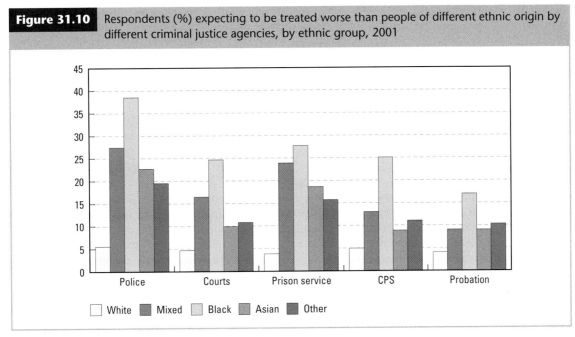

Source: Hearnden and Hough (2004).

Table 31.3   Beliefs about police malpractice: % saying the police treat ethnic minorities unfairly

Ethnic group	1981 (PPL) – %	2000 (PFL) – %
Black	48	53
Asian	36	39
White	20	34

Source: Hough (2007).

treated ethnic minorities unfairly, the proportion had increased to over a third (36%) by the PFL survey in 2000. Moreover, a comparison of the surveys according to the ethnicity of respondents shows that black and Asian respondents not only hold more negative views of the police, but that these have deteriorated over the past 20 years (though it is important to note how substantially the views of white respondents have also declined) (see Table 31.3).

From Scarman to Lawrence

In the aftermath of the 1981 riots, Lord Scarman was appointed to inquire into the causes of the unrest in Brixton and to make recommendations (Scarman, 1982) (see also Chapter 25). Scarman was critical of the policing of Brixton and especially the heavy-handed 'Swamp 81' 'street saturation' operation. Almost 950 'stops' had been made in the course of this operation, resulting in 118 arrests. More than half the people stopped were black. A total of 75 charges were brought, though only one was for robbery, one for attempted burglary, and 20 for theft or attempted theft. As a result of his inquiry, Scarman concluded that the lack of consultation with community representatives prior to 'Swamp 81' was 'an error of judgement' (Scarman, 1982: 4.73), that the whole operation 'was a serious mistake, given the tension which existed between the police and local community' (*ibid*, 4.76) and that 'had policing attitudes and methods been adjusted to deal fully with the problems of a multi-racial society, there would have been a review in depth of the public order implications of the operation, which would have included local consultation'.

In relation to the nature of the policing service being delivered to minority communities, Scarman explicitly rejected 'institutional racism' as an explanation for the problems that had precipitated the Inquiry. However, in the careful language of an eminent lawyer, he went on to note that if 'the suggestion being made is that practices may be adopted by public bodies as well as private individuals which are *unwittingly discriminatory* against black people, then this is an allegation which deserves serious consideration, and, where proved, swift remedy' (Scarman, 1981, *emphasis added*).

As Stuart Hall noted at the time (1982: 68) 'the idea that oppressive policing is not a set of fortuitous events but a process, a structural condition, is beyond [Scarman's] grasp. The concept of "institutional racism" is not merely repugnant to his sympathies. It is unthinkable within his discourse. This is one limit-point to his reformism.' Nevertheless, the report emphasised the need for change and, despite its limitations, 'was the trigger for a reorientation of policing on a wide front. Indeed by the late 1980s, [Scarman's] ideas had become the predominant conception of policing philosophy amongst Chief Constables' (Reiner, 1991). Although, from today's perspective, elements of the Scarman Report may seem somewhat timid, at the time they constituted something of a 'wake-up call' for both the police and the government.

A little over ten years later, on 22 April 1993, 18 year-old Stephen Lawrence was stabbed to death in Eltham, South London. Stephen Lawrence was by no means alone in being subject to a vicious racist assault. There were numerous other cases at the time and, of course, they continue (Bowling, 1999). However, partly because of the way in which the case was handled, and partly because of the public campaign that was subsequently mounted by family and supporters, the case focused attention on racist victimization and, once again, on the attitudes and behaviour of the police.

Attacked at a bus stop by a small group of hostile and abusive white youths, Stephen Lawrence was

Stephen Lawrence, stabbed to death in Eltham, South London, on 22 April 1993. The subsequent inquiry into his murder found that the police investigation had been 'marred by a combination of professional incompetence, institutional racism and a failure of leadership by senior officers'.

stabbed twice and died within a short period of time. The police investigation found no witnesses to the attack other than Stephen Lawrence's friend, Duwayne Brooks, who was with him at the time of the attack, and 'other sound evidence against the prime suspects [was] conspicuous by its absence' (Macpherson, 1999: para 2.2). A private prosecution was launched against five suspects in 1996 but failed because of lack of evidence (two suspects were discharged at the committal stage and the other three, who went to trial, were acquitted). Ominously the verdict of the inquest jury was that 'Stephen Lawrence was unlawfully killed in a completely unprovoked racist attack by five white youths'. It is still the case that no one has been successfully charged with Stephen Lawrence's murder.

The Home Secretary met with Stephen Lawrence's parents in June 1997 and afterwards said that 'it is not an option to let this matter rest. I recognise that a strong case has been made by Mrs Lawrence for some form of inquiry and I am actively considering what she put to me' (Macpherson, 1991, Appendix 1). The decision to establish an inquiry, chaired by Sir William Macpherson of Cluny (formerly a High Court Judge), was announced on 31 July 1997, the terms of reference of which were: 'To inquire into the matters arising from the death of Stephen Lawrence on 22 April 1993 to date, in order particularly to identify the lessons to be learned for the investigation and prosecution of racially motivated crimes'.

The inquiry reported in February 1999 and memorably said that:

> The conclusions to be drawn from the evidence in connection with the investigation of Stephen Lawrence's racist murder are clear. There is no doubt but that there were fundamental errors. The investigation was marred by a combination of professional incompetence, institutional racism and a failure of leadership by senior officers. A flawed MPS [Metropolitan Police Service] review failed to expose these inadequacies. The second investigation could not salvage the faults of the first investigation. (Macpherson, 1991: para 46.1)

The 'professional incompetence' included a lack of direction and organisation in the hours after the murder, little or no pursuit of the suspects, insensitive treatment of both the Lawrence family and Duwayne Brooks, inadequate processing of intelligence, ill-thought-out surveillance and inadequate searches. At least as, if not more damningly, the inquiry concluded that incompetence could not alone account for the failure of the Metropolitan Police. Rather, it suggested that the very fact that the victim was black led directly to less competent behaviour on the part of officers, in particular with regard to their actions at the scene of the crime, in connection with family liaison, the treatment of Duwayne Brooks and in the use of inappropriate and offensive language. The Service, the inquiry suggested, was 'institutionally racist'. This it defined (para 6.34) as:

> The collective failure of an organisation to provide an appropriate and professional service to people because of their colour, culture or ethnic origin. It can be seen or detected in processes, attitudes and behaviour which amount to discrimination through unwitting prejudice, ignorance, thoughtlessness, and racist stereotyping which disadvantage minority ethnic people.

The inquiry made 70 recommendations which covered:

- the monitoring and assessment of police performance;
- the reporting and recording of racist incidents and crimes;
- the investigation and prosecution of racist crime;
- family liaison;
- the treatment of victims and witnesses;
- first aid;
- training;
- employment, discipline and complaints;
- stop and search;
- recruitment and retention.

These recommendations amounted 'to the most extensive programme of reform in the history of the relationship between the police and ethnic minority communities' (Bowling and Phillips, 2002: 16). At the centre of the recommendations was a proposed Ministerial Priority for the police to seek to 'increase trust and confidence in policing among minority ethnic communities'.

The vast majority of the inquiry's recommendations were accepted by the Home Office (56 were accepted in full, five in part and seven were referred to the Law Commission for further examination); the Home Secretary published an action plan for their implementation and has subsequently published two annual reports detailing the progress that

has been made. The climate of policing has changed since Lawrence. The HMIC Thematic Inspection on Police and Community Relations (1999: 9), for example, found evidence 'on this inspection that many officers partly due to publicity around Sir William Macpherson's Inquiry have race issues in the forefront of their minds'. However, the thematic also reported 'that whilst a number of forces are at the cutting edge of progress in this field, the approach by a large section of the police service is less than satisfactory' (HMIC, 1999: 3).

Though the pace of change within the police service may be relatively slow, the Lawrence case did have an appreciable impact on the political climate. As Reiner (2000: 211) notes, 'the Macpherson Report ... has transformed the terms of the political debate about black people and criminal justice ... what had not [previously] featured in public awareness and political debate was the disproportionate rate at which black people suffered as victims of crime'. In this, the Macpherson Inquiry achieved something that Scarman hadn't. Moreover, as Bowling and Phillips (2002: 18) note:

> Where Scarman was hesitant on the question of accountability, Macpherson was strident. Since the Lawrence Inquiry had concluded that the failings of the police were systemic and the result of insufficient accountability, it recommended the introduction of lay oversight into all areas of police work, and the creation of a fully independent complaints system. Crucially, the Inquiry recommended bringing the police into the ambit of race relations law, a proposal that had been roundly rejected two decades earlier.

Cautioning, arrest and sentencing

Cautioning rates are roughly similar for those of white, Asian and other ethnic origin, but are almost three times higher for black people. However, such data are difficult to interpret as they can be influenced by a number of factors such as willingness to plead guilty, the attitude of the police toward different groups and, relatedly, the possibility that the police are more willing to take action against some groups than others. The disproportionality between ethnic groups is not as great for arrests as it is for stops but it remains sizeable nonetheless. The incidence of arrests per 1,000 population is now about three times higher for black than for white people. Similarly, the arrest

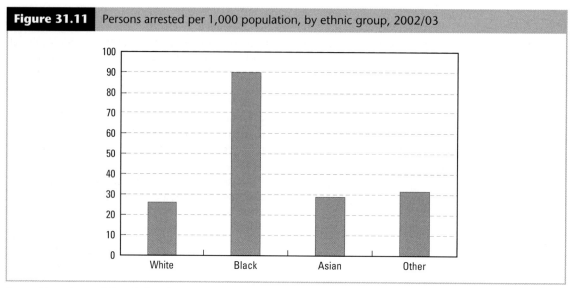

Figure 31.11   Persons arrested per 1,000 population, by ethnic group, 2002/03

Source: Hearnden and Hough (2004).

rate is greater for Asian people than for white people, but the difference is not as great as it is in relation to stops (see Figure 31.11).

Similarly, information on decisions by police concerning whether or not to remand suspects or release them on bail is generally insufficient to make judgements about possible differences between ethnic groups, and the same is largely true in relation to conviction data (Hearnden and Hough, 2004). A study conducted in the 1980s (Walker, 1989) found that black suspects were much more likely to be held at the police station prior to the initial court hearing than was the case for either white or Asian suspects. Similarly, Phillips and Brown (1998) found that ethnicity was an important factor in the police decision to grant or refuse bail, though other studies have raised the possibility that the differential rate is actually a product of the seriousness of the offence concerned (Bucke and Brown, 1997). Court decisions also result in a much higher proportion of black suspects being remanded into custody rather than bailed, though again it is possible that there are some intervening explanatory factors which might explain some of this difference.

Apart from stop and search, sentencing is the other area that has received some rigorous, serious research attention. The most significant study, by Roger Hood (1992), used data from five Crown Court centres in the West Midlands. Overall, Hood found that 40% of Asian defendants, 48% of white defendants, and 57% of black defendants received a custodial sentence. The research involved the construction of 'probability of

custody scores' – statistical estimates of the likelihood of a prison sentence – which could then be compared with the actual sentence of the court. Overall, black defendants had an approximately five per cent greater probability of receiving a custodial sentence than white counterparts. The major differences were primarily the result of custodial sentences in offences of medium seriousness where, arguably, the greatest amount of discretion exists for judges. Hood (1992: 179) concluded:

> The best estimate that it is possible to make from this study is that 80% of the over-representation of black male offenders in the prison population was due to their over-representation among those convicted at the Crown Court and to the type and circumstances of the offences of which black men were convicted. The remaining 20%, in the case of males but not females, appeared to [be] due to differential treatment and other factors which influence the nature and length of the sentences imposed: two thirds of it resulting from the higher proportion of black defendants who pleaded not guilty and who were, as a consequence, more liable on conviction to receive longer custodial sentences.

In terms of differential treatment, Hood found that in some of the less serious cases it appeared that matters that might have been seen as mitigating factors (things which in some way reduced the overall seriousness of the offence) were less likely to be taken into account if the defendant was black compared with the likelihood had they been white.

Furthermore, in four of the five Crown Court centres Hood found significant racial differences in the use of custody – both in terms of the likelihood of custody and in the length of sentence. He concluded, 'When one contrasts the overall treatment meted out to black Afro-Caribbean males one is left wondering whether it is not a result of different racial stereotypes operating on the perceptions of some judges' (1992: 188).

More recent research by Shute *et al.* (2005) found there to have been some apparent improvement in this area, with a lower than expected proportion of defendants (between one-quarter and one-third) from ethnic minorities reporting that they felt that they had been treated in a racially biased way. There is no room for complacency, they conclude, for among those minority ethnic defendants who feel they have been unfairly treated, six out of ten attribute this to racial bias.

Ethnicity and imprisonment

The indisputable end product of the criminal justice system is the jailing of proportionately more black people than people of other ethnic origins (see Figure 31.12). Historically, such over-representation has been even greater in the remand than in the sentenced prison population. The reasons for this, as we have seen above, are by no means entirely clear. Using census data and information from a national prison survey, Fitzgerald and Marshall (1996) have explored this question. They argue that it is possible to identify a number of important socio-economic differences between the main ethnic groups and, crucially, that it is possible that these differences help explain at least part of the disproportionate visibility of minorities in prison. The differences they focused on included:

- employment history (likelihood of being in semi-skilled or unskilled manual occupations);
- family disruption (growing up with only one parent and spending time in local authority care);
- educational difficulties (particularly absence from school through truancy).

Their conclusion is that the evidence they present adds weight to socio-economic arguments, though they by no means discount the possibility that racism at various stages of the criminal justice process may also play a part.

The black prison population rate per 1,000 population is over four times higher than that for whites and about seven and a half times that for Asians. Such disproportionality has existed for some time. However, there is evidence that within the rise in the overall incarceration rate that has been taking place over the past decade, the differences between different ethnic groups are quite marked (see Figure 31.13).

The final stage of the criminal justice process is *parole* – the release of prisoners on licence at a certain point in their sentence (sometimes referred to as discretionary conditional release) if they have been serving at least four years in prison. A Home Office study of over 6,000 parole decisions taken in

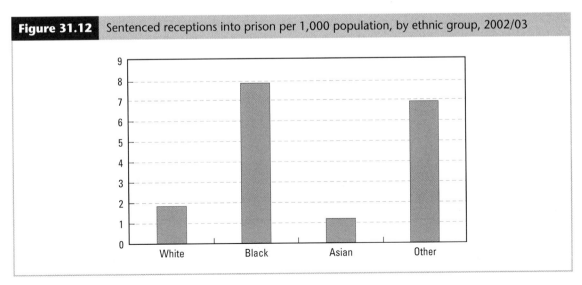

Figure 31.12   Sentenced receptions into prison per 1,000 population, by ethnic group, 2002/03

Source: Hearnden and Hough (2004).

Figure 31.13 Prison population, percentage change since 1993, by ethnic group, 1994–2002

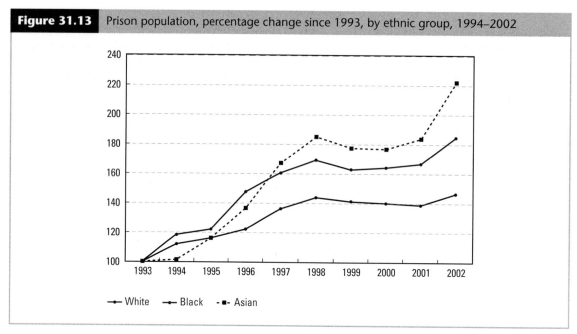

Source: Hearnden and Hough (2004).

1999/2000 (Moorthy *et al.*, 2004) found that women were far more successful in parole hearings than men, and that South Asians and people of Chinese/other ethnic origin were also more likely to be granted parole (see Table 31.4).

The authors built a predictive model to attempt to explain how parole decisions were made. An initial model which included such factors as: behaviour during sentence; location of the applicant; type of offence; age; offending history, etc. was successfully able to predict approximately three-quarters of the outcomes. Interestingly, adding ethnicity to the model didn't improve its accuracy, leading the authors to conclude that there was 'no evidence of differential treatment of minority ethnic prisoners by the parole board, and that differences in parole release rates between ethnic groups were likely to result from other characteristics associated with release' (2004: 6).

Treatment in custody

Of course, it is not just the brute fact of over-representation, there is also the question of how people are treated whilst in prison service custody. A number of high profile cases in recent years have drawn attention to some very significant problems of racism and the absence of appropriate protection for vulnerable prisoners. Research conducted in the 1980s by Genders and Player (1989) used qualitative methods to explore the impact of the Prison Department's new policies on race, and found the issue of 'race relations' to be very low on the agenda of most prison staff. However, they found some clear evidence of the application of racial stereotypes by prison staff – consistently categorising black prisoners as uneducated, for example – together with other forms of discrimination. Prison service race relations policies have been reformed

Table 31.4 Prisoners considered and released on parole in 1999/2000 by ethnic group

	White	Black	South Asian	Chinese/other	Total
Considered	4,775	1,023	244	166	6,213
Released	1,879	438	156	88	2,561
Release rate	39%	43%	64%	53%	41%

on several occasions since they were first formally introduced in 1986. Nevertheless, research (Burnett and Farrell, 1994; NACRO, 2000) has continued to find fairly clear evidence of both direct and indirect discrimination, including:

- Verbal and physical abuse, threats and harassment in relations between prisoners and prisoners and staff. In Burnett and Farrell's (1994) study, for example, one-third of Asian respondents and one-quarter of African-Caribbean respondents reported being racially abused or attacked by other inmates.
- Differential use by prison officers of discretion over offences, punishments and complaints.
- Lack of specialist products (food, hair products, magazines, etc.).
- Differential allocation to cells, wings and other prisons.
- Differential access to jobs and training (see Ellis *et al.*, 2004).

One of the areas that ties together inadequate health care provision and questions of racism is sickle cell anaemia. An inherited blood disorder that affects people of African, Caribbean, Indian, Mediterranean and Arab descent, sickle cell anaemia is one of many conditions that appears to be poorly dealt with in the prison system (Dyson and Boswell, 2006). Moreover, it has been misused by various commentators as a means of explaining sudden deaths, particularly those associated with forced restraint. In 1998 the then Director General of the Prison Service, Richard Tilt, questioned an inquest verdict of unlawful killing after the death of a black prisoner, Alton Manning, in prison service custody. Tilt raised the possibility that sickle cell anaemia may have played a role in the relatively high number of deaths in custody of African-Caribbeans. However, sickle cell anaemia affects about 1 in 300 people of African-Caribbean descent, making it rather implausible that it is precisely these people who not only end up in custody, but are the ones who are subject to extreme forms of restraint. More likely, Dyson and Boswell (2006) argue, it is a convenient means of drawing attention away from the possibility of institutional racism in the provision of services.

Deaths in custody

One area of the treatment of minorities in the criminal justice system that has caused some controversy for years now is the issue of deaths in custody. There have been a number of high profile cases that have raised concerns about the care and treatment of suspects in custody, whether by the police or by the prison service, a great many of which have involved black and minority ethnic victims. One of the first concerned a young man, Stephen McCarthy, arrested in Islington in November 1970 after a violent confrontation. Allegedly assaulted by police officers during his arrest, McCarthy's condition deteriorated during the seven weeks he spent in custody in Wormwood Scrubs and Dover Borstal (Benn and Worpole, 1986) and he was admitted to hospital in early January 1971 with violent headaches and vomiting. He went into a coma and died on 26 January. The subsequent inquest brought in a verdict of 'death by natural causes', but noted that there had been insufficient care given at Wormwood Scrubs. McCarthy's family and friends, convinced that there had been a serious miscarriage of justice, mounted a vigorous campaign. Demands for a public inquiry fell on deaf ears despite the vociferous public protests:

> The march to the police station [in Islington]; disbelieving outbursts in court; the repeated calls for a Public Inquiry that are then peremptorily dismissed; the demonstrations and unnecessary sometimes violent arrests; all these elements of the McCarthy case were to be repeated in subsequent years with increasingly serious political consequences. (Benn and Worpole, 1986: 18)

The death of Liddle Towers in 1976 is a clear illustration of this point. Towers, aged 39 at the time, was arrested outside a nightclub in Gateshead early in 1976. Eyewitnesses alleged that he was severely beaten by the eight arresting officers. He was also kept in the police station overnight and then released but 'was so ill and badly injured that he could hardly move' (Scraton and Chadwick, 1987: 72). Towers died three weeks after his arrest. No police officers were prosecuted, no breach of force discipline was held to have taken place, and the subsequent inquest returned a verdict of 'justifiable homicide'. More recently, the case of Christopher Alder, who died in police custody in Hull in 1998, led to an investigation by the Independent Police Complaints Commission (IPCC). The IPCC described Alder's death as 'unnecessary, undignified and unnoticed' and its chairman, Nick Hardwick, went on to say that his 'grim conclusions' were 'not that Mr Alder mattered enough to those who dealt with him on that night nearly eight years ago for them to conspire to kill him – but that he did not matter enough for them to do all they could to save him' (http://www.ipcc.gov. uk/christopher_alder_review.htm).

The reason for raising this issue here is that there is some evidence of ethnic differences in relation to this most extreme end of the treatment of suspects in custody. Home Office research conducted in the late 1990s (Leigh *et al.*, 1998) examined the causes of death in police custody between 1990–96, as well as exploring the nature of the cases concerned and the backgrounds of the offenders. Although the number of cases involved (275) was not large enough to provide statistically significant results, the authors nevertheless found some potentially important differences:

- a smaller proportion of black than white detainees were arrested for alcohol-related offences;

- a larger proportion of white than black detainees died from in-custody deliberate self-harm or from medical conditions;

- over one-third of cases in which a black detainee died occurred in circumstances in which police actions may have been a factor (the proportion rises to almost one-half if the cases of accidental death where the police were present were added) – this compared with only four per cent of cases where the detainee was white.

Views of the criminal justice system

Research evidence on views of the criminal justice system among different ethnic groups reveals some interesting findings. We will begin by looking at criminal justice generally, and consider perceptions of *effectiveness, confidence* and *fairness,* before moving on to consider minority ethnic views of the police in particular.

Zahid Mubarek

Among all the recent cases involving racism within prisons, arguably it was the death of Zahid Mubarek which raised the greatest concerns. Mubarek, a 19 year-old Asian man, was in Feltham Young Offenders' Institution serving his first prison sentence of 90 days having been found guilty of theft and interfering with a motor vehicle. He was placed in a cell with another young offender, Robert Stewart, who held extreme right-wing views and had spent the bulk of the previous three years in custody for a range of offences, including violence.

On the night of 21 March 2000, Stewart attacked Mubarek with a table leg, hitting him between seven to 11 times on the head. He died later of the injuries sustained in the attack. An inquiry by the Commission for Racial Equality in the case found that at the 'subsequent trial in Kingston Crown Court, the evidence, which included letters recovered from the cell and from recipients by the police, showed clearly that Stewart was a seriously disturbed and unstable young man. His lurid and confused letters were pervaded with crude racial hatred and expressions of violence' (CRE, 2003). The CRE Inquiry concluded:

> The conclusion of the investigation is that, had proper practice been followed in the specific failure areas the investigation identified, then the murder would not have taken place ... The cumulative effect of these failures meant that Zahid Mubarek,

as an ethnic minority prisoner in Feltham, was not provided with the equivalent protection available to prisoners who were white. Had [he] been white he would not have experienced a racially motivated assault by Robert Stewart.

The CRE Inquiry lends further confirmation to Bowling and Phillips' (2002: 208) conclusion that the 'deaths of ethnic minorities while in prison custody indicates a pattern of excessive physical restraint, misdiagnosis, disbelieving inmates' claims concerning their health, or the provision of inadequate or inappropriate medical treatment by prison officers and medical staff'.

For further information go to: http://www.zahidmubarekinquiry.org.uk/article.asp?c=374&aid=2848

Figure 31.14 Criminal justice agencies felt to be doing a 'good' or 'excellent' job (%), by ethnic group, 2002/03

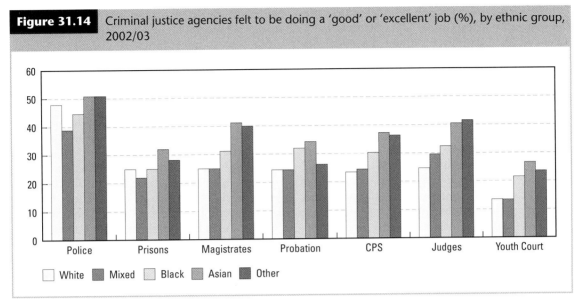

Source: Hearnden and Hough (2004).

British Crime Survey data on the question of effectiveness suggest that Asian respondents and, in relation to most agencies, those in the 'other' category, give the criminal justice system higher ratings than do other ethnic groups. In addition, a higher proportion of black than white respondents consider the Probation Service, CPS, judges and the youth court to be doing a 'good' or 'excellent' job. Prisons are rated equally, and a very slightly higher proportion of white than black respondents rate police performance highly. Those of mixed origin rated the police lowest, and also tended to have the lowest estimation of most criminal justice agencies (see Figure 31.14).

Figure 31.15 Confidence (% very or fairly confident) in the criminal justice system, by ethnic group, 2002//03

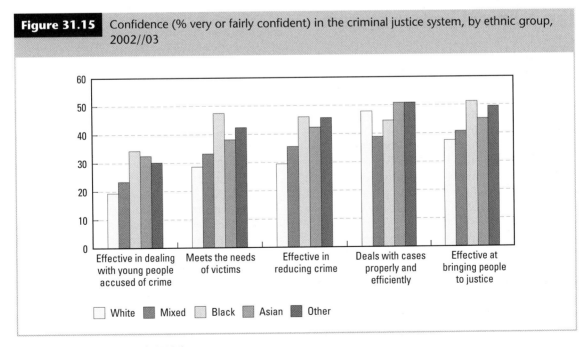

Source: Hearnden and Hough (2004).

Interestingly, confidence in criminal justice agencies generally appears to be higher among black, other and Asian respondents to the BCS when compared with white respondents. This was true in relation to all five major questions asked by the survey (see Figure 31.15). Interestingly, it seems that confidence in criminal justice agencies among minorities is higher in Britain than in some other countries. In the US, whereas 24 per cent of white respondents in 2004 expressed low levels of confidence in the criminal justice system, the figure was 38 per cent for black respondents (Hough and Roberts, 2005). Indeed, the differences in confidence levels in criminal justice agencies in America have been described by Sherman (2002) as a 'racial divide'.

Although, as the two figures above show, minority ethnic groups tend to have relatively positive views of the criminal justice system when asked about its effectiveness, the same cannot be said when questions are asked about fairness. The BCS finds that a smaller proportion of black respondents (65%) express confidence that the criminal justice will respect the rights of people accused of crime compared with white respondents (78%), and a number of surveys have identified experiences of, and attitudes towards, the police as being of central importance in this relative lack of confidence.

Minority representation in the criminal justice system

Of all the areas of criminal justice, it is policing that has seen the most long-standing debate over minority representation. Certainly since the Scarman Inquiry in the early 1980s there has been considerable concern about both the general under-representation of minorities in the police service, and the lack of visibility of minorities at senior levels. Though this issue has been pretty much an ever-present concern over the past two decades and longer, it was forcefully brought to public attention once again by the Macpherson Inquiry established in the aftermath of the murder of Stephen Lawrence and by the broadcasting of the *Secret Policeman* television programme by the BBC in 2003.

In the programme, filmed in a police training centre in Warrington, recruits to the police service were filmed by an undercover reporter and seen to be making extreme racist remarks. Eight officers were identified in the programme as holding unacceptable views: 'In the course of a series of "private" conversations between [the reporter] and

these officers they convey a visceral hatred of Asians, show a willingness to discriminate on racial grounds as soon as they were assigned to operational duties, and disclose strong sympathy for far right political groups' (McLaughlin, 2007: 29). The programme was particularly shocking for a police service that was still seeking to recover from the aftermath of the Stephen Lawrence Inquiry. As a consequence of this exposure, ten officers resigned and a further 12 were disciplined.

In the aftermath of the Lawrence Inquiry and the *Secret Policeman* revelations, two further inquiries were established to examine race relations in policing: one conducted by the Commission for Racial Equality (CRE) and led by Sir David Calvert-Smith, former director of the CPS, and one undertaken by the Metropolitan Police Authority (MPA) chaired by Sir Bill Morris, former general secretary of the Transport and General Workers Union. The Morris Inquiry ranged widely, covering management, governance and accountability, professional standards – including reviewing two very high-profile disciplinary cases involving Superintendent Ali Dizaei and Sergeant Gurpal Virdi – and employment matters. The inquiry concluded that: 'Having considered the evidence on complaints and discipline, we are concerned that some managers lack the confidence to manage black and minority ethnic officers without being affected by their race. The statistics indicate clear disproportionality in the way black and minority ethnic officers are treated in relation to the management of their conduct. This represents a serious issue of discrimination which must be tackled as a matter of priority' (Morris, 2004).

The CRE Inquiry report was similarly critical, concluding that the police service was 'like a perma frost – thawing on the top, but still frozen solid at the core'. Calvert-Smith commented:

> There is no doubt that the Police Service has made significant progress in the area of race equality in recent years. However, there is still a long way to go before we have a service where every officer treats the public and their colleagues with fairness and respect, regardless of their ethnic origin. Willingness to change at the top is not translating into action lower down, particularly in middle-management where you find the ice in the heart of the Police Service. For example, managers are not properly supported or fully trained on how to handle race grievances, so relatively minor issues are often unnecessarily escalated.
> (www.cre.gov.uk/Default.aspx.LocID-0hgnew058. RefLocID-0hg00900c001001.Lang-EN.htm)

Mike Fuller, the first black chief constable in England and Wales. He was appointed Chief Constable, Kent Police, in January 2004, having previously been a deputy assistant commissioner in the Metropolitan Police Service.

Table 31.5	Minority ethnic officers in the police service, by rank	
Rank rank	**Number**	**% of all in**
ACPO	7	2.6
Superintendent	38	2.4
Inspector	236	2.6
Sergeant	569	2.6
PC	4449	4.0

Source: Clegg and Kirwan (2006).

Home Office (2002) figures suggest that there have been some improvements in both overall recruitment from minority ethnic groups to the police service, and more generally in the criminal justice system. Nevertheless, there continue to be some very clear problems and all black and minority ethnic groups, for example, are under-represented in the police service. Figures on the ethnic composition of the police service as a whole show that there are 2.6 white officers per 1,000 population. The figures for other groups are 1.3 for those of 'mixed' ethnic origin, 1.2 Asian and other, and only 0.5 per 1,000 for those classified as black (Hearnden and Hough, 2004). Furthermore, the available evidence suggests that there is even greater under-representation at senior ranks. Thus, by March 2006, only seven of the 226 ACPO rank officers and only 38 of the 1,601 superintendents or chief superintendents were from ethnic minorities (see Table 31.5).

Stone and Tuffin's (2000) research on the attitudes of ethnic minorities toward working in the police service uncovered a range of factors that served to make such a prospect unattractive. They included:

- The thought of having to work in a racist environment and having to face prejudice from colleagues and the public.
- The prospect of having to deny their cultural identity in order to fit in.
- The anticipated reactions of friends or family.
- Concerns about pressures from the local community over loyalties.
- A perception that minority ethnic police officers have little or no promotion prospects.

It is not just difficulties in recruitment to the police service but, once recruited, there are also considerable problems in retention. The 'wastage rates' in the police service (trained officers resigning from the force) are greatest for ethnic minority officers. Indeed, resignation accounts for the single largest group of ethnic minority 'leavers' from the police and, if retirement, transfer and death are controlled for, resignation accounts for over three-fifths of ethnic minority leavers compared with under a third of white leavers (see Figure 31.16).

One of the areas of the police service that has experienced much greater success in the recruitment of minorities is that of police community support officers. Research by Johnston (2006) on the Metropolitan Police Service in 2002/03 found that around 44 per cent of applicants and about 32 per cent of recruits were from ethnic minorities. As many recruits to the ranks of PCSOs join because they wish eventually to become police officers, the greater minority representation among such officers

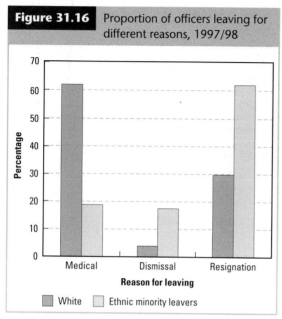

Figure 31.16 Proportion of officers leaving for different reasons, 1997/98

Source: Bland *et al.* (1999).

has been held out by some senior police commentators as indicating some potential for subsequent improvements in minority recruitment to the police

service itself. However, Johnston's research found that ethnic-minority PCSOs were doing less well than their white colleagues in the 'fast track' process that leads to becoming a police officer. The danger in the longer-term, he argued, 'is that a particularly unbalanced form of two-tier policing might emerge over time in which a predominantly white, male, regular police service works alongside a body of PCSOs made up, disproportionately, of female and minority ethnic personnel' (2006: 399).

S.95 data provide information on all the main criminal justice agencies and suggest that such under-representation is not typical across criminal justice. Both the police and the prison service have proportionately fewer minority ethnic employees than the equivalent in the population as a whole, but the other major agencies fare rather better in this regard. However, people from minority ethnic groups are under-represented at senior levels in all the main criminal justice agencies, and this under-representation is particularly well illustrated in the case of circuit judges (see Figure 31.17).

The proportion of black and minority ethnic officers in the prison service in 2004/05 was 4.4 per cent. Although this is an increase on previous years, it remains disproportionately low. Black and minority ethnic groups accounted for almost eight per cent of

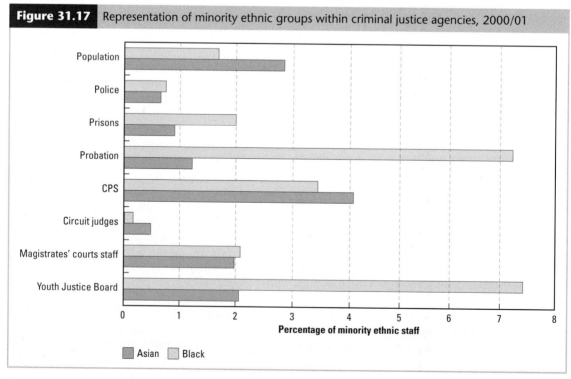

Figure 31.17 Representation of minority ethnic groups within criminal justice agencies, 2000/01

Source: Home Office (2002).

all recruits to the prison service in 2004/05, but also accounted for approximately seven per cent of those that left prison service employment. A study of ethnic-minority staff in the prison system conducted by the Commission for Racial Equality and the Prison Reform Trust (2003) found that:

- Covert and structural racism were more widespread causes of concern than blatant racist discrimination.

- Over three-fifths (61%) said that they had experienced direct racial discrimination while employed in prisons.

- Minority ethnic prison staff were more likely to have experienced direct racial discrimination from their colleagues than from prisoners or managers.

- Two-thirds of respondents felt that institutional racism was a problem in their workplace, with 15 per cent feeling that the problem was severe.

- Over half of those who experienced racism chose not to report it.

Under-representation in criminal justice professions – particularly at senior levels – and over-representa-tion as suspects, arrestees, defendants and among those serving sentences in prison and in the community, perhaps captures the central problem confronting us when considering the area of ethnicity and criminal justice. There are important, ongoing debates about how over-representation is to be understood and how under-representation is to be tackled. Moreover, with the emergence of new tensions around immigration and asylum and the highly racialised ways in which the threat of international terrorism is often understood and discussed, these are likely to be areas of increasing rather than decreasing concern in coming years.

> **Review questions**
>
> 1   What are the main barriers to increasing minority representation in the police?
>
> 2   What is meant by 'available population' in relation to stop and search?
>
> 3   What is meant by the phrase 'over-policed and under-protected'?

Questions for further discussion

1   To what extent do self-report data match up with the presentation of race and crime in the media?

2   What are the main patterns of offending and victimization in terms of race and ethnicity?

3   What are the arguments for and against treating 'hate crimes' more seriously than other offences?

4   What might be the shortcomings of a focus on 'community cohesion' in responding to the types of disturbance that occurred in Oldham, Burnley and elsewhere?

5   Is the over-representation of ethnic minorities in stop and search figures an illustration of institutional racism?

Further reading

The starting point for following up any of the areas covered in this chapter should be:

Bowling, B. and Phillips, C. (2002) *Racism, Crime and Justice,* Harlow: Longman (and see also the chapter by the same authors in the 4th edition of *The Oxford Handbook of Criminology*)

Webster, C. (2007) *Understanding Race and Crime,* Maidenhead: Open University Press

Then there are a number of useful books of specific aspects of this topic:

Hood, R. (1992) *Race and Sentencing,* Oxford: Oxford University Press

Rowe, M. (2005) *Policing, Race and Racism,* Cullompton: Willan

Rowe, M. (ed.) (2007) *Policing Beyond Macpherson,* Cullompton: Willan

A lot of useful information on minority over-representation in the criminal justice system has recently been produced by the Home Affairs Committee:

Home Affairs Committee (2007) *Young Black People and the Criminal Justice System,* London: The Stationery Office

Finally, anyone wishing to look at the international position would do well to start with:

Tonry, M. (ed.)(1997) *Ethnicity, Crime and Immigration: Comparative and cross-national perspectives,* Chicago: University of Chicago Press

Websites

There is a lot of useful material contained on the Home Office website drawing on s.95 data: http: //www.homeoffice.gov.uk/rds/pubsstatistical.html

There are a number of official reports available on the web including:

The Stephen Lawrence Inquiry: http: //www.archive.official-documents.co.uk/document/cm42/4262/sli-00.htm

The IPCC report into the death of Christopher Alder: http: //www.official-documents.gov.uk/document/hc0506/hc09/0971/0971_i.asp

The report of the Zahid Mubarek Inquiry: http: //www.zahidmubarekinquiry.org.uk/

The Cantle Report can be found at www.oldham.gov.uk

Chapter outline

Female and male offending 806
  Reasons for offending 808

Women and the criminal justice process 810
  Cautioning, arrest and prosecution 810
  The use of custody 811
  Women in prison 813
    Mothers in prison 815
  Understanding women and criminal justice 817
  Women in the criminal justice system: the future 818

Victimization 818
  Fear of crime 819
  Violence against women 819
    Domestic violence 820
    The perpetrators 821
  Policing rape and domestic violence 822
    Policy changes 823
  Attrition 825

Women's role in social control 828
  Women in the police 828
  Women in the probation service 830
  Women as prison officers 830
  Women and the legal professions 830

Masculinities, men and victimization 831
  Male victimization 832
  Conclusion 833

Questions for further discussion 834
Further reading 834
Websites 834

32

Gender, crime and justice

CHAPTER SUMMARY

Earlier in the book we explored in some detail the question what is 'crime'? One of the things that discussion revealed was that crime is something which varies historically and culturally. Moreover, our understanding of crime and our responses to it are highly 'gendered'. That is to say, we appear to take somewhat different approaches to male and female offending. Thus, for example, it has generally been male homosexuality rather than lesbianism that has been subject to regulation through the criminal law. The laws surrounding prostitution have been designed primarily with the regulation of women in mind. These and other differences raise a number of questions and we will return to the differential application of the law throughout this chapter.

This chapter is about:

● *sex* and *gender* and crime;

● innate characteristics of men and women (sex);

● the socially constructed ways of being that we associate with men and women (gender) and how these relate to what we know about crime.

Female and male offending

One of the most regularly-observed features of the criminological landscape is that the bulk of crime appears to be undertaken by boys and men (Gottfredson and Hirschi, 1990). Indeed, 'sex differences in criminality are so sustained and so marked as to be, perhaps, the most significant feature of recorded crime' (Heidensohn, 1996: 11). Relatively speaking, however measured, women tend to be much less involved in most sorts of offending. The proportion of women with a conviction is lower at all ages than that for males. Using data from a cohort of people born in 1953, the Home Office estimated that by the age of 46, 33 per cent of males had received at least one conviction compared with nine per cent of women. The difference is similar for younger age groups. Of females born in 1958, nine per cent had received a conviction by the age of 40, compared with 32 per cent of males. By their mid-40s, approximately one per cent of all women will have received a prison sentence compared with seven per cent of men (Barclay and Tavares, 1999).

Research conducted by the Home Office in the mid-1990s found that over half of males and almost one-third of females aged between 14 and 25 admitted to committing one or more criminal offences at some point in their lives (Home Office, 1995a). A more recent self-report study found that ten to 17 year-olds were responsible for 35 per cent

of the incidents measured even though they comprised only 14 per cent of the sample (Budd *et al.*, 2005). The same study found that approximately one-third of young males and just under one-fifth of young females aged between ten and 25 reported having committed at least one offence in the past year (see Figure 32.1).

Estimates of the peak age of offending vary, but generally place it somewhere between 15 (MORI, 2004) and 18 (Criminal Statistics, 2004). The estimated peak age of offending is higher for males than it is for females. Home Office self-report survey data identifies the 16–17 year age group as that with the highest prevalence of offending for males, with that for females being slightly younger at approximately 14–15 (see Figure 32.2). Official statistics also suggest that the peak age of known male offending has increased; it was 14 years in 1971, 15 in 1980, and increased to 18 by 1990, where it has since remained.

The location of the peak age of offending in the mid- to late-adolescent years has traditionally been taken as indicating that a significant proportion of young people will simply 'grow out of crime' (Rutherford, 1992). Again, however, there are important differences between males and females. A far higher proportion of female offenders are convicted only once by their mid-40s (74%) compared with male offenders (50%). Similarly, whereas approximately four-fifths of female offenders have criminal careers of less than one year (as measured by their lifetime criminal convictions), this is the

Figure 32.1 10–25 year-olds committing offences in last 12 months, by sex (%)

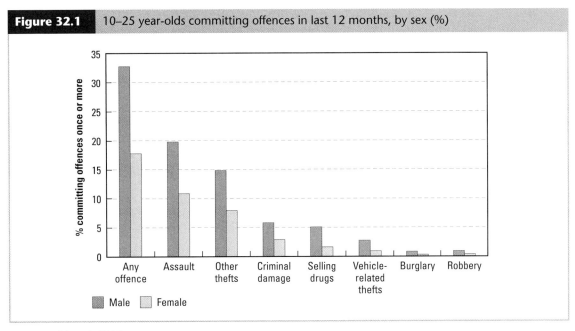

Source: Budd *et al.*, 2005.

Figure 32.2 Last year prevalence of offending, by age (%)

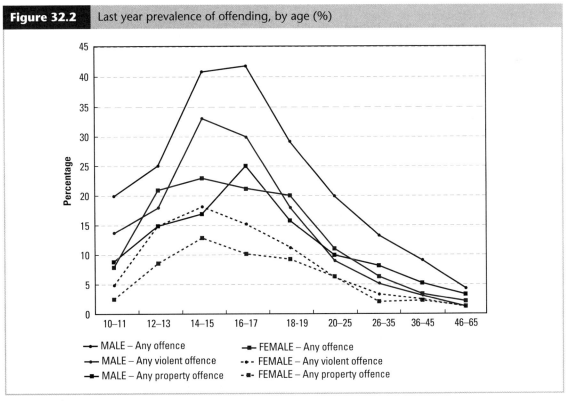

Source: Budd *et al.*, 2005.

case for only 55 per cent of male offenders. As Heidensohn (1996: 8) puts it, 'it does seem that women commit fewer serious crimes and are rather less likely to be recidivists'.

The predominance of property crime among those offences committed by young people is confirmed by official statistics and by self-report studies. Juveniles, irrespective of age or sex, are most likely to be cautioned or convicted for theft and handling stolen goods. Until relatively recently, burglary was the second most common source of cautions and convictions for male juvenile offenders, but the rise in recorded violent offending has seen such offences displace burglary in second place. Table 32.1 below shows the proportions of male and female juveniles in selected age categories found guilty or cautioned of a range of offences (calculated as a proportion of all those males or females in that age group who were cautioned or convicted of an offence).

Self-report data confirm the general picture available from *Criminal Statistics* and help provide a little more detail about patterns of male and female offending. The first point to make is that self-report data appear to indicate that the gap between male and female rates of offending is not as great as official statistics would suggest. Both male and female juvenile offenders are more likely to commit a violent offence than a property offence, albeit that males have considerably higher prevalence rates

than females. Official data put the peak age of violent offending at around 14 to 15 for both males and females, with 33 per cent of males and 18 per cent of females having committed such an offence in the previous year. The peak age of property offending remains 14 to 15 for females, and peaks at around 13 per cent, whereas it is both slightly older (16–17 years old) and higher (25%) for males. According to such surveys, after the age of 16 most of these offences decline in frequency, though fraud and buying stolen goods tend to become more common among females (Flood-Page *et al.*, 2000).

Reasons for offending

Do men and women offend for similar reasons? We focus here on empirical research in this area. However, it is worth reminding ourselves that there are important theoretical debates in this area, stimulated in large part by the failure of traditional sociological criminology to consider female offending. As we saw in Chapter 15, the failure to consider female offending necessitated something of an overhaul of criminological theory. In the view of feminist criminology, the bulk of criminological theory – from Chicago, via strain, anomie, control and even more recent radical approaches – had not only been dominated by a concern with male offending, but had drawn whatever insights it had gathered from the study of male offending. As Albert Cohen (1955: 44) put it, 'delinquency is

Table 32.1	Offenders found guilty or cautioned, by offence type, sex and age (%)					
	Male 10–11	**Female 10–11**	**Male 12–14**	**Female 12–14**	**Male 15–17**	**Female 15–17**
Theft and handling	52	78	45	70	34	60
Violence against the person	19	11	19	17	18	18
Burglary	13	4	13	3	10	3
Criminal damage	10	4	8	3	5	4
Robbery	2	1	3	1	4	2
Fraud and forgery	0	1	1	1	2	3
Sexual offences	1	0	2	0	1	0
Drug offences	1	0	6	2	18	6
Other (excl. motoring)	2	1	4	2	8	5
Motoring	0	0	0	0	1	0

Source: *Criminal Statistics*, 2004.

mostly male delinquency'. Feminist scholars argued, consequently, that much criminological theory was of little relevance to an understanding of female criminality – sometimes referred to as the issue of 'generalisability' (Miller, 2000).

Why should this be so? Heidensohn (1996) argues that in part it simply reflects the male-dominated profession of criminology and its male preoccupations with macho working-class deviance. She argues further that there is a real sense in which female offenders are relatively more invisible – there are actually fewer of them and they are consequently more difficult to study. What follows here is a brief survey of some of the studies in this area but, again, it should be read in conjunction with the discussions in Chapter 15.

Although offending rates differ, often markedly, by sex it remains the case that women offenders are to be found in all offence categories: from terrorism and homicide to domestic abuse and burglary. It is in relation to property crime that women feature most heavily, however. This has led some commentators to argue that many women become involved in criminal activity for largely instrumental reasons; to provide for children or family in circumstances where there are limited legitimate opportunities – referred to by Walklate (2004: 7) as the 'feminisation of poverty' thesis. And, indeed, a survey of over 1,000 mothers in prison which examined the most common reasons for offending appears to provide some support for this argument. The most common reasons were given as follows (Caddle and Crisp, 1997):

- Having no money (54%).
- Mixing with the wrong crowd (46%).
- Need to support children (38%).
- Drink or drugs (35%).
- Family problems (33%).
- Having no job (33%).

During the 1970s and 1980s there was something of an increase in female offending, according to official statistics, though for the most part this trend has been reversed from the mid-1990s. However, recent years have again seen questions raised about what appears to be some diminution in the gap between male and female offending.

One popular and, in some respects, persuasive argument has suggested that this trend is in some way connected with female 'emancipation'. Early work by Simon (1975) and Adler (1975) (see also Chapter 15) suggested that the changes taking place in the labour market and within the home were having an impact not only on women's legitimate activities, but also on their illegitimate activities. Though heavily criticised, such views continue to exert some influence. Carol Smart (1976) among others was critical of Simon's argument, suggesting, for example, that there is evidence that increases in female offending long pre-date anything that might be identified as a liberation movement. Box and Hale (1983) argue that the increasing female crime rate was almost entirely made up of property crime. To the extent that there had been increased recorded female violent crime, they argued that this was largely a consequence of the labelling of female offenders. The significantly-increased property offending was most likely a consequence of economic marginalisation. Further, the increasing proportion of crimes attributed to women in criminal statistics appear, in part at least, to be a product of greater numbers being prosecuted for drugs offences (Woodbridge and Frosztega, 1998) and possibly to the prosecution of greater numbers of minor offences of violence by girls and women (Alder and Worrall, 2004). Moreover, because the numbers of women being prosecuted are relatively small compared with the numbers of men, they are particularly susceptible to changes in policing and prosecution practices (Burman, 2004).

Moral panics about youth crime have tended to centre on boys and men. Increasingly, the media contain stories about female gangs and violence. Is violence by women on the increase?

Women and the criminal justice process

As many feminist scholars have argued, the bulk of criminological attention is focused on male offending. Although this chapter has the general title *gender and crime,* the bulk of the focus will be upon women. This is not to equate *gender* with *women,* merely to recognise that a great number of important debates that have arisen within criminology over the past 30–40 years have concerned women's treatment and experiences. Towards the end of the chapter we look briefly at the issue of masculinity and how that is beginning to be utilised in relation to offending and criminal justice. We begin, however, by looking at female offending, exploring women's experiences of the criminal justice system and, more particularly, how those experiences differ from those of male offenders.

Cautioning, arrest and prosecution

Data on cautioning suggest that a far higher proportion of women are cautioned than of men. Thus, in 2003, 43 per cent of young men (those aged ten to 20) and 61 per cent of young women were cautioned for indictable offences (as a proportion of all those cautioned or found guilty). Figure 32.3 illustrates the cautioning rates for young male and female offenders.

Studies since the 1980s, however, suggest that the sex of the young person has little or no effect on police decision-making in relation to cautioning (see Landau and Nathan, 1983; Evans, 1994). Predictably, given what we have learned above about male and female offending, women are much less likely than men to be arrested for notifiable offences: in 2002/03 16 per cent of all those arrested were women. Proportionately, it is offences

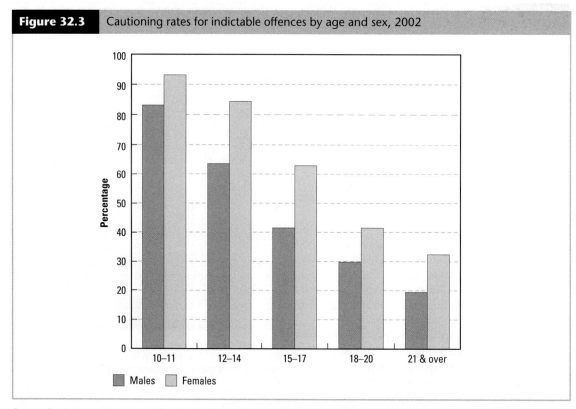

| **Figure 32.3** | Cautioning rates for indictable offences by age and sex, 2002 |

Source: *Statistics on Women and the Criminal Justice System 2003*, Home Office.

such as fraud and forgery (27%) and theft and handling (22%) for which women are most likely to be arrested. Women's higher cautioning rate, it is generally argued, is a product of the increased likelihood that they will admit their offences (a prerequisite of receiving a caution) and that they are also more likely to be arrested for relatively minor offences such as shoplifting.

Women are less likely than men to be remanded in custody during proceedings at magistrates' courts or on committal to the Crown Court and, if remanded, are less likely than men to receive a custodial sentence (41% as against 50%). With regard to sentencing, a similar pattern holds. For indictable offences, females of all ages are more likely than males to be discharged or given a community sentence (see Figure 32.4).

The use of custody

For much of the twentieth century the numbers of women in prison was in decline (Heidensohn, 1996). In recent times, custody rates for women have been rising (Hedderman, 2004). Nevertheless, as we have seen, women make up a relatively small minority of the prison population. In 1992 women comprised 3.5 per cent of the prison population in England and Wales. By 2000 this had risen to 5.2 per cent (at the time of writing – June 2007 – it was 5.4 per cent). Although the numbers are small this nevertheless represents a dramatic increase in women's imprisonment. One question to consider therefore is, apart from the fact that the numbers are increasing, and doing so more quickly than men, why we should be concerned about women's imprisonment. Walklate (2004) identifies five reasons:

- In the main, the crimes that result in imprisonment for women are of a more minor nature than those for men.
- The relatively small numbers of women in prison mean that they should be well catered for.
- Arguably, women react to prison differently from men (self-harming is particularly high).
- Being sent to prison has consequences for more than just the woman – she may have dependent children.
- Women suffer 'double discrimination' on release: they face the discrimination that all ex-prisoners face, but it is overlaid by further prejudice because they are women.

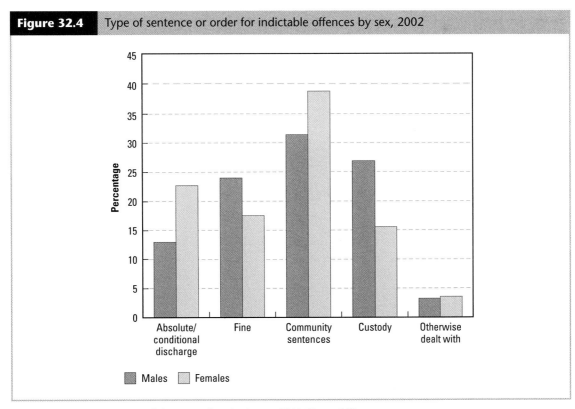

Figure 32.4   Type of sentence or order for indictable offences by sex, 2002

Source: *Statistics on Women and the Criminal Justice System 2003*, Home Office.

And, as already stated, the custody rate for women is rising, and doing so quite steeply. Thus, whereas just under 30 per cent of women sentenced in the Crown Court in 1994 received a custodial sentence, this had risen to over 43 per cent by 2002. The respective rates in the magistrates' courts were 3.5 per cent in 1994 and 10.7 per cent in 2002. Why is this occurring? The numbers being dealt with by the courts has been increasing. However, the proportion being dealt with by the Crown Court has remained fairly stable and the most likely explanations are either that the seriousness of the offending has increased, or that there has been a more general ratcheting-up of sentencing overall. An assessment by Hough and colleagues (Hough *et al.*, 2003) of sentencing trends generally (based mainly on data on male offenders) suggested that there was little evidence of an overall increase in offence seriousness, and that it appeared that offences that previously would have been dealt with in other ways are now more likely to attract a prison sentence (see Chapter 28). The available evidence suggests that a similar trend has characterised the treatment of women in the criminal justice system. Hedderman (2004: 93) in her review of recent trends concludes that 'Overall, the evidence suggests that sentencing has simply got more severe since 1992'.

Given that the custody rate has been rising, it is not surprising, therefore, to find that the number of women in custody has also been increasing markedly in the past decade or more (see Figure 32.5). Indeed, the female prison population has been growing significantly faster than the male prison population. Between 1992 and 2002 the average female population in custody increased by 173 per cent while that of males increased by 50 per cent. A look at the number of receptions into prison of men and women sentenced to immediate custody illustrates the trend (see Figure 32.5).

The most common offence type for which women are received into prison is theft and handling accounting for two-fifths (40%) of female receptions into prison compared with 23% of males (see Figure 32.6). In 2002, greater proportions of females than males entered custody under sentence for theft and handling, fraud and forgery and drugs offences, whilst a greater proportion of males arrived after being sentenced for violence against the person, sexual offences and burglary.

The length of prison sentences received by men and women also differs markedly, with women's prison sentences being shorter on average. In recent times there has been a substantial increase in the proportion of women sentenced to terms of imprisonment of a year or less and, overall, there has been

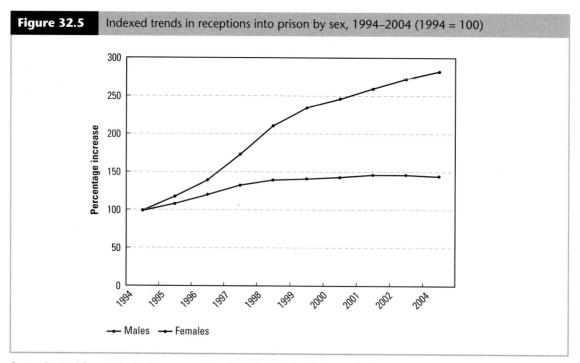

| **Figure 32.5** | Indexed trends in receptions into prison by sex, 1994–2004 (1994 = 100) |

Source: Derived from *Offender Management Caseload Statistics 2004*, Home Office.

| **Figure 32.6** | Receptions into prison by type of offence and sex, 2002 |

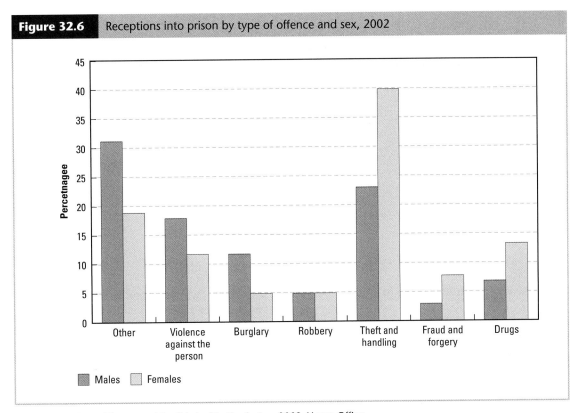

Source: *Statistics on Women and the Criminal Justice System 2003*, Home Office.

a decrease in the proportion of women received into prison with long sentences (see Table 32.2). Given that it has long been argued that short sentences are especially inefficient, and that prison should be reserved for those committing grave offences, the increasing number of short sentences for female offenders is itself a further indicator of the increasingly punitive climate that is affecting the criminal justice system, and which appears to be having a particularly dramatic impact on female imprisonment. Almost three-quarters (71%) of women sent to prison receive sentences of less than one year. The majority of the remainder (23%) receive sentences of between one and four years, and six per cent receive sentences of over four years. Women make up a small proportion of those serving life sentences. In 2002 just over three per cent of the life sentence population was female offenders, and the majority of these were in prison for murder.

Differences in the length of sentence received for different offences means that the make-up of the female prison population by offence type differs somewhat from the picture painted by using data on 'receptions' into prison. Thus, in the female prison population in 2002, the main offence groups were drugs offences (41%), violence against the person (16%) and theft and handling (14%). One of the often-mentioned characteristics of female imprisonment is that the population contains a substantial number of fine defaulters. The numbers have in fact been declining in recent times, from a total of 1,370 in 1995 to 372 in 1997 and 79 in 2002.

Women in prison

It was not until the work of Elizabeth Fry (see the box below) that the idea took hold that women prisoners might have needs that differed from those of men. Even so, the reality of the penal system in the nineteenth century, and arguably ever since, has been that it was designed and run with the needs of men in mind (Zedner, 1991). Heidensohn (1996) argues that there were two likely explanations for the failure to do more than adapt male systems and techniques of confinement

Table 32.2	Immediate imprisonment by length of sentence by sex, 1990 and 2000			
	1990		**2000**	
Length of sentence	**female prisoners %**	**male prisoners %**	**female prisoners %**	**male prisoners %**
Up to 1 year	66	57	79	57
1 year to 3 years	25	31	13	31
Over 3 and up to 5 years	6	7	5	7
Over 5 years	3	5	2	5
Life	0.5	0.5	0.3	0.5

Source: Gelsthorpe and Morris (2002).

and punishment when seeking to address female prisoners:

1. Women were in many respects regarded as incorrigible. Once they had 'fallen' there was considered to be little hope of reformation.

2. They lacked 'champions' – or at least sufficient champions. Elizabeth Fry, Josephine Butler and others had an important impact, but the more general exclusion of women from public life at this period limited what could be achieved.

So, what does the make-up of the female prison population look like? Ethnic minority groups make up approximately 29% of the female prison population compared with 22% of the male prison population. Over 75% of female prisoners are single (including those who are separated, widowed or divorced), just over 25% were living as lone parents prior to imprisonment (compared with 3% of adult males) and, though estimates vary, at least 66% of female prisoners have children and 39% of young female offenders are mothers (Niven and Olagundoye, 2002). A report from the Chief Inspector of Prisons in 1997 suggested that at least 20% of female prisoners had been in the care of a local authority at some stage in their childhood, and nearly 50% reported having suffered some form of abuse (a third reported sexual abuse, the remainder, physical abuse) (HMIP, 1997). The generally-marginalised position of the women who end up in prison is well illustrated via the following research findings and by the data in Table 32.3:

- 47% of female prisoners report having used crack cocaine in the year before coming to prison and 57% report having used heroin (Home Office Research Findings: 173).

- 40% of female prisoners received help or treatment for a mental or emotional problem in the year prior to imprisonment (the proportion is twice that of males).

- 50% of females had some form of personality disorder (compared with 78% of males).

- 14% of female prisoners were assessed as having suffered from a functional psychosis in the past year.

- 15% of female sentenced prisoners had previously been admitted to a mental hospital (Singleton *et al.*, 1998).

- 60% of female prisoners rated their own health as fair, poor, or very poor (Marshall *et al.*, 2000).

- Female prisoners report higher rates of asthma, epilepsy, high blood pressure, anxiety and depression, stomach complaints, period and menopausal problems, sight and hearing difficulties and kidney and bladder problems, than women in the general population (Marshall *et al.*, 2000).

- 74% of females in prison left school at age 15 or 16 compared with 32% in the general population.

- 39% of female prisoners had an educational qualification compared with 82% of the general population and 51% of the male prison population (Hamlyn and Lewis, 2000).

- 37% of sentenced female prisoners had previously attempted suicide (Singleton *et al.*, 1998).

- 20% of female prisoners report never having had paid employment (compared with 12% of male prisoners); in the 12 months before custody

10% of females were unemployed and not seeking work, 17% were looking after home and family, 12% were long-term sick or disabled, and 22% were living off crime (Niven and Olagundoye, 2002).

Mothers in prison

One of the ways in which the penal treatment of men and women differs is that, under limited circumstances, the Home Secretary may allow a woman to have her baby with her in prison, and specialist facilities are provided for this. The Prison Service in England and Wales currently runs seven Mother and Baby Units (MBUs).

Two prisons, New Hall and Holloway, keep babies with their mothers up to the age of nine months. Bronzefield, Peterborough, Styal, Eastwood Park and Askham Grange accommodate babies with their mothers up to the age of 18 months. Askham Grange is the only open prison with an MBU. According to the Prison service, 'each application for admission is assessed on an individual basis by a multi-disciplinary team, whose focus will be the best interests of the child. Every women's prison has an appointed Mother and Baby Liaison Officer, who offers help and advice to applicants' (www.hmprisonservice.gov.uk/adviceand-support/prison_life/femaleprisoners/).

Elizabeth Fry

In December 1816, Elizabeth Fry led an apprehensive committee of wives of Quaker businessmen and bankers into the women's wards at Newgate [prison]. As one of them later recalled, they felt they were going into a 'den of wild beasts'. As the gate clanged shut behind them, they were surrounded by a 'promiscuous assemblage' of 'half-naked' prisoners, begging for money, swearing, and fighting with each other to get closer. When the Quaker matrons succeeded in securing silence, Elizabeth Fry announced that the sheriff had given her permission to reform the wards and introduce new rules of discipline ...

With their apparent agreement, the Quaker women set about imposing order upon the prisoners. First, the tried and untried, the young and the old, the first offender and the 'hardened, drunken prostitute' were divided and placed in separate wards. The women's children were placed in a school within the prison ...

Soon, Fry had set the women to work sewing. She adopted the monitorial system of discipline used by her close friend and fellow Quaker Joseph Lancaster in his school for poor children in South London. The prisoners were divided into groups of thirteen each under the eye of a monitor chosen by them. Over the whole female wing she appointed a working-class woman as full-time matron ...

The results of Fry's work were dramatic. Passers-by noticed that the women had stopped begging from the cell windows. The keepers discovered that when the first batch of 'Mrs Fry's' prisoners were sent down to the ships to be transported to Australia they did not smash up their cells. Fry had convinced them to abandon this 'saturnalia' ...

Within a year, Fry had become one of the celebrities of Regency London. When Queen Charlotte stopped to talk to her during a public gathering, 'a murmur of applause' rippled through the assembled crowd watching this encounter between royalty and philanthropy. Fry's Sunday services at Newgate chapel became one of the major philanthropic venues of the city, attended by such personages as the Duke of Gloucester and the Home Secretary, Lord Sidmouth.

Source: Ignatieff (1978: 143–144).

Elizabeth Fry (1780–1845) was involved in a range of humanitarian activities, but is best known for her work as a prison reformer. Her portrait can currently be found on the back of £5 notes.

Table 32.3	Types of stressful life events experienced by sentenced prisoners		
		Male	**Female**
Violence at home		25	48
Bullying		30	26
Sexual abuse		8	31
Serious illness/injury		14	13
Violence at work		6	4
Relationship breakdown		45	46
Death of close friend or relative		47	47
Death of parent or sibling		29	30
Death of spouse or child		6	15
Stillbirth of baby		7	11
Expelled from school		49	33
Running away from home		47	50
Homelessness		37	34
Serious money problems		50	48
Sacked or made redundant		49	31

Source: *Psychiatric morbidity among prisoners in England and Wales*, ONS, 1998.

According to the reform group, *Women in Prison* (WIP): 'Places are limited, demand outstrips supply and there is no automatic eligibility. The upper age limit is 18 months at the open prison and nine months at the others, so there will always be babies

A women prisoner with her baby in the mother and baby unit at Holloway prison in London – one of seven women's prisons in the UK which have this facility.

who are forcibly separated from their mothers when this threshold is reached' (see www.womeninprison.org.uk). There is controversy over the necessity of MBUs. On the one hand it is possible to argue that they are important in ensuring that babies can be cared for by their mothers when, in their absence, they would be separated and, potentially, taken into care. However, as WIP have also argued, there are concerns about how well babies develop in the prison environment, and whether it may even be the case that the provision of such services provides encouragement to courts to impose custodial sentences when they might otherwise be reluctant.

As we saw earlier in the chapter, the prevalence of mental disorder in prisoners is considerably higher than that found in comparable non-incarcerated groups (Singleton *et al.*, 1998). Moreover, the highest rates of psychiatric morbidity are found amongst women prisoners and, although rates of mental disorder are apparently lower among women in mother and baby units, this remains a particular concern. A study by the Royal College of Psychiatrists (RCOP) found that three-fifths of the 55 women prisoners interviewed in MBUs had one or more of the five diagnostic categories of mental disorder (psychosis, personality disorder, neurotic disorders, drug abuse and hazardous alcohol use). Only three participants were receiving any treatment for mental health problems. They went on to argue that 'Some mothers with treatable mental disorders may not have obtained places on MBUs. The inmate medical record appeared to contain very little information about the mother's mental health' (www.rcpsych.ac.uk/pressparliament/press-releasearchive/pr708.aspx).

The RCOP found that almost one-third (30%) of mothers in the study suffered from undiagnosed depression and that, without treatment, this would have affected their ability to function effectively, with potentially adverse effects on the child's development. Thirteen women (24%) of the 55 women said that they had tried to kill themselves at some point in their life and ten (18%) reported a history of deliberate self-harm (Birmingham *et al.*, undated). A Home Office study undertaken a decade ago concluded that the existing research evidence 'suggests that imprisoned mothers are, in a sense, doubly penalised – they are serving a sentence and at the same time trying to make provision for their children with all the associated difficulties and strains. Fathers, on the other hand, generally serve their sentence in the knowledge that their partners will continue to care for their children, albeit with difficulty' (Caddle and Crisp, 1997: 55).

Understanding women and criminal justice

How are we to understand the treatment of women in the criminal justice system? Heidensohn (1996) identifies two contrasting themes. The first suggests that the justice system tends to be lenient in its treatment of women. This is a long-standing theme as illustrated by an observation made by Hermann Mannheim over 60 years ago (1940: 343):

> It can, of course, be taken for granted that the female offender – if punished – meets on the whole with greater leniency on the part of the courts than the male. Speaking generally, the percentage of women decreases in conformity with the severity of the particular method of penal treatment.

Such views have been summarised as the 'chivalry thesis' (see also Chapter 15); implying that the criminal justice system tends to take a protective and partriarchal view of female offending. In this vein Mary McIntosh (1978, quoted in Heidensohn 1996: 33) argued that:

> The general pattern of non-interference and relative benevolence comes out most clearly in the exercise of the criminal law. Most laws apply to men and women alike – yet far more men are convicted of crimes than women ... the differences are so gross that there can be no doubt that the main reason is that there are more laws against the kinds of thing that men and boys do than against the kind of thing that women and girls do.

By contrast, there is the view that the courts are actually much harsher on women than they are on men. In relation to the potential 'harshness' of the criminal justice system, there is now considerable evidence, for example, that women tend to find the criminal courts more intimidating, unsympathetic and bewildering than do men (Parker *et al.*, 1981). In this regard, although Farrington and Morris' (1983) study of decision making in a magistrates' court found that the sex of the defendant had no bearing on the severity of the sentence, it provided no support for the 'chivalry' thesis. Indeed, they detected no leniency towards female defendants and argued that women's lower likeli-

hood of reconviction was entirely due to the less serious nature of the offences they committed. Whilst general differences in severity may not be clear-cut, it has been argued that the use of the criminal law as a means of controlling women's sexuality is a clear illustration of one key difference between the sexes. Heidensohn (1996: 48) suggests such arguments can be summarised in four points:

- The courts operate a 'double standard' with respect to sexual behaviour, controlling and punishing girls, but not boys, for premature and for promiscuous sexual activities.

- The courts – and probation officers and social workers – 'sexualise' normal female delinquency and thus over-dramatise the offence and the risk.

- 'Wayward' girls can come into care and thence into stigmatising institutions without ever having committed an actual offence.

- Deviant women who deviate as women, that is, women who do not conform to accepted standards of monogamous, heterosexual stability with children, are over-represented amongst women in prison because the courts are excessively punitive to them. Recent research by Steward (2006: 143) on remand decision-making concluded:

Magistrates' perceptions of female defendants' characters were found to be significantly structured around normative gender roles. Women were typically perceived to be more 'troubled' than men, which encouraged magistrates to use the remand decision in cusp cases as an opportunity to help and support defendants ... Although this was found to benefit [some] women ... those 'troublesome' women whose defence representatives failed to reconstruct their characters in the eyes of the magistrates were not afforded the same latitude.

Hedderman and Hough's (1994) conclusion from their comparison of the treatment of men and women in the criminal justice system was that there was very limited evidence to suggest that women were dealt with in a systematically more severe manner. Indeed, they suggested, there is some evidence that women are treated somewhat more leniently under some circumstances. This would be consistent with elements of the chivalry thesis. However, they quickly move on to observe that, although it is possible that women are being treated leniently, it is equally possible that their treatment is not as lenient as their less serious offending warrants. Moreover, as they recognise, just because systematic discrimination remains unproven, does not mean to say that *some* women receive unusually harsh treatment at the hands of the criminal justice system.

Women in the criminal justice system: the future

In 2004 the government launched the Women's Offending Reduction Programme (WORP) which was scheduled to run for three years. The initial action plan described the programme as co-ordinating 'work across departments and agencies to ensure that policies, services, programmes and other interventions respond more appropriately to the particular needs and characteristics of women offenders' (Home Office, 2004). It sought to improve practices across the criminal justice process, as well as focusing on drugs treatment, mental health provision and problems of resettlement. Though receiving some endorsement from the Corston Review of women with particular vulnerabilities in the criminal justice system (Corston, 2007) such approaches have also been criticised for drawing greater numbers of women into the criminal justice 'net' (Carlen, 2002). The Corston Review (2007: 2) concluded:

> ... that it is timely to bring about a radical change in the way we treat women throughout the whole of the criminal justice system and this must include not just those who offend but those at risk of offending ... Women have been marginalized within a system largely designed by men for men for too long and there is a need for a 'champion' to ensure that their needs are properly recognized and met.

Accordingly, among its many recommendations it included:

- Every agency within the criminal justice system must prioritise and accelerate preparations to implement the gender equality duty and radically transform the way they deliver services for women.

- The government should announce within six months a clear strategy to replace existing women's prisons with suitable, geographically dispersed, small, multi-functional custodial centres within ten years.

- Custodial sentences for women must be reserved for serious and violent offenders who pose a threat to the public.

- Women unlikely to receive a custodial sentence should not be remanded in custody.

- Community solutions for non-violent women offenders should be the norm.

- There must be a strong consistent message right from the top of government, with full reasons given, in support of its stated policy that prison is not the right place for women offenders who pose no risk to the public.

Review questions

1 Why might the cautioning rates for women be higher than those for men?

2 Given that, historically, imprisonment rates for women have been lower than for men, why should we be concerned about women's imprisonment?

3 Why are women's imprisonment rates increasing?

4 What are the two main approaches to understanding women's experiences of criminal justice?

Victimization

The British Crime Survey (BCS) provides considerable evidence on criminal victimization and allows us to compare the experiences of men and women. Baldly put, in general terms men are at much greater risk than women, at least according to estimates derived from victimization surveys. Thus, according to the 2004/05 BCS, women aged 16–24 had a 6.3% chance of becoming a victim of violence in the previous year compared with the 14.6% chance faced by men of the same age. Domestic violence was the only category of violence for which the risks for women (0.7%) were higher than for men (0.2%) (Nicholas *et al.*, 2005). Risks of stranger and acquaintance violence were greater for men than for women (2.3% of men were victims of stranger violence compared with 0.6% of women). By contrast, 77% of victims of domestic violence were women while 78% of victims of stranger violence were men. However, this latter finding points to the important fact that much of women's victimization has tended to occur within the home and, consequently, has often largely been hidden from view (Walker *et al.*, 2006).

Feminist scholarship and campaigning, which has progressively increased the attention paid to the subject of women's experience of abuse and violence, has questioned the overall picture that is derived from large-scale victimization surveys. More particularly, feminist scholars have been sceptical of some of the assumptions about knowledge that underpin such survey techniques and have been critical of the notion of scientific detachment or 'objectivity', preferring to highlight the importance of normative engagement with the subject matter. Similar debates have taken place in the area of understanding fear of crime.

Fear of crime

Walklate (2004) identifies three conflicting views of the relationship between rationality, risk and fear. First, she says, there is the view based on the measurement of differences between levels of risk and levels of fear and which suggests that those who display levels of fear greater than their 'objective' risk are somehow irrational in their beliefs. Such views tend to be based on judgements about levels of crime as they are experienced in public, and to underplay the risks faced, for example, by women in private. The second view, which seeks to recognise the private as well as the public domain, and which is much influenced by left realism (see Chapter 13), argues that people are generally good judges of their levels of risk and that their levels of fear are generally commensurate with the risks they face. The third viewpoint, associated particularly with the work of Betsy Stanko (1985; 1996; 2000) challenges the whole idea of 'fear' and how such a notion might be measured. Rather, it views safety (or its absence) as being central. Walklate (2004: 100) sums up such a position in the following terms:

> If we take as our starting point, then, that women's 'fear' of crime needs to be connected to their experience and knowledge of what might happen to them, that is, if we take account not only of the expressed fear of crime as measured by victimization surveys but also the nature and extent of 'domestic' violence including 'wife' rape, 'date' rape, and murder, it is clear that women are exposed to much greater levels of

risk of criminal victimization than men. If we add to this women's experiences of what Crawford *et al.* (1990) called 'public' abuse, i.e. sexual harassment in the street and at the workplace, it is clear that the main offenders under all these circumstances are men.

In recent years, criminologists have begun to move away from a concern with 'fear of crime'. Holloway and Jefferson (1997), for example, have used psychoanalytical theory to focus on the idea of anxiety. In a slightly different vein, researchers such as Farrell *et al.* (2000) have been critical of the dominance of sociological theory in this area and have argued for greater use to be made of social psychological ideas. Perhaps most interestingly and importantly, the work of Jason Ditton and colleagues has argued that 'anger' rather than 'fear' is a more useful focus for our concerns (Ditton *et al.*, 1999).

Violence against women

In relation to 'intimate violence' women are clearly at greater risk than men. Across all categories of such crime women are more likely to have experienced intimate violence than men, though the differences in relation to family abuse (non-sexual) are less marked than other categories (see Figure 32.7).

Non-sexual partner abuse is the most common form of intimate violence reported with 28 per cent of women and 18 per cent of men reporting such victimization. Almost one-quarter of women (23%) report having experienced sexual assault and a similar proportion report having been stalked. These very high levels are lifetime measures (since age 16). However, even taking victimization within the last year only, the figures remain significant. According to the 2004/05 BCS, six per cent of women report non-sexual partner abuse, three per cent report having been sexually assaulted and nine per cent have been stalked (Finney, 2006).

As with other areas of victimization (see Chapter 17) some women experience considerably more violence than others. According to the BCS, a half of all women who had experienced at least one incident of intimate violence since the age of 16 had experienced more than one type in that time. The majority of these (30% of all victims) had experienced two types. Nevertheless, 16 per cent had experienced three of the main types of intimate violence and four per cent had experienced all four types. In particular, female victims of partner abuse

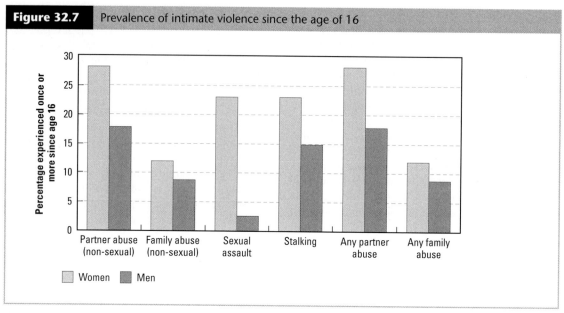

Figure 32.7 Prevalence of intimate violence since the age of 16

Source: Finney (2006).

were particularly likely to have experienced more than one type of intimate violence. Among female victims of intimate violence, the most serious violence was more likely to be committed by partners than strangers, and one in five respondents reported that it was a current partner who had been an offender (19%) (Finney, 2006).

Such victimization, as we have seen in relation to other types of crime (see Chapter 17), is demographically unevenly distributed. First of all, prevalence decreases with age. The younger one is the more likely one is to experience intimate violence. Similarly, according to the BCS, increased prevalence is also linked to marital status – being single is associated with all types of intimate violence among women, and being separated with higher rates of partner abuse. Finally, higher prevalence rates were also found among women who report poor health and were also linked inversely with socio-economic status: higher rates of victimization being found among the lower socio-economic groups.

Recent research for the Home Office (Kelly *et al.*, 2005: 16–17) summarised the existing state of knowledge about the extent of this particular form of crime in the following way:

- A 1991 UK survey found that one in four women had experienced rape/attempted rape in their lifetime, with current/ex-partners the most common perpetrators, and the vast majority not disclosing the crime at the time.

- Findings from the BCS 2001 revealed the prevalence rate for rape of women over 16 was 0.3 per cent for the year prior to interview, and an estimated 47,000 adult female victims of rape. The prevalence rate since the age of 16 is one in 27 women suffering at least one incident of rape.

- The BCS confirms that women are most likely to be raped by men they know, and that a considerable proportion had experienced repeat incidents by the same perpetrator.

Domestic violence

In early literature terms such as 'wife battering' were frequently used (Pizzey, 1974; Walker, 1979) and although the term 'family violence' has sometimes been advanced as a means of capturing many of the offences experienced by women, 'domestic violence' has come to be the predominant term. That said, this too is a term that has had a far from uncritical reception (Mullender, 1996). According to the Home Office (Circular 19/2000) domestic violence is 'any violence between current or former partners in an intimate relationship wherever and whenever it occurs. The violence may include physical, sexual, emotional, or financial abuse.'

According to some estimates, domestic violence accounts for approximately one-fifth of all violent incidents. Two-thirds of cases of domestic violence result in physical injury and research suggests

14 per cent of incidents result in some form of medical attention. Mooney, in her (1993) research in Islington, attempted to produce a 'composite' estimate of the extent of domestic violence. This she put at 30 per cent: that is, almost one in three of the women surveyed reported having experienced some form of domestic abuse. Using an innovative methodology which involved gathering data on all calls made to the police in a single day, Stanko (2001) was able to provide an unusual and thought-provoking picture of domestic violence in the UK. She found that:

- Between 1.1 and 4.9% of all calls to the police for assistance by the public are for domestic violence.

- On the day in question, one in four crimes of violence in London were for domestic violence.

- The police receive over 570,000 calls per year, or the equivalent of one almost every minute, in connection with domestic violence.

- The data available suggested:
  - 81% of cases involved female victims and male perpetrators;
  - 8% involved male victims and female perpetrators;
  - 4% involved female victims and female perpetrators;
  - 7% involved male victims and male perpetrators.

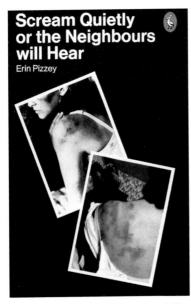

In *Scream Quietly* Erin Pizzey, the founder of Women's Aid, tells the story of the struggle to open the first Women's Refuge, in Chiswick, West London, in the early 1970s.

The perpetrators

A Home Office study (Gilchrist *et al.*, 2003) examined the histories of 336 male offenders from six probation areas. There is no offence of 'domestic violence', although all 336 offenders had been involved in offences that could be classified as involving domestic violence. The offences recorded for the sample included:

- Assault occasioning actual bodily harm (38%).
- Common assault (37%).
- Criminal damage (11%).
- Harassment (6%).
- Threats to kill (6%).
- Affray (5%).
- Grievous bodily harm (2%).

The researchers (Gilchrist *et al.*, 2003) distinguish what they referred to as various sub-types of offender. These they called 'anti-social/narcissistic' and 'borderline/emotionally dependent'. They suggest that narcissistic and anti-social offenders tended to display hostile attitudes towards women and attitudes which condoned domestic violence. However, they argued that such offenders may also explicitly display socially desirable attitudes and only reveal their endorsement of violence against women with a skilled interviewer. Borderline/emotionally dependent offenders, they argue, tend to be psychologically distressed, emotionally volatile and depressed. Such offenders tend to have high levels of jealousy and stormy intense relationships. Such personality traits are argued to originate from insecure attachment in childhood and early shaming. As a result, anger is experienced as an unavoidable part of intimacy and the researchers found this group of offenders to have very high levels of anger.

The researchers also provided a breakdown of the different behaviours reported by the perpetrators' partners, and link this to the different offender 'types' identified above (see Table 32.4).

Where much feminist literature focuses on women's social position, and more particularly their relatively disadvantaged position within the home and elsewhere when compared with men, the Home Office research above takes a rather different approach to understanding offending. As Walklate (2004: 134) puts it, such research has an 'inherent tendency ... to pathologise these men rather than render masculinity itself as being part of the problem'. In other words, it suggests that such behaviours are entirely atypical and abnormal,

Table 32.4	Types of behaviour reported by partners of offenders	
Type of abuse and incidence	**Anti-social/narcissistic**	**Borderline/emotionally volatile**
Economic abuse	Money not a big issue, more a matter of jealousy, e.g. wife away working with men	Very controlling over money
Emotional abuse	Very emotionally abusive	Only at time of assault
Male privilege	Does not do much work about the house. Expects gratitude	If takes an active role in the house, it is for his own reasons, e.g. will do the shopping to stop her going out
Isolation	Lets partner go out (unless impinges on him, e.g. childcare)	Actively stops partner going out. Wants to stop family and friends visiting and partner seeing them
Coercion and threats	Threatening and attempting suicide	Threats to kill children, family members, smashing property
Minimising	Apologising, blaming and denying	Apologising, blaming and denying
Intimidation	Uses looks to make her feel afraid, smashes property, uses children	Limited use of intimidation
Using children	Threats to take children, emotional blackmail, arguing with children, emotional abuse towards children. Insulting partner through children. Refusing to see children to hurt partner	Threats to take children, emotional blackmail, arguing with children, emotional abuse towards children. Insulting partner through children. Refusing to see children to hurt partner.

Source: Gilchrist *et al.* (2003).

rather than being integral to male domination within a patriarchal society. She continues, 'in this sense the perpetration of sexual violence is just one way in which the expression of "doing gender" by men is accomplished in relation to women'.

Policing rape and domestic violence

The last 30 years have seen a significant increase in awareness of issues surrounding the role and status of women. Much of this has focused on sexual discrimination and disadvantage. A substantial body of work has also been devoted to women's experiences of crime and criminal justice. Much of this has focused on the way in which the criminal justice system deals (or fails to deal) with sexual violence against women. Considerable attention has been devoted to encouraging a more sympathetic and respectful treatment of the victims of crimes of sexual violence. Increasing scrutiny around the policing of violence against women has its roots in the re-emergence of the feminist move-

ment in the 1970s. Until that point it appears there was considerable reluctance within the police to become involved in what were often termed 'domestic disputes'. There were at least four main reasons for this reticence (Smith, 1989):

- There were concerns about officer safety – some early American research suggested that up to a third of all assaults against police officers occurred during domestic incidents, though this was later challenged by other studies.

- That it was not considered to be 'real' police work – often being perceived as 'trivial'. One senior Metropolitan police officer was quoted in the press (*Times*, 4 October 1983) as suggesting that 'domestic disputes' might be categorised with 'stranded people, lost property and stray animals' as work to be handed over to other agencies to enable the police to focus on 'crime prevention, detection and community policing – real crime work'.

- That it is not really 'criminal' – that it is not really like other forms of violence because it is a 'family' or 'private' matter.

- That victims are reluctant to co-operate or are unreliable – there were seemingly strongly-entrenched police views that complainants would either be unwilling to press charges against abusive partners or, if they did, would withdraw them in due course. Again, these views were strongly challenged by feminist researchers (Stanko, 1985).

It has been argued that the agents of the criminal justice system have often tended to treat women complainants in a way that amounts to 'secondary victimization', especially in the case of sexual assault. There is evidence from the late 1970s (see for example Katz and Mazur, 1979) and early 1980s (Chambers and Millar, 1983) that women who reported sexual assault to the police often had their character and morality questioned in such a way as to imply some responsibility for their victimization. Similarly, Chambers and Millar (1987) detail a range of tactics used by prosecution lawyers to imply that women complainants were somehow to blame for their victimization or to throw doubt on the credibility of the case.

Indeed, many sources suggest that, at least until this point, the police were often highly unsympathetic to women complainants: 'Women were told not to get upset, not to get things out of proportion, not to go out alone, not to go out at night, to avoid "dangerous areas", not to put themselves at risk' (Benn, 1985, quoted in Walklate 2004: 150–1). As Smith (1989: 27) noted, traditional advice to women about avoiding the risk of sexual attack 'tended to be of the "Don't … " variety':

- Don't go out on your own at night.
- Don't travel on public transport late at night.
- Don't take shortcuts.
- Don't cross commons or parks on your own or use alleyways.
- Don't walk down badly lit streets; and so on.

This type of advice has been heavily criticised, in part because of the restrictions it seeks to place on women's freedom and independence, but also because of its implication that any woman failing to heed such advice is somehow at fault if she is attacked – that she has been *negligent* and has *contributed* to her own victimization.

Public attention was drawn to the frequently unsympathetic approach taken by the police to female victims by a case in which a man convicted of rape was fined – rather than imprisoned – on the grounds that the victim was guilty of 'contributory negligence'. Subsequently, a now famous BBC television documentary on the Thames Valley Police featured an episode in which investigating officers interviewed a female rape victim in an especially hostile and intimidating manner (see Chapter 17). As Adler (1987) put it, 'All but the most transparently flawless victim was liable to be bullied by interrogators and prosecutors, exposing her to a form of secondary victimization.' Feminists argued that sexual and domestic assault, and the failure of the criminal justice system to deal effectively with such phenomena, was a reflection of the subjugation of women's rights to male supremacy in society more generally (Rape Research and Counselling Project, 1981).

Policy changes

In some respects policing policy was slow to develop in this area. Following Roger Graef's documentary in 1982 and research by the Scottish Office (Chambers and Millar, 1983), the Home Office issued a circular to chief constables which contained advice on how investigations should be conducted, on the timing and conduct of medical examinations, the number of officers involved in an investigation and, where possible, the importance of having female officers centrally involved.

The following year a governmental advisory group, the Women's National Commission, set up a working party to examine violence against women with a view to bringing about some practical changes, in particular to attempt to improve the legal, medical, social and psychological help available to women. Its final report criticised the police for 'reluctance to interfere in domestic disputes and, in particular, for their reluctance to arrest and prosecute the perpetrators of violence' (Women's National Commission, 1985). Many accounts of the development of domestic violence as a social problem show the phenomenon as rooted in the traditional unequal power relationship between men and women.

English common law clearly outlined the rights that a man had over his wife, including the complete control over her property and of her daily affairs. This notion that a woman could be a man's property was fundamental to the idea that a husband had the right to administer physical 'punishment' to his wife. Similar arguments have been made in relation to the police approach to domestic violence as have been made for sexual assault: that the police have traditionally failed to treat the victims of domestic assault with the requisite degree of sympathy, that they have often failed to take a sufficiently serious view of the offence of domestic violence (indeed, may often not have regarded it as a criminal offence at all), and that they may often have regarded the victim as in some way responsible for what has happened to her. These are themes that have arisen from a body of research into the policing of domestic violence from both the USA and the UK.

One of the earlier, and most influential, pieces of research in this area was the 'Minneapolis experiment' in the USA (Sherman and Berk, 1983). This project attempted to allocate domestic incidents randomly to one of three alternate police responses: arresting the man, sending the man away for a cooling off period of a few hours, or giving advice and counselling. The conclusion was an apparent clear-cut 'success' for the arrest option, as over a six-month period, repeat calls fell much more when this option was used. The authors of the study favoured a policy of presumption of arrest – officers should arrest unless there were clear-cut reasons for not doing so. This led a number of US police departments to adopt more active arrest policies in relation to domestic violence. However, subsequent research has cast some doubt on the approach. Sherman himself (Sherman *et al.*, 1992) has argued that in some cases the effect of arrest may be to exacerbate the violence experienced by women rather than reduce it.

Research in the UK context has also provided support for a more active arrest policy, though some have argued that the most effective response will likely be a coordinated effort amongst a number of concerned agencies (Levens and Dutton, 1980; Hester and Westmarland, 2005). There continues to be some disagreement over the most appropriate role for the police in this area, and although it has been argued that inadequate police responses result in only a very low proportion of incidents of sexual assault and domestic violence being reported to the police, it is neither completely clear how a higher reporting rate would be encouraged, nor is it self-evidently the case that this would be unequivocally a good thing.

There have been numerous practical developments in these areas; indeed, Walklate (2004: 153) concludes that 'it is clearly the case that there has been a remarkable change of direction in terms of policing policy in this issue'. The Women's

A Georgian door leads to a house used as a rape crisis centre. Established in the 1970s, they expanded rapidly but have since been in decline because of lack of funding.

Movement was instrumental in the establishment of rape crisis centres and women's refuges in many towns and cities across the UK. The first refuge was set up in 1971 (Pizzey, 1974) and there were over 150 by 1978 (Binney *et al.*, 1981). The Parliamentary Select Committee on Violence in Marriage signalled government support for refuges. A few years behind domestic violence refuges, the Rape Crisis Movement began in the mid-1970s with the opening of the London Rape Crisis Centre in 1976 (though this has now closed due to lack of funding). The Rape Crisis Movement grew throughout the late 1970s and early 1980s, but has declined in number ever since due to a chronic lack of funding. In 1984 there were 68 Rape Crisis Centres but by 2005 there were only 32 (Women's Resource Centre, 2006). This is despite a massive increase in the number of rapes reported to the police – 1,842 in 1985 compared with 14,449 in 2005 (Women's Resource Centre, 2006). The campaign group Women Against Rape also opened in 1976 and was joined more recently by other campaign groups (Campaign to End Rape and the Truth About Rape).

Following an important Home Office circular (69/1986), and the establishment by the Metropolitan Police of a dedicated Domestic Violence Unit (DVU), the Home Office urged other forces to follow suit. Such units offer support to victims, liaise with other agencies and monitor the work of the police. Although it appears the trend began before such initiatives, there is little doubt that they contributed also to the rising rate of reporting of domestic violence that occurred at this time (Davidoff and Dowds, 1989). In addition to such developments in relation to domestic violence, around this time and again following the lead of the Metropolitan Police, many forces began to introduce 'rape suites', in which women could be medically examined and where they could be interviewed away from the unforgiving surrounding of traditional police interview rooms. There has been considerable debate as to the overall impact of these changes. Overall, there appears to have been progress, even though significant shortcomings remain. As one London study concluded:

> Over the past decade the facilities for dealing with victims have improved ... rape examination suites are available in all areas. Most complainants ... were on the whole satisfied with the way they were personally dealt with by the women police ... There was, however, much less satisfaction with the way the case was investigated and followed up. A quarter of the women were still not satisfied with attitudes of the male police officers investigating their case and pointed to the unsympathetic way they had been treated. (Gregory and Lees, 1999, quoted in Heidensohn, 2003: 574)

Understanding such changes needs to be placed in its wider context. Although changing policing policy in this area is undoubtedly largely a response to increased recognition of the ill-treatment of women – both in terms of the growing understanding of the very real threat and reality of violence within the home, and in uncovering the hitherto unsympathetic, even dismissive, response they had tended to receive from official bodies when making a complaint – there were broader changes underway which sought to make the police service more responsive to its customers. Indeed, the use of the words *service* and *customers* is itself illustrative of the process.

As we saw in Chapter 25, around this time the police came under greater financial scrutiny and pressure from government. Internally, partly as a result of the Scarman Inquiry and related developments, there was also concern about the quality of police–public interaction. The consequence was a set of changes that were encouraged both by government and by senior police figures which sought to make the police generally more responsive to the needs of local communities. This was reflected in part in the growing tendency in the 1980s and 1990s for the police to refer to themselves, or present themselves, as a *service* rather than a *force,* and for government progressively to impose a whole raft of changes on them aimed at improving the quality of this service and enabling central government to observe and measure these improvements.

More recently, the 2004 Domestic Violence, Crime and Victims Act further extended police powers, allowing them to make arrests for common assault, which previously hadn't been an arrestable offence (though the distinction between arrestable and non-arrestable offences was removed by the Serious Organised Crime and Policing Act, 2005). The new powers were accompanied by new national police guidance which stated that where a power of arrest exists, the alleged offender should normally be arrested and police officers should be prepared to justify a decision not to arrest. Elsewhere in this book we have referred to these changes, which affected the whole of criminal justice, not just the police, as *managerialism.* Heidensohn's (2003: 574) overall conclusion is that 'Police and policing remain gendered in the twenty-first century. The macho culture is still alive in some forces even now, although it is also a source of embarrassment.'

Attrition

This term is generally used within criminology (see Chapter 3) to refer to the process by which the total volume of crimes committed is gradually whittled away to leave only a very small proportion that ever reach court, and a smaller proportion that result in a criminal conviction. This process of 'attrition' has caused particular controversy in the area of sexual violence against women because it has been taken as an illustration of the lack of seriousness with which criminal justice agencies have traditionally treated such incidents or, more conservatively, of the problems that confront women when looking for resolution via the criminal justice system. More recently, it has emerged that attrition is also a problem in relation to domestic violence as well as rape, with only five per cent of domestic violence incidents resulting in a conviction (Hester and Westmarland, 2006).

A study in the early 1990s by Grace *et al.* (1992) examined 335 alleged cases of rape or attempted rape. They found three main attrition points in the criminal justice process:

● The police decision whether or not to 'no-crime' the incident.

● The police/CPS decision whether or not to proceed to prosecution.

● The jury decision whether or not to convict a defendant of rape.

Only one-quarter of the 335 cases resulted in a conviction for rape and the authors went on to examine the reasons why there was such an attrition rate. First, they found that a quarter (24%) of all incidents were 'no-crimed' by the police (this refers to cases in which, officially at least, information received subsequent to the incident being reported results in the police determining that no notifiable crime has been committed). The most common reason was the woman withdrawing the complaint (43%) and a further nine per cent were unwilling to testify or co-operate with police inquiries. In one-third (34%) of no-crimed cases they believed the allegation to be false or malicious, and in a further 12 per cent of cases there was insufficient evidence to proceed. They found that acquaintance attacks were least likely to result in a conviction – they were most likely to have a not guilty plea, and to be the most likely cases for women to withdraw their complaints. Similarly, cases in which there was some degree of consensual contact were almost twice as likely to be no-crimed than cases where there was no such contact. The cases which did result in a conviction for rape 'were most likely to involve young, single women who had never seen their attacker before and were physically injured during the attack' and they conclude that 'the "classic" rape was still the most likely to result in a conviction' (1992: 27).

What has happened since that time? Kelly *et al.* (2005) argue that Figure 32.8 below illustrates clearly the two primary trends in reported rape cases in England and Wales over the past 20 years. First, there has been a continuous and unbroken increase in reporting. Second, there has been a 'relatively static' number of convictions. They go on

(2005: 25) to say that the 'combination of these two trends, which began in the 1970s, means that whilst in 1977 one in three reported rapes resulted in a conviction, by 2002 this had fallen to one in 18 (32% versus 5.6%)'. This illustrates both the extent of attrition in rape cases and highlights the fact that it has increased markedly in recent years. Indeed, they point out that these figures actually underestimate the attrition rate because they don't take account of cases that are 'no-crimed' by the police.

Kelly *et al.* (2005: 31–2) identify a wide range of reasons associated with the non-reporting of rape. The main ones include:

● Not naming the event as rape (and/or 'a crime') oneself.

● Not thinking the police/others will define the event as rape.

● Fear of disbelief.

● Fear of blame/judgement.

● Distrust of the police/courts/legal process.

● Fear of family and friends knowing/public disclosure.

● Fear of further attack/intimidation.

● Divided loyalty in cases involving current/ex-intimates.

● Language/communication issues for women with disabilities and/or whose first language is not that of the country where they were assaulted.

They go on to note that the reasons given by victims or survivors for why they chose to report are less varied and the primary ones include:

● Acting automatically/it seeming the 'right' thing to do.

● Wanting to prevent attacks on others.

● Wanting protection for oneself.

● A desire for justice/redress.

What then are we to conclude from the current evidence on attrition in rape cases? It appears that there are evidential problems in a proportion of cases, leading to proceedings being dropped. The difficulties include: problems arising when the complainant has learning difficulties, mental health issues or, for some other reason, is unable to give a clear account of the incident; the absence of DNA testing; and, a failure to trace the alleged offender. Victim reluctance to continue or victim

Figure 32.8   Attrition in rape cases, England and Wales 1985–2002

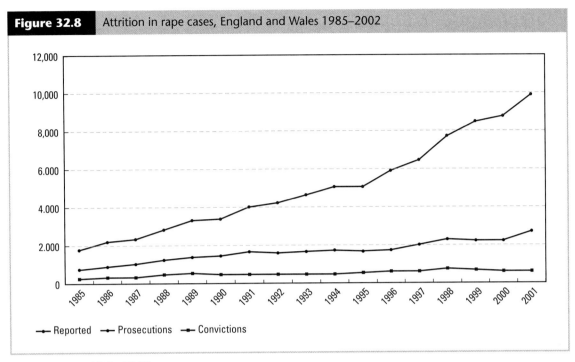

Source: Regan and Kelly (2003).

withdrawals account for around one-third of cases lost at the police stage. Research shows that concerns about being disbelieved and fear of the criminal justice process are important in such decisions. Only about 14 per cent of cases reach trial and some of these do not proceed. Approximately half the cases that result in a conviction do so as a result of a guilty plea. Where full trials are held, acquittals are more likely than convictions. The researchers concluded that there remain a number of aspects of the interaction between complainants and the criminal justice system that increase rather than mitigate the chances of cases falling (Kelly *et al.*, 2005):

● There is a 'culture of scepticism' in the police which leads to poor communication and a lack of confidence.

● Officers' assessments of the difficulties involved in prosecution and conviction can be seen by complainants as discouragement to continue.

● There is some evidence of poor investigative practice and poor understanding of the law.

As we noted earlier in this chapter (see also Chapter 15), a number of commentators have regularly observed that there are elements of the criminal justice process which act in such a way as

to make women's experiences amount to something close to 'secondary victimization'. One of the clearest illustrations of this, and something which undoubtedly feeds into the distrust of the system mentioned above, is the experiences that many rape victims have had in court. As Walklate (2004: 182) summarises it:

> In rape trials the way in which corroborating evidence is used and interpreted, alongside the performance of the complainant in the face of frequently very close interrogation by the defence barrister, can prove to be crucial elements in the acquittal or conviction of the defendant. This process, then, self-evidently puts the complainant – the woman – on trial.

Review questions

1 What are the main ways of understanding levels of fear of crime among women?

2 What have been the main policy changes in the policing of sexual violence against women?

3 How might high levels of attrition in rape cases be understood.

Women's role in social control

Our focus so far has been upon the experiences of women as victims of crime, as offenders and the relationship women have with the criminal justice system in these two 'roles'. There is another perspective we mustn't ignore. In her work over many years Frances Heidensohn (1992) has examined women's role *in* social control. There have been four crucial arenas, she suggests, in which women have played an important role in ordering the behaviour of others:

- The traditional domestic sphere of the home – 'the angel in the house'.
- The traditional community – the village street or tribe – 'the wisewoman and her kin'.
- The world of early modern welfare – the 'patriarchal feminine'.
- The world of modern welfare, of the feminine semi-professional.

In these and other ways women have been central to social ordering: from the maintenance and organisation of family life to involvement in the 'socially-controlling semi-professions' of health, teaching and social work, women 'have an enormous stake in perpetuating that society and its institutions' (1996: 173) albeit within structures dominated by men. In this section we turn our attention briefly to women's role in the criminal justice system.

Women in the police

It is only relatively recently – in 1995 – that Pauline Clare became the first female chief constable to be appointed in England and Wales. Others have followed, but women still make up a relatively small proportion of the highest ranks of the police service. In fact, it was not until the First World War that women were first formally used as police officers – and then it was only as volunteers. It was after the War that women were first paid as professional police officers. By the late 1970s the Commissioner of the Metropolitan Police, Sir Robert Mark, could write in his autobiography (though note the language he uses):

> I had always recognised that women were biologically necessary for the continuance of the force and were better able to persuade the public of our virtues as a service. In Leicester I had boldly ignored all the various Home Office exhortations and equipped them with court shoes, short skirts, air hostess tunics and shoulder bags. The effect was electric – our recruitment rocketed. So also did our matrimonial wastage rates. (quoted in Brown and Heidensohn, 2000: 62)

Home Office circular 87/1989 (*Equal Opportunities Policies in the Police Service*) stated that police policies 'should ensure that the best use is made of the abilities of every member of the force' and show 'that all members of the service are firmly opposed to discrimination within the service and in their professional dealings with members of the public' (quoted in Walklate, 2004: 161).

Although women were progressively integrated into the police service, concerns about discrimination and harassment continued to be widely heard. In the early 1990s an important case was brought by Alison Halford against Merseyside Police. Halford had been an Assistant Chief Constable, and claimed that it was because she was a woman that she had been passed over for further promotion. This was an unpleasant case in which the police authority and others attempted to use Halford's sexuality as a

Pauline Clare, who became the first female chief constable in England and Wales when she was appointed to head the Lancashire Police in 1995.

means of undermining her credibility and her case served to highlight there was still 'a very florid version of machismo flourishing at the highest levels' (Heidensohn, 2003: 565).

Policing in the UK is now inconceivable without the presence of women officers. Nevertheless, women currently represent just over one-fifth of police service strength, but tend to be concentrated in the lower ranks (see Table 32.5). By contrast, women make up 33% of special constables, 42% of police service civilian staff (including traffic wardens) and 66% of police community support officers.

In general women also tend to be under-represented in the high-status specialist roles such as criminal investigation and anti-terrorist policing, and research by Silvestri (2003) found that many high-ranking female officers felt themselves to be especially isolated, having to outsmart their male colleagues in a male-dominated world. In this vein, Walklate (2004: 160) argues that the mechanisms underpinning the continued under-representation of women in key roles 'relate to the "cult of masculinity" which surrounds policing and the notion of what constitutes the central policing task'. In this context, campaigning bodies such as the British Association of Women Police (BAWP) play an important role. In this regard, perhaps most important is *The Gender Agenda,* a document published in 2001 by the BAWP, which sets out a series of long-term aims for the police service:

1. For the service to demonstrate consistently that it values women officers.

2. To achieve a gender, ethnicity and sexual orientation balance across the rank structure and specialisms consistent with the proportion of women in the economically active population.

3. To have a woman's voice in influential policy for focusing on both internal and external service delivery.

4. To develop an understanding of the competing demands in achieving work/life balance and a successful police career.

5. To have a working environment and equipment of the right quality and standards to enable women officers to do their job professionally.

(www.bawp.org/New/Documents/gender.pdf)

Women police constables from the Hampshire Police.

Table 32.5	Women in the police service, England and Wales, March 2006			
Rank	**Male**	**Female**	**Total**	**% Female**
ACPO ranks	198	26	226	12
Chief supt	478	42	521	8
Superintendent	983	97	1,060	9
Chief inspector	1,771	225	1,995	11
Inspector	6,296	855	7,150	12
Sergeant	18,435	3,057	21,493	14
Constable	83,385	27,420	110,806	25
All ranks	111,548	31,723	143,271	22

Source: Clegg and Kirwan (2006)

Table 32.6	Women in the probation service, 2002		
	Total staff	**Female**	**Male**
Probation officers (main grade)	5,663	3,660 (65%)	2,003 (35%)
Probation officers (senior grade)	1,320	675 (51%)	645 49%)
Total (probation officers)	6,982	4,334 (62%)	2,648 (38%)
Other staff (inc. hostel managers)	9,160	6,598 (72%)	2,562 (28%)
Total staff	16,142	10,932 (68%)	5,210 (32%)

Source: Home Office (2003).

Women in the probation service

With its roots in the voluntary sector, and its historic social work orientation, one would expect the profile of the probation service to be rather different from other parts of the criminal justice system. As Table 32.6 shows, women make up over two-thirds of all probation staff, and though the proportion lessens the more senior the rank, female representation at senior levels is significant.

At the time these data were concerned, 18 (out of 42) chief officers were women, and there were a further 87 female assistant chief officers. Recent proposals, of course, have suggested a merger of the Probation and Prison Service (see Chapter 27) to create a new National Offender Management Service (NOMS) and although this hasn't as yet fully come into being, when it does it is likely to change the character of probation, not least in shifting it further away from its social work origins (Raynor, 2007). It will undoubtedly raise further questions about recruitment and retention of staff, not least female staff.

Women as prison officers

As we saw earlier, it was largely as a result of Elizabeth Fry's work in Newgate that the idea was established that women prisoners should be looked after by women rather than men. By contrast the idea of 'women guarding men' took much longer to become established. The histories of the gradual entry of women to the police and to male prisons are different – the influence of legislative requirements forcing administrators to integrate women officers being stronger in the prisons area – but the general outcome has been similar, with considerable subcultural resistance to women (Heidensohn, 1992). As Heidensohn (1996: 79) notes, 'Just as

women prisoners tend on the whole to suffer because of poorer facilities and lack of flexibility because there are so few of them, so do the staff of women's prisons.'

Research by Liebling and Price (2001) found that women's representation within prison officer grades is similar to their distribution within the police service: they make up a substantial minority of officers, but their representation falls with seniority of position. Overall, 17 per cent of prison officers are women. However, the proportion falls to about ten per cent of senior officers and 7.5 per cent of principal officers. However, and in contrast with the police service, the highest levels of female representation are found at the highest ranks. Overall 19 per cent of staff in governor grades are women as are two-thirds of governors on the Prison Service's accelerated promotion scheme.

The majority of female officers work in women's prisons. Research on female staff in men's prisons has tended to focus on women's integration into what is a typically macho culture. Liebling and Price's (2001) research found continuing concerns among male colleagues about the presence of women in the prison but, by contrast, prisoners were overwhelmingly positive, viewing women officers as being easier to talk to than their male colleagues and as 'bringing a human touch' to prison.

Women and the legal professions

The first woman to become a solicitor and first woman called to the bar (becoming a barrister) both occurred in 1922. As Figure 32.9 shows, women now represent two-fifths of all solicitors and almost one-third of barristers. However, research by the Law Society found that women law graduates tend to earn less than their male counterparts, and that this gap is widening (Fawcett Society, 2004).

Figure 32.9 Women's role in the courts and judiciary

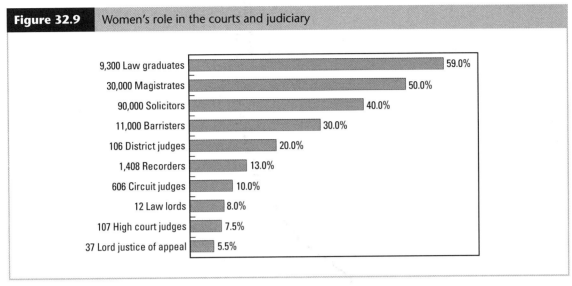

Source: Fawcett Society (2004).

Furthermore, as the bar chart also indicates, there appears still be something of a 'glass ceiling' when it comes to senior positions in the legal professions. Women make up only eight per cent of QCs and similarly small proportions of the various arms of the judiciary. This led the Commission for Judicial Appointments to note: 'We have built up a picture of a wider systemic bias in the way that the judiciary and the legal profession operate that affects the position of women, ethnic minority candidates and solicitors in relation to Silk [i.e. Q.C.] and judicial appointments.'

Research has also shown there to be significant earnings differences between white males and others. Men earn almost ten per cent more than women, and ethnic minority women earn 27.2 per cent less than white men. Although there are now more female than male trainee solicitors, during their careers men are much more likely to become partners than women (78% men compared with 45% women) (Thomas, 2005).

Beyond the issue of the principle of equality, the danger inherent in female under-representation in senior legal positions is that inappropriate and outdated attitudes toward female offenders may go unchallenged. The Fawcett Society (2004: 34) quote one of the respondents to their inquiry into women and the criminal justice system as arguing, 'Whilst there has been some (welcome) change, the age, sex and social experience of many of the judiciary means that they continue to judge women on the basis of stereotypes and mistaken "common sense" – such as battered women should just leave, and

young women should be more careful who they associate with, how much they drink, etc. This means that directions to the jury may explicitly or implicitly reinforce stereotypes about both femininity and masculinity which are a form of prejudice.'

Masculinity, men and victimization

We considered the issue of masculinity, and some of the theoretical developments associated with the work of people like Connell and Messerschmidt, in Chapter 15. We return to it here in order to remind ourselves that the subject of *gender and crime* is not simply about women (though given the general bias within criminology, focusing on women's experiences is surely more than justified).

Some years ago, Maureen Cain (1989: 4) noted that, 'Men as males have not been the objects of the criminological gaze. Yet the most consistent and dramatic findings from Lombroso to post-modern criminology is not that most criminals are working-class – a fact which has received continuous theoretical attention – but that most criminals are, and always have been, men.' This might seem an odd observation at first sight, given that the bulk of criminological theory appears to have focused almost exclusively on *male* delinquency. However, Cain's point here is that although this is the case, criminology has tended not to ask what it is about being male that leads men to behave in the ways that they do. As Walklate (2004: 32) puts it, 'while criminology might have thought a good deal about sex differences, it has roundly failed to think gender'. This is perhaps somewhat overstated, however, for as Downes and Rock (2007) note, masculine consciousness as a means of legitimising crime and delinquency has been a constant in criminological theorising since the work of the Chicago School.

For Edwin Sutherland, differential association in part involved processes in which boys' socialisation privileged the values of toughness and aggression and which allowed them greater freedom than that offered girls. Similarly, Albert Cohen (1955) in his work on delinquency focused on the status frustration the boys experienced and how gangs operate collectively within a (masculine) value system with its own ways of behaving and dressing. More recently, Paul Willis' study of the culture of bikers detailed various aspects of masculinity and masculine imagery including 'domination of women, humiliation of the weaker [and] aggression toward the different' (Willis, 1978: 29–30). Phillipe Bourgois (2003) in his ethnography of drugs and Latino culture in New York examines the relationship between highly masculinised Latino males and their successful and economically dominant female counterparts – a relationship often characterised by considerable violence. Finally, in this very brief overview, one might draw attention to the increasing number of studies of what has come to be called the 'night-time economy' and the masculinised (and feminised) forms of leisure and pleasure this involve (see for example Hobbs *et al.*, 2003; Winlow and Hall, 2006).

Male victimization

There have been few studies, relatively speaking, of male victimization. Early victimological research focused on victims as a largely undifferentiated group and more recently, of course, attention has rightly focused on uncovering and understanding the impact of male violence against women. In this regard much criminological attention has focused on violence within the home and although men also experience violence in this context, they do so much less frequently than women. Outside the home men are both more likely to be offenders but also, especially where violence is concerned, are also more likely to be victimized. Despite this, relatively little is known about men's experiences of victimization.

Some of this neglect is a product of one widely held belief about 'manliness': that men are reluctant or even unwilling to talk about or admit 'weakness'. As Stanko and Hobdell (1993: 400) put it, 'Criminology's failure to explore men's experience of violence is often attributed to men's reluctance to report "weakness". This silence is, we are led to believe, a product of men's hesitation to disclose vulnerability.' In the study of the fear of crime, of which gender is a very significant feature, there is considerable discussion of the difference in women's and men's reported levels of fear. A tendency, at least until relatively recently, to assume that men will be unwilling to disclose vulnerability has reinforced an inclination to focus almost exclusively on women's experiences of physical and sexual assault.

This is despite the fact that there has existed for some time evidence that indicates that a proportion of men are often profoundly affected by their experiences of crime. Research in the 1980s by Maguire and Corbett (1987) found that a considerable number of men *were* willing to admit to being severely emotionally affected by crime. Over half of all victims reported intense fear and:

> 'shaking and shivering' and feeling 'dazed, confused or unreal', symptoms associated with shock as well as fear, were at high levels among … both sexes in the case of assault. This latter finding, together with the fact that there was no significant difference in these reactions by age in the case of male victims, helps to underline one of the key points to emerge from this exercise: *the effects of violent crime are severe for a high proportion of men, as well as for women.* (Maguire and Corbett, 1987: 56)

In a small-scale study of male victims of sexual assault, King exploded a number of the myths about the impact of crime on men. He concluded (1992: 8) that despite its limitations, 'the results of this study demonstrate that male sexual assault is a frightening, dehumanising event, leaving men who have been assaulted feeling debased and contaminated, their sense of autonomy and personal invulnerability shattered'. Sexual assaults on men have the potential to strike at the heart of what Connell (1987) has called 'hegemonic masculinity': a model of being male in which men are in control, are invulnerable and are heterosexual. As Stanko (1990: 26–7) put it, using slightly different language: 'a "real" man is a strong, heterosexual, male protector, capable of taking care of himself and, if necessary, guarding his and others' safety aggressively. He is the man who will stand up in a fight, but will not abuse his power by unnecessarily victimizing others.' It is not difficult to see how sexual assault might challenge such a view of self. As Adler (1992: 128) has observed:

> Where the victim is male, any claim that he consented projects onto him a homosexual identity. Where the victim is homosexual, this can lead to considerable feelings of guilt, which tend to act as a deterrent to reporting. Where the victim is heterosexual, the very fear of being thought a homosexual may well stop him from reporting. Indeed, the reasons for not reporting for male victims are much the same as they are for female victims, and include shock, embarrassment, fear, self-blame, and a high degree of stigma.

There are significant parallels between the experience of sexual assault as described by men and women. Now, this is not to suggest of course that the socio-political context in which such offences take place is equivalent for men and women. It clearly is not. It is merely to note that the experience may be similar on other levels. Work by Stanko and Hobdell (1993) reinforces this point. They conducted a study of 33 male victims of assault by other men, many of whom reported fear, phobias, disruption to sleep and social patterns, hypervigilance, aggressiveness, personality change and a considerably heightened sense of vulnerability. They argued that not only was masculinity an important factor in helping make sense of the consequences of victimization for these men, but the ways in which offers of support were made, together with the victim's ability to look for, or accept, help and support were also crucially affected by the way they and others perceived them as 'men', within a context of what masculinity means more generally.

Such work raises important questions about how men cope with violence, how they order their lives as a result of violence, and how criminal justice professionals and support organisations view male victims. More generally, the neglect of masculinity also obscures other crimes against men: racist and homophobic attacks, and domestic violence between gay men, as well as men's experiences of attack by women which, although it constitutes a very minor element in men's experiences of violence, is still something reportedly experienced by 16 per cent of men (Finney, 2006).

Conclusion

The bulk of this chapter has focused on women's offending, and women's experience of the criminal justice system. The central theme has concerned the differences between men and women in these two main regards. To conclude, one can do no better than echo some of the observations made by the recent Corston Review (2007):

- Most women do not commit crime.

- Women with histories of violence and abuse are over-represented in the criminal justice system and can be described as victims as well as offenders.

- Women commit a different range of offences from men. They commit more acquisitive crime and have a lower involvement in serious violence, criminal damage and professional crime.

- Relationship problems feature strongly in women's pathways into crime.

- Drug addiction plays a huge part in all offending and is disproportionately the case with women.

- Mental health problems are far more prevalent among women in prison than in the male prison population or in the general population.

- Self-harm in prison is a huge problem and more prevalent in women prisoners.

- Women prisoners are far more likely than men to be primary carers of young children and this factor makes the prison experience significantly different for women than for men.

- Because of the small number of women's prisons and their geographical location, women tend to be located further from their homes than male prisoners, to the detriment of maintaining family ties, receiving visits and resettlement back into the community.

- Prison is disproportionately harsher for women because prisons and the practices within them have for the most part been designed for men.

- Women and men are different. Equal treatment of men and women does not result in equal outcomes.

Questions for further discussion

1 Are women generally treated leniently by the criminal justice system?

2 Are levels of fear of crime among women rational or irrational?

3 Are high attrition rates in rape cases an example of the criminal justice system working badly or working well?

4 What further policy changes do you think are necessary in order to improve women's experiences of criminal justice?

5 Is the use of imprisonment for women justified?

6 In what ways might male victimization be an important subject for criminologists to study?

Recommended reading

The best single text remains Frances Heidensohn's (1996) *Women and Crime*, 2nd edn (Basingstoke: Macmillan).

Carol Smart's *Women, Crime and Criminology* (London: Routledge and Kegan Paul, 1976) is the book that established and framed many of the arguments in this chapter.

Other books to consult are:

Walklate, S. (2004) *Gender, Crime and Criminal Justice*, 2nd edn, Cullompton: Willan

Stanko, B. (1986) *Intimate Intrusions: Women's experiences of male violence*, London: Routledge

Gelsthorpe, L. and Morris, A. (eds) (1990) *Feminist Perspectives in Criminology*, Milton Keynes: Open University Press

On imprisonment see:

Carlen, P. and Worrall, A. (2004) *Analysing Women's Imprisonment*, Cullompton: Willan

Heidensohn, F. (ed.) (2006) *Gender and Justice*, Cullompton: Willan, contains an interesting range of articles by a new generation of feminist scholars.

An up-to-date treatment of many of the issues discussed in this chapter can be found in: Heidensohn, F. and Gelsthorpe, L. (2007) Gender and crime, in Maguire, M. *et al.* (eds) *The Oxford Handbook of Criminology*, 4th edn, Oxford: Oxford University Press.

There is also a relatively new journal called *Feminist Criminology*, published by Sage, which contains useful, up-to-date articles.

Websites

There is interesting material on the Fawcett Society website: www.fawcettsociety.org.uk/

The campaigning organisation *Women in Prison* maintains a website with data on women's experiences and campaigning material: www.womeninprison.org.uk/

Other campaigning organisations with useful sites are Southall Black Sisters: www.southallblacksisters.org.uk/ and Justice for Women: www.jfw.org.uk/

There is a lot of useful material in the Corston Review (2007): www.homeoffice.gov.uk/documents/corston-report/

The Home Office publishes a lot of relevant material, not least the s.95 publications in its Statistical Publications website: www.homeoffice.gov.uk/rds/pubsstatistical.html

Chapter outline

Psychology and criminology   838
History of psychology and criminology   839

Individual factors in crime   840
Risk and protective factors   841
Individual risk factors   841
Family factors   841
Socio-economic, peer, school and community factors   842
Developmental or life course criminology   843
Sampson and Laub   843
Moffitt's theory of offending types   844

Mental disorder and crime   845
The prevalence of mental disorders   845
Mental disorder and offending   846
Understanding mental disorder and crime   846

Policing and psychology   847
Offender profiling   847
Assessing profiling   850
Legal and ethical issues   851
Interrogation   852
Confessions   853
Lying and lie detection   854
Statement validity analysis   856

The courtroom and psychology   856
Recall/eyewitness testimony   856
Vulnerable witnesses   857
Children as witnesses   858
Juries   859
Juries and evidence   859
Juries and other influences   860
Jury composition   860
Decision-making   861

Treatment of offenders and 'What Works'   861
Cognitive skills programmes   862

Questions for further discussion   864
Further reading   864
Websites   864

33

Criminal and forensic psychology

Psychology and criminology

James McGuire (2004) opens his textbook on psychology and crime with a tale about a conversation with a well-known criminologist who tells McGuire that he had never had much use for psychology. McGuire's first reaction is to assume that this is an unusual comment – it not being a view that he has heard before. However, he then goes on to say that the more familiar he became with criminology and criminologists, the more he came to see how widespread such views seemed to be. There is something about psychology, or what some think psychology is, or stands for, that turns certain types of criminologists against the discipline.

Indeed, as McGuire, Hollin (2007) and others have noted, the relationship between criminology and psychology has been far from straightforward, certainly in recent decades. The primary reason for this, he suggests, is probably to be found in what is perceived to be psychology's over-emphasis on individuals and individualised explanations within psychology. He suggests that this is partly because sociology and sociologists have exerted such a strong influence over contemporary British criminology. McGuire (2004: 9) suggests that 'there has been a mutual suspicion between those with fundamentally different approaches to criminological research'. In particular, he suggests that criminologists have often wrongly categorised psychological approaches to crime as being overly deterministic and biologically-oriented, when in practice contemporary psychological approaches generally pay significant attention to the social and environmental contexts of crime.

In thinking about different approaches to theorising and understanding crime, McGuire uses the metaphor of a compound microscope. Such instruments have a number of lenses which allow objects to be viewed with progressively greater power. Thus, he argues, 'using our first, but least powerful lens, crime can be studied on a large scale as an aspect of society at an aggregate or "macro" level. Alternatively, taking our next lens, its relative distribution across different places or times can be explored. Using a psychological approach we are, as it were, deploying the sharpest lens, to look closely at individual acts of crime and the people who have committed them.' Though this is a somewhat unfortunate metaphor – there is no good reason for suggesting that studying individuals requires greater 'power' than studying 'society' – it nevertheless conveys a sense of the different approaches, or levels, at which one might plausibly attempt to understand crime.

McGuire identifies what he says are four obstacles that have tended to limit broader acceptance of psychological approaches to crime:

- *Positivism* – Psychological approaches are often assumed to be positivistic in character. The term is often misunderstood and has come to be seen as a largely pejorative concept. The idea (see Chapter 5) is often associated with a philosophical position which argues that it is only that which can be directly experienced that can be 'known'. Approaches which seek an 'interpretive' understanding of human behaviour, such as those that underpin all interactionist sociology (and therefore much criminology), are rejected. In fact, McGuire argues that most contemporary psychology is better thought of as deriving from a *critical realist* perspective in which both social structures and personal, subjective experiences are considered central, and in which experimental and quantitative, as well as qualitative, methods are used.

- *Individualism* – Psychology is also hampered by the assumption that it locates the causes of crime within the individual – thereby ignoring social causes. In part, such assumptions possibly derive from earlier psychological work, such as that by Eysenck, which focused on personality traits and sought to link measurable differences in such traits to various forms of conduct, including offending. Again, however, McGuire says that contemporary psychology recognises both personality and situational factors in seeking to explain behaviour.

- *Biologism* – Again, there is an assumption in some circles that psychological approaches, because they focus on individuals, have a tendency towards assuming that biological differences are an important part of any explanation. From the work of Lombroso in the nineteenth century (see Chapter 6) through Eysenck and others, there is much in the history of psychology to support such assumptions (or prejudices). Though biologically-informed approaches continue to have some purchase within psychology, McGuire (2004: 15) suggests that 'most current theorizing and research in psychology adopts a much broader, psycho-social orientation'.

- *Determinism* – This, in many respects, is the logical outcome of the previous three obstacles; it assumes that certain individual features can be identified as the *cause* of offending behaviour. There are numerous reasons, he argues, why this charge is false:

  - Few psychologists would assume that straightforward *causes* could be found for something as complex as *crime*.

  - Most psychological research deals in probabilities or risk factors, rather than the kinds of certainties that straight cause–effect would imply.

  - Even where cause–effect is discussed, most psychologists work within a framework of 'reciprocal determinism' (where personality, behaviour and context influence each other).

  - Moreover, McGuire (2004: 54) argues, 'To locate the causes of crime exclusively in factors external to individuals is simply to adopt a different but equally unworkable form of crude determinism'.

- *Reductionism* – An implicit criticism, allied to *individualism* and *biologism*, is that such approaches are reductionist; that is, in this particular case, they seek to explain social phenomena by reference to either individual personality or biology. McGuire's response to this is to agree that, in many respects, psychology is a 'reductionist science'. However, whilst it seeks explanation at the individual level this should not, he suggests, be confused with the idea that this is the *only* level of explanation.

History of psychology and criminology

Criminology and psychology have strong connections and parallels in their respective histories. Both have their origins in the nineteenth century. The late nineteenth century and early twentieth centuries were a period of rapid expansion for psychology, which discipline is generally accepted as having its origins in the establishment of the psychological laboratory in Leipzig University in 1879. Though early pioneers explored the possibility of finding explanations in individual physiological differences, by the early twentieth century the use of mental tests and, later, intelligence tests became a standard approach to study. Such tests were used by the US military to manage the selection and classification of recruits and, indeed, by the US government as part of its assessment of potential immigrants.

It was at roughly this time that *legal* and *criminal psychology* also began to develop, with early studies focusing on the 'criminal mind' and later moving on to examine numerous aspects of the relationship between psychology and the law. In this connection, McGuire distinguishes three separate terms:

- *Criminological psychology* (sometimes referred to as *criminal psychology*) – Described as the application of psychology to the study of criminal conduct.

- *Legal psychology* – The study of psychological factors in the operation of the law.

- *Forensic psychology* – 'That branch of applied psychology which is concerned with the collection, examination and presentation of evidence for judicial purposes' (Gudjonsson and Haward, 1998: 1).

So far as the relationship between psychology and criminology is concerned, Hollin (2007) identifies three phases: an early accord in the second half of the nineteenth century; a parting of the ways as sociological criminology gradually came to dominate from the emergence of the Chicago School in the 1930s onward; and, what he detects to be a 'return to cordiality' in the 1980s and 1990s. The return to something approximating friendly relations is related to the rise of a number of individually-oriented approaches to criminology. We return to these below. Although there is a tendency to talk of 'forensic psychology' when discussing criminological topics, this is somewhat inaccurate (Hollin, 2007). Forensic psychology, as above, is effectively a form of applied psychology and there are many psychologists engaged in this area (Howitt, 2002):

- A clinical psychologist working, for example, as a consultant to the police.

- A mediator psychologist working for a law firm on dispute resolution.

- A social psychologist dealing with commercial litigation (employed to test and discover what might work in a trial).

- A counselling psychologist – working for the security services, examining risks and threats.

- A correctional psychologist, assessing prisoners and making recommendations for treatment.

Howitt illustrates the major components of forensic psychology as shown in Figure 33.1.

According to Hollin (2007) there are two areas of scholarly activity that have prompted renewed interest in some of the potential applications of psychology to criminology. One concerns the treatment of offenders and the role that psychology has in it; we consider this toward the end of the chapter. The other concerns the previously-mentioned focus on the individual within various strands of criminological research, notably those areas generally referred to as 'developmental' and 'life course' criminology. It is to these we turn next.

Individual factors in crime

Much work has explored and sought to identify those individual characteristics that are associated with offending. A large body of research evidence has now been accumulated as a result of longitudinal and life-course research. Within developmental criminology there have been a number of influential studies (for an overview see Farrington and Welsh, 2007: 29–36), two of the better-known being the Cambridge Study in Delinquent Development (Farrington, 1995) (see also Chapter 29) and the Pittsburgh Youth Study (Loeber et al., 2003). In recent years these and related studies

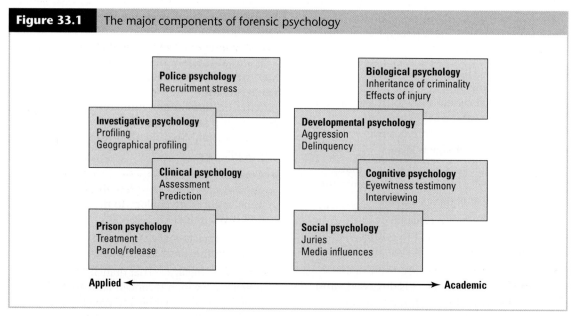

Figure 33.1   The major components of forensic psychology

Source: Howitt (2002).

have given rise to some apparently generally-applicable results which help isolate a number of factors that appear to be important in explaining increased likelihood of youthful offending.

Risk and protective factors

This approach, one that is increasingly visible and popular within criminology, identifies what it refers to as *risk* and *protective factors*. *Risk factors*, along the lines of those in the bullet points below, are variables that predict an increased probability of later offending (Kazdin *et al.*, 1997). Risk factors work cumulatively and in interaction with each other – though the precise nature of such interaction is only partially understood. In contrast, there are also *protective factors* which, as the name implies, increase an individual's protections against, or resistance to, 'undesirable outcomes' such as criminal careers. Whilst quite a lot is now known about risk factors, as Farrington and Welsh (2007: 3) note, 'disappointingly, less is known about protective factors against offending'.

Farrington and Welsh (2007) distinguish between *individual, family* and *socio-economic, peer, school and community factors*.

Individual risk factors

- *Low intelligence and attainment* – In the Cambridge Study low scores on non-verbal intelligence tests were associated with a raised likelihood of juvenile conviction and low school attainment predicted chronic offenders. Farrington and Welsh (2007: 41) argue that the key explanatory factor 'may be the ability to manipulate abstract concepts' with those doing badly in such tests having 'poor ability to foresee the consequences of their offending and to appreciate the feelings of victims'.

- *Personality* – Most research in this area has used Eysenck's theory of personality (see Chapter 7) and a review of studies in the early 1980s found that officially-recorded offending was linked with high scores of the N (neuroticism) dimension but not high E (extraversion), and that self-reported offending was associated with high E, but not N (Farrington *et al.*, 1982) (for further details see Chapter 7).

- *Temperament* – Effectively the childhood equivalent of personality, research tends to be based on parents' rating of children. A longitudinal study in Dunedin, New Zealand,

however, rated temperament by observing children during a testing session and found that being 'undercontrolled' (restless, impulsive and having poor attention) was linked with later aggression, self-reported delinquency and criminal convictions.

- *Empathy* – It is possible to distinguish between *cognitive empathy* (understanding people's feelings) and *emotional empathy* (experiencing other people's feelings). Jolliffe and Farrington (2004) found that low cognitive empathy was strongly associated with offending, but that low emotional empathy was only weakly so. Moreover, once intelligence and socio-economic status were taken into account, the impact of empathy was much lessened.

- *Impulsiveness* – Described by Farrington and Welsh (2007: 48) as 'the most crucial personality dimension that predicts offending', studies in this area are complicated by the vast array of terms used: impulsiveness, hyperactivity, restlessness, clumsiness, low self-control, sensation-seeking and risk-taking. The Pittsburgh Youth Study (White *et al.*, 1994), for example, found that impulsiveness as rated by teachers ('acts without thinking') and self-reported impulsiveness ('unable to delay gratification') were strongly related to self-reported delinquency between the ages of ten and 13.

- *Social cognitive skills* – This relates to the suggestion that offenders display poor decision-making and problem-solving skills in interpersonal situations. This risk factor relates to previously mentioned problems associated with abstract thinking.

Family factors

- *Crime runs in families* – Put at its simplest, this risk factor emerges from research which shows that 'criminal and anti-social parents tend to have delinquent and anti-social children' (Farrington and Welsh, 2007: 57). In the Cambridge Study almost two-thirds (63%) of boys with convicted fathers had convictions themselves, compared with under one-third (30%) of the remainder (Farrington *et al.*, 1996). They offer six (overlapping) possible explanations for this link:

  - There may be exposure to particular risk factors (such as poverty) across the generations.

- People tend to marry others like themselves in personality terms, and having two parents who offend disproportionately increases the likelihood of children offending.

- Socialisation and imitation may lead younger family members to resemble older ones.

- Parents engaged in offending tend to live in poorer neighbourhoods, be less consistent as parents and be more likely to engage in authoritarian forms of discipline – all associated with teenage offending.

- There is some genetic predisposition transmitted down the generations (see discussion of twins studies in Chapter 7).

- The criminal justice system monitors and labels particular families (as 'problem families'), raising the likelihood that children in those families will get in trouble with the authorities.

- *Large family size* – According to data from the Cambridge Study, boys with four or more siblings by the time of their tenth birthday were twice as likely to be convicted as a juvenile as those with fewer siblings (West and Farrington, 1973).

- *Child-rearing methods* – Research suggests that both harsh or punitive discipline (Haapasalo and Pokela, 1999) and erratic and inconsistent discipline are predictive of later delinquency (West and Farrington, 1973). Similarly, an absence of parental warmth (McCord, 1979) and low parental involvement in the child's activities (Lewis *et al.*, 1982) have also been found to be associated with youthful offending.

- *Child abuse and neglect* – There is some evidence that abuse and neglect in early childhood are linked with later (often violent) offending (Malinosky-Rummell and Hansen, 1993; McCord, 1983). There are numerous potential reasons for such a link:

  - Physical consequences of victimization, e.g. brain injury.

  - It may encourage impulsive or dissociative coping styles which, in turn, may be linked to poor school performance.

  - It may affect self-esteem.

  - Child abuse may have a direct impact on family functioning and family make-up.

  - Via a process of social learning, victims may develop forms of abuse behaviour themselves.

  - Abuse may lead to low attachment and thereby to low self-control.

- *Parental conflict and disrupted families* – Bowlby's theory (see Chapter 7) posits that attachment is vital in normal development, and that deprivation – caused by disruption of the relationship between mother and child – is associated with delinquency. Research evidence seems to point to a relationship between parental conflict and interpersonal violence and childhood anti-social behaviour (Kolbo *et al.*, 1996) and delinquency (Farrington and Loeber, 1999).

Socio-economic, peer, school and community factors

- *Socio-economic deprivation* – We considered a range of sociological theories earlier in the book (see Chapters 8 to 13), many of which place some emphasis at least on socio-economic deprivation as a factor in crime. Some longitudinal research shows that low socio-economic status of parents is associated with delinquency among their children (Elliott *et al.*, 1989), though such results are by no means found in all studies and are, anyway, sometimes argued to be affected by other factors such as parenting styles and discipline.

- *Peer influences* – Delinquency is not usually committed as a sole activity, but rather in small groups. Associating with delinquent friends is a good predictor of offending (Farrington, 1986), though to what extent this is peer influence (being influenced by friends) or peer selection (choosing friends who have similar interests and values) is not entirely clear.

- *School influences* – We have already seen that low educational achievement is associated with delinquency. To what extent, however, is the 'culture' of the school important? This is again a difficult matter to assess for, just as it is possible for pupils' behaviour to be influenced by school culture, so, similarly, it is also possible for the nature of school culture to reflect the nature of the student intake.

- *Community influences* – From the Chicago School research onwards, studies have sought to assess the influence of area on crime. There are essentially two major fields of activity here: one that explores the geographical distribution of offen*ces*, and one which looks at the geographical distribution of offen*ders*. Both offending and offenders are unevenly distributed and there are attempts both to explain why this might be so and, increasingly, to integrate both questions into a unified project (see Bottoms, 2007).

In the literature, a distinction is also drawn between *static* and *dynamic* risk factors. The former are generally demographic variables (sex, age, family background) or other aspects of criminal history (age at first offence, offending history). They are 'static' because they are unchanging. By contrast, 'dynamic' risk factors, such as attitudes, beliefs, emotions, and various forms of behaviour such as drug and alcohol use are more variable. One of the great challenges in this area is turning the evidence about risk (and protective) factors into practical and effective preventive strategies with individuals. There are a number of problems related to this:

- Some risk factors are impossible to alter – demographic variables such as gender and race, and others such as poverty, are not easily transformed.

- It is far from straightforward to separate correlation and cause in relation to factors identified by research as being statistically related to certain forms of offending.

- Research suggests that interventions that target multiple risk factors have the greatest impact, yet such ('multi-modal') interventions are often difficult to design and sustain.

- Risk factor research is largely based on measuring differences between individuals in large samples. Reducing offending requires change *within* individuals. However, risk-factor research tends to have rather less to say about how individuals change, or can be persuaded to change.

Developmental or life course criminology

A second strand of criminological research which has brought the study of the individual firmly back into the mainstream is what is increasingly being referred to as *developmental criminology*, or the study of crime and the life course. It is called developmental criminology because it explores the within-individual changes in offending over time (Loeber and LeBlanc, 1990). Such work explores how the nature and pattern of offending are affected by age. Now, there is a very clear pattern to the relationship between age and offending with the prevalence of offending increasing during the teenage years, peaking somewhere in the late teens and declining thereafter. This is often referred to as the 'age–crime curve' (see Chapter 29). Indeed, so predictable is this relationship that Gottfredson and

Hirschi in their general theory of crime described it, somewhat controversially, as being *invariant* (being the same in different cultures and historical periods), a claim that is disputed by many others (see Smith, 2007). We can illustrate elements of the contribution of research in this area by looking briefly at two influential pieces of work: Sampson and Laub's *Crime in the Making* and Terrie Moffitt's theory of offender types.

Sampson and Laub

The first unusual fact about this study (Sampson and Laub, 1993) is that it is based on the re-analysis of data that were originally collected between the 1940s and 1960s by Sheldon and Eleanor Glueck in the United States. In *Crime in the Making* Sampson and Laub re-analyse the data to examine the patterns of offending among the 500 males included in the original study. In follow-up work published ten years later (Laub and Sampson, 2003) they used criminal records to follow the group through to the age of 70. From these data they developed what they refer to as an 'age-graded theory of informal social control'. This they summarise in the following way (1993: 7):

> The basic thesis [is] threefold in nature: (1) structural context mediated by informal family and school social controls explains delinquency in childhood and adolescence; (2) in turn, there is continuity in antisocial behaviour from childhood through adulthood in a variety of life domains; and (3) informal social bonds in adulthood to family and employment explain changes in criminality over the life span despite early childhood propensities.

Sampson and Laub's argument suggests that weak social bonds are a key factor in understanding the link between adolescent delinquency and adult criminality. Having weak social bonds in early life is strongly associated with juvenile delinquency, and both predict later crime and deviance. Notwithstanding this close connection, it is possible for offending to begin later in life where there are weak social bonds in adulthood and, conversely, the development of strong bonds in adulthood will likely lead to a diminution of, or desistance from, offending. Thus, it is not necessarily the timing of life events that is crucial to Sampson and Laub's theory as much as the nature and strength of social bonds and related informal social controls.

Moffitt's theory of offending types

Another body of work which is having an increasing influence on studies of crime over the life course concerns Moffitt's distinction between 'life-course persistent' and 'adolescent-limited' offenders. Elsewhere in this book (see Chapters 20 and 29), in discussing patterns of offending, we have come across the finding that some offenders are substantially more involved in crime than the majority. So much so, in fact, that this relatively small proportion of offenders – often referred to as 'persistent', 'repeat' or 'chronic' – account for a substantial proportion of overall crime. In part, Moffitt's work picks up on this criminological truism. Looking at crime over the life course, Moffitt argues that there are two distinct patterns that may be identified:

- *Life-course persistent* – Here offending behaviour tends to begin early and continues throughout life.
- *Adolescence-limited* – Offending begins later, increases rapidly in early adolescence, and then declines quite sharply after the age of 18 or thereabouts.

Although the two groups are quite difficult to distinguish in adolescence, they clearly display very different patterns of offending in adulthood. The importance of distinguishing between the two groups, however, lies in the potential of this model to explain one of developmental criminology's major conundrums. This is that, on the one hand, there is substantial stability of offending over the life course: the best predictor of adult offender is childhood delinquency. On the other hand, there are also very significant changes in rates of offending by age – the age–crime curve showing that rates of offending drop markedly in adulthood. Moffitt's argument, in essence, is that stability over time is accounted for by the existence of life-course persistent offenders and a significant element of the changing rates of offending is accounted for by adolescence-limited offenders. When the patterns of offending of the two groups are put together they produce the age–crime curve, as illustrated in Figure 33.2.

Where Moffitt's theory becomes more controversial – at least in the eyes of sociological criminology – is in its proposition that part of the explanation for life-course persistent offending lies not only in early family risk factors and cognitive deficits, but also in neurological abnormalities and genetic factors. Using a range of studies, she argues that there is a significant heritable component to life-course persistent behaviour, particularly in relation to aggression in childhood. There is a

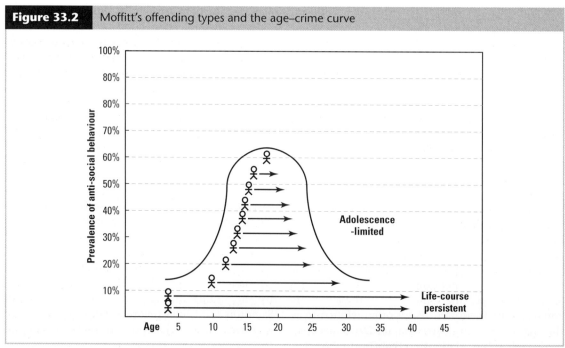

Figure 33.2   Moffitt's offending types and the age–crime curve

Source: Moffitt, T. (1993)

fairly strong contrast therefore, between Moffitt's theory of offending trajectories and that offered by Sampson and Laub. In effect, Moffitt's is a more individual-oriented theory positing, at least in relation to life-course persistent offenders, that the building blocks for such behaviour are set in place early in life and are almost inevitably acted out thereafter. By contrast, Sampson and Laub's approach, which also acknowledges the importance of certain early life factors, suggests that offending trajectories are more contingent. That is to say, they are subject to much greater influence by a range of factors during the life course which may reinforce offending behaviour, may diminish it, or may even lead to desistance.

Mental disorder and crime

In 1857, John Gray published work suggesting a link between mental illness and homicide. The idea that there is a link between violence and mental ill-health is widespread, and popular fiction is replete with narratives resting on the often appallingly violent criminal activities of the 'mentally unbalanced'. How realistic is this? An analysis of 500 homicide cases in England and Wales in the mid-1990s found that over two-fifths of offenders (44%) had a record of mental disorder at some point in their lifetime. Fourteen per cent had symptoms of mental illness at the time of the offence, and eight per cent had contact with mental health services in the year before the offence (Shaw *et al.*, 1999).

Looking at crime more generally, there is some research evidence that suggests that criminality may be both more widespread and more extensive among the mentally ill. Swedish research (Hodgins, 1992) found an association between the development of a severe mental disorder and the likelihood of committing a criminal offence by age 30. One-third (32%) of men with no mental disorder had a criminal conviction compared with half (50%) of those with a major mental disorder. However, a very sizeable American study (Monahan *et al.*, 2001) suggests that neighbourhood disadvantage may be an important explanatory variable in the levels of violence associated with people with mental disorders. Moreover, substance abuse or dependence may also be a significant linked factor.

Nevertheless, Prins (1990: 256) concluded that 'most psychiatric disorders are only very occasionally associated with criminality' and recent large-scale research found, for example, no evidence that schizophrenia was a risk factor for violence (Monahan *et al.*, 2001). Reinforcing this, Peay (2007) suggests that there are two crucial matters that must always be considered when discussing this issue:

- The complexity of the causes of violence among the mentally disordered – indeed, most likely among all violent offenders – means that there is no simple solution or treatment.
- Mental disorders account for only a tiny proportion of violence.

The prevalence of mental disorders

How widespread is mental disorder in the offending population? This is far from a straightforward question to answer. As Peay (2007: 504) points out:

… surveys of the incidence of mental disorder at the earliest stages will be an under-representation as the police, the Crown Prosecution Service, and the courts are likely to identify only those with the most obvious symptomatology, while surveys of custodial populations are likely to be an over-representation since they will include those whose disorders have been exacerbated, or brought about, by the process of prosecution and punishment, and those who would not be sufficiently disordered to bring them within the ambit of the 1983 [Mental Health] Act's definition.

Furthermore, the tendency of the courts to remand people into custody for psychiatric reports is likely further to exacerbate such over-representation. Bearing these important caveats in mind, let us look at some of the data. Early research by Gunn *et al.* (1978) found that one-fifth of prisoners – from a sample of 600 – had a marked or severe psychiatric condition and, subsequently (1991), they found that over a third (37%) of the sentenced male population had a diagnosable mental disorder. A more recent survey in the UK (ONS, 1998) found that seven per cent of male sentenced prisoners and 14 per cent of female sentenced prisoners met the diagnosis of psychotic illness.

Approximately half of male prisoners (49%) and one-third (31%) of female prisoners met the diagnosis for anti-social personality disorder and 40 per cent and 76 per cent respectively met the diagnosis for neurotic disorders. This is a particularly vulnerable population. We have seen in other chapters (28 and 29) the extent of suicide in prison.

Singleton *et al.* (1998) found that two per cent of the male remand population reported having attempted suicide in the week prior to interview, and other research has found that one-third of 'successful' prison suicides have some history of mental disturbance (quoted in Peay, 2007).

Mental disorder and offending

Just as 'crime' is socially constructed and difficult to define, so 'mental disorder' is a difficult term to be precise about. The difficulty, as Ainsworth (2000: 99) puts it, is that 'there is a blurred line between "normality" and "abnormality"'. It is this that lies behind Peay's (2007: 501) question: 'Should mentally disordered offenders be treated as a separate topic, in the same way that gender, race, youth, and victims are isolated from the mainstream?' Her answer is that they should not 'since mental disorder is not a fixed characteristic of an offender'. The Mental Health Act 1983 defines mental disorder as 'mental illness, arrested or incomplete development of the mind, psychopathic disorder and any other disorder or disability of the mind'.

Complex systems of diagnosis and classification have now been established, such as the Diagnostic and Statistical Manual of Mental Disorders (DSM-IV; American Psychiatric Association, 2000). According to this system of classification, a number of different forms of disorder can be identified, among the more important of which for our purposes are developmental disorders and personality disorders. Developmental disorders range from specific problems to do with speech, motor skills and the like through to various disruptive behaviour disorders such as *Attention-Deficit Hyperactivity Disorder* (ADHD) and *conduct disorder*.

Personality disorders concern psychological problems that arise 'from personal dispositions rather than breakdown or discontinuity in psychological functioning' (Blackburn, 1993: 76). According to McGuire (2004: 127) anti-social personality disorder is characterised by 'a pattern of disregarding the rights of others, which shows itself in such features as repetitive involvement in criminal behaviour, deceitfulness, impulsiveness, irritability and aggressiveness, irresponsibility and lack of remorse'. As he goes on to note, however, the nature of the argument involved is circular – the disorder being partly defined by the behaviour (criminality) it is being linked with.

A certain amount of controversy and confusion is also associated with the concept of psychopathy.

Originally put forward by Checkley (1941), it was used to indicate 'a lack of normal socio-emotional responsiveness that resulted in a pattern of social deviance characterised by features such as lack of remorse, an absence of close relationships, egocentricity, and a general poverty of affect' (Rutter *et al.*, 1998: 109). Since then research on so-called 'criminal psychopaths' has been used as the basis for the development of a Psychopathy Checklist (Hare, 1980). It is suggested that, in practice, the concept of psychopathy consists of two linked sets of factors – one relating to interpersonal features or personality traits and the other to anti-social behaviour. The relationship between psychopathy and violence appears to derive from the second of these sets of factors (Monahan *et al.*, 2001) and any 'underlying emotional pathology appears less important' (Peay, 2007: 517). There have been numerous criticisms of the use of the term psychopathy; in particular the view that it is tautologous (the identification of dangerous individuals being made on the basis of their dangerous behaviour rather than any other factors which might differentiate them from others in the population).

Understanding mental disorder and crime

Most commentators accept that, at times, mental disorder and criminal behaviour do co-exist (Hollin, 1992). The relationship, however, is generally far from clear and is difficult to analyse. Psychological research in this area has identified a number of difficulties in unpicking the relationship between mental disorders and violent crime:

- There is something of an overlap between 'mental illness' and violent crime in definitional terms. That is to say, one of the diagnostic criteria often used for identifying mental illness is violence (Howitt, 2006).

- It is possible that, for some, prescribed medication may increase the propensity to violence (at least blurring the boundaries of cause/effect).

- Much research evidence is drawn from clinical samples – which are likely to include a relatively high proportion of people who have come to attention because of violence.

- There has also been a tendency to rely upon studies of prisoners where it is possible that any measured problems may (wholly or partially) be the result of the experience of imprisonment itself.

- It is by no means always certain that the identification of 'mentally ill' people for the purposes of research is accurate.

- There may be important intervening factors, such as the de-institutionalisation of the mentally ill in recent decades, which precipitate violence under some circumstances (either by increasing opportunity and/or increasing pressures).

We acknowledged earlier that the nature of any relationship between mental disorder and crime is far from straightforward. Even at the most basic level of connection – prevalence of certain behaviours within different populations (those identified as mentally disordered versus the general adult population) – the evidence is weak:

- The vast majority of people with a mental disorder are not dangerous.

- The types of offences committed by 'disordered offenders' are largely similar to those in 'normal' populations (Peay, 2007).

- The available evidence suggests that people diagnosed with fairly severe mental disorders are no more likely to commit criminal offences than are adults generally.

- Moreover, research suggests that mentally ill people committed fewer homicides than the 'mentally ordered' (Taylor and Gunn, 1999).

- Restricted patients discharged from hospital pose a lower risk of serious re-offending than comparable individuals released from prison (Ly and Foster, 2005).

- Home Office (2007) research found a two per cent re-offending rate for violent and sexual offences (involving 16 restricted patients who re-offended out of a total of 843 discharged) between 1999 and 2003.

Policy in the area of mentally disordered offending is characterised by a number of interrelated problems. There has been an ongoing absence of appropriate treatment facilities, and this has led to large numbers of people with mental health problems languishing in the prison system. The government's own five year plan (Home Office, 2006) to reduce re-offending stated:

> We continue to imprison too many people with mental health problems. Dangerous people with mental health problems must be kept secure, and treatment is available for severe personality disorders in prison. Those with the most serious problems can also be transferred to secure hospital places. But the majority of offenders with

lower level disorders are not dangerous and could be better treated outside the prison system without any risk to the public.

On the other hand, contemporary obsessions with risk and risk management have led to proposals that would allow for compulsory detention and forced medication. Beyond the immediate human rights concerns raised by such proposals, they also carry a number of risks, not least that they will actually decrease public safety by driving people away from the services rather than bringing them into contact with them, and that they will further stigmatise already deeply socially-excluded members of the community.

Review questions

1 What are 'risk' and 'protective factors'?

2 What are the main categories of risk factors?

3 What are the differences between 'adolescence-limited' and 'life-course persistent' offenders?

4 What are the possible links between mental disorder and crime?

Policing and psychology

There are many aspects of policing to which psychological theory and research have made substantial contributions. In what follows we look at what, in recent years, has become one of the more publicised aspects of psychological work – the profiling of offenders – and then at the interrogation of suspects by the police and the psychology of investigative interviewing.

Offender profiling

Offender profiling is a somewhat controversial technique used in some criminal investigations. It has developed relatively quickly in recent years and versions have been popularised, if exceedingly misleadingly so, in TV shows such as *Cracker* and *CSI*. Attempting to identify the characteristics of a suspect has a long genealogy. According to Alison *et al.* (2007), in the 1880s Dr Thomas Bond attempted to profile the personality of Jack the Ripper, and in the Second World War the American government asked a psychoanalyst, Walter Langer, to develop a 'profile' of Adolf Hitler as part of their tactical planning in the War. In this profile it was argued that Hitler's need to prove himself derived from an Oedipal complex. Moreover, he was described as 'fearing syphilis, germs and moonlight, and that he loved severed heads. He also showed strong streaks of sadism and tended to speak in long monologues rather than have conversations, and he had difficulty establishing close relationships with anyone' (Alison *et al.*, 2007: 470).

The media has had a fascination with offender profiling and its (often exaggerated) efficacy – not least the popular American series *CSI*. This scene is from the episode 'What scenes may come'.

The formal origins of profiling are sometimes described as lying in the work of a psychiatrist, James Brussel, who became involved in the investigation of a series of crimes in 1956 attributed to an offender known as the 'New York bomber'. From studying the crime scene, and using his training in psychoanalysis, Brussel speculated that the bomber was likely to be: middle-aged; male; single; heavy; and living with a sibling. The man who was eventually convicted, George Metesky, was of course indeed male, and was also to be found to be living with two siblings.

If this case forms one possible beginning of activities described as 'profiling' then much of the work subsequently undertaken to develop this line of work was done at the FBI's academy in Quantico, Virginia, outside Washington DC. The Agency did much work by investigating the behaviour, motivations and personality of serial killers, particularly those involved in sexual crimes. The FBI's approach has been defined as an 'educated attempt to provide investigative agencies with specific information as to the type of individual who committed a certain crime … a profile is based on the characteristic patterns or factors of uniqueness that distinguish certain individuals from the general population' (Hazelwood and Douglas, 1980: 5). The major characteristics of the FBI approach to profiling are:

- A willingness to encompass experience and intuition as a component of profiling.
- A relatively weak empirical database which is small in comparison with use of the method.
- A concentration on the more serious, bizarre and extreme crimes, such as serial sexual murder.
- It tends to involve an extensive contact with the investigating team of police officers at all levels of the investigation rather than simply providing a profile. For example, the profiler may make recommendations on how to respond to letters and similar communications from what appears to be the offender. (Howitt, 2002: 1999)

The FBI approach has four main stages:

1 *Data assimilation* – The collation of major sources of information such as police reports, crime scene photographs, witness statements, pathologists' reports, and so on.

2 *Crime scene classification* – Here FBI profilers distinguish between *organised* and *disorganised* crime scenes. In the former there is evidence of planning, whereas in the latter the scene is more likely to appear chaotic. The nature of the crime scene may also then be linked to certain offender types (see Figure 33.3) – in terms both of their personal characteristics ('organised offenders' are more likely to be living with a partner, for example) and their behaviour in the aftermath of the offence ('organised offenders' are more likely to move the body, for example).

3 *Crime scene reconstruction* – Though the term *crime scene* implies something fairly static or fixed, clearly crimes are processes involving unfolding behaviour. Crime scene reconstruction involves attempts to recreate these behaviours in order to clarify both the nature and the order of events.

Figure 33.3	Examining crime scene and perpetrator characteristics		
Crime scene characteristics		**Perpetrator characteristics**	
Organised	*Disorganised*	*Organised*	*Disorganised*
Planned offence	Spontaneous offence	High intelligence	Below average intelligence
Controlled conversation	Minimal conversation	Socially adequate	Socially inadequate
Scene reflects control	Scene is random/sloppy	Sexually competent	Unskilled occupation
Demands submissive victim	Sudden violence	Harsh discipline	Harsh/inconsistent discipline
Restraints used	Minimal use of restraints	Masculine image	Lives alone
Body hidden	Body left in view	Charming	Poor personal hygiene
Transports victim	Body left at scene	Geographically mobile	Nocturnal habits

Source: adapted from Alison *et al.* (2007).

4 *Profile generation* – This is the stage at which various hypotheses are generated and brought together in order to build up a picture of the offender. The characteristics included will most likely be: sex, age, social class, type of employment, personality characteristics and behavioural activities.

Alison (2005) is critical of the assumptions underpinning such approaches, arguing that they tend not to make clear the behavioural or psychological principles that allow deductions to be made. He cites the work of the British profiler Paul Britton, author of *The Jigsaw Man*, as one example of work that implies that great expertise is involved without providing the basis by which this might be judged (see also box on the Rachel Nickell case below). It is not surprising that this type of 'profiler' has become popular in cinema and television, he suggests, for the 'idea of an expert who has special insight into the minds of killers and who can, through the examination of the crime scene, draw conclusions about the type of person who committed it, is an enticing prospect' (2007: 473). In fact, he argues, by and large such 'traditional trait-based' profiling has little 'operational utility beyond what might reasonably be expected of any competent detective' (2007: 473).

The next development in profiling occurred in the UK in the 1980s and 1990s. Often referred to as 'statistical' or 'actuarial' profiling, this approach, as the name implies, places less emphasis on the subjective aspects of identifying offender characteristics, and focuses more on analysing available evidence for patterns. Thus, it tends to involve using statistical techniques in the analysis of crime scenes and offender characteristics and is also broader than the

FBI approach in terms of the range of crimes that it will consider profiling. This somewhat more straightforward approach to profiling, nevertheless, also rests on the idea that it is possible to link characteristics of the crime scene with aspects of the features of the offender – the difference being that it takes a statistical approach to the task of exploring whether groups of crime scene characteristics can reveal aspects of the characteristics and character of the offender. According to Howitt (2006: 218), the statistical approach to profiling is characterised by:

● A greater emphasis on the need for a research base for profiling.

● A statistical approach to the relationship between crime scene evidence and offender characteristics.

● A rejection of clinical intuition as an important aspect of profiling.

● A willingness to encompass a greater range of crimes in profiling than the FBI profilers had.

Thus, one of the best-known profilers working in this mode, David Canter, has explored the relationship between murder crime scenes and the characteristics of murderers. This work, based on murders where the offender was unknown to the police at the time of the offence – so-called 'stranger murders' – identified a range of variables through which the crime could be classified, including the characteristics of the victim, traces of behaviours left at the scene and things done by offender to the victim (Salfati and Canter, 1999). They found that, on average, offenders were considerably younger than victims, they were mainly male, that murder mainly occurs in the evening, and that nearly half of victims were found in their own home (there were many other characteristics besides these). They then used 'smallest space analysis' – a technique which uses graphs to plot the likelihood of two phenomena (say a particular *crime scene characteristic* and a particular *offender trait*) being related. Ainsworth (2000: 113) describes the general approach saying:

> Canter believes that during the commission of a crime, vital clues are left behind and the distinctive personality of the offender shows through in some way. Thus, it is thought that the way in which the crime is committed is in part a reflection of the everyday traits and behaviour of the individual. The interaction between the offender and victim is thus studied closely and categorised along a number of dimensions, e.g. sexuality, violence and aggression, impersonal sexual gratification, interpersonal intimacy and criminality. Canter believes that by this careful study of offence behaviour, patterns can be established and variations between offenders identified. However, unlike the FBI's approach, Canter does not attempt to place offenders into rigid typologies, but rather suggests that their behaviour will mirror other aspects of their day-to-day life.

Professor David Canter, founder of the Centre for Investigative Psychology at Liverpool University, and a leading British authority on offender profiling.

Both of the major approaches to profiling outlined above are underpinned by two key assumptions (Alison and Kebbell, 2006). These are:

● *The consistency assumption* – Offenders' actions tend to be consistent across offences or 'the variance in the crimes of serial offenders must be smaller than the variance occurring in a random comparison of different offenders' (Alison, 2005: 3). A profile can hardly be constructed if any pattern identified in the offending is just as likely, or more likely, to be a product of multiple offenders. Alison *et al.* (2007: 475) conclude that 'while there is some evidence that certain crime scene behaviours *are* associated with certain background characteristics, there is no

compelling evidence that *clusters* of behaviours can be closely matched with particular *clusters* of background characteristics'.

● *The homology assumption* – That similar offence styles are associated with similar offender background characteristics. One example might be that offenders who destroy evidence at the scene of the crime are associated with previous convictions for the same offence.

Assessing profiling

In assessing profiling, Howitt (2002: 215) observes that 'purely in terms of psychological research methods, the issue might be thought of as a simple technical exercise in evaluation research'. Many of the difficulties, or complexities, are akin to those we might come across in any other form of evaluation research. Profiling tends to be used in the more extreme cases and, not least in popular media, of course, it has had some very positive coverage. Indeed, some of those academics who have become involved in profiling have frequently been also significantly involved in the promotion of the idea or process. This in itself may be something of a problem for profiling – raising expectations that cannot be met and, indeed, there have been a few high profile cases in which such expert help has rather backfired. Other difficulties with profiling include the possibility that such work may divert resources away from other forms and types of inquiry and, potentially therefore, may reduce the chances of success in investigation. Howitt (2002) asks a number of other questions about the nature and effect of profiling:

● It is very difficult to assess the efficacy of profiling: much of what we know, or think we know, depends upon publicity from single successful, or unsuccessful, cases.

● Are we clear about the purpose of profiling? Is it simply to do with detections or, rather, might it reasonably concern broader issues as to tactics to take in cases, assessment of the validity of evidence, and so on?

● Linked with this, might the results of profiling have uses beyond the individual case from which they were drawn?

Research by Alison *et al.* (2003) sought to assess the appropriateness of 21 offender profiles drawn mainly from the US and the UK, including the work of many prominent profilers. They identified a total of 780 statements in these profiles containing claims about the characteristics of the offender and found 92 per cent of these to be unsubstantiated, i.e. there was a claim made without any justification being given. They concluded that 'the majority of these profiles can be defined as not actually having anything to do with outlining the characteristics of the offender' (2003: 157).

Despite this largely negative conclusion, Alison and others (Alison *et al.,* 2003; Alison, 2006; Alison *et al.,* 2007) conclude that there remains a place for such activity in criminal investigation. In particular, they argue (2007: 477) that profilers can make investigations more efficient by:

- reducing the time spent on wholly irrelevant suspicions;
- providing police officers with a view of the style in which an offence has been committed;
- assisting in the construction of databases and advising how data might most fruitfully be collected, stored and utilised;
- assisting on interview strategies by preparing police officers for what they might expect psychologically from a given offender;
- assessing the credibility of statements, evaluating interviewer performance and advising on what aspects of accounts might most fruitfully be challenged or explored in more detail.

This is undoubtedly a rather less exciting portrayal of the activity of profilers than one finds in popular fiction – and, indeed, in the biographical accounts of some profilers – but it is almost certainly a more realistic presentation of the way that psychology can be brought to bear on police work in the area of criminal investigation.

Legal and ethical issues

There are no legal limits on the work of profilers, though there are clear rules about the presentation of expert evidence in court. The purpose of profiling information appears to be the crucial determinant in decisions about the admissibility of such evidence. In circumstances where the purpose is to identify the offender, profiles are likely to be excluded. By contrast, profiles are more likely to be deemed admissible when their purpose falls under one or more of the following categories (Alison *et al.,* 2007):

- The profiler may be able to testify about the crime scene.
- Profiles may be admitted as comparative crime scene analyses.
- The accused seeks to establish his or her own personality and its incompatibility with the police profile.
- When the question is whether it is more likely that defendant A rather than defendant B committed the crime with which they are both charged.

The Rachel Nickell murder inquiry

Rachel Nickell was murdered on Wimbledon Common in 1992. The Metropolitan Police employed a profiler, Paul Britton. On the basis of the profile he constructed, together with apparent positive identification from an e-fit shown on the BBC's *Crimewatch* programme, a particular suspect – Colin Stagg – was identified. Later in the case the psychologist was asked by the police to help design an undercover operation, based on the profile of the suspect, aimed at testing whether Stagg would implicate himself in the murder. The operation involved an undercover Metropolitan Police officer befriending Stagg – contacting him via a lonely hearts' club – and then building up a relationship with him. During a lengthy relationship – much of it conducted via letters – Stagg was progressively persuaded to talk about various sexual fantasies. Eventually, elements of these were close enough to aspects of the Nickell murder to persuade the police that Stagg was indeed the offender.

However, when the case reached the Old Bailey 'the judge said that the police had shown "excessive zeal"

and had tried to incriminate a suspect by "deceptive conduct of the grossest kind". Britton's evidence was thrown out and the prosecution withdrew its case against Stagg.' Stagg later admitted that he had made up many of the things that he had said to the undercover officer in order to impress her: 'Well that's why I had to make up this story because like at one point I thought I was going to lose her because I kept saying I didn't do this murder so you know I'm not like you [the officer had fabricated stories about being involved in human sacrifice] but yes we can still give it a go you know. But … erm … it … was after one of the meetings when I got back home I thought to myself you know I've got a feeling I'm not going to see her again' (quoted in Alison and Canter, 2005: 223). In 2005 it was revealed that DNA evidence pointed to the possibility that the real killer was already in custody in Broadmoor having been convicted of a number of other serious attacks.

Sources: http://www.guardian.co.uk/g2/story/0,3604,404994,00.html and Alison and Canter (2005).

The ethical issues connected with profiling link with the issue raised by Howitt earlier: that such activities, if not carefully managed, might well lead the police in an unhelpful direction, focusing attention and resources on a suspect where there is actually insufficient evidence to do so. In Britain it is the Rachel Nickell murder case, and the police targeting of one particular suspect, Colin Stagg, that perhaps best illustrates some of the problems that can occur when such activity is not properly regulated.

Interrogation

Once a suspect has been arrested and brought to a police station the next step is that they be interviewed and a statement taken (it is worth remembering that in practice it is not just the police who conduct interrogations in relation to criminal offences, but also HM Revenue and Customs, the military and the security services). Although it has often been suggested that the focus of interrogations is the extraction of confessions from suspects (Putwain and Sammons, 2002) – and this was the traditional goal of police interviews – since the early 1990s the focus has shifted toward the central goal of evidence gathering. Indeed, this difference is partly captured in the terms *interrogation* and *interview*: the former implies confrontation and the search for confession; the latter is less conflictual and is more concerned with eliciting information.

The nature of interrogation or interview depends, in part, on whether it is a suspect, a witness or a victim who is being questioned. Whereas suspects will often be questioned under caution – and the search for confession may be a realistic goal – clearly this doesn't apply to victims and witnesses. However, one strategy adopted by the police may be to begin by interviewing a suspect and only later beginning a more thorough and, perhaps, combative interrogation under caution. Traditional police interrogation training was guided by manuals whose authors argued:

> ... that most criminal suspects are reluctant to confess because of the shame associated with what they have done and the fear of the legal consequences. In their view, a certain amount of pressure, deception, persuasion and manipulation

is essential if the 'truth' is to be revealed. Furthermore, they view persuasive interrogation techniques as essential to police work and feel justified in using them. (Gudjonsson, 2003: 7)

Increasing concerns about the potentially adverse consequences of such approaches, together with increasing research evidence that traditional police investigative techniques were relatively ineffective, led to the emergence of a new approach, generally referred to as 'investigative interviewing'. The approach has seven basic principles (Gudjonsson, 2007: 470):

1 The objective of the investigative interview is to obtain accurate and reliable accounts from victims, witnesses and suspects in order to discover the truth about the subject matter under investigation.

2 The officer should approach the interview with an open mind and test the information obtained against what is already known or what can be reasonably established.

3 The interviewer must always act fairly in the circumstances of each case.

4 The interviewer is not obliged to accept the first answer given and persistent questioning does not have to be seen as unfair.

5 The officer has the right to put questions to the suspect, even in cases where the suspect chooses to exercise his or her right to silence.

6 During interviews officers are free to ask questions to ascertain the truth, except in cases of child victims of sexual or violent abuse, which are to be used in criminal proceedings.

7 Victims, witnesses and suspects who are vulnerable must always be treated with special consideration.

Investigative interviewing is now a compulsory part of the training of all police officers in England and Wales and advanced-level training is also available for more experienced officers. Despite the improvements that have undoubtedly been made, there remain concerns about the effectiveness of police officers' interviewing skills (Clarke and Milne, 2001) and one study has suggested that as many as one in ten interviews may be in breach of PACE codes of practice (Griffiths and Milne, 2006).

As Gudjonsson (2003) notes, poor technique or failing to stay within the law during interview can lead to a number of adverse outcomes:

- A confession, even if true, is ruled inadmissible during a pre-trial hearing.
- The eliciting of a false confession and a miscarriage of justice.
- Unfair pressure resulting in resentment and causing the suspect to retract the confession, even if true, and failing to co-operate in the future.
- Pressure or coercion leading to the suspect developing post-traumatic stress disorder.
- The undermining of public confidence in the police due to publicised cases of miscarriages of justice.
- Poor interviewing resulting in suspects failing to give a confession when they would otherwise do so.
- The 'boomerang effect' in which suspects who have confessed retract the confession because they feel pressurised to provide too much further information.

Confessions

As we saw in Chapter 26, there have been numerous cases in which false confessions have led to miscarriages of justice. Famously, the case of Maxwell Confait resulted in the wrongful convictions of three defendants and, indirectly, to the establishment of an official inquiry and later to a Royal Commission on Criminal Procedure. One of the important facets of this case concerned the vulnerability of the suspects and their particular susceptibility to intimidatory interviewing. The official inquiry concluded:

> Notoriously, a confession may be extracted by physical violence, or fear of physical violence; by a hectoring, bullying approach and a kind understanding approach. It may also be extracted by a promise of favours if a confession is made. It is conduct of that kind which renders a confession inadmissible. (Fisher, 1977, para 12.127)

In addition to reviewing and amending the legal rules concerning the conduct of interviews, the Royal Commission also prompted research into the psychological processes involved in investigative processes. There are now a number of models relating to interrogation and confession:

- *The decision-making model* – This model involves a form of rational choice, or limited rationality, theory to explore how suspects come to evaluate the options available to them, such as probability of conviction, estimation of punishment, and also including the nature of their 'relationship' with the interviewing officer(s) (Hilgendorf and Irving, 1981). Under such circumstances the social, psychological and environmental context of decision-making can be very important, and police interrogators can manipulate these in ways that affect the suspect's behaviour. Examples of this might include manipulating the suspect's perception of the likely outcome by stressing or minimising the seriousness of the offence, and affecting the suspect's ability to manage their decision-making by increasing their anxiety or stress levels.

- *The 'Reid' model* – Is similar to the decision-making model, but places greater emphasis on manipulating the interview in order to increase the likelihood of information being revealed or a confession being offered (Inbau *et al.*, 1986). In this model (originated by John E. Read Associates in 1947) 'interrogation is construed as the psychological undoing of deception' (Gudjonsson, 2007: 478). There are four major criteria which can affect the suspect's perceptions and understanding:
  - The credibility and sincerity of the interrogator.
  - Understanding of the suspect's attitudes and identifying weaknesses that can be used to break down resistance.
  - The suspect needs to agree with the interrogator's suggestions – the more suggestible the suspect, the easier it will be to extract a confession.
  - The interrogator has to check whether or not the suspect is accepting the theme suggested, whether the suspect needs to be placed under more pressure and if the timing of the presentation of an alternative theme is right.

- *Psychoanalytic models* – Argue that feelings of remorse and the need to elevate it are the primary cause of confession. Greater emphasis in such models is placed on subconscious processes in which the confession is a means of resolving internal conflicts, or a sense of guilt associated with a punitive super-ego.

- *An interaction model* – Which examines the interaction between such factors as the context of the offence, the strength and nature of police evidence and the skills of the interrogator, and adds to the decision-making model by acknowledging ways in which the interaction between interviewer and suspect may change over time.

- *A cognitive-behavioural model* – In which confessions are 'construed as arising through the existence of a particular relationship between the suspect, the environment and significant others within that environment' (Gudjonsson, 2007: 480). The relationship is examined by looking at the *antecedents* (events that occur prior to the interrogation) and the *consequences* (immediate and long-term impacts) of confession.

Criminal interrogations are by their nature stressful. The stressful features of such interviews include confinement, social isolation, physical discomfort, a sense of helplessness and lack of control, and the fear and anxiety surrounding both the process of interview and its possible outcome (Davis and Leo, 2006). These may be increased where the suspect is already anxious as a result of events that occurred prior to interview, where they are tired or intoxicated, and where they are psychologically or physically vulnerable. In particular, mentally disordered suspects and juvenile suspects are especially vulnerable to the pressures of accusatorial investigation (Gudjonsson, 2003). Such stress is one of the major sources of false confessions among suspects more generally, with research showing that some people confess simply in order to end the process of interrogation (Kassin and Gudjonsson, 2004).

The empirical evidence suggests that offenders are significantly more likely to confess when they believe that there is strong and accurate evidence against them. The positive implication of this is that the police should set about collecting evidence and establishing a solid case before beginning the interview process (see also Chapter 25). This also guards against miscarriages of justice in that weak cases – those with the greatest likelihood of having an innocent suspect – are weeded out early. However, a negative reading of the evidence might include the proposition that the police exaggerate the extent of the evidence at their disposal in order to convince suspects that the case against them is strong. Although there is much anecdotal evidence which suggests that police officers do, on occasion, behave in this manner, the research evidence shows that suspects'

likelihood of confessing is reduced when they believe that evidence has been fabricated (Kebbell *et al.*, 2006).

Psychological evidence, Gudjonsson (2003) argues, has perhaps had a greater impact on judicial decision-making and police practice in Britain than anywhere else in the world. He reviews 23 murder cases between 1989–2002 in which disputed confessions led eventually to the convictions being quashed, and suggests that the primary explanation in 14 of these cases was 'psychological vulnerability', and in nine cases 'police impropriety or malpractice'. Moreover, 'in 13 of the cases psychological or psychiatric evidence was the most important new evidence that resulted in the conviction being overturned' (2002: 336). There are a host of factors that can have an adverse effect on whether a suspect can cope with the circumstances of police custody and interrogation, and psychological research has shown that 'it is wrong to assume that only persons with learning disability or those who are mentally ill make unreliable or false confessions' (2002: 338).

Davis and Leo (2006: 145) suggest four primary strategies for avoiding false confessions:

- Interrogation only of those for whom there is sufficient evidence of probable guilt.

- Educating police officers concerning the potential for and causes of false confessions.

- Avoiding practices known to promote false confession.

- Greater training and sensitivity to the psychological vulnerabilities that render some suspects unusually susceptible to influence, and adjustment of police interrogation policies and practices based on these vulnerabilities.

Lying and lie detection

The attempt to detect lies is an important part of the work of many professional psychologists. That said, relatively few are formally trained to do such work and, moreover, there is quite strong evidence to suggest that professionals such as psychologists, police officers, and lawyers are only able to detect lies at roughly a rate that would be predicted by chance (Ekman, 1996). A review of research exploring police officers' abilities in this area found that:

- There are no substantial differences between experienced and newly-recruited police officers in their ability to detect lies/truth.

- Similarly, there are few substantial differences between police officers and members of the public in this regard.
- Officer confidence in their ability is not directly correlated with their ability.
- Experienced officers tend toward over-confidence in their abilities.

Detecting lying within an interrogation is far from straightforward. Officers must process extremely large quantities of data (facial expressions, language, verbal cues, other physical movements/ attributes) and must also be aware of the very different relationships certain cues have to lying. It is suggested, however, that there are what might be thought of as *leakages*, which can help reveal the existence of lying (Ekman, 1992). Such leakages include:

- Raised pitch of speech or raised voice (both associated with anger).
- Pauses and errors in speech – which may indicate either fear and/or some attempt to construct a story during the interview.
- Changes in breathing patterns, sweating, frequent swallowing.

Seemingly, there are also a number of facial cues that may indicate lying. These include asymmetrical facial expressions, the abrupt onset of emotion, and emotional expressions at inappropriate parts of the story. Helpful though these and related indicators from research undoubtedly are, their nature also gives a sense of just how tricky this territory is. Many of the indicators listed above are merely that – indicators – and are clearly far from easy to be certain about. More importantly, a quick scan of the list will also identify a number of indicators that will be immediately be recognised as occurring in other situations, i.e. ones that don't necessarily involve lying. Thus, anyone who has done much public speaking will recognise physical responses such as changes in breathing patterns, frequent swallowing and sweating! Once again, we find ourselves in territory where media images of police work are probably rather unhelpful in their somewhat unrealistic portrayal of the importance of the experienced and savvy detective breaking down the suspect in interview, having 'known all along' that they were lying.

Another area in which a degree of mythology exists concerns the use of the 'polygraph' or 'lie-detector tests'. The polygraph emerged in the 1930s, though an earlier machine that measured breathing

A polygraph, or lie detector, in operation – shown here being used by the FBI with one of their new recruits (all of whom have to undergo a lie-detector test before being accepted into the agency).

patterns was constructed, for the same purpose, around 1914. The polygraph, using a number of receptors attached to different parts of the body, simply measures a number of physical responses during a period of questioning. The major physical responses measured are (Madsen *et al.*, 2004):

- Sweating in the palms of the hands.
- Changes to blood pressure.
- The rate and amplitude of breathing.

The underlying assumption is that lying is associated with certain physical reactions and the reading of the multiple graphs (poly-graph) that are produced is used as a means of measuring physiological responses and thereby forming judgements about the veracity of the account being given by the person being questioned.

Polygraph use is most common in the United States and there are many practitioners who are convinced of its effectiveness. Needless to say, its practical use is far from unproblematic. Crucially, it is perfectly possible that intense questioning may produce intense reactions in anyone subject to it, guilty or innocent. Thus, one assessment of polygraph tests found that it was extremely successful (a 98% success rate) in identifying the guilty, but much less good at correctly identifying the innocent (down to 55%) (Patrick and Iacono, 1991). Like a number of other practices we have considered, such as profiling, it is perfectly possible that the notable successes are remembered, but the more egregious failures are simply forgotten, hence its continuing popularity in some quarters. In its defence, however, even in the absence of robust, scientific evaluation, it may nevertheless be the case that the polygraph may contribute in some small way to an increased level of confessions – if only through the extra pressure it helps apply on suspects.

It is worth adding at this point that the polygraph has potential uses beyond the assessment of the accuracy of statements by suspects in criminal cases. Thus, in the growing area of risk assessment, particularly in relation to sex offenders, the polygraph is used as a means of increasing the likelihood of truthful accounts being given (rather than testing truthfulness *per se*) (Gannon *et al.*, 2007). Much risk assessment activity is dependent at least in part upon self-report information provided by the offender, and there is considerable concern about the honesty of such disclosures. Under these circumstances the polygraph is felt to have considerable utility as a truth *facilitator* (Grubin, 2005), and up to one-third of probation management services use the polygraph in this way in the United States (Gannon *et al.*, 2007).

Statement validity analysis

Another approach to assessing the veracity of evidence has emerged in forensic psychology in the last decade or so. Known as *statement validity analysis* it involves content analysis of victims' accounts together with psychological assessment of the victim to estimate the likelihood that they might be motivated to lie. This approach has been used particularly in sexual abuse cases, especially against children, where there is often little or no physical evidence. At the heart of the approach is the assumption that there are some important differences in the nature of truthful and fictitious accounts of such events. Broadly speaking, the more truthful accounts tend to include more detail of context, conversations and interactions related to the incident and also to have more irrelevant detail and be somewhat disorganised.

Significant claims are made for the success of this approach with a number of cases in Germany, where statement validity analysis originated, involving acquittals on appeal in court using such evidence. However, as Howitt (2002) argues, the proportion of cases where there are false allegations of child abuse is probably less than one in ten and, consequently, an 'allegation is a good sign of guilt' (though this would be little comfort to those who are falsely accused). More problematic for the approach would appear to be two more trenchant queries, first concerning the absence of

information about the number of 'false negatives' (cases where the analysis suggests that the allegation is false when it is actually true) the approach produces, the second raising the possibility that the apparent success of the approach has been inflated because it has generally been used in cases where there is already sufficient evidence to make reliable judgements about truth/falsehood.

Review questions

1 What are the main differences between 'statistical profiling' and the FBI's approach?

2 What is 'investigative interviewing'?

3 What are the main models for understanding confessions?

4 How does a polygraph work?

The courtroom and psychology

Popular representations of the courtroom – from crime fiction through to television drama – play heavily on aspects of courtroom psychology. They focus heavily on the dramatic potential of the courtroom – the questioning of witnesses, the reliability of witnesses and the ability of lawyers to question those in the dock in such a way as to reveal things that otherwise might have remained hidden. As with most fiction, much of this, if not entirely fanciful, represents something of a distortion of what takes place in most criminal trials. Nevertheless, there are a number of important aspects of what occurs in some criminal trials – remember only a very small minority of cases are tried in front of a judge and jury in a Crown Court and the vast majority are dealt with in the much more mundane surroundings of magistrates' courts.

Recall/eyewitness testimony

Memory, as we should all be well aware, is far from infallible. How much of what you have read in the last few minutes can you remember, and even when you think you can recall something, how accurate is your memory? A significant body of knowledge has been developed in the general area of the cognitive psychology of memory (Braisby and Gellatly, 2004), and one application of this has been in relation to assessing evidence presented in criminal trials (both in terms of helping to convict the guilty and helping to protect the innocent). There are a number of stages that can be identified in relation to the recall of criminal events (indeed all events): witnessing the act or incident; the period in between the event and being asked to recall it; and, the process of giving evidence – often referred to as *acquisition, retention* and *retrieval* respectively.

- *Acquisition* – Three main factors affect eyewitness memory:
  - *Time* – The longer an event takes to witness, the better the eyewitness memory of it. Psychological research has compared witness recall of events that are very similar, but that differ in their duration (Clifford and Richards, 1977).
  - *Violence* – Witnesses tend to have better recall of non-violent events than violent ones (Clifford and Hollin, 1981).
  - *Weapons* – Witness recall is less good in relation to events in which weapons are used (Loftus *et al.*, 1987).
- *Retention* – Here two factors have been investigated in some detail:
  - *The period between the event and having to recall it* – With the exception of facial recognition, most memories deteriorate over time.
  - *Discussion of the event with others* – There is mixed evidence here which suggests on the one hand that discussion with other witnesses prior to testimony may lead to a fuller account of the event but, on the other hand, may also increase the chances of unreliable details being added to the account.
- *Retrieval* – This is the point at which testimony is given, i.e. the memories are accessed. Research in this area has explored the extent to which retrieval of memories is affected by the nature of the questions asked and the ways in which they are asked. In particular, what are known as 'leading questions' may influence what or how things are remembered (implying an answer or style of answer in the question itself such as 'How often did you hit him?' rather than 'Did you hit him?'). The implication of some of this research is that the memory is malleable and that recall can be (re)structured somewhat according to the nature of the questions that are asked. Hollin (1989) gives the example of research by Loftus in which groups of witnesses

were shown a filmed automobile accident. They were all asked to estimate the speed of the cars in the accident using the same question, but with the verb in the sentence changed to indicate differing levels of severity: 'contacted', 'hit', 'bumped' or 'smashed'. Loftus found that the estimated speeds given increased according to the severity of verb used: witnesses who were asked what speeds the cars were going when they 'hit' estimating significantly less than those asked what speed they were going when they 'smashed'. More recent research has shown similarly how the presentation of false information can prompt people to recall events in their past that have never occurred, such as being attacked by an animal (Porter *et al.*, 1999) or being rescued by a life guard (Heaps and Nash, 1999).

How reliable is such research, however? Much work of this kind is laboratory-based or is undertaken in other conditions that are dissimilar to those in which testimony would be given in practice. Howitt (2006: 209) outlines a critique of such research by Konecni and colleagues in which they identify a number of factors that limit the usefulness of research in this area:

- Research on eyewitness testimony is by no means consistent in its outcomes.
- Most research in this area is done using college students, rather than the general population.
- There is a huge difference in exposure to events in real life (averaging between five and ten minutes) and in the research context (often only about six seconds).

Despite possible limitations, research in this area has undoubtedly undermined some long-held misconceptions about the reliability of memory and has enabled those representing defendants in court, for example, to challenge the evidence presented against them. A now famous example of such influence is to be found in the Innocence Project in the United States (see box below).

Vulnerable witnesses

There has been considerable change in recent times in relation to the treatment of certain types of witnesses in court. In the previous chapter we discussed some of the changes to the treatment of women in court and, in particular, to the rules governing the cross-examination of rape and sexual assault

The Innocence Project

The Innocence Project was founded in 1992 by Barry C. Scheck and Peter J. Neufeld at the Benjamin N. Cardozo School of Law at Yeshiva University to assist prisoners who could be proven innocent through DNA testing. To date, 205 people in the United States have been exonerated by DNA testing, including 15 who served time on death row. These people served an average of 12 years in prison before exoneration and release.

Eyewitness misidentification

Eyewitness misidentification is the single greatest cause of wrongful convictions nationwide, playing a role in more than 75 per cent of convictions overturned through DNA testing.

Despite 30 years of strong social science research that has proven eyewitness identification to be frequently unreliable, it is highly persuasive to judges and juries. Contrary to what many people believe, research shows that the human mind is not like a tape recorder; we neither record events exactly as we see them, nor recall them like a tape that has been rewound. Instead, witness memory is like any other evidence at a crime scene; it must be preserved carefully and retrieved methodically, or it can be contaminated.

When witnesses get it wrong

In case after case, DNA has proven what scientists already know – that eyewitness identification is frequently inaccurate. In the wrongful convictions caused by eyewitness misidentification, the circumstances varied, but judges and juries all relied on testimony that could have been more accurate if reforms proven by science had been implemented. The Innocence Project has worked on cases in which:

- Witnesses' confidence was artificially inflated after the police informed them that they had selected the suspect, information which also led witnesses to recall having had a better opportunity and ability to view the suspect during the event itself and to change substantially their description of a perpetrator (including key information such as height, weight and presence of facial hair) at trial.

- Witnesses only made an identification after viewing multiple photo arrays or lineups inclusive of the suspect – and then made only hesitant identifications (saying they 'thought' the person 'might be' the perpetrator, for example), but at trial demonstrated confidence in their identification in front of juries who were never told that the witnesses wavered in their identifications.

- A witness made an identification in a 'show-up' procedure from the back of a police car hundreds of feet away from the suspect in a poorly lit parking lot in the middle of the night.

- A witness in a rape case was shown a photo array where only one photo – of the person police suspected was the perpetrator – was marked with an 'R'.

Source: The Innocence Project.

victims. Traditionally, it is children who have been treated as being in need of some protection and/or particularly sensitive treatment when in court. For some time children, for example, have been able to give video-recorded evidence prior to a case for use in court, but since the Youth Justice and Criminal Evidence Act 1999 this has been extended to other 'vulnerable' witnesses. These include:

> ... people with a psychopathic or any other personality disorder, schizophrenia or any other mental disorder. In some circumstances, this might include a clinical diagnosis of depression; people with learning disabilities; people with Alzheimer's Disease or other forms of dementia; people suffering from impairments of hearing or speech. (Milne and Bull, 2006: 13)

Children as witnesses

There have been some sizeable changes in the treatment of children in court over the past century or so. From a period when children were widely perceived to be unreliable witnesses, more recently many changes have been made to courtrooms and courtroom practice to accommodate children and what are perceived to be their specific needs. Much of this change has been driven by the increasing recognition of certain types of crime involving children – most notably child sexual abuse. Howitt (2006) identifies a number of reasons why special procedures are often considered necessary for children in court (drawn from a study of children who had experienced sexual abuse, but quite likely applicable to other child witnesses):

- *Language and questioning styles* – Including the use of complex words and questions.
- *Cognitive issues* – Relating to the amount of information being asked for in court, particularly if the incident happened some time ago.
- *Personal issues* – Relating personal information may be difficult, and reprisals may be feared.
- *Motivational issues* – The presence of particular adults may be difficult.
- *Social characteristics of the interviewer* – In particular the way they treat the child may be important.

He then goes on to report research by Lamb *et al.* (1999) which highlights a range of factors that may have a bearing on the nature and quality of children's evidence:

- *Fantasy* – Questions as to at what age children are able effectively to separate fact from fantasy (there has been particular controversy that the use of anatomical dolls with children who, it is believed, may have suffered sexual abuse, may encourage children to fantasise through play).
- *Language* – Children tend to talk in short sentences and passages, without a lot of detail.
- *Interviewers* – As discussed above, it is easy for interviewers to use language that is difficult for children to understand or follow.
- *Memory* – The brevity of children's accounts, as discussed above, is not an illustration of any necessary problem with memory.
- *Suggestibility* – Research suggests that even very young children are less suggestible than is sometimes thought.
- *Interviewer characteristics* – May affect how a child responds to questions.

Both children and other vulnerable witnesses often require more time when being questioned in order to understand what they are being asked, to think about questions, to retrieve information from their memory, to articulate what they are thinking, and to speak (Milne and Bull, 2006). A number of procedures or changes have been made in order to make the court experience less adult in orientation and better suited to enabling children to be effective witnesses. These include preparation for court, professional support, video-link evidence and closure of the court to the press and/or public. Although there has been much progress in this area, it remains the case that 'recognizing and responding

to the fact that witnesses are embedded in particular social contexts which strongly shape their decision-making with respect to co-operating with police investigations and, at a later stage, giving evidence in court, remain crucial challenges for UK criminal justice policy' (Fyfe and Smith, 2007: 463).

Juries

The Contempt of Court Act has made it impossible to undertake research on real life juries in the UK. By and large the best that can be done is to attempt to replicate some of the circumstances a group of persons approximating a jury might find themselves in and then test various aspects of their behaviour. Psychologists have long been interested in this area and have tended to focus on four aspects of the jury: the impact of evidence on jury decision-making; the impact of other factors on juries; the composition of juries; and the process of decision-making itself (Hollin, 1989).

Juries and evidence

The bulk of research has examined the impact of eyewitness evidence. Research suggests that jurors are highly influenced by eyewitness evidence. Despite the evidence we have already reviewed in relation to the problems associated with memory, jurors tend to assume that people are generally accurate in their recall of events. Moreover, this seems to be limited to positive identifications: non-identifications appear to have less impact on perceptions of guilt than to positive identification or forensic evidence, such as fingerprints (McAllister and Bregman, 1986). This leads to the possible conclusion that juries are insufficiently attuned to the strengths and weaknesses of particular types of evidence.

One potential corrective is the use of expert testimony in court cases. Research on mock juries comparing cases with and without expert testimony (attesting as to the reliability of particular types of evidence) found substantial drops in 'conviction rates' in cases where information had been provided about the reliability of eyewitness testimony. Although, one argument suggests that juries might be positively influenced by the status of an expert (Kocsis and Heller, 2004), at least one set of commentators (Egeth and McCloskey, 1984) has questioned whether the impact of such expert testimony isn't to make juries overly-sceptical.

Juries and other influences

Research has also explored what are generally referred to as 'extra-evidential' factors in criminal cases. These include such matters as pre-trial publicity, the confidence expressed or shown by a witness, the confidence and approach of the lawyers involved (Bartlett and Memon, 1995), jurors' attitudes and perceptions and, in particular, their views of others in the courtroom. There is a body of research evidence which suggests that witness confidence is important. More particularly, it appears that juries are more likely to place trust in evidence delivered by witnesses who appear confident and vice versa (Wells and Lindsay, 1983). Penrod and Cutler (1987) have suggested that witness confidence may be the most important factor in influencing mock juries. On the assumption that some prosecution witnesses – such as the police – are experienced and therefore likely to be confident in their delivery, such findings have potentially important consequences for criminal trials.

It is also possible that juries may be influenced by other features of those appearing in court. Factors such as the presentation of the defendant and witnesses, their attractiveness, their status, and their ethnicity and gender can all have an impact on jury members' views in experimental studies (Elwork *et al.*, 1981). What is less well-established is to what extent these same factors actually have a bearing on the outcome in court, though one study (Visher, 1987) suggested that they were less impor-

tant than the evidence itself. Prejudicing juries through pre-trial publicity is one of the abiding concerns in criminal trials. Research has consistently shown that prejudicial information appears to have an impact on jury decision-making – making them more likely to convict than where such information is absent. This makes the question of screening juries potentially a very important one.

Jury composition

In the UK, juries are made up of 12 adults chosen at random from the electoral register. Candidates may not qualify for jury service if they: are currently on bail; have ever been sentenced; suffer from mental illness; are a priest or a judge; know the defendant, a witness, the judge, an advocate or solicitor involved in the trial. Beyond this, and unlike the situation in the United States, there is very little by way of a selection process. In America, unsuitable jury candidates are screened using a variety of criteria including their attitudes toward the offence, their knowledge of pre-trial publicity as well as any personal connection with anyone in the case.

In the 1970s something called 'scientific jury selection' emerged in the US in which potential jurors were screened for a variety of characteristics to help identify whether or not they were likely to be suitable. Social scientists – often psychologists – are hired by defence, prosecution or both to make judgements about the likely views of potential

Scene from the classic courtroom drama *Twelve Angry Men* (1957). Did the 18 year-old defendant murder his father? Henry Fonda (*centre left*) persuades the eleven other jurors of his innocence and secures the unanimous verdict necessary for his acquittal.

jurors, often by using surveys or focus groups to assess the range of views among the local population. Such work is controversial, not least because there is little evidence that it has a particularly substantial effect or, relatedly, that it is any more 'scientific' than the less formal procedures used by attorneys (Hollin, 1989). Research in the UK has found that peremptory challenges to jurors (to have them removed and replaced – something which was abolished in the late 1980s) did not appear to increase the number of cases ending in acquittal (Lloyd-Bostock, 1996).

Decision-making

Studies of 'mock juries' have found that they do change their mind during the course of cases, though not to the extent of arguably the most famous of all films about jury deliberation – *Twelve Angry Men* – in which Henry Fonda, the only juror not to be convinced of the guilt of the defendant, gradually shifts the whole jury to his way of thinking.

In practice, although research suggests that as much as one-third of a jury may change their minds during the course of a case, the most likely outcome remains the one that reflects the balance of opinion in the jury at the outset (Hastie *et al.*, 1983). Another major question asked in jury research is to what extent do they reach the right/wrong decision? Yet again, of course, this is difficult if not almost impossible to research, and psychologists have tended to rely upon approaches such as comparing jury decisions with the views of judges in the case. Hollin reports research by Kalven and Zeisel (1966) which found that in 3,576 trials, there was agreement between judge and jury in 78 per cent of cases. Where there was disagreement, in 19 per cent of cases the jury acquitted where a judge would have convicted, and in only three per cent of cases did a jury convict where a judge would have acquitted. Research by Baldwin and McConville (1979) also found that judges and juries agreed in the majority of cases, and that where they did not, juries were less likely to convict (see also Zander and Henderson, 1993).

Treatment of offenders and 'What Works'

In a number of other chapters we have discussed how the dominant philosophies of punishment changed during the course of the twentieth century and how, in particular, during the second half of the century the goal of rehabilitation came to be seen as increasingly problematic. In 1974 Robert Martinson published what is now a famous essay entitled 'What Works? Questions and answers about prison reform'. In it Martinson sought to assess the impact of interventions with offenders and found relatively few examples of significant impact. Although his conclusions were by no means entirely as pessimistic as they were subsequently portrayed, his work has become associated with the emergence of widespread pessimism about rehabilitative efforts, often now referred to as the 'nothing works' philosophy.

Subsequently, however, there has been something of a revival of interest in rehabilitation, though the current political preference is to talk of 'crime reduction' and 'reducing re-offending'. At the time that the 'nothing works' mood was fairly dominant in the UK, a body of work was being undertaken in Canada in particular which challenged such pessimism and which has been highly influential in the emergence of the more recent 'What Works?' movement in the UK and elsewhere. Much of the work was based on what are known as 'meta-analyses' – essentially a technique which enables statistical analysis of a large number of different empirical studies to be undertaken, and which allows the findings from them to be integrated. A series of meta-analyses were undertaken which apparently identified a number of substantial 'treatment effects', suggesting a number of ways in which offending might be reduced.

Much of the work undertaken in Canada, and which has subsequently become influential elsewhere, was heavily influenced by psychological approaches to understanding offending behaviour. In particular, work by Andrews and Bonta (1998) outlined a theory of offending which sought to integrate social structural factors with cognitive and personality characteristics in treatment models. Goggin and Gendreau (2006: 211) describe the approach of the Canadian psychologists at this time as follows:

> In their roles as clinical and community psychologists, this group was involved in implementing, administering, and evaluating offender assessment and treatment programmes within correctional and governmental jurisdictions that, fortunately, were generally supportive of rehabilitation policies. Professionally they were [familiar and up-to-date] with learning theory as well as related behavioural treatments, and championed

the perspective that criminal behaviour, like most social behaviours, is largely learned and can, therefore, be modified through the use of ethical and appropriate behaviour reinforcement contingencies (rewards and punishers).

The model which emerged from Canada is known as the 'risk-need-responsivity' model. As will be clear, the model contains three separate concepts, or principles, of rehabilitation:

- *Risk* – Which seeks to identify the match between the levels of risk posed by offenders with the actual amount of treatment they receive.

- *Need* – The principle is that programmes should target criminogenic needs (in effect the dynamic risk factors that are associated with recidivism).

- *Responsivity* – This is a programme's ability to engage with its participants in order to maximise the likelihood that the content of the programme will have its expected impact.

According to Ward and Maruna (2007: 64) the 'primary treatment implication of these models is that interventions ought to be focused on modifying or eliminating dynamic risk factors (criminogenic needs)'. Andrews and Bonta (2003) suggest that successful rehabilitation, informed by the risk-need-responsivity model, should be based on six principles. They should be:

- Cognitive-behavioural in orientation.

- Highly structured with a clear statement of aims and objectives.

- Implemented by trained and supervised staff.

- Delivered in the intended manner (treatment integrity).

- Manual-based.

- Housed within institutions committed to the ideals of rehabilitation with appropriate management support. (Ward and Maruna, 2007)

An alternative to the risk-needs-responsivity approach is to be found in what is known as the 'Good Lives' model (Ward and Brown, 2004). Though taking aspects of Andrews and Bonta's approach, this model seeks to move beyond the emphasis on risk factors:

> We argue the management of risk is a necessary but not sufficient condition for the rehabilitation of offenders. We propose that the best way to lower offending recidivism rates is to equip individuals with the tools to live more fulfilling lives rather than to simply develop increasingly sophisticated risk management measures and strategies. At the end of the day, most offenders have more in common with us than not, and like the rest of humanity have needs to be loved, valued, to function competently, and to be part of a community. (Ward and Brown, 2004: 244)

At heart, therefore, the major difference in emphasis is that the Good Lives model, though acknowledging the importance of dealing with risks and deficits with the aim of reducing anti-social behaviour, also places substantial – arguably equal – emphasis on offender welfare, seeing this not as a means to an end, but as a positive end in itself. Ward and Maruna (2007: 173) conclude their comparative review of these two approaches by suggesting that the strength of the risk-responsivity model is that there is by now quite of lot of supporting evidence as to its impact. Its weakness, they argue, lies in its inability to deal with offender motivation and identity. By contrast, the Good Lives model is stronger theoretically, but the research evidence base is still being developed.

Cognitive skills programmes

In Britain, from the early 1990s onwards, a series of 'What Works' conferences were held and the prison and probation services both began to show great interest in the models and programmes being promoted by the Canadian psychologists. Slowly, a number of programmes were developed. One of the first of these, Reasoning and Rehabilitation, was a cognitive-behavioural programme delivered by probation and prison staff and focused on problem-solving skills, critical reasoning and challenging attitudes and beliefs supportive of offending. A variant of this, Straight Thinking on Probation (STOP), adopted the same approach and reported some success at a 12 month follow-up with offenders who completed the programme (Raynor and Vanstone, 1997).

Such programmes generally fall into the category of cognitive skills programmes, and focus on attempts to enable participants to acquire skills and capacities in relation to thinking and problem-solving – hence their title. A model developed by Ross and Fabiano (1985) – the *cognitive model of offender rehabilitation* – has been particularly influential in the development of cognitive skills programmes subsequently. McGuire (2004) suggests that the skills and capacities that such programmes aim to develop include the ability to:

- Identify and tell yourself exactly what the problem is.

- Control the impulse to act on the first idea that comes into your head.

- Generate alternative solutions – consider other things you could do.

- Think in a flexible, rather than a rigid, way about the problem.

- Look ahead and anticipate the possible consequences of your actions.

- Understand the perspective of other people affected by the problem.

The theoretical model that has been most influential in the UK in the last decade has been cognitive behaviouralism. Cognitive-behavioural interventions use a range of structured methods which seek to develop and build cognitive skills where there are deemed to be existing deficits or, alternatively, to restructure cognition where offenders' current patterns of thinking are somehow distorted. The methods include cognitive skills training, anger management and a series of related approaches which seek to improve social skills, assertiveness, reasoning and moral development.

Although the results of early programmes like STOP were far from unequivocally positive, by the late 1990s government was pressing full-steam ahead with its 'What Works' programme across a range of areas, but particularly in connection with rehabilitative activity undertaken by the Prison and Probation services. As we saw in Chapter 27 an accreditation panel was established both to monitor and to promulgate interventions that were deemed to be sufficiently successful. In addition, a series of what became known as 'Pathfinder' projects were established, working in four priority areas. These were:

- Offending behaviour programmes (involving the delivery of cognitive-behavioural programmes to offenders under supervision).

- Basic skills (using supervision as an opportunity to train educationally disadvantaged offenders in basic literacy and numeracy skills which might help them to get jobs).

- An enhanced version of Community Service (aiming to teach offenders more pro-social attitudes and behaviour as well as useful skills).

- Resettlement projects for short-term prisoners (often persistent offenders with a high risk of reconviction, but not subject to compulsory post-release supervision and increasingly unlikely to be offered services on a voluntary basis) (Raynor, 2004: 311).

In the event, although there have been numerous positive reported results in relation to cognitive-behavioural therapeutic approaches (McGuire, 2002; Andrews and Bonta, 2003), the outcome of many of the UK programmes has been disappointing, with difficulties of implementation, of practice and of evaluation (Raynor and Vanstone, 2002).

According to Raynor (2007) the pace of implementation in some cases led to shortcuts being taken, including changing the targets set for the number of offenders completing particular programmes. The creation of the national probation service (see Chapter 27) also drew some energy away from the new programmes and disrupted implementation. Projects were often slow to start and there were several cases where they were insufficiently developed or embedded at the time evaluation was to begin. There were considerable problems of 'attrition' (offenders dropping out before completing the programme) in some of the Pathfinders and this limited what research was able to say about impact. The outcome of the whole initiative has therefore been rather disappointing, though Raynor (2007: 1083) notes that the 'three year implementation timescale, with a major reorganization [of the probation service] in the middle, was never likely to be long enough to show clear benefit from such a complex process of change'.

Such an outcome might be viewed as especially disappointing given the weight of evidence that has been building in relation to offending behaviour programmes around the world. A recent Home Office review of evidence in this area, though acknowledging the limitations of some of the research, concluded that: 'International evidence from systematic reviews of effective practice on reducing re-offending tends to support the use of cognitive-behavioural offending behaviour programmes and interventions with offenders' (Harper and Chitty, 2004: 51). Much of this type of support comes from what are referred to as meta-analyses – a methodological technique for analysing and combining the results of a range of studies. However, although 'the meta-analyses have highlighted an overall treatment effect ... this effect is an aggregated statistical effect across different treatment modalities rather than a consistent effect of a single approach' (Hollin and Palmer, 2006: 21–2). This is an area, therefore, in which further careful evaluation of individual programmes is required (something that proved to be problematic in the case of some of the recent Pathfinders), together with the development of further theoretical models along the lines of the approach outlined earlier in the work by Ward and Maruna (2007).

Review questions

1 What are the three main stages involved in understanding the process of remembering information?

2 How can vulnerable witnesses be protected?

3 What is 'scientific jury selection'?

4 What are the basic facets of cognitive behavioural approaches to treatment?

Questions for further discussion

1 Why has British criminology been reluctant to embrace psychological approaches to offending?

2 What are the strengths and weaknesses of risk factor theory?

3 Are compulsory detention and forced medication a necessary response to mentally disordered offending?

4 Is it realistic to suggest that the primary aim of police interrogation should be something other than the search for a confession?

5 What ethical issues are raised by the use of offender profiling?

6 Under what circumstances should jury selection be allowed?

Further reading

There are a number of helpful introductions – of differing sizes and levels – which will provide more complete discussions of the topics contained in this chapter. They include:

Ainsworth, P. (2000) *Psychology and Crime: Myths and reality*, Harlow: Longman

Hollin, C. (1989) *Psychology and Crime*, London: Routledge

Howitt, D. (2006) *An Introduction to Forensic and Criminal Psychology*, 2nd edn, Harlow: Longman

On developmental criminology I would recommend: Farrington, D. and Welsh, B. (2007) *Saving Children from a Life of Crime*, Oxford: Oxford University Press, and Smith, D.J. (2007) Crime and the life course, in Maguire, M. *et al.* (eds) *The Oxford Handbook of Criminology*, 4th edn, Oxford: Oxford University Press.

On profiling, a range of good articles is contained in: Alison, L. (ed.) (2005) *The Forensic Psychologist's Casebook*, Cullompton: Willan.

On mentally disordered offenders you should begin with: Peay, J. (2007) Mentally disordered offenders, mental health and crime, in Maguire, M. *et al.* (eds) *The Oxford Handbook of Criminology*, 4th edn, Oxford: Oxford University Press, and Prins, H. (2005) *Offenders, Deviants or Patients?* 3rd edn, London: Routledge.

On treatment programmes for offenders: Hollin, C. and Palmer, E. (eds) (2006) *Offending Behaviour Programmes*, Chichester: Wiley. For a critical review of the impact of 'what works' see: Mair, G. (ed.) (2004) *What Matters in Probation*, Cullompton: Willan; and the special issue of the journal *Criminology and Criminal Justice* (vol. 4, no. 3, 2004, London: Sage Journals) which examines the government's Crime Reduction Programme.

On the general issue of rehabilitation see Ward, T. and Maruna, S. (2007) *Rehabilitation*, London: Routledge.

Websites

The Centre for Investigative Psychology: www.i-psy.com
British Psychological Society: www.bps.org.uk

There is a wealth of interesting information about evidence at the Innocence Project website: http://www.innocenceproject.org

Chapter outline

Globalisation 868
  Globalisation and criminology 869
  Criminalising migration 869

Terrorism 871
  What is terrorism? 871
  Terrorism in Britain 872
  The new international terrorism 873
  Special powers for special circumstances? 874
    Control orders and the PATRIOT Act 875
  Terrorism and the 'new wars' 875
    Private military industry 876
    Privatised security in Iraq 877

State crime 878
  Genocide 879
    Cambodia 880
    Rwanda 880
    Bosnia 881
  War as crime and war crimes 882

Human rights 883
  Origins of human rights 883
    Human rights in the twentieth century 884
  Human rights in Britain 886
    The Human Rights Act 1998 886
    The impact of the Human Rights Act 888
  Criminology and human rights 890
  Dealing with human rights abuses 891
  Advantages and disadvantages of different tribunals 892

Questions for further discussion 892
Further reading 893
Websites 893

34

Globalisation, terrorism and human rights

CHAPTER SUMMARY

'Globalisation' is a term that has now entered the everyday language. It is generally used as a short-hand way of referring to a set of changes that give the feel of a shrinking world: much faster, internationalised means of communication; much greater movement of goods and peoples; and a perceived reduction in the importance of national boundaries in everything from trade to politics.

In this chapter we consider some of the most important ways in which globalisation affects crime and justice; we explore:

● the term itself, considering what it means and how it is applied;

● issues of terrorism;

● the growth of international terrorism;

● some of the issues and threats posed by such activities.

Although we are used to thinking and talking about the state as a guarantor of security, as critical criminologists in particular remind us, it is important not to lose sight of the fact that the state can also act in illegal ways. We explore the idea of state crimes and then conclude the chapter by looking at what has become the dominant way of talking about protections against contemporary abuses: human rights.

Globalisation

The German sociologist, Ulrich Beck, among others, argues that just as modernisation produced the transition from feudalism to industrialism, so it is now dissolving industrial society and a new form of modernity is coming into being. This new form, if that is what it is, has numerous attributes which in various combinations have given rise to a number of partly overlapping and competing labels, including postmodernity, late modernity, disorganised capitalism (Lash and Urry, 1994), risk society (Beck, 1992), reflexive modernisation (Beck, 1992; Giddens, 1990), and globalisation. For the purposes of the discussion in this chapter we will stick with the term *globalisation*. What is meant by this? Globalisation is 'the intensification of worldwide social relations which link distant localities in such a way that local happenings are shaped by events occurring many miles away and vice versa' (Giddens, 1990: 64).

In essence the term refers to a set of processes that have the consequence of bringing otherwise distant places into fairly close and immediate contact with each other, and in ways in which what happens in one place may have very significant consequences for the other. An example of this would be the way in which a recession in the United States or a dramatic failure in, say, the Chinese or Indian economies would have very sizeable and lasting consequences in many parts of the world – and very clearly in the UK. More particularly, there are a number of core elements that help explain the nature of globalisation. These include:

● The spread and connectedness of communication, production and technologies across the world. These enable you to see events from the other side of the world almost instantaneously. Thus, when a war begins, a disaster strikes or some other major event occurs, there is very often a camera there and the ability now exists to see events as they happen from the other side of the globe (how many of you were watching television as the second plane went into the World Trade Center on 11 September 2001?)

● The speed and power of technological innovation. Thus, for example, the number of online internet users grew from zero in 1985 to 605 million by 2002; the number of mobile phones in the UK grew from zero in 1978 to 24 million by 2000, with an estimated 400 million worldwide; and, the number of international air travellers increased from 25 million to 400 million between 1950 and 1996.

- The emergence, growth and spread of multinational corporations. You might quickly check now where your clothes, shoes or trainers were made.

- The development of, or attempts to create, a global free market.

- Developments meaning that matters that would once have been dealt with face-to-face can now can be managed across huge distances in real time (these processes have been referred to as de-localisation and supraterritoriality).

- The increasing ease of movement of people – with the associated tensions this may bring.

Globalisation and criminology

Why is the subject of globalisation of importance or relevance to criminology? We can identify at least four main reasons:

1 Globalisation affects the nature of the nation state and therefore has consequences for the organisation of policing and criminal justice (which you might see described as changes in the nature of 'sovereign authority').

2 It leads to new opportunities for crime, or new means by which criminal activities can be conducted.

3 It gives rise to new insecurities and inequalities.

4 It has been argued that one of the consequences of globalisation is that it gives rise to a new 'mentality' which prioritises assessments of risk as a central way of organising social and political life (see Chapter 16).

The bulk of the discussion of crime, criminal justice and penal policies in this book has focused on Britain, though we have looked at issues and trends elsewhere from time to time. And, indeed, much crime and crime control continue to make sense at the national level. However, processes of globalisation which involve the creation of supranational bodies and jurisdictions, international laws, trade agreements and protocols, mean that there is a level of activity and action beyond the nation state, and which cannot be reduced to the actions of one or more nation states. Some of this activity concerns crime, security and order and needs to be understood in its transnational or global context (see Chapter 19). Second, the revolution in communication technologies which allows people and signals to be transported around the globe far more easily than hitherto, opens up new possibilities for criminal activity.

Little of this is entirely new – internet fraud, for example, is just another form of fraud. However, the internet makes new forms of fraud, and new techniques for fraud, possible. Third, arguably, globalising changes give rise to new insecurities. The centrality of electronic communication in modern lives has focused attention on such matters as computer-based fraud and identity theft, for example. More concretely, globalisation has brought forth new patterns of migration. The last decade or so has seen issues such as asylum and immigration become linked with concerns about crime and security. 'Protecting our borders' is one very clear illustration of globalisation-induced insecurities. We will return to this below. Finally, the processes of globalisation result in the progressive rise of a risk-oriented mentality. Risk is no longer tied to place; it is global in its potential in (at least) two important ways. First, as commentators such as Beck argue, the last century has seen the emergence of risks that have localised consequences, but also threaten the globe – from nuclear weapons to environmental catastrophe. Second, the 'shrinking' of the globe through ease of communication and movement of people means that matters occurring on one side of the world can have enormous, and all but immediate, consequences for people and places on the other side. Finally, and crucially, the idea of *risk* in the context of Beck's risk society thesis has a forward-looking element in it, placing emphasis on attempting to calculate the likelihood of future occurrences and acting accordingly (see Chapter 16).

These processes have had profound consequences in the field of crime control – shifting attention from crimes that have been committed to the risks of future crimes. They have also led to the criminalisation of new areas of activity as 'new threats' are identified. Under conditions of globalisation, as ease of movement increases, and particularly with current concerns around security (which we come to below), one of these areas is migration.

Criminalising migration

For the reasons described above, and others, in recent decades immigration has become a somewhat fraught area of public policy. How is immigration to be managed and controlled? Should limits be set and, if so, how should they be monitored and policed? What is the appropriate response to people arriving and claiming asylum? One of the responses in individual nation states, and indeed in Europe more generally, has been to attempt to strengthen border controls. Germany imposed visa requirements on people from specific countries (traditionally associated with asylum-seeking) as early as 1980, and Britain and others did so not long afterward. Several states, including Britain, Canada and the US, and now all EU member states, have imposed sanctions on airlines and others who bring in undocumented or falsely-documented passengers (Webber, 2004).

In addition to border controls and immigration checks, a series of situational measures have been used, including night vision aids, thermal imaging, and closed-circuit and video surveillance to protect and secure some of the more common points of entry. Apparently, in 1999, the border between Germany and its neighbours Poland and the Czech Republic had the highest density of border guards in the world (quoted in Webber, 2004).

One of the greatest concerns currently is the issue of immigrant detention. Concern about the potential for people to 'disappear' once they have crossed borders has led to the establishment in many countries of immigration detention centres where people can be held whilst their case is heard and resolved. In both the UK and the US, immigration detention was the basis for the first experiment in privatising custodial institutions (see Chapter 28) and there have been repeated concerns voiced about the conditions in such centres.

In a now infamous case at Yarl's Wood detention centre, what was perceived to be the overly-aggressive restraint of a 52 year-old female detainee led to a protest and to the burning of large parts of the centre, with damage estimated at least at £40 million. Though police arrived within ten minutes of the emergency call, they were not let on site by the private security company that guarded the site, and fire brigade officials also later criticised the company for locking inmates into an unsafe site. Two men were eventually convicted of offences relating to the fire. In the UK, unlike much of the rest of Europe, there are no legal limits on the time a person may be held in such a detention centre. Existing statistics suggest that about two-fifths of detainees are held for less than a month, but that almost one-fifth may be held for four months or more (Welch and Schuster, 2005).

Controversy has also surrounded the eventual ejection of refuges and asylum seekers who have not been given leave to stay. This is far from a new area

Yarl's Wood detention centre near Bedford was the largest immigration detention centre in Europe when it opened in 2001. Less than three months later, half of it was destroyed by fire following a protest about the treatment of a woman detainee.

of concern, however. In 1993 the Metropolitan Police raided a house in North London in order to serve a deportation order. The order was for the removal of a 40 year-old woman, Joy Gardner. She was restrained by officers who handcuffed her and wound several metres of tape round her head in order to stop her screaming. Joy Gardner was taken to hospital in a coma, but never regained consciousness. Three officers were prosecuted, but acquitted. A study by the Medical Foundation for the Care of Victims of Torture examined 14 more recent cases of alleged abuse in cases linked with deportation. The methods of restraint that had been used in these cases included 'being dragged along the ground, being kicked or kneed, being punched – including to the head and face, being elbowed, having the thumb forcibly bent back, pressure being applied to the angle of the jaw, pressure exerted on the neck, being sat on (thorax and abdomen), and assault to the genitals' (Granville-Chapman et al., 2004). The study concluded that 'There appears to be misuse of normally accepted restraint methods, which in some cases would seem to be deliberate and intended to cause pain or suffering'.

In addition to questions being raised about the general treatment by the state of refugees and those seeking asylum, there is also the broader context of the impact of the often-negative coverage of immigration in public life (Pickering, 2001). The image of benefit-scrounging, illegal immigrants 'flooding' the country can be found implicitly and, sometimes, explicitly in media and political discussions of asylum and immigration.

The consequence is in some ways a fairly classic 'moral panic'. As Stan Cohen has observed:

> Assume we know, that over the last three years, (i) that X% of asylum seekers make false claims about their risk of being persecuted; (ii) that only a small proportion (say 20%) of this subgroup have their claims recognized and (iii) that the resultant numbers of fake asylum seekers are about 200 each year. Surely then the claim about 'the country being flooded with bogus asylum seekers' is out of proportion. (2002: xxviii)

There is some evidence of a rise in the level of hate crime in the UK, and more broadly in Europe, and many have argued that an element of this – directed at people perceived to be 'outsiders' – is linked to the tenor of public discussion. The European Commission in 2001 commented that, 'Problems of xenophobia, racism and discrimination persist and are particularly acute *vis-à-vis* asylum seekers and refugees. This is reflected in the xenophobic and intolerant coverage of these groups of persons in the media, but also in the tone of the discourse resorted to by politicians in support of the adoption and reinforcement of increasingly restrictive asylum immigration laws' (quoted in Block and Schuster, 2002).

Moreover, research shows that the government policy of 'dispersal', introduced following the Immigration and Asylum Act 1999, in which people seeking asylum are often sent to live in quite deprived areas around the UK, results in relatively high levels of both physical and verbal abuse (Anie *et al.*, 2005). As we will see below, the tendency to respond to the movement of people through criminal justice measures of surveillance and detention has only increased since 11 September 2001, and the 'war on terror' has seemingly exacerbated some existing tensions, as well as creating some new ones.

Terrorism

If any one thing captures the way in which issues associated with globalisation have affected the territory in which criminologists have an interest, it is surely the emergence of *international terrorism* as a key issue of our times. Theorists of globalisation view the range of changes identified under this heading as collectively resulting in the emergence of a new political order. This order has a number of characteristics, but they include the growing importance of sources of political power and authority beyond individual nation states, consequent changes to the nature of citizenship, much greater freedom of movement, and very significant changes in the nature of conflict (in part what we will discuss later under the heading of 'new wars'). One aspect of this changing global order can be seen in the activities of relatively small groups of terrorists whose links are primarily ideological rather than territorial, and whose communications are as likely to be conducted via internet and satellite phones as face-to-face.

Terrorism is not a matter that criminologists have traditionally spent much time researching or writing about. In the main, this has been left to political scientists and international relations specialists. However, for reasons we have already explored (the blurring of domestic and international security issues; arguments about the changing role of the state in the maintenance of order; and the impact of international security concerns on domestic policing and law and order), criminologists are belatedly taking an interest in this area.

Terrorism is not unique to the modern era. The terms 'terrorism' and 'terrorist' date back to the late eighteenth century (Lacquer, 1987). Prior to the 1960s most terrorist activity was localised. It was either confined within specific geographic jurisdictions or limited to certain regions. However, the rapid advances in transportation and communication technology associated with globalisation have brought about a shift in the nature and scale of the terrorist threat. Some commentators have suggested that such advances heralded a new form of terrorism – what has been called 'non-territorial terrorism' (Sloan, 1978), and certainly the use of the term nowadays of 'international terrorism' is a reflection of the fact that some of the most extreme terrorist threats come from loose networks of small groups that are not based in any particular country or region. In what follows we will consider four main questions: what is terrorism; what experience of terrorism do we have in Britain; does responding to terrorism require special measures; and what impact and relevance has all this for criminology?

What is terrorism?

Terrorism is hard to define. However, for our purposes here, the legal definition contained in section 1 of the Terrorism Act 2000 is sufficient.

The Act covers actual or threatened acts of violence against people and/or property designed to influence the government, to intimidate the public or a section of the public, or to advance a political, religious or ideological cause. Wilkinson (2006: 328) suggests that terrorism can be distinguished from other forms of violence in the following way:

● It is premeditated and designed to create a climate of extreme fear.

● It is directed at a wider target than the immediate victims.

● It inherently involves attacks on random or symbolic targets, including civilians.

● It is considered by the society in which it occurs as 'extra-normal', that is in the literal sense that it violates the norms regulating disputes, protest and dissent.

● It is used primarily, though not exclusively, to influence the political behaviour of governments, communities or specific social groups.

A number of distinctions can be drawn in order to differentiate forms and types of terrorist activity. Increasingly important is the distinction between *domestic* terrorism, which occurs within national boundaries and doesn't involve people from other states, and *international* terrorism which involves people from several states. Wilkinson also distinguishes between four types of non-state terrorist movements or groups:

● *Ethno-nationalist* groups – Groups identified by ethnicity and political motivation such as ETA, the Basque separatist organisation.

● *Ideological* groups – Such as the Red Brigade in Italy in the 1970s and 1980s, which sought to create a communist state.

● *Religio-political* groups – Such as Hamas in Palestine, which aims to create an Islamic republic.

● *Single issue* groups – Including animal rights groups such as the Animal Liberation Front.

Terrorism in Britain

Until recently, for the police and security services in the UK, the major anti-terrorist activity has been as a result of the Troubles in Northern Ireland since 1969. Since 1969 over 3,000 people have died because of political violence in Northern Ireland, and the conflict has affected people far beyond the borders of the region, leading to the deaths of

approximately 200 people in Great Britain, the Republic of Ireland, and elsewhere in Europe (O'Leary and McGarry, 1993; McKittrick *et al.*, 1999). Put crudely, the terrorist campaigns emanated from two primary sources: republican groups (the provisional IRA, the Irish National Liberation Army, and the 'dissident groups', the 'real' IRA, and the Continuity IRA) and loyalist paramilitary organisations (primarily the Ulster Volunteer Force, the Ulster Defence Association, and the Loyalist Volunteer Force). The terrorist activities included: attacks on members of the police and the army; political assassinations and attempted assassinations (such as the bombing of the Conservative Party Conference in Brighton in 1984); bombings of shops, pubs, hotels and other targets in city centres in Northern Ireland and in England; as well as sectarian-inspired violence and murder.

There have been two other sources of domestic political violence in Britain in recent times: so-called 'animal rights extremists' and the activities of far right political groups, such as Combat 18.

Front of the Grand Hotel in Brighton after the bombing by the Provisional IRA during the Conservative Party's annual conference in 1984. Five people were killed in the explosion. Margaret Thatcher, the Prime Minister, escaped unharmed.

Terrorism 873

Established in the early 1990s, Combat 18 was 'a by-product of the rising militancy within the British National Party' which by that time had replaced the National Front as the main far right party in the UK (Lowles, 2001). In addition to its involvement in numerous violent attacks, Combat 18 was also believed to be linked to Loyalist paramilitaries in Northern Ireland, in particular the Ulster Defence Association (and also the Ulster Volunteer Force).

The extreme end of the animal rights movement has been involved in various forms of civil disobedience, some of which have been held to constitute a form of terrorism. These include: industrial sabotage, destruction of property, raids on premises associated with animal exploitation (to gather evidence, to sabotage, to free animals), together with the intimidation of, and attacks upon, individuals held to be in breach of 'animal rights'. Professor Colin Blakemore, at one time the director of Oxford University's Centre for Cognitive Neuroscience, for example, has been sent letter bombs, attacked, received kidnap threats against his family and is accompanied by a police escort when travelling.

Much of the international terrorism in the UK has been connected to the Middle East, though with links far beyond, particularly to Africa. In 1970, the Black September group assassinated the Jordanian ambassador in London, and in June 1982 the Abu Nidal group killed the Israeli ambassador in London. The Israeli Embassy in London, and other Jewish targets, were bombed in 1994, and there were a number of incidents in the mid-1990s involving Sikh terrorists (Taylor, 2002). Overseas, terrorism-related activities include the kidnappings of Terry Waite, John McCarthy and others in Beirut in 1986–87, as well as other incidents in Yemen, Chechnya, and the murder of the British military attaché in Athens in June 2000.

Of course, this all changed, initially on 11 September 2001, with the attacks in New York and Washington DC when at least 65 Britons were among the 2,000 or more who were killed. The bombings in London on 7 July 2005 marked a new development. The bombs, which exploded on three tube trains and a bus, killed 52 people and injured as many as 700 others. They were detonated by suicide bombers, the first time such an approach to terrorism had been used in western Europe. Moreover, though many aspects of the bombings had the characteristics of an al-Qaeda attack, it was soon established that the young Muslim men involved were British.

Wreckage of a London double-decker bus shortly after being blown up in Tavistock Square, 7 July 2005 – the fourth of the four terrorist bomb explosions in London that day which killed 52 people.

The new international terrorism

Globalisation is argued by some to have brought with it a shift in the nature of terrorism. Political developments – the end of the Cold War and the emergence of new conflict, as well as the growing impact of environmental change – together with new technological advances are held to have resulted in the emergence of new threats such as those posed by weapons of mass destruction and by cyber-terrorism. Taylor and Horgan (1999: 84) predict three fundamentally different sources of future terrorism:

- *International sources* – Which will relate to the absorption of terrorism within conventional warfare.

- *Focused issue-based terrorism* – Which might be local in character like the Oklahoma bombing (in April 1995), or narrow but international in character, such as anti-abortion terrorism.

- *Organised crime-related terrorism* – Where the techniques of terrorism may be used for political ends to achieve financial gain.

It is argued that, increasingly, the traditional constraints that inhibited high impact/high casualty methods no longer apply, so that whereas it was once the case that 'terrorists wanted a lot of people watching, not a lot of people dead. Now they evidently want both, or so it is widely believed' (Weinberg and Eubank, 1999: 94). This does not mean that the principles of terrorism have changed, possibly just its scale.

A number of authors have argued that contemporary conditions make terrorism more threatening and states less able to cope with it. Philip Bobbit (2002) has advanced one of the more pessimistic visions of modern times. He argues that the new threats will lead to a fundamental reworking of the state. The fact that loosely-knit groups involving relatively small numbers of people can pose a threat to nation states is part of the problem. So is the fact that such attacks can be disguised so that it is difficult to know, as he puts it, 'whether they are the result of a terrorist's attack, or a strategic assault by another state, or just the afternoon diversions of a teenager in California' (2002: 812). As a result we will see what previously were the majority 'certainties' of national security – that security is national not international, that it is public rather than private, and that it seeks victory not stalemate – being turned upside down. The implication is that we will respond to these threats differently and, in particular, that much less concern will be shown for civil liberties and the rule of law.

Special powers for special circumstances?

Two competing arguments can be identified. One holds that the most successful policing and security strategies in relation to terrorism are precisely those that use normal policing methods. By contrast, there are many who would argue the reverse: that the very nature of terrorism requires special tactics and approaches. Taking the example of the Troubles in Northern Ireland, it is clear that a broad range of counter-insurgency tactics were used including:

- internment without trial;
- the abolition of trial by jury;
- brutal methods of interrogation;
- alleged abuse of army and police powers of arrest, stop and search;
- the use of 'supergrasses' to obtain convictions; and (at its most extreme),
- the adoption of an alleged 'shoot to kill policy'.

Although emergency legislation was passed on several occasions extending police powers, some critics have argued that the majority of terrorist arrests in England, Wales and Northern Ireland could have been made under normal provisions (Hillyard, 1997).

Northern Ireland became a favoured site for testing and developing an array of new technology, including helicopter monitoring equipment fitted with surveillance and night vision cameras, telephone taps, advanced communications and automatic vehicle tracking systems, computerised data intelligence banks with remote access to terminals in police vehicles and at border check points. On the British mainland, there has also been a greatly increased emphasis on the use of technology in the attempt to prevent terrorism. After the first major bombing in 1992 in the City of London, the ideas of private responsibility for security and the creation of 'defensible space' were heavily promoted both by the local police and by the City of London Corporation and the Home Office. In parallel with the use of technical intelligence-gathering systems there has also been a growing reliance on 'human intelligence'. The infiltration of political groups, or the encouragement of informants within them, has become another standard tactic in anti-terrorist activity (Stevens, 2003) and this has certainly been used with some success against groups like Combat 18.

Finally in relation to police powers and tactics, recent years have seen increasing emphasis placed on forfeiture and asset seizure as a means of hampering the work of terrorist organisations. The successes the FBI in America had in their use of the Racketeer Influenced Corrupt Organizations (RICO) legislation passed in 1970 were a significant boost to this kind of policing. Prior to 9/11 the link between crimes for economic gain with terrorism was not high on the agenda of the USA or of many of the major international investigative bodies. Subsequently, however, in the UK the National Terrorist Financial Investigation Unit, based within the Metropolitan Police Special Branch, has trebled its staff resources and, according to the Cabinet Office (2002), assets worth over $100 million have been frozen since 9/11. There are a number of suggested differences between the funding of terrorism and other forms of 'organised' criminal activity:

- Some forms of terrorism may be state-sponsored.
- Some terrorist organisations can rely for their funding wholly, or in part, on donations and contributions from supporters.
- Many terrorist organisations engage in legitimate business activities as a means of supporting themselves, though the latter is certainly true of much organised crime, too.

In the past 20 years or more, a gradual accretion of powers has occurred through the passage of special legislation designed, on the surface at least, to deal with the policing of terrorism. The emergency powers that were introduced in the first half of the twentieth century were largely incorporated into the Emergency Powers Act 1973 (Walker, 2000). Police powers have increased time and again as new legislation has been passed, most usually in response to specific terrorist activities, initially Irish republican terrorism. Legislation has broadened the definition of terrorism, created new acts of conspiracy, extended police powers of arrest without a warrant and, via the Anti-Terrorism, Crime and Security Act 2001, considerably increased powers of detention of immigrants suspected of terrorism (Matassa and Newburn, 2003), and more recent legislation has further increased police powers (Walker, 2005).

Control orders and the PATRIOT Act

Particular concern in the UK has been expressed in relation to the recently introduced 'control orders'. The restrictions that can be applied under a control order include 'prohibitions on the possession or use of certain items, restrictions on movement to or within certain areas, restrictions on communications and associations, and requirements as to place of abode', the most restrictive of which would be indefinite 'house arrest'. The extent to which such orders run counter to human rights legislation is illustrated by their name: the most restrictive orders are referred to as 'derogating control orders', effectively in recognition that special dispensation was required for the government to avoid its responsibilities under Article 5 of the European Convention. As we have seen, criminologists have been writing for some time now about a perceived shift toward a more future-oriented, risk-focused form of crime control, and control orders are, perhaps, recent and extreme examples of this type of development.

Similar developments are visible in the United States. The PATRIOT Act (the acronym stands for the Uniting and Strengthening America by Providing Appropriate Tools Required to Intercept and Obstruct Terrorism), passed in the aftermath of 9/11, vastly extends US law enforcement agencies' powers to monitor internet use, to conduct clandestine physical searches, and to access financial records. Thus, for example, it:

- increases the power of agencies to use wiretaps on individuals 'proximate' to the primary person being tapped, to use such 'roving

wiretaps' to monitor all communications transmitted through particular facilities, such as public libraries and internet cafés;
- significantly expands their ability to conduct secret searches for material that 'constitutes evidence of a criminal offence in violation of the laws of the US' (i.e. is not limited to investigations in connection with terrorism);
- increases powers available to compel the production of business, medical, employment and library records without showing 'probable cause' (i.e. information showing a link with a suspected crime) by simply linking it to an ongoing terrorist investigation.

British legislation – such as the Anti-Terrorist, Crime and Security Act 2001 – doesn't go nearly as far.

Nevertheless, the Prevention of Terrorism Act 2005, together with other changes made as part of the 'security agenda', is perhaps the clearest illustration that, since 9/11, there appears an increased willingness on the part of government to extend policing powers in a fairly radical manner, whilst apparently being less concerned with how such powers should be regulated. Police actions in the aftermath of the 7 July 2005 bombings in London might potentially also be seen in this light. Indeed, the process of 'normalisation' that occurred in relation to the gradual incorporation of emergency powers into the armoury of everyday policing in Northern Ireland and beyond during the Troubles (Hillyard, 1994) can, arguably, be seen occurring once again in the response to the more recent terrorist threats.

Terrorism and the 'new wars'

In Chapter 25 we looked at the pluralisation of policing and the growth of private security. In addition, at several stages we have noted how both public and private policing organisations working in this field have begun increasingly to work across national boundaries. Such activity is nowadays commonly referred to as *transnational policing*. These processes of pluralisation and transnationalisation are argued to be having a dramatic impact on the nature and structure of contemporary policing. In parallel with these developments in the area of policing it is also possible to see a number of important shifts in the field of international security and conflict which have taken place largely since the end of the Cold War (usually considered as occurring with the fall of the Berlin Wall in 1991). One of the outcomes of these changes has been the very rapid emergence of a privatised military industry. Thus, just as domestic security is increasingly policed by an amalgam of public and private agencies, so a similar mixture is visible in the international security arena.

As Rothe (2006: 215) notes, the 'intersection of state and corporate interests during times of war is a fundamental part of the war-making process'. However, recently the integration of state interests with those of the private corporation has intensified. The private military industry has grown and spread extraordinarily quickly. In part this was a result of the end of the Cold War and the removal of any immediate threat of war between East and West. Consequently, many countries reduced the size of their standing armies, navies and air forces. This had two important consequences. It reduced state military capacity and made it more difficult for them to respond to international crises, and it produced a ready supply of trained military personnel looking for jobs. Despite the fact that many countries slimmed down their military, other developments increased the demand for troops. Most importantly, there was an increase in global instability which led to the emergence of a series of bloody conflicts in Africa and Eastern Europe in particular.

This led some commentators to remark on what seemed to be the changing nature of warfare in which the characteristics of the conflicts concerned are quite different from *traditional* wars. Increasingly, wars are not waged in the national interest. They are less and less likely to result from established rivalries between hostile nation states. And, frequently, rather than being the product of strong states threatening others, they are the result of the weakening or weak*ness* of particular nation-states. As a consequence, many now talk of the emergence of the 'new wars' (Kaldor, 1999), 'post-national wars' (Beck, 2005) or 'network wars' (Duffield, 2005).

Private military industry

There are at least three main reasons why the rise of the private military industry is associated with globalisation:

- Following the work of the sociologist Max Weber, the central defining characteristic of the modern nation state is often taken to be its monopolisation of the legitimate use of force. The rise of the private military may, therefore, indicate that the role and/or power of the nation state are changing.

- Many of the conflicts around the world that have involved the private military are viewed as being partially a consequence of globalisation.

- The shift toward the greater use of non-state bodies, especially the private sector, is seen as a central characteristic of neo-liberalism – the spread of market and private sector mentalities – itself closely associated with globalisation.

Despite some novel aspects, it is important to recognise that the private contracting of military services has a lengthy history, much of which concerns the murky activities of mercenaries. However, in the last ten to 15 years, a vast international network of privatised military operators has emerged to become an established part of modern warfare. The new private military industry is largely made up of a complex web of large corporate providers, many working in direct partnership with established military forces. The industry consists of three main sectors (Singer, 2004):

- Military support firms which provide logistical and intelligence services.

- Military consulting firms that provide strategic advice and training.

- Military provider firms which offer tactical, military assistance including the defence of key installations and individuals, together with combat services. This latter sector is sometimes referred to as 'private security'.

One of the consequences of the nature of the 'new wars', not least their messiness, has been that Western powers have become increasingly reluctant to intervene, producing situations in which transnational bodies such as the United Nations (UN), non-state actors such as NGOs and, increasingly, private corporations became involved. Thus, for example, every multilateral peace operation conducted by the UN since 1990s has included private security companies (Avant, 2005: 7). Additionally, even when the military have been involved in peacekeeping or other frontline operations, more and more often they act with the support of, or in partnership with, private military suppliers of various forms.

Finally, as mentioned earlier, the rise of the private military has been promoted by a set of economic changes associated with the increasing influence of neo-liberal policies in America, Europe and beyond. A significant element of such economic programmes has involved the promotion of policies of privatisation as a means of generating greater efficiency and effectiveness through the use of the market as a means of managing competition. In Britain these changes affected the military rather later than a number of other sectors. Nevertheless the changes have been quite dramatic and nowhere have some of the consequences of this trend been more visible than in the recent conflict in Iraq (Whyte, 2007).

Privatised security in Iraq

According to Singer (2005) Iraq was the site of the largest deployment of private military firms ever. By 2005 there were over 60 firms employing more than 20,000 private personnel engaged in military activities in Iraq (and, of course, thousands more private operators providing non-military services). The UK Foreign Office confirmed that it alone had paid £30m during 2004 to private security companies (about two-thirds of it in Iraq, *Independent on Sunday*, 19 March 2005) having paid £20m in 2003. Three groups dominated the market in such work: Control Risks Group, Armor Group, and Pegasus Security (*Independent on Sunday*, 27 March 2005).

Armor, a private security company listed in London, chaired by ex-Foreign Secretary, Sir Malcolm Rifkind, is estimated to have earned over £50m during 2004 alone – almost half its total revenue – through its guarding activities in Iraq (*Evening Standard*, 24 January 2005). By early 2006 it was employing around 1,300 people in Iraq. The largest private security contract went to another London-based company, Aegis Defence Services, headed by Col. Tim Spicer (whose previous company, Sandline, was involved in breaking the UN arms embargo in its private military work in Sierra Leone in 1998) (*The Independent*, 5 January 2005).

All three major forms of Private Military Firm (PMF) activity have been in plentiful supply in post-war Iraq (Whyte, 2007). The American company Halliburton, for example, is reckoned to have undertaken at least $6 billion worth of business providing military logistical support activity (Singer, 2004; Rothe, 2006). Similarly, a number of companies have secured large contracts to provide military consulting services, such as creating the new Iraqi police force and army. But, as Singer (2004) notes, 'the most dramatic and controversial expansion of PMF involvement is in the combat realm' through tactical PMFs like Custer Battles and Control Risks. One company, Blackwater, provided protection and transport to the chief of the Coalition Provisional Authority, Paul Bremer (this contract alone being worth $21 million). Far from

the everyday image of private security, these corporations are engaging in activity that is very similar to, and undoubtedly carries the same risks as, the military:

> Blackwater, the firm that lost the four men in Fallujah, just days later defended the CPA [Coalition Provisional Authority] headquarters in Najaf from being overrun by radical Shiite militia. The firefight lasted several hours, with thousands of rounds of ammunition fired, and Blackwater even sent in its own helicopters twice to resupply its commandos with ammunition and to ferry out a wounded U.S. Marine. (Singer, 2004b)

The notorious prison at Abu Ghraib near Baghdad, run at various times by American private corporations – and originally built by British contractors in the 1960s.

The entire conflict has been book-ended by the activities of the private military. The invasion of Iraq was launched from Camp Doha, built, operated and guarded by number of private corporations led by a consortium called Combat Support Associates (Singer, 2004b). Detainees have been held in camps and prisons similarly built, and often run, by private corporations, including infamously both Abu Ghraib and Guantanamo Bay military prison which was built by the Kellogg, Brown and Root division of Halliburton at a cost of $45 million (Singer, 2003: 17). Such private corporations are involved in a broad range of activity. Their promotional literature is fascinating, for it provides a very clear insight into how another key attribute of globalisation – the rise of risk discourses and mentalities – is an important organising principle of this type of work. The example of the company Custer Battles, reproduced below, captures this well.

CUSTER BATTLES

Transforming risk into opportunity

Securing framework to rebuild Iraq
Iraq is a nation and marketplace wrought with challenges, obstacles, and malevolent actors. However, Iraq offers contractors, traders, entrepreneurs as well as multi-national enterprises an unprecedented market opportunity. The ability to identify, quantify, and mitigate this myriad of risks allows successful organizations to transform risk into opportunity. Terrorist, sophisticated criminal enterprises, political and tribal turmoil, and a lack of modern infrastructure present formidable challenges to companies operating in all areas of Iraq. Organizations that have a comprehensive understanding of the threats facing their efforts, combined with a flexible strategy for overcoming these obstacles, will have a far greater chance of success. Risk management is not just about identifying hazards and implementing control measures to keep people safe. The Custer Battles approach to risk is about seeking opportunities, and designing solutions to enable these opportunities to be exploited. The greatest threat to success is failure to manage risk.

Source: http://www.custerbattles.com/iraq/index.html (accessed 20/4/07).

A number of concerns have been raised about the activities of the private military industry (Singer, 2003; Newburn, 2007; Whyte, 2003). Some argue that there should be a complete ban on the activities of 'mercenaries'. Others argue that, at the very least, there should be much more highly developed systems for the monitoring, controlling and holding such companies to account. Recent events in Iraq have reinforced such concerns. There has been no shortage of stories of human rights abuses emerging during the 'war on terror'. Among them the allegations of the mistreatment of prisoners – including the widespread publication of photographic evidence – has become one of the best known. At a

number of locations, including the notorious Abu Ghraib detention centre in Iraq, there have been scandals involving personnel from private security companies as well as the military. In the vast majority of these no one was prosecuted, or even dismissed from their job (Newburn, 2007). We return to Iraq and the 'war on terror' below as we consider the notion of 'state crime' and its growing visibility within contemporary criminology.

Review questions

1 What are the main characteristics of globalisation?

2 What is meant by 'criminalisation' in the context of migration?

3 What are the main characteristics of terrorism?

4 What are the main differences between 'old' and 'new' wars?

State crime

We observed in previous chapters in relation to such topics as white-collar crime and organised crime that one of the frequent observations made by critical criminologists of the discipline in which they work is that, in its traditional forms, it tends to focus on the crimes of the powerless, rather than the crimes of the powerful – on crimes of the 'streets', rather than the crimes of the 'suites'. A good illustration of this observation is the general failure of criminology to have much to say about 'state crime'. This is despite the fact that states can often be responsible for harms which far exceed those traditionally defined as 'criminal'. Thus, Green and Ward (2004) give the example of the late Nigerian dictator, Sani Abacda, who was accused of stealing $4 billion from his country – a sum that far exceeds the total stolen and damaged in domestic and commercial burglary in England and Wales in a single year. As we saw in Chapter 20, there are somewhere in the region of 800–900 homicides each year in England and Wales. By contrast, estimates of the numbers murdered in Cambodia by the Khmer Rouge range from 300,000 to two million. Michalowski and Kramer (2006: 1) put it most succinctly when they say, 'Great power and great crimes are inseparable'. They continue:

> We contend that criminology's focus on interpersonal crimes is largely responsible for its general inattention to the ways that economic

and political elites can bring death, disease, and loss to tens of thousands with a single decision, and can affect entire human groups through the creation of criminal systems of oppression and exploitation. (2006: 5)

It is not just the scale of some crimes committed by those in powerful positions that makes such activities important to the criminologist; it is precisely because it is *the state* that is involved that makes it a particular concern. It is states and governments that ordinarily determine what is to be considered criminal or otherwise and that manage and direct the justice system. Prosecutions are generally brought *by* the state against transgressors. It is for this reason that corruption, malfeasance and criminal activity by the state is so important, for it potentially undermines the system of justice. Green and Ward (2005: 431) define 'state crime' as 'illegal or deviant acts perpetrated by, or with the complicity of, state agencies'.

If the core of the definition is that such crimes involve offences perpetrated by or on behalf of the state, the limit of what can be included under this rubric is that such activities do not cover acts that benefit only individual office holders, such as individual cases of the acceptance of bribes or violence by a police officer (Chambliss, 1989). As such, therefore, it includes: genocide, war crimes, political corruption, state terrorism, state-supported piracy (see below), state corporate crime (Michalowski and Kramer, 2006), *organised* crimes by state agencies such as the police, and the systematic abuse of human rights – say through torture – by the state. Chambliss (1989: 184) illustrates this

last point when he says that the 'policies of torture and random violence by the police in [apartheid] South Africa are incorporated under the category of state-organised crime because, apparently, those practices are both state policy and in violation of existing South African law. On the other hand, the excessive use of violence by the police in urban ghettoes is not state-organised crime for it lacks the necessary institutionalised policy of the state.'

Genocide

Though its definition is subject to dispute, genocide is generally taken to refer to mass murder directed at particular peoples because of their membership of a specific ethnic group, with the aim of eliminating that group. The euphemism 'ethnic cleansing' has been used in recent times to describe the genocidal intent of certain groups in particular conflicts. The 1948 UN Convention on the Prevention and Punishment of Genocide defines it as 'any of the following acts committed with intent to destroy, in whole or in part, a national, ethnical, racial or religious group, as such':

(a) Killing members of the group.
(b) Causing serious bodily or mental harm to members of the group.
(c) Deliberately inflicting on the group conditions of life calculated to bring about its physical destruction in whole or in part.
(d) Imposing measures intended to prevent births within the group.
(e) Forcibly transferring children of the group to another group.

Piracy

Sir Richard Hawkins and his apprentice, Francis Drake, were issued 'letters of marque' from the Admiralty directing governors of British colonies and captains of British warships to give safe passage and every possible assistance to Hawkins and Drake as they were acting 'under orders of the Crown'. Their 'orders' were to engage in piracy against Spanish and Portuguese ships. Thus, the state specifically instructed selected individuals to engage in criminal acts. The law, it must be emphasised, did not change. Piracy remained a crime punishable by death, but some pirates were given licence to murder, rape, plunder, destroy and steal ...

On one voyage (between 1572 and 1573), Drake returned to England with enough gold and silver to support the government and all its expenses for a period of seven years. Most of this wealth came from Drake's attack on the town of Nombre de Dios, which was a storage depot for Spanish gold and silver ...

Drake was knighted for his efforts, but the Spanish were not silent. They formally challenged Britain's policies, but the Queen of England denied that Drake was operating with her blessing (after, of course, taking the gold and silver that he brought home) and Drake was tried as a criminal. He was publicly exiled, but privately he was sent to Ireland, where he re-emerged several years later (in 1575) serving under the first Earl of Essex in Ireland.

Source: Chambliss (1989: 186–7).

The best-known modern example of what would fall under this definition of genocide is the holocaust in which the Nazi regime in Germany under Adolf Hitler planned the mass extermination of Jews across Europe. One difficulty with the definition is that it is limited in scope (though for an alternative view see Green and Ward, 2004). As Robertson (2002: 245) notes:

> This definition reflects contemporary preoccupation with genocidal Nazi policy towards the Jews as revealed at Nuremberg: it is wide enough to cover ethnic cleansing and religious pogroms, but it does not address Stalin's extermination of a particular economic class (the kulaks) or the millions he liquidated for suspected dissidence or disloyalty. It would cover gypsies or Rastafarians, but not homosexuals or members of a political or social organisation unless membership was confined to a particular tribe, race or nationality.

As we shall see later in the chapter, human rights legislation has emerged with regularity since the end of the Second World War with the hope of preventing genocide and other abuses from occurring again. Our recent history, however, is littered with examples of attempts at mass extermination.

Cambodia

Cambodia, in South East Asia, gained independence in 1953 having previously been a French colony. In 1970, backed by the US, a right-wing military coup ousted the existing Cambodian government. For the best part of a decade, a guerrilla army, the Khmer Rouge, led by Pol Pot, had been attempting to destabilise the Cambodian leader Prince Sihanouk. When Sihanouk was ousted by the military he joined forces with his old adversary Pol Pot. The Vietnam War, and American bombings of what were believed to be Vietnamese strongholds in Cambodia, further destablised the country. The withdrawal of American troops from Vietnam in 1975 and military support for the Cambodian military government provided an opportunity for Pol Pot to take control.

Inspired by the Maoist revolution in China, Pol Pot set about creating a communist agrarian utopia in Cambodia (now renamed Kampuchea). All foreigners were expelled, foreign languages banned and cities closed down as the Cambodian people were forced back into rural areas. Two million Cambodians were forcibly removed from Phnom Penh, the largest city in the country. People were set to work on the land, working under the most

extreme conditions in what became known as the 'killing fields'. As with other examples in this chapter, the mass murder that took place in Cambodia under the Khmer Rouge was characterised by both an explicit political ideology (in this case a particular form of communism) and ethnic antagonism.

The Cambodian dictator Pol Pot (1925–1998), one of the worst mass murderers in history.

Professionals, the educated, and anyone perceived to be unsympathetic to the new regime were murdered. All leading Buddhist monks were also executed and minority groups – Chinese, Vietnamese and Thai – were targeted. In all it is estimated that almost two million people, or over one-fifth of the entire population of the country, died in the period of under four years prior to the overthrow of the Khmer Rouge in 1978.

Rwanda

Rwanda is a country that had an estimated population of slightly over eight million in 1991, of whom eight to ten per cent were Tutsi, the remainder being Hutu. This distinction originally reflected social status and occupation, with Tutsi being landowners and Hutu labourers or commoners. Gradually it took on the form of a more entrenched, ethnic division as marriage was generally – though not entirely – confined within each group. Rwanda was a German colony in the early twentieth century, and became a Belgian colony after the First World War. Under Belgian rule, the Tutsi were installed in power and the Hutu were prevented from taking official positions. To enable this, everyone had to be registered according to which group they belonged to, further reinforcing the divisions that were building. In the early 1960s, after growing conflict, the Hutu majority took power. Conflicts continued but in the mid-1970s Rwanda officially became a one-party state.

The genocide that occurred there took place in 1994. The ethnic division in the country was between the Hutu and the Tutsi. The lead-up involved the declining power of the incumbent president and increasingly violent attempts to shore up his position by targeting the Tutsi minority and dissident Hutu. There were several massacres of Tutsi between 1990–94, some also directed against Hutu opposed to President Habyarimana. Habyarimana died in a plane crash in 1994 – though who was responsible for the murder is not known – and power was seized by a military leader, Colonel Bagosora. Genocide directed at Tutsis had been in planning for some years and with the removal of Habyarimana its architects were able to take control of the state. Although soldiers and police were involved in the slaughter, much of it involved Hutu civilians, sometimes willingly, sometimes having been persuaded or bribed, and sometimes under threat of death if they refused. Estimates of the death toll vary markedly. There is some consensus that at least half a million people died, the majority of them Tutsi, and that upwards of 75 per cent of the Tutsi population of Rwanda was slaughtered in a matter of months.

Bosnia

The term 'ethnic cleansing' came to international prominence as a result of the conflict in Bosnia in the early 1990s. Part of the former Yugoslavia, Bosnia had a population of approximately three million, of whom about 1.3 million were Bosnian Serbs, one million were Sunni Muslim, and the remainder were Bosnian Croats. The break-up of Yugoslavia led to civil wars in its various constituent parts: Croatia, Serbia and Bosnia. In the aftermath of a vote for independence in 1992 war broke out in Bosnia. Described by some as a civil war, by other as a war of aggression by Serbia, many of the initial conflicts involved Serb paramilitaries attacking villages and towns in northern and eastern Bosnia in the spring and summer of 1992 and, area by area, seizing control and expelling or murdering local Muslims. Some of this 'ethnic cleansing' was undertaken without much conflict. On other occasions it involved extraordinary levels of violence and cruelty. Its purpose 'went far beyond the sadistic gratification of the perpetrators, beyond, even, the desire to send hundreds of thousands of people fleeing. It was designed to render the territory ethnically pure, and to make certain, by instilling a hatred and fear that would endure, that Muslims and Serbs could never again live together' (Silber and Little, 1996: 245).

Slobodan Milosovic (1941–2006), former President of Serbia and Yugoslavia. He was indicted for a range of war crimes including genocide in Bosnia and crimes against humanity in Kosovo, but died before the conclusion of his trial at the Hague by the International Criminal Tribunal for the former Yugoslavia.

The worst massacre of the conflict occurred at Srebrenica in 1995. Bosnian Serb forces laid siege to an enclave where tens of thousands of Muslim refugees had taken refuge. They were being guarded by 600 Dutch infantry forces. The area was shelled by Serb forces and the Dutch peacekeepers requested UN support. As the shelling worsened, many refugees fled. The Serbs then attacked and initially took about 30 Dutch soldiers hostage. There was a brief UN air strike on Serb positions but when the Serbs threatened to kill both the refugees and the Dutch peacekeepers, air support was withdrawn. It was at this stage that the Bosnian Serb commander, Ratko Mladic, entered Srebrenica. Although there were 'negotiations between Mladic and the leader of the Dutch peacekeeping force, in effect the Serbs took control of Srebrenica. In return for the return of the Dutch captives, the peacekeepers handed over about 5,000 Muslims to Mladic. In the guise of moving the Muslim women and children to a safe haven, and interrogating Muslim men in order to identify 'war criminals', a massacre began. At least 5,000 Muslim men are believed to have been killed in the week after the Dutch handed over control.

War as crime and war crimes

As the sub-heading indicates, there are two broad issues for us to consider briefly here. The first is the proposition that war itself can be illegal and those that instigate such acts be prosecuted for doing so. The second concerns the behaviour of combatants during times of war and the rules and conventions that are supposed to guide the conduct of the military and the treatment of prisoners of war.

In the name of the so-called 'war on terror', major conflicts have occurred in Afghanistan and in Iraq. In both cases commentators have questioned the legality of the wars, and some have called for them to be treated as state crimes. Thus, Mandel (2002: 77) argued that, 'The US-led war on Afghanistan is a violation of international law and of the express words of the Charter of the United Nations. As such it is illegal. It is also immoral and it won't prevent terrorism.' His argument about the UN Charter is that it states, explicitly, that decisions about going to war are to be made by the Security Council of the UN in all cases except those characterised by the strictly limited right of self-defence. The UN resolutions passed in the aftermath of the 11 September attacks in Washington DC and New York condemned the attacks, agreed a range of measures to tackle terrorism, but did not mention or sanction military force. No reasonable definition of 'self-defence', he argues, would possibly accommodate the military action that has been taken. If Mandel and other commentators are right that the war in Afghanistan is illegal, does it matter? His answer is twofold (2002: 83):

> In the first place, this attack is not wrong just because it is illegal. On the contrary, like murder itself, it is illegal because it is wrong ... Furthermore, it is illegal because it has sidelined the real international community, as represented by the United Nations. If we allow the system of international legality as designed in the UN Charter to be overthrown ... there will be nothing left to limit international violence but the power, ruthlessness and cunning of the perpetrators.

In a similar manner, Kramer and Michalowski (2005) make the same argument in relation to the invasion of Iraq. Iraq had not attacked the United States and therefore they argue that Article 51 – the right to self-defence – could not apply as a justification for the war. Moreover, they argue that the justifications that were advanced by the Bush government – in particular alleging links between the Saddam Hussein regime in Iraq and Al Qaeda – were not only false, but were known to be false. The Bush administration's argument came to be that America had a right to attack any state which it considered to be a *potential* threat to US interests. The now well-worn arguments on both sides of the Atlantic about weapons of mass destruction and the alleged ability of Iraq to launch attacks against the West have similarly been largely discredited (Butler, 2004). Moreover, Kramer and Michalowski (2005) argue, the one remaining possible justification for invasion – that of humanitarian concerns – is also not supported by international law.

According to commentators such as Kramer and Michalowski, not only is the war itself an illegal act, but its conduct has also been characterised by the commission of a variety of 'war crimes'. In this connection they suggest that under international humanitarian law, four types of war crimes were committed by coalition forces during the occupation of Iraq:

- The failure to secure public safety and protect civilian rights.
- The illegal transformation of the Iraqi economy (see also, Whyte, 2007).
- Indiscriminate responses to Iraqi resistance actions resulting in further civilian casualties.
- Torture and abuse of Iraqi prisoners.

We have already considered (in Chapter 28) the treatment of those held at Camp Delta in Guantanamo Bay in Cuba. Before moving on, let us look a little closer at the fourth of the charges listed above: the torture and abuse of prisoners taken during the course of the war. During the course of the war in Iraq there were quite widespread allegations of torture. Nowhere was there clearer evidence, however, than at Abu Ghraib prison, 20 miles west of Baghdad. One of the most notorious Iraqi prisons prior to the war, Abu Ghraib was taken over by the coalition authorities. In 2004 an internal inquiry report by Major General Antonio M. Taguba found that in late 2003 there were numerous instances of 'sadistic, blatant, and wanton criminal abuses' at Abu Ghraib (Greenberg and Dratel, 2005). Little might have come of this were it not for the publication of photographs detailing elements of the abuse against Iraqi prisoners. The American investigative journalist Seymour Hersh (2004) described the photographs as follows:

The photographs tell it all. In one, Private England, a cigarette dangling from her mouth, is giving a jaunty thumbs-up sign and pointing at the genitals of a young Iraqi, who is naked except for a sandbag over his head, as he masturbates. Three other hooded and naked Iraqi prisoners are shown, hands reflexively crossed over their genitals. A fifth prisoner has his hands at his sides. In another, England stands arm in arm with Specialist Graner; both are grinning and giving the thumbs-up behind a cluster of perhaps seven naked Iraqis, knees bent, piled clumsily on top of each other in a pyramid. There is another photograph of a cluster of naked prisoners, again piled in a pyramid. Near them stands Graner, smiling, his arms crossed; a woman soldier stands in front of him, bending over, and she, too, is smiling. Then, there is another cluster of hooded bodies, with a female soldier standing in front, taking photographs. Yet another photograph shows a kneeling, naked, unhooded male prisoner, head momentarily turned away from the camera, posed to make it appear that he is performing oral sex on another male prisoner, who is naked and hooded.

As so often happens in cases of corruption, the Abu Ghraib scandal was blamed on a 'few bad apples'. Rather than being viewed or treated as an institutionalised problem, prosecutions – few in number – were brought against a small number of soldiers, primarily from the lower ranks. In total nine US Army soldiers were court-martialled and convicted of crimes committed at Abu Ghraib prison. Of these, seven were military police and two were from military intelligence. All were enlisted soldiers, the highest ranking being a staff sergeant. No commanding officers were prosecuted. Similarly, although personnel from private corporations working at Abu Ghraib were also implicated in the prisoner abuse by several of the official reports conducted in its aftermath, not a single prosecution was brought (Newburn, 2007). Welch (2006) reports one soldier's admission that even after the scandal at Abu Ghraib, similar abuses continued. The documents painstakingly collected by Greenberg and Dratel (2005) show in detail how the US government prepared the ground for the use of torture in Afghanistan, Iraq and beyond (we return to the issue of torture below). It is precisely the organised and institutionalised nature of such practices which makes them 'state crimes' rather than the misconduct of a few soldiers, and which also helps to explain why such practices appear to have continued despite the public outcry after Abu Ghraib.

> **Review questions**
>
> 1 What types of activity are classified as 'state crime'?
>
> 2 What is meant by the term 'genocide'?
>
> 3 What are we referring to when we talk of 'war crimes'?

Human rights

'Human rights' is a group of ideas, a set of moral claims and an international discourse of growing power. As we will see, these claims are often expressed in legal terms. Indeed, until relatively recently the bulk of writing on human rights has been legalistic and it has been a subject that had largely been ignored by social science. However, this has begun to change and the influence of human rights discourses can increasingly be seen across the social sciences, including criminology. So powerful is this new discourse that Stan Cohen (1993: 491) has described human rights as a 'secular religion' and Michael Ignatieff (2001: 53) has suggested that human rights discourses are the '*lingua franca* of global moral thought'.

Origins of human rights

Echoing Cohen and Ignatieff, Freeman argues that the concept of human rights is now 'one of the most potent in contemporary politics' (2002: 32). The Second World War and, more particularly, the holocaust, are the most immediate source of this transformation. In the aftermath of the War, Winston Churchill spoke of the 'great principles of freedom and the rights of man which are the joint inheritance of the English-speaking world and which, through Magna Carta, the Bill of Rights, the Habeas Corpus, trial by jury and the English common law, find their most famous expression in the American Declaration of Independence':

> We hold these truths to be self-evident, that all men are created equal, that they are endowed by their creator with certain unalienable rights, that among these are life, liberty and the pursuit of happiness – that to secure these rights, governments are instituted among men, deriving their just powers from the consent of the governed. That whenever any form of government becomes destructive of these ends, it is the right

of the people to alter or abolish it. (quoted in Freeman, 2002: 23)

Within 20 years of independence, the 1791 Bill of Rights had been incorporated into the US Constitution. Similarly, after the French revolution of 1789, the new National Assembly proclaimed the Declaration of the Rights of Man and the Citizen as the basis of the new constitution of France. Such ideas were picked up by British radicals such as Thomas Paine. Opposition to conceptions of natural rights came from different parts of the political spectrum: conservatives finding it too egalitarian; radicals too accepting of financial and social inequality. Edmund Burke, for example, viewed such ideas as posing an unreasonable challenge to the social order. Jeremy Bentham, by contrast, viewed the term as being vague and not providing the basis for rational laws. During the nineteenth century, the concept of natural rights was largely overtaken by utilitarianism (see Chapter 22). Though ideas of rights remained, they were generally defended not as being 'natural', but rather as being conducive to, or supportive of, the common good.

Human rights in the twentieth century

Much of the modern idea of human rights derives from John Locke's theory of 'natural rights' – rights deriving from nature rather than government or laws. In its modern guise, human rights discourses focus primarily on the rights of citizens in their relationship with the state. Relationships between states are governed by international law. International law has, at its heart, the idea of state sovereignty – the principle that no state should interfere in the matters of another. Though human rights were imported into international law by the UN the matter of state sovereignty remained and for much of the period after the Second World War the UN did little to implement human rights. It was the author, but generally not the guarantor, of human rights standards: 'The UN has, therefore, been the central institution where international human-rights law and politics meet, and often clash, and where the gap between human-rights ideals and realities is especially apparent' (Freeman, 2002: 9). Nevertheless, as we will see, human rights remain very much a matter of politics.

As we have noted, in the twentieth century it was the Nazi holocaust that precipitated the move toward the creation of what were portrayed as universal human rights standards. The holocaust was the clearest possible example of what Theodore Roosevelt meant by a 'crime against humanity'

which he described in his 1904 State of the Union address in which he said:

> There are occasional crimes committed on so vast a scale and of such peculiar horror as to make us doubt whether it is not our manifest duty to endeavour at least to show our disapproval of the deed and our sympathy with those who have suffered by it ... in extreme cases action may be justifiable and proper. (quoted in Robertson, 2002: 15)

The United Nations was established in the aftermath of the Second World War to oversee the construction of a new world order. The Universal Declaration on Human Rights – the 'fountain-head of human rights law' (Freeman, 2002: 3) – was passed on 10 December 1948 (48 states voted in favour, none against, and eight abstained). The declaration did not impose legal obligations on states, but rather standards toward which they were expected to aspire.

As a 'declaration', the UN document outlines and describes human rights, but does not provide a means by which they might be implemented and protected. Indeed, Gearty (2003) describes the document as 'intentionally unenforceable, self-consciously a mission statement for humanity rather than an immediately realizable set of goals for the people who read it'. Particular attention has been paid to states such as South Africa, Israel and Chile, whereas others with arguably equally serious human rights issues have been largely ignored by the UN. During the Cold War, little was done to challenge the human rights records of many communist states and, indeed, there was equally little challenge to those western states that provided support for regimes that had poor human rights records (Chomsky, 2000). The UN General Assembly and the Human Rights Commission became more active in the aftermath of the Cold War with interventions in, for example, Somalia, El Salvador, Haiti, Nicaragua and elsewhere.

Robertson (2002) argues that, after the holocaust, the other great influence on post-war human rights legislation was the show trials in Moscow which were used by Stalin as part of the process of legitimating his purge of his opponents. The trials were held in public, in front of international witnesses, the defendants all having admitted guilt, having been tortured until they signed confessions that had already been written for them. Robertson (2002: 21) suggests that 'Stalin's show trials came to haunt later generations because they proved how a system of law, with procedural forms and rituals calculated to impress, could be vulnerable to political manipulation by an all-powerful state ... These "purge" trials with their inevitable conclusion for "enemies of the people" – a bullet in the head, followed by burial in an unmarked grave – cast a long, historical shadow.' It is the frame-ups in these trials, for example, that led to the protections that were inserted in UN and International Criminal Court legislation enabling defendants to refuse to testify without adverse inference being drawn. In the last half century since the signing of the Universal Declaration on Human Rights, a series of other Conventions have been established:

- *Convention on the Prevention and Punishment of the Crime of Genocide 1951* – As we saw earlier this covers a variety of physical harm aimed at destroying a national, ethnic, or religious group.

- *Convention on the Elimination of all Forms of Racial Discrimination 1966* – Condemns racial segregation, apartheid and racial propaganda and provides for a wide range of rights including treatment in the justice system, security, freedom of movement, marriage, property, work and trades union rights, housing and health.

- *Convention on the Elimination of All Forms of Discrimination Against Women 1981* – In ratifying this Convention, signatory states accept that sexual equality principles should be incorporated into domestic law; any discriminatory laws should be abolished; and there should be specific tribunals created to protect the rights of women.

- *Convention Against Torture and Other Cruel, Inhuman and Degrading Treatment or Punishment 1987* – Torture is forbidden and the Convention requires states to make torture a domestic extraditable crime. Torture is defined as:

  - any act by which severe pain or suffering, whether physical or mental, is intentionally inflicted on a person for such purposes as obtaining from him or a third person information or a confession;

  - punishing him for an act he or a third person has committed or is suspected of having committed;

  - intimidating or coercing him or a third person;

  - when such pain or suffering is inflicted by or at the instigation of or with the consent or acquiescence of a public official or other person acting in an official capacity;

  - but not including pain or suffering arising only from, or inherent in or incidental to lawful sanctions.

- *Convention on the Rights of the Child 1989* – Under the Convention, children are defined as every human being aged under 18 and that the best interests of children must always have primacy (this has particular implications for criminal justice). Children must be protected from violence, injury, neglect and abuse. Article 37, for example, states that the 'arrest, detention or imprisonment of a child shall be in conformity with the law and shall be used only as a measure of last resort and for the shortest appropriate period of time'.

Each and all of these have relevance for contemporary criminology, not just in relation to state crimes, but also in connection with the operation of domestic criminal justice systems. Consider, for example, to what extent criminal justice systems are characterised by discriminatory practices against women and ethnic minorities. Similarly, human rights protocols provide us with the basis upon which international comparisons can be made in relation to the treatment of suspects arrested by the police or detained in custody. The Convention on the Rights of the Child ought to form a binding framework for the operation of juvenile justice systems.

Although the twentieth century has seen some successes on the humanitarian front, there have also been some very significant failures, such as those described earlier in the former Yugoslavia. Equally, as Freeman (2002: 50) notes, despite the good work undertaken by the United Nations High Commissioner for Refugees (UNHCR) 'the problem of refugees is becoming worse, not better'. The new migratory patterns and rapidly expanding numbers of people seeking asylum appear a direct consequence of globalisation, and such pressures have begun to shift the emphasis in human rights campaigning toward social and economic rights. Freeman (2002: 51) summarises the situation:

Since 1945 the UN has done a lot of 'standard setting', institution-building and human-rights promotion. The concept of human rights is one of the most influential of our time, and many poor and oppressed people appeal to it in their quest for justice. The capacity of the UN to implement its own standards is still modest, however. The concept of state sovereignty and the realities of international power politics still make the implementation of human-rights standards uneven, and generally weak.

Human rights in Britain

It is only relatively recently that we have come to talk of 'human rights' in Britain. It has only been for a decade or so that we have had formal human rights legislation. The origins of many of the freedoms that we seek to defend today lie centuries back. The advances secured between the seventeenth and nineteenth centuries were often secured through a combination of civil disobedience and other acts close to what today might be described as 'terrorism', as well as parliamentary action such as the passage of the Reform Acts of 1832 and 1867 (Gearty, 2003). The protesters wished to exercise their rights in the knowledge that they could do so without interference from the state. As Gearty (2003) puts it, 'they wanted to protest without being shot and to publish pamphlets without being jailed'.

In the late 1980s Ronald Dworkin wrote that 'liberty is ill in Britain'. The concern he was expressing was illustrated by a number of events, and Ewing (2004) lists the case of Sarah Tisdall, a Foreign Office official imprisoned in 1983 under the Official Secrets Act for leaking information to a newspaper about the arrival of US cruise missiles to the UK, the ban on union membership for members of GCHQ in 1984, the 'paramilitary' policing of the miners' strike, and the alleged 'shoot to kill' policy used against the IRA in Northern Ireland. These and other cases were indicative, Dworkin argued, of the tension that exists between the rule of law and the power of government to override it. Indeed, he says, this tension was by no means confined to the 1980s, but has been ever-present throughout the last century and continues into this (despite the Human Rights Act). As examples he lists:

- The forced feeding of the suffragettes in the first decade of the twentieth century.
- The intolerance of anti-war activists during the First World War.
- The persecution and prosecution for sedition of communists in the 1920s.
- The brutal policing of the General Strike in 1926.
- The crackdown on unemployed marchers in the 1930s.
- The internment of various groups during the Second World War.
- The exclusion of communists and the prosecution of peace activists during the Cold War.
- The secrecy surrounding the activities of the security services in the 1960s and 1970s.

Arguably, the most significant development in the UK in recent times has been the passage of the Human Rights Act. According to the former Lord Chancellor, Lord Irvine (2004), the Act 'has transformed our system of law into one of positive rights, responsibilities and freedoms, where before we had only the freedom to do what was not prohibited'.

The Human Rights Act 1998

Lord Irvine (2004) suggests that there were two primary reasons why it took half a century for the European Convention on Human Rights to be incorporated into British domestic law. First, the view that rights could most effectively be protected through political accountability, i.e. via democracy and, second, a concern about the prospect of undermining parliamentary sovereignty through increasing the power of unelected judges. It is important to note, therefore, that the 1998 Act did not simply incorporate the European Convention into domestic law, rather it was intended 'to give further effect to the rights and freedoms guaranteed under the European Convention on Human Rights'. It does this in two ways: by seeking to ensure that the courts should interpret the law in a way that is compatible with Convention rights; and, by placing an obligation on public authorities to act compatibly with Convention rights.

The 'rights' contained in the Act are of three types, what are referred to as 'absolute', 'limited' and 'qualified' rights:

- *Absolute rights*, such as the right to protection from torture, inhuman and degrading treatment and punishment (Article 3), the prohibition on slavery and enforced labour (Article 4) and protection from retrospective criminal penalties (Article 7) upon which there are no limits.

- *Limited rights*, such as the right to liberty (Article 5) which are limited under explicit and finite circumstances, set out in the Convention itself (the circumstances under which one can reasonably be arrested and detained).

- *Qualified rights*, which include the right to respect for private and family life (Article 8), religion and belief (Article 9), freedom of expression (Article 10), assembly and association (Article 11), the right to peaceful enjoyment of property (Protocol 1, Article 1) and, to some extent, the right to education (Protocol 1, Article 2). It is possible to interfere with these rights under limited circumstances:

  – this interference has its basis in law; and

- is done to secure a permissible aim set out in the relevant Article, for example for the prevention of crime, or for the protection of public order or health; and

- is necessary in a democratic society, which means it must fulfil a pressing social need,

pursue a legitimate aim and be proportionate to the aims being pursued.

Each right is set out under a separately numbered paragraph of the European Convention, known as an *article* (see box below for a description of the main articles set out in the 1998 Human Rights Act).

The Human Rights Act 1998 (Main articles)

Article 2: The right to life
You have the absolute right to have your life protected by law.

Article 3: Freedom from torture or inhuman or degrading treatment
You have the absolute right not to be tortured or subjected to treatment or punishment that is inhuman or degrading.

Article 4: Freedom from slavery or forced labour
You have the absolute right not to be treated like a slave or forced to perform certain kinds of labour.

Article 5: Personal freedom
You have the right not to be deprived of your liberty – 'arrested' or 'detained' – even for a short period. However, this right is a limited right and it does not apply where this detention is lawful and it is for one of six specified reasons:

- Lawful detention following a conviction by a criminal court.

- Lawful arrest or detention to make you comply with a legal obligation such as a court order to pay maintenance money or to submit to a medical examination, but not necessarily to punish you for not complying with the order.

- Lawful arrest or detention to ensure you attend at court, if there is a reasonable suspicion that you have committed a crime, or to prevent you from committing further crimes or escaping while you are under investigation if you are under 18.

- Lawful detention to ensure that you are subject to educational supervision or to ensure you attend court, even where this is not because you are suspected of having committed a crime.

- If you are shown to be of unsound mind, an alcoholic, a drug addict or a vagrant or to prevent you from spreading an infectious disease and your detention in these circumstances is provided for in law.

- Where this is necessary to prevent you from unlawfully entering the UK, or to allow your deportation to another state or extradition for a crime you face there.

Article 6: Right to a fair trial
You have the right to a fair trial. This includes the right to a:

- *fair* hearing;
- *public* hearing;
- hearing before an *independent and impartial tribunal*;
- hearing *within a reasonable time*.

Article 7: No punishment without law
You normally have the right not to be found guilty of a criminal offence arising out of an action that, at the time that you did it, was not criminal. You are also protected against any increase in the possible sentence for an offence that has taken place as a result of the law changing since the date of your action.

Article 8: Private life and family
You have the right to respect for your private and family life, your home and your correspondence.

Article 9: Freedom of belief
This protects rights in relation to a broad range of views, beliefs, thoughts and positions of conscience as well as to your faith in a particular religion.

Article 10: Free expression
This protects your right to hold opinions and express your views singly or in dialogue.

Article 11: Free assembly and association
You have the right to assemble with others in a peaceful way. You also have the right to associate with others and to form a trade union.

Article 12: Marriage
Men and women have the right to marry and found a family.

Article 14: Freedom from discrimination
People have the right not to be treated differently because of race, religion, sex, political views or any other status, unless this can be justified objectively. Everybody must have equal access to Convention rights, whatever their status.

Source: Department for Constitutional Affairs.

The impact of the Human Rights Act

The passage of the Human Rights Act was welcomed by a very broad range of commentators and, as we saw in the quote from Lord Irvine earlier, has often been presented by government as being illustrative of a profound shift in relation to the protection of personal freedom in the UK. However, the Act has been by no means without its critics. Gearty (2005) suggests that, in the aftermath of 11 September, the Human Rights Act has come under attack on two fronts. The first challenge has been that of politicised religious faith – initially a particular form of Islam and, subsequently, a form of fundamentalism linked to Christianity. The second challenge is linked, he argues, with the reassertion of state sovereignty and power over international, cosmopolitan values and goals (as evidenced by the USA PATRIOT Act).

There has been considerable debate in recent years around where the boundary is to be drawn in relation to the tension between individual rights and the interests of the state. The debate has perhaps been clearest in relation to the renewed discussion of the use of torture. Indeed, a number of highly influential commentators such as Alan Dershowitz and Michael Ignatieff (see below) have recently attempted to defend the necessity of the use of torture as a response to the threat of international terrorism.

Torture and terror: is one a lesser evil?

In introducing the Human Rights Bill in the House of Lords in November 1997, Lord Irvine said that he expected that it would 'deliver a modern reconciliation of the inevitable tension between the democratic right of the majority to exercise political power and the democratic need of individuals and minorities to have their human rights secured'. The Lord Chancellor's optimistic vision was that the new legislation would establish an acceptable balance between the need to govern and the rights of individuals to enjoy certain freedoms. This goes to the heart of some of the key human rights questions of our time. What, for example, can be justified as being part of the democratic right of the majority? Where and why must the right of government to govern be restricted in the interests of protecting the rights of individual citizens?

A controversial contribution to such debates has recently been made by Michael Ignatieff, Professor of Human Rights at Harvard University. His central question in his book, *The Lesser Evil,* concerns the limits of what democratic governments might reasonably do in the battle against terrorism. 'Defeating terror', he says, 'requires violence. It may also require coercion, secrecy, deception, even violation of rights.' The question for us is how can democracies use such means without undermining the values on which they are established? In other words, is it possible to 'resort to the lesser evils without succumbing to the greater?'

Ignatieff's answer is a heavily qualified 'yes'. For example, he examines the case for using torture. The exclusion of torture, he says, has long been the hallmark of free government. He goes on to note what seem to be three overwhelming arguments against the use of torture even in the most extreme cases (where its use might result in information leading to the saving of thousands of lives). First, a 'thin end of the wedge' argument: if torture is expressly allowed under very limited circumstances, little by little its use will increase. Second, there is no evidence that information extracted through torture is reliable and, third, that the use of torture is more likely to *create* terrorists than *prevent* terror.

Ignatieff's conclusion is then complex. He begins by arguing that 'an outright ban on torture, rather than an attempt to regulate it, seems the only way a democracy can keep true to its ideal of respecting the dignity even of its enemies'. However, in proceeding to outline the importance of regulating the limits of coercive interrogation, he argues that 'permissible duress might include forms of sleep deprivation that do not result in lasting harm to mental or physical health, together with disinformation and disorientation (like keeping prisoners in hoods) that would produce stress'.

He concludes, 'keeping a war on terror under democratic scrutiny is critical to its operational success. A lesser-evil approach permits preventive detention, where subject to judicial review; coercive interrogation, where subject to executive control; preemptive strikes and assassination, where these serve publicly defensible strategic goals. But everything has to be subject to critical review by a free people: free debate, public discussion, Congressional review, in camera if need be, judicial review as a last resort.'

[An article by Ignatieff on 'The Lesser Evil' can be found at: http://www.ksg.harvard.edu/news/opeds/2004/ignatieff_less_evils_nytm_050204.htm]

There have been a number of responses. In particular you should look at: Gearty, C. (2005) With a little help from our friends, *Index on Censorship*, 1, 46–51.

Gearty asks, 'how, if at all, our concern for the equal dignity of all – of which the Human Rights Act is our clearest legal symbol – can survive in a contemporary political and legal culture that has become so deeply preoccupied with matters of war, politicised religious belief, and national security'? In this, Keith Ewing appears to agree. Ewing's (2004) view of the post-Human Rights Act situation in the UK, far from being characterised by new and enhanced protections of our basic freedoms, is a 'period of unparalleled restraint on our liberty'. In part, this is a consequence of the unusual circumstances that have prevailed since the attacks in New York and Washington DC on 11 September 2001. But it is not entirely traceable to those events for, of the three major statutory initiatives affecting liberties in the UK since the passage of the Human Rights Act, one was passed prior to 2001. All three initiatives contained provisions which significantly curtailed particular civil liberties. Take, for example, the Anti-terrorism, Crime and Security Act 2001, which contains (Ewing, 2004):

- *The right to liberty* – Powers to imprison indefinitely without trial people who the Home Secretary believes to be a danger to national security (this power has subsequently been revoked).

- *The right to privacy* – Powers enabling government departments and public bodies to exchange confidential information acquired for one purpose so that it can be used for another purpose.

- *The right to respect for private property* – Powers authorising the seizure of assets and freezing of bank accounts of suspected terrorists.

Section 19 of the Human Rights Act requires a Minister responsible for a Bill in Parliament to make a 'statement of compatibility' between it and the Human Rights Act. As a consequence, much of the parliamentary discussion of the draft legislation was couched in the language of rights. How much difference did the Human Rights Act make to the eventual shape of the legislation? Gearty's (2005: 23–4) view is that it 'was able to bite where there was already strong background unease about government proposals, but that it was not effective where no such concerns existed, and that it was not even guaranteed to affect outcomes in cases of pre-existing high controversy where the government showed itself determined to act'. The most controversial powers are the powers of detention contained in the Act, powers which have been subject to much judicial debate and critical comment.

Again, Gearty's view is that the 'rights formulation proved helpful in framing the discussion as one in which it was necessary to seek to balance freedom and security, rather than to allow an entirely blank cheque to the latter'.

Ewing argues that there are at least three important paradoxes to be found in the current state of affairs. The first is that, despite the fact that Britain has long-standing procedures enabling the courts to protect the vulnerable and the persecuted, 'it remains the case that the courts have typically looked the other way when called upon to balance liberty against security'. The second paradox is that it is precisely those who are identified as being the source of the likely cure for this problem – judges using the Human Rights Act – who were responsible for many of the difficulties in the first place (by privileging security over freedom, the interests of the state over individual citizens and executive discretion over due process). According to Ewing, the irony of our current circumstances, and therefore the third paradox, is that the passage of the Human Rights Act does not appear to have changed this balance.

There have been a number of decisions in recent times that illustrate the limits of human rights considerations in an era of the 'War on Terror'. A Court of Appeal judgement in 2004 (*R (Gillan) v. Metropolitan Police Commissioner [2004] E.W.C.A. Civ. 1067*), for example, upheld the use of stop and search powers provided by the Terrorism Act 2000 against a man on his way to demonstrate at an arms fair in London's Docklands. Both this man, and a journalist who had been stopped and searched and ordered to stop filming outside the event, were held not to have had their human rights infringed. The development that has, arguably, caused the most concern relates to the decision in *A v. Secretary of State for the Home Department (no 2)*, in which the Special Immigration Appeals Commission considering the case of a detained person suspected of terrorism would be allowed to take into consideration evidence from a third party allegedly obtained by torture (*The Guardian*, 14 August, 2005).

Although the Human Rights Act represents a potentially important moment in relation to civil liberties and their protection in the UK, the impact of the attacks in the United States on 11 September 2001 have given enormous impetus to those who would emphasise the security paradigm. As Gearty (2003: 205) puts it, 'Human rights may be a trump in the pack of political cards, carrying all before it, but the interests of national security is the trump of trumps, carrying all before it'.

Criminology and human rights

As we have already noted, much academic discussion of human rights has been dominated by lawyers. Until recently, criminologists, with one or two notable exceptions, had paid relatively little attention to the subject. One of the earliest criminological articles on the subject was written by Herman and Julia Schwendinger in which they argued that criminologists should broaden their attention beyond those crimes defined by the criminal statutes of particular nation states:

> The abrogation of these rights certainly limits the individual's chance to fulfil himself (*sic*) in many spheres of life. It can be stated that individuals who deny these rights to others are criminal ... imperialism, racism, sexism and poverty can be called crimes according to the logic of our argument. (1975:148)

Since that time a particular group of critical criminologists has sought to focus criminology's attention on crimes of the state and, indeed, on the criminology of war (Jamieson, 1998). Although in some ways they were successful, as Cohen (1993) notes, in the discussion of state crimes 'the human rights connection became lost'. By the mid-1980s when left realism (see Chapter 13) appeared, 'we had moved entirely from "crimes of the state" back to the "state of crime"'. According to Cohen (1993), however, the combination of the growth of the international human rights movement outside criminology, and the growth of victimology within it, helped to raise the profile of human rights-related issues.

Writing in the early 1990s, and surveying criminological work in this area, Stan Cohen (1993) identified three major gaps. First, he noted that there existed little comprehension that a major source of law making at national and international levels draws on human rights rhetoric. Second, scholarship seems to be preoccupied with America and American 'problems' such as, for example, the disreputable practices of the CIA, rather than violations in other parts of the world. Third, there is an absence of focus on victimization. That is, the gross violations of human rights around the world had hitherto stimulated little criminological interest – and, indeed, this largely remains the case. One of the main barriers to greater criminological interest in the area of human rights abuses, state crimes, and so on has, arguably, been the restrictive nature of the conception of 'crime' that

traditional criminology works with. Thus, two of the main objections to focusing on 'crimes' by the state are similar to the objections often raised in relation to corporate crime:

- That the state (or the corporation) is not an actor and therefore it is not possible to identify individual criminal responsibility.
- The actions of the state (or the corporation) are, therefore, not really 'crime'.

In relation to the first argument, Braithwaite and Fisse (1990) have argued that, on the contrary, corporations *do* engage in rational goal-seeking behaviour. They act, have intentions and, therefore, commit crimes. The same might be said of the nation state. In relation to the second point, as we have seen there are now various international agreements and statutes setting out in detail the nature of state crimes/crimes against humanity and, indeed, many of the actions concerned (e.g. torture) are likely to be 'criminal' by the standards of domestic law. And, yet, crimes by states regularly occur, but remain 'hidden'. This leads Cohen (2001) to the subject at the heart of his more recent work: 'denial'. In totalitarian states, he says, where there is no freedom of speech, denial of activities like torture is straightforward: 'you do it, but say you do not'. In democratic-type societies there is an altogether more complicated vocabulary of denial, which goes through three stages:

- It doesn't happen here.
- If it does, 'it' is something else.
- Even if it is what you say it is, it is justified.

Cohen's primary interest, however, is in another form of 'denial': this is the question of why people who 'know' about atrocities are not supportive of such policies and practices, and yet do not condemn. In search of answers, Cohen turns to various forms of literature, including Sykes and Matza's (1957) classic work on 'neutralisation techniques' (see Chapter 8). He applies their five major neutralisation techniques to the subject of human rights violations:

- *Denial of injury* – They exaggerate, they don't feel it, they are used to violence.
- *Denial of victim* – They started it, they are terrorists, we are the real victims.
- *Denial of responsibility* – I was only following orders, only doing my duty.

- *Condemnation of the condemners* – Why are we being picked on, it's just double-standards, it's worse elsewhere, they are anti-semitic/anti-Islamic.

- *Appeal to a higher loyalty* – Such as the army, nation or 'the cause' (Islam, Zionism, free trade, world security, etc.)

Cohen's (2001) work shows not only how the individual perpetrators of atrocities can rationalise and normalise what they do but, equally if not more importantly, how governments and states can both justify and deny human rights abuses on a significant scale. A central question he poses throughout this work concerns how we make such abuses known when there is so much investment in keeping them hidden. A final issue for us in this chapter is what is to be done about state crimes and other human rights abuses once they become known?

Dealing with human rights abuses

Towards the end of the Second World War, Churchill began to make plans for the summary execution of a number of Nazi leaders. A list was compiled of 50 prominent Nazis who were to be executed without trial once the war was over. The Foreign Secretary, Anthony Eden, argued that 'the guilt of such individuals as Himmler is so black that they fall outside and go beyond the scope of any judicial process' (quoted in Robertson, 2002: 227). In the event, American and Russian objections to such summary justice (Stalin apparently wanted show trials) led to the establishment of public tribunals in Nuremberg at which Nazi war criminals were prosecuted for their actions. The charter establishing the Nuremberg tribunal defined crimes against humanity and, indirectly, led to the establishment of the International Criminal Court half a century later.

Though a permanent tribunal in which those who are alleged to have abused human rights could be prosecuted was suggested in the aftermath of the Second World War, it was only in the 1990s when *ad hoc* international tribunals were established to deal with the genocides in Rwanda and Yugoslavia that this became a realistic prospect. In the interim, the main response by the UN and other bodies was to impose sanctions, embargoes or, occasionally, to use military force. However, in many cases such approaches were far from effective, many civilians were injured and killed, and there remained a frustrating inability to

Nazi war criminals on trial at the International Military Tribunal at Nuremberg, set up in 1945 at the end of the Second World War in Europe. The Nuremberg trials were a key influence on the development of international criminal law.

bring any perpetrators to justice. In the event, the International Criminal Court (ICC) was established in 1998 and came into force in 2002. Although the ICC is by no means yet universally supported – the United States, China, Turkey and India have not signed up to it – it is nevertheless regarded as an important development in relation to the enforcement of international criminal law.

The ICC may be contrasted with another relatively recent development that has emerged to deal with major abuses of power: truth commissions. Truth commissions were first used in Latin America to examine human rights abuses in Argentina, Chile, El Salvador and Guatemala. The South African Truth and Reconciliation Commission, chaired by Archbishop Desmond Tutu in the late 1990s, is the best known such tribunal. As Roche (2005) notes, there is the potential for conflict between the ICC and truth commissions, should the case arise that amnesties from prosecution are granted to individuals appearing before a truth commission (as happened in South Africa). However, he concludes that there is no reason, in principle, why the two should not be compatible, and argues that it should be perfectly possible for the ICC to work with states to prosecute those who don't satisfy the conditions for the granting of a truth commission amnesty. Such arguments are also applied, for example, in relation to the use of restorative justice techniques side-by-side with the existence of more formal justice processes, particularly in relation to their potential application to areas such as varied as domestic violence and corporate crime (see Chapter 30).

Advantages and disadvantages of different tribunals

Criminal trial	Truth commission
Advantages	*Advantages*
– Able to establish a version of events	• Builds up more complete picture
– Helps shape collective memory	• Can cope with complexity
– Drama makes process compelling	• Flexible rules about 'evidence'
	• Can consider 'complicity'
Disadvantages	*Disadvantages*
– May only get at part of the 'story'	• May depend upon 'amnesties'
– Focused on innocence/guilt, not 'truth'	• Doesn't involve punishment
– Limited use of witnesses	• Insufficient support for victims

Source: Roche (2005)

Although it may not be immediately obvious that approaches such as truth commissions are compatible with the operation of the ICC, Roche (2005: 579) argues that it should, in principle, be possible for them to work co-operatively whereby 'the ICC would work with states to prosecute perpetrators who fail to satisfy the conditions for the granting of a truth commission amnesty. Such an approach would enhance the legitimacy and effectiveness of both institutions: ICC support would enable truth commissions to hold out a more credible threat of prosecution to those who refuse to confess and to make amends for their crimes, while the Court's own legitimacy may be enhanced by its demonstrating a willingness to support states' efforts to address human rights abuses.'

Review questions

1 Not all human rights are absolute. What are the other two main forms of rights in the Human Rights Act?

2 What are the main neutralisation techniques in relation to human rights abuses?

3 What are the advantages and disadvantages of truth commissions?

Questions for further discussion

1 Has globalisation really had any appreciable impact on the nature of crime and its control?

2 Does the threat posed by terrorism require that we provide the police with special powers?

3 Is it really possible for a state to commit crimes?

4 Are there circumstances under which the use of torture may be justified by the ends it accomplishes?

5 What have been some of the main successes and failures of the Human Rights Act 1998?

Further reading

On globalisation a short introduction can be found in: Loader, I. and Sparks, R. (2007) Contemporary landscapes of crime, in Maguire, M. *et al.* (eds) *The Oxford Handbook of Criminology*, 4th edn, Oxford: Oxford University Press. Those wanting a fuller discussion should turn to Held, D. *et al.* (1999) *Global Transformations*, Cambridge: Polity Press, or other titles by Held on the subject.

On state crime, a good place to start is either with Green, P. and Ward, T. (2004) *State Crime: Governments, violence and corruption,* London: Pluto Press, or the special edition of the *British Journal of Criminology,* also edited by Penny Green and Tony Ward (vol. 45, no. 4, 2005), Oxford: Oxford Journals.

For a timely, up-to-date discussion of state crimes and the war on terror I recommend Michael Welch's (2006) *Scapegoats of September 11th: Hate crimes and state crimes in the war on terror,* New Brunswick NJ: Rutgers University Press. The issue of state-corporate crime is dealt with in a stimulating and provocative manner in: Michalowski, R. and Kramer, R. (eds) (2006) *State-Corporate Crime: Wrongdoing at the intersection of business and government,* New Brunswick, NJ: Rutgers University Press.

There are a number of fine introductions to the issue of human rights. Perhaps the best place to start is with Freeman, M. (2006) *Human Rights,* 2nd edn, Cambridge: Polity Press, and, subsequently, with Robertson, G. (2002) *Crimes Against Humanity: The struggle for global justice,* 2nd edn, London: Penguin.

Finally, anyone wanting to consider how globalising influences relate to the ways in which criminological ideas change might look at: Newburn, T. and Sparks, R. (eds) (2004) *Criminal Justice and Political Cultures,* Cullompton: Willan.

Websites

A number of NGOs, such as Amnesty International and Human Rights Watch, often carry much useful information on their website: www.amnesty.org and www.hrw.org

The organisation *Statewatch* is a vital source of information about state crime, human rights, espionage, and private profiteering: www.statewatch.org

More specifically on the Human Rights Act, there is a very good guide available on the website of the Ministry of Justice: http://www.justice.gov.uk/guidance/humanrights.htm

On the 'war on terror' there is also a useful website maintained by the Oxford Research Group: http://www.oxfordresearchgroup.org.uk/work/global_security/war_on_terror.php

Part 6
Doing Criminology

35 **Understanding criminological research**
36 **Doing criminological research**

Chapter outline

Introduction	898
Research methods	898
Surveys	899
Questionnaire design	901
Interviews	903
Focus groups	905
Ethnography	907
Documentary analysis	910
Case studies	911
Sampling	911
Random (or probability) sampling	912
Stratified sampling	912
Quota sampling	913
Purposive sampling	913
Convenience sampling	913
Snowball sampling	913
Statistics	914
Descriptive statistics	914
Numerical and categorical data	914
Normal distribution	915
Correlation	916
Probability and significance	916
Controversy: evaluation and experimentation	917
Experimental methods	917
Quasi-experimental methods	918
Evaluation research	918
Questions for further discussion	921
Further reading	921
Websites	922

Understanding criminological research

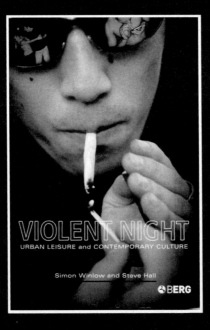

As a student of criminology you have to read and analyse criminological research. You may well also need to undertake a small-scale piece of research yourself – for a long essay or dissertation. Both of these tasks require you to develop the ability to assess, in a critical manner, how research is undertaken and what it is (and is not) able to tell us.

In this chapter we:

- take a quick journey through research methods, exploring the differences between 'quantitative' (numerical) and 'qualitative' (non-numerical) methods;

- look at each of the main research methods in turn, exploring the basic techniques and looking at the strengths and limitations of each.

Most research involves some sort of 'sampling' – selecting respondents from a larger population – and we explore the main methods of making such selections.

Although we won't look at statistical techniques in any detail, it is, nevertheless, important to understand the most frequently-used terms and we briefly consider some of the most common bits of statistical language – the things you are most likely to come across when reading criminological books and articles.

Research methods can occasionally cause controversy and we finish by looking at one such: the debate over evaluation in criminological research and, more particularly, the place of what are often referred to as 'experimental methods'.

Introduction

The purpose of this and the following chapter is not to provide you with everything you need for the purpose of doing your first piece of criminological research – a long essay or a dissertation. Rather, it is to give you an overview of some of the important things you will probably need to take into consideration; to provide a short overview of a number of things – such as research methods – that you will undoubtedly need to read about in much greater detail in due course; to provide some tips about how to go about the task in front of you and, perhaps, to save you from one or two of the difficulties you might otherwise face. So, what follows is not a *how to* guide. It is not all the nuts and bolts of doing criminological research – that would require another textbook, quite possibly as large as this one. What I want to do here is walk you through some of the main features of research so that you have a general feel for what is involved and know where to go next in search of further information.

Research methods

Broadly speaking, we may distinguish between *quantitative* and *qualitative* research. Quantitative research tends to be relatively large-scale and uses numeric data and statistical procedures to analyse such data and reach conclusions. Research strategies that employ quantitative methods tend to be more heavily influenced by models of inquiry derived from the physical sciences than are qualitative methods. They also tend to be *deductive* in approach, with the testing of theories or hypothesis being a favoured approach in such research studies (see Chapter 36). By contrast, qualitative research is often based on relatively small samples – and is therefore often smaller in scale than quantitative research. It is also more likely to be used in the generation of hypotheses, or an *inductive* approach to the research/theory relationship. In broad terms, where quantitative research focuses its attention on the search for representative samples and generalisable findings, qualitative research

Table 35.1	Contrasting quantitative and qualitative research	
Quantitative	**Qualitative**
Numbers	Words
Point of view of researcher	Points of view of participants
Researcher distant	Researcher close
Theory testing	Theory emergent
Static	Process
Structured	Unstructured
Generalisation	Contextual understanding
Hard, reliable data	Rich, deep data
Macro	Micro
Behaviour	Meaning
Artificial settings	Natural settings

Source: Bryman (2001).

tends to be more concerned with understanding the world through the eyes of its human subjects. That said, all such distinctions are tentative rather than definitive, for there is much that quantitative and qualitative methods have in common.

Many researchers seem to specialise in one type of research or the other, preferring to use qualitative or quantitative methods. Whilst this is understandable, there is much to be gained from a working knowledge of a range of methods and, indeed, in many cases some of the most useful research will involve a combination of qualitative and quantitative approaches. Sometimes you will see this referred to as *triangulation*. Essentially, this term refers to the idea of looking at a particular phenomenon from a number of different points – as one might do in surveying or navigation – and using these together to produce a more accurate understanding than would be possible with only a single viewpoint.

In effect, this general assumption is also largely true in social research. It is often helpful to be able to look at things from different angles, and using different methods. Not only does this help refine one's position, but it is also very helpful in checking the validity of one data source against another. Though both are quantitative methods, we came across a very good example in Chapter 3 of how different data sources may complement each other. There we looked at trends in crime and discovered that on the surface police-recorded crime statistics and the British Crime Survey appeared to indicate differing

trends in crime in the mid- to late-1990s. However, the BCS enabled us to assess the impact of changes in reporting practices on police-recorded crime trends. Taking these changes into account, together with changes in recording practices, indicated that the underlying trends were rather different than recorded crime statistics alone suggested.

Surveys

Much large-scale (and, indeed, smaller-scale) quantitative research is undertaken using survey research methods. We are all used to the idea of surveys. Most of us will have been interviewed at one time or another – on the street, at home or elsewhere – as part of a survey. Moreover, terms like 'opinion polls', which are now an everyday part of the political landscape, are just another way of talking about surveys. Surveys are generally fairly large research instruments that obtain data through the use of a standardised questionnaire. In the main, because of their size and the nature of the questions that can be asked effectively in this manner, surveys are used for gathering quantitative data, though this is not exclusively the case, and often researchers will also include a small qualitative component.

Two terms you may come across in connection with surveys (and with other research methods also) are those of the *dependent* and *independent* variable. Put simply, the independent variable is the *cause* in the cause and effect relationship; the dependent variable is the effect. So, as a criminologist, it is highly likely that the dependent variable in your study will be offending or crime; the independent variable might be anything from unemployment to school under-achievement. Some other factor that might interfere with the relationship between the independent and the dependent variable is likely to be referred to as an *extraneous* or *confounding* variable.

Surveys can be undertaken in a number of ways. They may be conducted by post, face-to-face interview or, as is now the case with the British Crime Survey, through a combination of face-to-face interview and computer-assisted personal interviewing. Computers are used for particularly sensitive questions so that respondents can answer questions directly on to a laptop computer without the interviewer knowing how they have answered (see Chapter 3).

Postal surveys have the advantage that they are cheap. It is obviously much simpler and cheaper to send questionnaires out through the post, with a stamped addressed envelope, asking people to complete them and return them to you. Because there is no interviewer present, the instruments used in postal surveys (and in other circumstances where appropriate) are called *self-completion questionnaires*. The downside, and it is a major one, is that the *response rate* for postal surveys tends to be very low. Questionnaires arrive and many people, even if they show some interest in responding initially, may simply forget, or forget within the time period that has been set, to complete and return it. The presence of an interviewer for *face-to-face interviews* tends to ensure much greater compliance and can also have the advantage of sorting out any misunderstandings should they arise.

A further method that can be used which contains more of a personal element than the postal survey, but involves less expense than face-to-face interviews, is to conduct a *telephone survey*. Response rates are rarely as good as face-to-face interviews, and there are certain questions that are more difficult to ask over the phone than personally. In addition, there are practical issues such as getting hold of telephone numbers for those in the sample. In earlier times one of the shortcomings of telephone surveys was the limitation placed on sampling by the fact that not everyone had access to a telephone. This is much less of a problem these

---

Advantages and disadvantages of the self-completion questionnaire

Advantages

- They are relatively cheap to produce and to administer.
- The low cost potentially allows large samples to be surveyed.
- Large territories can be covered – if the questionnaire is posted or emailed.
- The absence of an interviewer potentially means:
  - sensitive topics can be addressed;
  - the respondent won't be affected by the personal characteristics of an interviewer (interviewer effects);
  - there can be no interference in the process of answering the questions (interviewer bias).

Disadvantages

- Response rates tend to be poor – without an interviewer present there is no opportunity to build rapport with the respondent. In the absence of some other reminder, questionnaires will often remain uncompleted.
- In order to encourage reasonable response rates it is often necessary to ensure that:
  - questionnaires are kept short;
  - questions are very simple;
  - there are few opportunities for 'open' questions: most have to be 'closed'.
- The absence of an interviewer may mean:
  - any misunderstanding of questions goes uncorrected;
  - any misunderstanding of the structure of the questionnaire – the routing of questions, etc. – goes uncorrected;
  - there is a response bias as potential respondents with, say, literacy problems will be less likely to complete the questionnaire.

days, but has been replaced by a number of practical difficulties relating to the growing use of mobile phones: phones being turned off or turned to voicemail and the problem that some mobile phone networks charge the call recipient for particular types of call. All of these may limit the researcher's ability to make contact with potential respondents.

Finally, there is the *internet-based survey*. The advantages of this approach are obvious, for it is relatively cheap and, in principle, a great many people can be reached and followed-up fairly easily and quickly. Like telephone surveys, it is necessary to have the contact information (an email address rather than phone number in this case) in order to make the survey possible. The major limitation is the same as the postal survey. My university conducts internet surveys of students. Unfortunately, the response rates are generally so poor that the results are often barely usable. Most people reading this will, like me, no doubt already receive more emails than they feel they can easily deal with. It is easy to understand why extra ones, especially those that require an investment of time, might be discarded or ignored. I certainly don't fill in every email questionnaire I receive – even though as a researcher I feel pangs of guilt whenever I decline to do so. Finally, as with telephone surveys, there is the issue of coverage in such surveys, in that not everybody has access to the internet. Moreover, the fact that it is particular segments of the population that are disproportionately likely to be in the group without access (e.g. the elderly) means that there is a high probability of systematic bias in the survey.

Questionnaire design

There are a number of basic features of questionnaires that you should bear in mind when thinking about their construction. First of all, they should be set out clearly and simply. Your aim is to elicit information from respondents. You need to make this as straightforward as possible. Most people are busy, have probably been asked to fill in questionnaires before and will, in all likelihood, be fairly easily put off. You need to think about what will make them, and keep them, interested in your survey. At the outset you need to explain, in plain English, the aims of the study, why you are doing it and hoping to achieve, and outline any confidentiality agreement that there may be.

Second, and linked with this, you need to think through what it is vital to ask and what not. It is all too easy to throw everything in and end up with a questionnaire that is too long. Think about

how much time you can reasonably expect an interview to take, and what is the minimum number of questions you need to ask? Keeping things short will almost certainly increase your response rate (i.e. increase the proportion of people you approach who complete a questionnaire).

What sorts of questions will you ask? You will almost certainly need to know some details about the respondent, such as their age, sex, ethnicity and some other demographic details. There are some fairly standard ways of doing this, and one example is shown in Figure 35.1.

Because the questionnaire-based survey is primarily a method of eliciting quantitative data, you need to think carefully about the phrasing of questions and the range of answers that will be necessary or allowed. Most questions will be *closed*. That is to say, they will only offer respondents a limited range of possible answers. You may occasionally include a small number of more *open* questions such as 'what was the most positive/negative aspect of your experience?' There are two main reasons for including such questions: first, in order to gather some more detailed information about particular aspects of what is being studied and, second, to give the respondent some space in which to express themselves. Page after page of closed questions can feel a little constricting. It is important to bear in mind, however, that open questions are both difficult and time-consuming to analyse.

The majority of questions should generally remain closed. Some of these may be a simple 'yes/no/don't know'. In such cases, you should almost always include a 'don't know' category, for it is important not to force people into answering in ways that might be misleading. Others may involve scales of one sort or another in order to allow respondents to differentiate between, say, the strength of their opinion about something, or the frequency with which they have done or felt something. There are a number of different scales, but one of the most common is that which is called a *Likert scale*. This is mainly used to gather data on attitudes and opinions and will tend to look something like:

Strongly agree (2)	Agree (1)
Neither agree nor disagree (0)	
Disagree (–1)	Strongly disagree (–2)

As you can see there are an equal number of positive and negative statements, as well as a neutral one, and this allows mean (average) scores to be calculated as well as the proportions answering in each category, or positively/negatively, and so on.

| **Figure 35.1** | An example of standard demographic questions in a self-complete survey |

1   Are you male or female?

Male ☐   Female ☐

2   How old are you? ☐☐

3   Which of the following best describes you?

White		*Asian*	
British	☐	Indian	☐
Irish	☐	Pakistani	☐
European	☐	Bangladeshi	☐
White other (describe)	☐	Chinese	☐
		Asian other	☐

Black			
British	☐	*Mixed Race/Dual Heritage (describe)*	☐
African	☐		
Caribbean	☐		
Black other (describe)	☐		

Source: Shiner *et al.* (2005).

The wording of questions is vitally important to the potential success of surveys. The words and phrases one chooses to use in questionnaires will affect, often very profoundly, the answers that one receives. As we saw in Chapter 17, for example, for some years the BCS has asked questions about 'fear of crime'. This has generated a vast literature and some interesting debates and findings. However, in recent years some criminologists have come to question the usefulness of the term 'fear of crime' and have argued that by beginning to ask different questions it appears that one of the primary responses to criminal victimization is not *fear* but *anger*. On a more mundane level, it is important in questionnaire design that careful consideration is given to the meaning of questions and how they are likely to be interpreted by respondents. There are a number of basic rules, including (May, 2001):

- *Don't use leading questions* – 'By how much do you think prison numbers will go up next year?' (they may go down).

- *Use simple language wherever possible.*

- *Don't ask two questions in one* – 'Are you in favour of the government's recent proposals on youth crime, and do you think they will be successful?'

- *Be very careful about asking personal questions* – especially in a questionnaire.

- *Ask questions that the respondent can answer* – In a survey of police officers there is no point in asking relatively new recruits what they think of the changes in operational policing over the last ten years.

- *Remember that there are limits to what people may be able to remember.*

As we have seen, the style in which questions are asked determines the type of data that are forthcoming. In surveys it is usual to ask 'closed' questions and then produce numerical tallies summarising the results. This is done by *coding* the data – essentially assigning a numerical code to a particular answer (so in the example above 'Strongly agree' might be 2, 'Agree' 1 and so on). Answers are usually pre-coded allowing the results to be entered swiftly and accurately into SPSS or a similar statistical package for analysis. In thinking about the coding of potential answers there are two vital considerations:

- Answers must be *mutually exclusive* – It should not be possible for an answer to fall into more than one of the categories offered. You would be falling into this trap if you asked respondents:

'How often do you go to the pub?' and then offer the following categories as possible answers: Very often; often; occasionally; seldom; never. Although on the surface, the scale looks reasonable, there is no easy way of differentiating 'occasionally' and 'seldom', and no guarantee that respondents with very similar habits will answer the question in the same way.

- Answer categories should be *exhaustive* – In response to the pub question it would be insufficient simply to have 'daily', '3–4 times per week', 'once or twice a week' and 'never' as the categories don't cover the full range of possible answers to the question.

Interviews

We have already briefly come across interviews in our discussion of survey methods. Interviews may be used in a variety of research settings and have uses well beyond survey research. In general terms, interviews may be divided into three main types: *structured; semi-structured* and *unstructured*. Different types are used depending on whether the research is largely quantitative or largely qualitative in nature.

The ideal type of a *structured* interview is one in which the same questions are asked of all participants, the questions are asked in the same way, and they are generally closed in nature. As such,

How leading questions can affect the outcome of a poll

To my mind, one of the funniest, and most instructive, examples of the use and abuse of 'leading questions' is from an episode of the BBC TV series Yes, Prime Minister. *The exchange is between the fictional Cabinet Secretary, Sir Humphrey Appleby, and the Prime Minister's Private Secretary, Bernard Woolley.*

Sir Humphrey: 'You know what happens: nice young lady comes up to you. Obviously you want to create a good impression, you don't want to look a fool, do you? So she starts asking you some questions: Mr. Woolley, are you worried about the number of young people without jobs?'
Bernard Woolley: 'Yes'
Sir Humphrey: 'Are you worried about the rise in crime among teenagers?'
Bernard Woolley: 'Yes'
Sir Humphrey: 'Do you think there is a lack of discipline in our Comprehensive schools?'
Bernard Woolley: 'Yes'
Sir Humphrey: 'Do you think young people welcome some authority and leadership in their lives?'
Bernard Woolley: 'Yes'
Sir Humphrey: 'Do you think they respond to a challenge?'
Bernard Woolley: 'Yes'
Sir Humphrey: 'Would you be in favour of reintroducing National Service?'
Bernard Woolley: 'Oh … well, I suppose I might be.'
Sir Humphrey: 'Yes or no?'
Bernard Woolley: 'Yes'

Sir Humphrey: 'Of course you would, Bernard. After all you said you can't say no to that. So they don't mention the first five questions and they publish the last one.'
Bernard Woolley: 'Is that really what they do?'
Sir Humphrey: 'Well, not the reputable ones no, but there aren't many of those. So alternatively the young lady can get the opposite result.'
Bernard Woolley: 'How?'
Sir Humphrey: 'Mr. Woolley, are you worried about the danger of war?'
Bernard Woolley: 'Yes'
Sir Humphrey: 'Are you worried about the growth of armaments?'
Bernard Woolley: 'Yes'
Sir Humphrey: 'Do you think there is a danger in giving young people guns and teaching them how to kill?'
Bernard Woolley: 'Yes'
Sir Humphrey: 'Do you think it is wrong to force people to take up arms against their will?'
Bernard Woolley: 'Yes'
Sir Humphrey: 'Would you oppose the reintroduction of National Service?'
Bernard Woolley: 'Yes'
Sir Humphrey: 'There you are, you see Bernard. The perfect balanced sample.'

Source: Yes, Prime Minister ('The Ministerial Broadcast', first broadcast BBC, January 1986)

http://www.yes-minister.com/ypmseas1a.htm

therefore, it is fairly clear that it is typically the structured interview that is used in large-scale quantitative research. By contrast, within highly qualitative research, or work that borders on ethnography (see below), where the concern is to understand certain things in detail and in depth and to hear how respondents perceive matters, one is much more likely to use *unstructured* interviews. Here the questions are open-ended and there is no set structure for the ordering of questions, no necessary wording for questions, and no necessity that all questions be asked of all respondents. Such interviews are much closer to conversations, though they will be steered by the interviewer who, perhaps by using a *topic guide,* will use their skills and experience to explore various issues with the respondent. Lying in between these two ends of the interviewing spectrum are *semi-structured interviews*, where there may be some form of fairly formal interview schedule, but where there remains sufficient freedom for the interviewer to follow up things that they are especially interested in, and room for the respondent to talk at some length about what concerns them.

By definition, structured interviews are guided by a set of standardised questions. But how are unstructured interviews undertaken? For this approach you will need to construct what is referred to as an 'interview guide' or 'topic guide'.

This is the unstructured version of the interview schedule. It will contain the areas you will, in principle, want to cover. It may even contain one or two specific questions. But, in the main, its phrasing and ordering are relatively inconsequential. The nature of the research process here means that it is much more important to form some type of relationship with the respondent, to get them to talk, and to allow them to do so in a way that they are comfortable with. This means following their physical and verbal cues, allowing and enabling a more organic interview to take place.

That said, unstructured interviews are neither 'formless' nor without rigour. You will want to think carefully about what you are trying to investigate. When interviewing you will have to be alive to what is important to the respondent, to how they see and talk about things, and you will have to adapt your approach to the situation you are confronted with. Being adaptable takes skill. There is security in a structured interview that disappears when one is faced with a more free-flowing approach. Thinking about how to phrase questions is important, and being able to use open questions, and clear follow-up questions, is crucial. You will almost certainly need a variety of neutral prompt questions. You must be careful not to push respondents into answering in particular ways because of the nature of the prompts you use. Also, vary what

The advantages and disadvantages of telephone interviews

Advantages

- The fact you don't have to travel potentially means:
  - they are cheaper than face-to-face interviews;
  - samples can be larger;
  - geographical spread can be greater.
- The 'anonymity' of the telephone potentially means that there are fewer 'interviewer effects' (the respondent being affected by the personal characteristics of the interviewer).
- There is no issue of 'interviewer safety' (interviewing in people's homes, for example, raises questions of safety).

Disadvantages

- It is more difficult to establish rapport between interviewer and interviewee.
- Response rates may be lower – especially now that 'cold-calling' is such a common sales technique.
- With closed questions it is difficult to use scales (1 = very much; 2 = quite a lot, etc.) as they are difficult to remember, are time-consuming, and can become very tedious.
- Open questions can be a problem as people may not wish to speak at length on the phone, or feel uncomfortable doing so.
- Interviewers find it more difficult to judge how 'well' the interview is going when they can't see the respondent.
- The growing use of mobile phones makes telephone interviews more difficult.

you say – it will get terribly boring for your interviewee if you use the same prompt question the whole time. Irrespective of the nature of your interview, but especially where they are semi- or unstructured, your aim is to build rapport with your respondent – to reach a sufficient level of trust that your interviewee feels that it is safe to share information with you.

How should you capture the data in an unstructured interview? Unless you have mastered shorthand, you are faced with having to try to take notes whilst conducting the interview or, alternatively, recording the interview. If you are going to write notes then some practice is important. It is not easy to conduct an interview, ask questions, listen to the answers and write notes simultaneously. Without shorthand, you will only be able to capture a proportion of what is said and so you need to think carefully about what it is you are trying to capture and what implications the missing material has for your research.

In many cases recording will be preferable. Again, you will often need to have established a degree of rapport with your interviewee prior to using a tape recorder. If you are going to record an interview, make sure that your recording equipment works, that you have spares (batteries, tapes, minidisks, etc.) and that you are comfortable working the machinery. Every experienced researcher has at least one horror story of the equipment not working or, worse still, some failure to operate it efficiently themselves. I have a vivid memory of a researcher I worked with coming back from one very important interview. It was important in two senses. The respondent was crucial to the study, but was also an important person. The researcher concerned was pleased to have secured the interview. Having settled into the interview, and secured agreement that it be recorded, about half way through the interview he realised that he hadn't turned on the tape recorder. Showing great presence of mind, he made some excuse to mess with the recorder, turned it on, and carried on with the interview. Knowing that a lot had been missed he decided to try to go over some of the questions covered earlier, but to do so in as subtle a manner possible. Again, this worked well, the interview proceeded without further mishap and some considerable time later the interviewer drew the session to a close, packed up the equipment and left, happy about a situation saved. When he got back to the office and checked the tape he realised that for the whole time the microphone had been plugged into the wrong socket and so nothing had recorded anyway! The moral of the tale is, be familiar with the equipment and sufficiently so that you can operate it without having to double-check.

The choice between these three basic approaches to interviewing will very much depend upon the aim of the research. To summarise what we've covered so far: where a core objective concerns the testing of a hypothesis, it is the *survey methodology* that tends to be most appropriate. Where the concern is with attitudes, beliefs and perceptions, then *qualitative* or *semi-/unstructured interviews* will tend to fare better. The choice of approach will have a knock-on effect on sample size, and quite likely sampling method – a matter we come to in more detail below. Because of their suitability to quantitative research, structured interviews will demand much larger sample sizes than qualitative interviews. The nature of data collected via unstructured or in-depth interviews is such that it is generally only possible to make use of a relatively limited number of cases. Often researchers will argue that 40–70 interviews is the optimum number using this type of method (though often there will be fewer). Any more and it is difficult to deal with the data.

As suggested, where large samples are concerned it will generally be *structured interviewing* that is required. However, there are still choices to be made. Which will be best: the telephone interview, the face-to-face interview, or a self-completion questionnaire? Self-completion questionnaires and telephone interviews are significantly cheaper than face-to-face interviews, with postal surveys being cheapest of all. However, postal questionnaires tend to have significantly poorer response rates. A comparison of the characteristics of structured interviews and self-completion questionnaires can be found in Table 35.2.

Focus groups

A focus group is, in effect, a form of group interview, or a 'group discussion exploring a specific set of issues' (Kitzinger and Barbour, 1999). Rather than simply interviewing a single person, the focus group involves several people. The group is asked a series of questions and the data gathered are a combination of the answers individuals give to these questions as well as any discussions the group has collectively. It is this interactional element that distinguishes focus groups from group interviews more generally. Like one-to-one

Table 35.2	Comparing qualitative interviews with self-administered questionnaires	
Characteristics	**Qualitative interviews**	**Self-administered questionnaires**
Provide information about …	As questionnaires, but in greater depth	Attitudes, motivation, opinions, events
Best at…	Exploring informants' stories and perspectives	Checking whether sample share research hypothesis
Also useful for…	Surveys: closed questions can be asked, as in opinion polls	Open-ended questions allow researcher to investigate informants' stories/views
Richness of response …	Dialogue between researcher and informant allows nuances to be captured and questions to be clarified. Long interviews quite common	Questions cannot be modified once printed, nor can nuances of respondents' views be easily detected
Sensitive to …	Informants. Good for finding out about the individual, specific and particular	The research literature and the range of responses amongst groups
Anonymity …	Some things can be difficult to say face-to-face	Sensitive questions may be more acceptable
Ethics …	Although interviewers know who they have spoken to, transcripts can be anonymised	Anonymous questionnaire responses easily ensured
Sample size …	With exception of telephone interviews, less suitable for wide coverage	Can be very large, and as generalisation is often the aim, samples may need to be big
Time costs …	Devising interview guide, piloting, arranging interviews, establishing rapport, transcription and data analysis	Devising and distributing questionnaire, checking data, analysing data
Money costs …	Travel, transcription, equipment, phone bills	Printing, distributing and retrieving questionnaires, especially where response rates are low.

Source: Arksey and Knight (1999).

interviews, focus groups may vary considerably in the extent to which they are structured. They are a relatively efficient and rich way of getting information from a number of people. There are obviously limits to what can be discussed in focus groups and personal matters are rarely likely to be best explored in this type of context, though there are circumstances where focus groups have been used in researching sensitive topics such as sexual health (Farquhar and Das, 1999).

Focus groups have become an increasingly popular method of obtaining feedback and eliciting views – for market research as well as social and political opinion surveys.

According to Kitzinger and Barbour (1999: 5) focus groups are best used in the exploration of people's 'experiences, opinions, wishes and concerns'. More particularly, they are useful 'for allowing participants to generate their own questions, frames and concepts and to pursue their own priorities on their own terms, in their own vocabulary'. The term 'vocabulary' is key here, for it points to an important quality of focus groups. This method is especially good when one's interest is in understanding the terminology and language people use in describing and evaluating particular phenomena. Thus, if the aim of a piece of research is to gauge how popular a particular politician is, then the most suitable method is almost certainly a survey. However, if you want to explore how people think about, and the ways in which they talk about, that politician, then the focus group may well be the appropriate way forward. Similarly, if you want to explore group norms, values and attitudes then group interviews/focus groups may be particularly useful.

What size should focus groups be? To some extent this depends on the subject being investigated. Often it is assumed that the standard group will contain somewhere between six and 12 people, but in social research – as opposed to market research – the group may be smaller, more usually between four and eight. Any more than eight to 12 people and the group can easily become unmanageable. The make-up of the group, again, will depend on what is being investigated. Sampling is generally purposive (see below), and groups will tend either to be made up of people from a range of backgrounds – in order to stimulate discussion and possibly disagreement – or from largely the same background, in which any comparisons tend to arise *between* rather than *within* focus groups. The great skill in focus groups lies in *facilitation* (sometimes called *moderation*) – stimulating and managing interaction between the members of the group. The other great challenges concern data analysis. Here, as with all qualitative research, a computer package, such as *NUD*IST* or *Ethnograph*, is likely to be helpful in the process of identifying themes, and manipulating and summarising data.

There are a number of limitations to focus groups that need to be borne in mind:

- As indicated above, they are not necessarily an appropriate setting for dealing with sensitive topics.

- They are time-consuming and sometimes tricky to organise.

- One or two members of the group may dominate or, alternatively, the group may veer toward consensus with the more unusual views in the group being partly suppressed.

- They can be difficult to 'control' and may be more resistant to management by the interviewer/moderator than individual interviewees.

- The data can be difficult to analyse, both in terms of the quantity of material that is collected, and because of the interaction between members of the group.

Ethnography

When discussing ethnography we move about as far from large-scale quantitative methods as it is possible to go. Interpretive sociologists from Max Weber onwards have noted that the very fact that humans are reflexive beings, capable of giving meaning to their actions, requires us to consider this in our attempts to understand the social world. We cannot simply rely upon observation, but need to consider the meaningfulness of the behaviour to human actors. One way in which this can be done is via interviews or indeed through questionnaire-based surveys. However, there are clear limitations to such approaches. Let's say we wish to study the interaction between prison officers and prisoners. We could conduct interviews and ask both sets of actors their impression of how they interact with each other, and we could use survey techniques to gather information on officers' and inmates' attitudes and perceptions of conduct within the prison. Though potentially of great value, however, neither approach would necessarily tell us all that much about the ways in which interaction unfolds, and how different circumstances affect what occurs. For this, we really need to be able to observe what happens, and this is where ethnography comes in.

Ethnography, certainly as I shall use the term here, is closely associated with the types of fieldwork undertaken by cultural anthropologists such as Margaret Mead whose studies were often based on lengthy periods of time spent living among particular tribal peoples. Through observation and close social relationships, Mead, and other anthropologists, including Malinowski and Radcliffe-Brown, sought to understand the cultural and interior life of the communities in which they temporarily lived. Though criminologists may rarely immerse themselves to quite this extent, the underlying principles are the same. Willis and Trondman (2000: 5) describe ethnography as 'a family of methods involving direct and sustained social contact with agents, and of richly writing up the encounter, respecting, recording, representing at least partly *in its own terms*, the irreducibility of human experience. Ethnography is the disciplined and deliberate witness-cum-recording of human experience.'

At the heart of much ethnographic research, therefore, is some form of observational data gathering. This activity is generally broken down into two major categories (Gold 1969) – *participant observation* or *non-participant observation* – or a continuum in which there are four main categories:

complete participant — participant-as-observer — observer-as-participant — complete observer

The complete participant role occurs where the researcher effectively lives or functions as part of a particular community. This is sometimes referred to as 'covert participation' because it is usually undertaken without the knowledge of the other members of the community. The greatest danger – methodologically – in such research is of completely losing

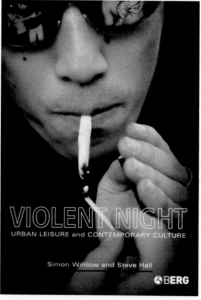

Books based on different kinds of ethnographic research (see Table 35.3): Dick Hobbs' *Doing the Business* (criminality and policing in London's East End) and Simon Winlow and Steve Hall's *Violent Night* (violence and the night-time economy). What ethical dilemmas can be encountered in research of this kind?

critical distance, or 'going native' as it is sometimes called. Covert research also raises a number of tricky ethical issues (see Chapter 36).

The participant-as-observer role is very similar, except that it is not undertaken covertly. Here, the researcher is known to be just that but, nevertheless, joins the group they are studying and participates in many of their activities. Close to this, the observer-as-participant role is where there is more limited interaction with those being studied – they are observed, but there is relatively little participatory activity. The final role is the complete observer, where there is no participation as a member of the group, although there is interaction with the group. Again, this may be overt or covert.

There are undoubtedly occasions when research has to be conducted covertly. Nigel Fielding's (1981) study of the National Front is a case in point. Equally, however, there are others where the necessity to hide the fact that research is being undertaken is more open to question, and where some awkward moral dilemmas must be considered. In addition to

whether the ethnographer's role is overt or covert, such studies may also be distinguished by the nature of the setting in which the research takes place – in particular, whether the situations are 'open' or 'closed' (or 'public'/'private'). Table 35.3 below gives examples of ethnographies carried out under these different conditions.

One obvious question is what sort of data does ethnography generate? The answer, often, is *field notes*. These are reflections written at the time, or shortly after, by the researcher, who records what they have witnessed and heard, together with some thoughts or observations about what this might mean and how it fits with other observations. How to take field notes can sometimes be a problem for the covert researcher. Williams *et al.*'s (1989) study of football hooliganism, for example, required frequent visits to the toilet to scribble down memorable snippets of conversation and a similar technique was used by Jason Ditton in his wonderful study of petty pilfering (see box below).

Table 35.3	Ethnographic research	
	Open/public setting	**Closed setting**
Overt role	Taylor's (1993) study of intravenous drug users; Maher's (1997) study of drug use and sex work	Punch's (1979) study of police corruption in Amsterdam
	Willis's (1977) study of working-class 'lads'	Smith and Gray's (1983) study of police and people in London
	Hobbs's (1988, 1993) research on the East End	Ditton's (1977) study of pilfering in a bakery (strictly speaking, Ditton was 'partially open' about his research)
	Whyte's (1955) classic study of street-corner life in Boston	
Covert role	Patrick's (1973) study of a violent Glasgow gang (though he was 'known' by one of the gang members)	Holdaway's (1982, 1983) study of a police force in which he worked
	Parker's (1974) study of the Roundhouse boys in Liverpool	Fielding's (1981) study of the National Front
		Winlow's (2001) study of bouncers

Source: adapted from Bryman (2004).

An ethnography of fiddling and pilferage

Right from the start , I found it impossible to keep everything that I wanted to remember in my head until the end of the working day (some of the shifts were over twelve hours long) and so had to take rough notes as I was going along. But I was stuck 'on the line', and had nowhere to retire to privately to jot things down. Eventually, the wheeze of using innocently provided lavatory cubicles occurred to me. Looking back, all my notes for that third summer were on Bronco toilet paper! Apart from the awkward tendency for pencilled notes to be self-erasing from hard toilet paper (sometimes before I could even get home), my frequent requests for 'time out' after interesting happenings or conversations in the bakehouse and the amount of time that I was spending in the lavatory began to get noticed. I had to pacify some genuinely concerned work-mates, give up totally undercover operations and 'come out' as an observer, albeit in a limited way. I eventually began to scribble notes more openly, but still not in front of people when they were talking. When questioned about this, as I was occasionally, I coyly said that I was writing things down that occurred to me about 'my studies'.

Source: Ditton (1977: 5).

In practice field notes may take many different forms. They may be highly formal, full notes written whilst under little or no pressure after a period of observation has been completed. By contrast, they may be some scribbled or jotted notes written, as in Ditton's and Williams's experiences – whenever there is a 'convenient' moment.

In practice, qualitative studies using ethnography often combine a range of approaches – most likely interviews of various sorts – including some observational fieldwork, possibly some documentary analysis (see below) of the local press and other materials, and also even bits and pieces of quantitative fieldwork. Winlow and Hall's recent study of urban leisure is a good example of just such an approach. As they described it (2006: 13):

> Drawing upon our sympathies for ethnographic method in depicting social and cultural life in all its richness, we set out to develop a range of key contacts, whom we hoped would become portals to contemporary youth culture. Our aim was to observe and engage with young people in a nat-ural everyday setting, and, to the researchers' eternal gratitude, this occasionally involved going out drinking. Our primary method of data collection was, however, semi-structured and unstructured interviews, the majority of which we recorded. We also conducted quite lengthy observational work, primarily to add depth and insight into how young people's night-life tends to be organized and performed.

Documentary analysis

Many research projects will involve some analysis of documentary records alongside other approaches such as interviews, surveys and the like. For students writing dissertations or long essays, the limited resources available often mean that primary research involving interviews is extremely difficult, and documentary analysis is an attractive option. The focus of such analysis may be very varied, but might include:

- Official documents such as parliamentary debates, policy documents, political speeches, statistical series, official inquiries, etc.

- Media output, such as newspaper reports, magazine articles, television or radio programmes.

- Internet-based resources.

- Personal documents such as diaries, autobiographies, letters, etc.

In thinking about how to assess the quality of documents, Scott (1990) suggests that four criteria be considered:

- *Authenticity* – Do the documents appear to be genuine and of unquestionable origin?

- *Credibility* – Is the evidence free from error and distortion?

- *Representativeness* – Is the evidence typical of its kind and, if not, is the extent of untypicality known?

- *Meaning* – Is the evidence clear and comprehensible?

How are such materials to be analysed? The most usual systematic method is known as *content analysis*. This means applying some set categories to particular texts in order to count the number of occasions particular things appear or occur. These could be particular words or, more often, they will be particular themes that you are looking for.

These themes may be known from the start or, more likely, will in part be generated as the analysis proceeds. The effectiveness of such analysis depends partly on the thoroughness of the process, but also on the authenticity, credibility and reliability of the sources. Other less quantitatively-oriented approaches to analysis may involve a similar process of identifying themes, but will be less concerned with assessing the frequency with which particular things appear, and is more focused upon the way in which things are said/written and the messages that are conveyed.

Case studies

This approach can be used in quantitative or qualitative research, but is most usually associated with the latter. It rests on a single case or a small number of cases and is characterised by intensive investigation of the setting (Bryman, 2004). These cases may be an individual person, a particular group of people, a neighbourhood or community, an event, an area or even a country. As such, therefore, the choice being made is not actually a methodological one, but a design one – something akin to sampling. It is a choice about the object of research, and is usually undertaken for one or more of the following reasons:

- The phenomena being studied involve relationships and links that would be unlikely to be understood using experimental or survey approaches.

- There is little or no concern with generalisation from the results.

- Understanding the social context of the matters being studied is vital.

- It is the only practical way of undertaking research in the area concerned – e.g. in relation to community responses to drug use, or in the day-to-day operation of police authorities.

A number of famous examples within criminology illustrate the potential of the case study approach:

- Clifford Shaw's (1930) study, *The Jack Roller*, of a single 'delinquent boy'.

- Edwin Sutherland's (1937) *The Professional Thief* is a case study of a single individual: 'Chic Conwell'.

- Stan Cohen's (1972/2002) study of moral panics was based around a case study of reactions to the mods and rockers during the 1960s.

- Bill Chambliss' (1978) study of organised crime was based on a case study of a single city: Seattle.

Review questions

1 For what types of research might you select primarily quantitative methods?

2 For what types of research might you select primarily qualitative methods?

3 What are the differences between 'open' and 'closed' questions?

4 What is a leading question? Why are leading questions problematic in the context of research?

5 What are the main differences between structured, semi-structured and unstructured interviews?

Sampling

Having spent a little time outlining the basic parameters of some of the major research methods used by criminologists, we need briefly to consider one or two more technical issues. Once again, the intention is not to provide the nuts and bolts, rather to sketch out elements of the general territory so that you have a sense of some of the key issues and can make some educated decisions about where to go next with your reading and your studies.

When conducting research you will almost always have to give some thought to sampling. Who will you be researching? Is it possible for you to include the whole *population*? If so, then you don't need to worry about sampling. However, if you are only able to, say, survey or interview a proportion of the population you are interested in, then you will need to think about sampling. Thus, you might decide that you want to do some research on the drinking habits of undergraduate students at your university. However, there are almost certainly several thousand undergraduates and you haven't the time or the means to speak with them all. Consequently, you need to choose a more limited group to interview or send questionnaires to. The process by which you make this selection is *sampling*. Your *sampling frame* is provided by a list of the population from which you will select your respondents. There are then a number of sampling techniques you can use, depending on the nature of your study and what you are trying to achieve.

Random (or probability) sampling

This approach selects people randomly for inclusion in the research and is used to eliminate systematic bias so that the eventual sample is as representative as possible of the overall population. There are various types of probability sampling. The most straightforward is a *simple random sample* where everyone in a particular population has an equal chance of being selected for inclusion in the sample. If you wish to interview a random sample of adults in a particular neighbourhood, then so long as you have the names of all adults in that neighbourhood you can create a random sample. You allocate numbers to all the adults and then using a table of random numbers you can select the number of adults according to the sample size you have decided upon.

Stratified sampling

However, things are usually more complex than this. Let's say that you are still conducting your survey in the same neighbourhood, but it is a fairly mixed neighbourhood and you are concerned to ensure that particular groups are included. You may be worried that because you are doing most of the interviews during the daytime you will over-sample those not going out to work and under-sample those with full-time jobs. Moreover, because of the nature of your survey you may want to hear from people who are owner-occupiers, people living in rented accommodation and those who are in local authority-owned housing. Immediately, you can see that the application of random numbers to your sampling frame may not produce a sample that will necessarily have all the features you need. You are going to need to rework it a little. In which case, what you may well need to do is construct a *stratified sample*.

You can do this so long as you have the information that would allow you to stratify the sample according to the characteristics you are interested in – home ownership or by other demographic characteristics. In order to ensure that your sample is selected in proportion to the overall totals of adults falling into each of the home ownership categories in the population, you randomly sample within each of the strata. Within criminology, the best-known example of this type of sampling is the British Crime Survey. The intention behind the BCS is to be representative of two linked populations:

- Households in England and Wales living in private, residential accommodation.
- Adults aged 16 and over living in such accommodation.

The sample size is now approximately 40,000 and the sampling frame is provided by the Postal Address File (PAF) which is the most comprehensive database of private residential accommodation in the country. Because a certain number of interviews in each police force area in England and Wales is required and this cannot be achieved naturally in the smaller police force areas, some over-sampling (increasing the numbers in other areas) is undertaken to meet this requirement.

The BCS also employs a process called *clustering*. A random sample – even one as large as 40,000 – of the whole population would inevitably be geographically very dispersed and, consequently, very expensive to interview. To manage this process, cluster sampling produces what are called *primary sampling units* which are effectively sub-groups of the population, from which the eventual sample is constructed. In the BCS the primary sampling units are postcode areas. Within the eventually selected postcode areas (selected according to complex criteria) households are ranked and then randomly selected. Within the selected households an interviewee is randomly selected from all household members aged 16 or over. No substitution is allowed if the person selected is unavailable or refuses. In addition to this procedure, a *booster sample* (an extra sample) of non-white respondents is generally added. This is done by identifying areas with high minority ethnic populations, randomly selecting households, and then screening potential respondents face-to-face. The booster sample is added in order to ensure that the number of people from ethnic minority groups in the survey is large enough to support meaningful analysis.

The reason for discussing this in some detail is merely to illustrate some of the complexities that can be involved in producing a sample that researchers can be reasonably confident reflects the general make-up of the population. We have briefly discussed probability sampling. However, there are a number of other ways of sampling for research purposes which are not based on random selection, and these are generally referred to as *non-probability sampling*. We begin with *quota sampling*.

Quota sampling

Quota sampling is probably the best-known form of non-probability sampling. On the surface it looks very like stratified random sampling. However, it has one major difference. It does not involve any randomisation. If you have ever been interviewed as part of a market research study, or for a political opinion poll, you will almost certainly have been part of a quota sample. Thus, for example, if you have been stopped on the street by someone with a clipboard and asked questions about your shopping habits, you were most likely initially asked questions which screened you for matters like your age or other demographic details. Your answers to such questions are used both for the usual purpose of analysing the eventual data, but also as a means of deciding whether or not to ask you to continue with the interview after the initial questions have been asked. This is because the interviewer will usually be working to a quota sample; they will be trying to interview a specific number of people with certain characteristics, rather than simply approaching anyone who happens to pass them on the street and agrees to be interviewed. Thus, if the questionnaire is about beer sales and preferences, it is highly likely that men in certain age categories will form the bulk of the intended sample. But the main reason is to ensure that the sample approximates to the general population as, for example, with opinion polls.

The great advantage of quota sampling is that it is reasonably efficient and therefore a comparatively cheap method of constructing a varied and *broadly* representative sample. However, the word *broadly* here gives the game away. Often the apparent representativeness of the sample is illusory, and the fact that decisions about who to approach for interview are left to the interviewer leaves considerable room for bias. Moreover, the way in which such surveys are conducted – often, as in the example above, outside shops during the daytime – means that there may be systematic bias in the sample – excluding all those not shopping at particular times of day, or days of the week, for example.

Purposive sampling

This form of sampling will tend to be used in qualitative studies, particularly when relatively small numbers are being selected for inclusion in a sample. In essence, it is a form of selective sampling designed by the researcher to reflect a range of experiences or attributes. In effect, it is a little like a quota sample in survey research – it enables the researcher to ensure that certain types of people, or people with certain experiences, are included within the sample frame. Thus, you might wish to undertake a qualitative study of defendants' experiences in court. As you are conducting in-depth interviews, you might decide that 40 interviews is the upper limit of what you can reasonably manage. However, you are concerned to ensure that your sample includes both male and female defendants, people of different ages, and defendants who were in court for different reasons, as well as ensuring that you include people found guilty and not guilty. The only way that this can successfully be achieved is through purposive sampling.

Convenience sampling

This is what it says: a sample that is accessible or available. You might do a small piece of research using your fellow students as your sample – perhaps those from your tutor group, from your course or from your hall of residence. This is a convenience sample. Its strength lies in the ease of access that you have. It is fairly easy for you to find respondents, and the chances are you'll get a decent response rate. Its limitation is that whilst it should tell you quite a lot about this particular group of students, the findings cannot be generalised to any larger group because it is not representative. •

Given this limitation, is it best to avoid convenience sampling? The answer to this question is, no, not necessarily. It may be the only way you can do research in a particular area. Let's say you want to do a small study of people who are rough sleeping. Because of the nature of homelessness there is no obviously available sampling frame (a list of homeless people that you can select from randomly). You may be constrained in other ways also, and find that the only way you can do the research is to interview anyone you happen to be able to find sleeping rough. This is a convenience sample and whilst not necessarily representative of the homeless population generally, it may still tell you quite a lot about the experience of homelessness.

Snowball sampling

Rather like convenience sampling – or perhaps even a form of it – the metaphor is of the snowball gathering size as it is rolled. In snowball sampling one starts with one or more respondents and then, using their recommendations/contacts, gradually increase the size of the sample. Howard Becker's classic study of marijuana users began with interviews with people he knew in the music business and progressed from there. His sample 'snowballed' from his initial contacts.

Sampling marihuana users

I conducted fifty interviews with marihuana users. I had been a professional dance musician for some years when I conducted this study and my first interviews were with people I had met in the music business. I asked them to put me in contact with other users who would be willing to discuss their experiences with me. Colleagues working on a study of users of opiate drugs made a few interviews available to me which contained, in addition to material on opiate drugs, sufficient material on the marihuana to furnish a test of my hypothesis. Although in the end half of the fifty interviews were conducted with musicians, the other half covered a wide range of people in the professions. The sample is, of course, in no sense 'random'; it would not be possible to draw a random sample, since no one knows the nature of the universe from which it would have to be drawn.

Source: Becker (1963: 45–6).

This is, in effect, a convenience sample, as it is exploiting a situation that presents itself in order successfully to manage a research problem. As such, it has much to commend it. Its shortcoming, as with all convenience sampling, is that it produces a sample that is very far from representative. It is, predictably enough, generally used within qualitative research studies, where the aim is not to make statistical generalisations to a wider population.

Statistics

Depending on what sort of student you are, this may be the point at which you stop reading. I would urge you not to do so, however. Unfortunately, there seems to be a mindset within British education which leads some people to recoil from all things statistical. Even if you never plan to

do any quantitative research you should still be able to understand the basics. How can you form a judgement about it otherwise? Now, there is not the space here to do any more than introduce one or two ideas, but these are the basic building blocks that will give you a start. Anyone wishing to take this further – and, again, I would urge you to do so – can follow up the suggested reading at the end of the chapter. All I intend to cover in this short section is the difference between *numerical* and *categorical data,* introduce the idea of a *normal distribution* and the linked term *standard deviation,* and briefly discuss the terms *probability* and *significance.* If you understand this much, then you will be able to make sense of basic quantitative data that you will undoubtedly come across in your studies.

Descriptive statistics

As the term suggests, descriptive statistics are used in a general way to describe or outline information about a particular subject. I might be able to tell you a number of things about my university using descriptive statistics such as the number of students, their age range, average qualifications and so forth. You might be able to do the same for your university and then the two could be compared. As I have implied, one of the commonest forms of descriptive statistic is to talk of *averages.* Most people understand what this means. In common terms, it is generally thought of as the figure you get when, say, you add the ages of everyone in a particular class, and then divide the total by the number of people in the class. This will tell you their average age. In fact, there are three types of average, and the one just described is known as the *mean.* The other two ways of calculating averages are called the *mode* and the *median.* The mode tells you which is the most commonly occurring value in any group, and the median tells which value occurs at precisely the mid-point in a group of values (see box below).

Numerical and categorical data

Categorical data, as the names implies, divide things into categories. Such data come in two basic forms: *nominal* and *ordinal.* Nominal data are found when the categories do not have any inherent order. There can be any number of categories, but where there are only two the data are said to be binary. Examples include male/female; black/white;

Mean, mode and median

Take the following list of values, representing the ages of an imagined group of 35 undergraduate students, already ordered so that the mid-point can easily be seen:

42, 39, 38, 32, 26, 26, 23, 23, 22, 22, 22, 21, 21, 20, 20, 20, 20, 19, 19, 19, 19, 19, 19, 19, 18, 18, 18, 18, 18, 18, 18, 18, 18, 18, 18

What is the average age? Well, the *mean* is 22. The *mode* is 18 and the *median* is 19. Each of these measures tells you something slightly different about that group of students, but each is an *average*.

provides a classic example, with the numeric data going 0, 1, 2, 3, 4 ... and so on. These are referred to as *ratio data*. There is a further subset of numeric data, called *interval data,* and these occur where there is no zero point – such as the measurement of temperature – but such scales are extremely rare. Just to complicate matters there is a further subdivision of numeric data: *discrete data* are those expressed on whole numbers only (age in years would, again, be an example); *continuous data* are those where a decimal division is possible (e.g. per capita alcohol consumption in litres).

Normal distribution

The mathematical calculation of what is called the *normal distribution* is generally associated with Karl Friedrich Gauss and is sometimes referred to as the Gaussian curve (see Figure 35.2). This distribution plays a key role in statistics and the application of quantitative methods and relates to numeric data.

Under these conditions the value of the mean, mode and median will be the same. Where this is not the case and the mean, mode and median have different values (as in the Mean, mode and median box above), the data are said to be *skewed*. How much variation is there in the data around the mean point? The answer to this question is usually made using the *standard deviation*. Suppose, for example, your survey told you that the average

young/old, etc. Ordinal data refers to situations where the data are organised into categories that can be ranked in some form of order: very satisfied/quite satisfied/quite dissatisfied, etc. By contrast, numeric data generally refer to scales where the data are in rank order from a zero point and are based on a consistent unit of measurement where the categories are equally spaced. Because of this, differences between categories can be specified numerically – we can say, for example, somebody with a score of 20 has twice as much of something as somebody with a score of 10 but half as much as someone with a score of 40, and so on. Age in years

Figure 35.2   Normal distribution

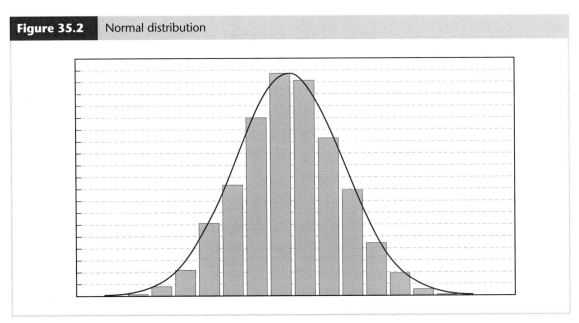

Source: derived from www.statsdirect.com/help/statsdirect.htm (2007).

alcohol consumption of a particular group was 20 units per week. Without another measure you cannot know whether, for example, most people in the group drank between 15–25 units or whether the variation in drinking patterns was much greater. *Standard deviation* is one way of indicating the extent of variation – in this case of drinking patterns – around the average.

The other term you may hear in this connection is *confidence interval*. This is a descriptive statistic which indicates the degree of certainty/uncertainty associated with a particular finding. Thus, survey data may suggest that in a particular local population 20 per cent of people think that the police do a 'very good job'. Because the finding is based on the answers drawn from a sample of the local population, there is a continuing possibility of measurement error. The confidence interval describes the range within which the 'true' value (i.e. that which exists in the population) is likely to lie.

Correlation

In research, one of the standard things we investigate is the relationship between two variables. We may wish to look at a group of juveniles and their offending patterns and see, for example, to what extent their offending is related to age. We shall probably find that it is – for research tends to do so pretty consistently. What do we mean when we say that these things are *related*? Generally, we mean they are *positively correlated*. That is, if the data were plotted on a graph, for example, the level of offending might increase as age increases. If the reverse were the case – offending decreased as age increased – there would still be a relationship, but this would be described as an inverse relationship and would give rise to a *negative correlation*. The extent or degree of correlation refers to how close this relationship is. In statistics, the strength of a relationship is usually indicated using a *correlation coefficient* – generally presented within a range from –1.0 (which indicates a perfect negative correlation) to 1.0 (which indicates a perfect positive correlation).

Probability and significance

If we find a measurable difference between two groups as a result of a survey we have conducted, how do we know whether this is meaningful or not? One of the ways in which we make such assessments is through calculating *probability*.

Probability, in the way it is used here, expresses the likelihood that the findings displayed might have arisen as a result of chance. Assuming we have a random sample, probability values or p-values show the probability of finding a relationship at least as strong as the one observed in our data when there is no such relationship in the population:

- The smaller the p-value, the less likely it is that the relationship we have observed could have occurred by chance.
- When the p-value is quite large, say 0.20, we would say that a relationship at least as strong as the one observed could occur quite often when there is no such relationship in the population.
- If the p-value is very small, say less than 0.01, then it is very unlikely that a relationship as strong as the one observed would occur simply by chance.

Statistical convention dictates that a cut-off is chosen for assessing probability values and this is called the *critical value*. Although the choice of cut-off is arbitrary, 0.05 is conventionally used and 0.01 is sometimes used. When the p-value falls below the critical value, the relationship is said to be *statistically significant*, and when it falls above the critical value it is said to be *not significant*. This simply provides a judgement about whether the relationship we have observed in a sample is likely to exist in the population.

A finding of statistical significance doesn't guarantee that a relationship was not observed by chance, but suggests that this was probably not the case.

There is a wide range of statistical tests that can be used to generate p-values. This is not the place to begin to describe them all, but you may see or read reference to such things as *t-tests*, and the *chi-squared test*. Different tests are appropriate under different circumstances and depend, for example, on the level of measurement of the data (nominal, ordinal or numeric). Each test produces a p-value, however, and the basic interpretation of this value is the same across the various tests. As you begin to manipulate data you will need to know the difference between the tests and understand why one rather than the other is considered appropriate under certain circumstances. If you use a statistical package such as *SPSS*, it is possible to produce results with such tests of significance without understanding their relevance. This is unwise and either a methods course in your university, or one of the good textbooks listed at the end of this chapter, will guide you through basic statistical tests of significance and how they should be used. Understanding such things is actually quite straightforward and you will quickly discover that you don't need to be Stephen Hawking to make sense of this stuff. Once you have mastered the basics, it will give you considerable confidence in discussing all manner of research findings. Moreover, it may well help to get you a job when you graduate!

Controversy: evaluation and experimentation

I want to close this chapter by looking briefly at an area of methodological debate that is currently causing something of a stir within British criminology. In short, it concerns the value of what are generally referred to as 'experimental methods'. As we will see, experimental methods have rarely been used in British criminological research, but the government has recently shown an increasing interest in their use, particularly in evaluations of interventions with offenders. This has been the cause of some debate. I don't wish to give a blow-by-blow account of this dispute, merely outline some of the basic points of departure between scholars who hold differing views on how to conduct rigorous evaluation research.

Experimental methods

Experimental methods are commonly associated with medical research, particularly the evaluation of a new treatment or a new drug. The use of such methods probably dates back to the late nineteenth century, though it was relatively rare at this stage, and only grew in popularity in the early twentieth century (Oakley, 1998). At the heart of experimental research is the process of randomisation which is used in an effort to eliminate extraneous factors in the search for cause and effect relationships. Under experimental conditions, random sampling is usually achieved by allocating research subjects to two groups: a *treatment* group that will be receiving whatever intervention is being evaluated (a new drug, for example) and a *control* or *non-treatment* group that receives no intervention, or just a placebo. Subjects are allocated to the groups randomly in order to ensure that there is no consistent feature (e.g. age, sex, ethnicity, criminal history) that might distinguish the two groups. On the basis that they can, therefore, be assumed to be equivalent in every other respect except for the fact that one receives the treatment and one does not, any measurable differences between the groups at the end of the research can safely be attributed to the effects of the treatment.

The best known experimental design is known as the *Randomised Controlled Trial (RCT)*. The standard basic design of such trials can be seen below (Figure 35.3).

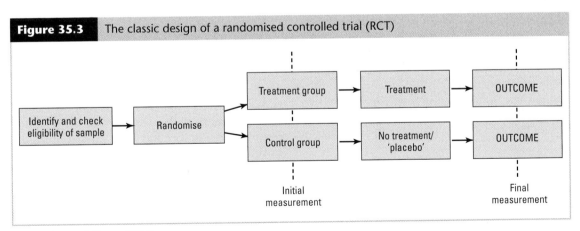

| Figure 35.3 | The classic design of a randomised controlled trial (RCT) |

Source: Clegg and Kirwan (2006).

The model above is generally referred to as the standard 'pre- and post-test' in which measurements are taken before and after the intervention and are then compared in order to assess the impact of that intervention (see, for example, the discussion of Bandura's Bobo Doll experiment in Chapter 7). There is also a simpler post-test measurement design in which, as implied, it is only the outcome measurements that are taken. This approach is more usual when there is the possibility that pre-test research – say the use of a questionnaire – will provide information to participants that would affect the 'blindness' of the process.

In some studies, researchers may attempt to reduce any biases through a process called *blinding*. There are two main types. *Single blinding* is where the subjects in the research don't know whether they are in the treatment or the control group. *Double blinding* is where neither the subjects of the research nor those providing treatment – which usually means administering the drug – know which group they are in. There is a further option for RCTs in which those participants who have a preferred treatment option are allocated to that group and the remainder are randomly allocated between the two groups (sometimes referred to as a *preference trial*).

The RCT is often referred to as the 'gold standard' in research methods, implying that it is the ideal to be striven for. This is unfortunate, because it rather glosses over the important point that the appropriateness of any research method depends upon the thing being studied and the questions being asked. Thus, there are clearly areas of inquiry to which the RCT is ideally suited, and where it might reasonably be referred to as the gold standard – the testing of pharmaceuticals, for example. However, there are many other areas where such a methodology would be entirely unsuitable. The study of police culture would be one. Such a study would almost certainly be better undertaken using a range of other approaches, some of which would quite likely be qualitative. The implication that such approaches are not the 'gold standard' devalues their worth.

Quasi-experimental methods

This range of approaches has many but not all of the attributes of the full experimental design outlined above. Generally, it is randomisation that is absent and researchers use a variety of techniques in an attempt to generate a situation that is as close to the effect that randomisation would have as is possible. Thus, in *matched pairs* designs, the sample to be studied is matched into twos along a set of key characteristics – which could involve such things as age, sex, ethnicity, education, occupation, medical history, offending history, and so on – in an attempt to control for the influence of these factors. That is, if people are matched on a whole range of potentially important variables, then any differences between them after 'treatment' are more likely to be as a result of that intervention (and not age, sex, ethnicity, etc.). The major difficulty with such an approach is that it is extremely difficult to match across a sufficient number of factors to be certain that one has 'controlled' for all major extraneous variables.

A second approach is to compare *non-equivalent* groups using a treatment group and a comparison group. In such research there is no randomisation, merely a group of subjects who are subject to an intervention and another group that is not. Often, great efforts are made to try to ensure that the two groups are as similar as possible to each other. However, it is accepted that the groups will inevitably differ. The approach taken thereafter is usually to attempt to control for any major differences between the groups using statistical techniques at the analytical stage. The data are *weighted* to take account of identified disparities between the groups, helping to increase the likelihood that any statistically significant differences between the intervention and non-intervention groups can be attributed to the intervention itself. Weighting refers to a process of adjustment whereby the emphasis that is placed on each case varies according to certain criteria. This process is generally used to take account of bias and to increase accuracy.

Evaluation research

Like so many other features of the British social world, much of what we understand by 'evaluation' derives from the United States. Evaluation research has a longer and more privileged history in the US than it does in the UK, dating back to the post-war Keynesian reconstruction and the major social programmes of the 1950s and 1960s. Initially, at least, evaluation was dominated by experimental and quasi-experimental approaches, with the period from the 1960s to the 1980s sometimes being referred to as the 'golden age' of evaluation (Rossi and Wright, 1984).

A large number of experimental evaluations of major policy initiatives were undertaken during this period covering such areas as welfare, health, education, housing, fiscal and penal policy – and federal spending in this area grew six-fold between 1969 and 1972. A number of factors influenced this development. Public services were widely perceived to be poorly organised and inefficient; there was no dominant model of public policy decision-making that offered an easy solution of how this problem of inefficient public services might be resolved. Into this breach stepped the new 'science' of evaluation (Oakley, 1998). For many in the field, experimental methods were not only dominant at this time but, in Campbell and Stanley's (1963:3) phrase, were considered to be 'the only available route to cumulative progress'.

Whilst experimental methods have remained important, they have been gradually superseded by evaluations that were tailored more to informing or influencing decision-making processes (Robson, 2000). Weiss (1987) described this as being a shift from knowledge-driven to use-led approaches to evaluation, or towards what Patten called 'utilization-focused' evaluation. One consequence of this was that a diversity of evaluation practice began to emerge, with methodological pluralism becoming increasingly visible.

What then happened to experimental and quasi-experimental methods? In fact, something rather interesting. Whereas, as I have suggested, the early days of evaluation were dominated by experimental methods – at least in the US – this is now much less the case. Or, rather, there are certain fields of inquiry – health and medicine, for example – where such methods continue to enjoy a dominant position, and others – social welfare, for example – where, despite the continued assumption that experimental methods represent the so-called 'gold standard' in evaluation, they are hardly ever used.

Why should this be? Oakley (1998:94; see also Oakley, 2000) points to five 'reasons' that have often been advanced against the use of experimental methods:

- That prospective experimental designs are often not feasible in social situations (you cannot easily randomly assign serious offenders to prison on the one hand and some other form of intervention on the other).

- That they are inappropriate for assessing complex, multi-level interventions, especially those that take place in community settings.

- That 'withholding treatments' from a control group is unethical.

- That such designs are too expensive, take too long and are too remote from the policy-making process.

- Such research tends to be method-driven and atheoretical; it tends to ignore subjective meanings and under-emphasises human agency.

It is as much the last point as any other that is, arguably, key. This has been part of a paradigm shift within social sciences over the past 20–30 years. From the 1970s onwards, just as social science generally was gripped by a debate over the limits of positivism (Giddens, 1974 – and see Chapters 5 to 13), so experimental methods in evaluation were subjected to a critique from what became known as 'constructivism'. As Pawson and Tilley (1997:17) summarise it, this approach 'urges us to consider again the nature of what it is we are evaluating. The argument goes as follows: that the initiatives and programmes which go under the microscope cannot and should not be treated as "independent variables", "things", "treatments", or as "dosages". Rather, all social programmes are constituted in complex processes of human understanding and interaction. [Such programmes] work through a process of reasoning, change, influence, negotiation, battle of wills, persuasion, choice increase (or decrease), arbitration or some such like.'

One of the consequences of this critique was to place much greater emphasis on 'process' in evaluation: 'instead of concentrating on questions such as "does the program improve reading standards?" … research is directed primarily to the internal dynamics of such schemes, by seeking the views of those present on why (if at all) the implicit ideas behind a scheme' have influenced them (Pawson and Tilley, 1997:17–18). A much greater emphasis was placed on 'stakeholders' in evaluation.

Perhaps the most lasting contribution of the constructivist critique was to point to the absence of theory (understanding of process) in much (quasi-) experimental evaluation. Such evaluation, the critics suggested, even where it was capable of identifying success, which did not appear to be often, could not explain why such success occurred. The paradigm war between experimentalists and constructivists has led to the development of various alternative approaches which seek to deal with both agency and structure in explanation. One of the most recent, and best known, of these is what is now referred to as 'realistic evaluation' (see Figure 35.4).

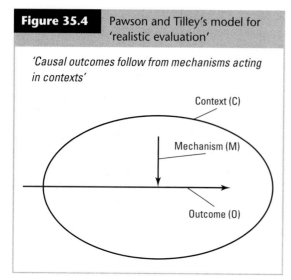

| **Figure 35.4** | Pawson and Tilley's model for 'realistic evaluation' |

Source: Pawson and Tilley (1997).

'Realistic evaluation', as outlined in the diagram above, focuses on explaining how particular outcomes (O) are produced by interventions (the way in which an intervention produces an outcome they call a 'mechanism' (M)) within particular salient conditions, or the 'context' (C). Crucially, realistic evaluation is theory driven: having at its core both hypotheses about 'mechanisms' and the influence of variations in 'context'.

Just as there was something of a paradigm shift and experimental methods fell out of favour in the evaluation field, so are they now beginning to re-emerge. As I have suggested, this has proved controversial in some quarters. A number of semi-official sets of research guidelines have begun to appear which rank evaluation methods in terms of their reliability and rigour. One of the more influential, generally referred to as the 'Scientific Methods Scale' (Sherman *et al.*, 1997), places experimental methods at the top of a hierarchy of approaches to evaluation and such rank-ordering of approaches to research has drawn considerable criticism (Hope, 2006). The danger both in the promotion of hierarchies in this fashion, and in the disputes between the proponents of such a position and scholars who take a different view – the

Evaluation research – a hot topic?

Much academic debate is pretty dry and often fairly tame. However, occasionally, scholars are brave enough to take the gloves off and engage in vigorous debate (though they can sometimes stray beyond reasonable limits). Intriguingly, evaluation research is one of those areas that has occasionally stimulated such debate. Two examples are outlined below, both involving the 'realists' Pawson and Tilley.

The first debate took place in the *British Journal of Criminology* between Pawson and Tilley and Trevor Bennett, then of the Institute of Criminology, Cambridge. Pawson and Tilley responded critically to an article written by Bennett on a police fear-of-crime reduction strategy. Bennett responded and then Pawson and Tilley replied to Bennett. The relevant articles are:

Bennett, T. (1991) The effectiveness of a police-initiated fear-reducing strategy, *BJC*, 31, 1, 1–14 (http://bjc.oxfordjournals.org/cgi/reprint/31/1/1)

Pawson, R. and Tilley, N. (1994) What works in evaluation research?, *BJC*, 34, 3, 291–306 (http://bjc.oxfordjournals.org/cgi/reprint/34/3/291)

Bennett, T. (1996) What's new in evaluation research?, *BJC*, 36, 4, 567–573 (http://bjc.oxfordjournals.org/cgi/reprint/36/4/567)

Pawson, R. and Tilley, N. (1996) What's crucial in evaluation research: A response to Bennett, *BJC*, 36, 4, 574–578 (http://bjc.oxfordjournals.org/cgi/reprint/36/4/574)

The second debate concerns methods for the evaluation of complex, multi-site community initiatives. In this case the original article was published by David Farrington. That article, and the ensuing debate, can be found at:

Farrington, D.P. (1997) Evaluating a community crime prevention programme, *Evaluation*, 3, 1, 57–73

Pawson, R. and Tilley, N. (1998) Caring communities, paradigm polemics, design debates, *Evaluation*, 4, 1, 73–90

Farrington, D.P. (1998) Evaluating communities that care: Realistic scientific considerations, *Evaluation*, 4, 2, 204–210 (http://evi.sagepub.com/cgi/reprint/4/2/204)

Pawson, R. and Tilley, N. (1998) Cook book methods and disastrous recipes: A rejoinder to Farrington, *Evaluation*, 4, 2, 211–213 (http://evi.sagepub.com/cgi/reprint/4/2/211)

so-called 'paradigm wars' – is that we lose sight of the two important lessons that apply in relation to social scientific – in this case, criminological – research. First, that the choice of method will very often depend upon the nature of the questions being asked, as well as the resources available to the researcher. Second, whatever the method employed, it is the responsibility of the social scientist to ensure that the work is conducted to the highest standards and utmost rigour.

Review questions

1 What are the main differences between probability and non-probability sampling?

2 What is quota sampling and where might it be used?

3 What is the difference between numerical and categorical data?

4 What is the primary difference between experimental and quasi-experimental methods?

Questions for further discussion

1 Do different standards apply to quantitative and qualitative research?

2 What are the pros and cons of interview-based and postal surveys?

3 Why is sampling important?

4 What is the value of qualitative research?

5 Is it appropriate to talk of a 'gold standard' in relation to research methods?

Further reading

I have said on several occasions during the course of this chapter that it is designed very much as an introduction to some important issues and ideas. Its aim is to help guide you towards further study. There are a huge number of 'methods' books out there, many of them terrific. Arguably, an almost equivalent number are either deadly dull, or just too much like plain hard work without much reward. Learning about how to do research (well) can be fun, but it is important to find the right books. In my opinion, the following are all reliable and interesting:

Bryman, A. (2004) *Social Research Methods*, 2nd edn, Oxford: Oxford University Press

Healey, J.F (2005) *Statistics: A tool for social research*, London: Wadsworth Press

May, T. (2001) *Social Research: Issues, methods and process*, Buckingham: Open University Press

Pawson, R. and Tilley, N. (1997) *Realistic Evaluation*, London: Sage

Robson, C. (2002) *Real World Research*, 2nd edn, Oxford: Blackwell Publishing

There are also some useful articles by criminologists reflecting on the task of research in:

King, R. and Wincup, E. (eds) (2007) *Doing Research on Crime and Justice*, 2nd edn, Oxford: Oxford University Press

In addition to reading books about how to do research there's nothing like reading original research using the methods themselves. So, possibly, you might care to try:

Surveys

Hough, M. and Mayhew, P. (1983) *The British Crime Survey*, London: Home Office; and

Jones, T. *et al.* (1986) *The Islington Crime Survey*, Aldershot: Gower

Interviews and focus groups

Heidensohn, F. (1995) *Women in Control*, Oxford: Oxford University Press

Reiner, R. (1991) *Chief Constables*, Oxford: Oxford University Press

Worrall, A. (1990) *Offending Women*, London: Routledge

Ethnography

Hobbs, D. (1988) *Doing the Business*, Oxford: Oxford University Press

Maher, L. (1997) *Sexed Work*, Oxford: Clarendon Press

Documentary analysis

Reiner, R. *et al.* (2000) No more happy endings? The media and popular concern about crime since the Second World War, in Hope, T. and Sparks, R. (eds) *Crime, Risk and Insecurity*, London: Routledge

Case studies

Cohen, S. (1972/2002) *Folk Devils and Moral Panics*, London: Routledge

Websites

Apart from doing research yourself, one of the most straightforward ways of learning about research is to read first-hand accounts. The best source is to look at the main journals:

British Journal of Criminology – http://bjc.oxfordjournals.org/archive/

Criminology and Criminal Justice – http://crj.sagepub.com/

Howard Journal – http://www.blackwellpublishing.com/journal.asp?ref=0265-5527&site=1

Punishment and Society – http://pun.sagepub.com/

Theoretical Criminology – http://tcr.sagepub.com/

There are also some specialist journals worth looking at:

Ethnography – http://www.sagepub.com/journalsProdDesc.nav?prodId=Journal200906

Evaluation – http://www.sagepub.co.uk/journalsProdDesc.nav?prodId=Journal200757

The Social Research Association maintains a website with information about developments in particular areas: http://www.the-sra.org.uk/index.htm

Chapter outline

Introduction	926
Choosing a topic	926
Doing a literature review	929
Selecting methods	931
Theory and research	931
Hypothetico-deductive theory	931
Grounded theory	932
Negotiating access	933
Research governance/ethics	935
Pilot research	936
Writing	937
Beginning to write	938
Write clearly	938
Decent prose	938
Plagiarism	940
Time management	941
Further reading	942

Doing criminological research

In the previous chapter we looked at some of the nuts and bolts of criminological research. We outlined the bases of the main research methods, looked at sampling and some key statistical terms, and considered some of the competing claims in respect of experimental and other approaches to evaluation research.

In this chapter we turn our attention to the practical matter of putting some of this into practice. As students most of you will have to undertake a small research project, most likely for the first time. This can be a daunting prospect. Although the circumstances you are working within mean that certain approaches to research are ruled out – you are most unlikely to be undertaking a large-scale sample survey, for example – many of the problems that face you are precisely the same as those that face us when doing large-scale professional research. They concern such apparently basic things as how to relate theory and method, how to undertake a literature review and, most basic of all, but arguably also most challenging, how to write. It is these things we will discuss in the coming pages, looking at techniques that will, I hope, help you to cut through some of the difficulties.

Introduction

Doing research for the first time is quite a challenge. Indeed, doing research under any circumstances can be challenging. However, it is a challenge well worth taking on, for research can be both exciting and fulfilling. Even with limited resources – such as are most likely to be available to you – you can do interesting and original research, exploring the social world and producing evidence about how people see it and experience it, about how it operates and the consequences it has. You need a bit of confidence to get started and one of the aims of this chapter, in combination with the previous one, is to give you the basis for that confidence. We begin with what often seems to be a thorny question – choosing the topic for your research.

Choosing a topic

Sometimes this can be very straightforward – somehow you just know that there is a particular area that you would like to investigate. Other times, perhaps most commonly, it is not that easy. Certainly, I can remember as an undergraduate being faced with having to write a 10,000 word dissertation and finding that the most difficult issue was finding something to do it on. I just didn't know what a research question looked like. I thought I would have less of a problem with my PhD thesis, but it still took me the best part of a year to hone down my general 'idea' into something that was genuinely researchable.

Part of choosing a topic for your study involves some basic, practical decisions. Crucially, you need to think carefully about what it is that you are interested in. Your long essay or dissertation is a substantial piece of work, and if your interest is to be sustained then you will need to select something that excites or stimulates you in some way. From here you need to narrow this down to a manageable piece of research. There are a number of things that you can do to help in the process of finding a topic:

- Does your department have copies available of previous years' dissertations/long essays? If so, have a look at a few. What did people do them on? How do these things relate to what you've been learning? Is there something related you are interested in?

- On the internet, look up the most recent issues of the major journals (say *British Journal of Criminology; Criminology and Criminal Justice; Punishment and Society; Theoretical Criminology;* and the *Howard Journal* for a start). You only need look at the contents pages and article abstracts. A quick skim will give you a very good idea of what people are currently writing about, and possibly arguing about.

- What have been the major debates/issues covered in the lectures that you've found most interesting? Is there something relating to those that you might be able to do some research on?

Perhaps the biggest problem we all confront, however, is turning a general topic into a specific researchable idea. An old sociology professor of mine used to confront new PhD students with the inquiry, 'What is your question?' This was a pretty tough introduction to the department and, delivered with a fairly strong Germanic accent and an unsmiling face, it was doubly terrifying. All he was doing, however, was getting straight to a point that a rather more subtle supervisor or tutor might have come to by a slightly more circuitous route. 'Do you have a question?' is *the* question. To do research you need to be able to interrogate something. So, in previous chapters we have looked at research which has asked questions like:

- Is crime going up or down?
- What is the nature of police culture?
- Are women treated differently from men in the criminal justice system?
- Are stop and search powers used in a discriminatory manner?

These are all bigger or broader questions than you can address in a small-scale piece of research, but they indicate the importance of having a question at the heart of your research enterprise. Essentially what is required is that the focus of your study should go beyond being simply descriptive, into something which is analytical. So, rather than a dissertation exploring *what* is happening in a particular city in response to anti-social behaviour, it looks more like a research question if one frames the descriptive task (what *is* happening) within the broader question of *why*, or a comparative one, such as *compared with other local practices,* or *compared with government policy,* and so on. Questions framed in this way then take you directly to the core issue: how will you go about collecting information with which to answer your question? If the answer is that you cannot imagine where such information might exist, or collecting it is beyond your means, then you will need to rethink your question. We will return to the question of selecting data and methods below.

At the heart of your project there is usually the assessment of a *claim*. So, for example, you might be interested in the introduction of new restorative justice practices in youth justice, but this is not in itself a *problem* for you to research. There are, however, some claims buried in what is otherwise a rather bland statement. They include:

- Youth justice practices have been changing in some areas.
- Elements of the new youth justice practices are *restorative.*
- Presumably, such changes are intended to have some beneficial consequences.

Each of these provides you with the basis for the beginnings of a research study. You can assess one or more of these claims. Your very general research question might therefore become, say:

- To what extent have youth justice practices been changing?
- To what extent are new youth justice practices *restorative*?
- To what extent do the changes result in the benefits claimed for them?

Now, each of these may sound like a big question, but each can quite easily then be further refined and cut down to size to fit the scale of your study. So, you might focus on one part of any new initiative that has been introduced rather than the whole thing. You will undoubtedly also limit it geographically. Thus, you can quickly rein in your study by adding 'in Borsetshire Youth Offending Team' at the end of your research question.

So, to recap, your first major task is to identify a research question. Underlying your main question are three subsidiary ones you can ask yourself:

- What am I doing?
- How am I doing it?
- Why is it important or valuable?

Each of these will help you focus on the core issue, and to relate it to any broader criminological issues that provide the context. There are a number of ways you can test whether or not you have a researchable question (apart from the obvious and most highly recommended one of checking with your tutor/supervisor). One I shall call 'the party', the other is the 'radio interview':

- *'The party'* – Here you have to imagine that you are at a party. You find yourself talking to a stranger who asks you about yourself and finds out you're studying criminology. They know little or nothing about the subject (though they will almost inevitably assume that you are being trained to help the police to crack the latest serial killer problem) and ask you about it. You start to tell them about your research. Can you explain it in lay terms? Is it meaningful and do you think the person you're speaking to understands *why* you are doing this research (or are they saying '*So what?*')?

- '*The radio interview*' – Similarly, here you simply imagine you are appearing on a local radio programme. The interviewer is friendly – this is not *Newsnight* – and genuinely interested in what you have to say. However, they have no knowledge of criminology. You are one of several students, from different courses at the

local university, invited to talk about your studies. The presenter wants to know about your research. Again, can you talk about it for a couple of minutes, using only everyday language, in a way that conveys both *what* you are doing and *why* you are doing it?

Once you feel confident that you can outline what you are doing and why you are doing it in this manner, then carry on and try to boil it down to a maximum of two to three sentences (you can practise on friends doing other courses, or family

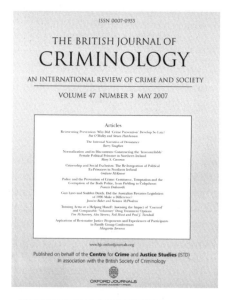

Four of the leading British criminological journals – looking at recent issues of these on the internet or in the library will give you a good idea of what research has been going on.

members, perhaps). Once you've managed that, print it out and stick it somewhere where you will see it regularly when you are working on your research project. Having found your 'problem', there are now likely to be a number of other issues for you to consider, such as selecting methods. Before we get to that there is the question of the literature review.

Doing a literature review

In writing a long essay or a dissertation you are very likely to need to review a body of literature. If you have not done this before, it can feel a very intimidating prospect. What should you read? How much should you read? How do you decide what to say about the things you do read? Luckily, especially in this electronic age, there are number of things that you can do to make the task slightly less frightening than it might at first appear. First, we need to think about why you are doing this in the first place:

- The subject you are studying and writing about will almost certainly have been considered in some form by someone else previously. You need to see what they have said/not said.

- The review will both help you identify gaps in current knowledge, and will give you pointers as to how you might undertake your own research.

- The review should also provide you with some analytical equipment with which to interrogate any data you collect. What sorts of questions should you be asking?

There are a number of ways in which you can do fairly simple searches of social science literature. First, and straightforwardly, why not browse through the major journals for the last few years? You don't have to read more than the titles of most of the articles, and then the abstracts of those that might be interesting and relevant (if you followed my advice earlier you will have done some of this when trying to identify your research question). You can mark those that seem relevant for future reference. This is one way that you can fairly easily move beyond the reading lists you will have been provided with. Reading lists are generally good introductory guides to work in a particular area, but they are not designed, for example, as guides to the reading you will need for a long essay or dissertation. If you are looking to do a good,

thoughtful and original piece of work, then looking at recent journal articles is likely to be a huge help (there is a list of useful criminology journals and their URL addresses at the end of this chapter).

When going through the journals, don't forget the book reviews. Why go to all the trouble of scouring through all the books yourself, when someone may well have done some of the reading for you? Look through the reviews, and read all those that seem at all relevant to the subject you're writing about. See what others have to say. You may not agree, if and when you come to read the book yourself, but at least it will give you something to start from. Just remember to keep an open mind. There is no reason why something that is in print is necessarily right!

Now, before we move on, a bit of advice that I will repeat later on (probably several times). You need to be disciplined about making a record of the references you consult. It is important to have a record of what you have looked at, what you found useful, or not, as the case may be. Should you stumble across ideas or other references or quotes that you want to keep, then you must make sure you know the origin of them. There are two crucial reasons for this. First, if you use material, directly or otherwise, in your work you will need to acknowledge it. There will need to be a citation (e.g. 'Bloggs *et al.*, 2000') and a reference in the bibliography. Other researchers, supervisors, markers and so on need to know what your source materials are.

Second, and related to this, there is the question of plagiarism (which we will come to in greater detail below). You cannot, or must not, quote other people's work as your own. Consequently, it becomes vital to keep a full and accurate record of your sources. Your university department will generally have guidance on how it likes references and bibliographies to be presented. Sticking to these guidelines is part of being a scholar and you should take it seriously. There is precious little excuse for failing to abide by basic guidelines in this area. In the absence of such guidelines, I would recommend sticking with what is called the 'Harvard' referencing system. This is the one that is used in this book and is now fairly standard for most social science journals. Now, back to searching literature.

If you have access to BIDS (Bath Information and Data Services – www.bids.ac.uk), for example, you can do searches of a wide range of journals simply by typing in keywords (there are lots of search systems – check with your library which you have access to). BIDS, for example, will find articles that have those keywords in the title or abstract, or will find other articles by a specified author, if that's what you're looking for. Then, use the skills you've developed over the years on the internet in the search for whatever it is you use the internet for, to search around the subject you're studying. Type keywords into Google, Google Scholar or another search engine and see what comes up. Follow leads. You'll be surprised. You'll find all sorts of material – academic articles, newspaper articles, political speeches, blogs by academics, journalists and policy-makers, and much else besides. At the very least, this will provide some grounding for the formal review that you do. Once again, with websites make sure that you keep an accurate record of the full URL address and when you accessed it.

When you move on to reading materials try not to get bogged down early on:

- Do some skim reading:
  - If it's an article look at the abstract, then skim over the introduction and conclusion.
  - If it's a book, read the opening pages, a few bits on method, and the conclusions.
- When you've decided something is important to what you're studying, then read it carefully, perhaps several times.
- Make notes.
- Use your own experience, and things you've learned from other reading, to compare with what this particular author has to say.
- If anything occurs to you, write or type it up. Just keep a file called 'odds and sods' or some such. You'll be surprised how useful these snippets are.
- As I said earlier, always, without fail, keep a note of any references [the details of the books/articles you have been reading] and if you pull out any quotes, make sure you have noted the page number. You can waste an enormous amount of time searching through things you've read for a sentence you've quoted in your own work. I say this from painful experience (you can imagine how many references there are in a book this size).

In terms of assessing existing research, there are a number of questions you might ask:

- What methods have been used?
  - Are they appropriate to the questions being asked?
  - Were they faithfully implemented?
  - Was the response rate adequate?
  - What analysis has been undertaken?
  - What is the nature of the sample?
  - Does it have any limitations and, if so, how serious are they?
- What are the main concepts used?
  - Are they clear?
  - Are they used consistently?
- What are the key theoretical ideas informing this research?
  - Why these ideas and not others?
  - Are there other literatures/ideas that might have been useful?
- What are the major findings?
  - Are they new?
  - Do they confirm/contradict existing knowledge?
- What are the gaps?
  - Is there further research that needs to be done in this area?

Finally, remember that the literature review serves a number of purposes. Primarily it helps to locate your piece of work in the larger body of criminological inquiry. It shows that you have read some of the most important, relevant work. Try to avoid any temptation to include everything that appears

Doing your literature review – don't be intimidated, be selective!

relevant. Even if you had the space to include it – which you almost certainly won't – it would be deadly dull to read. In essence, what you are trying to do is present a picture of the current state of knowledge in a particular area, or outline the major arguments. You can do this by selecting some of the more important or, possibly, definitive pieces of work, and using them to illustrate the contours of the bit of the subject you are exploring. You can always use supporting references to show that you have read other pieces of work even though you are not making direct use of them.

Selecting methods

Choosing methods is generally a question of 'horses for courses'. The kinds of questions one wants to ask and the nature of the problem being researched can frequently have a determining impact on the choice of methods. So, for example, as Dick Hobbs (1994: 442) notes, 'until gangsters, armed robbers, fraudsters and their ilk indicate their enthusiasm for questionnaires or large-scale social surveys, ethnographic research, life histories, oral histories, biographies, autobiographies and journalistic accounts will be at a premium'. The nature of your research question determines in large part what methods you will use. If you want to examine the ways in which people experience some aspect of criminal justice, you are more likely to use qualitative than quantitative methods. On the other hand, if you want to analyse patterns of behaviour within a group then the reverse is probably true.

In the previous chapter we looked at the main research methods and their strengths and limitations. As I have just outlined, these strengths and limitations will be primary determining factors for you in deciding which methods you use for your work. In addition, however, there are a number of quite practical things you need to take into consideration. Indeed, it is vital that you remain focused on the practical questions relating to your choice of research methods. Thus, for example:

- *Time* – How much time do you have? The answer to this question will have an important impact on your choice and, within that, also on certain other decisions, such as sample size. It will limit how many people you can interview, or how long you can spend doing observational work, and so on. There may be other practical issues relating to timing. If your work has to be

done, say, in July and August, then it is most unlikely that research in schools is going to be practical (they will be on holiday).

- *Resources* – If you are thinking about doing a postal survey, have you thought about the cost of doing so? There is the printing of the questionnaires, the postage, the stamped addressed envelopes, and so on. What about a tape recorder or mini-disk recorder? Do you need one for your interviews?

- *Access* – We will come to this in greater detail below but, for now, we simply need to note that in selecting methods there is always a question of access:

  - *Surveys* – Do you have a *sampling frame?* Do you have relevant names and addresses, etc?

  - *Interviews* – How will you make contact? Will your potential respondents want to talk about the subject of your research? Will they be able to do so at the right time for you?

  - *Observation* – On what basis are you going to observe some activity – say, the work of a local magistrates' court or Youth Offending Team? Whose permission do you need and how will you seek it?

  - *Skills* – Do you have the requisite skills to do the planned research and, if not, are you able to acquire them in time?

Theory and research

In this final section of the book we have been looking at research methods, and some of the issues that may arise in the course of your own research study. Earlier, in Chapters 5 to 16, we looked in some detail at various theoretical approaches to understanding crime or offending. In undertaking your own research project, one question that immediately arises is what is the relationship between theory and research? Bottoms (2000) makes a very useful comparison between two contrasting approaches to the relationship between theory and research: *hypothetico-deductive theory* and *grounded theory*.

Hypothetico-deductive theory

In essence, this approach to the production of knowledge involves a few simple-to-identify steps: collection of current information about a particular substantive matter; the generation of an hypothesis or theory based on deduction that might help explain the information we have; the conduct of further research with the aim of testing and refining the existing theory, and so on. This approach is, perhaps, most commonly associated with the philosophical work of Karl Popper. Bottoms identifies three main difficulties or shortcomings with this approach:

1 The hypotheses that are tested in such work tend to be relatively narrowly focused and specific. Consequently, hypothetico-deductive approaches often have great difficulty in engaging with general social theory.

2 Once generated, hypotheses may restrict the focus of the inquirer; arguably one's concerns concentrate on the detail of a particular hypothesis, cutting down the possibility of innovative and unusual observation.

3 The emphasis on verification/falsification has tended to privilege quantitative over qualitative data.

Grounded theory

Associated with Glaser and Strauss, grounded theory begins from a very different position from hypothetico-deductive theory. That is to say, rather than using data to test the veracity of a particular theory, its central proposition is that theory should emerge from data, and only then should the process of refinement begin. Glaser and Strauss (1967: 3–4) argue:

> [W]e suggest as the best approach an initial, systematic discovery of the theory from the data of social research. Then one can be relatively sure that the theory will fit and work. And since the categories are discovered by examination of the data, laymen involved in the area to which the theory applies will usually be able to understand it, while sociologists who work on other areas will recognise an understandable theory linked with the data of a given area.

They see this as having several advantages over hypothetico-deductive theory. They argue that the latter tends only to leave the researcher with 'at best a reformulated hypothesis or two and an unconfirmed set of speculations; and at worst a theory that does not seem to fit or work'. Furthermore, it helps overcome the second criticism of hypothetico-deductive reasoning listed above, by giving greater freedom to the researcher

to respond to the unusual and the unexpected. However, grounded theory also has a number of limitations:

1 The notion of theory being derived from the data implies that it is possible in the first instance to have data that are 'theory-free'. However, for example, it is not possible to collect any data on 'crime' that is theory neutral, for the very notion of 'crime' itself contains a number of assumptions.

2 The fairly 'pure' model of grounded theory outlined by Glaser and Strauss closes down any possibility of building general social theory into the process.

3 Because of its nature, grounded theory tends to privilege qualitative data over quantitative. In general terms this is no more justifiable than the reverse.

Rather, what we should probably be looking to do is to build on the best of both these approaches. Layder (2005) calls this 'adaptive theory', in which induction and deduction play an equal part – or at least are treated as if they each have equal claim as a means for producing social scientific knowledge. Bottoms (2000: 44) proposes six key features of an integrated approach to the theory–research relationship:

i A firm acceptance that there are no theory-neutral facts, and that the process of empirical research is therefore inextricably involved with theoretical issues from the outset of the inquiry.

ii A willingness to refine and test hypotheses rigorously where appropriate, but not in such a way that one becomes blind to the implications of fresh data that do not readily 'mesh' with the pre-existing line of inquiry.

iii A willingness to employ to the full the benefits of the 'comparative analysis' method of grounded theory, while nevertheless accepting the two key points listed above.

iv An unwillingness to foreclose inquiry too quickly, recognising with Glaser and Strauss that theory is indeed a 'process … an ever-developing entity'.

v A constant willingness and ability to be open to the relevance of concepts from general social theories at all stages of the developing theoretical analysis.

vi A genuine willingness to utilise appropriately both quantitative and qualitative data-sources.

Negotiating access

How do you gain access to the information you require for your research? For some, this will be no more than the relatively straightforward task of securing the documents that are to be analysed, or perhaps getting hold of a quantitative dataset from a data archive so that secondary analysis can be undertaken. However, for others it means negotiating access to people and organisations, and this is not necessarily easy.

Methods textbooks tend to distinguish between 'open' and 'closed' settings (Bryman, 2001 and see Chapter 35). Open settings (e.g. studying a group of local youths) are less formal than closed ones (e.g. doing research in a school), though the boundary between the two is not always clear-cut. In open settings there is often a premium placed upon the researcher's 'presentation of self'. Access to the people they wish to research – young lads, football 'hooligans', drug users, sex workers – is quite likely to be significantly affected by the personal appearance and other characteristics of the researcher. Age, for example, may well be crucial. Sadly there's nothing we can do about that.

The same is true of sex. To what extent does this have a bearing on what one can research? Well, gender dynamics may open up or restrict certain settings so far as particular people are concerned. Researching groups of women, for example, may well be easier for a female researcher. Similarly, as we saw in Chapter 32, there are areas of criminology that have been dominated by male concerns, and by studies of and by men. Whilst this does not restrict what women criminologists can do in prin-

ciple, in practice it may well *feel* as if it does. Finally, personal safety restricts what researchers can reasonably do, and there may be a gender aspect to this, too.

There are other aspects of personal style and appearance that can, within reason, be manipulated or used in order to aid access. Here's James Patrick (1973: 13) on his first encounter with the Glasgow gang he is introduced to by one of its members, 'Tim', and which he went on to study for some months:

> I was dressed in a midnight-blue suit, with a twelve inch middle vent, three inch flaps over the side pockets and a light blue handkerchief with a white polka dot (to match my tie) in the top pocket. My hair, which I had allowed to grow long, was newly washed and combed into a parting just to the left of centre. My nails I had cut down as far as possible, leaving them ragged and dirty. I approached the gang of boys standing outside the pub and Tim, my contact, came forward to meet me, his cheeks red with embarrassment.
>
> 'Hello, sur, Ah never thoat ye wid come'
>
> Fortunately, the others had not heard the slip which almost ruined all my preparations.

Howard Parker (1974), in his study of the Liverpool 'Roundhouse boys', describes a not dissimilar circumstance. He is older, but not so much older than the street kids that he looks incongruous. A number of other general features are important to his acceptance by the group:

> Although I was twenty-two gone (The Boys were sixteen) there was little difference in our

Examples of 'open' and 'closed' research settings – teenage boys in a skate park (*left*) and pupils in a secondary school classroom (*right*). What strategies might you adopt in securing access to them for research purposes?

appearance ... By the time I came down town I was established as OK – that is, amongst other things, boozy, suitably dressed and ungroomed, playing football well enough to survive and badly enough to be funny, 'knowing the score' about theft behaviour and sexual exploits.

In both the examples above, male researchers are using aspects of masculinity in order to attempt to blend in with those they study. As many female researchers have noted, however, there are often a number of very specific challenges facing them in the field. As an example, a brief extract from Laura Piacentini's wonderful study of Russian prisons:

> The process of conforming (to some degree) did involve what Rawlinson (2000) describes as 'bending gender' – that is, wearing cosmetics and different jewellery depending on whom I was interviewing and where I was conducting the interview, adapting social skills to either blend in or stand out ... On one occasion, before the interview, I was told forcibly to return to my accommodation and wear cosmetics because 'the governor liked that'.

> Initially I resisted colluding with such gender constructions that expect women to look their best and behave in a subservient and passive manner (for men). I always dressed casually and comfortably in clothes that I would wear every day. But, in the end, I reconciled the feelings of guilt that others too have expressed when faced with the realisation that utilising their gender may be advantageous to the research and, instead, I embraced the expectation to look youthful and attractive. (Piacentini, 2004: 20–21)

In relation to formal, closed settings in criminal justice there are a number of things you need to bear in mind:

- Note-taking in court generally requires permission in advance as, indeed, does research in courts generally (even though there is public access most of the time). (Noaks and Wincup, 2004)
- Research on juries is prohibited by law.
- The Prison Service manages research access to all prisons in England and Wales.

There are always 'gatekeepers' in organisations who manage access, and it is important to think about who they are and how best to approach them. These gatekeepers include such people as chief constables, chief probation officers, prison governors, youth offending team managers (or possibly the Youth Justice Board) or a Crown Court manager or magistrates' court committee. In relation to access to closed settings, Bryman (2001) suggests that the following strategies have been used with some success:

- Using friends, contacts, colleagues to help you gain access.
- Locating someone within the organisation who will act as your 'champion'.
- It is usual to try to secure permission from the top, or close to the top of the hierarchy. In order to do research within a police force it would be usual to write to the chief constable in the first instance. However, there may be occasions where it would be possible or appropriate to make an approach via another means (particularly if one has a contact one can use).
- Offering something in return may be useful – possibly a report of what you have done. Research can often feel rather exploitative: asking lots of people for help and then not giving anything back – very directly at least. Equally, however, be realistic about what you are able to offer in return.

The Zhilaya Zona (prison living zone) at Omsk in Russia, where Laura Piacentini carried out part of her doctoral research – adapting to local conditions was essential to the process. Your own research is likely to be closer to home!

- Be clear about what you want to do and why you want to do it.
- Be prepared to negotiate.
- Remember, people are generally busy, often very busy, and you should endeavour to be appreciative of their generosity in giving up time and providing any other help.

In the majority of cases, formal approaches to organisations will need to be done by letter. There are a number of basic rules for such approaches that most methods books appear to agree upon. First, the letter should outline, briefly, what you hope to do by way of research, and should do so in plain English. Avoid complicated, academic descriptions and, at all costs, abstruse theory. Second, be honest and straightforward. You must be clear about what you are going to do. Deception is occasionally used in research, but it is an ethically problematic area and certainly not something to be used lightly, or by the inexperienced. Wherever possible, indicate a willingness to be flexible and to negotiate. You may wish to be able to offer things like guaranteeing anonymity. If so, you need to have thought this through in advance. So, a brief checklist for you if you are going down this road:

- Establish your points of contact.
- Prepare an outline of your study.
- Discuss with as many interested parties as possible.
- Attempt to identify any particularly sensitive issues (and means of overcoming them).
- Make a formal approach first (begin at the top unless there is very good reason not to).
- Be prepared to modify what you want to do in the light of the response that you get.

Research governance/ethics

When talking about access, particularly in relation to open settings, we touched on issues that raised potential moral or ethical dilemmas. These are numerous in research and it is important that you think carefully about the ethics of any research you plan to do.

These days, much academic research, particularly in clinical fields such as medicine, is conducted within frameworks that set out general standards of practice. Should you ever wish to conduct research within a medical setting – exploring victimization within an NHS Trust, for example – you would have to submit your research to detailed scrutiny by an ethics committee. Indeed, increasingly across the social sciences, there is now much greater formal attention being paid to ethical questions, and all the major professional societies such as the British Society of Criminology (BSC), the British Sociological Association, and the British Psychological Society all have their own published ethical guidelines.

As an example of the general approach taken in such statements, the BSC's code of ethics begins with an overview of the general responsibilities. Criminological researchers, it says, should endeavour to:

i   Advance knowledge about criminological issues.

ii   Identify and seek to ameliorate factors which restrict the development of their professional competence and integrity.

iii Seek appropriate experience or training to improve their professional competence, and identify and deal with any factors which threaten to restrict their professional integrity.

iv   Refrain from laying claim, directly or indirectly, to expertise in areas of criminology which they do not have.

v   Take all reasonable steps to ensure that their qualifications, capabilities or views are not misrepresented by others.

vi   Correct any misrepresentations and adopt the highest standards in all their professional relationships with institutions and colleagues whatever their status.

vii Respect their various responsibilities as outlined in the rest of this document.

viii Keep up to date with ethical and methodological issues in the field, for example by reading research monographs and participating in training events.

ix   Check the reliability of their sources of information, in particular when using the internet.

(The full code of ethics is available at: http://www.britsoccrim.org/ethical.htm)

In relation to the subjects of research, ethical considerations generally cover such matters as respecting the privacy and interests of research participants, and ensuring that participation only occurs where there is 'informed consent' – which implies making sure that a full and clear explanation of the study is made to the participants, covering what the research is about, who is undertaking and financing it, why it is being undertaken, and how any research findings are to be disseminated. This also usually involves making it clear that participants can withdraw from the research at any stage.

There are also a set of ethical issues to do with the handling of research data. Guarantees of anonymity mean great care must be taken when storing information, and particularly when sharing it with other researchers. Data protection requirements must be respected, including thinking about the potential for circumstances to arise when confidentiality might have to be breached because of legal requirements to divulge information to legal or other authorities. It is increasingly likely that your university will have ethics scrutiny procedures. You need to think about the issues that they will consider, and also build time into your timetable for the committee to make its deliberations.

Pilot research

So far, then, we have talked a bit about some important preliminary aspects of your research: choosing a topic and selecting methods; reviewing literature and thinking about the relationship between theory and your empirical inquiry. Now, you might reasonably think that having done all this that you are ready to dive in to the main bit of

your research. This is almost the case, but there is one further thing that you may well need to think about: a pilot stage.

For many research studies, a pilot phase is very important. In essence, this is the period in which you test out some or all of your research tools and approaches. If you are conducting a survey, you will need to check to see that the questions you are using are easily understood by your respondents. You will want to check that the answers you get can be straightforwardly interpreted and are consistent with what you thought you were asking about. You may be thinking of conducting your research within a particular institutional setting – a school, police station or prison, for example. What are the practical constraints on this research? Are there particular institutional procedures that might affect what you do? Pilot research will help you check this. Sometimes this element of the research may be described as a feasibility study and, in many ways, this captures what is being attempted. The purpose of the pilot study is to check that the research can actually be undertaken in the way that is planned, and the research instruments, whatever they may be, actually work.

Piloting is absolutely vital in relation to questionnaires. Horror stories abound in research circles. One example will suffice. In one organisation in which I worked, a very large survey was conducted – for the purposes of the story we'll say

---

Specification for 'fully informed consent' form

The form needs to be designed before you make contact with the organisation or individuals who will 'host' or be the subject of your research. At the very least it should contain:

1 The name, address and telephone number of the person and/or organisation seeking consent.

2 An outline of the purpose of the study. This should be sufficient to convey a sense of how the research will be undertaken, why it is being undertaken and what will happen to the information collected.

3 Specific consent should be gained (where appropriate); include:

   a intention to maintain confidentiality and anonymity;

   b measures to be taken to prevent data being linked with a specific informant and to limit access to the data;

c note that the respondent has the right to withdraw from the study at any time;

d note that participation is entirely voluntary unless the respondent has already agreed, as a part of a prior research contract, to participate in legitimate studies

4 A sign-off space for the participant in which they acknowledge that they have read and agreed to the stipulations set out in the form, with a space for their signature and the date.

5 A further sign-off space to indicate that the person agrees to their being quoted (should this be appropriate).

6 A copy of the signed form should be given to the respondent.

Source: Robson (1993: 298).

it was looking at young people's experiences of education, training and employment. Although a lot of very careful design work went into the preparation of the questionnaire and the design of what was a quite complex stratified sample of young people, the person in charge of the study did not pilot it. The questionnaire was mailed out and pretty soon the responses started to come in. The response rate was very good indeed and all seemed set fair for a most successful study. Unfortunately, no one had thought to put an identification number on each of the questionnaires and, therefore, it was impossible to know who had responded and who had not. This in turn made it impossible to check the representativeness of the sample and almost entirely undermined the validity, and therefore purpose, of the research. Moreover, as it meant the survey had to be redone, and the cost of this borne by the organisation, it was an enormously expensive mistake to make. A small pilot study would have identified the problem and enabled the researcher quickly to fix it.

Piloting your questionnaire enables you to avoid major problems like this, but also to check out other important matters:

- Do respondents understand why the research is being undertaken?
- Can they understand and follow the instructions on the questionnaire?
- Is the 'routing' on the questionnaire clear? For example, you may want people who have answered 'no' to question 2 to jump to question 4, but people who answered 'yes' to question 2 to go on to question 3, and so on.
- Are the questions clear and free of ambiguity? You may be surprised how easy it is to construct questions that can be interpreted in several ways. You may also find that your first draft of a question is actually two questions.
- Are there any ethical problems in asking the questions you have done?
- Is there anything missing from the survey?
- How long did it take to complete? This, again, is often crucial. If you are conducting face-to-face interviews and ask for 20 minutes of someone's time, you may never get to the end of your questionnaire if, in practice, it takes 40 minutes to complete. If so, you risk either aggravating your respondents and/or missing out on important data.

However, it is not just surveys where piloting is important. It can also be a vital stage in both other types of interview situation as well as in observational research. Thus, both semi-structured and unstructured interviews can benefit from a feasibility or pilot stage. There are all sorts of issues that can crop up:

- Where and when are interviews to be held? Are the locations convenient/appropriate?
- How long will the interviews take? Are they too long/do you need to be more focused?
- Are there particular areas that are sensitive and where the wording of the questions, the timing of the questions, or just the appropriateness of the questions need further thought?
- Do you have the appropriate equipment to record the interviews?
- How will you record data from your observational work?
- Are there practical issues relating to observation? The police, for example, tend to work in shifts. Are there particular shifts you wish to observe? What will you do when arrests are being made?

Writing

Having successfully collected some or all of your data, and analysed it, the time has come to write it up. You will notice that I have not talked about the data analysis stage in this chapter. The reason is straightforward. Data analysis, especially in relation to quantitative data, is a technical matter often involving software packages. If you are analysing quantitative data you may well use *SPSS*, or an equivalent. If you are analysing qualitative data, it is increasingly likely that you will use *NVivo* or *NUD*IST*. The analytical packages are terrific these days and there are a number of very good introductory and advanced guides as to how to use them. Here, I want to focus on one of the things that gives all of us who do research many of our most painful headaches – writing.

Now, earlier I implied that once your analysis was finished, or was at least underway, that it was time to start writing. This is misleading. If you have a long piece of work to do – a dissertation or long essay – the sooner you start writing the better. From the moment you start thinking about your potential topic, and particularly once the process of reading and reviewing literature is underway, you should be writing. There is no necessity for anything you write to be terribly coherent, or to be part of your final product. Rather, you are simply setting down thoughts and ideas, possibly summaries of things you have read, quotes you especially like and so on.

Beginning to write

Don't worry about the quality of your prose when you begin to write something. When you write, if you can avoid thinking of what you are doing as being the final product so much the better. It is easy to get bogged down in the minutiae of a sentence. Is this word right? Can I think of a better way of saying this? When you are beginning a piece of work, I think these questions are among the least helpful you can ask yourself. It is much better to say, 'How much can I write in the next hour?', and then bash away at the keyboard for as long as you can, than to become preoccupied with the state of your prose. So, whenever possible, think about 'drafts', not the finished product (most of the time).

Write clearly

Try to write clearly. Do not be seduced into thinking that the more complex your writing the more of an 'academic' you will appear to be. If you doubt this advice, I suggest you read the second chapter of Howard Becker's (1986) *Writing for Social Scientists* in which he recounts his discussions with Rosanna Hertz on this subject. Her thoughts on academic expectations are highly revealing and, to my eye, especially helpful. As the famous American sociologist, and very clear writer, C. Wright Mills once put it (1959: 219), 'To overcome the academic prose you first have to overcome the academic pose'.

I was lucky enough to receive a number of important bits of advice as an undergraduate student. One, offered by a tutor in my second year, concerned academic writing. Each week we were given something to read and then had to discuss it at the next tutorial. One week we arrived, sat down, and in turn the tutor asked each of us what we thought of the article he had given us. After we had all struggled to offer something coherent and academic-sounding, he stopped us and asked us to estimate, as honestly as we could, how much of the article we understood. The estimates varied,

but few of us suggested we understood more than about half of what had been written. In every case I'd imagine that was a substantial overstatement. He then asked why we thought that was. I can't remember the answers, but am sure they were all variations on the theme of 'the article is very dense and complex, and was just a bit beyond me, etc.'. At this he looked quite pleased, having clearly received the answers he was looking for. 'Rubbish', he said, 'you may not be the brightest students I've ever had, but that's nothing to do with making sense of this article. You didn't understand it because it's badly written. And, next time you have a similar problem, tell yourself the same thing is happening. Unfortunately, you probably won't have to wait too long!' I don't know whether I quite believed him at the time, but I do now.

I try to say something similar to my students. If you read academic material and find it off-putting, it is highly likely that is because it is poorly written. Test it. Find things you do like, that inspire you in some way, and compare them with things you're not so keen on. What is the difference between them? I suspect at least one of the factors is the quality of the prose. Everyone will have slightly different ideas about what good writing looks like. Nevertheless, I think there are a few things on which we can probably agree.

Decent prose

Good writing will speak to its readers. So, when you write, think about your audience. Who are you writing for? To whom is it supposed to be clear? Who will read what you write? What do they have to know so that they will not misread or find what you say obscure, unintelligible or simply dull? All these questions, if you ask them of yourself, will help you draft something that will likely appeal to the person/people you are writing for. So, how can you find out what readers will understand? One simple way is to give your early drafts to sample members of your intended audience and ask them what they think' (Becker, 1986). A few other pointers:

- Wherever you can, use simple words. I keep coming back to this, but don't be misled by the idea that simple writing is not academic writing. It may not be *typical* academic writing. If it looks like good journalism, then it is almost certainly good writing. Good journalism conveys complex ideas straightforwardly. Try to do the same if you can.

- Try to keep sentences short. Take words out if they add little. Stephen King talks about one of the best bits of advice he ever received being 'Formula: 2nd draft = 1st draft – 10%. Good luck.'

  If you have followed my advice about not worrying too much what your first draft looks like, then you will certainly have written more than you first thought you would, or even intended to. The job then becomes the much easier one (much easier than starting to write, that is) of tidying up and editing. Follow King's advice and aim to take out ten per cent, or more if appropriate.

- There are a number of books written by experts on the craft of writing. All authors will have their personal favourites. Two of mine are Stephen King's *On Writing* and Howard Becker's *Writing for Social Scientists*. At one level you'd be hard pressed to find two more different people: a best-selling author of horror fiction on the one hand, and one of our pre-eminent social scientists on the other. And, indeed, their books are very different from each other. Yet they also say very similar things, albeit in very different ways. Both writers clearly love writing, and both have great skill. The consequence is that not only are both books full of good advice, but they also are beautifully written and a real pleasure to read.

So, in relation to the task of writing clearly don't forget to:

- Keep paragraphs short.
- Try to plan (and write a plan).
- Use sub-headings liberally.
- Where appropriate, use bullets, diagrams, and other devices to aid understanding.
- Don't worry about having to rewrite (that's what we all do).

When you come to rewrite:

- Read through and then read through again.
- Check for a 'narrative'. Whatever you're writing as a researcher you are telling a story. In simple terms it must have a recognisable beginning, middle and end. As importantly, its message must run through from beginning to end in a way that the reader can easily follow.
- If necessary, as you are going through on a separate piece of paper, or on screen, list the major points you make in the order in which they are made in your essay/dissertation/thesis. When you read back over your draft, the line of argument should be clear or, alternatively, you should be able to spot where there are missing bits of the jigsaw.
- Take out the extraneous bits and the unnecessary words.
- Make sure you have referenced work fully and properly. Each institution will have its own preferred method for references and citations. Check the instructions carefully and then follow them.

The other major problem that people have with writing – and the one that I find that I have the greatest number of conversations about – is what is sometimes referred to as 'writer's block'. This rather misleadingly makes it sounds like some sort of treatable condition. Nurse – the tablets please! In fact, it is the psychological hurdle associated with a task that can be hard work, that often requires that you give quite a lot of yourself to it and, eventually, that you have to display publicly in some form. This can put the most experienced of writers off – and does. In my experience of writing and of supervising a lot of other people's writing, I have come across a great deal of what can only be called procrastination. The reasons for not writing come in all shapes and sizes:

- I can't get started.
- There is too much to write.
- I haven't done this before.
- I'll do it tomorrow when I'm feeling better.
- It'll be easier if I've had a few drinks first.
- It's too noisy.
- I've only got an hour.
- I don't know what to write.
- There's that programme on TV I meant to watch.
- I don't know what I'm going to say.
- I'll just read one more book/article first.
- Someone has said this all before (and said it better than me).
- My partner/children are going to be unhappy if I go back to the computer again.

You can add your own to the list. Now, I'm not wishing to diminish the importance of many of these things. However, they can be used as excuses and they need to be overcome. How can you overcome them? Part of the answer is discipline. You just need to take a deep breath and get on with it some of the time. One writer wryly observed that he wrote when he was inspired, but saw to it that he was inspired at nine o'clock every morning! You need to be aware of your own strengths and weaknesses. Some people work well in the early hours of the morning, some late at night. It is generally best to try to exploit the hours of the day when you are at your best, and not try to force yourself to work when you are flagging (though sometimes you can't avoid it). In addition, however, I have found that there are a number of very practical things that you can do to get the process of writing started and leave the procrastination behind:

- Make notes – you may not feel like writing, so just type out some notes or any thoughts you may have about what you're working on.

- Draft a contents page – make it as detailed as you can. What are you going to write in each chapter/sub-section? This may make you write a paragraph or two.

- Do the references/bibliography – again, an important task and well worth keeping on top of.

- Type out quotes/illustrations – it's not quite writing, but sometimes can be the next best thing. Have you found some good bits from other people's work that you may wish to draw upon? Good, then type them out, order them, and perhaps write a sentence or two around them (and don't forget to have full references).

- Construct a timetable – or another timetable. We will come to this below, but you should always have a timetable for your work. Rewriting it, because one often needs to, is again another method of getting you to sit in front of the screen and working on something connected with your research.

- Write anything (almost anything) – if you really can't face writing about the research, then write about something else (perhaps about not wanting to write). This can spur you into action.

- Rewrite something – this is the failsafe. Once you have started writing, then you can always rewrite. Tell yourself that. I don't fancy/feel up to writing just now, so I'll sit down and play with those paragraphs/pages I wrote yesterday. Nine times out of ten you'll find you end up writing something new.

- Offer yourself rewards. Perhaps tea and biscuits if you keep going for an hour or more. Work all morning and then have that walk/break that you've been promising yourself.

The bottom line is that there is no substitute for actually writing. Not sitting in front of the computer screen deliberating over each word, but simply trying to type as quickly as you can without any reference to any other materials. It really doesn't matter what comes out. You will undoubtedly rewrite. But then you would do that even if you spent a lot of time struggling over the words. As I said earlier, the great thing about a bit of furious writing is that it gets a lot of words on the page. The screen is no longer white. There's nothing worse, sometimes, than the blank screen or the blank page. Many of the things I listed above are simple ways of getting rid of them. Moreover, once you've knocked out some words you will find that there's probably quite a lot of good stuff there. You may want to chop it up, re-order it, and fill in some gaps. If so, great, that's called writing.

Plagiarism

In essence, plagiarism is passing someone else's work off as one's own. This can be intentional, as in those cases where someone simply copies out bits of published work, buys essays off the internet and so on. It can also be unintentional, as in cases where someone has failed properly to reference work they intended to cite, but end up simply appearing to have inserted it in their text as if they had written it themselves. With electronic access to materials so easy now, and with the ability simply to cut and paste work from the internet straight into documents, plagiarism has become a major problem. There are essentially two things that you need to do:

- Consult the guidelines or protocols at your institution. Every university, college or school will now have published guidance about plagiarism. You will almost certainly have this drawn to your attention at the beginning of an academic year or at the beginning of a course. Heed the advice in it. If you have any doubts, consult with tutors or supervisors.

- Make sure that you are very careful with the materials you collect. If, as I have suggested, you type out sections of books or articles you have read and feel you may want to use again, then ensure that any excerpts are accompanied by a full reference, including the page number. Then, should you ever use such material in an essay or dissertation, make sure that any direct quotation has inverted commas around it, and has the citation details next to it and the full reference at the end of your work.

Do not underestimate the seriousness of plagiarism. As I say, all universities will have guidelines and policies, and these will generally include very serious penalties for anyone that is caught. Be aware that some fairly sophisticated computer programmes are now available that can be used to check students' work. Such software is increasingly used within universities and is becoming more sophisticated all the time.

Time management

Finally, we come to the issue of timetables and time management. This is always a big issue. Most of us are very busy and have many competing pressures. You may well have exams to do as well as your research. You may be working and studying at the same time. You may have family or other responsibilities to juggle also. All this means that you undoubtedly need to be careful with your time and to try to manage it. However, especially if you have not done research before, you may have some difficulties in working out how long things are going to take. Here again you should, obviously, talk it through with a tutor or supervisor. They should be able to help you estimate and to plan.

In thinking about a research project I have always found it helpful to do the following:

- Think about the various stages your work is going to go through. We've covered most of them in this chapter: literature review; selection of methods; piloting; fieldwork; analysis and writing up.
  - What do you need to do to achieve them?
  - How long might each of them reasonably take?
  - Alternatively, how much time do you have available and how best can this be tailored to suit your study?
- Divide the project up into weeks and months. What are you hoping to achieve in each? Put together a rough outline timetable.
- The timetable below is the most general one. It is well worth constructing one which breaks down each of the tasks further and also has the schedule in weeks rather than months. The more detailed you can be, the better.
- The one thing you can take for granted in research is that you can take nothing for granted. With good fortune and good planning your research will most likely go pretty much as you anticipated. However, it almost certainly will proceed slightly differently in some respects from how you imagined it at the outset. Because of the nature of the world you are working in, it is easy for things to take an unexpected turn (one of your key respondents falls ill; the school you are doing research in has an unannounced inspection, and so on). The consequence is 'slippage' – your research will take longer than

	June	July	Aug	Sept	Oct	Nov	Dec
Discussion and project design	⟶						
Literature review	⟶						
Interviews		⟶					
Questionnaire design and piloting			⟶				
Survey distribution			⟶				
Data analysis			⟶				
Draft report					⟶		
Final report						⟶	

you anticipated. How will you cope? One way is to try to build in a little 'extra' or 'slack' time to your timetable. Researchers will differ on how much this should be. I would suggest about ten per cent.

- Research is not neat, but try to plan.
- Writing up takes a long time. Setting targets and deadlines will take away some of the pain.
- Try to write something every week.
- Set yourself small and manageable targets.

- Try to update your timetable once a month. The more you can get used to thinking about, looking at, and rewriting your plan, the more likely you will be to stick to reasonable deadlines. The great thing about timetables for research is that, barring the end date, you can fiddle with them and alter them according to how things are going.

All of this should help you keep roughly on track and to deliver whatever it is you have to deliver on time. Good luck!

Further reading

In terms of the practical issues discussed in this chapter I recommend the following:

In relation to writing: Becker, H. (1986) *Writing for Social Scientists,* Chicago: University of Chicago Press; and King, S. (2000) *On Writing,* London: New English Library

On doing research: Booth, W.C. *et al.* (2003) *The Craft of Research,* 2nd edn, Chicago: University of Chicago Press; and, Robson, C. (1993) *Real World Research,* Oxford: Blackwell Publishing

A hugely stimulating read is: Bottoms, A.E. (2007) The relationship between theory and data, in King, R. and Wincup, E. (eds) *Doing Research on Crime and Justice,* 2nd edn, Oxford: Oxford University Press (there are plenty of other chapters in this volume that will give you a nice insight into some of the realities and practicalities of criminological research).

In the chapter I recommended that you use any access to journals you have (electronically or otherwise) to see what has been published recently. Among the journals you may wish to consult are:

British Journal of Criminology – http://bjc.oxfordjournals.org/archive/

Crime, Media, Culture – http://cmc.sagepub.com/

Crime Prevention and Community Safety – http://www.palgrave-journals.com/cpcs/index.html

Criminology and Criminal Justice – http://crj.sagepub.com/

European Journal of Criminology – http://euc.sagepub.com/

Howard Journal – http://www.blackwellpublishing.com/journal.asp?ref=0265-5527&site=1

Policing – http://policing.oxfordjournals.org/

Policing and Society – http://www.tandf.co.uk/journals/titles/10439463.html

Punishment and Society – http://pun.sagepub.com/

Theoretical Criminology – http://tcr.sagepub.com/

Youth Justice – http://www.sagepub.co.uk/journalsProdDesc.nav?prodId=Journal201769

Publisher's acknowledgements

The author and publishers are very grateful to the following individuals and agencies for the use of the photographs throughout the book. All photographs are under copyright and may not be reproduced, stored in a retrieval system, or transmitted in any form, without prior permission from the copyright holder.

Alamy: 39, 58, 151, 179, 203, 265, 318, 329, 351, 360, 370, 381, 391, 454, 468, 475, 487, 494, 499, 517, 568, 578, 609, 622, 630, 629, 650, 666, 674, 686, 702, 708, 687, 700, 742, 816, 872, 880, 891, 895, 907, 924, 933

Albert Bandura: 146, 154

American Society of Criminology: 189

American Sociological Association: 178, 189, 190, 217, 230, 373

Archives, University at Albany, SUNY: 134

Bart Jonker: 532

Bridgeman Art Library: 25, 111, 172, 189, 257, 528

CCJS: 658, 662

Carol Smart: 307

Charles Murray: 274

Colin Rogers: 578

Corbis: 141, 142, 177, 233, 236, 252, 258, 326, 381, 382, 396, 411, 412, 414, 418, 421, 428, 434, 440, 446, 449, 484, 514, 517, 574, 625, 620, 685, 779, 804, 809, 824, 855, 930

David Canter: 850

Gerald Suttles: 189

Getty: 26, 27, 103, 130, 186, 193, 197, 203, 294, 298, 312, 441, 460, 462, 507, 513, 596, 615, 625, 629, 682, 689, 714, 717, 723, 756, 877

Goldsmiths College: 205

Hampshire Constabulary: 829

Howard Becker: 216

Howard Zehr: 752

IISG: 125, 249

Innocence Project: 858

Jill Dando Institute: 278, 291

John Braithwaite: 763

Kent Police: 799

Laura Piacentini: 934

Lincolnshire Archives: 24

Marcus Felson: 287

Mary Evans: 24, 32, 34, 36, 37, 40, 70, 116, 122, 123, 124, 161, 175, 177, 247, 815

NAPO: 679

New York University: 189

Nils Christie: 745

PA Photos: 208, 551, 540, 636, 656, 712, 750

Reuters: 82, 101

Rex: 10, 11, 14, 56, 105, 202, 215, 217, 269, 304, 334, 336, 362, 343, 383, 380, 388, 410, 427, 448, 494, 497, 503, 544, 592, 605, 687, 694, 699, 729, 735, 736, 790, 796, 828, 836, 848, 860, 870, 873, 866, 881

Rochdale Observer: 592

Ronald Clarke: 281

Sage Publications: 928

Science Photo Library: 51, 127, 159, 240, 321, 491, 529

The Sun: 2, 16
The Guardian: 108
University College London: 119
University of Chicago: 189, 211

Glossary

Accountability Generally, though somewhat crudely, thought of as a system for controlling agencies and individuals. In relation to policing a distinction is often drawn between individual forms of accountability ('controlling the constable') and organisational accountability (oversight of the policies and processes of constabularies).

Actuarial justice A term that refers to the increasing use of risk assessment and other forms of calculation to manage offending populations.

Administrative criminology A term originally coined by Jock Young to capture a trend within criminology which focused on increasing the efficiency of the criminal justice system, particularly via situationally-based crime prevention.

Adversarialism A particular style of criminal justice, which treats the process as a competition. In particular, in the criminal trial the defence and prosecution oppose each other, each seeking to establish the strength of their own case, or contradict or undermine the other. This approach is generally contrasted with what are described as inquisitorial criminal justice systems.

Anomie As a shorthand, often referred to as a state of 'normlessness'. Associated originally with Emile Durkheim, and developed by Robert Merton, within criminology the term has been used to draw attention to the ways in which the limited access to approved social goals (wealth, success, fame) through legitimate means may lead some to adopt illegitimate means.

Anti-social behaviour Defined in law as behaviour that causes or is likely to cause harassment, alarm or distress. Since 1998 a large number of measures – most notably anti-social behaviour orders (ASBOs) – have been introduced to deal with such sub-criminal conduct.

ASBO Anti-Social Behaviour Order. Introduced by the Crime and Disorder Act 1998 and extended by further legislation, in particular the Anti-Social Behaviour Act 2003.

Attrition A term used to refer to the process by which only a proportion of crimes committed eventually find their way into the criminal justice process and into the criminal courts. The main reasons that crimes don't reach the courts include non-reporting, non-recording, failure to identify a suspect and insufficient evidence to proceed with charges.

Biological positivism Along with other forms of 'positivism', approaches human behaviour as something that is largely *determined* by external factors. In the case of biological positivism, the search for explanation lies in human biology and physiology – these factors being held to play a significant influence in particular forms of behaviour.

Bipartisan consensus Indicating that there is close agreement in some important area of public policy between the main political parties. In criminology, the term tends to be used to describe aspects of the period prior to the mid- to late-1970s; a period in which there was a generalised political consensus around issues of crime and punishment. With the gradual politicisation of law and order this consensus was fractured and disappeared. Some would argue that the period since the mid-1990s has seen the emergence of a new bipartisan consensus – this time around populist punitiveness.

British Crime Survey (BCS) A victimization survey, first conducted in 1982, and now conducted annually (on a rolling basis). Asks respondents – aged over 16 – a series of quite detailed questions about any crimes they might have experienced in the previous 12 months, as well as exploring their perceptions of crime locally and nationally. One of our two (with police-recorded crime statistics) methods of measuring trends in crime.

Broken windows The title of an article by James Q. Wilson and George Kelling, published in 1982, in which they argued that successful community crime prevention must involve a focus on relatively 'minor' forms of disorder – such as vandalism and graffiti – as well as targeting more serious offences. It is the low-level incivilities, they argue, that undermine local social cohesion, with the likelihood that more serious crime will flourish. This 'philosophy' is closely associated with so-called zero-tolerance policing in New York City and with the British government's anti-social behaviour agenda.

Burglary An offence of burglary is recorded by the police if a person enters any building as a trespasser and with intent to commit an offence of theft, grievous bodily harm or unlawful damage. Burglary does not necessarily involve forced entry; it may be through an open window, or by entering the property under false pretences (e.g. impersonating an official). A distinction is drawn between 'domestic' burglary, where the premises are a dwelling (or connected outhouse or garage), and 'non-domestic' burglary for other kinds of premises (including detached garages, sheds, commercial premises, schools, hospitals, etc.). A burglary does not entail forced entry or actual loss of goods.

Caution An offence is deemed to be detected if an offender has been cautioned by the police or given a reprimand or warning under the Crime and Disorder Act 1998. A caution may be given by, or on the instructions of, a senior police officer when an offender admits guilt, where there is sufficient evidence for a realistic prospect of conviction, where the offender consents, or where it does not seem in the public interest to instigate criminal proceedings. The Crime and Disorder Act 1998 reformed the youth cautioning system introducing what are known as 'reprimands' and 'final warnings'.

Chicago School A term used to refer to a particularly influential group of sociologists based at the University of Chicago in the first half of the twentieth century. Noted for their 'ecological' approach to the explanation of crime in the city, Chicago School sociology had a profound influence on the use of ethnographic approaches to research and to the development of what these days tends to be referred to as environmental criminology.

Classical criminology An early criminological school based upon the assumption that criminals

are rational actors capable of choosing between different courses of action. Models of punishment influenced by such approaches tend, therefore, to argue that the extent of the penalty involved should only be what is sufficient to modify behaviour.

Cognitive behaviourism An approach to treatment or therapy which focuses both upon how people think and how they behave – and assumes that these things interact. In relation to criminality such approaches may, for example, seek to work on the decision-making strategies that offenders engage in.

Community orders (sentences) A term used to refer to penalties imposed by a criminal court which involve some form of supervision – most usually by the Probation Service. Thus, imprisonment is excluded as are penalties such as fines, compensation orders and discharges that tend not to involve supervision. Until the Criminal Justice Act 2003, which introduced a single Community Order with different requirements, these penalties were known by a variety of different names such as probation order, community service order and combination order among others.

Community policing A police organisational strategy that decentralises policing, seeks to be responsive to local citizen demands and to incorporate a general problem-oriented approach to policing, and to helping communities solve crime problems collaboratively, often through partnership working.

Community safety A term that came into common usage in the 1990s to indicate a broader, community-based approach to prevention than typically associated with the term 'crime prevention'. Where crime prevention had been closely associated with the police, those using the term community safety sought to emphasise the importance of the involvement of a broader range of agencies in preventative activity, as well as extending the potential focus of such activities beyond crime to other forms of disorder and other hazards.

Corporate crime Refers to crimes committed by corporations, or by influential individuals within corporations, where the illegal act is carried out with the intention of furthering the goals of that organisation.

Crime and Disorder Reduction Partnership (CDRP) Local bodies in England and Wales with statutory responsibility for crime and disorder issues, set up under the terms of the Crime and Disorder Act 1998. Their responsibilities have subsequently been reformed by the Police and Justice Act 2006.

Crime prevention Measures aimed at preventing crime. In recent times the term has become particularly associated with police and physical security/situational crime prevention measures.

Crime reduction A term favoured by Labour governments since 1997, in part to distinguish activities from the difficult task of *preventing* crime on the one hand, and from the looser focus on *community safety* on the other.

Crime science A field of academic endeavour that seeks to distinguish itself from the broader subject of criminology by narrowing its focus to the aim of preventing or reducing crime. Much influenced by rational choice and opportunity theories, crime science tends to be hostile to sociologically-informed criminology.

Criminal damage Criminal damage results from any person who without lawful excuse destroys or damages any property belonging to another, intending to destroy or damage any such property or being reckless as to whether any such property would be destroyed or damaged.

Criminalisation The processes by which certain acts, or particular people or groups, are defined as criminal.

Cultural criminology A recently emerging strand of criminological theory that combines traditional sociological theories with aspects of cultural studies. Dominated by ethnographic, 'appreciative' understandings of crime, the approach in much cultural criminology is resonant of aspects of earlier sociologies of deviance.

Deterrence (general and specific) An approach to punishment which rests on the belief that it will prevent future offending. It may do so in two ways: either by persuading those who are punished not to engage in such behaviour again (referred to as specific or

individual deterrence) or by the broader impact that the existence of a system of punishment has upon the population at large (referred to as general deterrence).

Developmental (crime) prevention An approach to the prevention of crime through the study and application of interventions at various stages in the life course. Often focused on individuals or groups perceived to be at risk, developmental prevention often seeks to prevent the 'onset' (the start) or the progression of offending.

Deviancy amplification A term which conveys the idea that deviant conduct may be exacerbated by intolerant social responses. Linked in particular with labelling theory.

Differential association Associated with Edwin Sutherland, differential association concerns the idea that our behaviour is heavily influenced by those with whom we interact. More particularly, Sutherland argued that a person becomes delinquent in circumstances in which the attitudes of the people with whom they associate tend, on balance, to favour the violation of the law rather than the reverse.

Displacement Often thought to be the Achilles heel of crime prevention, the term displacement refers to the possibility that crimes are simply 'moved around' (in time, space and so on) rather than prevented by activities such as increased street lighting, CCTV and the like.

Domestic violence Violence within the household – in particular, though not exclusively, domestic violence is used to refer to the physical, sexual or emotional abuse of women by male partners.

Due process and crime control Terms associated with Herbert Packer to distinguish two ideal typical approaches to criminal justice. Each is characterised by different values and objectives: crime control approaches tending to emphasise the importance of convicting the guilty and due process approaches placing greater emphasis upon the importance of protections against the wrongful conviction of the innocent.

Electronic monitoring Often called 'tagging', such monitoring generally involves the use of a 'tag' or bracelet worn around the ankle. The systems allow the Probation Service or other body to monitor the whereabouts of offenders and to encourage compliance with the terms of community orders or the terms of release from prison.

Evaluation An approach to research that seeks to assess particular programmes, policies or interventions. Evaluation may focus on *process* (how things work or are implemented), *outputs* (what is produced) and *outcomes* (the impact of the programme, policy or intervention).

Governance A term from political science and sociological literature that focuses on the systems of regulation and ordering (governing) contemporary societies. Where this once might have focused on the agencies/institutions of the state, the term is now generally taken to refer to strategies of governing both within and beyond the state.

Harm reduction An approach to prevention, particularly in relation to drugs policy, that emphasises the importance of focusing on the reduction of the social- and health-related harms that are associated with such behaviour (by contrast with approaches which emphasise either abstinence and/or law enforcement).

Home Office The government department that historically has been responsible for internal affairs in England and Wales (http://www.homeoffice. gov.uk). Restructuring of government in 2007 saw the creation of a Ministry of Justice and the passing of responsibilities for much of criminal justice, including probation and prisons, from the Home Office to the new department.

Homicide Comprises the recorded crimes of murder, manslaughter and infanticide.

Human rights Basic entitlements that are argued to be general in their application (i.e. applicable to citizens of all nations). There are a number of formal human rights protocols, the most important of which is arguably the European Convention. The Convention on Human Rights was incorporated into UK law as a result of the Human Rights Act 1998.

Incapacitation An approach to punishment which stresses the importance of prevention through incarceration/imprisonment or other restriction (it is worth remembering that imprisonment doesn't prevent crimes being committed within prisons).

Incarceration rate A means of indicating the extent of the use of imprisonment. The incarceration rate is normally expressed as the number of people per 100,000 population that are subject to imprisonment in a year.

Incidence This refers to the number of crimes or, alternatively, the number of crimes in relation to a particular population. Incidence and prevalence are arguably the two commonest measurements of crime levels.

Inquisitorialism By contrast with adversarialism, inquisitorialism is held to place greater emphasis in the justice process on the search for truth. Rather than two sides in a context, such systems are suggested to be more concerned with examining the likelihood of events having happened, or having occurred in a particular way.

Institutional racism A term applied by the Lawrence Inquiry to the Metropolitan Police and defined by the Inquiry as 'The collective failure of an organisation to provide an appropriate and professional service to people because of their colour, culture or ethnic origin. It can be seen in processes, attitudes and behaviour which amount to discrimination through unwitting prejudice, ignorance, thoughtlessness and racist stereotyping which disadvantage minority ethnic people' (1999: 6.34).

Intelligence-led policing Essentially, a model which seeks to increase the effectiveness of policing through greater emphasis on the collection and analysis of intelligence and the development of targeted responses to that analysis.

Just deserts A sentencing philosophy which argues that discretion should be limited and that punishment should be proportionate to the seriousness of the offence committed.

Labelling (theory) The application of a label or identity to a person or a group in a way that has some consequential effect on behaviour. Labelling theory focuses upon the way that deviant activity may be understood as the application of labels and, at least in part, as the reaction to such processes.

Left realism An approach to criminological theory which was, in part, a reaction to and criticism of existing radical theories in the 1970s and 1980s. Left realism argued that radical theories had underestimated the impact of crime on ordinary people and had romanticised offending. Using local crime surveys, early left realist criminology sought to measure the extent and impact of crime in local, predominantly working-class neighbourhoods.

Limited or bounded rationality A term used to indicate that even though individuals may make poor decisions, often based on incomplete or simply inadequate information, they are nonetheless rational actors.

Managerialism (or 'new public management') A term associated with the shift in government policy towards 'new public management' characterised by, among other things: elements of privatisation; marketisation; the increased use of performance indicators; a growing emphasis on outputs and outcomes; partnership working; and the redesignation of clients as 'customers'.

Mandatory sentence Where sentencers (judges or magistrates) have little or no discretion, and legal guidelines impose an obligation to impose a particular type of sentence, or a particular length of sentence. Though relativey unusual in UK law, there have been increasing examples of mandatory sentencing in recent years from the 'three strikes'-style sentences included in the Crime (Sentences) Act 1997 to the restorative justice-influenced initiatives in the Youth Justice and Criminal Evidence Act 1999.

Moral panic (and folk devil) A term now lastingly associated with Stanley Cohen. His definition is still the most apposite. Periods of moral panic, he suggested occur when a 'condition, episode, person or group of persons emerges to become defined as a threat to societal values and interests (these are the 'folk devils'); its nature is presented in a stylized and stereotypical fashion by the mass media...'.

Morgan Report A report from the Standing Committee on Crime Prevention published in 1991 which had a significant impact on crime prevention and community safety policy, notably when New Labour came to power in 1997.

National Crime Victimization Survey (NCVS) A victimization survey conducted in the USA since the early 1970s. It is the US counterpart of the British Crime Survey.

National Offender Management Service (NOMS) An amalgam of the Prison and Probation Services. The National Offender Management Service (NOMS) was established in 2004 following a review of 'corrections' by Sir Patrick Carter the previous year. The intention behind this amalgamation is to provide seamless services to offenders before, during and after imprisonment. However, the creation of NOMS has been beset by difficulties.

Neighbourhood Watch (NW) Undoubtedly the best known and most widely adopted crime prevention programme in the UK (in which local residents take responsibility for watching each other's property and generally remaining alert to local crime opportunities and problems). NW first appeared in the early 1980s, was promoted initially by the Metropolitan Police and has now spread nationwide.

Offender profiling Offender profiling is a set of techniques used by law enforcement agencies to try to identify perpetrators of serious crime. There has been a rapidly growing interest in this subject over recent years both within the police service and in the media through films like *Silence of the Lambs* and television programmes such as *Cracker*.

Organised crime Sometimes referred to as 'syndicated crime', such activities are organised in the sense that they involve criminal collaboration, take place over an extended period of time, and tend to use violence or other forms of coercion to maintain discipline. Associated with gangsterism, organised crime is a staple of popular entertainment where portrayals of the mafia have long been a central element of television and cinema. Increasingly, organised crime is treated as a feature of globalisation, with criminal networks (involved for example in smuggling and trafficking of people and products) extending across the world.

Panopticon A plan for a particular style of prison, primarily associated with the utilitarian philosopher Jeremy Bentham. The institution was to be designed with a central inspection tower around which cells would be arranged so that prisoners could, in principle, be viewed at all times without knowing whether they were being watched. The intention behind this 'inspection principle' was to inculcate discipline through self-control.

Parole Early release from prison on licence (and a promise of good behaviour). The system is administered by the Parole Board, a non-departmental public body (NDPB) established in 1967 to advise the Home Secretary (now the Minister of Justice).

Partnerships Criminal justice agencies are increasingly expected to work jointly with other organisations and agencies in preventing and reducing crime. Thus, for example, the Crime and Disorder Act 1998 established crime and disorder reduction partnerships comprising representatives of the police, local authorities, and health and probation services. It also established multi-agency youth offending teams including representatives of a range of agencies and, more recently, the prison and probation services have been progressively merged into a single body: NOMS.

Penal populism The term (and its near neighbour populist punitiveness) refers to the rise of a new politics of crime from the early 1990s onward. In particular, it refers to the growing politicisation of crime control and to the apparent increasing desire of politicians to defer to public opinion (or certain forms of public opinion) when making decisions on crime policy. Such populism has coincided with a growing punitiveness in penal policy, captured in such phrases as 'prison works' and 'tough on crime'.

Performance indicators A target against which 'performance' can be gauged. The police are subject to an increasing array of performance indicators, including those contained in the National Policing Plan, local policing plans and as part of Best Value.

Plural policing Policing has become increasingly complex and the set of activities we understand as 'policing' is clearly delivered by a broad, and increasing, array of providers. These include the commercial security sector; new public sector provision such as local authority patrol, municipal police forces and wardens (as

well as informal policing such as vigilantism); the range of regulatory agencies within local and national government; together with those transnational policing agencies that operate beyond individual states.

Police-recorded crime statistics Until the early 1970s in America and the early 1980s in Britain, these were the main source of information about crime. The data are a reflection of crimes that are reported to, and are recorded by, the police. As many crimes are never reported to the police such statistics are incomplete and, in part, it is this shortcoming that led to the search for other sources of data and, in particular, the development of victimization surveys.

Prevalence The number of people or places that are victimized. The prevalence rate is generally presented as the number of people or places per hundred, thousand or hundred thousand that have been victimized at least once. Prevalence rates are thus to be distinguished from incidence rates.

Primary crime prevention This generally refers to action that is targeted at a general population and which aims to prevent crime before it occurs (see also 'secondary prevention' and 'tertiary prevention').

Primary and secondary deviance Terms associated with Edwin Lemert. Primary deviance refers simply to acts that are defined as deviant. Secondary deviance occurs when someone begins to employ their deviant identity as the basis for their actions.

Privatisation At its simplest, the shift of ownership and control from the public to the private sector. In practice, privatisation can cover a range of policies including civilianisation, 'contracting out', the increasing use of sponsorship and private finance and the establishment of public–private partnerships.

Psychological positivism An approach to explaining criminality which focuses on the psychological orientations and dispositions of those committing crimes. Referred to as psychological positivism as such approaches traditionally saw individual behaviour as being largely determined by such factors.

Punishment In general, the system of sanctions imposed by criminal courts in response to offending. More particularly, the term may be used to refer to specific penalties imposed as a result of such wrongdoing.

Radical criminology A body of criminological theory, influenced by Marxist sociology, which emphasises the importance of social inequalities and power relationships in the processes by which certain forms of behaviour, and particular groups in the population, are criminalised. More particularly, such approaches tend to view the criminal justice system as part of a broader system by which relatively powerless groups – the working classes – are kept in a subordinate position.

Rational choice A theory which emphasises the importance of rationality in human action, even if this is limited (or 'bounded'). Rational choice theories of crime emphasise the decision-making processes involved in the choices made by offenders, and tend to seek means by which to manipulate those processes, i.e. to persuade offenders or potential offenders to make different decisions (generally by attempting to alter the balance between the costs of particular actions as against potential rewards).

Rehabilitation Rehabilitation is a treatment-based process, intervention or programme to enable individuals to overcome previous difficulties linked to their offending. Belief in the 'rehabilitative ideal' – i.e. that law-breaking tendencies could be changed by criminal justice interventions – peaked in the 1960s but declined in the 1970s and 1980s when the belief that 'nothing works' became the prevailing orthodoxy.

Reintegrative shaming A theory, associated with John Braithwaite, which proposes that, used positively, shaming may form a central part of work with offenders in the process of reintegration. Such process are contrasted by Braithwaite with 'labelling' which tends to be negative in its connotations and impact, and which he refers to as 'disintegrative shaming'.

Repeat victimization The observation, based largely on data drawn from victimization surveys, that criminal victimization is not evenly distributed, but is concentrated in particular places and on particular people. The fact that some places and people are likely to be repeatedly victimized has given rise to a substantial body of work examining the crime prevention impact of focusing resources on those who are most likely to be the victim of further offences.

Responsibilisation A term referring to a set of strategies adopted by governments where the aim is to redistribute the crime control and crime prevention activities beyond the state. It is associated with terms such as partnership, multi- and inter-agency co-operation, active citizenship and active communities.

Restorative justice (RJ) One of the most significant social movements in criminal justice reform in recent times. Often viewed simply in opposition to formal justice, the most commonly used definition is of a 'process whereby the parties with a stake in a particular offence come together to resolve collectively how to deal with the aftermath of the offence and its implications for the future' (Marshall, 1996: 37).

Retributivism In relation to punishment, the term refers to a justification based on vengeance – of society 'getting its own back' for offences committed. Punishment from such a position need not seek to rehabilitate or deter – it merely involves retribution.

Right realism Just as left realism was in part a response to perceived shortcomings of existing radical theories, right realism also rejected such explanations for criminality. In this case, it sought explanation in moral decline, in the failures of welfarism and in the inadequacy of current systems of punishment.

Risk factors Factors which research suggests are statistically associated with increased likelihood of engagement in crime or other forms of anti-social conduct. It is generally thought that such factors are not akin to individual 'causes' of crime but, rather, in combination elevate the chances that particular individuals will engage in criminal conduct.

Robbery An incident or offence in which force or the threat of force is used either during or immediately prior to a theft or attempted theft.

Routine activities theory A theory, associated primarily with Marcus Felson, which suggests that for crime to occur three factors must be present: a motivated offender; a suitable victim; and the absence of capable guardians.

Secondary crime prevention Secondary prevention is action targeted at known offenders in order to reduce offending and/or the harms associated with offending (see also 'primary' and 'tertiary prevention')

Situational crime prevention According to Ron Clarke (1992: 4) this refers to: 'a pre-emptive approach that relies, not on improving society or its institutions, but simply on reducing opportunities for crime…Situational prevention comprises opportunity-reducing measures that are (1) directed at highly specific forms of crime, (2) that involve the management, design or manipulation of the immediate environment in as specific and permanent way as possible (3) so as to increase the effort and risks of crime and reduce the rewards as perceived by a wide range of offenders.'

Social control theories Theories which take various forms but which, at heart, assume that everyone would commit crimes given the opportunity, but are prevented from doing so by a variety of controls – some external (i.e. social) and some internal (i.e. psychological).

Social crime prevention By contrast with situational crime prevention, such approaches tend to focus on informal controls that are held to inhibit offending behaviour most of the time.

Sociological positivism A theoretical approach within criminology that places emphasis on the social determinants of behaviour, and pays little regard to individual deicision-making or choice.

Strain theory Linked with the notion of anomie, strain theory focuses upon the failure to achieve socially approved goals and the problems this creates. Such 'strain' may result in a variety of adaptations, one of which is to engage in deviant activity.

Subcultural theory Sociological theories that traditionally focused on working-class subcultures and the ways in which alternative value systems might form the basis for deviant activity. Subcultural theory tends to proceed from the assumption that behaviour may be understood as a largely rational means of solving problems (possibly only symbolically) thrown up by existing social circumstances.

Techniques of neutralisation A term associated with Sykes and Matza, and referring to a set of justifications that may be used to 'neutralize' the deviant character of certain behaviours. These include (among others): denial of responsibility (I wasn't to blame); denial of injury (they were insured anyway); denial of the victim (they were asking for it); and appeal to higher loyalties (I was only obeying orders).

Terrorism Another term that is highly problematic to define but, in shorthand, is often referred to simply as 'political violence'. The definition of terrorism in s. 1 of the Terrorism Act 2000 includes actual or threatened acts of violence against people and/or property designed to influence the government, to intimidate the public or a section of the public, or to advance a political, religious or ideological cause.

Tertiary crime prevention Tertiary crime prevention tends to be targeted at known offenders in order to reduce offending and/or harms associated with offending (see also 'primary prevention' and 'secondary crime prevention').

Tripartite structure A reference to the system of governance established originally by the Police Act 1964; 'tripartite' because it has three pillars: chief constables, local police authorities and the Home Secretary. The system has subsequently been reformed, in particular by the Police and Magistrates' Courts Act 1994 and by the Police Act 2002.

Utilitarianism A philosophy often summarised as involving concern with promoting the sum of human happiness (the greatest happiness of the greatest number). In relation to punishment, therefore, utilitarian philosophy tends to focus upon the goal of the prevention or reduction of crime.

Vehicle crime Recorded vehicle crimes include offences of theft of or from a vehicle, aggravated vehicle taking, vehicle interference and tampering, and criminal damage to a vehicle. Theft of a vehicle includes offences of theft of a vehicle and aggravated vehicle taking.

White-collar crime Defined originally by Edwin Sutherland as offences committed by high status individuals within the workplace or in the interests of the organisation.

Zemiology A term used by some critics of traditional criminology. Such critics argue that the socially constructed nature of crime means that the subject of criminology lacks coherence. By contrast, they advocate the study of social harms (zemiology) rather than crimes.

Zero tolerance A term that has become associated with a particular style of policing – notably that adopted by the New York Police Department in the 1990s. Influenced by Wilson and Kelling's broken windows thesis, this approach involves concentrated initiatives against low-level offences, the use of civil remedies against those perceived to be involved in crime, and aggressive action against street crimes.

Bibliography

Adler, F. (1975) *Sisters in Crime*, New York: McGraw-Hill

Adler, J. (1992) *The Urgings of Conscience*, Philadelphia: Temple University Press

Adler, P.A. and Adler, P. (1987) *Membership Roles in Field Research*, Newbury Park, CA: Sage

Adler, Z. (1987) *Rape On Trial*, London: Routledge

Aebi, M.F. *et al.* (2006) *European Sourcebook of Crime and Criminal Justice Statistics*, Den Haag, The Netherlands: Boom Juridische uitgevers

Agnew, R. (1992) 'Foundation for a general strain theory of crime and delinquency', *Criminology*, 30, 47–87

Agnew, R. (2000) 'Strain theory and school crime', in Simpson, S. (ed.) *Of Crime and Criminality*, Thousand Oaks, CA: Pine Forge Press

Agnew, R. (2001) 'Building on the foundation of general strain theory: Specifying the types of strain that are likely to lead to crime and delinquency', *Journal of Research in Crime and Delinquency*, 36, 123–155

Agnew, R. (2006) *Pressured into Crime: An overview of general strain theory*, Los Angeles: Roxbury

Ainsworth, P.B. (2000) *Psychology and Crime: Myths and reality*, Harlow: Longman

Akers, R. (1967) 'Problems in the sociology of deviance: Social definitions and behaviour', *Social Forces*, 46, 455–465

Akers, R.L. (1998) *Social Learning and Social Structure: A general theory of crime and deviance*, Boston: Northeastern University Press

Albini, J.L. (1971) *The American Mafia: Genesis of a legend*, New York: Appleton-Century-Crofts

Alder, C. and Worrall, A. (eds) (2004) *Girl's Violence: Myths and realities*, Albany, NY: State University of New York Press

Alison, L. (2005) 'From trait-based profiling to psychological contributions to apprehension methods', in Alison, L. (ed.) *The Forensic Psychologist's Casebook*, Cullompton: Willan

Alison, L. and Canter, D.V. (2005) 'Rhetorical shaping in an undercover operation: the investigation of Colin Stagg in the Rachel Nickell murder enquiry', in Alison, L. (ed.) *The Forensic Psychologists Casebook*, Cullompton: Willan

Alison, L. and Kebbell, M.R. (2006) 'Offender profiling: limits and potential', in Kebbell, M.R. and Davies, G.M. (eds) *Practical Psychology for Forensic Investigations and Prosecutions*, Chichester: Wiley

Alison, L., McLean, C. and Almond, L. (2007) 'Profiling suspects', in Newburn, T., Williamson, T. and Wright, A. (eds) *Handbook of Criminal Investigation*, Cullompton: Willan

Alison, L., Smith, M.D., Eastman, O. and Rainbow, L. (2003) 'Toulmin's philosophy of argument and its relevance to offender profiling', *Journal of Psychology, Crime and Law*, 9, 2, 173–181

Allatt, P. (1984) 'Fear of crime: the effect of improved residential security on a difficult to let estate', *The Howard Journal of Criminal Justice*, 23, 170–182

Allen, C. (2005) *Fair Justice: The Bradford disturbances, the sentencing and the impact*, Richmond: Forum Against Islamophobia and Racism

Allen, F. (1981) *The Decline of the Rehabilitative Ideal*, New Haven: Yale University Press

Allen, F.A. (1960) 'Raffaele Garofalo', in Mannheim, H. (ed.) *Pioneers in Criminology*, London: Stevens

Allen, H. (1984) 'At the mercy of her hormones: Pre-menstrual tension and the law', *M/f*, 9, 4, 19–44

Allen, J., Livingstone, S., and Reiner, R. (1997) 'The changing generic location of crime in film', *Journal of Communication*, 47, 4, 1–13

Allen, J.P. (2005) 'Ethnic geography dynamics: Clues from Los Angeles', *Yearbook of the Association of Pacific Coast Geographers*, 67, 97–116

Amir, M. (1971) *Patterns in Forcible Rape*, Chicago: University of Chicago Press

Anderson, B. and O'Connell Davidson, J. (2004) *Trafficking: A demand-led problem?* Stockholm: Save the Children Sweden

Anderson, E. (1990) *Code of the Street*, New York: W.W. Norton

Anderson, M. (1989) *Policing the World: Interpol and the politics of international police co-operation*, Oxford: Clarendon Press

Anderson, P. and Mann, N. (1997) *Safety First: The making of New Labour*, London: Granta

Anderson, S., Kinsey, R., Loader, I. and Smith, C. (1990) *The Edinburgh Crime Survey*, Edinburgh: Scottish Office

Andreas, P. and Nadelmann, E. (2006) *Policing the Globe: Criminalization and crime control in international relations*, New York: Oxford University Press

Andrews, D.A. and Bonta, J. (1998) *The Psychology of Criminal Conduct,* Cincinnati, OH: Anderson Publishing

Andrews, D. A., and Bonta, J. (2003) *The Psychology of Criminal Conduct,* 3rd edn, Cincinnati, OH: Anderson Publishing

Andrews, D.A., Zinger, I., Hoge, R.D., Bonta, J., Gendreau, P., and Cullen, F.T. (1990) 'Does correctional treatment work? A clinically relevant and psychologically informed meta-analysis', *Criminology,* 28, 3, 369–404

Anie, A., Daniel, N., Tah, C. and Petruckevitch, A. (2005) *An exploration of factors affecting the successful dispersal of asylum seekers,* Home Office online report 50/05, London: Home Office

Aries, P. (1973) *Centuries of Childhood,* Harmondsworth, Penguin

Arksey, H. and Knight, P. (1999) *Interviewing for Social Scientists,* London: Sage

Arlacchi, P. (1988) *Mafia Business: The mafia ethic and the spirit of capitalism,* Oxford: Oxford University Press

Ashworth, A. (1983) *Sentencing and Penal Policy,* London: Weidenfeld and Nicolson

Ashworth, A. (1992) *Sentencing and Criminal Justice,* 1st edn, London: Weidenfeld and Nicolson

Ashworth, A. (1993) 'Victim impact statements and sentencing', *Criminal Law Review,* 498–509

Ashworth, A. (1995) *Sentencing and Criminal Justice,* 2nd edn, London: Butterworths

Ashworth, A. (2000) *Sentencing and Criminal justice,* 3rd edn, London: Butterworths

Ashworth, A. (2002) 'Responsibilities, rights and restorative justice', *British Journal of Criminology,* 42, 3, 578–95

Ashworth, A. and Redmayne, M. (2005) *The Criminal Process,* 3rd edn, Oxford: Oxford University Press

Association of Chief Police Officers (1985) *Drug-related crime: The Broome Report,* London: ACPO

Audit Commission (1996) *Misspent Youth,* London: Audit Commission

Audit Commission (1999) *Safety in Numbers,* London: Audit Commission

Audit Commission (2004) *Youth Justice 2004,* London: Audit Commission

Auld, R.E. (2001) *Review of the criminal courts of England and Wales,* London: The Stationery Office

Avant, D.D. (2005) *The Market for Force: The consequences of privatizing security,* Cambridge: Cambridge University Press

Aye Maung, N. (1995) *Young People, Victimisation and the Police: British Crime Survey findings on experiences and attitudes of 12 to 15 year olds,* Home Office Research and Planning Unit, London: HMSO

Ayres, I. and Braithwaite, J. (1992) *Responsive Regulation: Transcending the deregulation debate,* Oxford: Oxford University Press

Bailey, R., Knight, C. and Williams, B. (2007) 'The probation service as part of NOMS: fit for purpose?' In Gelsthorpe, L. and Morgan, R. (eds) *Handbook of Probation,* Cullompton: Willan

Bailey, V. (ed) (1981) *Policing and Punishment in Nineteenth Century England,* London: Croom Helm

Baker, E. and Clarkson, C.M.V. (2002) 'Making punishments work? An evaluation of the Halliday Report on Sentencing in England and Wales', *Criminal Law Review,* 81

Baldwin, J. and Bottoms, A.E. (1976) *The Urban Criminal: A study in Sheffield,* London: Tavistock Publications

Baldwin, J. and McConville, M.J. (1979) *Jury Trials,* Oxford: Oxford University Press

Bandura, A. (1975) *Social Learning and Personality Development,* New Jersey: Holt, Rinehart & Winston

Bandura, A. (1977) *Social Learning Theory,* Englewood Cliffs, NY: Prentice Hall

Bandura, A., Ross, D. and Ross, S.A. (1961) 'Transmission of aggression through imitation of aggressive models', *Journal of Abnormal and Social Psychology,* 63, 3, 575–582

Barclay, G. and Tavares, C. (1999) *Information on the Criminal Justice System in England and Wales: Digest 4,* London: Home Office

Barkan, S. (1997) *Criminology: A sociological understanding,* Upper Saddle River, NJ: Prentice Hall

Barker, M. (1984) *A Haunt of Fears: The strange history of the British horror comics campaign,* London: Pluto Press

Barker, P. and Little, A. (1964) 'The Margate offenders – a survey', *New Society,* 4, 96, 6–10

Barr, R. and Pease, K. (1990) 'Crime placement, displacement, and deflection', in Tonry, M. and Morris, N. (eds) *Crime and Justice: A Review of Research, Vol. 12,* 277–318, Chicago: University of Chicago Press,

Bartlett, D. and Memon, A. (1995) 'Advocacy', in Bull, R. and Carson, D. (eds) *Handbook of Psychology in Legal Contexts,* Chichester: Wiley

Bartol, C. (1999) *Criminal Behaviour: A psychosocial approach,* 5th edn, Upper Saddle River, NJ: Prentice Hall

Barton, A. (2005) *Fragile Moralities and Dangerous Sexualities,* Aldershot: Ashgate

Bayley, D. (1994) *Police for the Future,* Oxford: Oxford University Press

Bayley, D.H., and Shearing, C. (1996) 'The future of the police', *Law and Society Review*

Bazemore, G. and Umbreit, M.S. (2001) *A Comparison of Four Conferencing Models,* Washington, DC: Office of Juvenile Justice and Delinquency Prevention, U.S. Department of Justice

Bean, J.P. (1981) *The Sheffield Gang Wars,* Sheffield: D & D Publications

Bean, P. (2004), *Drugs and Crime,* 2nd edn, Cullompton: Willan

Beattie, J. (1986) *Crime and Courts in England 1660–1800,* Oxford: Clarendon Press

Beccaria, C. (1764/1963) *An Essay on Crimes and Punishments,* Indianapolis: Bobbs-Merrill.

Beccaria, C. (1767/1995) *On Crimes and Punishments and Other Writings,* (translated by Richard Bellamy), Cambridge: Cambridge University Press

Beck, U. (1992) *The Risk Society,* Cambridge: Polity Press

Beck, U. (2005) *Power in the Global Age: A new global political economy,* translated by Kathleen Cross, Cambridge; Malden, MA: Polity Press

Becker, G. (1968) 'Crime and punishment: An economic approach', *Journal of Political Economy,* 76, 169–217

Becker, H. (1963) *Outsiders: Studies in the sociology of deviance,* London: Macmillan

Becker, H. (1974) 'Labelling theory reconsidered', in Rock, P. and McIntosh, M. (eds) *Deviance and Social Control,* London: Tavistock

Becker, H. (1986) *Writing for Social Scientists,* Chicago: University of Chicago Press

Beckett, K. (1997) *Making Crime Pay: Law and order in contemporary American politics,* New York: Oxford University Press

Beckett, K. and Sasson, T. (2000) 'The war on crime as hegemonic strategy: A neo-Marxian theory of the new punitiveness in U.S. criminal justice policy', in Simpson, S. (ed.) *Of Crime and Criminality,* Thousand Oaks, CA: Pine Forge Press

Beckett, K. and Sasson, T. (2003) *The Politics of Injustice,* 2nd edn, Thousand Oaks, CA: Pine Forge Press

Beirne, P. (1993) *Inventing Criminology: Essays on the rise of Homo Criminalis,* Albany, NY: State University of New York Press

Bell, D. (1973) *The Coming of Post-Industrial Society,* New York: Basic Books

Benn, C, and Worpole, K. (1986) *Death in the City,* London: Canary

Bennett, T. (1989) 'The neighbourhood watch experience', in Morgan R. and Smith, D. (eds) *Coming to Terms with Policing,* London: Routledge

Bennett, T. (1991) 'The effectiveness of a police-initiated fear-reducing strategy', *British Journal of Criminology,* 31, 1, 1–14

Bennett, T. (1996) 'What's new in evaluation research?', *British Journal of Criminology,* 36, 4, 567–573

Bennett, T. (2000) *Drugs and crime: the results of the second development stage of the NEW-ADAM programme,* Home Office Research Study No. 205, London: Home Office

Bennett, T. and Holloway, K. (2004) 'Gang membership, drugs and crime in the UK', *British Journal of Criminology,* 44, 305–323

Bennett, T. and Holloway, K. (2005) *Understanding Drugs, Alcohol and Crime,* Maidenhead: Open University Press

Bennett, T., Holloway, K. and Williams, T. (2001) 'Drug Use and Offending', *Findings,* 148, London: Home Office

Bennett, T. and Sibbett, R. (2000) *Drug Use among arrestees,* London: Home Office

Bennett, T. and Wright, R. (1984) *Burglars on Burglary: Prevention and the offender,* Brookfield: Gower

Bennett, W.J., DiIulio, J.J., and Walters, J.P. (1996) *Body Count: Moral poverty and how to win America's war against crime and drugs,* New York: Simon and Schuster

Bentham, J. (1789/1973) *An Introduction to the Principles of Morals and Legislation,* New York: Hafner Press

Berk, R.A. and Rossi, P.H. (1990) *Thinking About Program Evaluation,* Newbury Park, CA: Sage

Binney, V., Harknell, G. and Nixon, J. (1981) *Leaving Violent Men: A study of refuges and housing for battered women,* London: Women's Aid Federation

Birkland, T.A. (1997) *After Disaster: Agenda setting, public policy and focusing events,* Washington DC: Georgetown University Press

Birmingham, L., Gregoire, K., Kamal, M., Mulee, M. and Coulson, M. (undated) *Psychiatric morbidity and mental health treatment needs among women in prison mother and baby units,* Southampton: Department of Forensic Mental Health, University of Southampton

Bittner, E. (1980) *The Functions of the Police in Modern Society: A review of background factors, current practices and possible role models,* Cambridge, MA: Oelgeschleager, Gunn & Hain, Publishers, Inc

Blackburn, R. (1993) *The Psychology of Criminal Conduct: Theory, research and practice,* Chichester: Wiley

Blagg, H. (1997) 'A Just Measure of Shame?', *British Journal of Criminology,* 37, 481–501

Bland, N., Mundy, G., Russell, J. and Tuffin, R. (1999) *Career Progression of Ethnic Minority Police Officers,* London: Home Office

Block, A. (1983) *East Side – West Side: Organizing crime in New York 1930 – 1950*, New Brunswick, NJ: Transaction

Block, A. and Chambliss, W. (1981) *Organising Crime*, New York: Elsevier

Block, A. and Schuster, L. (2002) 'Asylum and welfare: contemporary debates', *Critical Social Policy*, 22, 3, 393–414

Block, B.P and Hostettler, J. (1997) *Hanging in the Balance: A history of the abolition of capital punishment in Britain*, Winchester: Waterside Press

Blumer, H. (1969) *Symbolic Interactionism: Perspective and method*, Englewood Cliffs, NJ: Prentice Hall

Bobbitt, P. (2002) *The Shield of Achilles: War, peace and the course of history*, New York: Alfred A. Knopf

Bohman, J. (1995) 'Public reason and cultural pluralism', *Political Theory*, 23, 2, 253–279

Bohman, M. (1978) 'Some genetic aspects of alcoholism and criminality': A population of adoptees', *Arch Gen Psychiatry*, 35, 3, 269–276

Bondeson, U.V. (2005) 'Levels of punitiveness in Scandinavia: description and explanations', in Pratt, J., Brown, D., Brown, M., Hallsworth, S. and Morrison, W. (eds) *The New Punitiveness: Trends, theories, perspectives*, Cullompton: Willan

Bonger, W. (1969) *Criminality and Economic Conditions*, Boston: Little, Brown and Co.

Booth, A. and Osgood, D.W. (1993) 'The influence of testosterone on deviance in adulthood', *Criminology*, 31, 1, 93–117

Booth, C. (1902) *Life and Labour of the People in London*, London: Macmillan

Booth, M. (1996) *Opium: A history*, New York: St Martin's Press

Boreham, R. and Blenkinsopp, S. (eds) (2004) *Drug use, smoking and drinking among young people in England in 2003*, London: The Stationary Office

Boreham, R., Fuller, E., Hills, A. and Pudney, S. (2006) *The Arrestee Survey Annual Report, Oct 2003 – Sept 2004*, London: Home Office

Bosworth, M. (1999) *Engendering Resistance: Agency and power in women's prisons*, Aldershot: Ashgate

Bottomley, K. (1984) 'Dilemmas of parole in a penal crisis', *The Howard Journal of Criminal Justice*, 25, 1, 24–40

Bottomley, K. and Pease, K. (1986) *Crime and Punishment: Interpreting the data*, Milton Keynes: Open University Press

Bottoms, A.E. (1974) 'On the decriminalization of the English juvenile courts', in Hood, R. (ed.) *Crime, Criminology and Public Policy*, London: Heinemann

Bottoms, A.E. (1983) 'Neglected features of contemporary penal systems', in Garland, D. and Young, P. (eds) *The Power to Punish: Contemporary penality and social analysis*, Aldershot: Gower

Bottoms, A.E. (1987) 'Limiting prison use: The experience of England and Wales', *The Howard Journal of Criminal Justice*, 26, 2, 177–202

Bottoms, A.E. (1995) 'The philosophy and politics of punishment and sentencing', in Clarkson, C. and Morgan, R. (eds) *The Politics of Sentencing Reform*, Oxford: Oxford University Press

Bottoms, A.E. (1999) 'Interpersonal violence and social order in prisons', in *Crime and Justice: A Review of Research, Vol. 26*, Chicago: University of Chicago Press

Bottoms, A.E. (2000) 'The relationship between theory and research in criminology', in King, R. and Wincup, E. (eds) *Doing Research on Crime and Justice*, Oxford: Oxford University Press

Bottoms, A. (ed.) (2007) *Victims in the Criminal Justice System*, Cullompton: Willan Publishing

Bottoms, A.E. and Costello, A. (2001) *Offenders and victims of property crimes in a deindustrialised city*, Presentation at the First Annual Conference of the European Society of Criminology, Lausanne, Switzerland

Bottoms, A.E. and Light, R. (1987), *Problems of Long-term Imprisonment*, Aldershot: Gower

Bottoms, A. and McWilliams, E. (1979) 'Non-treatment paradigm for probation practice', *British Journal of Social Work*, 9, 2

Bottoms, A.E., Mawby, R. and Walker, M. (1987) 'A localised crime survey in contrasting areas of a city', *British Journal of Criminology*, 27, 125–54

Bottoms, A.E., Rex, S. and Robinson, G. (eds) (2004a) *Alternatives to Prison: Options for an insecure society*, Cullompton: Willan

Bottoms, A.E., Rex, S. and Robinson, G. (2004b) 'How did we get here?', in Bottoms, A.E., Rex, S. and Robinson, G. (eds) *Alternatives to Prison: Options for an insecure society*, Cullompton: Willan

Bouffard, J., Exum, M.L. and Paternoster, R. (2000) 'Whither the beast? The role of emotions in a rational choice theory of crime', in Simpson, S. (ed.) *Of Crime and Criminality*, Thousand Oaks, CA: Pine Forge Press

Bourgois, P. (2003) *In Search of Respect*, Cambridge: Cambridge University Press

Bowling, B. (1993) 'Racial harassment and the process of victimisation', *British Journal of Criminology*, 33, 2, 231–250

Bowling, B. (1999) *Violent Racism: Victimisation, Policing and Social Context*, revised edition, Oxford: Oxford University Press

Bowling, B. and Phillips, C. (2002) *Racism, Crime and Justice,* London: Longman

Box, S. (1981) *Deviance, Reality and Society*, 2nd edn, Eastbourne: Holt, Rinehart and Winston

Box, S. (1983) *Power, Crime and Mystification,* London: Tavistock

Box, S. and Hale, C. (1983) 'Liberation and female criminality in England and Wales', *British Journal of Criminology,* 23, 1, 35–49

Brain, K., Parker, H. and Carnwath, T. (2000) 'Drinking with design: young drinkers as psychoactive consumers', *Drugs: Education, prevention and policy,* 7, 1, 5–20

Braisby, N. and Gellatly, A. (2004) *Cognitive Psychology,* Oxford: Oxford University Press

Braithwaite, J. (1984) *Corporate Crime in the Pharmaceutical Industry,* London: Routledge and Kegan Paul

Braithwaite, J. (1985) 'White Collar Crime', *Annual Review of Sociology,* 11, 1–25

Braithwaite, J. (1989) *Crime, Shame and Reintegration,* Cambridge: Cambridge University Press

Braithwaite, J. (1991) 'Poverty, power, white-collar crime and the paradoxes of criminological theory', *Australian and New Zealand Journal of Criminology,* 24, 40–58

Braithwaite, J. (1995) 'White-collar crime', in Geis, G. *et al.* (eds) *White Collar Crime: Classic and contemporary views,* New York: The Free Press

Braithwaite, J. (1996) 'Restorative justice for a better future?'. *Dalhousie Law Review,* 76, 1, 9–32

Braithwaite, J. (1997) 'Charles Tittle's control balance and criminological theory', *Theoretical Criminology,* 1, 1, 77–97

Braithwaite, J. (1999) 'Restorative Justice: Assessing optimistic and pessimistic accounts', in Tonry, M. and Morris, N. (eds) *Crime and Justice: A Review of Research, Vol. 25,* Chicago: University of Chicago Press

Braithwaite, J. (2000) 'The new regulatory state and the transformation of criminology', in Garland, D. and Sparks, R. (eds) *Criminology and Social Theory,* Oxford: Oxford University Press

Braithwaite, J. (2003) 'Restorative justice and corporate regulation', in Weitekamp, G.M. and Kerner, H-J (eds) *Restorative Justice in Context,* Cullompton: Willan

Braithwaite, J. and Daly, K. (1994) 'Masculinities, violence and communitarian control', in Newburn, T. and Stanko, E.A. (eds) *Just Boys Doing Business: Men, masculinities and crime,* London: Routledge

Braithwaite, J. and Fisse, B. (1987) 'Self-regulation and the control of corporate crime', in Shearing, C. and Stenning, P. (eds) *Private Policing,* Thousand Oaks, CA: Sage

Braithwaite, J. and Fisse, B. (1990) 'On the plausibility of corporate crime theory', *Advances in Criminological Theory,* 2, 15–38

Braithwaite, J. and Petit, P. (1990) *Not Just Deserts: A republican theory of criminal justice,* Oxford: Clarendon Press

Braithwaite, R. (2001) *Managing Aggression,* London; New York: Routledge

Brake, M. and Hale, C. (1992) *Public Order and Private Lives: The politics of law and order,* London: Routledge

Brantingham, P. and Faust, F. (1976) 'A conceptual model of crime prevention', *Crime and Delinquency,* 22, 284–96

Bratton, W.J. (1998) *Turnaround: How America's top cop reversed the crime epidemic,* New York: Random House

Brennan, P., Grekin, E. and Mednick, S. (1999) 'Maternal smoking during pregnancy and adult male criminal outcomes', *Archives of General Psychiatry,* 56, 216–219

Bresler, F.S. (1980) *The Trail of the Triads: An investigation into international crime,* London: Weidenfeld & Nicolson

Brienen, M.E.I. and Hoegen E.H. (2000a) *Victims of Crime in 22 European Juridictions: The implementation of recommendation 85 (11) of the Council of Europe on the position of the victim in the framework of criminal law and procedure,* Tilburg: Wolf Legal Productions

Briere, J. (1984) *The Effects of Childhood Sexual Abuse on Later Psychological Functioning: Defining a post-sexual-abuse syndrome,* paper presented at the 3rd National Conference on Sexual Victimization of Children, Los Angeles

British Associaton of Women Police (2001) *The Gender Agenda,* London: BAWP

British Beer and Pub Association (2006) *The Statistical Handbook 2006,* London: British Beer and Pub Association

Broeders, A.P.A. (2007) 'Principles of forensic identification science', in Newburn, T., Williamson, T. and Wright, A. (eds) *Handbook of Criminal Investigation,* Cullompton: Willan

Brogden, M. and Nijhar, P. (2006) 'Crime, abuse and social harm: towards an integrated approach', in Wahidin, A. and Cain, M. (eds) *Ageing, Crime and Society,* Cullompton: Willan

Brookman, F. (2005) *Understanding Homicide,* London: Sage

Brookman, F. and Maguire, M. (2003) *Reducing Homicide: A review of the possibilities,* London: Home Office

Brown, J., Maidment, A. and Bull, R. (1992) 'Appropriate skill-task matching or gender bias in deployment of male and female police officers', *Policing and Society,* 2

Brown, J. and Heidensohn, F. (2000) *Gender and Policing: Comparative perspectives*, Basingstoke: Macmillan

Brown, J. and Heidensohn, F. (2006) *Gender and Policing: Comparative perspectives*, Basingstoke: Macmillan

Brown, R. (2003) 'Clausewitz in the age of CNN: Rethinking the military-media relationship', in Norris, P., Kern, M. and Just, M. (eds) *Framing Terrorism: The news media, the government and the public*, New York: Routledge

Brown, S.E., Esbensen, F-A. and Geis, G. (2004) *Criminology: Explaining crime and its context*, 5th edn, Cincinnati, OH: Anderson Publishing

Brownlee, I. (1998) *Community Punishment: A critical introduction*, Harlow: Addison Wesley Longman

Bryman, A. (2001) *Social Research Methods*, Oxford: Oxford University Press

Bryman, A. (2004) *Social research Methods,* 2nd edn, Oxford: Oxford University Press

Bucke, T. and Brown, D. (1997) *In police custody: Police powers and suspects' rights under the revised PACE codes of practice*, London: Home Office

Bucke, T., Street, R. and Brown, D. (2000) *The Right of Silence: The impact of the Criminal Justice and Public Order Act 1994,* London: Home Office

Buckley, K. and Young, K. (1996) 'Driving us crazy: Motor projects and masculinity', in Newburn, T. and Mair, G. (eds) *Working With Men*, Lyme Regis: Russell House

Budd, T. and Mattinson, J. (2000) *British Crime Survey Training Notes,* London: Home Office

Budd, T., Sharp, C., Weir, G., Wilson, D. and Owen, N. (2005) *Young People and Crime: Findings from the 2004 Offending, Crime and Justice Survey*, HOSB 20/05, London: Home Office

Burgess, A.W. (1984) *Child Pornography and Sex Rings*, Massachusetts/Toronto: Lexington Books

Burgess, A.W. and Holmstrom, L.L. (1974) 'Rape trauma syndrome', *American Journal of Psychiatry*, 131, 9, 981–986

Burgess, E.W. (1925) 'The growth of the city: An introduction to a research project', in Park, R.E. and Burgess, E.W. (eds) *The City*, Chicago: University of Chicago Press

Burgess, E.W. and Bogue, D.J. (1964) 'Research in urban society: A long view', in Burgess, E.W. and Bogue, D.J. (eds) *Contributions to Urban Sociology*, Chicago: University of Chicago Press

Burgess, R. and Akers, R. (1966) 'A differential association reinforcement theory of criminal behavior', *Social Problems*, 14, 128–47

Burman, M. (2004) 'Breaking the mould: Patterns of female offending', in McIvor, G. (ed.) *Women Who Offend*, London: Jessica Kingsley

Burnett, R. and Farrell, G. (1994) 'Reported and unreported racial incidents in prisons', *Centre for Criminological Research Occasional Paper No. 1,* Oxford University

Burney, E. and Rose, G. (2002) 'Racist offences – how is the law working?', Home Office research studies, 244, London: Home Office

Burney, E. (2005) *Making People Behave: Anti-social behaviour, politics and policy,* Cullompton: Willan

Bursik, R.J. (2000) 'The systemic theory of neighbourhood crime rates', in Simpson, S. (ed.) *Of Crime and Criminality*, Thousand Oaks, CA: Pine Forge Press

Butler, Lord (2004) *Review of Intelligence on Weapons of Mass Destruction,* London: The Stationery Office

Butler-Sloss, D.B.E. (1988). *Report of the inquiry into child abuse in Cleveland, 1987,* Presented to Parliament by the Secretary of State for Social Services by Command of Her Majesty, London: HMSO

Cabinet Office (2002) *The United Kingdom and the Campaign against International Terrorism,* London: Cabinet Office

Cabinet Office (2003) *Alcohol Use: How much does it cost?* London: Cabinet Office Caddle, D. and Crisp, D. (1997) *Imprisoned Women and Mothers,* London: Home Office

Cain, M. (1986) 'Realism, feminism, methodology and law', *International Journal of the Sociology of Law*, 14, 3/4, 255–67

Cain, M. (1989) *Growing Up Good: Policing the behaviour of girls in Europe*, London: Sage

Campbell, A (1993) *Out of Control: Men, women and aggression*, London: Pandora

Campbell, B. (1988) *Unofficial Secrets: Child sexual abuse – the Cleveland case*, London: Virago

Campbell, D. and Stanley, J. (1963) *Experimental and Quasi Experimental Designs for Research*, Chicago: Rand McNally

Campbell, D.T. and Stanley, J.C. (1966) *Experimental and Quasi-Experimental Designs for Research*, Boston: Houghton-Mifflin

Campbell, S. (2002) *A Review of Anti-Social Behaviour Orders*, London: Home Office

Cann, J., Falshaw, L., Nugent, F. and Friendship, C. (2003) *Understanding what works: Accredited cognitive skills programmes for adult men and young offenders*, Home Office Research Findings 226, London: Home Office

Cantle, T. (2001) *Community Cohesion: Report of an independent review team*, London: Home Office

Carlen, P. (1983) *Women's Imprisonment*, London: Routledge and Kegan Paul

Carlen, P. (1985) *Criminal Women*, Oxford: Polity Press

Carlen, P. (1992) 'Criminal women and criminal justice: the limits to, and potential of, feminist and left realist perspectives', in Matthews, R. and Young, J. (eds) *Issues in Realist Criminology*, London: Sage

Carlen, P. (1995) 'Virginia, criminology and the anti-social control of women', in Blumberg, T. and Cohen, S. (eds) *Punishment and Social Control*, New York: Aldine de Gruyter

Carlen, P. (ed.) (2002) *Women and Punishment: The struggle for justice*, Cullompton: Willan

Carlen, P. and Worrall, A. (eds) (1987) *Gender, Crime and Justice*, Milton Keynes: Open University Press

Carlen, P. and Worrall, A. (2004) *Analysing Women's Imprisonment*, Cullompton: Willan

Carrabine, E., Iganski, P., Lee, M., Plummer, K. and South, N. (2004) *Criminology: A sociological introduction*, London: Routledge

Carrington, K. (2002) 'Feminism and critical criminology: confronting genealogies', in Carrington, K. and Hogg, R. (eds) *Critical Criminology: Issues, debates, challenges*, Cullompton: Willan

Carter, P. (2003) *Correctional Services Review*, London: Home Office

Castells, M. (1996) *The Information Age: Economy, society and culture: Vol 1, The rise of the network society*, Oxford: Blackwell Publishing

Castells, M. (2002) *The Internet Galaxy: Reflections on the internet, business and society*, Oxford: Oxford University Press

Cavadino, M. and Dignan, J. (1992) *The Penal System, An Introduction*, London: Sage

Cavadino, M. and Dignan, J. (2005) *The Penal System, An Introduction*, 3rd edn, London: Sage

Cavadino, M. and Dignan, J. (2006) *Penal Systems: A comparative approach*, London: Sage

Central Statistical Office (1994) *Social Trends*, London: HMSO

Chaiken, J. and Chaiken, M. (1990) 'Drugs and predatory crime', in Tonry, M. and Wilson, J.Q. (eds) *Drugs and Crime*, Chicago: University of Chicago Press

Chaiken, J., Lawless, M. and Stevenson, K. (1974) *The Impact of Police Activity of Crime: Robberies on the New York City subway system*, Santa Monica, CA: Rand Corporation

Chakraborti, N. (2007) 'Policing Muslim communities', in Rowe, M. (ed.) *Policing Beyond Macpherson*, Cullompton: Willan

Chambers, G. and Millar, A (1983) *Investigating Sexual Assault*, Scottish Office Research Study, Edinburgh: HMSO

Chambers, G. and Millar, A. (1987) 'Proving sexual assault: Prosecuting the offender or persecuting the victim?', in Carlen, P. and Worrall, A. (eds) *Gender, Crime and Justice*, Milton Keynes: Open University Press

Chambliss, W. (1964) 'A sociological analysis of the law of vagrancy', *Social Problems*, 12, 1, 67–77

Chambliss, W. (1966) 'The Deterrent Influence of Punishment', *Crime and Delinquency*, 12, 70–75

Chambliss, W. (1975) 'Toward a political economy of crime', *Theory and Society*, 2, 149–170

Chambliss, W. (1978) *On the Take: From petty crooks to presidents*, Bloomington: Indiana University Press

Chambliss, W. (1988) *On the Take: From petty crooks to presidents*, 2nd edn, Bloomington: Indiana University Press

Chambliss, W. (1989) 'State-organised crime – the American society of criminology, 1998 Presidential address', *Criminology*, 27, 183–208

Chambliss, W. and Siedman, R. (1971) *Law, Order and Power*, Massachusetts: Addison-Wesley

Chan, J. (1997) *Changing Police Culture: Policing in a multicultural society*, Cambridge: Cambridge University Press

Checkley, H. (1941) *The Mask of Sanity*, St Louis, MO: Mosby

Chelimsky, E. (1997) 'Thoughts for a new evaluation society', *Evaluation*, 3, 1, 97–118

Cheney, D., Uglow, S., Dickinson, L. and Fitzpatrick, J. (2001) *Criminal justice and the Human Rights Act 1998*, Bristol: Jordans

Chesney-Lind, M. (1997) *The Female Offender: Girls, women and crime*, Thousand Oaks, CA: Sage

Chesney-Lind, M. (2006) 'Patriarchy, crime and justice: Feminist criminology in an era of backlash', *Feminist Criminology*, 1, 1, 6–26

Chibnall, S. (1977) *Law and Order News*, London: Tavistock

Chomsky, N. (2000) *Rogue States*, New York: South End Press

Christiansen, K.O. (1977) 'A preliminary study of criminality among twins', in Mednick, S. and Christiansen, K.O. (eds) *Biological Causes of Human Behaviour*, New York: Gardner Press

Christie, N. (1977) 'Conflicts as property', *British Journal of Criminology* 17, 1–15

Christie, N. (1982) *The Limits of Pain*, Oxford: Martin Robertson

Christie, N. (1986) 'The ideal victim', in Fattah, E.A. (ed.) *From Crime Policy to Victim Policy*, New York: St. Martins Press

Christie, N. (2004) *A Suitable Amount of Crime*, London: Routledge

Clare, E. and Bottomley, K. (2001) *Evaluation of Close Supervision Centres*, London: Home Office

Clarke, A. (1999) *Evaluation Research*, London: Sage

Clarke, C. and Milne, R. (2001) 'National evaluation of the PEACE investigative interviewing course', *Police Research Award Scheme*, Report Number PRAS/149

Clarke, J. (1976a) 'The skinheads and the magical recovery of community', in Hall, S. and Jefferson, T. (eds) *Resistance through Rituals*, London: Hutchinson

Clarke, J. (1976b) 'Style', in Hall, S. and Jefferson, T. (eds) *Resistance through Rituals*, London: Hutchinson

Clarke, M. (1990) *Business Crime: Its nature and control*, Cambridge: Polity Press

Clarke, R.V.G. (1980) '"Situational" crime prevention: theory and practice', *British Journal of Criminology*, 20, 2, 136–147

Clarke, R.V.G. (1983) 'Situational crime prevention: Its theoretical basis and practical scope', in Tonry, M. and Morris, N. (eds) *Crime and Justice: An Annual Review of Research, Vol. 4*, Chicago: Chicago University Press

Clarke, R.V.G. (ed.) (1992) *Situational Crime Prevention: Successful Case Studies*, 1st edn, New York: Harrow and Heston

Clarke, R.V.G. (1995) 'Situational crime prevention', in Tonry, M. and Farrington, D. (eds) *Building Safer Communities*, Chicago: Chicago University Press

Clarke, R.V.G. (1997) *Situational Crime Prevention Successful Case Studies*, 2nd edn, New York: Harrow and Heston

Clarke, R.V.G. (2004) 'Technology, criminology and crime science', *European Journal on Criminal Policy and Research*, 10, 55–63

Clarke, R.V.G. (2005) 'Seven misconceptions of situational crime prevention', in Tilley, N. (ed.) *Handbook of Crime Prevention and Community Safety*, Cullompton: Willan

Clarke, R.V.G. and Cornish, D. (1985) 'Modelling offenders' decisions: A framework for research and policy', in Tonry, M. and Morris, N. (eds) *Crime and Justice: A Review of Research*, Chicago: University of Chicago Press

Clarke, R.V.G. and Cornish, D. (2001) 'Rational choice', in Paternoster, R. and Bachman, R. (eds) *Explaining Criminals and Crime: Essays in contemporary criminological theory*, Los Angeles: Roxbury

Clarke, R.V.G. and Harris, P. (1992) 'Auto-theft and its prevention', in Tonry, M. (ed.) *Crime and Justice: A Review of Research*, Chicago: University of Chicago Press

Clarke, R.V.G. and McGrath, G. (1990) 'Cash reduction and robbery prevention in Australian betting shops', *Security Journal*, 1, 160–63

Clarke, R.V.G. and Mayhew, P. (eds) (1980) *Designing Out Crime*, London: HMSO

Clarke, R.V.G. and Mayhew, P. (1988) 'The British Gas suicide story and its criminological implications', in Morris, N. and Tonry, M. (eds) *Crime and Justice: A Review of Research, Vol. 10*, 79–116, Chicago: University of Chicago Press

Clegg, M. and Kirwan, S. (2006) *Police Service Strength 2006*, HOSB 13/06, London: Home Office

Clifford, B.R. and Hollin, C.R. (1981) 'Effects of the type of incident and the number of perpetrators on eyewitness memory', *Journal of Applied Psychology*, 66, 364–370

Clifford, B.R. and Richards, V. (1977) 'Comparison of recall by policemen and civilians under conditions of long and short durations of exposure', *Perceptual and Motor Skills*, 45, 503–12

Clinard, M. (1946) 'Criminological theories of violations of wartime regulations', *American Sociological Review*, 11, 258–70

Clinard, M. (1964) 'The theoretical implications of anomie and deviant behaviour', in Clinard, M. (ed.) *Anomie and Deviant Behaviour*, New York: The Free Press

Clinard, M. and Yeager, P. (1980) *Corporate Crime*, New York: The Free Press

Cloward, R. and Ohlin, L. (1960) *Delinquency and Opportunity: A theory of delinquent gangs*, New York: The Free Press

Coggans, N. and McKellar, S. (1994) 'Drug use amongst peers: Peer pressure or peer preference?', *Drugs: Education, Prevention and Policy*, 1, 1, 15–26

Coggans, N. and McKellar, S. (1995) *The Facts about Alcohol, Aggression and Adolescence*, London: Cassell

Cohen, A.K. (1955) *Delinquent Boys: The culture of the gang*, New York: The Free Press

Cohen, A.K. and Short, J. (1961) 'Juvenile delinquency', in Merton, R. and Nisbet, R. (eds) *Contemporary Social Problems*, New York: Harcourt, Brace and World

Cohen, E.S. (2001) *The Politics of Globalization in the United States*, Washington DC: Georgetown University Press

Cohen, J. M. (2002) *Inside Appellate Courts: The impact of court organization on judicial decision making in the United States Courts of Appeals*, Ann Arbor: University of Michigan Press

Cohen, L.E. and Felson, M. (1979) 'Social change and crime rate trends: A routine activities approach', *American Sociological Review*, 44, 588–608

Cohen, P. (1972) 'Subcultural conflict and working class community', in Hall, S., Hobson, D., Lowe, A. and Willis, P. (eds) *Culture, Media, Language*, London: Hutchinson

Cohen, S. (1972) *Folk Devils and Moral Panics: The creation of the Mods and Rockers,* London: MacGibbon and Kee

Cohen, S. (1980) *Folk Devils and Moral Panics,* 2nd edn, London: Martin Robertson

Cohen, S. (1980) *Folk Devils and Moral Panics,* 3rd edn, London: Routledge

Cohen, S. (1981) 'Footprints in the sand: A further report on criminology and the sociology of deviance in Britain', in Fitzgerald, M., McLennean, G., and Pawson, J. (eds) *Crime and Society,* London: Routledge and Open University Press

Cohen, S. (1985) *Visions of Social Control,* Cambridge: Polity Press

Cohen, S. (1986) 'Community Control: To demystify or to reaffirm?', in Bianchi, H. and van Swaaningen, R. (eds) *Abolitionism: Towards a non repressive approach to crime,* Amsterdam: Free University Press

Cohen, S. (1988) *Against Criminology,* New Brunswick, NJ: Transaction

Cohen, S. (1993) 'Human rights and crimes of the state: The culture of denial', *Australian and New Zealand Journal of Criminology,* 26, 2, 97–115

Cohen, S. (1996) 'Crime and politics: spot the difference', *British Journal of Sociology,* 47, 1–21

Cohen, S. (2002) *Folk Devils and Moral Panics,* 30th anniversary edition, London: Routledge

Cohen, S. and Young, J. (eds) (1973) *The Manufacture of News: Deviance, social problems and the mass media,* London: Constable

Coleman, A. (1985) *Utopia on Trial,* London: Hilary Shipman

Coleman, C. and Moynihan, J. (1996) *Understanding Crime Data: Haunted by the dark figure,* Buckingham: Open University Press

Coleman, K., Jansson, K., Kaiza, P. and Reed, E. (2007) *Homicides, Firearm Offences and Intimate Violence 2005/06* (Supplementary volume 1 to *Crime in England and Wales 2005/06*), HOSB 02/07, London: Home Office

Coleman, L. and Cater, S. (2005) *Underage 'risky' drinking: Motivations and outcomes,* York: Joseph Rowntree Foundation

Collier, R. (1998) *Masculinities, crime and criminology: Men, heterosexuality and the criminal(ised)other,* London: Sage.

Commission for Racial Equality (2003) *The Murder of Zahid Mubarek,* London: CRE

Conklin, J. (1977) *Illegal but not Criminal: Business crime in America,* Englewood Cliffs, NJ: Prentice Hall

Connell, R. (1987) *Gender and Power: Society, the person and sexual politics,* Cambridge: Polity Press

Connell, R. and Messerschmidt, J. (2005) 'Hegemonic masculinity: Rethinking the concept', *Gender and Society,* 19, 6, 829–59

Cookson, H. (1992) 'Alcohol use and offence type in young offenders', *British Journal of Criminology,* 32, 3, 352–60

Cope, N. (2003) 'Crime analysis: principles and practice', in Newburn, T. (ed.) *Handbook of Policing,* Cullompton: Willan

Corbett, C. (2003) *Car Crime,* Cullompton: Willan Publishing

Cordray, D.S. and Lipsey, M.W. (1986) 'Program evaluation and program research', *Evaluation Studies: A Review Annual,* Beverley Hills, CA: Sage

Cornish, D. and Clarke, R.V.G. (1986) *The Reasoning Criminal,* New York: Springer Verlag

Cornish, D.B. and Clarke, R.V.G. (1987) 'Understanding crime displacement', *Criminology* 25, 4, 933–47

Cornish, D. and Clarke, R.V.G. (2006) 'The rational choice perspective', in Henry, S. and Lanier, M. (eds) *The Essential Criminology Reader,* Boulder, CO: Westview Press

Corston, Baroness J. (2007) *The Corston Report,* London: Home Office

Coser, L.A. (1977) *Masters of Sociological Thought: Ideas in historical and social context,* New York: Harcourt Brace Jovanovich

Coser, L.A. (1979) 'American trends', in Bottomore, T. and Nisbet, R. (eds) *A History of Sociological Analysis,* London: Heinemann

Cottle, S. (2006) *Mediatized Conflict,* Maidenhead: Open University Press

Council of Europe (2005) *Report by Mr Alvaro Gil-Robles, Commissioner for Human Rights on his visit to the United Kingdom, 4–12 November 2004,* Strasbourg: Council of Europe

Court of Appeal (2005) *Review of the Legal Year 2004/05,* Court of Appeal: Criminal Division (available at: www.hmcourts-service.gov.uk/cms/files/crim_div_review_2004_05.pdf)

Cowie, J., Cowie, V. and Slater, E. (1968) *Delinquency in Girls,* London: Heinemann

Cox, S., Lesieur, H.R., Rosenthal, R.J. and Volberg, R.A. (1997) *Problem and Pathological Gambling in America: The National picture,* Washington, DC: National Council on Problem Gambling

Coyle, A. (2002) *A Human Rights Approach to Prison Management: A handbook for prison staff,* London: International Centre for Prison Studies

Coyle, A. (2005) *Understanding Prisons: Key issues in policy and practice,* Maidenhead: Open University Press

Craig, J. (undated) *Almost adult: Some correlates of alcohol, tobacco and illicit drug use among a sample of 16 and 17 year olds in Northern Ireland,* NISRA Occasional Paper No. 3, Belfast: Northern Ireland Statistics and Research Agency

Crawford, A. (1997) *The Local Governance of Crime,* Oxford: Clarendon Press

Crawford, A. (1998) *Crime Prevention and Community Safety,* Harlow: Longman

Crawford, A. (2001) 'Joined up but fragmented: contradiction, ambiguity and ambivalence at the heart of New Labour's "third way"', in Matthews, R. and Pitts, J. (eds) *Crime, Disorder and Community Safety,* London: Routledge

Crawford, A. (ed.) (2002) *Crime and Insecurity: The governance of safety in Europe,* Cullompton: Willan Publishing

Crawford, A. (2003) 'The pattern of policing in the UK: Policing beyond the police', in Newburn, T. (ed.) *Handbook of Policing,* Cullompton: Willan

Crawford, A. (2007) 'Crime prevention and community safety', in Maguire, M., Morgan, R. and Reiner, R. (eds) *Oxford Handbook of Criminology,* 4th edn, Oxford: Oxford University Press

Crawford, A., Jones, T., Woodhouse, T. and Young, J. (1990) *Second Islington Crime Survey,* London: Middlesex Polytechnic

Crawford, A., Lister, S., Blackburn, S. and Burnett, J. (2005) *Plural Policing: The mixed economy of visible patrols in England and Wales,* Bristol: Policy Press

Crawford, A. and Newburn, T. (2002) 'Recent developments in restorative justice for young people in England and Wales: community participation and restoration', *British Journal of Criminology,* 45, 2, 476–95

Crawford, A. and Newburn, T. (2003) *Youth Offending and Restorative Justice,* Cullompton: Willan

Crawley E. (2004) *Doing Prison Work: The public and private lives of prison officers,* Cullompton: Willan

Cressey, D. (1953) *Other People's Money: A study in the social psychology of embezzlement,* Glencoe, IL: The Free Press

Cressey, D. (1969) *Theft of the Nation: The structure and operations of organized crime in America,* New York: Harper and Row

Cressey, D. (1972) *Organized Crime and Criminal Organizations,* Cambridge: Heffer

Cretney, A. and Davis, G. (1995) *Punishing Violence,* London: Routledge

Critchley, T.A. (1970) *The Conquest of Violence: Order and liberty in Britain,* London: Constable

Croall, H. (1992) *White Collar Crime,* Milton Keynes: Open University Press

Croall, H. (2001) *Understanding White Collar Crime,* Buckingham: Open University Press

Croall, H. (2007) 'Food crime, in Beirne, P. and South, N. (eds) *Issues in Green Criminology: Confronting harms against environments, humanity and other animals,* Cullompton: Willan

Cromwell, P. (1991) 'The burglar's perspective', in Roberts, A. (ed.) *Critical Issues in Criminal Justice,* London: Sage

Crowe, R. (1974) 'An adoption study of anti-social personality', *Archives of General Psychiatry,* 31, 785–91

Crown Prosecution Service (2006) *Annual Report 2005–06* (available at: http://www.cps.gov.uk/Publications/reports/index.html)

Cullen, F.T. and Agnew, R. (2006) *Criminological Theory: Past to present,* New York: Oxford University Press

Cullen, F.T., Gendreau, P., Jarjoura, G. and Wright, J. (1997) 'Crime and the bell curve: lessons from intelligent criminology', *Crime and Delinquency,* 3, 4, 387–411

Currie, E. (1974) Review of *The New Criminology, Issues in Criminology,* 9, 123–142

Currie, E. (1985) *Confronting Crime: An American challenge,* New York: Pantheon

Dahrendorf, R. (1959) *Class and Class Conflict in an Industrial Society,* London: Routledge and Kegan Paul

Dalgaard, O.S. and Kringlen, E.A. (1976) 'A Norwegian Twin Study of Criminality', *British Journal of Criminology,* 16, 213–232

Dalton, K. (1977) *The Premenstrual Syndrome and Progresterone Therapy,* London: Heinemann

Daly, K. (1997) 'Different ways of conceptualizing sex/gender in feminist theory and their implications for criminology', *Theoretical Criminology,* 1, 1, 25–51

Daly, K. (2000) 'Revisiting the relationship between retributive and restorative justice', in Strang, H. and Braithwaite, J. (eds) *Restorative Justice: Philosophy to practice,* Aldershot: Dartmouth/Ashgate

Daly, K. (2003) 'Mind the gap: restorative justice in theory and practice', in von Hirsch, A., Roberts, J., Bottoms, A.E., Roach, K. and Schiff, M. (eds) *Restorative justice and criminal justice: Competing or reconcilable paradigms?* 219–36, Oxford: Hart Publishing

Daly, K. and Chesney-Lind, M. (1988) 'Feminism and criminology', *Justice Quarterly,* 5, 497–538

Darbyshire, D. (2002) 'Magistrates', in McConville, M. and Wilson, R. (eds) *Handbook of the Criminal Justice Process,* Oxford: Oxford University Press

Davidoff, L. and Dowds, L (1989) *Recent trends in violence against the person in England and Wales,* Home Office Research and Planning Unit, Research Bulletin, No. 27, London: Home Office

Davies, J.B. (1992) *The Myth of Addiction*, Philadelphia: Harwood Academic Publishers

Davis, D. and Leo, R. (2006) 'Strategies for preventing false confessions and their consequences', in Kebbell, M.R. and Davies, G.M. (eds) *Practical Psychology for Forensic Investigations and Prosecutions*, Chichester: Wiley

Davis, M. (1990) *City of Quartz*, London: Vintage

D'Cruze, S., Walklate, S. and Pegg, S. (2006) *Murder*, Cullompton: Willan

DeKeseredy, W. and Schwartz, M. (1991) 'British and U.S. left realism: a critical comparison', *International Journal of Offender Therapy and Comparative Criminology*, 35, 248–262

Denham, J. (2002) *Building Cohesive Communities: A report of the ministerial group on public order and community cohesion*, London: Home Office

Dennis, N. and Mallon, R. (1997) 'Confident policing in Hartlepool', in Dennis, N. (ed.) *Zero Tolerance: Policing a free society*, London: Institute for Economic Affairs

Denton, B. (2001) *Dealing: Women in the drug economy*, Sydney: University of New South Wales Press

Department of Health (2002) *Prevalence of HIV and Hepatitis Infections in the UK*, London: Department of Health

Department of Health (2004) *Alcohol Harm Reduction Strategy*, London: Department of Health

Dhami, M.K. (2002) 'Do Bail Information Schemes Really Affect Bail Decisions?', *The Howard Journal of Criminal Justice*, 41, 3, 245–262

Dhami, M.K. and Ayton, P. (2001) 'Bailing and jailing the fast and frugal way', *Journal of Behavioral Decision Making*, 14, 141–168

Dignan, J. (1999) 'The Crime and Disorder Act and the Prospects for Restorative Justice', *Criminal Law Review*, 48

Dignan, J. (2000) *Youth Justice Pilots Evaluation Interim Report of Repartive Work and Youth Offending Teams*, London: Home Office

Dignan, J. (2005) *Understanding Victims and Restorative Justice*, Maidenhead: Open University Press

Dillon, L., Chivite-Matthews, N., Grewal, I., Brown, R., Webster, S., Weddell, E., Brown, G. and Smith, N. (2006) *Risk, Protective Factors and Resilience to Drug Use: Identifying resilient young people and learning from their experience*, London: Home Office

Di Nicola, A. (2005) 'Trafficking in human beings and smuggling of migrants', in Reichel, P. (ed.) *Handbook of Transnational Crime and Justice*, Thousand Oaks, CA: Sage

Dingwall, G. (2006) *Alcohol and Crime*, Cullompton: Willan

Dinsmor, A. and Goldsmith, A. (2005) 'Scottish Policing – A historical perspective', in Donnelly, D. and Scott, K. (eds) *Policing Scotland*, Cullompton: Willan Publishing

Ditchfield, J. (1997) 'Actuarial prediction and risk assessment', *Prison Service Journal* 113

Ditton, J. (1975) *Contrology: Beyond the new criminology*, New York: Macmillan

Ditton, J. (1977) *Part-Time Crime*, London: Macmillan

Ditton, J. (1979) *Controlology*, London: Macmillan

Ditton, J. and Duffy, J. (1983) 'Bias in newspaper reporting of crime news', *British Journal of Criminology*, 23, 1, 159–165

Ditton, J. and Farrall, S. (2000) *The Fear of Crime*, Aldershot: Ashgate

Ditton, J., Farrall, S., Bannister, J., Gilchrist, E. and Pease, K. (1999) 'Reactions to victimization: why anger has been ignored', *Crime Prevention and Community Safety*, 1, 3, 37–54

Dixon, B. and Gadd, D. (2006) 'Getting the message? "New Labour" and the criminalization of hate', *Criminology and Criminal Justice*, 6, 3, 309–328

Dobash, R.E. and Dobash, R.P. (1979) *Violence Against Wives*, Basingstoke: Macmillan

Dobash, R.E. and Dobash, R.P. (1992) *Women, Violence and Social Change*, London: Routledge

Dobash, R., Cavanagh, K., Dobash, R., and Lewis, R. (2001) *Homicide in Britain: Risk factors, situational contexts and lethal intentions*, ESRC report, University of Manchester

Dobash, R., Dobash, R., and Gutteridge, S. (1986) *The Imprisonment of Women*, Oxford: Blackwell Publishing

Dobrin, A. (2001) 'The risk of offending on homicide victimization: A case control study', *Journal of Research in Crime and Delinquency*, 41, 3–36

Dodd, T., Nicholas, S., Povey, D., and Walker A. (2004) *Crime in England and Wales 2003/04*, HOSB 10/04, London: Home Office

Doig, A. (2006) *Fraud*, Cullompton: Willan

Donzelot, J. (1980) *The Policing of Families*, London: Hutchinson

Dorling, D. (2004) 'Prime Suspect: Murder in Britain', in Hillyard *et al.* (eds) *Beyond Criminology: Taking harm seriously*, London: Pluto Press

Dorn, N. (1983) *Alcohol, youth and the state*, London: Croom Helm

Dorn, N. and South, N. (1982) 'Of males and markets: A critical review of youth culture theory', *Research Paper 1, Centre for Occupational and Community Research*, London: Middlesex Polytechnic

Dorn, N., Levi, M. and King, L. (2005) *Literature Review on Upper Level Drug Trafficking,* Home Office Online Report 22/05, London: Home Office

Dorn, N., Murji, K. and South, N. (1992) *Traffickers,* London: Routledge

Douglas, M. and Wildavsky, A. (1982) *Risk and Culture,* Los Angeles: University of California Press

Downes, D. (1966) *The Delinquent Solution: A study in subcultural theory,* London: Routledge and Kegan Paul

Downes, D. (1979) 'Praxis makes perfect', in Downes, D. and Rock, P. (eds) *Deviant Interpretations: Problems in criminological theory,* Oxford: Martin Robertson

Downes, D. (1989) 'Thatcherite values and crime', *Samizdat,* May/June

Downes, D. and Hansen, K. (2006) 'Welfare and punishment in comparative perspective', in Armstrong, S. and McAra, L. (eds) *Perspectives on Punishment,* Oxford: Oxford University Press

Downes, D. and Morgan, R. (1994) 'Hostages to Fortune? The politics of law and order in post-war Britain', in Maguire, M., Morgan, R. and Reiner, R. (eds) *The Oxford Handbook of Criminology,* 1st edn, Oxford: Oxford University Press

Downes, D. and Morgan, R. (2007) 'No turning back: the politics of law and order into the millennium', in Maguire, M., Morgan, R. and Reiner, R. (eds) *The Oxford Handbook of Criminology,* 4th edn, Oxford: Oxford University Press

Downes, D. and Rock, P. (1982) *Understanding Deviance,* Oxford: Oxford University Press

Downes, D. and Rock, P. (2003) *Understanding Deviance,* 4th edn, Oxford: Oxford University Press

Downes, D. and Rock, P. (2007) *Understanding Deviance,* 5th edn, Oxford: Oxford University Press

Dubber, M. (2002) *Victims in the War on Crime,* New York: New York University Press

Dubois, D. (2002) 'The attacks of 11 September: EU-US cooperation against terrorism in the field of justice and home affairs', *European Foreign Affairs Review,* 7, 317–335

Duff, P. (1998a) 'Crime control, due process and the "case for the prosecution"', *British Journal of Criminology,* 38, 611–15

Duff, P. (1988b) 'The "victim movement" and legal reform', in Maguire, M. and Ponting, J. (eds) *Victims of Crime: A new deal?* Milton Keynes: Open University Press

Duff, R.A. (2003) *Punishment, Communication and Community,* Oxford: Oxford University Press

Duff, R.A. and Garland, D. (eds) (1994) *A Reader on Punishment,* Oxford: Oxford University Press

Duffield, M. (2005) *Global Governance and the New Wars,* London: Zed Books

Dugdale, R. (1895) *The Jukes: A study in crime, pauperism, disease and heredity,* New York

Dunning, E., Murphy, P., Newburn, T. and Waddington, I. (1987) 'Violent disorders in twentieth century Britain', in Gaskell, G. and Benewick, R. (eds) *The Crowd in Contemporary Britain,* London: Sage

Durkheim, E. (1938) *The Rules of Sociological Method,* New York: The Free Press

Durkheim, E. (1964/1972) *The Division of Labour in Society,* New York: The Free Press

Durkheim, E. (1970) *Suicide: A study in sociology,* London: Routledge and Kegan Paul

Dyson, S. and Boswell, G. (2006) 'Sickle cell anaemia and deaths in custody in the UK and USA', *The Howard Journal of Criminal Justice,* 45, 1, 14–28

East, K. and Campbell, S. (1999) *Aspects of Youth Crime: Young Offenders 1999,* London: Home Office

Eaton, M. (1986) *Justice for Women?,* Milton Keynes: Open University Press

Edgar, K., O'Donnell, I. and Martin, C. (2003) *Prison Violence: The dynamics of conflict, fear and power,* Cullompton: Willan

Edmunds, M., Hough, M. and Urquia, N. (1996) *Tackling local drug markets,* London: Home Office

Edwards, A. and Gill, P. (eds) (2003) *Transnational Organised Crime,* London: Routledge

Edwards, S. (1984) *Women on Trial,* Manchester: Manchester University Press

Edwards, S.M. (1981) *Female Sexuality and the Law,* London: Martin Robertson

Egeth, H.E. and McCloskey, M. (1984) 'Expert testimony about eyewitness behavior: Is it safe and effective?', in Wells, G.L. and Loftus, E.F. (eds) *Eyewitness Testimony: Psychological Perspectives,* Cambridge: Cambridge University Press

Eisner, M. (2001) 'Modernization, self-control and lethal violence: The long-term dynamics of European homicide rates in theoretical perspective', *British Journal of Criminology,* 41, 618–38

Ekblom, P. (2005) 'Designing products against crime', in Tilley, N. (ed.) *Handbook of Crime Prevention and Community Safety,* Cullompton: Willan

Ekblom, P. and Pease, K. (1995) 'Evaluating crime prevention', in Tonry, M. and Farrington, D.P. (eds) *Building a Safer Society: Crime and Justice: A Review of Research, Vol. 19,* Chicago: University of Chicago Press

Ekman, P. (1992) *Telling Lies: Clues to deceit in the marketplace, politics and marriage*, New York: W.W. Norton

Ekman, P. (1996) 'Why don't we catch liars?', *Social Research*, 63, 3, 801–817

Eley, T., Lichtenstein, P. and Stevenson, J. (1999) 'Sex differences in the etiology of aggressive and nonaggressive antisocial behaviour: results from two twin studies', *Child Development*, 70, 1, 155–168

Elias, N. (1978) *The Civilizing Process: The history of manners*, Oxford: Blackwell Publishing

Elias, N. (1982) *State Formation and Civilization*, Oxford: Blackwell Publishing

Elliot, D.S. *et al.* (1989) *Multiple Problem Youth: Delinqunecy, substance use, and mental health problems*, New York: Springer-Verlag

Ellis, T., Tedstone, C. and Curry, D. (2004) *Improving race relations in prisons: what works?* Home Office Online Report 12/04, London: Home Office

Elwork, A., Sales, B. and Suggs, D. (1981) 'The trial: a research review', in Sales, B. (ed.) *The Trial Process*, New York: Plenum

Emsley, C. (1983) *Policing and Its Context, 1750–1870*, New York: Schocken

Emsley, C. (1996) *The English Police: A political and social history*, Harlow: Longman

Emsley, C. (2003) 'The birth and development of the police', in Newburn, T. (ed.) *Handbook of Policing*, Cullompton: Willan

Engels, F. (1969) *The Condition of the Working Class in England*, London: Panther

Ennis, P. (1967) *Criminal Victimization in the United States: A report of a national survey*, Washington DC: President's Commission on Law Enforcement and Administration of Justice.

Ericson, R. (1991) 'Mass media, crime, law and justice', *British Journal of Criminology*, 31, 3, 219–49

Ericson, R., Baranek, P. and Chan, J. (1987) *Visualising Deviance*, Milton Keynes: Open University Press

Ericson, R., Baranek, P. and Chan, J. (1991) *Representing Order*, Milton Keynes: Open University Press

Ericson, R. and Carriere, K. (1994) 'The fragmentation of criminology', in Nelken, D. (ed.) *The Futures of Criminology*, London: Sage

Ericson, R. and Haggerty, K. (1997) *Policing the Risk Society*, Oxford: Clarendon Press

Erikson, K.T. (1963) 'Notes on the sociology of deviance', *Social Problems*, 9, 307–314

Erikson, K.T. (1966) *Wayward Puritans: A study in the sociology of deviance*, New York: Wiley

Estabrook, A. (1916) *The Jukes in 1915*, Washington DC: Carnegie Institute of Washington

European Monitoring Centre for Drugs and Drug Addiction (2003) *The State of the Drugs Problem in the EU and Norway*, Luxembourg: EMCDDA

Evans, R. (1994) 'Cautioning: Counting the cost of retrenchment', *Criminal Law Review*, 566–575

Ewing, K.D. (2004) 'The futility of the Human Rights Act', *Public Law*, 829–852

Eysenck, H.K. (1970) *The Structure of Human Personality*, London: Methuen

Eysenck, H.K. (1977) *Crime and Personality*, 3rd edn, London: Routledge and Kegan Paul

Eysenck, H. and Gudjonsson, G. (1989) *The Causes and Cures of Criminality*, New York: Plenum Press

Farquhar, C. with Das, R. (1999) 'Are focus groups suitable for "sensitive" topics?' in Barbour, R. and Kitzinger, J. (eds) *Developing Focus Group Research*, London: Sage

Farrall, S. and Gadd, D. (2004) 'The frequency of the fear of crime', *British Journal of Criminology*, 44, 1, 127–132

Farrell, G. (1995) 'Preventing repeat victimization', *Crime and Justice*, 19, 469–534

Farrell, G. (2005) 'Progress and prospects in the prevention of repeat victimization', in Tilley, N. (ed.) *Handbook of Crime Prevention and Community Safety*, Cullompton:Willan

Farrell, G., Edmunds A., Hobbs L. and Laycock G. (2000) 'RV Snapshot: UK Policing and Repeat Victimisation', *Crime Reduction Research Series, Paper 5*, London, UK: Home Office

Farrell, G. and Pease, K. (2006) 'Criminology and Security', in Gill, M. (ed.) *The Handbook of Security*, Basingstoke: Macmillan

Farrington, D.P. (1986a) 'Explaining the link between problem drinking and delinquency', *Addiction*, 91, 4, 498–501

Farrington, D.P. (1986b) 'Stepping stones to adult criminal careers', in Olweus, D., Block, J., and Radke-Yarrow, M. (eds) *Development of Antisocial and Prosocial Behavior*, New York: Academic Press

Farrington, D.P. (1995) 'The development of offending and antisocial behaviour from childhood: key findings from the Cambridge Study in Delinquent Development', *Journal of Child Psychology and Psychiatry*, 36, 929–964

Farrington, D.P. (1997) 'Evaluating a community crime prevention programme', *Evaluation*, 3, 2, 157–173

Farrington, D.P. (1998) 'Evaluating "communities that care": Realistic scientific considerations', *Evaluation*, 4, 2, 204–210

Farrington, D.P. and Loeber, R. (1999) 'Transatlantic replicability of risk factors in the development of delinquency', in Cohen, P., Slomkowski, C. and Robbins, L.N. (eds) *Historical and Geographical Influences on Psychopathology*, Mahwah, NJ: Lawrence Erlbaum

Farrington, D.P., Barnes, G. and Lambert, S. (1996) 'The concentration of offending in families', *Legal and Criminological Psychology,* 1, 47–63

Farrington, D.P., Biron, L. and LeBlanc, M. (1982) 'Personality and delinquency in London and Montreal', in Gunn, J. and Farrington, D. (eds) *Abnormal Offenders, Delinquency and the Criminal Justice System,* Chichester: Wiley

Farrington, D.P. and Lambert, S. (1994) 'Differences between burglars and violent offenders', *Psychology, Crime and Law,* 1, 107–116

Farrington, D.P., Langan, P., and Tonry, M. (2004) *Cross-National Studies in Crime and Justice,* Washington DC: US Department of Justice

Farrington, D.P., Loeber, R., Van Kammen, W.B. (1990) *Straight and Devious Pathways from Childhood to Adulthood,* Cambridge: Cambridge University Press

Farrington, D.P. and Morris, A. (1983) 'Sex, sentencing and reconviction', *British Journal of Criminology,* 23, 229–48

Farrington, D.P. and Welsh, B. (2007) *Saving Children from a Life of Crime,* New York: Oxford University Press

Fattah, E.A. (1991) *Understanding Criminal Victimization,* Scarborough, Ontario: Prentice Hall

Fattah, E.A. (1992) *Critical Victimology,* London: Macmillan

Faulkner, D. (1998) 'A principled response', *Criminal Justice Matters,* 31, 3–4

Fawcett Society (2004) *Women and the Criminal Justice System: Report of the Commission on Women and Criminal Justice System,* London: Fawcett Society

Federal Bureau of Investigation (2005) *Financial Crimes Report to the Public* (available at: http://www.fbi.gov/publications/financial/fcs_report052005/fcs_report052005.htm)

Feeley, M. (2006) 'Origins of actuarial justice', in Armstrong, S. and McAra, L. (eds) *Perspectives on Punishment,* Oxford: Oxford University Press

Feeley, M. and Little, D. (1991) 'The vanishing female: The decline of women in the criminal process, 1687–1912', *Law and Society Review,* 25, 4, 719–57

Feeley, M. and Simon, J. (1992) 'The new penology: notes on the emerging strategy of corrections and its implications', *Criminology,* 30, 4, 449–474

Feeley, M. and Simon, J. (1994) 'Actuarial justice: The emerging new criminal law', in Nelken, D. (ed.) *The Futures of Criminology,* London: Sage

Feilzer, M. and Hood, R. (2004) *Differences or discrimination? Minority ethnic young people in the youth justice system,* London: Youth Justice Board

Felsen, D. and Kalaitzidis, A. (2005) 'A historical overview of transnational crime', in Reichel, P. (ed.) *Handbook of Transnational Crime and Justice,* Thousand Oaks, CA: Sage

Felson, M. (2000) 'The routine activity approach as a general crime theory', in Simpson, S. (ed.) *Of Crime and Criminality,* Thousand Oaks, CA: Pine Forge Press

Felson, M. (1998) *Crime and Everyday Life,* 2nd edn, Thousand Oaks, CA: Pine Forge Press

Felson, M. (2002) *Crime and Everyday Life,* 3rd edn, Thousand Oaks, CA: Pine Forge Press

Felson, M. and Clarke, R.V.G. (1998) 'Opportunity makes the thief: Practical theory for crime prevention', in Webb, B. (ed.) *Police Research Series,* paper 98

Ferguson, D., Lynskey, M. and Horwood, J. (1996) 'Alcohol misuse and juvenile offending in adolescence', *Addiction,* 91, 4, 483–94

Ferraro, K.F. (1995) *Fear of Crime: Interpreting victimization risk,* Albany, NY: State University of New York Press

Ferri, E. (1900) *Socialism and Modern Science: Darwin, Spencer, Marx,* (translated by La Monte, R. R.), New York: Hutchinson

Ferri, E. (1917) *Criminal Sociology,* (translated by J.I. Kelly and J. Lisle and edited by W.W. Smithers), Boston: Little, Brown and Company

Field, S. (1990) *Trends in Crime and their Interpretation: A study of recorded crime in post-war England and Wales,* London: Home Office

Fielding, N. (1981) *The National Front,* London: Routledge and Kegan Paul

Finch, E. (2002) 'Stalking the perfect stalking law: An evaluation of the efficacy of the Protection from Harassment Act 1997', *Criminal Law Review,* 703–718

Finney, A. (2004a) *Alcohol and sexual violence: key findings from the research,* Home Office Research Findings 215, London: Home Office

Finney, A. (2004b) *Alcohol and intimate partner violence: key findings from the research,* Home Office Research Findings 216, London: Home Office

Finney, A. (2006) *Domestic Violence, sexual assault and stalking: findings from the 2004/05 British Crime Survey,* Home Office Online Report 12/06

Fisher, Sir, H. (1977) *The Confait Case: Report,* London: HMSO

Fitzgerald, M., Hough, M., Joseph, I. and Qureshi, T. (2002) *Policing for London,* Cullompton: Willan

Fitzgerald, M. and Marshall, P. (1996) 'Ethnic minorities in British prisons: Some research implications', in Matthews, R. and Francis, P. (eds) *Prisons 2000,* Basingstoke: Macmillan

Gibson, E. (1975) *Homicide in England and Wales 1967–1971,* Home Office Research Study, No. 31, London

Gibson, M. (2002) *Born to Crime: Cesare Lombroso and the origins of biological criminology,* New York: Praeger Press

Giddens, A. (ed.) (1974) *Positivism and Sociology,* London: Heinemann

Giddens, A. (1981) *A Contemporary Critique of Historical Materialism,* Basingstoke: Macmillan

Giddens, A. (1990) *The Consequences of Modernity,* Cambridge: Polity Press

Gilchrist, E., Johnson, R., Takriti, R., Weston, S., Beech, A. and Kebbell, M. (2003) *Domestic violence offenders: Characteristics and offending related needs,* Home Office Research Findings 217, London: Home Office

Gill, M.L. (2000) *Commercial Robbery: Offenders' perspectives on security and crime prevention,* London: Blackstone Press

Gill, O. (1977) *Luke Street: Housing policy, conflict and the creation of the delinquent area,* London: Macmillan

Gilling, D. (1997) *Crime Prevention: Theory, policy and practice,* London: Routledge

Gilling, D. (1997) *Crime Prevention and Community Safety: New directions,* London: Sage

Giordano, P.G. and Rockwell, S.M. (2000) 'Differential association theory and female crime', in Simpson, S. (ed.) *Of Crime and Criminality,* Thousand Oaks, CA: Pine Forge Press

Giuliani, R. (2002) *Leadership,* New York: Little Brown

Glaser, B.G. and Strauss, A.L. (1967) *The Discovery of Grounded Theory: Strategies for qualitative research,* Hawthorne, NY: Aldine de Gruyter

Glueck, E. and Gleuck, S. (1950) *Unraveling Juvenile Delinquency,* New York: The Commonwealth Fund

Glueck, E. and Gleuck, S. (1956) *Physique and Delinquency,* New York: Harper

Glidewell, Rt Hon Sir I. (1998) *Review of the Crown Prosecution Service,* London: The Stationery Office

Gobert, J. and Punch, M. (2003) *Rethinking Corporate Crime,* London: Butterworths

Goddard, E. (1998) *Young Teenagers and Alcohol in 1997,* London: The Stationery Office

Goddard, H.H. (1913) *The Kallikak Family: A study in the heredity of feeble-mindedness,* New York: Macmillan

Godfrey, B. and Lawrence, P. (2005) *Crime and Justice 1750–1950,* Cullompton: Willan

Goffman, E. (1961) *Asylums: Essays on the social situation of mental patients and other inmates,* Harmondsworth: Penguin

Goffman, E. (1963) *Behavior in Public Places: Notes on the social organization of gatherings,* Glencoe, Il: The Free Press

Goffman, E. (1968) *Asylums: Essays on the social situation of mental patients and other inmates,* Harmondsworth: Penguin

Gofton, L. (1990) 'On the town: Drink and the new lawlessness', *Youth and Policy,* 29, 33–9

Goggin, C. and Gendreau, P. (2006) 'The implementation of quality services in offender rehabilitation programs', in Hollin, C.R. and Palmer, E.J. (eds) *Offending Behaviour Programmes: Development, application, and controversies,* Chichester: Wiley

Gold, R. (1969) 'Roles in sociological field observation', in McCall, G. and Simmons, J. (eds) *Issues in Participant Observation,* London: Addison Wesley

Goldblatt, P. and Lewis, C. (1998) *Reducing Offending: A review of research evidence on ways of dealing with offending behaviour,* Home Office Research Study 187, London: Home Office

Goldson, B. and Coles, D. (2005) *In the Care of the State? Child deaths in penal custody in England and Wales,* London: Inquest

Goode, E. and Ben-Yehuda, N. (1994) *Moral Panics: The social construction of deviance,* Oxford: Blackwell Publishing

Goodey, J. (2005) *Victims and Victimology: Research, policy and practice,* Harlow: Longman

Gordon, R. (1987) 'SES versus IQ in the Race-IQ-Delinquency model', *International Journal of Sociology and Social Policy,* 7, 3, 30–96

Görgen, T. (2006) '"As if I just didn't exist" – elder abuse and neglect in nursing homes', in Wahidin, A. and Cain, M. (eds) *Ageing, Crime and Society,* Cullompton: Willan

Goring, C. (1913) *The English Convict: A statistical study,* London: His Majesty's Stationery Office

Gottfredson, M.R. and Hirschi, T. (eds) (1987) *Positive Criminology,* Newbury Park, CA: Sage Publications

Gottfredson, M. and Hirschi, T. (1990) *A General Theory of Crime,* Stanford: Stanford University Press

Götz, M., Johnstone, E. and Ratcliffe, S. (1999) 'Criminality and antisocial behaviour in unselected men with chromosomal abnormalities', *Psychological Medicine,* 29, 953–962

Gould, S.J. (1995) 'Mismeasure by any measure', in Jacoby, R. and Glauberman, N. (eds) *The Bell Curve Debate,* New York: Times Books

Goulden, C. and Sondhi, A. (2001) *At the margins: drug use by vulnerable young people in the 1998/99 youth lifestyles survey,* Home Office Research Study No. 228, London: Home Office

Gouldner, A. (1968) 'The sociologist as partisan: Sociology and the welfare state', *American Sociologist*, 3, 103–16

Gouldner, A. (1973) Foreword, in, Taylor, I., Walton, P. and Young, J. *The New Criminology: For a social theory of deviance*, London: Routledge and Kegan Paul

Grabosky, P. and Braithwaite, J. (1986) *Of Manners Gentle: Enforcement strategies of Australian business regulatory agencies*, Melbourne: Oxford University Press

Grace, S., Lloyd, C. and Smith, L. (1992) *Rape: From recording to conviction*, London: Home Office

Graham, J.G. and Bowling, B. (1995) *Young People and Crime*, Home Office Research Study No. 145, London: HMSO

Granville-Chapman, C., Smith, C. and Moloney, N. (2004) *Harm on Removal: Excessive force against failed asylum seekers*, London: Medical Foundation for the Care of Victims of Torture

Graycar, A. (2002) 'Trafficking in human beings', in Freilich, J., Newman, G., Giorna Shorham, S. and Addad, M. (eds) *Migration, Culture, Conflict and Crime*, Aldershot: Ashgate

Green, G.S. (1990) *Occupational Crime*, Chicago: Nelson-Hall

Green, P. and Grewcock, M. (2007) 'The war against illegal immigration: State crime and the construction of a European identity', *Current Issues in Criminal Justice*, 14, 1

Green, P. and Ward, T. (2004) *State Crime: Governments, violence and corruption*, London: Pluto Press

Green, P. and Ward, T. (2005) 'Special issue on State Crime', *British Journal of Criminology*, 45, 4

Greenberg, K.J. and Dratel, J.L. (2005) *The Torture Papers: The road to Abu Ghraib*, New York: Cambridge University Press

Greer, C. (2003) *Sex Crime and the Media*, Cullompton: Willan

Greer, C. (2005) 'Crime and media', in Hale, C., Hayward, K., Wahidin, A., and Wincup, E. (eds) *Criminology*, 152–82, Oxford: Oxford University Press

Greer, C. (2007) 'News media, victims and crime', in Davies, P., Francis, P. and Greer, C. (eds) *Victims, Crime and Society*, London: Sage

Gresswell, D.M., and Hollin, C.R. (1994) 'Multiple murder: A review', *British Journal of Criminology*, 34, 1

Griffiths, A. and Milne, B. (2006) 'Will it all end in tiers? Police interviews with suspects in Britain', in Williamson, T. (ed.) *The Handbook of Knowledge Based Policing: Current conception and future directions*, Chichester: Wiley

Gudjonsson, G.H. (2002) *The Psychology of Interrogations and Confessions: A handbook*, Chichester: Wiley

Gudjonsson, G.H. (2003) *The Psychology of Interrogations and Confessions: A handbook*, Chichester: Wiley

Gudjonsson, G.H. (2007) 'Investigative interviewing', in Newburn, T., Williamson, T. and Wright, A. (eds) *Handbook of Criminal Investigation*, Cullompton: Willan

Gudjonsson, G.H. and Hayward, L.R.C. (1998) *Forensic Psychology: A guide to practice*, London: Routledge

Gunn, J. and Bonn, J. (1971) 'Criminality and violence in epileptic prisoners', *British Journal of Psychiatry*, 118, 554, 337–43

Gunn, J. (1978) *Psychiatric Aspects of Imprisonment*, London: Academic Press

Gurr, T.R. (1976) *Rogues, Rebels and Reformers*, Beverley Hills, CA: Sage

Gurr, T.R. (1981) *Handbook of Political Conflict*, New York: Macmillan

Gurr, T.R. (1989) *Violence in America, Vol.1, The history of crime*, Newbury Park, CA, London: Sage

Haapasalo, J. and Pokela, E. (1999) 'Child-rearing and child abuse: Antecedents of criminal behaviour', *Aggression and Violent Behavior*, 4, 107–127

Hagell, A. and Newburn, T. (1994a) *Persistent Young Offenders*, London: Policy Studies Institute

Hagell, A. and Newburn, T. (1994b) *Young Offenders and the Media*, London: Policy Studies Institute

Hagan, J. (1987) *Modern Criminology*, Toronto: McGraw Hill

Hakim, S. and Rengert, G. (1981) *Crime Spillover*, Beverley Hills, CA: Sage

Hale, C. (1996) 'Fear of crime: A review of the literature', *International Review of Victimology*, 4, 79–150

Hall, S., Critcher, C., Jefferson, T., Clarke, J. and Roberts, B. (1978) *Policing the Crisis: Mugging, the state and law and order*, Basingstoke: Macmillan

Hall, S. and Jefferson, T. (eds) (1976) *Resistance through Rituals: Youth subcultures in post-war Britain*, New York: Holmes & Meier

Hall, S. (1982) 'The rediscovery of "ideology": Return of the repressed in media studies', in Gurevitch, M., Bennett, T., Curran, J. and Woolacott, J. (eds) *Culture, Society and the Media*, London: Methuen

Hamlyn, B. and Lewis, D. (2000) *Women Prisoners: A survey of their work and training experiences in custody and on release*, Home Office Research Study No. 208, London: Home Office

Hammersley, R., Marsland, L. and Reid, M. (2003) *Substance Use By Young Offenders: The impact of the normalization of drug use in the early years of the 21st century,* Home Office Research Study 261, London: Home Office

Hannah-Moffat, K. (2002) 'Creating choices? Reflecting on the choices', in Carlen, P. (ed) *Women and the Struggle for Justice,* Cullompton, Devon: Willan

Hanmer, J., Radford, J. and Stanko, E.A. (1989) *Women, Policing and Male Violence,* London: Routledge

Hansen, K. (2006) 'Gender differences in self-reported offending', in Heidensohn, F. (ed.) *Gender and Justice: New concepts and approaches,* Cullompton: Willan

Harcourt, B. (2001) *Illusion of Order,* Cambridge, MA: Harvard University Press

Harding, R. (1997) *Private Prisons and Public Accountability,* New Brunswick, NJ: Transaction

Harding, R. (2007) 'Inspecting prisons', in Jewkes, Y. (ed.) *Handbook on Prisons,* Cullompton: Willan

Harding, S. (1987) *Feminism and Methodology,* Milton Keynes: Open University Press

Hare, R.D. (1980) *The Hare Psychopathy Checklist,* North Tonawanda, NY: Multi-Health Systems

Harper, G. and Chitty, C. (2004) *The Impact of Corrections on Offending: A review of 'what works',* Home Office Research Study 291, London: Home Office

Harrington, R. *et al.* (2005) *Mental Health Needs and Effectiveness of Provision for Young Offenders in Custody and in the Community,* London: Youth Justice Board

Harris, R. (1994) 'Continuity and change: probation and politics in contemporary Britain', *International Journal of Offender Therapy and Comparative Criminology,* 31, 1

Harrison, K. (2007) 'The high risk sex offender strategy in England and Wales: Is chemical castration an option?', *The Howard Journal of Criminal Justice,* 46, 1, 16–31

Hartless, J., Ditton, J., Nair, G. and Phillips, S. (1995) 'More sinned against than sinning: A study of young teenagers' experiences of crime', *British Journal of Criminology,* 35, 1, 114–33

Harvey, D. (1989) *The Condition of Postmodernity,* Cambridge: Polity Press

Harvey, J. (2007) *Young Men in Prison,* Cullompton: Willan

Hastie, R., Penrod, S.D., and Pennington, N. (1983) *Inside the Jury,* Cambridge, MA: Harvard University Press

Hatt, K., Caputo, T. and Perry, B. (1992) 'Criminal justice policy under Mulroney, 1984–90: Neo-Conservatism eh?', *Canadian Public Policy,* 18, 245–60

Hauser, R. (1995) Review of *The Bell Curve, Contemporary Sociology,* 24, 149–153

Hawkins, K. (2002) *Law as Last Resort: Prosecution decision-making in a regulatory agency,* Oxford: Oxford University Press

Haxby, D. (1978) *Probation: A changing service,* London: Constable

Hayden, D. (1995) *Young People and Alcohol-related incicents,* London: Centre for Research on Drugs and Health Behaviour

Hayman, S. (2006) 'The reforming prison: A Canadian tale', in Heidensohn, F. (ed.) *Gender and Justice: New perspectives,* Cullompton: Willan

Hazel, N., Hagell, A. and Brazier, L. (2002) *Young Offenders' Perceptions of their Experiences in the Criminal Justice System,* London: Policy Research Bureau

Hazelwood, R.R. and Douglas, J.E. (1980) 'The lust murderer', *FBI Law Enforcement Bulletin* 49, 4, 18–22

Health Protection Agency (HPA) Health Protection Scotland, National Public Health Service for Wales, CDSC Northern Ireland and CRDHB (2006) *Shooting Up: Infections among injecting drug users in the United Kingdom 2005,* London: HPA

Heal, K. and Laycock, G. (eds) (1986) *Situational Crime Prevention: From theory to practice,* London: Home Office

Healy, P. and Palepu, K. (2003) 'The fall of Enron', *Journal of Economic Perspectives,* 17, 2, 3–26

Heaps, C. and Nash, M. (1999) 'Individual differences in imagination inflation', *Psychonomic Bulletin and Review,* 6, 313–318

Hearn, J. (1996) 'Is masculinity dead? A critique of the concept of masculinity/ masculinities', in Mac an Ghail, M. (ed.), *Understanding Masculinities: Social relations and cultural arenas,* Buckingham: Open University Press

Hearnden, I. and Magill, C. (2004) *Decision-making by burglars: Offenders' perspectives,* Home Office Findings 249, London: Home Office

Hearnden, I. and Hough, M. (2004) *Race and the Criminal Justice System: An overview to the complete statistics 2002–2003,* London: Home Office

Hearold, S. (1986) 'A synthesis of 1043 effects of television on social behaviour', in Comstock, G. (ed.) *Public Communications and Behaviour Vol. 1,* 65–133, New York: Appleton Century

Hebenton, B. and Thomas, T. (1995) *Policing Europe: Co-operation, conflict and control,* London: Macmillan

Hedderman, C. (2004) 'Why are more women being sentenced to custody?', in McIvor, G. (ed.) *Women Who Offend,* London: Jessica Kingsley

Hedderman, C. and Hough, M. (1994) *Does the criminal justice system treat men and women differently?* Home Office Research Findings 10, London: Home Office

Hedderman, C. and Moxon, D. (1992) *Magistrates or Crown Court? Mode of trial decisions and their impact on sentencing*, London: Home Office

Heidensohn, F. (1968) 'The deviance of women: a critique and an inquiry', *British Journal of Sociology*, 19, 2, 160–73

Heidensohn, F. (1985) *Women and Crime*, London: Macmillan

Heidensohn, F. (1987) 'Women and crime: Questions for criminology', in Carlen, P. and Worrall, A. (eds) *Gender, Crime and Justice*, Milton Keynes: Open University Press

Heidensohn, F. (1989) *Crime and Society*, London: Macmillan

Heidensohn, F. (1992) *Women in Control? The role of women in law enforcement*, Oxford: Oxford University Press

Heidensohn, F. (1996) *Women and Crime*, 2nd edn, Basingstoke: Macmillan

Heidensohn, F. (2002) 'Gender and crime', in Maguire, M., Morgan, R. and Reiner, R. (eds) *The Oxford Handbook of Criminology*, 3rd edn, Oxford: Oxford University Press

Heidensohn, F. (2003) 'Gender and policing', in Newburn, T. (ed.) *Handbook of Policing*, Cullompton: Willan

Heidensohn, F. (ed.) (2006a) *Gender and Justice: New concepts and approaches*, Cullompton: Willan

Heidensohn, F. (2006b) 'New perspectives and established views', in Heidensohn, F. (ed.) *Gender and Justice: New concepts and approaches*, Cullompton: Willan

Heidensohn, F. and Gelsthorpe, L. (2007) 'Gender and crime', in Maguire, M., Morgan, R. and Reiner, R. (eds) *The Oxford Handbook of Criminology*, 4th edn, Oxford: Oxford University Press

Held, D., McGrew, A., Goldblatt, D. and Perraton, J. (1999) *Global Transformations*, Cambridge: Polity Press

Hendrick, G. (1977) 'When television is a school for criminals', *TV Guide*, 29 January, 118

Hennigan, K.M., Delrosario, M.L., Heath, L., Cook, J.D., and Calder, B.J. (1982) 'Impact of the introduction of television crime in the United States: empirical findings and theoretical implications', *Journal of Personality and Social Psychology*, 42, 3, 461–77

Henry, B., Caspi, A., Moffitt, T. and Silva, A. (1996) 'Temperamental and familial predictors of violent and non-violent criminal convictions: Age three to age eighteen', *Developmental Psychology*, 32, 614–623

Henry, A. (2007) 'Looking back on "Police and People in London"', in Henry, A. and Smith, D.J. (eds) *Transformations of Policing*, Aldershot: Ashgate

Henry, S. and Lanier, M. (eds) (2005) *The Essential Criminology Reader*, Boulder, CO: Westview Press

Herrnstein, R. and Murray, C. (1994) *The Bell-Curve: Intelligence and class structure in American life*, New York: The Free Press

Hersh, S.M. (2004) 'Torture at Abu Ghraib', *The New Yorker*, May 10th 2004

Hester, M. and Westmarland, N. (2005) *Tackling Domestic Violence: Effective interventions and approaches*, Home Office Research Study 290, London: Home Office

Hester, M. and Westmarland, N. (2006) *Service Provision for Perpetrators of Domestic Violence*, Bristol: University of Bristol

Hibell, B. *et al.* (2004) *Alcohol and other Drug Use among Students in 35 European Countries*, The ESPAD Report, 2003, Stockholm: Swedish Council for Information on Alcohol and Other Drugs

Hickman, M., Carnwath, Z., Madden, P., Farrell, M., Rooney, C., Ashcroft, R., Judd, A. and Stimson, G. (2003) 'Drug-related mortality and fatal overdose risk: Pilot cohort study of heroin users recruited from specialist drug treatment sites in London', *Journal of Urban Health – Bulletin of the New York Academy of Medicine*, 80, 2, 274–287

Hilgendorf, E. and Irving, B. (1981) 'A decision-making model of confessions', in Lloyd-Bostock, M.A. (ed.) *Psychology in Legal Contexts: Applications and limitations*, London: Macmillan

Hill, P. (2003) 'Heisei Yakuza, Burst Bubble and Botaiho', *Social Science Japan Journal*, 6, 1, 1–18

Hillyard, P. (1994) 'The normalization of special powers', in Lacey, N. (ed.) *A Reader on Criminal Justice*, Oxford: Oxford University Press

Hillyard, P. (1997) 'Policing divided societies: trends and prospects in Northern Ireland and Britain', in Francis, P. *et al.* (eds) *Policing Futures: The police, law enforcement and the Twenty-first century*, Basingstoke: Macmillan

Hillyard, P., Pantazis, C., Tombs, S. and Gordon, D. (eds) (2004a) *Beyond Criminology: Taking harm seriously*, London: Pluto Press

Hillyard, P., Pantazis, C., Tombs, S. and Gordon, D. (2004b) 'Introduction', in Hillyard, P., Pantazis, C., Tombs, S. and Gordon, D. (eds) *Beyond Criminology: Taking harm seriously*, London: Pluto Press

Hillyard, P. and Tombs, S. (2004) 'Beyond criminology?', in Hillyard, P., Pantazis, C., Tombs, S. and Gordon, D. (eds) *Beyond Criminology: Taking harm seriously*, London: Pluto Press

Hindelang, M.J., Gottfredson, M.R., and Garofalo, J. (1978) *Victims of Personal Crime: an empirical foundation for a theory of personal victimization*, Cambridge, MA: Ballinger Publishing Co

Hinds, L. (2005) 'Crime control in Western countries, 1970–2000', in Pratt, J., Brown, D., Brown, M., Hallsworth, S. and Morrison, W. (eds) *The New Punitiveness: Trends, theories, perspectives,* Cullompton: Willan Publishing

Hirschi, T. (1969) *Causes of Delinquency,* Berkeley: University of California Press

Hirschi, T. and Hindelang, M. (1977) 'Intelligence and Delinquency: A revisionist view', *American Sociological Review,* 42, 4, 571–587

Hirschi and Gottfredson, M. (1983) 'Age and the explanation of crime', *American Journal of Sociology,* 89, 552–84

Hirschi, T. and Gottfredson, M. (1993) 'Commentary: Testing the general theory of crime', *Journal of Research in Crime and Delinquency,* 30, 1, 47–54

Hirschi, T. and Gottfredson, M.R. (2000) 'In defense of self-control', *Theoretical Criminology,* 4, 1, 55–69

Hirst, P. (1975a) 'Marx and Engels on law, crime and morality', in Taylor, I., Walton, P. and Young, J. (eds) *Critical Criminology,* London: Routledge and Kegan Paul

Hirst, P. (1975b) 'Radical deviancy theory and Marxism: a reply to Taylor, Walton and Young', in Taylor, I., Walton, P. and Young, J. (eds) *Critical Criminology,* London: Routledge and Kegan Paul

Hitchens, P. (2003) *A Brief History of Crime,* London: Atlantic Books

HM Chief Inspector of Prisons (2000) *Unjust Deserts: A thematic review of the treatment and conditions for unsentenced prisoners in England and Wales,* London: Home Office

HM Chief Inspector of Prisons (2005) *Annual Report, 2003–04,* London: HMIP

HM Government (2004) *Cutting Crime, Delivering Justice: A strategic plan for criminal justice 2004–2008,* London: Stationery Office

HM Government (2007) *Safe, Sensible, Social: The next steps in the National Alcohol Strategy,* London: HM Government

HM Inspectorate of Constabulary (1997) *Women in Prison,* London: HMIC

HM Inspectorate of Constabulary (2000) *Calling Time On Crime,* London: HMIC

HM Inspectorate of Prisons (1997) *Women in Prison: A Thematic Review,* London: Home Office

HM Inspectorate of Prisons (2005) *Women in Prison,* London: HMIP

HM Inspectorate of Prisons and YJB (2005) *Juveniles in Custody 2003–4: An analysis of children's experiences of prisons,* London: HMIP

HM Prison Service and Metropolitan Police Service (2006) *Corruption in the Prison Service,* unpublished

Hobbs, D. (1988) *Doing the Business,* Oxford: Oxford University Press

Hobbs, D. (1994) *Interpreting the Field,* Oxford University Press

Hobbs, D. (1995) *Bad Business,* Oxford: Oxford University Press

Hobbs, D. (1998) 'Going down the glocal: the local context of organised crime', *The Howard Journal of Criminal Justice,* 37, 4, 407–422

Hobbs, D., Hadfield, P., Lister, S. and Winlow, S. (2003) *Bouncers: Violence and governance in the night-time economy,* Oxford: Clarendon Press

Hobsbawm, E. (1959) *Primitive Rebels,* Manchester: Manchester University Press

Hodgson, J. (2004) 'The role played by the juge in the protection of the suspect's rights during the police investigation', in Feuillée-Kendall, P. and Trouille, H. (eds) *Justice on Trial: the French 'juge' in question,* Bern: Peter Lang

Hodgson, J. (2005) *French Criminal Justice: A comparative account of the investigation and prosecution of crime in France* Oxford: Hart Publishing

Hoggart, R. (1957) *The Uses of Literacy,* Harmondsworth: Penguin

Hollin, C.R. (1989) *Psychology and Crime: An introduction to criminological psychology,* London: Routledge

Hollin, C.R. (1992) *Criminal Behaviour: A psychological approach to explanation and prevention,* London: Falmer Press

Hollin, C. (2002) 'Criminological psychology', in Maguire, M., Morgan, R. and Reiner, R. (eds) *The Oxford Handbook of Criminology,* 3rd edn, Oxford: Clarendon Press

Hollin, C. (2007) 'Criminological psychology', in Maguire, M., Morgan, R. and Reiner, R. (eds) *The Oxford Handbook of Criminology,* 4th edn, Oxford: Clarendon Press

Hollin, C.R., and Palmer, E.J. (eds) (2006) *Offending Behaviour Programmes: Development, application and controversies,* Chichester: Wiley

Holloway, W. and Jefferson, T. (1997) 'The Risk Society in an age of anxiety: situating fear of crime', *British Journal of Sociology,* 48, 255–266

Holloway, K. and Bennett, T. (2004) *The results of the first two years of the NEW-ADAM programme,* London: Home Office

Holmes, R.M., and Holmes, S.T. (1998) *Serial murder,* 2nd edn, Thousand Oaks, CA: Sage

Home Affairs Committee (2007) *Young Black People and the Criminal Justice System,* London: The Stationery Office

Home Office (1965), *The Child, the Family and the Young Offender,* London: Cmd.2742, HMSO

Home Office (1979) *The Use and Safekeeping of Tranquillising Weapons,* London: Home Office

Home Office (1984a) *Criminal Justice: A working paper,* London: Home Office

Home Office (1984b) *Tougher Regimes in Detention Centres: Report of an evaluation by the Young Offender Psychology Unit,* London: Home Office

Home Office (1986) *Violence Against Women,* Home Office circular 69/1986, London: Home Office

Home Office (1987) *Efficiency Scrutiny of HM Probation Inspectorate,* London: Home Office

Home Office (1988) *Punishment, Custody and the Community,* London: Home Office

Home Office (1995a) *Criminal careers of those born between 1953 and 1973*, Home Office Statistical Bulletin 14/95, London: Home Office

Home Office (1995b) *Strengthening punishment in the community,* London: Home Office

Home Office (1996) *Victim's Charter,* London: HMSO

Home Office (1997) *Getting to Grips with Crime: A new framework for local action,* London: Home Office

Home Office (1998) *Joining Forces to Protect the Public,* London: Home Office

Home Office (1999) *The Correctional Policy Framework,* London: Home Office

Home Office (2001a) *Making Punishments Work,* London: Home Office

Home Office (2001b) *Review of the Victims Charter,* London: Home Office

Home Office (2002) *Race and the Criminal Justice System,* London: Home Office

Home Office (2003) *Statistics on Women and the Criminal Justice System – 2003,* London: Home Office

Home Office (2004a) *Building Communities, Beating Crime,* London: Home Office

Home Office (2004b) *Women's Offending Reduction Programme,* London: Home Office

Home Office (2005a) *Hearing the Relatives of Murder and Manslaughter Victims: Consultation Document,* Criminal Justice System, 28, London: Home Office

Home Office (2005b) *Rebuilding Lives: Supporting victims of crime,* London: Home Office

Home Office (2005c) *Victims' Code of Practice,* London, HMSO

Home Office (2005d) *Probation Circular 25/2005: Criminal Justice Act 2003: Implementation on 4 April,* London: Home Office

Home Office (2005e) *Sentencing Statistics 2003,* HOSB 05/05, London: Home Office

Home Office (2006a) *Review of the partnership provisions of the Crime and Disorder Act,* London: Home Office

Home Office (2006b) *Statistics on Race and the Criminal Justice System – 2005,* London: Home Office

Home Office (2007) *Sentencing Statistics 2005,* HOSB 03/07, London: Home Office

Homel, R. (2005) 'Developmental crime prevention', in Tilley, N. (ed.) *Handbook of Crime Prevention and Community Safety,* Cullompton: Willan

Hope, T. (1995) 'Community crime prevention', in Tonry, M. and Farrington, D. (eds) *Building Safer Communities,* Chicago: University of Chicago Press

Hope, T. (2001) 'Crime victimization and inequality in a risk society', in Matthews, R. and Pitts, J. (eds) *Crime, Disorder and Community Safety,* London; Routledge

Hope, T. (2005) 'Pretend it doesn't work: The "anti-social" bias in the Maryland scientific methods scale', *European Journal on Criminal Policy and Research,* 11, 3–4, 275–296

Hope, T. (2006) 'What do crime statistics tell us?', in Hale, C., Hayward, K., Wahidin, A. and Wincup, E. (eds) *Criminology,* Oxford: Oxford University Press

Hope, T., Bryan, J., Trickett, A. and Osborn, D.R. (2001) 'The phenomena of multiple victimization: The relationahip between personal and property crime risk', *British Journal of Criminology,* 41, 4, 595–617

Hope, T. and Foster, J. (1992) 'Conflicting forces: changing the dynamics of crime and community', *British Journal of Criminology,* 32, 488–504

Hood, R. (1992) *Race and Sentencing,* Oxford: Oxford University Press

Hood-Williams, J. (2001) 'Gender, masculinities and crime: From structures to psyches', *Theoretical Criminology,* 5, 1, 37–60

Horgan, J. and Taylor, M. (1999) 'Playing the green card: Financing the provisional IRA Part 1', *Terrorism and Political Violence,* 11, 1, 1–38

Horowitz, I.L. and Leibowitz, M. (1968) 'Social Deviance and Political Marginality: Toward a Redefinition of the Relation between Sociology and Politics', *Social Problems,* 15, 3, 280–296

Hough, M. and Mayhew, P. (1983) *The British Crime Survey: First Report,* London: HMSO

Hough, M. (1996) 'People talking about punishment', *The Howard Journal of Criminal Justice,* 35, 3

Hough, M., Jacobson, J. and Millie, A. (2003) *The Decision to Imprison,* London: Prison Reform Trust

Hough, J. and Roberts, J. (2004) *Youth Crime and Youth Justice: Public opinion in England and Wales,* Bristol: Policy Press

Hough, M. and Roberts, J.V. (2005) 'Just how punitive is the public?', *Criminal Justice Matters,* 60, 10–11

Hough, M., Allen, R. and Padel, U. (eds) (2006) *Reshaping Probation and Prisons: The new offender management framework*, Researching Criminal Justice Series Paper No. 6, Bristol: Policy Press

Hough, M. (2007) 'Policing London 20 years on', in Henry, A. and Smith, D.J. (eds) *Transformations of Policing*, Aldershot: Ashgate

Hough, M. and Maxfield, M. (eds) (2007) *Surveying Crime in the 21st Century* Cullompton: Willan Publishing

Hough, M., Mirrlees-Black, C. and Dale, M. (2005) *Trends in violent crime since 1999/2000*, London: Kings College

House of Commons (1990) *Practical Police Co-operation in the European Community*, Home Affairs Committee Report (7th Report) Session 1989–90, London: HMSO.

Howarth, C., Kenway, P., Palmer, G. and Street, C. (1998) *Monitoring Poverty and Social Exclusion*, York: Joseph Rowntree Foundation

Howe, A. (1994) *Punish and Critique: Towards a feminist analysis of penality*, New York: Routledge

Howitt, D. (2002) *Forensic and Criminal Psychology*, Harlow: Longman

Howitt, D. (2006) *Introduction to Forensic and Criminal Psychology*, 2nd edn, Harlow: Prentice Hall

Howson, G. (1985) *Thief-taker General: Jonathan Wild and the emergence of crime and corruption in eighteenth century England*, New Brunswick, NJ: Transaction

Hoyle, C., Cope, E., Morgan, R. and Sanders, A. (1998) *Evaluation of the One Stop Shop and Victim Statement Pilot Projects*, London: Home Office

Hsu, L., Wisner, K., Richey, E. and Goldstein, C. (1985) 'Is juvenile delinquency related to abnormal EEG?', *Journal of the American Academy of Child Psychiatry*, 24, 310–15

Hudson, B. (1993) *Penal policy and social justice*, Basingstoke: Macmillan

Hudson, B. (1998) 'Restorative justice: the challenge of sexual and racial violence', *Journal of Law and Society*, 25, 2, 237–56, reprinted in Johnstone, G. (ed.) (2003) *A Restorative Justice Reader*, Cullompton: Willan

Hudson, B. (2003a) *Justice in the Risk Society*, London: Sage

Hudson, B. (2003b) *Understanding Justice*, 2nd edn, Maidenhead: Open University Press

Hughes, G. (2007) *The Politcs of Crime and Community*, Basingstoke: Palgrave

Hughes, G., McLaughlin, E. and Muncie, J. (eds) (2002) *Crime Prevention and Community Safety*, London: Sage

Hughes, R. (2003) *The Fatal Shore*, London: Vintage

Hutchings, B. and Mednick, S. (1977) 'Criminality in adoptees and their adoptive and biological parents: A pilot study', in Mednick, S. and Christiansen, K. (eds) *Biosocial Bases of Criminal Behaviour*, New York: Gardner Press

Ianni, F.A. and Ianni, E.R. (1972) *A Family Business*, London: Routledge and Kegan Paul

Ignatieff, M. (1978) *A Just Measure of Pain: The penitentiary in the industrial revolution, 1750–1850*, New York: Pantheon Books

Ignatieff, M. (2001) *Human Rights as Politics and Idolatry*, Princeton, NJ: Princeton University Press

Ignatieff, M. (2004) 'Lesser Evils', *New York Times Magazine*, May 2nd 2004

Inbau, F., Reid, J. and Buckley J. (1986) *Criminal Interrogation and Confessions*, Baltimore, MD: Williams and Wilkins

Indermaur, D. (1995) *Violent Property Crime*, Sydney: Federation Press

Institute of Community Cohesion (2006) *Challenging Local Communities to Change Oldham*, Coventry: Institute for Community Cohesion

Irvine, D. (2004) 'The Human Rights Act: Principle and Practice', *Parliamentary Affairs*, 57, 4, 744–753

Jacobs, J. (1961) *The Death and Life of Great American Cities*, New York: Random House

Jacobs, J. and Potter, K. (1998) *Hate Crimes: Criminal law and identity politics*, New York: Oxford University Press

Jacoby, J. (2004) *Classics of Criminology*, 3nd edn, Long Grove, Il: Waveland Press

James, A., Bottomley, K., Liebling, A. and Clare, E. (1997) *Privatizing Prisons: Rhetoric and reality*, London: Sage

Jamieson, R. (1988) 'Towards a criminology of war in Europe', in Ruggiero, V., South, N. and Taylor, I. (eds) *The New European Criminology*, London: Routledge

Jarvis, F.V. (1972) *Advise, Assist and Befriend : A history of the probation and after-care service*, London: National Association of Probation Officers

Jeffery, C.R. (1965) 'Criminal behaviour and learning theory', *Journal of Criminal Law, Criminology and Police Science*, 56, 294–300

Jeffery, C.R. (1971) *Crime Prevention Through Environmental Design*, Beverly Hills, CA: Sage Publications

Jenkins, P. (1988) 'Serial murder in England, 1940–1985', *Journal of Criminal Justice*, 16

Jenkins, P. (1992) *Intimate Enemies: Moral panics in contemporary Britain*, New York: Aldine de Gruyter

Jensen, A.R. (1968) 'Social class, race and genetics: implications for education', *American Educational Research Journal*, 5, 1, 1–42

Jessop, B. (1995) 'The regulation approach, governance and post-fordism', *Economy and Society*, 24, 3, 307–333.

Jewkes, Y. (2003a) *Dot.Cons: Crime, deviance and identity on the internet*, Cullompton: Willan

Jewkes, Y. (2003b) 'Policing cybercrime', in Newburn, T. (ed.) *Handbook of Policing*, Cullompton: Willan

Jewkes, Y. (2003c) 'Policing the Net: crime, regulation and surveillance in cyberspace', in Jewkes, Y. (2003a) *Dot.Cons: Crime, deviance and identity on the internet*, Cullompton: Willan

Jewkes, Y. (2004) *Media and Crime*, London: Sage

Jewkes, Y. (2007) *Crime Online*, Cullompton: Willan

Jewkes, Y. and Johnstone, H. (eds) (2006) *Prison Readings: A critical introduction to prisons and imprisonment*, Cullompton: Willan

Johnson, P. (2003) *Inner lives: Voices of African American women in prison.* New York: New York University Press

Johnston, L. (2006) 'Diversifying police recruitment? The deployment of police community support officers in London', *The Howard Journal of Criminal Justice*, 45, 4, 388–402

Johnston, V., Leitner, M., Shapland, J. and Wiles, P. (1994) *Crime on industrial estates*, Crime Detection and Prevention Series, 54, London: Home Office

Johnstone, G. (2002) *Restorative Justice: Ideas, values, debates*, Cullompton: Willan

Johnstone, G. (2003) *A Restorative Justice Reader*, Cullompton; Willan

Joint Prisons/Probation Accreditation Panel (2001) *What works: second report*, London: Home Office

Jolliffe, D. and Farrington, D. (2004) 'Empathy and offending: a systematic review and meta-analysis', *Aggression and Violent Behaviour*, 9, 441–476

Jones, P., Rodgers, B., Murray, R. and Marmot, M. (1994) 'Child development risk factors for adult schizophrenia in the British 1946 birth cohort', *The Lancet*, 344,1398–1402

Jones, T. (2003) 'Police governance and accountability', in Newburn, T. (ed.) *Handbook of Policing*, Cullompton: Willan

Jones, T. and Newburn, T. (1998) *Private Security and Public Policing*, Oxford: Clarendon Press

Jones, T. and Newburn, T. (2002) 'Learning from Uncle Sam? Exploring U.S. Influences on British Crime Control Policy', *Governance*, 15, 1

Jones, T. and Newburn, T. (2006) *Plural Policing: A comparative perspective*, London: Routledge

Jones, T. and Newburn, T. (2007) *Policy Transfer and Criminal Justice*, Buckingham: Open University Press

Jones, T., Maclean, B. and Young, J. (1986) *The Islington Crime Survey: Crime, victimization and policing in inner-city London*, Aldershot: Gower

Joseph, J. (2003) 'Cyberstalking: an international perspective', in Jewkes, Y. (2003a) *Dot.Cons: Crime, deviance and identity on the internet*, Cullompton: Willan

Joseph Rowntree Foundation (2004) *Drug Testing in the Workplace*, York: Joseph Rowntree Foundation

Kahan, D.M. (2006) *What's really wrong with shaming sanctions*, Yale Law School, Public Law Working Paper No. 116 (available at SSRN: http://ssrn.com/abstract=914503)

Kaldor, M. (1999) *New and Old Wars*, Cambridge: Polity Press

Kalven, H. Jr. and Zeisel, H. (1966) *The American Jury*, Boston: Little Brown

Kamin, L. (1985) 'Is crime in the genes?', *Scientific American*, 22–25

Kandel, E. and Mednick, S.A. (1991) 'Perinatal complications predict violent offending', *Criminology*, 29, 3, 519–529

Karmen, A. (2001) *New York Murder Mystery: The true story behind the crime crash of the 1990s*, New York: New York University Press

Karp, D., and Walther, L. (2001) 'Community reparative boards: theory and practice', in Bazemore, G. and Schiff, M. (eds) *Restorative Community Justice: Cultivating common ground for victims, communities and offenders*, Cincinnati, OH: Anderson

Karstedt, S. and Farrell, S. (2007) *Law-abiding majority? The everyday crimes of the middle classes, Briefing 3*, London: Centre for Crime and Justice Studies

Kassin, S. and Gudjonnson, G. (2004) 'The psychology of confessions: A review of the literature and issues', *Psychological Science in the Public Interest*, 5, 2, 33–67

Katz, J. (1988) *Seductions of Crime: Moral and sensual attractions in doing evil*, New York: Basic Books

Katz, J. and Abel, C. (1984) 'The medicalization of repression: eugenics and crime', *Contemporary Crises*, 8, 227–241

Katz, S. and Mazur, M. (1979) *Understanding the Rape Victim*, New York: Wiley

Kauffman, K. (1988) *Prison Officers and their World*, Harvard, MA: Harvard University Press

Kazdin, A.E., Kraemer, H., Kessler, R., Kupfer, D. and Offord, D. (1997) 'Contributions of risk factor research to developmental psychopathology', *Clinical Psychology Review*, 17, 375–406

Kebbell, M., Hurren, E. and Roberts, S. (2006) 'Mock suspects' decisions to confess: Accuracy of eyewitness evidence is crucial', *Applied Cognitive Psychology*, 20, 477–486

Kefauver, E. (1951) *United States Congress, Senate Special Committee to Investigate Organized Crime in Interstate Commerce*, Third Interim Report, Washington DC: Government Printing Office

Kellett, S. and Gross, H. (2006) 'Addicted to joyriding?: An exploration of young offenders' accounts of their car crime', *Psychology, Crime and Law*, 12, 1, 39–59

Kelling, G. and Coles, C.M. (1996) *Fixing Broken Windows*, New York: Touchstone

Kelly, A. (1978) 'Feminism and research', *Women's Studies International Quarterly*, 1, 225–232

Kelly, L. (1988) *Surviving Sexual Violence*, Cambridge: Polity Press

Kelly, L., Lovett, J. and Regan, L. (2005) *A Gap or a Chasm? Attrition in reported rape cases*, Home Office Research Study 293, London: Home Office

Kelly, L. and Regan, L. (2000) *Stopping Traffic: Exploring the extent of, and responses to trafficking of women for sexual exploitation in the UK*, London: Home Office

Kemshall, H. and Maguire, M. (2001) 'Public protection, partnership and risk penality: The multi-agency risk management of sexual and violent offenders', *Punishment and Society: The International Journal of Penology*, 5, 2, 237–64

Kemshall, H. (2003) *Understanding Risk in Criminal Justice*, Buckingham: Open University Press

Kennedy, D., Braga, A. and Piehl, A. (2001) 'Developing and implementing operation ceasefire', in *Reducing Gun Violence: The Boston Gun Project's Operation Ceasefire*, Washington DC: US Department of Justice

Kershaw, C., Budd, T., Kinshott, G., Mattinson, J., Mayhew, P. and Myhill, A. (2000) *The 2000 British Crime Survey*, Home Office Statistical Bulletin 18/00, London: Home Office

Kershaw, C., Chivite-Matthews, N., Thomas, C. and Aust, R. (2001) *The 2001 British Crime Survey*, Home Office Statistical Bulletin 18/01, London: Home Office

King, M. (1991) 'The political construction of crime prevention', in Stenson, K. and Cowell, D. (eds) *The Politics of Crime Control*, London: Sage

King, M. (1992) 'Male sexual assault in the community', in Mezey, G. and King, M. (eds) *Male Victims of Sexual Assault*, Oxford: Oxford University Press

King, R. (2007) 'Security, control and the problems of containment', in Jewkes, Y. (ed.) *Handbook on Prisons*, Cullompton: Willan

Kinsey, R. (1984) *Merseyside Crime Survey: First Report*, Liverpool: Merseyside Metropolitan Council

Kitsuse, J. (1962) 'Societal reaction to deviant behaviour: Problems of theory and method', *Social Problems*, 9, 247–256

Kitzinger, J. and Barbour, R.S. (1999) 'Introduction: The challenge and promise of focus groups', in Barbour, R. and Kitzinger, J. (eds) *Developing Focus Group Research*, London: Sage

Kleiman, M. and Smith, K. (1990) 'Research on Drugs and Crime', *Crime and Justice: A Review of Research, Vol. 13*, Chicago: University of Chicago Press

Klockars, C. (1979) 'The contemporary crises of Marxist criminology', *Criminology*, 16, 4

Kocsis, R.N. and Heller, G.Z. (2004) 'Believing is seeing II: Beliefs and perceptions of criminal psychological profiles', *International Journal of Offender Therapy and Comparative Criminology*, 48, 313–329

Kolbo, J., Blakely, E. and Engleman, D. (1996) 'Children who witness domestic violence: A review of empirical literature', *Journal of Interpersonal Violence*, 11, 2, 281–293

Kolvin, I., Miller, F., Fleeting, M. and Kolvin, P. (1988) 'Social and parenting factors affecting criminal-offence rates: Findings from the Newcastle thousand family study', *British Journal of Psychiatry*, 152, 80–90

Kramer, R.C. (2006) 'The space shuttle *Challenger* explosion', in Michalowski, R. and Kramer, R. (2006) *State-Corporate Crime: Wrongdoing at the intersection of business and government*, New Brunswick, NJ: Rutgers University Press

Kramer, R.C. and Michaelowski, R.J. (2005) 'War, aggression and state crime', *British Journal of Criminology*, 45, 4, 446–469

Labour Party (1996) *Tackling the Causes of Crime*, London: Labour Party

Labour Party (1997) *New Labour – Because Britain Deserves Better*, London: Labour Party

Lacey, N. (1988) *State Punishment: Political principles and community values*, London: Routledge

Lacey, N. (2007) 'Legal constructions of crime', in Maguire, M., Morgan, R. and Reiner, R. (eds) *The Oxford Handbook of Criminology*, 4th edn, Oxford: Oxford University Press

Lader, D., Singleton, N. and Meltzer, H. (1997) *Psychiatric Morbidity among Young Offenders in England and Wales*, London: Office for National Statistics

Lacey, N. (2002) 'Legal constructions of crime', in Maguire, M., Morgan, R., Reiner, R. (eds) *The Oxford Handbook of Criminology*, 3rd edn, Oxford: Oxford University Press

Lacquer, W. (1987) *The Age of Terrorism,* Boston, MA: Little, Brown and Co.

Lamb, M., Sternberg, K. and Orbach, Y. (1999) 'Forensic interviews of children', in Memon, A. and Bull, R. (eds) *Handbook of the Psychology of Interviewing,* Chichester: Wiley

Landau, S. and Nathan, G. (1983) 'Detecting delinquency for cautioning in the London Metropolitan area', *British Journal of Criminology,* 23, 2, 128–149

Lange, J. (1929) 'Verbrechen als Schicksal: Studien an kriminellen Zwillingen', 96, *Crime and destiny,* (trans. by C. Haldane), Leipzig

Lanier, M.M. and Henry, S. (1998) *Essential Criminology,* Boulder, CO: Westview Press

Lash, S. and Urry, J. (1994) *Economies of Signs and Space,* London: Sage

Laub, J (1983) *Criminology in the Making: An oral history,* Boston: Northeastern University Press

Laub, J. and Sampson, R. (1991) 'The Sutherland-Glueck Debate: On the sociology of criminological knowledge', *American Journal of Sociology,* 6, 1402–40

Laub, J. and Sampson, R. (2003) *Shared Beginnings, Divergent Lives: Delinquent boys to age 70,* Cambridge, MA: Harvard University Press

Lavranos, N. (2003) 'Europol and the fight against terrorism', *European Foreign Affairs Review,* 8, 259–75

Laycock, G. (2005) 'Defining crime science', in Smith, M.J. and Tilley, N. (eds) *Crime Science: New approaches to preventing and detecting crime,* Cullompton: Willan

Laycock, G. and Tilley, N. (1995) *Policing and Neighbourhood Watch: Strategic issues,* Crime Prevention and Detection Series paper 60, London: Home Office

Layder, D. (2005) *Understanding Social Theory,* 2nd edn, London: Sage

Lea, J. and Young, J. (1984) *What is to be Done About Law and Order?,* London: Penguin Books

Lee, M. (2007) *Inventing Fear of Crime: Criminology and the politics of anxiety,* Cullompton: Willan

Leigh, A., Read, T. and Tilley, N. (1998) 'Brit pop II: Problem orientated policing in practice', *Police research Series Paper 93,* London: Home Office

Leishman, F., Cope, S. and Starie, P. (1995) 'Reforming the police in Britain: New public management, policy networks and a tough "old bill"', *International Journal of Public Sector Management,* 8, 4, 26–37

Leishman, F. and Mason, P. (2003) *Policing and the media: Facts, fictions and factions,* Cullompton: Willan

Lemert, E.M. (1967) *Human Deviance, Social Problems, and Social Control,* Englewood Cliffs, NJ: Prentice Hall

Lemert, E.M. (1972) *Human Deviance, Social Problems, and Social Control,* 2nd edn, Englewood Cliffs, NJ: Prentice Hall

Leng, R., Taylor, R. and Wasik, M. (1998) *Blackstone's Guide to the Crime and Disorder Act 1998,* London: Blackstone Press

Leonard, E. (1982) *Women, Crime and Society: A critique of criminology theory,* New York: Longman

Levens B. and Dutton D. (1980) *The Social Service Role of the Police: Domestic crisis intervention,* Canada: Ministry of Supply and Services

Levi, M. (1987) *Regulating Fraud: White collar crime and the criminal process,* London: Tavistock

Levi, M. (1988) *The Prevention of Fraud,* Crime Prevention Unit Paper 17, London: Home Office

Levi, M. (1994) 'Violent crime', in Maguire, M., Morgan, R., Reiner, R. (eds) *The Oxford Handbook of Criminology,* 1st edn, Oxford: Oxford University Press

Levi, M. (1995) 'Serious fraud in Britain: Criminal justice versus regulation', in Pearce, F. and Snider, L. (eds) *Corporate Crime: Contemporary debates,* Toronto: University of Toronto Press

Levi, M. (1998) 'Perspectives on "Organised Crime: An Overview"', *The Howard Journal of Criminal Justice,* 37, 4, 335–345

Levi, M (2002) *Money Laundering and its Regulation,* The Annals of the American Academy of Social and Political Science, July 2002

Levi, M. (2007) 'Lessons for countering terrorist financing from the war on serious and organized crime', in Biersteker, T. and Eckert, S. (eds) *Countering the Financing of Terrorism,* London: Routledge

Levi, M., Burrows, J., Fleming, J. and Hopkins, M. (2007) *The Nature, Extent and Economic Impact of Fraud in the UK,* London: ACPO

Levi, M. and Maguire, M. (2002) 'Violent crime', in Maguire, M, Morgan, R. and Reiner, R. (eds) *The Oxford Handbook of Criminology,* 3rd edn, Oxford: Oxford University Press

Lewis, D.O., Pincus, J.H., Shanok, S.S. and Glaser, G.H. (1982) 'Psychomotor epilepsy and violence in a group of incarcerated adolescent boys', *American Journal of Psychiatry,* 139, 882–887

Leyton, E. (1995) *Men of blood: Murder in modern England,* London: Constable

Liebling, A. (2007) 'Prison suicide and its prevention', in Jewkes, Y. (ed.) *Handbook on Prisons,* Cullompton: Willan

Liebling, A. and Price, D. (2001) *The Prison Officer,* London: The Prison Service

Light, R., Nee, C. and Ingham, H. (1993) *Car Theft: The offender's perspective,* Home Office Research Study 130, London: HMSO

Lilly, J.R., Cullen, F.T. and Ball, R.A. (2002) *Criminological Theory: Context and consequences,* 3rd edn, Thousand Oaks, CA: Sage

Lipsey, M. (1992) 'Juvenile delinquency treatment: A meta-analytic inquiry into the variability of effects', in Cook T.D., Cooper, H., Cordray, D.S., Hartmann, H., Hedges, L.V., Light R.J., Louis T.A. and Mosteller, F. (eds) *Meta-Analysis for Explanation: A Casebook*, New York: Russell Sage Foundation

Livingstone, S. (1996) 'On the continuing problem of media effects', in Curran, J. and Gurevitch, M. (eds) *Mass Media and Society,* 305–24, London: Arnold

Lloyd, C. (1998) 'Risk factors for problem drug use: identifying vulnerable groups', *Drugs: education, prevention and policy,* 5, 3, 217–232

Loader, I. (1996) *Youth, Policing and Democracy,* London: Macmillan

Loeber, R., Farrington, D., Stouthamer-Loeber, M., Moffit, T., Capsi, A., White, H., Wei, E. and Beyers, J. (2003) 'The development of male offending: key findings from 14 years of the Pittsburgh Youth Study', in Thornberry, T. and Krohn, M. (eds) *Taking Stock of Delinquency: An overview of findings from contemporary longitudinal studies,* New York: Kluwer

Loeber, R. and LeBlanc, M. (1990) 'Toward a developmental criminology', in Tonry, M. and Morris, N. (eds) *Crime and Justice, A Review of Research, Vol. 12,* Chicago: University of Chicago Press

Loftus, E.F. and Schneider, N.G. (1987) '"Behold with strange surprise"; Judicial reactions to expert testimony concerning eyewitness reliability', *UMKC Law Review,* 56, 1–45

Lombroso, C. and Ferrero, G. (1893/2004) *Criminal Woman, the Prostitute and the Normal Woman,* translated, and with a new introduction, by Rafter, N.H. and Gibson, M., Durham: Duke University Press

Lowe, G., Foxcroft, D.R. and Sibley, D. (1993) *Adolescent Drinking and Family Life,* Amsterdam: Harwood Academic

Lowles, N. (2001) *White Riot: The violent story of combat 18,* Bury: Milo Books

Lyman, M. and Potter, G. (2004) *Organized Crime,* 3rd edn, New York: Prentice Hall

Ly, L. and Foster, S. (2005) *Statistics of mentally disordered offenders 2004 England and Wales,* London: Home Office

Lyon, D. (2001), *Surveillance Society: Monitoring everyday life,* Buckingham: Open University Press

McAllister, H.A. and Bregman, N. (1986) *Effects of victim and bystander testimony on juror decision-making,* paper presented at the annual meeting of the American Psychology-Law Society, Tucson, AZ

McConville, M., Sanders, A. and Leng, R. (1991) *The Case for the Prosecution.* London: Routledge

McConville, M., Sanders, A. and Leng, R. (1997) 'Descriptive or critical sociology: The choice is yours', *British Journal of Criminology,* 37, 3, 347–458

McConville, M. and Shepherd, D. (1992) *Watching Police, Watching Communities,* London: Routledge

McCord, J. (1979) 'Some child-rearing antecedents of criminal behavior in adult men', *Journal of Personality and Social Psychology,* 37, 1477–1486

McCord, J. (1982) 'A longitudinal view of the relationship between paternal absence and crime', in Gunn, J. and Farrington, D. (eds) *Abnormal Offenders, Delinquency and the Criminal Justice System,* Chichester: Wiley

McCullough, D., Schmidt, T. and Lockhart, B. (1990) *Car theft in Northern Ireland, Cirac Paper 2,* Belfast: The Extern Organisation

McDermott, K. and King, R. (1989) 'A fresh start: The enhancement of prison regimes', *The Howard Journal of Criminal Justice,* 28, 3, 161–76

McEvoy, K. (2003) 'Beyond the metaphor: political violence, human rights and "new" peacemaking criminology', *Theoretical Criminology,* 7, 3, 319–346

McGallagly, J., Power, K., Littlewood, P. and Meikle, J. (1998) *Evaluation of the Hamilton Child Safety Initiative,* Edinburgh: The Scottish Office

McGarry, J. and O'Leary, B. (1993) *The Politics of Ethnic Conflict Regulation: Case studies of protracted ethnic conflicts,* New York: Routledge

McGhee, D. (2005) *Intolerant Britain: Hate, citizenship and difference,* Maidenhead: Open University Press

McGowen, R. (1995) 'The Well-Ordered Prison: England, 1780–1865', in Morris, N. and Rothman, D. (eds) *The Oxford History of the Prison,* Oxford: Oxford University Press

McGuire, J. (ed.) (2002) *Offender Rehabilitation and Treatment: Effective programmes and policies to reduce re-offending,* Wiley Series in Forensic Clinical Psychology, Chichester: Wiley

McGuire, J. (2004) *Understanding Psychology and Crime: Perspectives on theory and action,* Maidenhead: Open University Press

McGuire, J. (2005) 'The Think First programme', in McMurran, M. and McGuire, J. (eds) *Social Problem-Solving and Offenders: Evidence, evaluation and evolution,* Chichester: Wiley

McIvor, G. (1992) *Sentenced to Serve: The operation and impact of community service by offenders,* Aldershot: Avebury

McIvor, G. and McNeill, F. (2007) 'Probation in Scotland: Past, present and future', in Gelsthorpe, L. and Morgan, R. (eds) *Handbook of Probation*, Cullompton: Willan

McKay, G. (1996) *Senseless Acts of Beauty: Cultures of resistance since the 60s*, London: Pluto

McKechnie, R.J., Cameron, D., Cameron, I.A., Drewery, J. (1977) 'Teenage drinking in south west Scotland', *British Journal of Addiction*, 72, 287–95

McKittrick, D., Kelters, S., Feeney, B. and Thornton, S. (1999) *Lost Lives: The stories of the men, women and children who died through the Northern Ireland troubles*, Edinburgh: Mainstream

McLaughlin, E. (2001) 'The crisis of the social and political materialization of community safety', in Hughes, G., McLaughlin, E. and Muncie, J. (eds) *Crime Prevention and Community Safety*, London: Sage

McLaughlin, E. (2007) 'Diversity or anarchy? The post-Macpherson blues', in Rowe, M. (ed.) *Policing Beyond Macpherson*, Cullompton: Willan

McLaughlin, E., Muncie, J. and Hughes, G. (2001) 'The permanent revolution', *Criminology and Criminal Justice*, 1, 3, 301–318

McLaughlin, E., Muncie, J. and Hughes, G. (2003) *Criminological Perspectives: Essential Readings*, 2nd edn, London: Sage

McMurran, M. and Hollin, C. (1989) 'Drinking and delinquency: another look at young offenders and alcohol', *British Journal of Criminology*, 29, 4, 386–94

McRobbie, A. (1980) 'Settling accounts with subcultures: A feminist critique', *Screen Education*, 39

McRobbie, A. (1982) 'The politics of feminist research: Between talk, text and action', *Feminist Review*, 12, 46–57

McRobbie, A. (1991) *Feminism and Youth Culture: From Jackie to Just Seventeen*, London: Macmillan

McRobbie, A. and Garber, J. (1976) 'Girls and subcultures: An exploration', in Hall, S. and Jefferson, T. (eds) *Resistance through Rituals*, London: Hutchison

McRobbie, A. and Garber, J. (1991) 'Girls and Subcultures', in McRobbie, A. (ed.) *Feminism and Youth Culture: From Jackie to Just Seventeen*, London: Macmillan

McRobbie, A. and Thornton, S. (1995) 'Rethinking "moral panic" for multi-mediated social worlds', *British Journal of Sociology*, 46, 4, 559–574

McSweeney, T., Stevens, A., Hunt, N. and Turnbull, P.J. (2007) 'Twisting arms or a helping hand? Assesing the impact of "coerced" and comparable "voluntary" drug treatment options', *British Journal of Criminology* 47, 3, 470–490

McWilliams, B. (1981) 'The probation officer at court: From friend to acquaintance', *The Howard Journal of Criminal Justice*, XX, 97–116

McWilliams, B. (1983) 'The mission to the English Police Courts 1876–1936', *The Howard Journal of Criminal Justice*, XXII, 129–147

McWilliams, B. (1985) 'The mission transformed: professionalisation of probation between the wars', *The Howard Journal of Criminal Justice*, 24, 4, 257–74

McWilliams, B. (1986) 'The English probation system and the diagnostic ideal', *The Howard Journal of Criminal Justice*, 25, 4, 241–260

McWilliams, B. (1987) 'Probation, pragmatism and policy', *The Howard Journal of Criminal Justice*, 26, 2, 97–121

MacDonald, D.I. and Blume, S.B. (1986) 'Children of Alcoholics', *American Journal of Diseases of Children*, 140, 750–754

Maas, P. (1969) *The Valachi Papers*, London: Panther

Maas, W. (2005) 'Freedom of Movement inside "Fortress Europe"', in Zureik, E., and Salter, M.B. (eds) *Global Surveillance and Policing: Borders, security, identity*, Cullompton: Willan

Maccoby, E.E. and Jacklin, C.N. (1975) *The Psychology of Sex Differences*, Stanford: Stanford University Press; London: Oxford University Press

Macpherson, W. (1999) *The Stephen Lawrence inquiry*, Report of an Inquiry by Sir William Macpherson of Cluny, advised by Tom Cook, The Right Reverend Dr John Sentamu and Dr Richard Stone, Cm 4262-1, London: The Stationery Office

Madsen, L., Parsons, S. and Grubin, D. (2004) 'A preliminary study of the contribution of periodic polygraph testing to the treatment and supervision of sex offenders', *Journal of Forensic Psychiatry and Psychology*, 15, 682 –695

Maguire, E.R. (2003) *Organizational Structure in American Police Agencies: Context, complexity and control*, Albany: State University of New York Press

Maguire, K. (1992) *Prison Industry: The effect of participation on inmate disciplinary adjustment*, Albany: State University of New York

Maguire, M. (1980) 'The impact of burglary upon victims', *The British Journal of Criminology*, 20, 3, 261–275

Maguire, M. (1982) *Burglary in a Dwelling*, London: Heinemann

Maguire, M. (2002) 'Crime statistics: The "data explosion" and its implications', in Maguire, M., Morgan, R. and Reiner, R. (eds) *The Oxford Handbook of Criminology*, 3rd edn, Oxford: Clarendon Press

Maguire, M. (2004) 'The crime reduction programme in England and Wales: Reflections on the vision and the reality', *Criminology and Criminal Justice*, 4, 3, 213–238

Maguire M. (2007) 'Crime data and statistics', in Maguire, M., Morgan, R., and Reiner, R. (eds) *The Oxford Handbook of Criminology*, 4th edn, Oxford: Oxford University Press

Maguire, M. and Corbett, C. (1987) *The Effects of Crime and the Work of Victims Support Schemes*, Aldershot: Gower

Maguire, M. and John, T. (2006) 'Intelligence led policing, managerialism and community engagement: competing priorities and the role of the national intelligence model in the UK', *Policing and Society*, 16, 1

Maher, L. (1997) *Sexed Work*, Oxford: Oxford University Press

Mair, G. (1995) 'Developments in probation in England and Wales, 1984–1993', in McIvor, G. (ed.) *Working with Offenders*, London: Jessica Kingsley

Mair, G. (2000) 'Creditable accreditation?', *Probation Journal*, 47, 688–71

Mair, G. (ed.) (2004) *What Matters in Probation*, Cullompton: Willan

Mair, G., Cross, N. and Taylor, S. (2007) *The use and impact of the Community Order and the Suspended Sentence Order*, London: Centre for Crime and Justice Studies

Malinosky-Rummell, R. and Hansen, D. (1993) 'Long-term consequences of childhood physical abuse' *Psychological Bulletin*, 114, 68–79

Malleson, K. (1991) 'Miscarriages of justice and the accessibility of the Court of Appeal', *Criminal Law Review*, 323

Mandel, E. (1984) *Delightful Murder: A social history of the crime story*, London: Pluto

Mandel, M. (2002) 'This war is illegal and immoral, and it won't prevent terrorism', in P. Scraton (ed.) *Beyond September 11: An Anthology of Dissent*, London: Pluto Press

Mannheim, K (1940) *Man and Society in an Age of Reconstruction*, New York: Harcourt, Brace

Manning, P. (ed.) (2007) *Drugs and Popular Culture*, Cullompton: Willan

Maple, J. (1999) *Crime Fighter*, New York: Doubleday

Mark, Sir R. (1977) *Policing a Perplexed Society*, London: George Allen and Unwin

Marsh, P. and Fox Kibby, K. (1992) *Drinking and Public Disorder*, London: Portman Group

Marshall, T.F. (1996) 'The evolution of restorative justice in Britain', *European Journal on Criminal Policy & Research* 4, 4, 21–43

Marshall, T.F. (1998) *Restorative Justice: An overview*, Minnesota: Centre for Restorative Justice and Peacemaking

Marshall, T.F. and Merry, S. (1990) *Crime and Accountability: Victim/Offender Mediation in Practice*, London: Home Office

Marshall, T., Simpson, S. and Stevens, A. (2000) *Healthcare in Prisons: A healthcare needs assessment*, Department of Public Health and Epidemiology, University of Birmingham (available at: http://www.hsmc.bham.ac.uk/prisonhealth/Tom%20Marshall2.pdf)

Martinson, R. (1974) 'What works? Questions and answers about prison reform', *The Public Interest*, 35, 22–54

Marx, K. (1976) Preface and introduction to *A Contribution to the Critique of Political Economy*, Peking: Foreign Languages Press

Matassa, M. and Newburn, T. (2003) 'Policing and terrorism', in Newburn, T. (ed.) *Handbook of Policing*, Cullompton: Willan

Mathieson, D. (1992) 'The Probation Service', in Stockdale, E. and Casale, S. (eds) *Criminal Justice Under Stress*, London: Blackstone Press

Matrix Research and Consultancy and NACRO (2004) *Evaluation of Drug Testing in the Criminal Justice System*, London: Home Office

Matsueda, R.L. and Anderson, K. (1998) 'The dynamics of delinquent peers and delinquent behaviour', *Criminology*, 36, 269–308

Matthews, R. and Young, J. (eds) (1992) *Rethinking Criminology: The realist debate*, London: Sage

Matthews, R. (1999) *Doing Time*, Basingstoke: Macmillan

Matthews, R. (2002) *Armed Robbery*, Cullompton: Willan

Matthews, R. and Young, J. (eds) (1986) *Confronting Crime*, London: Sage

Matthews, R. and Young, J. (eds) (1992a) *Issues in Realist Criminology*, London: Sage

Matthews, R. and Young, J. (1992b) 'Reflections on realism', in Matthews, R. and Young, J. (eds) *Rethinking Criminology: The realist debate*, London: Sage

Matsueda R. and Anderson, K. (1998) 'The dynamics of delinquent peers and delinquent behaviour', *Criminology*, 36, 269–308

Matza, D. (1964) *Delinquency and Drift*, New York: Wiley

Matza, D. (1969) *Becoming Deviant*, Englewood Cliffs, NJ: Prentice Hall

Matza, D. and Sykes, G. (1961) 'Juvenile delinquency and subterranean values', *American Sociological Review*, 26, 5, 712–719

Mawby, R.C. (2002) *Policing Images: Policing, communication and legitimacy,* Cullompton: Willan

Mawby, R.C. and Wright, A. (2003) 'The Police Organisation', in Newburn, T. (ed.) *Handbook of Policing,* Cullompton: Willan

Mawby, R.I. (1977) 'Defensible space: a theoretical and empirical appraisal', *Urban Studies,* 14, 169–80

Mawby, R.I. (1979) 'The victimization of juveniles: A comparative study of three areas of publicly owned housing in Sheffield', *Journal of Research in Crime and Delinquency,* 16, 98–113

Mawby, R.I. and Walklate, S. (1994) *Critical Victimology,* London: Sage

Mawby, R.I. (2001) *Burglary,* Devon, UK: Willan Publishing

May Report (1979) *Report of the Committee of Inquiry into the United Kingdom Prison Services,* HMSO, Cmnd 7673

May, C. (1992) 'A burning issue? Adolescent alcohol use in Britain 1970–1991', *Alcohol and Alcoholism,* 27, 2, 109–15

May, J. and Pitts, K, (eds) (2000) *Building Violence: How America's rush to incarcerate creates more violence,* Thousand Oaks, CA: Sage

May, T., Duffy, M., Warburton, H. and Hough, M. (2007) *Policing Cannabis as a Class C Drug,* York: Joseph Rowntree Foundation

May, T. (1994) 'Probation and community sanctions', in Maguire, M., Morgan, R. and Reiner, R. (eds) *The Oxford Handbook of Criminology,* Oxford: Oxford University Press

May, T (2001) *Social Research, Issues, Methods and Process,* Buckingham: Open University Press

May, T. and Hough, M. (2004) 'Drug markets and distribution systems', *Addiction Research and Theory,* 12, 6, 549–63

May, T., Warburton, H., Turnbull, P. and Hough, M. (2002) *Times they are a-changing: Policing of cannabis,* York: Joseph Rowntree Foundation

Mayhew, P., Clarke, R., Sturman, A., and Hough, M. (1976) *Crime as opportunity,* London: HMSO

Mayhew, P., Elliott, D. and Dowds, L. (1989) *The 1988 British Crime Survey,* London: Home Office

Mayhew, P. (1979) 'Defensible space: The current status of a crime prevention theory', *The Howard Journal of Criminal Justice,* 150–159

Mayhew, P. and Hough, M. (1988) 'The British Crime Survey: Origins and Impact', in Maguire, M. and Ponting, J. (eds) *Victims of Crime: A New Deal?,* Milton Keynes: Open University Press

Mayhew, P. and Mirrlees-Black, C. (1993) *The 1992 British Crime Survey,* Home Office Research Study No. 132, London: Home Office

Mead, G.H. (1934) *Mind, Self, and Society,* Chicago: University of Chicago Press

Measham, F., Newcombe, R. and Parker, H. (1993) 'The post-heroin generation', *Druglink,* May/June, 16–17

Measham, F., Newcombe, R. and Parker, H. (1994) 'The normalization of recreational drug use amongst young people in North-West England', *British Journal of Sociology,* 45, 2, 287–312

Mednick, S.A. (1977) *Biosocial Bases of Criminal Behaviour,* New York: Gardener

Mednick, S.A., Gabrielli, W.F. and Hutchings, B. (1983) 'Genetic influences in criminal convictions: evidence from an adoption cohort', in Van Dusen, K.T. and Mednick, S.A. (eds) *Prospective Studies of Crime and Delinquency,* Hague: Kluwer-Nijhoff

Mednick, S.A., Gabrielli Jr. W.F. and Hutchings, B. (1984) 'Genetic influences in criminal convictions: evidence from an adoption cohort', *Science,* 224, 4651, 891–894

Melossi, D. and Pavarini, M. (1981) *The Prison and the Factory: Origins of the penitentiary system,* London: Macmillan

Merikanges, K.R. (1990) T'he genetic epidemiology of alcoholism', *Psychological Medicine,* 20, 11–22

Merrington, S. and Stanley, S. (2000) 'Doubts about the what works initiative', *Probation Journal,* 47, 272–5

Merton, R.K. (1938) 'Social Structure and Anomie', *American Sociological Review,* 3, 672–682

Merton, R.K. (1949) 'Social Structure and Anomie: Revisions and extensions', in Anshen, R. (ed) *The Family,* New York: Harper Brothers

Merton, R.K. (1968) *Social Theory and Social Structure,* 2nd revised edn, New York: The Free Press

Merton, R.K. (1969) 'Social structure and anomie', reprinted in Cressey, D. and Ward, D. (eds) *Delinquency, Crime and Social Process,* New York: Harper and Row

Messerschmidt, J. (1993) *Masculinities and Crime: Critique and reconceptualisation of theory,* Lanham, MD: Rowman and Littlefield

Messner, S. and Rosenfeld, R. (2001) *Crime and the American Dream,* 3rd edn, Belmont, CA: Wadsworth

Meyer, J. and O'Malley, P. (2005) 'Missing the punitive turn? Canadian criminal justice, "balance" and penal modernism', in Pratt, J., Brown, D., Brown, M., Hallsworth, S. and Morrison, W. (eds) *The New Punitiveness: Trends, theories, perspectives,* Cullompton: Willan Publishing

Meyrowitz, J. (1985) *No Sense of Place: The impact of electronic media on social behavior,* New York: Oxford University Press

Michalowski, R. and Kramer, R. (2005) 'War, aggression and state crime: A criminological analysis of the invasion and occupation of Iraq', *British Journal of Criminology,* 46, 4, 446–469

Michalowski, R. and Kramer, R. (2006a) 'Enron-era economics versus economic democracy', in Michalowski, R. and Kramer, R. (eds) *State-Corporate Crime: Wrongdoing at the intersection of business and government,* New Brunswick, NJ: Rutgers University Press

Michalowski, R. and Kramer, R. (eds) (2006b) *State-Corporate Crime: Wrongdoing at the intersection of business and government,* New Brunswick, NJ: Rutgers University Press

Michalowski, R. and Kramer, R. (2007) 'State-corporate crime and criminological inquiry', in Pontell, H. and Geis, G. (eds) *International Handbook of White Collar and Corporate Crime,* New York: Springer

Miers, D. (1989) 'Positivist victimology: a critique', *International Review of Victimology,* 1, 1, 1–29

Miers, D. (1990) *Compensation for Criminal Injuries,* London: Butterworths

Miers, D., Maguire, M., Goldie, S., Sharpe, K., Hale, C., Netten, A., Uglow, S., Doolin, K., Hallam, A., Enterkin, J. and Newburn, T. (2001) *An Exploratory Evaluation of Restorative Justice Schemes,* London: Home Office

Miers, D (2007) 'Looking beyond Great Britain: The development of criminal injuries compensation', in Walkate, S. (ed.) *Handbook of Victims and Victimology,* Cullompton: Willan

Miller, E. (1999) 'The neuropsychology of offending', *Psychology, Crime and Law,* 5, 515–36

Miller, J. (2000) 'Feminist theories of women's crime: Robbery as a case study', in Simpson, S. (ed.) *Of Crime and Criminality,* Thousand Oaks, CA: Pine Forge Press

Miller, J., Bland, N. and Quinton, P. (2000) *The Impact of Stops and Searches on Crime and the Community,* Police Research Series Paper 127, London: Home Office

Miller, P. and Plant, M. (1996) 'Drinking, smoking and illicit drug use among 15 and 16 year olds in the United Kingdom', *British Medical Journal,* 313, 394–7

Miller, W.B. (1958) 'Lower-class culture as a generating milieu of gang delinquency', *Journal of Social Issues,* 14, 3, 5–19

Miller, W. (1975) 'Cops and Bobbies 1830–1870', *Journal of Social History,* IX, 73–88

Millie, A., Jacobson, J., McDonald, E. and Hough, M. (2005) *Anti-social Behaviour Strategies: Finding a Balance,* York: Joseph Rowntree Foundation

Mills, C.W. (1956) *The Power Elite,* Oxford: Oxford University Press

Mills, C.W. (1959) *The Sociological Imagination,* New York: Oxford University Press

Milne, R. and Bull, R. (2006) 'Interviewing victims of crime, including children and people with intellectual disabilities', in Kebbrell, M. and Davies, G. (eds) *Practical Psychology for Forensic Investigations and Prosecutions,* Chichester: Wiley

Mitchell, B. (1990) *Murder and Penal Policy,* London: Macmillan

Mokhiber, R. (1988) *Corporate Crime and Violence,* San Francisco: Sierra Club

Moffitt, T.E. 92005) 'The new look of behavioural genetics in developmental psychopathology: gene-environment interplay in antisocial behaviours', *The Psychological Bulletin,* 131, 4, 533–554

Monahan, J. *et al.* (2001) *Rethinking Risk Assessment: The MacArthur Study of Mental Disorder and Violence,* Oxford: Oxford University Press

Mooney, J. (1993) *The Hidden Figure: Domestic violence in North London,* Middlesex University Centre for Criminology

Moore, D. and Hannah-Moffat, K. (2005) 'The liberal veil: revisiting Canadian penality', in Pratt, J., Brown, D., Brown, M., Hallsworth, S. and Morrison, W. (eds) *The New Punitiveness: Trends, theories, perspectives,* Cullompton: Willan Publishing

Moore, R., Gray, E., Roberts, C., Taylor, E. and Merrington, S. (2006) *Managing Persistent and Serious Offenders in the Community,* Cullompton: Willan

Moorthy, U., Cahalin, K. and Howard, P. (2004) *Ethnicity and Parole,* Home Office Research Findings 222, London: Home Office

Morgan, J. (1987) *Conflict and Order: The police and labour disputes in England and Wales, 1900–1939,* Oxford: Clarendon Press

Morgan, J. and Zedner, L. (1992) *Child Victims: Crime, impact and criminal justice,* Oxford: Oxford University Press

Morgan, P.M. and Henderson, P.F. (1998) *Remand decisions and offending on bail: evaluation of the Bail Process Project,* London: Home Office

Morgan R. (1983) 'How resources are used in the prison system', *A Prison System for the 80's and Beyond (The Noel Buxton Lectures 1982–3),* London: NACRO

Morgan, R. (1992) 'Following Woolf – The Prospects for Prison Policy', *Journal of Law and Society,* 19, 2

Morgan, R. (1994) 'Imprisonment', in Maguire, M., Morgan, R. and Reiner, R. (eds) *The Oxford Handbook of Criminology,* 1st edn, Oxford: Clarendon Press

Morgan, R. (2006) 'With respect to order, the rules of the game have changed: New Labour's dominance of the "law and order" agenda', in Newburn, T. and Rock, P. (eds) *The Politics of Crime Control,* Oxford: Oxford University Press

Morgan, R. and Evans, M. (1999) *Protecting Prisoners: The standards of the European Committee for the Prevention of Torture in Context,* Oxford: Oxford University Press

Morgan, R. and Russell, N. (2000) *The Judiciary in the Magistrates' Courts,* Home Office and LCD Occasional Paper 66, London: Home Office/LCD

Morgan, R. and Newburn, T. (2007) 'Youth Justice', in Maguire, M., Morgan, R. and Reiner, R. (eds) *The Oxford Handbook of Criminology,* 4th edn, Oxford: Oxford University Press

MORI (2004) *MORI Youth Survey 2004,* London: Youth Justice Board

Moriarty, M. (1977) 'The policy-making process: how it is seen from the Home Office', in Walker, N. and Giller, H. (eds) *Penal Policy-Making in England,* Cambridge: Insitute of Criminology

Morris, A. and McIsaac, M. (1978) *Juvenile justice? The practice of social welfare,* London: Heinemann Educational

Morris, A. and Maxwell, G. (2000) 'The practice of family group conferences in New Zealand: Assessing the place, potential and pitfalls of restorative justice', in Crawford, A. and Goodey, J. (eds) *Integrating a Victim Perspective within Criminal Justice,* Aldershot: Ashgate

Morris, A. and Giller, H. (1987) *Understanding Juvenile Justice,* London: Croom Helm

Morris, N. (1974) *The Future of Imprisonment,* Chicago: University of Chicago Press

Morris, N. and Rothman, D. (eds) (1997) *The Oxford History of the Prison,* Oxford: Oxford University Press

Morris, T. and Blom-Cooper, L. (1979) *Murder in England and Wales since 1957,* London: Observer

Morris, W. (2004) *The Report of the Morris Inquiry: The case for change: people in the Metropolitan Police Service,* London: Metropolitan Police Authority

Mott, J. and Mirrlees-Black, C. (1993) *Self-reported Drug Misuse in England and Wales: Main Finding from the 1992 British Crime Survey,* London: Home Office

Mountbatten Report (1966) *Report of the Inquiry into Prison Escapes and Security,* Cmnd 3175, London: HMSO

Moxon, D., Hedderman, C. and Sutton, M. (1990) *Deductions from benefit for fine default,* London: Home Office

Mulcahy, A. (1994) 'The justifications of justice', *British Journal of Criminology,* 34, 411

Mullender, A. (1996) *Rethinking Domestic Violence,* London: Routledge

Muncie, J. (1984) *'The trouble with kids today': Youth and crime in post-war Britain,* London: Hutchinson

Muncie, J. (2000) 'Pragmatic realism? Searching for criminology in the new youth justice', in Goldson, B. (ed.) *The New Youth Justice,* Lyme Regis: Russell House

Muncie, J. (2001) 'The construction and deconstruction of crime', in Muncie, J. and McLaughlin, E. (eds) *The Problem of Crime,* London: Sage

Muncie, J. (2004) 'Youth justice: Globalisation and multi-modal governance', in Newburn, T. and Sparks, R. (eds) *Criminal Justice and Political Cultures,* Cullompton: Willan

Murray, C. (1990) *The Emerging British Underclass,* London: IEA Health and Welfare Unit

MVA and Miller, J. (2000) *Profiling Populations Available for Stops and Searches,* Police Research Group Paper 131, London: Home Office

Mwenda, L. (2005) *Drug Offenders in England and Wales,* Statistical Bulletin, 23/05, London: Home Office

Mythen, G. and Walklate, S. (2006) *Beyond the Risk Society: Critical reflections on risk and human security,* Maidenhead: Open University Press

NACRO (2000) *Race and Prisons: A snapshot survey in 2000,* London: NACRO

Nadelmann, E. (1993) *Cops Across Borders: The internationalization of U.S. criminal law enforcement,* University Park, PA: Pennyslvania State University Press

Narey, M. (1997) *Review of Delay in the Criminal Justice System,* London: The Home Office

Nash, M. and Savage, S. (1994) 'A criminal record? Law, order and Conservative policy', in Savage, S., Atkinson, R. and Robins, L. (eds) *Public Policy in Britain,* Basingstoke: Macmillan

National Audit Office (1997) *The Crown Prosecution Service,* London: National Audit Office

National Audit Office (2004) *The Management of Sickness Absence in the Prison Service,* London: National Audit Office

National Criminal Intelligence Service (2005) *Annual Report 2004/05,* London: The Stationery Office

National Economic Research Associates (2000) *The Economic Cost of Fraud,* London: National Economic Research Associates

Nee, C. and Taylor, M. (1988) 'Residential Burglary in the Republic of Ireland: A Situational Perspective', *The Howard Journal of Criminal Justice,* 27, 105–116.

Nelken, D. (1994) 'White collar crime', in Maguire, M., Morgan, R. and Reiner, R. (eds) *The Oxford Handbook of Criminology*, 1st edn, Oxford: Oxford University Press

Nelken, D. (2005) 'When is a society non-punitive? The Italian case', in in Pratt, J., Brown, D., Brown, M., Hallsworth, S. and Morrison, W. (eds) *The New Punitiveness: Trends, theories, perspectives,* Cullompton: Willan Publishing

Nelken, D. (2007) 'White collar and corporate crime', in Maguire, M., Morgan, R. and Reiner, R. (eds) *The Oxford Handbook of Criminology*, 4th edn, Oxford: Oxford University Press

Nellis, M. (1991) 'The last days of "juvenile" justice', in Carter, P., Jeffs, T. and Smith, M. (eds) *Social Work and Social Welfare Yearbook 3*, Milton Keynes, Open University Press

Nellis, M. (2006) 'NOMS, contestability and the process of technocorrectional innovation', in Hough, M., Allen, R. and Padel, U. (eds) *Reshaping probation and prisons: The new offender management framework*, London: Centre for Crime and Justice Studies

Nellis, M. (2007) 'Humanising justice: the English Probation Service up to 1972', in Gelsthorpe, L. and Morgan, R. (eds) *Handbook of Probation*, Cullompton: Willan

Newburn, T. (1991) *Permission and Regulation: Law and Morals in Post-War Britain*, London: Routledge

Newburn, T. (1999) 'Understanding and Preventing Police Corruption: Lessons from the literature', London: Home Office

Newburn, T. (2003) *Handbook of Policing*, Cullompton: Willan

Newburn, T. (2006) 'Contrasts in intolerance: Cultures of control in the United States and Britain', in Newburn, T. and Rock, P. (eds) *The Politics of Crime Control: Essays in Honour of David Downes*, Oxford: Clarendon Press

Newburn, T. (2007) 'Tough on crime: Penal policy in England and Wales', in Tonry, M. and Doob, A. (eds) *Crime and Justice: A review of research,* Chicago: Chicago University Press

Newburn, T. and Jones, T. (2007) 'Symbolising crime control: reflections of zero tolerance', *Theoretical Criminology*

Newburn, T. and Rock (eds) (2006) *The Politics of Crime Control: Essays in Honour of David Downes*, Oxford: Clarendon Press

Newburn, T. and Shiner, M. (2001) *Teenage Kicks: Young people and alcohol*, York: Joseph Rowntree Foundation

Newburn, T. and Shiner, M. (2005) *Dealing with Disaffection*, Cullompton: Willan

Newburn, T., Shiner, M. and Hayman, S. (2004) 'Race, crime and injustice: Strip search and the treatment of suspects in custody', *British Journal of Criminology*, 44, 677–694

Newburn, T. and Souhami, A. (2005) 'Youth diversion', in Tilley, N. (ed.) *Handbook of Crime Prevention and Community Safety*, Cullompton: Willan

Newburn, T. and Sparks, R. (2004) *Criminal Justice and Political Cultures*, Cullompton: Willan

Newburn, T. and Stanko, E.A. (1994) *Just Boys Doing Business: Men, masculinities and crime*, London: Routledge

Newman, O. (1972) *Defensible Space: Crime prevention through urban design*, New York: Collier

NFER (2007) *Smoking, drinking and drug use,* London: Department of Health

Nicholas, S. *et al.* (2005) *Crime in England and Wales*, HOSB 11/05, London : Home Office

Nieuwbeerta, P. (ed.) (2002) *Crime Victimization in comparative perspective: Results from the International Crime Victims Survey, 1989–2000,* Den Haag, The Netherlands: Boom Juridische uitgevers

Nisbett, R.E. (1995) 'Race, IQ and Scientism', in S. Fraser (ed.) *The Bell Curve Wars: Race, Intelligence and the Future of America,* New York: Basic Books

Niven, S. and Olagundoye, J. (2002) *Jobs and Homes – A survey of prisoners nearing release*, Home Office Research Findings 173, London: Home Office

Niven, S. and Stewart, D. (2005) *Resettlement Outcomes from Release from Prison 2003*, Home Office Findings 248, London: Home Office

Noaks, L. and Wincup, E. (2004) *Criminological Research: Understanding qualitative methods*, London: Sage

Nobles, R. and Schiff, D. (2000) *Understanding Miscarriages of Justice: Law, the media and the inevitability of a crisis*, Oxford: Oxford University Press

Nordberg, L., Rydelius, P. and Zetterstrom, R. (1993) 'Children of alcoholic parents: health, growth, mental development and psychopathology until school age', *Acta Paediatrica Supplement*, 387, 1–24

Norris, C. and Armstrong, G. (1999a) 'CCTV and the rise of mass surveillance society', in Carlen, P. and Morgan, R. (eds) *Crime Unlimited? Questions for the 21st Century,* Basingstoke: Macmillan

Norris, C. and Armstrong, G. (1999b) *The Maximum Surveillance Society: The rise of CCTV,* London: Berg

Nussbaum, M. 2004) *Hiding from Humanity: Disgust, shame and the law*, Princeton, NJ: Princeton University Press

Nutt, D., King, L., Saulsbury, W. and Blakemore, C. (2007) 'Development of a rational scale to assess the harm of drugs and potential misuse', *The Lancet*, 369, 1047–1053

Nye, F.I. (1958) *Family Relationships and Delinquent Behaviour*, New York: Wiley

Oakley, A. (1998) 'Public Policy Experimentation: Lessons from America', *Policy Studies*, 19, 2, 93–114

Oakley, A. (2000) *Experiments in Knowing: Gender and method in the social sciences*, Cambridge: Polity Press

O'Connor, M., Sigman, M. and Brill, N. (1987) 'Disorganization of attachment in relation to maternal alcohol consumption', *Journal of Consulting and Clinical Psychology*, 55, 831–6

Office for National Statistics (1998) *Psychiatric Morbidity Amongst Prisoners in England and Wales*, London: Stationery Office

Office of National Statistics (2001) *Health Survey for England 2000*, London: ONS

Oliver, J. (1985) 'Successive generations of child maltreatment: Social and medical disorders in the parents', *British Journal of Psychiatry*, 147, 484–90

O'Malley, P. (1992) 'Risk, power and crime prevention', *Economy and Society*, 21, 3, 251–268

O'Malley, P. (2000) 'Risk societies and the government of crime', in Brown, P. and Pratt, J. (eds) *Dangerous Offenders: Punishment and social order*, London: Routledge

O'Malley, P. (2001) 'Policing crime risks in the neo-liberal era', in Stenson, K. and Sullivan, R. (eds) *Risk and Justice: The politics of crime control in liberal democracies*, Cullompton: Willan

O'Malley, P. (2006) 'Criminology and risk', in Mythen, G. and Walklate, S. (eds) *Beyond the Risk Society: Critical reflections on risk and human security*, Maidenhead: Open University Press

Orford, J. (1985) *Excessive Appetites: A psychological view of addictions*, Chichester: Wiley

Osborn, S. and West, D. (1979) 'Conviction records of fathers and sons compared', *British Journal of Criminology*, 19, 120–133

Osborne, R. and Kidd-Hewitt, D. (eds) (1995) *Crime and the Media: The Postmodern Spectacle*, East Haven, CT: Pluto Press

Osborne, D. and Gaebler, T. (1992) *Reinventing Government*, New York: Penguin

Olweus, D., Block, J. and Radke-Yarrow, M. (1986) *The Development of Antisocial and Prosocial Behaviour*, Orlando, FL: Academic Press

Packer, H. (1968) *The Limits of the Criminal Sanction*, Stanford: Stanford University Press

Painter, K.A., Farrington, D.P. (1997) 'The crime reducing effect of improved street lighting: the Dudley Project', in Clarke, R.V.G. (ed.) *Situational Crime Prevention: Successful Case Studies*, 2nd edn, 209–26, New York: Harrow and Heston

Palmer, E. (2003) *Offending Behaviour: Moral reasoning, criminal conduct and the rehabilitation of offenders*, Cullompton: Willan

Pape, H. and Hammer, T. (1996) 'How does young people's alcohol consumption change during the transition to early adulthood?', *Addiction*, 91, 9, 1345–1358

Park, R.E. (1915) 'The City', *American Journal of Sociology*, 20, 577–612

Park, R.E. (1925) 'Community, organization and juvenile delinquency', in Park, R. and Burgess, E. (eds) *The City*, Chicago: Chicago University Press

Parker, E.S., Morihisa, J.M., Wyatt, R.J., Schwartz, B.L., Weingartner, H. and Stillman, R.C. (1981) 'The alcohol facilitation effect on memory: A dose-response study', *Psychopharmacology*, 74, 88–92

Parker, H. (1974) *View from the Boys*, London: David and Charles

Parker, H., Newcombe, R. and Bakx, K. (1988) *Living With Heroin: The Impact of Drugs 'Epidemic' on an English Community*, Milton Keynes: Open University Press

Parker, H. (1996) 'Young adult offenders, alcohol and criminological cul-de-sacs', *British Journal of Criminology*, 36, 2, 282–298

Parker, H. and Measham, F. (1994) 'Pick 'n mix: changing patterns of illicit drug use among 1990's adolescents', *Drugs, Education, Prevention and Policy*, 1, 1, 5–13

Parker, H., Aldridge, J., and Measham, F. (1998) *Illegal Leisure: The normalization of adolescent recreational drug use*, London: Routledge

Parker, H., Measham, F. and Aldridge, J. (1995) *Drug Futures: Changing patterns of drug use amongst English youth*, London: ISDD

Parker, H., Williams, L. and Aldridge, J. (2002) 'The normalization of "sensible" recreational drug use: further evidence from the North West England longitudinal study', *Sociology*, 24, 291–311

Passas, N. and Nelken, D. (1993) 'The thin line between legitimate and criminal enterprises: Subsidy frauds in the European community', *Crime, Law and Social Change*, 19, 223–44

Patrick, J. (1973) *A Glasgow Gang Observed*, London: Methuen

Patrick, C.J. and Iacono, W.G. (1991) 'Validity of the control question polygraph test: The problem of sampling bias', *Journal of Applied Psychology*, 76, 2, 229–238

Patton, M.Q. (1981) *Creative Evaluation*, Newbury Park, CA: Sage

Patton, M.Q. (1986) *Utilization-Focused Evaluation*, 2nd edn, Newbury Park, CA: Sage

Pawson, R. (2006) *Evidence-Based Policy*, London: Sage

Pawson, R. and Tilley, N. (1994) 'What works in evaluation research?', *British Journal of Criminology*, 4, 3. 291–306

Pawson, R. and Tilley, N. (1996) 'What's crucial in evaluation research: A reply to Bennett', *British Journal of Criminology*, 36, 4, 574–578

Pawson, R. and Tilley, N. (1997) *Realistic Evaluation*, London: Sage

Pawson, R. and Tilley, N. (1998) 'Caring communities, paradigm polemics, design debates, evaluation', *The International Journal of Theory, Research and Practice*, 4, 1, 73–90

Pawson, R. and Tilley, N. (1998) 'Cookbook methods and disastrous recipes: A rejoinder to Farrington's evaluation', *The International Journal of Theory, Research and Practice*, 4, 2, 211–213

Pearce, D. (1978) 'The feminization of poverty: women, work and welfare', *Urban and Social Change Review*, 11, 28–36

Pearce, F. (1976) *Crimes of the Powerful*, London: Pluto

Pearce, F. and Tombs, S. (1992) 'Realism and corporate crime', in Matthews, R. and Young, J. (eds) *Issues in Realist Criminology*, London: Sage

Pearson, G. (1975) *The Deviant Imagination: Psychiatry, social work and social change*, London: Macmillan

Pearson, G. (1983) *Hooligan: A history of respectable fears*, Basingstoke: Macmillan

Pearson, G. (1984) 'Falling standards: A short, sharp history of moral decline', in Barker, M. (ed) *The Video Nasties: Freedom and censorship in the media*, London: Pluto Press

Pearson, G. (1987) 'Social deprivation, unemployment and patterns of heroin use', in Dorn, N. and South, N. (eds) *A Land fit for Heroin? Drug policies, prevention and practice*, Basingstoke: Macmillan

Pearson, G. (2001) 'Normal drug use: ethnographic fieldwork among a recreational network of adult drug users in inner-London', *Substance Use and Misuse*, 36, 1/2, 167–200

Pearson, G. (2007) 'Drug markets and dealing from "street dealer" to "Mr Big"', in Simpson, M., Shildrick, T. and Macdonald, R. (eds) *Drugs in Britain: Supply, consumption and control*, Basingstoke: Palgrave

Pearson, G. and Hobbs, D. (2001) *Middle market drug distribution*, London: Home Office

Pearson, G., Sampson, A., Blagg, H., Stubbs, P. and Smith, D. (1989) 'Policing racism', in Morgan, R. and Smith, D. (eds) *Coming to Terms with Policing*, London: Routledge

Pease, K. (1991) 'The Kirkholt Project: Preventing burglary on a British public housing estate', *Security Journal*, 2, 2, 73–7

Pease, K. (1997) 'Crime prevention', in Maguire, M., Morgan, R. and Reiner, R. (eds) *The Oxford Handbook of Criminology*, 2nd edn, Oxford: Oxford University Press

Peay, J. (2007) 'Mentally disordered offenders, mental health and crime', in Maguire M., Morgan, R., and Reiner, R. (eds) *The Oxford Handbook of Criminology*, 4th edn, Oxford: Oxford University Press

Pellew, J. (1982) *The Home Office 1848–1914: From clerks to bureaucrats*, London: Heinemann

Pengelly, R. (1999) 'Crimewatch: A voyeur's paradise or public service?', *Police Magazine*, January

Penrod, S.D. and Cutler, B.L. (1987) 'Assessing the competency of juries', in Weiner, I. and Hess, A. (eds) *The Handbook of Forensic Psychology*, New York: Wiley

Persky, H., Smith, K.D., and Basu, G.K. (1971) 'Relation of psychologic measures of aggression and hostility to testosterone production in man', *Psychosomatic Medicine*, 33, 265–278

Phillips, C. and Brown, D. (1998) *Entry into the Criminal Justice System: A survey of police arrests and their outcomes*, Home Office Research Study No. 185, London: Home Office

Philips, D. (1978) *Crime and Authority in Victorian England: the Black Country 1835–1860*, London: Croom Helm

Philips, D. (1983) 'A just measure of crime, authority, hunters and blue locusts: The "revisionist" social history of crime and the law in Britain, 1780–1850', in Cohen, S. and Scull, A. (eds) *Social Control and the State*, Oxford: Blackwell Publishing

Phillips, C. and Brown, D. (1998) *Entry into the criminal justice system: A survey of police arrests and their outcomes*, Home Office Research Study 185, London: Home Office

Phillips, C. (2002) 'From voluntary to statutory status', in Hughes, G., McLaughlin, E. and Muncie, J. (eds) *Crime Prevention and Community Safety: New directions*, 163–81, London: Sage

Phillips, O.H. (1978) *Constitutional and administrative law*, 6th edn, by O.H. Phillips and Paul Jackson, London: Sweet and Maxwell

Piacentini, L. (2004) *Surviving Russian Prisons*, Cullompton: Willan

Piaget, J. (1952) *The Origins of Intelligence in Children,* New York: International Universities Press

Pickens, R.W., Svikis, D.S., McGue, M., Lykken, D.T., Heston, L.L. and Clayton, P.J. (1991) 'Heterogeneity in the inheritance of alcoholism: A study of male and female twins', *Archives of General Psychiatry,* 48, 19–28

Pickering, S. (2001) 'Common sense and original deviancy: News discourses and asylum seekers in Australia', *Journal of Refugee Studies,* 14, 2, 169–186

Piquero, A., Farrington, D. and Blumstein, A. (2007) *Key Issues in Criminal Career Research,* Cambridge: Cambridge University Press

Piquero, A. and Hickman, M. (1999) 'An empirical test of Tittle's control balance theory', *Criminology,* 37, 319–342

Pizzey, E. (1974) *Scream Quietly or the Neighbours Will Hear,* London: Penguin

Plant, M. and Plant, M. (2006) *Binge Britain: Alcohol and the national response,* Oxford: Oxford University Press

Plomin, R. (1990) *Nature and Nurture,* Pacific Grove, CA: Brooks/Cole

Plotnikoff, J. and Woolfson, R. (2001) '*A Fair Balance'? Evaluation of the operation of disclosure law,* London: Home Office

Plummer, K. (1979) 'Misunderstanding labelling perspectives', in Downes, D. and Rock, P. (eds) *Deviant Interpretations,* Oxford: Oxford University Press

Police Foundation (2000) *Drugs and the Law: Report of the Independent Inquiry,* London: Police Foundation

Police Foundation (2002) *Policing the possession of cannabis: Residents views on the Lambeth experiment,* London: The Police Foundation

Polk, M. (1994) *When Men Kill: Scenarios of masculine violence,* Cambridge: Cambridge University Press

Pollak, O. (1961) *The Criminality of Women,* New York: A.S. Barnes

Pollard, C. (1996) 'Public safety, accountability and the courts', *Criminal Law Review,* 152

Porporino, F.J. and Fabiano, E.A. (2000) *Theory Manual for Reasoning and Rehabilitation,* London: Joint Prison Probation Service Accreditation Panel

Porter, S., Yuille, J.C., and Lehmna, D.R. (1999) 'The nature of real, implanted and fabricated memories for emotional childhood events: Implications for the recovered memory debate', *Law and Human Behaviour,* 23, 5, 517–537

Power, A. (1997) *Estates on the Edge,* Basingstoke: Macmillan

Poyner, B. (1983) *Design against Crime: Beyond defensible space,* London: Butterworths

Poyner, B. (1991) 'Crime prevention in two car parks', *Security Journal,* 2, 96–101

Poyner, B. and Webb, B. (1997) 'Reducing theft from shopping bags in city centre markets', in Clarke, R.V.G. (ed.) *Situational Crime Prevention Successful Case Studies,* 2nd edn, 83–9, New York: Harrow and Heston

Pratt, J. (2007) *Penal Populism,* London: Routledge

Pratt, J., Brown, D., Brown, M., Hallsworth, S. and Morrison, W. (eds) (2005) *The New Punitiveness: Trends, theories, perspectives,* Cullompton: Willan

Presdee, M. (2000) *Cultural Criminology and the Carnival of Crime,* London: Routledge

President's Commission on Law Enforcement and the Administration of Justice (1967) *The Challenge of Crime in a Free Society,* Washington DC: Government Printing Office

Price, W.H., Strong, J.A., Whatmore, P.B. and McClemont, W.F. (1966) 'Criminal patients with XYY sex-chromosome complement', *The Lancet,* 1, 565–6

Prins, H. (1990) 'Dangerousness: A review', in Bluglass, R. and Bowden, R.(eds) *Principle and Practice of Forensic Psychiatry,* Edinburgh: Churchill Livingstone

Prison Reform Trust (2003) 'Experiences of Minority Ethnic Employees in Prisons', London: Prison Reform Trust

Punch, M. (1996) 'Dirty Business: Exploring corporate misconduct', London: Sage

Putwain, D. and Sammons, A. (2002) *Psychology and Crime,* London: Routledge

Pynoos, R. S., Frederick, C., Nader, K., Arroyo, W., Steinberg, A., Eth, S., Nunez, F., and Fairbanks, L. (1987) 'Life threat and posttraumatic stress in school-age children', *Archives of General Psychiatry,* 44, 1057–1063

Quaker Peace and Social Witness (2005) *Circles of Support and Accountability in the Thames Valley: The first three years,* London: Quaker Communications (available at: www.quaker.org.uk)

Quinney, R. (1970) *The Social Reality of Crime,* Boston: Little, Brown

Quinney, R. (1974) *Critique of the Legal Order,* Boston: Little, Brown.

Quinney, R. (1977) *Class, State and Crime,* New York: Longman

Quinney, R. (1980) *Class, State and Crime,* 2nd edn, New York: Longman

Quinney, R. (1997) 'Socialist humanism and critical/peacemaking criminology: The continuing project', in Maclean, B. and Milovanovic, D. (eds) *Thinking Critically About Crime,* Vancouver, BC: Collective Press

Quinney, R. (2000) *Bearing Witness to Crime and Social Justice*, Albany: State University of New York Press

Radzinowicz, L. (1948) *A history of English criminal law and its administration from 1750*, 1, London : Stevens & Sons

Radzinowicz, L. (1962) *In Search of Criminology*, London: Heinemann

Radzinowicz, L. (1966) *Ideology and Crime: A study of crime in its social and historical context*, London: Heinemann Educational

Rafter, N. (1985) 'Chastizing the unchaste: Social control functions of a women's reformatory', in Cohen, S. and Scull, A. (eds) *Social Control and the State*, Oxford: Blackwell Publishing

Rafter, N. (1992) 'Criminal anthropology in the United States', *Criminology*, 30, 4, 525–36

Rafter, N.H. (1998) *Creating Born Criminals*, Champaign, IL: University of Illinois Press

Rafter, R.H. and Stanko, B. (1982) *Judge, Lawyer, Victim, Thief: Women, gender roles and criminal justice*, Boston: Northeastern University Press

Raine, A. (1993) *The Psychopathology of Crime*, San Diego, CA: Academic Press

Raine, A. (1996) 'Autonomic nervous system factors underlying disinhibited, antisocial, and violent behavior: Biosocial perspectives and treatment implications', *Annals of the New York Academy of Sciences*, 794, 1, 46–59

Raine, A., Brennan, P., Farrington, D.P. and Mednick, S.A. (eds) (1997) *Biosocial Bases of Violence*, New York: Plenum

Raine, A., Buchsbaum, M., Lottenberg, S., Abel, L. and Stoddard, S. (1994) 'Selective reductions in prefrontal glucose metabolism in murderers', *Biological Psychiatry*, 36, 365–73

Raine, J.W. and Willson, M.J. (1993) *Managing Criminal Justice*, New York, London: Harvester Wheatsheaf

Ramazanoglu, C. and Holland, J. (2002) *Feminist Methodology: Challenges and Choices*, London: Sage

Ramsay, M. (1990) *Lagerland Lost: An experiment in keeping drinkers off the streets in Coventry and elsewhere*, Crime Prevention Unit Paper 22, London: Home Office

Ramsay, M. (1991) *The influence of street lighting on crime and fear of crime*, Crime Prevention Unit Paper 28, London: Home Office

Ramsay, M., Baker, P., Goulden, C., Sharp, C. and Sondhi, A. (2001) *Drug misuse declared in 2000: Results from the British crime survey*, Home Office Research Study 224, London: Home Office

Ramsbotham, D. (2005) *Prisongate: The shocking state of Britain's prisons and the need for visionary change*, London: The Free Press

Rape Research and Counselling Project (1981) *Submission to the Criminal Law Revision Committee*, November

Rauchs, G. and Koenig, D.J. (2001) 'Europol', in Koenig, D.J. and Das, D.K. (eds) *International Police Co-operation: A world perspective*, Lanham, MA: Lexington Books

Rawlings, P. (1992) 'Creeping privatization? The police, the Conservative government and policing in the late 1980s', in Reiner, R. and Cross, M. (eds) *Beyond Law and Order: Criminal justice policy and politics into the 1990s*, Basingstoke: Macmillan

Rawlings, P. (1995) 'The idea of policing: a history', *Policing and Society*, 5, 2, 129–149

Rawlings, P. (1999) *Crime and Power: A history of criminal justice 1688–1998*, London; New York: Longman

Rawlings, R. (2002) *Delineating Wales: Constitutional, legal and administrative aspects of national devolution*, Cardiff: University of Wales Press

Rawlinson, P. (2000) 'Mafia, methodology and "alien" culture', in King, R. and Wincup, E. (eds) *Doing Research on Crime and Justice*, New York: Oxford University Press

Ray, L. and Smith, D. (2001) 'Racist offenders and the politics of "hate crime"', *Law and Critique*, 12, 3, 203–221

Raynor, P. (1988) *Probation as an Alternative to Custody*, Aldershot: Avebury

Raynor, P. (2004) 'The probation service "pathfinders": Finding the path and losing the way?', *Criminology and Criminal Justice*, 4, 3, 309–325

Raynor, P. (2007) 'Community penalties: Probation, 'what works' and offender management', in Maguire, M., Morgan, R. and Reiner, R. (eds) *The Oxford Handbook of Criminology*, 4th edn, Oxford: Oxford University Press

Raynor, P. and Vanstone, M. (1997) *Straight thinking on probation (STOP): The Mid Glamorgan experiment*, Probation Studies Unit Report No. 4

Raynor, P. and Vanstone, M. (2002) *Understanding Community Penalties; Probation, Change and Social Context*, Buckingham: Open University Press

Raynor, P. and Vanstone, M. (2007) 'Towards and correctional service', in Gelsthorpe, L. and Morgan, R. (eds) *Handbook of Probation*, Cullompton: Willan

RDS NOMS (2006) *Offender Management Caseload Statistics 2005*, Home Office Statistical Bulletin 18/06, London: Home Office

Reckless, W.C. (1967) *The Crime Problem*, 4th edn, New York: Appleton-Century-Crofts

Redhead, S. (1990) *The End of the Century Party: Youth and pop towards 2000,* Manchester: Manchester University Press

Redmayne, M. (2004) 'Disclosure and its discontents', *Criminal Law Review,* 61, 684

Redshaw, J. and Mawby, R. (1996) 'Commercial burglary: Victims' views of the crime and the police response', *International Journal of Risk, Security and Crime Prevention,* 1, 3, 185–193

Reed, G.E. and Yeager, P.C. (1996) 'Organizational offending and neoclassical criminology: Challenging the reach of a general theory of crime', *Criminology,* 34, 3, 357–382

Regan, L. and Kelly, L. (2003) *Rape: Still a forgotten issue,* London: Child and Woman Abuse Studies Unit, London Metropolitan University (available at: http://www.rcne.com/)

Reiman, J.H. (1979) *The Rich get Richer and the Poor get Prison,* New York: Wiley

Reiner, R. (1991) *Chief Constables,* Oxford: Oxford University Press

Reiner, R. (1994) 'The dialectics of Dixon: The changing image of the TV cop', in Stephens, M. and Becker, S. (eds) *Police Force, Police Service,* Basingstoke: Macmillan

Reiner, R. (2000) *The Politics of the Police,* 3rd edn, Oxford: Oxford University Press

Reiner, R. (2002) 'Media-made criminality', in Maguire, M., Morgan, R. and Reiner, R. (eds) *The Oxford Handbook of Criminology,* 3rd edn, Oxford: Clarendon Press

Reiner, R. (2003) 'Policing and the media', in Newburn, T. (ed.) *Handbook of Policing,* Cullompton: Willan

Reiner, R. (2007) 'Media-made criminality', in Maguire, M., Morgan, R. and Reiner, R. (eds) *The Oxford Handbook of Criminology,* 4th edn, Oxford: Clarendon Press

Reiss, A. (1951) 'Delinquency as the failure of personal and social controls', *American Sociological Review,* 16, 196–207

Reiss, A. and Roth, J. (eds) (1993) *Understanding and Preventing Violence,* Washington DC: National Academy Press

Renzetti, C.M. (1993) 'On the margins of the malestream (or, they *still* don't get it, do they?): Feminist analyses in criminal justice education', *Journal of Criminal Justice Education,* 4, 2, 219–234

Repetto, T. (1974) *Residential Crime,* Cambridge, MA: Ballinger

Repetto, T. (2005) *American Mafia: A history of its rise to power,* New York: Owl Books

Reuter, P. (1983) *Disorganized Crime: Illegal markets and the mafia,* Cambridge, MA: MIT Press

Reuter, P. and Petrie, C. (eds) (1999) *Transnational Organised Crime: Report of a workshop,* Washington DC: National Academy Press (available at: http://fermat.nap.edu/books/0309065755/html/R1.html)

Reuter, P. and Stevens, A. (2007) *An Analysis of UK Drug Policy: A monograph prepared for the UK Drug Policy Commission,* London: UKDPC

Rex, S. and Tonry, M. (eds) (2002) *Reform and Punishment: The future of sentencing,* Cullompton: Willan

Rhee, S.H. and Waldman, I.D. (2002) 'Genetic and environmental influences on antisocial behaviour: A meta-analysis of twin and adoption studies', *Psychological Bulletin,* 128, 3, 490–529

Richardson, H. (1969) *Adolescent Girls in Approved Schools,* London: Routledge and Kegan Paul

Roberts, J.V. (2002) 'Public opinion and the nature of community penalties: international findings', in Roberts, J. and Hough, M. (eds) *Changing Attitudes to Punishment,* Cullompton: Willan

Roberts, J.V. and Hough, M. (2005) *Understanding Public Attitudes to Criminal Justice,* Maidenhead: Open University Press

Roberts, R. (1971) *The Classic Slum: Salford life in the first quarter of the century,* Manchester: Manchester University Press.

Robertson, G. (1999) *Crimes Against Humanity: The struggle for global justice,* London: Penguin

Robertson, G. (2002) *Crimes Against Humanity: The struggle for global justice,* 2nd edn, London: Penguin

Robson, C. (1993) *Real World Research,* Oxford: Blackwell Publishing

Robson, C. (2000) *Small-scale Evaluation,* London: Sage

Roche, D. (2005) 'Truth commission amnesties and the International Criminal Court', *British Journal of Criminology,* 45, 565–581

Roche, D. (2006) 'Dimensions of restorative justice', *Journal of Social Issues,* 62, 2, 217–238

Rock, P. (1973) 'News as eternal recurrence', in Cohen, S. and Young, J. (eds) *The Manufacture of News. Deviance, social problems and the mass media,* London: Constable

Rock, P. (1983) 'Law, order and power in late seventeenth and early-eighteenth century England', in Cohen, S. and Scull, A. (eds) *Social Control and the State,* Oxford: Blackwell Publishing

Rock, P. (1990) *Helping Crime Victims: The Home Office and the rise of victim support in England and Wales,* Oxford: Clarendon Press

Rock, P. (1993) *The Social World of an English Crown Court,* Oxford: Clarendon Press

Rock, P. (1994) *A History of British Criminology,* Oxford: Clarendon Press

Rock, P. (2004a) *Constructing Victims' Rights: The Home Office, New Labour and victims,* Oxford: Clarendon Press

Rock, P. (2004b) 'Victims, prosecutors and the state in nineteenth century England and Wales', *Criminal Justice,* 4, 4, 331–354

Rock, P. (2005) 'Victims' policies as contingent accomplishments', in Vetere, E. and Pedro, D. (eds) *Victims of Crime and Abuse of Power: Festschrift in honour of Irene Melup,* Bangkok: United Nations

Rock, P. (2007) 'Cesare Lombroso as a signal criminologist', *Criminology and Criminal Justice,* 7, 2, 117–134

Roe, S. and Man, L. (2006) *Drug Misuse Declared: Findings from the 2005/6 British Crime Survey,* London: Home Office

Rook, C. (1899) *The Hooligan Nights,* London: Grant Richards

Rose, D. (2004) *Guantanamo: America's war on human rights,* London: Faber and Faber

Rose, N. (1999) *Powers of Freedom,* Cambridge: Cambridge University Press

Rose, N. (2000) 'The biology of culpability: Pathological identity and crime control in a biological culture', *Theoretical Criminology,* 4, 5–34

Rosenbaum, D.P. (1988) 'Community crime prevention: a review and synthesis of the literature', *Justice Quarterly,* 5, 3, 323–93

Roshier, B. (1973) 'The selection of crime news by the press', in Cohen, S. and Young, J. (eds) *The Manufacture of News: Deviance, social problems and the mass media,* London: Constable

Ross, R. and Fabiano, E. (1985) *Time to Think: A cognitive model of delinquency prevention and offender rehabilitation,* Johnson City, TN: Institute of Social Sciences and Arts

Ross, R., Fabiano, E. and Ewles, C. (1988) 'Reasoning and rehabilitation', *International Journal of Offender Therapy and Comparative Criminology,* 32, 29–36

Rossi, P.H. and Wright, J.D. (1984) 'Evaluation Research: An assessment', *Annual Review of Sociology,* 10, 331–352

Rossow, I., Pape, H. and Wichstrom, L. (1999) 'Young, wet and wild? Associations between alcohol intoxication and violent behaviour in adolescence', *Addiction,* 94, 7, 1017–31

Rothe, D. (2006) 'Iraq and Halliburton', in Michalowski, R. and Kramer, R. (eds) *State-Corporate Crime: Wrongdoing at the intersection of business and government,* New Brunswick, NJ: Rutgers University Press

Rowlingson, K., Newburn, T. and Hagell, A. (1997) 'A drop in the ocean? The discharge grant and the immediate needs of prisoners on release from custody', *The Howard Journal of Criminal Justice,* 36, 3, 293–304

Royal College of Physicians and British Paediatric Association (1995) *Alcohol and the Young,* London: Royal College of Physicians

Royal Commission on Criminal Justice (1993) *Report,* Cmnd.2263, London: HMSO

Royal Commission on Criminal Procedure (1981) *Report,* Cmnd 8092, London: HMSO

Ruggiero, V. (1992) 'Realist criminology: A critique', in Matthews, R. and Young, J. (eds) *Rethinking Criminology: The realist debate,* London: Sage

Ruggiero, V. (1996) *Organised and Corporate Crime in Europe,* Aldershot: Ashgate

Rumgay, J. (1998) *Crime, Punishment and the Drinking Offender,* Basingstoke: Macmillan

Rumgay, J. (2007) 'Partnerships in probation', in Gelsthorpe, L. and Morgan, R. (eds) *Handbook of Probation,* Cullompton: Willan

Rusche, G. and Kirchheimer, O. (1968) *Punishment and Social Structure,* New York: Russell and Russell

Rutherford, A. (1992) *Growing Out of Crime: The new era,* Winchester: Waterside Press

Ruthven, D. and Seward, L. (2002) *Restricted Access: Legal information for remand prisoners,* London: Prison Reform Trust

Rutter, M. (1972) *Maternal Deprivation Reassessed,* Harmondsworth: Penguin

Rutter, M. and Giller, H. (1983) *Juvenile Deliquency: Trends and perspectives,* Harmondsworth: Penguin

Rutter, M., Giller, H. and Hagell, A. (1998) *Antisocial behaviour by young people,* Cambridge: Cambridge University Press

Ryan, M. (1983) *The Politics of Penal Reform,* London: Longman

Ryan, M. and Ward, T. (1989) *Privatization and the Penal System,* Milton Keynes: Open University Press

Salfati, C.G. and Canter, D.V. (1999) 'Differentiating stranger murders: Profiling offender characteristics from behavioural styles', *Behavioural Sciences and the Law,* 17, 391–406

Salisbury, H. and Upson, A. (2004) *Ethnicity, victimisation and worry about crime: findings from the 2001/02 and 2002/03 British Crime Surveys,* Home Office Research Findings 237, London: Home Office

Samenow, S.E. (2006) 'Forty years of the Yochelson/Samenow work', in Henry, S. and Lanier, M. (eds) *The Essential Criminology Reader,* Boulder, CO: Westview Press

Sampson, A., Blagg, H., Stubbs, P. and Pearson, G. (1988) 'Crime, localities and the multi-agency approach', *British Journal of Criminology*, 28, 478–93

Sampson, A. and Phillips, C. (1992) *Multiple victimization: Racial attacks on an East London estate*, Crime Prevention Unit Paper No. 36, London: Home Office

Sampson, R. and Laub, J. (1990) 'Crime and deviance over the life course: The salience of adult social bonds', *American Sociological Review*, 55, 609–627

Sampson, R. and Laub, J. (1993) *Crime in the Making: Pathways and turning points through life*, Cambridge, MA: Harvard University Press

Sampson, R. and Laub, J. (2003) 'Life-course desisters? Trajectories of crime among delinquent boys, followed to age 70', *Criminology*, 41, 555–92

Sampson, R and Laub, J. (2005) 'A life-course view of the development of crime', *The Annals*, 602, 12–45

Sampson, R., Raudenbush, S. and Earls, F. (1997) 'Neighborhoods and violent crime: A multilevel study of collective efficacy', *Science* 277, 918–24

Sanders, A. and Jones, I. (2007) 'The victim in court', in Walklate, S. (ed.) *Handbook of Victims and Victimology*, Cullompton: Willan

Sanders, A. and Young, R. (2007) *Criminal Justice*, 3rd edn, Oxford: Oxford University Press

Savage, M. and Warde, A. (1993) *Urban Sociology, Capitalism and modernity*, Basingstoke: Macmillan

Savage, S. and Milne, B. (2007) 'Miscarriages of justice', in Newburn, T., Williamson, T. and Wright, A. (eds) *Handbook of Criminal Investigation*, Cullompton: Willan

Savelsberg, J.J. (1999) 'Controlling violence, criminal justice, society, and lessons from the US', *Crime, Law, and Social Change*, 30, 185–203

Scarman, Lord (1981) *The Scarman Report*, London: HMSO

Scherdin, M.J. (1986) 'The halo effect: psychological deterrence of electronic security systems', *Information Technology and Libraries*, 5, 232–235

Schlesinger, P. and Tumber, H. (1992) 'Crime and criminal justice in the media', in Downes, D. (ed.) *Unravelling Criminal Justice*, Basingstoke: Macmillan

Schlesinger, P. and Tumber, H. (1994) *Reporting Crime: The media politics of criminal justice*, Oxford: Clarendon Press

Schlesinger, P., Tumber, H. and Murdock, G. (1991) 'The media politics of crime and criminal justice', *British Journal of Sociology*, 42

Schoenthaler, S.J. (1983) 'Diet and crime: an empirical examination of the value of nutrition in the control and treatment of incarcerated juvenile offenders', *International Journal of Biosocial Research*, 4, 25–39

Schramm, W., Lyle, J. and Parker, E.B. (1961) *Television in the Lives of Our Children*, Stanford, CA: Stanford University Press

Schur, E. (1969) *Our Criminal Society*, Englewood Cliffs, NJ: Prentice Hall

Schur, E. (1971) *Labeling deviant behaviour: Its sociological implications*, New York: Harper and Row

Schur, E. (1973) *Radical Nonintervention: Rethinking the delinquency problem*, Englewood Cliffs, NJ: Prentice Hall

Schwendinger, H. and Schwendinger, J. (1970) 'Defenders of order or guardians of human rights?', *Issues in Criminology*, 5, 123–57

Scott, J. (1990) *A Matter of Record: Documentary sources in social research*, Cambridge: Polity Press

Scraton, P. and Chadwick, K. (1987) *In the Arms of the Law: Coroners' Courts and deaths in custody*, London: Pluto Press

Scraton, P. and Chadwick, K. (1991) 'The theoretical and political priorities of critical criminology', in Stenson, K. and Cowell, D. (eds) *The Politics of Crime Control*, London: Sage

Scriven, M. (1967) 'The methodology of evaluation', in Tyler, R.W., Gagne, R.M. and Scriven, M. (eds) *Perspectives on Curriculum Evaluation*, Chicago: Rand McNally

Scott, J. (1990) *A Matter of Record*, Cambridge: Polity Press

Scott, D. (2006) 'The caretakers of punishment', *Prison Service Journal*, November

Sellin, T. (1937) 'The Lombrosian Myth in Criminology' (letter to the editor), *American Journal of Sociology*, 42, 897–99

Sellin, T. (1938) *Culture Conflict and Crime*, New York: Social Science Research Council

Sellin, T. (1960) 'Enrico Ferri', in Mannheim, H. (ed.) *Pioneers in Criminology*, London: Stevens

Sellin, T. (1970) 'A sociological approach', in Wolfgang, M.E. *et al.* (eds) *The Sociology of Crime and Delinquency*, New York: Wiley

Shaftoe, H. and Read, T. (2005) 'Planning out crime: The appliance of science or an act of faith?', in Tilley, N. (ed.) *Handbook of Crime Prevention and Community Safety*, Cullompton: Willan

Shapiro, S.P. (1990) 'Collaring the crime, not the criminal: Reconsidering the concept of white-collar crime', *American. Sociological Review*, 55, 346–365

Shapland, J. and Cohen, D. (1987) 'Facilities for victims: Role of police and courts', *The Criminal Law Review,* January 1987, 28–38

Shapland, J. (1985) *Victims in the Criminal Justice System,* London: Gower

Shapland, J. and Vagg, J. (1988) *Policing by the Public,* London: Routledge

Sharp, C. and Budd, T. (2005) *Minority Ethnic Groups and Crime: Findings from the Offending, Crime and Justice Survey 2003,* Home Office Online Report 33/05, London: Home Office

Sharpe, J. (1990) *Judicial Punishment in England,* London: Faber and Faber

Sharpe, J. (2001) 'Crime, order and historical change', in Muncie, J. and McLaughlin, E. (eds) *The Problem of Crime,* London: Sage

Shaw, C.R. (1930) *The Jack-Roller: A delinquent boy's own story,* Chicago: University of Chicago Press

Shaw, C.R. and McKay, H.D. (1942) *Juvenile Delinquency and Urban Areas,* Chicago: University of Chicago Press

Shaw, J., Appleby, L., Ames, T., McDonnell, R., Harris, C., McCann, K., Kiernan, K., Davies, S., Biddey, H. and Parsons, R. (1999) 'Mental disorder and clinical care in people convicted of homicide: national clinical survey', *British Medical Journal,* 318, 1240–4

Shearing, C. and Stenning, P. (1981) 'Modern private security: Its growth and implications', in Tonry, M. and Morris, N. (eds) *Crime and Justice: A review of research,* Chicago: University of Chicago Press

Shearing, C. and Stenning, P. (1983) 'Private security: Implications for social control', *Social Problems,* 30, 5, 493–506

Shearing, C. and Stenning, P. (1987) 'Say "Cheese"! The Disney order that is not so Mickey Mouse', in Shearing, C. and Stenning, P. (eds) *Private Policing,* Newbury Park, CA: Sage

Shepherd, J. (1996) 'Significant connections', *Addictions,* 91, 4, 501–2

Shepherd, J. and Brickley, M. (1996) 'The relationship between alcohol intoxication, stressors and injury in urban violence', *British Journal of Criminology,* 36, 4, 546–66

Shepherd, J., Robinson, L. and Levers, B. (1990) 'The roots of urban violence', *British Journal of Criminology,* 36, 4, 546–66

Sheptycki, J. (2000) *Issues in Transitional Policing,* London: Routledge

Sherman, C. (2002) 'The police', in Wilson, J. and Petersilia, J. (eds) *Crime: Public policies for crime control,* Oakland, CA: Institute for Contemporary Studies Press

Sherman, D., Iacono, W. and McGue, M. (1997) 'Attention-deficit hyperactivity disorder dimensions: A twin study of inattention and impulsivity-hyperactivity', *Journal of the American Academy of Child & Adolescent Psychiatry,* 36, 6, 745–753

Sherman, L.W. (1993) 'Defiance, deterrence, and irrelevance: A theory of the criminal sanction', *Journal of Research in Crime and Delinquency,* 30, 4, 445–473

Sherman, L. and Berk, R. (1983) 'The Minneapolis Domestic Violence Experiment', *Police Foundation Reports,* July

Sherman, L. et al. (1992) 'The variable effects of arrest on criminal careers: the Milwaukee Domestic Violence Experiment', *The Journal of Criminal Law and Criminology,* 83, 1, Spring

Sherman, L., Gottfredson, D., MacKenzie, J., Reuter, P. and Bushway, S. (1999) *Preventing Crime: What Works, What Doesn't, What's Promising – A report to the United States Congress,* Maryland: National Institute of Justice, University of Maryland

Sherman, L. and Strang, H. (2007) *Restorative Justice: The evidence,* London: The Smith Institute

Shiner, M., Young, T., Groben, S. and Newburn, T. (2005) *Mentoring Disaffected Young People,* York: Joseph Rowntree Foundation

Shiner, M. and Newburn, T. (1997) 'Definitely, maybe not: the normalisation of recreational drug use amongst young people', *Sociology,* 31, 3, 511–529

Shiner, M. and Newburn, T. (1999) 'Taking tea with Noel: drugs discourse for the 1990s', South, N (ed.) *Drugs: Cultures, controls and everyday life,* London: Sage

Shury, J., Speed, M., Vivian, D., Kuechel, A. and Nicholas, S. (2005) *Crime against retail and manufacturing premises: findings from the 2002 Commercial Victimisation Survey,* Online Report 37/05, London: Home Office

Shute, S., Hood, R. and Seemungal, F. (2005) *A Fair Hearing? Ethnic minorities in the criminal courts,* Cullompton: Willan

Sibbitt, R. (1997) *The perpetrators of racial harassment and racial violence,* Home Office Research Study No. 176, London: HMSO

Silber, L. and Little, A. (1996) *The Death of Yugoslavia,* revised edition, London: BBC Books

Silverstri, M. (2003) *Women in Charge: Policing, gender and leadership,* Cullompton: Willan

Sim, J. (1994a) 'Reforming the penal wasteland? A critical review of the Woolf Report', in Player, E. and Jenkins, M. (eds) *Prisons After Woolf: Reform through riot,* London: Routledge

Sim, J. (1994b) 'Tougher than the rest? Men in prison', in Newburn, T. and Stanko, E. (eds) *Just Boys Doing Business: Men, masculinities, and crime,* 100–117, London: Routledge

Sim, J. (2007) 'An inconvenient truth: pain, punishment and prison officers', in Crew, B., Bennett, J. and Wahidin, A. (eds) *Understanding Prison Staff,* Cullompton: Willan

Simester, A. and von Hirsch, A. (2006) *Incivilities: Regulating offensive behaviour,* Oxford: Hart Publishing

Simmel, G. (1997) *Simmel on Culture: Selected writings,* Frisby, D. and Featherstone, M. (eds) London: Sage

Simmons, J. and Dodd, T. (eds) (2003) *Crime in England and Wales 2002/2003,* Home Office Statistical Bulletein 07/03, London: Home Office

Simon, I. (1975) *The Contemporary Woman and Crime*, Washington, DC: National Institute of Mental Health

Simon, J. (1997) 'Governing through crime', in Friedman, L. and Fisher, G. (eds) *The Crime Conundrum: Issues in criminal justice,* Boulder, CO: Westview Press

Simon, J. (2006) *Governing Through Crime,* New York: Oxford University Press

Simpson, M., Shildrick, T. and MacDonald, R. (eds) (2007) *Drugs in Britain: Supply, consumption and control*, Basingstoke: Palgrave

Singer, P. (2004) *One World: The ethics of globalization*, 2nd edn, Yale: Yale University Press

Singer,P. (2004) *The Private Military Industry in Iraq; What have we learned and where to next?,* Geneva: DCAF

Singer, P.W. (2004) *Corporate Warriors: The rise of the privatized military industry*, Ithaca, NY: Cornell University Press

Singer, P.W. (2005) *Outsourcing war*, Foreign Affairs, March/April

Singleton, N., Meltzer, H., Gatward, R., Coid, J. and Deasy, D. (1998) *Psychiatric Morbidity among Prisoners in England and Wales,* London: ONS

Singleton, N., Bumpstead, R., O'Brien, M., Lee, A. and Meltzer, H. (2001) *Psychiatric Morbidity Among Adults Living in Private Households,* London: The Stationery Office

Skinner, B.F. (1953) *Science and Human Behaviour,* New York: Macmillan

Skinner, B.F. (1974) *About Behaviourism,* New York: Alfred Knopf

Skogan, W. (1990) *The Police and Public in England and Wales,* Home Office Research Study No. 117, London: Home Office

Skogan, W. (2006) 'Asymmetry in the impact of encounters with police', *Policing and Society,* 16, 2, 99–126

Slapper, G. and Tombs, S. (1999) *Corporate Crime,* Harlow: Longman

Sloan, S. (1978) *The Anatomy of Non-territorial terrorism: An analytical essay,* Gaithersburg: International Association of Chiefs of Police

Smart, C. (1976) *Women, Crime and Criminology: A feminist critique,* London: Routledge and Kegan Paul

Smart, C. (1990) 'Feminist approaches to criminology or postmodern woman meets atavistic man', in Gelsthorpe, L. and Morris, A. (eds) *Feminist Perspectives in Criminology,* Milton Keynes: Open University Press

Smith, A. (2007) *Review of Crime Statistics,* London: Home Office

Smith, C. and Allen, J. (2004) *Violent crime in England and Wales,* Home Office online report 18/04, London: Home Office

Smith, D.J. (1997) 'Case construction and the goals of criminal process', *British Journal of Criminology,* 37, 3, 319–346

Smith, D.J. (1998) 'Reform or moral outrage: The choice is yours', *British Journal of Criminology,* 38, 4, 614–622

Smith, D.J. (2007) 'Crime and the life course', in Maguire, M., Morgan, R. and Reiner, R. (eds) *The Oxford Handbook of Criminology,* 4th edn, Oxford: Oxford University Press

Smith, D.J., Gray, J. and Small, S. (1983) *Police and People in London,* London: Policy Studies Institute

Smith, I. (1990) 'Alcohol and crime: the problem in Australia', in Bluglass, R. and Bowden, P. (eds) *Principles and Practice of Forensic Psychiatry,* Edinburgh: Churchill Livingsone

Smith J. (2003) *The nature of personal robbery,* Home Office Research Study No. 254, Home Office: London

Smith, L.J.F. (1989) *Domestic Violence,* Home Office Research Study No. 107, London: Home Office

Smith, M., Clarke, R. and Pease, K. (2002) 'Anticipatory benefits in crime prevention', in Tilley, N. (ed.) *Analysis for Crime Prevention: Crime Prevention Studies No. 13,* Monsey, NY: Criminal Justice Press

Smith, P. and Natalier, K. (2005) *Understanding Criminal Justice: Sociological perspectives,* London: Sage

Smith, R. (2003) *Youth Justice: Ideas, policy, practice,* Cullompton: Willan

Social Exclusion Unit (2000) *National strategy for neighbourhood renewal: Report of the Policy Action Team,* London: Social Exclusion Unit

Social Exclusion Unit (2002), *Reducing Re-offending by Ex-Prisoners,* London: Social Exclusion Unit

Solivetti, L. (2004) *Italian Prison Statistics*, Rome: Department of Statistics, La Sapienza

Solomon, E., Eades, C., Garside, R. and Rutherford, M. (2007) *Ten years of criminal justice under labour: An independent audit,* London: Centre for Crime and Justice Studies

Soothill, K. and Walby, S. (1991) *Sex Crime in the News,* London: Routledge

Soothill, K., Francis, B. and Ackerley, E. (1998) 'Paedophilia and paedophiles', *New Law Journal,* June, 882–3

Sopel, J. (1995) *Tony Blair: The moderniser,* London: Michael Joseph

South, N. (1994) 'Drugs and crime', in Maguire, M., Morgan, M. and Reiner, R. (eds) *The Oxford Handbook of Criminology,* 1st edn, Oxford: Oxford University Press

South, N. (2002) 'Drugs, alcohol and crime', in Maguire, M., Morgan, M. and Reiner, R. (eds) *The Oxford Handbook of Criminology,* 3rd edn, Oxford: Oxford University Press

South, N. (2007) 'Drugs, alcohol and crime', in Maguire, M., Morgan, M. and Reiner, R. (eds) *The Oxford Handbook of Criminology,* 4th edn, Oxford: Oxford University Press

Sparks, R. (1982) *Research on Victims of Crime: Accomplishments, issues and new direction,* Washington, DC: Government Printing Office

Sparks, R. (1992a) 'Reason and unreason in "left realism": some problems in the constitution of the fear of crime', in Matthews, R. and Young, J. (eds) *Issues in Realist Criminology,* London: Sage

Sparks, R. (1992b) *Television and the Drama of Crime,* Buckingham: Open University Press

Sparks, R., Genn, H. and Dodd, D. (1977) *Surveying Victims: A study of the measurement of criminal victimization,* London: Wiley

Spierenburg, P. (1984) *The Spectacle of Suffering: Executions and the evolution of repression,* Cambridge: Cambridge University Press

Spitzer, S. (1975) 'Toward a Marxian theory of crime', *Social Problems,* 22, 368–401

Spitzer, S. (1979) 'Notes toward a theory of punishment and social change', *Law and Sociology,* 2, 207–29

Squires, P. and Stephen, D. (2005) *Rougher Justice: Anti-social behaviour and young people,* Cullompton: Willan

Stalans, L. (2002) 'Measuring attitudes to sentencing', in Roberts, J. and Hough, M. (eds) *Changing Attitudes to Punishment,* Cullompton: Willan

Standing Conference on Crime Prevention (1991) *Safer Communities: The local delivery of crime prevention through the partnership approach,* (The Morgan Report), London: Home Office

Stanko, E. (1985) *Intimate Intrusions: Women's experiences of male violence,* London: Virago

Stanko, E. (1990) *Everyday Violence: How women and men experience sexual and physical danger,* London: Pandora

Stanko, E. (1996) 'Warnings to women: Police advice and women's safety in Britain', *Violence Against Women,* 2, 1, 5–24

Stanko, E. (2000) 'Naturalising danger: Women, fear and personal safety', in Brown, M. and Pratt, J. (eds) *Dangerous Offenders: Punishment and social order,* London: Routledge

Stanko, E. (2001) 'The day to count: Reflections on a methodology to raise awareness about the impact of domestic violence in the UK', *Criminal Justice,* 1, 2, 215–226

Stanko, E. and Hobdell, K. (1993) 'Assault on men: Masculinity and male victimization', *British Journal of Criminology,* 33, 3, 400–15

Stanko, E., O'Beirne, M. and Zaffuto, G. (2002) *Taking Stock: What do we know about interpersonal violence?,* Swindon: ESRC

Stanley, E. (2005) 'Truth commissions and the recognition of state crime', *British Journal of Criminology,* 45, 582–597

Stanley, L. and Wise, S. (1979) 'Feminist research, feminist consciousness and experiences of sexism', *Women's Studies International Quarterly,* 2, 259–279

Stanley, L. and Wise, S. (1983) *Breaking Out: Feminist consciousness and feminist research,* London: Routledge and Kegan Paul

Steedman, C. (1984) *Policing the Victorian community: The formation of English provincial police forces, 1856–80,* London: Routledge and Kegan Paul

Steffensmeier, D. (1989) 'On the causes of "white collar" crime: An assessment of Hirschi and Gottredson's claims', *Criminology,* 27, 2, 345–358

Stern, V (1989) *Bricks of Shame: Britain's prisons,* 2nd edn, Harmondsworth: Penguin

Stevens, Sir J. (2003) *Stevens Inquiry: Summary and recommendations,* London: Metropolitan Police

Stevenson, J. (1979) *Popular Disturbances in England 1700–1870,* London: Longman

Stevenson, J. (1992) *Popular Disturbances in England 1700–1870,* Harlow: Longman

Steward, K. (2006) 'Gender decisions in remand decision-making', in Heidensohn, F. (ed.) *Gender and Justice,* Cullompton: Willan

Stone, L. (1979) *The Family, Sex and Marriage in England 1500–1800,* Harmondsworth: Penguin

Stone, V. and Tuffin, R. (2000) *Attitudes of People from Minority Ethnic Communities toward a Career in the Police Service,* London: Home Office

Storch, R.D. (1976) 'The Policeman as Domestic Missionary: Urban discipline and popular culture in Northern England, 1850–80', *Journal of Social History,* 9, 4, 481–809

Strategy Unit (2003) *Alcohol Harm Reduction Project: Interim analytical report,* London: Cabinet Office

Stufflebeam, D.L. and Shinkfield, A.J. (1985*) Systematic Evaluation: A self-instructional guide to theory and practice,* Dordrecht: Kluwer Nijhoff

Suchman, E.A. (1967) *Evaluative Research: Principles in public service and action programs,* New York: Russell Sage

Sutherland, E.H. (1937) *The Professional Thief: By a professional thief,* Chicago: University of Chicago Press

Sutherland, E.H. (1939) *Principles of Criminology,* 3rd edn, Philadelphia: J.B. Lippincott

Sutherland, E.H. (1947) *Principles of Criminology,* 4th edn, Philadelphia: J.B. Lippincott

Sutherland, E. H. (1949) *White Collar Crime,* New York: Dryden

Sutherland, E.H. (1983) *White Collar Crime: The Uncut Version,* New Haven: Yale University Press

Sutherland, E.H. and Cressy, D.R. (1947) 'Minority group criminality and cultural integration', *Journal of Criminal Law and Criminology,* 37, 498–510

Sutton, M. (2005) 'Complicity, trading dynamics and prevalence in stolen goods markets', in Tilley, N. (ed.) *Handbook of Crime Prevention and Community Safety,* Cullompton: Willan

Sykes, G. (1958) *The Society of Captives,* Princeton, NJ: Princeton University Press

Sykes, G. and Matza, D. (1957) 'Techniques of neutralization: A theory of delinquency', *American Sociological Review,* 22, 6, 664–670

Sykes, G. (1971) *The Society of Captives,* Princeton, NJ: Princeton University Press

Tannenbaum, F. (1938) *Crime and the Community,* New York: Columbia University Press

Tappan, P.W. (1947) 'Who is the criminal?', *American Sociological Review,* 12, 96–102

Tarde, G. (1903) *The Laws of Imitation,* New York: H. Holt

Taylor, D. (1998) *Crime, policing and punishment in England, 1750–1914,* New York: St. Martin's Press

Taylor, I., Walton, P. and Young, J. (1973) *The New Criminology: For a social theory of deviance,* London: Routledge and Kegan Paul

Taylor, I., Walton, P. and Young, J. (1975) *Critical Criminology,* London: Routledge and Kegan Paul

Taylor, L. (1971) *Deviance and Society,* London

Taylor, M. and Horgan, J. (1999) 'Future developments of political terrorism in Europe', *Terrorism and Political Violence,* 11, 4, 83–93

Taylor, M. and Horgan, J. (2000) *The Future of Terrorism,* London: Frank Cass

Taylor, P.J. and Gunn, J. (1999) 'Homicides by people with mental illness: myth and reality', *British Journal of Psychiatry,* 174, 9–14

Taylor, R. (1998) *Forty Years of Crime and Criminal Justice Statistics, 1958–1997,* London: Home Office

Taylor, T. (2002) 'The truth about globalization', *The Public Interest,* 47, 24–44

Thomas, C. (2005) *Judicial Diversity in the UK and other Jurisdictions,* London: Commission for Judicial Appointments

Thomas, D. and Loader, B. (2000) *Cybercrime: Law enforcement, security and surveillance in the information age,* London: Routledge

Thomas, J. and Pooley, R. (1980) *The Exploding Prison: Prison riots and the case of Hull,* London: Junction Books

Thomas, W.I. (1923) *The Unadjusted Girl,* Boston, MA: Little, Brown

Thomas, W.I. and Thomas, D.S. (1928) *The Child in America: Behavior problems and programs,* New York: A.A. Knopf

Thomas, W.I. and Znaniecki, F. (1918) *The Polish Peasant in Europe and America,* Boston: Gorham Press

Thompson, E.P. (1972) *The Making of the English Working Class,* Harmondsworth: Penguin

Thompson, E.P. (1975) *Whigs and Hunters: The origin of the Black Act,* London: Allen Lane

Thompson, E.P. (1994) *Customs in Common,* New York: The Free Press

Thompson, K. (1998) *Moral Panics,* London: Routledge

Thornton, A., Walker, D. and Erol, R. (2003) *Distraction burglary amongst older adults and minority ethnic communities,* Home Office Findings 197, London: Home Office

Thorpe, D.H., Green, C. and Smith, D. (1980) *Punishment and welfare: Case studies of the workings of the 1969 Children and Young Persons Act,* Lancaster: Centre of Youth, Crime and Community, Centre of Social Administration, University of Lancaster

Thrasher, F.M. (1927) *The Gang: A study of 1,313 gangs in Chicago,* Chicago: University of Chicago Press

Thrasher, F. (1963) *The Gang,* Chicago: Phoenix Press

Tierney, J. (1996) *Criminology: Theory and context,* London: Harvester Wheatsheaf

Tierney, J. and Grossman, J. (1995) *Making a Difference: An impact study of Big Brothers/Big Sisters,* Philadelphia, PA: Public/Private Ventures

Tilley, N. (1993) *After Kirkholt: Theory, method and results of replication evaluations,* Police Research Group, Crime Prevention Unit Series Paper 47, London: Home Office

Tilley, N. (2000) 'Doing realistic evaluation of criminal justice', in Jupp, V., Davies, P. and

Francis, P. (eds) *Doing Criminological Research,* London: Sage

Tilley, N. (2003) 'Community policing, problem-oriented policing and intelligence-led policing', in Newburn, T. (ed.) *Handbook of Policing,* Cullompton: Willan

Tilley, N. and Ford, A. (1996) *Forensic Science and Crime Investigation,* Crime Detection and Prevention Paper 73, London: Home Office

Tilley, N. and Laycock, G. (2002) *Working out what to do: Evidence-based crime reduction,* Crime Reduction Series Paper 11, London: Home Office

Timmer, D.A. and Eitzen, S. (1989) *Crime in the Streets and in the Suites,* Boston, MA: Allyn and Bacon

Tittle, C. (1995) *Control-Balance: Toward a general theory of deviance,* Boulder, CO: Westview

Tittle, C. (2000) 'Refining the control-balance theory', *Theoretical Criminology,* 8, 395–428

Toby, J. (1983) 'Crime in the schools', in Wilson, J.Q. (ed.) *Crime and Public Policy,* San Francisco: Institute for Contemporary Studies

Tombs, S. (2004) 'Workplace injury and death: Social harm and the illusions of law', in Hillyard *et al.* (eds) *Beyond Criminology: Taking harm seriously,* London: Pluto Press

Tombs, S. and Whyte, D. (2007a) 'Researching corporate and white-collar crime in an era of neo-liberalism', in Pontell, H. and Geis, G. (eds) *International Handbook of White Collar and Corporate Crime,* New York: Springer

Tombs, S. and Whyte, D. (2007b) *Safety Crimes,* Cullompton: Willan

Tonry, M. (ed.) (2007) *Crime, Punishment and Politics in Comparative Perspective,* Chicago: University of Chicago Press

Triplett, R. (2000) 'The dramatization of evil: Reacting to juvenile delinquency during the 1990s', in Simpson, S. (ed.) *Of Crime and Criminality,* Thousand Oaks, CA: Pine Forge Press

Tufts New England Medical Center (1984) *Sexually exploited children: service and research project,* Washington DC: US Department of Justice

Tunnell, K.D. (1992) *Choosing Crime: The criminal calculus of property offenders,* Chicago: Nelson Hall

Tuormaa, T.E. (1994) 'The adverse effects of food additives on health', *Journal of Orthomolecular Medicine,* 9, 4, 224–243

Turk, A. (1969) *Criminality and Legal Order,* Chicago: Rand McNally

Turnbull, P., McSweeney, T. and Hough, M. (2000) *Drug treatment and testing orders: the 18 month evaluation,* London: Home Office

Tyler, T. (1990) *Why People Obey the Law,* New Haven, CT: Yale University Press

Tyler, T. and Huo, Y.J. (2002) *Trust in the law: Encouraging public cooperation with the police and courts,* New York: Russell-Sage Foundation

Turning Point (2006) *Bottling it Up: The effects of alcohol misuse on children, parents and families,* London: Turning Point

Uglow, S. (2002) *Criminal Justice,* 2nd edn, London: Sweet and Maxwell

United Nations Office on Drugs and Crime (2006) *Trafficking in Persons: Global Patterns* (available at: http://www.unodc.org/pdf/traffickinginpersons_report_2006ver2.pdf)

Unnever, J., Cullen, F. and Pratt, T. (2003) 'Parental management, ADHD and delinquent involvement: Reassessing Gottfredson and Hirschi's general theory', *Justice Quarterly,* 20, 3, 471–500

U.S. Department of State (2004) *Office to Monitor and Combat Trafficking in Persons, Trafficking in Persons Report,* Washington DC: Department of State

Valier, C. (1998) 'True Crime Stories: Scientific methods of criminal investigation, criminology and historiography', *The British Journal of Criminology,* 38, 88–105

Valier, C. (2002) *Theories of Crime and Punishment,* Harlow: Longman

van Andel, H. (1989) 'Crime prevention that works: The case of public transport in the Netherlands', *British Journal of Criminology,* 29, 47–56

van Bemmelen, J.M. (1960) 'Willem Adriaan Bonger', in Mannheim, H. (ed) *Pioneers in Criminology,* London: Stevens and Sons

Van Dijk, J. (2007) 'The international crime victims survey and complementary measures of corruption and organised crime', in Hough, M. and Maxfield, M. (eds) *Surveying Crime in the 21st Century,* Cullompton: Willan

Van Ness, D. and Strong, K. (2006) *Restoring Justice,* 3rd edn, Cincinnati, OH: Anderson Publishing

van Swaaningen, R. (1997) *Critical Criminology: Visions from Europe,* London: Sage

Varese, F. (2001) *The Russian Mafia: Private protection in a new market economy,* Oxford: Oxford University Press

Varese, F. (2006) 'How Mafias migrate', *Law and Society Review,* 40, 2, 411–444

Veblen, T. (1912) *The Theory of the Leisure Class,* New York: Macmillan

Visher, C.A. (1987) 'Juror decision making: The importance of evidence', *Law and Human Behavior,* 11, 1, 1–17

Vold, G. (1958) *Theoretical Criminology,* New York: Oxford University Press

Vold, G., Bernard, T.J. and Snipes, J. (2002) *Theoretical Criminology,* 5th edn, New York: Oxford University Press

Von Hentig, H. (1948) *The Criminal and His Victim,* New Haven, CT: Yale University Press

von Hirsch, A. (1976) *Doing Justice,* New York: Hill & Wang

von Hirsch, A. (1993) *Censure and Sanctions,* New York: Oxford University Press

von Hirsch, A. (1995) 'Proportionality and parsimony in American sentencing guidelines: The Minnesota and Oregon standards', in Clarkson, C. and Morgan, R. (eds) *The Politics of Sentencing Reform,* Oxford: Oxford University Press

von Hirsch, A., Bottoms, A.E., Burney, E. and Wikstrom, P-O (1999) *Criminal Deterrence and Sentence Severity,* Oxford: Hart Publishing

von Hofer, H. (2003) 'Prison populations as political constructs: The case of Finland, Holland and Sweden', *Journal of Scandinavian Studies in Criminology and Crime Prevention,* 4, 1, 21–38

von Knorring, A-L. (1991) 'Children of alcoholics', *Journal of Child Psychology and Psychiatry,* 154, 677–82

Waddington, P.A.J. (1991) *The Strong Arm of the Law,* Oxford: Clarendon Press

Waddington, P.A.J. (1999) 'Police (canteen) sub-culture. An appreciation', *British Journal of Criminology,* 39, 2, 286–308

Waddington, P.A.J., Stenson, K. and Don, D. (2004) 'In proportion: Race and police stop and search', *British Journal of Criminology,* 44, 889–914

Wahidin, A. and Cain, M. (eds) (2006) *Ageing, Crime and Society,* Cullompton: Willan

Walby, S. and Allen, J. (2004) *Domestic violence, sexual assault and stalking: Findings from the British Crime Survey,* Home Office Research Study No. 276, London: Home Office

Walker, A., Kershaw, C. and Nicholas, S. (2006) *Crime in England and Wales 2005/06,* Home Office Statistical Bulletin 12/06, London: Home Office

Walker, C. (2000) 'Briefing on the Terrorism Act 2000', *Terrorism and Political Violence,* 12, 2, 1–36

Walker, C. (2005) 'Terrorism and the law', *Criminal Law Review*

Walker, L. (1979) *The Battered Woman,* New York: Harper and Colophon

Walker, M.A. (1989) 'The court disposal and remands of white, Afro-Caribbean, and Asian men (London, 1983)', *British Journal of Criminology,* 29, 4, 353–67

Walker, N. (2003) 'The pattern of transnational policing', in Newburn, T. (ed.) *Handbook of Policing,* Cullompton: Willan.

Walker, S. (1988) *Popular Justice: A history of American criminal justice,* New York: Oxford University Press

Walklate, S. (1989) *Victimology: The victim and the criminal justice process,* London: Unwin and Hyman

Walklate, S. (1992) 'Appreciating the victim: conventional, realist or critical victimology?', in Matthews, R. and Young, J. (eds) *Issues in Realist Criminology,* London: Sage

Walklate, S. (2004) *Gender, Crime and Criminal Justice,* 2nd edn, Cullompton: Willan

Walklate, S. (2007) *Imagining the Victim of Crime,* Maidenhead: Open University Press

Wall, D. (1998) 'Policing and the regulation of the Internet', *Criminal Law Review,* special edition, 79–91

Wall, D. (2001) *Crime and the Internet,* London: Routledge

Walters, G. (1994) *Drugs and Crime in Lifestyle Perspective,* London: Sage

Warburton A.L. and Shepherd, J.P. (2006) 'Tackling alcohol related violence in city centres: Effect of emergency medicine and police intervention', *Emergency Medicine Journal,* January, 23, 1

Warburton, C. (1932) *The Economic Results of Prohibition,* New York: Columbia University Press.

Ward, T. and Brown, M. (2004) 'The good lives model and conceptual issues in offender rehabilitation', *Psychology, Crime and Law,* 10, 243–57

Ward, T. and Maruna, S. (2007) *Rehabilitation,* London: Routledge

Wasik, M. and Munro, C. (1992) *Sentencing, judicial discretion and training,* London: Sweet & Maxwell

Weatheritt, M. (1986) *Innovations in Policing,* London: Croom Helm

Webber, F. (2004) 'The war on migration', in Hillyard, P., Pantazis, C., Tombs, S. and Gordon, D. (eds) *Beyond Criminology: Taking harm seriously,* London: Pluto Press

Webster, C. (1995) *Youth Crime, Victimization and Racial Harassment: The Keighley crime survey,* Bradford: Bradford and Ilkley College Corporation/ Centre for Research in Applied Community Studies,

Webster, C. (1996) 'Local heroes: Violent racism, localism and spacism among Asian and white young people', *Youth and Policy,* 53, 15–27

Webster, C. (2003) 'Race, space and fear: Imagined geographies of racism, crime, violence and disorder in Northern England', *Capital and Class,* 80, 95–122

Webster, C. (2007) *Understanding Race and Crime,* Maidenhead: Open University Press

Weinberg, L. and Eubank, W. (1999) 'Terrorism and the shape of things to come', *Terrorism and Political Violence*, 11, 4, 94–105

Weiner, M.J. (1998) 'The Victorian criminalization of men', in Spierenberg, P. (ed.) *Men and Violence: Gender, honour and rituals in modern Europe and America*, Columbus, OH: Ohio State University Press

Weisburd, D., Wheeler, S., Waring, E. and Bode, N. (1991) *Crimes of the middle-classes: White collar offenders in the federal courts*, New Haven: Yale University Press

Weisburd, D., Waring, E. and Chayet, E. (1995) 'Specific deterrence in a sample of offenders convicted of white-collar crimes', *Criminology*, 33, 587–607

Weisburd, D. and Eck, J. (2004) 'What can police do to reduce crime, disorder, and fear?', *Annals of the American Academy of Political and Social Science*, 593

Weisburd, D. and Braga, A. (2006) *Police Innovation: Contrasting perspectives*, New York: Cambridge University Press

Weiss, C.H. (1987)' The circuitry of enlightenment', *Knowledge, Creation, Diffusion, Utilisation*, 8, 274–81

Weiss, R. (1987) 'Humanitarianism, labour exploitation, or social control? A critical survey of theory and research on the origin and development of prisons', *Social History*, 12, 3

Welch, M. (2006) *Scapegoats of September 11th: Hate crimes and state crimes in the war on terror*, New Jersey: Rutgers University Press

Welch, M. and Schuster, L. (2005) 'Detention of asylum seekers in the US, UK, France, German and Italy: A critical view of the globalizing culture of control', *Criminal Justice*, 5, 4, 331–356

Wells, G.L. and Lindsay, R.C.L. (1983) 'How do people infer the accuracy of memory? Studies of performance and a meta-memory analysis', in Lloyd-Bostock, S. and Clifford, B.R. (eds) *Witness Evidence: Critical and empirical papers*, New York: Wiley

Wender, P.H. (2002) *ADHD: Attention-deficit hyperactivity disorder in children and adults*, New York: Oxford University Press

West, D.J. and Farrington, D.P. (1973) *Who Becomes Delinquent?*, London: Heinemann

West, D.J. and Farrington, D. (1977) *The Delinquent Way of Life*, London: Heinemann

West, M. and Prinz, R. (1987) 'Parental alcoholism and childhood psychopathalogy', *Psychological Bulletin*, 102, 214–18

White, H. and Hansell, S. (1998) 'Acute and long-term effects of drug use on aggression from adolescence into adulthood', *Journal of Drug Issues*, 28, 4, 837–58

White, J., Moffitt, T., Capsi, A., Bartusch, D., Needles, D. and Stouthamer-Loeber, M. (1994) 'Measuring impulsivity and examining its relationship to delinquency', *Journal of Abnormal Psychology*, 103, 192–205

White Paper (1997) *No More Excuses: A new approach to tackling youth crime in England and Wales*, Cm 3809, London: HMSO

White, R. and Haines, F. (2004) *Crime and Criminology: An introduction*, Melbourne: Oxford University Press

Whitehead, P. and Statham, R. (2006) *The History of Probation: Politics, power and cultural change, 1876–2005*, Crayford: Shaw and Sons

Whitman, J. (1998) 'What's wrong with inflicting shame sanctions?', *Yale Law Journal*, 107, 1055–92

Whitman, S., Coleman, T., Patmon, C., Desai, B., Cohen, R. and King, L. (1984) 'Epilepsy in prison: Elevated prevalence and no relationship to violence', *Neurology*, 34, 775

Whyte, B. (2000) 'Between two stools: Youth justice in Scotland', *Probation Journal*, 47, 2, 119–25

Whyte, D. (2003) 'Lethal regulation: State-corporate crime and the United Kingdom Government's new mercenaries', *Journal of Law and Society*, 30, 575–600

Whyte, D. (2007) 'The crimes of neo-liberal rule in occupied Iraq', *British Journal of Criminology*, 47, 2, 177–196

Wiles, P. and Costello, A. (2000) *The 'Road to Nowhere': The evidence for travelling criminals*, Home Office Research Study No. 207, London: Home Office

Wiley, J. and Weisner, C. (1995) 'Drinking in violent and non-violent events leading to arrest: Evidence from a survey of arrestees', *Journal of Criminal Justice*, 23, 5, 461–76

Wilkins, L. (1960) *Delinquent Generations*, London: HMSO

Wilkins, L. (1964) *Social Deviance: Social policy, action and research*, London: Tavistock

Wilkinson, C. (1995) *The Drop Out Society: Young people on the margin*, Leicester: Youth Work Press

Wilkinson, P. (2006) 'Terrorism', in Gill, M. (ed.) *The Handbook of Security*, Basingstoke: Palgrave

Williams, J.E. and Holmes, K. (1981) *The Second Assault: Rape and public attitudes* Westport, CT: Greenwood Press

Williams, J., Murphy, P. and Dunning, E. (1989) *Hooligans Abroad*, London: Routledge

Williams, K.S. (2004) *Textbook on Criminology*, 5th edn, Oxford: Oxford University Press

Williams, P. and Dickinson, J. (1993) 'Fear of crime: Read all about it? The relationship between newspaper crime reporting and fear of crime', *British Journal of Criminology*, 33, 1, 33–56

Williams, R. (1958) *Culture and Society 1780 – 1950,* Harmondsworth: Penguin.

Williams, R. and Johnson, P. (2007) 'Trace biometrics and criminal investigations', in Newburn, T., Williamson, T. and Wright, A. (eds) *Handbook of Criminal Investigation,* Cullompton: Willan

Willis, P. (1977) *Learning to Labour: How working class kids get working class jobs,* Farnborough: Saxon House

Willis, P. (1978) *Profane Culture,* London: Routledge

Willis, P. and Trondman, M. (2000) 'A manifesto for ethnography', *Ethnography,* 1, 1, 5–16

Willmott, P. (1966) *Adolescent Boys in East London,* Harmondsworth: Penguin

Wilson, D., MacKenzie, D. and Mitchell, F. (2005) *Effects of correctional boot camps on offending,* A Campbell Collaboration systematic review (available at: http://www.aic.gov.au/campbellcj/reviews/titles.html)

Wilson, J.Q. (1975) *Thinking about Crime,* New York: Vintage

Wilson, J.Q. and Herrnstein, R. (1985) *Crime and Human Nature,* New York: Simon and Schuster

Wilson, J.Q. and Kelling, G. (1982) 'Broken windows: the police and neighbourhood safety', *Atlantic Monthly,* March, 29–38

Winlow, S. and Hall, S. (2006) *Violent Night: Urban leisure and contemporary culture,* Oxford: Berg

Wolfgang, M.E. (1958) *Patterns in Criminal Homicide,* Philadelphia: University of Pennsylvania Press

Wolfgang, M.E. (1960) 'Cesare Lombroso', in Mannheim, H. (ed.) *Pioneers in Criminology,* London: Stevens

Wolfgang, M.E. (1996) 'Preface', to Beccaria, C., *Of Crimes and Punishments,* New York: Marilio Publishers

Wolfgang, M.E. and Ferracuti, F. (1967) *The Subculture of Violence,* London: Tavistock

Wolfgang, M., Figlio, R.M. and Sellin, T. (1972) *Delinquency in a Birth Cohort,* Chicago: University of Chicago Press

Women's National Commission (1985) *Violence Against Women,* London: Cabinet Office

Women's Resource Centre (2006) *Statistics About Women in the UK,* London: Women's Resource Centre (available at: http://www.wrc.org.uk/resources/policypubs.htm)

Woodbridge, J. and Frosztega, J. (1998) *Recent Changes in the Female Prison Population,* London: Home Office

Woodiwiss, M. (2003) 'Transnational organised crime: The global reach of an American concept', in Edwards, A. and Gill, P. (eds) *Transnational Organised Crime,* London: Routledge

Woodiwiss, M. (2005) *Gangster Capitalism: The United States and the global rise of organised crime,* London: Constable

Woolf, Lord Justice (1991) *Prison Disturbances April 1990: Report of an Inquiry by the Rt. Hon. Lord Justice Woolf (Parts I and II) and His Honour Judge Stephen Tumin (Part II),* Cm 1456, London: HMSO

Wootton, B.F. (1959) *Contemporary Trends in Crime and its Treatment,* London: Clarke Hall Fellowship

Working Group on Fear of Crime (1989) *Final Report,* London: Home Office

Worrall, A. (1990) *Offending Women,* London: Routledge

Worrall, A. (2002) 'Rendering them punishable', in Carlen, P. (ed) *Women and Punishment: The struggle for justice,* Cullompton: Willan

Worrall, A. (2004) 'Twisted sisters, ladettes and the new penology: The social construction of violent girls', in Alder, C. and Worrall, A. (eds) *Girl's Violence: Myths and realities,* Albany, NY: State University of New York Press

Wright, L. (1999) *Young People and Alcohol: What 11–24 year olds know, think and do,* London: Health Education Authority

Wright, A (2006) *Organized Crime,* Cullompton: Willan

Wright, R. and Decker, S. (1997) *Armed Robbers in Action: Stickups and street culture,* Boston: Northeastern University Press

Yar, M. (2006) *Cybercrime and Society,* London: Sage

Yates, D. (1987) 'The detection of problem drinkers in the accident and emergency department', *British Journal of Addiction,* 82, 163–7

Young, A. (1996) *Imagining Crime: Textual outlaws and criminal conversations,* London: Sage

Young, J. (1973) 'The amplification of drug use', in Cohen, S. and Young, J. (eds) *The Manufacture of Deviance,* London: Constable

Young, J. (1975) 'Working class criminology', in Taylor, I., Walton, P. and Young, J. (eds) *Critical Criminology,* London: Routledge and Kegan Paul

Young, J. (1986) 'The failure of criminology: The need for a radical realism', in Matthews, R. and Young, J. (eds) *Confronting Crime,* London: Sage

Young, J. (1988a) 'Radical criminology in Britain', *British Journal of Criminology,* 28, 159–183

Young, J. (1988b) 'Risk of crime and fear of crime: a realist critique of survey-based assumptions', in Maguire, M. and Pointing, J. (eds) *Victims of Crime: A new deal?* Milton Keynes: Open University Press

Young, J. (1992) 'Ten points of realism', in Young, J. and Matthews, R. (eds) *Rethinking Criminology: The realist debate,* London: Sage

Young, J. (1997) 'Left realist criminology: Radical in its analysis, realist in its policy', in Maguire, M., Morgan, R. and Reiner, R. (eds) *The Oxford Handbook of Criminology*, 2nd edn, Oxford: Oxford University Press

Young, J. (1999) *The Exclusive Society,* London: Sage

Young, J. (2007) *The Vertigo of Late Modernity,* London: Sage

Young, J. and Matthews, R. (1992) *Issues in Realist Criminology,* London: Sage

Young, R. and Goold, B. (1999) 'Restorative police cautioning in Aylesbury – from degrading to reintegrative shaming ceremonies?', *Criminal Law Review,* 126–138

Young, R. (2000) 'Integrating a multi-victim perspective into criminal justice through restorative justice conferences', in Crawford, A. and Goodey, J. (eds) *Integrating a Victim Perspective Within Criminal Justice,* Aldershot: Ashgate

Young, R. (2002) 'Testing the limits of restorative justice: the case of corporate victims', in Hoyle, C. and Young, R. (eds) *New Visions of Crime Victims,* 133–72, Oxford: Hart Publishing

Youth Justice Board, ACPO and Home Office (2005) *Anti-social behaviour: A guide to the role of Youth Offending Teams in dealing with anti-social behaviour,* London: Youth Justice Board

Zander, M. and Henderson, P.F. (1993) *Crown Court Study, Royal Commission on Criminal Justice,* Home Office Research Study No.19, London: HMSO

Zedner, L. (1991) *Women, Crime and Custody in Victorian England,* Oxford: Oxford University Press

Zedner, L. (2002) 'Dangers of dystopias in penal theory', *Oxford Journal of Legal Studies,* 22, 2, 341–366

Zedner, L. (2004) *Criminal Justice,* Oxford: Oxford University Press

Zedner, L. (2005) 'Policing before and after the police', *British Journal of Criminology,* 46, 1, 78–96

Zedner, L. (2006) 'Opportunity makes the thief-taker: The influence of economic analysis on crime control', in T. Newburn and P. Rock (eds) *The Politics of Crime Control,* Oxford: Clarendon Press

Zehr, H. (1985) 'Retributive Justice, Restorative Justice, Occasional Paper No.4, New Perspectives on Crime and Justice series', MCC Canada Victim Offender Ministries Program and MCC US Office on Crime and Justice, reprinted in Johnstone, G. (ed.) (2003) *A Restorative Justice Reader,* Cullompton: Willan

Zhang, S. and Chin, K.L. (2002) 'Enter the dragon: Inside Chinese human smuggling organisations', *Criminology,* 40, 4, 737–768

Zimring, F. (2001) Review of 'The Culture of Control', *Criminology and Criminal Justice,* 1, 4, 465–467

Zimring, F. (2003) *The Contradictions of American Capital Punishment,* New York: Oxford University Press

Zimring, F. and Hawkins, G. (1993) 'Crime and justice in the savings and loan crisis', in Tonry, M. and Reiss, A. (eds) *Beyond the Law,* Chicago: University of Chicago Press

Zimring, F. and Hawkins, G. (1995) *Incapacitation: Penal confinement and the restraint of crime,* New York: Oxford University Press

Zimring, F. and Hawkins, G. (1997) *Crime is Not the Problem: Lethal violence in America,* New York: Oxford University Press

Zimring, F., Hawkins, G. and Kamin, S. (2001) *Punishment and Democracy: Three strikes and you're out in California,* New York: Oxford University Press

Index

Abel, C. 133
abnormal behaviour 139
Abu Ghraib prison 882–3
Adams family 419
adaptive theory 932
ADHD (attention-deficit hyperactivity disorder)
   139–40
Adler, F. 305, 809, 823, 833
adolescent-limited offending 844
adoption studies 136–7
adversarial, and inquisitorial (criminal justice)
   systems 557–9
aetiological crisis 266
Agnew, R. 181–2, 183
Ainsworth, P. 138, 846
Akers, R. 155–6, 194–5, 222
Albini, J.L. 414
alcohol 140, 498–511
   background 474, 498
   binge drinking 504
   consumption 475 *Fig.*
   costs of misuse and crime 508, 509 *Table*
   and crime 505–8
   government policy 508–9
   impact of Licensing Act 2003 510
   legal situation 504–5
   patterns of consumption 498–501
   and young people 501–4
Alder, C. 305
Alderson, J. 612
Alison, L. 847, 849, 850–1
American dream 175–8, 182
American radicalism 250–4
   conflict
      and peacemaking 252–4
      theories 250–1
   criminalisation 250
   explicitly Marxist 251–2
Amir, M. 345
Anderson, E. 182, 200
Andreas, P. 432
Andrews, D.A. 861
anomie 184, 198, 199, 203, 229, 231, 241, 246, 248,
   259, 269, 808
   and American dream ideology 175–8, 182
   institutional theory 182–3
   and Merton 174–5, 178–9
   and subcultural theory 205
   and suicide 172–4
ANS (autonomic nervous system) 141
anti-social behaviour 574–7, 732–3, 735–7
   background 574
   'broken windows' issues 575–6, 732
   criticisms of agenda 735–7
   and ethnicity 783–4

and respect agendas 576–7
   types 733
Aries, P. 725
armed robbery 446–7
arrest
   powers 607–8
   and women 810–11
Ashworth, A. 366, 639, 641, 647, 648, 663, 765
attachment 232
attention-deficit hyperactivity disorder (ADHD)
   139–40
Attorney General (UK) 545
Auld Review 639, 668
automatism 139
autonomic nervous system (ANS) 141
Ayres, I. 402, 765

bail 645–7
   offending while on 648–9
Baker, E. 669
Baldwin, J. 861
Bandura, A. 153–5
Banton, M. 602, 629
Barker, M. 90
Barr, R. 582
Batchelor, William 41
Bayley, D. 603, 632
Bean, P. 417, 485, 494
Beccaria, Bonesana, C, Marchese di 116–17, 518
Beck, U. 329–30, 868, 869
Becker, G. 281
Becker, H. 9, 939
   'Becoming a marijuana user' 215–16
   Outsiders 214–16, 223, 409
Beckett, K. 257–8
behaviourism 152
   and media 91–2
belief 233
Bell Curve, The 164, 272–3, 274
Bell, D. 320
Bennett, T. 479, 920
Bennett, W. 274, 456
Bentham, J. 38, 115, 117–18, 119, 324–5, 518
Bentley, Derek 686
Ben-Yehuda, N. 219
Bhopal 383
Big Brothers/Big Sisters Programme 587
Binet, A. 164
binge drinking 504
biochemical factors 138–43
   ADHD 139–40
   central nervous system 138–9
   hormones/testosterone 141–2
   laterality 141
   neurotransmitters 140
   nutrition 142–3

biological positivism 132, 143–4
biologism 839
biosocial theory 161–3
bipartisan consensus 12–13, 331
Bittner, E. 602
Blackburn, R. 136, 150
Blagg, H. 765
Blair, Tony 14, 108, 545, 557, 729
blinding, single/double 918
Block, A. 414, 415, 416
Blom-Cooper, L. 439, 442
Bloody Code 35, 36
Blumer, H. 210
Blunkett, David 691
Bobbit, P. 874
Bobo doll study 154–5
Bogue, D.J. 190
Bond, Dr T. 847
Bonger, W. 248–9
Bonn, J. 139
Bonta, J. 861
Boston Gun Project 585–7
Bottoms, A. E. 17, 328, 663, 674, 765, 932
boundaries
    blurring 328
    maintenance 170
Boutros-Gali, B. 428
Bow street Runners 25
Bowlby, J. 149, 150–1, 842
Bowling, B. 773, 781, 791, 796, 801
Box, S. 78, 179, 387, 809
Boy George 217
Brady, Ian 440–1
Brain, K. 503
Braithwaite, J. 219–20, 222, 223, 241, 322, 387, 397, 400, 402, 748, 750–1, 760–5, 890
Bratton, W. 620
Brickley, M. 506
British Crime Survey (BCS) 51, 62–5, 70–3, 355–8, 899, 912
British Journal of Criminology 17, 745, 926
British Journal of Sociology 303
British radicalism 254–8
    background 254–5
    contemporary 256–8
    new criminology 255–6
British Society of Criminology (BSC) 18
Brittan, Leon 728
Britton, P. 849
Broeders, A.P.A. 605, 606
'broken windows' 269, 290, 574–8, 620, 732
Brookman, F. 440, 442
Brussel, J. 848
Bryman, A. 934
Bulger, James 441, 666, 729–30
Burgess, E. 155–6, 190, 191, 192, 354
burglary 460–5
    commercial 463–5
    crime prevention 591–3
    distraction 462
    risk factors 461
    trends 460–1

Bursik, R.J. 195–6
Burt, C. 129
Butler, R. A. 567

Cain, M. 307–8, 831–2
Calvert-Smith, Sir D. 798
Cambridge Study in Delinquent Development 78, 841–2
cannabis 55, 67, 97, 216, 419, 475–489, 496–8, 507, 511, 722–23
Canter, D. 849–50
capital punishment
    history 35–7
    international trends 698–700
Capone, Al 409–10, 411
car crime 465–9
    measurement 466–7
    road injuries/deaths 465–6
carceral clawback 312–13
Carlen, P. 307, 311–13, 314–15
Carriere, K. 329
Carter Review 678
case studies 911
Castells, M. 320
Cater, S. 504
cautioning 663, 666, 728, 731–4
    and ethnicity 791–2
    restorative cautioning 752–4, 764
    and women 810–11
CDRP (Crime and Disorder Reduction Partnerships) 547
central nervous system (CNS) 138–9
centralisation 13–14
Centre for Contemporary Cultural Studies (CCCS) 202
Chaiken, J. and Chaiken, M. 487
Chakraborti, N. 780
Challenger space shuttle 384
Challinger, D.O. 467
Chambliss, W. 251–2, 253, 407, 415–16, 431
Chan, J. 619
charge bargaining 651–2
Checkley, H. 846
chemical castration 522
Chesney-Lind, M. 306
Chibnall, S. 85–6
Chicago area Project 193
Chicago School 151, 170, 175, 188–96, 199, 201, 210, 248, 256, 303, 832, 840, 842
    assessment 195–6
    cultural transmission 192–3
    differential association 151–2, 193–5
    differential reinforcement 153, 194–5
    influence 188–90
    social ecology 190
    zonal hypothesis 191
child abuse 361–3, 842
childhood, and punishment 725–6
Christiansen, K.O. 135
Christie, N. 9, 342–4, 744–5
chromosomal anomalies 137–8
citizens' panels 757–8

Clarke, Kenneth 729–30
Clarke, R.V.G. 281–5, 290, 292–3, 294, 386, 399, 476, 578, 581–2, 583
Clarkson, C.M.V. 669
classicism 114–20
    see also contemporary classicism
    Beccaria 116–17
    Bentham 38, 115, 117–18, 119
    impact 118–20
    and positivism 122 *Fig.*
    and punishment 114–16
Clinard, M. 385, 393–5
Cloward, R. 180–1, 198–9
CNS (central nervous system) 138–9
cognitive-behavioural model
    and confessions 854
    programmes 862–4
    theories 157–61
    therapies 153
Cohen, A. 178, 180, 196, 197–8, 808–9, 832
Cohen, L. 286–7
Cohen, P. 202, 203, 459
Cohen, S. 95–7, 100, 199, 206, 228–9, 327–8, 663, 871, 883, 890–1, 911
    Folk Devils and Moral Panics 218–19
Coleman, A. 291
Coleman, L. 504
Colquhoun, P. 25–6
commercial burglary 463–5
commitment 232
community
    crime prevention 583–8
        background 585
        mentoring 587–8
        Operation Ceasefire 585–7
    influences 842
    late modern 322
    policing 612
    punishment 661–2, 670–2, 674–6
    and restorative justice 749–50
    safety
        and crime prevention 569–70
        and crime reduction 570–3
    and youth justice 739
Community Order 662, 670
Community Punishment Order 661–2
Community Rehabilitation Order 661, 670
community reparative boards 757–8
COMPSTAT 621
conditioning 151
Confait case 639, 853
confessions 852, 853–4
confidence interval 916
conflict theories 249
Conklin, J. 394
Connell, R. 315–16, 832
consumer offences 381–2
containment theory 229–30, 231
contemporary classicism 280
    see also classicism
    assessment 295–7

control
    culture 330–3
    ratio 238
    theory 228–9, 241
control orders 875
control-balance theory 238–40
    and deviance 239–40
convenience sampling 913
Cooley, C. 213
Corbett, C. 465–6, 832
Cornish, D. 281–5, 582
corporate crime *see under* white-collar crime
Corsten Review 818, 833
Cosa Nostra 410, 411–13, 414, 416
Coser, L. 195
Court Administration, HM Inspectorate 555
court process
    see also juries
    appeals 654–5
    children as witnesses 858–9
    defendants' rights 650–1
    evidence *see* evidence
    miscarriages of justice 655–7
    mode of trial decision 649–50
    pleas *see* pleas and bargaining
    pre-trial decisions 645–9
    and psychology 856–61
    recall/eyewitness testimony 856–7, 858
    vulnerable witness 857–9
court system, development 33
court-ordered compensation 359
Coyle, A. 684, 695
CPTED (crime prevention through environmental design) 291
Crawford, A. 567, 630, 751
Cressey, D. 385, 410–13, 415–16
crime 6–16
    approaches 6–8
    and criminal law 8
    fiction 87
    general theory *see* general theory of crime
    historical levels 42–3
    historical perceptions 43–6
    and opportunity 292–4
    and politics *see* politics
    as social construct 8–11
    square 266 *Fig.*
    state 878–83
    surveys *see* victimization surveys
crime control, and due process 559–61
Crime and Disorder Act 1998 570, 573, 574
Crime and Disorder Reduction Partnerships (CDRP) 547
crime prevention 334, 566–93
    analysis 588–93
    community *see under* community
    and community safety 569–70
    definitions 566
    hot spots 589
    key developments 571
    Kirkholt Burglary Prevention Project 591–3

policy issues 566–73
practice 577
repeat victimization 589–91
situational *see* situational crime prevention
social *see* criminality prevention
theory and volume crime analysis 588–9, 590 *Table*
crime science 294–5
and criminology 295 *Fig.*
methodology stages 567
crime trends 69–76
all crime 71 *Fig.*
London/New York 456 *Fig.*
overall recorded crime rate 71 *Fig.*
and routine activity theory 286–8
violent crime 72 *Fig.*
Crimewatch UK 105
Criminal Cases Review Commission (CCRC) 547, 656–7
Criminal courts 546–7
criminal injuries compensation 358–9
criminal investigation 427, 430, 432, 546, 558–9, 603–4, 605, 623, 624, 829, 847, 851
criminal justice 542–61
adversarial v inquisitorial systems 557–9
agencies/organisations 546–8
cooperation 549–50
due process v crime control 559–61
emergence 22–3
and ethnicity 785–98, 796–8
expenditure/employment 551, 553
flows through 552 *Fig.*
and government 542–4
inspectorates 555–6
management/oversight 553–6
new public management 553–4
politics and reform 556–7
process 550–1
and restorative justice 746–7
Scotland 548
and victims 365–7
volunteers 548–9
and women 810–18
Criminal Justice Act 1991 664–7
Crime(Sentences) Act 1997 667
post-1991 reform 666–7
sentencing framework 665 *Fig.*
Criminal Justice Act 2003 669
criminal law
and crime 8
historical variation 9–11
Criminal Statistics, England and Wales 52, 70
criminal types 123–4
criminalisation 9, 248–9, 250, 251, 258, 310, 313, 315, 383, 401, 432, 474, 479, 487, 488, 557, 869
of women 313
criminality prevention 583–5
background 583
Perry Pre-School Project 584–5
risk-focused prevention 584
criminology 4–6
background 4–5

in Britain 17–18
definitions 5–6
disciplines 5
Croall, H. 378, 382–3, 386, 399
Crowe, R. 136
Crown Court 643–50
defendants 643 *Table*
judiciary 643–4
juries 644–5
reasons for preference 649 *Table*
Crown Prosecution Service 23, 638–41
background 638–9
discontinuance 641
downgrading of charges 641
HM Inspectorate 555
public interest 640–1
sufficient evidence 639–40
Cullen, F. T. 163
cultural criminology 204
cultural transmission 192–3
culture of control 330–3, 336, 338
cultures and subcultures 196–9
see also subcultural theory
delinquency 196–9, 204
Currie, E. 237, 255, 264, 386
custody *see* imprisonment
cybercrime 104–7

Dahrendorf, R. 250–1
Dalgaard, O.S. 135
Dalton, K. 302
Daly, K. 306, 308–9, 761–2, 765, 766
Darwin, C. 121, 123, 125
data 48–79
see also statistics
background 50
crime trends 69–76
and ethnicity 772
measurement methods 50–1
official *see* official statistics
recorded crime statistics 51
standard 73–4
victimization *see* victimization surveys
Davis, M. 321, 854
D'Cruze, S. 441
Decker, S. 447, 462
defendants' rights 650–1
delinquency 196–9, 204
determinism 259, 839
developmental criminology 843–5
deviance
amplification 218–19
changing focus 212–13
outsiders 214–16, 221–3
primary/secondary 213–14
deviant identification 149
Dick, P. K., *Minority Report* 336
differential association 151–2, 193–5
and white-collar crime 385
differential reinforcement 153, 194–5
diffusion of benefits 583
Dignan, J. 344, 358, 364, 747–8, 749, 759, 766
Dilulio, J. 274

Dinkins, D. 620
direct-contact predatory violations 287
discharges 661
Disney World 328–9
displacement 296, 582–3, 590
Ditton, J. 223, 378, 910
diversion 220–1
DNA identification 858
Dobash, R. 440
Dobrin, A. 344
doli incapax 732–3
domestic violence 761–3, 820–7
    attrition 825–7
    background 820–1
    perpetrators 821–2
    and policing 822–3
    policy issues 823–5
    types 822 *Table*
dopamine 140
Dorling, D. 445
Dorn, N. 504
Downes, D. 5, 17, 18, 178, 183–4, 195, 198, 201–4,
    206, 210, 214, 228, 264, 268, 269, 315, 832
drift theory 231
Drug Abstinence Order (DAR) 492
Drug Treatment and Testing Order (DTTO) 489–91,
    670
drugs 474–98
    background 474, 511
    causing crime 485–6
        no causal relationship 487
    and crime 484–5
    and criminal justice 488–9
    drug courts 490–1
    and ethnicity 784
    legal classification 475–6
    legalisation 479–80
    mean harms 476, 477 *Fig.*
    medicalisation 477
    normalisation debate 482–4
    official attitudes 477–80
    penalties 488 *Table*
    pharmacological categories 475
    and policing 493–8
    sentences 489 *Fig.*
    testing 491–3
    use 480–4
        caused by crime 486
        and deviancy amplification 97–8
    and youth crime 721–4
drugs trafficking 408, 420, 425–8, 432, 433
    forms of organisation 427
    routes 425–7
    structures 425
    war on drugs 427–8
Dubber, M. 367
Dubois, D. 430
due process, and crime control 559–61
Duff, A. 358, 765
Duff, P. 561
Dugdale, R. 133

Dunlap, A. 486
Durkheim, E. 170–4, 229, 517, 744
    assessment 174
    and crime 170–1, 183
    and punishment 527–9
    and social change 171–2
    suicide and anomie 172–4, 179, 231–2
Dworkin, R. 886

Eaton, M. 306
Edwards, A. 306
EEG (electroencephalogram) 139
ego 149
electroencephalogram (EEG) 139
electronic tagging 583, 648, 666, 709, 739
Elias, N. 45, 457–8
    and punishment 531–2
embezzlement 378
empathy 841
employment offences 380–1
Emsley, C. 26, 34, 36
enforcement pyramid 765
Engels, F. 248
England and Wales, *Criminal Statistics* 52, 70
Enron collapse 390
environmental crime 383–4
Ericson, R. 86, 329
Erikson, K.T. 86
essentialism 269
ethnicity
    anti-social behaviour 783–4
    background 772
    cautioning 791–2
    and community 779–80
    and criminal justice system 785–98, 796–8
    data sources 772
    deaths in custody 795–6
    drug use 784
    fear of crime 774
    and imprisonment 793–6
    and offending 780–4
    and policing 788–91, 798–800
    prison officers 800–1
    self-reported offending 781–3
    and sentencing 792–3
    stop and search 785–8
    treatment in custody 794–6
    and victimization 773–80
ethnomethodology 211
eugenics, negative 133–5
Europol 430
evaluation research 918–21
evidence 653–4
    disclosure 653–4
    exclusion 654
    forms 652
Ewing, K. 889
expected utility 280–1
experimental methods 917–18
extroversion 162
eyewitness testimony 856–7, 858
Eysenck, H. J. 161–3, 841

Fabiano, E.A. 159, 862
family factors 841–2
family group conferencing 753–5
Farrall, S. 357
Farrell, G. 377
Farrington, D. 78, 139, 506, 718, 817, 841
Fattah, E.A. 344
fear of crime 62, 63, 93, 94, 268, 271, 276, 331, 352,
    351, 355–8, 462, 537, 554, 568, 630, 696, 819, 827,
    832, 902, 920
    and women 819
Feeley, M. 334–5, 336–7
Feilzer, M. 648
Felson, M. 286–90, 292–4, 347, 459, 580
female born criminal 302
feminist criminology
    see also women
    assessment 314–16
    background 300
    contemporary 308–9
    criminalisation of women 313
    development 305–8
    early criminology 301–4
    and female emancipation 305–6
    methodology 313–14
    nature of female offending 309–11
    and penology 311–13
    secondary victimization 359–61
    and sociological criminology 205, 303–4
    victimology 314
Ferguson, D. 506
Ferracuti, F. 200
Ferraro, K.F. 301–2
Ferri, E. 125–6
fiddling 379
    ethnography 910
Fielding, Henry 24–5, 36
fines 661
firearms offences 454–6
Fisse, B. 890
fixed-penalty notices 551
Fletcher, H. 679
focus groups 905–7
food offences 382–3
Ford , Gerald 523
Forensic psychology 839, 840, 842, 856
forensic science 605–6
Forensic Science Service (FSS) 547–8
Foucault, M. 323–9, 336, 532–5
    Discipline and Punish 324–5, 684–5
    dispersal of discipline 327–8
    impact 534–5
    instrumental discipline 328–9
    nature of government 325–7
    power and knowledge 323
fraud 378–80
    cost 394–5
    victims 390–2
Freeman, M. 885
Freilich, J. 421
Freud, S. 149
Friedrichs, D.O. 375

Fry, Elizabeth 815
Fryer, P. 774–9
Fuller, J. 254
fully informed consent form 936

Gadd, D. 357
Gambetta, D. 409
gang delinquency 196–7, 204
Garfinkel, H. 211, 212
Garland, D. 4, 50, 114, 174, 295–6, 321–2, 554
    Culture of Control 330–3, 336, 338, 525, 528
Garofalo, R. 4, 125–6
Gatrell, V.A.C. 35, 44
Gaussian curve 915
Gearty, C. 884, 886, 889
Geis, G. 385
Gelsthorpe, L. 305, 307, 313–14
gender, male/female offending 806–9
Gendreau, P. 861
general theory of crime 234–7
    assessment 237
    background 234
    low self-control 234–6
genetic factors 132–8
    adoption 136–7
    chromosomal anomalies 137–8
    eugenics, negative 133–5
    and offending 138
    twin studies 135–6
Genn, H. 350
genocide 879–81
    definition 879–80
    Bosnia 881
    Cambodia 880
    Rwanda 880–1
Gesch, C.B. 143
Giddens, A. 320
Giller, H. 521
Glaser, B.G. 932
globalisation 10, 172, 320, 321, 323, 389, 408, 420,
    868–71, 872, 873, 874, 876, 878, 885
    and criminology 869
    definitions 868–9
    migration issues 869–71
Glueck, E. 128, 843
Gobert, J. 401, 402
Godfrey, B. 23, 31, 33, 34, 39
Goffman, E. 217
Goften, L. 504
Goggin, C. 861
Goldstein, H. 612
Goode, E. 219
Goody, J. 353–4, 356, 363
Goold, B. 754
Görgen, T. 353
Goring, C. 126–7, 128
Gottfredson, M. 138, 231, 234–7, 275, 385, 717
Götz, M. 138
Gould, S. J. 272
Gouldner, A. 223, 256
governmentality see Foucault, and governmentality
Grade, M. 93
Graef, R. 823

Gramsci, A. 256–8
Gray, J. 845
Graycar, A. 424
Green, P. 878, 879
Greer, C. 86
Gross, H. 467–8
grounded theory 932
Grünhut, M. 17
Guantánamo Bay 712
Gudjonsson, G.H. 853, 854
Guiliani, Rudolph 620
gun crime 454–6
Gunn, J. 139, 845
Gurr, T. G. 43, 457
Gusfield, J. 195

Haines, F. 120
Hale, C. 356, 809
Hall, S. 86, 98–9
Halliday Report 668–9
Hammer, T. 504
Hansen, K. 183
Harrington, R. 448
Harris, R. 467
Harvey, D. 320
Hauser, R. 164
Hawkins, K. 455–6
Heal, K. 582
healing circles 756
Hebenton, B. 429, 430
Hedderman, C. 651, 817
hegemonic masculinity 315–16
Heidensohn, F. 205, 300, 303, 304, 309–11, 314,
    315, 806, 809
Henderson, P.F. 648
Hennigan, K.M. 92
Henry II 23
Henry, A. 150
Herald of Free Enterprise 395
Herrnstein, R. 163, 164, 272–3, 275
Hill, P. 409
Hindelang, M.J. 163–4, 165
Hindley, Myra 440–1
Hirschi, T. 138, 163–4, 165, 231–2, 234–7, 275, 385,
    717
Hirst, P. 259
HM Inspectorates 555
Hobbs, D. 431–2
Hobdell, K. 832, 833
Hobsbawm, E. 408
Hollin, C. 139, 141, 156, 506, 838, 840, 861
Holloway, K. 456, 479
Holmstrom, L.L. 354
Home Office 543–5
    Home Secretaries 544–5
homicide 438–46
    categories 438–9
    historic trends 456–8
    method of killing 444 *Fig.*
    motive 442
    offenders 439–41

serial killers 444–6
and social status 444
trends 439
use of weapons 442
victim/offender relationship 442, 443 *Table*
victims 441–2
Hood, R. 648, 792
Hooton, E. 127
Hope, T. 459
hormones 141–2
Horowitz, I.L. 246
hot spots 299, 333, 589, 590, 591, 613
Hough, M. 74–5, 817
Howard, John 39, 420, 667, 684
Howard, Michael 14, 74–5, 522, 545, 694, 730, 775
Howitt, C. 140, 148, 849, 850, 856, 858–9
Hudson, B. 520, 521, 664
human interactionism 210–12
human rights 883–92
    abuses 891–2
    background 883
    in Britain 886
    Conventions 885
    and criminology 890–1
    and imprisonment 711–13
    origins 883–4
    tribunals 891–2
    in 20th C 884–5
Human Rights Act 1998 886–9
    impact 888–9
    main articles 887
human trafficking 421–5
    activities 421
    factors 421–2
    groups 424
    methods 424
    profile of victims 422 *Fig*
    recruitment methods 423
    stages 422–3
    transportation 423–4
Hurd, Douglas 688
Hutchings, B. 136
hypothetico-deductive theory 931–2

Ianni, F.A. and Ianni, E.R. 408–9, 414–15
id 149
idealism 259
Ignatieff, M. 888
imprisonment
    see also prison
    in Britain 685–6
    and ethnicity 793–6
    history 38–42
    and human rights 711–13
    international trends 695–7
    mass 535–7
    and non-custodial sentencing 670–2
    and penal politics 694
    and social exclusion 705
    suspended sentences 662–3
    trends 690–4

and women 811–13
and young people 737–9
impulsiveness 841
inappropriate behaviour 139
incapacitation 521–3
incarceration *see* imprisonment
Independent Police Complaints Commission (IPCC)
543, 556, 795
individual factors 840–5
background 840–1
developmental/life course theories 843–5
risk factors 841–3
individualism 839
inner containment 230
Innocence Project 858
innovation 176–7
inquisitorial, and adversarial (criminal justice)
systems 557–9
Institute for the Study and Treatment of
Delinquency (ISTD) 17, 18
instrumental discipline 328–9
intelligence 163–5, 272–3
low 841
interactionism 210–12, 221–3
International Crime Victim Survey (ICVS) 51, 67
international terrorism 107–9
internet crime *see* cybercrime
Interpol 429
interrogation 852–4
approaches 852
and confessions 852, 853–4
investigative interview techniques 852–3
interviews 903–5
and questionnaires 906 *Table*
involvement 232–3
IQ *see* intelligence
Iraq, privatised security 877–8
Custer Battles 878
Irvine, Lord 886

Jacklin, C.N. 302
Jacobs, J. 290, 776
Jacques, M. 95
Jarvis, F.V. 42
Jeffery, C.R. 153
Jewkes, Y. 100
Jill Dando Institute of Crime Science 294
Johnstone, G. 758, 765
Jones, T. 632–3
joyriding 467–9
Jukes family 133
juries 859–61
composition 860–1
Crown Court 644–5
decision-making 861
and evidence 859
extra-evidential factors 860
just deserts 331, 524–7, 664, 668, 675
Justice for All, White Paper 669

Kallikak family 133–4
Kalven, H. Jr. 861

Kandel, E. 139–40
Karstedt, S. 377
Katz, J. 133, 309, 387–8
Kellett, S. 467–8
Kelling, G. 269–70, 290–1, 574
Kelly, L. 826
Kemshall, H. 453
Keynesian State 322
Kidd-Hewitt, D. 85, 95
King, R. 832
King, S. 939
Kirchheimer, O. 39
Kirkholt Burglary Prevention Project 591–3
Kirkholt Project 351
Kleiman, M. 494
Klochars, C. 259
Knapp Commission 624
Kohlberg, Lawrence 159–60
Kramer, R. 384, 878, 882
Kray twins 418–19

labelling theory 9, 95, 171, 178, 203, 204, 229, 246,
251, 255, 304, 342, 347, 728, 749, 750
assessment 220–3
and deviance *see* deviance
emergence 213–14
outsiders 214–16
self-fulfilling prophecy 218
shaming, disintegrative, reintegrative 219–20,
221 *Fig.*
stigma 217–18
Lacey, N. 5
Lamb, M. 859
Lambeth cannabis experiment 496–7
Langer, W. 847–8
late modernity, transition 320–3
background 320
regulatory state, new 322–3
surveillance 320–1
laterality 141
Laub, J. 128, 237, 843–5
law and order, approach to 267
Lawrence Inquiry 616, 774–5, 790–1
Lawrence, P. 23, 31, 33, 34, 39
Laycock, G. 582
Layder, D. 932
Lea, J. 267, 269
leading questions 902, 903
learning theories 151–7
background 151
differential association 151–2
operant learning 152–3
rational choice 156–7
routine activity theory 157
social learning theory 153–6
Leeson, Nick 380
left idealism 265–6
left impossibilism 265
left realism 178, 259, 264–70, 271, 308, 347, 386,
819, 890
approach to law and order 267
assessment 268–70

background 264–5
critique of left idealism 265–6
local crime surveys 267–8
nature of 266–7
and right realism 270–2
Legal Services Commission (LSC) 546
Leibowitz, M. 246
Lemert, E. 213, 218
Leng, R. 560
Leonard, E. 308
Levi, M. 390, 394, 397, 400–1, 413, 417, 436
lie detection 854–7
Liebling, A. 830
life-course
persistent offending 844
theories 843–5
Light, R. 468–9
Likert scale 901
Lilly, J.R. 275
limited retributivism 668
literature review 929–31
Livingstone, S. 92, 93
local crime surveys 267–8
Locke, J. 884
Lombroso, C. 4, 50, 122–5, 126, 138, 139, 831
and female offender 301–2
Lowe, G. 503
Luciano, Charley (Lucky) 412, 414
Lyman, M. 407

McCold, Paul 759
McConville, M. 560, 608, 861
McCullough, D. 467
McDaniel, Stephen 32
McGuire, J. 153, 165, 838, 839, 846
McIntosh, M. 817
McKay, H. K. 191, 192–3
McLaughlin, E. 554, 573
McMurran, M. 506
Macpherson Inquiry 774–5, 790–1
see also Lawrence Inquiry 616, 774–5, 790–1
McRobbie, A. 100, 205, 304
McSweeney, T. 485, 487
McWilliams, B. 41, 674
Maccoby, E.E. 302
Mafia 408–9, 409–10, 411, 414
Magill, C. 462
Magistrates' courts 41, 52, 60, 359, 398, 454, 542,
546, 547, 548, 551, 555, 627, 628, 639, 641–3, 644,
648, 649, 650, 651, 652, 654, 661, 668, 692, 725,
727, 733, 800, 811, 812
magistracy 642–3
Maguire, M. 69, 70, 79, 354, 436, 453, 572, 604, 832
Maher, L. 306
male/female offending 806–9
males, conviction rates 76–7
Malinowski, Bronisław 908
Malleson, K. 655
managerialism 13
mandatory minimum sentences 519
Mannheim, H. 17, 817
manslaughter 438–9

manufacturing premises, crimes against 463–5
Maple, J. 621
marihuana 98, 215–16
sampling users 914
Mark, Sir R. 101–2
Marshall, A. 747
Martinson, R. 521, 861
Maruna, S. 521, 862, 864
Marx/Marxism 246–9
and punishment 530–1
masculinity
see also women
and crime 831–2
and victimization 832–3
mass society approaches 91
Masseria, Guiseppe (Joe) 410, 411, 412
maternal deprivation 150–1
Matthews, R. 259, 270–1, 446–7
Matza, D. 128, 191, 199, 201, 230–1, 233, 385–6,
890
Mawby, R. C. 102, 347, 462, 463
May Report 687, 688, 710
May, T. 503
Mayhew, P. 448–9, 581–2
Mayne, R. 26, 120
Mays, J. B. 201
Mead, G. H. 193, 210, 211, 213
Mead, L. 275
Mead, M. 908
media 84–109
academic study of 84–5
background 84
content 86–8
criminogenic effects 90–4
exaggeration/distortion 96
and fear of crime 93–4
and international terrorism 107–9
newsworthiness 85–6
primary/secondary definers 99
relationship with police 101–2
representation of police 102–4
representations of crime 85
and sex crime 88–90
and violent crime 88
and young offenders 93
Mednick, S.A. 136, 139–40
Megan's Laws 333, 334, 343
Mendelsohn, B. 344
mental disorder 845–7
background 845
links with crime 846–7
and offending 846
prevalence 845–6
mentoring 548, 587–8
Merton, R. K. 174–9, 183, 184, 196, 218
assessment 178–9
mesh thinning 328
Messner, S. 182–283
Messerschmidt, J. 309, 315–16
Michalowski, R. 384, 878–9, 882
Miers, D. 346, 347, 359
migration issues 869–71

Millbank penitentiary 39
Miller, J. 306
Miller, W. B. 200
Milosovic, Slobodan 881
Ministry of Justice (UK) 545
Minnesota sentencing guidelines 525, 526 *Table*
Mirrlees-Black, C. 722
miscarriages of justice 655–7
Mitchell, B. 440, 441–2
modernity *see* late modernity, transition
mods and rockers 95–7, 219
Moffitt, T. 135, 140, 844–5
Mooney, J. 821
moral development 159–61
moral entrepreneurship 214–15
moral panics 85, 90, 94–100, 264, 503, 773
   criticisms of theory 99–100
   deviancy amplification 97–8, 218–19
   key elements 95
   signification spiral 95–7, 98–9
   use of term 94–5
Morgan, J. 354, 642, 648
Morgan Report 569–70
Moriarty, M. 544
Morris Inquiry 798
Morris, N. 523
Morris, T. 17, 201, 307, 439, 442, 521, 817
motivation 153–4, 232
Mott, J. 722
Mountbatten Report 687
Moxon, D. 651, 652
Mubarek, Zahid 796
mugging panics 98–9, 721
Mulcahy, A. 651
Multi-Agency Public Protection Arrangements (MAPPA) 523
murder 36, 43, 86, 88, 90, 91, 95, 118, 122, 344, 355, 364, 438–9, 440–6, 457, 526, 639, 657, 729–30, 774–5, 790, 849, 851, 879, 880, 881
Murphy, Patrick V. 625
Murray, C. 163, 164, 272–5

Nadelmann, E. 432
naïve anti-empiricism/abolitionism 265
Narey Report 649
Natalier, K. 174
National Association of Pretrial Service Agencies (NAPSA) 337
National Crime Reporting Standard (NCRS) 73–4
National Crime Victimization Survey (NCVS) (US) 51
National Deviancy Conference (NDC) 18
National Offender Management Service (NOMS) 13, 678–80
nature v nurture debate 135, 136
negative eugenics 133–5
Neighbourhood Watch 332, 548, 568, 592
Nelken, D. 375
Nelson, George 41
net-widening 328, 739, 766
neuroses 149
neuroticism 162
neurotransmitters 140
neutralisation 230–1

   and white-collar crime 385–6
new criminology 255–6
new penology 334–6, 336–7
new public management, criminal justice system 553–4
New Public Management (NPM) 13
new regulatory state 322–3
'new wars' 875
Newburn, T. 14, 90, 93, 309, 320, 351, 352, 484, 504, 523, 576, 583, 587, 625, 632–3, 663, 670, 695, 696, 718, 719, 720, 730, 736, 739, 740, 744, 747, 751, 753, 754, 758, 787, 876, 878, 883
Newman, O. 290–1, 566
Newman, Sir K. 612
Nickell, Rachel 849, 851, 852
Nightwatchman State 322
nominal data 914
normal distribution 915–16
Northern Ireland Crime Survey (NICS) 65
nutrition 142–3
Nye, F. I. 229, 232

offenders
   data 76–9
      self-report studies 77–9
   male/female 806–9
   persistent 523
   racist 778–9
   reintegration 750–1
   treatment 861–4
   types 844–5
Offenders Index 76
offender profiling 847–52
   assessment 850–1
   FBI approach 848–9
   legal/ethical issues 851–2
   origins 847–8
Offending, Crime and Justice Survey (OCJS) 78
official statistics 51–61
   assessment 53–60
   attrition 56–60
   background 51–2
   categories of offences 54–5
   England and Wales, *Criminal Statistics* 52, 70
   impact of legislation 55–6
   limitations 60–1
   recording practices 58–9
   reporting practices 56–8
   US, *Uniform Crime Reports* 51, 52–3
   and victimization surveys 68–9
Ohlin, L. 178, 180, 198–9
Oliver, Jamie 142
Olweus, D. 165
O'Malley, P. 327, 333
ordinal data 914
organised crime 9, 67, 97, 104, 176, 251, 252, 269, 382, 406–32, 600, 602, 604, 608, 873
   in America 409–17
      alien conspiracy theory 413
      ethnic succession theory 413
      organisation 412–13, 414–17
      portrayal 409–10
      and prohibition 409, 411, 412

in Britain 417–20
critical issues 431–2
definition 406–8
traditional forms 408–9
trafficking *see* drugs trafficking; human trafficking
transnational 420–8, 431–2
control/policing 429–30
Osborn, D. R. 133, 135
outsiders 214–16

Packer, H. 559, 608
paedophile notification schemes 333, 334
panopticon 38, 324–5
Pape, H. 504
parental conflict 842
Park, R. E. 190, 196
Parker, H. 203, 482, 484, 506, 507, 722, 933
Parole Board 548
Patrick, J. 933
PATRIOT Act 875
Pavlov, I. 151
Pawson, R. 920
Payne, Sarah 454
Pearson, G. 90, 246, 351, 448
Pease, K. 582, 593
Peay, J. 845, 846
Peel, Sir R. 26, 44, 102, 120, 622
peer influences 842
penal populism 14–15, 331
penal-welfarism 332
penology 201, 338, 516, 517, 534
and feminist criminology 311–13
new 334–6, 336–7
Pepinsky, H. 254
Perry Pre-School Project 584–5
Persky, H. 142
personality 841
phenomenology 211
Philips, D. 35
Phillips, C. 781, 791, 796
Phillips, M. 94
phrenology 122
physiognomy 122
Piacentini, L. 934
Piaget, J. 159
PICTS (Psychological Inventory of Criminal Thinking Styles) 159
pilferage 910
plagiarism 940–1
Plant, M. and Plant, M. 498
pleas and bargaining 651–3
charge bargaining 651–2
options 651–2
plea bargaining 652–3
pleasure principle 149
Plummer, K. 223
police court missionaries 41–2
policing 598–633
accountability 627 *Fig.*, 628
arrest powers 607–8
centralisation 616–17
commercial 632, 633 *Table*

community 612
confessions 852, 853–4
corruption 622–6
background 622–3
causes 623–6
gratuities, arguments 624 *Fig.*
types 623 *Fig.*
criminal investigation 603–4
culture 617–19
and cybercrime 107
detention at station 608–10
and domestic violence 822–3
and drugs 493–8
ethnic minority officers 600 *Fig.*
and ethnicity 788–91
forensic science 605–6
functions 602–3
governance 626–9
history 23–30, 613–17
centralisation 616–17
early history 23–6
legitimacy problems 615–16
new police 26–7, 613–14
resistance and reform 27–9
Royal Commission 614–15
in Scotland 29
20th century 29–30
HM Inspectorate of Constabulary 555
intelligence-led 612–13
legitimacy problems 615–16
models 611–13
municipal 631–2
national forces 600–2
National Intelligence Model (NIM) 604–5
officer strength 598 *Table*
organisation 546, 598–602
plural 629–32
powers 606–11
problem-orientated 292, 612
profiling *see* offender profiling
and psychology 847–56
rank structure 599 *Fig.*
rape 822–3
relationship with media 101–2
representation by media 102–4
revolution 632–3
right to silence 610–11
risk-orientated practices 334
Royal Commission 614–15
stop and search 607, 785–8
strategies 613 *Fig.*
studies 602–6
transnational 429–30, 875–6
tripartite structure 627 *Fig.*
volunteers 548
women's role 828–9
zero-tolerance 619–22
politics 11–16
background 11–12
bipartisan consensus 12–13, 331
Pollak, O. 302–3
pollution 384
polygraphs 855–6

positivism
  background 120–1
  biological 132, 143–4
  and classicism 122 *Fig.*
  definition 121–2, 838–9
  Ferri/Garofalo 125–6
  Garland 50, 114
  Goring 126–7, 128
  impact 128–9
  Lombroso 4, 50, 120–9, 122–5, 126
  somatypes 127–8
  types of criminal 123–4
post-Fordism 320
Potter, G. 407, 776
power and knowledge 323
Poyner, B. 291
preference trial 918
Price, D. 830
primary social control 633
primitive rebellion thesis 248
Prins, H. 845
prison 684–713
  see also imprisonment
  complaints 711 *Fig.*
  disciplinary role 324–5
  governance 709–13
  grievance/complaints procedures 710
  historical development 684–90
  HM Inspectorate 555
  independent inspection 710
  inmates 703–6
  life 702–3
  and mothers 815–17
  officers 707–9
  Ombudsman 556, 710
  overcrowding 689–90
  population 536 *Figs*
  private 701–2
  release 709
  security 686–8
  statistics 691–4 *Figs*
  and stressful life events 816 *Table*
  system 546
  types 700–2
  violence 705–6
  volunteers 548
  and women 311–13, 813–17
  women officers 830
private military industry 876–7
probability 916–17
probability sampling 912
probation 673–80
  and community punishment 674–6
  history 40–2, 673–4
  HM Inspectorate 555
  National Offender Management Service (NOMS)
    678–80
  national service 677–8
  and New Labour 676–80
  Ombudsman 556
  Probation Service 546

  and punitive policies 675–6
  volunteers 548
  and 'what works' 676–7, 861–2, 863
  women's role 830
problem-orientated policing 292
profiling *see* offender profiling
prohibition 409, 411, 412
property crime 459–60
  categories 458, 459 *Fig.*
  factors 459–60
  trends 459
property relations, changes 321–2
proportionality 524–5
prosecution, history 31–5
  decline of profit motive 33–5
  development of court system 33
  formalisation of process 31–3
  private actions 30–1
prudentialism 327, 525
psychoanalysis 148–51
Psychological Inventory of Criminal Thinking Styles
  (PICTS) 159
psychological positivism 148, 165
  types/theories 148 *Fig.*
psychology
  approaches 838–9
  and court process 856–61
  and policing 847–56
  relevant areas 839–40
psychopathy 846
psychoticism 162
public interest
  Crown Prosecution Service 640–1
  immunity 653–4
Punch, M. 376, 387, 389, 401, 402
punishment
  see also sentencing
  and childhood 725–6
  and classical criminology 114–16
  community 661–2, 670–2, 674–6
  criteria 516
  general deterrence 518–19
  history 36–42
  incapacitation 521–3
  individual deterrence 519–20
  just deserts 524–7
  key questions 516–17
  mass incarceration 535–7
  proportionality 524–5
  rehabilitation 520–1, 674
  retributivism 524–7
  sociology 527–35
  utilitarian/consequentialist approaches 518–23
purposive sampling 913
Pynoos, R. S. 355

quasi-experimental methods 918
questionnaire
  design 900, 901–3
  and qualitative interviews 906 *Table*
Quetelet, A. 51, 121

Quinney, R. 252–4
quota sampling 913

race *see* ethnicity
radical criminology 246
    see also American radicalism; British radicalism
    assessment 258–9
radical victimology 347
Radzinowicz, L. 17, 33, 120
Rafter, H. H. 133
Raine, A. 140
random sampling 912
randomised controlled trial (RCT) 917–18
rape 822–7
    attrition 825–7
    policing 822–3
    policy issues 823–5
    press coverage 88 *Fig.*
    secondary victimization 359–61
rational choice theory 156–7, 280–6, 296
    bounded rationality 282–3
    continuing involvement model 285 *Fig.*
    crime scripts 283–5
    desistance model 286 *Fig.*
    expected utility 280–1
    initial involvement model 284 *Fig.*
    propositions 281–2
Rawlings, P. 23, 32, 38
Raynor, P. 863
Read, J. E. 853
Reagan, Ronald 265, 323
realism *see* left realism; right realism
reality principle 149
rebellion 178
Reckless, W. C. 229–30, 231
Redergard, Silje 441
Redmayne, M. 366, 639, 641, 647, 648
reductionism 839
Regional Crime Squads 600
regulatory state, new 322–3
rehabilitation 520–1, 674
Reid, John 543
Reiman, J. 120
Reiner, R. 28, 84–5, 87–8, 94, 101, 102, 602, 617–18, 627, 791
Reiss, A. 229
relative deprivation 179
release from prison 709
remand 645–6, 647–9
Renzetti, C. M. 315
reparation orders 752
research
    fully informed consent form 936
    governance/ethics 935–6
    literature review 929–31
    methods 898–911
        see also interviews; questionnaire
        case studies 911
        ethnography 907–10
        focus groups 905–7
        quantitative/qualitative 898–9

selection 931
    surveys 899–903
    negotiated access 933–5
    pilot 936–7
    plagiarism 940–1
    theory 931–2
    time management 941–2
    topic choice 926–9
    writing 937–40
respect agendas 576–7
responsibilisation 327, 333
restorative justice 744–66
    assessment 763–6
    background 744
    cautioning 752–4, 764
    citizens' panels 757–8
    community boards 757–8
    community involvement 749–50
    conflicts as property 744–5
    and corporate crime 760–1
    court-based measures 751–2
    and criminal justice 746–7
    definitions 747–8
    and domestic violence 761–3
    enforcement pyramid 765
    family group conferencing 753–5
    healing/sentencing circles 756–7
    limits 760–3
    objectives 748–51, 763
    offender reintegration 750–1
    optimistic/pessimistic view 30
    pyramid 748 *Fig.*
    and restorativeness 758–9
    types 751–8
    victim involvement 748–9, 766
    victim-offender mediation (VOM) 752–3
    and youth justice 739–40
restorativeness 758–9
retail premises, crimes against 463–5
retreatism 177–8
retributivism 524–7
right realism
    assessment 275
    background 270
    biosocial approach 272–3
    and left realism 270–2
    underclass 273–4
right to silence 610–11
risk 329–34, 841–3
    and criminal justice 333–4
    culture of control 330–3, 336, 338
    factors in offending 841–3
    modernisation 459
    society 329–30, 337–8
    static/dynamic 843
risk-need-responsivity model 862
ritualism 177
road injuries/deaths 465–6
robbery 437
    armed 446–7
    street 448–50

Robertson, G. 884
Roche, D. 766, 892
Rock, P. 33, 178, 184, 195, 206, 210, 228, 264, 268, 269, 315, 346, 832
romanticism 265
Rosenfeld, R. 182-3
Ross, R. 159, 862
Rossow, I. 507
Rothe, D. 876
routine activity theory 157, 286–90
    and concept modification 289 *Fig.*
    crime elements 287–8
    and crime trends 286–8
    elaboration 288–9
    target criteria 289–90
Rowan, C. 26, 120
Rusche, G. 39
Russell, N. 642
Rutter, M. 150–1

Safer Cities project 568
Samenow, S. 157–9
sampling 911–14
    background 911
    convenience 913
    purposive 913
    quota 913
    random 912
    snowball 913–14
    stratified 912
Sampson, R. 128, 196, 237, 843–5
Sanders, A. 560, 561, 651, 654
Sasson, T. 257-8
Savelsburg, J.J. 240
Scarman Inquiry 622, 789–90
Schengen Convention 429
Schleisinger, P. 94
Schmidt, T. 467
school influences 842
Schramm, W. 93
Schur, E. 8–9, 221
Schutz, A. 211
Scientific Methods Scale 920
Scotland, criminal justice system 491, 548
Scottish Crime Survey (SCS) 65
Seattle, crime network 416 *Fig*, 431
secondary social control 633
self-control
    low 234–6
    and white-collar crime 385
self-fulfilling prophecy 218
Sellin, T. 5, 124, 125–6, 199–200, 248
sentencing 519, 521, 523, 524, 525, 526, 660–80, 694, 791–2, 811–2
    see also punishment
    background 660
    conclusion 680
    for indictable offences 671 *Fig.*
    and New Labour 667–9
    non-custodial 670–2
    and plea bargaining 652
    policy 663–9

probation *see* probation
    suspended 662–3
    types 660–3
    and women 811
sentencing circles 756–7
serial killers 444–6
serotonin 140
sex crime, and media 88–90
sexual offences 437, 450–4
    data 450–1, 452 *Table*
    definition 450
    offenders 333–4
        monitoring 453–4
    stalking 451, 453
shaming, disintegrative, reintegrative 219–20, 221 *Fig.*, 751
Sharp, C. 503
Sharpe, J. 43, 44, 115
Shaw, C. R. 191, 192–3, 911
Shawcross, A. 137
Shearing, C. 321, 328–9, 632
Sheldon, W. 127–8, 161–2, 843
Shepherd, J. 506
Sherman, L. 222, 223, 587, 798
Shipman, Harold 445–6
Short, J. 228-9
Sibbitt, R. 778
signification spiral 95–7, 98–9
Simmel, G. 190
Simon, J. 334–5
Simon, R. 305, 809
Simon, T. 164
Singleton, N. 846
situational crime prevention 290–4, 296–7, 578–83
    action research 578
    background 290
    defensible space 290–1
    and displacement 582–3
    examples 578–82
    opportunity and crime 292–4, 578
    problem-orientated policing 292
    techniques 579 *Table*
    and washrooms 580 *Table*
skinheads 202–3
Skinner, B.F. 152, 153
Slapper, G. 374, 382, 386, 389, 394
Smart, C. 305–7, 809
Smith, D. J. 560, 608
Smith, P. 174, 448, 449
snowball sampling 913–14
social bond theory 231–4
    elements 232–3
    testing 233–4
social change 171–2
social cognitive skills 841
social constructionism 8–11, 211–12
social control
    secondary/primary 633
    women's role 828–31
social democratic approach 264
social disorganisation 192–3, 195
social ecology 190

social interactionism 210–12
social learning theory 153–6
    and social structure 156
socio-economic deprivation 842
somatypes 127–8, 132
Sparks, R. 94, 268, 321–2
Sparks, R. Snr. 61–2, 345, 348–50
Spitzer, S. 248-9
square of crime 266 *Fig.*
Stanko, B. 314, 356, 821, 832, 833
state crime 878–83
state, new regulatory 322–3
state-corporate crime 372, 378, 384, 431, 879
statement validity analysis 856
statistics 914–17
    see also data; official statistics
    background 914
    correlation 916
    descriptive 914
    mean/mode/median values 915
    normal distribution 915–16
    numerical/categorical 914–15
    probability/significance 916–17
Steffensmeier, D. 385
Stenning, P. 321, 328–9
Stevenson, J. 44
stigma 217–18
Stone, L. 799
stop and search 607, 785–8
Storch, R.D. 29
Straight Thinking on Probation (STOP) 862, 863
strain theory 180–4
    assessment 183–4, 199
    background 180
    differential opportunity 180–1
    general theory 181–2
Strangeways disturbance 689–90
stratified sampling 912
Strauss, A. L. 932
Straw, Jack 574, 667
street robbery 448–50
Strong, K. 758
structuralist theory 249
subcultural theory 199–206
    see also cultures and subcultures
    American 199–201
    assessment 204–6
    background 199
    British 201–4
    feminist critique 205
suicide
    and anomie 172–4
    typology 173 *Fig.*
superego 149
surveillance 39, 44, 157, 289, 290, 291, 296, 320–1,
    324, 325, 327, 329, 334, 459, 523, 533, 569, 580,
    581, 592, 604, 606, 870, 871
surveys 899–903
suspended sentences 662–3
Sutherland, E. 5–6, 8, 151–2, 153, 155, 180, 193–5,
    198, 832, 911
    and Marxism 248

and white-collar crime 373–6, 385, 393–4
Sykes, G. 199, 217, 230–1, 233, 385–6, 890
syndicated crime *see* organised crime

Tannenbaum, F. 213
Tappan, P. W. 8, 374
Tarde, G. 153, 193
Tatchell, P. 215
tax fraud 379–80
Taylor, I 43, 119–20, 221, 255–6
Taylor, H. 457
Taylor, L. 184
teenagers, perceptions 716
teleology 258–9
telephone interviews 904
temperament 841
terrorism 871–8
    background 871
    in Britain 872–3
    definition 871–2
    international 873–4
    and 'new wars' 875
    special powers 874–5
    and torture 888
testosterone 141–2
Thatcher, Margaret 12, 13, 265, 323, 519, 599, 728
theft at work 378
Thomas, W. I. 191, 211
    and female offender 302–3
Thompson, E. P. 259
Thompson, K. 94, 95, 100
Thornton, S. 100, 462
Thrasher, F. 194, 196–7
Tierney, J. 266, 345
Tilley, N. 207, 463, 569, 571, 605, 612, 919, 920
Tittle, C. 238–40
Toby, J. 229, 232
Tombs, S. 346, 380, 382, 386, 389, 394, 398, 401
Topinard, P. 4
torture 888
Toynbee, P. 74–5
trafficking *see* drugs trafficking; human trafficking
transnational policing 429–30, 875–6
transportation 37–8, 39
Triads 409
Trondman, M. 908
truth commissions 891–2
Tuffin, R. 799
Tumber, H. 94
Tunnell, K. D. 296
Turk, A. 250–1
twin studies 135–6

underclass 273–4
Uniform Crime Reports (US) (UCR) 51, 52–3
United States, *Uniform Crime Reports* (US) (UCR) 51,
    52–3
utopianism 265

Valachi, Joseph 410–412, 416
Valier, C. 125, 148
Van Ness, D. 758

Veblen, T. 373
vehicle-related crime *see* car crime
vice dynamics 208–9
Victim Support 355, 363–4
Victim–offender mediation (VOM) 752–3
victimization
    behavioural impact 354
    and elderly 352–3
    emotional/psychological impact 354–5
    and ethnicity 773–80
    extent 51, 61–8, 348–9
    financial impact 355
    and homeless 351–2
    impact 353–4
    physical impact 354
    in prison 706 *Table*
    repeat 349–51, 589–91
    secondary 359–61
    vulnerable groups 351–3
    and youth crime 724–5
victimization surveys 51, 61–8, 348–9
    assessment 67–8
    British Crime Survey (BCS) 51, 62–5, 70–3
    commercial 67
    International Crime Victim Survey (ICVS) 67
    local 65–7
    and official statistics 68–9
    purposes of crime surveys 62
    strengths/weaknesses 68
victimology
    approaches 346–8
    critical 347–8
    emergence 344–8
    positivist 346–7
    radical 347
    victim-blaming 346
    victim-precipitation 345–6
victims
    child abuse 361–3
    court-ordered compensation 359
    criminal injuries compensation 358–9
    and criminal justice system 365–7
    fraud 390–2
    historical role 30–1
    homicide 441–2, 443 *Table*
    ideal 342–4
    policy 358–67
    rights 364–7
    statements 365
    support 363–4
    women 359–61
Victims Charter 364–5
violent crime
    concept 436–8, 469
    contemporary trends 458
    crime trends 72 *Fig.*
    data 72 *Fig.*, 437, 438 *Figs*
    and media 88
    and weapons 454–6
VIVA 289
Vold, G. 250

Von Hentig, H. 345, 346
von Hirsch, A. 524–5

Walker, S. 409, 429
Walklate, S. 346, 347, 809
Walters, G. 487
Walters, R. 274
Walton, P. 255–6
war
    as crime 882
    crimes 882–3
'War on Terror' 107–9
Ward, T. 521, 862, 864, 878, 879
waste dumping 383–4
Weatheritt, M. 566
Weber, Max 529, 876, 907–8
Webster, C. 780
Weiner, M. J. 44
Welsh, B. 841
Wertham, F. 344–5
'what works' 676–7, 861–2, 863
West, D. 133, 135, 718
White, R. 120
white-collar crime 372–402
    case studies 396–7
    categories 397
    control 397–9
    and corporate crime 376–7
    and criminology 372–3
    critical theory 386–7
    cultural factors 387
    and differential association 385
    elements 377–8
    extent 393–4
    impact 394–7
    individual/organisational offenders 389
    and neutralisation 385–6
    offenders, typology 388–9
    qualitative impacts 395–7
    regulation 399–402
    regulatory agencies 400
    and restorative justice 760–1
    and self-control 385
    self-regulation 401–2
    social/psychological factors 387
    and stigmatisation 387–8
    structural factors 387
    Sutherland's concept 373–6
    victims, typology 390–2
Whitehouse, Mary 215
Whitelaw, William 519, 728
Whyte, D. 346, 380, 389, 398
Wild, Jonathan 25
Wilkins, L. 97, 218
Williams, R. 202, 910
Willis, P. 908
Willmott, P. 201
Wilson, James Q. 248, 269–70, 272, 274–5, 290–1, 574
witnesses
    children as 858–9

eyewitness testimony 856–7, 858
vulnerable 857–9
Wolfgang, M. 123, 200, 344, 718
women 806–33
  see also feminist criminology; masculinity
  cautioning sentencing 810–11
  and criminal justice 810–18
  criminalisation 313
  fear of crime 819
  and imprisonment 811–13, 814 *Table*
  and legal professions 830–1
  male/female offending 806–9
  in police 828–9
  and prison 311–13, 813–17
  prison officers 830
  in probation service 830
  social control, role 828–31
  victimization 359–61, 818–27
  violence against 819–22
    see also domestic violence; rape
Woodiwiss, M. 410, 420, 428
Woolf Report 689–90, 709–10
Wootton, B. 150
Worrall, A. 305, 311–12, 314–15, 921
Wright, A. 425, 447, 462, 503

Yakuza, 409
Yarl's Wood detention centre 870
Yochelson, S. 157–9, 255–6
Young, A. 561
Young, Jock 18, 66, 95, 97, 178, 255–6, 259, 264, 266–9, 270–1
  fear of crime 355–6
young people
  crime and justice 740–1
  and imprisonment 737–9
  perceptions of 716
Young, R. 651, 655, 754, 760

youth crime 717–25
  distribution 719 *Fig.*
  and drug use 721–4
  and ethnic minorities 720–1
  male/female offending 806–9
  patterns of offending 717–18
  persistent offenders 718–20
  profile of offending 719 *Fig.*
  trends 720
  victimization 724–5
youth justice 725–40
  see also anti-social behaviour
  childhood and punishment 725–6
  community approach 739
  contemporary 734–5
  and diversion 727–8
  emergence of system 726–7
  managerialism 730–1
  and New Labour 731
  non-custodial penalties 731
  and punitiveness 728–31
  referral orders 733–4, 739–40
  restorative 739–40
  volunteers 549
Youth Justice Board 554–5
Youth Lifestyles Surveys (YLS) 78
Youth Offending Panels (YOPs) 734, 755
Youth Offending Teams 546, 731

Zeisel, H. 861
Zedner, L. 8, 354, 516, 520, 633
Zehr, H. 752
zemiology 258
zero-tolerance policing 576, 619–22
Zimbardo, P. 575
Zimring, F. 455–6
Znaniecki, F. 191
zonal hypothesis 191